Early Modern Conceptions of Property

Consumption and Culture in the 17th and 18th Centuries

Consumption and the World of Goods
Edited by John Brewer and Roy Porter

Early Modern Conceptions of Property
Edited by John Brewer and Susan Staves

The Consumption of Culture, 1600–1800
Edited by Ann Bermingham and John Brewer

Early Modern Conceptions of Property

Edited by

John Brewer and Susan Staves

London and New York

First published 1996
Reprinted and first published in paperback 1996
by Routledge
11 New Fetter Lane, London EC4P 4EE

Simultaneously published in the USA and Canada
by Routledge
29 West 35th Street, New York, NY 10001

Routledge is an International Thomson Publishing company

This collection © 1995, 1996
The Regents of the University of California

Typeset in Palatino by
Florencetype Ltd, Stoodleigh, Devon

Printed and bound in Great Britain by
T. J. Press (Padstow) Ltd., Padstow, Cornwall

British Library Cataloguing in Publication Data

A catalogue record for this book is available from the British Library

Library of Congress Cataloguing in Publication Data

A catalogue record for this book has been requested

ISBN 0-415-10533-1 √
    0-415-15314-X (pbk)

Contents

Tables

Plates

Preface

The papers in this volume were part of the three-year research project mounted by the Center for Seventeenth and Eighteenth Century Studies and the Clark Library at UCLA on "Culture and Consumption in the Seventeenth and Eighteenth Centuries." This project was partially funded by grant no. RO-21623-88 from the Interpretive Research Division of the National Endowment of the Humanities. Additional resources came from the Dean of the Division of Humanities at UCLA, the Center and the Clark Library.

The project director, John Brewer, would like to thank not only all the scholars who took part as paper-givers and discussants but the staff of the Center and Library whose efforts made the project possible.

The editors and publishers would like to thank the following:

Oxford University Press for permission to reprint David Solkin's chapter, which was previously published in John Barrell (ed.) *Painting and the Politics of Culture*, Oxford, Oxford University Press, 1992, pp. 73–99; *Political Theory* for permission to reproduce Ian Shapiro's chapter, which was previously published in *Political Theory* 2/91; *Romance Quarterly* and the University Press of Kentucky for permission to reprint material from "Property and personality in *Emile*," *Romance Quarterly* 38 (1991), in Patrick Coleman's chapter.

Notes on contributors

Donna T. Andrew is Associate Professor in the Department of History, University of Guelph, Ontario, Canada. She is the author of *Philanthropy and Police: London Charity in the Eighteenth Century* and *London Debating Societies, 1776–1799* (1989) and is completing a book entitled *The Attack on Aristocratic Vice, 1680–1850*. She plans to extend her study of Lady Spencer's charities in a volume, *Noblesse Oblige: Female Benevolence in an Age of Sentiment*.

Richard Ashcraft is Professor of Political Science at the University of California, Los Angeles. He is the author of *Revolutionary Politics and Locke's Two Treatises of Government* (1986), *Locke's Two Treatises of Government* (1987), and editor of *Critical Assessments: John Locke* (1991).

Hilary Beckles holds a Chair in Economic and Social History at the Cave Hill Campus (Barbados) of the University of the West Indies and is currently Dean of the Faculty of Arts and Chair of the History Department. He has published three books and dozens of essays on the history and sociology of Caribbean slave systems. He is an editor of the *Journal of Caribbean History*.

David D. Bien is Professor of History at the University of Michigan. The present article is an offshoot of a work-in-progress on French state borrowing and the reinforcement of privilege and corps under the old regime.

Carol Blum is Research Professor of Humanities at the State University of New York at Stony Brook. She is the author of *Rousseau and the Republic of Virtue: The Language of Politics in the French Revolution* (1986). In 1994 she held a National Endowment for the Humanities Fellowship for a project entitled "History of a Delusion: Depopulation Rhetoric in Eighteenth-Century France."

John Brewer is Professor of Cultural History at the European Institute in Florence. He is the author of *Party Ideology and Popular Politics at the Accession of George III* (1976) and *The Sinews of Power: War, Money and the English State, 1688–1783* (1989). He has also co-edited *The Birth of a Consumer Society: the Commercialization of Eighteenth-Century England* (1982) and the first volume of the present series, *Consumption and the World of Goods* (1993).

Patrick Coleman is Professor of French at the University of California, Los Angeles. He is the auithor of *Rousseau's Political Imagination* (1984) and *The Limits of Sympathy: Gabrielle Roy's "Bonheur d'occasion"* (1993). He has edited Rousseau's *Discourse on Inequality* (1994) and is preparing an edition of Rousseau's *Confessions*.

Michael Craton, an English-born Canadian, has taught British Imperial and West Indian History at the University of Waterloo since 1966. His published work has ranged over the Caribbean in general, and all aspects of colonial slavery and plantations. Currently, he is completing (with Gail Saunders) a two-volume social history of the Bahamas entitled *Islanders in the Stream*; his renewed interest in the foundations of Caribbean colonies and "slave societies" is a spin-off from the first volume, published in October 1992.

Barbara B. Diefendorf is Professor of History at Boston University. She is the author of *Paris City Councillors in the Sixteenth Century: The Politics of Patrimony* (1983) and *Beneath the Cross: Catholics and Huguenots in Sixteenth-Century Paris* (1991) and editor, with Carla Hesse, of *Culture and Identity in Early Modern Europe* (1993). She is currently working on female spirituality in Counter-Reformation France.

Nina Rattner Gelbart is Professor of History and Chair of the History Department at Occidental College in Los Angeles. She is the author of *Feminine and Opposition Journalism in Old Regime France: Le Journal de dames* (1986). Currently, she is preparing a full-length biography of Mme du Coudray. Two essays from this project include "Midwide to a Nation: Mme du Coudray serves France" in *The Art of Midwifery: Early Modern Midwives in Europe*, ed. Hilary Marland (1993), and "Books and the Birthing Business: The Midwife Manuals of Mme du Coudray," will appear in Dena Goodman and Elizabeth Goldsmith, eds, *Going Public: Women and Publishing in Early Modern France* (forthcoming, Cornell University Press).

Dena Goodman is Associate Professor of History at Louisiana State University. She is the author of *Criticism in Action: Enlightenment Experiments in Political Writing* (1989) and *The Republic of Letters: A Cultural History of the French Enlightenment* (1994).

Robert W. Gordon is Sweet Professor of Law at Stanford University.

John Guillory is Professor of English at The Johns Hopkins University. He is the author of *Poetic Authority: Spencer, Milton, and Literary History* (1983) and *Cultural Capital: The Problem of Literary Canon Formation* (1993).

Tim Keirn teaches in the History Department and Social Science Credential Program at California State University, Long Beach. He is the co-editor and a contributor to *Stilling the Grumbling Hive: The Response to Economic and Social Problems in England, 1689–1750* (1922) and has published articles iu *The Journal of British History, Parliamentary History* and *Historical Research*.

Lawrence E. Klein, an Associate Professsor in the History Department at the University of Nevada, Las Vegas, is the author of *Shaftesbury and the Culture of Politeness: Moral Discourse and Cultural Politics in Early Eighteenth-Century England* (1994).

David Lieberman is a Professor in the Jurisprudence and Social Policy Program of the Boalt Hall School of Law, University of California, Berkeley. He is the author of *The Province of Legislation Determined: Legal Theory in Eighteenth-Century Britain* (1989).

P. J. Marshall is Professor of History Emeritus, King's College, London. He is the author of *East India Fortunes: The British in Bengal in the Eighteenth Century* (1976),

Bengal: the British Bridgehead: Eastern India, 1740–1828 (1988), and the associate editor of *The Writings and Speeches of Edmund Burke.*

Mario Pastore is a visiting fellow at the Latin American Studies Program, Cornell University. He has published "State-led Industrialization: The Evidence on Paraguay, 1852–1870," in the *Journal of Latin American Studies* (May 1994) and "Trade Contraction and Economic Regression. The Agrarian Economy of Paraguay, 1810–1840" in the *Journal of Latin American Studies* (October 1994).

J. S. Peters, Associate Professor of English and Comparative Literature at Columbia University, is working on a book about the relations between European theater and printing from 1500 to 1900. She is the author of *Congreve, the Drama, and the Printed Word* (1990), as well as a number of essays on seventeenth- and eighteenth-century culture, and on the theory and history of performance.

James Raven is Fellow and Director of Studies in History at Magdalene College, Cambridge. He is author of *Judging New Wealth: Popular Publishing and Responses to Commerce in England 1750–1800* (1992), co-editor of *The Practice and Representation of Reading in England* (1994) and *The Commercialization of the Book* (forthcoming, Oxford University Press).

Harriet Ritvo is Professor of History at Massachusetts Institute of Technology and the author of *The Animal Estate: The English and Other Creatures in the Victorian Age* (1987). She is currently at work on a cultural history of animal classification in eighteenth- and nineteenth-century Britain.

Laura J. Rosenthal is Assistant Professor of English at Florida State University. She has published essays in Renaissance Drama, *The Eighteenth Century: Theory and Interpretation*, and the *Journal of Dramatic Theory and Criticism*. She is currently finishing a book on adaptation, appropriation, plagiarism, and gender in Restoration and Augustan drama.

Ian Shapiro is Professor of Political Science at Yale University, where he specializes in early modern and contemporary political philosophy. He is author of *The Evolution of Rights in Liberal Theory* (1986), *Political Criticism* (1990) and, with D. Green, *Pathologies of Rational Choice Theory* (1994). His contribution to the present volume is an expanded version of an article by the same title that appeared in *Political Theory*, Vol. 19, No. 1 (February 1991), pp. 47–72. A controversy about the original article appeared in *Political Theory*, Vol. 20, No. 2 (May 1992), pp. 319–31.

David Solkin is Reader in the History of Art at the Courtauld Institute of Art, University of London. He is the author of *Richard Wilson: The Landscape of Reaction* (1982) and *Painting for Money: The Visual Arts and the Public Sphere in Eighteenth-Century England* (1993).

Margaret R. Somers teaches in the Department of Sociology at the University of Michigan, Ann Arbor. Her recent publications include articles on the meaning of citizenship in the *American Sociological Review* and *Law and Social Inquiry*, as well as an essay, "Where is Sociology After the Historic Turn? Knowledge Cultures, Narrativity, and Historical Epistemologies," in *The Historic Turn in the Human Sciences*, ed. Terrence J. Mcdonald (forthcoming, University of Michigan Press). She is currently completing a manuscript titled *The People and the Law: Political Cultures, Civil Societies, and the Place of the Public Sphere in the Making of Modern Citizenship Rights* (forthcoming, Cornell University Press).

Susan Staves is Paul Proswimmer Professor of the Humanities at Brandeis University. She is the author of *Player's Scepters: Fictions of Authority in the Restoration* (1979) and *Married Women's Separate Property in England, 1660–1833* (1991). Among her recent articles on property is "Chattel Property Rules and the Construction of Englishness, 1660–1800," in *The Law and History Review* (1994).

David Sugarman is Professor of Law and Director of the Law in History Programme at Lancaster University. He is the author of *Law and Social Change in England, 1780–1900* (1993), editor of *Legality, Ideology and the State* (1983), and co-editor of *Law, Economy and Society, 1750–1914: Essays in the History of English Law* (1984), *Regulating Corporate Groups in Europe* (1990), and *Professional Competition and Professional Power: Lawyers, Accountants and the Social Construction of Markets* (1994). He is currently completing *Law in History* (forthcoming, Dartmouth, 1995).

Ronnie Warrington has recently completed a novel on the relationship between music and language.

1
Introduction

John Brewer and Susan Staves

Now, in the 1990s, America and Western Europe watch in astonishment as the peoples of the former Soviet Union move to reintroduce private property in land. In Poland and other Eastern European countries, Western economists offer advice about how to turn state enterprises into competitive private businesses. Considering the reunification of Germany, political experts and business people alike debate whether the East Germans, having lived for more than a generation under a communist regime, will emerge psychically incapable of entrepreneurship or even incapable of the disciplined hard work and craftsmanship formerly supposed to be characteristic of German workers. Every day, reading the newspapers, we are reminded in one way or another how profoundly particular property regimes are expressions of particular political ideologies and how even "personality" itself is constructed in relation to a particular regime of ownership.

In the Anglo-American political and popular imaginations "property" has been a resonant word. To Englishmen, Magna Carta gave a precious right not to have one's body or one's land taken by the king without due process, a right that in the English-speaking world exfoliated into a more general right to be secure in one's property. As many commentators have observed, the United States Constitution promises no explicit rights of personhood, yet these – including the right to privacy – have been constructed from provisions of the fourth, fifth, and fourteenth amendments that protect "persons" and "property" (bound together in the language of each amendment) from state searches and seizures without due process of law. The private ownership of land especially has seemed to hold out the hope of encouragement to honest labor, of high levels of productivity from which all can benefit, and – politically – of an independent and free republican citizenry. Oliver Goldsmith in his popular poem *The Deserted Village*, imagined this idyll of property in land in terms that would have made equal sense to Thomas Jefferson:

> A time there was, ere England's griefs began,
> When every rood of ground maintained its man;
> For him light labour spread her wholesome store,
> Just gave what life required, but gave no more.

Yet, as we shall suggest, this idyll of personal independence sustained by private property obscures important aspects of what property is – indeed, of what personhood is.

While property in land is a crucial early form of property and a fundamental model for later conceptions of property, modern property also appears in much more variegated, intangible, and peculiar forms. The chapters in our collection consider a number of these newer forms of property constructed in the early modern period; for example, literary property, genetic property, and the franchise property of brokers of government debt obligations (that is, of dealers in financial instruments comparable with twentieth-century United States Treasury bills, notes, and bonds). In considering these newer forms of property, our chapters shed light both on the nature of modern intangible forms of property and on the processes of reification and legitimation that were required to produce them.

Our chapters explore the meaning of "property," especially property in the early modern period, from a wide variety of disciplinary perspectives: political theory, law, sociology, history, economics, literature, and art history. Perhaps especially within the disciplines of political and legal theory, property is often considered in quite abstracted and generalized ways. Indeed, it is a normal aim of theory to propound general truths. Yet both the political theory and the legal theory of property have been significantly determined by the paradigm of property in land, unsurprisingly, since the older basis of political representation was property in land. Thus, it seems useful to attend more carefully to important alternative forms of property to test the explanatory power and satisfactoriness of those theories. The paradigm of property in land is powerfully linked with images of virtuous republican labor yielding crops that need to be secured from thieving wastrels. But suppose we abandon the paradigm of property in land to look instead at the property in persons sanctioned by early modern slave law? When an economic historian analyzes the debates over the Royal African Company, a private English monopoly in the African slave trade, then legitimizing rationales about the benignity of private ownership of property may look a bit different. Moreover, the resistance of some "things" – like slaves or literary property or genetic property – to being subjected to a private property regime of individual ownership is perhaps particularly well appreciated by specialists in other disciplines that study those "things." We believe that theory can profit by being confronted with a more contextualized practice and with a more particularized account of important early modern forms of property in things other than land. It is worthwhile, too, to expose the more particular and disciplinarily based accounts of specific kinds of property to broadly ranging theoretical debates about ownership.

Unlike some considerations of private property, our collection is also concerned to understand the crucial role of state power in securing private ownership. How, for instance, do modern states come to believe that it is in the state's interest to protect private rights to copyright or patent property? Although the due process rights of Magna Carta and the United States Constitution present themselves as rights against the state, state police powers guarantee the security of individual owners and can be invoked by owners to exclude "trespassers," whether literal trespassers on land or less material trespassers on license privileges or copyrights. Property rights are, by definition, legitimated rights, yet again and again the use of state force on behalf of some owners to exclude other trespassers or to confer on some owners rights to the labor (or even the personhood) of others raises profound questions of contradictions between legitimacy and violence.

Property and political theory

Our collection begins with three chapters that explore important arguments in the political theory of property. Each of these chapters demonstrates different limitations to the ideas of "absolute ownership" and "absolute property" and each also considers crucial arguments legitimating private ownership. "Property," after all, in civil society, cannot be simply what we are able to take and to keep by force, it must also be what we are "entitled" "legitimately" to possess. Ian Shapiro, in a very broadly ranging chapter considers the power of "the workmanship ideal," that is, the principle that we are entitled to possess the fruits of our own labor. This ideal is importantly associated with John Locke, but, Shapiro demonstrates, variants of it appear in Marx and in the twentieth-century philosophers John Rawls and Ronald Dworkin. Attractive as this ideal is, it is also problematic. As Shapiro suggests, once theological beliefs about how different people come to have different productive capacities are abandoned, a new burden of "fairness" seems to be placed on society either to justify or to remedy the consequences of one person's being born blind and mentally retarded and another's being born sighted and mentally gifted. Furthermore, an individual's productive capacity is not such an isolated and autonomous phenomenon as some economic and political theory has supposed. As twentieth-century divorce settlements giving stay-at-home wives percentages of their husbands' professional earnings are intended to indicate, an individual's productive capacity itself is the product of a complex social milieu.

Although the idea of private property suggests individual autonomy, property is necessarily relational, conceivable only in the context of communities of people; property rights are rights "against" other people, rights to exclude them from the use and enjoyment of the thing owned. Also invoking Locke, Richard Ashcraft sees him not as the founder of "possessive individualism" (as C. P. Macpherson does), but rather as retaining certain natural law ideas about individuals' rights to subsistence. Private individuals own property, in this view, not absolutely, but subject to liens that can be claimed by their more necessitous neighbors if and when those neighbors are in danger of perishing. Even in the later eighteenth century when the newer views of Adam Smith that poverty was a sign of social pathology and misconduct began to prevail, Locke's older views continued to find expression in contemporary debate, including in 1782 a call by William Ogilvie for the nationalization of land.

Both Shapiro's ideas about the socialization of the capacity to produce and Ashcraft's vivid sense of property as embedded in social relations find expression in Margaret R. Somers's account of what "property in skill" meant to English artisans who were guild members. Amongst these artisans, Somers finds an older idea of property as social membership which, she argues, continued well into the nineteenth century to provide support for workers' assertions of their rights against a newer idea of property as produced solely from autonomous individual labor. When an artisan possessed "the art and mystery" of a craft after an apprenticeship, what he possessed was not so much a technical skill as political membership in a group, membership on which his citizenship also depended. His rights as an Englishman were not so much rights against the state as rights to substantive justice (for example, in the public fixing of wages and prices) and rights to administrative participation.

Property and legal ideology

Next, three practitioners of critical legal history consider property as it has appeared to lawyers' eyes. Agreeing with the political theorists that "it requires a heroic act of reification" to conceive of things as absolutely owned and that property relations are inevitably collaborative relations of mutual dependency, Robert W. Gordon explores some of the conflicting rationales that have been used to legitimate private ownership. Despite the continuing appeal of the idea of ownership as enabling personal autonomy and liberty, Gordon argues, we must also acknowledge that one person's property rights are apt to impose burdens on another person, and so invariably restrict freedom for some while creating it for others. Rather than increasing security in the world, property rights "merely redistribute uncertainty away from the owner to those who will be subject to his rights' exercise": if my property rights in my farm allow me to build a dam on my brook, my neighbor's alfalfa field may be flooded. In the eighteenth century, as property in contracts (mortgages, debt-instruments, stock) grew, the creditor's property in his debt also increasingly seemed to give him a disturbing sort of property in his debtors. Thus, looking at the relation of English merchant bankers and Virginia tobacco-growers who were their debtors, Thomas Jefferson observed bitterly that these debts "had become hereditary from father to son, for many generations, so that the planters were a species of property annexed to certain mercantile houses in England."

Gordon considers a wide variety of legal property relations, while David Sugarman and Ronnie Warrington concentrate on one very important but little studied kind of legal property: the equity of redemption. (An equity of redemption is the legal interest a mortgagor of real property has in his mortgaged property even after he ceases payments on his mortgage.) The equity of redemption protects the current owner against foreclosure by his mortgage creditor despite the failure of the current owner to live up to his side of the contractual bargain. Understanding even the technicalities of classical real property law as a "way of social imagining" and as "a potent and institutionalized privileged way in which society presents the world to itself," Sugarman reveals how the judges' treatment of the equity of redemption supported the interests of landowners against those of mortgage creditors and how, especially after the threats of instability posed by the stock speculation of the South Sea Bubble, the judiciary conceived of this support of the landed interests as a way of promoting the continued possession of land "by its rightful owners." Consequently, because land was the basis of political power, the judiciary thought of itself as promoting continuity of governance, even ultimately the stability of the nation itself. Despite the developing rhetoric about contract rights as themselves important property and despite the wide variety of newly important contract property that Gordon's chapter surveys, Sugarman and Warrington strikingly observe how willingly the judiciary turned deaf ears to the contract claims of mortgagors in conflict with their landed debtors. Not until the late nineteenth century, when the landed also usually had other forms of capital, when the value of land fell, and when the electoral franchise had been dissociated from the ownership of land, did these lenders' pleas for contract enforcement against the landed meet with much judicial sympathy.

Historians have generally neglected the study of seventeenth- and eighteenth-century private law, in part because it has seemed that until the high-profile legislative battles of the nineteenth century, not much happened with the common law. Both the chapter by Sugarman and Warrington and the next essay by David Lieberman help to remedy this neglect. Lieberman turns his attention to commercial law and the judicial interventions of Lord Mansfield, which were perceived by many contemporaries to be a crucial form of legal modernization. Lieberman's analysis of Mansfield's position raises the question of how long the more conservative land law could remain insulated from the different, more "modern" approach to commercial law in a world in which, as Adam Smith proclaimed, "every man . . . lives by exchanging, or becomes in some measure a merchant, and the society itself grows to be what is properly a commercial society." For no matter how brilliantly Mansfield strove to create a system of commercial law that was simple, rational, and "certain," as Gordon's chapter so eloquently suggests, the ownership of commercial property itself proved to be "only a ticket of entry to a condition of vulnerability."

Property and the family

Until quite recently, when considering questions of owners and ownership, political and legal theory tended to be gender-blind. Yet, in the early modern period, as liberal political philosophies figuring citizens as autonomous private owners were developed, the sorts of ownership that were imagined typically conferred citizenship on males, not on females. Quite striking tensions emerged between how property was understood in the context of the state and how it was understood in the context of the family. In a provocative chapter on Montesquieu and Diderot, Carol Blum reminds us of the eighteenth-century French fears of depopulation, then proceeds to argue that these *philosophes* had a variant on the workmanship ideal: as men's ownership of land is legitimated by men's labor on the land, so a man's possession of a woman is legitimated by his fertilization of her. Barbara B. Diefendorf, focusing on French practice rather than on theory, investigates the division of property within families in Paris, where customary law prevailed, and Dauphiné, where civil law governed. Her chapter complicates the too often heard assertion that women were the property of men by displaying the range of property rights belonging to daughters, wives, and widows. Despite the assertions of traditional patriarchal ideology that women were not competent owners, Diefendorf is particularly struck by evidence she uncovers of wives' and, even more, of widows' understanding their husbands' business affairs and being entrusted with management and administration of family property.

Continental civil law systems gave daughters and younger sons forced share rights to family property (the *légitime*), rights children did not enjoy under the English common law system which Susan Staves examines in the final chapter in this section. Individual upper-class English families, nevertheless, often conferred on children some rights to shares by means of parents' marriage settlements. How the courts dealt with disputes over such rights reveals, among other things, how forcefully the English state was willing to project what it saw as its own interests (for example, disadvantaging Roman Catholics and Jews) in the "private" sphere of the family. Staves's chapter also considers how weakly the "legitimate," supposedly "natural" family, the family often deferred to by the state as pre-existing the state and immune from state scrutiny, could correspond to the biological family, which was apt to include a variety of persons the state was content to disadvantage, not only Roman Catholics, Jews, or aliens, but also bastards.

Property and the construction of a self

That different entitlements to property or the ownership of different kinds of property are apt to produce different sorts of people is a familiar idea: the confident, perhaps presuming heir of primogeniture in contrast to the worried, perhaps envious, younger brother; or the independent-minded, public-spirited landowner in contrast to the servile, self-interested city lawyer or stockbroker. Early modern commentators were exquisitely conscious not only of the emergence of new forms of property like stocks or government paper, but also of new sorts of persons, perhaps most notably the new men of commerce and money. The very characterization of "the landed interest" itself seems to have arisen in the earliest years of the eighteenth century, by way of contrast with the interests of the new owners of the government paper created by the Bank of England and of those who made markets in this paper. Traditionally, the influential periodical produced by Joseph Addison and Richard Steele, the *Spectator*, has been seen as one of the earliest expressions of a new commercial ideology, offering explicit propaganda defending modern commercial men like their fictional hero Sir Andrew Freeport, and, ever so gently, poking fun at the old-fashioned, country-squire values of "Sir Roger de Coverley," a lovable enough character, but one whose day seems to have passed. Lawrence E. Klein, however, argues that what the *Spectator* actually aimed at, and accomplished, was the overcoming of this contrast between the landed man and the commercial man, inventing a new ideal of politeness that could include both. Fundamental to the *Spectator*'s resistance to the dichotomy was its realization that "commerce was not a sector of the economy, but a fundamental form of the entire economy" and that land itself was not so insulated from commerce as the mythology of the landed interest pretended. Emerging notions of self thus could be released from dependence on the kind of property that materially supported a particular self, indeed, reference to the material bases of selfhood became a vulgarism in polite society. Instead, the polite self could be imagined as freely constructed, perhaps in accordance with the directions of the *Spectator*, and, potentially at least, universally available. The ideals of politeness Klein sees the *Spectator* developing, in fact, aim to repress partiality and difference with a genuinely new construction of self; they are not simply intended to force commercial men to imitate the landed elites, nor are they simply a way of domesticating a traditional elite to the more pacific norms of commercial men.

David Solkin's art historical essay presents a related contrast between images of personalities based on landed property and personalities created by commerce, through readings of two paintings: Closterman's picture of the Earl of Shaftesbury and his brother, as contrasted to Joseph Wright's picture of a group of much more modest Englishmen, women, and children clustered around a scientific demonstration in *The Air Pump*. In Wright's emphatically modern picture, Solkin argues, we see not classicized transhistorical types, but a very particular private set of people, in a very particularized historical moment. They visibly inhabit a world so subject to division of labor and individual difference that acts of imagination are required to produce empathy. Wright's image of the cockatoo apparently on the verge of expiring in the vacuum jar, its suffering the occasion of scientific enlightenment and entertainment, seems to make problematic the progression from industry to knowledge, and, even as it honors the refinement visible in the polished surfaces of the painting, to raise the question of whether improvements may also be corruptions.

Proceeding further into the dark places of personality hinted at by Wright's chiaroscuro, Patrick Coleman offers a subtle analysis of Rousseau's insights into the relation of property and personality. Coleman's readings of the *Discourse on Political Economy* and *Emile* develop some of the paradoxes of property earlier identified by Robert W. Gordon. In Rousseau's account of the development of civil society, the division of land implies mutual dependency, yet the individual's experience of the regime of private property for Rousseau arouses concomitant anger and resentment at this very fact of dependency. In contrast to the cheerier Anglo-American notions of property as enabling individual autonomy and self-assertion, Rousseau here is read to reveal the individuation resulting from private property as a dispossession and as a form of alienation requiring "an involuntary and permanent preoccupation with other people."

The last two chapters in this section consider the implications of appearing to have "too little" or "too much" property; how does the construction of self depend upon the possession of a certain quantum of property? Donna T. Andrew's "*Noblesse oblige. Female charity in an age of sentiment*" presents, among others, a set of persons who, psychically, feel themselves genteel, yet, materially, lack the resources to maintain genteel personhood. They, therefore, write begging letters to Margaret, Lady Spencer, seeking her charity and attempting to explain why she ought to use her material resources to sustain their psychic senses of entitlement to gentility (or, in some cases, merely a more modest respectability). Lady Spencer set about fulfilling her own sense of aristocratic and Christian duty in responding to these letters by creating an investigative network to test their truthfulness. Ironically, her investigations could threaten the credit of applicants who were, tenuously, sustaining themselves on nothing but the appearance of gentility. Thus, one distressed clergyman wrote indignantly to Lady Spencer after one of her investigators had called at his lodgings: "If it was Curiosity alone that led this Lady to such an Enquiry, it was a little uncharitable, as it laid open my sores to a Creditor." In the transactions between Margaret, Lady Spencer and her begging clientele, many of whom claimed some kind of familial relationship or at least personal connection (like that of former servants or tenants) with the Spencers, she seems to recognize a duty to give not only to maintain the credit of her own family, but, sometimes, more generally, to maintain the appearance of the upper classes themselves. Lady Spencer, at least, understood many of the deserving poor to have a lien on her wealth. She also developed a rather sophisticated sense of herself as a trustee or guardian of wealth for the benefit of the deserving and for the credit of her own family and class. The idea that it is a special cruelty to bring up a child with expectations of wealth – a clerical admonition to parents noted in Staves's chapter – recurs here in the self-representations of Lady Spencer's claimants, who urge that their original gentility, now that they lack the material means to support it, makes their suffering a more severe distress, a more bitter anguish, than if they had been born poor.

James Raven directs attention to early modern versions of an ancient ethical dilemma: how much property is enough for one person, how much is "too much"? As he explores English magazine debates over luxury in the second half of the eighteenth century, he discovers some modern contradictions that seem still with us: the press denounced overconsumption as a dreadful vice, yet increasingly developed a nice (and often desperate) distinction between the good luxury of the tasteful and the bad luxury of the vulgar. Moreover, the education necessary to make such a distinction itself became a new product (or property) manufactured and sold by the same press that denounced luxury. Magazines simultaneously featured anti-fashion tirades and tempting descriptions of the latest dresses, nosegays, and cuisine. Engaged in a "competitive and often desperate discrimination" between the polite and impolite, the magazines simultaneously sold new models for ladies and gentlemen who aspired to proper modes of consumption, and proper understandings of the responsibilities of wealth.

Literary property

One of the most notable features of the early modern period was the development of modern ideas of literary property. It is not obvious that a single person ought to own a story; indeed, twentieth-century literary theory, in its emphasis on intertextuality, the inextricability of stories from each other, has made the idea of private ownership of literary property quite sharply paradoxical. From an older point of view that imagined poetry as divinely inspired, to attempt private ownership of a poem and to sell that poem in the market could look like a form of simony. Nevertheless, the English Copyright Act of 1714 was a landmark not only in the private ownership of property, but also – and inevitably, given what we have already said about the relation of property and personhood – in the construction of the modern conception of "the author." Selecting a rich textual example, Laura J. Rosenthal looks at Nahum Tate's version of *King Lear* (1681). Why, she asks, should Shakespeare's use of the early text, *Leir*, have been received as an authentic play of Shakespeare's, while Tate's version became an "adaptation" of Shakespeare? Why does Shakespeare not perceive *Leir* as anyone's private property, but Tate have to consider *Lear* as peculiarly Shakespeare's? Also figuring in Rosenthal's account of Shakespeare's fate in the early modern period is Lewis Theobald, who probably deserves the title of Shakespeare's first modern editor, but who, as an adaptor of what he thought was another play by Shakespeare, *The*

Double Falshood, was accused of having "forged" the play, attaching Shakespeare's name to a play of his own in order to "steal" fame that properly belonged to the name of Shakespeare.

From the early modern period to the present the personal letter has been one form of literary property (or potential literary property) that has tended to raise fundamental questions about literary property itself and about the nature of the public interest in protecting such property. Currently, for example, a literary scholar has been prohibited from using material from J. D. Salinger's letters in a critical book about Salinger by an American court's ruling that the letters are the private property of the Salinger estate; historians of the twentieth century who have retrieved letters relevant to their work under Freedom of Information statutes or by other means have nevertheless been prevented from publishing them by the original writers or their representatives, even when those letters have been written by individuals who were clearly "public figures." Copyright statutes proclaimed that it was in the public interest to guarantee authors' property in their published works in order to encourage authors to produce books and to reap profits from sales. This rationale, of course, cannot be simply applied to the writers of private letters. Dena Goodman examines the position of one French lawyer, Michel de Servan, who argued that letters ought to be understood as the communal property of both the writer and the recipient. Like several students of the periodical press of this period (a press of which letters were an important staple), Goodman sees the emergence of a new civil sphere, differentiable from the public sphere of the state and from the private sphere of the individual. In this civil sphere, healthy and constructive criticism of private manners and of the state ought to flourish, protected from censorship. If the state takes a long view of its own best interests, *Avocat* Servan argues, its post office will deliver the correspondence of its critics to one another, refrain from breaking the seals that guarantee privacy, and even protect the privacy of one party to a correspondence who wishes to decline making a correspondence in which he has been a participant part of the printed public record.

Sometimes property seems to depend on technology: technology can invent new kinds of value worth owning, make things previously considered worth owning valueless, or, indeed, change the nature of ownership itself. With respect to literary property, what it meant to own a text was fundamentally different in earlier manuscript cultures than it became after the introduction of printing. Goodman quotes Servan's observation on the impact of printing on intellectual property:

> The thoughts of a man are surely the most incontestable of properties; but before the invention of printing, it was the least solid: a mouse could nibble away in a week thirty years of reflections. Since [the invention of] printing, on the contrary, ideas are the most durable property; not a building on earth is more imperishable than a good work, and the most fertile soil will be buried beneath the sand before a good work is buried in oblivion.

J. S. Peters further considers the implications of printing for property, developing analogies that appear between printed literary texts, especially dramatic texts, and the printed paper money issued by the new Bank of England in the 1690s. The mechanical reproduction of printing, she argues, produced a crisis of representation in which the ephemerality and insubstantiality of representation itself were made apparent. Just as letters, part of a correspondence, can be seen as a form of communal property resistant to the ownership of a single individual, so even more evidently theatrical representations seem to make plays a kind of communal property, in which writers, managers, stagehands, actors, and audience are all sharers, even co-creators. Yet playwrights like Congreve, Beaumarchais, and Sheridan discerned the possibilities of using vigilant control over the printed texts of their dramatic works to make them private possessions, ways of resisting the apparent ephemerality and communal character of theatrical representation itself.

Finally in this section, John Guillory considers a way in which the oldest literary form, poetry, comes to be understood in the eighteenth century not as the property of the poet who produced it, but, instead, as a kind of cultural capital or commodity newly valuable to the upwardly mobile middle classes. Moving away from earlier rhetorical conceptions of poetic texts, new anthologies – and even poems themselves constructed by a compositional method akin to that of the commonplace book or anthology – enable a different way of consuming texts to emerge in a transformed culture of book production.

Reification: the invention and institution of special forms of property

Unlike property in such material things as land or animals, literary property and other species of intellectual property depend on reification, that is, on regarding an abstraction (or, in some uses of the word, a person) as a thing. According to copyright law doctrines, the owner of textual property owns neither the manuscript nor the physical book in which his or her text has been printed, nor the ideas it expresses; instead, the owner owns the particular sequence of words he or she has "created" to express those ideas. Similarly, the owner of patent rights in a machine owns neither a particular machine nor the model or drawings of the machine submitted to the patent office, but rather the rights to control the use of his or her design for the machine. Immaterial, even "nonexistent" entities can be subjugated to property regimes, if they are believed to have value, if they can be clearly conceptualized, and if they can be "constructed" in such a way as to make property rights in them administrable. For instance, the laws of slander and libel have been made to protect something as immaterial as a businessman's "property in reputation."

Several important insights into the nature of reification are offered by Harriet Ritvo's entertaining chapter on Robert Bakewell, a man who deserves some credit as a pioneer of biotechnology. Ritvo reveals Bakewell, a legendary hero of the agricultural revolution famed for his New Leicester or Dishley sheep, to be a more inventive entrepreneur than tradition suggests. In 1760 he began renting out tups (stud rams) at a fee of 17s 6d per animal per season; by 1789 he was asking and receiving £300–£400 per animal per season. Bakewell convinced his customers that they were purchasing something like a design patent: "a template for the continued production of animals of a special type." The worth of a stud animal's template was not necessarily visible in the animal's own physical characteristics; furthermore, Bakewell treated the lineage of his stud animals as a trade secret, refusing to disclose it to customers. Given the relatively weak understanding of genetics in this period, Bakewell's marketing successes must certainly be considered, to borrow a phrase from Robert W. Gordon's essay, "heroic acts of reification."

Ritvo also explores how reliant Bakewell's success was on the invention of new kinds of administration, notably on changing the perception of farm animals like sheep as undifferentiated from each other into an awareness of them as unique individuals by giving them names and pedigrees and recording those names and pedigrees in stud books. Among the fundamental paradoxes of property that appear in Bakewell's career is the tension between a desire for secrecy so that private property (especially such intangible private property as a design or template) may be protected as private, and a need for publicity and some sort of "registry" so that the public value of the private property can be established and the property protected by the state. Biotechnology firms to this day are frightened of filing for patent protection lest the descriptions of the processes they file be stolen by rivals, yet their descriptions must have sufficient detail to establish the originality and uniqueness of the process and to enable administrative protection of the limited-term monopoly rights they request.

The possibility of subjecting living things to property regimes has raised some of the most fundamental concerns about property. Living things, things apparently created by nature not by man, have often seemed to have autonomous qualities that make them in practice resistant to being treated as chattel property; indeed, qualities that in theory seem to demand a respect for their natures not consistent with models of ownership as absolute dominion. Unlike land or bonds, living things are often able to move of their own volition; moreover, many of them are self-reproducing. Thus, the law concerning cattle is rich with puzzles concerning responsibility for damage done when they stray, and, as soon as entrepreneurs like Bakewell established the value of genetic templates, problems of what to do about unauthorized matings of stud animals arose.

Within the law of living things, the state has shown special interest in setting limits on the absolute dominion of owners in the interest of the thing owned, construing ownership more as delimited use-rights and, in some cases, moving all the way to a model of ownership as guardianship or trusteeship. Thus owners of farm animals or pets are now apt to have their prerogatives constrained by anti-cruelty statutes, and, although animals have not achieved a standing in modern legal systems that allows them to appear as plaintiffs in their own right, courts have been prepared to strike down owners' wills ordering the destruction of animals and to allow trusts (with human trustees) for the benefit of an animal or animals. Social (or political) and state-enforced definitions of what constitutes legitimate and responsible use of a "thing" owned thus permit some kinds of commodification and reification of animals – allowing owners to sell them, for instance – but constrain others, requiring the "owner," once he or she has elected to enter in the relationship of owner with the "thing owned," to act in some respects as a guardian protecting the interests of "the thing." This model of ownership as guardianship is actually a very old one, familiar enough in the provisions of medieval English land law that require "owners" of forests to preserve them as forests and "owners" of meadows to preserve them as meadows. Similar notions of ownership as guardianship have been revived in laws that protect the environment by restricting the ownership rights of those who hold wetlands or desert land. The guardianship model is a way of recognizing the non-equivalency of "things" that could conceivably be subjected to a free market of unrestrained alienation and interchangeability. It offers an alternative to a model of absolute ownership that would permit the destruction of the thing owned by the owner. This model also can express a moral resistance to reification.

Moral indignation about the treatment of living beings as "things owned" has been most vivid with respect to slavery. Yet slaves were an important form of property in the early modern period, and it is important to understand how slavery could be fitted into the political rationales legitimating private ownership. Tim Keirn contributes a study of the English Royal African Company from the perspective of an economic historian. Recipients of an exclusive monopoly patent from the Crown, the shareholders of this company and their licensees had an exclusive right to provide African slaves for West Indian sugar plantations, a right to make war in Africa for the purpose of securing their human product, and a right to erect courts in Africa. Since by 1700 sugar accounted for more than 10 percent of the value of English imports and roughly 15 percent of all exports, the company's product was an important one. The state granted a monopoly to the company for the same reason that states now grant patents to pharmaceutical companies: in order to attract sufficient capital to a high-risk venture thought to be in the public interest.

Keirn explores the contemporary political debate over the company as it was prompted by regulatory legislation and as it appeared, not in treatises, but in a very large and more representative pamphlet literature. Effective opposition to the monopoly came especially from West Indian planters who complained that the company failed to deliver slaves in sufficient quantity. When the monopoly was threatened, shareholders protested that their property interests were "equal with any Subject's rights to his Freehold." Their opponents denounced the monopoly as violating other subjects' liberty to engage in free trade (in slaves), artificially raising prices (of slaves), and restricting the supply of (slave) "goods."

In order for reification to work, not only does the "thing" in question have to be conceptualized in such a way that it can become part of an administrable system of property law, but the state also must consider that the "thing" has sufficient value to be worth state protection. As Blackstone's *Commentaries* remind us, in 1765 "base animals" not good for food or kept merely for a whim were not protected as property. Nina Rattner Gelbart's chapter introduces an intriguing example of one of the most important kinds of immaterial property in the early modern period: property in an office or a profession. (As academics enjoying tenure ought to appreciate, this is still a valuable kind of property.) Some early modern professions took the form of monopolies; for instance, the Royal College of Physicians in England was a kind of monopoly company, possessing a royal charter, permitted to license practitioners, and able to seek redress from the state should unlicensed practitioners poach upon its domain of practice. Gelbart has discovered a more unusual medical practitioner: Mme du Coudray, a French midwife whose apparent expertise was rewarded by the state with *brevets* granting her an annual salary, permitting her to teach throughout the realm (and to issue her own certificates to those she trained), and, apparently, also giving her rights against unlicensed midwives.

As Carol Blum's earlier chapter has indicated, the French in the eighteenth century were extraordinarily concerned about depopulation. In its transactions with Mme du Coudray, an entrepreneur of biology worthy to rank alongside Bakewell, the French government was interested in promoting the birth of as many live infants as possible among the rural poor, not because the rural poor wanted more children, but because the state wanted more citizens. Like Diefendorf's essay on French women and family property, Gelbart's helps to complicate over-simple notions of women as property; here, while the female bodies of peasant mothers were in one sense treated as national property, Mme du Coudray, inventing a job for herself as a mediator between the medical establishment and peasant women, succeeded in creating new forms of property which she herself owned.

An exceptionally sophisticated kind of intangible property was invented by the French state for a class of men called *agents de change*; these brokers possessed an exclusive right to negotiate government and other paper, a right for which they paid a capital sum, rather as one would today buy a seat on a stock exchange. David D. Bien uncovers the delicate dance of negotiation between the French government, possessed of a low credit rating and hungry for capital, and the *agents de change*, who were willing to part with some of their own capital in the expectation of profiting from fees on the transactions they were exclusively licensed to execute. The government, of course, retained the powers to tax or to increase the taxes on these fees, as well as to lessen or to increase the value of an individual's privilege by narrowing or expanding the number of "franchisees." Many similar complex kinds of reification were essential to the success of the various national debt schemes that were hallmarks of the early modern "financial revolution." Public debt and the availability of stock in entities like the English East India Company, in turn, supported these nation-states in their imperial projects.

Colonial and imperial property

Historians are becoming increasingly conscious that early modern history must be understood not only as a history of nationalism in European nation-states and of various forms of enlightenment progress, but also as a history of European imperial projects. Rationales legitimating private property, having a certain common-sense appeal when considered in the at-home contexts of farmers, artisans, or even authors, become more complex and more disturbing when they are played out on the larger field of empire. Indeed, one of the trickiest moves of European political philosophy entailed erasing the personhood of non-Europeans, to whom the positive incentives of the workmanship ideal were said not to apply. Non-European lands, to European eyes, appeared "wastes": barren and uncultivated regions and also lands used so inefficiently that their value was being dissipated. Thus, in *Two Treatises of Civil Government*, Locke manages to read the non-European indigenous inhabitants of these wastes out of the social contract, making their land available for European colonization: "yet there are still great tracts of land to be found, which the inhabitants thereof, not having joined the rest of mankind in the consent of the use of their common money, lie waste, and are more than the people who dwell on it, do, or can make use of, and so still lie in common; though this can scarce happen amongst that part of mankind that have consented to the use of money." A principal stigma of the inhabitants of these wastes was frequently said to be a "barbaric" indifference to the civilized advantages of private property.

Colonization could thus be construed – in a purely secular sense – as a rescue of indigenous peoples from barbarism by conferring upon them the benefits of private property as understood by Europeans. Even the colonization of Ireland was justified after this fashion. According to David Hume's popular *History of England*, native Irish custom ("which supplied the place of law") was "calculated to keep that people for ever in a state of barbarism and disorder." Particularly annoying was the Irish system of sharing property among the lineage and allowing elected chieftains to decide the descent of land. Hume scolded: "As no man, by reason of this custom, enjoyed the fixed property of any land; to build, to plant, to enclose, to cultivate, to improve, would have been so much lost labour."

Recent scholarship has also become newly sensitive to ways in which Europeans failed to perceive both the property rights and the personhood of women among the indigenous peoples whom they encountered. From a feminist point of view, there is a poetic justice in Robert Hughes's account of how the English in Australia attempted to learn the secrets of flax production from the inhabitants of New Zealand. Knowing of Maori linen, they had two Maori tribesmen kidnapped from New Zealand and brought to Norfolk Island – only to discover that men in the tribe had no idea of how to make flax, the production of which was controlled by women. Subtle and adaptive customs of land use and rights in land and animals among Australian Aborigines and American Indians remained equally invisible to European eyes, as European force was used to impose European systems of private ownership.

What is more remarkable, in India, where Europeans had to acknowledge that they had encountered another "civilization," quite complex systems of Indian property law were similarly stigmatized as dysfunctional, "barbaric," "arbitrary," and "tyrannical." The inhabitants of India, understood by the English to have a high civilization, learned literatures, commercial as well as subsistence crops, skilled artisans – even banks, bullion, and tax collectors – hardly seemed to inhabit a Lockean waste available to any civilized cultivator for the taking. Indian civilization, in fact, was rich in variations on the whole range of conceptions of property we have been considering here. One of the most memorable, a very valuable monopoly in the opium trade, figured amongst the impeachment charges against Warren Hastings. Indian opium was shipped to China (although it was illegal there), in exchange for money to purchase tea that was, in turn, shipped to England. No one in England or India objected to the trade itself, but it was alleged against Hastings that he had sold the monopoly to a favorite of his below the market price without advertisement of its availability to other potential purchasers.

In India, the English found a group of people called *zamindars* who had rights to collect taxes and the duty to pass part of what they collected on to the government. The rights of the *zamindars* included some kinds of authority over the people who paid taxes to them, but the *zamindars* were not in the English sense landlords with tenants. The rights which they held were themselves property rights that could be inherited or bought and sold. Bankers acted as brokers between the *zamindars* and the government, handling revenue payments in many different species of currency and remitting bills of exchange to the central treasury. Hardly, one would think, an "uncivilized" system; indeed, since taxation was on the order of one-half or one-fourth of the value of crops, it appears to be an even more powerful revenue-extracting system than the emerging English one John Brewer has described in *Sinews of Power*. Nevertheless, although the

English relied very heavily on these *zamindars* to turn taxes over to them, they came to attack the system as "barbaric" and replaced it with a reconceptualized system. Among the English complaints was the charge that the nature of *zamindars'* property rights was defective, lacking adequate security, and, hence, in the English analysis, not adequately providing incentives to improvement. *Zamindars* were thus in "The Permanent Settlement of Bengal" in 1793 given more absolute property rights in their lands, contingent on providing fixed revenue and subject to forfeiture if for any reason they failed to pay. This was supposed to favor efficient proprietors and lead to large-scale land sales. The older patterns of taxation were attacked as "arbitrary" and "tyrannical" – just as the customary tributes of Irish chieftains had been – allowing the English also to congratulate themselves on saving the native masses from oppression.

Because of the obvious complexity and advanced development of India the creation of English rationales for its conquest is of particular interest. In the eighteenth century, as the work of P. J. Marshall and others makes clear, the principal object of the East India Company and of the British government was the promotion of trade and the collection of revenue; contrary to what one might suppose, missionary activity to convert the inhabitants to Christianity was not yet of much importance. Despite the bitter debates about British policy in India that occurred during the long impeachment trial of Hastings, there was general agreement that the British should stay in the subcontinent. Edmund Burke, Hastings's most savage and persistent opponent, pontificated: the English are placed in India "by the Sovereign Disposer, and we must do the best we can with our situation. The situation of man is the preceptor of his duty." Burke wanted profit for Englishmen without oppression to the Indians. Few at the time would have agreed with the harsher realism of Thomas Erskine in Hastings's defense: "if our dependencies have been secured, and their interest promoted . . . it is mad and preposterous to bring to the standard of justice and humanity, the exercise of a dominion founded upon violence and terror." British belief in the value of private property systems like their own was again and again invoked to legitimate conquest and force used against others.

In this set of chapters on the property of empire we have an opportunity to consider three different kinds of constituencies created by European imperial projects: the stay-at-homes, the European colonizers and settlers in non-European "wastes," and the indigenous peoples whose lives were transformed (or, in too many cases, extinguished). Michael Craton's comparative study of the English settlement of three West Indian islands – Bermuda, Barbados, and Jamaica – allows us to consider the clashes in interests between English colonists and their government back home. From the colonists' point of view, they considered that they were bringing English rights, including rights under English property law and rights to local self-government, with them to their new settlement. From the point of view of London, though, such rights were not always convenient. To the displeasure of its settlers, Jamaica, much the largest of these islands and the only one inhabited when the English arrived, was, at first, said by London to be a "conquered" land where English law did not come into force. Moreover, Craton points out, in the colonies two quite different models of landownership were in conflict: on the one hand, a model of free socage and local self-government that appealed to smallholders drawn by the hope of available land, and, on the other hand, an older, more feudal model which gave chief proprietors governance rights, including rights to collect rents and to appoint officials. As the West Indian colonies were developed, especially as large sugar plantations were established, the interests of large owners often failed to coincide with those of their fellow colonists. And the more reliant the planters became on African slave labor for the cultivation of their sugar, the more they were required to depart from English law by having their local legislatures invent and adopt elaborate slave codes. Ironically, Craton concludes, the colonists' victories in winning their rights to self-legislation against London became opportunities to treat Africans as chattel property.

P. J. Marshall's wide-ranging essay on a crisis of property rights in the English empire of the eighteenth century considers conflicts that broke out between home interests, as represented by Parliament, newly attempting to exercise unprecedented power, and colonists dispersed across this vast empire. In theory, as Craton notes, a distinction was supposed to be observed between the rights of inhabitants in "colonies of conquest," where the law of the conquered country was, essentially, to be preserved, and "colonies of settlement," to which Englishmen were to transport their own laws and privileges; in practice, however, this distinction proved very difficult to maintain. From far-flung points of empire, from New England, from Quebec, and from India, British subjects insisted that they were being deprived of rights belonging to them as British subjects, including rights in property, sometimes lamenting that they had been induced to participate in the imperial project relying on the security of those rights. These cries, though, often fell on deaf parliamentary ears, or, worse, were stigmatized as the pleas of selfish special interests. Instead, Parliament attempted to promote what it believed to be conditions and rules that would maximize the benefits of world trade at home.

Studying early modern Paraguay, Mario Pastore finds Spanish colonists equipped by the Spanish Crown with rights to Indian labor that were roughly analogous to those the English Crown bestowed on the Royal African Company in African labor. The development of the West Indies and of Central America were both joint state-private ventures. Like Keirn an economic historian, Pastore analyzes two different systems of property rights in Indian labor, aiming to explain the conditions under which each was likely to prevail. In this Spanish context, the Pope had granted American lands to the Spanish Crown in exchange for the Crown's undertaking to protect the Indians and to convert them to Christianity. The Crown in turn delegated these functions to Spanish *encomienderos*, compensating the *encomienderos* by rights to Indian labor. Left to their own ways, the Indians did not produce enough saleable surplus to be worth taxing, but when they were coerced into producing crops for export, then the products of their labor could be made to yield tax revenue for the Crown. Under the conditions of land abundance in Paraguay, only labor was scarce, and, Pastore argues, Indian labor (and hence Indians) was like a natural resource that was "overfished" and consequently depleted, despite various efforts of the state to regulate its exploitation.

The construction of some people's property rights in other people's forced labor is further developed in Hilary Beckles's chapter on "white slavery" in the West Indies. It has been customary to draw a sharp distinction between slavery, on the one hand, and indentured servitude, on the other. Yet, as Beckles's chapter demonstrates, there was a much richer variety of rights in labor than this dichotomy would suggest. Property, as the lawyers say, is a "bundle of rights," and a considerable variety of bundles of rights in others' labor was available in the early modern world. Owners' rights might or might not be limited to terms of years, might or might not include the right to control the movements or the total day of the laborer, might or might not include rights to severe corporal discipline of the laborer, and so on. Beckles demonstrates that a category of white "servants" in the West Indies – some there voluntarily (initially), some involuntarily – found themselves subject to laws and customs that had many of the features normally supposed to characterize slavery. To the planter owners, the "white niggers" were a form of capital: they were included in property inventories, used as security for mortgages, bequeathed, sold, and taken by government in lieu of unpaid debts or taxes. Although an Interregnum petition from a number of Englishmen sold as political prisoners to Barbados prompted some affecting parliamentary rhetoric about the offensiveness of selling men, the petitioners were not released from their forced labor alongside the Africans. Racism explains much about the relationships of empire, yet Beckles's research suggests that even the concept of racism has limited explanatory power. Powerful as the workmanship ideal might have been to inspire European philosophers and politicians, it clearly did little for the Indians of Paraguay, for the Africans sold in the West Indies, or even for these "white niggers."

Conclusion

These twenty-six detailed studies of topics in early modern property, we have been suggesting, illuminate theoretical issues of the nature of property that are still of enormous consequence now in fields ranging from labor law to environmental law to the law of intellectual property. From a more purely historical point of view, these studies also demonstrate the inadequacy of an important current view of the nature and significance of changes in the forms of property-holding in the early modern period. It cannot be the case, as many now suppose, that in this period older, multiple use-rights to property were simply supplanted by a rise of absolute property rights. Older ideas that owners held property subject to moral liens by their fellow citizens in need of subsistence persisted throughout the period. Indeed, they were strengthened and elaborated in the late eighteenth century by thinkers and activists like William Ogilvie and Thomas Paine, as Ashcraft's chapter makes clear. Nor, despite some political and legal rhetoric, were absolute property rights ever really practicable, as Gordon demonstrates. In the seventeenth and eighteenth centuries, even interests in land were divided among owners and renters, mortgagors and mortgagees, owners with life estates and remaindermen, or owners with legal interests and owners with equitable interests.

In the newer, emergent kinds of property treated in several of our chapters – the slave-trading monopoly, the literary property of authors, the genetic property of Bakewell, the professional property of Mme de Coudray, the franchises of the *agents de change* – not only were interests fractionated, but nation-states were apt to appear more as interested co-participants, sometimes even co-creators, with the individual entrepreneurial citizen right-holder than as mere passive protectors of individuals' pre-existing goods. Instead of a rise of absolute ownership being the hallmark of early modern property, our chapters seem to point to a more active presence of rival European nation-states, each carefully formulating its own interests and attempting to craft a system of property rights designed to advance them. Thus, in our separate studies, we see state force used to help coerce unfree labor to add to national revenues, state protection of authors' literary property to increase national cultural productivity and glory, state creation of a monopoly on teaching midwifery designed to increase the numbers of citizens, and state-sanctioned monopolies in trading in government paper to help fund government indebtedness and thus to fund more expensive state ambitions. A handy partner for some inventive and entrepreneurial citizens, the early modern state could also be alarmingly predatory toward others.

Yet, even if it weakly described actual systems of property-holding, the rhetoric of absolute private property was politically important. The idea that absolute private property was the best way to incentivize owners and to maximize productivity was used not only to legitimate the enclosing of commons, but also, as we have seen, to legitimate the taking of land from foreign peoples with different systems of property. And the rhetoric of absolute ownership provoked a powerful eighteenth-century counter-rhetoric of human rights in America, in France, and in England.

The Enlightenment in Europe shattered ancient and classical dreams of permanent intelligibility and value, relentlessly insisting on historical and geographical difference. Enlightenment historians accepted that, in some ways at least, despite the most vigorous scholarly efforts, the past would remain irremediably other, irremediably inaccessible and irrelevant. Joseph Wright's human figures in *The Air Pump*, dressed according to the English fashion of the 1760s, cannot effortlessly be resituated in the old stories of Greece and Rome – or in the laboratories of our own day.

Yet, ironically, the old dreams of universal values and significance seem to have been reincarnated, not in aesthetics or philosophy, but in economists' dreams of rational markets populated by profit-maximizers interacting in a one-world economy "from China to Peru." Adam Smith in *An Inquiry into the Nature and Causes of the Wealth of Nations* certainly made a contribution to the progress of mankind when he insisted: "it is but equity, besides, that they who feed, cloath and lodge the whole body of the people, should have such a share of the produce of their own labour as to be themselves tolerably well fed, cloathed and lodged." Yet worship of the mysterious wisdom of "markets" and the promotion of ideas of absolute property and maximum alienability, a legacy from classical economics, can seem like a nightmare reincarnation of the ancient dreams of universal value, dreams that stubbornly deny a real lesson of the Enlightenment about differences in the world. As stewards, rather than "owners," of the world, we cannot treat cattle and literary plots, beaches and stock certificates, uranium mines and mouse genes, all indifferently as interchangeable assets. We need property rules attentive to the use-value of things. As the poet Gerard Manley Hopkins reminds us, we ought to respect and to celebrate the quiddity of things in a world where

> each tucked string tells, each hung bell's
> Bow swung finds tongue to fling out broad its name;
> Each mortal thing does one thing and the same:
>   Deals out that being indoors each one dwells;
>   Selves – goes it self; *myself* it speak and spells,
> Crying *What I do is me; for that I came.*

Part I
Property and political theory

2
Resources, capacities, and ownership
The workmanship ideal and distributive justice

Ian Shapiro

Though the Earth, and all inferior Creatures be common to all Men, yet every Man has a *Property* in his own *Person*. This no Body has any Right to but himself. The *Labour* of his Body, and the *Work* of his hands, we may say, are properly his. Whatsoever then he removes out of the State that Nature hath provided, and left it in, he hath mixed his *Labour* with, and joyned it to something that is his own, and thereby makes it his *Property*. It being by him removed from the common state Nature placed it in, it hath by this *labour* something annexed to it, that excludes the common right of other Men. For this *Labour* being the unquestionable Property of the Labourer, no Man but he can have a right to what that is once joyned to, at least where there is enough, and as good left in common for others.

(John Locke, *Second Treatise of Government*, Section 27)

Human beings generate much of what they want and need by mixing their productive capacities with other resources, producing objects and services of value. This fact about human creativity has been incorporated into Western thinking about distributive justice via the workmanship ideal of ownership. It revolves around the conviction that so long as the resources with which people mix their productive capacities are justly acquired they may legitimately own the product of the conjunction. Just how to organize things so that the caveat embedded in the workmanship ideal is not violated has been subject to vituperative debate for centuries, as have the meaning of and justification for the premise that a people may be said to own their productive capacities in the first place. In a number of idioms both intellectual and political the workmanship ideal sets the terms of debate about the just distribution, ownership, and even definition of property.[1]

The enduring intensity of arguments about this ideal signifies that it retains a powerful hold on the Western political imagination and it is the hold as much as the ideal that concerns me in this chapter. In a deconstructionist spirit I try to account for our collective inability to let go of the ideal, despite major conceptual difficulties it confronts. In a constructive spirit I try to adduce support for the view that partly because of its internal tensions the workmanship ideal can defensibly be part of our thinking about distributive justice only in a limited and conditional way; we must not expect too much from it, nor should we attribute to the rights it spawns a necessary trumping power with respect to competing justice values.

In the first section I argue that the workmanship ideal first formulated in its modern form by Locke was part of an internally cohesive view of just ownership that derived part of its intellectual appeal from the fact that it situated the rights of workmanship in a complex moral scheme that left room for other demands of social justice. I also argue, however, that the attractiveness and coherence of Locke's view depended on theological assumptions that have long since been jettisoned in the dominant intellectual traditions of the West. Yet because of the powerful appeal of the intuitions that drive the workmanship ideal many have tried to formulate secular variants of it; they have sought historical linking strategies that can be used to tether legitimate property rights to the work of productive agents. Sections II and III are devoted to analysis of the two main variants of such strategies that have grown out of the Marxist and neoclassical traditions of political economy. This leads to a discussion – in section IV – of why historical linking strategies invariably fail, running into insuperable problems of over-determination and threatening perpetually to swamp the competing values with which property regimes are bound to coexist in any intellectually compelling account of social justice. This conclusion seems naturally to counsel abandoning historical linking strategies altogether, a possibility I examine in section V via a discussion of recent attempts by John Rawls and Ronald Dworkin to displace them with socialized views of human productive capacities. But the proposal that we should abandon the workmanship ideal turns out to be as troublesome as are the difficulties created by embracing secular variants of it. In section VI I discuss two possible ways out of the conundrum thus generated: one involves embracing a variant of the workmanship ideal on consequentialist grounds although conceding it to rest partly on causal and moral fictions; the second, which need not be inconsistent with the first, requires us to treat the workmanship ideal as part of a democratic conception of distributive justice. I suggest briefly in conclusion that this latter course is better.

I   Theological foundations of the classical workmanship ideal

Locke's theory of property was elegant, coherent, and – if one accepts the premises to which he was committed – compelling.[2] He thought that human labor is the main source of value, but he believed that natural resources make an independent – if comparatively minor – contribution to the value of produced goods and services.[3] Against Filmer (who had insisted that God gave the world to Adam and his heirs via an hierarchical system of inheritance), Locke argued that God gave the world to mankind in common, subject to two constraints: that it not be wasted, and that any individual's use of the common to produce his own property was subject to the restriction that "enough, and as good" remain available to others to use in common.[4]

Locke's treatment of human capacities was linked to his theology in a different way.

It rested on his categorial distinction between natural right and natural law which explained human autonomy. Natural law, Locke tells us, "ought to be distinguished from natural right: for right is grounded in the fact that we have the free use of a thing, whereas law enjoins or forbids the doing of a thing." Right, then, is a different kind of thing from law, the former indicating a capacity for autonomous action, and the latter externally imposed obligatory constraints.[5] It is through acts of autonomous making that rights over what is created come into being: making entails ownership so that natural law is at bottom God's natural right over his creation.[6] Locke's frequent appeals to metaphors of workmanship and watchmaking in the *Two Treatises* and elsewhere make it fundamental that men are obliged to God because of his purposes in making them. Men are "the Workmanship of one Omnipotent, and infinitely wise Maker. . . . They are his Property, whose Workmanship they are, made to last during his, not one another's pleasure."[7]

For Locke human beings are unique among God's creations because he gave them the capacity to make, to create rights of their own. Natural law may dictate that man is subject to divine imperatives to live in certain ways, but within the limits set by the law of nature men can act – as Tully notes – in a godlike fashion: "[m]an as maker . . . has analogous maker's knowledge of, and a natural right in his intentional actions." Provided we do not violate natural law, we stand in the same relation to the objects we create as God stands in to us; we own them just as he owns us.[8] This is not to say that for Locke all our capacities are God-given or that their development is uninfluenced by social arrangements; he thought that productive capacities could be bought and sold in ways that increased productivity and there is some evidence that he believed workers' productivity to be influenced by mercantile workhouse discipline.[9] Certainly there was potential for tension between these causal beliefs and the workmanship ideal; we will see that arguments that human activity and organization shape productive capacities would eventually be pressed into the service of an explosive immanent critique of that ideal.[10] But so long as human creative power was seen as a gift from God this possibility could be staved off; even if productive capacities are influenced by human agency, this agency finds its genesis and limits in the will of a beneficent deity.

Locke conceived of the range of human activities free of God's sanctions quite broadly; certainly it included most of what is conventionally thought of as the realm of the production and consumption of goods.[11] But the existence of natural law constraints on human autonomy meant that there were circumstances in which the exercise of otherwise legitimate rights of appropriation would be curtailed. If Locke's provisos were violated, for instance, the right to appropriate from nature would be limited. Likewise someone starving and disabled would have the right to another's plenty based on the natural law requirements of the right of preservation, and someone starving and able-bodied would have the right to the means of preservation – the right to materials to work on to preserve oneself, whether by means of the workhouse system or coerced labor for a landowner. In addition, there were limits, for Locke, to the reparations a conqueror could legitimately demand in wartime having to do with the subsistence rights of the wives and children of defeated soldiers.[12]

The existence of Locke's natural law constraints thus meant that not all rights were of the same kind; property rights occupied a circumscribed space in an hierarchical system. Productive human actions issue in rights and obligations that are binding on human beings, but these are not the only types of moral claims to which Locke believed us subject. Although not independent of the workmanship model (natural law was argued to be valid as God's workmanship) these other moral claims were conceived of as prior to claims of human workmanship.[13] To be sure, there would be disputes about when and how the natural law requirements are triggered and about the degree to which they limit property rights in particular instances which the natural law theory could not by itself resolve; as Ashcraft has shown with respect to eighteenth-century English debates about poor relief, the scope of what subsistence requires could be expanded and pressed into the service of a radical Lockean critique of the claims of capital.[14] But if the theory left balancing the claims of the competing requirements of natural law and human workmanship open to interpretation and political argument at least at the margins, it also undermined the presumption that rights of human appropriation necessarily trump competing just claims.

II   Secularizing the workmanship ideal: Marxism

Marx's labor theory of value was in many respects more sophisticated than Locke's. He famously distinguished labor from labor-power, and developed the concepts of abstract human labor and socially necessary labor time, and from them the theory of exploitation of labor by capital. Yet Marx held onto the basic logic of the workmanship ideal, even though he transformed it radically by secularizing it and locating it in a dynamic theory of historical change.

Since Locke's treatment of both resources and capacities had been linked to his theology, both would now have to be treated differently. For Marx resources cease to be of independent moral significance; the value of a natural resource is determined by the socially necessary labor time required for its appropriation from nature or the value concealed in it as a consequence of its earlier appropriation. God is no longer needed as the giver of natural resources since they are by definition without value apart from the human capacities needed for their appropriation. Not until the marginalists' rejection of the labor theory of value in the late nineteenth century would natural resources re-enter the explanatory and moral calculus as an independent unit of value, and by then the theory of markets would offer different conceptual tools for dealing with them.

If resources are secularized by being reconceptualized as moral proxies for capacities, what of the treatment of capacities themselves? Are we still the ultimate owners of our capacities for Marx, and if so, why? In *The Critique of the Gotha Program* Marx offers his most elaborate discussion of his views about the ultimate basis of entitlements in the course of a discussion of fair socialist distribution. Defining the cooperative proceeds of labor as the "total social product" he argues that after various deductions have been made by the state, the balance of the surplus becomes available for consumption.[15] Because distribution in the early stages of communism is "still stamped with the birth marks of the old society from whose womb it emerges," it will continue to be based on work. The individual producer receives back from society, after the deductions have been made, "exactly what he gives to it."[16] In these circumstances "the same principle prevails as that which regulates the exchange of commodities," but it is nonetheless an advance on capitalism because "under the altered circumstances no one can give anything except his labour," and "nothing can pass into the ownership of individuals except individual means of consumption." Thus although "equal right" continues to mean "bourgeois right" under socialism, "principle and practice are no longer at loggerheads."[17]

Marx concedes that this principle will generate inequalities by virtue of the fact that actual work becomes the basic metric of equality. Since labor must be defined either by duration or intensity to function as a measure at all, and since people differ from one another in physical and mental capacities, the right to each according to his work is unavoidably "an unequal right for unequal labor." He also notes that these inequalities will be exacerbated by the differing social circumstances of different workers.[18] Such defects are inevitable through the early stages of communism, but in a "higher phase" of it "after the enslaving subordination of the individual to the division of labor, and with it also the antithesis between mental and physical labor, has vanished" and the "springs of cooperative wealth flow more abundantly," then the "narrow horizon of bourgeois right" can be "crossed in its entirety" and distribution can be based on needs. The transcendence of every regime of right is seen as necessary for the triumph of genuine equality; the work-based regime of socialism is not special in this regard; it is "a right of inequality, in its content, like every right."[19]

The workmanship ideal plays a role throughout Marx's account, but it should not be confused with his formulation of the labor theory of value. This is the causal thesis that only living human labor-power creates exchange-value, and that exchange-value determines price in a capitalist economy. Marx believed it explained the phenomenon of exploitation under capitalism by generating an account of how exchange-value accrues to the capitalist as a byproduct of the difference between the value of the wages he pays his workers and the value of the products those workers produce. In Marx's hands the labor theory of value thus became a vehicle for incorporating the moral appeal of the workmanship ideal into arguments about the production and distribution of wealth in a different way than had been the case with Locke; it rested on a different variant of the labor theory of value. Yet in neither case is the workmanship ideal part of or reducible to the labor theory of value. The ideal rests on the moral thesis that the legitimate basis of entitlement lies in productive action, and it is only because of the intuitive moral appeal of this thesis that the labor theory of value was thought to be pregnant with moral significance.

It is not surprising, therefore, that Marxists who have abandoned the labor theory of value nonetheless affirm variants of the workmanship ideal. G. A. Cohen argues that exploitation under capitalism derives not from the problematical thesis that the workers alone produce value, only that the workers alone produce the product.[20] Conceding that capitalists may *act productively* by investing, he distinguishes this from *producing goods*, which, he argues, is exclusively done by workers. Whether Cohen is right about this we need not settle now; that he makes the argument at all exhibits his reliance on the intuitive moral pull of the workmanship ideal.[21] This reliance becomes explicit in two essays on the relations between self-ownership and world-ownership where Cohen advances criticisms of Nozick that rely on affirming the idea that we own our productive capacities and the goods, in certain circumstances, which they are instrumental in generating.[22]

Likewise, John Roemer assumes that people own their productive capacities, and defines exploitation and unfairness (for him these two are not the same) in terms of distribution of the alienable means of production that force or supply incentives to workers to produce goods that become the property of capitalists.[23] To pack any moral punch such arguments must rest on the claim that such class monopoly is unjustifiable, and when we ask why, the answer turns out to rely either on the claim that the monopoly was achieved via illicit appropriation of the proceeds of the work of others or on an argument that the class monopoly prevents workers' realizing at least some of the potential fruits of their own labor, or both. Thus Roemer resists the possibility that the class monopoly might have come about as a result of differences in natural abilities or propensities toward risk on historical and probabilistic grounds, and he defines unfairness and exploitation by reference to counterfactuals in which individuals or classes would produce more goods by as much work as or less work than is the case when the class monopoly obtains.[24]

If the workmanship ideal is implicated in Marxist critiques of capitalist exploitation whether or not these rest on the labor theory of value, what is its role in Marx's positive argument for the superiority of socialism over capitalism and of communism over socialism? His appeal to the workmanship ideal might be interpreted as an *ad hominem* polemical charge that socialism is an advance on capitalism because under it those who actually do the work are rewarded as bourgeois ideology requires. Yet to claim that what is wrong with capitalism is that it fails to live up to a standard that cannot, anyhow, be independently justified is to say less than Marx wanted or needed to say. One has only to think of other systems to which he objected – notably feudalism – that were not subject to the particular defect of hypocrisy as capitalism allegedly is, to realize that Marx's critical arguments were intended to have more far-reaching moral impact.[25] Throughout his writings human beings are described as productive creatures, creating their means of subsistence in ways that decisively shape other aspects of their lives and identities as persons. Even a communist society, where the existence of a superabundance of wealth frees people from necessity, is described by the mature Marx as a society of free *producers*.[26] The workmanship ideal thus captured something in Marx's positive conception of the human condition that motivated his attack on modes of production that alienate people from their productive natures. Certainly the ideal was much changed in Marx's hands; it took on a dynamic character deriving from the romantic expressivist notion that human beings produce not only the means for their subsistence but also, and as a result of that fact, themselves. This meant that the distributive implications of the ideal were more complex than in Locke's mechanistic view of the relation between the producer and his product, more complex – as will become plain in section IV – than even Marx realized. But the workmanship ideal remained, nonetheless, the basic legitimating ideal of human ownership.[27]

Workmanship diminishes in significance for Marx when we turn attention to the argument that socialism is merely transitional to a needs-based communist regime of superabundance, although even here it retains a residual influence on his view. First there is the negative pole in Marx's implicit justificatory argument: a communist utopia is conceived of as the only possible regime in which there is no exploitation of one class by another. By thus requiring its own negation the theory of exploitation leaves an indelible stamp on the depiction of communism, and so, inevitably, does the workmanship ideal which gives the theory of exploitation its critical moral bite. Second there is the assumption driving Marx's defense of collective allocation of the productive surplus in *The Critique of the Gotha Program* and elsewhere, namely that under conditions of advanced division of labor private allocation is not defensible, and collective allocation is, on the grounds that the surplus is collectively produced.[28] This assumption has only to be stated for its reliance on the workmanship ideal to become plain. If making was not thought to entail ownership there would be no basis for arguing that the relations of mutual reliance and enhanced productivity resulting from the division of labor both reveal private appropriation as illegitimate and justify collective allocation of the collectively produced surplus. Unless we interpret superabundance to mean that a situation could arise in which no distributive choices of any kind would ever have to be made (because everyone could always have everything that they wanted or needed) Marx would presumably continue to embrace some variant of this workmanship-based defense of collective decision-making.[29] In this way Marx's speculations about the post-capitalist future affirm the justificatory power of the workmanship ideal, even if he often relies on a mixture of *ad hominem* argument and intuitionist appeal – rather than principled justification – in its defense.

III Secularizing the workmanship ideal: neoclassical views

Like most Marxists, neoclassical political and economic theorists exhibit an abiding commitment to the workmanship ideal that has long survived the marginalists' abandonment of the labor theory of value. Indeed, the labor theory was rejected partly on the grounds that, since the causal story it tells was thought by the marginalists to be false, attempts to use it as a basic yardstick for thinking about distributive fairness violate the ideal; such attempts were argued not to take into account the productive contributions of capitalists. Modern neoclassicists thus retain a commitment to the notion that the act of working creates entitlements in the object or service produced by the relevant work; indeed they typically defend acquisition of goods through exchange by reference to the claim that an agent is entitled to dispose of what she has produced however she likes. It is no accident that Robert Nozick's critique of redistributive taxation reduces to the claim that it is "forced labor."[30]

The principal neoclassical strategy for secularizing the workmanship ideal replaces the Lockean theology with a foundational appeal to the value of individual autonomy, whether for more or less Kantian reasons. Its proponents link property rights over the products of one's productive capacities to the preservation of autonomy, as in Nozick's claim that everyone has an inviolable right to what he has himself produced or received as a consequence of voluntary exchange. It is an open secret that where these rights come from is never fully accounted for in such arguments, and that the freedoms they preserve are purely formal.[31] Typically, as in Nozick's case, there is some appeal to Locke, but without grappling with the issues inevitably raised once Locke's limited defense of private appropriation is detached from its theological moorings. Thus Richard Posner embraces a variant of the Kantian argument when arguing that no injustice results from the fact that in a market system "people who lack sufficient earning power to support even a minimally decent standard of living are entitled to no say in the allocation of resources unless they are part of the utility function of someone who has wealth." He resists the Rawlsian critique of this view (taken up in section V below), insisting that treating the more and less well endowed as equally entitled to valuable resources "does not take seriously the differences between persons," and indeed that any redistributive taxation policy "impairs the autonomy of those from whom redistribution is made."

Posner concedes that this procedure has the implication that "if an individual happens to be born feeble-minded and his net social product is negative, he would have no right to the means of support even though there was nothing blameworthy in his inability to support himself." Yet he insists that although this conclusion might be argued to violate the autonomy of the feeble-minded, there is no escape from it "consistent with any of the major ethical systems." This is a view he shares with John Harsanyi who asserts against Rawls and without argument that our abilities "are parts of our own inner selves and belong to us as a matter of sheer natural fact." That such declarations are deemed sufficient to bridge the fact/value gap and to legitimate secular variants of the workmanship ideal is testimony to its captivating power; no principled argument is thought to be needed in their defense.[32]

IV   Difficulties confronting secular variants of the workmanship ideal

In both Marxist and neoclassical traditions, then, the workmanship ideal has exhibited a staying power that has long outlived both its theological origins and the labor theories of value to which it was initially linked. Yet in its secular form the workmanship ideal confronts two major types of conceptual difficulty. These combine to throw into sharp relief the difficulties in determining the nature of and limits to human-produced entitlements once we are without Locke's natural law limiting constraints such as the provisos, the requirements of charity, and the legitimate demands of dependants.

First, luck in the genetic pool and in the circumstances into which one happens to be born plays a substantial role in what kind of productive capacities people develop and are able to develop. The resulting inequalities seem to be deeply at odds with what is attractive in the logic of the workmanship ideal, since these are only the proximate result of the work of the relevant producing agent. If two people work equally hard but one is twice as productive because of her more effective natural capacities or her better nurtured capacities, it seems that in a deeper sense it is not her work but her superior genetic or nutritional luck that is at the basis of her relative advantage. If differences deriving from natural capacity or social condition were traceable ultimately to the will of God, they need not seem unjustifiable, nor need it be the responsibility of human society to counteract their effects. Once these differences are thought about by reference to secular understandings of workmanship, however, they are bound to become morally controversial.

Second, because human productive capacities are themselves partly produced by human work, it seems arbitrary to treat a given producing agent as the "final" owner of his productive capacities to begin with. Locke saw our productive capacities as God-given, so the question of why we might be said to own them never arose for him; indeed their very existence was part of what marked off the ultimate moral boundaries among persons. But in the absence of a theology which dictates this assumption, defenders of secular variants of the workmanship ideal have to confront the difficulty of how to specify the morally relevant boundaries among persons *qua* productive creatures. American courts have begun to recognize how complex this can be in divorce settlements in recent years. The domestic labor performed in support of a spouse attaining a professional qualification is treated as part of the relevant work in creating the capacity to generate the income that the qualification brings. For this reason, the divorcing spouse who performed the domestic labor is given a property interest in the stream of future income that the now qualified divorcing spouse is newly capable of generating.[33] As a philosophical matter the intuition behind this type of example has been generalized by feminist theorists to make the point, for instance, that it was morally arbitrary for Marx to try to measure the rate of exploitation by exclusive reference to the relation between the surplus produced and the money wage paid to the worker. Any such calculation ignores the contributions of the worker's spouse to his capacity to work which he rents to the capitalist, and which Marx arbitrarily takes to be the worker's "own." From this standpoint Marx's argument can be turned on the worker's relationship with his spouse to reveal *it* in certain circumstances to be exploitative.[34] It is indeed surprising that Marxists have attended so little to the significance of produced productive capacities, both for the coherence of the self-ownership thesis which they generally embrace and for its distributive implications.[35]

In short, if the use of productive capacities generates entitlements, and if productive capacities are themselves partly produced by the work of others, then tracing the moral reach of a particular productive capacity exercised in the production of a particular nonhuman object becomes exceedingly complex, arguably impossible even in principle. For the feminist point can itself be generalized: the productive capacities a conventional wife "has" that she expends in her husband's attainment of a professional qualification were no doubt themselves partly produced by the work of others: parents, perhaps children, Sunday school teachers who drummed into her a particular mixture of the work ethic and conventional family values, and so on. If one pushes to the limit the idea of productive capacity as the moral basis for entitlement, it seems to point in the direction of a tangled and indecipherable web of overdetermined entitlements, and indeed to reveal a deep tension at the core of the workmanship ideal itself. The claim that we own what we make in virtue of our ownership of our productive capacities undermines the claim that we own our productive capacities, once it is conceded that those capacities are themselves produced partly by the work of others. Yet if we want to employ a variant of the workmanship ideal without pushing it to the limit, and in the absence of a theological limiting device such as Locke's, then the difficulty remains of how to do the pertinent line-drawing without inviting charges of arbitrariness.

V   The workmanship ideal and the socialization of capacities strategy

These formidable difficulties lend seriousness to the suggestion that we abandon the workmanship ideal altogether. This possibility has been most fully explored by John Rawls and Ronald Dworkin in different ways as part of a larger debate about whether resources, welfare, or some intermediate metric should form the basic unit of account of theories of distributive justice. The initial impetus for their turn to resource-based theories was the perceived defects of welfarist views like utilitarianism which seem to require either too little or too much in the way of interpersonal judgments of utility to be morally satisfying. In classical (objective) welfarism, where cardinal scales and interpersonal comparisons of utility are permitted, welfarist theories are vulnerable to the charge that they fail to take seriously the differences among persons, since paternalistic judgments may be employed to increase one person's welfare at the expense of another's. Yet if the neoclassical move toward subjective welfarism is made and interpersonal comparisons are disallowed, welfarism either requires information about mental states on which it seems impossible to rely without generating perverse incentives for the systematic misrepresentation of preferences or it is managed through the market-based theory of revealed preference. This latter strategy runs into the disquieting fact that people have different resources to express preferences in a market system, neatly summed up in Anatole France's quip that the poor are free to sleep under the bridges of Paris.[36] These difficulties with welfarism are no less intractable than they are oft repeated; resourcism is attractive because it appears to open up the possibility of avoiding them. Its motivating idea is that some set of instrumental goods – such as Rawls's primary goods – can be thought of as valuable for all rational individual conceptions of the good life, and it is those that should be justly distributed without reference to the mental states (or welfare otherwise construed) that they allegedly engender.[37]

Rawls and Dworkin both argue that like other resources human capacities should for certain purposes be regarded as social goods. This socialization of capacities strategy may be thought of as a mirror image of the classical Marxian one: where for Marx nonhuman resources cease to be of independent moral interest, being reducible to the capacities necessarily expended in their creation or their separation from nature, on this view capacities cease to be of independent moral interest: they are treated as social resources like any other. Thus Rawls argues forcibly that differences both in natural abilities and in contingencies of upbringing are morally arbitrary factors that should not in principle determine the rewards people receive, usefully rendering the nature/nurture debate beside the point for arguments about distributive justice.[38] Similarly, Dworkin treats human capacities and external material resources as moral equivalents from the standpoint of distributive justice, arguing that although there may be good reasons for resisting the redistribution of physical and mental resources (insofar as this is technologically feasible), a case might nonetheless be made for compensating those with inferior physical and mental resources for their relative incapacities.[39]

Given the preceding discussion of luck and produced capacities it might be suggested that there is no way genuinely to link entitlements to work other than via some variant of the socialization of capacities strategy, that it alone can consummate the workmanship ideal. This is true, I think, but the variant of the ideal thus saved is so thin that it dispenses with a good part of what gives it its intuitive appeal. This has to do with the psychological side of workmanship, with the sense of subjective satisfaction that attaches to the idea of making something that one can subsequently call one's own. We all know the feeling, and it is not easily argued that it can apply to a generalized notion that there is a sense in which I, along with everyone else, own everything that everyone appears at a given time and place to make. And for a species so critically reliant as is ours on productive activity for survival it seems self-defeating to deny the legitimacy of so powerful a spur to productive activity as the psychic activity which producing something that one can own brings.

This may be why theorists like Rawls and Dworkin balk at the implications of the socialization of capacities strategy. Rawls supplies a list of primary goods which are held to be desirable for any rational life-plan but he explicitly refuses to confront the implications of his account of the moral arbitrariness of differing capacities, when he holds that the effectiveness with which people are able to use resources, or choose to use them, is not a relevant consideration in deciding how resources should be distributed. There are two different issues here, both of which raise internal tensions in the Rawlsian account. One derives from Amartya Sen's point that if we really want justly to distribute what people of greatly different capacities are enabled to do, then we cannot use Rawlsian primary goods; we need a different metric which takes account of how different people employ capacities and resources, as basic.[40] Second, there is the point made by Cohen, Nagel, Arneson and others, that different people have different preferences and goals, some more expensive and more difficult to satisfy than others. Rawls's attempt to sidestep this problem by arguing that these are not afflictions but are chosen scarcely meets the objection because, as Scanlon and others have noted, often they are not.[41]

Dworkin also balks at the implications of the socialization of capacities strategy. He invites us to speculate on how resources might in principle be equalized by use of a hypothetical auction in which all parties begin with the same finite number of bargaining chips.[42] As part of this he argues that human capacities should be thought of as resources, yet there are two ways in which he dodges the full implications of the socialization of capacities strategy. First he claims that although capacities (his term is "physical and mental powers") are resources and as a consequence legitimate objects of a theory of distributive justice, they should nonetheless be treated differently from "independent material resources." With physical and mental powers, the goal should not be to strive to distribute them justly (which, for Dworkin, means equally). Instead the problem is construed as one of discovering "how far the ownership of independent external resources should be affected by differences that exist in physical and mental powers, and the response of our theory should speak in that vocabulary."[43] For this reason he argues that people should be compensated by reference to a standard arrived at by our speculations concerning whether and to what extent people would, on average, have insured against the particular handicap or disability or lack of talent *ex ante*, assuming that insurance rates would be set in a competitive market.[44]

Notice that Dworkin supplies no principled argument for why physical and mental powers should be treated differently from material resources, from the standpoint of distributive justice. The assertion that they "cannot be manipulated or transferred, even so far as technology permits" is not further explained or justified, but since Dworkin has chosen to treat powers *as* resources an explanation is surely in order.[45] This is so not least because compensation in any amount will sometimes be inadequate to equalize a power – or capacity – deficiency (as in the case of blindness), as Dworkin elsewhere notes, yet equality of resources is his basic criterion of distributive justice. In such circumstances compensation based on a standard set by a hypothetical insurance auction cannot be said to equalize the resources of two persons, one blind, one sighted.[46] Yet it is not always true, *pace* Dworkin, that their powers of sight *could not* be equalized.[47] The state might forcibly transplant an eye from a sighted person to the blind one in order to equalize their resources, or, for that matter, simply blind the sighted person. Less callously and more interestingly, it might invest billions of dollars on research into and development of artificial eyes, financed by a tax on the sighted. If Dworkin is to avoid such unpalatable results, he must supply an argument for why we may be said to be entitled to our powers and capacities (and in some sense responsible for having or lacking them) in different (and trumping) ways than we can be said to be entitled to material resources, given his equation of the two. In the absence of such an argument it is difficult to see how Dworkin can adopt the socialization of capacities strategy in principle, yet simply assert that people are entitled to, and responsible for, their capacities and incapacities in fact.

The second way in which Dworkin refuses to live with the socialization of capacities strategy which he otherwise embraces concerns his discussion of how our conception of a person should be distinguished from our conception of her circumstances. Dworkin argues that we need a view of distributive justice that is "ambition-sensitive," which requires a view of equality in terms of which people "decide what sorts of lives to pursue against a background of information about the actual costs that their choices impose on other people and hence on the total stock of resources that may fairly be used by them." This he tries to achieve by assigning "tastes and ambitions" to the person, and "physical and mental powers" to his "circumstances," arguing that the former are not relevant considerations in deciding how resources should be distributed.[48] In this way he hopes to redeem an island of creative autonomy for the individual agent. He wants to rescue the kernel of what is intuitively attractive in the workmanship ideal, the idea that when people conceive of and put into practice productive plans, the benefits from the resulting actions should flow back to them. Yet he wants to do this without being swamped by the difficulties of overdetermination that flow from the Rawlsian claim that the distribution of physical and mental powers is morally arbitrary.[49]

Dworkin's strategy fails. The volitions we are able to form, the ambitions it occurs to us to develop: these are greatly influenced, perhaps even determined, by our powers and capacities. To "think big," to "resolve to go for broke," to steel oneself through self-control to perform demanding acts: do these reflect ambition or capacity? When we describe someone as ambitious, are we not describing something more basic to her psychology and constitution than her tastes? There are certainly circumstances in which we would say that lack of confidence is an incapacity that prevents the formation (not just the attainment) of particular ambitions. Different people have different capacities to form different ambitions, and those different capacities must be as morally tainted from Dworkin's point of view as any other capacities. That Donald Trump is able to develop more far-reaching ambitions than Archie Bunker is due at least partly to luck in the genetic pool and in the circumstances of his upbringing.[50]

Similar arguments can be made about the different abilities to form (or refrain from forming) different kinds of tastes, whether expensive, compulsive, or both, as Dworkin is aware. The case Dworkin considers is where a person might have an incapacitating obsession that he wishes he did not have, and Dworkin deals with this by arguing that such cravings may be thought of as handicaps and thus handled via his hypothetical insurance scheme.[51] But this is to sidestep the point being made here, which is that the obsession may itself incapacitate a person from forming the relevant second-order desire to make Dworkin's hypothetical insurance solution work. Are we to say of an alcoholic whose affliction is so severe that he cannot even form the desire not to be an alcoholic that his preference for alcohol results from his *taste* rather than his *incapacity*? I think not.[52]

With all acquired tastes (not just the expensive), experiencing the taste is by definition conditional on the exercise of pertinent capacities. A taste for good beer, or even just for beer, a taste for a particular kind of music, perhaps even for any music, these can be developed only through the exercise of relevant capacities. We would not say of a deaf woman that she could have a taste for music of a particular sort, or even a taste for music of any sort (although of course we could intelligibly say that such a person might perhaps wish that she was able to have such a taste). Likewise with beer and someone who had no functioning tastebuds or sense of smell. The idea that we form our tastes and ambitions in some way that is independent of our resources and capacities is too whiggish, as would be revealed to anyone who tried to perform a thought-experiment in which she was required to decide on her future tastes and ambitions while kept in ignorance of her powers and capacities. Surely we have learned this much from two decades of debate about the veil of ignorance. What drives Dworkin's intuition here is the notion that people should be held responsible only for the choices they make in life, not for things over which they have no control. A variant of this thesis might be defensible, but Dworkin's treatment of it is unpersuasive. His replacement of the resources versus capacities distinction with the ambitions and tastes versus physical and mental powers distinction fails to rescue the Lockean notion of an autonomous agent, of whom rights and responsibilities may legitimately be predicated.

To sum up: like Rawls, Dworkin is unable to live with the deterministic implications of the socialization of capacities strategy. This, I have suggested, is partly because when taken to its logical conclusion this strategy undermines what is attractive in the workmanship ideal. Yet reluctant as Rawls and Dworkin both are to abandon their intuitive commitments to the idea of moral agency that informs the ideal, neither has supplied an account of how this can be rendered consistent with the socialization of capacities strategy which both feel compelled to endorse. This reflects deep tensions within the secular variant of the workmanship ideal itself; it presses relentlessly toward a determinism which its very terms suggest we ought to be able to deny.

VI Productive fictions: consequentialist and democratic considerations

Historical linking strategies fail to tie regimes of entitlement to the work of productive agents in morally satisfying ways, yet theorists who have explored the full implications of junking them find the consequences too threatening to the idea of personal responsibility, even of personal identity, to stomach. This is partly because once the labor theory of value has been rejected there is no evident method to assess which work performed by whom ought to be compensated in what amount when a given object or service is produced. Liberal theorists have often argued or assumed that the market generates the appropriate system of rewards, but we saw in section III that this is not so; neoclassical variants of the workmanship ideal take for granted prevailing distributions of resources and capacities as matters of "sheer natural fact" without justificatory argument. However, the failure of the traditional contending theories to generate a metric by reference to which we might plausibly assess productive contributions does not undermine the intuition that there are productive contributions and that these should play some role in just distribution; this fact at least partly accounts for the inability of people like Rawls and Dworkin to stick consistently to the socialization of capacities strategy.

The difficulty runs deeper than a problem of measurement, however. The tensions internal to the workmanship ideal are partly reminiscent of this paradox of free will: a person may find it both rationally undeniable and psychologically impossible to accept that all his actions are determined. In a similar spirit it might be argued that for both individual and species some fictions about workmanship may be required for reproduction and well-being even if we know them to be fictions. The belief that autonomous productive action is possible may be indispensable to the basic integrity of the human psyche and necessary for generating and sustaining the incentive to work on which human beings are, after all, critically reliant. As a result, although facts about moral luck and produced productive capacities conspire – when confronted – to enfeeble the workmanship ideal, people may nonetheless be powerless to abandon it.

These considerations might reasonably be thought to counsel embracing a variant of the workmanship ideal on consequentialist grounds while conceding it to rest partly on causal and moral fictions. There is much to be said in support of such a view, but rather than explore it at length here I will take brief note of three difficulties it is bound to confront. To some extent these will already be obvious from my repeated use of "may" and its cognates in the preceding paragraph.

First, although a wide consensus might be possible on the principle of a consequentialist defense, it seems inevitable that there would be an equally wide dissensus over what it entails in practice. It is not only the labor theory of value and neoclassical price theory that fail to reward work impartially; no neutral system of rewards has ever been developed. As a consequence, whatever fiction is employed will work to the disproportionate benefit of some and be subject to endemic political controversy – as Marx noted so perspicaciously in his discussion of rights under socialism.[53]

Second, distributive questions aside, the consequentialist benefits of workmanship are not beyond legitimate controversy. If it gets out of control the work ethic can be subversive of psychological well-being and promote morally unattractive kinds of acquisitiveness, and the realization that invisible hands can as often be malevolent as benign suggests that the consequentialist effects of embracing the workmanship ideal will not always be beneficial. A legitimating ethic that encourages productive action can easily thus become too much of a good thing, and it can have external effects (on the environment, for instance) that are bound to be controversial politically.

Third, if a variant of the workmanship ideal is embraced on consequentialist grounds questions must arise concerning its appropriate range, given the inevitability of its conflict with other justice values. Once it is conceded that the rights of human workmanship have no natural status or special trumping moral power, then there is bound to be controversy about where they fit into a governing distributive scheme that must cope with multiple demands on scarce resources – from redressing the effects of historical disadvantage, to caring for the sick and elderly, to supporting just causes in other countries. In short, it seems unlikely that a consequentialist scheme could be developed that would or should be beyond the bounds of political controversy.

These are not intuitions about mere implementation. Once it is conceded, in a world of endemic scarcity, that there is neither a theological model nor a calculus of contribution from which correct distributive injunctions can be "read off," we have to come to grips with the primacy of politics to arguments about distributive justice. It is remarkable, in this light, that so little attention has been paid by justice theorists to how and by whom their principles should be implemented – particularly given the dismal historical records of both *laissez-faire* and statist distributive regimes.[54] The idea that what is just in the distribution of social goods can be reasoned about independently of how such justice might practically be achieved rests on inappropriate expectations from philosophy, thrown into sharp relief by the undergraduate who insisted on knowing why, now that Rawls's difference principle had "been established," the Constitution had not yet been changed to incorporate it. Although few academic theorists will permit themselves such revealing directness, much of the debate I have been discussing here proceeds on the assumption that there is a correct answer, that Rawls, Dworkin, Nozick, Cohen, or someone else will eventually get it right. But if the reasoning being pressed here is accepted, whether and to what degree the workmanship ideal should be institutionalized is a political question not a philosophical one, and as a consequence rights of workmanship cannot fairly be thought of as anterior to the political process.

The research agenda opened up by this conclusion is to explore ways of developing and grappling with the implications of democratic distributive principles. To attempt such exploration now would take us too far from the scope of the present chapter. Here let me note in conclusion that Cohen and other justice theorists may be right that in democratic systems there is the permanent possibility for tyranny of the majority, but the risks of this should be evaluated not against some unspecified ideal of a just social order (which Cohen, among others, has done much to undermine) but against the alternative feasible systems of ordering social relations.[55] In this light I would venture that the question should not be whether or not democracy carries with it the threat of majority tyranny, but whether or not this threat is better to live with than systems that carry with them the threat of minority tyranny. I have suggested elsewhere that it is, a suggestion I hope in the future to elaborate into a full defense of a democratic conception of social justice, conceived of as a third way between statist and market-based accounts.[56]

Notes

Earlier versions of this chapter were presented at the annual meeting of the American Political Science Association in Atlanta, Georgia in September 1989 and at the workshop on changing conceptions of property at the Clark Library, University of California, Los Angeles in November 1989. Helpful comments have been received from an anonymous reader for *Political Theory*, Bruce Ackerman, Joyce Appleby, Richard Arneson, Richard Ashcraft, John Brewer, Jeffrey Isaac, Douglas Rae, Alan Ryan, Debra Satz, Steven Smith, Susan Staves, Tracy Strong, and Sylvia Tesh. While working on this chapter I have received financial support from the Social Science

Faculty Fund at Yale, the Guggenheim Foundation, and the Center for Advanced Study in Palo Alto. Part of my support at the center was paid for by the National Science Foundation, grant number BNS87–00864.

1 I take the term "workmanship ideal" from James Tully, *A Discourse Concerning Property* (Cambridge and New York: Cambridge University Press, 1980).

2 The following discussion of Locke incorporates and builds on aspects of my account in *The Evolution of Rights in Liberal Theory* (Cambridge and New York: Cambridge University Press, 1986), pp. 86–118.

3 Locke minimizes the independent contribution of resources by arguing that the world which has been given us in common is God's "Waste." It is "*Labour* indeed that *puts the difference of value* on every thing" and thus "Labour, in the Beginning, *gave a right to Property*." A hunter owns his catch because in laboring to remove it from the state of nature wherein it "was common" he "hath *begun a Property*." John Locke, *Two Treatises of Government* (Cambridge, UK: Cambridge University Press, 1970), p. 331. Even in gathering foods that have grown wild, "[t]hat labour puts a distinction between them and the common." Locke is famously vague about the exact contributions of labor and nature to the value of property, although "*labour makes* the far greater part." ibid., pp. 337, 338, 341, 330.

4 ibid., p. 329. To this moral theory Locke added two dubious empirical claims which combined to get him from the theory of use-rights in the common to something like the view of property that twentieth-century libertarians often wrongly designate as Lockean. First was the claim that with the introduction of money the injunction against waste, although not in principle transcended, for practical purposes became obsolete. Locke believed that as well as itself not being subject to physical decay money made possible the comparatively more productive use of natural resources through trade and productive work. See Richard Ashcraft, *Locke's Two Treatises of Government* (London: Allen & Unwin, 1987), pp. 123–50, and Richard Ashcraft, *Revolutionary Politics and Locke's Two Treatises of Government* (Princeton, NJ: Princeton University Press, 1986), pp. 270–85, and, for the view (which Ashcraft criticizes) that Locke thought the proviso was transcended with the introduction of money, C. B. Macpherson, *The Political Theory of Possessive Individualism: Hobbes to Locke* (Oxford: Clarendon Press, 1962), pp. 203–21. Second was the claim that the productivity effects of enclosing common land would be so great that the "enough, and as good" proviso could in practice also be dispensed with (thereby legitimating private ownership). By committing himself to these empirical claims Locke formulated an early version of the trickle-down justification for unlimited private accumulation. It is possible to reject either or both of the empirical claims without rejecting Locke's basic moral argument, although any such move would jeopardize his defenses of unlimited accumulation and private property.

5 By following Hobbes and Pufendorf in this formulation of the distinction, Locke was embracing an important departure from the Thomist tradition, rooted in Grotius's revival of the Roman law conception of a right as one's *suum*, a kind of moral power or *facultas* which every man has, and which has its conceptual roots, as Quentin Skinner has established, in the writings of Suarez and ultimately Gerson and the conciliarist tradition; *The Foundations of Modern Political Thought* (Cambridge and New York: Cambridge University Press, 1978), Vol. II, pp. 117, 176–8. See also Richard Tuck, *Natural Rights Theories: Their Origin and Development* (Cambridge and New York: Cambridge University Press, 1979). This "subjective" view of natural rights as "essentially something someone *has*, and above all (or at least paradigmatically) a *power* or *liberty*" involved a shift in perspective that carried the right-holder, and his right, "altogether outside the juridical relationship which is fixed by law (moral or posited) and which establishes *jus* in Aquinas's sense: 'that which is just' [or fair]"; John Finnis, *Natural Law and Natural Right* (Oxford: Clarendon Press, 1980), pp. 207–98.

6 John Locke, *Essays on the Law of Nature*, ed. W. von Leiden (Oxford: Clarendon Press, 1958), pp. 111, 187. Locke's view of natural law was more many-sided and contradictory than the above summary implies, as is discussed in Shapiro, *Evolution*, pp. 100–18, but these complex-

ities concern the nature and basis of natural law, not the constraints it generates for human acts of appropriation once the natural law theory is embraced.

7   Parents are thus obliged to provide for their children "not as their own Workmanship, but the Workmanship of their own Maker, the Almighty, to whom they were to be accountable for them" (Locke, *Two Treatises*, pp. 311, 347). For further discussion see Tully, *Discourse*, pp. 35–8, and John Dunn, *The Political Thought of John Locke* (Cambridge, UK: Cambridge University Press, 1969), p. 95.

8   Tully, *Discourse*, pp. 109–10, 121.

9   Evidence that capacities may be bought and sold can be found in Locke's insistence that "the turfs my servant has cut . . . become my *property*," and his account of wage-labor which states that "a free man makes himself a servant to another, by selling him for a certain time, the service he undertakes to do, in exchange for wages he is to receive." That Locke thought wage-labor enhanced productivity is evident from his defense of enclosure partly on the grounds that this would replace less efficient forms of subsistence production from the common. *Second Treatise*, pp. 330, 365–6, 90–7, 290, 292–3. On Locke on discipline and productivity, see James Tully, "Governing conduct," in E. Leites (ed.), *Conscience and Casuistry in Early Modern Europe* (Cambridge and New York: Cambridge University Press, 1988), pp. 12–71.

10   On the implicit tensions between the causal argument and the workmanship ideal in Locke's formulation, see David Ellerman, "On the labor theory of property," *Philosophical Forum* 16, 4 (Summer 1985): 318–22.

11   For further discussion see Patrick Riley, *Will and Political Legitimacy* (Cambridge, MA: Harvard University Press, 1982), pp. 64 ff. and Shapiro, *Evolution*, pp. 105–7.

12   On the role of the provisos in the theory of individual appropriation, see Locke, *Two Treatises*, pp. 327–44, on charity, ibid., p. 206, and on the natural law limits to conqueror's rights to just reparations, ibid., p. 438.

13   On the hierarchical priority of Locke's natural law requirements see Ashcraft, *Locke's Two Treatises*, pp. 123–50.

14   See Richard Ashcraft, "Locke and eighteenth-century conceptions of property: the politics of interpretation," the Clark Lecture delivered at the UCLA Center for Seventeenth- and Eighteenth-Century Studies, November 3, 1989, Chapter 3 of the present volume.

15   The following must be deducted: costs of replacing the means of production that have been used up, additional costs of expanding production, funds to be kept in reserve for insurance against accidents, administrative costs, costs of the provision of such public goods as schools and health services, and funds "for those unable to work"; Karl Marx, *The Critique of the Gotha Program*, in Karl Marx and Frederick Engels, *Selected Works* (Los Angeles, CA: Progress Publishers, 1970), Vol. III, pp. 15–17.

16   "What he has given to it is his individual quantum of labor. For example, the social working day consists of the sum of the individual hours of work; the individual labor time of the individual producer is the part of the social working day contributed by him, his share in it. He receives a certificate from society that he has furnished such and such an amount of labor (after deducting his labor for the common funds), and with this certificate he draws from the social stock of the means of consumption as much as the same amount of labor costs. The same amount of labor which he has given to society in one form he receives back in another." ibid., p. 17.

17   Ibid., p. 18.

18   "[O]ne worker is married, another not; one has more children than another, and so on and so forth. Thus, with an equal performance of labor, and hence an equal share in the social consumption fund, one will in fact receive more than another, one will be richer than another, and so on." ibid., p. 19.

19   Ibid., pp. 19, 18.

20   "What raises a charge of exploitation is not that the capitalist gets some of the value of what the worker produces, but that he gets some of *what* the worker produces." G. A. Cohen, "The labor theory of value and the concept of exploitation," *Philosophy and Public Affairs* 8, 4 (1979): 338–60 (354), Cohen's italics.

21   Cohen does concede that in some circumstances capitalists may also work productively, but not in their prototypical roles as capitalists. Ibid., pp. 355–6. I do not mean to suggest that Cohen believes that the workmanship ideal is the only or most important basis for distributive entitlements. Indeed, his recent advocacy of equality of "access to advantage" suggests a different basis for distributive justice, that people should not be held responsible for unchosen disadvantages. It is not yet possible to assess how the imperatives generated by this injunction should affect other rights, including rights of workmanship, in Cohen's view because he defends equality of access to advantage only as what he dubs a weak form of egalitarianism; he explicitly refrains from saying to what extent we should equalize that equality in his sense, or even how conflicts between his kind of equalization and other kinds that egalitarians might prize should be settled. G. A. Cohen, "On the currency of egalitarian justice," *Ethics* 99, 4 (July 1989): 906–44 and G. A. Cohen, "Equality of what? On welfare, goods and capabilities," forthcoming in a volume of papers presented at the WIDER symposium on the quality of life and referred to here in manuscript form. Some of these issues are taken up briefly in my *Political Criticism* (Berkeley, CA: University of California Press, 1990), pp. 217–19.

22   G. A. Cohen, "Self-ownership, world ownership and equality I," in Frank S. Lucash (ed.), *Justice and Equality Here and Now* (Ithaca, NY: Cornell University Press, 1986), pp. 108–35, and G. A. Cohen, "Self-ownership, world ownership and equality II," *Social Philosophy and Policy* 3, 2 (Spring 1986): 77–96. In "Self-ownership I" Cohen appeals to the idea that "value adders merit reward" to attack Nozick's defense of private ownership of external resources by demonstrating (ingeniously) that different forms of ownership of external resources may in some circumstances reward value adders more often or more accurately than a private property regime of the sort Nozick advocates. See especially pp. 128–30. In fairness to Cohen it should be noted that in these essays he professes some discomfort with the self-ownership thesis (deriving from the inequalities it must inevitably generate given that some people are more productive than others) and he promises at a future time to show how and why the self-ownership thesis should be undermined. To say that one owns oneself is to say something broader than that one owns one's productive capacities, and it may be that both Cohen and I would eventually want to say that productive capacities should be distinguished from other dimensions of personal identity and given less, or at any rate different kinds of, protection.

23   John Roemer, "Property relations versus surplus value in Marxian exploitation," *Philosophy and Public Affairs* 11, 4 (Fall 1982): 281–313. More generally, see his "Should Marxists be interested in exploitation?", *Philosophy and Public Affairs* 14, 1 (Winter 1985): 30–65 and his *A General Theory of Class and Exploitation* (Cambridge, MA: Harvard University Press, 1982).

24   Roemer, "Property relations," pp. 284–92, 305–10. Roemer also insists that even when differential ownership is necessary for reasons of productivity, if it is the differential distribution of assets as such, "rather than the skills of capitalists, which brings about incentives, competition, innovation, and increased labor productivity which benefit even the workers, then the capitalists do not deserve their returns." By its terms this reasoning concedes the moral force of the workmanship ideal: were it, by contrary hypothesis, the differences in skill rather than the distribution of assets as such, that counted for greater productivity, etc., presumably the capitalist would deserve the differential benefit. Roemer does not face this possibility because he assumes equality of skill and propensity toward risk.

25   For a useful discussion of how Marx's critique of capitalism differs from his critique of feudalism, see Jürgen Habermas, "Technology as science and ideology," *Toward a Rational Society* (Boston, MA: Beacon, 1970), pp. 62–80.

26   Thus in *The German Ideology*: "Men can be distinguished from animals by consciousness, by religion, or by anything else you like. They themselves begin to distinguish themselves from animals as soon as they begin to produce their means of subsistence. . . . By producing their means of subsistence men are indirectly producing their actual material life." Marx and Engels, *Selected Works*, Vol. I, p. 20. See also pp. 26–30, 38–50, and 62–73. For Marx's description of communism as a society of free producers see *Capital* (London: Lawrence & Wishart, 1974), Vol. I, pp. 82–3.

27 The difficulties inherent in trying to pin down just what work has been done by which worker in a given cycle of production have been well explored by Cohen, "The labor theory of value," and by Roemer, "Property relations versus surplus value" and "Should Marxists be interested in exploitation?"

28 *Selected Works*, Vol. III, pp. 17–19; *Capital*, Vol. I, p. 83.

29 For reasons elaborated elsewhere I do not regard Marx's notion of a superabundance that transcends scarcity as coherent or even consistent with his own account of human needs, and nor do I regard as plausible attempts by Cohen and others to reason about distribution without taking account of endemic scarcity by referring to the idea of "relative abundance." If I am right, those who continue to insist that the moral force of Marx's critique of capitalism depends on the possibility of a communist economy of superabundance are committed to the view that it has no force at all. See *Political Criticism*, pp. 217–19.

30 Robert Nozick, *Anarchy, State, and Utopia* (New York: Basic Books, 1974), pp. 169–72, 265–8.

31 Cohen usefully points out that despite the much-trumpeted commitment to freedom behind libertarian thinking, in philosophies like Nozick's freedom is derivative of self-ownership. "[Nozick's] real view is that the scope and nature of the freedom we should enjoy is a function of our self-ownership. That is why he does not regard the apparent unfreedom of the proletariat . . . as a counterexample to his view that freedom prevails in capitalist society. For the proletarian forced daily to sell his labor power is nevertheless a self-owner, indeed must be one in order to sell it, and is, therefore, nevertheless free, in the relevant sense." "Self-ownership II," p. 77.

32 Richard Posner, *The Economics of Justice* (Cambridge, MA: Harvard University Press, 1981), pp. 76–87; John Harsanyi, "Democracy, equality, and popular consent," in Ian Shapiro and Grant Reeher (eds), *Power, Inequality, and Democratic Politics: Essays in Honor of Robert A. Dahl* (Boulder, CO: Westview Press, 1988), p. 279. In the face of arguments about the prima-facie moral arbitrariness of their secular variants of the workmanship ideal, neoclassical theorists often shift to consequentialist justificatory grounds, arguing that treating productive capacities and what they generate as privately owned and alienable via the market maximizes productive efficiency. In such formulations it is often difficult to pin down whether the consequentialist consideration is thought to justify the secular variant of the ideal or vice versa, as in Posner's defense of whatever distributions markets generate on the grounds that they simultaneously maximize the production of wealth and generate outcomes in which "the wealthier people will be those who have the higher marginal products, whether because they work harder, or are smarter, or for whatever reason." *Economics of Justice*, p. 81. See also Nozick, *Anarchy, State, and Utopia*, pp. 149–82, 232–76. These justifications become yet more difficult to disentangle when a trickle-down causal theory of market-based appropriation is embraced. For criticism of the causal assumptions embedded in Posner's account see my "Richard Posner's Praxis," *Ohio State Law Journal* 48, 4 (1987): 999–1047.

33 See *O'Brien v O'Brien* 66NY 2d 576 (1985), in which the Appellate Division of the Supreme Court in the Second Judicial Department of New York upheld a decision that a husband's license to practice medicine was marital property on the grounds that "[t]he contributions of one spouse to the other's profession or career . . . represent investments in the economic partnership of the marriage and the product of the parties' joint efforts." Thus although New York is not a community property state the divorcing wife was awarded 40 percent of the estimated value of the license to be paid over eleven years and the divorcing husband was ordered to maintain a life insurance policy for the unpaid balance of the award, with the divorcing wife as the beneficiary.

34 See Nancy Folbre, "Exploitation comes home: a critique of the Marxian theory of family labor," *Cambridge Journal of Economics* 6, 4 (1982): 317–29.

35 As Cohen notes, in this respect so-called liberals like Rawls and Dworkin, who reject self-ownership as a basic moral commitment, must be accounted to the left of Marxists, who generally embrace it. "Self-ownership I," pp. 113–15.

36 This difficulty inevitably rears its head when a theory designed for the purpose of predicting prices becomes the normative basis of arguments about distribution. I discuss this reduction at length in "Three fallacies concerning majorities, minorities and democratic politics," in

John Chapman and Alan Wertheimer (eds), *NOMOS XXXII: Majorities and Minorities* (New York: New York University Press, 1990), pp. 79–125 (pp. 81–94).

37 Difficulties with pure resourcism, some of which are touched on in section VI below, have led some theorists to defend a middle ground consisting of resourcist views that take limited account of what agents are able to achieve with the resources that they have. Thus we get Amartya Sen's basic capability equality (which rests on the idea of a people having the capacity to fulfill their potential through activity), Richard Arneson's equality of opportunity for welfare (which includes in the definition of resource-egalitarianism information about the welfare that different distributions of resources make possible), and Cohen's equality of access for advantage, which is a similar "midfare" idea (although access is more broadly defined than Arneson's opportunity, and advantage is more broadly defined than Arneson's welfare). For a useful account of what is at issue between resourcist and welfare egalitarians, see Amartya Sen, "Equality of what?", in *The Tanner Lectures on Human Values*, ed. Sterling M. McMurrin (Salt Lake City, UT: University of Utah Press, 1980), pp. 197–220, and Ronald Dworkin, "What is equality? Part I: Equality of welfare," *Philosophy and Public Affairs* 10, 3 (Summer 1981): 185–246, and "What is equality? Part II: Equality of resources," *Philosophy and Public Affairs* 10, 4 (Fall 1981): 283–345. For the middle ground theories, see Sen, "Well-being, agency and freedom," the Dewey Lectures 1984, *Journal of Philosophy* 82, 4 (April 1985): 169–221; Richard Arneson, "Equality and equal opportunity for welfare," *Philosophical Studies* 56 (1989): 77–93; and Cohen, "Currency of egalitarian justice," and Cohen, "Equality of what?"

38 See John Rawls, *A Theory of Justice* (Cambridge, MA: Harvard University Press, 1971), pp. 12, 15, 72–3, 101–3, 507–11.

39 Ibid., pp. 12, 18 f., 137 f., 172, 200, and Dworkin, "What is equality? I," pp. 300–1.

40 See Sen, "Equality of what?", pp. 212–20 and Sen, "Well-being, agency and freedom," pp. 185–221.

41 Rawls's most explicit statement of the view that people must be regarded as responsible for their preferences can be found in "Social unity and primary goods," in Amartya Sen and Bernard Williams (eds), *Utilitarianism and Beyond* (Cambridge and New York: Cambridge University Press, 1982), pp. 168–9. For discussion of the tensions between this claim and the argument that differences in capacity are arbitrary, which Rawls defends most fully in *A Theory of Justice* at pp. 101–4, see Thomas Scanlon, "Equality of resources and equality of welfare: a forced marriage?", *Ethics* 97, 1 (1986): 116–17; Thomas Scanlon, "The significance of choice," *The Tanner Lectures on Human Values* (Salt Lake City, UT: University of Utah Press, 1988), Vol. VIII, pp. 192–201; Arneson, "Equality and equal opportunity," and Richard Arneson, "Primary goods reconsidered," *Nous* 24 (1990): 429–54; and Cohen, "Equality of what?", pp. 7–10.

42 Ronald Dworkin, "What is equality? I and II." For reasons that I here lack the space to expound at length, I think Dworkin's hypothetical auction, described at "What is equality? II," pp. 283–90, fails in its own terms as a device for deciding on what could count as an equal initial allocation of resources. An example of one of the difficulties, which will be intelligible only to initiates of these debates, is that in the hypothetical auction Dworkin describes it would be quite possible for some player or players to bid up the price of some good which he, she or they did not want, but which he, she or they knew someone else had to have at all costs (such as the available stock of insulin on the island in Dworkin's example, assuming there was one diabetic). In this way the diabetic either could be forced to spend all (or at least a disproportionate quantity) of his initial resources on insulin, thereby making other bundles of goods relatively cheaper for the other inhabitants, or might be forced to buy it at an artificially high price from whomever had bought it in the initial auction. The more general point is that Dworkin's hypothetical story assumes that people do not have different strategic resources and powers to bargain, and that they will not have reasons to misrepresent their preferences during the initial auction. But there is no good reason to suppose that either of these assumptions is true, and as a result there is no reason to believe that a hypothetical auction of the kind he describes can be a device which equalizes resources in the way that he claims.

43 Ibid., pp. 300–1.

44 As a result insuring against the possibility of not having an extremely rare skill would be far more expensive than insuring against the possibility of not having a widely shared capacity such as sight. In this way Dworkin hopes to come up with a theory of equality of resources that does not itself make implicit judgments about welfare and avoids the "slavery of the talented" problem which any theory that permits compensation for differences in capacities must confront. See Dworkin, *ibid.*, pp. 292–304. Again for initiates only: notice that for the hypothetical insurance market argument to work it has to be assumed not only that each of the ex-ante choosers has equal initial resources (see the preceding notes), but also that none of them has any incapacity or absence of talent (since otherwise the question of whether or not to insure against the possibility of not having it could not arise). This latter I take to be an unthinkably incoherent speculation, given that talents and incapacities are treated as analytical equivalents from the standpoint of the hypothetical insurance market.

45 Ibid., p. 301.

46 See ibid., p. 300, where he notes in opposition to the idea that there can be a view of "normal" human powers, that no amount of initial compensation could make someone born blind or mentally incompetent equal in physical or mental resources with someone taken to be "normal" in these ways.

47 "Someone who is born with a serious handicap faces his life with what we concede to be fewer resources, just on that account, than others do. This justifies compensation, under a scheme devoted to equality of resources, and though the hypothetical insurance market does not right the balance – *nothing can* – it seeks to remedy one aspect of the resulting unfairness." ibid., p. 302, italics added.

48 Ibid., pp. 311, 288, 302.

49 Ibid., pp. 311 ff.

50 I should not be understood here to be saying that people always have the capacities to achieve their ambitions, or even that we cannot develop ambitions which we know we cannot achieve, although I suspect that sustained analysis would reveal part of the difference between an ambition and a fantasy to reside in the fact that the former is generally a spur to action in a way that the latter need not be. Here I want only to establish that it is not credible to believe that our ambitions are developed independently of our capacities, which Dworkin's categorial distinction requires.

51 Dworkin, "What is equality? II," pp. 302–3 ff.

52 Cohen has tried to minimize the extent of such difficulties by suggesting that we should not confuse the true claim that our capacities for effort are "influenced" by factors beyond our control with the false claim that people like Nozick mistakenly attribute to egalitarians like Rawls, that those capacities are "determined" by factors beyond our control. Preserving this distinction enables him to say that although not all effort deserves reward it is not the case that no effort deserves reward, that effort "is partly praiseworthy, partly not," although he concedes that in practice "we cannot separate the parts." Cohen, "Equality of what?", pp. 8–10. Yet once it is conceded that the very decision to choose to expend effort is influenced by factors that are conceded to be morally arbitrary, one suspects that difficulty becomes one of principle rather than practicality; certainly Cohen offers no account of how that component of effort meriting reward might in principle be singled out.

53 Marx and Engels, *Selected Works*, Vol. III, pp. 15–18.

54 For instance, in his only discussion of democratic decision-making in the "Self-ownership" articles (in which he devotes a single paragraph to it), Cohen remarks that traditional socialist hostility to bills of rights has to be disavowed. The socialist reply to the liberal constitutionalist that "socialism is complete democracy, that it brings within the ambit of democratic decision issues about production and consumption which capitalism excludes from the public agenda" is now believed by Cohen to be inadequate. A defensible socialist constitution, he argues, "must contain a bill of individual rights, which specifies things which the community cannot do to, or demand of, any individual." The proffered reason derives from the fact that socialist democratic decisions require either a unanimous or a majority vote. If they require unanimity, then they have the potential to destroy individual

freedom of action and trivialize self-ownership (since any action might require unanimous consent before legitimately being undertaken), and majority rule without a bill of rights "also legitimates unacceptable tyranny over the individual." "Self-ownership II," p. 87. Yet he does not address the much-argued-over issues of what the content of this bill should be and how the difficulties of unanimity and majority rule should be managed in the business of constitution-making. For discussion of some of these see my "Three fallacies," pp. 81–113. In fairness to Cohen it must be said that he claims not to have done full justice to these issues, which he promises to take up more fully in the future (although to my knowledge he has not done so).

55   Cohen may be wise to insist that a socialist constitution should protect individual freedoms via a bill of rights (see the preceding note), but as the *Lochner* era in the United States demonstrated all too clearly, bills of rights can be used to facilitate what Cohen would regard as exploitation as well as to prevent it – whatever the intentions of those who create them. This is not to say that bills of rights are undesirable, only that their benefits from the standpoint of achieving and maintaining social justice are not self-evident. Whether such bills are desirable, what their scope and content should be, who should be empowered to alter and implement them, are all controversial questions that cannot be declared beyond politics (and, I would argue, beyond democratic politics). For an empirically based argument that democratic systems have best protected individual rights historically, see Robert Dahl, *Democracy and its Critics* (New Haven, CT: Yale University Press, 1989), pp. 135–92.

56   For the suggestion, see Chapter 9 of *Political Criticism*. The first installment of the positive argument is my "Three ways to be a democrat," *Political Theory* 22, 1 (February 1994): 124–51.

3

Lockean ideas, poverty, and the development of liberal political theory

Richard Ashcraft

Although it may be true that "the poor ye shall always have with you," the existence of mass poverty in eighteenth-century England was such a striking and shocking social phenomenon that it called forth thousands of tracts, sermons, pamphlets, and books that attempted to explain and/or justify the existence of poverty as a feature of the most economically developed society in the world.

My object in this chapter is to offer a conceptual and historical analysis of the most significant arguments pertaining to poverty during the period from the end of the seventeenth century to the beginning of the nineteenth century. As the literature on this subject is enormous, let me indicate more specifically the parameters within which I shall formulate the argument of the chapter. Viewed as a whole, the reconstruction of the eighteenth-century debate concerning poverty would appear as a complex totality, not only in the sense that there were numerous specific arguments, but also because they were of different "types" (religious/secular, political/economic, etc.) and because some arguments presupposed permanent aspects of social relations, while other arguments appeared and/or disappeared, according to the changing conditions of eighteenth-century society.

In these circumstances, one must exercise considerable methodological caution in developing what, at first glance, appears to be a contradictory position. On the one hand, certain arguments, such as God's providential wisdom in assigning individuals to the differential ranks of rich and poor, or the claim that poverty reflects defective moral discipline on the part of the poor, were made in the seventeenth and in the nineteenth centuries, and thus appear as persistent and unchanging elements of the debate. On the other hand, at the same time, arguments associating poverty with trade cycles, demographic shifts in population, or bad harvests, are much more contingent in character. Other arguments analyzing poverty in terms of a structured set of social relations are meant to be more than merely contingent but perhaps less than permanent features of human existence. The point, then, is that general characterizations, such as the claim that there was a movement away from religious-based to secular explanations for the existence of mass poverty, are misleading when, as is usually the case, such observations are extracted from what is a much more complex historical totality.[1] At the same time, there are "progressive" developments with respect to this debate. Some arguments, if not refuted, are abandoned. Other arguments whose formal nature may seem unchanged take on new meanings in relation to changing social circumstances. And a few arguments are truly novel in relation to previously accepted beliefs or assumptions underlying the discourse about poverty. Hence, it has to be possible to speak of both change and persistence, and to make some evaluative but plausible assessment of the relative importance over time of particular arguments in the context of the debate as a whole.

Moreover, in considering attitudes toward poverty over such a long period, it is difficult to provide sufficient detail to characterize the fluctuating intensity of the debate arising from the perceived financial burden of poverty in the face of escalating poor rates or from a recognition of the extent to which changes in the political situation in England transformed the discussion of poverty as a social problem into a polemical critique or defense of the existing political regime.

Even if these methodological guidelines were adopted, without further discrimination, the reader might be presented with little more than a catalogue of arguments concerning poverty indiscriminately assembled. In this chapter therefore, I propose to focus upon certain assumptions and arguments contained in the thought of John Locke as a baseline for questions such as the following: How were these arguments employed and developed by eighteenth-century thinkers with respect to the problem of poverty? How did the meanings of Lockean arguments change over time? What significance did Lockean ideas and arguments have in the context of the debate over poverty, viewed as a whole, and to what extent can one speak of Lockean arguments being "replaced" by other arguments concerning poverty?

I have focused upon Lockean concepts or arguments not merely because one needs some axis from which to view the debate concerning poverty, but also because I wish to illustrate the importance of this debate to the development of the political theory of liberalism. Political theory, in my view, has a dualistic nature. In its narrowest sense, political theory is constituted by the arguments and beliefs directed toward the recognition and resolution, generally through engagement in collective action, of a specific concrete problem, such as the extension of the franchise, religious toleration, slavery, or poverty. In its broadest sense, political theory provides a framework for understanding how and why the social relations between members of a particular society came to be what they are, and what actions have been or are necessary in order to effect a restructuring of those social relations. Of course, this is purely an analytical distinction, but it supplies a standpoint for assessing the political theory of a particular thinker. Since I have argued at length elsewhere that John Locke's political theory provides an illustration of both meanings of political theory, I shall take it as given that those who employed his arguments did so in ways which both illuminate the significance of a particular social problem in eighteenth-century England and provide a critical perspective from which to assess the social relations of that society.[2]

Employing the traditional language of natural law, Locke argues in the *Two Treatises of Government* that everyone has an "equal right" or "a right in common . . . [to] provide for their subsistence."[3] This right to subsistence is defended by Locke as a necessary means to fulfill the general obligation laid upon each individual by the Law of Nature to act so as to preserve all mankind.[4] Thus, an individual has "a right to the surplusage" of another's goods because natural law "gives every man a title to so much out of another's plenty, as will keep him from extreme want, where he has not means to subsist otherwise."[5] The natural right to subsistence is both a primary rights claim, and a theoretical presupposition underlying any Lockean definition of "property."

In considering a conflict between two "rightful" claims, that of a just conqueror to the spoils of war and that of the subsistence needs of the women and children residing in the defeated country, Locke insists that the rights claim of the latter to subsistence takes precedence, an assertion defended in terms of "the fundamental Law of Nature being, that all, as much as may be, should be preserved."[6] More generally, Locke's position is that the natural right to subsistence is a legally enforceable right within any post-subsistence form of society, and within seventeenth-century England in particular. In the memorandum he drafted for a revision in the English poor laws as a member of the Board of Trade, Locke declared as a political policy that "everyone must have meat, drink, clothing, and firing. So much goes out of the stock of the kingdom, whether they work or no."[7] Indeed, Locke believes that it should be a crime chargeable against those responsible for administering poor relief within the parish to allow anyone to die for want of due relief.[8] Since governments are instituted to protect the life, liberty, and property of individuals, it could be argued from the way in which Locke employs his fundamental assumptions, that no government could be adjudged to be employing political power for the common good – the preservation of mankind – which failed to preserve all members of society through guaranteeing their subsistence.

Turning to another set of arguments in the *Two Treatises*, Locke maintains that "God commanded" man to labor, "to subdue the earth, i.e., improve it for the benefit of life," so that whoever "in obedience of this command of God, subdued, tilled and sowed any part of it" could rightfully claim the land as the product of his productive labor.[9] But if some individual in the state of nature simply appropriated, enclosed, or fenced the land but did not cultivate it or improve it, then, Locke argues, the land "notwithstanding his enclosure, was still to be looked on as waste, and might be the possession of any other."[10] Productive labor, and not simply appropriation of property, is the key concept in Locke's understanding of economic development as well as an element in his theologically structured political theory.[11]

Not surprisingly, Locke maintains that a large population of laborers is much more important with respect to the production of national wealth than "largeness of dominions."[12] This preference for labor over land is, of course, consonant with Locke's mercantilist position that trade is the means by which both individuals and countries accumulate wealth and power.[13] Exchange of commodities for money thus allows individuals to employ their productive labor beyond the natural familial limits of consumption, and, in so doing, individuals are acting in accordance with the basic precept of natural law, for they are enhancing the objective circumstances under which mankind may be preserved. For reasons which will become evident later, it is important to emphasize the point that Locke believes that trade, or life in a commercial society, benefits every member of that society.[14]

Locke's views on other matters relevant to the discussion of poverty will emerge in the context of a consideration of the arguments advanced by eighteenth-century thinkers. But it is essential to keep in mind as these views are presented the natural law-natural right to subsistence, divine authority for productive labor, political power directed toward the preservation of mankind, and the universally beneficial features of commerce as the structuring, if skeletal, elements of Locke's political-economical thought.

II

Among the many traditional beliefs drawn from Christian doctrine which shaped people's attitude toward the poor, I would emphasize the efficacy and persistence of the notions of providential design, moral depravity, and stewardship. With regard to the first belief, the title of a pamphlet by Robert Moss published in 1708 – *The Providential Division of Men into Rich and Poor, and the Respective Duties Thence Arising, Briefly Considered* – virtually says it all. Moss has little to say concerning the duties of the rich, but, as for the poor man, he is instructed "to rest contented with that state or condition in which it hath pleased God to rank him."[15] This counsel of submission to a higher design was still being offered at the end of the century by those who took the time between tea and supper to ruminate upon the Deity's wisdom.[16]

Since the focus of this chapter is upon political theory and political action, there is little to be said concerning this perspective except to note its persistence and persuasiveness as a counsel of nonaction. A version of providential design does, however, structure Locke's argument in *The Reasonableness of Christianity*, where Locke maintains that God designed Christianity for and Jesus preached its doctrines to the poor.[17] Yet the fact that even the poorest individual is rational enough to comprehend and carry out – ought implies can for Locke – his or her religious duties, viewed as an attack upon the authority of the clergy, leads not to inaction, but rather to a more democratic conception of authority in religion and politics, though I shall not pursue that point here.[18]

That poverty is the consequence of moral depravity is an attitude that also persisted throughout the eighteenth century. Indeed, that poverty reflects "fraud, indolence, and improvidence" on the part of the poor was the primary conclusion offered for its existence in the Report of the Poor Law Commission in 1834.[19] In a more general sense, without the Calvinist undertones, various writers maintained throughout this

neighbors." Locke accepted such a distinction, and for him as well as for his friend Thomas Firmin education and coerced employment supplied the disciplinary remedy for idleness. Not only the state, but also individual employers, bore some responsibility for the solution of the problem of poverty, viewed as a defective exercise of self-discipline.[22]

That the rich are "general stewards to employ and relieve . . . the poor" was another precept of Christian doctrine, and a prominent theme in sermons preached throughout the eighteenth century.[23] People who believed that their wealth was "not a stewardship, but [was] given only to gratify their own appetites and enrich their posterity, without regard to others, and particularly to the poor," John Bellars declared, "show their religion to be vain."[24] Because riches were "entrusted" to the individual by God, a wealthy individual had an "indispensable duty to be very liberal in acts of public and private charity."[25] Locke accepted the doctrine of stewardship in general, and in his will he made a number of bequests to provide for the poor.[26]

The moral force of stewardship was upon private acts of charity freely given, but religion was also an integral feature of the social order, and the role of steward could therefore be easily associated with the responsibility of authority. It could hardly be otherwise in a paternalistic, hierarchically structured, and largely rural society. The congruence between wealth, social status, and political authority provided, for most of the eighteenth century, a basis for hoping that the claims of the poor would be met by local stewards. Yet, these claims were frequently not met, in part because the numbers of the poor were constantly increasing, but also, it was argued, because the social relationship between rich and poor was undergoing a significant change.

To account for this change, a myth was created of a disappearing society where "old English hospitality" flourished and rich and poor lived like "families in mutual care of each other."[27] In the early nineteenth century, it was still being argued that "the ties of relationship and neighborhood" as the basis for charity had been replaced "by the operations of the coercive system of parochial aid." From this perspective, the poor rates were attacked as impersonal and compulsory legal obligations laid upon property-owners in place of relations of deference, gratitude, and charity that had once pre-vailed.[28] The idea of stewardship as the "conscious responsibility" to provide for the poor was undermined, it was argued, by a "system of compulsory provision" of poor relief.[29] The image of that "happy nation" where "people live in natural love and dependence . . . [and] rich and poor are attached to each other by the reciprocal good offices of kindness and gratitude" was increasingly invoked by eighteenth-century writers in proportion to the obviousness of its nonexistence.[30]

III

Whatever the degree of reality one accords to the familial or Christian framework as a way of viewing acts of charity by individuals, the underlying premise of statutory poor relief from the Elizabethan period to the nineteenth century was largely, though not exclusively, a punitive one. That is, vagabonds, beggars, and idle individuals were either to be whipped or to be put to work in order to cure their "vicious habits."[31] What was needed, Locke and his contemporaries argued, were public workhouses where the idle poor could acquire "a habit of industry" through labor.[32] Workhouses, in short, were designed to be "nurseries of religion, virtue, and industry."[33] Notwithstanding the punitive language and the moral value attached to labor as an essential feature of the human condition, the argument for workhouses in the seventeenth century also reflected a *de facto* recognition of the poor's claim to a right to subsistence.[34]

Toward the end of the seventeenth century, however, an argument for the establishment of workhouses as industrial and profitable enterprises, that is, as sources of national wealth and not merely as nurseries of virtue, became increasingly popular. In his speech to Parliament in 1689, William III supported the building of more workhouses, not only because they were charitable institutions but also as "effectual expedients for increasing our manufactures."[35] In a number of tracts, John Bellars championed this view, that employment of the poor could be made a profitable and self-supporting enterprise. Bellars predicted that not only would the workhouse scheme he had devised produce a profit, but also the income generated by the poor would make the poor rates unnecessary.[36] The Workhouse Act of 1723 encouraged the building of workhouses, and in some parishes they were constructed by or leased to local manufacturers eager to avail themselves of the supply of cheap labor.[37]

In order to appreciate why the idea of employing the poor for profit was so enticing we need to grasp the meaning of labor from the standpoint of a mercantilist view of the world, as expressed, for example, in Locke's thought. The basic argument was simple: all goods are produced by labor; wealth is gained through trading one good for another. Hence, what a trading nation requires is a large supply of cheap labor engaged in the production of goods.[38] Since "it's only the labor of the poor that increases the riches of a nation," Bellars declared, "there cannot be too many laborers in a nation."[39] Sixty years later (1759), this was still the dominant view. Since it is "the intent of the state to cherish the numerous offspring of the poor," the author of *Populousness with Oeconomy, the Wealth and Strength of a Kingdom* reasoned, "let every poor man that has a numerous family be looked upon as a great benefactor to his country."[40] With a constant supply of cheap labor, English manufacturers and merchants would be able to undersell their competitors in the international market.[41]

Of course this argument for the "utility of poverty" assumed that what was crucial was not the number but the employment of the poor. Unemployed individuals receiving poor relief were "the dead stock of the nation," i.e. a wasted resource, unless their labor, like other commodities, was sold in the marketplace.[42] With respect to the latter, however, the poor constituted a special case, for, in order for the workhouse to be a profitable undertaking, the cost of maintaining the poor had to be kept below the prevailing wage of those already employed in producing that commodity. Since those

further consideration. The workhouse as a means of enforcing virtue with respect to the poor required, in addition to strict discipline, the separation of husbands from wives, the break-up of families, and, in general, an administrative regime resembling that of a prison.[44] John Bellars recognized the legitimacy of the complaints of the poor against the tyrannical administration of the poor law. "A workhouse," he wrote, "bespeaks too much of servitude." He preferred to call them "colleges of industry," because he envisioned the resident poor as constituting "a community, something like the example of primitive Christianity, that lived in common." Bellars admitted that "community" implied "a greater unity in spirit" than could be realized in his "college," but he was convinced that "an outward fellowship" among the workhouse poor was possible.[45] Other reformers echoed this view that a workhouse should not be looked upon as a prison but as a "college of artificers" where "the work would be cheerfully carried on."[46] But the idea that you could "force the slothful poor to work" *and* make them cheerful was not widely held, certainly not amongst the poor, who fiercely resisted being sent to the workhouse.[47] As one overseer of a workhouse reported, "we have many here who would choose to starve, rather than be maintained in . . . [the] house of correction, as they call it."[48]

It is not only that the developing manufacturing economy depended upon voluntary contractual and not upon forced labor, but also, as even its supporters recognized, the workhouse symbolized a rupture in the "spirit of the community" insofar as parish life in any period in English history could be characterized in those terms. The eighteenth-century workhouse stood as an incomplete bridge between the world of religiously inspired discipline enforced by the Tudor government and the world of industrial capitalism driven by the profitability of manufactured goods.

From the outset, the idea that workhouses were "nurseries of virtue" was dismissed by many as a fiction. With the publication of a number of reports on the actual operations of workhouses throughout the country, by the middle of the eighteenth century, there was considerable empirical evidence to support the view that workhouses had failed to realize their moral objective.[49] Moreover, the evidence demonstrated, overwhelmingly, that workhouses were not profitable enterprises either.[50] Nevertheless, characteristically undeterred by the empirical evidence, Jeremy Bentham still entertained thoughts at the beginning of the nineteenth century of a massive network of workhouses generating huge profits, and he drew a general map of pauperland, as he called it.[51]

The failure of workhouses to provide a solution to the problem of poverty in accordance with mercantilism's insistence upon the importance of productive labor not only showed that poor relief could not be administered according to the laws of the competitive economic market, it also disclosed a much more disturbing problem; namely, as

Defoe's remarks implied, the employed laborer was already a poor man. What the numerous surveys and reports concerning poor relief undertaken during the eighteenth century revealed was that most poor relief was paid to individuals living outside the workhouse, and that a significant proportion of those individuals were employed but were receiving wages that were inadequate to maintain their families.[52] In other words, it was not merely a question of putting the idle poor to work as the Elizabethan poor law had assumed. The eighteenth century discovered a new dimension of the problem of poverty and a new category to describe it – "the laboring poor."[53]

Locke assumed, as did most of his contemporaries, that wage laborers maintained a subsistence-level existence.[54] Given the generally held belief that individuals would work only for reasons of immediate necessity, and that if the worker received wages above this subsistence level, he would cease to work, preferring leisure, the proposition was regarded as a self-evident truth. Hence, the poverty line, and the economic rationale for poor relief, had to be set at a level below the income of the able-bodied employed worker.[55] If the latter were included within the definition of poverty, it not only meant that large numbers of individuals might be added to the rolls of poor relief – with a correspondingly huge increase in the poor rates, already on the rise – but also that the problem of poverty, seen from this perspective, might prove to be insoluble.

Yet, it was undeniable, as the surveys showed, that the wages of hundreds of thousands of workers were insufficient to provide for their families. With a sense of paternal responsibility, local magistrates who had the authority to regulate wages sometimes awarded relief payments to workers as wage supplements. Outdoor relief and family wage supplements were widespread responses to the poverty of the laboring poor decades before this practice was later made notorious as the Speenhamland system.[56] In fact, this practical response to poverty only increased the awareness of people that the system of poor relief failed to solve the problem of poverty.

In addition to the moral and economic arguments concerning poverty, the latter was recognized to be a problem for which the state assumed responsibility. Given the Elizabethan poor law, this is hardly surprising, but I shall put aside the straight-forward legal/historical references to state policy in order to concentrate on the broader political arguments, i.e., those which focused upon the nature and objectives of government. These arguments, of course, could be, and were, phrased in the language employed by Locke. Such arguments carried with them radical implications because the rights claim to poor relief could not be defeated on the basis of the empirical evidence of the failure of the system to execute its obligations to provide for the poor. On the contrary, given such a right, the evidence could be turned against the state itself. In other words, the very existence of mass poverty reflected the failure of the government to provide for the common good, thereby threatening the legitimacy of the political order.

The failure of poor relief efforts, the author of a tract published in 1767 argued, "has not been owing to any natural depravity peculiar to the low people of this country . . . and, if this be admitted . . . the causes . . . must be looked for solely in our laws and polity."[57] That the deplorable condition of the poor was the consequence of "bad government" was a commonplace by the end of the eighteenth century.[58] However, to place the blame for poverty upon defective political institutions, framed in the language of Lockean political theory, drastically narrowed the alternatives, for the failure of the

was not given up with the contractual formation of political society. Hence, every individual has a "claim on the community" for a portion of "the public patrimony" necessary to sustain his family. How, Woodward asked, could property-owners expect their "right" of property to be recognized "unless they consent in return to provide for the subsistence of the poor?"[61] William Paley advanced a similar argument, going so far as to maintain that there was no natural right to property in land, an assertion which, at the very least, rendered nugatory the complaints of landowners concerning the poor rates when weighed against the existence of mass poverty.[62]

Some individuals, including William Cobbett, extended the natural law argument to its logical consequences; namely, that with the dissolution of government, all obligations on the part of the poor to obey the government ceased, and they were entitled, *en masse*, to take whatever action they believed would secure their preservation. If the poor are oppressed and made miserable, James Murray warned, they will certainly reclaim their natural right to relief through riots and violence. In short, revolution was a legitimate response to the state's failure to provide subsistence for the poor.[63] Of course, parallel to and largely independent of such justificatory arguments, there were riots and uprisings by the poor during periods of economic depression and famine. No facile explanation relating these actions to the theoretical argument I have outlined is acceptable, notwithstanding the fact that Cobbett's political ideas were widely disseminated amongst the laboring poor. Yet, neither can such disturbances of the political order be viewed merely as instinctual responses to contingent economic circumstances. Not only is the constancy of low wages a reasonable element of any explanation for the actions of the poor, but also the fact that, in many instances, their attacks were directed specifically at the workhouses or the local overseers of the poor indicates that, on some level, it is plausible to draw a connection between what the poor believed they were rightfully entitled to receive for their labor and the failure of the system, symbolized by the workhouse, to recognize such a right.[64] Such a connection was certainly drawn by the political opponents of the poor law, and, in particular, by the Poor Law Commissioners who wrote the 1834 report.[65]

The prospect of revolution did not, however, exhaust "the radical possibilities" within Lockean political theory, as viewed by eighteenth-century thinkers. Not only did Paley's observation that land ownership was a conventional and not a natural right reflect Locke's position, but, as Locke had maintained in the *Two Treatises*, uncultivated or "waste" land represented a failure to realize God's intentions that individuals should engage in productive labor. When the natural right to subsistence was linked, as it was in numerous eighteenth-century tracts, with the existence of millions of acres of "waste" land, it was clear to both proponents and opponents of the poor law that this Lockean argument could be deployed as an attack upon the landed aristocracy and especially upon absentee landlords who allowed their property to become "waste" land.[66] Most scholars have assumed, incorrectly, that such "levelling" schemes with respect to solving the problem of poverty arose in England in the wake of the French Revolution or were due to the influence of Thomas Paine's ideas. In fact, the connection between a right to poor relief and the use of uncultivated land was not only a longstanding one, but it was recognized by numerous individuals who had never heard of the Diggers or read the works of Paine.[67]

Addressing himself to "the general causes of poverty," an anonymous author observed that if "those extensive tracts of land" that are uncultivated were "more equally distributed," there would be sufficient employment for the poor.[68] Richard Price, who explicitly identified himself as a follower of Locke, also associated poverty and oppression with the unequal distribution of property as contrasted with that "natural and simple life" in a Lockean state of nature where "property is equally divided" and "the wants of men are few."[69] William Ogilvie, in his *Essay on the Right of Property in Land* (1782), followed Locke's argument closely, frequently citing passages from the *Two Treatises* in support of the "natural rights" of "the laborious poor" against oppressive landowners. Giving "the industrious poor" uncultivated land, Ogilvie argued, was not only a necessary reform of but also a preferable alternative to the existing system of poor relief.[70] This point was further developed by Thomas Spence, who also cited passages from Locke in defence of the natural rights of the laboring poor, and advanced a scheme whereby counties could reclaim unused land for the employment of the poor. For Spence, as for many other radicals, the primary issue of politics was not "about what form of government is most favorable to liberty." Rather, he argued, it was "which system of society is . . . capable of delivering us from the deadly mischief of great accumulations of wealth" counterposed to the existence of mass poverty.[71] The argument linking poverty and unemployment with waste land of property-owners, accompanied by citations from Locke, became an increasingly prominent feature of the defense of the right to poor relief. It was taken up by the Chartists, and later, in the 1870s, by advocates of the nationalization of all land as a common resource of society.

Nevertheless, although it was an important and a constant element of radical thought from the seventeenth century to the nineteenth, the redistribution of landed property was a minority-held view within the larger perspective of radical political theory. Most radicals focused upon political reform, believing that the defects of the social system, including poverty, could be remedied through the passage of new laws. This, of course, presupposed a shift in the distribution of political power toward the working class through the institution of manhood suffrage. Major Cartwright, Thomas Paine, and other radicals defended manhood suffrage, employing the natural rights/consent argument which Locke formulated in the *Second Treatise*.[72] Indeed, passages from that work were frequently reprinted in nineteenth-century radical newspapers, such as *The Black Dwarf* or *The Northern Star*, in the context of arguments for manhood suffrage.[73]

James Burgh, claiming Locke as a mentor, specifically relied upon Locke's broad definition of property – "life, liberty, and property" – and, citing the paragraph from the *Second Treatise* which maintained that the government "must not raise taxes on the property of the people, without the consent of the people, given by themselves, or their deputies . . . to be from time to time chosen by themselves," Burgh argued that the

The employment of Locke's ideas by radicals in defense of the rights of the poor in the eighteenth and nineteenth centuries is a subject that could be pursued at much greater length, but, in the final section of this chapter, I want to discuss, briefly, the arguments directed against this radical perspective. In the end, they scored a decisive political victory with respect to the latter insofar as their presuppositions were reflected in the legislation reforming the franchise and the poor laws enacted by Parliament in the 1830s.

IV

In rejecting the Lockean concepts of natural law, natural rights, state of nature, and the theological and philosophical assumptions underlying such concepts, David Hume laid the philosophical foundations for an alternative response to the problem of poverty, one which did not presuppose a rights claim to poor relief. As a general proposition, Hume argued that it was "fruitless" to "seek in the laws of nature a stronger foundation for our political duties than interest and human conventions."[76] Hume was not interested in questions concerning the origins of property or society, since even if these were or could be known in a strictly historical sense, that information, Hume maintained, was neither likely nor sufficient to establish the legitimacy of property ownership or government.[77] Both property ownership and government, Hume asserted, were social practices and/or institutions whose legitimacy was a function of time and "constant possession."[78]

Not surprisingly, the objective of such an argument was to emphasize the importance of social stability, and this, in turn, depended upon acceptance of the proposition that, with respect to property, it was best "that every one continue to enjoy what he is at present possessed of."[79] Hence, even if one could imagine a more equitable distribution of property according to a utilitarian standard of justice, Hume argued, the collective action required to bring about such a restructuring of social relations would produce more pain than benefit to society, and so ought not to be undertaken.[80] Nevertheless, the policy implications of Hume's general argument with respect to poverty are not unequivocally clear. For, while there could be no Humean natural right to poor relief, the latter was a longstanding custom and legal practice, and Hume's position supplied no compelling reason for its abandonment.

It was Hume's friend, Adam Smith, who played a critical role in reformulating the eighteenth-century debate concerning poverty. Although Smith declared in the *Wealth of Nations* that, "civil government . . . is in reality instituted for the defence of the rich against the poor, or of those who have some property against those who have none at all," he also maintained in that work that "no society can surely be flourishing and happy, of which the greater part of the members are poor and miserable. It is but equity, besides, that they who feed, clothe and lodge the whole body of the people, should have such a share of the produce of their own labor as to be themselves tolerably well fed, clothed and lodged."[81] Smith advocated "a liberal reward of labour" because, he argued, high wages for the laboring poor were a "natural symptom of increasing national wealth," while a "scanty maintenance of the labouring poor" was a sign of economic stagnation.[82] In rejecting Mandeville's assertion that national wealth "consists in a multitude of laborious poor" whose wages were to be kept at the level of bare subsistence – a basic assumption of the utility of poverty argument – Smith transformed poverty from being a precondition for economic development into a symptom of economic decline.[83] It is all the more amazing that Smith advanced this argument during a period (1750–76) when the poor rates doubled and the level of anxiety amongst taxpayers concerning the costs of poverty was greatly intensified.[84]

Yet, how was it possible for a commercial nation paying high wages to remain competitive in the world of international trade? And how could the extreme inequality in the distribution of property characteristic of a commercial society be compatible with the satisfaction of the laborers' needs? To these questions, Smith gave a simple answer: it was the division of labor in the process of production that explained the productivity of labor and, therefore, the wealth of the nation. "The division of labour by which each individual confines himself to a particular branch of business," Smith wrote, "can alone account for the superior opulence which takes place in civilized societies and which, notwithstanding the inequality of property, extends itself to the lowest members of the community."[85] In lowering the unit labor costs of manufactured goods for export through the division of labor, Smith argued, it was possible for the real wages of the laboring poor to rise so long as the economic system as a whole remained in a state of dynamic expansion.

Smith specifically linked the progressive advancement of society to improvements in the condition of the laboring poor, and not simply to an increase in per capita income. It was a brilliant, if radical, move in the long debate over poverty, for it offered a chance to escape from the marshy ground of morality, religion, or politics by placing the social problem of poverty on the solid terrain of economics. If Smith was right, a free market economy would generate sufficient wealth to satisfy the needs of the laboring poor, thus obviating any debate over the "right" to poor relief or the empirically grounded objections to the high poor rates paid by property-owners.[86] How this solution to the problem of poverty fits into Smith's social thought, viewed as a whole, is the subject of an ongoing debate amongst interpreters of his thought, but the point I want to stress is that Smith took the bold step of linking poverty with the dynamic workings of the economic system of production. Thereafter, the continued existence of poverty could be viewed – as it was by Marx – as a structural defect of the economic system, i.e., capitalism.

Despite the generally favorable reception accorded to the *Wealth of Nations*, the fact is that most of Smith's contemporaries were not willing to make his leap of faith with respect to the problem of poverty. It is true that, by the end of the eighteenth century, the utility of poverty argument was generally discredited, and the importance of the division of labor as a technique of production was generally conceded, but other aspects

learn to accept their condition with patience and submission.[88] Doubtless Burke believed he was following Smith in stating that "labor" was a "commodity" subject to the "rules of commerce" like any other commodity. But Burke not only went on to argue that those rules could not be suspended in order to accommodate the needs of the poor arising from unemployment or a large family, but also, unlike Smith, to maintain that poverty was not a social problem at all.

Frederick Eden, in his influential three-volume work *The State of the Poor*, published in 1797, agreed with Burke that to suggest that an individual had a right to food, lodging, or clothing was to propagate "an idea that undermined the strongest ties of civil society." The poor, Eden warned, should not be deceived: "the best relief they can receive must come from themselves."[89] In *The State of Indigence, and the Situation of the Casual Poor in the Metropolis Explained* (1799), Patrick Colquhoun also reformulated Burke's argument, maintaining that if those who labored were poor, then poverty was not a problem but merely a normal feature of society. Only those unable to labor, the indigent, Colquhoun wrote, could be regarded as having needs to be met through private or public relief.[90]

Jeremy Bentham, who, like all those cited above, viewed himself as an adherent of Smith's political economy, also rejected the concept of the laboring poor, reinstating the traditional distinction between the idle and the industrious poor. The latter, Bentham argued, were to be excluded from the discussion of poverty. Those who labored for their subsistence might be poor, Bentham wrote, but if so, their condition was "the general, and the *unchangeable* lot of man."[91] The idle poor – or paupers as Bentham preferred to call them – on the other hand, were undeserving of public assistance; what they required was to be put to work. Bentham devised a scheme modeled after his prison reform plan to establish large "Houses of Industry" through-out the country where the conditions of strict discipline would make residency in the workhouse "less desirable" than the conditions of the poorest individuals living outside it.[92]

Like Hume, Bentham recognized that greater equality in the distribution of property represented a closer approximation to a utilitarian standard of justice than could be derived from the socioeconomic inequalities characteristic of eighteenth-century Britain. Yet, like his predecessor, Bentham could not accept "forced equalization" through political action as a remedy, nor could he accept Smith's reliance upon the market as a systemic solution to the problem of poverty. Instead, Bentham reasserted the Humean – and Burkean – priority of social stability as the fundamental principle of a theory of justice.[93] Not only did such a theory exclude any notion of a natural right to poor relief on the grounds that all natural rights claims were a "fiction," but also, as Bentham and his contemporaries recognized, such natural rights arguments were especially dangerous as a practical threat to social stability when they were disseminated amongst the poor.[94] As the author of *A Short Treatise on the Dreadful Tendency of Levelling Principles* (1793) observed, it was the language of natural law and natural rights that led the poor to believe that violence against the rich could be justified as the reclaiming of a natural right to poor relief.[95] Whatever the alleged defects of Smith's economic argument, after 1776, there were convergent political reasons for rejecting his positive and "democratic" view of the laboring poor.[96]

All the themes of the counterattack expressed in a flood of pamphlets published in the 1790s denouncing the dangerous leveling doctrine of a right to poor relief were given their most dramatic and influential formulation in Thomas Malthus's *Essay on Population*. "No possible contributions or sacrifices of the rich," Malthus observed, "could for any time prevent the recurrence of distress among the lower members of society." Thus, poor relief was not only a misnomer – it could not raise the standard of living of the poor – but also, Malthus argued, it was a "check to productive industry." Poor relief encouraged idleness and vicious habits among the poor.[97] Malthus attacked the workhouses and the general assumption underlying their existence, namely, that the government could provide employment for the poor. He denied that individuals possessed a natural right to subsistence, insisting that the poor would simply have to accept their condition as an "absolutely irremediable" feature of society.[98] This was the case, Malthus argued, not merely for the philosophical or theological reasons advanced by Bentham, Burke, and others, but also – and here Malthus supplied the compelling argument missing in a Humean analysis which defended the importance of custom or tradition – for reasons of scarce economic resources. "The sole reason why I say the poor have no claim of *right* to support," Malthus wrote, "is the physical impossibility of relieving this progressive population [growth]."[99]

Moreover, Malthus, like Bentham, invoked an older view, suggesting that poverty "ought to be held disgraceful." Prosperity was simply an expression of virtue providentially directed.[100] Hence, as one of the Commissioners of the New Poor Law of 1834 remarked, in compelling the idle poor to be "industrious, sober, provident . . . the workhouse" represented "the law of necessity imposed by Providence upon mankind."[101]

Indeed, in the 1834 Report of the Poor Law Commissioners, the authors candidly admitted that if poverty "had been principally the result of unavoidable distress, we must have inferred the existence of an organic disease," that is, some defect in the structure of social relations. Instead, the commission viewed poverty as the consequence of the "fraud, indolence, and improvidence" of the poor themselves. Poverty, they assumed, was a consequence of "misconduct," not "misfortune."[102] Naussau Senior, one of the Poor Law Commissioners, attacked the belief in "the rights of the poor" to relief as one of those "monstrous and anarchical doctrines" which threatened to destroy "the relation between the employer and the laborer," which was a contractual relationship. For Senior, as for most classical political economists, there was no naturalistic, pre-political form of social relations, such as Locke had postulated. Rather, Senior insisted, the contractual relations of the market were "the most extreme and most important of all *political* relations."[103] Thus, whether the laws of the market were identified with providential design or were politicized to the point of being the essence of all contractual social relationships, poverty ceased to be a social problem. The very

and that the poor possessed no rights, either to relief or to be free from the strict discipline and loss of privacy associated with residence in the workhouse. Even if one accepts the judgment of a respected economic historian that the Poor Law Commissioners' "analysis of the problem of poverty was defective, their diagnosis inaccurate, and the recommendations ineffectual," the fact remains that a certain conception of poverty acquired considerable social significance as a consequence of being incorporated into and enforced by the 1834 poor law.[106]

Notes

I wish to thank John Brewer for his helpful comments on this essay.

1 See, for example, Daniel A. Burgh, "Poverty, Protestantism, and political economy: English attitudes toward the poor, 1660–1800," in *England's Rise to Greatness, 1660–1763*, ed. Stephen B. Baxter (Berkeley, CA: University of California Press, 1983), pp. 63–107 (p. 83).

2 See Richard Ashcraft, *Revolutionary Politics and Locke's Two Treatises of Government* (Princeton, NJ: Princeton University Press, 1986); and Richard Ashcraft, *Locke's Two Treatises of Government* (London: Unwin Hyman, 1987).

3 Locke, *First Treatise*, pars 86–93, 97; *Second Treatise*, par. 25.

4 *Second Treatise*, pars 7, 16, 135, 171, 183.

5 *First Treatise*, par. 42.

6 *Second Treatise*, par. 183.

7 Locke's memo is reprinted in H. R. Fox-Bourne, *The Life of John Locke*, 2 vols (London: 1876), Vol. 2, p. 382.

8 Ibid., Vol. 2, p. 390.

9 *Second Treatise*, pars 32, 35.

10 Ibid., pars 38, 184.

11 For a discussion of this point and a critique of C. B. Macpherson's interpretation of Locke (*The Political Theory of Possessive Individualism* [Oxford: Oxford University Press, 1962), see Richard Ashcraft, "The politics of Locke's *Two Treatises of Government*," in John Locke's *Two Treatises of Government*, ed. Edward J. Harpham (Lawrence, KS: University Press of Kansas, 1992), pp. 14–49.

12 *Second Treatise*, par. 42.

13 For a good discussion of Locke's mercantilist views, see Mark Blaug, *Economic Theory in Retrospect* (Homewood, IL: R. D. Irwin, 1962), pp. 10–21.

14 See Locke's statement that an Indian king in America is worse off than a daylaborer in England (*Second Treatise*, par. 41) and Adam Smith's paraphrase of this point in *An Inquiry into the Nature and Causes of the Wealth of Nations*, 2 vols, ed. Edwin Cannan (London: Methuen, 1950), Vol. 1, p. 14.

15 Robert Moss, *The Providential Division of Men* . . . (London: 1708), p. 11; *An Essay on Public Industry* (1724), p. 2.

16 George Hill, *The Present Happiness of Great Britain* (Edinburgh: 1792; 2nd edn), p. 10;

Raymond G. Cowherd, *Political Economists and the English Poor Laws* (Athens, OH: Ohio University Press, 1977), p. 40.

17 John Locke, *The Works of John Locke*, 9 vols (London: 1824; 12th edn), Vol. 6, pp. 157–8.

18 I have discussed this point in "Radical anticlericalism and the problem of authority in Locke's thought," presented to a conference at Le Moyne College, Syracuse, NY, September 25–7, 1991.

19 Peter Dunkley, "Whigs and paupers: the reform of the English poor laws, 1830–1834," *Journal of British Studies* 20 (1981): 124–49 (134); J. R. Poynter, *Society and Pauperism* (London: Routledge, 1969), pp. 29–30.

20 Roger North, *A Discourse of the Poor* (1753), pp. 40–1; *Considerations on Fatal Effects* (1763), p. 2; J. W., *Letter to a Member of Parliament* (1767), p. 14.

21 *An Inquiry into Management* (1767), pp. 78, 91–2; Samuel Carter, *Legal Provisions for the Poor* (1710), p. 2; George Nichols, *A History of the English Poor Law*, 3 vols (London: 1854), Vol. 1, pp. 196–7; Paul Slack, *Poverty and Policy in Tudor and Stuart England* (London: Longman, 1988), p. 23.

22 For Locke's memo on the poor laws, see Fox-Bourne, *Life of Locke*, Vol. 2, pp. 377–91; Thomas Firmin, *Some Proposals for the Employment of the Poor* (1681).

23 *Letter to a Conscientious Man* (1720), p. 11; Richard Woodward, *An Argument in Support of the Right of the Poor* (Dublin: 1768), p. 29; Thomas Mangey, *The Wise Steward* (1716).

24 John Bellars, *Abstract of George Fox . . .* (1724), p. 9, cf. p. 3; John Bellars, *Essays About the Poor, Manufactures, Trade, Plantations, and Immorality* (1699), p. 15; Mangey, *Wise Steward*, pp. 9–10.

25 *Letter to a Conscientious Man*, p. 11; Slack, *Poverty and Policy*, pp. 19–22.

26 Peter, Lord King, *The Life of John Locke: with Extracts from his Correspondence, Journals, and Common-place Books*, 2 vols (London: R. Bentley, 1830), Vol. 2, p. 58; John Locke, *Essays on the Law of Nature*, ed. W. von Leyden (Oxford: Clarendon Press, 1954), p. 203; Fox-Bourne, *Life of Locke*, Vol. 2, p. 536; see Locke's will, appendix to Jean LeClerc, *An Account of the Life and Writings of John Locke* (1714; 3rd edn).

27 *Considerations on Fatal Effects*, pp. 10, 31–2; North, *Discourse*, p. 37; Poynter, *Society and Pauperism*, p. 33; Peter Dunkley, "Paternalism, the magistracy and poor relief in England, 1795–1834," *International Review of History* 24, pt 3 (1979): 371–97.

28 William Bayly, *The State of the Poor* (1820), p. 12; *The Poor Laws England's Ruin* (1817; 2nd edn), pp. 2–3.

29 Bayly, *State of Poor*, pp. 60–1.

30 Poynter, *Society and Pauperism*, p. 40; *Poor Laws England's Ruin*, pp. 2–3; M. A. Crowther, *The Workhouse System, 1834–1929* (Athens, GA: University of Georgia Press, 1982), p. 22.

31 *Particular Answers . . . for Relieving . . . the Poor* (1722), p. 56; Firmin, *Some Proposals*, pp. 14, 21, 25; *An Essay on Public Industry*, pp. 5–7. On the punitive character of the poor laws, see A. L. Beier, *The Problem of the Poor in Tudor and Early Stuart England* (London: Methuen, 1983), pp. 13–14.

32 Richard Haines, *England's Weal and Prosperity Proposed* (1681), p. 4; Richard Haines, *Proposals for Building . . .* (1677), p. 7.

33 *An Account of Several Workhouses* (1732; 2nd edn), p. iii; Crowther, *Workhouse System*, p. 41.

34 See, for example, *A Method Concerning the Relief and Employment of the Poor* (1699), pp. 3, 9; Poynter, *Society and Pauperism*, p. 4; Edgar S. Furniss, *The Position of the Laborer in a System of Nationalism* (New York: Houghton Mifflin, 1920), p. 83.

35 *Account of Several Workhouses*, p. iii. In his *History of the Poor Laws* (1764), pp. 213–14, Richard Burn noted the shift in attitudes toward the poor from an Elizabethan concern for the maintenance of the poor to the employment of the poor which occurred at the end of the seventeenth century. For a discussion of this debate concerning employment of the poor, workhouses, and the advancement of trade, see Furniss, *Position*, pp. 85–95.

36 Bellars, *Essays About the Poor*, p. 5; John Bellars, *An Essay for Employing the Poor to Profit* (1723); Haines, *England's Weal*, p. 12; Haines, *Proposals for Building*, p. 7; *Particular Answers*, p. 14; *Considerations on Fatal Effects*, p. 39.

37 *Account of Several Workhouses*, p. vi.

Importance . . . , 2 vols (1767), Vol. 2, pp. 122, 162; Furniss, *Position*, pp. 31, 140–2, 173–5.

42   *Enquiries into the Principal Causes of the General Poverty* . . . (Dublin: 1725), pp. 16, 23; *Essay on Public Industry*, pp. 2–3; Furniss, *Position*, pp. 32, 41, 117–19.

43   Daniel Defoe, *Giving Alms No Charity* (1704), p. 23.

44   Crowther, *Workhouse System*, pp. 42–3.

45   John Bellars, *Proposals for Raising a College of Industry* (1695), pp. 13–14, 23; Bellars, *Essays About the Poor*, p. 4.

46   Carter, *Legal Provisions*, p. 87.

47   Ibid., preface.

48   *Account of Several Workhouses*, p. 127; cf. pp. 143, 145, 159.

49   North, *Discourse*, p. 18. The "crammed, noxious workhouses of Britain" lacked all sense of "decency"; cited in Thomas Horne, *Property Rights and Poverty: Political Argument in Britain, 1605–1834* (Chapel Hill, NC: University of North Carolina Press, 1990), p. 212.

50   North, *Discourse*, p. 18; Poynter, *Society and Pauperism*, p. 16; Furniss, *Position*, p. 109; Crowther, *Workhouse System*, p. 27.

51   Gertrude Himmelfarb, *Idea of Poverty: England in the Early Industrial Age* (New York: Vintage, 1985), pp. 79–80; Poynter, *Society and Pauperism*, pp. 107–9, 129–30; Horne, *Property Rights*, p. 159.

52   Dorothy Marshall, *English Poor in the Eighteenth Century* (London: Routledge, 1926), pp. 104–5; Mark Neuman, "Speenhamland in Berkshire," in *Comparative Development in Social Welfare*, ed. E. W. Martin (London: Allen & Unwin, 1972), pp. 85–127 (p. 100).

53   Bernard Mandeville uses the term in the *Fable of the Bees* (Himmelfarb, *Idea of Poverty*, p. 30), but Defoe may have used it even earlier; cf. Hanaway, *Letters*, Vol. 2, p. 73; *Inquiry into Management*, pp. 78, 91–2; Paul Slack, *The English Poor Law, 1531–1782* (London: Macmillan, 1990), p. 12.

54   Locke, *Works*, Vol. 4, p. 24.

55   North, *Discourse*, p. 60; J. W., *Letter to MP*, p. 10; Furniss, *Position*, p. 48.

56   Poynter, *Society and Pauperism*, pp. 48–9; George R. Boyer, *An Economic History of the English Poor Law, 1750–1850* (Cambridge: Cambridge University Press, 1990), pp. 8, 23–4, 43, 69; Marshall, *English Poor*, pp. 104–5; Neuman, "Speenhamland in Berkshire," p. 100.

57   *Inquiry into Management*, p. 2.

58   Poynter, *Society and Pauperism*, pp. 199, 262–3; P. M. Ashraf, *The Life and Times of Thomas Spence* (Newcastle upon Tyne: Frank Graham, 1983), p. 23; Peter Dunkley, *Crisis of the Old Poor Law in England, 1795–1834: An Interpretive Essay* (New York: Garland Publications, 1982), p. 117; *An Enquiry into the Causes* . . . *of the Poor* (1738), p. 3.

59   Ashcraft, *Revolutionary Politics*, Ch. 7.

60   *An Enquiry into the Nature* . . . *of Public Credit* (1747?), pp. 10–11.

61   Woodward, *An Argument*, pp. 24, 28. For other linkages of the natural right to subsistence with a state of nature and with Locke's argument in particular, see [James Murray] *The Teacher of Common Sense; or, Poor Man's Advocate* (Newcastle: 1779), pp. 1, 22; Brian Inglis, *Poverty and the Industrial Revolution* (London: Panther Books, 1972), p. 442.

62   Poynter, *Society and Pauperism*, p. 34; Horne, *Property Rights*, pp. 136–8; M. L. Clarke, *Paley: Evidences for the Man* (Toronto and Buffalo: University of Toronto Press, 1974), pp. 14–17, 65–6.

63   Horne, *Property Rights*, pp. 230–3; James Murray, *Sermons to Asses* (London: 1768; 2nd edn),

pp. 48, 50, 153; Nicholas C. Edsall, *The Anti-Poor Law Movement, 1834–44* (Manchester: Manchester University Press, 1971), p. 24.

64 Dunkley, "Whigs and paupers," p. 143; Edsall, *Anti-Poor Law*, p. 35; E. P. Thompson, "The moral economy of the English crowd in the eighteenth century," *Past and Present* 50 (February 1971): 76–136, see 123; Slack, *English Poor Law*, p. 44; Crowther, *Workhouse System*, p. 21.

65 Dunkley, "Whigs and paupers," p. 139; Dunkley, *Crisis of Old Poor Law*, pp. 97–100, 112, 122, 136; Crowther, *Workhouse System*, pp. 20–1.

66 Horne, *Property Rights*, pp. 125, 217, 230, 239.

67 *Observations on Misery of the Poor*, pp. 31–4; William Ogilvie, *An Essay on the Right of Property in Land* (1782), pp. 193–5, 229. For a discussion of tracts published in 1734 and 1756, see Furniss, *Position*, pp. 27, 186–7.

68 *Observations on Misery of the Poor*, pp. 32–3.

69 Richard Price, *Postscript to . . . Additional Observations* (1773), pp. 380–1; Murray, *Teacher of Common Sense*, pp. 1–49.

70 Ogilvie, *Right of Property*, pp. 14–15, 188, 229.

71 Ashraf, *Life and Times of Spence*, p. 132; Olive Rudkin, *Thomas Spence and His Connections* (London: n.p., 1927), p. 102.

72 Horne, *Property Rights*, p. 146.

73 Ibid., pp. 246–8. For a further discussion of this point, see Richard Ashcraft, "Liberal political theory and working-class radicalism in nineteenth-century England," *Political Theory* 21, 2 (May 1993): 249–72.

74 Carla H. Hay, "The making of a radical: the case of James Burgh," *Journal of British Studies* 78 (1979): 90–117 (96, 109–10).

75 Josiah Tucker, *A Treatise Concerning Civil Government* (1781), pp. iii, 25–7, 257, 358–9.

76 *Hume's Moral and Political Philosophy*, p. 104.

77 Ibid., pp. 360–2, 368; cf. p. 117.

78 Ibid., pp. 116, 124, 363; cf. pp. 71, 75.

79 Ibid., p. 71.

80 Horne, *Property Rights*, p. 97.

81 Smith, *Wealth of Nations*, Vol. 1, p. 80.

82 Ibid., pp. 75, 83.

83 Ibid., pp. 83–4; Istvan Hont and Michael Ignatieff, "Needs and justice in the *Wealth of Nations*," in *Wealth and Virtue: The Shaping of Political Economy in the Scottish Enlightenment*, ed. I. Hont and M. Ignatieff (Cambridge and New York: Cambridge University Press, 1983), pp. 2, 14–15.

84 Slack, *English Poor Law*, pp. 31, 33–4.

85 Smith, *Wealth of Nations*, Vol. 1, p. 12.

86 Hont and Ignatieff, "Needs and justice," pp. 2–4, 8, 14–15, 25; Himmelfarb, *Idea of Poverty*, p. 46.

87 Poynter, *Society and Pauperism*, pp. 52–3; Himmelfarb, *Idea of Poverty*, pp. 68–71.

88 Horne, *Property Rights*, pp. 162–3; Himmelfarb, *Idea of Poverty*, pp. 67–8; Poynter, *Society and Pauperism*, p. 54.

89 Poynter, *Society and Pauperism*, pp. 114–17; Horne, *Property Rights*, p. 164.

90 Poynter, *Society and Pauperism*, p. 202.

91 Ibid., p. 119.

92 Horne, *Property Rights*, p. 159; Himmelfarb, *Idea of Poverty*, pp. 79–80; Poynter, *Society and Pauperism*, pp. 124, 129–30.

93 Horne, *Property Rights*, pp. 152–4.

94 Poynter, *Society and Pauperism*, p. 122.

95 John Somers Cocks (1st Earl of Somers), *A Short Treatise on the Dreadful Tendency of Levelling Principles* (1793), pp. 10, 23, 27.

96 Himmelfarb, *Idea of Poverty*, pp. 62–3.

97 Poynter, *Society and Pauperism*, p. 152.

98 Ibid., pp. 156–7, 171, 300–1; Himmelfarb, *Idea of Poverty*, p. 122.

............that unemployment would disappear, see Boyer, *Economic History*, p. 64.

105   Dunkley, "Whigs and paupers," p. 129.

106   A. W. Coats, "The classical economists, industrialization, and poverty," in *The Long Debate on Poverty*, ed. R. M. Hartwell and G. E. Mingay (n.p.: Institute of Economic Affairs, 1972), pp. 143–68 (p. 167); Mark Blaug, "The poor law report reexamined," *Journal of Economic History* 29, 2 (June 1964): 229–45 (p. 243); cf. Cowherd, *Political Economists*, p. 239; Boyer, *Economic History*, p. 64.

4

The "misteries" of property
Relationality, rural-industrialization, and community in Chartist narratives of political rights

Margaret R. Somers

Property has long held a foundational place in political theories of rights. The idea that the private and autonomous sphere of property offers rights and protections against the omnipresent potential tyranny of the public state can readily be traced back to Locke's treatises on property, labor, and rights in which he argues that the sole purpose for which government exists is to protect and secure its subjects' property.[1] Most crucially, he insists that the right to this property – which he defines as "lives, liberties and estates" – is a *natural* right rather than an arbitrary one contingent on the will of a ruler (p. 368). For Locke what makes these property rights natural is their rootedness in the deeply private sphere of human labor, more specifically by "mixing our labour" with God's common ground (p. 308).[2] A different republican strand of influence reaches back to Machiavelli's celebration of small agricultural property as the source of political virtue and liberty.[3] Only the capacity for self-support which such property provides can secure for people the material conditions for *independent* political participation, that is, political rights beyond the influence of corruption. The absence of such property conduces to *dependence* as the propertyless are vulnerable to corruption by the rich – the bloated property-owners who will inevitably use money to politically influence weaker citizens.[3] Again, the privacy of ownership is assumed to found the rights to public liberty.

Finally, yet another influential variant on property and rights can be found in Marx.[4] Marx begins from the presupposition that freedom is rooted in the autonomous human capacity for *free* labor; inexorably this points to waged-labor capitalist control over the means and ends of production as the source of unfreedom. Capitalism's exponential dependence on the creation of surplus value demands (beyond the will of individual capitalists) a comparable continual increase in the exploitation and alienation of human labor. Combined with the labor theory of value, discussed by Ian Shapiro in the second chapter in this volume, a powerful claim emerges in Marx for political freedom to lie in the expropriation of capitalist property at the point of production.

Strikingly, these ideologically dissimilar theories clearly converge on a single episte-

citizenship, for example, documents the growth of citizenship as a product of the developmental logic of private property and its social consequences.[7] He argues that the needs of the seventeenth-century landed gentry for waged labor on the land and bourgeois demands for mobile property set the motor in gear for the movement toward civil rights. Subsequent contradictions between property relations and the exclusions and inequalities of class kept the engine going. Political citizenship was a product of the nineteenth-century ascendancy of the middle class, while social citizenship came in the twentieth century with the power of the working class.

This approach to property has a long pedigree. It can be found at the heart of the *social naturalism* of the private sphere from which the growth of the social sciences can be traced.[8] In eighteenth-century England, for instance, we find William Townsend, a statesman and policy-maker, propounding an apocryphal allegory about a desert island "society" of "goats" and "dogs" comprised of only two "races" – property-owners and laborers – who lived in perfect harmony with each other.[9] Counter to prevailing political wisdom, however, this naturalistic social utopia would thrive as a self-regulating (private) economy precisely because of the *absence* of public state interference in the productive sphere. Deprived of poor relief (public welfare) the propertyless would be *naturally* – that is, harmoniously – driven to labor. Dubbed the "theorem of the goats and dogs," the allegory was widely popularized in the (successful) cause of exhortation to repeal the Elizabethan poor laws in 1834. Following Locke, however, Townsend does find one purpose for government on his island. Historically constructed public laws *would* be needed to protect the propertied from theft by the propertyless.

In Townsend, then, and later in Malthus and Ricardo on whom he was a direct influence, the relationship of property and the private sphere was not only foundational and autonomous, but natural and, metaphorically, *biological* – in the sense that the classes are so different by nature that the differences among them are like differences among species. And while its crudity has been long surpassed, the fable still highlights the *conceptual link* between property and political rights. Against the inexorable force of natural law, political forms can be posed as *social* constructions which will either interfere with the harmony of nature (e.g., the poor laws) or be a necessary complement of that same natural force (e.g., laws to protect property).[10]

Two historical periods in particular have played center stage in the story of property's foundational place in liberty and rights-formation. Locke's seventeenth century is of course the first when the landed gentry used their claims to the natural rights of property to demand inclusion in the polity and, when that was consistently denied, to seize power and later to settle on a constitutional monarchy. The second historical period is the second quarter of the nineteenth century, marked first by the combined struggle of the working and middle classes for the vote – culminating in the limited

1832 Reform Bill – and subsequently by the massive growth and ultimate defeat of Chartism. This chapter will focus on these nineteenth-century Chartist claims to political rights and present a counter-foundational approach to the relationship between property and rights. Against the mainstream, I will argue that the private sphere of property – whether in land or in labor – was not perceived to be the precondition for political rights and thus the ultimate protection against public tyranny. By contrast, I will argue that the *public realm of social relations and membership* was the precondition for what the Chartists and the working people defined as property in the first place. The first section of this chapter will address prevailing and recent arguments concerning Chartism and property; the second will present my alternative conception of the Chartists' political culture of property; and the third, fourth, and fifth will explore the historical meaning of that culture in the lives of the Chartists' early modern urban and proto-industrial ancestors.

The underlying method of analysis is one which replaces ideas of class formation and interest with the idea of *narrative identity*.[11] This reflects my effort to find a concept capacious and historically sensitive enough to capture the connectivity of social action. Identities are not formed by interests imputed from a stage of social development (be it pre-industrial or modern), or by "experience" imputed from a social category (such as traditional artisan, factory laborer, or working-class wife), but by a person's "place" in a relational setting comprised of (breakable) rules, (variable) practices and discourses, and binding (and unbinding) institutions. This setting must be conceived as a network of temporal and spatial relationships. The concept of narrative identity, therefore, makes action not an event but an *episode* – one that is shaped by both memory and anticipation. This makes identities both malleable and contested, but nonetheless intelligible only through the narratives of their past. Narrativity also eliminates the notion that certain actions are rational while others are irrational or "backwards-looking"; the relationships which give meaning, contingency, and historicity to identity have no teleology. Thus the development of identity must be explored over the long term, and the problem of understanding the political meaning of property posed afresh as a problem of discovering the complexities of narrative identities and political cultures.

I   Chartism and rights-claims: the rights of property in labor?

The Chartist movement of the second quarter of the nineteenth century bears particular significance for political theory. It is well known that in the face of the 1832 Reform Bill which extended the franchise to the propertied middle classes, working people lost little time in building Chartism, the first and largest autonomous working-class suffrage movement (roughly 1836–48). Because this autonomous movement of propertyless working people went down to defeat against Parliament, now widely enlarged by the newly enfranchised middle classes, the conclusions to be drawn regarding property and rights have long confirmed the foundational approach. As an historical exemplar, however, one aspect of the Chartist period remains for historians and theorists especially intriguing. Although no longer allied with the propertied middle classes, this working-class movement continued to justify its claims to suffrage rights on the basis of

teenth century, these radicalized versions of the labor theory of value were most clearly expressed in the writings of J. F. Bray, William Thompson, John Gray, and Thomas Hodgskin. The "people's science," as it was called, turned Ricardo on his head by appropriating the concept that labor was the source of all value as a reason for workers to be entitled to rights rather than exposed to a commodified labor market.[12] Following the Marxist variant, some historians have since used these writings to prove that the Chartist movement was in fact a class-conscious movement which demonstrated an explicit comprehension that the suffering of working people derived from the point of production and the alienation of their property in labor.

Although this Marxist view had long been challenged by Weberian and neo-Durkheimian perspectives, more recently Gareth Stedman Jones has presented a persuasive and highly influential alternative interpretation of these nineteenth-century working-class claims.[13] It is one that reads a radical Lockeanism into the popular link between property and rights. Drawing from a revisionist approach to Locke in political theory,[14] Stedman Jones was the first to argue that this radical Lockeanism could be applied to the Chartist period. His main argument was with the long-prevalent "social" analyses of Chartism which essentially imputed a socioeconomic causality and meaning to the explicitly *political* language of the Charter. Using what he defined as a political and linguistic approach to Chartism, he argued that people actually *meant what they said*. That is, when working people said that the solution to their distress was political – i.e., in winning the vote – it was because the discursive tradition of radical Lockeanism defined social distress as a political problem, namely, in the monopoly of political power held by the ruling political classes, rather than a problem founded in the production process or the alienation of labor. In the words of Chartist O'Brien:

> Knaves will tell you that it is because you have no property, you are unrepresented. I tell you on the contrary, it is because you are unrepresented that you have no property . . . your poverty is the result not the cause of your being unrepresented.[15]

Stedman Jones takes us back to the eighteenth-century "Country Party" – an important tradition of disaffected smallholding Tories who challenged the great propertied Whig "Court Party" for the corrupting effects of their political monopoly and those gentry practices of exclusion Tories associated with the settlements of 1688 and 1714.[16] In the 1790s, at the beginning of the Reform Movement, this quasi-populist tradition was transmuted into a plebeian phenomenon; it provided a popular political analysis for ruling-class corruption and a constitution-focused solution centering on the demand for more inclusive political representation.[17] Although most historians had argued that with political repression and industrialization, radicalism had faded and by the 1830s been transformed into the beginnings of a truer class-consciousness, Stedman Jones argues instead that the Chartist platform and mass appeal can be explained only by the robust continuity of radicalism and its political critique well into the 1840s. Indeed, the rise and fall of Chartism, according to Stedman Jones, can be made much more intelligible by tracking the actual behavior of the English state. After all, if the concentration of parliamentary power and its legislative consequences were the source of popular distress, it was only logical that the political appeal of radicalism would no longer resonate in the face of actual legislative reform such as the 1847 Factory Act, a statute which, although limited, finally met working-class demands for a ten-hour limit on the working day for women and children.

That it was their *property in labor* which provided working people with the *natural* right to political representation is, of course, the Lockean element in this tradition of radicalism. Indeed, a "reasonable" reading of Locke suggests that "as St Paul and Lenin agreed, the man who did not work had no right to eat"; it is *only* working people who have such a natural right.[18] It was precisely such a reading of Locke, channeled through Paine and Cobbett, to which the Chartists held, according to Stedman Jones, citing their belief that the poverty of the working classes was the result of a process of "legal robbery, made possible by the monopoly of law-making" by aristocratic robbers, "parasites," and "idlers" who lived off wealth that in truth should belong to the workers themselves. Through political corruption these idlers "reaped" the rewards of workers' labor. Despite being viewed as a threat to the propertied by the propertyless, the Chartists "did not regard the working classes as propertyless. For since the only legitimate source of property was labor, laborers were in possession of the most fundamental form of all property" (pp. 108–9). The solution, then, to this problem would *not* be one aimed at expropriating the means of production. On the contrary, it would be one that focused on transforming through universal manhood suffrage a corrupt and unfairly exclusive political system in which "all other forms of property were afforded political and legal support, while that of labor was left at the mercy of those who monopolized the state and the law."[19]

In this reading of Chartism, Stedman Jones launched a significant critique of the socio-centrism which had been characteristic of political analysis in nineteenth-century social history. It is one which gives the workers back their own words and their own lives. For all the strengths and contributions of his revisionism, however, in its fundamentals his reading is still firmly grounded in a familiar epistemological tradition: that in which property as a foundational natural object assumes the role of a private buttress against public tyranny by legitimating political rights.[20] If his reading of political monopoly, for example, is correct, it is still only the *proximate* cause of distress; the ultimate source of political monopoly would have to be in the distinction contemporaries made between landed and other sorts of property. According to the power-holders only fee simple *landed and real property* guaranteed political rights, while the Chartists contested with the equally foundational claim that since labor is the *natural* source of all property, nature demands that laborers should be included in Parliament. Stedman Jones still attributes the political meaning of Chartist claims to their possession of property in labor.

basis for their claims to the right of political participation, these nineteenth-century working people nonetheless clearly articulated that their *very conception of property was itself founded on the preconditions and practices of socially constructed rights and obligations of public membership, social networks, and institutional association.* In this epistemological inversion, the property supporting public rights was not the property of autonomous private labor, but the property of membership. In this we can also read an inverted understanding of the relationship between property and personality. The social identity of freedom and independence was only proximately derived from the autonomy of property. More fundamentally, it was derived from the rights and obligations of membership on which property itself was founded.

This reading of Chartist claims suggests a very different conception of the terms "property," labor," "rights," "freedom," and "liberty," and, above all, of that which most embodied their definition of property, namely that of "skilled" and "fair" labor. Skill was articulated as a property by factory workers and artisans alike. But in the social and narrative identities of these working people, skill was only marginally a technical practice – indeed, through various extra-relational methods many "unskilled" and "dishonorable" workers had obtained technical ability. More fundamentally, skill referred only to those whose work was rightfully exercised within the bonds and bounds of the strict practices of membership. In practical terms, this meant that a person was skilled only if he or she had served an apprenticeship (formal or informal); apprenticeship was the process by which the line was demarcated between inclusion and exclusion of membership.[22] People were included in the freedoms and rights of the skilled community only if they operated within the largely unwritten but well-understood rules and practices of their trade and only if they maintained the "misteries" of their labor associations.[23]

The property of skill was thus a *relational practice* rather than an individual attribute. Not the *capacity* to work a trade but the *right* to do so was endowed by virtue of membership in a skilled community. To ground these abstract arguments about property, labor, and rights, I will briefly revisit the social practices of the Chartists and other contemporary movements. In doing so it should become clear that the right to participate politically (universal suffrage) at both the national and local level was only one of a bundle of liberties that the property of skilled labor was understood to guarantee – others included the substantive regulation of markets in prices, wages, and commodities, and a necessary link between these freedoms and the cohesion of families and communities. Rather than a "moral economy," however, this bundle of rights tied up with property as membership signified a commitment to a form of *regulative liberty* as a form of citizenship. For like citizenship, this was a conception of property tied to rights which were not free-floating and natural but which were connected only with a particular membership in a particular polity of relationships, rules, and obligations.[24]

During the Chartist era English working people marched peacefully to Parliament and they mobbed unpopular workhouses; they petitioned to retain or reinstitute apprenticeship and wage regulations and they demanded new forms of state intervention into the length of the working day; they tenaciously fought for the right to outdoor poor relief and for local control over its administration and they waged militant strikes; they formed self-help and community-based educational organizations and families "huddled" and exercised political influence by boycotting selected merchants; throughout, they linked these practices to the demand for participation in Parliament through universal manhood suffrage.[25] Through all these social practices one central narrative ran like a thick thread. Quite simply, this narrative theme was that working people had inviolable *rights* to a particular *political* and *legal* relationship between *the people* and *the law*. They claimed these rights through a particular understanding of the law, a particular understanding of the people and their membership in the political community, and a particular conception about the rightful relationship between the people and the law. This conception of rights defined independence and autonomy as inexorably linked to the property rights of working people, but only minimally to the fruits of individual labor. The rights rested primarily on membership in the political community. Let us first look briefly at each of the two components, the people and the law, to better understand how they fit together as a single animating principle.

The claims put to the law were composed of three interlocking languages of legal and political rights: one of civil, one of participatory, and the third of substantive and regulative rights. The claim to participatory rights is the one with which we are most familiar. It was salient first in the Reform Movement of the 1820s and then in Chartism during the 1830s and 1840s. In their claims for participatory rights, as Stedman Jones has argued, the Chartists ascribed blame for the social inequities and poverty of the working classes to the political "arrangements" of "that house" (Parliament), arrangements which excluded working people. The second language was that of substantive justice and the claim to regulative law. It was expressed through the consistent demand for the right, the obligation, and the necessity of laws to regulate markets, whether in labor, commodities, machinery, or currency. These two discourses were joined together by a third, the language of civil rights and independence which assumed that *freedom* and *access to law* were rights of all freeborn English people.[26] But the critical conjoining thread among the three was the understanding that because *laws and rules were the infrastructural elements of the social world, then participatory and substantive legal rights were the preconditions of independence and freedom.*[27] This meant that participatory rights were unequivocally understood to be linked to regulative and redistributive issues; that substantive laws were appealed to not by a deferent lower class seeking paternalism or protection, but in the name of liberty and independence, and – as perhaps the strongest indicator – that the Chartists insisted that regulative laws were not to be administered from central state inspection committees. Without exception, each demand to the state for regulation was complemented by the insistence on *local control over the process of implementation*. The anti-poor law movement, for example, railed as much against administrative centralization as against the dreaded workhouse, just as the factory implied that the people were all of those who worked a trade honestly, those who were not idlers (parasites, placemen, capitalists, and aristocrats), and those who had the right to be independent in the "true" sense of the word, that is, on the basis of property rightfully held in labor.[30] Coexisting with this radical Lockeanism, however, was an insistence that *membership rules were the key to self-rule*. This was a conception of the people based neither on the capacity to work, nor on ownership of property in labor, but on actual engagement in "honest labor," skilled labor, and cooperative labor. The people, in this conception, were those who worked *according to membership rules*.[31] The property of labor in this language was not conceived of as an individual attribute but as one consequent on self-regulation *among* the people. Indeed, the very property that gave people the right to be skilled was the property of a formal or informal apprenticeship. Colluders with a competitive and free labor market were excluded.[32] Finally, within this conception of membership and independence, a third language understood the people as those who were equal democratic participants in the practices of self-rule. As Clive Behagg has convincingly documented, an "active form of popular democracy" operated within workshops and trade societies; it found expression in, among other things, trade courts and continually rotating participation in trade responsibilities.[33]

What joined together these three conceptions of the people was that they all defined "the people" in *relational* and *exclusionary* terms. Social and narrative identities were derived not from roles in production, or in terms of their class "interests," but from social and political *relationships*. The line between the people and the oppressors was thus not a strictly horizontal one but a circular one which circumscribed those who had a fictitious independence, whether it was the despised independence of wealth gained from depriving working people of their true property in labor or the fraudulent independence of those who broke the rules of cooperation. Just as the condition of the people was explained in part by political exclusion, the basis of exclusion was in turn explained as the people being deprived of their rightful property in honorable labor, itself defined, in turn, in exclusionary terms. The vocabulary of exclusion was inseparable from the self-identity of workers as independent property owners in their relational rules of association.

This characterization does not prioritize either a language of class or one of politics. There is no question that a language of class developed from the 1830s on, just as there is no question but that that same language identified the state as controlling the levers of social power.[34] But most significant is that the language of *rights* embraced both politics and class; it was the explanatory prism through which class issues and other aspects of social distress were mediated and made intelligible. Rights-claims were thus political in the broadest sense – they established the claim to empowerment deriving not only from constitutional and "natural" rights, but from community cohesion and autonomy in membership. Because they conjoined artisanal conceptions of property-based citizenship rights, these rights-claims also conjoined our usually separate notions of social and political rights. Rights-bearing identities included class rights as one part of a bundle of rights attached to political membership under law; they combined social power, politics, individual rights, and membership.[35]

Thus the prevailing public narrative of the Chartists, and the plot-line by which it was configured, was that of a *political culture of rights*.[36] The history and projected future of this rights culture was the theme through which events were evaluated, explained, and given meaning.[37] The political culture of English working people was based upon political *rights*, *obligations*, and *rules* – rules of law and rules among the people – not upon a conception of their place or function in the sphere of production. I am not asserting that this political culture had nothing to do with Locke. Rather I want to show how radical Lockeanism was overdetermined by a far more deeply institutionalized and highly adaptable set of practices which long preceded Locke and which endured in protean form well into the twentieth century. Let us now explore the narrative identities and relational settings of the Chartists' ancestors.

III   Rural-industrialization: the Chartists' ancestry

The recent body of literature on proto-industrialization would seem to have especially far-reaching importance for understanding nineteenth-century working-class identities since we now know that it was from these regions of rural-industrial concentration that the "industrial revolution" and its working peoples emerged. Although the existence and continual growth of English domestic industry in the countryside from as early as the thirteenth century have long been recognized, the renamed concept of "proto-industrialization" or "industrialization before industrialization" has now moved rural industry to center stage in the analysis of Western European industrialization. The new model, most notably associated with Franklin Mendels, Rudolph Braun, Hans Medick, Peter Kriedte *et al.*, and Chuck Tilly, has large aims (in its more clearly Marxist version, it purports to be no less than the most recent contribution to the extended debate over the transition from feudalism to capitalism), and has had wide influence in revising ideas of economic and social development.[38] Not surprisingly it has generated a small academic revolution in its theoretical challenge to the conventional causal arguments and periodization of European development.[39] No one who speaks of textile work in the rural areas of Western Europe before the nineteenth century can refer to this mode of production in the quaint old terms of the "putting-out industry," "cottage industry," or the "domestic system" without either adopting or explicitly rejecting the new term.[40] And since we now know that the industrial villages of the early nineteenth century sprouted from the labors and lands of proto-industrial families, we can now ask: to what extent can the narrative identities of the Chartists now be understood as a product of an earlier period of proletarianization and propertylessness?

The model's central claim is that industrialization was ultimately successful thanks to the proletarianization of pre-nineteenth-century rural-industrial families. These putting-out working families are said to have comprised the first "modern" labor

The proto-industrial theory depends upon three propositions about the lives and livelihoods of the ancestors of nineteenth-century industrial working people. First, the core of most explanations for the development of rural industry is that it was the *absence* of skilled labor practices that attracted merchants in the first place to areas outside the regulative reach of urban guilds and skilled workers. Second, proto-industrial theorists have readily followed Adam Smith's lead in assuming that little if any technical skill was necessary for the weaving and spinning of textiles. Since textile work did not require technical skill, employers hired unskilled women and children whose cheap labor, he argued, was one of the reasons for the economic success of rural-industrial textile production. And third, rural-industrial workers were completely without self-defensive organizational resources. Analysts following the Webbs' *History of Trade Unionism* have rejected any possible links between guilds, rural labor disputes, and nineteenth-century industrial trade unions; they label earlier appearances of labor conflict "primitive" and "ephemeral," lacking the continuity that fortifies organization.[41] Accordingly, they do not discern the economic preconditions for true organization until the industrial revolution.

Yet English evidence from the countryside challenges the proto-industrial theory. This evidence points to notable labor market power, restrictive practices, the highest European rural-industrial wages, and an extraordinary capacity to use the law to the advantage of working peoples.[42] In England's textile communities (in contrast to agricultural regions) this evidence suggests that clothworkers were not defenseless to a free labor market or the perils of self-exploitation. There is also considerable evidence to suggest that in English textile communities (this time in contrast to rural-industrial workers in continental regions) clothworkers displayed a striking capacity for regulative intervention into the labor market and an impressive – although, to be sure, not invincible – capacity to counter the threats of a free labor market. Although outside of the regulated urban guilds, it appears they nonetheless were able to restrict entry to their trade by regulating the acquisition of skills necessary to work in textile production. Although without formal organization, they were able to prevent fellow workers from accepting "unfair" wages. Although without representatives, they often seized the advantage over employers by demanding higher wages and restricting labor supply in times of labor demand. And although without unions, they were able to provide social security relief for each other in order to prevent the drive of hunger from forcing fellow workers to accept low wages during trade slumps.[43] In fact, rather than wage labor signaling the triumph of an unregulated labor market, powerful regulative practices appear to have been a major force in shaping the nature of English rural-industrial labor relations. Through restrictive and regulative practices, rural-industrial artisans exercised a competing and countervailing set of rules over and against the rules of the free labor market – the supply-demand-wage-price mechanism – of the merchant capitalist employers.

Restrictive labor practices, community empowerment, occupational monopolies, and organized rules among the rural-industrial labor force? Surely such practices are those we associate with skilled artisanal workers. How are we to explain such a pattern among a "propertyless" and fully "proletarianized" community? One answer points to the empirical limitations of the theory. For example, the exclusive utilization of unskilled women and children by rural-industrial employers was not nearly as universal as either Adam Smith or the theorists of proto-industrialization have suggested. David Levine writes that rural industry was "dependent upon the artisanal mode in which the arduously accumulated skills of the craftsman, not the authority of the employer, were the pre-eminent determinants of the method and pace of work." Successful production was therefore built not upon technological complexity and fixed capital, but rather on the "craftsman's experience, intellect, skill, diligence and training." This presents a picture of an independent worker who forced employers to accept the "high cost of craftsmen" in the production process. These judgments are supported by Sidney Pollard's findings that rural industry developed most successfully in those regions notable for their local accumulation of artisanal skills. Buchanan Sharp, referring to the seventeenth century, also rejects the idea that textile work was by-employment, insisting instead on the "artisanal status" of rural clothworkers.[44]

But this addresses only one aspect of the problem. The attempt fully to understand the regulative capacities of rural-industrial people takes us to the serious limitations of the proto-industrial model, especially its theoretical and methodological premises.[45] For all of its breadth of argument and its analytical power, the entire causal sequence of explanation hinges upon the single lynchpin of the "free" and totally unregulated character of the rural-industrial labor market. This, however, is an example of what Karl Polanyi has called "the economistic fallacy," namely, the assumption that economic relations are prior to and hence analytically discrete from institutional and social relationships.[46] Economic sociology can provide an important alternative framework for analyzing rural-industrial labor markets. The approach involves analyzing labor relations not through abstract "economic" functions, but as "an instituted process" of interactive rules and cultural, rather than abstract, relations. In economic sociology we do not ask *whether* markets exist within institutional boundaries, but, instead, of what *nature* are the institutional and cultural frameworks of the market and what are the different *effects* of these frameworks in actual historical *practice*? Economic sociology assumes that *all* labor relations are structured through contested rules of authority, and rights and obligations in regard to the productive use of persons and things.[47] The challenge is to understand empirically the impact of those rules, rights, and obligations. Only this will help us to understand the lives of the rural-industrial predecessors to those nineteenth-century workers who comprised the ranks of the Chartists.

When rural-industrial workers are described as a defenseless proletarianized labor force, it is with the base-line of the regulated urban guilds that they are being compared. Theorists of proto-industrialization argue that it was precisely because urban artisanal guild workers were able to control and restrict labor relations that merchant capitalists sought out and created a free labor market from impoverished rural families outside the guilds in the countryside. But the importance of understanding more fully

of labor but in the nature of the social relations among artisanal workers themselves.[48] I will first explore these institutional surroundings in which urban labor markets were embedded in order to contrast them to those of the rural-industrial countryside. After so doing, I will make the strong and controversial case that English rural-industrial communities were the only ones among European countries that had functionally similar institutional foundations,[49] *and thus that alone among European rural-industrial families, English clothworkers had the capacity to maintain a significant degree of regulative power over their labor markets*. It was this unique capacity which goes a fair way to explain the nature of the political claims and expectations later expressed by their Chartist progeny.

IV   Urban roots of artisanal property in skill

In popular lore, medieval and early modern cities are most renowned for having been a refuge for personal liberty in an age of arbitrary feudal power and insecurity. "A year and a day" was the customary amount of "city air" an escaped serf needed to gain freedom from a manorial lord. But equal in importance to this negative liberty of the freed serf was the positive liberty of citizenship rights to which a surprising number of the population laid claim. Not just elites and bourgeois merchants, but numerous artisans as well "possessed" the freedom of the city and hence the rights of citizenship – the right to law (civil), the right to participate (political), and the right to livelihood (social). This freedom, moreover, was a form of property; it was possessed by those who held rights to its claim. The hallmark of these urban "freedoms" was their rooting in the property of membership.[50] How did this property develop and why did so many urban working people have relatively broad rights long before their "proper" structural cause?

The answer lies in the place of the guild in the urban political culture.[51] In a process of struggle lasting almost half a century, guilds battled local elites of merchants and authorities and eventually won both official recognition and notable power in local governance. The triumph occurred in 1319 by royal charter under King Edward II: all "inhabitants to be admitted [into the freedom] shall be of some *mistery*"; anyone seeking to obtain the freedom who did not belong to a guild "shall then only be admitted with full assent of the commonality assembled."[52] In translation, that meant that to become a citizen one had to enter into or "possess" the "freedom" of the town or city. Yet entry to the freedom and thus to citizenship *could be achieved only through membership in a guild* (the *mistery*).[53] Thus was forged a mighty bond between guild membership and citizenship. It was not the division of labor or the mode of production that shaped artisanal rights and created this political culture. Rather it was the political culture of the guild which gave artisans access to the public sphere of citizenship. In order to make sense of this it is necessary to reconstruct the practices and institutions of that political culture, its civil rules and codes of membership. For therein lay its power.

In a medieval and early modern town more was required for a skilled artisan to ply the trade than knowledge of a technical skill. To practice the "arte and mystery" of a craft required guild membership. Only members of a guild could legally practice their craft in a town, but guild membership in turn required the possession of a crucial kind of property – the property of an apprenticeship.[54] Apprenticeship, of course, is generally thought of as a period of training for a skill, but the meaning of an apprenticeship was not primarily in its technical training. Seven years was the standard time required to serve as an apprentice but at the end of the service the artisan did not "leave behind" the apprenticeship. Only in part did it represent the journeyman's training and investment of time. More significantly, the credential of an apprenticeship signified the new "ownership" of a set of social and political relations and connections, a guaranteed place in a network of attachments, as well as all the rights and obligations consequent to those attachments. The apprenticeship now became the artisan's "property" – a permanent credential belonging to the artisan guaranteeing benefits as long as these were exercised within the guild. This was not mobile property that attached to the individual craftsperson.[55] The property acquired during an apprenticeship was in fact the property of social membership; the exercise of apprenticeship rights was thus *predicated* on the practice and maintenance of institutionalized social relations.

The key to this relational conception of property is in the original English word for skill. The word is *"mistery,"* as in the "arte and mistery of weaving." One reason skill was a *mistery* was because knowledge of a craft was viewed as a specialized and symbolic secret that should take time and trust to acquire.[56] But *mistery* had another meaning and use that prevailed over the first: a *mistery* was also the medieval word for the craft guild itself, the social body, the fellowship, the corporate and instituted group.[57] Unlike the word "skill" which is singular and individual, *mistery* was simultaneously individual and corporate. To possess the *mistery* was to simultaneously "possess" knowledge and membership.[58] By contrast, in modern social science and economics, skill is defined as "human capital," a technical capacity which provides economic power to an individual. But in the political culture of the guild an "unskilled" worker was not defined as such because he or she was technically incompetent. *Indeed, through a wide array of illegal practices many "unskilled" workers, in fact, were technically trained.* The definition of an "unskilled," "dishonorable," and "illegal" worker was one who worked without the property of an apprenticeship, that is, who worked without a *mistery*, without *relational obligations*, without the bounds and the bonds of association, and without the political culture of membership. The attachments of membership, not training or ability alone, conferred legality and the property of skill.[59]

The property of apprenticeship and skill was therefore a form of *cultural capital*. It was a social and cultural *"mistery,"* not a technical or individual attribute. At the end of the service, the crafts-person (now a journeyman) was taken through a public ceremony in which he or she swore by oath to follow the guild's rules and obligations.[60] With that oath the artisan was entitled and obligated to the connections and the powers embodied in the property of apprenticeship. This included citizenship, livelihood,

dence and autonomy suggests the importance of distinguishing the normative from the institutional conception of relationality. The right to the freedom of practicing one's skill, as well as that of citizenship, achieved the goal of individual empowerment. But this empowerment only had viability when rooted in the institutional foundations of attachments and membership. Only the possession of membership allowed for individual empowerment and the meaningful exercise of rights. Clearly the practices of relationality were matched by those of exclusion, thus preventing citizenship rights from being automatically conferred upon all people. But this is the important point: among "the people" inclusion and exclusion (including gender exclusion) were based less on class divisions or land ownership than on the political contingencies and powers of membership.

V   Rural-industrialization, property, and skill

On the face of it, these urban practices would seem to have little to do with rural-industrial labor markets and livelihoods. After all, it was precisely to avoid this political culture of skill and property that merchant capitalists sought out the rural countryside. But to accept this proposition is to assume exactly that which economic sociology urges us to question – namely the very possibility that economic relations and labor markets can ever operate outside of any cultural and institutional environment. English rural-industrial labor markets, contrary to this assumption, most assuredly did *not* exist outside of any institutional framework. In fact, through different means rural-industrial communities existed within a political culture functionally parallel to that of the urban guilds. I have considered the first two institutional foundations elsewhere.[63] In this final section I will concentrate on the third – the rural-industrial possession of property in membership on which an essential part of their political culture was grounded.

We have seen that the regulative labor power of guild workers in large part was dependent upon the networks of association among members themselves. What this presupposed, however, and what the enforcement of sanctions required, was the continuity of an independent and self-disciplined community. Independent, because the community had to be free from potentially countervailing elite sanctions and rules. And self-disciplined, because workers chose the public relations of the laboring community over private interests whether through apprenticeship, "fair" and "just" wage levels, or participation in formal and informal mutual social security associations. Recall that the right to acquire skill – and so to have the "attributes" necessary for employment – was the *result* of an individual's inclusion and rootedness within the community that controlled the right to be trained. A skilled community, therefore, was a particular kind of community. It was one that conferred independence upon the working person – we can think of it as a "willed community" rather than a "traditional community" – and it certainly did not preclude, but negotiated with, commodity and labor markets.[64] The independence of the willed community was based not on the freedom of the individual labor contract, but on the freedom gained by the exercise of rights and expectations, of *public and relational* protection against private economic power. Through the individual's alliance with a set of social and public relationships, skill and independence became rights of membership. The network or community of the skilled was the precondition for restrictive labor market practices.

If rural-industrial workers were also able to exercise such practices, it must be explained by the political and institutional relationships of their communities. But we must be careful not to make the mistake of looking for evidence of "proto-bureaucracies." The Webbs' approach suffered from an excessive formalism; as long as they were looking for something which resembled modern unions, they surely could not find it in rural-industrial countryside. If we turn their arguments inside out, however, a different proposition can be considered. Regulative power was not the cause, but the result, of workers' association. This allows us to consider textile communities from a different perspective. It was not formal trade unionism that created workers' association, but the reverse: by maintaining relationality over time and space, English rural clothworkers were able to organize without formal guilds. As in the case of urban skilled artisans, this regulative solidarity was contingent upon community institutions and practices of association which promoted the power of sanction and the conferring of collective rights. Like urban skilled artisans, rural-industrial textile workers nego-tiated with market forces through cohesive political association. Association *preceded* organization; indeed, it was its foundation. Yet a question still remains. Association required the continuity of a settled population, and such continuity cannot be taken for granted in the face of the potentially corrosive impact of the market. It is not enough to explain association by relying on *gemeinschaft* notions of "habit," or to claim that association was a "natural . . . part of the life of the community."[65] The capacity for association or community cannot be invoked or assumed; it must be explained.[66]

To understand the capacity for association, it is the relational "infrastructure" of rural-industrial life that must be the subject of analysis.[67] English textile communities differed from agricultural communities in their conditions and rules. Along two axes English rural textile communities resembled urban communities: 1) in the degree of spatial and political independence from authority; and 2) in the degree of self-regulated cooperation among themselves. Along the first axis, rural-industrial communities had both a relatively less powerful, smaller, and more diffused manorial presence as well as an employer class which did not live locally. These communities, therefore, enjoyed greater collective independence than did agrarian communities. And along the second axis, textile communities had more tightly regulated kin relationships. These two interrelated characteristics combined to create the sociological hybrid of self-regulating independent communities which linked independence not to freedom *from* the public sphere but *to* public participation, self-rule, and membership rules binding people to each other.

Among the several factors that supported rural-industrial life was the ownership of a kind of property with which we should now be familiar – the property of skill. By

labor "much above what is due to the nature of their work."[68] Just as with urban apprenticeship, rural apprenticeship required of the young person a mandatory seven years of association with an adult worker. It was intended to prevent people from acting out of individual interest and to check the balance of employer demand over worker supply by restricting the numbers of available working people. Preventing gluts of labor by controlling entry was only one of the benefits of apprenticeship. Through apprenticeship the customs of the trade were passed on and preserved, and the practice became part of the "school of public life" in which rights and obligations were taught and given renewed life.[69] Those who violated these became "unskilled" and "unfair" workers. Skilled working people were not skilled because they had been apprenticed; they were apprenticed only because they were already "skilled," which is to say, participants in a network of social relations that practiced obligation and exclusion.

Apprenticeship was not only a right of participation in the collectivity; it was also in no uncertain terms conceived of as a property right. Where Smith viewed apprenticeship as a violation of the "most sacred and inviolable" property which every man had in his own labor, skilled workers viewed the right that a formal or informal apprenticeship conferred upon them as the true kind of property – the kind defined by the social relations and the institutional association of which they were a part.[70] Thus, one weaver claimed in defense of the practice: "The weaver's qualifications may be considered as his property and support. It is as real property to him as buildings and land are to others. Like them his qualification cost time, application and money" as well as "the care and purchase of their parents and friends."[71] This property right, moreover, was sanctioned by the state. English rural-industrial workers were *not* excluded from regulative policies; the 1563 Statute of Artificers made apprenticeship a national legal right throughout town and country. But – and this is crucial – the state was only codifying an existing practice and institution which long predated and in fact informed the Act of 5 Elizabeth. Thus, while it was an essential by-law of all guild and chartered companies, apprenticeship was no less deeply embedded in the strictly regulated networks and by-laws of the rural-industrial countryside and the textile villages where it was a long-established custom. Accordingly, when defending the putatively inviolate customary status of the threatened law in 1814, craftspeople would frequently cite the legal definition of custom in claiming that apprenticeship had been a right of working people "from time, to the contrary whereof the memory of man runneth not."[72]

The right to become skilled by means of an apprenticeship was thus a right given only to those already included in associated networks. In cities, the guilds determined who was to be included. But in the absence of formal urban guilds, the question must arise as to what could play the same role of defining who was to be included and who was to be excluded from the right to apprenticeship.

The rural-industrial family was the guild of the countryside. In the 1970s and 1980s, building on the pathbreaking work of earlier scholars such as Ivy Pinchbeck and Alice Clark, scholars developed an influential "household economics" theory to address the relationship between the family and early capitalist development.[73] The household economics approach begins from a set of Marxist assumptions about the logic of capitalist production. The chief one concerns the transmutation of potentially resistant workers into "factors of production." Applied to proto-industry, this assumption points to the commodification of the family unit by the process of capitalization in the countryside. Most important to this claim is the assumption of the propertyless condition of these family units. Without ownership of production it is assumed that the family had no resources to resist total exploitation. In contrast to the militancy of an organized urban artisanry, rural-industrial families are thus portrayed principally as powerless victims to the invincible logic of accumulation. But there is a different angle of vision from which to view the relationship between the rural-industrial family and textile production for a waged labor market. This perspective would begin with the "logic" of the family itself.

Rural clothworkers were the progenies of earlier peasant families who tenaciously practiced partible inheritance in the pastoral regions of England. Dividing the land among heirs ensured generational bonding over time and space and so institutionalized in inheritance patterns the rights and obligations of social security and family cohesion. When early modern rural families confronted the new conditions of rural-industrial production and the potential threats of an open labor market, this "logic" of partibility was not superseded by the logic of accumulation. Instead, the pastoral-cum-rural-industrial family flexibly transformed the rights that land inheritance guaranteed to a new form of inheritance adapted to the new conditions: *it converted the rights of partible inheritance into the rights of the inheritance of skill.* This conversion explains the rural-industrial family's jealous control over its power to confer apprenticeship: as long as children were dependent upon the acquisition of apprenticeship to enter on fair terms the associated laboring collectivity, they were equally bound to their families. The practice of transmitting and distributing skills among children served, like the practice of partible inheritance, as a *transgenerational trust*.

Because it established the boundaries of social inclusion, membership in a family was the prerequisite for apprenticeship. In a process comparable to guilds (and guilds were originally nothing more than households), clothworking families regulated and distributed apprenticeships.[74] It all looked deceptively simple and natural: apprenticeships were usually carried out either in the home, where both father and mother instructed their children, or in a neighbor's or relative's home, or even in a small workshop.[75] In rural-industrial regions, family continuity in the trade was the rule. Parentally trained children either worked in the family home until they inherited it, or set up their own family home when they married; their parents were likely to help them purchase their own looms. Weaving, for example, was always taught to children by a parent or sibling:

> My mother taught me (while too young to weave) to earn my bread carding and spinning cotton, winding linen or cotton weft for my father and elder brothers at the loom, until I became of sufficient age and strength for my father to put me into a loom.[76]

Threatened with the potentially corrosive impact of a wage-labor market, apprenticeship became the glue of the rural-industrial family's cohesion. The right to apprenticeship, like the right to land, was an institutional relationship. And like all institutional relationships with any binding power, it was composed of a right and an obligation: apprenticeship conferred the right to full membership in the laboring community while it simultaneously obliged the child to the family. This generational bonding over time was as essential for the parents as for the young. It ensured support for parents when their old age significantly reduced their earning power.[77]

But rights and obligations need sanctions to work effectively. Like the ownership of land, the "ownership" of the "property" of apprenticeship was an entitlement that was conditional upon fulfilling family and community obligations. Because the right to the property of industrial skill required familial bonding, the sanction and the expectation of apprenticeship maintained familial cohesion and stability. One could not go out and simply buy an apprenticeship; apprenticeships were available only to those already within the family system. As a social right, apprenticeship could be acquired only through the networks of inheritance and familial transmission. Apprenticeship was thus a thoroughly *relational idiom*. It was both acquired in the first place through the relationships, the rights, and the duties of family membership; and it was only *useful* as an institutional relationship, to entitle the owner to the right of inclusion in the working community.

If the loss of land threatened to loosen parental control over children,[78] the transmission of skill came to substitute for land with an equally iron-like grip and maintained the geographical stability of rural-industrial villages.[79] Unlike children in agricultural regions, children of rural-industrial families did not normally leave home for service in another household.[80] Instead they stayed at home to serve their apprenticeship. And when rural-industrial children did leave home after apprenticeship to set up their own households, they did not go far. Even among those who moved, it was rarely more than fifteen miles from the place of birth. Marriage partners were usually from the immediate area and families entrenched themselves by spreading out in their regions so that networks of families, kin, and kindred could absorb and redistribute resources.[81] What mobility did take place, moreover, was orchestrated through networks of kin, former workers, or neighbors, and "extended" families of lodgers, neighbors, and kin were so common in these households that they have been described as "eating up labour."[82]

Family practices had a direct impact on social relations in the community at large, producing a denser network of kinship ties – hence community-wide rights and obligations – than in the non-textile regions.[83] The density of actual blood-kinship relations varied across rural communities; people in rural-industrial communities were more closely related than people in rural-agricultural communities. This is not difficult to explain: because they produced more children, and because these children tended to stay within their immediate place of birth, it is not surprising that over time rural-industrial communities would have denser kinship networks. These denser kinship relationships among people promoted stronger social sanctions and interdependent expectations of rights and obligations than among non-blood-related neighbors. They reinforced the distribution of skills, regulated the level of acceptable wages, and countered the pull of hunger by providing alternative sources of livelihood to those of "illegal" wages. The consequences were likely to be swift and direct for those who violated kinship pressures, most likely the severing of the social relations on which individual survival was based. But the normal sanctions of kinship ties more than likely pre-empted many violations even before they happened.

While clothworking families thus imposed their own cohesive practices against the corrosive impact of the labor market, these practices were not, however, geared toward familial isolation from the working community at large. Woven into the fibers of intra-familial relationships, apprenticeship throughout the wider community was equally "woven into the fabric of domestic industry" in all of the rural-industrial regions.[84] Familial practices of apprenticeship set the standard (if not always the reality) for a closed labor market not only in the older textile regions of the West Country, East Anglia, or the West Riding of Yorkshire but also in Lancashire's newest cotton regions where apprenticeship was formally excluded from Eliz 5. Community control over apprenticeship was usually much stronger than that of formal law and a fully competitive labor market was hard pressed to "take off" even in the nation's number one growth industry of cotton. Apprenticeship was the chief emblem of participatory rights in the labor community. It denoted initiation in and commitment to the common ethics and obligations of that community, and it conferred the right to independence characteristic of skilled labor.

Family practices were also at the heart of self-regulation in work. The family basis of labor supported a structure of production that depended upon coordination, cooperation, and mutual interdependence. Because rural textile production operated on a domestic basis, it is often thought to have been a non-disciplined, almost idiosyncratic activity that took place in spurts. But even when compared to the more notorious aspects of early factory discipline, the degree of anomie among rural-industrial working people has been greatly exaggerated.[85] Mutual interdependence was necessary to rural-industrial production, and the familial and community bases of production ensured the enforcement of this interdependency. Mutual interdependence in work relations began in the family itself. As a unit of labor, the family was observed to have been like a disciplined machine made up of interconnected parts. This was so pronounced in the domestic textile industry that in the Napoleonic wars, the government was reluctant to conscript family members out of concern that the disruption to family units of production would be of greater damage to the productive capacity of the nation than the military benefits.[86] Women and children did not de-skill the workforce. On the contrary, the interdependency of the working unit reinforced the skilled practices of association.

Coordination and cooperation not only characterized a single producing family but also integrated the multiple family units in the rural-industrial community. The

The direct link between family practices and the regulation of the labor supply of the larger community was forged through the currency of a political culture of membership. The rightful and "fair" membership in the networks of textile working families which apprenticeship demanded was an induction into the social experience of the community.[88] To violate these values in favor of individual gain was in these terms an absolute loss; to be deprived of the association was a total deprivation. That dishonor and enforced isolation befell one who took on work as an "illegal," who accepted lower than customary wages under the temptation of unemployment, who refused to support a strike or to give mutual assistance to a fellow worker, may well have been experienced as group tyranny. But that cooperation in the ethics of regulative solidarity was identified by contemporaries as a *right* and a *freedom* is not in doubt.

The picture of rural-industry my argument offers is as different from the picture presented in the proto-industrialization model as my picture of community independence is from the *gemeinschaft* models of traditional communities. Theories of proto-industrialization substitute merchant capitalist wealth for landed wealth as the labor market mechanism shaping society, and argue that because they lived beyond the bounds of urban regulated guilds, rural producers were unorganized and overpopulated and thus defenseless victims of the market forces of supply and demand. If the proto-industrialization theory is correct, the rural-industrial community should have been utterly corroded by the capitalization of the countryside. But the wage-labor market was itself confronted by the strength of institutional relationality and social networks. The bundle of rights and obligations embodied in apprenticeship – the relationality bound up in the right to the property of skill – was a formidable force against any inherent logic of capital production.

Conclusion

We have seen many social practices in action; but can we identify a logic to them? In many ways they appear to be a jumble of incompatible ideas. The notion that individual freedom was rooted in social and institutional relationships is incompatible with foundational ideas which locate freedom in the private realm of an individual's right to freedom from the tyranny of the public sphere – the group, the despot, the church, or the community. The "customs of the trade" were surely part of the lexicon of the "traditional craftsman," and so seem oddly cloaked in the modern language of liberty, freedom, and rights. Apprenticeship is another "traditional" idea which may fit with pre-industrial society before the age of new model unionism,[89] but which seems incompatibly linked with the idea of property right. Wage demands, on the other hand, are surely modern demands that seem out of place with the more traditional ideas of solidarity (it was E. P. Thompson who spoke of the transition from the eighteenth to the nineteenth century as one reflected in the transition in demands from the "bread nexus" to the "wage nexus").[90] And finally the principle of freedom in associations seems equally odd: traditional (urban) guilds are identified with mutual associations, but the redistribution of wages and the inter-local alliances of these rural-industrial textile workers seem distinctly like the modern "citizen wage" of the welfare state. We may have identified the connections among skill, property, and rights but have we unraveled their meaning?

The relationship among these activities strongly suggests that livelihoods did not depend on the reproduction or even the ownership of productive processes; rather, livelihood was constituted through the rules of social networks and their political cultures. The property of membership and the rights it endowed reflected the insepar-able connection between individual freedom and participatory embeddedness within the ties of social relations. Freedom and independence – both of which were highly valued and articulated goals of Chartists – were thus not conceived as "freedom from" the community, the family, the state, or the law. On the contrary, freedom, independence, even property itself, were explicitly linked to the relationship of the individual to the variety of ways that institutional relationships were expressed.

Nineteenth-century workers who were to fill the rank and file of the Chartist move-ment brought with them this political culture of property, rights, and membership – one at odds with the ideas of liberal, Marxist, and communitarian theories which have long dominated theories of class formation. In their political culture, to maintain skill was to maintain the associated and regulative character of the working community, to maintain its capacity for association. The aim was to prevent the metaphorical separ-ation of each person's public associations – of family, of kin, of community, of the public – from the individual person's private wage contract. For if the associated character of skill preserved independence, the reverse was also true: detachment led to free agency, competition, and labor glutting through "de-skilling" – in short, to collec-tive discontinuity. The degree to which textile workers saw wage levels as a means of corporate mutuality is a lucid example of the simultaneity of "modern" waged labor relations and "traditional" corporate solidarity. Wage demands are viewed by many sociologists as "reformist" demands indicating an acceptance of modern capitalism, the modern market and its ancillary social attributes – primarily that of self-interest. "Traditional" behavior, on the other hand, is supposed to be "qualitative"; traditional workers allegedly focus on non-monetary forms of moral solidarity. Neither of these presuppositions can account for the relationship between a waged labor market and the cooperative use of wages on the part of the workers. The explanation is simple: wage demands in the interest of relationality reflected the flexible readjustment of a collective identity based on association to the reality of waged labor. A waged labor market did not fragment and corrode the community of producers into abstract free agents divested of their sociality; nor did that community only "look backward" to a non-market and non-waged system of labor relations. In a world where production was primarily one of wage-labor, association required harnessing the currency of the cash-nexus. Wage levels, to be sure, were central issues, but in a non-utilitarian context they were "citizen wages."

larger public sphere. It was not property that *caused* political rights; it was the political culture of membership that produced property, and the rights of property were expressed through the cultural capital of membership rights. Property could take the form of land, the house, or, most importantly, skill. But regardless of its form, its meaning was relational. The rights of property in effect existed only within the context of institutional relationships and the political culture of which they were a part. Beginning in the seventeenth century, this relational concept of property was forced to compete with a newly developed idea of liberty based solely on the individual rights of property produced from autonomous labor. Since then these Lockean ideas of natural rights have dominated the social history of politics.[91] But not only did the former public conception of rights and freedom prove remarkably robust in its competition with Locke's ideas; arguably, it was more significant in shaping modern popular conceptions of and claims to political rights.

Finally, I want to argue that this study suggests a radical amendment to a common thread underlying recent historiographical and sociological moves to abandon economic relations and instead to concentrate principally on culture, discourse, and ideology. These revisions have been invaluable. Paradoxically, however, they have often had the unintended consequence of reinforcing (by neglect) the "economism" of social history. Stressing culture or even politics as separate spheres from the economy leaves intact the fiction that markets are self-regulating, autonomous systems. It locates labor and property and material life on one side, and cultural and political concerns on the other. But the challenge to the "economistic fallacy" must be twofold: it must not only reject the idea that the state (or culture, or ideas) is driven by the logic of the economy. More fundamentally, it must challenge the idea that there can exist a "logic" of the economy that is not itself institutionally and culturally constituted.[92]

Notes

An earlier version of this chapter was first presented as a paper in 1989 at the UCLA Clark Library symposium, "Conceptions of property," sponsored by the Center for Seventeenth- and Eighteenth-Century Studies. I am grateful to members of the seminar for their engaged responses to the paper. In addition I would like to thank John Brewer, Gloria Gibson, Tom Green, Rick Lempert, Bill Sewell, Susan Staves, Marc Steinberg, and Lawrence Stone for their comments on a previous version. The research was carried out in part under the auspices of a 1989–90 fellowship at the Shelby Cullom Davis Center for Historical Studies, Princeton University. I thank Lawrence Stone for making that support possible.

1   John Locke, *Two Treatises of Government* (Cambridge, UK: Cambridge University Press, 1970; 2nd edn).

2   Not only do we therefore not need a ruler's permission to exercise those rights, but the duty of the government is above all to secure those "natural rights" through the consent of all rational men (p. 344). Among the many recent studies which address theoretically and historically the nature and influence of Locke's views on property see especially John Dunn, *The Political Thought of John Locke* (Cambridge, UK: Cambridge University Press, 1970); J. G. A. Pocock, *Virtue, Commerce and History* (Cambridge, UK: Cambridge University Press, 1985); Richard Ashcraft, *Locke's Two Treatises of Government* (London and Boston, MA: Allen & Unwin, 1987); James Tully, *A Discourse on Property* (Cambridge, UK: Cambridge University Press, 1980); Alan Ryan, *Property* (Minneapolis, MN: University of Minnesota Press, 1987); Alan Ryan, *Property and Political Theory* (Oxford: Blackwell, 1984); H. T. Dickinson, *Liberty and Property* (London: Weidenfeld & Nicolson, 1977); and Ian Shapiro, *Political Criticism* (Berkeley, CA: University of California Press, 1990).

3   Niccolò Machiavelli, *The Discourses* (Harmondsworth, Mx: Penguin, 1970), pp. 102–4.

4   Karl Marx, *Writings of the Young Marx on Philosophy and Society*, ed. Lloyd Easton and Kurt Guddat (New York: Doubleday, 1967); Karl Marx, "The German ideology," in *Karl Marx: Selected Writings*, ed. David McLellan (Oxford: Oxford University Press, 1977), pp. 159–91; Karl Marx, *Capital*, Vol. III (London: Lawrence & Wishart, 1974); Karl Marx, *Capital*, Vol. I (Harmondsworth, Mx: Penguin, 1976), Ch. 26.

5   On the significance of social naturalism in defining the private sphere as a foundational natural object, see Margaret R. Somers, "The political culture concept: the empirical power of conceptual transformation" (paper presented at the American Sociological Association meetings, Cincinnati, OH, 1991).

6   See also Reinhard Bendix, *Nation-Building and Citizenship* (Berkeley and Los Angeles, CA: University of California Press, 1977 [1967]); Charles Tilly, *Coercion, Capital, and European States, A.D. 990–1990* (Oxford: Blackwell, 1990); Charles Tilly, "Where do rights come from?" Working Paper #98, Center for Studies of Social Change, New School for Social Research (New York: 1990); Anthony Giddens, *The Constitution of Societies* (London: Macmillan, 1985); J. M. Barbalet, *Citizenship* (Minneapolis, MN: University of Minnesota Press, 1988); and Bryan S. Turner, *Citizenship and Capitalism* (London: Allen & Unwin, 1986). For an important exception see Michael Walzer, *Spheres of Justice* (New York: Basic Books, 1982).

7   T. H. Marshall, *Citizenship and Social Class* (Cambridge, UK: Cambridge University Press, 1950).

8   See Margaret R. Somers, "Where is sociology after the historic turn? Knowledge, cultures and historical epistemologies," in Terrence J. McDonald (ed.), *The Historic Turn in the Human Sciences* (forthcoming); and Somers, "The political culture concept."

9   William Townsend, *Dissertation on the Poor Laws 1786 by a Well-Wisher of Mankind* (Berkeley and Los Angeles, CA: University of California Press, 1979 [1786]).

10 Which is why in modern economic theory, institutions are defined as market "impairments" which must be bracketed for analytical purposes and only factored back in after the natural formula of the market is analyzed.

11 Margaret R. Somers, *The People and the Law: Narrative Identity and the Place of the Public Sphere in the Making of Modern Citizenship Rights* (Ithaca, NY: Cornell University Press [the Wilder House series in Politics, History and Culture, University of Chicago], forthcoming); Margaret R. Somers, "Narrativity, narrative identity, and social action; rethinking English working-class formation," *Social Science History* 16 (Winter 1992): 591–630; and Margaret R. Somers and Gloria Gibson, "Reclaiming the epistemological 'other': narrative and the social constitution of identity," in Craig Calhoun (ed.), *Social Theory and the Politics of Identity* (Oxford: Blackwell, 1994).

12 Noel W. Thompson, *The People's Science: the Popular Political Economy of Exploitation and Crisis, 1816–1834* (Cambridge, UK: Cambridge University Press, 1984).

13 H. L. Perkin, *The Origins of Modern English Society 1790–1880* (London: Routledge & Kegan Paul, 1969); Neil J. Smelser, *Social Change in the Industrial Revolution: an Application of Theory to the Lancashire Cotton Industry, 1770–1840* (Chicago: University of Chicago Press, 1959); Craig J.

17   E. P. Thompson opens his *The Making of the English Working Class* (New York: Vintage, 1966) with a discussion of English radicalism in the 1790s through the Napoleonic Wars.

18   "It is going too far to say that Locke either said or implied in the Second Treatise that 'he who does not work, neither shall he eat,' but it is not going too far to say that what Locke wrote implied it. [And] Works outlive their authors." Ryan, *Property and Political Theory*, p. 4, original emphases.

19   Stedman Jones, *Languages of Class*, pp. 108–11.

20   The concept of the epistemologically privileged place of a "natural object" is taken up at length in Somers, "The political culture concept."

21   Paraphrased from Jack Goody, *Death, Property, and the Ancestors* (Stanford, CA: Stanford University Press, 1962): "A man without social relations is a man without property," p. 287.

22   On the surprising number of women who served apprenticeships see K. D. M. Snell, *Annals of the Labouring Poor: Social Change in Agrarian England 1660–1900* (Cambridge, UK: Cambridge University Press, 1985); Maxine Berg, "Women's work, mechanisation and the early phases of industrialization in England," in Patrick Joyce (ed.), *The Historical Meanings of Work* (Cambridge, UK: Cambridge University Press, 1987), pp. 64–98.

23   See below for a full discussion of the relational meaning of the word "mistery."

24   For a full discussion of this conception and the development of nineteenth-century citizenship claims see Somers, *The People and the Law*; Margaret R. Somers, "Rights, relationality, and membership: rethinking the making and meaning of citizenship," *Law and Social Inquiry* 19, 1 (1994): 1301–50; and Margaret R. Somers, "Citizenship and the place of the public sphere: law, community, and political culture in the transition to democracy," *American Sociological Review* 58, 5 (1993): 587–620.

25   On machine-breaking and Luddism, see Thompson, *The Making of the English Working Class*, Ch. 14; E. Hobsbawm, *Labouring Men* (London: Weidenfeld & Nicolson, 1964); J. R. Dinwiddie, "Luddism and politics in the northern counties," *Social History* 4, 1 (1979): 33–63; Charlotte Brontë, *Shirley* (Oxford: Clarendon Press, 1979).

     On the petitioning of Parliament and Chartism, see Clive Behagg, *Politics and Production in the Early Nineteenth Century* (London: Routledge, 1990); Asa Briggs, "The background of parliamentary reform in three English cities (1830–32)," *Cambridge Historical Journal* 10 (1952): 293–317; Asa Briggs, "The language of 'class' in early nineteenth-century England," in Asa Briggs and John Saville (eds), *Essays in Labour History* (London: Macmillan, 1960), pp. 43–73; James Epstein, *The Lion of Freedom: Feargus O'Connor and the Chartist Movement, 1832–1842* (London: Croom Helm, 1982); James Epstein and Dorothy Thompson (eds), *The Chartist Experience: Studies in Working-Class Radicalism: 1830–60* (London: Macmillan, 1982); J. C. Belchem, "Henry Hunt and the evolution of the mass platform," *English Historical Review* 93 (1978): 739–73; J. C. Belchem, "Radical language and ideology in nineteenth-century England: the challenge of the mass platform," *Albion* 20 (1988): 247–59; J. C. Belchem, "Republicanism, popular constitutionalism and the radical platform in early nineteenth-century England," *Social History* 6 (1981): 1–32; Dorothy Thompson, *The Chartists: Popular Politics in the Industrial Revolution* (New York: Pantheon, 1984); R. G. Gammage, *The History of the Chartist Movement* (New York: Augustus M. Kelley, 1969); M. Hovell, *The Chartist Movement* (Manchester: Manchester University Press, 1966); Stedman Jones, *Languages of Class*; James Epstein, "Understanding the cap of liberty: symbolic practice and social conflict in early nineteenth-century England," *Past and Present* 122 (1989): 75–118.

On storming workhouses, see A. Digby, *Pauper Palaces* (London: Routledge & Kegan Paul, 1978); Charles Tilly, "Proletarianization and rural collective action in East Anglia and elsewhere," *Peasant Studies* 10, 1 (1982): 5–34.

On the fight to retain apprenticeship and wage regulations, see J. Rule, *The Labouring Classes in Early Industrial England, 1750–1850* (London: Longman, 1986); I. Prothero, *Artisans and Politics in Early Nineteenth-Century London: John Gast and His Times* (Folkestone, Sx: Dawson, 1979); J. Hammond and B. Hammond, *The Skilled Labourer 1760–1832* (London, New York: Longman, Green, 1920 [1967]); P. Mantoux, *The Industrial Revolution in the Eighteenth Century: An Outline of the Beginnings of the Modern Factory System in England* (New York: Harper & Row, 1961).

On fighting for a ten-hour day, see J. T. Ward, *The Factory Movement 1830–1850* (London: Macmillan, 1962); Cecil Driver, *Tory Radical: The Life of Richard Oastler* (New York: Oxford University Press, 1946); Robert Gray, "The languages of factory reform in Britain, *c.* 1830–1860," in Patrick Joyce (ed.), *The Historical Meanings of Work*, pp. 143–79; S. C. Deb, "The British factory movement in the early nineteenth century," *Indian Journal of Economics* 44 (1963); B. Hutchins and A. Harrison, *The History of Factory Legislation* (Westminster: King & Staples, 1926); Philip Grant, *The Ten Hours' Bill: The History of Factory Legislation* (Manchester: Manchester University Press, 1866); Samuel Kydd, *The History of the Factory Movement from the Year 1802 to the Enactment of the Ten Hours' Bill in 1847* (London: Simpkin, Marshall, 1857).

On fighting for the right to outdoor poor relief, see Norman Edsall, *The Anti-Poor Law Movement* (Manchester: Manchester University Press; Totowa, NJ: Rowman & Littlefield, 1971); M. E. Rose, "The anti-Poor Law movement in the north of England," *Northern History* 1 (1974): 70–91; M. E. Rose, "The anti-Poor Law agitation," in J. T. Ward (ed.), *Popular Movements c. 1830–1850* (London: Macmillan, 1971); Driver, *Tory Radical*, Chs 22, 24, 25; Ward, *Popular Movements c. 1830–1850*.

On strikes, see R. G. Kirby and A. E. Musson, *The Voice of the People, John Doherty, 1798–1854: Trade Unionist, Radical and Factory Reformer* (Manchester: Manchester University Press, 1975); J. Foster, *Class Struggle and the Industrial Revolution: Early Industrial Capitalism in Three English Towns* (London: Weidenfeld & Nicolson, 1974); A. E. Musson, *British Trade Unions, 1800–1875* (London: Macmillan, 1972); Rule, *The Labouring Classes*; I. Prothero, "William Benbow and the concept of the general strike," *Past and Present* 63 (1974):132–71; Clive Behagg, "Custom, class and change: the trade societies of Birmingham," *Social History* 4 (1979): 455–80; Clive Behagg, "Secrecy, ritual and folk violence: the opacity of the workplace in the first half of the nineteenth century," in Robert D. Storch (ed.), *Popular Custom and Culture in Nineteenth-Century England* (New York: St Martin's, 1982), pp. 154–79; Clive Behagg, "Masters and manufacturers: social values and the smaller units of production in Birmingham, 1800–1850," in Geoffrey Crossick and Heinz-Gerhard Haupt (eds), *Shopkeepers and Master Artisans in Nineteenth-Century Europe* (London: Methuen, 1984), pp. 137–54; Behagg, *Politics and Production*.

On self-help, community education, and Owenism, Thompson, *The Making of the English Working Class*; Barbara Taylor, *Eve and the New Jerusalem: Socialism and Feminism in the Nineteenth Century* (New York: Pantheon Books, 1983); D. Vincent, *Bread, Knowledge and Freedom: A Study in Nineteenth-Century Working-Class Autobiography* (London: Europa Publications, 1981); Stedman Jones, *Languages of Class*; E. Yeo, "Robert Owen and radical culture," in S. Pollard and J. Salt (eds), *Robert Owen, Prophet of the Poor* (London: Macmillan, 1971).

On boycotting merchants, see Foster, *Class Struggle*.

On crowds in general, see the classic by G. Rude, *The Crowd in History* (New York: Wiley, 1964); R. J. Holton, "The crowd in history: some problems of theory and method," *Social History* 3 (1978): 219–33.

On Britain and social movements, see Charles Tilly, "Repertoires of contention in Britain and America," in Mayer N. Zald and John D. McCarthy (eds), *The Dynamics of Social Movements: Resource Mobilization, Social Control, and Tactics* (Cambridge, MA: Winthrop, 1979), pp. 126–55; Charles Tilly, "Britain creates the social movement," in James E. Cronin and

is the exorbitant rents, tithes, interests on money, profits on labor, and profits on trade, which are imposed on you by laws made by the land stealers, the merchants, the manufacturers, and the tradesmen in that house [Parliament] from which you are excluded, and by which exclusion you are prevented from making laws to regulate your wages." *Poor Man's Guardian*, April 14, 1932, cited in Stedman Jones, *Languages of Class*, p. 119.

28 Driver, *Tory Radical*, *passim*, and references to the anti-poor law movement in note 25.

29 On the concept of "the people," cf. C. Hill, "Parliament and people in seventeenth-century England," *Past and Present* 142 (1981): 100–24; D. T. Rogers, *Contested Truths: Keywords in American Politics Since Independence* (New York: Basic Books, 1987); Prothero, *Artisans and Politics*.

30 Stedman Jones, *Languages of Class*; Thompson, *The Making of the English Working Class*; Foster, *Class Struggle*. Independence and autonomy were sought by artisans and factory workers alike: "The object they sought to obtain," stated the industrial cotton-spinner John Doherty in 1834, "was that freedom and independence which had long been the characteristic of Englishmen, but of which at present only a small remnant was left." Cited in Kirby and Musson, *The Voice of the People*.

31 Activities against scabs, "knobsticks," and unapprenticed workers were common. Similarly, the massive support for Owenism among "modern" factory workers reflected the centrality of the cooperative principle. See Barbara Taylor, in Taylor, *Eve and the New Jerusalem*; Thompson, *The Chartists*; Kirby and Musson, *The Voice of the People*; Stedman Jones, *Languages of Class*; Hammond and Hammond, *The Skilled Labourer*.

32 Because of competition, John Gray declared, "the labourer who seeks employment, frequently finds enemies to his interest even among those who would otherwise be his friends." John Gray, *Human Happiness* (1915), p. 45, cited in Stedman Jones, *Languages of Class*, p. 121.

33 Behagg, "Secrecy, ritual, and folk violence."

34 The classic article on the language of class in the nineteenth century is still Briggs, "The language of 'class'." For recent discussion on "language of class," see Stedman Jones, *Languages of Class*; Joan Scott, "On, language, gender, and working-class history," in Joan Scott (ed.), *Gender and the Politics of History* (New York: Columbia University Press, 1988), pp., 53–67; Marc Steinberg, "Talkin' class: discourse, ideology, and their roles in class conflict," in Scott G. McNall, Rhonda F. Levine, and Rick Fantasia (eds), *Bringing Class Back In: Contemporary and Historical Perspectives* (Boulder, CO: Westview, 1991), pp. 261–84; Robert Gray, "The deconstructing of the English working class," *Social History* 11 (1986): 363–73; Gray, "The languages of factory reform in Britain"; John Belchem, "Radical language and ideology in early nineteenth-century England: the challenge of the mass platform," *Albion* 20 (1989): 247–59; Gregory Claeys, "Language, class, and historical consciousness in nineteenth-century Britain," *Economy and Society* 14 (1985): 239–63; James E. Cronin, "Language, politics and the critique of social history," *Journal of Social History* 20 (1986): 177–83; James Epstein, "Rethinking the categories of working-class history," *Labour/ Travail* 18 (1986): 195–208.

35 For the convergence of constitutional and natural rights rhetoric, see Thompson, *The Making of the English Working Class*; Epstein, "Understanding the cap of liberty"; Belchem, "Republicanism."

On the link between artisanal skills, property, and political rights, Stedman Jones, *Languages of Class*; J. Rule, "The property of skill in the period of manufacture," in Patrick

Joyce (ed.), *The Historical Meanings of Work*; E. J. Hobsbawm, "Artisan or labour aristo-crat?" *Economic History Review* 37 (1984): 355–72; Joan Scott, "L'ouvrière! Mot imle, sordide: women workers in the discourse of French political economy, 1840–1860," in Scott (ed.), *Gender*, pp. 139–63; Joan Scott, "Work identities for men and women: the politics of work and family in the Parisian garments trades in 1848," in ibid., pp. 93–113; William H. Sewell, Jr, *Work and Revolution in France* (New York: Cambridge University Press, 1980).

See Scott, "On language, gender, and working-class history," in Scott (ed.), *Gender*, for a critique of Stedman Jones's opposing of political and class claims.

For critiques of the opposition of rights-claims and community membership identities, see especially Michael Walzer, *Spheres of Justice: A Defense of Pluralism and Equality* (New York: Basic Books, 1983); Martha Minow, "Interpreting rights: an essay for Robert Cover," *Yale Law Review* 96 (1987): 1860–1915; S. Hall and D. Held, "Left and rights," *Marxism Today* (June 1989):16–22.

For an especially important view of rights-formation, cf. Tilly, "Where do rights come from?".

36   See Somers, "Narrativity, narrative identity and social action."

37   On workers' self-narratives and autobiographies see John Burnett, David Vincent, and David Mayall (eds), *The Autobiography of the Working Class: An Annotated, Critical Bibliography*, 3 vols (Hemel Hempstead, Herts: Harvester Wheatsheaf, 1984; 1987; 1989) and Vincent, *Bread, Knowledge and Freedom*.

38   Hans Medick, "The transition from feudalism to capitalism: renewal of the debate," in Raphael Samuel (ed.), *People's History and Socialist Theory* (London and Boston, MA: Routledge & Kegan Paul, 1981), pp. 120–30; Hans Medick, "Plebeian culture in the transition to capitalism," in Raphael Samuel and Gareth Stedman Jones (eds), *Culture, Ideology and Politics: Essays for Eric Hobsbawm* (London and Boston, MA: Routledge & Kegan Paul, 1983), pp. 84–113.

39   Franklin Mendels, "Proto-industrialization:the first phase of the industrialisation process," *Journal of Economic History* 32, 1 (1972): 241–61; Peter Kriedte, Hans Medick, and J. Schlumbohm, *Industrialization Before Industrialization* (Cambridge, UK: Cambridge University Press, 1982); Rudolf Braun, "Early industrialization and demographic change in the canton of Zurich," in Charles Tilly (ed.), *Historical Studies of Changing Fertility* (Princeton, NJ: Princeton University Press, 1978), pp. 289–334; Rudolf Braun, "The impact of cottage industry on an agricultural population," in David Landes (ed.), *The Rise of Capitalism* (New York: Macmillan, 1966); Charles Tilly, "Flows of capital and forms of industry in Europe, 1500–1900," *Theory and Society* 12, 2 (1983): 123–42.

40   For one of the cleverest rejections of the new term, see Donald Coleman, "Proto-industrialization: a concept too many?" *Economic History Review*, 2nd series, 36 (1983): 435–48; see also Lawrence Stone, "The new eighteenth century," *New York Review of Books* 31, 5 (1984): 42–7.

41   Sidney Webb and Beatrice Webb, *The History of Trade Unionism* (London, New York, and Bombay: Longman, Green, 1907).

42   See Somers, *The People and the Law*, for extended details supporting this claim.

43   For the eighteenth century, see Rule, *The Experience of Labour*; J. Rule, *The Labouring Classes in Early Industrial England, 1750–1850*; C. B. Dobson, *Masters and Men* (London: Croom Helm, 1980); Snell, *Annals of the Labouring Poor*; Roy Porter, *English Society in the Eighteenth Century* (Harmondsworth, Mx: Penguin, 1982). For the seventeenth century see K. Wrightson, *English Society, 1580–1680* (London: Hutchinson, 1982); Snell, *Annals of the Labouring Poor*; and David Underdown, *Revel, Riot and Rebellion: Popular Politics and Culture in England 1603–1660* (New York: Oxford University Press, 1985). For the sixteenth century, see Buchanan Sharp, *In Contempt of All Authority: Rural Artisans and Riot in the West of England, 1586–1660* (Berkeley, CA: University of California Press, 1980). For the fifteenth and fourteenth centuries see R. H. Wawney, "The assessment of wages in England by the Justices of the Peace," in W. E. Minchinton, *Wage Regulation in pre-Industrial England* (Newton Abbot, Devon: David R. Charles, 1972), pp. 37–92; R. Webber, *The Peasants' Revolt*,

45 It is difficult to separate the empirical and the theoretical critiques since most cover both aspects, but see especially Rab Houston and K. D. M. Snell, "Proto-industralization? Cottage industry, social change, and industrial revolution," *Historical Review* 27 (1984): 473–92, and Charles Sabel and J. Zeitlin, "Historical alternatives to mass production: politics, markets, and technology in nineteenth-century industrialization," *Past and Present* 108 (1985): 136–76; Charles Sabel, "Protoindustry and the problem of capitalism as a concept: response to Jean H. Quataert," *International Labor and Working-Class History* 33 (Spring 1988): 30–7; Jean H. Quataert, "A new view of industrialization: 'protoindustry' or the role of small-scale, labor-intensive manufacture in the capitalist environment," *International Labor and Working-Class History* 33 (Spring 1988): 3–22; Jean H. Quataert, "The politics of rural industrialization: class, gender, and collective protest in the Saxon Oberlausitz of the late nineteenth century," *Central European History* 20 (June 1987): 91–124; Frank Perlin, "Proto-industrialization and pre-colonial South Asia," *Past and Present* 98 (1983): 30–95; but for the very strongest argument for the importance of the thesis, see Geoff Eley, "The social history of industrialization: 'proto-industry' and the origins of capitalism," *Economy and Society* 13, 4 (1984): 519–39.

46 Karl Polanyi, *The Livelihood of Man*, ed. Harry Pearson (New York: Academic Press, 1977).

47 This framework is variably known as the "sociology of labor markets" or simply "institutional economics." This is of course a paraphrase of Karl Polanyi's "The economy as an instituted process." As Polanyi argues, it is the "social organization of appropriational power [which] locates the institutional matrix which orders man-to-man economic relations." Harry Pearson, "Editor's Introduction," in Polanyi, *The Livelihood of Man*, pp. xxx, xxxii.

48 G. Unwin, *The Guilds and Companies of London* (London: Frank Cass, 1908); G. Unwin, *Industrial Organization in the 16th and 17th Centuries* (London: Frank Cass, 1904); W. Cunningham, *The Growth of English Industry and Commerce*, 2 vols (Cambridge: Cambridge University Press, 1890–2); S. Kramer, *The English Craft Gilds and the Government* (New York: Columbia University Press, 1905); Lujo Brentano, *On the History and Development of Gilds, and the Origin of Trade Unions* (London: Trubner, 1870); Lujo Brentano, "Gilds," in Sylvia L. Thrupp (ed.), *Early Medieval Society* (New York: Appleton-Century Crofts, 1961); Lujo Brentano, "On the history and development of guilds and the origin of trade-unions," preliminary essay in Joshua Toulmin Smith (ed.), *English Gilds: The Original Ordinances of More than One Hundred Early English Gilds* (London and New York: Oxford University Press for the Early English Text Society, 1963); Robert A. Leeson, *Travelling Brothers: The Six Centuries' Road from Craft Fellowship to Trade Unionism* (London: Allen & Unwin, 1979).

49 These were institutional foundations which are conventionally identified with but had no logically exclusive links to urban settings.

50 Alan Harding, "Political liberty in the Middle Ages," *Speculum* 55, 3 (1980): 442–7; Toulmin Smith (ed.), *English Gilds*; M. Bloch, *Feudal Society*, 2 vols, trans. L. Manyon (Chicago: University of Chicago Press, 1961); Anthony Black, *Guilds and Civil Society in European Political Thought from the Twelfth Century to the Present* (London: Methuen, 1984).

51 On guilds see Sylvia L. Thrupp, "The gilds," in M. M. Posten, E. E. Rich, and Edward Miller (eds), *The Cambridge Economic History of Europe* (Cambridge, UK: Cambridge University Press, 1963), Vol. III, pp. 230–80; Brentano, *On the History and Development of Gilds*; Philip Abrams and E. A. Wrigley (eds), *Towns in Societies: Essays in Economic History*

and Historical Sociology (Cambridge, UK: Cambridge University Press, 1977); Susan Reynolds, *An Introduction to the History of English Medieval Towns* (Oxford: Oxford University Press, 1977); P. Corfield, "Urban development in England and Wales in the sixteenth and seventeenth centuries," in D. C. Coleman and H. H. Johns (eds), *Trade, Government, and Economy in Pre-Industrial England* (London: Weidenfeld & Nicolson, 1976); Black, *Guilds and Civil Society*; Steve Rappaport, "The extent and foundations of companies' powers in sixteenth-century London," paper presented at Social Science History Association meeting (Chicago: 1988); Steve Rappaport, *Worlds Within Worlds: Structures of Life in Sixteenth-Century London* (Cambridge, UK: Cambridge University Press, 1989); Laurie Nussdorfer, "Urban politics and the guilds in early modern Europe: guilds and government in baroque Rome," paper presented at Social Science History Association meeting (Chicago: 1988); Gail Bossenga, "Regulating the local economy: guilds and the town council in eighteenth-century Lille," paper presented at Social Science History Association meeting (Chicago: 1988); Pamela Nightengale, "Capitalists, crafts and constitutional change in late fourteenth-century London," *Past and Present* 124 (August 1989): 3–35.

52 Cited in Rappaport, *Worlds Within Worlds*, p. 31.

53 The merchant guild preceded the crafts guild, but the latter (composed of masters and journeymen) became far more important.

54 On apprenticeship, see especially E. Lipson, *An Introduction to the Economic History of England*, 3 vols (London: A. & C. Black, 1920), Vol. I, Ch. 8.

55 Tramping, one of the most important forms of labor migration, was contained within social membership networks; see Leeson, *Travelling Brothers*.

56 *Oxford English Dictionary* s. v. "mistery." In ancient Greece, the craftsmen were, like priests and doctors, believed to possess some secret power; see M. Godelier, "Work and its representations: research proposal," *History Workshop Journal* 10 (1980): 167–74.

57 *Oxford English Dictionary*, op. cit.; Brentano, *On the History and Development of Gilds*, p. cxxxii.

58 For various references to "mystery," "mistery," "misterium," "misterium artis," or "mestera, misteria, from ministerium," as the collective body of the craft guild (rather than the skill itself) see A. B. Hibbert, "The economic policies of towns," in Postan *et al.* (eds), *The Cambridge Economic History of Europe*, Vol. III, pp. 157–229; Harold J. Berman, *Law and Revolution: The Formation of the Western Legal Tradition* (Cambridge, MA: Harvard University Press, 1983), p. 391; Reynolds, *English Medieval Towns*, p. 165; Black, *Guilds and Civil Society*, p. 14; Leeson, *Travelling Brothers*, p. 26.

59 On illegal shops as unapprenticed ones, see Lipson, *The Economic History of England*, Vol. II, p. 41.

60 On women in guilds, see Lucy Smith, "Introduction," in Toulmin Smith (ed.), *English Gilds*; Leeson, *Travelling Brothers*, pp. 27–8. On oaths and obligations, see Prothero, *Artisans and Politics*, p. 37; Thrupp, "The gilds," pp. 184, 232–3; Hibbert, "The economic policies of towns"; Leeson, *Travelling Brothers*.

61 C. Adams-Phythian, "Ceremony and the citizen: the communal year at Coventry 1450–1550," in P. Clark (ed.), *The Early Modern Town* (New York: Longman, 1976), pp. 106–7.

62 For the strongest evidence on this point, see Black, *Guilds and Civil Society*, as well as the numerous guild documents collected in Toulmin Smith, *English Gilds*.

63 Somers, *The People and the Law*; Somers, "Rights, relationality, and membership"; Somers, "Citizenship and the place of the public sphere."

64 See Berg, "Women's work," on the false dichotomy between markets and communities.

65 H. A. Turner, *Trade Union Growth* (Toronto: University of Toronto Press, 1962), p. 86. Inspired by Turner, Hobsbawm, and Thompson, and challenging what was considered to be the Webbs' overemphasis on formal "modern" labor institutions, social historians in the last twenty-five years have tended to explain the presence of collective action by the absence of formal institutions. In Turner's words, early labor organizations were simply part of community life, part of "the habit of association" that was "natural . . . without artificial contrivance" – an autonomy which was later lost when bureaucracies emerged to divide the rank and file from the formal leadership of new trade unions. But, if the Webbs' approach suffered from an institutional excess, the new autonomist one suffers from a sociological

... but rather further illustrates – the continuity of association.

67 This argument supports to some degree that of recent sociological contributions to the "social foundations of collective action"; see, for example, Craig Calhoun, "Community: toward a variable conceptualization of comparative research," *Social History*, 5, 1 (1980): 105–29. As is evident, however, it differs in focusing on the institutional character of those foundations; see Somers and Gibson, "Reclaiming the epistemological 'other.'"

68 M. Davies, *The Enforcement of English Apprenticeship 1563–1642* (Cambridge, MA: Harvard University Press, 1956); Rule, *The Experience of Labour*, p. 95.

69 Thompson, *The Making of the English Working Class.*

70 Montesquieu (as paraphrased by William Cobbett) wrote: "A man ought not to be called poor, merely because he has neither land, nor house, nor goods; his labour is property; it is better than an annuity; the mechanic who gives his art to his children has left them a fortune." G. Himmelfarb, *The Idea of Poverty* (New York: Vintage Press, 1985).

71 Cited in Rule, *The Experience of Labour*, p. 107.

72 Ibid., p. 114.

73 M. Anderson, *Approaches to the History of the Western Family, 1500–1914* (London: Macmillan, 1980); F. Collier, *The Family Economy of the Working Classes in the Cotton Industry* (Manchester: Manchester University Press 1964); A. Clark, *Working Life of Women in the Seventeenth Century* (London: Routledge & Kegan Paul, 1982); I. Pinchbeck, *Women Workers and the Industrial Revolution* (London: Routledge, 1930 [1981]).

74 Cunningham, *The Growth of English Industry*, Vol. I.

75 K. Wrightson, *English Society, 1580–1680* (London: Harvester Press, 1982); Rule, *The Experience of Labour.*

76 Pinchbeck, *Women Workers*, p. 115.

77 M. Anderson, *Family Structure in Nineteenth-Century Lancashire* (Cambridge, UK: Cambridge University Press, 1971) discusses how the family replaces apprenticeship in the nineteenth century.

78 Braun, "The impact of cottage industry."

79 To be sure, a son could abandon his family and seek individual fame and fortune, but the only difficulty with such hubris of self-will was that sooner or later such an effort would backfire. In the absence of family and neighborly networks, he would be potentially an "illegal worker" – unapprenticed and vulnerable to blacklegging.

80 L. Stone, "Social mobility in England, 1500–1700," *Past and Present* 33 (1966): 16–55; Medick, "The transition from feudalism to capitalism."

81 A. Redford, *Labour Migration in England* (Manchester: University of Manchester Press, 1964); Wrightson, *English Society*, p. 87; Pinchbeck, *Women Workers*, pp. 112, 160, 168, 179; David Levine, *Family Formation in an Age of Nascent Capitalism* (London: Academic Press, 1977).

82 ibid.; Roy Porter, *English Society in the Eighteenth Century* (Harmondsworth, Mx: Penguin, 1982).

83 Wrightson, *English Society*, p. 42; Hans Medick, "The proto-industrial family economy: the structural function of household and family during the transition from peasant society to industrial capitalism," *Social History* 3 (1976): 291–315. Social historians have drastically reduced their assessment of kinship density in the pre-factory communities; K. Wrightson, "Household and kinship in sixteenth-century England," *History Workshop Journal* 12

(1981):151–8; Peter Laslett (ed.), *Household and Family in Past Time* (Cambridge, UK: Cambridge University Press, 1972).

84 H. Heaton, *The Yorkshire Woollen and Worsted Industries* (Oxford: Oxford University Press, 1920).

85 M. Berg, P. Hudson, and M. Sonenscher (eds), *Manufacture in Town and Country Before the Factory* (Cambridge, UK: Cambridge University Press, 1983).

86 Medick, "The proto-industrial family economy," p. 61.

87 D. Gregory, "The process of industrial change 1730–1900," in R. A. Dodgshon and R. A. Butlin (eds), *A Historical Geography of England and Wales* (London and New York: Academic Press, 1978), pp. 291–312.

88 Heaton, *The Yorkshire Woollen and Worsted Industries*; Thompson, *The Making of the English Working Class*; Rule, *The Experience of Labour*.

89 Webb and Webb, *The History of Trade Unionism*.

90 E. P. Thompson, "Eighteenth-century English society: class struggle without class?" *Social History* 4 (1979): 133–66.

91 See note 2 for several influential discussions of property.

92 See A. Hirschman, *Rival Views of Market Society and Other Recent Essays* (New York: Viking, 1986); A. Hirschman, "Against parsimony," *American Economic Papers and Proceedings* (1984): 89–96; K. Polanyi, *The Great Transformation* (New York: Rinehart, 1944); M. Granovetter, "Economic action and social structure: the problem of embeddedness," *American Journal of Sociology* 91 (1985): 481–510; Fred Block, *Post-Industrial Possibilities: A Critique of Economic Discourse* (Berkeley and Los Angeles, CA: University of California Press, 1989); Richard Swedberg, "Economic sociology," *Current Sociology* 35 (1987): 1– 221; Margaret R. Somers, "Karl Polanyi's intellectual legacy," in Kari Polanyi-Levitt (ed.), *The Life and Work of Karl Polanyi* (Montreal and New York: Black Rose Books, 1991), pp. 152–8; F. Block and M. R. Somers, "Beyond the economic fallacy: the holistic social science of Karl Polanyi," in T. Skocpol (ed.), *Vision and Method in Historical Sociology* (Cambridge, UK: Cambridge University Press, 1984), pp. 47–84; D. Bell, "Models and reality in economic discourse," in D. Bell and I. Kristol (eds), *The Crisis in Economic Theory* (New York: Basic Books, 1981), pp. 46–80; M. Sahlins, *Culture and Practical Reason* (Chicago: University of Chicago Press, 1976); Donald N. McCloskey, *The Rhetoric of Economics* (Madison, WI: University of Wisconsin Press, 1985); B. Roberts, R. Finnegan and D. Gallie (eds), *New Approaches to Economic Life*, (Manchester: Manchester University Press, 1985); S. Gudeman, *Economics as Culture: Models and Metaphors of Livelihood* (London: Routledge & Kegan Paul, 1986). And for an important introduction of the ideas of economic sociology to social history see Patrick Joyce, "The historical meanings of work: an introduction," in Patrick Joyce (ed.), *The Historical Meanings of Work*, pp. 1–30.

Part II

Budgets and local strategies

Property is one of the central tropes of eighteenth-century public discourse, crucial to debates in public law, political argument, political economy, and moral philosophy. And not property of any and every kind, but a peculiar form of property: property as individual absolute dominion, "that sole and despotic dominion which one man claims and exercises over the external things of the world, in total exclusion of the right of any other individual in the universe."[1] In this form all the potential sticks in the bundle of property rights are gathered in a single owner, the rights to enjoy and to exploit the owned resources without restriction, to exclude others from access to them for any or no reason, and to alienate them without restraint – all secured by fixed, stable, predictable rules of law against diminution or encroachment. The ideology of property as absolute dominion has, of course, many different sources: Lockean natural rights to appropriation and improvement; the pseudo-medievalism of the ancient Gothic constitution with its "allodial" Saxon tenures; Scottish evolutionary history and political economy, showing separate property emerging at the shepherd's stage of development, and edging out competing forms of tenure in the commercial stage; or civic humanism, with its independent yeoman freeholders forming the necessary social basis of self-governing republics. Yet in general political rhetoric these very different sources promiscuously intermingle, tending to converge however sloppily in the modal form of property as absolute individual right, the legally guaranteed security of private possession, disposition, and alienation required for individual happiness, self-government, political stability, and economic improvement. This modal form of property as dominion, which as Blackstone says "so generally strikes the imagination, and engages the affections of mankind," is hardly confined to property in land and chattels. It is rapidly and recklessly generalized to intangibles, then to any type of potentially valuable expectancy, and ultimately to public, political rights as well. As John Reid has exhaustively shown in his study of American Revolutionary rhetoric, liberty itself was property. To be free was to have a "freehold" in rights of which one could not be "dispossessed" by arbitrary action, as opposed to being a villein or "tenant at will," holding, as John Dickinson put it, by "the precarious tenure of the will of others."[2]

What strikes the backward-looking observer as curious is simply this: that in the midst of such a lush flowering of absolute dominion talk in theoretical and political discourse, English legal doctrines should contain so very few plausible instances of absolute dominion rights. Moreover, it is curious that English and colonial social practices contained so many property relations that actually seemed to traduce the ideal of absolute individual rights. The real building-blocks of basic eighteenth-century social and economic institutions were not absolute dominion rights but, instead, property rights fragmented and split among many holders; property rights held and managed collectively by many owners; property relations of dependence and subordination; property subject to arbitrary and discretionary direction or destruction at the will of others; property surrounded by restriction on use and alienation; property qualified and regulated for communal or state purposes; property destabilized by fluctuating and conflicting regimes of legal regulation. Blackstone's *Commentaries* themselves are a compendious catalogue of "relative" and qualified property relations. His general definitions of property and bodily security, as Duncan Kennedy has nicely put it, "were not fountainheads of more specific rights; they were more like barriers at the border, designed to deal with extreme cases . . . not to aid in the day-to-day task of elaborating rule systems."[3] It is true that many eighteenth-century rules and practices could be accounted for as the obsolescing remnants of "feudal" policy or of what E. P. Thompson has called the "moral economy" of pre-commercial custom. Among such survivals were the wage and price regulations like the "assize of bread," or the common rights of open fields, pasture, and the forest; indeed, the great bulk of the land law might be accounted for as a feudal remain. But many more early modern rules could not be so explained; they represented *emerging* property relations of the new commercial society. Furthermore, the limited sphere of absolute dominion rights – or "liberal" rights if we may agree to give them that somewhat reductive label – was riddled with ambiguities and conflicts that were full of potential for disruption to any scheme of rights that prized consistency, as Anglo-American law in its aspirations to "scientific," systematic status sporadically did.

To illustrate this point let me attempt a brief catalogue, by general type, of some of the major systemic deviations from, and conflicts within, absolute dominion property rights. Most of these examples come from American colonial practices, partly because I know the literature somewhat better, partly because everybody stipulates that liberal-individualist institutions and *mentalités* were likely to be more evolved in America than in England – with the huge exception of slavery.

Let us first consider deviations from the model of absolute dominion, important instantiations of non-absolute rights, or of the total "ownership" bundle dispersed among various holders. Technically, the deviations would include all real property, since only the king held absolute ownership of land; but it is hardly necessary to rely on technicalities to make the case. We can also afford to omit from this catalogue almost everything that might savor of a mere feudal relic, including virtually everything in Blackstone's relative rights of persons, indeed, also most of his rights of things. My focus will be on major functioning institutions at the end of the eighteenth century.[4]

The best-known as well as historically oldest deviations from the property regime of

milldams. In the northeastern and middle colonies, common grazing was on its way out by the end of the eighteenth century.[6] New England fishermen were vigorously and more successfully protecting through politics a legal balancing of millowners' and common fishing rights in the rivers.[7] In the south, open-range grazing remained the norm in the face of all attempts to regulate it. As it turned out, regimes of common or "inherently public" property, so far from fading into anachronism, were to undergo a revival and an expansion in the nineteenth and again in the twentieth centuries with the development of "public rights" and "public trust" doctrines that protect recreation and environmental as well as commercial use-rights. Some of these public rights regimes were presented as inroads upon or qualifications of a presumed set of individual property rights. More often, they were conceptualized as something the proprietor had never "owned," or fully owned, to begin with. The right was simply redefined to leave out the bits "dedicated to" or "reserved for" common or public use.[8]

Property taken or regulated for public convenience or necessity constitutes a related legal category of deviant rights, one often blurred into that of commons or public property. The main thing to be said about this category is once again that as old forms of community claims on property fade out, new ones take their place. The "organic communitarianism" of New England towns gives way to acquisitive individualism (or, more accurately, familism), common meadowlands are appropriated to private use, mercantilist regulations of trades and staple commodity prices and various sumptuary laws become increasingly unenforceable and are then repealed. Nevertheless, the eighteenth-century law of "police" was still a vital function of local government. As various scholars have shown, this police power had at its core a notion of community happiness promoted through distributive justice. In the words of John Erskine's *Institutes of the Laws of Scotland* the power was "calculated for the providing of all members of the community with a sufficient quantity of the necessaries of life at reasonable rates, and for the preventing of dearth."[9] Eventually, it receded before the political economists' norm of market distribution and happiness realized privately rather than publicly.[10] Yet the idea that the public good and commercial development might be promoted by forced transfers of property accomplished through aggressive use of the eminent domain power and restrictions on uses through what is becoming known as the general "police power" to regulate health, safety, and morals was about to embark on a brilliant nineteenth-century career, as legal powers to regulate were reassigned from intermediate associations and local government to state administrative bodies.[11]

The most common and most important examples that deviate from the model of the absolute dominion property regime are property regimes in which rights of formal ownership or of management and control are split among or held collectively by several proprietors. All family property belongs in this category, because it is shared by dependants (wives, children, servants, day-laborers, indentured servants, slaves) who all (though to some extent part of the household property themselves) have some legal claim on it. Strict absolute dominion theory would vest family property in a single owner, with full powers of control and disposition, fee simple interest in the owner, and to one or more of the heirs upon his death. Even putting aside the many pseudo-feudal remnants tortured into commercial manageability by legal fictions and equitable evasions of the feudal rules, the actual regimes of family landholding, as we know, were far more complex than strict theory could suggest. There was dower, the widow's life estate, and women's separate equitable estates. In England, there was also dynastic property protected by the strict settlement, the conveyance to trustees to preserve contingent remainders from destruction by heirs anxious to convert land to cash. In America, dynastic trusts were not permitted until the late nineteenth century, though some 20 percent of plantation owners still used the entail at the end of the eighteenth century.[12] Much more important were the regimes of shared and fragmented power over family property created by testamentary dispositions, the "extended cognate practices" or "favored-heir-plus burdens" regimes described by family historians:

> Adults inheriting homesteads shared their use with parents and unmarried brothers and sisters. Favored heirs routinely assumed obligations to care for parents and to provide legacies for both single and married sisters; when their married siblings died prematurely, these obligations extended to nieces and widowed sisters-in-law. . . . There are glimpses of co-heirs cooperatively working farms, brothers and brothers-in-law jointly running mills and tanneries. In short, inheritance practices reinforced extended family relations through the creation of overlapping rights.[13]

Family property is an example of a fragmented collective rights regime created by the disposing power of an owner, the testator. Another regime of this kind, created by the state, was the corporation. With the "freedom of contract" permitted by a market society, such regimes were also increasingly created by contract among proprietors themselves. The corporation, for most purposes, ultimately was in this category. Often, farm tenancy was also a regime of this kind. Absolute dominion generalized to everybody, or at least to all white adult males, would have had everyone a yeoman freeholder. But even in America, though the myth prevailed at times that almost every white male farmer was a freeholder – and more actually were than in other major Western countries – most were tenants or landless laborers. Colonial tenancy was not very "feudal," however. It was a means whereby the landless could secure cheap interests in land, often, as in the "developmental lease," baited with initial low rents and subsidies for equipment and materials in exchange for a rising share for the landlord of the crop and its profits. In some places the demand for scarce tenants gave them enough bargaining power to gain for themselves such normally proprietary rights as the rights to improvements, or even rights to convert long leases to freeholds for themselves. In others, tenants never accumulated enough under the terms of their leases to escape extreme dependence. The point is simply that farm tenancies were a ubiquitous type of joint venture among co-proprietors, landlords, and tenants, characterized by partial and collective rights, some created by law, others by contract.[14]

Moreover, contracts plainly create relations of dependence on the will of others. Classical contract talk tries to obscure this by formally bounding the rights transferred: I give up only a discrete limited property in my thing, in exchange for a discrete limited property in yours; we have traded a little clod of our island for a slightly bigger and better clod; otherwise we are much the same as before. But that was not the real world of commercial contract, where transactions were conventionally part of long-term relations sustained by credit. Local attorneys ran regional credit markets supplying small business loans, masters gave credit to apprentices, big merchants to small, shopkeepers to customers. To be in business at all, as John Brewer has pointed out in describing the web of commercial credit in eighteenth-century England, was to surrender a large discretionary authority over one's person and property. For it was the creditor, "in effect, who determined when the credit that he had extended transmuted itself into a debt for which one had a legal liability."[15] The creditor, like the employer in the wage bargain, acquires not a discrete limited power over the other, but a potentially vast discretionary power over an extensive range of the other's assets, decision-making discretion, and time. (If the debt is large enough, of course, the creditor is similarly in the debtor's power.) And not only over the debtor, but over the debtor's debtors, over the debtor's friends who must stand surety for his debts, and over the debtor's descendants who inherit his liabilities. "These debts," said Jefferson bitterly of the commercial credit extended to tobacco-growing Virginia gentlemen by British merchants, "had become hereditary from father to son, for many generations, so that the planters were a species of property annexed to certain mercantile houses in Britain."[16]

Finally, the intangible and speculative nature of the new contract property deprived it of any fixity or solidity, thus fatally threatening, one might have thought, the notion of property as security. Even if the legal system had been able to protect contract property by clear, fixed, enforceable rules, its value remained dependent on world economic conditions, on vagaries of public policy, on the surface tension of speculative bubbles, and on sudden shifts in the business cycle that no single trader could control, or even adequately insure or hedge against. Legal enforcement does little good against a debtor without assets; even against a debtor with assets, enforcement may be unpalatable if taking them deprives him of his future income stream and destroys the possibility of a continuing commercial relationship. To escape the fantastically chancy world of individual property trades, one did well to participate in various kinds of collective ventures, an ethnic or co-religionary trading clan, a risk-pooling mutual benefit society or political lobby. Some of the most valuable forms of trade property were wholly evanescent, like the bubble property of trade credit reputation, which could drive merchants into conspicuous consumption well beyond their means to maintain their public image of easy property. As John Brewer puts it, "Presentation of self as sober, reliable, candid and constant was not merely a question of genteel manners, but a matter of economic survival."[17] Commercial property is not security, only a ticket of entry to a condition of vulnerability.

To a significant extent, legal theorists could handle the deviations between absolute dominion ideology and the unruly pluralism of much lesser rights recognized in legal practice by reification. They redefined each lesser form of right as an "estate" or as a "thing" in itself, so that even if one held only the lesser right, one held it absolutely. If there were limits to what one could do with one's reified, partial "thing," they said that those limits simply inhered in the "nature" of the right that was held. But the most severe problems for legal theory would be raised not by deviations from the absolute dominion ideal, but by ambiguities and conflicts arising from within the ideal itself.

In real life, and in real lawsuits, even relatively "absolute" rights must come into inevitable conflict. The most obvious case is nuisance: I do something on my land that affects the value of yours. With the rise of industrial uses noxious to abutting land-owners, milldam construction that flooded meadows or interfered with watercourses, mining or roadbuilding that undercut lateral support to land, manufacturing that polluted neighboring streams or air and frightened off game, and building construction that cut off light, nuisance was rapidly becoming more frequent. There are really only three ways for a legal system to handle such conflicts. The first is to constitute some arbitrarily chosen proprietor, usually the first in time to appropriate, as the absolute right-holder. The maxim, "So use your own, as not to injure anyone else's," is then addressed to latecomers who infringe upon turf already owned. The first comer is permitted to protect his accustomed bundle of rights by injunction and self-help abatement, as well as by rights to damages. Generally, this approach has the effect of protecting traditional or static uses at the expense of developmental or dynamic uses. It seems to have been the dominant regime of eighteenth-century nuisance law, though there are not many reported cases. An important statutory modification, which one sees in the American Milldam Acts, is to change the "property" into a "liability" rule, to take away the first owner's right to self-help and to injunction (and often the right to jury-assessed damages as well), giving him only the right to damages. The latecomer can then continue to flood or to pollute or to build, so long as he is willing to pay.

The second way to deal with conflicts of rights in nuisance law is to address the maxim, "So use your own, as not to injure anyone else's," to *all* users, so that each is required to limit his uses at the point where they conflict with others. In reality this solution creates a kind of regulated commons of relative rights, in which the courts arbitrate the balance of "reasonable" uses. In some areas of nineteenth-century law the balance struck comes strongly to favor active industrial uses over passive agrarian or *rentier* property.[18] Recent scholarship, however, has shown that this preference was by no means uniform, and we still have no idea how much industry had to pay privately for the right to foul the countryside, or whether it mostly never had to pay anything because access to the courts was so difficult.[19]

The third kind of solution to conflicts in nuisance law is to convert use-rights into what the legal theorist Wesley Hohfeld called "privileges," rights imposing no correlative duties.[20] Such rights-holders inhabit a virtual state of nature in which all the owners may do as they will with their own without regard to the damage they may

especially hard pressed to rationalize utilitarian or other preferred uses tradeoffs in the language of rights. The standard ways of doing this come to be: 1) focusing on the protected user as the absolute right-holder, simply ignoring the other party; 2) redefining the property right so that it remains absolute, though considerably narrower, as by saying that it extends only to "natural" uses of the property; or 3) acknowledging the harm to property, but denying that it constitutes legally recognizable injury, saying that it is merely "indirect" or "consequential" damage, *damnum absque injuria*.

When the language of rights is left behind for the language of policy and commercial convenience, the problem rapidly arises that the policy rationales still all conflict with one another. Moving to the language of policy and convenience, like moving to the language of "natural justice" in hopes of a source of tie-breaking considerations for use in hard cases, is apt merely to recast disputes in a different vocabulary, not to resolve them. The policy of promoting labor and investment by securing reasonable expectations gave no useful guidance, for example, on how to resolve the enormous number of land disputes in the eighteenth and early nineteenth centuries between, on the one hand, settlers, squatters, and adverse possessors making Lockean use and occupancy claims to title and, on the other hand, absent or distant claimants to formal title through Crown or proprietary grants or shares in land companies. In America, in both colonial and post-Revolutionary litigation, the answer one got depended largely on the forum.[22] Elizabeth Mensch has identified two very different models of economic development underlying convenience and utility arguments urged in New York legal and political disputes over colonial land titles. One model favored independent freeholds as an incentive to settle and cultivate. The other favored large proprietary grants as a vehicle for capital accumulation of a surplus for investment in manufactures and improvements, through developmental leasing, and for the superior efficiency of hierarchical collective modes of production with a large dependent labor force.[23]

It is truly a tribute to the power of ideology to structure perceptions of reality that in public speech "property," except among the propertyless, could come to be presented as unambiguously a condition of personal autonomy and liberty, without having the audience immediately summon to mind its authoritarian connotations as well. Despite the assiduous efforts of Marxist and legal realist critics, "property" is still to this day heard as univocally expressive of autonomy and liberty. Yet the authoritarian connotations of property ought to be familiar enough, for instance, in the idea of property as lordship over one's demesne or household. While this is still formalized as jurisdiction, or governance rights, it is not (at least in ideal supposition) raw command or power without restraint, but right limited by some correlative obligations of protection and support to those governed, and even to some extent to be exercised through the forms of due process. But as property becomes reified and redefined as power over things rather than over people, the public law constraints upon *patria potestas* or mesne lord are gradually removed, except with respect to dependants plainly not *sui juris*, such as wives, servants, or bound labor. Thus, absolute dominion is left unrestrained within a sphere of right, an unreviewable *fiat* authority defined as freedom. The power of property also extends well beyond the household economy. It imposes burdens on *everyone* to refrain from infringing on the right, and so invariably restricts freedom while creating it. Most important, it gives the holder the power to dictate terms to others who may want or need access to his property, and this is, again, an arbitrary and unreviewable discretion backed by the trespass sanction and, consequently, by the coercive power of the state. To endow someone with a full private property right does not increase the sum of security in the world. It merely redistributes uncertainty away from the owner to those who will be subject to his rights' exercise.

Absolute dominion is paradoxical at the core. The freedom to do anything one likes with property implies the freedom to create restraints on it, and thus to bind one's own hands or the hands of one's transferees. In the early modern period perhaps the most severe form of the paradox was that of intergenerational restraints, the problem of the "dead hand." As soon as the great sixteenth-century statutes of Uses (1536) and of Wills (1540) increased the freedom to dispose of land, the current generation of disposing owners began using that freedom to tie up property in the hands of the next generation. That in turn set off the famous protracted struggle between common law and equity courts over *which* parties must be restrained to protect the freedom of others, the donors or donees. Later, judges and legal theorists made heroic attempts to try to fit the zig-zagging doctrine of restraints on alienation into the general historical story of progress as the lifting of all restraints.[24] The same paradox appeared elsewhere in the tangled law of married women's equitable estates, among other places in the argument over whether to enforce "restraints upon anticipation" clauses by which fathers sought to disable their daughters from converting their trusts into capital, and, as Susan Staves and James Oldham have documented, in the doctrine of separate maintenance contracts between estranged couples.[25] Here the courts were first inclined to treat the wife's allowance under the contract as property of which she could freely dispose; then, in 1800, in sharp reaction against this encouragement to an unbecoming individuation within the patriarchal family, even the separated one, the courts refused to allow a wife with such an allowance to contract with or be sued by creditors as a *feme sole*. Finally, they reached a sort of compromise between disapproval of and accommodation to the maintenance contracts that were now in widespread use.[26] Quite aside from the wife's freedom, one of the issues raised here was whether even the husband's freedom to dispose of property included the freedom to contract it away to his wife, a question that continued to perplex the courts late into the nineteenth century, well after Married Women's Property and Earnings Acts (granting to married women the capacity to contract and the right to retain and manage as their own separate property what they had acquired before marriage and earned during it) might have been supposed to have settled it.[27]

So the paradox, as the examples show, is everywhere. The problem for the legal system is not merely whether the owner may create restraints in others by transfers from his bundle of rights or whether the legal system ought to restrain him to prevent his doing so. It is also the problem potentially present in any contract, any partial communal object of society which is subject to the technical disposal of a smaller or larger number of persons, and by means of the market, subject to the economic disposal of the whole of society."[28] The power to alienate, as it expresses autonomy, becomes the instrument for the subversion of autonomy. There is a wonderful moment in the early nineteenth-century state conventions on suffrage qualifications, where in response to the standard republican argument that only men of property can be sufficiently independent to cast their votes free of domination, a reformer says:

> The gentleman yesterday objected to tenants being voters, because, said he, the landlord held them by their very heart-strings: could distrain [i.e. seize their animals or goods for non-payment of rent] upon them, sell their last cow, and even the cradle on which their infants reposed. If the gentleman's argument be a good one, I think it will prove too much. . . .
>
> Will not the reasons assigned . . . for the exclusion of tenants, operate in equal degree to exclude his own favorite freeholders? Will it not furnish a good reason for excluding every man that is indebted, and for putting the Government in the hands of the creditor class of the community? And if this be the rule of exclusion, how many of the freeholders, think you, will be excluded? I venture to affirm at least one half or three-fourths: is there not that proportion indebted to their neighbours, their merchants, to the Banks, &c., by account, by bond, and by trust deed, or otherwise; and will not a debt have the same influence upon a freeholder, as upon a tenant or other non-freeholders? Indebtedness is, in substance, the reason assigned for excluding the tenant; and can it be a matter of any importance what sort of debt it be, whether it be for rent or any other consideration; whether it be collectable by distress-warrant, or by fieri facias [i.e. a writ for the seizure and sale of property], whether the cow or the cradle be sold by the constable, the sheriff, or a trustee or marshal, or whether the person indebted be turned out of possession by notice, to quit if a tenant, or by a *habere facias possessionem*, or *sesinam* [both writs ordering the sheriff to give actual possession of property to plaintiffs who have established their rights to recover it] if a mortgaged freeholder?[29]

The security of absolute property was necessarily dependent on fixed and certain legal rules, marking the boundaries between right and right, *meum* and *tuum*, and also dependent on the availability of processes giving remedies for every violation of right. The developing theories of property rights in political economy similarly emphasized the importance of fixed and definite boundaries. To translate into more modern terms: when the proprietor gets to reap the fruits of his own labor, security of possession may be called a "production incentive." Free alienability, it may be said, makes possible "rapid reallocation to highest and best uses." Similarly, sole ownership is supposed "to facilitate trades" because it is easier for outsiders to identify the person with whom they have to trade, and to cut a deal with one rather than with many. Clear legal rules defining entitlements also "facilitate trade" by aiding parties to plan their deals in advance, to ensure that what is bought stays bought, and to discourage people from taking advantage of one another by manipulating the legal system. So speaks our modern policy language.

It is, to put it mildly, exceedingly difficult to maintain that eighteenth-century English law defined and enforced such a fixed and functional system of rights. This is not merely on account of its appalling technicality and cost, but because of a built-in instability resulting from conspicuous struggles over principles and working methods. These have been discussed by David Lieberman and James Oldham, so I can very briefly summarize them here. There was a split between common law and equity. In consequence, in some important areas of social life, competing jurisdictions recognized conflicting rights in the same property and pursued quite distinct property policy agendas. For instance, while the common law promoted alienability, equity promoted dynastic preservation. More globally, there were the inherent conflicting choices that any legal system must make between adherence to bright line rules or to open-ended standards, between technicality and liberality in the construction of legal instruments. Is it best to adhere to strict requirements of form even where the results are manifestly unjust, arbitrary, and absurd in individual cases, and to rely on justification by precedent and positive rule as against appeals to utility and morality? A legal system at different periods in its history may find ways of disguising this conflict between technicality and liberality, as by doing its equitable justice interstitially through the manipulation of technical forms. But in the eighteenth century we have at least one great judge, Mansfield, adopting during one phase of his career the method of liberality in adjudication with a bold and overt appeal to commercial convenience. He thus introduced the tough question of whether the norm of certainty might not often be defeated entirely by resting on lawyers' rules, and much better served by resting on customary expectations, or some legally stabilized codification of them.[30]

The problem of instability in adjudication was especially acute for the new forms of commercial rights, precisely because, as earlier mentioned, the bundle of property rights tended to be split up among many holders, and because every action of any of the parties to a multi-party transaction could alter the legal rights and expectancies of all the others. As Lord Kames put it, speaking of equitable interests:

> It is commonly observed, that equitable rights are less steady and permanent than those of common law: the reason will appear from what follows. A right is permanent or fluctuating according to the circumstances upon which it is founded. The circumstances that found a right at common law, being always few and weighty, are not variable: a bond of borrowed money, for example, must subsist till it be paid. A claim in equity, on the contrary, seldom arises without multiplicity of circumstances; which make it less permanent, for if but a single circumstance be withdrawn, the claim is gone.[31]

To illustrate, take an utterly commonplace commercial transaction: a merchant mortgages his stock-in-trade to a creditor to secure a debt. The mortgage conveys all

appearances shall agree with the real state of things, but also that the real state of things shall be honest and consistent with public policy, and that it afford no unnecessary facility to deception."[32] The law "abhors" a lien existing separately from possession. Even the presumption does not end the difficulty, however, for the presumption is only that, and may be rebutted by proof that retention of possession is for a "fair, honest and necessary purpose." Note that the property, the claim to the stock in case of default, does a good bit of shuttling back and forth between the first and second creditors.

For an even more dramatic example of instability in adjudication resulting from the splitting of interests in new forms of commercial property among several holders, consider the evolving law of preferences in bankruptcy, of which Lord Mansfield was one of the chief pioneers. If a debtor knows or thinks he may be about to face bankruptcy, he is not allowed to favor any particular one of his creditors by paying off that debt, but must preserve the assets for the benefit of all his creditors. Any "preferential" conveyance to a favorite creditor will be voided, and snap back into the bankrupt estate. But what, and when, was a preference? One of Mansfield's contributions to this hideously intractable problem was to make the matter turn on the debtor's "intent" in paying off the favorite: had he been pressured into doing so (in which case the transfer was valid), or had he conspired with the favorite against the creditor community? The debtor's lawyers proposed a different moral test: whether the debt paid off was to a "faithful friend, and for a just debt lent in extremity," rather than to a ruthlessly pressing creditor.[33] The property was at one moment the debtor's to dispose of at will to his favorite, then, at the faintest scented whiff of his subtly improper motives, the community property of his trade creditors.[34]

After thus cataloging some of the major deviations from, and conflicts within, the absolute dominion ideal of property, we must ask: how on earth did the managers of this system respond to this rampant incongruity? In asking this, we are, of course, raising a question interesting to us, but one hardly so to most eighteenth-century lawyers. The imperative to bring accustomed practices into line with generally asserted abstract rhetorical norms is hardly ever very urgent, especially among lawyers. Mansfield, Kames, and Bentham, even Blackstone, are in this regard exceptional lawyers indeed. Theorists of a higher order – political theorists, moral philosophers, political economists – were certainly concerned with the integrity of their systems, but at such a level as not to worry much about the details of legal regulations. As David Hume put it with magnificent insouciance in the *Enquiries Concerning Understanding and Concerning the Principles of Morals*:

> we must ever distinguish between the necessity of a separation and constancy in men's possession, and the rules, which assign particular objects to particular

persons. The first necessity is obvious, strong, and invincible: the latter may depend on a public utility more light and frivolous, on the sentiment of private humanity and aversion to private hardship, on positive laws, on precedents, analogies, and very fine connexions and turns of the imagination.[35]

(Hume, I might remark parenthetically, was surely overstating his case. It is not a light or frivolous matter, in his scheme, if property rights in practice are not generally "separate" at all; or if their boundaries are blurry or they are in continual flux among their potential owners.)

But legal theory did have a number of conventional methods for mediating or suppressing these dissonances. Some devices have been mentioned already. To protect the notion of absolute ownership in a world in which actual ownership rights are fragmented, simply redefine each fragment as a species of property and assign it to an owner. If the owner cannot do much with it, that limit may be said to be inherent in the thing owned, "repugnant," as the lawyers say, "to its nature." Or óne can frankly recognize the partial nature of the right, but suppose that it flows from some contract, either a real or fictitious contract, or one implied for the convenience of civil society, among owners to surrender some share of their full rights. Alternatively, apparent dissonance could be avoided by suppressing the collective, by not recognizing some of the people involved in the collectively managed property at all. Or, if they were recognized, their subordinate status to a master, a chief rights-holder in charge, might be naturalized.

History could also be invoked to account for dissonances. Anomalies, it might be said, were on the point of disappearing or had already disappeared because of the genius of a legal system that was self-reforming according to the evolutionary logic of the history of liberty and commerce. The modern system of free disposition and alienability could thus be defined, by looking not so much at what it was, but at what it was not, the communal property of prehistoric times or the feudal property of the Norman invaders, just as later it could be defined by contrast to the communal property and arbitrary rule of communist states. "Feudalism" could figure in these histories either as a set of excrescences grafted onto the ancient constitution, an interruption in English liberty; or as a stage in the evolution of English society toward a free commercial society; or even (as in Blackstone) as both at once. In the third chapter in this part David Lieberman considers Blackstone's famous metaphor of an ancient castle gradually adopted for modern commodious use by means of an intricate machinery of fictions and evasions. What Anglo-Norman law was to Blackstone, British law became to John Adams: "The canon and the feudal systems, tho' greatly mutilated in England, are not yet destroyed. Like the temples and palaces, in which the great contrivers of them, once worshipped and inhabited, they exist in ruins; and much of the domineering spirit of them remains."[36] Yet in America, increasingly, the feudal law had been left behind and the "allodial" tenures recovered; symbolic remnants like primogeniture and entail could be symbolically decapitated with all the satisfactions, and none of the real hurt, of a slaughter of kings and nobles. Moreover, to legal theorists most of the actual rule-system in force was merely relative and contingent, adopted for the convenience of the moment, rather than sacralized as permanent and immutable, or as the necessary consequence of an abstract right of property: it was reformable, and

of their property to provide for their children, an obligation in some ways recognized by the legal system, and, on the other hand, privatizing rules that appointed parents judges of the amount of maintenance appropriate to each of their children and rules allowing such extreme testamentary freedom that parents could disinherit their children completely. These conflicts were partly denied by insistence on the naturalness of parents' love for their children, which supposedly rendered it unnecessary for the legal system to enforce natural law obligations, and partly suppressed by allowing the poor law system to deal with cases of extreme need. David Lieberman's chapter concluding this part offers another example, the denial that law and equity were rival systems with rival principles, which by the end of the nineteenth century had reached its ultimate *reductio* in the denial that equity confers any property rights at all, or is anything but a supplementary, wholly miscellaneous, system of remedies.

One further possibility for dealing with the anomalies remained: to transform the world so that it seemed to fit the theory better, to make war on anomalies like primogeniture, entail, restraints on alienation, and the other obvious limitations on the untrammeled powers of owners. The power of the absolute dominion trope in political discourse, in fact, put tremendous pressure on the legal system to identify a single "owner" of every species of property, and then to transfer to that owner as many sticks of the bundle of rights as possible. The logic of absolute property eventually called into question all the customary and traditional relations of civil society that Blackstone folded under the law of persons. All special privileges and special disabilities incident to status relationships become suspect: indentured servitude, slavery, coverture, and the special charter corporation. At the same time, the generalization of the property trope to every conceivable type of commercial expectancy had, by the end of the end of the nineteenth century, expanded into a full panoply of rights to intangibles, including the freedom to contract, the right to a reasonable return on investment in public utility property, the right to management of one's business without interference, the right to advantageous contractual relations. By virtue of being called "property," these have all been alchemized into "natural" entitlements protected against even legislative attempts to revise them.

Yet every expansion of the concept of property as absolute dominion has threatened to explode the concept entirely. The uncontrollable expansion of the absolute individual property trope continues to pose serious problems because of the continuing difficulty of reconciling absolute property with the evident facts of economic life. The institutions of modern capitalism, especially the business corporation, with its modes of collective production and fragmentary rights distributed among innumerable owners and controllers, should – legal writers and social theorists keep predicting – lead to general abandonment of "property" as a strong normative term of public discourse, to acknowledgment of the "disintegration" of property.[37] But of course nothing of the sort has happened. The core image of absolute dominion, the owner in undisturbed enjoyment of his physical things, is too compelling. It still offers something to everyone: security, autonomy, expressive freedom, protection from arbitrary encroachment or restraint, participation as an equal in economic and civic life, both apology for the status quo and a promise of emancipation from it. For the great, it symbolizes protection from expropriation and regulation; for the smallholder, independence and a patrimony to trade into wealth; for the artisan, control over work and its product; even for the propertyless, a claim for more equal distribution, or at least for secure entitlement to welfare benefits. Yet the price that has been paid for the compulsive power of the absolute dominion trope has been a heavy one, a maddeningly persistent tendency to suppress and to deny the collective and collaborative elements, the necessity of mutual dependence, inherent in social endeavor, and a consequently enormous distortion in our common capacities to understand and regulate our social life.

Notes

1 William Blackstone, *Commentaries on the Laws of England: A Facsimile of the First Edition of 1765–1769*, ed. Stanley N. Katz, 4 vols (Chicago: University of Chicago Press, 1979), Vol. 2, p. 2.

2 John Phillip Reid, *Constitutional History of the American Revolution: The Authority of Rights* (Madison, WI : University of Wisconsin Press, 1986), p. 99. Strictly speaking the property in liberty was a form of tenancy-in-common, inalienable without the consent of all the co-tenants; or a kind of estate in possession, inherited at birth and "entailed upon" or "held in trust for" the next generation.

3 Duncan Kennedy, "The rise and fall of classical legal thought" (unpublished course materials, Harvard Law School, 1978), Vol. 1, p. 135.

4 For lists with similar intent, but somewhat differing content, see Forrest McDonald, *Novus Ordo Seclorum: The Intellectual Origins of the Constitution* (Lawrence, KS: University Press of Kansas, 1985), pp. 9–15; G. R. Rubin and David Sugarman, *Law, Economy and Society. 1750–1914: Essays in the History of English Law* (Abingdon, Oxon: Professional Books, 1984), pp. 23–42.

5 Carol Rose, "The comedy of the commons: custom, commerce, and inherently public property," *University of Chicago Law Review* 53 (1986): 711–81.

6 McDonald, *Novus Ordo Seclorum*, p. 31.

7 Gary Kulik, "Dams, fish and farmers: defense of public rights in eighteenth-century Rhode Island," in Steven Hahn and Jonathan Prude (eds), *The Countryside in the Age of Capitalist Transformation* (Chapel Hill, NC: University of North Carolina Press, 1985), pp. 25–50 (p. 25).

8 Harry N. Scheiber, "Public rights and the rule of law in American legal history," *California Law Review* 72 (1984): 217–51; Molly Selvin, "The public trust doctrine in American law and economic policy, 1789–1920," *University of Wisconsin Law Review*, No. 6 (1980): 1403–42.

9 John Erskine, *An Institute of the Laws of Scotland*, ed. Alexander Macallan (Edinburgh: 1838 [1775]; rev. edn), p. 1095, as cited in W. G. Carson, "Policing the periphery: the development of Scottish policing, 1795–1900, Part I," *Australian and New Zealand Journal of Criminology* 17 (December 1984): 210; I owe this valuable reference to Christopher Tomlins.

10 Istvan Hont and Michael Ignatieff, "Needs and justice in the *Wealth of Nations*: an introductory essay," in *Wealth and Virtue: The Shaping of Political Economy in the Scottish Enlightenment* (Cambridge, UK: Cambridge University Press, 1983), pp. 1–44; Christopher Tomlins, "Police: the pursuit of happiness," in *Law, Labor and Ideology in the Early American Republic* (Cambridge, UK: Cambridge University Press, 1993), pp. 35–59.

13   Toby L. Ditz, *Property and Kinship: Inheritance in Early Connecticut, 1750–1820* (Princeton, NJ: Princeton University Press, 1986), p. 159. For an extended discussion of the thesis that property relations in colonial society were embedded in a mesh of household and community obligations, see James Henretta, "Families and forms: *mentalité* in pre-industrial America," *William and Mary Quarterly*, 3rd series, 35 (1978): 3–32.

14   On colonial tenancy, see Sung Bok Kim, *Landlord and Tenant in Colonial New York: Manorial Society, 1664–1775* (Chapel Hill, NC: University of North Carolina Press, 1978); Dennis P. Ryan, "Landholding, mobility and opportunity in revolutionary New Jersey," *William and Mary Quarterly*, 3rd series, 36 (1979): 571–8; Jack P. Greene, *Pursuits of Happiness: The Social Development of Early Modern British Colonies and the Formation of American Culture* (Chapel Hill, NC: University of North Carolina Press, 1988), pp. 126–9; Lucy Simler, "Tenancy in colonial Pennsylvania: the case of Chester County," *William and Mary Quarterly*, 3rd series, 43 (1986): 542–69; Gregory A. Stiverson, *Poverty in a Land of Plenty* (Baltimore, MD: Johns Hopkins University Press, 1977).

15   John Brewer, "Commercialization and politics," in Neil McKendrick, John Brewer, and J. H. Plumb, *The Birth of a Consumer Society: The Commercialization of Eighteenth-Century England* (Bloomington, IN: Indiana University Press, 1982), p. 211.

16   T. H.-Breen, *Tobacco Culture: The Mentality of the Great Tidewater Planters on the Eve of Revolution* (Princeton, NJ: Princeton University Press, 1985), p. 141.

17   Brewer, "Commercialization and politics," p. 214.

18   Willard Hurst, *Law and the Conditions of Freedom in the Nineteenth-Century United States* (Madison, WI: University of Wisconsin Press, 1967), p. 24; Morton J. Horwitz, *The Transformation of American Law, 1780–1860* (Cambridge, MA: Harvard University Press, 1977), pp. 30–53.

19   John P. S. McLaren, "Nuisance law and the industrial revolution: some lessons from social history," *Oxford Journal of Legal Studies* 3 (1983): 155–221; Robert Bone, "Normative theory and legal doctrine in American nuisance law: 1850 to 1920," *Southern California Law Review* 59 (1986): 1101–1226.

20   Wesley N. Hohfeld, *Fundamental Legal Conceptions as Applied in Judicial Reasoning* (New Haven, CT: Yale University Press, 1923).

21   Horwitz, *Transformation of American Law*, pp. 104–6.

22   Elizabeth Mensch, "The colonial origins of liberal property rights," *Buffalo Law Review* 31 (1983): 635–735; Paul W. Gates, *Landlords and Tenants on the Prairie Frontier* (Ithaca, NY: Cornell University Press, 1973), pp. 13–47; Ryan, "Landholding, mobility and opportunity."

23   Mensch, "Colonial origins," pp. 678–90.

24   Gregory S. Alexander, "The dead hand and the law of trusts in the nineteenth century," *Stanford Law Review* 37 (1985): 1189–1266.

25   Susan Staves, "Separate maintenance contracts," *Eighteenth-Century Life*, new series, 11, 2 (1987): 78–99; James Oldham, "Lord Mansfield's imprint on eighteenth-century English property concepts" (workshop paper, Clark Library: December 1989).

26   Staves, "Maintenance contracts," pp. 90–9.

27   Amy Dru Stanley, "Conjugal bonds and wage labor: rights of contract in the age of 'emancipation'," *Journal of American History* 75 (1988): 471–500.

28 Karl Renner, *Institutions of Private Law and their Social Functions* (London: Routledge [1949]), p. 196.

29 *Proceedings and Debates, Virginia State Convention of 1829–30* . . . (Richmond, VA: 1830), quoted in Robert J. Steinfeld, "Property and suffrage in the early American republic," *Stanford Law Review* 41 (1989): 359–60.

30 *Perrin* v. *Blake*, 1 W Bl 671, 4 Burr 2579 (1770); Francis Hargrave, *Law Tracts* (London: 1787), p. 487; Francis Hargrave, *Collectanea Juridica* (London: 1791), Vol. 1, p. 283. Cf. Oldham, "Lord Mansfield's imprint"; David Lieberman's chapter in this volume; and David Lieberman, *The Province of Legislation Determined: Legal Theory in Eighteenth-Century Britain* (Cambridge, UK: Cambridge University Press, 1989), pp. 133–41.

31 Henry Home, Lord Kames, *Principles of Equity* (Edinburgh: 1800; 4th edn), pp. 18–19.

32 *Clow* v. *Woods*, 5 *Sergeant & Rawle's Reports* 275 (Pa 1819).

33 *Worseley* v. *De Mattos*, 96 *English Reports* 1160 (King's Bench, 1758); *Alderson* v. *Temple*, 96 *English Reports* 384 (King's Bench, 1768).

34 On the history of preferences, see Robert Weisberg, "Commercial morality, the merchant character, and the history of the voidable preference," *Stanford Law Review* 39 (1986): 3–138.

35 David Hume, *Enquiries Concerning Human Understanding and Concerning the Principles of Morals*, ed. L. A. Selby-Bigge, rev. P. H. Nidditch (Oxford: Clarendon Press, 1975), section 259, note 1.

36 John Adams, "A dissertation on the canon and the feudal law," in Robert J. Taylor, Mary-Jo Kline, and Greg L. Lint (eds), *Papers of John Adams* (Cambridge, MA: Belknap Press of Harvard University Press, 1977), Vol. 1, p. 127.

37 See, for example, the excellent essay by Thomas C. Grey, "The disintegration of property," in J. Roland Pennock and John W. Chapman (eds), *Nomos XXII: Property* (New York: New York University Press, 1980), pp. 69–85.

of redemption

David Sugarman and Ronnie Warrington

In one favourite conceit . . . [England] was in essence a family, squabbling over inessentials, but pulling together when there was trouble. . . . Practical and down-to-earth, the English were nevertheless romantically attached to tradition, to the "unchanging beauty" of the English countryside, to the "cottages small" "beside a field of grain". Crack shots when it came to confronting the enemy . . . they were for the rest hopelessly old-fashioned and at odds with the modern world.[1]

Introduction

In the strange, half-timeless world of the traditional English landed estate, feudal concepts blissfully lingered long after feudal relations had been eradicated. Whether or not satisfied with their semi-feudal position, most landowners treated their landed estates with the same reverence as a miser was supposed to treat gold. Land was not just the most valuable form of property; both to its owners and to non-owners it was a social-political nexus, a way of life.

The law also treated land with peculiar devotion. If for no other reason, the enormous complexities of the pre-twentieth-century land transfer system[2] meant that the sale of land was not undertaken lightly. One of the protections the legal system developed to safeguard land was the equity of redemption, a seemingly unshakeable branch of mortgage law. Largely the creature of the seventeenth and eighteenth centuries, this intricate body of legal doctrine minimized the possibility that landowners would lose their land when they mortgaged it in order to raise cash, or used it as security for the debts they incurred. The courts applied the equity of redemption irrespective of the terms of the agreement between the parties and their manifest intentions. The rights of the landed were thus entrenched as against lenders, even though this might involve the courts rewriting the transactions between the parties.

Only in 1914 did the courts substantially recast the doctrine.[3] In this chapter we argue that the rise and tenacity of the equity of redemption highlight some of the paradoxical ways in which certain areas of property law privileged the rights of the landed for a longer time-span than is often assumed, yet, at the same time, fostered the extension of commercial contracts sustained by credit. From an economic perspective, the equity of redemption created a legal bulwark safeguarding land (and the landed) from the encroachments of capital, while helping to fashion the mortgage as a major vehicle for economic development. From a legal perspective, although the creation and development of the equity of redemption has been taken as exemplifying the law's increasing commitment to the notion of property as individual absolute dominion, it also illustrates the extent to which the law routinely fostered the qualification of property and restraints on alienation. Although the ideology of absolute private property denied those social and collaborative dimensions intrinsic to human endeavor, in practice the law continually threatened to undo the ideology of absolute private property and its atomistic conception of human relations. These are some of the paradoxes that we hope to address.

In this chapter we have sought to emphasize the complex interplay between the legal, economic, political, and cultural dimensions of the equity of redemption in ways that dissolve these disciplinary divisions. Under this wider optic the law of property was, amongst other things, an important form of story-telling. It provided *post-hoc* explanations for particular relationships between people. Certain forms of property relations, and therefore the ability to exercise power over other people, were rendered more natural than other types of relations. The equity of redemption not only enhanced the rights of the landowning classes while facilitating the extension of credit and business, but, in the context of other cognate areas of property law, it was also an important narrative discourse, like religion, history, or literature, a discourse which helped to explain how property relations developed in a way that was both necessary and inevitable.

The creation and development of the equity of redemption was part of a wider trend within land law concerned with the preservation and consolidation of landed wealth. This topic has already received extensive treatment within the context of the debates surrounding the strict family settlement and primogeniture. Historians have also acknowledged the importance of mortgages in the expansion of aristocratic indebtedness and as a flexible and widely available means of borrowing often overseen by an attorney. In these ways historians have extended our sense of the economic importance of mortgages and the legal order that sustained it.[4] Nonetheless, the nature and significance of the equity of redemption have been neglected by all but legal historians.[5] More generally, the larger cultural and political significance of property law, in the sense of inventing and policing certain ideas of "Englishness," property, justice, citizenship, and, therefore, the legitimate distribution of power, merits greater attention. It is these facets of property law, as exemplified by the development of the equity of redemption, that we hope to illuminate.[6]

In the first part of this chapter, we explain what lawyers meant by the equity of redemption, its relationship to mortgages and property, and its legal implications. We then analyze the battle waged by judges and jurists to create, extend, and, occasionally, hold in check, this new jurisprudence. While we have sought to render this technical

privileged position of the landed aristocracy and gentry and its role in English society. In economic terms, land had become almost another species of property, largely shorn of its sacredness. The law of property helped to constitute these changes, and even the equity of redemption was not exempt from a process which transformed the "natural" relations of property and, therefore, modern notions of justice and Englishness.

I The rise and persistence of the equity of redemption

1 Mortgages and the equity of redemption: an introduction and overview

Historically, a mortgage arose where an owner of property (usually land) required money and arranged to transfer the property to a lender as security in return for a loan. The loan agreement would generally provide for a reconveyance of the property to the borrower at a specific date on repayment of the money borrowed and the interest due. If the loan was not repaid, the property became forfeited to the lender.[7] At common law, the date for repayment had to be strictly adhered to. A single day's delay in tendering repayment could result in the borrower losing the entire property to the lender, even though the amount of the loan might be far less than the value of the land.[8]

Now the interpretive stance adopted by the common law courts was challenged by the courts of equity. Dating from at least the turn of the seventeenth century, the courts of equity determined that the strict date for repayment was somewhat irrelevant. Accordingly, the lender's claim to the property became subject

> to a right called the equity of redemption, which arose from the court's consideration that the real object of the transaction was the creation of a security for the debt. This entitled the [borrower] to redeem (or recover the property), even though he had failed to repay by the appointed time.[9]

Time was not to be the essence of the agreement. Although the mortgagor's legal right to redeem the property was lost after the expiration of the time specified in the contract, in equity the mortgagor had an equitable right to redeem on payment within a reasonable period of the principal, interest, and costs. A reasonable period could in some cases span many years.

The rights of the mortgagor were further enhanced by the rules governing foreclosure. Equity developed the decree of foreclosure, an order of court, made on application by the mortgagee, declaring the equity of redemption at an end and thus leaving the mortgagee with the fee simple absolute. But if the property was worth more than the amount owed by the mortgagor, the court would order a sale of property, the mortgagee taking the money owed to her/him, the remainder going to the mortgagor.

The discretion to allow the borrower to get back property notwithstanding the contractual term soon hardened into a right.[10] In addition to this right (the fully fledged equity of redemption), the courts developed various analogous protections for borrowers. Partly under the umbrella of that seemingly tautological maxim of equity, "once a mortgage always a mortgage," the courts also laid down that the borrower's right to get property back could not be rendered ineffective either by postponing the right for some unacceptable period or by making the right subject to some penalty, such as the borrower being deprived of some or all of the property mortgaged on exercising the right to redeem.[11] What became known as a "collateral advantage," that is, the lender asserting a claim to some or all of the borrower's property irrespective of repayment of the loan, was outlawed.

2   The establishment of the equity of redemption

It is generally agreed that the exact origin of the equity of redemption in its modern form is probably lost. A. W. B. Simpson suggested that the Chancery courts were prepared to relieve mortgagors from strict forfeiture conditions from the fifteenth century.[12] But although there are examples to support this, these probably relate to what Simpson calls "peculiarly scandalous cases." The most common example of this would be where the mortgagee was repaid entirely from the rents and profits of the property and still refused to reconvey the property to the mortgagor. Richard Turner, the leading historian of the equity of redemption, concluded that the equity of redemption arose during the reign of Elizabeth I.[13] While the Court of Chancery did grant relief to mortgagors during this period, there are only two reported decisions where relief was given after a forfeiture. It was probably not until the start of the seventeenth century that courts began to grant relief to borrowers as a matter of course, without looking for the special circumstances that would have previously been necessary to activate equity's conscience. The courts gradually extended the list of circumstances that they regarded as causing the special hardship necessary for them to give protection. Thus, the jurisdiction to intervene which had originally operated only in exceptional circumstances became the rule; and the cases where no relief was granted became the exception.[14]

In the mid-seventeenth century the courts also announced two principles which were an inevitable product of the increasing confidence of mortgagors in obtaining the return of their property notwithstanding the strict terms of mortgaged deeds. In *Emmanuel College* v. *Evans* (1625)[15] the courts first elaborated the principle that a pledge of property was a "mere" security; and a few years later, in *Duchess of Hamilton* v. *Countess of Dirlton* (1654),[16] the actual formulation of the "equity of redemption" itself was first enunciated.[17] Turner pointed out that in both these cases the judgments were not actually reported until many years after the cases were decided.[18] There is, therefore, the danger of a later reporter reading back into the decisions the ideas of a succeeding age by finding rules that were not yet established but which the reporter wished to discover. But even if this were the case, the concept that the land in a mortgage transaction is merely a security, a concept fundamental to the equity of redemption, is

the common lawyers made one final effort to cut back the growth of the equity of redemption, in *Roscarrick v. Barton* (1672).[20]

According to Turner, this was the last reported decision of an attempt to defeat the equity of redemption on the grounds that it was only a mere chose in action, that is, not a real property interest but merely a personal right recoverable by a suit at law.[21] In this case, Chief Justice Hale acknowledged both the extent of the equity of redemption by this date and the threat that it posed to the common law:

> "And it hath gone far enough already," he said, "and we will go no further than Precedent in the Matter of the Equity of Redemption, which hath too much favour already. . . . [There should be] no Decree for the Plaintiff in respect of the antiquity, and if he will redeem, he must come in Time."[22]

As a leading nineteenth-century commentary observed, this was soon rejected and replaced by the "sound principles" of treating the equity of redemption as an estate in land with the "person entitled to it the real owner of the land and the mortgage personal assets."[23] In short, despite the occasional expression of concern, it was during the latter half of the seventeenth century that the courts firmly established the equity of redemption. And having created it, judges and jurists then sought to consolidate it into a major equitable jurisdiction, one testifying to the care and attention that equity lavished upon the owners of land. On the other hand, some dissidents within the legal community sought to contain what they perceived to be "an unruly horse" unleashed in the name of justice.

3 The jurisdiction consolidated

The courts quickly established that the mortgagor (the borrower) could not be prevented from redeeming, either before or after the contractual redemption date.[24] Put simply, the date was fully effective against the lender, but rather less than effective against the borrower. Although later courts stressed that in certain circumstances the mortgagor might be prevented from redeeming early,[25] the vital principle that a mortgagor cannot be prevented from seeking the return of the mortgaged property has been taken to be established in the seventeenth century by Lord Nottingham.

Lord Nottingham was instrumental in starting the shift of the equity of redemption from a "thing" to an "estate" in equity, that is, in conceptualizing the equity of redemption as a kind of real property rather than as a kind of chattel property. Increasingly, a mortgagor's claims were given precedence over other interests to which they had earlier been postponed: for example, a mortgagor's claims came to take precedence even over a real property claim like the wife's right to dower. In *Attorney*

General v. *Pawlett* (1667),[26] Lord Hale first characterized the equity of redemption as a title in equity. According to Lord Hale, a trust was contractual in nature, while the equity of redemption was proprietorial. Lord Nottingham took this further by distinguishing the trust (binding in particular) from the equity of redemption (binding in general).[27] Lord Nottingham wrote that equity suffers no land to be lost, "if in a convenient time it may be redeemed," and that equity would always allow a mortgage to be redeemed.[28] "No words of Scrivener nor any invention of Counsel can make that which was intended as a mortgage to work as an absolute assurance."[29] And in *Jason* v. *Eyres* (1680), as judge rather than historian, Lord Nottingham declared: "That no Mortgage by any artificial words can be altered, unless by subsequent agreement."[30]

Although the principle in *Jason* v. *Eyres* was clear enough, an early nineteenth-century commentator, R. H. Coote, argued that the decision should have gone against the mortgagor on the same principle on which Lord Nottingham was reversed in the case of *Newcombe* v. *Bonham* (1681).[31] The history of this important decision is of some interest. In his version of the case, Lord Nottingham is reported as not only using the maxim "once a mortgage always a mortgage," but as stating that the agreement "being but a security, the same could not be extinguished by any covenant or agreement at the time of making the mortgage."[32] Yet the decision was, after some hesitation, reversed by Lord North. The agreement in the case was part of a family settlement where the mortgagor was permitted to redeem during his own lifetime only. Lord North thought that, therefore, on the original borrower's death, the right to redeem was at an end since otherwise interfamily arrangements might be upset because of the "indefinite" possibility of redemption.

Lord North's decision on the grounds of family security illustrates the problems that might be caused by a mechanistic interpretation of the equity of redemption and the rules made in its name. It foreshadowed difficulties equity would face with its own creation at a much later period. The point at issue was how far should courts take on themselves the duty to interfere in private arrangements. Two years later in *Howard* v. *Harris* (1683),[33] on similar facts, Lord Nottingham made the same decision. This time Lord North upheld the judgment, but again dropped hints that in cases of family settlements the courts might not interfere.

Other decisions which seem to prevent redemption such as *Isham* v. *Cole* (1639),[34] where, confronted with a 33-year mortgage, it was stressed that "this Court doth hold it a dangerous Precedent to relieve Mortgages after so long an Elapse of Time,"[35] or *Floyer* v. *Lavington* (1714),[36] where redemption was not permitted after sixty years, or *Mellor* v. *Lees* (1742),[37] where the court appeared to accept the perpetual mortgage of rent charge, were equally bypassed as either erroneous or decided on "special circumstances."[38]

There were other instances where the exceptions appear to have almost challenged the basic equitable jurisdiction itself, although, significantly, until the end of the nineteenth century none of them actually did so. For example, from an early date the courts accepted that the mortgagor could release the equity of redemption to the mortgagee absolute if a separate agreement to this effect was entered into after the mortgage was created.

But despite these and other exceptional areas,[39] the move to establish a strong equity of redemption became too powerful to resist. To put it as Turner would, in terms of

Lord Nottingham was also responsible for settling that mortgagees' (that is, the lenders') rights were mere personality. In *Thornborough* v. *Baker* (1675) he explained this by saying: "For in natural justice and equity the principal right of the mortgagee is to the money, and his right to the land is only as a security for the money."[42] The property, that is, the land, really belonged to the borrower; the lender was only entitled to the money. Even Lord Mansfield seems to have had no doubts that in this area of the law the position of the landed gentry should be privileged irrespective of the intentions of the parties. "In the eye of this Court," he said in *Burgess* v. *Wheate* (1750), "the equity of redemption is the fee simple of the land."[43] Again, this development helped to legitimate the view that the fee simple should be returned to the "true owner" wherever possible, that is, the owner of the equity of redemption.

Despite these legal developments, numerous lenders tried to circumvent the equitable protections, a practice possibly encouraged for a while by the final outcome of *Newcombe* v. *Bonham* (1681). But time and again the courts stressed that they would strike down the actual terms of a contract, especially where the lender attempted to limit the potential for redemption to the life of the individual borrower only. In *Spurgeon* v. *Collier* (1758), for example, Sir Robert Henley said: "The policy of this court is not more complete in any part of it than in its protection of mortgages; and, as a general rule for that purpose, a mortgage once redeemable continues so until some act is done afresh by the mortgagor to extinguish the redemption; and a man will not be suffered in conscience to fetter himself with a limitation . . . of redemption. It would ruin the distressed and unwary and give unconscionable advantage to greedy and designing persons."[44]

Similar claims that the mortgage had subsisted for too long to permit a redemption were also rejected.[45] Nor were the courts impressed when the mortgagee claimed to have suffered particular hardship or taken unusual risks. In *Newton* v. *Langham* (1675),[46] the plaintiff had mortgaged a somewhat risky share in an East India Company venture. "This Court declared, That notwithstanding the Hazzard and Contingency of the said Adventure mortgaged, and the Length of Time since the Mortgage, the Plaintiff ought to be admitted to a Redemption of the said Adventure."[47]

It is important to stress just how "fair" this striking down of bargains was thought to be. Commenting on another attempt to restrict redemption to the life of the mortgagor,[48] Coote opined that equity protects borrowers "justly considering it would throw open a wide door to oppression, and enable the creditor to drive an inequitable and hard bargain with the debtor who is rarely prepared to discharge his debt at the specified time."[49] This justice was not an abstract principle. It turned upon the assumptions of those who were deciding what was or what was not "just." And for most judges most of the time, justice in this context meant the restoration of landed property to the original owner.

As already suggested, Turner reduces much of his history of the equity of redemption to the "personality" of the Chancellors. This allows him to move straight from Lord Nottingham, the father of the equity of redemption, to Lord Hardwicke, who became the most important figure in the story by "consolidating" the work of Lord Nottingham. Lord Hardwicke's influential tenure as Lord Chancellor from 1736 to 1756 helped to settle equity as a system of general rules. His apparent respect for precedent and his careful and comprehensive statements of the law provided valuable ammunition to those who sought to defend Chancery practice against contemporary charges that it was arbitrary and uncertain. With respect to the equity of redemption, Lord Hardwicke did more than settle the law; he constructed new, enhanced foundations upon which to secure the doctrine by establishing the equity of redemption as an "estate" in its own right. If nothing else, Lord Hardwicke's claim to the central position in the story is assured by his famous decision in *Casborne* v. *Scarfe* (1735).[50] In this case, he determined that a husband was entitled to be a tenant by the curtesy of property of his wife, that is, to acquire his wife's life-interest where she predeceased him, notwithstanding that the property was in mortgage at her death, and therefore apparently not seised by the wife at the relevant time. Lord Hardwicke argued vehemently in favour of a strong equity of redemption. Once again, the lender's interest was seen as merely personality. The manuscript notes for his judgment were preserved, and nearly three-quarters of a century later they were published. These show him in little doubt as to the outcome of the decision. He said that the equity of redemption was considered an estate in land which may be granted or devised. "This proves that it is not considered as a mere right, but as such an estate whereof in the consideration of the Court, there may be a seisin, for without such seisin, a devise could not be good."[51] He clinched the argument to his own satisfaction by writing: "The true grounds of this is, that the ownership of the land doth, in equity, remain in the mortgagor, and therefore it shall pass by his devise though made precedent to the mortgage."[52]

While this case is by no means the first to define the equity of redemption as an estate,[53] the importance of the equity of redemption as the equivalent of ownership limited through time is fundamental. It provided the legal foundation to underpin the "fairness" of the courts' interference in contract. Not only was this just, it was technically correct. Although doubts lingered in the minds of some judges for a century or more as to the accuracy of characterizing the equity of redemption as an estate, for practical purposes they were of no further significance.[54] By 1822, Thomas Coventry could write as incontrovertible: "And equity of redemption will follow the custom as to the legal estate."[55]

A similar transformation took place in the rules governing what were termed "collateral advantage." These rules policed any additional benefit that the mortgagee had extracted from the mortgagor, additional, that is, to the interest and the principal owed to the mortgagee. Here again, the courts went out of their way to interfere with bargains which to the late nineteenth-century and early twentieth-century courts seemed, on paper, perfectly "fair." As with the rules relating to attempts to limit rights to redeem, anything that allowed the mortgagee the slightest opportunity of obtaining the mortgaged property itself was, by definition, oppressive or unjust.

Hardwicke was what shocked the aristocracy and landed gentry.[57]

In summary, the general effect of the rules governing the equity of redemption was to protect the owners of landed wealth as far as possible. The rules never purported to allow borrowers to escape from the actual debts they contracted, but the courts took it upon themselves to decide the limits beyond which lenders of money secured on landed estates could not go. The rights developed, summarized in the rules of "once a mortgage always a mortgage," the prohibitions on collateral advantages, and the prohibitions against clogging or fettering the equity of redemption, the "three catchphrases" as Turner called them,[58] were all part of what was, in essence, one paternal jurisdiction. In the mid-nineteenth century, the jurisdiction was seemingly incontrovertible. Even as late as 1912, Lord Halsbury spoke of "this equitable doctrine which, I agree, is now part of the jurisprudence of this country."[59]

4   Little short of ideal

As we have seen, the equity of redemption was a highly interventionist jurisdiction. Why was this jurisdiction fair; and how was it justified? Judges and jurists tended to adopt two intersecting rationales for this special jurisdiction. First, one distinctive strand of equity's broad and highly discretionary jurisdiction in fraud concerned the protection of young heirs. In these cases it would be argued that landed heirs should be relieved from their bargains to borrow money, convey land, buy horses, jewellery, etc., because these bargains were unconscionable and fraudulent. They were fraudulent and unconscionable because the young heirs concerned were in "necessitous circumstances," often shorthand for meaning that they had more money than sense! Because they felt impelled to undertake the sort of bargains that others would scorn, they were the obvious targets of what were characterized as "unscrupulous moneylenders" or "rogues" selling goods at a high price. There were other similar cases in which lenders to young heirs attempted to avoid the statutes of usury. It was coextensive with these developments that equity developed and consolidated the equity of redemption.

Thus, judges and jurists alike often asserted that when landowners pledged their property they did so "out of necessity" and were subject to all sorts of pressures from "crafty" lenders. The equity of redemption was intended to protect the landowner from the money-hungry activity of commercial interests. According to Lord Hardwicke in *Toomes* v. *Conset* (1745), to enforce the original agreement strictly would be to put "the borrower too much in the power of the lender who, being distressed at the time, is too inclined to submit to any terms proposed on the part of the lender."[60] The borrower here was by definition a landowner, something Lord Macnaghten recognized over 150 years later in 1904 when he too was faced with the claim that the borrower ought to be protected automatically. Speaking of the jurisdiction he said: "It seems to have had its origin in the desire of the Court of Chancery to protect embarrassed landowners from imposition and oppression."[61] But by then Lord Macnaghten was beginning to have doubts as to the justice of the doctrine. No such scruples had troubled Lord Henley, who was satisfied that the rule was based on the highest principles. "And there is great reason and justice in this rule for necessitous men are not, truly speaking, free men, but to answer a present exigency, will submit to any terms the crafty may impose upon them."[62] The anomalous character of this protection for the "necessitous" is evident when one considers the many other instances in which starker necessitousness did not postpone debts due. In other words, the equity of redemption was the product of a jurisdiction which in important respects turned on the status of a party before the court, by reason of infancy, lunacy, or the fact that a party was a married woman or landowner.

Secondly, it was emphasized that the court's function was to ensure that ultimately land was returned to its "rightful" (often meaning historical or traditional) owner. Even when the terms of the contract unequivocally pointed to an agreement to transfer the ownership of the land in exchange for money, goods, or services, the courts were seemingly loath to accept it at face value. It was as if it were inconceivable that an English gentleman would give up his land, save in wholly exceptional circumstances. Thus the courts conceived the mortgagee's right as a right to money rather than land. From this perspective, for Englishmen to bargain away their land in these circumstances, and for "moneylenders" and "rogues" to acquire significant landholdings, was suspect, if not downright un-English.

As the story was told by Turner, the development of the equity of redemption was a minor miracle. Speaking of Lord Hardwicke's role in the development, he could hardly contain his enthusiasm. His Lordship had created a body of law that was "fair," "rational," and "noble," "a structure which soon became one of the most important features of English land law, having a far-reaching effect upon the internal economic position of the country."[63] Although Turner conceded that the end result was not quite up to the high standard of Roman law, "The conceptions upon which the rules in application are based are sound in character and little short of the ideal."[64] He even allowed his enthusiasm to go so far as to suggest a comparison between the creation and development of the equity of redemption and the development of new symbols in mathematics making possible further advances into "unknown realms of mathematical speculation."[65] Here was a doctrine that could indeed perform miracles.

Ironically, Turner completely failed to comprehend that this near perfect doctrine had been substantially recast by the House of Lords in *Kreglinger* v. *New Patagonia Meat & Cold Storage* (1914),[66] a case which he describes but whose significance escaped him. Turner had become so enamored of the judicial process which he wished to admire that he was incapable of realizing that, by 1931, when his own legal history was published, the Chancery lawyers had transformed the equity of redemption. One conception of fairness (the fairness needed to protect and entrench the superior position of the landed oligarchy) had been largely supplanted by another conception of fairness (the fairness demanded by the financier) which appeared to demand the rigorous enforcement of the letter of contracts. Since Turner treated the development of the equity of redemption as intrinsically natural, desirable, and superior, thereby abstracting the history of the

Land gives so much more than the rent. It gives position and influence and political power, to say nothing of the game.[67]

1   England's patrician polity, the law of real property and mythmaking

What were the particular circumstances that sustained the construction and expansion of the equity of redemption, and enabled the landed elite to exploit it? First and foremost was the fact that until the 1870s England was a "patrician polity."[68] While comparative work is problematic, most commentators are agreed that England's landed elite were collectively more wealthy, powerful, and exclusive relative to their continental counterparts; and that the correlation between the property, position, and power of the landed elite was probably more intense in England than elsewhere in Europe. On the Continent, each time land was inherited by a new generation it tended to be subdivided into smaller and more numerous units. Continental estates were therefore smaller in size, while the landed establishment tended to be somewhat larger in number. The ranks of the titled were further swollen as honors were bestowed on other groups, notably that service class which lacked a landed base but played a crucial role in the administration of the state. In these circumstances it was relatively more difficult to maintain the elite status of the landed. England's landed oligarchy was small in number compared with the landed elites of other European countries, and it seems to have exercised a more tenacious hold on power, wealth, and status. Until the 1870s, the landed establishment owned about four-fifths of the land in the British Isles. Their political, economic, and cultural hegemony is exemplified by their pre-eminence in government, Parliament, the law, the Church, the civil service, and the armed forces. Despite Britain's unique status as the "first industrial nation," it was only from the last quarter of the nineteenth century onwards that the hitherto superior position of the landed establishment was gradually eroded.[69]

In Britain, land was sacred. Above all, land denoted status and citizenship. As David Spring put it, "Land in England had long been something more than a mere commodity to be bought and sold at the highest price the market could afford."[70] Many landowners spent huge sums on the improvement of the most obvious trappings of conspicuous consumption, their homes and their parks. The real returns on such investments "were not visible in monetary terms."[71] Moneymaking as an activity in its own right became respectable, albeit gradually and unevenly; yet the retention of semi-feudal relations of deference and hierarchy was still regarded as a priority. Many landowners were prepared to countenance some economic development of their lands provided their parks were unaffected, their hunting undisturbed, and their physical peace and seclusion guaranteed.[72] Some (but by no means all) landowners were lucky enough to avold or delay the unpleasant prospect of industrialization on their doorstep. For example, C. R. M. Talbot, the wealthy Welsh landowner and MP, was able both to receive handsome returns from his railway investment, and to keep the railways out of the Gower Peninsula and off his estate. "Whilst allowing the railways to pass over his land, Talbot stipulated that he did not wish to hear the sound of passing trains from his mansion at Margam."[73] In an age of rationalization and scientific discovery, exaggerated social deference patterns lingered on many of the old estates. The 1847 funeral procession of the third Duke of Northumberland brought all activity on the estate to a standstill. "In this procession we can see the County and the Northumbrian tenantry bidding farewell to their feudal chief."[74]

Most landowners were faced at some time or other with pressure to sell their land. Until the end of the nineteenth century, however, they tended to be reluctant to sell at times when the rational economic thing to do would have been to abandon their estates. Writing in 1827, Sir James Graham recognized the problems that heavy indebtedness caused many country gentlemen, and conceded that sale was a possibility:

> But what agony of mind does that word convey? The snapping of a chain, linked perhaps by centuries; the destruction of the dearest attachments, the dissolution of the earliest friendships, the violation of the purest feelings of the heart.[75]

This reluctance to sell was part of a larger ethos: namely, the landowners' desire to create and maintain a dynasty. For England's landed elite, righteousness came to be defined in terms of their devotion to the sanctity of the estate as the interests of the family took precedence over those of the individual. As Edmund Burke put it, landownership was "a partnership not only between those of the living, but between those who were living, those who were dead, and those who are to be born."[76] Most large landowning families schemed with varying degrees of success to insure that the interests of future generations were secure.

The legal system played a decisive role in these developments. At the most general level, England's patrician polity was defined and constituted by and through the law.[77] It was the rights, privileges, and responsibilities *in law* that characterized social relations (who could own, inherit, participate in government, etc.); in other words, it was the law that made people "landowners," "tenants," "masters," "servants," "husbands," "wives,"[78] and so on, albeit that in practice this was mediated and refracted by a diffuse series of *de facto* constraints, not least the uncertain state of the law itself. Constitutional rights and land law were closely connected. It was Maitland who observed that "our whole constitutional law seems at times to be but an appendix to the law of real property."[79]

The landed elite and the law were intensely bound together. From 1621 until 1844, the kingdom's supreme judges were not the professional lawyers of King's Bench or Chancery but England's nobility assembled in Parliament. Although the law remained the law of the Crown, the largest owners of property became the highest judges of the law of property. Even after 1844, England's most senior judges and law officers continued to be peers, in part because the House of Lords remained the kingdom's supreme court of judicature.[80]

middle classes, for example, tended to divide family wealth on a more equal footing, having "no sense of the elder son's importance in carrying on the line."[95]

The Chancery refinements of mortgage law encouraged many landowners to borrow to the limits of their security and beyond, but they did not apparently discourage the lending of money. Mortgages were increasingly treated as a safe and popular form of investment.[96] In his pioneering study of capital formation in Lancashire, B. L. Anderson concluded that the practice of borrowing and lending on mortgages "had taken deep root amongst all classes from the beginning of the [eighteenth] century."[97] So also in Bath; R. S. Neale argued that the opulent development of Bath in the eighteenth century was possible partly because a wide, local, national, and even international credit market was easily available to the owners of landed property. The increasing sophistication of land law encouraged lenders, and most of Bath's building architects and landowners relied heavily on mortgage finance.[98] In short, the eighteenth-century development of mortgage law, the decline in the rate of interest, the growth of specialized lending institutions, and the expansion of the mortgage market outside London, all helped encourage borrowing, and none more so than aristocratic borrowing.[99]

Most large landowners were therefore familiar with mortgages. As Powell put it: "There are few men possessed of either real or personal estate, who are not more or less concerned in that species of property called a mortgage."[100] Although a series of law lectures delivered in the early nineteenth century, presumably to the sons of men who possessed either real or personal estate, discussed mortgages only in relation to the distinction between real and personal property, it is significant perhaps that the one substantive point of mortgage law that the lecturer thought fit to mention was that the mortgaged estate "was merely a pledge and not to be meddled with."[101] If nothing else, sons of gentlemen were reminded that land was not just any form of wealth. Mortgagees were the servants of the landowner, not the other way round.

The attitude that it was the landowners' natural privilege to take loans on security and then be relieved from the terms of the bargain, persisted until well into the nineteenth century. Lord Guildford borrowed money at 60 percent when an expectant heir and then successfully claimed that the strict terms of the bond that he gave against the expectancy should not be upheld. The exchange between counsel for the lender and Lord Guildford shows His Lordship denying that he even understood the meaning of "60 percent." "I did not know whether it was high or low interest; I thought money-lenders always charged that amount," he said. Asked whether he thought the rate too high, he replied: "I think they ought to have let me have money at a lower interest; because they knew perfectly well that I was certain to come into the property, and that I could pay them and I was quite right to borrow the money if I wanted it."[102]

2   The narratives of the equity of redemption

The forging of national identity is a theme which has been taken up and illuminated in several recent historical studies.[103] The thrust of much of this work is the socially constructed character of nationalism and the nation-state. The important role played in the construction of a common identity by invented traditions, propaganda, symbols, the languages of history and religion, as well as the experience of warfare and the fear of impending attack, has rightly received much attention. Much of this work has emphasized the ways in which identity and community are created and recreated in opposition to a common enemy or "others" – whites against blacks, Protestants against Catholics, men against women, the West against the Orient, etc. Building upon work in anthropology, hermeneutics, and literary theory, this literature has illuminated the crucial role played by narratives – stories, fictions, and myths – in the making and remaking of subjectivity. Telling stories is a universal way in which people make sense of the world and their place in it. In our endeavor to transform chaos into order, we use the narrative form of language to render social relations coherent, stable, and fixed, albeit provisionally. Narrative serves a host of functions. It renders certain forms of social relations more plausible, natural, and moral than others; it provides comfort and meaning, fostering agency and/or complacency; it generates a sense of Utopian destiny, helping to create an imagined unity; and it helps to bind citizens into nations.[104]

With certain notable exceptions, the role and significance of law, lawyers, and legal narratives in the formation of national identity and community have not received much attention within this important literature.[105] In the remainder of this chapter, therefore, we shall examine the role played by the narratives of the equity of redemption in privileging the position of the landed elite and helping to fabricate a particular conception of the English nation, one of the several forms of "Englishness" that were fostered by the languages of the law.

Law is an influential story: it is one of the privileged ways through which society presents and defines the world to itself. Being normative in nature and a partially intelligible description and prescription for action, law's narratives predispose their writers, actors, and audiences to certain interpretive choices and social stances. This is to recognize that one of the important ways in which the law seemingly naturalizes certain types of social relationships is through its narratives; and that the legal community creates and transmits some of our most important political and social discourses.[106] Law is more than a structure of restraint, setting the boundaries within which individuals pursue their self-interest. It is one of the major processes by which the dominant representations of society are created and justified. These representations of society may become accepted as that society itself.[107] Law is, therefore, one of the major languages through which ideas are expressed.

In addition to being an important instrument for preserving and consolidating landed wealth, the equity of redemption was also a set of political and cultural codes. It was a repository of stories signifying the central importance of the landed aristocracy and gentry to English society. It assumed a certain ordering of preferences and rights: of what was proper and what was illicit; and who and what should be recognized, protected, or excluded. What we see here is the construction of memory, consciousness, and identity, a process binding together and privileging particular conceptions of "justice" and "Englishness." To stress the interaction of the legal, economic, and cultural in this way is to direct attention away from questions about the effect of law on society or even the effect of society on law toward conceptualizing a more complex and interactive relationship between law, economy, politics, and culture. Instead of mutual influences between the two separate entities, this perspective sees the boundaries between law, economics, politics, and culture as so blurred that they are best perceived as participating in the same social field.[108]

In order to appreciate the intimate links between the equity of redemption and the invention and policing of a particular conception of Englishness, we need to consider how the equity of redemption exemplified a wider language and imagery, melding religious, historical, and legal symbols and tropes into a reservoir of political language which embodied a particular national mythology. The close association of Protestantism, the sanctity of property, and a unique legal order with the English (and British) nation was the product of the seventeenth and eighteenth centuries. The translation of the Old Testament into the vernacular and its dissemination, along with other leading Protestant texts (Bunyan's *Pilgrim's Progress*, Foxe's *Book of the Martyrs*, etc.), helped to forge a national discourse among rich and poor alike in which the English became God's chosen people, the defenders of Protestantism, forever locked in battle with the forces of Satan, Catholicism, and despotism.[109] As Hilaire Belloc observed, "The modern English were cast and set in the mould of the English Old Testament."[110] As the Israelites had been delivered up from Egypt and led to a promised land, so the English were building a "Jerusalem,/In England's green and pleasant land."[111] In Britain's militantly Protestant polity, "time past was a soap opera written by God, a succession of warning disasters and providential escapes which they [Britons] acted out afresh every year [in the Protestant calendar] as a way of reminding themselves who they were."[112] The great meta-narratives were often superimposed onto biblical narratives, telling stories of steady progress, or of a once simple, golden age now debased, or of loss, struggle, and redemption.

Other languages coexisted and interacted with this discourse.[113] Particularly relevant here is the language of precedent and the ancient constitution: the idea of English law as immemorial custom, rooted in the distant past, the feudal law, the only law that England had known, the great palladium of individual freedom and liberty.[114] In this brogue, rights were largely determined by appeals to the past. The sanctity of the law of real property, for instance, derived from the insistence of the common lawyers that this branch of law was specially privileged because its authority could be sought in time immemorial. In these ways the longevity and sanctity of England's religion, law, and history were interwoven to create a common identity.

These discourses easily lent themselves to apocalyptic interpretations of history; they also exercised a significant hold on the language of politics during the period which spawned and sustained the equity of redemption. For the most part, religious, historical, and legal narratives were allied together, sharing similar forms of symbolism and rhetoric. Together, they helped to constitute England's national identity and destiny. These stories told of how Protestantism, the law, and the constitution had delivered up the people of England from tyranny at home and the threat of tyranny from abroad. Central, here, was the idea that the English were exceptionally fortunate – bathed in the King's Peace, sustained by Magna Carta, and thereby secure in the protection of their property and person.[115] England was a land where every Englishman's home was his castle. As it was put in the leading case of *Entick* v. *Carrington* (1765), "No man can set his foot upon my ground without my licence."[116] In the face of the wars in and against the continent of Europe, not to mention the arbitrary and uncertain protection of property and the person in foreign parts, England alone was safe. England's exceptionalism was attributable in part to her "splendid isolation,"[117] an isolation mirrored and reinforced by the relatively insular and arcane world of the common law, an antique, indigenous world, resolutely resistant to Romanization.[118]

The forms and symbols of the law were also closely connected with those customs that denoted good breeding and manners. As Goodrich and Hachamovitch discern:

> The unwritten constitution, the English constitution, is a court-based custom, a series of conventions transmitted through an unwritten knowledge of the forms and tacit rules of behaviour associated with the better classes, the better educated, the honourable and the gentle. Just as the court has its place, namely London, so the people have their place with "every man in his room of honour according as his place requires". The distinction of blood, of breeding, of genealogy has been as important as (possibly more important than) any particular behaviour. . . . It was the lawyers in the main who systematised and spelled out the system of honours, manners, proper speech and social law. . . .
>
> As Sir John Ferne defines it, nobility is derived as a word from the Latin *nobilitas* which in turn has a root in *nosco*, to know. By extension we might argue that the system of nobility not only signifies . . . nobility, of blood and degree . . . but it is also a form of codification, an encoding of knowledge, a hidden language or initiate wisdom even if that wisdom is of manners and mores and little else.[119]

This imbrication of the languages of religion, history, and law is significant with respect to narratives of the equity of redemption. To redeem has long meant to buy back a thing formerly possessed. But it also has other meanings touching upon the honor, status, and liberty of the redeemer which may be relevant in understanding why equity sought to intervene in the private world of agreement and accord. Thus, it was honorable people who sought to redeem their pledges, that is, buy back a thing formerly possessed; and the act of redemption was itself a symbol of their honor and gentility. To disable a person of standing from redeeming his pledge would therefore touch the position and honor of that individual. If the law placed obstacles in the way of the redemption of land, previously honorable people would be dishonored and bondage might ensue. In this sense to redeem one's land was an act of liberation, akin to the paying of a ransom, and yet another meaning of "to redeem."

Even more potent was the image of the aristocracy and landed gentry, clothed in the title associated with Christ himself, as the redeemers of English society. Viewed from this optic, the landed gentry embodied the same elevated role in secular society as that performed by Christ in the spiritual world. The redeemer was someone especially worthy of or especially entitled to deliverance from sin and damnation. In the context of the equity of redemption, the law incorporated the imperative that the landed should be saved from excommunication; that is, losing their land and therefore their souls. Moreover, their curse might be ours too. Thus, to grant redemption to the landed gentry was to preserve and redeem English society as a whole. Ultimately, their ownership interests were imagined as having a sacred quality: the preservation of the rights of the landed oligarchy guaranteed the continuance of divine favor, stability, and national identity.

3 Property, citizenship, and the constitutional idiom

The legal community, personified above all by Lord Mansfield, had exhibited great ingenuity in developing a commercial common law sensitive to the needs of commercial society.[120] But coexisting uneasily alongside these innovations was England's law of real property; and it was here that Mansfield locked horns with Blackstone. It was Blackstone who led the attack on what he and other judges regarded as Lord Mansfield's innovatory approach to real property, an approach that others stigmatized as Scottish, Romanist, and alien.[121] In Blackstone's view:

> the law of real property in this country is now formed into a fine artificial system, full of unseen connections and nice dependencies, and he that breaks one link of the chain endangers the dissolution of the whole.[122]

Here, Blackstone coupled reassurance and national pride with a chilling warning. England had a unique heritage: liberty, private property, stability, continuity, and the common law were intricately woven together like the fabric of a garment. The landed elite were entitled to their privileged status because they were part of an elaborate structure that held the nation together. Significant tinkering with the law of real property and the rights of the landed threatened to destroy English society.

Blackstone's passionate defense of the sanctity of land, with its attendant celebration of the common law, was reiterated by Edmund Burke.[123] For both Blackstone and Burke, any erosion of property opened the floodgates to radical reform, leveling, and anarchy. In his celebrated *Reflections on the Revolution in France*, Burke argued that the concentration of large tracts of landed wealth in the hands of the few was both necessary and desirable; and that land must remain unfettered for such consolidation created "a natural rampart about the lesser properties in all their gradations."[124] Again, the rhetorical thrust of these narratives was to demonstrate that the privileged position of the landed was just, and that its special prerogatives also served the best interests of the nation. The power of the landed elite and the constitutional settlement of 1688 were thereby canonized, while the case for reform was rendered suspect.

From this perspective, the narratives, symbols, and rhetoric of the equity of redemption were part of a larger, conservative discourse which confined citizenship to the owners of real property, idolizing an "independent" aristocracy mindful of all "the people." And in so doing it designated some categories of persons as different from others, implicitly negating certain individuals and social relations, while claiming to be neutral. For example, it was defined against more inclusive notions of citizenship such as plebeian and radical notions of common law rights to land as public or communal property;[125] and those customary use-rights in commons pertaining to gleaning, grazing, hunting, wood-gathering, etc., rights which were increasingly attacked in the eighteenth and nineteenth centuries by more exclusive uses of land.[126]

The common law also starkly distinguished between the British subject, who could own real property, and the alien, who could not. In law, if not always in practice, the limits to religious toleration were narrowly confined. Throughout the eighteenth century, Catholics and Jews were treated as un-British. Such was the popular hostility to the removal of their legal disabilities that the Jewish Naturalization Bill of 1753 had to be repealed; and the Catholic Relief Act of 1778 was the pretext for the bloody Gordon

Riots. In Scotland, the 1778 Act was unenforceable.[127] Immigration controls were properly installed by 1793, and the liberalization of naturalization was frustrated until 1836. Only with the passing of the Test and Corporation Act of 1828 and the Catholic Emancipation Act of 1829 did Catholics become part of the British nation.[128]

Of course the most obvious exclusion from the languages of property and citizenship was women. Much of the law (like much elite and popular culture) was intensely patriarchal, and the equity of redemption was no exception. As the Bible and the classic European texts, like Homer's *Odyssey* and Plato's *Symposium*, told and retold the heroic tale of how males took charge of heaven and earth, so the narratives of the equity of redemption were part of an exclusionary canon which celebrated "manliness." Joined with a mass of similar images in history and fiction, and those godlike representations of the Crown and aristocracy on coins and medals and in paintings, tapestries, and sculptures, they provided "a composite manual of language as well as behaviour."[129] Manliness was a fundamental value which animated much of the law of property and the languages of citizenship.[130] This was contrasted with women, who were represented as different human subjects within a particular hierarchy. For instance, married women's property was a contradiction in terms; it was only sometimes recognized as "property." According to the legal doctrine of coverture, the husband and the wife were one person in law, and that person was the husband.[131]

4   Room for maneuver

The equity of redemption was one of the legal institutions that supported landed power. And it continued to do so until 1914, when the doctrine was significantly recast by the House of Lords.[132] However, it exemplified but one of the several languages that together characterized the law of real property and contemporary debates concerning personhood.

It was the much vaunted British constitution, with its checks and balances and separations of power limiting the power of the monarch, which contemporaries and subsequent commentators alike have celebrated as the distinguishing hallmark of England's polity. More recently it is the paradoxical, pluralistic, and contested political structures of governance, and the interface between state and civil society, which have begun to receive serious attention: for example, the coexistence of a powerful, central state alongside a mass of semi-autonomous realms, long-standing traditions of local government and self-help.[133] Also significant was the expansion of the public sphere through the proliferation of new forms of associational activities (clubs, coffee-houses, theaters, societies, etc.).[134] Coinciding with the rapid growth of commerce, these new institutions were particularly associated with the effort of the middle classes to wrest greater independence from the landed elite. They reflected and sustained the burgeoning aspirations of the middle classes, reconstituting "gentility" so that it embraced industry, moral earnestness, and politeness, which together helped to reconstitute civil society.[135] It has also been shown that the legislative process, through the instrument of private bills and local legislation, could ensure a measure of responsiveness to regional needs and diverse interests.[136] The important role of the crowd as a political force in local communities has also been stressed, as has the moral economy of the crowd, emphasizing the moral responsibilities that might ground economic relations, at least in rural society.[137] The theater of popular politics in the Georgian era and its larger political importance have also been rescued from oblivion.[138]

The languages of religion, history, and the law had worked together to create a fixed and coherent conception of national identity through the narratives of their discourses. But as the Bible's stories had lent themselves to radically different interpretations, so also the narratives of history and the law. The languages of precedent, the common law, the ancient constitution and constitutionalism were together the major shared political idiom within which politics was spoken. But they were sufficiently elastic and ambiguous to be appropriated in different ways by unequally situated social groups. These groups sought to have their representations of the world recognized.[139] As James Epstein puts it, "the authority to give accent or meaning to . . . [such metanarratives] is an essential part of the exercise of power. Struggles to enforce or destabilize such meanings often define the contested terrain of politics."[140] Thus, liberals and radicals claimed more comprehenslve rights of political participation through expanded conceptions of property and citizenship.

"Of course, this sedative rhetoric of constitutional liberty . . . rationalized the hegemony of the great proprietors. Within this mythology, it was their guardianship of property rights that was in turn every Englishman's security against despotism and demagogy alike."[141] But it also had its own benefits. And it led those whom it mobilized to feel entitled to make new demands on the state. This was more so as the gulf between the rhetoric of English liberty and its practice widened in the 1790s, when fear of Jacobinism in Britain became intense. On the one hand, the free and prosperous English were juxtaposed with the French, a nation that was despotic and unfree. On the other hand, the British state sought to repress dissent, imposing new laws defining sedition and treason, and suspending habeas corpus. This suppression of certain features of British society and their transference onto "the other" created an unstable unity, Englishness, whose internal contradictions might be mobilized in new as well as conservative ways.[142]

But what the law made possible it also helped to foreclose. As James Vernon observes:

> the reason radicals failed to provide any feasible alternative to popular constitutionalism during the nineteenth century can be found largely in the political conditions of the 1790s. For it was then that Paine's republican and deist ideas became irretrievably associated with the "foreign and unchristian" creeds of the French Revolution. . . . As a result of both Pitt's terror and this populist reaction, radicals were forced underground and lumbered with equally damaging images of illegality and marginality. . . . Once again one is reminded of the importance of the state's use of the law in structuring the shape of political languages by limiting the choice of discursive strategies.[143]

The law was one, albeit the most authoritative, of several arenas within which property and personhood might be contested. While Coke and other common lawyers might claim that the constitution had a single and certain meaning, thereby marginalizing other notions of social relations and other interpreters of the constitution, others used the language of constitutionalism to posit different conceptions of power, rights, and Englishness. Writing of the early seventeenth century, Clive Holmes has illuminated the notorious ambiguity of the unwritten constitution, of contemporaries who spoke not of the English constitution but of England's *constitutions*, a complex and contradictory series of jurisdictions and rights. Rather than embodying the supposed certainties of the Cokeian constitution, politics was governed by a set of "inchoate conventions" permitting rival claims concerning the power of the Crown, Parliament, and the people.[144] In a similar vein, Charles Gray concludes that "Constitutional law in the seventeenth century was in a highly uncertain state."[145]

Even that central figure of eighteenth-century political discourse, individual private property, was undercut in practice by the variety of property regimes, regimes which were frequently qualified and collective in nature.[146] The notion of absolute private property became increasingly difficult to reconcile with the development of newer, more intangible forms of property. Both at its core and in its technical detail and practice, individual private property was not one notion but many different notions masked by the concept of absolute dominion.

Moreover, the moral justification for aristocratic rule could be turned on its head as liberals and radicals alike questioned its moral and economic basis in a world increasingly dominated by the language of economic freedom. From Adam Smith's criticism of strict settlements, to Ricardo's critique of unearned rents, from John Stuart Mill's advocacy of the reform of the law governing land tenure to Maitland's admonishment of primogeniture, the wisdom of limiting power in a landed elite was increasingly scrutinized in late Georgian and Victorian England. And from the 1870s to the First World War, "the land question" was revived, and the reform of primogeniture, entails, strict settlements, etc., became a major political issue.[147] By this time, the reasons for the equity of redemption – the strong desire of the owners of property to retain their hold over it – looked increasingly anachronistic. The rate of return on land significantly declined and the economic development of land fostered by coal, railways, urbanization, and the employment of professional land agents, all encouraged the landed to dispose of their land:

> Land started to come on the market during the 1880s and 1890s, but . . . much of the property available failed to find a purchaser. The real tidal change arrived in the years 1910–14, when the prices [of land] recovered and owners took the opportunity to sell. In one week during June 1910 over 72,000 acres in thirty-six counties were offered for sale in England, and during the corresponding week a year later the total rose to 98,000 acres. In 1912 no fewer than nineteen peers were believed to have property for sale, and by the outbreak of the First World War it was calculated that perhaps 800,000 acres had changed hands over the previous five years. The real collapse was postponed until after the First World War.[148]

5   The metamorphosis of the equity of redemption

As we have seen, there have always been some members of the judiciary who took issue with the doctrine of the equity of redemption even in its seventeenth- and eighteenth-century heyday. These misgivings grow louder from about the middle of the nineteenth century. Those elements of resistance within the discourse itself were galvanized anew as a more middle-class judiciary found itself privileging a social group, the landed, who no longer seemed to need or merit this privileging. The intellectual conviction that the judiciary's function was, at least in part, to protect the owners of landed property against other forms of property, had long since ceased to be the most emphatically articulated viewpoint of any section of the makers of "public opinion." The courts had played a crucial role in articulating and sustaining the "broad church" liberalism that pervaded much British political thought in the period after the 1790s, a liberalism founded in the notion of economic freedom. As Patrick Atiyah has pointed out, "The period 1770–1870 saw the emergence of general principles of contract law closely associated with the development of the free market and the ideals of the political economists. The period saw the shift in emphasis from property law to contract."[149] The effects of this were considerable: "[The] equation of general principles of contract law with the free market economy led to an emphasis on the framework within which individuals bargained with each other and a retreat from interest in substantial justice or fairness."[150]

Law was one of several discursive processes which helped to forge these new representations of the social world and personhood, determining who could speak and how. These narratives celebrated commerce, the crucial economic role played by the middle classes, the freedom of the market, self-help, and a less aristocratic notion of manliness. Freedom of contract served to fuse the tradition of the ancient constitution, a new emphasis on business and the town as the expressions of a liberal sense of evolutionary progress and national advance.[151] In the context of the declining political and economic power of the landed establishment, these narratives presented the middle classes as the real guardians of society. As Patrick Joyce has said in a different context: "[What] emerges may be broadly termed a liberal view of the present and a liberal construction of the past. Past and present were intrinsically linked in the advance of liberal culture."[152]

The members of the judiciary closely involved with the equity of redemption at the end of the nineteenth century and the beginning of the twentieth century had lost their aristocratic bias and were strong advocates of the new contract orthodoxy. Lord Jessell, for example, thought it unarguable that freedom of contract was necessary for property-owners. "I have always thought," he proclaimed:

> that it is of the utmost importance as regards contracts between adults – persons not under disability and at arm's length – that the Courts of Law should maintain the performance of the contracts according to the intention of the parties; that they should not overrule any clearly expressed intention on the grounds that Judges know the business of people better than they know it themselves . . . Judges have no right to say that people shall not perform their contracts which they have entered into deliberately and put a different meaning on the contracts from that which the parties intended.[153]

The mortgagor, it was argued, was "usually a grown-up man, with a very clear vision of his own interests, and quite able to take care of himself even without the Solicitor who is generally found at his elbow."[154] Hence, presumably, there was no need for the classic equity of redemption.

It was almost inevitable that this would produce a conflict with the traditional doctrines of the equity of redemption. For these judges, their role was not to protect one species of property, land, but to protect contractual rights generally, that is, to protect forms of property including rights in land but not to privilege rights in land. If the courts were still to interfere with bargains freely made as the equity of redemption demanded, what would happen to sacred *laissez-faire* doctrines? If, on the other hand, it was permissible to downgrade the equity of redemption, one of Chancery's most revered, almost mystical creations would be strangled. Faced with these two apparently conflicting positions, the courts decided, after some hesitation, that freedom of contract as they understood it meant more to them than anything else, including the classic form of the equity of redemption. From this perspective, the metamorphosis of the equity of redemption was part of a late exorcism of sixteenth-, seventeenth-, and eighteenth-century notions of the place of land and the landed in English property-holding and a manifestation of alternative conceptions of justice and Englishness.

The victory of freedom of contract over property had less to do with the intrinsic superiority of the arguments concerned than the circumstances in which they were expressed, which enabled certain groups to exploit them. From the Third Reform Act to the First World War, debates concerning citizenship intensified and progressive liberals sought to transcend the atomistic individualism of classic liberalism. In the eyes of Old Liberals like the constitutional lawyer Albert Venn Dicey, the much-feared age of collectivism had arrived.[155] From this perspective, the upholding of freedom of contract with respect to the equity of redemption, and by implication minimal state interference, was itself an attempt to entrench the individualism of classic liberalism in a period when it seemed increasingly under attack. Such, then, was the context within which the equity of redemption was reformulated by the House of Lords in 1914.[156]

Conclusion

The belated metamorphosis of the equity of redemption, and therefore of the transformation of property, from older monopolistic forms of ownership grounded in the privileges of status to newer contractual, individualistic, and free-market forms of ownership, testifies to the tenacity of what some commentators have called the backward or feudal dimensions of modern English society.[157] Yet as with so much of English property law, its pre-modern form was deceptive and paradoxical.[158] The tenacity of the equity of redemption demonstrates that in some areas of property relations commercial prosperity was parasitic upon the stability, strength, and survival of the landed gentry. The mortgage, and the doctrine of the equity of redemption which accompanied it, facilitated both the qualification, alienation, and fragmentation of property, on the one hand, and also the concentration of landed wealth and more absolute and exclusive property rights, on the other. In these ways it could be both feudal and modern.

In a society where there were few legal restrictions with regard to who might buy and sell land, and where land was seldom in short supply, the law facilitated the preservation and consolidation of what the landed already possessed. Historians have devoted considerable attention to certain legal safeguards constructed to facilitate this preservation, namely, primogeniture and the strict family settlement. What they have tended to neglect, however, is the important role of the equity of redemption in furthering the dynastic ambitions of landowners. Thus, the construction of the equity of redemption should be seen as part of a wider movement throughout most of Western Europe during the sixteenth and seventeenth centuries when legal devices of various sorts were introduced to prevent estate fragmentation. What distinguishes England from much of continental Europe is that these rules were enforced until the end of the nineteenth century, and, in the case of the equity of redemption, up to the First World War. Of course, these efforts at preservation and extension did not invariably work, despite the nineteenth-century belief in a land monopoly. Thus, they were also important as symbols of power, knowledge, justice, and Englishness, of what was legitimate and illegitimate, conceivable and inconceivable, public and private.

Much has also been made of the deference to the aristocracy and its values by the rising business and professional classes, and the cohesive self-confidence of the aristocracy until at least 1914.[159] Insofar as this is correct, it requires that further consideration be given to the law of property as an instrumentality and as a symbol which isolated and privileged certain groups so as to make their actions intelligible and legitimate. Within the dynamic field of political struggle, significant tracts of the law of property and, therefore, the core of the common law helped to generate "knowledges" that tended to render aristocratic rule natural and essential. Other branches of property law, however, were more openly supportive of "commerce." It is, perhaps, this contradictory juxtaposition that helps to explain England's distinctive route toward modernity.[160]

Notes

David Sugarman was largely responsible for the Introduction, section II and the Conclusion of this chapter; and Ronnie Warrington was largely responsible for section I. We are grateful to Susan Staves for her editorial assistance and enthusiasm, to James Vernon for his helpful comments on an early draft, and to Viviene Brown and Leonie Sugarman for their support and encouragement.

1   R. Samuel, "Introduction: exciting to be English," in R. Samuel (ed.), *Patriotism: the Making and Unmaking of British National Identity* (London: Routledge, 1989), Vol. I, pp. xxiv.
2   For one account of the nineteenth-century legal problems facing buyers and sellers of land, and suggestions for improvements, some of which were subsequently to be taken up, see J. Williams, *On the True Remedies for the Evils which Affect the Transfer of Land* (London: H. Sweet, 1862).
3   In *Kreglinger* v. *New Patagonia Meat & Cold Storage* [1914] AC 25.
4   See, generally, B. English and J. Saville, *Strict Settlement: A Guide for Historians* (Hull, Yorks: Hull University Press, 1983); L. Bonfield, *Marriage Settlements, 1601–1740* (Cambridge, UK: Cambridge University Press, 1983); the essays by M. R. Chesterman ("Family settlements on trust: landowners and the rising bourgeoisie," pp. 124–67, i–xii), B. English ("The family settlements of the Sykes of Sledmere, 1792–1900," pp. 209–40, i–xi), and E. Spring ("The family, strict settlement, and historians," pp. 168–91, i–vi), in G. Rubin and D. Sugarman (eds), *Law, Economy and Society, 1750–1914: Essays in the History of English Law* (Abingdon, Oxon: Professional Books, 1984); G. E. Mingay, *English Landed Society in the Eighteenth Century* (London: Routledge, 1963); D. Spring, *The English Landed Estate in the Nineteenth Century: Its Administration* (Baltimore, MD: Johns Hopkins University Press, 1963); F. M. L. Thompson, *English Landed Society in the Nineteenth Century* (London: Routledge, 1963) and F. M. L. Thompson, "English landed society in the nineteenth

century," in P. Thane *et al.* (eds), *The Power of the Past: Essays for Eric Hobsbawm* (Cambridge, UK: Cambridge University Press, 1984), pp. 195–214; L. Stone and J. Fawtier Stone, *An Open Elite? England, 1540–1880* (Oxford: Oxford University Press, 1983); W. D. Rubinstein, "New men of wealth and the purchase of land in nineteenth-century England," *Past and Present* 92 (1981): 125–47; E. Spring, "Landowners, lawyers and land law reform in nineteenth-century England," *American Journal of Legal History* 21 (1977): 40–59; G. S. Alexander, "The dead hand and the law of trusts in the nineteenth-century," *Stanford Law Review* 37 (1985): 1189–1286; S. Staves, *Married Women's Separate Property in England, 1660–1833* (Cambridge, MA: Harvard University Press, 1990); A. L. Erickson, "Common law versus common practice: the use of marriage settlements in early modern England," *Economic History Review*, 2nd series, 43 (1990): 21–39; D. Cannadine, *Lords and Landlords: The Aristocracy and the Towns, 1770–1967* (Leicester: University of Leicester Press, 1980); D. Cannadine, "Aristocratic indebtedness in the nineteenth century: a restatement," *Economic History Review*, 2nd series, 33 (1980): 47–60; D. Cannadine, *Patricians, Power and Politics in Nineteenth-Century Towns* (Leicester: Leicester University Press, 1982); D. Cannadine, *The Decline and Fall of the British Aristocracy* (New Haven, CT: Yale University Press, 1990); B. English, *The Great Landowners of East Yorkshire 1530–1910* (London: Harvester/Wheatsheaf, 1990); B. A. Holderness and M. Turner (eds), *Land, Labour and Agriculture, 1700–1920* (London: Hambledon Press, 1990); J. V. Beckett, *The Aristocracy in England, 1660–1914* (Oxford: Blackwell, 1986); A. Offer, *Property and Politics 1870–1914* (Cambridge, UK: Cambridge University Press, 1981); P. Langford, *Public Life and the Propertied Englishman, 1689–1798* (Oxford: Clarendon Press, 1991); J. S. Anderson, *Lawyers and the Making of English Land Law 1832–1940* (Oxford: Clarendon Press, 1992).

5   On mortgages, see the valuable discussion in D. E. C. Yale, "Introduction: an essay on mortgages and trusts and allied topics in equity," in *Lord Nottingham's Chancery Cases*, Vol. II (London: Seldon Society, Vol. 79, 1961); and J. L. Barton, "The common law mortgage," *Law Quarterly Review* 83 (1967): 229–39.

6   This chapter is part of a larger study of the economic, political, and cultural significance of law and lawyers in early modern and modern England. See, also, D. Sugarman and G. R. Rubin, "Introduction: towards a new history of law and material society in England, 1750–1914," in Rubin and Sugarman (eds), *Law, Economy and Society, 1750–1914*, pp. 1–123; D. Sugarman, *In the Spirit of Weber: Law, Modernity and "the Peculiarities of the English"* (Madison, WI: Institute of Legal Studies, 1985); D. Sugarman, "'A fear of disorder': liberalism, legal science and imperialism," in P. Fitzpatrick (ed.), *Dangerous Supplements: Resistance and Renewal in Jurisprudence* (London: Pluto, 1992), pp. 34–67; D. Sugarman, "Simple images and complex realities: English lawyers and their relationship to business and politics, 1750–1914," *Law and History Review* 11 (Fall 1993): 257–301; D. Sugarman, "'The best organised and most intelligent trade union in the country': the private and public life of the Law Society, 1815–1914," in E. Skordaki (ed.), *Solicitors and Social Change* (Oxford: Oxford University Press, 1995), forthcoming.

7   While the form has changed (see the Law of Property Act 1925, s.85 *et seq.*), this centuries-old concept is still the basis of the law today.

8   In the landmark decision in *Kreglinger* v. *New Patagonia Meat & Cold Storage* [1914] AC 25, the leading judgment of Lord Parker surprisingly appears to get this wrong. He says: "The mortgagor might pay the money on the specified date, in which case, equity would specifically perform the contract for reconveyance" (p. 47). But if the loan was repaid on the due date then equity was irrelevant; the common law rights of the borrower enabled the borrower to claim reconveyance or re-entry when necessary. We discuss this important case in greater detail below.

9   *Fisher and Lightwood's Law of Mortgages*, ed. E. L. G. Tyler (London: Butterworth, 1977), p. 7.

10   See, generally, R. W. Turner, *The Equity of Redemption: its Nature, History and Connection with Equitable Estates Generally* (Cambridge, UK: Cambridge University Press, 1931); Ronnie Warrington, "Law and property: the equity of redemption re-examined, an essay in socio-legal history" (PhD thesis, University College, London University: 1982).

11 In the classic language of traditional mortgage law: "The Court does not permit any stipulation in a mortgage which 'clogs' or 'fetters' the equity of redemption; in other words, any stipulation in a mortgage is invalid if it prevents the mortgagor from redeeming or allows the mortgagee to retain for his own benefit any part of or any interest in the mortgaged property after the mortgage has been discharged." W. Ashburner, *A Concise Treatise on Mortgages, Pledges and Liens* (London: William Clowes, 1911), p. 341.

12 A. W. B. Simpson, *An Introduction to the History of Land Law* (Oxford: Clarendon Press, 1961), p. 227.

13 Turner, *The Equity of Redemption*, p. 26.

14 Ibid., pp. 26–7. Our account of the development of the equity of redemption in section I of this chapter is largely derived from Warrington, "Law and property," Chs 7–9.

15 1 Ch Rep 18.

16 1 Ch Rep 165.

17 See also *Smith* v. *Valance* 1 Ch Rep 169, decided the following year (1655), where the report refers to "the title of redemption" and to "the equity of redemption."

18 Turner, *The Equity of Redemption*, p. 56.

19 *Manning* v. *Burgess* (1663) 1 Ch Cas 29 at 29.

20 1 Ch Cas 216.

21 Turner, *The Equity of Redemption*, p. 57.

22 1 Ch Cas 216 at 220.

23 R. H. Coote, *A Treatise on the Law of Mortgages* (London: Butterworth, 1821), pp. 41–2.

24 See, for example, *Talbot* v. *Braddil* (1681) 1 Vern 394.

25 *Brown* v. *Cole* (1845) 14 Sim 427.

26 Hardres 465.

27 See, further, Turner, *The Equity of Redemption*, pp. 54–5.

28 *Lord Nottingham's Manual of Chancery Practice and Prolegomena of Chancery and Equity*, ed. D. Yale (Cambridge, UK: Cambridge University Press, 1975), p. 280.

29 Ibid., p. 282.

30 2 Ch Cas 33 at 35.

31 Vern 7; 1 Vern 214; 1 Vern 232; 2 Vern 264.

32 at 266.

33 1 Vern 33, affirmed 1 Vern 190.

34 1 Ch Rep 127.

35 at 528.

36 1 P Wms 268.

37 2 Atk 494.

38 See, for example, Coote, *A Treatise on the Law of Mortgages*.

39 A major exception was created in the nineteenth century in relation to mortgages on West Indian estates.

40 See, also, *Manlove* v. *Bale & Burton* (1688) 2 Vern 84.

41 1 Vern 33, affirmed 1 Vern 190.

42 3 Swans 628; 36 ER 1000 at 1001.

43 1 Eden 177; 96 ER 67 at 84. Lord Mansfield's attachment to an equitable, discretionary approach to decision-making was apparently influenced by Lord Hardwicke, a judge whom Lord Mansfield much admired: see C. H. S. Fifoot, *Lord Mansfield* (Oxford: Clarendon Press, 1936), p. 168. Lord Hardwicke adopted a liberal approach in the consolidation of the equity of redemption, a process which Mansfield was therefore likely to find congenial. In his later judgments in the field of real property, however, Lord Mansfield increasingly stressed the importance of certainty and predictability rather than discretion and equity.

44 1 Eden 56; 28 ER 605 at 606.

45 See, for example, *Cornel* v. *Sykes* (1660) 1 Ch Rep 193.

46 2 Ch Rep 108; 21 ER 630.

47 21 ER 630 at 630.

48 In *Price* v. *Perrie* (1702) 2 Freen 258.

49   Coote, *A Treatise on the Law of Mortgages*, p. 127.
50   1 Atk 598; for the notes , see 2 J & W 194; 37 ER 600. On Lord Hardwicke's contribution to the law, the best modern account is C. E. Croft, "Philip Yorke, first Earl of Hardwicke – an assessment of his legal career" (PhD thesis, Cambridge University: 1982) and C. E. Croft, "Lord Hardwicke's use of precedent in equity," in T. G. Watkin (ed.), *Legal Records and Historical Reality* (London: Hambledon Press, 1989), Ch. 8. See also R. Browning, *Political and Constitutional Ideas of the Court Whigs* (Baton Rouge, LA: Louisiana State University Press, 1982), Ch. 6; D. Lieberman, *The Province of Legislation Determined: Legal Theory in Eighteenth-Century Britain* (Cambridge, UK: Cambridge University Press, 1989), pp. 81–3; Philip C. Yorke, *The Life and Correspondence of Philip Yorke, Earl of Hardwicke, Lord High Chancellor of Great Britain*, 3 vols (Cambridge, UK: Cambridge University Press, 1913).
51   37 ER 600 at 600.
52   Ibid.
53   Lord Hardwicke's own notes refer to several earlier decisions.
54   See Turner, *The Equity of Redemption*, pp. 71–87.
55   J. J. Powell, *A Treatise on the Law of Mortgages*, ed. T. Coventry (London: Brooke, 1822; 5th edn), Vol. 1, p. 265.

The landowner's right was so strong and so well established that in 1802, when trying to explain the difference in attitude to compliance with time limits between law and equity, Lord Eldon could think of no better example than the law of mortgages:

> At law the mortgagee is under no obligation to re-convey [after the contractual redemption date]; and yet this Court says that, though the money is not paid at the time stipulated, if paid with interest at the time a re-conveyance is demanded, there shall be a re-conveyance; upon this ground: that the contract is in this Court considered a mere loan of money, secured by a pledge of the estate. But that is a doctrine upon which this Court acts against what is the prima facie import of the terms of the agreement itself; which does not import at law, that once a mortgage, always a mortgage; but Equity says that . . . (*Seton* v. *Slade* 7 Ves 265; 32 ER 108 at 111)

Nor could Lord Eldon envisage the parties being permitted to enter into different terms in a mortgage: "You shall not by special terms alter that which this Court says are the special terms of the contract": *Seton* v. *Slade* 7 Ves 265; 32 ER 108 at 111.

56   *Biggs* v. *Hoddinott* [1898] 2 Ch D 307 at 321; see also 320.
57   Lord Hardwicke's relation to the landowners of his time is vividly described in E. P. Thompson, *Whigs and Hunters: the Origin of the Black Act* (London: Allen Lane, 1977), especially at p. 208 *et seq*. Thompson's account damns Lord Hardwicke's hypocrisy, as the person responsible for drafting the Black Act in Parliament, and then as a judge enforcing it far beyond its strict terms.
58   Turner, *The Equity of Redemption*, p. 175.
59   *De Beers Consolidated Mines* v. *British South Africa* [1912] AC 52.
60   (1745) 3 Atk 261; 26 ER 952 at 952–3.
61   *Samuel* v. *Jarrah Timber and Wood Paving Ltd* [1904] AC 323 at 326.
62   *Vernon* v. *Bethell* (1762) 2 Eden 110; 28 ER 838 at 839.
63   Turner, *The Equity of Redemption*, p. 136.
64   Ibid., p. 137.
65   Ibid., pp. 137–8.
66   [1914] AC 25.
67   Trollope's Archdeacon Grantly, cited Stone and Stone, *An Open Elite?*, p. 14.
68   Cannadine, *Decline and Fall of the British Aristocracy*, p. 37.
69   Thompson, *English Landed Society in the Nineteenth Century*; Beckett, *The Aristocracy in England, 1660–1914*; M. L. Bush, *The English Aristocracy: A Comparative Synthesis* (Manchester and Dover, NH: Manchester University Press, 1984); Cannadine, *Decline and Fall of the British Aristocracy*.

70   D. Spring, "The English landed estate in the age of coal and iron, 1830–1880," *Journal of Economic History* 11 (1951): 3–24 (16).

71   Thompson, *English Landed Society in the Nineteenth Century*, p. 96.

72   R. Sturgess, "Landowners, mining and urban development in nineteenth-century Staffordshire," in J. T. Ward and R. G. Wilson (eds), *Land and Industry* (London: David & Charles, 1971), pp. 162–84 (p. 174).

73   J. V. Hughes, *The Wealthiest Commoner: C. R. M. Talbot (1803–1890)* (Aberavon, Glam.: published by the author, 1977), p. 26.

74   Thompson, *English Landed Society in the Nineteenth Century*, p. 80.

75   J. Graham, *Corn and Currency* (London: James Ridgway, 1827), p. 25.

76   Quoted in Beckett, *The Aristocracy in England, 1660–1914*, p. 49.

77   Cf. M. Bloch, *Feudal Society*, trans. L. A. Manyon (London: Routledge & Kegan Paul, 1961).

78   E. P. Thompson, "The grid of inheritance," in J. Goody *et al.* (eds), *Family and Inheritance* (Cambridge, UK: Cambridge University Press, 1976), pp. 86–140.

79   F. W. Maitland, *Constitutional History of England* (Cambridge, UK: Cambridge University Press, 1913).

80   J. S. Hart, *Justice upon Petition* (London: Routledge, 1992); R. Stevens, *Law and Politics: the House of Lords as a Judicial Body, 1800–1976* (London: Weidenfeld & Nicolson, 1979).

81   C. M. Gray, "Parliament, liberty, and the law," in J. H. Hexter (ed.), *Parliament and Liberty* (Stanford, CA: Stanford University Press, 1992), pp. 155–200 (pp. 179–80).

82   W. Blackstone, *Commentaries on the Laws of England: a Facsimile of the First Edition of 1765–1769*, ed. Stanley N. Katz, 4 vols (Chicago: Chicago University Press, 1979), Vol. 1, Introduction, p. 7.

83   B. Abel-Stevens and R. Stevens, *Lawyers and the Courts* (London: Heinemann, 1967), pp. 53–77, 187–209; Cannadine, *The Decline and Fall of the British Aristocracy*, pp. 250–5.

84   L. Colley, *Britons: Forging the Nation, 1707–1837* (New Haven, CT and London: Yale University Press, 1992), pp. 64–5.

85   D. Hay *et al.*, *Albion's Fatal Tree* (London: Allen Lane, 1975); Thompson, *Whigs and Hunters*; M. Ignatieff, *A Just Measure of Pain* (London: Macmillan, 1978): D. Garland, *Punishment and Welfare* (Aldershot, Hants: Gower, 1975); M. J. Wiener, *Reconstructing the Criminal* (Cambridge, UK: Cambridge University Press, 1990); E. P. Thompson, *Customs in Common* (London: Merlin Press, 1991); P. Linebaugh, *The London Hanged* (London: Allen Lane, 1993); R. J. Steinfeld, *The Invention of Free Labor* (Chapel Hill, NC: University of North Carolina Press, 1991), Chs 2–4.

86   Gray, "Parliament, liberty, and the law", p. 176.

87   See, generally, L. Sheridan, *Fraud in Equity: A Study in English and Irish Law* (London: Pitman, 1957).

88   *Freeman* v. *Bishop* (1740) 2 Atk 39, 39 cited in Croft, "Lord Hardwicke's use of precedent in equity," p. 146, note 158.

89   *Brooke* v. *Gally* (1740) Barn C.1, 6 cited in ibid.

90   J. P. Dawson, "Coke and Ellesmere disinterred: the attack on Chancery in 1616," *Illinois Law Review* 36 (1941): 127–52; J. H. Baker, *The Legal Profession and the Common Law: Historical Essays* (London: Hambledon Press, 1986), Ch. 13, "The common lawyers and the Chancery: 1616."

91   On the claims of the common lawyers in the period up to 1616, see J. G. A. Pocock, *The Ancient Constitution and the Feudal Law* (Cambridge, UK: Cambridge University Press, 1987), p. 292.

92   Gray, "Parliament, liberty, and the law," pp. 177–9.

93   See, generally, English and Saville, *Strict Settlement*; Bonfield, *Marriage Settlements, 1601–1740* (Cambridge, UK: Cambridge University Press, 1983); the essays by Chesterman, English, and Spring in Rubin and Sugarman (eds), *Law, Economy and Society, 1750–1914*; Thompson, *English Landed Society in the Nineteenth Century*; Stone and Stone, *An Open Elite?*; Beckett, *The Aristocracy in England, 1660–1914*, pp. 58–65; Erickson, "Common law versus common practice", 21.

94   See, generally, C. S. Kenny, *The History of the Law of Primogeniture in England* (Cambridge, UK: Cambridge University Press, 1878).

95   Cannadine, *Decline and Fall of the British Aristocracy*, p. 12.

96   G. E. Mingay, *The Gentry* (London: Longman, 1976), pp. 83–4.

97   B. L. Anderson, "Provincial aspects of the financial revolution of the eighteenth century," *Business History* 9 (1969): 11–22.

98   R. S. Neale, *Bath 1680–1850* (London: Routledge, 1981).

99   D. Cannadine, "Aristocratic indebtedness in the nineteenth century: the case reopened," *Economic History Review* 2nd series, 30 (1977): 624–50 (624–7).

100 J. J. Powell, *A Treatise upon the Law of Mortgages* (London: Puriel and T. Whieldon, 1785), p. v.

101 J. A. Greed, *Property Law in Stage-coach Days* (London: St Trillo Publications, 1976), p. 14.

102 See *Aylesford* v. *Morris* (1872) 42 LJ Ch 146, 151–2.

103 See, for example, E. Hobsbawm and T. Ranger (eds), *The Invention of Tradition* (Cambridge, UK: Cambridge University Press, 1983); E. Gellner, *Nations and Nationalism* (Ithaca, NY and London: Cornell University Press, 1983); E. Said, *Orientalism* (Harmondsworth, Mx: Penguin, 1985); S. Schama, *The Embarrassment of Riches: An Interpretation of Dutch Culture in the Golden Age* (London: Knopf, 1987); T. Todorov, *The Conquest of America* (New York: Harper & Row, 1987); T. Nairn, *The Enchanted Glass: Britain and its Monarchy* (London: Radius, 1988); B. Anderson, *Imagined Communities* (London: Verso, 1991; enlarged edn); E. Hobsbawm, *Nations and Nationalism since 1780* (Cambridge and New York: Cambridge University Press, 1990); P. Sahlins, *Boundaries: the Making of France and Spain in the Pyrenees* (Berkeley, CA: University of California Press, 1989); H. Bhabha (ed.), *Narrating the Nation* (London: Routledge, 1990); Colley, *Britons*. For the increasing body of work on "Englishness" see, for example, R. Colls and P. Dodd (eds), *Englishness* (London: Croom Helm, 1986) and R. Porter (ed.), *Myths of the English* (Cambridge, UK: Polity, 1992).

104 See, for example, F. Jameson, *The Political Unconscious: Narrative as a Socially Symbolic Act* (Ithaca, NY: Cornell University Press, 1981); P. Ricoeur, *Time and Narrative*, 3 vols (Chicago: Chicago University Press, 1985); N. Z. Davis, *Fictions in the Archives* (Cambridge, UK: Polity, 1987); P. Joyce, *Visions of the People* (Cambridge, UK: Cambridge University Press, 1991); J. Vernon, *Politics and the People* (Cambridge, UK: Cambridge University Press, forthcoming), esp. Ch. 8. On the narrativity of historical writing see H. White, *Metahistory* (Baltimore, MD: Johns Hopkins University Press, 1973) and H. White, *Tropics of Discourse* (Baltimore, MD: Johns Hopkins University Press, 1978).

105 An important exception being Pocock, *The Ancient Constitution and the Feudal Law*. See, also, P. Fitzpatrick, *The Mythology of Modern Law* (London: Routledge, 1992).

106 On law and narrative see, for example, R. Cover, "Foreward: nomos and narrative," *Harvard Law Review* 97 (1983): 4–68 (4); R. West, "Narrative, responsibility and death: a comment on the death penalty cases from the 1989 term," *Maryland Journal of Contemporary Legal Issues* 1 (1990): 161–77; M. Minow, "Law turning outward," *Telos* 73 (1987): 79–99; V. Schultz, "Telling stories about women and work," *Harvard Law Review* 103 (1990): 1749–1843; and P. J. Williams, *The Alchemy of Race and Rights* (Cambridge, MA: Harvard University Press, 1991). On completing this chapter we discovered a valuable essay on property which complements the approach adopted here: see Carol M. Rose, "Property as storytelling: perspectives from game theory, narrative theory, feminist theory," *Yale Journal of Law and the Humanities* 2 (1990): 37–57 (37). On the links between property and personhood see M. J. Radin, "Property and personhood," *Stanford Law Review* (1982): 957–1015.

107 G. Peller, "The metaphysics of American law," *California Law Review* 73 (1985): 1151–1290; R. J. Coombe, "Room for manoeuvre," *Law and Social Inquiry* 14 (1989) 69–121; and R. J. Coombe, "Contesting the self," *Studies in Law, Politics and Power* 11 (1991): 3–40.

108 Cf. S. E. Merry, *Getting Justice and Getting Even* (Chicago: Chicago University Press, 1990).

109 O. Smith, *The Politics of Language, 1791–1819* (Oxford: Oxford University Press, 1984); D. Cressy, *Bonfires and Bells* (Berkeley, CA: University. of California Press, 1989); Joyce, *Visions of the People*, pp. 173–4; Colley, *Britons*, Ch. 1.

110 H. Belloc, *An Essay on the Nature of Contemporary England* (New York: Sheed & Ward, 1937), p. 57.

111 William Blake, cited in Colley, *Britons*, p. 30.

112 Ibid., p. 19.

113 Other significant idioms which influenced political discourse include the languages of commercial society, republicanism, and humanism.

114 See Pocock, *The Ancient Constitution and the Feudal Law*.

115 F. Thompson, *Magna Carta: Its Role in the Making of the English Constitution, 1300–1629* (Minneapolis, MN: University of Minnesota Press, 1948); A. Pallister, *Magna Carta* (Oxford: Oxford University Press, 1977).

116 (1765) 19 State Tr 1029.

117 Samuel, "Introduction: exciting to be English," in Samuel (ed.), *Patriotism*, pp. xxii–xxviii.

118 See Pocock, *The Ancient Constitution and the Feudal Law*, esp. pp. 280–305 on the debate that it has generated with respect to the role of civil law in the culture and thought of the common law.

119 P. Goodrich and Y. Hachamovitch, in P. Fitzpatrick (ed.), *Dangerous Supplements* (London: Pluto Press, 1992) pp. 172–3.

120 See C. H. S. Fifoot, *Lord Mansfield* (Oxford: Clarendon Press, 1936).

121 See, for example, *Lord Camden's Argument in Doe on the Demise of Hindson . . . Wherein Lord Mansfield's Argument in Wyndham v Chetwind is Considered and Answered* (London: 1766).

122 Fifoot, *Lord Mansfield*, p. 159, note 2, citing Justice Blackstone in *Perrin* v. *Blake* (1772). See, further, D. Lieberman, "Property, commerce and the common law: attitudes to change in the eighteenth century," Chapter 7 in this present volume.

123 Cf. J. G. A. Pocock, *Politics, Language and Time: Essays on Political Thought and History* (New York: Atheneum, 1971), Ch. 4, "Burke and the ancient constitution," pp. 202–32.

124 E. Burke, *Reflections on the Revolution in France . . .* ed. C. C. O'Brien (Harmondsworth, Mx: Penguin, 1968), p. 140.

125 On communitarian, radical, and other alternative conceptions of property and citizenship see: C. Hill, "The Norman yoke," in his *Puritanism and Revolution* (London: Secker & Warburg, 1955), pp. 50–122; R. J. Smith, *The Gothic Bequest: Medieval Institutions in British Political Thought, 1688–1863* (Cambridge, UK: Cambridge University Press, 1987); M. Chase, *The People's Farm: English Radical Agrarianism, 1775–1840* (Oxford: Oxford University Press, 1988); G. Claeys, *Machinery, Money and the Millennium, from Moral Economy to Socialism, 1815–1860* (Oxford: Oxford University Press, 1987); G. Claeys, *Thomas Paine's Social and Political Thought* (London: Routledge, 1989); and G. Claeys, *Citizens and Saints: Politics and Anti-Politics in Early British Socialism* (New York: Cambridge University Press, 1989); S. Yeo, "Socialism, the state, and some oppositional Englishness," in R. Colls and P. Dodd (eds), *Englishness: Politics and Culture, 1880–1920* (London: Croom Helm, 1986), p. 308–69; T. A. Horne, *Property Rights and Poverty* (Chapel Hill, NC: University of North Carolina Press, 1990).

126 Hay *et al.* (eds), *Albion's Fatal Tree*; Thompson, *Customs in Common*, Ch. III; Linebaugh, *The London Hanged*.

127 With respect to Catholics, see Colley, *Britons*, pp. 19, 325–33. See also N. Rogers, "Crowd and people in the Gordon riots," in E. Hellmuth (ed.), *The Transformation of Political Culture: England and Germany in the Late Eighteenth Century* (Oxford: Oxford University Press, 1990), pp. 39–55.

128 See, generally, H. S. Q. Henriques, *Law of Aliens and Naturalisation* (London: Butterworth, 1906); H. S. Q. Henriques, *The Jews and English Law* (London: Bibliophile Press, 1908); V. Bevan, *The Development of British Immigration Law* (London: Croom Helm, 1986), pp. 50–64.

129 M. Girouard, *The Return to Camelot: Chivalry and the English Gentleman* (New Haven, CT: Yale University Press, 1981), p. 13.

130 See L. Davidoff and C. Hall, *Family Fortunes* (London: Hutchinson, 1989); S. Collini, *Public Moralists* (Oxford: Clarendon Press, 1991), esp. Ch. 5; Colley, *Britons*, pp. 177–93.

131 See Staves, *Married Women's Separate Property in England, 1660–1833*. On the unequal position of women, see also: S. P. Menafee, *Wives for Sale* (Oxford: Oxford University Press, 1981); Davidoff and Hall, *Family Fortunes*; and A. Clark, *Women's Silence, Men's Violence: Sexual Assault in England, 1770–1845* (London and New York: Pandora, 1987).

132 In *Kreglinger* v. *New Patagonia Meat & Cold Storage* [1914] AC 25.

133 S. Webb and B. Webb, *English Local Government*, 2 vols (London: Benn, 1906–8); C. Tilly (ed.), *The Formation of Nation-States in Western Europe* (Princeton, NJ: Princeton University Press, 1975); D. Sugarman and G. Rubin, "Towards a new history of law and material society in England, 1750–1914," in Rubin and Sugarman (eds), *Law, Economy and Society, 1750–1914*, pp. 1–123, i–lxiii; R. Porter, *English Society in the Eighteenth Century* (Harmondsworth, Mx: Penguin, 1990, rev. edn), Ch. 3.

134 J. Money, "Taverns, coffee houses and clubs," *Historical Journal* 14 (1971): 13–47; J. Brewer, "Clubs, commercialization and politics," in N. McKendrick, J. Brewer, and J. H. Plumb (eds), *The Birth of a Consumer Society* (Bloomington, IN: Indiana University Press, 1982), pp. 197–262; Davidoff and Hall, *Family Fortunes* pp. 416–49; P. Langford, *A Polite and Commercial People* (Oxford: Oxford University Press, 1989).

135 Langford, *A Polite and Commercial People*.

136 Lieberman, *The Province of Legislation Determined*, pp. 13–28, 179–215; J. Innes, "Parliament and the shaping of English social policy," *Transactions of the Royal Historical Society* 40 (1990): 63–92.

137 Thompson, *Customs in Common*, Chs 4 and 5.

138 Ibid., Chs 2 and 8; J. Brewer, *Party Ideology and Popular Politics at the Accession of George III* (Cambridge, UK: Cambridge University Press, 1976).

139 See P. Bourdieu, "The force of law," *Hastings Law Journal* 38 (1987): 805–53.

140 J. Epstein, "Understanding the cap of liberty: symbolic practice and social conflict in early nineteenth-century England," *Past and Present* 122 (1989): 75–118.

141 R. Porter, *English Society in the Eighteenth Century* (Harmondsworth, Mx: Penguin, 1990; rev. edn), p. 115.

142 See, for example, the tactics adopted by Wilkes and his supporters as detailed in G. Rude, *Wilkes and Liberty* (Oxford: Clarendon Press, 1962); Brewer, *Party Ideology and Popular Politics at the Accession of George III*, and J. Brewer and J. Styles (eds), *An Ungovernable People* (London: Hutchinson, 1980).

143 Vernon, *Politics and the People*, p. 307. See, also, Staves, *Married Women's Separate Property in England, 1660–1833*, which analyzes the ways in which the ambiguities of contract theory might have made it possible to extend the rights of women; but in practice contract theory was used by the courts to serve other ends, such as the desire of landed families to maintain and consolidate their estates.

144 C. Holmes, "Parliament, liberty, taxation, and property," in J. H. Hexter (ed.), *Parliament and Liberty* (Stanford, CA: Stanford University Press, 1992), pp. 122–54.

145 Gray, "Parliament, liberty, and the law," p. 197.

146 Sugarman and Rubin, "Introduction . . . law and material society in England, 1750–1914," in Rubin and Sugarman (eds), *Law, Economy and Society, 1750–1914*; Sugarman, *In the Spirit of Weber*.

147 Offer, *Property and Politics, 1870–1914*.

148 Beckett, *The Aristocracy in England, 1660–1914*, p. 85. As the rationale for the equity of redemption was reworked from above, so it was also reworked from below with the democratization of the mortgage and the rise of building societies.

149 P. S. Atiyah, *The Rise and Fall of Freedom of Contract* (Oxford and New York: Clarendon Press and Oxford University Press, 1979), p. 388.

150 Ibid., p. 402. Here, Atiyah's argument parallels that of M. J. Horwitz, *The Transformation of American Law, 1780–1860* (Cambridge, MA: Harvard University Press, 1977).

151 Cf. Joyce, *Visions of the People*, p. 177.

152 Ibid., p. 185.

153 *Wallis* v. *Smith* (1882) 21 Ch D 243 at 266. See, too, his notorious celebration of freedom of contract in *Printing and Numerical* v. *Sampson* (1875) LR 19 EQ 462. In another case, his Lordship allowed a claim for interest at 60 percent against an alcoholic in the name of freedom of contract: see Atiyah, *The Rise and Fall of Freedom of Contract*, p. 388.

154 *Law Quarterly Review* 15 (1899): 3.

155 A. V. Dicey, *Law and Public Opinion* (London: Macmillan, 1914).

156 In *Kreglinger* v. *New Patagonia Meat & Cold Storage* [1914] AC 25. We hope to complete a detailed study of this case, and the context surrounding the metamorphosis of the equity of redemption, in the near future.

157 See, for example, P. Anderson, *English Questions* (London: Verso, 1992); Nairn, *The Enchanted Glass*; A. Mayor, *The Persistence of the Old Regime: Europe to the Great War* (New York: Pantheon, 1981); M. Wiener, *English Culture and the Decline of the Industrial Spirit, 1850–1980* (Cambridge, UK: Cambridge University Press, 1981); J. C. D. Clark, *English Society, 1688–1832* (Cambridge, UK: Cambridge University Press, 1985). Cf. E. P. Thompson, "The peculiarities of the English," in his *The Poverty of Theory and Other Essays* (London: Merlin, 1978), pp. 35–91, and E. M. Wood, *The Pristine Culture of Capitalism* (London: Verso, 1991).

158 Sugarman and Rubin, "Introduction . . . law and material society in England, 1750–1914," in Rubin and Sugarman (eds) *Law, Economy and Society, 1750–1914*; Sugarman, *In the Spirit of Weber*; Wood, *The Pristine Culture of Capitalism*, pp. 45–54.

159 See, for example, Anderson, *English Questions*; Nairn, *The Enchanted Glass*; Mayor, *The Persistence of the Old Regime*; Wiener, *English Culture and the Decline of the Industrial Spirit, 1850–1980*. Cf. Thompson, "The peculiarities of the English," in *Poverty of Theory*, and Wood, *The Pristine Culture of Capitalism*.

160 Sugarman and Rubin, "Introduction . . . Law and Material Society in England, 1750–1914," in Rubin and Sugarman (eds), *Law, Economy and Society, 1750–1914*; Sugarman, *In the Spirit of Weber*.

7
Property, commerce, and the common law
Attitudes to legal change in the eighteenth century

David Lieberman

In eighteenth-century commentary on the nature and condition of law in England, the topics of "property" and "commerce" figured conspicuously. The first term was especially prominent, given the established understanding of the distinctive moral excellence of the English legal system. As Sir William Blackstone enthusiastically explained at mid-century, "The idea and practice of . . . political or civil liberty flourish in their highest vigour in these kingdoms, where it falls little short of perfection." This political or civil liberty, itself, comprised "no other than natural liberty so far restrained by human laws (and no farther) as is necessary and expedient for the general advantage of the public." The core of natural liberty was constituted by the "absolute rights of man" which represented "one of the gifts of God to man at his creation, when he endued him with the faculty of free will." In England such divine benefactions had been preserved in the weighty body of legal provisions that secured to each individual "the right of personal security, the right of personal liberty, and the right of private property."[1] Thus, if it was found, for example, that the English legal system was more complex and more intricate than others, and seemed almost embarrassed by a singular "multiplicity of law," this was due to the law's proper concern to provide a full and particular remedy to every injury that might harm the subject's liberty and property.[2] And if such complexity and multiplicity, in turn, led to a no less intricate and time-consuming process of legal redress, this too was "the genuine offspring of that spirit of equal liberty which is the singular felicity of Englishmen." Quick judicial deliberations, as Montesquieu demonstrated, characterized the legal systems of despotic states, whereas "in free states, the trouble, expense and delays of judicial proceedings are the price that every subject pays for his liberty." And "from these principles" it naturally followed that justice in England ought to be slower than anywhere else, since the courts "set a greater value on life, on liberty, and on property."[3]

If property and its protection so stood at the moral center of England's particular fabric of law, commerce seemed no less central to the kingdom's particular fabric of property forms and exchange. "But nothing hath wrought such an alteration in this order of people," Henry Fielding maintained, "as the introduction of trade. This hath indeed given a new face to the whole nation, hath in a great measure subverted the former state of affairs, and hath almost totally changed the manners, customs, and habits of the people, more especially of the lower sort."[4] Given such momentous social changes, it was not surprising to find the impact of commerce also felt in England's courts of justice. When Lord Chancellor Hardwicke, who for twenty years presided over England's premier equity court, had occasion in 1759 to identify the major challenges for law and equity "since the Revolution," he naturally remarked upon the "new discoveries and inventions in commerce" which had produced "new species of contracts" and "new contrivances to break and elude them," and "for which the ancient simplicity of the common law had adapted no remedies." As a result, "courts of equity . . . have under the head, *adjuvandi vel supplendi juris civilis*, been obliged to accommodate the wants of mankind."[5] When, in 1794, Edmund Burke had occasion to instruct the House of Lords on the nature of the judicial achievement of Lord Mansfield, who for thirty years presided over the court of King's Bench, he promptly pointed to all the Chief Justice had done to adapt the law "to the growth of our commerce and of our empire."[6]

The impact of "commerce" on the cultural experience of eighteenth-century Britain is, of course, a familiar theme, important to the intellectual history of this period. For my purposes here, it is convenient briefly to recall two current lines of scholarship in which commerce has received its abundant due. The first of these concerns the now massive body of study on early modern republicanism, or what J. G. A. Pocock has taught us to call "civic humanism."[7] On Pocock's reading, early modern republican ideology centered on a deeply moralized ideal of citizenship, conceived as the active exercise of civic virtue and participation in the common good which alone enabled the individual to achieve full moral capacity and the community to maintain republican self-government. Civic virtue and republican association were ever vulnerable to the mortal diseases of corruption and self-interest, and the inevitable conflict between virtue and corruption featured as the organizing category of the republican perception of political life. In eighteenth-century England, following upon the seventeenth-century constitutional struggles and the Harringtonian tendency to identify the patriotic citizen with propertied independence, republicanism involved an intense disquiet over the perceived corrupting influence of commercial prosperity and the manner in which the institutional accompaniments of commercial life – in such forms as the national debt, government patronage, and the "monied interest" – threatened the preservation of constitutional balance and parliamentary independence. In the polemics of the Walpolean era and in the arguments against imperial policy in the American colonies, for example, such concerns informed and structured the standard criticisms of Whig leadership and the mechanisms of Whig political management: its financial system of public credit, excise, and national debt; its parliamentary system of an enlarged executive, placemen, and the Septennial Act; and its military system of standing armies and swollen navies. "From 1688 to 1776 (or after)," Pocock observes, "the central question in Anglophone political theory was not whether a ruler might be resisted for misconduct, but whether a regime founded on patronage, public debt, and professionalization of the armed forces did not corrupt both governors and governed; and corruption was a problem in virtue."[8]

A second area of recent scholarship concerns the early modern tradition of natural jurisprudence associated with Grotius and his successors (and, most familiarly in England, with Selden, Hobbes, and Locke), which again has served to highlight the category of commerce and commercial life. Here, though, the historiographic situation perhaps needs some unraveling. Recent studies have tended to undermine one well-known interpretive formula for establishing the importance of commerce for natural rights theory – such as that offered by C. B. Macpherson – whereby the developing commercial economy of the seventeenth century itself serves as the material basis for the theory, and whereby the capitalist market serves as the mostly unavowed model for the practice of rights. Work in criticism of the "Macpherson thesis" has been at pains to reveal the theoretic distance between "property" in the Grotian tradition and the absolute property right of bourgeois society, and to make clear how poorly capitalist accumulation could be served by the practice of rights endorsed by most rights theorists.[9] But while commerce in this respect has tended to recede in the discussion of natural law and natural rights theory, it has risen to prominence in those studies concerned to recover the jurisprudential foundations of eighteenth-century social theory, particularly in the case of Scottish sociology and political economy.[10] These studies have encouraged us to see such moralists as David Hume, Adam Smith, and John Millar as attempting to give greater historical content to the natural law jurists' speculations on consequences of human appetite and sociability and, as part of this enterprise, moving on to formulate an influential account of commercial society as a distinct and distinctly modern mode of cultural experience, naturally accompanied by its particular system of manners and politics, styles of sociability and forms of government. What began in the effort, in John Millar's terms, to develop the Grotian tradition into a "natural history of legal establishments" generated a powerful conceptualization of that form of life in which, in Adam Smith's terms, "every man thus lives by exchanging, or becomes in some measure a merchant, and the society itself grows to be what is properly a commercial society."[11]

In comparison with the Scottish creation of a sociology of commercial society, or with even the republican preoccupation with commerce's capacity to corrupt the public sphere, eighteenth-century English common law and legal thought often appear to present a rather pathetic specimen – the unfortunate case of an insular and over-confident intellectual tradition being struck down by arrested development. Merchant-improvers of the early modern period complained lavishly of limitations of English justice in handling their affairs. "It is well," Josiah Child explained in 1693, "if we can make our counsel, being common lawyers, understand one half of our case, we being amongst them as in a Foreign Country, our language strange to them, and theirs as strange to us."[12] And the tendentious thesis of the Victorian "Age of Reform" (here voiced by John Stuart Mill) – that a legal system originating among "a tribe of rude soldiers, holding a conquered people in subjection" had yet adequately to adjust to the circumstances of "an industrious, commercial, rich, and free people" – continues to echo in recent treatments.[13] Thus, many legal historians still regard the law's effective response to market capitalism as an essentially nineteenth-century story, one that required a full "transformation" of earlier common law doctrines and categories.[14]

Much of the discussion of the formal legal speculation of the period continues to stress the very halting and frequently confused manner in which common lawyers came to understand the newer forms of property in circulation in England. A classic instance has been found in the period's most celebrated and influential law book, Blackstone's four-volume *Commentaries on the Laws of England* (1765–9). In contrast to the remarkable clarity and comprehension he achieved in his account of the law of estates and tenures, Blackstone's presentation of commercial and mercantile matters seems abrupt and sketchy. He devoted a mere thirty pages to contract, in a chapter also treating grants and gifts. He discussed contracts of employment as part of the law of "masters and servants," essentially as a branch of feudal status. In his account of the law covering insurances, he frankly confessed his inability to reduce the leading court decisions "to any general heads."[15] As A. W. B. Simpson, recent editor of the *Commentaries*, concluded, "Blackstone's whole account of personal property . . . smells of the countryside; the law is the law of the country gentry, not Cheapside."[16]

This scholarly picture has not gone unchallenged,[17] and in what follows I want to suggest that a more complicated and interesting story deserves to be told about the manner in which eighteenth-century English lawyers understood commerce and legal change. Instead of neglecting commerce, or finding its arena of property relations confusing and foreign, they could easily discern and describe its impact on England's jurisprudence and legal development. And here, again, Blackstone's testimony is especially instructive. Not that Blackstone can be taken simply to personify the eighteenth-century "common law mind," or that his *Commentaries* can be received, as Henry Maine suggested, as "always a faithful index of the average opinions of his day."[18] Rather, it is the challenge of finding that Blackstone, notwithstanding the presumed inadequacy of his treatment of commercial law topics, expressly understood the legal order of his time to be the law of "a polite and commercial people," whose character and excellence were properly understood in part in terms of the modern social circumstances of the community it served.[19]

Blackstone, it must be admitted, may appear a singularly unpromising exponent of the legal world of "a polite and commercial people," not least on account of how avowedly "backward-looking" was so much of his attitude to English law. According to the formalities of English jurisprudence, the centerpiece of the legal system, the common law, comprised ancient customs of the realm "used time out of mind, or in the solemnity of our legal phrase, time whereof the memory of man runneth not to the contrary."[20] Common law, as was the case with "traditional laws in general," had of course changed and developed; although it was frequently "impossible to define the precise period" at which a particular alteration of law occurred, "we plainly discern the alteration of the law from what it was five hundred years ago."[21] And some of this legal alteration, such as the elaboration of many of the rules governing personal property, had plainly occurred outside the structure of the law's "ancient usage."[22] Nevertheless, the central feature of the kingdom's legal history remained much more intimately connected to the law's antique origins. These origins, Blackstone maintained, could be confidently located in the liberal Saxon laws and customs collected by Alfred and later consolidated by Edgar and Edward the Confessor.[23] But this "ancient constitution" of Saxon freedom had been nearly obliterated by the Norman monarchs' manipulation and abuse of feudal law. The major burden of English legal history thus became the labored process by which the law was cleansed of its Norman "excrescences" and "its pristine simplicity and vigour" restored.[24] The process began in earnest under Edward I, whom Blackstone hailed as the "English Justinian" and whose reforms were credited with having settled "the very scheme and model of the administration of common justice between party and party . . . [which] has continued nearly the same in all succeeding ages to this day."[25] With regard to matters of private law (though not, of course, in matters of constitutional practice), "all the principal grievances introduced by the Norman conquest" had been "shaken off" by the end of the reign of Elizabeth, and all that remained for later generations to do to complete the process of restoration was the final abolition of military tenures, secured under Charles II.[26]

Blackstone, as several commentators have emphasized, had a range of purposes to serve in producing this version of the "rise, progress, and gradual improvements" of England's law.[27] But for our purposes here, interest lies in how this picture of historical restoration might be thought to connect up – if it does at all – with Blackstone's other pronouncements on a developed legal order conditioned by the needs of "a polite and commercial people." A clue is found in one of the most eloquent passages of the *Commentaries*, where Blackstone again sought broadly to characterize the course of English legal change. In this instance his remarks followed a protracted account, of nearly 300 pages, of the common law's system of writs and civil remedies. Blackstone sought to show that the notorious "intricacy of our legal process" did not deserve the reproach it regularly attracted, and that the frequently ridiculed "fictions and circuities" of England's law ought properly to be regarded as a minor consequence of an otherwise wholesome process of judicially orchestrated legal improvement. When the "influence of foreign trade and domestic tranquillity" led to the decay of England's "military tenures," the common law judges "quickly perceived" that the "old feudal actions" were "ill suited" to the succeeding "commercial mode of property" which "required a more speedy decision of right, to facilitate exchange and alienation." But instead of "soliciting any great legislative revolution in the old established forms," they "endeavoured by a series of minute contrivances" to adapt the existing legal actions "to all the most useful purposes of remedial justice." These contrivances became "known and understood," and the "only difficulty" which remained "arose from their fictions and circuities." But once the necessary historical exposition was supplied, "that labyrinth [was] easily pervaded":

> Our system of remedial law resembles an old Gothic castle, erected in the days of chivalry, but fitted up for a modern inhabitant. The moated ramparts, the embattled towers, and the trophied halls, are magnificent and venerable, but useless, and therefore neglected. The inferior apartments, now accommodated to daily use, are cheerful and commodious, though their approaches may be winding and difficult.[28]

Here, for Blackstone, the course of legal change was unmistakably a matter of legal modernization, and the rationale of the change itself related directly to the legal requirements set by a new "commercial mode of property." To the extent that this process of liberalizing the "old feudal actions" represented a removal of Norman "excrescences," it was possible to speak of a restoration of Saxon simplicity. But the liberalization was expressly designed "to facilitate exchange and alienation" under the dictates of trade and commerce. As Blackstone reported the conventional legal wisdom elsewhere, "It is an object indeed of utmost importance in this free and commercial country, to lay as few restraints as possible upon the transfer of possessions from hand to hand."[29]

If Blackstone, then, did have a fairly specific sense of what commerce required of a legal order, what seems so surprising is his readiness to locate the relevant legal transformation in the history of real property law, and so to associate trade and commerce with the halting, convoluted, and generally unfathomable process by which his "old feudal actions" came to be supplanted by "replevin, detinue of title deeds, trespass *quare clausum fregit*, actions on the statutes of forcible entry, and ejectments."[30] We may in this context be moved to go beyond Simpson, and find the *Commentaries* not so much smelling as reeking "of the countryside." Yet, the Blackstonean linking of commerce and real property was perhaps less quaint and idiosyncratic than this allows. Adam Smith, after all, was soon to conjecture that no feature of English law had done more to promote commercial prosperity than the "action of ejectment" and the various "laws and customs" that preserved the property of tenants and proprietors.[31] Blackstone's decision in the *Commentaries* to present the laws governing "domestic commerce" as a branch of "the King's Prerogative" may convey the, by now, anticipated archaic approach.[32] Yet the legal topics there identified – public markets, weights and measures, coinage and money – were perhaps not all that distant from the concerns of the period's more self-consciously modern commentators "on commerce." For Blackstone, just as for Smith and Hume, eighteenth-century commerce is still far removed from nineteenth-century capitalism and its associated categories of industrialization, urbanization, and class formation.

And yet, all historical allowances allowed and all historical solecisms avoided, a fundamental inadequacy seems to remain in the *Commentaries*' embrace of commerce and law. For although Blackstone readily perceived commerce as the historical force behind sweeping changes in England's system of property law, it is much less clear that he had much sense of a commercial society as such. Commerce, in this sense, could so easily and organically be absorbed into English legal history because it was a social practice rather than a form of social experience. The common law judges who transformed the "old feudal tenures" may have served the interests of those involved in trade and commerce, but they had not participated in the creation of a new social universe in which everyone, as Smith famously put it, "becomes in some measure a merchant." Blackstone's investment in English legal continuities perhaps simply foreclosed any such conception of societal transformation. The resulting balancing act was well caught by the terms Blackstone deployed to introduce the rules of personal (as opposed to real) property. This was a topic scarcely mentioned in "our ancient law-books," which had only received legal attention "since the introduction and extension of trade and commerce." In developing the rights of personal property, the courts had adhered to considerations of "reason and convenience, adapted to the circumstances of the times," and had fashioned a "more enlarged and less technical mode of considering" personalty than realty. But even here the courts took care to preserve "withal a due regard to ancient usages and a certain feudal tincture."[33]

To the extent that eighteenth-century lawyers arrived at a sharper image of a break in legal development occasioned by commercial life, this occurred most commonly in their reflection on those branches of law directly tied to commerce and mercantile exchange. John Millar maintained that in a "mercantile age and country" the general manners of the people were displayed most conspicuously "in that part of the inhabitants who are actually engaged in trade."[34] The nature of property law in general in a commercial society might be supposed likewise to be revealed most clearly in the law specific to mercantile transactions, so that the more general character of commercial society's legal order might be identified in such law as that applying to bills of exchange and promissory notes, marine insurances and maritime transactions, contracts and quasi-contracts, and the like. In pursuing this line of speculation, the lawyers' task was considerably eased by their tendency to think of the establishment of England's "commercial law" as an extremely recent creation that could, for the most part, be directly attributed to the Chief Justiceship of Lord Mansfield. Even before his retirement from the court of King's Bench in 1788, Mansfield had been hailed as "the founder of the commercial law of this country."[35] The personal nature of his achievement thereafter became a standard element in the legal literature pertaining to merchants and trade. As George Joseph Bell observed in introducing his weighty treatise on *Mercantile Jurisprudence*, "in an uninterrupted period of thirty years," Mansfield had "devoted the strength of his great talents" to the "duty of building up, in a series of determinations, a system of mercantile jurisprudence."[36]

The publication in 1992 of James Oldham's long-awaited and important *The Mansfield Manuscripts and the Growth of English Law in the Eighteenth Century* by the University of North Carolina Press may perhaps excuse me from offering any comment on the accuracy of this contemporary evaluation of Mansfield's innovations, or from discussing the body of recent scholarship that has seen in his judicial labors a refinement and consolidation of common law experience rather than a departure from past practice (tasks which in any case are well beyond my talents and expertise). Instead of seeking to assess the extent of Mansfield's personal contributions to (say) the law of marine insurances or the law of negotiable instruments, I would like to consider briefly the broad implications for English legal thought of the contemporary conviction that the Chief Justice's decisions, taken "collectively," constituted "a complete code of jurisprudence . . . admirably suited to the genius and circumstances of the age."[37]

Mansfield himself, in his declarations from the bench, laid the groundwork for subsequent characterizations of his "system of mercantile jurisprudence." There was, first, the insistence that the appropriate law to govern commercial practices was the "law merchant," which, based on general mercantile custom and usage, applied equally to "foreigners as well as natives." In these cases the court did not look to "the principles of our municipal laws," but instead was guided "by the law of war and by the law of nature, that is, of right reason."[38] Second was the frequently invoked claim that "the great object" in "mercantile law" was "certainty";[39] and that this requirement demanded of law a system of "easily learned and easily retained" rules, freed from "subtleties and niceties."[40] Neither of these pronouncements was especially novel or controversial. Yet in the practice of these judicial precepts, Mansfield's court was seen to depart, and not without opposition and controversy, from the prior practices of common law. The goal of legal certainty, as understood by the Chief Justice, meant that decisions of "fact" previously left by the courts to the determination of a jury, had now to be settled as principles of law, so as to provide a certain guide for future transactions.[41] The reliance on the law merchant and foreign legal authorities meant that analogies and legal categories drawn from common law had to be repudiated. Thus, for example, to establish the principles of assignability that applied to instruments of credit it was necessary to insist on the irrelevance of the common law doctrine of "consideration" in mercantile usage.[42] The need to provide prompt and immediate legal remedies, so as better to support the purposes of owners, meant that the common law court would recognize rights and entitlements previously protected only by courts of equity.[43]

In a ruling of 1777, Mansfield declared: "I desire nothing so much as that all questions of mercantile law should be fully settled and ascertained."[44] And, as we have seen, for many of his contemporaries the Chief Justice had proved singularly triumphal in realizing this aspiration. The "law of merchants" had "been wonderfully elucidated, and reduced to rational and firm principles"; and these "certain general principles" could now effectively "serve as a guide to the future."[45] The content of Mansfield's "code of jurisprudence" had of course been determined by the nature of the economic practices it was designed to govern. The Scottish jurist Lord Kames reported that "no circumstance tends more to the advancement of commerce than a free circulation of the goods of fortune from hand to hand."[46] And the law merchant directly served to support that system of fluid and rapid exchange on which commerce depended. "Our courts," Joseph Chitty explained at the close of the century in his authoritative treatise on *Bills of Exchange*, "subservient, as it were, to the necessity and circumstances of the time, have, in favour of commerce, adopted a less technical mode of considering *personalty* than *realty*; and in support of commercial transactions have established the law-merchant."[47]

Mansfield's commercial code, on this pervasive eighteenth-century reading, thus presented itself as a newly settled body of legal principles, specifically shaped by the demands of commerce, and plainly unlike much of the main body of English law governing other areas of property and exchange. If mercantile law rejected "subtleties and niceties" in favor of "easily learned and easily retained" rules, how sharply it contrasted with common law, where, as Blackstone acknowledged, it was altogether "impracticable to comprehend many rules of the modern law, in a scholarlike scientifical manner" without referring to "the antiquities of our English jurisprudence."[48] If mercantile law was distinguished by its simplicity and rationality, how different was the situation in other branches of English jurisprudence, where, as Charles Butler conceded, property law was "singularly and surprisingly complicated."[49] According to English legal orthodoxy there was no special problem in the existence of a specific body of law, such as the law merchant, forming a distinct branch of the legal system and applying to a distinct area of economic practices. After all, the English legal system already incorporated in its operation such distinct and autonomous systems of law as the Roman law and the canon laws, whose authority in specific courts and over specific issues had been long sanctioned by the common law.[50] And yet the question remains as to why Mansfield's commercial code did not raise a more threatening challenge to established common law practices and principles. If the logic of commercial society was to transform "every man" into "some measure a merchant," then over how isolated an area of economic life could the commercial law be contained? Why did not the same social and economic developments which rendered Mansfield's founding of the commercial law such a necessary and apposite task, in turn establish the case for a more extensive overhaul of property rights at common law?

I have tried to suggest elsewhere that the challenges posed by these questions furnished the matrix for one of the period's most intriguing programs of law reform, that developed by Scottish philosopher and judge, Lord Kames, in his *Historical Law Tracts* (1758) and *Principles of Equity* (1760).[51] In these works, Kames critically surveyed Scots law, identifying a wide range of inherited legal practices that had been rendered obsolete and pernicious by the advent of commercial life. And on the basis of this diagnosis, he went on to identify general principles of legal modernization whose application would properly reshape Scots law according to altered and novel social conditions. There were good reasons, both political and intellectual, for a theory of this sort being produced in Scotland and not England. England enjoyed its own law reform traditions, and part of the reason for the absence of an English Kames perhaps lies in the English reformers' need to confront a less accommodating thesis regarding the appropriate legacy of commerce for native legal development.

To pursue this speculation further requires us to return to the law of estates and tenures, and to the antique learning of the common law. And for this purpose we can take advantage of the case of *Perrin* v. *Blake*, which provided the setting for one of Mansfield's most celebrated failures at legal improvement.[52] (As Professor Oldham might put it, we here explore the frustration of Mansfield's imprint on eighteenth-century property ideas.) The determination of *Perrin* v. *Blake* involved the legal construction of a technically flawed will. Such cases were the common currency of the courts, and at the level of legal principle the position of the law to them was plain. As Blackstone maintained from the bench, "the great and fundamental maxim upon which the construction of every devise must depend, is 'that the intention of the testator shall be fully and punctually observed, *so far* as the same is consistent with the established rule of law and *no farther*.'"[53] "The first rule of law in expounding wills," Lord Chancellor Hardwicke explained, meant that "the law will help an improper and unapt expression" where "the testator's intent appears plain."[54] Thus the courts were empowered to follow the testator's intention even in those cases where the legal instrument under dispute had been inaccurately or imprecisely drawn. "Courts of justice," Mansfield maintained, "are to construe the words of parties so as to effectuate their deeds, and not to destroy them."[55]

This legal principle, while allowing the courts considerable flexibility in interpreting the terms of a particular will or devise, restricted the courts to doing only what was "consistent with the established rule of law." In the first place, this simply indicated that the courts could never effect an illegal intention. Thus the courts would not support "an intention in the testator to create a perpetuity, or to limit a fee upon a fee, or to make a chattel descend to heirs," since in all these cases the avowed intention was "contrary to the rules of law."[56] But included under the rubric of the rule of law were also the more technical rules by which the courts construed those standard terms of legal art commonly employed in wills and conveyances. Such standard rules of construction were required to preserve the certainty of property law, since otherwise the authentic meaning of any particular instrument could only be established by individual judicial decision.

Unfortunately in the case of English law, these standard rules for interpreting devises had been formulated as part of the elaborate web of legal fictions through which the courts had gradually extended the individual's power to alienate property. As a result, they were enormously complex and technical, if not entirely unintelligible to the uninitiated. Blackstone had argued in the *Commentaries* that given the proper historical learning, it was not difficult to perceive the "clew" to this "labyrinth." Other legal writers proved more skeptical. Richard Wooddeson, one of Blackstone's first successors to the Vinerian chair at Oxford, acknowledged that the "necessary shifts and contrivances used in conveyancing" were "frequent and popular matters of complaint," and legal writer, Michael Nolan, maintained that if the professional conveyancer mastered the system, for "the rest of mankind it must remain unaccountable."[57] Even the most basic rules of construction, such as those relating to the distinction between real and personal property, were frequently unknown. As Mansfield observed in a typical ruling, "generally speaking, no common person has the smallest idea of any difference between giving a person a horse and a quantity of land. Common sense alone would never teach a man the difference."[58]

Given the technical demands of the conveyancing system, mistakes were easily made, and in the many cases concerning wills and devises which entered Westminster Hall, the courts were forced to determine between an interpretation which followed the testator's intent and one conforming to the technical rules of construction. The general policy of the courts was to sacrifice the rules to the intent where that intent was clearly stated, but to supply a more technical construction where the intent was unclear. In *Perrin* v. *Blake* the testator had stated in his will that "it is my intent and meaning that none of my children shall sell or dispose of my estate for a longer time than his life." He then left the estate to his son "for his natural life" with the remainder "to the heirs of the body of my said son."[59] By using this formula the will fell under the so-called "rule in Shelley's case," laid down in Coke's *Reports*.[60] According to this rule, the son received the estate as a tenant in tail in possession. He thereby enjoyed effective power to alienate the estate as he pleased, in violation of the testator's intention to limit his powers over the estate to his own lifetime. The rule in question had been formulated to prevent the evasion of feudal dues, and even when it appeared as a rule of construction in the sixteenth century, it represented a restrictive interpretation of rules originally designed to facilitate powers of alienation. By the eighteenth century, the application of the rule in cases like *Perrin* v. *Blake* virtually always prevented the testator's intention from being effected, even though the intention itself was perfectly legal.[61]

Perrin v. *Blake* came before the court of King's Bench in 1769, where it was decided in favor of the testator's intent. The court argued that in this particular case the testator had expressed his design so clearly that it was proper to exempt the devise from the rule in Shelley's case. In his judgment, Mansfield admitted that there were doubtless "lawyers of a different bent of genius" who would have "chosen to adhere to the strict letter of the law." But he insisted upon upholding the principle of law which "allowed a free communication of intention to the testator," stressing that "it would be a strange law to say, 'Now you have communicated that intention so as everybody understands what you mean, yet because you have used a certain expression of art, we will cross your intention . . . though what you mean to have done is perfectly legal, and the only reason for contravening you is because you have not expressed yourself as a lawyer.'"[62] The King's Bench ruling had not carried the unanimous opinion of the court, and was actively attacked by the conveyancers. A writ of error was brought against the judgment, and the suit was reheard in 1772 in the Exchequer Chamber where Mansfield's resolution was reversed. This action proved decisive. In later cases on the same point of law, Mansfield's court adhered to the technical rule in Shelley's case, and the rule never again underwent judicial examination.[63] Blackstone, then a judge in the court of Common Pleas, supplied the 1772 judgment in reversal. He argued that the disputed devise did not in fact provide "any such plain and manifest *intent* of the divisor" as was needed to exempt the will from the rule in Shelley's case.[64] Accordingly, the technical rule of construction prevailed.

In terms of these arguments the decisions of the two courts occupied rather narrow legal ground. What was disputed was whether the testator had recorded his intentions with sufficient clarity, both courts accepting that if this had been achieved, the intention was to override the relevant rule of construction. But to support their rulings, the two courts went on to address other questions, including issues regarding commerce and its meanings for the future development of property in English law.

Mansfield and his judicial supporters readily acknowledged that the rule in Shelley's case was "clear law." But, they needed to show that the rule did "not constitute a decisive uncontrollable rule" equivalent to a "general proposition" of law in order to justify the court's decision to restrict its application. The judges pursued this objective by supplying an historical analysis of the rule itself so as to demonstrate its anachronistic status in the laws of a commercial people. Mansfield's colleagues, Sir Richard Aston and Edward Willes, developed this position at length. Aston described the rule in Shelley's case as "an old rule of feudal policy, the reason of which is long since antiquated," and which accordingly "must not be extended one jot."[65] Willes echoed these comments in stressing that the rule "grew with feudal policy, and the reasons of it are now antiquated." He went on to insist that the strictness of feudal property law was essentially antithetic to the needs of contemporary society. "It is an universal notion," he claimed, "that in a commercial country all property should be freed from every clog which may hinder its circulation." In accord with these "motives of policy," he would "ever discountenance" as much as possible "anything which favours of ancient strictness" and "depart with justice from an old maxim the policy of which is now ceased." He went on to invoke Lord Cowper's telling formula that should the courts simply adhere "to the technical expressions without any deviation," then common law would be reduced to "mere matter of memory, instead of being a system of judgment and reason."[66] Mansfield himself did not explore this argument, aside from recording his complete agreement with Aston and Willes.[67] In previous cases, though, he had embraced the same position and treated the rule in Shelley's case as "an ancient maxim of law" to be restrictively applied because "the reason of this maxim has long ceased."[68]

Blackstone's judgment reversing the King's Bench decision contained a direct response to this argument. He admitted that the rule was not "to be reckoned among the great fundamental principles of juridical policy," and therefore would "give way" to the "plain intention of the testator." But while agreeing with the judges over the status of the rule, he was careful to eschew the historical reasoning through which they had contained it. What Blackstone clearly perceived was that the logic of commercial life embraced by the King's Bench threatened to introduce a far too corrosive element into the discussion of property in England. Hence, he examined the historical character of the rule in order to demonstrate its continued relevance to the vitality of common law, and thereby provided an elegant statement of the conservative implications of an historical approach:

> There is hardly an ancient rule of real property but what has in it more or less of a feudal tincture. The common law maxims of descent, the conveyance by livery of seisin, the whole doctrine of copyholds, and a hundred other instances that might be given, are plainly the offspring of the feudal system: but whatever their parentage was, they are now adopted by the common law of England, incorporated into its body, and so interwoven with its policy, that no court of justice in this kingdom has either the *power* or (I trust) the *inclination* to disturb them. . . . The law of real property in this country wherever its materials were gathered, is now formed into a fine artificial system, full of unseen connexions and nice dependencies; and he that breaks one link of the chain, endangers the dissolution of the whole.[69]

In his *Commentaries*, Blackstone had suggested that centuries earlier England's "old feudal tenures" had made their peace with trade and commerce, and that the resulting adjustments in the law of property effectively provided for modern "exchange and alienation." But the dispute and arguments in *Perrin* v. *Blake* raised the challenge of just how permanent and stable this past adjustment should be. In his response from the bench, Blackstone insisted that modernization of England's real property law in some sense for ever had to respect the structure and nature of its historical origins, even if such "modernization" now looked more to conservation than change. Yet this doctrine of legal conservatism was, after all, articulated in the face of an abortive effort at legal improvement, led by the judicial figure who seemed to his contemporaries to personify legal creativity and innovation. In this light, we might think of the eighteenth-century English legal experience as presenting at least two faces to the issue of legal change and modernization. There was the record of Mansfield and the founding of the commercial law which could be taken to demonstrate decisively the common law system's continued capacity to develop and advance as commerce and changing social circumstances dictated. And there was the law of real property where, notwithstanding obvious change and development, the law's antique origin properly continued to exercise its power. It was the labor of later proponents of English law reform to suggest that the latter was the definitive and authentic image of the common law. Given Blackstone's apt portrayal in 1772 of England's property law as a "fine artificial system" in which the removal of but "one link of the chain" threatened "the dissolution of the whole," we should not be surprised to find the advocates of modernization countering with alternative metaphors.[70] As Jeremy Bentham put it a decade later in considering the position of an enlightened legislator seeking to overcome the obstacles to reform furnished by established usage and past custom:

> [If] it be found impossible to untie the Gordian knot, you must e'en do at once like Alexander and cut it. The welfare of all must not be made a sacrifice of to the obstinacy of a few; nor the happiness of ages to the quiet of a day.[71]

156   David Lieberman

Notes

1   William Blackstone, *Commentaries on the Laws of England*, ed. Edward Christian, 4 vols (London, 1803 [1765–9]), Vol. I, 123–9; hereafter cited as, for example "1 *Comm* 123–9."

2   3 *Comm* 265–6, 327.

3   3 *Comm* 423–4.

4   Henry Fielding, *An Enquiry into the Late Increase of Robbers, with some Proposals for Remedying this Growing Evil*, in *The Complete Works of Henry Fielding*, ed. William Ernest Henley, 16 vols (London: 1903 [1751]), Vol. XIII, p. 14.

5   Philip C. Yorke, *The Life and Correspondence of Philip Yorke, Earl of Hardwicke, Lord High Chancellor of Great Britain*, 3 vols (Cambridge, UK: 1913), Vol. II, pp. 554–5.

6   Edmund Burke, "Report from the Committee of the House of Commons appointed to inspect the Lords' journals in relation to their proceedings on the trial of Warren Hastings, Esq." (1794), in *The Works of the Right Honourable Edmund Burke* (Boston, MA: 1884 [1865–7]; 8th edn), Vol. XI, p. 84.

7   Pocock himself surveys much of this scholarship in his essays in *Virtue, Commerce, and History. Essays on Political Thought and History, Chiefly in the Eighteenth Century* (Cambridge, UK: 1985), especially the closing chapter on "The varieties of Whiggism from exclusion to reform," pp. 215–310.

8   "Virtues, rights and manners. A model for historians of political thought," in ibid., p. 48.

9   A particularly strong version of the anti-Macpherson thesis is advanced by James Tully in *A Discourse on Property: John Locke and his Adversaries* (Cambridge, UK: 1980).

10   Important recent studies include the following volumes: Duncan Forbes, *Hume's Philosophical Politics* (Cambridge, UK: 1975); Knud Haakonssen, *The Science of a Legislator: The Natural Jurisprudence of David Hume and Adam Smith* (Cambridge, UK: 1981); Donald Winch, *Adam Smith's Politics. An essay in historiographic revision* (Cambridge, UK: 1978); Peter Stein, *Legal Evolution. The Story of an Idea* (Cambridge, UK: 1980); Istvan Hont and Michael Ignatieff (eds), *Wealth and Virtue: The Shaping of Political Economy in the Scottish Enlightenment* (Cambridge, UK: 1983).

11   John Millar, *An Historical View of English Government*, 4 vols (London: 1812 [1803]), Vol. IV, pp. 284–5; Adam Smith, *An Inquiry into the Nature and Causes of the Wealth of Nations*, ed. R. H. Campbell, A. S. Skinner, and W. B. Todd, 2 vols (Oxford: 1976 [1776]), Vol. I, p. 37.

12   Josiah Child, *A New Discourse of Trade* (London: 1693), pp. 113–14.

13   J. S. Mill, "Essay on Bentham" (1838), in *Essays on Ethics, Religion and Society*, ed. J. M. Robson (Toronto: 1969), p. 101.

14   For two significant recent instances, see Morton J. Horwitz, *The Transformation of American Law 1780–1860* (Cambridge, MA: 1977), and P. S. Atiyah, *The Rise and Fall of Freedom of Contract* (Oxford: 1979).

15   2 *Comm* 442–70, 1 *Comm* 422–32, 2 *Comm* 460. Milsom supplies an important rejoinder to the usual criticisms of Blackstone's handling of these topics in "The nature of Blackstone's achievement," *Oxford Journal of Legal Studies* 1 (1981): 7–8.

16   William Blackstone, *Commentaries on the Laws of England: A Facsimile of the first edition of 1765–1769*, intro. A. W. B. Simpson, 4 vols (Chicago: 1979), Vol. II, p. xii (editorial introduction).

17   Little, for example, survives of the version of the "pre-history" of nineteenth-century contract law advanced by Horwitz in *The Transformation* and Atiyah in *Rise and Fall*; see, for example, the critique offered in A. W. B. Simpson, "The Horwitz thesis and the history of contracts," *University of Chicago Law Review* 46 (1979): 533–601, and the excellent review and addition to the debate in James Oldham, "Reinterpretations of 18th-century English contract theory: the view from Lord Mansfield's trial notes," *Georgetown Law Journal* 76 (1988): 1949–91.

18   Henry Maine, *Ancient Law. Its Connection with the Early History of Society and its Relation to Modern Ideas*, intro. Raymond Firth (Gloucester, MA: 1970 [1861]; reprint of the Beacon Paperback edn), p. 244.

19   3 *Comm* 325–6.

20 1 *Comm* 67.
21 4 *Comm* 409.
22 2 *Comm* 385.
23 1 *Comm* 64–7, and see 4 *Comm* 408–14.
24 4 *Comm* 419–20.
25 4 *Comm* 425, 427. (Blackstone here, as elsewhere in the *Commentaries*, closely follows the account supplied by Matthew Hale in his *The History of the Common Law of England*.)
26 4 *Comm* 432; and see 4 *Comm* 438–40.
27 See Robert Willman, "Blackstone and the 'theoretical perfection' of English Law in the reign of Charles II," *Historical Journal* 26 (1983): 39–70; John W. Cairns, "Blackstone, the ancient constitution and the feudal law," *Historical Journal* 28 (1985): 711–17; and David Lieberman, "Blackstone's science of legislation," *Journal of British Studies* 27 (1988): 117–49.
28 3 *Comm* 267–8.
29 3 *Comm* 329.
30 The list is taken from J. H. Baker, *An Introduction to English Legal History* (London: 1979; 2nd edn), p. 203. The legal history in question is set out in detail in A. W. B. Simpson, *An Introduction to the History of Land Law* (Oxford: 1962).
31 See Smith, *Wealth of Nations*, Vol. I, p. 392: "Those laws and customs so favourable to the yeomanry, have perhaps contributed more to the present grandeur of England than all their boasted regulations of commerce taken together."
32 1 *Comm* 273–9.
33 2 *Comm* 384–5.
34 Millar, *Historical View of English Government*, Vol. IV, p. 238.
35 See the comments of Sir Francis Buller J., in *Lickbarrow* v. *Mason* (1787) 2 Term Rpts 63, 73.
36 George Joseph Bell, *Commentaries on the Laws of Scotland and the Principles of Mercantile Jurisprudence* (Edinburgh: 1810 [1804]; 2nd edn), pp. ix–x.
37 Charles Butler, *The Reminiscences of Charles Butler, Esq. of Lincoln's Inn* (London: 1822), p. 139. In what follows, I am drawing on material explored at greater length in my *The Province of Legislation Determined: legal theory in eighteenth-century Britain* (Cambridge, UK: 1989), Chs 5–6.
38 *Goss* v. *Withers* (1758) 2 Burrow 683, 689; for a similar ruling see *Anthon* v. *Fisher* (1782) 3 Douglas 166.
39 *Milles* v. *Fletcher* (1779) 1 Douglas 231, 232. For similar statements, see *Alderson* v. *Temple* (1768) 4 Burrow 2235, *Tyrie* v. *Fletcher* (1777) Cowper 666, *Bond* v. *Nutt* (1777) Cowper 601, *Drinkwater* v. *Goodwin* (1775) Cowper 251.
40 *Hamilton* v. *Mendes* (1761) 2 Burrow 1198, 1214.
41 See, for example, Mansfield's comments in *Medcalf* v. *Hall* (1782) 3 Douglas 113, 115: "Nothing is more mischievous than uncertainty in mercantile law. It would be terrible if every question were to make a cause, and to be decided according to the temper of a jury. If a rule is intended to apply to and govern a number of like cases, that rule is a rule of law." For his criticisms of earlier common law practice, see his comments in *Hankey* v. *Jones* (1778) Cowper 745, 751–2: "With regard to what passed at the trial in Wilson's case, with great respect to Lord Chief Justice Lee's memory, I think the jury asked him a very proper question: whether this drawing and redrawing [of notes] was, in point of *law*, a trading in merchandise within the statutes concerning bankrupts. . . . But the report says 'He told them it was a question of *fact* and *not* of *law*.' With all deference to his opinion, it was a question of law upon the fact. It may be proper to leave it to the jury whether the person gets a profit or remits other people's money; but the fact being established, the result is a matter of law."
42 See Mansfield's comments in *Pillans* v. *Van Mierop* (1765) 3 Burrow 1663, 1669: "This is a matter of great consequence to Trade and Commerce in every light. . . . If there be no fraud, it is a mere question of Law. The Law of Merchants, and the Law of the Land, is the same. . . . A *nudum pactum* does not exist in the Usage and Law of Merchants. . . . In commercial cases amongst merchants, the want of consideration is *not* an objection."
43 See the comments of Sir William Asshurst J., in *Winch* v. *Keeley* (1787) 1 Term Rpts 619, 622–3: "It is true that formerly the courts of law did not take notice of an equity or a trust;

for trusts are within the original jurisdiction of a court of equity. But of late years, as it has been found productive of great expense to send the parties to the other side of the Hall, wherever this court gave seen that the justice of the case has been plainly with the plaintiff, they have not turned round upon this objection." For earlier Mansfield pronouncements on this point, see *Robinson* v. *Bland* (1760) 2 Burrow 1077; *Darlington* v. *Pluteney* (1775) Cowper 260; *Rice* v. *Shute* (1770) 5 Burrow 2611.

44   *Buller* v. *Harrison* (1777) Cowper 565, 567.

45   Richard Wooddeson, *Elements of Jurisprudence* (London: 1783), p. 92; Francis Buller J., *Lickbarrow* v. *Mason* (1787) 2 Term Rpts 63, 73.

46   Henry Home, Lord Kames, *Principles of Equity* (Edinburgh: 1767 [1760]; 2nd edn, corrected and enlarged), p. 259.

47   Chitty, *Laws of Bills of Exchange*, p. 7.

48   2 *Comm* 44.

49   Butler, *Reminiscences*, p. 59.

50   See 1 *Comm* 79–84.

51   See my paper on "The legal needs of a commercial society: the jurisprudence of Lord Kames," in Hont and Ignatieff (eds), *Wealth and Virtue*, pp. 203–34.

52   In what follows I again draw on my discussion in *Province of Legislation Determined*, pp. 132–40.

53   Francis Hargrave, *A Collection of Tracts, Relative to the Law of England* (London: 1787), pp. 489–90.

54   *Bagshaw* v. *Spencer* (1743) 2 Atkyns 570, 580.

55   *Pugh* v. *Duke of Leeds* (1777) Cowper 714, 725.

56   Mansfield's examples in *Long* v. *Laming* (1760) 2 Burrow 1100, 1108.

57   Wooddeson, *Elements of Jurisprudence*, p. 106, and *Coulson* v. *Coulson* (1743) 2 Strange 1125 (Nolan's note).

58   *Hogan* v. *Jackson* (1775) Cowper 299, 306.

59   Francis Hargrave, *Collectanea Juridica, Consisting of Tracts Relative to the Law and Constitution of England*, 2 vols (London: 1787), Vol. I, p. 285.

60   For an account of the rule, see Simpson, *History of Land Law*, pp. 89–96. For contemporary discussions, see Edward Coke, *The First Part of the Institutes of the Laws of England, or, a Commentary upon Littleton*, ed. Francis Hargrave and Charles Butler, 2 vols (London: 1775–88; 13th edn), Vol. II, pp. 276–80 (Butler's note) and Hargrave, *Collection of Tracts*, pp. 549–78.

61   "In the cases in which the question arises, whether the rule shall govern or not, it almost ever occurs that the author of the entail doth not mean that the tenant for life, to the heirs of whose body the remainder is limited, should have power to defeat the succession to them by an alienation to their prejudice," Hargrave, *Collection of Tracts*, p. 556.

62   Hargrave, *Collectanea Juridica*, Vol. I, pp. 318, 321–2.

63   See *Hodgson* v. *Ambrose* (1780) 1 Douglas 337.

64   Hargrave, *Collection of Tracts*, p. 502.

65   Hargrave, *Collectanea Juridica*, Vol. I, p. 305.

66   Ibid., pp. 297–8, 301.

67   Ibid., p. 318.

68   *Long* v. *Laming* (1760) 2 Burrow 1100, 1106–7.

69   Hargrave, *Collection of Tracts*, pp. 494–5, 498.

70   Several of the issues considered here have recently received excellent treatment by Henry Horwitz in his "Law, liberty and property," in J. R. Jones (ed.), *Liberty Secured? Britain Before and After 1688* (Stanford, CA: 1992), pp. 285–98.

71   Jeremy Bentham, "Essay on the influence of time and place in matters of legislation" (1782), in *The Works of Jeremy Bentham, published under the supervision of his Executor, John Bowring*, 11 vols (Edinburgh: 1838–43), Vol. I, p. 182 (where a slightly different version of the passage is incorrectly given).

Part III
Property and the family

8
Of women and the land
Legitimizing husbandry

Carol Blum

If modern property in the West, generally speaking, consists of relations between people regarding ownership of things, this definition is by no means self-evident; it is rather a victory of the Enlightenment over older, more "organic" meanings of property that included the rights of persons over *other people*. Seignorial property in *ancien régime* France comprised many categories the validity of which we, as heirs of the Enlightenment, deny. Slavery, serfdom, *mainmorte* (seignorial death duties), the *corvée* (forced labour), the seignorial monopoly over *four, moulin, pressoir* (oven, mill, wine or oil press) are only the best-known types of personal "property" that can no longer be owned by one individual at the expense of another. In some cases, of course, analogous burdens (inheritance taxes, military service) are placed on the citizens of democratic societies, but as civic duties at least theoretically accepted and equally imposed. In this way one might see the *ancien régime*'s categories of seignorial and ecclesiastical property as merely anachronistic usages rendered inappropriate by the rise of the centralized absolute monarchy, as well as by bourgeois property as Marx has it, although these explanations are not altogether adequate to explain the shift.

Thus in the period under discussion property drags in its wake a swarmy retinue of living beings, tangled attachments, and evolving ideas. In the eighteenth century and up to our own time, defining property generates major questions about the nature of human personality in social, psychological, and legal terms:[1] who could be a legitimate person, what justified ownership, and whether or to what extent women were things, a form of property, or persons, proprietors in their own right? That these problems are still unresolved in our own world undoubtedly reflects the basic ambivalences adhering to the concept of property. That private property institutionalizes violence, as Marx held, does not negate Freud's assertion that it functions merely instrumentally in the expression of human aggression.[2]

Here I consider a moment in the slow and imperfect shift from an early concept of woman as a thing to be possessed to the modern model of an independent person. Two *philosophes* generally favorable to women's advancement, Montesquieu and Diderot,[3] wrote of exotic civilizations where attitudes toward women as property were startling from the perspective of Western Europe. Crucial antecedents of both *philosophes'* thought on women and property were to be found in two arguments in Locke's treatises of government, the one legitimizing the ownership of land by cultivation, the right of sweat in the dust, and the other legitimizing marriage by fecundation, the right of seed in the womb. This parallel between possessing land and possessing women, implicit but undeveloped in Locke,[4] takes on florid importance in the eighteenth century in France in the militant populationist debates and campaigns of the encyclopedists and physiocrats as well as others. The metaphor as used by Montesquieu and Diderot introduced an unprecedented erotic pragmatism into their critiques of French society, especially in the *Lettres persanes*, the *Encyclopédie*, and the *Supplément au voyage de Bougainville*.

In the course of his opposition to Robert Filmer's aggressively absolutist arguments in *Patriarcha*, Locke had held that labor, not scripture, produced rights over things between men. In opposition to a theologically buttressed theory awarding all land to the Crown, he used an extended agrarian metaphor to depict a hypothetical first farmer gaining legitimate ownership of land by his physical exertions in cultivating the soil. "He who . . . employed his Pains about any of the spontaneous Products of Nature, as any way to alter them, from the state which Nature put them in, by placing any of his Labour on them, did thereby acquire a Propriety in them."[5] This "propriety" had limits, in Locke's view; it had always to be balanced by the duty to charity and could not legitimately exceed what a man's family could consume, a family man constituting the proper subject of philosophical discourse on government. The one who wasted food offended Locke's vision of "propriety," for while he was entitled to the fruits of the earth he had worked to produce, "if they perished in his Possession, without their due use: if the Fruits rotted or the Venison putrefied, before he could spend it, he offended against the Common Law of Nature . . . for he had no Right, farther than his Use called for any of them, and they might serve to afford him Conveniences of Life" (p. 313).

By the same token, land claimed but not husbanded might not be said to be rightly owned; the accusation against absentee landlordship was lodged. Property that has been worked, however, does more than provide a human being and his family with sustenance, it is the necessary condition for an individuated personality, for being a subject in one's own right, for political existence.[6]

In Locke's attack on Filmer he took consistent aim at the "Patriarch" in *Patriarcha*, pointing out repeatedly that Filmer falsified or distorted scripture in order to eliminate the political personality of the mother and children, dependent people, reduced to the status of possessions. Filmer had asserted: "God has also given to the Father a Right or Liberty, to alien his Power over his children to any other; whence we find the Sale and Gift of Children to have been much in use in the Beginning of the World, when Men had their Servants for a Possession and an inheritance, as well as others Goods, whereupon we find the power of castrating and making Eunuchs much in use in Old Times. Law is nothing else but the Will of him that hath the Power of the Supreme Father." Locke expressed indignation that Filmer asserted without proving: "I could scarce believe my self, when upon attentive reading that Treatise, I found there so mighty a structure raised upon the bare supposition of this Foundation" (p. 167). Where Filmer read *father* in the Bible, Locke insisted upon *father and mother*, never separating the two parents in rights, reminding the reader that the commandment is to "honour thy father *and* mother," and denying the father's ownership of his family. Locke systematically refuted the exclusive patriarchal justification Filmer advanced for absolute monarchy.[7]

The form of government tracing right from God to king to father was naturally the absolutist monarchy; on the other hand, where slavery and serfdom were abolished or attenuated, where women and children were granted certain autonomous character-istics, and where larger numbers of people could be proprietors, the appropriate form of government inclined toward the representational. Since both polities could be but-tressed from comments in scripture, the debate in eighteenth-century unbelieving France took a new track: arguing not God's intentions for human affairs but rather the quantifiable results of various forms of government, land usage, and economic policy.

The period between 1685 and 1715 in France, the *"crise de conscience européenne,"* was marked by severe breakdowns in the operations and in the prestige of the absolutist state, disorders fully as grave as those occasioning the Revolution of 1789. The years of catastrophic wars, frequent famines, epidemics, and severe government deficits corre-sponded to the period of decrepitude of Louis XIV and the infancy of his successor. A surge of writing during those years of monarchical debility illuminated the beginnings of Enlightenment as the government was scathingly criticized for its bellicosity, so costly in human lives, for the persecution of Protestants after the revocation of the Edict of Nantes in 1685, and for archaic, unjust, and regressive systems of taxation. All three attacks might be said to be mounted on modern ground: *not* that of scriptural prescrip-tions, but rather that of mathematical calculations. The ominous numbers of men killed in war, the lost productive capacity of Protestants, the decreased revenues resulting from inefficient and irrational taxation, these subjects of accusation were textually represented as mathematical realities. This strategy of mathematical representation was politically adroit because the kingship had traditionally been held responsible for the size of the population. With the beginnings of demographic statistics, the glory of the sovereign himself came to be evaluated in numerical terms: "La grandeur des rois se mesure par le nombre des sujets," wrote Vauban.[8]

A calculus of population became the constant referent in eighteenth-century French discussions about government, the objective demonstration of political wisdom or its opposite. Yet this insistence was based upon a fundamental error, a curious mispercep-tion almost universally held throughout the century, that the human race was dimi-nishing in numbers, its fertility nearly exhausted. Where once great cities had held immense throngs of citizens, it was thought, now stood only ruins. The world was experienced as depleted and the future as ominously headed toward the extinction of the human race. This idea, that there are fewer of us now than there used to be, so antithetical to our contemporary sense of suffocation in pullulating humanity, extended to the rest of nature and to the earth itself, perceived as aged, infertile, and worn out. This *perception* that the world, and especially the kingdom, had become wasteland, had important consequences in the kinds of arguments brought against absolutism, argu-ments bolstered by an emotional logic accusing a withered despot of failing in his sacerdotal duty: to insure the fertility of the land. In fact one might speculate that the declining fertility fallacy, although factually incorrect, was psychologically irresistible to disappointed subjects of a faltering monarchy.

As the second volume of *La Population française*[9] makes clear, the population of Europe in the eighteenth century actually *increased* as did that of France. By the 1770s it was apparent that the depopulation so poignantly experienced was illusory,[10] yet a "natural" morality founded on this premise long continued to dominate mentalities, a morality with but one end in view, demographic expansion. The boldest and most brilliant attack on the *ancien régime* based on the depopulationary delusion was that of Montesquieu, in the *Lettres persanes*.

Montesquieu's elegant offensive against the absolutist state in the *Lettres persanes* offered Usbek's seraglio in Ispahan as an outrageous metaphor for the court at Versailles. For the theoretical pleasure of one man both Persia and France sacrificed the lives of numerous other people whose only existence was complementary to that of the privileged subject, the patriarch. Persia represented patriarchy morbidly engorged, its excesses casting by constant implication those of Versailles in bizarre but revealing light.

Montesquieu has a Persian describe the dearth of men in modern times: "Après un calcul aussi exact qu'il peut l'être dans ces sortes de choses, j'ai trouvé qu'il y a à peine sur la Terre la dixième partie des hommes qui y étaient dans les anciens temps. Ce qu'il y a d'étonnant, c'est qu'elle se dépeuple tous les jours, et, si cela continue, dans dix siècles elle ne sera qu'un désert" (lettre 112; Rhedi à Usbek).[11] For Montesquieu this conviction, whether sincerely held or merely very handy, permitted him to attack the Catholic Church and the Muslim religion alike as institutions leaving women to lie fallow, with deleterious effects on population. In Persia, Montesquieu informed his readers in brilliantly racy passages, women were viewed as commodities to be bought and sold; yet even as a commerce of desire and its fruit, it was neither consistent nor rational because once become the property of a fully autonomous male, the woman acquired ownership rights as well; the property becoming proprietor, the enslaved woman owning the eunuch who had purchased her. The purchased thing not only was gratified with gifts and marks of respect, but exercised rights of ownership over her purchaser, in this instance the Great Black Eunuch who buys Usbek a Circassian girl from Armenian merchants. First he examines her: "Je la déshabillai, je l'examinai avec les regards d'un juge." Once satisfied as to the value of his purchase, his attitude changes from connoisseur to slave, he places a ring on her finger and "Je me prosternai à ses pieds: je l'adorai comme la reine de ton coeur; je payai les Arméniens" (lettre 79). Montesquieu reduces *ad absurdum* the conflation of amorous language and mercantile mentality of Usbek's proxy; the crowning irony was that the eunuch could purchase but not possess, while Usbek, far from Ispahan, had acquired yet another expensive dependant he did not desire. Montesquieu depicted the Mohammaden family, faithful to the Koran, and the Catholic, faithful to Rome, as causing depopulation, the Mohammaden because of polygamy, the Roman Catholic because of monastic institutions and the prohibition of divorce.

The sterility in both these practices lies in the waste of *jus genitricem*, the right to women's reproductive capacity, although in entirely differing ways. The Mohammaden policy is based not on a mortification of the flesh as in the Christian religion, but, on the contrary, in an exaltation of erotic property for one privileged male. To the pleasure of the Persian patriarch, according to Montesquieu, are consecrated the lives of his four legitimate wives, his concubines, his female slaves, and those castrated male slaves necessary for the order and decorum of his household.

Usbek complains that the Koran demands a man be polygamous and also satisfy all his wives, leaving him exhausted. Revealing the true reason for his protracted voyage in the West, an overburdened Usbek confesses his incapacity to live up to the obligations placed upon him by his belongings: his wives. "Vos femmes sont vos labourages, dit encore le Prophète. Approchez-vous donc de vos labourages, faites du bien pour vos âmes, et vous le trouverez un jour."[12] Usbek describes the polygamous Muslim husband as "overwhelmed, exhausted," his generative powers weakened by the excessive demands put upon them by his property: "C'est dans cet état de défaillance que nous réduit toujours ce grand nombre de femmes plus propre à nous épuiser qu'à nous satisfaire."[13] The depleted patriarch cannot adequately husband his women, hence the seraglio contains few children. Not only are the women rebellious at their non-reciprocal station as things, and Usbek out of town as much as possible, but the institution fails the test of productivity as well as that of happiness.

Montesquieu has nothing to say about the comparative truth or moral value of the two great religious systems. Both, however, run counter to the one most central value: demographic expansion. Seraglios in the East are like convents and monasteries in the West, senseless institutions restricting optimal populationist output. An erotic physiocrat, Montesquieu points to the wisdom of a policy of sexual *laissez-faire*.

Similarly, Diderot's entire oeuvre, including his correspondence, is shot through with value-judgments based on the absolute supremacy of fertility as a goal in human affairs. It is the principle with which he replaces Christian morality in numerous allusions. In *La Religieuse*, for example, the convent is condemned on many grounds having to do with its effects on the individual; the primary denunciation, however, is that of waste: "Quel besoin a l'époux de tant de vierges folles? Ne sentira-t-on jamais la nécessité de rétrecir l'ouverture de ces gouffres, où les races futures vont se perdre?"[14] It is in the *Supplément au voyage de Bougainville* that Diderot mounts a full-blown campaign against Christianity as an anti-demographic institution by which the legitimate *use* of women has degenerated into a destructive *possession*. By the time this piece was written, in 1772, the depopulation delusion had been demonstrated to be false. Yet it has lost no purchase in his mind.

Diderot constructs his argument carefully. Tahiti is depicted as a land in constant need, not of things, but of people. A tribute owed to a neighboring island leaves the Tahitians, like the Cretans before Theseus, in permanent anxiety over a diminished younger generation. Their religion and mores are a transparent response to this constant drain on their youth: Tahitian life is structured to maximize the fertility of the inhabitants. Since the supreme value of this people is its birthrate, fortunes are measured not in numbers of objects, as in Europe, but in quantities of children.

Thus, young men and women are exhorted to begin their reproductive lives as soon as they are biologically optimal, the birth of a child being "an increase in fortune for the hut." Like Weber's Protestants assiduously working to accumulate wealth in the European way, Tahitians invest their energies in sexual labours. Orou, "bon père de famille" of the Tahitian type, recounts how his wife reproached their youngest daughter for her infertility: "Thia, à quoi penses-tu donc? Tu ne deviens point grosse; tu as dix-neuf ans; tu devrais avoir déjà deux enfants, et tu n'en as point."[15] In a world of such apparently Edenic promiscuity, men no longer own wives and sexuality is no longer envisaged as the "possession" of a woman by a man. The children themselves constitute a wealth scrupulously shared by the parents in an equality Locke might have approved. The needs of the country coincide exactly with this belief of the inhabitants, producing a moral harmony where civilized countries create only moderatable conflicts. "Tu ne saurais croire combien l'idée de richesse particulière ou publique, unie dans nos têtes à l'idée de la population, épure nos moeurs."[16] In Diderot's Tahiti children were always well cared for by the entire population since they were to the natives what money was to Europeans: "L'enfant étant par lui-même un objet d'intérêt et de richesse." Diderot imagines the avarice of aged European societies transformed into a greed for babies: "plus la famille du Tahitien est nombreuse, plus elle est riche."[17] It was the Europeans who introduced vice, theft, and violence into Tahiti, according to Diderot's tropical fantasy, by their perverted sense of property. "Nous ne t'avons point demandé d'argent;" says Orou, "nous ne nous sommes point jetés sur tes marchandises; nous avons méprisé tes denrées: mais nos femmes et nos filles sont venues exprimer le sang de tes veines."[18] The dialogue is framed by a discussion between two interlocutors, A and B, who reflect upon unnatural European society from the perspective of Tahitian sanity, a moral health resulting from a people "assez sage pour s'arrêter à la médiocrité."[19] Whereas in Europe property and sexuality had become so hatefully intertwined through the institution of marriage that happiness was the rarest of conditions, in Tahiti sexuality "naturally" produced property; joy and wealth flowed from each other. The inhibitions and complexes of the West, as Diderot expressed them, resulted from the attempt to convert sexual enjoyment into permanent possession. Interlocutor A formulates the great interrogation of the dialogue. How has sexuality become "la source la plus féconde de notre dépravation et de nos maux?"

Diderot underscores his response with a specific injunction to hear and retain the true answer: "C'est par la tyrannie de l'homme, qui a converti la possession de la femme en une propriété."[20]

Yet in Diderot's liberating Tahiti, woman has not been altogether dissociated from property. While he makes it abundantly clear that men and women do not belong to each other by reason of sexual union, and a seemingly rigorous symmetrical equality is established, there is another human bondage he cannot relinquish: the father's ownership of his daughters. The wish to *own* the daughter is revealed as a sort of afterthought to Orou's glowing tribute to Eros unbound. As he offers his daughters to the ship's chaplain, he exclaims: "Elles m'appartiennent et je te les offre: elles sont à elles, et elles se donnent à toi."[21] This chiastic paradox defines the young women as paternal possessions, to be offered with obvious pleasure to visitors, a hospitality ritual using the female as intermediary object between males. At the same time Diderot presents these young women as free subjects, belonging only to themselves. His contradictory "solution" consists of a statement of woman's simultaneous autonomy and perfect mimesis of the father's will.[22]

At one point in the dialogue Diderot descends from his basic exposition of a world where erotic "possession" is not synonymous with conjugal property. He slips from that modified patriarchalism to a more primitive idea, one that Rousseau had already alluded to in the *First Discourse*, one that Sade and eventually Fourier would develop, labeled as authentic liberation of male sexuality. In a truly free society men would not be subject to any sexual restraint at all. The primacy of the masculine subject and his desire leads Diderot to postulate a more extreme situation for women that, beneath a libertarian philosophical veneer, is brutal servitude of a non-European kind. In corrupt Europe, he explains, "on a consacré la résistance de la femme; on a attaché l'ignominie à la violence de l'homme; violence qui ne serait qu'une injure légère dans Tahiti, et qui devient un crime dans nos cités."[23] Calling rape a "trivial insult," Diderot conjures the fantasy of decriminalized sexual violence, a society where women are sexually available on demand.[24] "Possession" without "property" may be translated as forced copulation, morally justified because the man is not claiming proprietorship. In Sade's words, "l'homme peut contraindre momentément son semblable car il ne s'agit que de jouissance et non de propriété."[25] This possibility in the relations between the sexes emerges only fleetingly in Diderot; it does not play the central role in his thought that it does in Rousseau's, Sade's, and Fourier's.

The central metaphor Montesquieu and Diderot exploit equating woman with land, male sexuality with work, and fertility with legitimate ownership appears to liberate both partners from the tyranny of marriages at once dead and indissoluble. On the other hand, by positing demographic expansion as an absolute value, masculine desire and men's "reproductive labor" continue to dominate a hierarchy so internalized as to be experienced as biologically determined.

Notes

1 J. G. A. Pocock's chapter "Authority and property: the question of liberal origins" offers a convincing analysis of the emergence of the new individual in relation to property at the end of the seventeenth century in England. He provides an essential conceptual framework for the problem in eighteenth-century France as well. *Virtue, Commerce and History: Essays in Political Thought and History, Chiefly in the Eighteenth Century* (Cambridge, UK: Cambridge University Press, 1985), pp. 51–71.

2 Marx calls the list of feudal properties "this clutter of quasi-medieval services and dues, this natural history museum of the rottenest plunder of antediluvian times!" Karl Marx and Friedrich Engels, *Werke* (East Berlin: Dietz, 1956), Vol. 5, pp. 137–8. In *Civilization and its Discontents* Freud comments on the "second instinct": "In abolishing private property we deprive the human love of aggression of one of its instruments, certainly a strong one, though certainly not the strongest; but we have in no way altered the differences in power and influence which are misused by aggressiveness, nor have we altered anything in its nature. Aggressiveness was not created by property." Ed. James Strachey (New York: Norton, 1961), pp. 60–1.

3 Although much criticism has been leveled against both Montesquieu and Diderot in recent years for being less egalitarian than they claim in their attitudes, both public and private, toward women, it seems to me essential to place their texts within the context of eighteenth-century social thought as well as that of contemporary feminist theory. The volume edited by Samia I. Spencer, *French Women and the Age of Enlightenment* (Bloomington, IN: University of Indiana Press, 1984), contains several pertinent critiques, including Pauline Kra, "Montesquieu and women" (pp. 272–84), and Blandine McLaughlin, "Diderot and women" (pp. 297–308). See also: Katharine M. Rogers, "Subversion of patriarchy in *Les Lettres persanes*," *Philological Quarterly* 65 (1986): 61–78; Rita Goldberg, *Sex and Enlightenment, Women in Richardson and Diderot* (Cambridge, UK: Cambridge University Press, 1984).

4 Lorenne M. G. Clark places Locke's arguments concerning women and property within the context of the value he attaches to private property and "the absolute right of the uncle to

pass his property to his rightful heirs." However, she does acknowledge that "it is to Locke's credit that he saw even the possibility of contractual marriage, which at least opens up the possibility of a co-equal relationship." "Women and Locke: who owns the apples in the garden of Eden?," in *The Sexism of Social and Political Theory* (Toronto: University of Toronto Press, 1979), pp. 16–40 (pp. 26, 27); ibid., p. 33.

5 John Locke, *Two Treatises of Government*, ed. Peter Laslett (Cambridge: Cambridge University Press, 1988), p. 313.

6 As Peter Laslett summarized it: "it is through the theory of property that men can proceed from the abstract world of liberty and equality based on their relationship with God and natural law, to the concrete world of political liberty guaranteed by political arrangements" (intro. to *Two Treatises*, p. 103).

7 "The next place of Scripture we find our A. builds his monarchy of Adam on is 3. gen. 16. And thy desire shalle be to thy Husband, and he shall rule over thee. Here we have, he says, the Original Grant of Government, from whence he concludes . . . that the Supreme Power is settled in the Fatherhood, and limited to one kind of Government, that is, to Monarchy." Locke contradicts Filmer, holding that "The Mother cannot be denied an equal share in begetting of the Child, and so the Absolute Authority of the Father will not arise from hence" (p. 198). Of course Locke negates supernatural paternal authority in order to substitute natural domination. This, however, is based on force, not duty, a not inconsiderable distinction. See also Susan Moller Okin, *Women in Western Political Thought* (Princeton, NJ: Princeton University Press, 1979), pp. 199–201, and, for a discussion of Locke's motivation in invoking the figure of the mother and comments on the cultural context of this issue in the Filmer/Locke debate, see Susan Staves, *Player's Scepters: Fictions of Authority in the Restoration* (Lincoln, NB: University of Nebraska Press, 1979), Ch. 3, "Sovereignty in the family," pp. 111–89, esp. pp. 140–4.

8 *Projet d'une Dîme royale* (s.l., 1716), p. 25.

9 *De la Renaissance à 1789*, ed. Jacques Dupâquier, Guy Cabourdin *et al.*, 4 vols (Paris: PUF, 1988), especially Jean-Claude Perrot, Ch. XI, "Les Economistes, les philosophes et la population."

10 Jean-Claude Perrot describes the process by which reliable statistical information was established showing an actual increase in population in Chs IV and V of *Histoire de la population française*, Vol. 2, *De la Renaissance à 1789*.

11 "After a calculation as exact as it is possible to have in such matters, I have found that there is scarcely one-tenth the number of men on the earth that there was in ancient times. What is astonishing is that it is depopulating every day and if this continues, in ten centuries it will be a wilderness." *Lettres persanes* (Paris: Garnier-Flammarion, 1964), pp. 179–80.

12 "Your wives are your furrows, says the Prophet. Come therefore unto your furrows, do good for the benefit of your soul, and you will be rewarded one day."

13 "It is to such a state of collapse that we are always reduced by this great number of wives, more likely to enervate us than satisfy us."

14 "What does the bridegroom need with so many mad virgins? Will people never realize they must narrow the door to this abyss where future races go to be destroyed?" *La Religieuse* (Paris: Garnier, 1968), p. 120.

15 "Thia, are you dreaming? You don't get pregnant; you are nineteen; you should have two children by now and you don't have any." *Supplément au voyage de Bougainville. Oeuvres complètes* (Paris: Garnier, 1954), p. 498.

16 "You wouldn't believe how much the idea of private or public wealth, linked in our minds to the idea of population, purifies our morals" (ibid., p. 485).

17 "The child being by itself an object of interest and of richness." "The more numerous the Tahitian's family, the richer it is" (ibid., p. 485).

18 "We didn't ask you for money, we didn't throw ourselves on your merchandise; we had contempt for your things: but our wives and our daughters came to extract the blood from your veins" (ibid., p. 500).

19 "wise enough to come to rest at the middle level" (ibid.).

20 "The most fruitful source of our depravity and of our woes?" "Through the tyranny of man, who has converted the possession of woman into property" (ibid., p. 509).

21 "They are my property and I offer them to you: they belong to themselves and they give themselves to you" (ibid., p. 476).

22 Georges Van Den Abbeele analyzes the "perverse economy" of Diderot's Tahiti, remarking that "we are not dealing with a free circulation 'd'hommes, de femmes et d'enfants,' but rather with a restricted economy of women and children, who circulate between nodal points geographically designated as 'cabanes' and gender designated as 'men.'" "Utopian sexuality and its discontents: exoticism and colonialism in the *Supplément au Voyage de Bougainville*," *Esprit créateur* 24, 1 (Spring, 1984): 43–52 (48). Bernard Papin comments: "De tous les despotismes, le despotisme paternel, ou plus généralement masculin, est décidément le moins insupportable aux yeux du père de madame de Vandeul." *Sens et fonction de l'utopie tahitienne dans l'oeuvre politique de Diderot*, Studies on Voltaire and the Eighteenth Century 251 (Oxford: the Voltaire Foundation, 1988), p. 157.

23 "The resistance offered by women has been consecrated; ignominy has been attached to the violence of men; violence that would be but a trivial insult in Tahiti becomes a crime in our cities." *Supplément au voyage de Bougainville*, p. 509.

24 That this notion is not unknown in the modern world is illustrated by a recent news item from Kenya where 71 schoolgirls were raped and 19 died at the hands of their fellow students. The *New York Times* reported the deputy principal as commenting: "The boys never meant any harm against the girls. They just wanted to rape" (July 29, 1991, p. A7). The idea that rape constitutes *harm* may be less of a rule in the history of the world than a modern Western anomaly.

25 "The man may momentarily use force on his fellow being since it's only a question of pleasure and not of property." *La Philosophie dans le boudoir* (Paris: Garnier, 1976), pp. 221–2.

9
Women and property in *ancien régime* France
Theory and practice in Dauphiné and Paris

Barbara B. Diefendorf

Before the reform of the French legal system begun during the Revolution and completed by Napoleon, there were literally hundreds of distinct bodies of customary law for northern France. Even in the areas of civil, or statutory, law in the south, there was much diversity because of the influence of local customs. Moreover, as with most legal systems, there was often considerable distance between the theory of the law and common practice, and, of course, there was change over time. A general essay on "Women and property in *ancien régime* France" thus threatens to founder under the weight of contradictory evidence or to sink entirely from the holes in its generalizations. At the same time, a narrowly specific case study will be less useful in the context of this volume than one that adopts a broader view of the problem of women's access to and management of property in pre-Revolutionary France. In an attempt to resolve these difficulties, I have chosen to incorporate a case study of the theory and practice of women's property rights in the province of Dauphiné into a broader comparative framework that draws largely upon previous research into the practice of customary law in the region of Paris.

This may seem an odd comparison: little Dauphiné, whose capital city of Grenoble had some 20,000 inhabitants in the eighteenth century, with the metropolis of Paris. Yet the disparities of size and wealth between the two regions are less important here than the contrasts between their legal systems, which represent well the respective traditions of civil and customary law, the civil law descending from Roman law versus the customary law deriving from local French practices. When the impoverished Dauphin Humbert II sold his independent domain to the kings of France in 1349, he made it a condition that Dauphiné retain its independent legal system. Raised to the status of Parlement in 1456, the high court of Grenoble prided itself on its fidelity to Roman law. At the same time, the Grenoble Parlement accepted as a natural consequence of its status as a sovereign court its right to differ from Roman law where the magistrates saw fit.[1] As in all statutory law regions, the jurisprudence of the Parlement of Grenoble thus became a unique blend of civil law and local practice.

Paris, by contrast, represents a relatively pure customary law tradition. There was of course some gradual accretion of Roman law through the Middle Ages, but those charged with codifying and revising the Paris Coutumier in the sixteenth century resisted most attempts of legal reformers to introduce new Roman law concepts and clung firmly to the principle that "the true test of the law is local practice."[2] Highly regarded by *ancien régime* jurists, the Paris Coutumier became a model against which other customary laws were measured, and it exerted an important influence on the Civil Code that is still today the law in France. (In tolerating the plurality of laws represented by these alternative legal systems, France was by no means unique; early modern England similarly used not only its common law, but also civil law traditions in the ecclesiastical courts that dealt with some matrimonial disputes and its own customary law in manorial courts where some property issues arising from marriage were litigated.)[3] Since Grenoble and Paris represent the two major theoretical and applied legal traditions of early modern France that affected property, a comparison between them can provide a relatively solid basis for generalization about women and property in *ancien régime* France.

Ideally this comparison should be carried out over a period of three centuries – from the legal humanism of the sixteenth century through the French Revolution and the adoption of a unified Civil Code in 1804. The mass of evidence that would need to be analyzed for a comparison of legal practice in two different areas over a period of three hundred years is, however, truly forbidding, and I feel obliged to point out the limits of my research. Unlike many of the chapters in this book my own is not part of a long-term project nearing completion but is rather an exploration intended to define a future area of research. Ever since completing my studies of marriage, family property, and widowhood in sixteenth-century Paris, I have wanted to return to these subjects in a broader comparative framework. Other research interests have kept me from doing so until recently, when the chance to spend a year in Grenoble, with its rich archives for the study of civil law and family history, allowed me to return to this continuing interest.

As I explored the potential sources for such a study in the archives of the Department of the Isère, I found they were even richer than I had anticipated. In addition to the notarial records – primarily marriage contracts and wills – that first came to mind for a project of this sort, I found that there is a wealth of information in the records of both Parlement and the common court of Grenoble. The common court in particular was intimately involved in family affairs. Its judges oversaw the reading of wills and partitioning of inheritances, they called family assemblies to name guardians for orphaned minors and to authorize the sale of the minors' property, and they approved the accounts presented by these guardians when the heirs came of age. The records of these transactions provide valuable clues to the assumptions people made about the rightful disposition of family properties. The records of Parlement plunge us into another aspect of this question by showing us contested inheritances. Through the books of pleas, we can read the arguments lawyers made as they defended their clients' claims to the properties of their relatives.[4] These sources go back to the sixteenth century, but they are most complete for the seventeenth and eighteenth. This chapter relies most heavily on eighteenth-century materials, but I have also sampled sources from the late sixteenth and seventeenth centuries to get an idea of how much things might have changed. Even within these limits, it has not been possible to make much of a dent in the enormous mass of potential sources, and my conclusions are necessarily tentative ones. The initial evidence suggests that family practices did not change dramatically between the sixteenth century and the end of the *ancien régime* and that there is rather a remarkable continuity throughout this period. Only a more thorough and systematic study than this one, however, could prove that this was indeed the case.

There are three sets of problems that interest me in studying women's access to and management of property in *ancien régime* France. They relate to the position of women in their family of birth, in their marriages, and in widowhood respectively. The first is the relationship between the share of a parent's properties that normally went to a daughter and the share that went to a son. The second is the relationship between husband and wife with regard to the properties they brought to their marriage or acquired during it – who controlled this property, and what claim might each make upon it? Third and last, what was the role of the widow with regard to the management of her own properties, those of her deceased spouse, and those of her children? I shall take up each of these questions in turn and in terms of both theory and practice.

Daughters and the parental properties

Let us begin with the question of the patrimony that female children received from their parents. Common wisdom tells us that the traditional time for daughters to receive their share of the parental properties was at their marriage. Too often, however, this has been taken to mean that daughters were "dowered off" at marriage with whatever funds their parents chose to give them and thereafter cut off from any further claim to the parental estate. This generalization applies better to statutory than to customary law regions, but it is not entirely accurate with regard to either of them. Unlike the English and American legal traditions to be discussed by Susan Staves in the next chapter, continental legal traditions, like Roman law, normally gave all children some rights to shares in property owned by their parents at the parents' death. In French, the child's share was called a *légitime*. While these rights could be forfeited by the child's notoriously bad conduct, the basic assumptions about children's entitlements were different in France than in England.

In Paris, after 1510, when the customary law was first codified, dowered daughters had the right to return to the parental succession, that is, they retained their entitlement to share in the inheritance from their parents, unless they explicitly renounced this right in their marriage contracts.[5] The study of notarial records suggests that practice did indeed conform to the law. In the sixteenth century, at least, it was very rare for daughters to renounce their rights to a future inheritance at the time of their marriage. Only two of the 180 contracts used for my studies of marriage involved the renunciation of future inheritances, and one of these contracts was voided less than a year later by the donor, who wished to recall the child to her succession.[6] The norm was for dowered children of both sexes to participate fully in the parental succession, at which time they returned the sums advanced in their marriage portions or deducted them from their share of the inheritance.[7] Study of inheritance practices among the Parisian elite corroborated this conclusion. I found a strong tendency to adhere to the spirit of the customary laws of the region, laws that prescribed that children should share equally in the non-noble assets of their parents.[8] Even in noble families, the daughters often fared well. The eldest son had special rights in any noble lands the family possessed, but the non-noble sources of wealth – bonds and urban real estate, for example – were divided evenly among the children. At least during the sixteenth century, there is little reason to believe that Parisian daughters were disposed of cheaply in favor of the sons.

In statutory law regions, by contrast, the daughter did usually renounce any further claims when she received the dowry (*dot*) promised in her marriage contract. She retained the right to claim an additional share of her parents' properties, if it later proved that the dowry was less than her *légitime*, or share of the reserve that the law guaranteed to the nearest heirs, and she might also be recalled to the parental successions through a special clause in the parent's will.[9] The wills of Dauphinois heads of households confirm, however, that daughters married by their families in Dauphiné usually did receive their share of the family estate at the time of their marriage, whereupon they renounced all further claims to the parental properties. Unless there was some major change in the testator's financial circumstances between the daughter's marriage and the time of drawing up the will, the bequest made to a married daughter in this will was usually a token amount – seldom more than 30 pounds (*livres*), even in wealthy families.[10]

These wills do not, however, suggest that daughters were in any way "sacrificed" in order to preserve the family's greatest wealth for its sons. Indeed, they suggest that the greatest effort was made to balance the needs of all members of the family.[11] We can see this most clearly in large families where some of the children were already married and others remained unmarried at the time the will was drawn up. The married children tended each to have received the same amount of money, regardless of sex, and if there was any favoritism shown it was as likely to be directed toward the children who remained unmarried and at home as to an eldest son. To cite just one example, in a will drawn up in 1774, Etienne Berthrand made bequests of 5 sous each to a married son and a married daughter, each of whom had already received 3,000 *livres* at marriage, and he left a like sum of 3,000 *livres* to his eldest son, described as "currently absent." The remainder of the estate was to be divided equally among three unmarried daughters. Berthrand further specified that if one of these daughters were to marry, her third of the properties was to be evaluated at 6,000 *livres* and paid within the year. The same would hold if a second married. If the third married, she too would receive 6,000 *livres*, and the balance of the estate would be divided equally among the three "universal heirs" (see below). The financial advantage, if there was one, was thus to a daughter who remained unmarried, perhaps because she would need the money to keep living in the manner to which she was accustomed without a husband to contribute to the household expenses. This does not explain why the portions given to the three universal heirs, even if they married, were to be double those of the already established children, but such favoritism was well within the spirit of testamentary liberty allowed in civil law.[12]

The tendency to treat sons and daughters equally, with the exception of the "universal heir" (the person or persons designated to receive the remainder of the estate once the legacies and debts were all paid), is particularly evident in the testaments of parents whose children were still young at the time the will was drawn up. Thus, for example, Jean Martinon, a lawyer in the Parlement of Grenoble, left bequests of 1,000 *livres* to each of his four sons and five daughters. Any children born later to the couple were to receive a like bequest. Martinon named his wife, Anne Peyelle, as his universal heir and charged her with passing on the estate to whichever one or two of the children she wished to name. He added that, if Peyelle died without naming a universal heir, his eldest son, Pierre, currently a student in Lyon, was to be so designated. Martinon insisted, however, that he did not intend in any way to limit Peyelle's freedom to choose among the children and named Pierre only so that the legal requirement to name a universal heir would be fulfilled.[13] Similarly, François Giroud, a nobleman and secretary to the king in the chancellory of the Parlement of Grenoble, left bequests of 8,000 *livres* each to four sons and four daughters. He named his wife as his universal heir and charged her with surrendering the estate at the time of her choice to whichever of the sons she cared to choose.[14]

Other testaments confirm that, at least among wealthy families, there was some tendency to favor sons over daughters as "universal heirs," but there was not a strong bias in favor of the eldest.[15] The testament of Alexandre Oronce de Galbert exemplifies this frame of thought. Galbert did not have any children at the time he drew up his will, so his estate-planning was an abstract exercise uninfluenced by the personalities and behavior of potential claimants to that estate. He specified that each of the children he might have by his marriage to Marie-Magdaleine de Charney was to receive 6,000 *livres* from his estate, and then he named as his universal heir whichever of his male children his wife might care to choose. If she did not name an heir, then his oldest son was to be chosen, but this was to happen only by default and not as the preferred means of naming the universal heir. Galbert further specified that, if he had only daughters, they were to divide the estate equally.[16]

Members of noble or wealthy non-noble families occasionally used the "substitution," a legal device through which properties were to pass from one designated heir to another in an order specified by the testator, to favor not only an eldest son but also his lineal descendants.[17] This seems to have been relatively rare in Dauphiné, however, and individuals who did want to favor the masculine heirs were more likely to name younger sons in order of seniority as successors to the eldest than they were to skip a generation and favor the eldest son's descendants. While there was thus some tendency to favor sons, and among sons to favor the eldest, these were not central elements in the successional practices of Dauphiné.[18] It appears, moreover, that the bias in favor of sons was less pronounced in artisanal and mercantile families than it was among nobles and royal officers,[19] but only a systematic quantitative study of testamentary practices in different social groups could demonstrate if this was in fact the case.

Finally, it should be noted that the universal heir was not in fact always favored financially, because he or she was the one who had to pay off all of the debts on the estate. These debts included the legacies or dowries payable to the other children, and, if the decedent left a widow, the return of her dowry, and the increase in her dowry, or the payment of her pension or legacy. More than one universal heir discovered that there were so many charges against the inheritance that the portion that remained after the debts were paid was smaller than those received by the children who had earlier been given dowries.[20]

Husbands and wives

Any discussion of a woman's property rights during marriage inevitably revolves around the problem of her legal incapacity. A married woman was under the authority of her husband. He was, in the words of one of Grenoble's seventeenth-century barristers, "her head, her eye, her guardian, and her master."[21] Any legal actions she undertook without his explicit consent were null and void. The husband administered his wife's properties and in some areas could even dispose of them without her consent. There were certain exceptions to this incapacity. Some statutory law regions – Dauphiné was one of them – accepted the Roman law tradition that allowed women to administer non-dotal properties, and in certain areas women could have it written into their marriage contracts that they retained the right to administer even the properties that they brought to their husband in marriage. In some areas, women could also be qualified as *marchandes publiques*, a quality that allowed them validly to contract in matters relating to the trade they practiced. (Similarly, English law allowed certain married women to conduct trade independently of their husbands as *feme sole* traders.) On the whole, however, such exceptions were rare. The principle of women's legal incapacity seems to have been so thoroughly implanted in *ancien régime* France that the husband's permission for the alienation of his wife's property was almost always included in legal contracts, even in cases where it might not have been technically required.[22]

These rules did change over time. Some forward-looking commercial areas struggled against the older restrictions and gradually dismantled them, so that women would have more freedom to use their assets to further their husbands' business interests. By the late seventeenth century, the inhabitants of the Lyonnais had freed themselves of most of the laws that restricted the sale of dotal properties and rendered women legally incapable. The precocity of the Lyonnais in this regard was, however, unusual.[23]

Ancien régime jurists tended to justify women's legal incapacity on the ground of the inherently weak, frivolous, and light-headed nature of the female sex, but behind this apparent misogyny was a more fundamental assumption that the legal incapacity of women was a necessary adjunct to the marital and paternal authority of the head of the household. André Tiraqueau, whose treatise on the "laws of marriage" is peppered with statements that would outrage most twentieth-century women, nonetheless rests his argument on the essential premise that married women were legally incapable because they were married and not because they were women.[24] Guy Coquille, in a commentary on the customary law, came to the same conclusion. No one doubted, observed Coquille, that an unmarried woman who had reached the age of majority could assume legal obligations; rather, "it was the authority of the husband that prevented her from contracting."[25]

The need for marital authority must in turn be seen in the context of the fundamental structures of society in *ancien régime* France. The household, like the state, was hierarchical, and, like the state, could have only one head. Indeed, the same principle of hierarchical authority that gave the husband dominion over his wife during his lifetime allowed the widow to step into the role of the head of the household upon his death, and so, as we shall see, gave widows extensive rights to manage not only their own properties but also those of their deceased spouse and their children.[26]

Furthermore, the same laws that limited women's capacity to dispose of their properties served to protect these properties against dispersion through mismanagement on the part of the husband. The properties a woman brought in marriage were intended to help support her in widowhood, as well as to help pay the costs of the common household, and strict laws regulated the husband's right to dispose of these properties. In Grenoble, as in most civil law areas, a woman's dotal properties could only be alienated if the husband was unable to support his family and the alienation was necessary to feed and care for its members.[27]

In Paris, on the other hand, as in most other customary law areas, the division of the dowry into two distinct categories proved a means of resolving the tension between the need to provide for the common household and the need to protect the wife's patrimony. The marriage contract specified which of the assets the wife brought to the marriage were intended to help support the common costs of the household (her contribution to the marital *communauté*) and which were to be regarded as lineage properties (*propres*) that returned to her on widowhood or passed on to her nearest blood relations. The husband had full authority over the community properties; he could invest them or dispose of them as he pleased. He could not, however, alienate his wife's lineage properties without her consent, and even with her consent he was normally required to reinvest the proceeds of the alienation in assets that would henceforth acquire the status of lineage properties belonging to her and her heirs. (English common law treated land women brought into marriage or land they inherited while married as though it were similarly lineage property, allowing husbands to enjoy the profits from the land during their lives but then having the wife's land revert to her or to her family after the husband's death.)

A woman of modest background might enter everything she possessed into the marital community, but a wealthy woman was not allowed to bring only lineage properties to the marriage. It was considered essential that a woman (or a woman's relatives or friends on her behalf) contribute to the community funds. As a seventeenth-century guide for notaries explained the situation, a man could declare all of his possessions *propres* and exempt them from the community of goods if he chose, because he contributed to the community through his labor. On the other hand, a woman (her labor apparently being presumed to have no economic value) was ordinarily expected to enter at least a quarter if not a third of her assets as community property.[28] If she had no cash or personal property, a portion of her real property was declared personal property (*meubles*) by convention, so that the husband might have free disposition of it.

Although one might be tempted to say that the dotal system as practiced in Grenoble was more favorable to women than the community property system because it protected all of the property that a woman brought to a marriage, as opposed to only those assets that had explicitly been declared lineage properties, it must be recognized that these very protections – the prohibition on selling a wife's dotal properties – could hinder a family's ability to meet its economic requirements. The dotal system had developed to suit the needs and values of a landed aristocracy. It served quite well if the wife's dowry consisted largely of lands and investments, and if the husband and wife could enjoy the profits from these assets without ever needing to sell them. It was ill-adapted, however, to the economic needs of the mercantile classes, which required ready capital for investment and expansion. I have already noted that forward-looking commercial areas like the Lyonnais chafed under the legal restrictions that prevented women from using their assets to further their husbands' businesses, and gradually they dismantled these restrictions. Even so, the community property system, by allowing for both liquidity and stability, proved better suited than the dotal system to the needs of a changing society. It is not surprising that it was the community property system that triumphed in the Civil Code.

Widows and the family properties

The important administrative role assumed by widows contrasts sharply with the legal incapacity of married women and bears out the truth of the statement that married women were incapable because they were married and not because they were women. Before looking at the role that widows played in the management of their own and other people's properties, however, we need to understand the laws that governed the widow's economic rights on the death of her husband.

The Parisian widow had the right to the return of her lineage properties. She also received one-half of the community properties; the other half was divided among the husband's nearest heirs. In addition, she had a subsistence right that allowed her to claim the lifetime usage of certain lineage properties of her husband. The customary law allowed her the usufruct of one-half of her husband's lineage properties as her dower right (*douaire*), but a larger or smaller amount could be specified in the marriage contract. A woman whose marriage contract specified a fixed dower could not claim the customary dower unless this option was explicitly stated in the contract. The customary dower always returned to the husband's heirs on the widow's death; the fixed dower might be acquired by her in full property and pass on to her heirs. It all depended on the conventions specified in the marriage contract. Similarly, the customary dower right did not cease with remarriage (although a woman could be deprived of her dower for adultery or debauchery), but marriage contracts sometimes specified a reduction in the fixed dower if the widow married again.

The widow was permitted to renounce her share of the community property if she pleased. This right, originally permitted to noblewomen in order to free them from ransoms or other obligations contracted by husbands who went off to war, was extended to commoners in the sixteenth century. Commentators on the customary law explained the right to renounce the community property as a counterbalance to the wife's incapacity during marriage. Having had no say in the success or failure of the joint economic enterprise, she was free to disclaim the fruits or losses of her husband's labors. In the eyes of some commentators, these privileges benefited the wife unduly; she did not share in the risks her husband took but stood only to gain. This is something of a misconstruction, because a woman who renounced her community property rights stood to lose all of the community property that she had contributed to the marriage. The purpose of the rule was to prevent the wife's lineage properties from also being engulfed in the husband's losses.[29]

In statutory law regions, the laws regarding women's property rights at the dissolution of marriage worked very differently. There was no community property, and the widow was entitled to the return of all of the properties she had brought her husband in marriage (her dowry, or *dot*). The widow was also entitled to claim an additional amount (*augment*) specified by the husband in the marriage contract. The *augment* was normally set at one-third of the *dot* for commoners and one-half for nobles, but it did not exist by right in the way the *douaire* of the customary law regions existed and had to be specified in the marriage contract if it was later to be claimed.[30]

In practice, as we shall see, many widows in statutory law regions renounced the right to claim their *dot* and *augment* in favor of a testamentary bequest offered as an alternative by the husband. This was also sometimes the case in customary law regions, but less frequently. In the civil law tradition, the freedom of the testator was a cherished liberty.[31] In customary law regions, on the other hand, an individual's right to determine the disposition of his or her properties after death was strictly limited; even wealthy people often left their estates to be divided according to the rules of intestate succession. In Parisian law, for example, a person could dispose freely of all personal properties and acquired real properties but only one-fifth of all lineage properties (*propres*). The remainder had to be divided among the nearest blood kin according to the customary rules of succession. If the husband's wealth was largely inherited, as was so often the case in the *ancien régime*, he had only a limited ability to favor his wife with a testamentary bequest, and she was probably better off claiming her dowry and dower rights than accepting a bequest, even if one was offered.

Parisian law did allow for two circumstances under which a couple might seek to improve the financial circumstances of the party eventually left widowed. If there were no surviving children, the husband and wife were allowed to make a mutual donation (*don mutuel*) of the usufruct of all personal properties and acquired real properties left by the decedent. Couples with children were forbidden to make such a donation, but they were allowed to write a special clause into the marriage contracts of their children that forbade the division of the community property of the parents' marriage as long as one parent was still living and did not remarry.

My studies of the sixteenth-century Parisian elite suggested that both of these practices were commonly employed. In fact, some parents went beyond these limits and inserted clauses into their children's marriage contracts that allowed a widowed parent to maintain all or part of the lineage properties of the deceased spouse as well as the community property and assets acquired during the marriage. Even when there were no explicit agreements to this effect, it appears to have been possible for a surviving parent to continue to administer the properties of a deceased parent long after the children of the marriage had come of age.[32] These practices were also found by Jacques Le Lièvre in his study of notarial practice in late eighteenth-century Paris. Le Lièvre points out that the clauses by which parents had their children promise that they would not make any claims to the parental succession until both parents had died violated the law and would not have stood up in court, but, he adds, "the notaries seem to count on the good faith and loyalty of the dowered children."[33]

A husband who wished to avoid the customary partition of his properties at death in order to leave all or most of these properties in the hands of his widow could have had two principal motives for this wish. The first was to allow the widow to live in the same style and manner as she had during his lifetime; the second was to allow her the management of his estate for the benefit of his eventual heirs. Both motives, singularly or together, seem to have been important to Parisian husbands, but it is the second motive in particular that shows the faith these husbands reposed in the common sense and managerial skills of their wives. Sometimes this faith was expressed explicitly, as it was by the famous chancellor Michel de l'Hôpital, who made his wife the administrator of his estate by his will, even though his only child was a married woman in her thirties at the time. L'Hôpital stated in his will that he was confident that his wife's management would be to the profit of his heirs, and he forbade them to ask her to account for her stewardship.[34] In other cases this faith was implicit in the husband's nomination of his wife as the executor of his estate and the guardian of his children.

The widow was the preferred guardian of her minor children under Parisian law.[35] She could be excluded from the guardianship only for serious reasons or if the father had named another guardian in his testament, neither of which situations appears to have occurred with any frequency. If she was not yet of age herself, or if she remarried, a co-guardian had to be appointed, but this co-guardian could even be the new spouse.[36] As the children's guardian, the widow assumed official responsibility for their legal and financial affairs. In addition to administering the properties due them from the estate of their father, she was responsible for their education and preparation for a career or marriage. As the husband's executor, she was responsible for collecting monies owed him, paying his creditors, carrying out the charitable and religious bequests promised in his will, and seeing to the proper devolution of the remainder of his estate.

A study of notarial practice in Dauphiné reveals a similar tendency for men to entrust their widows with administrative and financial responsibilities that go far beyond what one might expect to find from the study of the law alone or from the prevailing discourse about the fragile and flighty nature of the female sex. The key document for Dauphinois practice was the last will and testament, a document that one seventeenth-century Grenoblois jurist described as a man's self-portrait, an opportunity to immortalize himself and his wishes beyond the tomb, and a "mirror of his life and actions."[37] With a frequency that is perhaps surprising, this "mirror" reflects the widow as the agent of her husband's immortality and the individual chosen to execute his wishes beyond the tomb.

There were several ways in which a husband might convey these responsibilities to his widow in his will. He could simply charge her with the administration of his properties until his legal heirs, his children, came of age. In this case, he also usually named her in his will as his children's guardian, but even if he did not, as long as he did not explicitly name another guardian, she was given this responsibility. As in Parisian law, the law of Dauphiné made the widow the guardian of choice for her minor children.[38] She could decline this responsibility if she chose, but in practice she rarely did, except in cases in which her own legal actions against her husband's estate made it best to assign someone else to look out for the interests of the children and heirs. Even in this case, it was possible for her to retain custody of the children and the broad direction of their affairs, except for those areas where her interests and those of the children might come into conflict.[39] A widow who remarried had to have a family assembly called to appoint a new guardian, but in fact the widow herself might be reappointed, in company with or exclusive of her new husband.[40]

In fact, fathers in Dauphiné commonly went beyond naming their wife as guardian of the children and administrator of their properties. They willed her the bulk of their estate by naming her as their universal heir. Indeed, this action occurs so frequently that it is a striking characteristic of Dauphinois testamentary practice, and one entirely overlooked by historians who study only legislative texts. I found this practice to be particularly common in cases in which there were young children in the family at the time the will was written. Naming his wife as his universal heir, the husband charged his widow with raising the children and insuring their education out of the funds left at his death. She was then to establish them appropriately through marriage and pro- fessional placement. In most cases, the husband specified the dowry he wanted paid on the daughter's marriage or the son's establishment. He further specified that when the children were all adult, at the wife's death, or at a moment she was free to choose, she was to pass on the estate to one or more chosen heirs.[41]

Sometimes this heir was named in the husband's will; more often the widow was left the responsibility for this choice. This was a deliberate tactic on the part of the husband and was designed to insure the children's obedience to their mother and their acquies- cence to her ultimate decision about how to dispose of the estate. Etienne Ducros explicitly instructed his wife to name as heir, in whole or in part, the son or daughter who proved "most submissive" to her.[42] Jean du Vache went still further. Asking his wife to choose which of their three married daughters should be named the universal heir, he stipulated that if any of the daughters should dispute the mother's choice, she was immediately to lose any advantages that had been offered her and be reduced to the portion that the parents could not by law deny her. The property she would have received was to be divided among the daughters who had "acquiesced to the testator's wishes."[43]

Not all husbands, of course, chose this practice. If the husband and wife were very old, he might prefer to give her an annual pension. To insure further her well-being, he might charge his universal heir with seeing that the widow was well cared for.[44] In some cases the husband even specified exactly what personal properties his widow was to enjoy on his decease – typically a bed, bedroom furniture, household linens, and silverware. The solution of a pension was also sometimes chosen in other circumstances – for example, by men whose only children and eventual heirs were born of a previous marriage, or by royal officers who felt the need to consolidate their holdings to promote the social ascension of a son – but it does not appear to have occurred nearly as often as the institution of the wife as the universal heir.[45]

Still less frequent was the simple return to the wife of her dowry and *augment*. Nearly every man who had a living wife at the time that he drew up his will made some sort of special provision for her in this will, even if he also left her the alternative of demanding her dowry and *augment* (as he had to do by law).[46] The reason for this is clear. After years of marriage, the husband's properties and those of his wife were often thoroughly confounded. To sort out her properties, the income due from them, and the charges against them was a complicated and potentially expensive process. It required the drawing up of inventories, the evaluation of repairs and improvements, and consul- tations with notaries or lawyers. If the couple had children and their properties were eventually to pass to the same heirs, why bother to sort them out for the widow? A pension could provide just as well for her needs – perhaps better – and with infinitely less complication and expense. Even when there were no children, however, the husband often named his wife as his universal heir.[47]

Although one reason for this practice was to permit the wife to maintain her accustomed style of living through widowhood, the nomination of the wife as universal heir could be fraught with financial hazards. If the husband was a spendthrift and deeply in debt, the widow might have been better off renouncing the inheritance and withdrawing her dowry and *augment*. If the husband's properties and wife's properties were tangled together, however, this was not always a practical solution. Besides, if there were children, the widow had also to consider their best interests. To reclaim her dowry and *augment* might pose an impossible burden for the remaining heirs.[48] A merchant's or artisan's widow might have little choice but to continue to try to run her husband's business after his death, because this was the only possible way to preserve – or to create – some sort of income for herself and her children. This was the argument that Luce Ritton made when she asked for custody of her five children and administration of their estate after her husband, a baker, died intestate. The husband had left very little property, Ritton explained in the custody hearing, and if she were to reclaim what was due her the bakery would have to be sold, which would leave her no way of providing a living for the family. As the children's guardian and administrator, she would be able to continue to work the shop, as she had done since her husband's death.[49]

Barbe Chazel was in a similar situation, although it was not immediately apparent when her husband, Pierre Acloque, made her his universal heir and left her his inn and catering business in Vienne. Acloque's will specified that Chazel was eventually to pass the estate to the couple's daughter, Jeanne. She was also required to pay legacies of 2,000 *livres* each to Acloque's three sons by a previous marriage when they came of age or established themselves in a career. Alternatively, if the sons chose to leave Chazel's household when their apprenticeships were finished, she was to pay them a stipend of 50 *livres* a year. Apparently all three sons did leave the household as soon as they were able, and for several years Chazel paid the stipends that were due them. Then, claiming that she could not afford the annual payments because of other debts with which the estate was burdened, Chazel stopped paying the stipends. In revenge, one of the sons invoked a clause in his father's will that stipulated that if Chazel sought to diminish the sons' inheritance rights in any way she was to forfeit her own claims to his estate. This dispute ended in a settlement, but when Jeanne Acloque married she and her husband revived the issue of her paternal inheritance, contending that her share of the estate had been unfairly diminished by the agreement between her mother and her stepbrothers. The documents produced in the ensuing lawsuit reveal the condition of the estate that Chazel had inherited. Pierre Acloque had left properties worth 24,667 *livres*, including the inn valued at 18,000 *livres*, but his outstanding debts had totaled 25,579 *livres*.[50] Jeanne Acloque's chances of enjoying her paternal inheritance had thus been entirely dependent upon Barbe Chazel's ability to pay off the debts left by her husband and make the inn function successfully. Perhaps this would have been possible, had she had the active cooperation of Acloque's three grown, or nearly grown, sons, but apparently the incentive offered the sons – 2,000 *livres* when they turned 26 – was not sufficient to convince them to continue to work on their stepmother's and stepsister's behalf. Without their help, it is not surprising that Chazel found herself sinking under the mass of debts her husband had left her.[51]

If we look at practice rather than theory, then, we can see that French widows exercised considerable economic power and administrative responsibility with regard to their young during the *ancien régime*. Not that the widow's situation should necessarily be seen in a favorable light. The husband's estate might well be burdened with debt, or it might be too small to support a numerous progeny without the father's daily labor. Nevertheless, it is significant that, in both Paris and Dauphiné, husbands often chose to provide for their wives in ways that went beyond the strict limits of the law. They chose to do this both because of the personal bond between them and because of the conviction that this was in the best interests of their children and heirs.

Women's wills

If a man's last will and testament was "a mirror of his life and actions," a woman's, too, was her self-portrait. Unlike English women, who, at common law, could make wills only with their husband's permission, for French women the power to make a will was one exception to the legal incapacity of the married woman. This was permitted on the ground that the will would not be carried out until after the woman's death, and, as such, until after the marriage was dissolved. What use did French women make of the testamentary liberty that they, like their husbands, enjoyed?

One might argue that a strong-minded husband could pressure his wife into leaving her property in ways that worked to the husband's advantage. This could, of course, happen. The ability to write a completely secret testament, a *"testament mystique,"* nevertheless worked against this sort of pressure. This secrecy could be used to revoke a will previously written at the husband's wishes; it could also be used explicitly to deny the husband any access to the properties left in his wife's estate.[52] It is unlikely, however, that most husbands had to use threats and blandishments to convince their wives to favor them in their wills. The study of common practice suggests that this favoritism was most often the product of a natural and reciprocal wish on the part of both husbands and wives.

Examination of testamentary practice suggests that women in Dauphiné made their husbands their universal heirs with approximately the same frequency as they were named universal heirs by their husbands. One difference, however, is that if there were unmarried children at the time the will was drawn up, there was less tendency on the part of the wife to specify the amount to be given to the children upon their marriage or establishment in careers. A woman was more likely to leave such matters to the discretion of her husband. She was also less likely than he to name the child who should become the universal heir on the spouse's death. This choice too was usually left to the husband's discretion. If the couple had no children, however, she was just as likely as he to say which of the collateral relatives – most often nieces and nephews – she wished to name as her eventual heir. In such circumstances, women were usually careful to specify that the husband's enjoyment of their properties throughout his lifetime was not to be hampered in any way by the eventual claims of the collateral heirs.[53] In some cases, they also gave the husband the authority later to adjust the legacies and nomination of heirs according to his best judgment.[54]

Moreover, women seem to have been neither more nor less likely than men to divide their properties evenly among their children rather than to name a universal heir.

Women, though, may have favored female heirs. If so, this is not a strong pattern, and only a quantitative study of inheritance patterns could determine its significance.[55] In any event, it is clear that women took full advantage of the testamentary liberty the law allowed them. In fact, one woman, named by her husband as his universal heir on the condition of passing on the estate at her death to one or more of their common descendants, made such active use of her right to choose which of their children should eventually receive the joint estate that she provoked a suit in Parlement to determine just which one of the three successive wills she had made should be considered valid. Surprisingly, the case was not initiated by a disgruntled heir but rather by a lawyer in Parlement who was "very disturbed" that the widow could prove so fickle as to rewrite her will every few years. Parlement upheld this right, however, ruling that by the terms of the husband's testament, the widow was to have full freedom throughout her lifetime to make her choice of heirs, and that her first nominations were not definitive if she subsequently changed her mind.[56]

Two sets of conclusions seem appropriate here. First, I have some suggestions about further research that needs to be done in order to understand how women managed the properties they possessed. Second, in keeping with the theme of this volume, it seems important to conclude by abandoning my pragmatic insistence on seeking out what families actually did with their properties in order to ask what broader "conceptions of property" underlay their behavior.

Some suggestions regarding further research

The contrast between the legal incapacity of married women and the relative autonomy of widows in at least some parts of *ancien régime* France raises important questions about the role of women in the family economy. Since it does not seem reasonable to assume that women were thrust totally unprepared into the important administrative tasks they assumed as widows, we need to look more closely at their roles as wives. Evidence from the families of the Parisian elite suggests that it was not uncommon for the husband virtually to abandon the day-to-day administration of the family's financial affairs to his wife.[57] The level of responsibility this could entail is well illustrated by a letter from a Parisian woman, Anne Baillet, to her daughter-in-law, Jeanne Luillier. These women were the widow and wife respectively of officers of the sovereign courts. Asking Jeanne to check up on her estates when she went out to the country to visit her own properties, Anne Baillet specified that Jeanne should oversee the winemaking, inspect some construction work in progress, meet with the principal tenants, interview new tenants, lease out the wine presses, insure that the laws against poaching were being enforced, compile inventories of personal properties, and draw up lists of the deserving poor on the estates.[58] The list is impressive, but it raises as many questions as it answers. Was this typical of the Parisian officer milieu, and did women elsewhere in France or in different social groups – the wives of the old nobility, for example – assume comparable responsibilities? We might also want to ask at what economic level families began to employ specialized agents to manage their financial affairs, and what was the relationship between these agents and the wives or widows whose families they served? What role did notaries play as advisors or financial counselors to widowed women?

At lower social levels, we must recognize that most women contributed to the family economy either by working at their own trade or through the assistance they offered in their husband's shop, and we must learn more about the conditions under which women worked and the ability they had to generate an income independent of their husbands' work. At what level were women in mercantile or artisanal families involved in the day-to-day operations of the husband's business? How prepared were they to take over the management of the shop if he died, and how often were they able to do this? Articles by Olwen Hufton, Natalie Davis, and, most recently, James Collins make an important start at answering these questions, but much remains to be done.[59] Admittedly, the sources for such research are problematic ones. Information on women and work can only be gathered piecemeal, from stray references in documents written for other purposes. It is particularly difficult to find information on women's work roles during marriage, because their legal incapacity makes them invisible in most legal records.

However difficult, it is worth pursuing these questions, even if we can only do this by patiently accumulating individual references while pursuing other subjects and themes. It is also worth investigating further the way that widows managed their own and their husband's properties once they received them. We need to seek out inventories that will show us a family's financial affairs at the death of the husband and later at the death of the wife. How much change does the husband's death bring about in his wife's standard of living, and is this change immediate or gradual? Is it the result of the division of property outlined in his will, or the result of a long-term decline in earning power? We must also ask about the widow's management of the estate she receives. How much change does she make in the sorts of assets the family holds? Does she tend to invest in annuities rather than real estate?[60] Is she more or less likely than her husband to loan out money to private parties? To borrow money from private parties? Lower court records can also provide revealing glimpses into women's work and their role in managing family finances. The creditors who turn up in court when a woman's estate is divided, for example, seem to include a disproportionately high number of female tradesmen – *marchandes de la mode*, *lingères*, and others described simply as "*marchandes*." Were female shopkeepers somehow forced by their marginal position to extend credit more often than men or to be less regularly paid?

Having discovered that women, at least when widowed, had a more independent and active role in the management of family finances than might have been expected, we need next to ask just what they did with this money once they had it. We also need to look at regional variations in these patterns. We cannot expect that women in progressive commercial communities like Lyon played the same economic role as women in the more traditional farming communities of Upper Provence. But just where along the spectrum from tradition to modernity do we place the women of Dauphiné or Paris? We cannot know until considerably more work has been done.

If I were to guess at the general outcome of such research, my prediction would be that further investigation will confirm that, on the whole, women in *ancien régime* France had a significantly greater measure of responsibility, autonomy, and equality within the family than has generally been assumed. This is not by any means to say that *ancien régime* France was egalitarian in its gender relations – most certainly, it was not – but rather to caution that we must be wary of painting gender relations in colors that are too stark. The image that we get from legal treatises and literary sources needs to be nuanced by the study of sources that bring us closer to the realities of family life in the *ancien régime*.

Conceptions of property in *ancien régime* France

Let us turn, however, from the question of what people actually did with their property to ask what broader conceptions of property and property rights guided their behavior. I have described in this chapter two distinct legal systems, one derived from the Roman, or civil law, tradition, and another derived from local practices, or customary law. If we look beyond the differences that characterize the two traditions, we can nevertheless delineate certain key premises common to both. These commonalities, I would venture, allowed the two systems to coexist – and even to interact fruitfully – throughout the *ancien régime*, each insisting upon the superiority of its own roots, while retaining a respect for local particularity.

As I see it, there were two complementary and often competing conceptions of property at play in the laws and practices that governed the use and transfer of possessions in the families of *ancien régime* France. The first was the conception of lineage property, which embodied the notion that one was less the owner of an asset than its custodian, privileged with its use but responsible for passing it on intact to one's descendants. The second conception was closer to our own notion of private property and allowed an individual great freedom in the use and disposition of his or her assets.

Readers familiar with Emmanuel Le Roy Ladurie's essay on "Family structure and inheritance customs in sixteenth-century France" may assume that I am going to go on to link the notion of lineage property with inheritance customs that favored a vertical conception of the family – one that flowed down from parent to child over the generations – and the notion of individual property to inheritance customs that favored a horizontal conception of the family – one created by and incarnated in the bonds of marriage.[61] I am not. Although there is a kernel of truth to this generalization, it leads not only to oversimplification but also to some badly misplaced assumptions about family priorities and values. In fact, the concepts of lineage and individual property in *ancien régime* France cannot be tidily separated. In both customary and civil law regions, the two concepts coexisted and overlapped. Under optimal conditions, they worked in complementary fashion to allow families to balance the needs of the current generation against the desire to preserve and extend the patrimony for generations to come. Under less optimal conditions, they entered into competition and provided the stuff of family quarrels and the fuel for costly lawsuits.

Their complementarity is perhaps best seen in the distinction made in customary law regions between the lineage properties and the community properties that a woman brought to marriage. The community properties were intended to serve the immediate needs of the household set up by the marriage, and the husband could dispose of them quite freely. The wife or her heirs might claim half of the community properties when the marriage was dissolved, but this eventual claim did not in any way hinder the husband's free use of them during the marriage. The lineage properties, by contrast, were intended to pass intact to the wife in widowhood or to her direct heirs, and the husband's freedom to dispose of his wife's lineage properties was consequently hedged about with restrictions. Indeed, as a guarantee of the wife's lineage property rights, the husband's own lineage properties were considered mortgaged in the same amount. In practice, this meant that his freedom to dispose of his own lineage properties was also limited.

This distinction between lineage and community properties was not made in civil law areas, but the principle of protecting the wife's dotal properties was nevertheless very strong. Except in extreme circumstances, the husband subject to a civil law regime could not dispose of *any* of his wife's dotal properties. At the same time, it was precisely in the civil law regions that a man had the greatest freedom to dispose of his own inherited or acquired properties, especially by testamentary bequest. Because of the complete separation of the properties of husband and wife, and because of the testamentary freedom allowed by the civil law, it is easy to leap to the conclusion that the underlying concept of property in civil law regions closely resembles our own notion of private property and at the same time contrasts radically with the conception of lineage property that is found in customary law regions. And it is true that lineage thinking is rather less pronounced in the south of France, where the civil law reigned supreme. We do not, for example, find here the laws that insured in customary law regions that the lineage properties of one spouse should never pass to the blood kin of the other spouse, unless it was to their common descendants. Nor, for the most part, do we find the *retrait lignager* that allowed blood relatives of an individual who alienated his or her lineage properties to buy them back for the price of the sale.

Civil law regions, however, were far from immune to the logic of lineage. The *légitime* that allowed children to claim a share of their parents' property, their right alternatively to claim the dower promised their mother, as well as the protections accorded the woman's dowry – all these spoke to the desire to protect the interests of the next generation by defining property rights in familial and not merely individual terms. Even the famous testamentary liberty of the civil law was conceived largely as a means of permitting a father to choose how best to use the patrimony to promote his family's fortunes in the generations to come.

The institution of the family assembly, formally convened by the magistrates to decide on matters of property that belonged by right to minor children, also attests to the importance of the notion of lineage property in civil as well as customary law areas. It is worth noting, for example, that even the patriarchal father of southern France, a father whom we tend to imagine reigning despotically over the tiny kingdom of his family, did not have the right to dispose of his deceased wife's properties even for the benefit of his children, the legitimate heirs to the property, without calling a family assembly to approve the sale. Take the case of Jean Bernard, a businessman in Grenoble, whose wife had died leaving two houses as the common property of the couple's four daughters. One of the daughters was married, and her husband, also a businessman, wanted to have the money for his wife's share of the houses, rather than a split title to the properties and a periodic income. Bernard agreed that, for his other daughters as well, ready money would make a more attractive dowry than a share of two houses, but before he could sell the houses he had to gather together representatives of both his and his wife's families to get their permission for the sale.[62] Another

Grenoblois father went to court to get permission to use the 600 *livres* income his son received from his maternal inheritance to pay for the son's upkeep and nourishment, the father's own resources being insufficient to this task.[63] We tend to think that legal protections accorded minors are something progressive and new, but in fact they were very much present in the *ancien régime*. The difference is that then it seems to have been only the property and not the person that was protected – a father could beat his children, but he could not touch their properties.

These same protections to the property of minors afforded a husband in civil law regions a very strong reason for naming his wife as his universal heir. This was in fact the most effective way to give her the freedom to manage the family's properties after his own death without having to make appeal to a court and a family council every time she turned around. In fact, as I have argued, there was a tendency in both civil and customary law regions to give a surviving spouse more control of the properties of the deceased spouse than the letter of the law – or at least intestate practice – allowed. The means for accomplishing this were different: in customary law regions, it was done primarily by postponing the division of the decedent's estate; in civil law regions, by testamentary nomination. But the end result and, I believe, the intentions were the same. They were to provide for the surviving partner in widowhood but also, and perhaps most importantly, to insure the best interests of the descendants and ultimate heirs. The horizontal and longitudinal bonds of family may appear distinct and separable if we take a structuralist view of the law; in practice this simply was not the case.

In fact, the most surprising result of my research for this chapter was the discovery of how often husbands in Dauphiné not only named their wives as their universal heirs but also made the wife responsible for choosing which child should ultimately receive a privileged share of the estate. This went directly against the grain of the inheritance practices that were familiar to me from my research on the Parisian elite – practices that mandated equality among children except for the special rights of the eldest son – but it was especially surprising for its seeming contradiction of the secondary and limited role that women were said to play in family affairs, especially in the patriarchal south. In the end, however, I have to see this very prerogative of naming the heir as a logical consequence of the patriarchal family of *ancien régime* France. It was the surest means for the husband to pass on his full authority to the one who would become head of the household on his decease.

Notes

1   T. A. Sabatery, *Précis de la jurisprudence du Parlement de Grenoble réduite aux questions qui peuvent se présenter encore, extraite des auteurs imprimés, des meilleurs recueils manuscrits et principalement de celui de M. Piat-Desvial* (Grenoble: 1825), pp. iii and vii.

2   The quotation is from Etienne Pasquier, *Lettres*, in his *Oeuvres* (Amsterdam: 1723), Book 6, letter 2. More generally, see François Olivier-Martin, *Histoire de la coutume de la prévôté et vicomté de Paris*, 2 vols (Paris: E. Leroux, 1922–30), Vol. 1, pp. 58–67, and René Filhol, *Le Premier Président Christofle de Thou et la réformation des coutumes* (Paris: Recueil Sirey, 1937), pp. 127–37.

3   See Susan Staves, *Married Women's Separate Property in England, 1660–1833* (Cambridge, MA, and London: Harvard University Press, 1990), pp. 18–25.

188 Barbara B. Diefendorf

4   A large number of pleas were eventually published and are available in the Bibliothèque municipale de Grenoble (hereafter, BMG). The more important mass, however, exists in unpublished form in the records of Parlement (B series) of the Archives départementales de l'Isère (hereafter, ADI).

5   My summary comments on laws relating to women's property in the customary law of the Paris region are largely drawn from the discussion of this subject in Barbara Diefendorf, *Paris City Councillors: The Politics of Patrimony* (Princeton, NJ: Princeton University Press, 1983), pp. 222–31 and 253–61. An excellent comparative study of the right to return to the parental succession in customary law is Jean Yver, *Egalité entre héritiers et exclusion des enfants dotés* (Paris: Sirey, 1966). See especially pp. 15–23 regarding the development of this privilege in the Parisian law.

6   Barbara B. Diefendorf, "Widowhood and remarriage in sixteenth-century Paris," *Journal of Family History* 7 (1982): 379–405 (383–4).

7   The laws concerning the return of these properties are set out in Charles-Antoine Bourdot de Richebourg, *Nouveau coutumier général* (Paris: 1724), Vol. 3, p. 23. The analogous English law of the *hotchpot* applied only to children's shares of parents' personal property that parents had not disposed of by will.

8   See Diefendorf, *Paris City Councillors*, Ch. 8.

9   In its simplest form, the *légitime* was calculated by dividing one-third of the decedent's properties by the number of surviving children, but in some areas the size of the reserve varied with the number of children. In the Lyonnais, for example, if there were more than four children, the *légitime* was calculated on half of the succession. Claude Aboucaya, *Le Testament lyonnais de la fin du XVe siècle au milieu du XVIIIe siècle*, Annales de l'Université de Lyon, 3rd series, Droit, no. 21 (Paris: Sirey, 1961), pp. 119–20. There were also other claims that might be made on the parental properties, unless these claims were explicitly renounced in the marriage contract. For example, the augmentation of dowry (*augment*) that a man promised his wife in their wedding contract was considered the inheritance of the children of that match, and a daughter who survived her mother could sue for her share of this *augment*, if it had not been previously paid.

10 Most wills specify that the dowry had in fact been paid as promised, but occasionally one reads that a daughter's bequest consists of the funds promised by the marriage contract but not yet paid. There is little, however, to suggest that in Dauphiné, as in the Lyonnais studied by Aboucaya, the dowry was tending to become "chimerical." See Aboucaya, *Le Testament lyonnais*, pp. 12–13; see also p. 23, on the legal position of a daughter who was "dowered off."

11 A similar conclusion is reached by Alain Collomp, *La Maison du père: famille et village en Haute Provence aux XVIIe et XVIIIe siècles* (Paris: Presses universitaires de France, 1983), p. 136; and by Gregory Hanlon and Elspeth Carruthers, "Wills, inheritance and the moral order in seventeenth-century Agenais," *Journal of Family History* 15 (1990): 149–61 (151 and 154–5). See also Margaret Darrow, *Revolution in the House: Family, Class, and Inheritance in Southern France, 1775–1825* (Princeton, NJ: Princeton University Press, 1989), p. 66 and, more generally, Ch. 3.

12 ADI, III E 3306*: testament mystique d'Etienne Berthrand, résident à Grenoble, August 22, 1774.

13 ADI, 13 B 441: testament mystique de Jean Martinon, avocat au Parlement, November 14, 1652.

14 ADI, III E 3306*: testament mystique de François Giroud, écuyer, conseiller et secrétaire du roy en la chancellerie près le Parlement de Dauphiné, July 14, 1742.

15 An interesting example here is the case of Alix de Stuart, who wrote a will in 1586 in which she named an unborn, "posthumous male child" as her universal heir even though she already had a son and at least one daughter. Three years later, de Stuart made a new will. A posthumous son had not been born to her, she wrote, and to avoid difficulties among her children, she was making a new will and naming her son Charles du Motet as her universal heir, substituting for him any children he might have, males before females. ADI, 3 E 1368/5: will of Alix de Stuart, wife of Charles du Motet, chevalier, seigneur de Champier

and Nantuy, and "gentilhomme de la chambre du roy," July 4, 1589, with citations from the previous will of July 15, 1586. A similar tendency to favor males but not necessarily the eldest occurs in the case of Claude Bruno. Like de Stuart, Bruno drew up two testaments. In the first, he named his third and youngest son as his universal heir and left 12,000 *livre* legacies to two other sons and a married daughter. Five years later, he wrote a new testament naming the eldest son as the universal heir and leaving only 10,000 *livre* legacies to the others. It would be interesting to know what caused the change in Bruno's thinking. ADI, III E 3306*: testament mystique de Noble Claude Bruno, maître correcteur honoraire en la Chambre des comptes de Grenoble, August 5, 1773; and 13 B 632: ouverture de testament, September 7, 1781. The testament itself is dated March 22, 1778.

16   ADI, III E 3306*: testament mystique de Messire Alexandre Oronce Constance de Galbert, August 2, 1775.

17   See ADI, 13 B 632: will of Claude Bruno, March 22, 1778.

18   Aboucaya, *Le Testament lyonnais*, p. 24, similarly found that the heir instituted by the father's testament was not necessarily the eldest son and that, indeed, fathers in the Lyonnais seemed "little concerned with reserving the family patrimony for the males, in the presence of daughters." Darrow, *Revolution in the House*, pp. 61–3, found that one-third of the testators in pre-revolutionary Montauban chose to favor the eldest male heir, but she qualifies this tendency towards primogeniture by noting first that this was the "most popular" but "by no means the majority choice" and, secondly, that critics of primogeniture have exaggerated the degree to which the eldest was favored.

19   See, for example, ADI, III E 1408/1: testament nuncupatif de Sieur Etienne Ducros, maître brodeur à Grenoble, September 20, 1740.

20   See, for example, ADI, 13 B 635: inventory made at the request of Sieur François Durand, marchand bijoutier à Grenoble, November 28, 1782.

21   Jean-Guy Basset, *Plaidoyez de Maistre Jean Guy Basset, advocat consistorial au Parlement de Grenoble. Ensemble divers arrests & reglemens du Conseil & dudit Parlement, sur plusieurs notables questions ès matières beneficielles, civiles & criminelles* (Grenoble: 1668), 3rd plaidoyé, p. 23.

22   See Paul Ourliac and Jehan de Malafosse, *Histoire du droit privé*, Vol. 3, *Le droit familial* (Paris: Presses universitaires de France, 1968), pp. 150–1 and 288. In Grenoble, women had the right to administer non-dotal properties that came into their hands after marriage (*adventifs*). See Nicolas Chorier, *La jurisprudence du célèbre conseiller et jurisconsulte Guy Pape dans ses décisions, avec plusieurs remarques importantes, dans lesquelles sont entr'autres employés plus de mille arrêts du Parlement de Grenoble* (Grenoble: 1769; 2nd edn), pp. 222–3. Nevertheless, the contracts that I found in Grenoble for the alienation of non-dotal properties all carried the husband's explicit consent. In my study of marriage practices in sixteenth-century Paris, I did find some women who inserted clauses allowing them to retain control of inherited properties, but in all cases these were widows who were remarrying and not first marriages.

Gérard Chinea notes that Grenobloise women could attach to their marriage contracts the clause guaranteeing their freedom to administer even their dotal properties, but his study is based on legislative texts and not on notarial practice, so he cannot tell us how often this clause was employed. See his "La mère et l'enfant dans le droit dauphinois de la fin de l'Ancien Régime (XVIIe–XVIIIe siècles)," extrait du *Recueil de mémoires et travaux publié par la Société d'histoire de droit et des institutions des anciens pays de droit écrit* 11 (1980): 113–36 (129).

23   Aboucaya, *Le Testament lyonnais*, pp. 12–17. Jurists in neighboring Dauphiné feared that Dauphinoise women, having legally contracted in the Lyonnais, might later renounce their obligations by claiming the legal incapacity that protected them in Dauphiné (called their rights of "*Velleian*," after the Roman law origin of the rights). This would be fraudulent, the judges decided; the validity of the contract must be judged according to the laws of the place where it was signed. Basset, *Plaidoyez*, Book 4, Title 1, Ch. 2, p. 277. On the *Velleian*, see Julien Brodeau, *Recueil de plusieurs arrests notables du Parlement de Paris. Pris des Mémoires de Monsieur Maître Georges Louet, conseiller du roy au même Parlement* (Paris: 1712; new edn), Vol. 2, p. 736. In the sixteenth century women normally waived their rights under the *Velleian* when they contracted. Henri IV, believing that the calculated inclusion or omission of these waivers was being used to allow people to renounce validly contracted obligations,

prohibited the inclusion of these clauses in contracts and annulled women's rights to appeal to the *Velleian* by an edict of August 1606. This right was nevertheless maintained in Dauphiné and certain other civil law areas.

24   Jacques Bréjon, *André Tiraqueau, 1488–1558* (Paris: Recueil Sirey, 1937), pp. 110–37, especially 110–11; and Ourliac and Malafosse, *Droit privé*, pp. 133–7.

25   Paulette Bascou-Bance, "La Condition des femmes en France et le progrès des idées féministes du xvie au xviiie siècles," *L'Information historique* 28 (1966): 139–44 (140), citing Coquille's *Questions et réponses sur les Coutumes de France.*

26   Olivier-Martin, *Coutume de Paris*, Vol. 2, p. 258, goes even further in drawing a parallel between "marital absolutism" and monarchical absolutism. Sarah Hanley also draws parallels between family priorities and those of the centralizing state in "Family and state in early modern France: the marriage pact," in *Connecting Spheres: Women in the Western World, 1500 to the Present*, ed. Marilyn J. Boxer and Jean H. Quataert (New York and Oxford: Oxford University Press, 1987), pp. 53–63; and "Engendering the state: family formation and state building in early modern France," *French Historical Studies* 16 (1989): 4–27. Hanley stresses the disadvantages women suffered under the "family-state compact," which "widened the gap in social entitlement by empowering male heads and placing females at risk." She argues that, in response to diminishing autonomy, women "fashioned a counterfeit culture both to suit themselves and to minimize the risks" the patriarchal system posed for them ("Engendering the state," p. 21). Without denying the gender biases that pervaded the structures of both family and state, my approach in this chapter is rather to emphasize the importance of the role that women, particularly widows, nevertheless retained within the early modern French family. I would agree with James Collins that "legal and social restrictions against women were never fully successful [in early modern France], because of the struggles against them by women and because of the survival of the household unit as an important economic and social institution." As Collins points out, "Widows did not really threaten this household-centered society, even when they gained control over the household. The critical private role played by the woman of the household was effectively disguised behind her public powerlessness. What is more, her private importance did not threaten the patriarchal power structure." See James B. Collins, "The economic role of women in seventeenth-century France," *French Historical Studies* 16 (1989): 436–70 (469 and 467).

27   Basset, *Plaidoyez*, Book 3, Title 5, Ch. 4, p. 286. More generally, see Xavier Benoît , *Traité de la Dot, ou Développement des principes exposés au chapître III du livre III du Code Civil*, Vol. 1 (Grenoble and Paris: 1829), pp. 244–400. Again Lyon appears to have been exceptional. According to Aboucaya, *Le Testament lyonnais*, pp. 13–16, the distinction between dotal and non-dotal properties in the Lyonnais tended to disappear and so did the inalienability of dotal properties.

28   Claude de Ferrière, *La science parfaite des notaires, ou le moyen de faire un parfait notaire* (Paris: 1682), p. 77.

29   The same principle applied to the children's right to renounce a parental inheritance that was overburdened by debt and reclaim instead the mother's dowry. French customary law tended to favor the conservation of family property.

30   Sabatery, *Précis de la jurisprudence*, p. 6.

31   As the next chapter makes clear, however, continental testators who wished to disinherit children were nevertheless more constrained than English common law testators, who were not restricted by the notion of a *légitime*.

32   See Diefendorf, "Widowhood and remarriage," pp. 385–6.

33   Jacques Le Lièvre, *La Pratique des contrats de mariage chez les notaires du Châtelet de Paris de 1789 à 1804* (Paris: Editions Cujas, 1959), pp. 74–5.

34   Cited in Diefendorf, "Widowhood and remarriage," p. 387.

35   Olivier-Martin, *Coutume de Paris*, Vol. 1, p. 195. Among the Parisian elite, at least, the only exceptions to this rule occurred when the mother was very young.

36   Ibid., Vol. 1, 195–9.

37   Basset, *Plaidoyez*, Book 5, Title 1, Ch. 1, p. 1.

38 Sabatery, *Précis de la jurisprudence*, p. 136; see also Chinea, "La mère et l'enfant," p. 124.

39 See, for example, ADI, 13 B 632: assemblée de famille for the estate of M. Louis De Bon, docteur en médecine, August 10, 1781, and 13 B 638: ibid., January 15, 1783. De Bon's widow, Anne Deville, at first refused guardianship of her son by De Bon because of lawsuits she had pending against the estate. She eventually accepted this guardianship, but only with the provision that another person serve as *curateur*, or financial administrator, to look after the son's interests with regard to her own suits for the separation of her properties from those of her deceased husband.

40 See, for example, ADI, 13 B 630: succession de Rose Didier, marchande, widow in first marriage of Sieur Noel Repellin (December 5, 1780). Chinea, studying only legislative texts, asserts that widows who remarried lost custody of their children, and it is true that the text he cites from Expilly does suggest that this was the case. A study of common court records for the family assemblies that met to name guardians does not, however, bear this out as a consistent practice. Cf. Chinea, "La mère et l'enfant," p. 124; and Claude Expilly, *Plaidoyez. Ensemble plusieurs arrests & reglements notables dudit Parlement* (Lyon: 1657 [6th edn]), p. 363.

41 See, for example, ADI, III E 1408/1: testament nuncupatif de François Gerboud, habitant à Grenoble, August 1, 1741; or III E 3306*: testament mystique de François Giroud, écuyer, conseiller et secrétaire du roy en la Chancellerie près le Parlement de Dauphiné, July 14, 1742. Examples from sixteenth- and seventeenth-century practice include ADI, III E 1368/5: testament de François Barot, fils de feu Ennemond, marchand cordonnier de la Bourgogne, habitant à Grenoble, November 12, 1589; 13 B 441: ouverture de testament for Jean Cosse, procureur en la cour du Parlement de Dauphiné, September 22, 1650; and 13 B 441: ouverture de testament for Jean Martinon, avocat au Parlement, November 14, 1652. This practice has also been noted in studies of testamentary practice in other written law areas of France. In Montauban, Darrow found that 16 percent of the testators whose wills she studied for the period of 1775–93 (N = 320) named their spouse as heir (*Revolution in the House*, p. 61). See also Hanlon and Carruthers, "Wills, inheritance, and the moral order," p. 153.

Sometimes, instead of actually naming his wife his universal heir, the husband specified that he wanted her to enjoy the revenues and profits from his estate during her lifetime and then to pass it to the heir of her choice on her death. This had somewhat different legal consequences; in particular, it meant that the widow could not dispose freely of her husband's properties. It reflects, however, much the same intention of holding the estate together under the widow's management during her lifetime. See ADI, III E 1408/1: testament nuncupatif de Claude Vallin, habitant de Grenoble, November 24, 1740.

42 ADI, III E 1408/1 testament nuncupatif de Sieur Etienne Ducros, maître brodeur à Grenoble, September 30, 1740. Similarly, Jean Cosse instructed his wife to choose as their heir a son or daughter who accorded her "honor, respect, and obedience." François Barot stipulated that his daughters were to remain obedient to their mother and to follow her advice; if they deviated from her advice, their inheritance was diminished by 20 *écus*. (See note 41 for Cosse and Barot citations.)

43 ADI III E 1368/2: testament nuncupatif de Monsieur Jean du Vache, conseiller du roi en sa cour de Parlement de Dauphiné, October 31, 1587.

44 See, for example, ADI, III E 1408/1 testament de Ennemond Perret Pollat, journalier vigneron, December 1, 1740.

45 See, for example, ADI, III E 1408/2: testament nuncupatif de Sieur Joseph Roux, marchand carrobanier of Voiron, August 10, 1742; and 13 B 632: ouverture de testament for Claude Bruno, September 7, 1781.

46 Susan Staves, discussing a somewhat similar situation in her book on *Married Women's Separate Property in England*, pp. 104–13, points out that "social, psychological, and moral inhibitions" could cause a woman to accept an estate willed to her by her husband even though it was significantly smaller than the dower the law promised her (pp. 111–12). The same situation could of course have occurred in France. The fact that there was significantly less emphasis in France on transmitting the bulk of an estate intact from father to eldest son

suggests that the pressure on a widow to step aside in favor of a male heir would also have been less, but only further research can tell if this was indeed the case.

47   See, for example, ADI, III E 1408/1: testament nuncupatif de Pierre Verney, jardinier aux Granges lez Grenoble, March 4, 1741.

48   Thus, for example, Claude Vallin recognized that if his wife claimed her debts against his estate, it would not suffice to cover them. He therefore left her the income from his properties for her lifetime but begged her to conserve the capital for the two daughters who would inherit on her death. ADI, III E 1408/1: testament nuncupatif de Claude Vallin, habitant de Grenoble, November 24, 1740.

49   ADI, 13 B 638: nomination de tuteur for children of Justin Laurent, boulanger à Grenoble, May 8, 1783.

50   This includes the 4,000 *livres* due to Chazel for the return of her dowry, a debt that she, of course, would not have to assume as Acloque's heir. Most of the outstanding debt did, however, consist of charges that she would have had to pay – such as the 4,000 *livres* still due for the purchase of the inn, the "Little Round Table."

51   BMG, 0.1176: Mémoire de griefs pour Sieur François Acloque, maître du logis de la Petite-Table-Ronde, de la ville de Vienne, appellant de sentence rendue au bailliage de la même ville, March 14, 1776.

52   See, for example, ADI, III E 3306*: testament mystique de Marie-Marthe-Catherine Garempet, wife of Victor Guard, 14 pluviose, An VII, in which she explicitly renounces the will she made simply to put an end to the "sollicitations importunes" of her husband; and III E 3306*: testament mystique de Louise Christinat, wife of Claude Moret, April 12, 1760, in which she institutes her only son as her universal heir and expressly prohibits her husband from profiting directly or indirectly from this inheritance.

53   See, for example, ADI, III E 3306*: testament mystique d'Anne Drier, femme de Sieur André Barthelemy, marchand droguiste à Grenoble, June 15, 1741.

54   See, for example, III E 3306*: testament mystique de Marie Josserand, femme de Jean-François Bache, négociant à Grenoble, March 14, 1786.

55   Cf. Stanley Chojnacki, "Patrician women in early Renaissance Venice," *Studies in the Renaissance* 21 (1974): 176–203, and Stanley Chojnacki, "Dowries and kinsmen in early Renaissance Venice," *Journal of Interdisciplinary History* 5 (1975): 571–600.

56   Basset, *Plaidoyez*, Book 5, Title 5, p. 31.

57   Diefendorf, *Paris City Councillors*, Ch. 5.

58   Arthur Michel de Boislisle, *Histoire de la Maison de Nicolay* (Nogent-le-Rotrou, 1873), no. 165: undated note from Anne Baillet to Jeanne Luillier.

59   Olwen Hufton, "Women and the family economy in eighteenth-century France," *French Historical Studies* 9 (1975): 1–22; Natalie Zemon Davis, "Women in the *Arts Mécaniques* in sixteenth-century Lyon," in *Lyon et l'Europe: Hommes et sociétés, Mélanges d'histoire offerts à Richard Gascon*, ed. Jean-Pierre Gutton (Lyon: Presses universitaires de Lyon, 1980), Vol. 1, pp. 139–67; Collins, "The economic role of women," pp. 436–70. Kathryn Norberg offers some telling details about women's economic position in eighteenth-century Grenoble in *Rich and Poor in Grenoble, 1600–1814* (Berkeley and Los Angeles, CA: University of California Press, 1985), pp. 182–92.

60   James Collins points out that women "often figure as owners of property but rarely show up as purchasers" ("The economic role of women," p. 457). His sample is small and largely rural; the subject requires further research. So does the question of investment in annuities (*rentes*), for which women appear to have provided a ready market. See, for example, Cissie C. Fairchilds, *Poverty and Charity in Aix-en-Provence, 1640–1789* (Baltimore, MD and London: Johns Hopkins University Press, 1976), pp. 66–7.

61   In *Family and Inheritance: Rural Society in Western Europe, 1200–1800*, ed. Jack Goody, Joan Thirsk, and E. P. Thompson (Cambridge, UK: Cambridge University Press, 1976), pp. 37–70. The article, originally published as "Structures familiales et coutumes d'héritage en France au XVIe siècle: Système de la coutume," *Annales: économies, sociétés, civilisations* 27 (1972): 825–46, is largely a summary and discussion of Jean Yver's *Egalité entre héritiers* (for Yver, see above, note 5). Neither Le Roy Ladurie nor Yver actually identifies the antithesis

between vertical and horizontal conceptions of the family with the contrasting notions of lineage versus individual property, but their analysis lends itself to this generalization.

62 ADI, 13 B 638: family assembly called by Jean Bernard, August 9, 1783.
63 ADI, 13 B 638: family assembly of February 8, 1783.

10
Resentment or resignation?
Dividing the spoils among daughters and younger sons

Susan Staves

I Introduction

In classical political theory the family tended to occupy a uniquely privileged position as the one social unit that preexisted the state. The family thus was figured as the pre-eminently "natural" social unit in contrast to the state, an artificial and later social creation. As opposed to the relation between husband and wife, which depended on an act of will and a verbal contract, the relation between parent and child appeared both the most "natural" of all possible human relationships and, as Blackstone put it, "the most universal relation in nature."[1] Blackstone, citing Pufendorf, derived the duty of parents to provide for their children from natural law: "an obligation . . . laid on them not only by nature herself, but by their own proper act, in bringing them into the world: for they would be in the highest manner injurious to their issue, if they only gave the children life, that they might afterwards see them perish."[2]

Despite this tradition of understanding the family as a social unit constructed by "nature," current work has emphasized seeing the family as a more artificial social, political, economic, and legal creation. In considering sharing property in the early modern English family here, I want to explore a variety of ways in which different biological children within the same family had different entitlements to share in family wealth. Primogeniture, the common law right of the eldest son to inherit all his father's land, although in strictness avoided by many family settlements and wills, nevertheless continued as an ideology that gave the elder brother a lion's share and other siblings smaller portions. Indeed, the biological division of children into male and female was in some ways supplanted by a different division between the heir and the others. So obvious was this non-biological opposition that when one clever lawyer contested a first-born daughter's rights to share in a portion fund designated for "younger children" arguing that the first-born of all the siblings could not be a "younger child," the court dismissed him rather curtly. The court pointed out: "Every one but the heir is a younger child in equity, and the provision which such a daughter will have is but as a younger child."[3]

The portions and legacies provided for many younger children were not necessarily, perhaps even usually, equal for all the younger children in a particular family. Nor were their entitlements guaranteed to younger children as publicly or legally forced shares; whatever shares they got were in a real sense private gifts members of private families elected to bestow on them.

Early modern English law, unlike civil law, allowed possessors of property unusual freedom to dispose of it as they wished, declining to enforce children's rights to shares. Just as the state permitted a father to disinherit any child he wished, the state itself created rules that disentitled certain biological children from shares in various kinds of family property. Thus, as we shall see, "natural" biological children of British property owners who happened to be Roman Catholic, alien-born, or illegitimate might find themselves banished from the family feast.

II   Primogeniture *v.* the rights of younger children

In the early modern English family, common law primogeniture struggled against a competing idea that all the children in a family deserved to be sharers in the family feast. Indeed, although by common law the eldest son inherited all the family land, under the 1670 Statute of Distribution setting out the rules for intestate succession to personal property, all children took equal shares of a parent's personal property.[4]

Primogeniture, many contemporaries understood clearly enough, was vital to the maintenance of the class structure. And the class structure was in turn vital to allow at least some men to live the best possible human lives. When that rather romantic American writer F. Scott Fitzgerald proclaimed, "The rich are different from you and me," Ernest Hemingway retorted, "Yes, they have more money." Hemingway's view was emphatically not that of early modern Englishmen. For them, the rich and the poor were, by nature, profoundly different sorts of persons. The rich were, by nature, generous, honorable, brave, refined, just, and public-spirited; the poor, by nature, mean, timid, coarse, and self-interested. The spectacle of someone born to wealth and privilege and then reduced to poverty contemporaries therefore found especially pitiful. Thus Dr. Johnson, not the most sentimental of writers, lamented the fate of Richard Savage, supposedly born the son of the Countess of Macclesfield, then bastardized and committed to the care of a poor woman to be brought up as her own: "Born with a legal claim to honour and to affluence he was in two months illegitimated by the parliament and disowned by his mother, doomed to poverty and obscurity, and launched upon the ocean of life, only that he might be swallowed by its quicksands or dashed upon its rocks."[5] While some twentieth-century critics have been puzzled at Johnson's sympathy for Savage's subsequent extravagance and refusal to work, Johnson, I think, honors Savage's insistence that the life of a rich person is the best and noblest life, Savage's refusal to accept the degradations of labor and economy, and Savage's insistence that his birth entitles him to the best life.

Yet if birth and blood were the grounds of entitlement to privilege, it could be difficult to grasp why one brother in a family was to be favored over all the other children. To be born into a rich family, to understand what it meant to be a rich person, to be taught that God had ordained that the few should enjoy luxury and the many hard toil, and then to understand that wealth was not to be your own lot, could be a disturbing discovery indeed. Yet primogeniture could mean that an elder brother was a rich person and his younger siblings poor ones. Even in the sixteenth century, therefore, a vigorous critique of primogeniture was developed, mostly by younger sons.[6] In the seventeenth century, when America began to be colonized, often by younger sons themselves, certain law reform ideas of the revolution, including partible inheritance, became American rules.[7] At the time of the Glorious Revolution, in 1688/9, the ideology of primogeniture suffered a more theoretical blow when the divine right of the eldest to rule in the state was repudiated, thus partially decoupling the ideology of state and the ideology of family. After 1688, even Church of England clerics were inclined to admit that the privilege of the eldest son was not divinely ordained. Arguments for primogeniture began to shift to more utilitarian claims that greatness itself, the greatness of some men in the state and the greatness of certain families, could not be maintained without primogeniture. Tom Paine, born and brought up in England, railed from below at primogeniture as the unjust and unnatural foundation of aristocracy. "Establish family justice," he wrote in *The Rights of Man*, "and aristocracy falls":

> Aristocracy has never more than *one* child. The rest are begotten to be devoured. They are thrown to the cannibal for prey, and the natural parent prepares the unnatural repast. . . . With what kind of parental reflections can the father and mother contemplate their younger offspring. By nature they are children, and by marriage they are heirs; but by aristocracy they are bastards and orphans. They are the flesh and blood of the parents in one line, and nothing akin to them in the other.[8]

In England, even softened, as we shall see, by settlements and testamentary devises, the ideology of primogeniture continued to make significant differences between the heir and his siblings.

While there certainly were many examples of happy and supportive relations between elder brothers and their younger siblings of both sexes in eighteenth-century families, younger brothers were more apt to resent any pretensions to superiority by their elder brothers while sisters were more likely to be resigned to them. As masculinity increasingly was constructed to mean independence, it is not surprising that younger brothers chafed at suggestions that they were or ought to be dependent on their elder siblings. Letters, diaries, and memoirs of younger brothers show something of the nature of such quarrels. William Hickey, for example, a younger brother apprenticed to an attorney in the 1760s, describes his response to his eldest brother's "calling him to account" for staying out all night: "But not feeling that his having come into the world a few years sooner than myself gave him any authority over me, I pertinaciously declined response, receiving his lecture and admonitions with contemptuous silence. When he ceased to speak, I, in peremptory tone, desired his right to censure or question me, and refused to satisfy his impertinent curiosity."[9]

But while the construction of masculinity in the eighteenth century was apt to make younger brothers uncomfortable with acknowledgments of subordination and dependency on elder brothers, the construction of femininity fit better with younger sisters' accepting such relationships. Among the better documented relationships of an elder brother and a younger sister at the period is that of Charles and Elizabeth Hamilton. From a family of struggling Scotch Jacobites with high principles and little cash, Charles got an education in Belfast, then in 1772 a cadetship in the East India Company. Eventually he achieved some fame by publishing a translation of the laws of India. Elizabeth saw little of her brother, but nevertheless maintained a very affectionate epistolary relationship with him, expressing her gratitude for his guiding her studies and her views. Portionless and living with an aunt and uncle, Elizabeth had little prospect of marriage at home. When her brother suggested that she come to live with him in India, she expressed doubts that she could get a husband even there, and worried "to throw such a burden" on his "generosity."[10] Although Elizabeth from time to time seems to wonder that her heroic brother cannot make more of a fortune in India and hasten his return home, her correspondence is mostly suffused with piety and resignation to her lonely fate. In a poem, "Anticipation," she contemplates herself as a 35-year-old spinster and imagines what her mirror will show in the future:

> But tho' deprived of youthful bloom,
> Free was my brow from peevish gloom.
> A cap, tho' not of modern grace,
> Hid my grey hairs and deck'd my face.
> No more I fashion's livery wear,
> But cleanly neatness all my care.
> Who e'er had seen me must have said,
> There goes one chearful, pleased, old maid.[11]

The disciplines of plain living and piety allow her to accept her portionless spinster-hood with a certain self-respect, even pride – and when her beloved Charles returns to London for a time before his early death, she enjoys those few, brief, blissful years living with him.

At least until quite recently, naked expressions of envy and greed for more wealth have not been considered respectable, so it is not surprising that the written self-representations of actual younger brothers more often complain about their poverty, their dependency, their inferiority, and their lesser entitlements to social goods than they demand more land or more pounds and pence.

Imaginative literature, however, is sometimes more willing to allow expression of unlovely feelings, since unlovely feelings can always be ascribed to bad characters rather than the author's having to take responsibility for them. In English literature, heroes, of course, most often come single, not accompanied by brothers, but there are a few texts in the Renaissance and early modern period that grapple with conflicts between heirs and younger brothers over property. The earlier texts, like Fletcher and Massinger's *Elder Brother* (1625), I think, tend to characterize envious younger brothers as villainous, while the mid- and late eighteenth-century texts, like Sheridan's *School for Scandal* (1777), tend to see the privileged elder brother as undeserving.

Of particular interest as a transitional text is Farquhar's *Twin-Rivals* (1702). Farquhar makes the chronological distinction between elder and younger as problem-atic as possible by making Young Benjamin Wou'dbee and the Elder Hermes Wou'dbee twins, born only one half-hour apart. Anticipating the style of analysis later popularized by Tristram Shandy, Benjamin jokes, "My Brother, 'tis true, was First-Born, but I believe from the bottom of my Heart, I was the First-Begotten."[12] Yet the two are physically very distinct; the younger boy's body is marred by a humpback, which he bitterly blames on his brother's crowding him in the womb. The Elder has just succeeded to an estate of £7,000 a year, while the younger has had a portion of about £1,500, all of which he has already spent.

Since the elder brother is abroad rather than actually in possession, the younger Benjamin proceeds to take possession and schemes to create a good title to the estate for himself. First a forged letter announces the death of Elder Wou'dbee to the estate servants, who consequently cooperate with Benjamin. Then, since Benjamin is not inclined to murder his brother, he secures the help of an attorney, Subtleman, who is willing to forge and procure witnesses to a will according to which their father has devised the property to Benjamin. Demonstrating scrupulosity and literal-mindedness, the witnesses insist that they will not swear to the words of the dead father unless they actually see them come out of his mouth, a phenomenon, they explain, that can be arranged by forcing open the corpse's mouth and putting in "a Bit of Paper." Benjamin objects that rigor mortis has set in and "his Teeth can't be got asunder." Subtleman, the attorney, replies: "But what occasion has your Father for Teeth now? I tell you what – I knew a Gentleman, three Day's Buried, taken out of his Grave, and his Dead Hand set to his Last Will, (unless some Body made him sign another afterwards) and I know the Estate to be held by that Tenure to this Day; and a firm Tenure it is; for a Dead Hand holds fastest; and let me tell you, Dead Teeth will fasten as hard." After this macabre little ritual to satisfy tender consciences, Benjamin soliloquizes:

> The Pride of Birth, the Heats of Appetite, and Fears of Want, are strong Temptations to Injustice – But why Injustice? – The World has broke all Civilities with me; and left me in the Eldest State of Nature, Wild, where Force or Cunning first created Right. I cannot say I ever knew a Father; – 'Tis true, I was begotten in his Life-time, but I was Posthumous Born, and Liv'd not till he Died – My Hours indeed, I numbred, but ne'er enjoy'd 'em, 'til this Moment – My Brother! What is Brother? We are all so; and the first two were Enemies.[13]

Benjamin's participation in the breaking of his dead father's jaw and the knocking out of his father's teeth seems a vivid enough emblem of the rage of a younger son at a father and the law of the father that has made a difference between two brothers born with equal needs and desires and raised with equal pride of class. Benjamin's plots (mostly suggested by characters considerably more malign than he is) are eventually defeated and he is shown to be unfit to be the heir. Yet his self-awareness, wit, and scruples make him a not entirely unsympathetic character.

The "facts" of birth, as Farquhar proceeds to show, can be alarmingly fragile; not only is paternity dependent on female testimony, but the fact of priority in time that is the ground of the privileges of primogeniture can also be difficult to demonstrate. When his brother reappears, Benjamin is in possession, attended by constables and reassured by Subtleman as to the "Benefit of Law . . . what an Advantage it is to the Publick for securing of Property."[14] The defection of one witness to the will threatens to topple Benjamin's plot, but his claim is shored up again by the clever testimony of one Mrs.

Midnight. Formerly a nurse in their family, she is now the proprietress of a brothel where women about to deliver infants of dubious parentage may do so privately. According to Mrs. Midnight's suddenly helpful testimony, Benjamin was actually the first-born, but his father, seeing Benjamin's deformity, bribed Mrs. Midnight to say that "the beautiful Twin, likely to be the greater Ornament to the Family, might succeed him in his Honour."[15] Hermes is consequently taken away by the constables. Eventually, of course, all Benjamin's schemes are blown up, Mrs. Midnight defects and tells the truth, the good and just Hermes is restored to his rightful place, and Benjamin walks off to "Poverty and Contempt."[16] Yet Farquhar's play gives expression to the anger of a younger brother at the felt injustice of his lot, and also very forcefully insists on the slipperiness of legal ownership and on the uncertainties of birth.

What Benjamin has failed to appreciate, fixated as he is on the difference made between elder and younger brothers, are the economic and social advantages younger siblings may derive from being members of a family raised by primogeniture. As one lawyer member of the great family of the Cecils commented after undertaking an historical investigation of primogeniture in England: "younger sons . . . owe their very social position and rank to the institution which is so bombarded in their names. It is just because they are members of a nobleman's or gentleman's family, which primogeniture has contributed to distinguish above others, just because they are 'known all about,' that they obtain that slight social start which is wanting to the ordinary mortal."[17] Furthermore, he was able to conclude, by creating some families of distinction primogeniture enriched the culture of England to the benefit of even the most disadvantaged Englishmen.

III Settlements and wills

So long as land simply "descended" from father to eldest son at common law, its descent at least seemed to have a certain inevitable, natural character. But when, after the Statute of Wills in 1544, the course of descent could be altered by a father's will, descent lost some of its apparent inevitability. By the late seventeenth century land and other wealth was normally apportioned among the various members of rich families, not by the general operations of common law, but by individualistic family settlements, usually made prenuptially, and by wills.

One of the most idiosyncratic features of English law in the early modern period was the extreme freedom of property owners to decide, as individuals, how family property would be divided among children. As far as common law was concerned, a father could divide all his real and personal property among his children in any way he liked; if he wished, he could utterly disinherit any one or even all of his children, including his eldest son. Such testamentary freedom would have been shocking to earlier English law, to early modern continental law (which followed Roman law in requiring some provision for all children), and even to twentieth-century English law, which now gives children disadvantaged by a parent's will an opportunity to make claims for more adequate shares.[18]

Extreme testamentary freedom violates the principle that parents, by nature, love all their children, and that they have a moral duty to provide for them all. A principal argument for fathers having such power to determine distribution was that this power helped fathers enforce proper discipline; a child who knew he was dependent on his father's goodwill for his fortune was supposed to be a well-behaved child.[19] Children who behaved badly, who failed in their duty to their parents or to their class, could be punished by economic deprivation. Thus, Edward Wortley Montagu, husband of Lady Mary Wortley Montagu, resisted settlements partly on the ground that he feared the prospect of an unsatisfactory eldest son. When he then had a quite spectacularly bad son, he left the vast bulk of his wealth to his daughter and a mere pension of £1,000 to the son; Lady Mary herself, when she later died, left her eldest son only a single guinea.[20] A principal disadvantage of the father's great testamentary power was that it encouraged siblings to jockey for favor, even to backbite in hope of diminishing the father's liking for a rival sibling, and thus increasing what was left for themselves. All the moral horrors of Roman legacy hunting, so brilliantly described in the satires of Horace, could also take place in the English family. Moreover, since settlements and wills could be, and often were, kept secret, fathers had opportunities to manipulate children with promises, sometimes false, of what might be done for them.

Legal intellectuals justified this extreme testamentary freedom in three ways. First, they asserted that nature had implanted in parents such love for their children and such a desire to provide for them that legal requirements would be superfluous.[21] Second, especially in the later eighteenth century, they claimed "every man has, or ought to have, by the laws of society, a power over his own property."[22] Although it certainly was not true that the right to dispose of particular property as one wished had always been an inherent part of ownership, increasingly in the eighteenth century the right to alienate, the *jus disponendi*, was coming to seem a crucial, even an essential, stick in the bundle of ownership rights. Third, legal intellectuals increasingly insisted that the family was a private sphere where delicate, subtle, even inexplicable decision-making went on, and that the courts neither should nor could intrude into this delicate sphere. Thus we get the principle that the father is to be the only judge of the quantum of provision for his children.

A number of historians have maintained that, although the problem of inequality between the eldest son and his siblings was severe in the early seventeenth century, it was more or less solved by the early eighteenth century in those classes that married with settlements through the provision of portions for younger children. Joan Thirsk, writing about younger sons in the seventeenth century, observes that in the mid-seventeenth century the term "younger son" virtually meant "an angry young man, bearing more than his share of injustice and resentment."[23] While there were a variety of possibilities for employing younger sons, including apprenticing them to merchants or sending them off to colonies, Thirsk believes that

> the habit of working for a living was not ingrained in younger sons of this class, and no amount of argument could convince them of the justice of treating them so differently from their elder brothers. The contrast was too sharp between the life of an eldest son, whose fortune was made for him by his father, and who had nothing to do but maintain and perhaps augment it, and that of younger sons who faced a life of hard and continuous effort, starting from

almost nothing. Many persistently refused to accept their lot, and hung around at home, idle, bored, and increasingly resentful.[24]

At the Restoration, however, she finds that the lot of younger sons improved markedly. Settlements made provision for them "in such a way that eldest sons were unable to frustrate it," and, since specific sums were "sealed" in settlements, the settlement "killed vain hope" and "at least guaranteed to younger sons a sum of money with which they could make a start in business or a profession." At the Restoration also, younger sons again found the court open to them, prospects within the Church brightened with the restoration of the episcopate, and a variety of new professions like medicine increasingly beckoned. Similarly, Lawrence Stone in *The Family, Sex and Marriage* argues that the father's authority was undermined after 1660 by strict settlements that stipulated the provision allocated to each unborn child at the time of the parents' marriage.[25] Randolph Trumbach, in a careful study of thirty aristocratic families, also finds that settlements improved the position of younger sons; he observes, correctly, that one purpose of settlements was "to secure sibling solidarity and to avoid generational conflict."[26] Trumbach, however, also noticed the difficulties that under-financed younger sons could have in making the kinds of marriages they wanted; he expresses skepticism – rightly, I think – about the notion that the new professions provided opportunities for aristocratic younger sons. When they failed to acquire fortunes through marriage, Trumbach contends, the real alternative for these younger sons was "to get into Parliament and look for a place."[27] Indeed, Trumbach's view is supported by the fulminations from below of Tom Paine, who snarled: "All the children which the aristocracy disowns . . . are, in general, cast like orphans on a parish, to be provided for by the public, but at a greater charge. – Unnecessary offices and places in governments and courts are created at the expense of the public, to maintain them."[28]

Although, as Trumbach says, it certainly was an aim of settlements "to secure sibling solidarity and to avoid generational conflict," it does not necessarily follow that they achieved this aim. Settlements might control to some extent the division of property among children, but they did not specify division among the children as much as is often supposed. And even in cases where younger children got sums specified in their parents' settlements, those sums were still very substantially less than what the elder brother got and, for younger brothers especially, often meant a markedly different and less desirable kind of life. Certainly Stone's claim that younger children were secured set amounts by their parents' settlements is misleading. It is true, as Lloyd Bonfield has shown in a careful and legally sophisticated study of 230 settlements executed in Kent and Northamptonshire between 1601 and 1740, that by the early eighteenth century conveyancers had developed forms for legally securing portions for younger children in settlements and that such forms began to be commonly used.[29] But it must be emphasized that eighteenth-century fathers did not all make trips to shops selling standard legal forms and all buy the same "settlement form A." Settlements were essentially contracts; they were drawn by individual conveyancers or attorneys of widely differing habits and abilities in order to satisfy individual client need.[30] When portions were contemplated, they might be secured by giving to trustees for a term of years a part of the patrimony to raise portions, a term that preceded the remainder in tail to the eldest son; alternatively, the settlement might simply give the father a power to charge the estate with portions, a power he might or might not elect to exercise. Conveyancers attempted to provide for a wide variety of demographic possibilities, but even the most astute conveyancer drawing up a new settlement on the marriage of the heir had no way of foretelling whether his client's son was likely to have no children or fourteen children, a fine heir or nothing but six daughters. It therefore usually did not make sense to specify an exact sum for each prospective child; instead, revenues from particular lands or specific lump sums might be set aside for portions, sometimes with a power allowing the father to determine the division. In other cases, a single fund might be equally divided among all the younger children, or, alternatively, separate funds might be provided, one for younger sons, one for daughters. Contemporary conveyancing books, settlement documents, and partial descriptions of settlements in litigation all demonstrate that parents often had opportunities to advantage one child over another.

Further evidence of insecurity in the portions of younger children can be teased out of what is known about legal and social practices. First, the elder brother enjoyed a number of legal and practical advantages over his siblings. When the heir came into physical possession of his estate he had the usual advantages of possession of land; as Midnight observes in *The Twin-Rivals*, "Possession gets you Money [and] that gets you Law."[31] An heir had additional legal advantages; for example, the right to have settlements and other papers delivered for his inspection. Since Parliament had resisted the registration of titles to land and since landowners took advantage of opportunities to set up secret trusts and unregistered mortgages, the issue of obtaining access to papers relevant to titles and claims was not trivial. It was not only in comedies like Congreve's *Way of the World* that people could be surprised by the sudden production of "writings" in black boxes, and fathers and elder brothers were most likely to have possession of family papers. Younger children, by contrast, might have to struggle to discover what their entitlements were. It was also very common for prenuptial settlements to be revised or supplemented by postnuptial agreements, including wills. These later documents sometimes appeared in conflict with settlements; such conflicts produced a good deal of litigation and the development of moderately elaborate legal doctrines concerning beneficiaries' election among apparently competing entitlements.[32] Again, disputable entitlements and entitlements based on documents kept among family papers tended to advantage elder brothers who could best afford to litigate and who had preferred access to the documents.

Fairly frequently, younger children had to scramble to persuade the father or the heir to disgorge the allowances to which they might be entitled under settlements or wills. Some fathers or heirs, who were supposed to pay, lacked assets or liquidity, some wanted to postpone payment until they acquired new cash (for example, from the payment of a bride's portion to them), and still others, who had resources or who could have obtained them by acquiring debt, decided to keep the resources for themselves. It is clear that the classes which made settlements had significant debt and cashflow problems. Even in the relatively cheap and simple milieu of South-West Wales, David Howell has found "a lack of good management of their incomes and a proclivity towards spending beyond their fortunes on the part of landowners of every rank."[33] A number of close studies of particular families or of particular gentry groups have shown that many fathers or elder brothers who were supposed to pay portions simply did not have cash in hand. Payments of portions to younger brothers and sisters were sometimes delayed until a cash-poor heir himself managed to marry a woman with a substantial portion of her own. For example, a private Act of 1733 on the occasion of the marriage of Anthony Henley with a daughter of the Earl of Berkeley shows £4,600 from the new bride's portion allotted to paying the unpaid balances of portions due Anthony's sister and younger brother, portions provided for in the father's settlement of 1699.[34] Similarly, A. P. W. Malcomson in a study of the Irish aristocracy finds incoming portions commonly used to pay the portions of the groom's siblings. "To the great majority of the class," he observes, "the idea of saving did not occur."[35] Peter Roebuck, in a very detailed and valuable study of the family finances of several generations of Yorkshire baronets, demonstrates "that as the period progressed the payment of a growing number of portions was via loans or by instalments and that the receipt of many was temporarily postponed or deferred indefinitely."[36] To cite only one of many examples he offers, we find three Liddell sisters, Anne, Cordelia, and Catherine, supposed to be getting from 1735 on 4$\frac{1}{2}$ percent interest on their still unpaid portions. Perhaps, Roebuck suggests, Sir John's sisters "were content to receive annual instalments of the interest, though this is difficult to believe of Catherine who married in 1743. The slow rate at which capital sums were realized probably accounts for her marrying a doctor, and for her sisters remaining, and dying, unmarried."[37] Finally, in 1750, Sir John had trustees give Anne £3,000, Cordelia £1,000, and Catherine £3,000.[38]

For daughters, portions unpaid or delayed for a decade could mean lesser marriages than they wanted or no marriages at all; for younger sons, portions unpaid or delayed could mean both lost marriages and lost opportunities for education and careers. Contemporaries were right to insist on the superior value of real property as security; in a conflict between a father or an elder brother in possession of an estate and younger children with portion claims, the possessor of the property had a secure estate and the younger children mere claims.

Moreover, moral younger children were supposed to have scruples about suing the heads of their families for portions, especially their fathers, but even elder brothers, who were also owed deference, and on whom siblings would continue to depend for a wide variety of favors. Moralists advised Christian forgiveness, patience, and submission, to children economically injured by parents rather than recourse to public contests at law: in "matters of Contract, Estate, Inheritance, or Money, it must not be for any small matter, nor for a light injury, nor for any thing easy to be born, that a Child can implead his Parent; the hardship must be near intollerable; the injustice great and pressing, when a wise indifferent Man or a Man's own Conscience can permit him to go to Law with his Father or Mother."[39] Even should a younger child dare to sue, being out of possession, no matter how worthy one's claim, could also mean lacking the resources for litigation. It is not surprising to see one daughter who had been denied a portion apparently keep quiet about it until she married an ambitious barrister, who seems to have enjoyed litigating.[40]

Giving younger children entitlement to larger portions than the family could realistically afford was, in fact, a form of conspicuous consumption in the eighteenth century. Few genteel families actually had the economic resources to establish many children in genteel life. By giving younger children expectations of generous portions, therefore, these families, far from eliminating sibling rivalry, actually set up struggles between fathers and elder brothers, who did not have the resources to pay portions, and younger children, who now considered themselves entitled to them. William Fleetwood, a Church of England clergyman, nicely identified the clash of interests between parents who wished "to be thought much richer than they truly are" and so bring up their children "as if they were all to inherit great Estates, when they are to inherit nothing but a Name, that does them mischief: This is not design'd a kindness to the Children, but generally proceeds from Pride and Vanity, which make the Children mean and miserable *indeed*, for fear the Parents should be *thought* so."[41] Partly Fleetwood wants parents to be more careful about their own expenditure, so that something would be left for the Children: "Parents who consume their whole Estate, with which they should provide for their Children, in Gaming, Drinking, Riot, Luxury, and sinful Pleasures, are in no better condition, nor do any better discharge their duty to their Children, than they who for little or no cause, Anger, Folly, or Humour . . . disinherit their Children, and cut them off from their Estates."[42]

Yet Fleetwood's additional advice that parents who could not afford fully genteel provision for some of their children should bring those children up with low expectations, mean education, and inured to industry was not practical. Demographic roulette meant that some younger sons would come to be heirs themselves and Fleetwood acknowledged that it was a "huge indecency" to give a "mean or sordid Education" to one who was to inherit an estate. Furthermore, he admitted, it was not "either fit, or decent, or at least not customary" to put people of quality "to Trades or settled Callings."[43] Congreve's Anthony Witwood was not the brightest fellow in the world, but when his half-brother Sir Willful taunts him with his former apprenticeship to "honest *Pumple Nose* the Attorney of *Furnival's* Inn," Anthony can offer his own indignant complaint about the degradation to which Sir Willful has subjected him: "I was glad to consent to that, Man, to come to *London*. He had the disposal of me then. If I had not agreed to that, I might have been bound Prentice to a Felt maker in *Shrewsbury*; this Fellow wou'd have bound me to a Maker of Felts."[44] So long as many income-producing occupations were considered degrading to the genteel, younger children born to gentility could resent them.

Even that one occupation considered by many the perfect solution to the problem of the impecunious younger son – the navy – was not without its drawbacks. The best features of the navy were that it was not socially degrading and that a young man required no capital to get into it. As Nicholas Rodger has argued, "The Navy was the only profession for a gentleman which did not require – indeed, did not admit – the application of money or influence."[45] According to Rodger, boys were generally enthusiastic about joining and many excess sons happily went away to sea as early as 10 and in few cases later than 14. Generous distribution of prize money allowed officers to dream of gaining an estate "in an afternoon."[46] On the other hand, conditions at sea were harsh and sea-service was extremely dangerous; some were killed in action, many more less gloriously by drowning or disease.[47] Fathers, even fathers who were themselves naval officers, considered the navy too dangerous a career for an eldest son: "eldest sons in the Navy were therefore confined to those families without property, or those whose fortunes were so badly damaged that they were prepared to run risks in the hope of recouping them."[48] The lives of eldest sons were worth more than the lives of younger sons, and every one knew it.

Parents provide for their children in two ways: while the parents are alive, they maintain and educate their children; after the parents die, they may also leave them some share of the family wealth. When dealing with rich families, legal intellectuals were generally content with the principle that fathers should judge both the level of maintenance for their children (and their wives, for that matter) and the quantum of provision after death.[49]

Early modern fathers were especially interested in controlling the marital choices of their children and not infrequently sought to accomplish this end by inserting into settlements or wills clauses that stipulated a child (perhaps most often a daughter) was to forfeit all or part of her portion if that child married without permission. The person or persons who were to give permission were named in the same instrument; they might be the father, the mother (if the father were dead), or other relatives or trustees. One of the most popular plays of the eighteenth century, Susanna Centlivre's *A Bold Stroke for a Wife* (1718), has as its hero a lover who has to win his lady by simultaneously pleasing her four highly idiosyncratic guardians. Her deceased father is said to have so "hated posterity" that he "wished the world were to expire with himself" and swore that if his daughter had been a son he would have "qualified him for the opera" by castrating him.[50] In an ultimate dead-hand gesture, this father has required his daughter to obtain consent to any marriage from four guardians "as opposite to each other as light and darkness": Sir Philip Modelove, an old beau; Perriwinkle, an obsessed virtuoso; Tradelove, a change-broker; and Obediah Prim, a Quaker.

It was not, however, obvious that such clauses depriving children of their portions for marrying without permission would be enforceable. According to civil law and also to English ecclesiastical law, conditions annexed to legacies in restraint of marriage were void because repugnant to the law of nature, contrary to the procreation of children, and detrimental to the commonwealth.[51] Thus, in *Peyton* v. *Bury* (1731), a girl received the residue of a testator's estate provided she married with the consent of two executors. One of the executors died and the girl married "a common mariner" without the consent of the surviving executor. The residuary legatee then sued on the ground that she had broken the condition and forfeited her legacy. While the Master of the Rolls could have accepted the residuary legatee's arguments that the girl ought to have obtained the consent of the surviving executor, instead he decided to say that satisfaction of the condition had become an impossibility, commenting, "which construction ought the rather to prevail, with regard to a condition so odious as that in the present case is, which restrains the freedom of marriage, and is void by the civil law, when annexed to a personal legacy."[52] In *Wrottesley* v. *Bendish* (1733), Sir Hugh Wrottesley had settled £8,000 to be divided among his daughters, payable at marriage or at 21, "provided, if any of his daughters should, after his death, marry under her age of twenty-one, and without consent of the mother," her share should be divided among the other daughters. Of four daughters, one was said to have married before 21 and without her mother's consent, so the other three sued, hoping that her share would be forfeit and distributed among them. The issue in equity was whether the allegedly disobedient daughter should be compelled to answer whether she had violated the condition. Invoking the equity principle that no one should be forced to give an answer leading to forfeiture, equity turned the three unhappy sisters away without a remedy.[53]

Other cases, however, enforced forfeitures for marrying without permission. In an important case finally decided in 1670 the Earl of Newport left his granddaughter Lady

Anne substantial real property on the condition that she marry with the consent of her grandmother and two earls. If she married without consent or if she had no children, then the property was to go to George Porter, Lady Anne's cousin. When Lady Anne was about 14, Charles Fry, according to the report, "stole" her "over the Garden Wall" at Newport House. Lady Anne had no notice of the condition. The two earls disliked the marriage, but declared in court that they consented to the marriage, adding, "*that they do not know but that if their Consents had been asked for before the Marriage, such Reason might have been given as they might have consented to it.*"[54] At first hearing, the Master of the Rolls found Lady Anne had not forfeited her legacy. On appeal, however, before five judges, Porter won. Chief Baron Hale reasoned that the devise was of land, that land was not governed by ecclesiastical law, and that the condition did not restrain her from marrying but simply annexed a penalty to marrying without consent. Lord Chief Justice Keeling added, "'Tis fit to keep those Bonds which Parents impose to hold their Children at Obedience, streight, and not fit for a Court of Equity to relax them." The Lord Keeper added that he was "glad to see that a Parent could settle his Estate, that it might be out of the Power of a Court of Equity."[55] Similarly, in 1698, one Stratton in a codicil to his will provided that if his daughter Eliza married before 21 without the consent of her brother and of two kinsmen, the father's executors, then £500 was to be deducted out of her share of his estate and paid to his son. The daughter, before 21 and without consent, married "a pawnbroker . . . of little or no property," and her brother sued for the £500.[56] He won, and, with the help of these precedents, the courts began distinguishing between clauses that decreed forfeits only, said to be merely *in terrorem* and not enforceable, and clauses that decreed the disobedient child should forfeit and another person succeed to the forfeited portion, these latter clauses becoming enforceable – and, consequently, more common.[57]

The issue of the extent to which parents could penalize children for marrying without permission by forfeiture clauses in wills or settlements was still not firmly settled in 1738. Thus siblings continued to have opportunities to challenge the portions of other siblings (although it should be said that most of these cases seem to have been initiated by husbands of siblings rather than siblings themselves). A leading case of 1738 featured the eight daughters of Sir Thomas Aston, all of whom were given portions under a settlement and legacies under a will, both on the condition that they marry with consent. Two daughters who married without consent nevertheless sued for their portions and legacies. In these instruments there was some possibility of arguing that no specific devises over had been provided, that is, that no successors to the supposedly forfeit portions had been named, and, thus, that the clauses were merely *in terrorem* and not enforceable. The court, however, decided that the condition was lawful and that the portions did not vest until a daughter married with appropriate consent; they therefore found against the disobedient sisters.[58] Discomfort was expressed that in several of these cases the person to consent and the residuary beneficiary were the same, an apparent conflict of interest, but this issue was not pursued. Lord Chief Justice Willis quoted with approval an earlier saying, "that men's wills by which they settle their estates are the laws that private men are allowed to make, and they are not to be altered even by the king in his courts of law or conscience."

IV   State control of family sharing

Judicial reverence for the will of the father and the privacy of the family, however, was overcome when certain state interests were at issue. Fathers with religious views considered obnoxious to the state were not necessarily credited with natural love of their children nor permitted to decide either how they should be raised or what quantum of provision those children ought to have. The early modern English state was quite uninhibited about exercising its prerogatives over children if parental prerogatives were producing unacceptable results. The rights of Protestant parents over their children were not extended to Jewish or to Roman Catholic parents. Jewish parents who attempted to control their children's religious allegiance by economic deprivation or disinheritance were met with a statute that allowed a Jewish child wishing to convert to Protestantism to apply to Chancery for a forced share of parental property.[59] In 1723, for example, we see one 22-year-old son, Moses Marcus, petition according to the statute, claiming that he had been educated "as a gentleman and a scholar with the dependence of a plentiful fortune from his father," that he then converted to Protestantism, and that, as a consequence of his conversion, his father had refused to maintain him. Chancery required the father to give £5,000 security to pay him an allowance and, subsequently, ordered the father to pay young Moses £60 a year. A few years later, Moses complained that his father had not paid. His father replied that Moses had returned to Jewish worship, even publicly done penance in a Dutch synagogue for his conversion, but the court, crediting a new declaration by Moses that he was indeed a Christian, again found for the son.[60] This statute and a similar one affecting Roman Catholics are interesting in part because they show an early – perhaps the earliest – example of legislative and judicial interference with a father's right to set the quantum of provision for the maintenance of a child. Not until very recently have doctrines emerged requiring well-to-do parents to provide such luxuries for children as university educations, and the application of those doctrines has so far been only to divorced parents, courts continuing to rely on natural affection so long as the marriage is ongoing.

Roman Catholic parents, more numerous and considered more subversive than the Jews, had their efforts to raise their children as Roman Catholics yet more seriously challenged by the state.[61] To send a child abroad to be educated as a Roman Catholic was a criminal offence, although many risked it. With respect to property, in England the Roman Catholic minority was subject to recusancy statutes according to which land held by Roman Catholics could neither descend nor be devised to their Roman Catholic children. In Ireland, where the majority of the inhabitants were Roman Catholics, the penal laws were more severe.[62] These penal laws established a very treacherous family dynamic. If the child of a Roman Catholic landowner converted to Protestantism, his father was immediately reduced to the status of a life tenant. If there were several brothers and all remained Roman Catholic, the land was gavelled, that is, divided into equal shares among all the sons. But if one brother converted, no matter whether an elder or a younger brother, that brother took all the land by primogeniture, all the other children being reduced to dependants on allowances. Clearly, neither the general principle of supporting paternal authority nor the public interest in promoting harmony in families dictated the statutes affecting the Jews or the Roman Catholics.

Nor was the principle that an owner of property ought to be allowed to dispose of it as he wished applied to Jews or to Roman Catholics. Not only were such parents' efforts to dispose of their property to their pious children and to disinherit children they considered impious resisted, but efforts made to bequeath money to charities for the education of children in Judaism or Catholicism were also void as legacies for "superstitious uses." One Jewish testator who bequeathed £1,200 to establish a yeshiva where boys could study the Talmud would presumably have been distraught to find his legacy declared "not good" by Lord Hardwicke and £1,000 of the funds given instead to support "a preacher and to instruct the children under their care in the Christian religion, and for other incidental expenses attending the said chapel."[63]

Certain features of the statutes affecting Roman Catholics may appear more peculiar to modern eyes than they actually were. When one statute provides that a younger brother who is a Protestant may take the estate from an older brother who remains a Roman Catholic or another prohibits freehold land from descending to a Roman Catholic heir, such provisions, in the minds of contemporary drafters, I suggest, treated Catholics as the common law treated aliens born outside the king's dominions. At common law, as it developed from feudal law, landowners were the liege subjects of their lord, owing fealty to him and him alone. At common law, if an eldest son happened to be born outside the king's dominions, he was necessarily the subject of another lord and incapable of taking land in England by descent; the land that would have been his passed to the next qualified to be heir in the line of descent (his younger brother born at home, if he had one). Roman Catholics, considered to owe allegiance to an alien lord, the Pope, were thus being treated as aliens. By the Restoration, Jews, earlier regarded by Coke as infidels and enemy aliens, were understood to have allegiance to no earthly sovereign other than the king and thus were privileged to hold land (although this privilege was sometimes doubted, even by the Jews themselves).

It is significant, however, that legislators were also beginning to see that the old common law of alienage was massively dysfunctional for a new colonial and imperial nation. Colonists and conquerors would hardly be encouraged to leave England for the West Indies or for India if any children born to them there were to be incapable of holding land in England, whether it be land their parents held before leaving or English land they might later acquire with the profits of empire. Children born abroad were also incapable of transmitting the right of inheritance through themselves to their own children who might be born in England.

Finding this common law of alienage unacceptable, Parliament changed it. In 1700 a new statute provided that all natural-born subjects might inherit as heirs and might trace their descent from any of their ancestors lineal or collateral, although such ancestors were born "out of the allegiance of the Crown." Subsequent statutes then provided that children and grandchildren born abroad of a father who was a natural-born British subject at the time of their birth were themselves given the status of natural-born British subjects, although that status was not transmissible to their descendants.[64] Certain other classes of individuals, born abroad, but deemed to have made important contributions to empire, were also statutorily given the benefits of natural-born British subjects. For example, foreign seamen serving on English ships during war for at least two years were entitled to British nationality. These statutes all changed existing rules about who counted as a family member for the purposes of sharing land. From the perspective of the law of alienage, one might even see the treatment of the Roman Catholics as kindly, since their land was permitted to go to their own Protestant descendants, while the lands actually held by aliens in England were forfeit to the Crown. Yet both the statutory modifications of the rights of natural-born Roman Catholics, in effect turning them into aliens, and the statutory modifications of common law disabilities of certain classes of the foreign-born, conferring on them the legal privileges of natives, show Parliament's willingness to change the supposedly natural course of descent of landed property in the family for reasons of state. Parliament understood clearly enough that land was the basis of political power, and, despite rhetoric about the naturalness of the family, exerted itself to tinker with and control the descent of landed property in families in ways that it believed congruent with the national interest. In this sense, land was understood to be the property of the nation, not the private property of individuals held independently of the state.

Although over the course of the eighteenth century the recusancy statutes were increasingly disused in England, they, nevertheless, affected behavior.[65] Some of these statutes were contradictory; one statute forbade Catholics to own land, and, while this statute was still in force and still sometimes applied, another required English Catholics to pay double the land tax on land they held. Wealthy Roman Catholics, like wealthy Protestants, resorted to trust instruments, often secret trusts, to evade the statutes; although religious tests were required for admission to the bar, a few Roman Catholics acquired legal training and practiced as unadmitted conveyancers, making specialties of drawing up trusts for their co-religionists.[66] Roman Catholics generally also seemed to have scorned breaking ranks by informing on one another. At the same time, as the threat of Jacobite uprisings faded, their Protestant neighbors became more tolerant. Some estates were forfeited, though. Even when the statutes were not used to procure official forfeiture, they created significant blackmail opportunities. For example, in a will of 1728 Henry Nevill left his eldest daughter £2,000 and his youngest daughter £10,000 in trust along with the guardianship and custody of his lunatic son. Sir Baldwin Conyers, the husband of the eldest daughter, contested the will by demanding another £6,000 from the favored daughter's share and arguing, correctly, that the statute of 11 & 12 William III disabled Roman Catholics from receiving legacies. When the Roman Catholic community apparently censured him severely, he dropped his attempt to destroy the will, instead privately accepting an extra £5,000.[67]

V   Illegitimacy

Let us consider finally the situation of illegitimate children. On the one hand, natural law arguments insisted that parents had an obligation to maintain all their children, legitimate and illegitimate, and the English poor laws provided mechanisms for enforcing parental contributions to the maintenance of illegitimate children. On the other hand, public policy interests were thought to require disadvantaging illegitimate children in various ways. With respect to property, an illegitimate child could not inherit either from its father or its mother.[68]

Exactly what percentage of all children were illegitimate, of course, it is impossible to say. Demographic studies of the whole population from parish registers suggest a rising rate from about 1 percent in 1660 to about 6 percent by 1780; such rates are certainly underestimates because about one-third of known births went unregistered and a disproportionate percentage of unregistered births were probably of illegitimate children. Among upper-class men in the second half of the eighteenth century, in what Roy Porter has celebrated as the sexual Eden of Enlightenment England, official monogamy was very often combined with unofficial polygamy.[69] Given what we know about the sexual practices of such men, and given the absence of effective birth control, it is hard to see why they should not have had roughly as many illegitimate children as legitimate ones. Pleasurable sex with no consequences was a male fantasy; Fanny Hill may never have got pregnant – but real women were not so lucky.

Both Roy Porter and Lawrence Stone take, I think, too cheerful a view of the situation of the illegitimate child of an upper-class parent in the eighteenth century. While there are certainly examples of such children being quite well provided for, it was not the typical practice of fathers to provide equally for legitimate and illegitimate children nor, given their difficulties in providing even for legitimate children, would such provision have been practicable in the majority of genteel families. Indeed, Stone himself cites Richardson's Lovelace as articulating one supposedly typical ethical code concerning mistresses: "to maintain a lady handsomely in her lying in, to provide for the little one, if he lived, according to the degree of the mother, if she died."[70] A follower of this code would thus provide for his illegitimate child not at his own economic level but rather at the level of its mistress mother, almost always lower. Furthermore, it is clear that men did not always acknowledge their children by established mistresses, much less their children by more casual liaisons or liaisons with prostitutes. Indeed, no matter how well disposed a gentleman might have been to take some responsibility for his children from casual liaisons, as common law insisted in its doctrine that a bastard was *filius nullus*, the child of no one, it was – in those days before DNA testing – not technologically possible to establish paternity.

Like legitimate younger children, only much more so, illegitimate children were extremely dependent on the willingness of their fathers to acknowledge and make provision for them. A father who wished to spend £10 or £15 to put such a child out to nurse, then to school for a few years, and finally into an apprenticeship might well have considered that he had added another person to the useful class of the laboring poor and done his duty. Some sense of how arbitrary and contingent a father's favor toward an illegitimate child might be is provided by the *Apology* of the actress George Anne Bellamy, an illegitimate daughter of Lord Tyrawley. Lord Tyrawley did provide for his daughter to be put at nurse, then sent her, at age 4, to a French convent. When she was 11, he summoned her to an audience. Not surprisingly, the child wanted to stay with the familiar nuns at school: "Having no knowledge of the nobleman to whom I was indebted for my being and subsistence . . . I had not the least desire to see [him]."[71] While she came to adore her father, he renounced her when she was 13 because she had disobeyed his order not to see her mother. Struggling for years to win her way back into his favor, she made progress in getting him to speak to her. Nevertheless, when Lord Tyrawley tells her she ought to leave the stage, an improper occupation for a child of his, George Anne cannot "help observing": "Notwithstanding his Lordship was reconciled to me, and he still continued to live at such an expense as to involve himself annually, although in receipt of immense sums from his employments and commissions

. . . he made no offer of furnishing me with a provision adequate to the emolument I reaped from my profession."[72]

Samuel Richardson introduced a question that was to become quite popular with women writers of the later eighteenth century: what should a good wife's attitude be toward her husband's illegitimate children? Pamela, after her marriage to Mr. B., is made to struggle with the problem of how she will treat Sally Godfrey, an illegitimate daughter of Mr. B. Like most of the problems in Part II of *Pamela* this is considered a difficult social question. Lady Davers, Pamela's new sister-in-law, warns her that Mr. B. loves the child and will "judge" Pamela by her conduct toward it. Lady Davers also observes that this will be "a trying part" of Pamela's conduct, one only a heroine like Pamela is capable of solving.[73] Pamela, disdaining to show signs of jealousy of Mr. B.'s former mistress, determines to be fond of the little girl, "as well for the sake of her unhappy mother . . . as for the relation she bears to the dear gentleman," Pamela's husband, whom she is "bound to love and honour."[74] Coyly proposing to Mr. B. that she work toward an understanding of Locke's *Some Thoughts Concerning Education* by taking in a child to practice on so that she will be a better mother for their legitimate son, Pamela amazes one and all by offering to take Sally into her house to raise. Sally is never told anything except that Mr. B. is her "uncle"; Sally's mother, having allowed her child to be put at nurse and to school by Mr. B., has married a man who believes she is a widow and that the relations of her supposed first husband are caring for the child of a supposed first marriage. Conveniently, she has nothing but extreme gratitude for Pamela's offer to care for the person she describes as "my poor, and, till now, *motherless* infant."[75] Sally, brought up by Pamela with firm warnings about the evils of rudeness to servants and improved by close study of the *Spectator* papers, is married at 18 to "a young gentleman of fine parts, and great sobriety and virtue"; whether this virtuous gentleman is informed that his bride is a bastard, we are not told.[76] The romance of the paragon wife who gladly includes her husband's bastards – or, more precisely, those of his bastards whose mothers had some claim to gentility – is repeated with moderate frequency in the sentimental drama and fiction of the later eighteenth century.

Later sentimental novels and plays also make much of the discovery of a previously unknown illegitimate child. Even the not very sentimental Smollett reunites forlorn Humphry Clinker with his biological father, Matthew Bramble, in his last novel of 1771. A less well-known play, Frances Sheridan's popular and sentimental *The Discovery* (1763), uses the discovery of a previously unknown illegitimate child to reveal contemporary anxieties about provision for children and to dramatize moral dilemmas about the relative entitlements to family wealth of fathers versus children and of legitimate children versus illegitimate children. The father of the family in *The Discovery*, Lord Medway, has spent most of his fortune on his own pleasures; he has nothing left for his son, Colonel Medway, or his unmarried daughter, Louisa, who wants to marry, but for whom he can provide no portion. "This is the curse of marrying early," Lord Medway complains, "to have our children tugging at our purse-strings, at a time when we have as quick a relish of the joys of life as they have, and ten times a better capacity for pursuing them."[77] In order to raise more cash, Lord Medway wants his son to marry the fabulously rich Mrs. Knightly, in hopes that her money can pay off their mortgages. Colonel Medway, however, loves Miss Richly, Mrs. Knightly's younger sister, who had a much smaller portion than her elder sister – and all of Miss Richly's small portion has now been lost because of "the breaking of a merchant, in whose hands her money lay." Still not having learned his economic lesson, Lord Medway suddenly loses another £2,000 gambling; this, "a debt of honor," he thinks he actually must pay. He pleads with his son to marry Mrs. Knightly "to save a father from disgrace" and a "mother . . . from penury."[78] Self-sacrificially, Colonel Medway agrees, but all then discover that Mrs. Knightly is actually an illegitimate daughter of Lord Medway by a woman he met in Portugal. Lord Medway's protestations of ignorance that he had such a child are plausible enough: "I was recalled to England early in my amour with her, I married soon after my return, and, thoughtless and young as I was, never inquired after her more."[79] What is less plausible, of course, is that such a daughter would ever be reunited with her father. Mrs. Knightly, to use the indelicate legal term Frances Sheridan avoids, is an "adulterine bastard." Her mother, pregnant with Lord Medway's child, quickly married a Portuguese merchant who was scheduled to be in India at the time of the child's birth and never suspected he was not her father. Ironically, the merchant favored this adulterine bastard, unknowingly robbing his own daughter, Miss Richly, of her rightful inheritance.

In Sheridan's sentimental comedy, thanks to this merchant's fortune, a personal estate of £50,000 and real estate of £3,000 a year, now in the possession of Mrs. Knightly, all the problems of the economically traumatized Medways can be solved. Mrs. Knightly begs a blessing from her natural father, Lady Medway graciously welcomes her into the family, and she promptly gives half her fortune to her younger sister, who is thereby enabled to marry Colonel Medway. Another character gives a generous portion to his nephew so he can marry Lord Medway's daughter Louisa. The now fortunate children will thus presumably unmortgage the estate and support their reformed father.

While there were a few real-life examples of wives who were as tolerant toward illegitimate children as Pamela and Lady Medway, it is more reasonable to regard these plots as romance rather than realism. The wife's acceptance of the husband's bastard is usually figured as an heroic transcendence of ordinary female jealousy, not as a specimen of ordinary morality. Questions of the fairness of taking family resources that would otherwise have gone to legitimate children and bestowing them on illegitimate children are not allowed to arise in these plots, where no economic scarcity ever mars the happy resolution. In women's fictions, especially, there is a desperate quality to these plots since only what is marked as superhuman goodness in the woman seems powerful enough to effect the conversions of libertine husbands into men of ordinary morality. Moreover, as sentimental tenderness toward children was emphasized as an important feminine quality in the later eighteenth century, it was difficult for a heroine to be shown as unsympathetic toward such a child.

An argument, of course, could be made that men bestowing more than subsistence maintenance on illegitimate children were subverting the moral order and defrauding legitimate children of their proper entitlements. This argument appears in litigation over legacies left to illegitimate children. When the Marquis of Annandale died, his wife was the administratrix of his estate. She refused to honor a bond for £2,000 that her husband had given to his mistress, the money to be laid out within a year after his death in an annuity for the support of his mistress and her illegitimate child; the bond also had had only one witness, instead of two, and that witness did not claim actually to have seen the bond sealed and delivered. The child had also died in the meantime. The marchioness argued that a court of equity should not help to enforce such a debt "as gained upon an unlawful and wicked consideration." (Contracts to pay mistresses are classic examples of contracts void as against public policy.) Equity, however, ruled against the marchioness, deciding, "If a man does mislead an innocent woman, it is both reason and justice he should make her a reparation; but this case is stronger in respect of the innocent child, whom the father has occasioned to be brought into the world in this shameful manner; and for whom in justice he ought to provide."[80] On the other hand, when a justifiably concerned grandfather, the Earl of Devonshire, devised £3,000 "*to all the natural children of his son the late Duke of Devonshire by Mrs.* Henage," the court determined that it was against public policy to permit an illegitimate child of the Duke of Devonshire born after the making of the will to take under the will. The earl, Lord Chancellor Parker decided, "could never intend that his son should go on in this course, that would be to encourage it; whereas it was enough to pardon what was passed; besides, bastards cannot take . . . until they have gained a name by reputation, for which reason, though I give to the issue of *J.S.*, legitimate or illegitimate, yet a bastard shall not take."[81] Hence we get the rule that bequests to a future illegitimate child are void.[82]

Many illegitimate children, fathered by men of high or low degree, led very wretched and very brief lives. Mortality among infants consigned to parishes ranged between 75 percent and 100 percent. The London Foundling Hospital, the very charity newly established to provide for abandoned infants, many of whom were illegitimate, tragically turned out to be less successful at providing for them than at killing them.[83] The holocaust of abandoned innocents in Ireland was even worse. In the first seven years of the Dublin Foundling Hospital and Workhouse, of 4,025 children received, 3,235 died. According to parliamentary investigators in 1758, the children lived in damp rooms with no glass in the dormitory windows and with holes in the roof; fires were provided only at Christmas and on Sundays. In the infirmary, "sixty sick children lay in indescribable filth, looked after by two elderly women." Boys who complained about maggots in the food were placed in the stocks and given twenty lashes; other offending children were locked up with lunatics in underground cells. Of 14,311 children admitted to this institution between 1756 and 1771, at least 10,000 died. Not all of these children were Irish. By 1770 a regular transport of illegitimate children from England to Ireland had been established. According to one indignant writer in the Irish *Freeman's Journal*: "Our masters on the other side of the water are not satisfied at the vast sums drawn from this poor kingdom, but are resolved that we should maintain their illegitimate offspring as well as their whores." But parliamentary investigations and journalistic railing did not reduce the death rates. Between 1781 and 1790, 19,368 infants were received, of whom 16,954 died.[84]

Despite considerable resistance, both from the state and from younger brothers, the male heads of families – the fathers and the elder brothers of the world – still retained considerable privilege by 1800. Their notable and traditional privileges included special opportunities to portion out family wealth and favors to their less privileged relatives. Among the less remarked upon of their privileges, perhaps, was this odd right to decide whether some of their biological children would get to be recognized members of their father's family at all, and, if recognized, on precisely what terms they would be sharers in the family feast. The privileges of an eighteenth-century patriarch might mean that Lord Chancellor Thurlow could live with a mistress he met when she was a barmaid at Nando's Coffee-House, then disinherit one of his illegitimate daughters when she married an innkeeper's son, then provide another illegitimate daughter with sufficient countenance and a sufficiently large inheritance that she married Alexander George, Baron Saltoun.[85] Alternatively, they might mean that Charles Dibden, successful author of the popular song "Dear me! How I long to be married!," could have two sons by a mistress with whom he lived for at least six years and make no provision for either of them.[86] Or, the privileges of an eighteenth-century patriarch might mean that a child of his, born outside marriage and unrecognized, was truly, as the lawyers said, *filius nullius*, nobody's child. That child was unlikely to have a narratable story or to leave much of a trace in the historical record. That child might do no more than anonymously swell the mortality statistics of a foundling hospital or a local parish poorhouse, never conscious enough to feel either resentment or resignation.

VI Conclusion

Appeals to the "natural affection" of parents for their children and to the "naturalness" of the relation between parents and children – a relationship imagined as more authentic than the relationship between the citizen and the state – were used to legitimate parents' control over the distribution of family assets within the family. The state and the law, it was claimed, ought to forbear intruding into the private sphere of the family where, in wills and settlements, as Lord Chief Justice Willis said, private men "were allowed to make . . . the laws." Yet, as we have seen, being the biological or "natural" child of a particular parent could constitute a relatively weak legal claim to be a sharer in family wealth: a younger child's claim could be trumped by an elder brother's primogeniture; a disobedient child's transgressive marriage could forfeit a portion or a legacy; a Roman Catholic child could be edged out by a sibling converting to Protestantism; a child born to parents who were not married could not be the heir of either parent. Such children, disadvantaged in relation to their biological siblings, were given weak claims because, as contemporaries sometimes acknowledged, the social order they desired, including the class structure and the establishment of the Protestant religion, trumped claims from nature. Contemporary invocation of the power and worth of natural affection to justify treating the family as exempt from public regulation was contradicted by willingness to impose both regulations to supply actual failures of natural affection (for example, legal requirements that fathers of illegitimate children pay the parish for the child's subsistence) and regulations that forbade the exercise of parental affection when it conflicted with state policy (as it could in Jewish or Roman Catholic families). Even when the twentieth-century British state recently improved the position of children born to unmarried parents by giving them new rights against putative fathers and better positions in intestate succession to parental property, the government still did not allow a child born outside of marriage to claim British nationality through its parents.[87] Despite the sentimental dream of families as unworldly places of true affection and hopes that families have riches enough to provide for all their members, even today, in a world of scarcity, the family and the state are still profoundly interdependent, and the family, legally regulated, still helps to maintain inequality by differentially distributing wealth and entitlement.

Notes

1 William Blackstone, *Commentaries on the Laws of England. A Facsimile of the First Edition of 1765–1769*, ed. Stanley N. Katz, 4 vols (Chicago: University of Chicago Press, 1979), Vol. 1, p. 434.
2 Ibid., Vol. 1, p. 435.
3 *Beale* v. *Beale* (1713), 1 P Wms 244.
4 "An Act for the better settling of intestates estates," 22 & 23 Car. II, c. 10 (1670).
5 Samuel Johnson, "Life of Savage," in *Lives of the English Poets*, ed. George Birkbeck Hill, 3 vols (Oxford: Clarendon Press, 1915), Vol. 1, p. 324.
6 Joan Thirsk, "The European debate on customs of inheritance, 1500–1700," in Jack Goody, Joan Thirsk, and E. P. Thompson (eds), *Family and Inheritance: Rural Society in Western Europe, 1200–1800* (Cambridge, UK: Cambridge University Press, 1976, pp. 177–91); Joan Thirsk, "Younger sons," *History* 54 (1969): 358–77.
7 George L. Haskins, "The beginnings of partible inheritance in the American colonies," *Yale Law Journal* 51 (1942): 1280–1315; George L. Haskins, "The beginnings of partible inheritance in America," in *Essays in the History of Early American Law*, ed. David H. Flaherty (Chapel Hill, NC: University of North Carolina Press, 1969), pp. 204–44; Stanley N. Katz, "Republicanism and the law of inheritance in the American revolutionary era," *Michigan Law Review* 76 (1977): 1–29; Carole Shammas, Mary Lynn Salmon, and Michel Dahlin, *Inheritance in America from Colonial Times to the Present* (New Brunswick, NJ: Rutgers University Press, 1987).
8 Thomas Paine, *The Thomas Paine Reader*, ed. Michael Foot and Isaac Kramnick (Harmondsworth, Mx: Penguin, 1987), p. 228.
9 *Memoirs of William Hickey*, ed. Peter Quennell (London: Routledge & Kegan Paul, 1975), p. 38. William was in his late teens at this time; his father was still alive, but abroad at the time of this scene.
10 *Memoirs of the Late Mrs. Elizabeth Hamilton. With a Selection from her Correspondence and other Unpublished Writing by Miss Benger*, 2 vols (London: 1818), Vol. 1, pp. 92–3.
11 Ibid., Vol.1, p. 95.
12 George Farquhar, *The Twin-Rivals* in *The Works of George Farquhar*, ed. Shirley Strum Kenny, 2 vols (Oxford: Clarendon Press, 1988), Vol. 2, act II, scene iii, ll. 115–17. A good critical essay on this play is Eric Rothstein, *George Farquhar* (New York: Twayne Publishers, 1967), pp. 57–71.
13 Farquhar, *Twin-Rivals*, act II, scene v, ll. 31–2, 35–41, 67–76.
14 Ibid., act IV, scene i, ll. 9–11.
15 Ibid., act IV, scene i, ll. 234–6.
16 Ibid., act V, scene iv, l. 148.
17 Evelyn Cecil [Baron Rockley], *Primogeniture: A Short History of its Development in Various Countries and its Practical Effects* (London: John Murray, 1895), p. 203.
18 Gareth Miller, "The Family Law Reform Act 1987 and the law of succession," *Conveyancer and Property Lawyer* (November–December 1988): 410–20.
19 For a very spirited argument that fathers ought to disadvantage badly behaved elder brothers (and a general plea on behalf of younger brothers), see John Ap Roberts, *The Younger brother His Apologie, or A Fathers Free Power disputed, for the disposition of his Lands, or other his Fortunes to his Sonne, Sonnes, or any one of them . . .* (Oxford: 1671).
20 Robert Halsband, *The Life of Lady Mary Wortley Montagu* (Oxford: Clarendon Press, 1956), pp. 15, 272–6, 285. For a lively account of some exceptionally badly behaved aristocratic children, many of whom were punished with economic deprivation, see Christopher Simon Sykes, *Black Sheep* (London: Chatto & Windus, 1982).

21 "The municipal laws of all well-regulated states have taken care to enforce this duty [of parents to provide for the maintenance of their children]: though providence has done it more effectually than any laws, by implanting in the brest of every parent that natural στοργη, or insuperable degree of affection, which not even the deformity of person or mind, not even the wickedness, ingratitude, and rebellion of children, can totally suppress or extinguish." Blackstone, *Commentaries*, Vol. 1, p. 435.

22 Ibid., Vol. 1, p. 436.

23 Thirsk, "Younger sons," p. 360.

24 Ibid., p. 367.

25 Lawrence Stone, *The Family, Sex, and Marriage* (New York: Harper & Row, 1977), pp. 89, 243–4.

26 Randolph Trumbach, *The Rise of the Egalitarian Family: Aristocratic Kinship and Domestic Relations in Eighteenth-Century England* (New York: Academic Press, 1978), p. 71.

27 ibid., p. 94.

28 Paine, *Reader*, p. 228 (in *The Rights of Man*).

29 Lloyd Bonfield, *Marriage Settlements, 1601–1740: The Adoption of the Strict Settlement* (Cambridge, UK: Cambridge University Press, 1983), pp. 102–20.

30 Bonfield, for example, finds that 73.1 percent of his settlements from the first two decades of the eighteenth century explicitly provide portions for younger children.

31 *Twin-Rivals*, act IV, scene i, l. 304.

32 For an interesting case which airs some of these issues, see *Pusey v. Sir Edward Desbouvrie* (1734) 3 P Wms 315. In this case, an unmarried daughter had accepted a legacy of £10,000 rather than take her orphanage part (according to the custom of London) amounting to about £40,000, a choice which advantaged the executor, her brother. She subsequently married an attorney, who litigated for the larger sum. The court commented: "the daughter might reasonably have a great regard for the intentions of her deceased father (for which she was to be highly commended), and might thereby be induced to comply with such intention, at the same time that she knew in strict justice there was more due to her by virtue of the custom" (at 319). The case was compromised.

33 David W. Howell, *Patriarchs and Parasites: The Gentry of South-West Wales in the Eighteenth Century* (Cardiff: University of Wales Press, 1986), p. 47.

34 Christopher Clay, "Property settlements, financial provision for the family, and sale of land by the greater landowners, 1660–1790," *Journal of British Studies* 21 (1981): 18–38 (30–1). Clay thinks portions amongst the greater landowners were "relatively secure" (p. 30).

35 A. P. W. Malcomson, *The Pursuit of the Heiress: Aristocratic Marriage in Ireland, 1750–1820* (Antrim: Ulster Historical Foundation, 1982), p. 330.

36 Peter Roebuck, *Yorkshire Baronets, 1640–1760: Families, Estates, and Fortunes* (Oxford: Oxford University Press for the University of Hull, 1980), p. 330.

37 Ibid., p. 242.

38 Ibid.

39 William Fleetwood, *The Relative Duties of Parents and Children, Husbands and Wives, Masters and Servants* (London: 1705; reprinted New York: Garland, 1985), p. 70. "Discourse VI" also contains a discussion of the morality and propriety of disinheriting particular children.

40 *King v. Withers* (1711) 26 Gilb Rep.

41 Fleetwood, *Relative Duties*, p. 128.

42 Ibid., pp. 161–2.

43 Ibid., pp. 130, 134.

44 William Congreve, *The Way of the World*, in *The Complete Plays of William Congreve*, ed. Herbert Davis (Chicago: University of Chicago Press, 1967), act III, scene i, ll. 549, 558–62.

45 N. A. M. Rodger, *The Wooden World: An Anatomy of the Georgian Navy* (London: Collins, 1986), pp. 253–4.

46 Ibid., p. 256.

47 "Of 443 captains made post before 1720 and 1750, more than 1/3 had by the end of the Seven Years' War ended their careers either in death or disgrace"; ibid.

48 Ibid., pp. 258–9.

49 See, e.g., *Cook* v. *Arnham* (1734), 3 P Wms 283.

50 Susanna Centlivre, *A Bold Stroke for a Wife*, ed. Thalia Stathas (Lincoln, NB: University of Nebraska Press, 1968), act I, scene i, ll. 78–80.

51 Henry Swinburne, *A Treatise of Spousals or Marriage Contracts* (New York: Garland, 1985), Pt 4, s. 12.

52 *Peyton* v. *Bury* (1731), 2 P Wms 626.

53 *Wrottesley* v. *Bendish* (1733), 3 P Wms 235.

54 *Fry* v. *Porter* (1669–70), 1 Chan Cas 138, at 139.

55 Ibid., 143, 144.

56 *Stratton* v. *Grymes et al.* (1698), 2 Vern 357.

57 *Wheeler* v. *Bingham* (1746) 3 Atk 364. Cf. *Underwood* v. *Mirris* (1741) 2 Atk 184, later attacked, 1 Bro Cha Rep 303, 2 Bro Cha Rep 488.

58 *Harvey* v. *Aston* (1738), 1 Atk 363.

59 1 Anne, c. 30 (1702), "An Act to oblige Jews to maintain and provide for their Protestant Children." For a general discussion of the treatment of Jews in English law, see H. S. Q. Henriques, *The Jews and the English Law* (London: J. Jacobs, [1908]; reprinted Clifton, NJ: Augustus M. Kelley, 1974), and on an episode in which a Jewish father attempted to deprive a converting daughter of maintenance, an episode that provoked the statute cited, see pp. 167–9.

60 Henriques, *The Jews and the English Law*, pp. 6–9.

61 1 & 2 Anne, c. 4, "An Act for the further preventing the growth of Popery"; 11 & 12 Wm. III, c. 4. Protestant children of Roman Catholic parents were also permitted to apply to Chancery for "a fitting Maintenance, suitable to the degree and ability of such parent, and to the age and education of such child."

62 J. G. Simms, "The making of a penal law (2 Anne, c. 6), 1703–4," *Irish Historical Studies* 12 (1960): 105–19. Henry Parnell, *A History of the Penal Laws against the Irish Catholics. From the Treaty of Limerick to the Union* (London: 1803).

63 *Da Costa* v. *De Paz* (1744), Ambler 228, note 2 quoting Register's Book, cf. Henriques, *Jews and the English Law*, pp. 19–23; cf. *Moggridge* v. *Thackwell*, 2 Swanston 487.

64 11 & 12 Wm. III, c. 6; 25 Geo. II, c. 39; 7 Anne, c. 5, 4, Geo. II, c. 21, 13 Geo. III, c. 21.

65 Sir Robert Chambers, *A Course of Lectures on the English Law Delivered at the University of Oxford, 1767–1773*, ed. Thomas M. Curley, 2 vols (Madison, WI: University of Wisconsin Press, 1986), in lecture 12, "Of offences against the Commonwealth and first of such as are committed against the established religion," observes, "It is apparent to common observation that many of these laws are at present dormant" (Vol. 1, p. 442). A useful local study is J. Anthony Williams, *Catholic Recusancy Statutes in Wiltshire, 1660–1791* ([London]: Catholic Record Society, 1968).

66 For the training of one of the most important of these conveyancers, see Nigel Abercrombie, "The early life of Charles Butler (1750–83)," *Recusant History* 14 (1978): 281–92.

67 Bernard Elliott, "A Leicestershire recusant family: the Nevills of Nevill Holt – II," *Recusant History* 17 (1985): 374–85.

68 Blackstone, *Commentaries*, Vol. 1, pp. 442–7. Some sense of how the poor laws were administered to provide for illegitimate children, as well as some citations of cases, may be gained from Richard Burn, *The Justice of the Peace and Parish Officer*, 4 vols (London: Cadell, 1800). Burn lived from 1707 to 1785; there were many earlier editions of this work, first published in 1755, and many later ones. Recently, major modifications have been made in the law of illegitimacy. In both the United Kingdom and the United States the law is moving toward abolishing the status of illegitimacy. Illegitimate children are gaining the same rights to maintenance and inheritance that legitimate children have, although certain rights to British nationality are still withheld (and rights to succeed to titles or the Crown are explicitly denied). DNA testing very recently has made it technically feasible to establish paternity with a certainty never before possible. For recent developments in England see: Frank Bates, "The presumption of legitimacy: a comparative analysis of its modern operation," *Anglo-American Law Review* 12 (1983): 78–88; the Law Commission, *Family Law: Illegitimacy*, no. 118 (London: HMSO, 1982); Jonathan Montgomery, "Children, status of (the Family Law

Reform Act 1987)," *Journal of Social Welfare Law* (1988): 320–3; Elizabeth W. Davies, "The Family Law Reform Act 1987 and DNA fingerprinting," *Family Law* 18 (1988): 221–3.

69 Roy Porter, "Mixed feelings: the Enlightenment and sexuality in eighteenth-century Britain," in Paul-Gabriel Boucé, *Sexuality in Eighteenth-century Britain* (Manchester: Manchester University Press, 1982), pp. 1–27.

70 Stone, *The Family, Sex and Marriage*, p. 535.

71 George Anne Bellamy, *An Apology for the Life of George Anne Bellamy, Late of Covent Garden Theatre, Written by Herself*, 6 vols (London: 1785), Vol. 1, p. 28.

72 ibid., Vol. 2, p. 46.

73 Samuel Richardson, *Pamela in Two Volumes* (London: Dutton, 1974), Vol. 2, p. 24.

74 Ibid., p. 38.

75 Ibid., p. 355.

76 Ibid., p. 472.

77 Frances Sheridan, *The Discovery*, in *The Plays of Frances Sheridan*, ed. Robert Hogan and Jerry C. Beasley (Newark, DE: University of Delaware Press, 1984), p. 43.

78 Ibid., p. 86.

79 Ibid., p. 94.

80 *Marchioness of Annandale* v. *Anne Harris* (1727), 2 P Wms 432, at 434.

81 *Metham* v. *Duke of Devonshire* (1718), 2 P Wms 529.

82 *Arnold* v. *Preston* (1811), 18 Ves 288; cf. *Wilkinson* v. *Adam* (1812), 1 V & B 422.

83 Ruth McClure, *Coram's Children: The London Foundling Hospital* (New Haven, CT: Yale University Press, 1981).

84 Joseph Robins, *The Lost Children: A Study of Charity Children in Ireland, 1700–1900* (Dublin: Institute of Public Administration, 1980).

85 A. W. B. Simpson, *Biographical Dictionary of the Common Law* (St. Paul, MN: Butterworth, 1984); Robert Gore-Browne, *Chancellor Thurlow; the Life and Times of an Eighteenth-Century Lawyer* (London: Hamish Hamilton, 1953).

86 Philip Highfill, Jr., Kalman A. Burnim, and Edward A. Langhans, *A Biographical Dictionary of Actors, Actresses, Musicians, Dancers, Managers and Other Stage Personnel in London 1660–1800* (Carbondale, IL: Southern Illinois University Press, 1973–), s. v. "Dibden, Charles."

87 Montgomery, "Children," p. 322.

Part IV

Property and the construction
of a self

11
Property and politeness in the early eighteenth-century Whig moralists
The case of the *Spectator*

Lawrence E. Klein

In early 1711, Parliament passed a bill establishing substantial requirements of land ownership for both county and borough members. The passage of such requirements, which had not previously been written in law, was a measure of the success of the Tory Party, in 1710 and 1711, in supplanting the Whigs in the queen's ministry and in Parliament.[1] The bill was also a measure of the anxiety felt by landed gentlemen in a changing historical landscape, an anxiety that they formulated in the distinction between the landed and the moneyed interests.

The language of landed and moneyed was a way of articulating the unsettling pressure to which post-1688 developments were exposing many landed gentlemen. Though they were feeling a keen fiscal pinch as a result of foreign policy and war finance, they also suffered a general malaise induced by the commercial drift of their times. Through the language of landed and moneyed, Tories mounted campaigns about government policy and practice. However, the distinction also had a broader reach, since it implied a politics of personal traits, in which the stable and autonomous personality of the landowner was juxtaposed to the malleable and dependent personality of the owner of mobile property.

The language of landed and moneyed was not, however, the only contemporary initiative in the politics of personality. During the spring of 1711, the three volumes of Shaftesbury's *Characteristicks* first made their way into print, and precisely one week after the passage of the landed qualification bill the first number of the *Spectator* appeared, on March 1, 1711. Addison, Steele, and Shaftesbury were all deeply involved in developing a distinctive language of moral and social personality, which offered a Whiggish politics of manners. These Whigs were well disposed toward modernity and, in various ways, toward commerce. While the language of landed and moneyed evoked the threats to moral personality posed by commerce, the Whig moralists developed ideas about constructing the personality under modern conditions.

One aspect of the ideological construction of commercial modernity was the formulation of an entrepreneurial ideal: an individual who, using integral resources (sense, initiative, industry) and motivated by the powerful incentive of material gain, strove to make his or her own fortune.[2] Shaftesbury was obviously opposed to the individualism and materialism of this ideal. However, political economy did not make much of an overt appearance in his writing. The case was different in the Whig periodical papers, which explicitly praised commerce and trading people. Still, economic man was not to be found in their pages. Their modernism took another form, which becomes visible by tracking the figures of land and commerce in the papers in relation to the notions of personality, manners, and politeness.

That politeness and the politics of manners, responding to the challenges of the country ideology, constituted a defense of commercial modernity in Britain has been pointed out by J. G. A. Pocock.[3] The Scottish phase of this development as well as some of its antecedents have been explored by Nicholas Phillipson.[4] While it is widely recognized that the early eighteenth-century Whig moralists were highly influential in this trajectory of ideas, the exact form of these ideas in the earlier writers still requires investigation. Here I will explore the contributions of the Whig periodicals, the *Tatler*, the *Guardian*, and especially the *Spectator*, to the rise of these new idioms.[5]

Though arguments involving the respective claims of land and trade featured significantly in Restoration political debate, the specific distinction between landed and moneyed interests appeared soon after the establishment of the National Debt and the founding of the Bank of England as a way of identifying those who profited from the new revenue devices: while the landed were those gentlemen whose income was entirely dependent on rents of land, the moneyed were the holders of public stocks and the stockjobbers who traded in them, those to whom Henry St. John referred, in 1709, as a "new interest" with "a sort of property, which was not known twenty years ago."[6]

However, since those who used the distinction between the landed and the moneyed were not very fastidious, this circumscribed use of the distinction was often accompanied by, when not entirely assimilated to, broader uses of it. The moneyed could encompass the varied population of commercial England. The Act prescribing landed qualifications for Members of Parliament had had as its targets, according to Gilbert Burnet, "Courtiers, military men, and merchants."[7] Though fear of placemen was one incentive for the Act, it also expressed anxiety about a range of forces in society, including commerce itself, that appeared to be undermining the landed order. The distinction between the landed and the moneyed raised questions about the continuing viability of the political order as forms of property were diversifying.

This vocabulary not only differentiated the landowning elite from those whose wealth derived from finance and commerce, but also endorsed a hostile opposition between the interests. Generalizing from the inequity of contemporary war finance, the landed ideology imagined that every gain of one interest was the detriment of the other. The paranoid dimension of this dichotomous view of society could be supported with historicizing theory in which the discontents of the landed gentlemen were lifted to a world-historical plane: the gentry, or their spokesmen, talked as if they were oppressed by the forces of history and menaced by the threat of imminent and radical decline.[8]

A premise of the landed argument was that the nature of property was connected operationally or analogically with the personality of its owner. Thus, the landed–moneyed distinction was posed, among other ways, as a moral and psychological distinction, implying a series of contrasts between the owner of land and the owner of other forms of wealth. The land stood still and palpable while other sorts of property were moving and invisible. Since land was pictured as an inheritance, it was firmly situated in time as well as in place. By contrast, mobile property lacked physical and temporal definition. While land was pictured as intrinsically valuable, passed in entirety from generation to generation, outside the exchanges and fluctuating values that constituted the market society, mobile property, always shifting hands and dependent on the market, lacked any such autonomy.[9]

The personalities associated with the divergent characters of property differed in two respects. First, land was seen as a form of wealth that insured the reliability of the owner. The permanence of land and its tangible reality were a guarantee of the owner's commitment to the nation since his wealth was physically part of the nation. Robert Molesworth's argument for landed parliamentary qualifications was that land made for a fixed and permanent stake in the kingdom, unlike "fleeting" forms of property, "which may be sent beyond Sea by Bills of Exchange by every Pacquet-Boat."[10] With the option of absconding with his wealth intact to another country, the owner of commercial wealth was depicted as unreliable. The nature of moveable wealth seemed to make its owner's relation to the polity contingent: the commercial human was too plastic a being.

Second, the fact that land was physically part of the nation meant that the landowner's wealth was entirely of a piece with the security and well-being of the nation. The landowner was ineluctably drawn to consider his own interests in the context of the interest of the nation as a whole. According to Lord Ashburnham, "whenever England comes to be settled and made happy it must be done by councils of such who love their country and value their estates beyond any thing else of any consideration whatsoever."[11] By contrast, the merchant, it was said, was motivated principally by an interest in his own moveable wealth and its fortunes. The landowner was capable of a comprehensive view of things and so of virtue and patriotism. "Possessed of a good estate," according to one contemporary, the landed gentleman "did not lie open to the temptations that might bias persons who had their fortunes to make against the interest of their country."[12] The commercial person's civic aptitude was limited by his self-interest, his narrow vision, and his partiality: his was a problem of specialization. Mobile property was a form of wealth that committed the owner to work to create new wealth whereas landed wealth freed the owner from such work and the narrowing interests associated with it.

In sum, the language of landed and moneyed conjured up a picture in which kinds of wealth constituted significant differences in society, differences of social and psychological as well as political resonance. In particular, the language elicited a politics of personal traits, indeed of personality, in which the landed asserted their autonomy and stability against the partiality and plasticity of the commercial person.

Though the Whig periodical papers all forswore politics or at least removed themselves from direct and routine partisanship, they bore numerous ideological traces, including a response to the distinction between the landed and the moneyed. In general, the periodicals explored the distinction while setting it in a new framework that undermined Tory arguments. The Whig periodicals emphasized social complexity rather than social dichotomy, so that the distinction between the landed and the moneyed became a source of value in the civil order, not of disruption.

However, the Whig periodicals did make some important adjustments in the treatment of land and commerce. Most important, they recognized that commerce was not a sector of the economy but the fundamental form of the entire economy. Given that recognition, problems of partiality and plasticity beset all individuals in modern society. With the help of religion and virtue, such problems could be mastered. Another remedy for such problems was politeness.

Of course, the periodicals addressed the distinction between the landed and the moneyed in economic as well as psycho-social terms. Answering anxieties about the innovations in government finance, the *Spectator* offered its well-known endorsement of public credit.[13] It also extolled the virtues of the Royal Exchange, which it peopled with merchants rather than stockjobbers.[14] This and the fact that the *Spectator* took an occasional swipe at the stockjobber[15] point to the broader construction of the distinction between the landed and the moneyed, with which the periodicals were principally concerned.

When the papers reiterated that England was a trading nation,[16] they neither exalted trade at the expense of land nor declared the victory of one interest over the other. Rather, they meant that commerce had penetrated the entirety of the nation's economy. According to the Spectator, "upon Reflection every Man will find there is a remote Influence upon his own Affairs, in the Prosperity or Decay of the Trading Part of Mankind."[17] The entirety of England had entered on a commercial career.

To support this idea, the Spectator was willing to situate his own moralist tasks within the framework of commerce. He pointed out that, in addition to any moral good he might have been doing the nation, his enterprise also consumed paper, furthered trade, and set the poor to work. He thereby applied to himself the language of projecting at no expense to his moral credentials.[18] Similarly, when the Stamp Act went into effect in August 1712, the Spectator advised readers to weigh his moral instruction against the increased expense of the paper. He admitted that contemporary conditions were commercial conditions, that his readership was a market, and that his paper was an item for sale.[19]

The *Spectator*'s recognition that the entire economy was moving in a commercial direction tended to undermine the distinction between land and money. However, this tendency is not so apparent if one pays attention only to the figures of Sir Roger de Coverley and Sir Andrew Freeport. Addison endowed de Coverley and Freeport with a certain iconic value, allowing each to be interpreted as an ideal type. De Coverley can be seen as the apotheosis of the old man (the gentleman who dominated a locality through his landed wealth and patronage and softened his dominance through varieties of paternalism, such as charity and hospitality); Freeport, as the apotheosis of the new man (the upwardly mobile merchant-turned-gentleman with strong business sense and a City fortune and the concomitant virtues of industry, reliability, and frugality). This contrast in types lends itself to an interpretation of the *Spectator* as representing the decline of one social group, with its peculiar ethic, in the face of a new soon-to-be dominant social group, with its own innovating set of values. In such an interpretation, the *Spectator* becomes the vehicle for hailing the arrival on the scene of Freeport.[20]

I am not satisfied with the simple dismissal of de Coverley as old-fashioned. However, more immediately to the point, it is important to see that the papers treated the landed and the moneyed as examples of interdependence rather than as independent alternatives. Land and commerce depended on each other economically.[21] So too they were mutually dependent in moral terms. Since the thrust of the papers was the exploration of moral complementarity and dependence, the values of the landed gentleman and of the commercial man, while commendable, could not be taken as self-subsistent.

It is easy to find in the papers illustrations of the Whig admiration of commercial values. What matters here is the way that commerce was said to affect the landed. The papers advertised commerce as a vocation for younger sons of landed families and thus as a remedy for genteel alienation or fecklessness.[22] More fundamentally, the papers proposed that the landed man himself had to have a commercial mentality in order to survive. In *Spectator* no. 174, Freeport challenged de Coverley's insinuation that the merchant's moral composition was inferior to that of the landed gentleman. Aside from pointing to such virtues as charity shared by both the landed and the moneyed, Freeport invoked the habits of the commercial mind (fastidiousness, frugality, and others) as virtues in themselves, virtues that the landed gentleman himself could not afford to ignore. In the words of Freeport, "This is the Oeconomy of the Merchant, and the Conduct of the Gentleman must be the same." In a similar vein, *Guardian* no. 9, describing the activities of a City merchant who retired and then purchased and improved a landed estate, illustrated the benefits resulting from the application of business sense to the rural economy. These numbers implied that land as property was not fundamentally different from the sorts of property usually manipulated by commercial men. Thus, the same commercial alertness was required of the landowner as of owners of the more mobile forms of property.

At the same time, the papers indicated the limits of a purely commercial ethos, since they asserted the inadequacies of gain and material ambition as autonomous schemes of value. Those whose "Hearts are wholly bent towards Pleasure, or intent upon Gain" were deaf to the claims of many values pitched in another key:

> When Mens Thoughts are taken up with Avarice and Ambition, they cannot look upon any thing as great or valuable, which does not bring with it an extraordinary Power or Interest to the Person who is concerned in it. But as I shall never sink this Paper so far as to engage with *Goths* and *Vandals*, I shall only regard such kind of Reasoners with that Pity which is due to so deplorable a degree of Stupidity and Ignorance.[23]

So, despite the congratulations offered the commercially minded in a commercial world, the papers did not endorse a possessive individualism. The commercial universe was not to be understood in terms of a collection of self-seeking individuals. Passions and interests in themselves were not a plausible basis for conceiving the modern world.

Thus, while the papers depicted the unviability of the landed gentleman divorced from the commercial life of the society, they condemned the merchant divorced from non-material sources of value. Undisciplined material ambition was a source of malicious behavior, but it also had other consequences, which are of particular interest here. In one scenario, as I have mentioned, the merchant retired to the country and, through his productive endeavors, illustrated the relevance of commercial values among the landed; but, in another, the merchant again retired to the country, surrounding himself with all manner of material appurtenances only to discover that he lacked any sense of how he should spend his time.[24] Such a commercial man was in need of the sort of education that *Tatler* no. 46 sketched for a City potentate: since

> Wealth and Wisdom are Possessions too solemn not to give Weariness to active Minds, without the Relief (in vacant Hours) of Wit and Love, which are the proper Amusements of the Powerful and the Wise: This Emperor therefore, with great Regularity, every Day at Five in the Afternoon, leaves his Money-Changers, his Publicans, and little Hoarders of Wealth, to their low Pursuits, and ascends his Chariot to drive to *Will's*; where the Tast is refin'd, and a Relish giv'n to Men's Possessions by a polite Skill in gratifying their Passions and Appetites.

This passage points in the direction that this chapter must now pursue: it invoked the complementary relations between the commercial life and the process of refinement and politeness; it linked politeness to the refinement of passions; and it pointed to the coffee-house Will's as a significant location in the moral landscape.

For the writers of the periodicals, the question of the landed personality and the moneyed personality was absorbed to a larger problem associated with modernity. Neither the landed gentleman nor the commercial man was presented in the papers as embodying a fully realized ethic. Nor were they alone, for the periodical papers presented a range of characters who were victims of their own moral incompleteness. These characters were partial in that they were incomplete and also in that their interest was vested too deeply and narrowly in their own concerns. They did not have enough distance from themselves and their settings to gauge moral matters coherently. Thus, the papers seem to agree with the fear of specialization informing the landed attack on commerce, but the papers did not regard the landed form of property as a plausible security against it.

This concern to recuperate wholeness bespoke the humanism of the periodical papers. Like civic and Tory humanism, this Whig humanism was concerned with the degradation of humanity under contemporary conditions.[25] However, it was optimistic because, in its view, modern conditions did not simply cast up impediments to human actualization but also offered opportunities for moral refinement. For instance, material progress was a feature of the modern world that could enhance moral possibilities: though such progress widened the traps of dissipation and luxury encountered by the wealthy, it freed many from the morally deadening effects of poverty.[26] However, the papers represented another feature of modernity with special effect, a feature that particularly illuminated the moral situation and moral opportunities of the modern world. This feature was diversity.[27]

The papers situated themselves in a diverse material, social, and moral world and engaged enthusiastically in the tasks of representing multiplicity in any number of domains. They pictured the manifold world of fashions, produced prodigious numbers of social groups and categories, sketched a wide range of individual characters, and multiplied moral cases. The remarkable *Spectator* no. 442, in which the Spectator requested submissions from readers, offers a dense sample of this interest in the multi-faceted modern world:

> I will invite all manner of Persons, whether Scholars, Citizens, Courtiers, Gentlemen of the Town or Country, and all Beaux, Rakes, Smarts, Prudes, Coquets, Housewives, and all sorts of Wits, whether Male or Female, and however distinguish'd, whether they be True-Wits, Whole, or Half-Wits, or whether Arch, Dry, Natural, Acquir'd, Genuine, or Deprav'd Wits; and Persons of all Sorts of Tempers and Complexions, whether the Severe, the Delightful, the Impertinent, the Agreeable, the Thoughtful, Busy, or Careless; the Serene or Cloudy, Jovial or Melancholy, Untowardly or Easy; the Cold, Temperate, or Sanguine; and of what Manners or Dispositions soever, whether the Ambitious or Humble-minded, the Proud or Pitiful, Ingenuous or Base-minded, Good or Ill-natur'd, Publick-spirited or Selfish; and under what Fortune or Circumstance soever, whether the Contented or Miserable, Happy or Unfortunate, High or Low, Rich or Poor (whether so thro' Want of Money, or Desire of more), Healthy or Sickly, Marry'd or Single; nay, whether Tall or Short, Fat or Lean; and of what Trade, Occupation, Profession, Station, Country, Faction, Party, Perswasion, Quality, Age or Condition soever, who have ever made Thinking a Part of their Business or Diversion.[28]

Gushy proliferation of this sort may have sprung from the particularly charged way that early modern humanistic writers could interpret the virtues of copiousness,[29] but it also arose in the attempt of the periodical writers to thematize the diversity of the contemporary world. This passage epitomized the practice found throughout the papers of inventing social categories. Aside from offering comic opportunities, the invention of social categories pointed up the problem of social variety. The papers delighted in the diversity but also worried about the moral consequences of narrow social identities. Diversity and partiality were intimately connected, it seemed. Against the background of this proliferation of social categories, the difference between the landed and the moneyed might be seen to lose its unique importance.

This interest in diversity can be related to the problem of commerce in a number of ways. First, commerce helped to create diversity, multiplying occupations and trades, goods, fashions, and diversions. Commerce multiplied the options for the expression of economic personality, since in "a trading Nation . . . there are very few in it so dull and heavy, who may not be placed in Stations of Life which may give them the opportunity of making their Fortune."[30] However, as the phenomenon of fashion illustrated, commerce also multiplied the options for the expression of many other aspects of personality.[31] Second, commerce was centered in the metropolis, which in the periodical papers was the particular locus of diversity. According to the Spectator, "my greatest Difficulty in the Country is to find Sport, and in Town to chuse it," since the latter offered so great a "Variety of odd Creatures in both Sexes." In another number, he remarked on "the strange variety of Faces and Persons which fill the Streets with Business and Hurry" and which fill successive numbers of the periodical.[32] Similarly, the gentlemanly personae of the *Tatler* and the *Guardian*, Isaac Bickerstaffe and Nestor Ironsides, were primarily residents in and commentators on London. A third and more intimate connection between this multiplicative bent of the periodical papers and commerce was simply the fact that they themselves were commercial entities being produced on a demanding schedule in order to take advantage of the ever-renewing appetites of an audience for literary consumption. The papers were self-conscious about their status as objects of commerce. In order to satisfy a market extended in time, the writers had to continue inventing copiously.

However, besides representing diversity and complexity, the *Spectator* also presented itself as an instrument for grasping a diverse and complex world and for tangling with its particular problems: disunity, disorientation, and partiality. If the diversity of modern life posed, in striking form, the problem of the partiality of moral agents, then a remedial strategy involved assuming a distance from those agents in order to achieve a more encompassing standpoint. The Spectator was engaged in precisely such a strategy. Though the Spectator frequently reminded readers that he loved solitude,[33] he did not hanker for isolation so much as contemplative distance. In fact, he wrote in one number: "A Man who is but a mere Spectator of what passes around him, and not engaged in Commerces of any Consideration, is but an ill Judge of the secret Motions of the Heart of Man."[34] His status, then, was in but not totally of the world. As he confessed, the key to his capacity for aloofness was an indifference to others' opinions and a lack of ambition, qualities that freed him from the constraints attached to a particular limited character.[35] He thus had the protean ability to engage with many different types of people and also to distance himself so as to acquire a perspective. This distance allowed him to be a moral oracle.

Of course, the Spectator was a privileged character, his moral authority deriving from the exaggerated way in which he sought to engage with others and remain aloof from them. Since most people were motivated by ambition and a keen sense of others' opinions,[36] the Spectator himself was hard to imitate. Nonetheless, his procedures were not entirely outside the range of ordinary social beings. What ordinary social beings needed was a mechanism for distancing themselves from themselves – or perhaps a certain plasticity of self – which would allow them to see themselves in a context of other selves. Politeness involved just such a mechanism.

The term "politeness" had a wide range of uses in this period, and it appeared with characteristic diversity in the periodical papers.[37] One relevant definition of "politeness" was the submission of the self to the disciplines of social interaction. These disciplines, explored throughout the periodical papers, had already been worked out in numerous courtesy books of the sixteenth and seventeenth centuries. The social disciplines aimed to enhance social interaction, making it more pleasurable and sometimes also more useful and instructive. They constituted an art of pleasing others in conversation and company often in ways that redounded to one's own pleasure or benefit. At its most humanistic, politeness was the means to bring out the best in others and in oneself. Among other capacities that such social discipline demanded was the ability to see oneself in the context of a complex social situation: one had to grasp one's own desires and interests while comprehending the legitimate desires and interests of others. The frequent exhortations in the *Spectator* to modesty, discretion, decorum, propriety, and politeness were demands that the moral agent recognize the social context of his or her actions and so integrate self and others, parts and wholes.

A revealing example of politeness in practice is found in *Spectator* no. 105, which takes off from remarks of Will Honeycomb, an older member of the Spectator's club who still pursued pleasures in the manner of the Restoration rake. In defense of his flagitious past and his enduring ignorance, Honeycomb asserted the superiority of "Knowledge of the World" to book learning and of the gentleman to the scholar. He also condemned "pedantry," a standard object of polite condemnation. Honeycomb's self-serving repetitions of courtesy-book commonplaces led the Spectator to his own reflections on the merits of learning, in which he reconstructed the idea of "pedantry": "A Man who has been brought up among Books, and is able to talk of nothing else, is a very indifferent Companion, and what we call a Pedant. But, methinks, we should enlarge the Title, and give it every one that does not know how to think out of his Profession, and particular way of Life." The ensuing catalogue of pedants – the Man of Town as pedant, the Military Pedant, the Law Pedant, the State Pedant, and the Book Pedant – comprised individuals who insisted on being specialists. Pedantry here stood for a commitment to one's own limits and a resistance to assuming a perspective broader than that available from one's daily profession. In other numbers, the Spectator mined the same vein, attacking prejudice, particularity, and partisanship.[38] To be polite, one had to repress differences; the aim, however, was not to consummate a love of uniformity (so opposite to the pleasures of diversity) but rather to allow the benefits of association. The Spectator praised the "Mind that lies open to receive what is pleasing to others, and not obstinately bent on any Particularity of its own," a mind "able to live with all Kinds of Dispositions."[39] It appears then that politeness was a way to take charge of the diversities of modern life. On one level, it provided practical suggestions for enhancing sociability among diverse individuals. On another, it offered a communal vision for a complex society.

Though the disciplines of politeness were invented in courtly circumstances, the Whig periodical writers suggested their appropriateness to a modern society. Among other things, politeness in the *Spectator* promised to integrate the landed gentleman and the commercial man since it was a discipline applicable to both types equally. It was not the point of politeness to force commercial men to submit to the cultural hegemony of the traditional elite; nor was politeness a way of domesticating a traditional honor-bound elite to the more pacific norms of commercial men. Rather, it was a way of reconstructing gentility for an age perceived to be novel.

It should be added that politeness made a virtue of human plasticity. Since, for the Whig moralists, passions were the motor of human actions, human moral development depended largely on shaping the passions, which were conceived as diverse and flexible in their orientation.[40] A passion of particular importance for the development of politeness was the human need for the approval of others. Of course, this need opened up the moral and social liabilities of posing – hypocrisy and deceit, on one hand, and moral timidity, on the other[41] – which the Spectator avidly chastised. Yet, the same need was a basis for civilization, because it forced the individual to situate and adjust his or her own actions and personality to the desires and interests of others. Building on the need for approval, politeness undermined the plausibility of human psychological autonomy at the same time that it mounted a campaign against the partialities to which the human tended.

Politeness was important as a model for transcending limitations and liabilities that selves were perceived as bound to have in a diverse, modern, and commercial society.

This role of politeness helps to explain the particular importance of conversation in the periodicals – as a topic for comment, as an object for representation, as a discursive practice of the papers themselves. Well-motivated conversation encapsulated the aspiration for social forms that admitted diversity and also distanced individuals from their particularities so that a public life could come into existence. A related theme in the papers was clubbability. The Spectator's own club created and regulated conversational opportunities through which moral interchange proceeded. As the scene for the negotiations of the landed de Coverley and the moneyed Freeport, that club had a "representative" quality; but the many other clubs confected in the Whig periodicals were exclusive, though not in the social sense. Composed of specialists dedicated to the elaboration of specialisms, usually of an idle or trivial sort, these clubs were the antithesis of polite sociability. The coffeehouse was obviously another device, used throughout the periodicals, to illustrate the possibilities or frustrations of polite interaction.

The instance that most compactly conveys the dynamic of politeness was a Spectatorial reflection on a Sunday in the country:

> if keeping holy the Seventh Day were only a human Institution, it would be the best Method that could have been thought of for the polishing and civilizing of Mankind. It is certain that Country-People would soon degenerate into a kind of Savages and Barbarians, were there not such frequent Returns of a stated Time, in which the whole Village meet together with their best Faces, and in their cleanliest Habits, to converse with one another upon indifferent Subjects, hear their Duties explained to them, and join together in Adoration of the supreme Being. *Sunday* clears away the Rust of the whole Week, not only as it refreshes in their Minds the Notion of Religion, but as it puts both the Sexes upon appearing in their most agreeable Forms, and exerting all such Qualities as are apt to give them a Figure in the Eye of the Village.[42]

Sermons were not, on the whole, a polite idiom; but other aspects of this scene are significant. Sunday worship drew people out of their routines; it forced them to talk about things other than the immediacies of their lives; it not only set them in a common place, but set each before the eyes of others. All these had the effect of dissolving apartness and partiality for the benefit of politeness and civilization.

I have proposed that, in the Whig periodicals, modern politeness depended on diversity as it sought to overcome partiality. Accordingly, the landed gentleman and the commercial man were on much the same moral footing. It therefore seems appropriate to end this discussion with a small defense of the role of Roger de Coverley in the papers. He was indeed the landed paternalist with a number of silly opinions. He also had a number of virtues which the Spectator found inestimable. One of these was companionship: while all the characters met in the club, it was de Coverley who accompanied the Spectator on expeditions in town and country.[43] Thus, while Freeport was a suitable vehicle for conjuring the diversities associated with the world of trade, de Coverley offered the Spectator opportunities to take in the diversity of the social world. De Coverley was comfortable in the town, and so he provided the Spectator access to a world that offered a necessary complement to both the country and the city.

De Coverley was no mere foxhunter, but he did hunt, and hunting, an arch-recreation of the landed man, made a number of significant appearances in the *Spectator*. Of course, like all enthusiasts, the hunter could be a pedantic destroyer of conversation, so that hunting illuminated the particular partialities and prejudices of the landed man.[44] Yet, the Spectator himself enjoyed hunting and saw in it a metaphor for his activities as the pursuer of social habits.[45] Thus, while the Spectator was capable of representing his activity in commercial terms, as the sale of a certain sort of moral goods to a volatile market, he was also capable of understanding it in a figure from the world of the landed gentleman. The commercial idiom explained the necessary relations of the papers to the readership. The gentlemanly metaphor explained the process of creation, the tact and selectivity required to produce a good periodical. The two idioms of explanation were complementary.

Notes

1 Similar measures had been twice defeated during William's reign and once early in Anne's. The "Act Imposing Property Qualifications on Members of the House of Commons" or the Landed Property Qualification Act (9 Anne, c. 5) and its context are discussed in Geoffrey Holmes, *British Politics in the Age of Anne* (London: Macmillan, 1967), Ch. 5, especially pp. 178–82. A more detailed account appeared in Edward Porritt, *The Unreformed House of Commons* (New York: Augustus M. Kelley, 1963 [1903]), Vol. 1, pp. 166–81.

2 For instance, Louis Dumont's account in *From Mandeville to Marx* (Chicago: University of Chicago Press, 1977), especially Chs 4 and 5, about Locke and Mandeville.

3 His most directly relevant statements appear in *Virtue, Commerce and History* (Cambridge, UK: Cambridge University Press, 1985): "Virtue, rights and manners," especially pp. 47–50; "The mobility of property and the rise of eighteenth-century sociology," especially pp. 107–15; "The varieties of Whiggism from exclusion to reform," especially pp. 230–9. See also J. W. Burrow, *Whigs and Liberals: Continuity and Change in English Political Thought* (Oxford: Clarendon Press, 1988), p. x. I have explored some aspects of the politics of "politeness" in "Liberty, manners, and politeness in early eighteenth-century England," *Historical Journal* 32 (1989): 583–605.

4 Nicholas Phillipson, *Hume* (London: Weidenfeld & Nicolson, 1989), pp. 23–30, and many other writings by Phillipson cited there.

5 The *Tatler* appeared in 271 numbers from April 12, 1709 to January 2, 1711 (Donald F. Bond [ed.], *The Tatler*, 3 vols [Oxford: Clarendon Press, 1987]). The *Spectator* appeared in 555 numbers from March 1, 1711 to December 6, 1712, with another 80 numbers from June 18 to December 20, 1714 (Donald F. Bond [ed.], *The Spectator*, 5 vols [Oxford: Clarendon Press, 1965]). The *Guardian* appeared in 175 numbers from March 12 to October 1, 1713 (John Calhoun Stephens [ed.], *The Guardian* [Lexington, KY: University Press of Kentucky, 1982]).

6 J. P. Kenyon, *Revolution Principles* (Cambridge, UK: Cambridge University Press, 1977), pp. 155–7; Henry St. John to Charles Boyle, Earl of Orrery, July 9, 1709, in "The letters of Henry St John to the Earl of Orrery 1709–1711," *Camden Miscellany*, 4th series, 14 (1975): 138; Holmes, *British Politics in the Age of Anne*, Ch. 5; H. T. Dickinson, *Liberty and Property: Political Ideology in Eighteenth-Century Britain* (London: Weidenfeld & Nicolson, 1977), pp. 85–9, 102 ff. On the earlier period, Richard Ashcraft, *Revolutionary Politics and Locke's Two Treatises of Government* (Princeton, NJ: Princeton University Press, 1986), Ch. 6.

7 On the applications of the distinction, both narrower and broader, Holmes, *British Politics in the Age of Anne*, pp. 169–70. Burnet is quoted in ibid., p. 149.

8 The theory underpinning the landed position is the subject of J. G. A. Pocock's *The Machiavellian Moment: Florentine Political Thought and the Atlantic Republican Tradition* (Princeton, NJ: Princeton University Press, 1975), Ch. 13.

9   The landed perspective conveniently ignored the economic interdependence of land and money. It also denied certain aspects of the nature of landed property in itself, such as the existence of a market in land, the use of land as a capital asset to raise money by mortgage, and the vulnerability of estates in land to forfeiture for breaches of condition (e.g. certain attempts to alienate, waste, put to superstitious uses). As we will see, the *Spectator* frequently pointed out that the landed proprietor had better be commercially minded or risk losing his estate.

10 Robert Molesworth, preface to François Hotman's *Francogallia* (London: 1721), p. xix.

11 Quoted in Holmes, *British Politics in the Age of Anne*, p. 163.

12 Quoted in ibid., p. 149.

13 *Spectator* no. 3. As William Speck points out, this number appeared in the run-up to the election of the directors of the Bank, in which subscribers were faced with Whig and Tory slates (*Society and Literature in England 1700–60* [Dublin: Gill & Macmillan, 1983], p. 62).

14 *Spectator* no. 69.

15 *Spectator* no. 114.

16 *Spectator* nos 69, 115, 443, 509.

17 *Spectator* no. 509.

18 *Spectator* no. 367. The language of projecting is in evidence throughout Joan Thirsk, *Economic Policy and Projects: The Development of a Consumer Society in Early Modern England* (Oxford: Clarendon Press, 1972). In no. 442, the Spectator called himself the "Projector of the Paper."

19 *Spectator* nos 445 and 488. For illuminating comments on how the conditions under which the periodicals were produced influenced their authors' rhetorical strategies, see Charles A. Knight, "Bibliography and the shape of the literary periodical in the early eighteenth century," *The Library*, 6th series, 8 (1986): 232–48. The double status of the *Spectator*, as a proliferating commercial vehicle and as a conceptually serious work of art, is a theme of Michael G. Ketcham's *Transparent Designs: Reading, Performance, and Form in the Spectator Papers* (Athens, GA: University of Georgia Press, 1985).

20 This is the approach of the major work on Addison, Edward A. Bloom and Lillian D. Bloom, *Joseph Addison's Sociable Animal* (Providence, RI: Brown University Press, 1971), which sees the periodical papers as middle-class documents in a situation of "submerged class rivalry" (p. 136). The approach is also common in general works, such as Maximillian Novak's *Eighteenth-Century English Literature* (New York: Schocken Books, 1984), in which de Coverley represents "the old landed interest" and "belonged to a quaint, dying world, as moribund as that of Sir Andrew Freeport was full of movement and energy" (p. 33). By contrast, Ketcham offers an interpretation of the *Spectator*'s "paradigm of social life" that is far less dichotomous and reductionist: *Transparent Designs*, pp. 163–71.

21 *Spectator* no. 69; *Guardian* no. 76.

22 *Spectator* nos 108, 123.

23 *Spectator* nos 248, 367; also, 224 and 352.

24 *Tatler* no. 176.

25 Aside from the references to Pocock above, see Paul Fussell, *The Rhetorical World of Augustan Humanism* (Oxford: Clarendon Press, 1965), Ch. 1.

26 *Spectator* nos 257, 464.

27 The treatment of the *Spectator* that follows is heavily indebted to the treatment of diversity in eighteenth-century Britain and the concomitant urgency for new forms of comprehension in John Barrell, *English Literature in History 1730–80* (New York: St Martin's Press, 1983). The tension between the "multiplying of perspectives" and the "movement toward consistency and closure" is also discussed in Ketcham, *Transparent Designs*, pp. 125–32.

28 *Spectator* no. 442. In *Tatler* no. 164, Steele commented on the diversity of his readership and the corresponding diversity of the *Tatler* material, which he could imagine sorted and repackaged for different segments of the readership: *ad aulum, ad academiam, ad populum, ad clerum*, and so forth.

29 Terence Cave, *The Cornucopian Text* (Oxford: Clarendon Press, 1979).

30 *Spectator* no. 21.

31 *Spectator* no. 478 related fashion and commerce. Since, as the papers point out, fashion could be politicized, commerce can be said even to help diversify the means of political expression.

32 *Spectator* nos 131, 193; also 403.

33 *Spectator* nos 4, 106, 110, 131.

34 *Spectator* no. 76.

35 *Spectator* no. 270.

36 *Spectator* nos 122, 188, 210, 255, among others.

37 Lawrence E. Klein, "Shaftesbury and the progress of politeness," *Eighteenth-Century Studies* 18 (1984–5): 186–214.

38 *Spectator* nos 432, 438, 445.

39 *Spectator* no. 386. For closely related reasons, the Spectator praised compassion as a particularly important passion and virtue: it brought individuals out of their own particular condition into contact with that of others; it served to "refine and civilize Human Nature"; and thereby it "knits Mankind together, and blends them in the same common Lot." *Spectator* nos 312, 397.

40 *Spectator* nos 255, 408. The Whig moralists participated in the general transvaluation of passion in the later seventeenth century, of which an excellent account appears in Norman Fiering, *Moral Philosophy at Seventeenth-Century Harvard* (Chapel Hill, NC: University of North Carolina Press, 1981). In *Spectator* no. 71, Steele wrote: "The entire Conquest of our Passions is so difficult a work, that they who despair of it should think of a less difficult Task, and only attempt to Regulate them. But there is a third thing which may contribute not only to the Ease, but also the Pleasure of our Life; and that is, refining our Passions to a greater Elegance, than we receive them from Nature."

41 *Spectator* nos 188, 386, 439.

42 *Spectator* no. 112.

43 *Spectator* nos 106–31, 269, 329, 335, 410.

44 *Spectator* no. 472.

45 *Spectator* no. 131.

12

ReWrighting Shaftesbury

The *Air Pump* and the limits of commercial humanism

David Solkin

Joseph Wright of Derby's best-known painting, *An Experiment on a Bird in the Air Pump* (1768; Plate 12.1), depicts a fashionable company in attendance at a lecture given by a natural philosopher, who is demonstrating the necessity of air to life by showing his audience (and us) a white bird struggling for breath in the partial vacuum that has been created within the glass receiver at the top of the pump. It is the climactic moment of the experiment, when the bird may die, or when the lecturer may restore it to health by opening the stopcock he grasps between the fingertips of his left hand. The suspense is heightened by the theatrical chiaroscuro, which highlights the various reactions of the spectators, ranging from the evident distress of the two young girls through to the calmer responses and apparent unconcern displayed by other members of the group.

This theme and its spectacular treatment add up to a kind of picture that defined Wright to his original audience as an artist who stood distinctly apart from eighteenth-century British norms – when an anonymous reviewer called him "a very great and uncommon genius in a peculiar way,"[1] he must have been registering an opinion that was generally shared at the time. Though large-size depictions of such highly particularized figures were usually only to be found in examples of group portraiture,[2] the *Air Pump* presented its human actors as contemporary types, and not as specifiable individuals;[3] and while thematically it stood in clear relation to a tradition of conversation-piece imagery, no other English painter had ever created so monumental an image of an elegant social gathering, or one with such powerful visual impact. The representation of a dramatic narrative enacted by numerous figures on the scale of life was supposed to fall within the province of history painting, the most noble of the pictorial genres; yet according to academic theory the dignity of historical art conventionally depended on the presence of an heroic action described in the elevated language of classical idealism – on a type of style and subject-matter, in other words, which was pointedly absent from Wright's work. His novel combination of different features taken from a range of standard pictorial types has prompted most modern scholars to treat

the *Air Pump* and Wright's other candlelight scenes from the 1760s as cultural oddities –
to explain their production by referring to certain special factors which apply to him
and him alone. Thus much has been made of Wright's provincial status (Wright "of
Derby"), of his links with an ostensibly enlightened Midlands bourgeoisie, and of his
sympathy with the nascent scientific, technological, and industrial revolutions, and so
on.[4] While I would be reluctant to dismiss these issues out of hand, I believe that
attempts to describe the *Air Pump* as a harbinger of great things to come have probably
done more to obscure than to clarify the historical significance of Wright's achievement. I do not see him acting simply as the spokesman for a marginal cultural
vanguard emerging north of the River Trent;[5] on the contrary, here I hope to show that
his most complex candlelight[6] addressed the basic concerns of an ideological project
which had for some time been of central importance to eighteenth-century British
culture as a whole. Broadly speaking we can perhaps best describe that project as
encompassing a range of attempts to describe the forms of modern social life – what
John Mullan has recently identified, in reference to the moral philosophers and writers
of imaginative literature working in the middle part of the century, as a recurrent
impulse to "*produce* society . . . on the page."[7] Though in Wright's case the medium was
a painted canvas, he likewise took it upon himself to construct an image – part
description, part projection, part critique – designed to instruct his audience about the
character of their own world, using a scientific experiment as the parabolic means of
achieving this larger moral end.[8]

To create a painting that sought to teach its viewers to know themselves was to
embrace a philosophical agenda for the visual arts that had first been proposed in
England at the beginning of the century, by Anthony Ashley Cooper, third Earl of
Shaftesbury. Taking his cue from Aristotle's *Poetics*, Shaftesbury asserted in his notes
for an unpublished essay on the plastic arts that their highest duty was to promote
"knowledge of the species, of our own species, of *ourselves*";[9] he followed much the same
line in his famous treatise on the *Judgment of Hercules*, which was first published in
English in 1713. Here of course Shaftesbury constructed a definition of historical art
that could not be applied to a picture like the *Air Pump*; but by the 1760s his aesthetic
theories had been substantially rewritten by subsequent writers, to the point where
they could now begin to accommodate forms of moral painting that would not have
fulfilled the criteria which the third earl had prescribed.

Among the various reworkings of Shaftesbury that appeared in the decades around
mid-century, one in particular speaks with quite remarkable directness to the formal
and thematic characteristics of Wright's scientific scenes. George Turnbull's *Treatise on
Ancient Painting*, which appeared in 1740, has recently been described as a "summary"
of Shaftesburian aesthetics,[10] and no doubt it is so in many basic respects. But on a
number of important issues Turnbull expressed opinions opposed to those of his
principal model; and for us his positive evaluation of scientific practice constitutes an
especially relevant case in point.

In his analysis of the highest purposes of art, Turnbull took his starting point from
Shaftesbury's contention that painting should contribute to the ethical instruction of
mankind by giving concrete form to abstract notions of morality. Both writers, in other
words, argued for a close alliance between the visual arts and moral philosophy. But in
a significant departure from Shaftesburian dogma, which had no time for the inductive

and empiricist premises of modern experimental science, the *Treatise* insisted that attempts to separate natural (i.e., Newtonian) philosophy from its moral counterpart were fundamentally flawed, and even pernicious. According to Turnbull, both aspects of philosophy should "be managed and carried on in the same way of Experiment; and in the one case as well as in the other, nothing ought to be admitted as fact, till it is clearly found to be such from unexceptionable Experience and Observation." He firmly believed, moreover, that "Conclusions derived from moral Powers and Affections, considered apart from sensitive ones, cannot make *Human Morality*, if Man really is a moral Being, intimately related to and connected with the Laws of the sensible World."[11] Drawing on the basic premises of Lockean epistemology, Turnbull defined painting as a form of cultural expression which could marshal the conjoined resources of moral and natural philosophy for the advancement of human understanding. No doubt certain pictures were primarily moral, and others primarily natural; but even works that fell into the second category, such as landscape paintings, were bound to promote an awareness of "the moral Ends or final Causes of Effects"[12] that were manifest in the physical world.

> In short, Pictures which represent visible Beauties, or the Effects of Nature in the visible World, by the different Modification of Light and Colours, in Consequence of the [Newtonian] laws which relate to Light, are Samples of what these Laws do or may produce. And therefore they are proper Samples and Experiments to help and assist us in the Study of those Laws, as any Samples or Experiments in the Study of the Laws of Gravity, Elasticity, or of any other Quality in the natural World. They are then Samples or Experiments in natural Philosophy.[13]

On the other hand, "Good moral Paintings" had to adhere to natural truths, if they were to serve "as proper Samples in moral Philosophy, [which] ought therefore to be used in teaching it, for the same Reason that Experiments are made use of in teaching natural Philosophy."[14] Such works provided lessons in human nature, whilst the former dealt with the nature of the universe; but ultimately their respective purposes, like those of the different aspects of philosophy to which each was linked, formed an inseparable whole – to teach men about themselves, the perceptible world, and the divinity responsible for all of creation.

The introduction of an empiricist component into the framework of Shaftesburian aesthetics forced Turnbull into the paradoxical position of subverting some of the most basic arguments of a discourse that he professedly admired. In modifying the third earl's views on philosophy – siding now with the moderns against the ancients[15] – he could not help but abandon his predecessor's strict definition of proper pictorial form. Instead of insisting that the highest truths could only be communicated in the idealizing language of classical art, the *Treatise on Ancient Painting* granted an importance to the representation of particular appearances which Shaftesbury himself would have rejected out of hand. Both writers were agreed that "Every Imitation ought to be performed with such Intelligence of human Nature, which is ever substantially the same, that it may be universally instructive and moving." "But," Turnbull proceeded to remark, "every Imitation being particular, or representative of a certain Action; the Action painted ought to be told with such a strict regard to the Accidental *Costume*, that the Subject and Scene must be easily distinguished by those who are versed in History."[16] The idea that historical actors should be shown in correct historical costumes went hand in hand with a belief in the precise rendering of detail as one (if not the only) standard of natural truth. To support his position Turnbull cited a statement by Socrates, to the effect that "A Picture must be a true Imitation, a true Likeness; not only the Carnation must appear red, but even the Stuffs, Silks, and other Ornaments in the Draperies. Without Truth no Imitation can please." And if a work of art gave pleasure in this manner, it could do so without endangering its "virtuous Effect" on the beholder – provided, of course, that the painter "made a fine and judicious Choice of Nature," and chose a subject capable of "exciting in our Minds great and noble Ideas of the moral kind."[17]

Yet even as he qualified certain fundamental assumptions of Shaftesbury's aesthetic enterprise, Turnbull refrained from directly challenging the conventional hierarchy of styles and genres. For him, as for the author of the *Hercules*, the sort of imagery that could best serve the purpose of inculcating virtue remained historical art in the grand style. In addition to the lost masterpieces of classical antiquity, Turnbull recommended the Raphael cartoons and Poussin's works as models for the most noble form of painterly practice. Presumably he would have been aware of the recent appearance in Britain of quite a different type of moral picture, which William Hogarth had been producing for the better part of a decade; but the *Treatise* offered no approval for representations of improper conduct, nor any explicit sanction for the depiction of contemporary scenes. Mind you, Turnbull nowhere ruled out the possibility of creating a modern-life *exemplum virtutis* – and despite its rather unpromising title (which does little justice to the range of its concerns), his *Treatise* could easily have been read as offering implicit support for just such an artistic project.

Whether Joseph Wright ever read or was inspired by Turnbull is probably incapable of proof, though it cannot be denied that their different endeavors occupied a considerable area of common ground. One imagines that a painter trained in the "particular" art of portraiture, and who enjoyed extensive contacts with his local scientific community, might have responded with considerable enthusiasm to the only art-theoretical text available to him which promoted an alliance between painting and natural philosophy, and legitimized the representation of "accidental" forms. But speculations of this sort, however tantalizing they might be, are really rather beside the point. I have looked at Turnbull primarily for the purpose of establishing some of the basic parameters of relevant mid-eighteenth-century thinking about morality and the visual arts so that when we begin to speak of the *Air Pump* as fulfilling a moral purpose, we can do so in historically specific terms. Obviously Wright sought to provide his viewers with something more than the straightforward representation of a scientific demonstration – and it would be entirely in keeping with the spirit of his grandest scientific candlelight if we were to regard it as a "sample or experiment in natural philosophy," not only by virtue of what it describes, but on account of its formal language as well. When Wright dramatizes the effect of light on color, in part he does so to assist our understanding of Newtonian laws; and when he portrays every object in meticulous detail, one point is to enable us to emulate the audience within the picture, who achieve an awareness of natural truth through close empirical observation. At the same time, the depiction of human actors acting in and upon nature at a moment of high drama, of life and death, takes the *Air Pump* into the province of moral philosophy. If the supreme purpose of such philosophy lay in the promotion of self-knowledge, then this was a purpose which Wright appears to have embraced in a much more literal sense than either Shaftesbury or Turnbull had had in mind: instead of describing some exemplary hero from the classical or Christian past, he showed his viewers people they could recognize as belonging to their own world. Wright's ambitions could hardly be better encapsulated than by the following passage from Turnbull's book: "The Design of moral Pictures is . . . to shew us to ourselves; to reflect our Image upon us, in order to attract our Attention the more closely to it, and to engage us in Conversation with ourselves, and an accurate consideration of our Make and Frame."[18] Thus it is with Turnbull and Shaftesbury in mind that we must try to determine what the *Air Pump* "reflected" onto its original viewers, how it engaged them in a "conversation" about themselves, and about the nature of the society in which they lived.

If this give and take had been in the nature of a direct and unmediated encounter, then the task I am proposing would be a relatively straightforward one. But one point requiring strong and immediate emphasis is that neither Wright nor his viewers would have been able to describe a social order, or even imagine its structure, outside an *a priori* conceptual framework. Here we must once again look back to Shaftesbury to see where and in what shape this framework emerged, and how it had first come to play a part in the arena of aesthetic discourse. As John Barrell has so convincingly shown,[19] Shaftesbury's writings on art both drew upon and supported the basic premises of a social and political theory – modern historians have called it civic humanism or classical republicanism[20] – which described an ideal polity according to a clearly defined set of terms that were challenged, revised, but never entirely abandoned as the eighteenth century went on. We know that those terms continued to carry paradigmatic force in formulations of art theory – for George Turnbull, to name but one obvious example, and in different ways for the early Reynolds. But I would go on to argue that Joseph Wright's ambitious attempts to "produce" the forms of contemporary society likewise worked within, even as in some respects they worked against, a set of civic paradigms. Thus in order to uncover the discursive assumptions which informed the *Air Pump*'s conversation with its audience, we shall need first of all to construct another dialogue, in this case between Wright and Shaftesbury, and between the different representations that each produced of contemporary society.

To analyze this relationship in a manner which will enable us to highlight the specifically pictorial issues at stake, I have decided to compare the *Air Pump* with an earlier painting which was authored, if not actually executed, by Shaftesbury himself:[21] the portrait of the third earl and his younger brother, Maurice Ashley Cooper, that the Anglo-German artist John Closterman painted *c.* 1700–1 (Plate 12.2).[22] I am not going to suggest that this directly influenced Wright (it is not an image that he could have known); instead I shall be considering Closterman's painting in the manner of a blueprint, a sort of ideological ground plan if you like, for the social edifice that the Derby artist was to construct in paint some seven decades later.

Closterman's full-length canvas portrays the two Shaftesbury brothers garbed in what was then considered Grecian fashion, conversing in a wooded grove which contains a temple with Ionic columns. The earl, on the right, appears to listen as Maurice expounds dramatically about the nature which surrounds them both. Its rugged, sylvan character corresponds quite closely to what Shaftesbury described as the "most sacred" order of natural scenery, filled with "pines, firs, and trunks of other aged trees . . . those sacred recesses, where solitude and deep retreat, and the absence of gainful, lucratible, and busy mortals, make the sublime, pathetic and enchanting, raise the sweet melancholy, the revery, meditation. 'Where no hand but that of time. No steel, no scythe, but that of Saturn's.'"[23] In the broadest sense, then, Closterman's painting reworks the familiar Horatian *topos* of virtuous rural retirement, setting up an implicit contrast between the wholesomeness of a tranquil country life on the one hand, and the active and self-interested pursuits associated with city or court on the other. At the same time, moreover, the rustic setting also recalls the tracts of woodland which covered much of Shaftesbury's Dorset estate – trees which then as now constituted an important part of its economic value. Yet I think we can fairly say that the picture mystifies the relationship between its two sitters and their paternal acreage. Land does not figure here as something owned, or as a resource to be exploited; rather, in its character of a classical retreat the forest signifies property as a moral and political phenomenon, as a piece of God's nature that has been entrusted to the Shaftesburys, and which supports them in their character of virtuous public men.

In common with other British political theorists of the period, Shaftesbury assumed that the character of any society, and of any individual as a social actor, rested on property as its material foundation. All his writings display an unswerving commitment to the most authoritative account of this relationship – the civic humanist account, that is – which specifically described land as the only possible basis for a truly virtuous polity, as the only sort of property that could guarantee its possessor true freedom of action and thought. Aside from granting him the leisure to study the workings of society, and thence to achieve wisdom, the ownership of a substantial piece of "real" estate also ensured that the landlord's concerns would coincide with the public interest at large. He alone could possess the "public" or "civic" virtues, those necessary for the exercise of heroism or statesmanship, and he was uniquely qualified to direct the nation's affairs. Thus landed property enabled the creation of an ideal society, in the form of a moral hierarchy ruled by an elite of disinterested masculine citizens. It was Closterman's brief to characterize Shaftesbury and his brother as members of this genuine "public," of that select group responsible for good government and social order.

Both iconographically and formally, Closterman's painting strives to represent its subjects as men of comprehensive vision, whose philosophical meditations range over the entire spectrum of things created by man as well as God. Their concern for spiritual matters is emphasized by the Greek inscription on the temple, which identifies it as dedicated "To the Pythian God": that is, to Apollo in his legendary and oracular connection with Delphi, the pre-eminent classical meeting place of the natural and supernatural worlds. Apollo being the divinity charged with responsibility for all the civilized arts, his stewardship embraced philosophy, which Shaftesbury ranked as the highest form of human intellectual endeavor. "It has not its name," he wrote, ". . . from the mere subtlety and nicety of the speculation, but by way of excellence, from its being superior to all other speculations, from its presiding over all other sciences and occupations, teaching the measure of each, and assigning the just value of everything in life."[24] Thus (moral) philosophy constituted the field of study *par excellence* for the man of public virtue, the arena in which he developed and displayed his capacity to rule. For Shaftesbury the citizen-philosopher had most to learn from the example of Socrates, who had shown how to transcend self-meditation to contemplate the public good.[25] The third earl could have found no better example to support his Stoic assertion that "real virtue and love of truth [are] . . . independent of opinion and above the world."[26]

In the arena of aesthetic judgment, the disinterested Shaftesburian virtuoso demonstrated his superior wisdom by confining his admiration to works which instantiated his own capacity to identify those higher, general truths which lay concealed from the view of lesser, particular men. Thus the genuine man of taste rejected what Shaftesbury called the "affectations" of most modern art in favor of the "natural grace" which he found expressed in the works of Greek and Roman antiquity[27]; it is for this reason that Closterman's portrait champions as emphatically as possible its commitment to the idealizing language of the classical tradition. Although the brothers' faces are sufficiently individualized to permit us to distinguish one from the other, their postures closely mirror the forms of an antique sculptural model – also describing two brothers, in this case Castor and Pollux.[28] The Shaftesburys, then, quite literally embody the universal character of the nature which surrounds them, and which supplies the object of their divinely inspired enthusiasm. Under his patron's direction Closterman produced what might justly be described as an historical portrait *avant la lettre*, a picture which not only could claim to be worthy of serious aesthetic appreciation, but which in its philosophical theme and its vocabulary of central forms demonstrated the capacity of its sitters to rise above their own particular interests in pursuit of the general good.

Of course, the Closterman is "historical" in another, more obvious sense, inasmuch as it incorporates a narrative dimension. While a momentary exchange between two brother-philosophers may not make for much of a story, or certainly not a terribly eventful one, its portrayal does activate the figures, and in so doing enhances the public character of the image as a whole. Its enlarged significance would have been particularly obvious, I imagine, to viewers who gained admittance into Shaftesbury's portrait gallery, where the Closterman must have stood out quite dramatically from the more static likenesses around it. But beyond forging a link between portraiture and history painting, the artist's introduction of a conversational element also operates on the philosophic level, indicating the means whereby individuals join together to become active builders of the social realm. Shaftesbury added his voice to a chorus of earlier moralists and religious thinkers when he claimed that contemplating the beautiful order of the cosmos could teach men how to pattern their lives in accordance with God's will. The earl added a new dimension to this doctrine, however, by stressing that an awareness of divine goodness prepared men psychologically for communal life. As Shaftesbury put it, "the admiration and love of order, harmony, and proportion, in whatever kind, is naturally improving to the temper, advantageous to social affection, and highly assistant to virtue, which is itself no other than the love of order and beauty in society."[29]

Although Shaftesbury placed the "social" or "natural affections"[30] beneath the level of virtue proper (i.e. public virtue), he insisted that "A public spirit can only come from a social feeling or sense of partnership with human kind."[31] Any leader who looked down upon the rest of mankind from a position of scornful superiority could only be an unnatural tyrant: for

> If eating or drinking be natural, herding is so too. If any appetite or sense be natural, the sense of fellowship is the same. If there be anything of nature in that affection which is between the sexes, the affection is certainly as natural towards the consequent offspring; and so again between the offspring themselves, as kindred and companions, bred under the same discipline and economy. And thus a clan or tribe is gradually formed; a public is recognised.[32]

Herein, I think, lies the primary reason why Shaftesbury made the unusual decision to commission an emphatically interactive portrait of himself and his younger brother.[33] No doubt he and Maurice liked one another, and we know they shared a common interest in Socratic philosophy;[34] but surely the crucial point was to represent the pair as men possessed of those "natural affections" which originated in the private confines of the family sphere and ultimately led "to the good of the public."[35] Closterman, in other words, has depicted his sitters experiencing the "pleasures of sympathy,"[36] which for Shaftesbury constituted the cornerstone of all human happiness. It was sympathy that Shaftesbury saw as the force in human nature which enabled the creation of a coherent and harmonious society; by "society" he meant that "company" of landed gentlemen, like himself and his brother, who came to agreement and mutual understanding by "sharing contentment and delight."[37] The third earl summed up this goal in one word: politeness.

To the term "politeness" Shaftesbury and a host of other contemporary English moralists assigned an importance and a range of meanings which would have come as a great surprise to earlier writers on the same subject. Politeness had traditionally been a matter of proper social form, that careful management of appearances which adorned the speech and actions of the virtuous man; according to the general consensus, it was "the art of pleasing in company," as Abel Boyer wrote in 1702.[38] By the early years of the century, however, this definition was already in the process of being radically amplified and transformed. The general tendency was to try to situate politeness within a moral framework, to find some way to forge the substance of virtue and its surface ornaments into an ideal of virtuous sociability. Shaftesbury sought to bridge this gap by arguing that philosophy arose out of politeness. "To philosophize," he wrote, ". . . is but to carry good-breeding a step higher. For the accomplishment of breeding is, to learn whatever is decent in company, or beautiful in arts: and the sum of philosophy is, to learn what is just in society, and beautiful in nature, and the order of the world. . . . Both characters [the well-bred man and the philosopher] aim at what is excellent, aspire to a just taste, and carry in view the model of what is beautiful and becoming."[39] Closterman's portrait of Shaftesbury and Maurice Ashley Cooper seeks to give this elision pictorial form. Here the two brothers figure as gentlemen-philosophers, as men of good manners as well as good morals. The enthusiasm they display for the highest beauties of the cosmos is conveyed by bodies which manifest the excellent taste of the truly well-bred. Disposed in harmony with the woods behind them, and in accordance with the dictates of classical art, their postures conjure up the early eighteenth-century vocabulary of polite values: naturalness, ease, freedom, elegance, and refinement are just some of the more obvious examples that spring to mind.[40]

According to Shaftesbury, such qualities could best be modeled on the gentlemanly art of conversation; thus Closterman's double portrait effectively joins the manner of politeness to its quintessential matter. Here, as in so many of Shaftesbury's own writings, the conversational ideal is defined as an exchange of discourse among men of equal rank who address themselves to topics of mutual concern. Acting on their sympathy for one another, and out of respect for the rules of propriety and decorum, they place all selfish impulses to one side, and display that quality of disinterestedness which not only guarantees their public spirit, but also sets them apart from their social inferiors. As the medium for perfecting taste, philosophy and the social affections, polite conversation builds the very foundations of the commonwealth of virtue. It is that commonwealth in microcosm – the classical republican ideal of society as a "mutual converse"[41] among masculine landowning citizens – which Closterman has portrayed.[42]

Equally to the point, perhaps, the double portrait also marks the intersection of a dialogue between Shaftesbury and his fellow citizens. Closterman's task was simply to execute the designs of his virtuoso patron, to play the mechanical hand to the earl's authorial mind. This was culture as created by and for the public man, both to demonstrate and to confirm the virtuous character which he possessed and shared with men of equivalent rank. But if these factors defined the conditions of cultural production and reception in an ideal Shaftesburian polity, it was an entirely different sort of world which produced Wright of Derby's *Air Pump*, and which his picture in turn reproduced.

The *Air Pump* was conceived by a professional artist operating independently of any patron;[43] Wright had established this brand of large-scale imagery, with its spectacular chiaroscuro, as his own particular specialty, one intended to attract maximum attention at an exhibition which attracted many thousands of viewers. Almost certainly, too, he designed the *Air Pump* with the reproductive print trade in mind. Under such circumstances the pressures to succeed demanded a sort of picture which had to appeal to a much larger and socially more heterogeneous audience than Shaftesbury's public of landed gentlemen; though Wright evidently had ambitions of producing a serious moral painting, he also wanted to make something that would sell, that would be both accessible and popular, even if this entailed ignoring the hierarchical imperatives of academic theory. To Shaftesbury all such considerations would have been anathema, symptomatic of the deleterious effects of commerce on the visual arts, and on the fabric of society in general. In his efforts to preserve public virtue, economic activity – we recall his scornful reference to "gainful, lucratible, and busy mortals" – figured only negatively, as the force which posed the greatest threat to a healthy and coherent social order. Commerce tended to promote private desires at the expense of public needs, to encourage the spread of avarice, and to stoke the flames of luxury, that pernicious agent of corruption responsible for the downfall of so many great civilizations. And at the same time the rising power of the marketplace brought about a corresponding decline in a nation's cultural achievements; if there were no true public, there could be no truly public art, but rather an art that expressed particular truths, and catered to private appetites and interests. Hence, according to Shaftesbury, a commercial society could produce only a corrupted form of painting – that of seventeenth-century Holland being an obvious case in point. Yet if for him the Dutch school exemplified all that was antithetical to a dignified art, Joseph Wright evidently saw no contradiction between seriousness of moral purpose and a Netherlandish style. The other major source for his candlelight scenes – the English conversation-piece tradition – was if anything even more problematic, both ethically and aesthetically, insofar as it focused on the trappings of opulence which were often charged with encouraging selfish passions and illegitimate desires. Furthermore, the *Air Pump* specifically belonged to that category of conversational imagery which featured contemporary types as opposed to specifiable portraits – the best-known earlier examples being Hogarth's modern moral subjects; Wright's viewers would have known that such high-life genre scenes typically described their human actors in situations of moral peril, tempted or trapped by those irrational fantasies of wealth and status engendered by the agency of commerce. And it is precisely the central theme of Hogarth's progresses – the character of social conditions and relations in a commercial world – that Wright's *Air Pump* asked its viewers to judge.

That act of judgment, however, could not take place in an ideological vacuum. As I have already suggested, it had to be shaped by a set of established criteria, which I would say were broadly identical to those that informed Wright's attempt to represent his society to itself. For him, as for other mid-eighteenth-century British artists and writers, the task of "producing society" had still to be conducted within the conceptual parameters defined by Shaftesbury and other civic humanist thinkers, even though at the same time Wright had to acknowledge – as the *Air Pump* surely does – that the actual circumstances of life in contemporary Britain no longer corresponded to the civic ideal. How, then, does the *Air Pump* inflect the discursive agenda which we have identified as the motivating force behind the Shaftesbury double portrait? What has happened to philosophy, politeness, conversation, sympathy, once these various attributes of classical citizenship have been deprived of their original enabling material foundation?

Shaftesbury and Closterman had represented property in its civic sense, as the material which guaranteed a citizen's autonomy: a solid and immoveable part of the natural world that was subject neither to improvement nor exchange. Wright's figures, on the other hand, inhabit a universe of circulating commodities, the fruits of wealth from an indeterminate source. Here we see property not as a share of the public stock which has fallen to an individual by dint of birth or fortune, and which in turn allows him to fulfill his political potential, but rather as things that have been purchased to satisfy personal desires, to enable a more pleasant life. Where Closterman includes a Delphic temple to conjure up the transcendent values of classical civilization, Wright shows a doorway ornamented in the most up-to-date pseudo-antique style; and rather than wearing the ostensibly timeless garb of the ancients, his figures are comfortably dressed according to the fashion of the later 1760s. Instead of trees we can just make out the bottom edge of an ornately framed landscape painting, in the upper left-hand corner; in place of an irregular "wilderness," the perfect geometry of a wood and metal cage, and a moonlit vista framed by the bars of a casement window. Of all the various items shown in the interior, one of the more costly was the air pump itself; if scientific instruments were meant to expand the boundaries of human knowledge, they also entered many eighteenth-century homes as part of a thriving trade in luxury goods. Most of the objects and articles of clothing that Wright has depicted would have originated in various parts of Britain, the one major exception being the white cockatoo, a rare and expensive bird from the East Indies which seems to have been quite unknown in Europe prior to 1760.[44] The bird is not the only living creature who has come into Wright's interior from the world outside; the same is true for the majority of his figures. While the scene appears to take place in the home of the incomplete family unit formed by a father with his two daughters, most of the remaining company would seem to consist of friends or relations gathered for this particular occasion. An even larger network of personal connections, and in this case of a distinctly commercial sort, is suggested by the presence of an itinerant natural philosopher, one of those traveling salesmen who peddled knowledge together with the tools of his trade. Thus the objects and activities contained within this candlelit space presuppose the existence of a complex network of production and exchange, involving a countless number of particular and interdependent interests, of manufacturers, consumers, and intermediaries.

The emphatic modernity of the scene which Wright has described also indicates that this is a world which is subject to change; his *Air Pump* acknowledges a history, in other words – and one might say a geography as well – which Closterman's portrait of the Shaftesburys effectively sought to deny. The classical citizen (here I am paraphrasing John Pocock) did not see himself as the mere product of historical forces, of a specific phase in the development of any individual nation, but as the personification of an ideal which transcended time and place.[45] As we have noted, Shaftesbury had believed that this world of value could be visualized only in the central forms of classical art; by abandoning that tradition in favor of painting in such a "peculiar way," and in so highly particularized a pictorial language, Wright located both his art and the figures he portrayed within the specialized conditions of social life that distinguished their world from the past.

The way in which the *Air Pump* insists on the individually distinctive characteristics of the various people and objects it portrays underlines the effect of commerce on social personality, how the whole figure of the public man has split into an array of human fragments. Wright shows men of various ages, a young woman, children[46] – each of whom manifests a different and partial response to the crucial phase of the experiment, and to its broader moral implications. None of the atomized individuals described in the *Air Pump* possesses the full rationality which had defined the character of the autonomous citizen; the unified construction of the gentleman-philosopher has succumbed to the division of labor, which has produced a world where philosophers are not gentlemen, and gentlemen are just as obviously not philosophers. While they all may aspire to understanding the workings of nature, for them its overall shape remains a mystery, a darkened cosmos which can be perceived only in discrete bits, by means of scientific rituals designed to demonstrate certain specific natural laws. The truths they seek to learn are those established by "unexceptionable Experience and Observation," as George Turnbull would have phrased it; from an experiment which by the 1760s had been performed repeatedly for more than a hundred years, they expect confirmation of what is already known. The air pump offers them a particular instance of the operation of a general principle, a law of nature, which they (like us) are then prompted to consider (though not all of them may do so) in its moral and religious dimensions. Hence Wright's invocation of the central human dilemma, concerning the temporal passage through life and into death; hence, too, his depiction of both earthly and heavenly light (candle and moon), which ask to be seen in relation to one another, as well as to the supreme and invisible author of enlightenment (in both the physical and spiritual senses of that word). That scientific demonstrations were meant to stimulate some degree of moral understanding was a commonplace notion in eighteenth-century educational literature. As Charlotte Lennox put it in 1760, "to the mind of clear and cool reflection [the] use [of studies in natural philosophy] is plain and evident; they lead by smooth and regular gradations to peace and happiness; they raise the thoughts to humanity and devotion, and, by a regular transition, convey our contemplation from the creature to its Creator."[47]

From observing particular phenomena, therefore, those who indulged in scientific study as a form of fashionable amusement strove to gain an intimation of general truths; but such truths could only be glimpsed from beneath, as it were, from the viewpoint of individuals with limited interests and experiences, of born subjects rather than born rulers – Lennox was speaking to an audience of women. To them she recommended natural philosophy for one reason above all: as a means of directing the dangerous female passion of curiosity into a safe and rational channel.

The *Air Pump* appears to support the opinion, voiced in numerous contemporary discussions of feminine education, that women could gain an understanding of natural laws only if male partners or fathers were there to act as intermediaries (would the same conditions have applied to an appreciation of the fine arts?). Yet the very fact that both sexes are present underlines the distance Wright has traveled from Shaftesbury's insistence that philosophical knowledge could follow only as a natural consequence of that genuine good-breeding which was confined to the community of public men. By the 1760s, now that scientific study had entered into the lives of a much larger constituency, this progression tended more often than not to be argued in reverse: a claim frequently voiced by the popular scientists of the period was that their products actually helped to make men and women well-bred. In the words of one of the most successful of these didactic entrepreneurs, "Knowledge is now become a fashionable thing, and philosophy is the science à la mode; hence, to cultivate this study is only to be in taste, and politeness is the inseparable consequence."[48] Under circumstances such as those described by Wright in his *Air Pump*, the discussion of philosophy could help inculcate the virtues of sociability – but it fell far short of producing or communicating the comprehensive wisdom of the classical citizen. Perhaps this is the most that one could expect of philosophy in a commercial society: that together with the other civilized arts, it could contribute to a process of refining the passions into manners.[49]

The *Air Pump* makes it clear that this is a process which works over time: while the distress shown by the two young girls may express a perfectly natural sympathy for the bird – this is an issue which I shall return to later on – their reactions transgress the rules of decorum to which all the older members of the group conform. Self-command comes about through the agency of education – or perhaps one might more accurately say thanks to social commerce, through the exchange of sentiments and opinions which defines the improving function of conversation. "It was not from Books, that I learned the most instructive affecting Lessons," speaks a fictive young woman in a mid-century pedagogic dialogue; rather, "It was by conversing with the better Part of the World."[50] There could have been no doubt in the minds of Joseph Wright's original viewers but that the *Air Pump* portrayed their world's "better part" – people "of quality," both materially and morally, gathered together for the laudable purpose of improving themselves and one another. Yet here conversation, like philosophy, lacks the public character that Shaftesbury had ascribed to the speech shared by masculine citizens; Wright's figures, unlike Closterman's, occupy an emphatically private space closed off from the world outside. The private character of the gathering around the air pump is underlined by the presence of the children, and also by the inclusion of a token female presence within a group dominated by adult men.

Contemporary moralists never tired of recommending the mixing of the sexes as a mutually beneficial conjunction. "The Man not only protects and advises, but communicates Vigour, and Resolution to the Woman," claimed an altogether typical writer on the subject; "She, in her turn, softens, refines, and polishes him."[51] One woman who appears to have done her job well is the unseen mother of Wright's two young girls, whose absence asks to be read, I believe, as a sign of her domestic virtue. In a conduct-book published in 1756, simply entitled *The Wife*, Eliza Haywood condemned the married woman who indulged in the "madness" of natural philosophy:

> it best becomes her to centre her whole studies within the compass of her own walls, – to enquire no farther than into the humours and inclinations of her husband and children, to the end that she may know how to oblige those she finds in him, and rectify what is amiss in them, and not to extend her speculations beyond her family, and those things that are entrusted to her management.[52]

It is because the mother has met all these obligations that the table in the *Air Pump* is so brilliantly polished, that the children are so well presented and so deferential, and her husband such a paragon of paternal benevolence. Yet at the same time his behavior points to a broader pattern of social amelioration. As John Millar was to state in 1771:

> The improvements in the state of society, which are the effects of opulence and refinement, will . . . dispose the father to behave with greater mildness and moderation in the exercise of his authority. As he lives in greater affluence and security, he is more at leisure to exert the social affections, and to cultivate those arts which tend to soften and humanize the temper. . . . Being less occupied with the care of his own preservation, he enters with more delicate sensibility into the feelings of others, and beholds their distresses and sufferings with greater sorrow and commiseration.[53]

While eighteenth-century British culture granted women an important role in the civilizing process, ultimately what made such improvement possible was the ease and opulence engendered by the rise of commerce.

David Hume, I think, may have best summarized this point of view in one of his moral *Essays* from the early 1740s. Defending the luxuries produced by commercial societies, he insisted:

> The more these refined arts advance, the more sociable men become. . . . They flock into cities; love to receive and communicate knowledge; to show their wit or breeding; their taste in conversation or living, in clothes or furniture. . . . Particular clubs and societies are every where formed: Both sexes meet in an

easy and sociable manner; and the tempers of men, as well as their behaviour, refine apace. So that, besides the improvements which they receive from knowledge and the liberal arts, it is impossible but they must feel an increase of humanity, from the very habit of conversing together, and contributing to each other's pleasure and entertainment. Thus *industry, knowledge*, and *humanity*, are linked together, by an indissoluble chain, and are found, from experience as well as reason, to be peculiar to the more polished, and what are more commonly denominated, the more luxurious ages.[54]

The *Experiment on a Bird in the Air Pump* manifests Wright's commitment to the ideology of refinement as much by virtue of its smoothly polished surface texture as through his choice of subject-matter, which would seem to describe the same "indissoluble chain" so highly praised by Hume. In his own way Wright, too, was trying to show that a commercial society could produce individuals (including artists) capable of sharing the citizen's disinterested sympathy for creatures beside himself. Yet if we look back to the Closterman double portrait, it becomes immediately obvious that Shaftesbury construed sympathy in a fundamentally different sense. Rooted in their fraternal origins, the fellow feeling displayed by the third earl and his younger brother expands outward to encompass the whole of creation; the natural affections, Shaftesbury had argued, built the foundations of public virtue. In the *Air Pump*, by contrast, sympathy works inward, and within much narrower constraints. The two girls are much affected by the plight of the struggling bird, and the father by the anxiety of his children; the young woman looks with some affection toward her husband or lover. But neither this couple nor anyone else, aside from the father, manifests any evident concern for the afflicted children or the cockatoo. As personal relationships become more distant, sympathy gives way to other reactions – the curiosity about science shown by the two seated figures on the left, and the apparently complete self-absorption enacted by the older man. This pattern of responses would seem to suggest that in a refined and opulent society, the workings of sympathy tend to be confined to circumstances of especial closeness. Adam Smith had made much the same point some nine years earlier in his *Theory of Moral Sentiments*: "Men," he claimed, "though naturally sympathetic, feel so little for another, with whom they have no particular connexion, in comparison with what they feel for themselves."[55] For Smith, as Jean-Christophe Agnew has remarked, "fellow-feeling was, more than anything else, a mark of the immense distance that separated individual minds rather than a sign of their commonality,"[56] as Shaftesbury had believed. The "mutual converse" that was his virtuous commonwealth had presupposed a fundamental congruence of interests among all members of the political republic. Social affection among citizens confirmed the fact that they knew themselves and one another in the identical character of public men; whereas in a world subject to the division of labor, it took an act of imagination for particular individuals to identify – if indeed they did so at all – with the passions experienced by others whose situation was quite different from their own.[57] Thus the sisters in the *Air Pump* enter into the sentiments of the bird by imagining what its feelings might be like; they respond as beholders to a dramatic spectacle of distress, just as we respond to the scene as a whole. From our privileged position in the audience, we can project ourselves into the position of Wright's various actors, up to and including the poor cockatoo. The highlit emphasis on the family group draws our attention to this touching vignette – Wright positions the spectator, in other words, as a connoisseur of admirable but exceptional feelings,[58] though in so doing he also invites us to take pleasure from distress. This may make an important contribution to the education of human sentiments, as numerous eighteenth-century moralists would have had their readers believe.[59] Yet the scene that Wright has described cannot help but raise certain ethical doubts: how virtuous are the people whom the painter has portrayed – and how virtuous the world "reflected" on his canvas?

The answers to these questions hinge around the feature which dominates Wright's pyramidal composition – the receiver containing the suffocating bird. We can, I think, be virtually certain that its treatment would have struck many eighteenth-century viewers as an unnecessary act of cruelty (or as morally problematic, at the very least); contemporary popular science texts frequently recommended the use of a bladder or a "lungs-glass" instead of a live animal, so as to avoid causing unnecessary pain both to the creature itself and to the human spectator.[60] And if we are to identify the cockatoo as a household pet, as at least one critic justifiably assumed in 1768,[61] then the exploitation of its suffering for the entertainment of an intimate sociable gathering cannot help but strike us as more than a little paradoxical. Here sympathy, then, together with the pursuit of knowledge, would appear to operate in a manner inconsistent with the dictates of morality; Hume's "chain" may not be quite so "indissoluble" after all. The progression from industry through knowledge to humanity may indeed be peculiar to the most polished societies; but judging by the *Air Pump*, such societies may be just as likely to tread a downward path, leading from commerce to luxury, and from self-interest to cruel indifference. Wright's philosopher plays a particularly problematic role in this regard: for in demonstrating his expertise for his own profit and for the benefit of his audience, he also assumes a power over life and death, a power which he cannot control with certainty, and which is not rightly his, but God's. There is danger here for all the actors in the *Air Pump*, a point underlined by the overtly religious character of Wright's image as a whole: that in pursuing their various and particular interests they will miss the true purpose of the experiment, which is to make mankind aware of the supreme wisdom of the divinity, and to encourage them to conduct themselves in accordance with His will, and in the knowledge that He holds their fate within His hands.[62] The fact that the bird may die at any moment underlines the transience of their earthly existence; and to drive this point home, Wright has described the murky shape of a decaying human skull in the jar which sits in the center of the table, where it is ignored by all but the oldest member of the company (he who is closest to death). The conjunction of skull and candle – we can just make out the taper's form along the left-hand side of the jar – functions here, as it had long done in Netherlandish art, as a sign of the vanity of human pleasures.[63] Prominent among those pleasures are philosophy, sympathy, and polite conversation; in the circumstances of private opulence, the corner-stones of what once had been the Shaftesburian ideal polity have lost their ethical moorings, and have taken on the mutable character of mobile forms of property, of refinements which may improve, but which can just as easily corrupt.

The *Air Pump*, then, differs in certain fundamental ways from the sort of moral picture which Shaftesbury or Turnbull had recommended. Among works of art, Turnbull claimed, it was those which excite our moral Affections, and call forth generous Sentiments, that yield us the highest and most satisfactory and lasting Entertainment . . . if those Imitations, which call forth our Pity and Compassion into Exercise, and interest us in behalf of Virtue and Merit, are indeed the Representations that give us the highest Satisfaction, it must be confessed that we are qualified by Nature to receive high Pleasure from social Affections, and virtuous Exercises; and that our Frame and Constitution is social and virtuous, or deeply interested by Nature in behalf of Worth and Merit.[64]

Although the *Air Pump* fulfilled many aspects of this agenda for history-painting, at the same time it played the admonitory role of a "modern moral subject" – it is Wright's own *Midnight Modern Conversation*, if you like.[65] Like Hogarth, though with a far greater degree of ambivalence, Wright withheld ethical sanction from the social order he had produced on canvas, and from the fashionable world which he addressed. Clearly there was a great deal to be said for a society which attended lectures on natural philosophy, or visited exhibitions of the fine arts; the exchange of opinions and material objects no doubt helped to refine the passions and to nurture social affections, but further work would have to be done before the task of building a commercial humanism could be brought to a successful conclusion. Together with many other products of mid-eighteenth-century British culture, the *Experiment on a Bird in the Air Pump* describes a new ideology in the making, albeit not yet entirely certain of its ground – an ideology inscribed with difficulty onto an older structure of civic and Christian values, which made it impossible to celebrate modern property relations without a profound sense of ethical unease. Perhaps Wright's picture can also offer us a timely word of warning, before we join the chorus of acclamation for those market forces we see marching in apparent triumph across the globe today.

Notes

1 "A lover of the arts," *The Gazetteer and New Daily Advertiser*, May 23, 1768, p. 4.
2 One important exception to this rule deserves to be mentioned here: the high-life genre scenes which figured as part of the series of supper-box paintings at Vauxhall Gardens, mainly designed by Francis Hayman and executed by him and his studio during the early 1740s. For an example of the sort of Vauxhall picture which might have been particularly useful to Wright, see the print after *Playing the Game at Quadrille* (designed by François Gravelot and painted by Hayman), in Brian Allen, *Francis Hayman* (New Haven, CT and London: Yale University Press, 1987), cat. no. 64, p. 135.
3 Since as far as we know no one in the eighteenth century regarded Wright's candlelights as portraits, I am at a loss to understand why modern scholars from Nicolson onwards have wasted so much time and energy trying to identify the individuals on whom his figures may be based. I imagine that he did use some of his friends as models, but surely the key point is that he depicted them as knowable unknowns; in so doing Wright allowed his viewers to consider his painted actors as surrogates for themselves, instead of regarding them as specific people whom they had simply never met.
4 An extreme example of this tendency may be found in Albert Boime's *Art in an Age of Revolution 1750–1800: A Social History of Modern Art*, Vol. 1 (Chicago: Yale University Press, 1987), pp. 233–60, where the author goes so far as to claim that "*Wright would do for the Industrial Revolution what David did for the French Revolution*" (p. 234). Boime's views take their

point of departure from the pioneering work of modern Wright scholarship, Benedict Nicolson's *Joseph Wright of Derby: Painter of Light*, 2 vols (London: Routledge & Kegan Paul; Pentheon Books, 1968). In a forthcoming book, from which he has kindly allowed me to read a draft of the chapter on Wright, Stephen Daniels traces the origins of this "progressive" interpretation back to the later nineteenth century.

5   Here I would emphatically agree with Daniels; see previous note.

6   Of course, much of what I shall be saying about the *Air Pump* might also be applied to Wright's other candlelights of the 1760s, and especially to *A Philosopher giving that Lecture on the Orrery, in which a Lamp is put in place of the Sun* (exhibited Society of Artists, 1766; now Derby Art Gallery), though the element of dramatic action featured in the *Air Pump* makes it a rather special case. The other major candlelights to which I refer (i.e., those depicting more than two figures) are Wright's *Three Persons Viewing the Gladiator by Candlelight* (Society of Artists, 1765; private collection), and his *Academy by Lamplight* (Society of Artists, 1769; Yale Center for British Art, Paul Mellon Collection). Good color reproductions, together with useful if rather unadventurous discussions of these and most other significant works by the artist, can now be easily found in Tate Gallery, *Wright of Derby*, cat. and intro. by Judy Egerton (London: 1990).

7   John Mullan, *Sentiment and Sociability: The Language of Feeling in the Eighteenth Century* (Oxford: Oxford University Press, 1988), p. 25.

8   Of course, I would not claim to be the first scholar to identify the *Air Pump* as a "moral" picture. The same assertion has been made by Egerton in the Tate Gallery catalogue (*Wright of Derby*, p. 61), and by William Schupbach (whose research provided Egerton with much of her information), in "A select iconography of animal experiment," *Vivisection in Historical Perspective*, ed. Nicolaas A. Rupke (London: Croom Helm, 1987), pp. 340–7. While I have drawn upon both of these sources, which broadly confirmed the views I had previously held, the basic thrust of my argument differs fundamentally from theirs, as I hope will become apparent. A more provocative discussion of the *Air Pump* – with which I agree in part, though it bears less specifically on my own concerns – can be found in Ronald Paulson, *Emblem and Expression: Meaning in English Art of the Eighteenth Century* (Cambridge, MA: Harvard University Press, 1975), pp. 184–98.

9   Anthony Ashley Cooper, third Earl of Shaftesbury, "Plastics: an epistolary excursion in the original progress and power of designatory art," in *Second Characters or the Language of Forms*, ed. Benjamin Rand (Cambridge, UK: 1914), p. 93.

10 John Barrell, *The Political Theory of Painting from Reynolds to Hazlitt: "The Body of the Public"* (New Haven, CT and London: Yale University Press, 1986), pp. 11, 18–20, and *passim*. I see more differences between Shaftesbury and Turnbull than Barrell seems prepared to acknowledge, though I would not dispute the fundamental similarities that he points out.

11 George Turnbull, *A Treatise on Ancient Painting* (London: 1740), p. x.

12 Ibid., p. 132.

13 Ibid., p. 146.

14 Ibid., p. 148.

15 For an important discussion of Shaftesbury's hostility to minuteness of pictorial detail in relation to the contemporary debates between the ancients and moderns in scientific discourse, see Harry Mount, "The reception of Dutch genre painting in England, 1695–1829" (PhD thesis, University of Cambridge, Cambridge, UK: 1990), pp. 109–42. Mount also briefly notes (on pp. 143–40) the different position adopted by Turnbull, and suggests that he may have been influenced by the English translation of Leonardo's *A Treatise on Painting*, which had been published in London in 1721. The idea of Joseph Wright self-consciously modeling his approach on Leonardo's example is an intriguing one, and not at all beyond the realm of possibility. I am grateful to Mount for permission to cite his research.

16 Turnbull, *Ancient Painting*, pp. 78–9.

17 Ibid., p. 81.

18 Ibid., p. 147.

19 See Barrell, *Political Theory*, esp. pp. 1–68.

20 Here the key work of modern historical scholarship remains J. G. A. Pocock, *The*

Machiavellian Moment: Florentine Political Thought and the Atlantic Republican Tradition (Princeton, NJ: Princeton University Press, 1975), esp. Chs 13 and 14.

21 In a letter written from Rome in May of 1699, referring to a conversation that had taken place prior to his departure from London, Closterman told Shaftesbury (or Lord Ashley as he then was) how pleased he had been to hear of his Lordship's "thoughts for a family picture," which the artist promised to paint as soon as he returned home. (The letter, now in the Public Record Office, London, is quoted in full in Edgar Wind, "Shaftesbury as a patron of art," *Journal of the Warburg and Courtauld Institutes* 2 [1938–9]: 187–8.) Though we do not know what those thoughts were, they presumably referred to the double portrait, which is the only work that Closterman produced depicting more than one member of the Shaftesbury family. Given Shaftesbury's exceptionally profound interest in the visual arts, and in the construction of his own self-image – together with the highly unusual character of the picture in question – we can be virtually certain that he would have devised a specific agenda for Closterman to follow. In January 1713, during the last months of his life, Shaftesbury wrote a series of three letters to the Neapolitan painter Paolo de Matteis, from whom he had earlier commissioned the *Judgment of Hercules*, asking him now to paint another picture, showing the earl himself as a dying philosopher and student of the arts. From the correspondence it is clear that Shaftesbury wished his artist to work to an extremely detailed iconographic and compositional program; furthermore, he described the project as one for "une Espèce de Portraiture moderne caracterisée et rendue Historique" – that is, for a type of modern portrait, in character and historical. I suspect that much the same notion, together with an equally specific list of demands, had emerged in his discussions with Closterman more than a decade earlier. In that instance, too, the third earl had set out to show how the wise direction of a man of taste could raise face-painting to the level of high intellectual dignity traditionally associated with historical art. For the correspondence documenting the Matteis portrait commission (which was never carried out), see J. E. Sweetman, "Shaftesbury's last commission," *Journal of the Warburg and Courtauld Institutes* 19 (1956): 110–16.

22 The picture is actually inscribed with the year 1702, but has been dated slightly earlier by Malcolm Rogers, whose conclusions are based on a combination of documentary and stylistic evidence. See Rogers, "John and John Baptist Closterman: a catalogue of their works," *The Walpole Society*, 49 (1983): 231–2, 258–9.

23 Rogers in ibid., p. 259, was the first to make the connection between Closterman's picture and this (undated) passage, which comes from Shaftesbury's unfinished "Plastics," *Second Characters*, p. 163. In the same note the earl recalls a time when he and Closterman had discussed the different species of landscape whilst in the woods around St. Giles's House, the Shaftesbury family seat; thus it seems highly likely that the forest shown in the picture would have specifically reminded the sitters of their own landed property.

24 Anthony Ashley Cooper, third Earl of Shaftesbury, *Characteristics of Men, Manners, Opinions, Times* (1711), ed. John M. Robertson, 2 vols in 1 (Indianapolis, IN and New York: 1964), Vol. 1, p. 193.

25 Lawrence Eliot Klein, "The rise of 'politeness' in England, 1660–1715" (PhD dissertation, Johns Hopkins University, Baltimore, MD: 1983), p. 437.

26 Shaftesbury, *Characteristics*, Vol. 1, p. 171.

27 Shaftesbury, *Second Characters*, pp. 110, 152.

28 Closterman's reference to the *Castor and Pollux* (which the artist would have seen in Rome; it is now in the Prado) was first pointed out by Alex Potts; see Rogers, "Closterman," p. 259. For a discussion of the various interpretations of the subject-matter of this sculpture, and its importance in the history of European taste, see Francis Haskell and Nicholas Penny, *Taste and the Antique: The Lure of Classical Sculpture 1500–1900* (New Haven, CT and London: Yale University Press, 1981), pp. 173–4 (the statue is reproduced on p. 175).

29 Shaftesbury, *Characteristics*, Vol. I, p. 279; for this point I am indebted to John Andrew Bernstein, *Shaftesbury, Rousseau, and Kant* (Rutherford, NJ: Fairleigh Dickinson University Press, 1980), p. 28.

30 Ibid., p. 286.

31 Ibid., p. 72.

32 Ibid., p. 74.

33 Shaftesbury also commissioned Closterman to paint two single portraits of himself and his brother, as types of the contemplative and active man respectively. For these two works see Rogers, "Closterman," pp. 231–2, 240, 259–60, cat. nos 5 and 86, Plates 57 and 58.

34 Both the third earl and Maurice were unusually fond of Xenophon, who had drawn upon the teachings of Socrates to trace a continuous path leading from family to friendship to polity, just as Shaftesbury did in the passage I have just quoted (see note 32). On Shaftesbury's admiration for Xenophon, whom he dared to rank even above Plato in importance, see Klein, "Rise of 'politeness'," p. 437. Just about all we know about Maurice Ashley Cooper, apart from the date of his death (1726), is that he translated Xenophon's *Cyropedia* into English. Closterman's single portrait of Shaftesbury (see previous note) actually includes a book by Xenophon, whose ideas also must have provided an important source for the double image we have been discussing.

35 Shaftesbury, *Characteristics*, Vol. I, p. 286.

36 Ibid., p. 300.

37 Ibid., p. 298. My discussion of Shaftesbury's views on sympathy owes a great deal to Mullan, *Sentiment and Sociability*, pp. 28–9.

38 Abel Boyer, *The English Theophrastus* (London: 1702), p. 106. This reference comes from Lawrence Klein, "The third Earl of Shaftesbury and the progress of politeness," *Eighteenth-Century Studies* 18, 2 (Winter 1984–5): 190. This excellent article and Klein's PhD thesis (see above) provided the primary bases for my discussion of Shaftesburian politeness.

39 Shaftesbury, *Characteristics*, Vol. II, p. 255.

40 See Klein, "Rise of 'politeness,'" p. 43.

41 Shaftesbury, *Characteristics*, Vol. I, p. 294.

42 I am acutely aware that the Closterman double portrait raises a number of important questions that I cannot explore within the context of this chapter; above all, it is not as "pure" a statement of Shaftesbury's civic ideals as my treatment of it here might lead one to believe. A more comprehensive account of this picture (and of Wright's *Air Pump* as well) has appeared in my *Painting for Money: The Visual Arts and the Public Sphere in Eighteenth-Century England* (New Haven, CT and London: Yale University Press, 1993).

43 It is quite possible that Dr Benjamin Bates – who had earlier purchased the *Gladiator* – bought the *Air Pump* prior to its going on exhibition. In the catalogue of the Society of Artists exhibition of 1768, Wright's title is not accompanied by the asterisk which denotes works that were available for purchase – though for the sake of preserving an aura of professional dignity (and success), painters were frequently reluctant to signal that they were on the lookout for potential patrons. In any case, given the usual pattern of transactions in the eighteenth-century English art market, a large subject-picture like the *Air Pump* is far more likely to have been painted and then purchased, as opposed to being commissioned in advance of its production.

44 The species of Wright's bird has been identified, and some of the implications of his choice discussed, in Schupbach, "Animal experiment," p. 346.

45 Pocock, *Machiavellian Moment*, p. 466.

46 It has often been suggested, and no doubt appropriately, that Wright selected his figure-types to invoke the traditional *topos* of the Ages of Man; see, for example, Paulson, *Emblem and Expression*, p. 186.

47 Charlotte Lennox, *The Lady's Museum*, 2 vols (London: 1760–1), Vol. I (1760), p. 136.

48 Benjamin Martin (1704/5–82), quoted in J. R. Millburn, *Benjamin Martin, Author, Instrument Maker, and "Country Showman"* (Leyden: 1976), p. 44.

49 For an extended discussion of this issue of refinement, see J. G. A. Pocock, *Virtue, Commerce, and History* (Cambridge, UK: Cambridge University Press, 1985), esp. Ch. 6.

50 David Fordyce, *Dialogues concerning Education*, 2 vols (London: 1745), Vol. II, p. 144.

51 David Fordyce, *The Elements of Moral Philosophy* (London: 1754), p. 157.

52 "Mira" [Eliza Haywood], *The Wife* (London: 1756), p. 29.

53 John Millar, *Observations concerning the Distinction of Ranks in Society* (London: 1771), pp. 102–3.

54   David Hume, "Of refinement in the arts," in *Essays Moral, Political and Literary* (1741–2), ed. Eugene F. Miller (Indianapolis, IN: Liberty Classics, 1987), p. 271.

55   Adam Smith, *The Theory of Moral Sentiments*, ed. D. D. Raphael and A. L. Macfie (Oxford: 1976 [1759]), Part II, section ii, ch. 3.4, p. 86.

56   Jean-Christophe Agnew, *Worlds Apart: The Market and the Theater in Anglo-American Thought, 1550–1750* (Cambridge, UK: Cambridge University Press, 1986), p. 178.

57   My discussion of the imagination as a vehicle for sympathetic feeling owes a good deal to Agnew, *Worlds Apart*, p. 178 and *passim*. Other useful treatments of this issue may be found in Mullan, *Sentiment and Sociability*, and in David Marshall, *The Figure of Theater: Shaftesbury, Defoe, Adam Smith, and George Eliot* (New York: Columbia University Press, 1986).

58   Cf. Mullan, *Sentiment and Sociability*, pp. 13–14.

59   For a good example of how popular science texts could promote the suffocation and electrocution of animals as a means of teaching children both to care for helpless creatures, and to appreciate the wisdom of God, see Benjamin Martin, *The Young Gentleman and Lady's Philosophy*, 2 vols (London: 1755), Vol. I, pp. 398–400, 311–12. The relevant passages from Martin are quoted in Schupbach, "Animal experiment," pp. 342–5.

60   This issue is discussed in Schupbach, "Animal experiment," pp. 341–2, and in David Fraser, "Joseph Wright of Derby and the Lunar Society," in Tate Gallery, *Wright of Derby*, p. 19. Here Fraser also points out that Wright appears to have based the figure of the boy lowering or raising the cage on the man pointing upwards to a skeleton on the left-hand side of Hogarth's *The Reward of Cruelty* of 1751. The connection between Wright and Hogarth deserves further thought, as I shall suggest below.

61   The anonymous author of *Critical Observations on the Pictures, which are now exhibiting at the Great Room, Spring-Garden, Charing-Cross, by the Society of Artists of Great Britain, 1768* (London: 1768), p. 15, singled out the "child whimpering for her pigeon" in the *Air Pump* as a "tender and ingenious" touch. The fact that the cage appears to form part of the permanent furnishings of the room indicates that the bird must be a family pet. Given the rarity of the cockatoo, it comes as no surprise to learn that at least one contemporary viewer mistook it for another species.

62   This might be the appropriate time to suggest that the actors in Wright's other large candlelights are also shown treading on morally dangerous ground – that by focusing so intently on the visible objects immediately in front of them, they may lose sight of larger, less tangible, but more important truths. In the *Air Pump*, however, where action is joined to contemplation, such dangers more overtly manifest their presence. Fraser makes something of a similar point, in reference to the general theme of the transience of life which also plays a part in the *Orrery*, in his "Lunar Society" essay, p. 20.

63   William Schupbach was the first to point this out, and to note that skulls are never mentioned in contemporary descriptions as present at scientific lectures of the sort portrayed by Wright; see "Animal experiment," p. 346.

64   Turnbull, *Ancient Painting*, pp. 141–2.

65   This is not an entirely frivolous analogy. If Wright's large candlelights had reminded their original viewers of any earlier depictions of nocturnal conviviality, then one could hardly think of a more likely candidate than the *Midnight Modern Conversation*. It may be just coincidence (though I am inclined to suspect otherwise) that Hogarth's work also features an outstretched hand (holding a glass) at the central apex of its composition, and a large bowl occupying a prominent position on the table – though the contrast between its contents and those of Wright's jar could hardly be more emphatic. There would also seem to be formal similarities between the poses of the two figures on the right-hand side of the *Modern Conversation*, and those of the grey-haired man and the older of the girls on the same side of the *Air Pump*. The possibility of Wright's borrowing pictorial ideas from Hogarth, and in so doing enhancing the semiotic richness of his work, has already been raised by David Fraser; see note 60 above.

13
Property, politics, and personality in Rousseau

Patrick Coleman

Like other social institutions, property is analyzed by Rousseau from two opposing perspectives. Looking at humanity's evolution away from the state of nature, he judges the invention of property to have marked a decisive step in the corruption of mankind. In the famous opening lines of the second part of the *Discourse on the Origin and the Foundations of Inequality* (1755), he declares:

> The first person who, having fenced off a plot of ground, took it into his head to say *this is mine* and found people simple enough to believe him, was the true founder of civil society. What crimes, what wars, what murders, what miseries, what horrors would the human race have been spared by someone who, uprooting the stakes or filling in the ditch, had shouted to his fellow-men: Beware of listening to this impostor; you are lost if you forget that the fruits belong to all and the earth to no one![1]

Yet, in his other political writings, Rousseau offers a very different judgment on property, one more suggestive of Lockean liberalism. Perhaps the most striking formulation occurs in a note included among the "Fragments politiques":

> For all civil rights being founded on that of property, as soon as the latter is abolished it is impossible for any other to survive. Justice would be no more than a delusion and the government no more than a tyranny, and public authority having no legitimate foundation, no one would be obliged to acknowledge it except insofar as he would be constrained to do so by force.[2]

These two points of view are not necessarily incompatible. Rousseau could argue that although bourgeois society rests on deceit and oppression, the state of nature is irrecoverable. One should try, therefore, to fashion a polity whose laws will be as fair and legitimate as possible. If property undermines personal independence by forcing men to respect geographical boundaries and social rules, this does not mean it should not be used to defend political freedom by limiting government intrusion into citizens' lives.

Rousseau's critique of the moral effects of property is too radical, however, to allow for easy compromise. And while in his political recommendations he professes to take "men as they are and the laws as they might be,"[3] the guiding purpose of *On the Social Contract* (1762) is not to protect citizens from the state but to bind them more closely together through a general will at odds with the divisive influence of property. For Rousseau, as for Hobbes, the sovereign power is absolute. Although the citizen "alienates through the social compact only that part of his power, goods, and freedom whose use matters to the community . . . it must also be agreed that the sovereign alone is the judge of what matters" (Book II, Ch. iv, p. 46).[4] Clearly the "liberal" interpretation of property sketched above, while grounded to some extent in the texts, fails to capture the thrust of Rousseau's thinking. His preoccupation with moral questions on the one hand, and the foundation of political legitimacy on the other, and in both cases with freedom of will above all else, leads him to neglect many of the practical issues regarding the extent and transfer of property rights that are addressed either by Locke or by the natural rights commentators such as Grotius and Pufendorf to whom he often refers. In those writings that do adopt a more practical perspective, such as the *Considerations on the Government of Poland* (written 1772; published 1782), Rousseau is more concerned with what he sees as the corrupting influence on public life of economic activity generally than with the relation between property and power.[5]

Even within the framework of Rousseau's thought, however, something seems to be missing. In a provocative article, James MacAdam identifies an important gap in the way Rousseau defines the relationship between property and human will. As he puts it, Rousseau tells us how men become slaves to property and how men could live in free association, but not how slaves could become free enough to establish and identify with such an association. MacAdam concludes that, despite Rousseau's many suggestive remarks, no coherent theory of property can be found in his political texts.[6]

The short answer to MacAdam's objection is that Rousseau is a pessimist who believes the corrupting effects of property – or of civilization itself – can never be undone. The political association depicted in the *Social Contract*, like the state of nature portrayed in the *Discourse on Inequality*, should be seen as representing a standard against which contemporary societies can be judged rather than a workable political blueprint.[7] But such a view implies that readers may still achieve a degree of psychological liberation by reading Rousseau's works. Of course, civilization for Rousseau is not only slavery. It fosters the development of human reason and imagination, whose "perfectibility" is made possible by the indeterminacy of human will. If these faculties lead to misery in the first instance, Rousseau does believe it possible to draw an antidote from the poison itself.[8]

Can the same treatment be applied to property? Rousseau's statement that property rights constitute a bulwark against tyranny suggests that it can, and yet MacAdam is right in claiming that Rousseau's conception of humanity's historical development does not clearly explain how the activity of will and labor enshrined in property might be rehabilitated. The discussion of property in the *Discourse on Inequality*, the *Discourse on Political Economy* (1755), and the *Social Contract* can, I think, be clarified by Rousseau's analysis of individual experience in *Emile* (1762). The treatise on education does not supply the missing link in the theory; rather, it helps explain why Rousseau believes there must be a gap.

In the second part of the *Discourse on Inequality*, having "proved that inequality is barely perceptible in the state of nature," Rousseau wants to show "its origin and progress in the successive developments of the human mind" (p. 140).[9] He begins by declaiming against the "first fencer," MacAdam's convenient name for the hypothetical first person to claim a particular piece of land as his own. He immediately adds, however, that by the time this imaginary villain is able to make his case, the institution of property has become inevitable. The first half of this part of the *Discourse* goes on to trace the development of property up to the institution of the first social contract while the last pages analyze the degeneration of this original polity into tyranny.

Rousseau's treatment of these issues is governed by his focus on inequality. This term encompasses much more than discrepancies in status, power, or wealth. For Rousseau, who defines the state of nature much more absolutely than his predecessors had done, inequality refers to any material or psychological difference that affects the way human lives are lived and the ways in which individuals understand themselves. Inequality is already present as soon as men start to notice differences (and then similarities) between things: humanity's cognitive and linguistic development begins with acts of comparison. So much so that Rousseau avoids specifying where on earth man in the pure state of nature might have lived, because "naturally" fertile areas such as the Nile valley owe their richness to floods. Any variation in the environment that affects the food supply would provoke the perception of difference and upset the balance of the state of nature. It is this extension of the idea of inequality that leads Rousseau to discuss the institution of property in terms of a much broader pattern of historical necessity. Thus, when he describes the establishment of family life in huts, he stresses the way the development of tools emerged from comparisons men made between themselves and the animals they hunted and, similarly, how the loose associations of hunters were based on recognizing the similar purposes of each individual hunter.

On the other hand, the "sort of property" (p. 146) that was created in these early families – basic huts along with rudimentary tools and other simple possessions – was not problematic because men were not forced to compare their lot with that of others. Competition was not a problem as long as it was easier for an individual to move away from his neighbor than to fight over a piece of land or its products. Only with the "permanent proximity [*voisinage permanent*]" (p. 148) established by the fusion of a group of families into a nation (a bond reinforced by the influence of a common climate and way of life) does comparison become inevitable and invidious. Here we find Rousseau adopting a much more restricted notion of inequality. If, at one level, it is practically coterminous with the entire process of alienation from the state of nature, within society it is limited to differences that are in fact perceived. This shift opens up new room for maneuver within the apparently impersonal course of human development. Social men and women may focus their attention on differences that are secondary from a material point of view, such as physical appearance. But this also suggests that they may be led, by circumstances or by persuasion, to overlook other, seemingly more serious disparities.

Thus, the first transformation of possessions into property (in the sense of possession explicitly acknowledged by other people) does not involve things but strength and beauty. In other words, the issue is the egotistical *amour-propre* that Rousseau had earlier distinguished from the more primitive and value-free *amour de soi* linked to simple self-preservation. Rousseau writes: "As soon as men had begun to appreciate one another, and the idea of consideration was formed in their minds, each one claimed a right to it, and it was no longer possible to be disrespectful toward anyone with impunity" (p. 149).[10] The peculiar twist Rousseau gives to the idea of property comes out at the end of the same paragraph in the way he misquotes Locke. Insisting that the vanity he has just analyzed does not characterize men in the state of nature but only those who have reached a relatively advanced stage of development, he declares that primitive men were gentle because "according to the axiom of the wise Locke, *where there is no property, there is no injury*" (p. 150; Rousseau's emphasis).[11] Locke's word was "injustice," not "injury."[12] The difference is important because although the French word *injure* was originally used to mean "injury," its primary meaning in modern French is "insult." The change (deliberate or not) reflects the priority Rousseau gives to the psychological over the less personal aspects of property, like its relation to material production. He invites the reader who agrees with Locke's statement (which had become a commonplace of natural rights thinking) to endorse its converse: a sense of injury is evidence that property exists. The property in question does not, however, seem to be the material possessions Rousseau called "a sort of property." Rather, it consists of the self-image or good name each individual wants others to respect. The conventions governing the right to one's reputation, Rousseau suggests, were the first systematic constraints on our independence. This shift in perspective prepares the way for the peculiar mixture of psychological and economic conflicts out of which the first social contract emerged. It also lays the groundwork for another, later move: the alienation and inequality associated with property can be mitigated just as appropriately by lessening the sense of injury as by reducing differences in wealth.

The next stage in the development of property begins for Rousseau with the invention of metallurgy and agriculture, which results in the production of a food surplus and allows the division of labor to become permanent. "From the cultivation of land its division necessarily followed; and from property once recognized, the first rules of justice" (p. 154). Rousseau's attitude is resolutely practical: "in order to give everyone what is his, it is necessary that everyone can have something."[13] Victor Goldschmidt points out that in deriving rules of justice from property rather than the other way round, Rousseau distinguishes himself from the Continental natural law tradition.[14] Of course, from the standpoint of the state of nature, the hallowed definition of justice in terms of giving to each his own is itself the product of a corrupt, socialized reason, to which Rousseau is here ironically deferring.

As in the workmanship theories of property discussed by Ian Shapiro in Chapter 2 of this book, Rousseau's theory derives a proprietor's moral right to his land and the produce of that land from his manual labor on the land. But while Rousseau follows Locke in speaking about the appropriation of things through the addition of one's labor to them, he is not really interested in exploring the kind of right labor creates. He agrees that "it is labor alone which, giving the cultivator a right to the product of the land he has tilled, gives him a right to the soil as a consequence,"[15] but the context is very different from Locke's. First, Rousseau views work primarily as a form of subjection. This is why he introduces the connection between labor and property only at the stage of organized agriculture. Rousseau might agree with Locke that gathering acorns requires labor, but only when there appears a gap between labor and its result (as in sowing and harvesting) and men have to worry about the future does the idea of property in things become relevant. But even more important than the loss of one's own labor is uncertainty about interpersonal relationships. "As men began to look to the future and as they all saw themselves with some goods to lose, there was not one of them who did not have to fear reprisals against himself for wrongs he might do to another" (p. 154).[16] We see here another reason for downplaying the self-centered view of a right arising from labor. Property not only restrains others from seizing what is mine, it also, and perhaps primarily, acts as a curb on my aggressive activity. If Rousseau takes for granted the link between the cultivation of land and its division, it is because this instability, which always existed, is now aggravated by men's greater interdependence.

True to the overall theme of the *Discourse*, Rousseau also emphasizes how, in this new stage of society, the natural inequalities of strength and intelligence that were of little importance in the state of nature produce more enduring effects. Like the vanity he discussed earlier, these differences can no longer be ignored. More abundant harvests, along with the negotiations of trade, give these differences a more enduring form, one that men cannot fail to notice. Property in land is also more oppressive than property in things because of the need to establish boundary lines between contiguous plots. This is why Rousseau highlighted the work of the "first fencer." The fence is the permanent sign both of individual appropriation and of the neighbor's *recognition* of that gesture. For Rousseau, it marks a deep form of alienation. It requires of men an involuntary and permanent preoccupation with other people, even when those people themselves are not present.

The stifling, noxious influence of property is reinforced by another factor that distinguishes Rousseau from Locke. The English writer often speaks of the improvement of "waste" land (at home or in the vast expanses of America) in arguing for the beneficial results of secure property rights. Rousseau, on the other hand, the citizen of a tiny republic surrounded by more powerful states, evokes a closed space already fully occupied. In the (perhaps rather Swiss) world of the *Discourse*, the hunting and gathering (and perhaps pastoral)[17] stage seems to coincide with the period of relatively open space; settled agriculture, with circumscribed fertile areas already crowded with people forced to interact.[18]

Still, the double oppression of division and interdependence does not destroy all independence. It encounters men's persistent self-centeredness, which finds new support in the very system that destroyed individual self-sufficiency. As Rousseau shows, the division of labor in a more complex economy ensures that even the richest man cannot avoid depending on those whose services he needs. Deceit and violence must be employed to "interest" men in each other's fate (p. 156). In the new world of property, men will only work for others if they "find their own profit" in doing so. Since at this point everyone, it would seem, is a property owner and the large surpluses that encourage extreme specialization have not yet been produced, we may infer that property provides a means for avoiding interaction. Individuals still have the option of working harder on their own land (or of accepting a lower standard of living) instead of consenting to further dependence. The rich themselves do not yet have to rely on others' cooperation. The "fervor to raise one's relative fortune" also arises from a search for psychological space. It arises "less out of true need than in order to place oneself above others" (p. 156).

While the regular labor that characterizes the emergence of agricultural society creates a right to property, that right in itself does not lead to a more elaborate system of legal or political rules. The latter emerge from the clash between two other forms of property right: "the right of the first occupant" and "the right of the stronger" (p. 157).[19] Political institutions became necessary because these rights led to "a perpetual conflict which ended only in fights and murders. . . . Nascent society gave way to the most horrible state of war."[20]

Now, Rousseau denies any legitimacy to the right of the stronger, at least when it takes the form of the right of conquest (p. 161).[21] In placing it on the same plane as the less controversial right of the first occupant, he reminds the reader of the dubious justice of all rights associated with property. At different moments in his historical account any right can be viewed as the consequence of humanity's corruption or as a defense against further decline. Rousseau's sometimes puzzling shifts between descriptive and evaluative language compel the reader to keep moving backward and forward in the story and thereby to appreciate the way words can be put to different purposes. Rousseau shows how arguments can be made on the basis of *each* of these rights as society grows and differences in wealth increase. His rhetorical strategy sharpens the clash between rights by robbing them of any stable differentiating context.

Those who have enriched themselves through talent or industry now feel tempted to expropriate from the poor. The latter must invoke the right of first occupant to defend their meager holdings against the "usurpations" (p. 157) of the rich, since the right they can invoke from labor no longer suffices to defend their property when differences of efficiency become more noticeable. But on the next page we find it is the poor who are attacking the rich men's right to *their* property. To the person who argues, "But I built this wall; I earned this field by my labor," the poor reply:

> Who gave you its dimensions . . . and by virtue of what do you presume to be paid at our expense for work we did not impose on you? Do you not know that a multitude of your brethren die or suffer from need of what you have in excess, and that you needed express and unanimous consent of the human race to appropriate for yourself anything from common subsistence that exceeded your own? (p. 158)[22]

This argument no doubt represents the answer Rousseau wished someone had given the first fencer. Its placement here, however, suggests Rousseau's peculiar image of the "first occupant." He is not a pioneer staking out a homestead on the frontier. Nor is he a Robinson Crusoe claiming a deserted island. The right of the first occupant arises – or rather, needs to be invoked – within an already integrated network of social relations whose equilibrium is being disturbed. Once again, Rousseau describes a closed, not an expanding, human space. Rousseau's overall view of the eighteenth-century world may be eccentric, but it does prevent him from accepting the seductive fiction of the wholly independent settler.

This passage also casts doubt on the unproblematic endorsement of property rights arising from labor. Unlike Locke, Rousseau does not begin with a man producing just enough for his sustenance and then go on to consider the legitimacy of his owning more. First we see the beginnings of labor. Then we see men who have become rich and others whose poverty has driven them to give up labor for "brigandage" (p. 157). This kind of sudden shift is typical of Rousseau. He only rarely portrays the moment of equilibrium between lack and excess; such moments belong to reverie rather than to history. As with other kinds of inequality, a difference in quantity brings about a qualitative change, which in turn requires a new conceptual framework. Once economic differentiation and interdependence have advanced to a certain point, the fear of reprisal that helped consolidate the first institution of property is no longer effective. Something more persuasive is required, a sanction better adapted to a more sophisticated society in which economic power actually makes the rich man more vulnerable than before. As Rousseau puts it: the rich man is "destitute of valid reasons to justify himself" (p. 158): ironically, a legitimizing reason is a "good" that riches (or labor) cannot buy.

The first social contract arises from the discursive stalemate between the right of first occupant and the right of the stronger. As Rousseau sees it, both "rights" are invoked by rich and poor alike to fight each other off. The rich are stronger individually, but when the poor unite they are the superior force. The poor do not have enough to protect to have made the sacrifice of their freedom attendant upon entering into the social contract worthwhile for them. The contract must, therefore, have been initiated by the rich. The poor go along in the belief that political union will restrain the rich from expropriating from them. At the same time Rousseau expresses wonder at the poor's willingness to give up their only valuable possession: freedom. The argument seems to rest on the crucial factor of "permanent proximity," which distinguishes the interaction of the *contractors* (if I may revive the early, now obsolete sense of the word) from relations between the inhabitants of different countries. This would explain why Rousseau denies that the contract could have arisen solely from a "union of the weak" (p. 161). Only when it is a question of the people of one nation (Rousseau is no doubt thinking of the Swiss confederation) uniting against another is it possible to imagine a union of the weak vis-à-vis the strong. Within a given nation the weak are not separate enough from the strong to establish a contract on their own.

The further development of political institutions only reinforces the constricting effects of this permanent proximity by adding to it the conceptual fusion of political, economic, and, ultimately, moral categories. Inequality gets worse as it becomes more stable and as the forms of dependence become more invasive at each stage in the "progress of inequality." Rousseau summarizes these developments toward the end of the *Discourse*:

> the establishment of the law and the right of property was the first stage, the institution of the magistracy the second, and the third and last was the changing of legitimate power into arbitrary power. So that the status of rich and poor was authorized by the first epoch, that of powerful and weak by the second, and by the third that of master and slave, which is the last degree of inequality and the limit to which all the others finally lead, until new revolu-

tions dissolve the government altogether or bring it closer to its legitimate institution. (p. 172)[23]

If these "new revolutions" are to succeed, or if the final descent of actual societies into the despotism described by the *Discourse on Inequality* is to be prevented, it would seem necessary to disentangle the different forms of power and the discourses that legitimate them.[24] Looking back on the early stages of society, we can say it is precisely because the rich and the strong were not the same, and the different rights invoked did not mesh, that tyranny was impossible in the first stage of inequality – even though there was constant strife. On the retrospective view Rousseau encourages us to take, that strife becomes a secondary consideration, just as the revenge killings that marked the first, loose associations of hunting and gathering families did not prevent that stage of humanity from having been its "happiest and most durable epoch" (p. 151). The stage seems to be set for Rousseau to present us with a political vision based on the idea of countervailing powers in which property rights play an important role. However dubious their origin, these rights would seem to create some valuable breathing room within the closed world of Rousseau's political economy. In his article on "Economie politique" for the *Encyclopédie*, Rousseau does move in this direction, but not whole-heartedly. For in moving from a retrospective to a prospective view, Rousseau cannot himself disentangle the assertion of rights from the aggression and violence that accompanied it. The desire to forestall tyranny will be tempered by a determination to avoid conflict in general.

In his *Encyclopédie* article, later published separately as a *Discourse on Political Economy*,[25] Rousseau introduces his key concept of the general will as the legitimate foundation of political law. But his focus is not so much on the citizen as on the government, which must respect the general will in its management of the "public economy" (p. 211). This economy is to be distinguished from that of the family. Whereas the goal of the latter is to "preserve and increase the father's patrimony," the aim of the prudent ruler is to "maintain private individuals in a state of peace and plenty" (p. 210). Yet, although he denies that political authority is modeled on patriarchal power, Rousseau defines "political economy" not as an expanding system of productive and commercial relations but in a more traditional, Aristotelian sense as a household to be managed wisely. Family members scatter and start new families; citizens should be led to love their country and remain within it (p. 221).

From this perspective, property rights are indeed a defense against arbitrary power. But even more important, they are an instrument through which the government fosters closer ties between the citizen and the state. In *Political Economy*, the "rules of conduct" outlined by Rousseau blur the distinction between rights and maxims of political prudence. Defending the eclecticism of his references to Locke and Jean Bodin, to Montesquieu and Plato, Rousseau claims that "whether the people can refuse or the sovereign should not require is indifferent in terms of right" (p. 230).[26] Many would argue the difference is a crucial one, but, as the next sentence shows, Rousseau is using "right" here solely as the opposite of "force," without distinguishing among kinds of right. "If it is only a question of force, it is completely useless to examine what is or is not legitimate."

Avoiding force becomes the guiding principle in Rousseau's specific recommendations regarding the public economy. Oppressive inequalities between rich and poor should be reduced. This is to be done "not by taking treasures away from those who possess them, but by removing the means of accumulating them from everyone; nor by building poorhouses, but by protecting citizens from becoming poor" (p. 222).[27] Commerce, which aggravates inequality, should be curtailed. So should the activity of the state, which leads to war and conquest, and hence to burdensome taxation. Demographic pressures are to be eased by a more equal distribution of people across the country. Measures such as these make conflict over property rights less likely.

Property rights themselves help in several ways to avoid the use of force. Indeed, property is said to be "the most sacred right of all the citizens, and more important in certain respects than freedom itself" (p. 224).[28] Rousseau offers three justifications for reversing what would seem to be the proper order of priority. Property may be more important than freedom "either because it is more closely connected with the preservation of life, or because, since goods are easier to usurp and more difficult to protect than one's person, greater respect should be accorded to what can more easily be stolen, or finally because property is the true basis of civil society and the true guarantee of the citizens' engagements" (p. 225).[29]

Each of these three justifications of property rests on the prevention of direct and potentially harmful clashes of will. The examples Rousseau chooses illustrate his unwillingness to distinguish between property as a shield against power and property as a buttress of political obligation. In the first case, Rousseau is referring not to individual self-preservation but to collective survival in a developed political economy. Because the state guarantees their lives and property, citizens will be willing to "contribute some of their goods to its upkeep" (p. 225) – for if they had to defend themselves they would jeopardize both. In contrasting goods that are hard to protect with a person's body that can more easily be protected, Rousseau suggests that a man can recover his freedom by fighting or running away and that the state needs to worry more about what individuals can less easily defend. Rousseau may be thinking about ordinary crimes from which the state protects the individual, but he may also be referring, in a rather roundabout way, to restraints on the state's intrusion into the citizens' lives. Property rights act as a buffer making personal independence possible.

In the third case, on the other hand, the same ability of the individual to escape others' grasp leads to the interesting idea that, because they do become dependent on their property, men will be forced to accept political obligation. But the result is not oppression, since here, too, property acts as a buffer. As Ramon Lemos has pointed out, if a man "had no property he could be compelled to comply with the laws of the body politic only by such means as threatening to deprive him of his life or his liberty; but if he has property he can also be compelled to comply by threatening to deprive him of his property."[30] This conclusion, which echoes the fragment I quoted at the beginning of this chapter, leads us to a kind of paradox: property becomes an obstacle to tyranny only if the citizen remains attached to (and thus alienated by) his material interests.

In *Political Economy*, MacAdam's dichotomy between irremediable enslavement and impossible freedom seems not to apply. In discussing a modern political economy – France is never named but the remarks about taxation and population clearly refer to that country – Rousseau assumes there is sufficient free room within the system to mitigate the effects of permanent proximity through a moderate redistribution of people and resources. On the theoretical level, too, his equation of right with almost any policy that minimizes compulsion allows him to negotiate the problem of dependence. However, in order to reach this happy result, Rousseau has to keep the problem of will – the psychological complexity of its assertion and restraint – in the background. Of course, he speaks of the need for "virtue," which includes self-denial and a commitment to equality on the part of the citizens and a special sense of duty in the ministers of government. But he also writes that it is not necessary for the citizens to assemble for the general will to be known. By definition, the true general will "is always for the side most favorable to the public interest – that is, for the most equitable; so that it is only necessary [for the government] to be just and one is assured of following the general will" (p. 216).[31] These statements must be understood within the context of the *Encyclopédie*'s program for reform within the context of monarchical institutions. A certain vagueness about popular participation was necessary. But one wonders if there is not a deeper connection between bracketing the exercise of will and contemplating without anxiety the contribution of property to the public good.

In the *Social Contract*, Rousseau declares explicitly that the general will can only be discovered and expressed through the deliberations of the assembled people. The sovereign power is inalienable and indivisible: it must rest in the body politic as a whole, and that body has "absolute power over all its members" (I, iv; p. 62). What restrains that power is not the buffer of a property right as such, but the stipulation that genuine law may only have a general object. The law may not burden one citizen over another (p. 64). And, since it would be contradictory for the general will to legislate against the interests of the people – for which citizen "does not think of himself as he votes for all?" – no general burden will be imposed "that is useless to the community" (p. 62). In this way, Rousseau attempts to preserve a space of freedom within the operation of will itself. What he calls the "double relationship" of the people to themselves (as individuals with private interests and as citizens seeking the common good) prevents the collapse of power into despotism, on the one hand, and into a mask for private privilege, on the other. In *Emile* he declares that this "double relationship" constitutes "the whole artifice [*jeu*] of the political machine."[32]

In practice, the proper play between private and public will is hard to maintain. Books III and IV of the *Social Contract* discuss the need for an agency, the "government," separate from the sovereign, to execute the general will. Yet, all governments in the end substitute their private will for that of the sovereign. Rousseau also declares that the possibility of political freedom depends in part on the climate and resources of different countries (III, viii). The activity of the general will should itself be shaped by the leaders' wise direction of public opinion and by the sovereign's own establishment of a civil religion (IV, vii–viii). Although Rousseau exalts the general will, the act of willing is always unstable, widening or narrowing the space of freedom beyond manageable limits.

Another kind of instability appears in the discussion of property rights. Property's origin in chance and violence can never be forgotten, although it must be overlooked if political society is to exist at all. The same chapter that describes how property is made legitimate (the only one in which property is discussed in detail) also stresses just how relative that legitimacy really is. Each man gives up everything to the sovereign, but he is immediately given back "the proprietorship of all he possesses" (I, viii; p. 56). And yet, what is this possession but "the effect of force or the right of the first occupant?" The parallel construction here is significant. Objectively speaking, that is, as far as outsiders are concerned, the transformation of possession into property secured by a "positive title" changes nothing.

> It is not that by this act possession, in changing hands, changes its nature and becomes property in the hands of the sovereign. But as the force of the City is incomparably greater than that of a private individual, public possession is by that very fact stronger and more irrevocable, without being more legitimate, at least as far as foreigners are concerned. For with regard to its members, the state is master of all their goods through the social contract, which serves the state as the basis of all rights. But with regard to other powers, it is master only through the right of the first occupant, which it derives from the private individuals. (I, ix; p. 56)[33]

Why should this matter to people establishing the internal constitution of their own state? First, keeping this external point of view in mind helps curtail the unwarranted expansion of any state. The right of the first occupant is limited by the extent of a man's actual needs. It is validated by his labor. When the explorer Balboa "took possession of the South Sea and all of South America in the name of the crown of Castile," his claim was therefore illegitimate (p. 57). But Rousseau also suggests that the illegitimacy of expansion is connected to the very act that made the right of the first occupant a "real right" *within* the bounds of the initial state. "Every man naturally has a right to everything he needs; but the positive act that makes him the proprietor of some good excludes him from all the rest. Once his portion is designated, he should limit himself to it, and no longer has any right to the community's goods" (pp. 56–7).[34] This principle properly refers to relationships within the state, but Rousseau inserts it immediately after introducing the foreigner's point of view and follows it with the example of Balboa. The principle of self-limitation seems to operate on two levels at once. Rousseau, I believe, justifies overlooking inequities in the distribution of property within the state by condemning those who upset patterns of possession around the globe.

It seems an odd move, at least for those who imagine that those most likely to protest inequality inside the country are not the same as those who seek foreign conquest. Whether or not this is true (and the relationship between internal class tensions and colonial expansion is by no means simple), for Rousseau resentment and aggressive self-assertion characterize rich and poor alike. As the *Discourse on Inequality* emphasized, they are the pervasive consequences of all social progress. But, just as in the *Discourse* the evil of the first institution of property was in part compensated by the possibility for the individual *not* to think of his neighbor, here the reference to international relations points to a similar kind of psychological benefit. The right of the first occupant is "respectable to every civilized man" because "one respects not so much what belongs to others as what does not belong to oneself" (p. 57).

The idea is plausible enough in relationships with strangers from whom we remain morally separate. Rousseau seems to want to import it into relationships among citizens of the same country. The outsider's point of view on the relativity of property rights helps preserve the space of free play within the political machine. Not becoming too interested in what belongs to another citizen prevents the eruption of domestic conflicts that could, in turn, lead to wars of conquest (which, as in the case of Spain, also led to internal ruin). Respect for what does not belong to oneself acts as a curb on individual aggression without fostering a preoccupation with other people, which can only foster aggression in other forms such as envy. By mitigating the "demand for consideration" that accompanies political as much as it does personal self-esteem, this contraction of self complements the double relationship between private person and citizen by adding to it a third aspect: that of the human being stepping back from involvement.[35]

But can any man actually play all these roles? The later books of the *Social Contract* argue that it is neither possible nor desirable to do so. Rousseau's inspired legislator, whose wisdom is required to draft a constitution, is an outsider but plays no role in the exercise of sovereignty. If the citizens themselves are to obey the laws they make, they must love them, and Rousseau's chapters on the molding of public opinion suggest that such love might be incompatible with intellectual detachment, except perhaps in some particularly virtuous statesmen. And yet, other republican thinkers have thought such versatility possible, at least for those whose property gave them both a stake in the public good and sufficient independence to resist being seduced by overweening power. Rousseau's political works, especially *Political Economy*, include elements from this tradition, but throughout his writing we also find a countervailing movement of revulsion that makes him shrink from adopting it. This reaction is obvious in the *Discourse on Inequality*, but it can be found in the *Social Contract* as well. For example, the happy notion that property provides a non-coercive instrument for ensuring obedience, a crucial element in *Political Economy*, is given a quite different cast in the later work, which praises those canny kings who call themselves masters of the country rather than leaders of the people. "By thus holding the land, they are quite sure of holding its inhabitants" (I, ix; p. 57).

Rousseau's revulsion clearly derives from his personal experience, as an artisan's son, of the pretension of and oppression by the propertied classes. It also reflects a persistent tendency in early modern French thought, especially the *moraliste* tradition, to consider virtue to be radically at odds with interest.[36] But these well-known attitudes do not fully account for Rousseau's reluctance to follow through on his intriguing comments about property's role in containing – that is, allowing for and at the same time restraining – the activity of will. To understand the nature of the difficulty, we need to look at the education of an autonomous and responsible individual as Rousseau describes it in *Emile*.

Contrary to common opinion, Rousseau's treatise on education does not portray a totally self-sufficient individual. Rather, its starting point is the question "What will a man raised uniquely for himself become for others?" (p. 41).[37] Since Emile is to receive his education from nature, things, and men (p. 38), and since these three educations must be harmonized, one expects Rousseau to show how property relations, which mediate between things and men, may be integrated into this scheme. Each of *Emile*'s five books does indeed include some discussion of property. What we find, however, is that while Rousseau is willing to speak of *property* as an economic fact, and of *possession* as enjoyment or consumption, he shies away from the psychological and social experience of *ownership*, which normally would furnish the vital connection between these two concepts.[38]

Rousseau believes that the young child should not own anything. In Book I, the child does have toys, but to prevent the development of vanity these are for him to use (although Rousseau does not at first explicitly specify the sex, it soon becomes clear that he means a boy) and are not to be identified as extensions of himself. Nor should he be expected to give anything away permanently. It is only in Book II that the pupil becomes acquainted with the notion of property. In order to introduce his pupil to the idea of property and to a first understanding of justice, Emile's tutor encourages him to grow a crop of beans on a plot of land already being cultivated (though Emile does not know it) by Robert the gardener. When Emile's delight in his crop and his sense of ownership of it have sufficiently developed, he arrives at the garden one day to find his prized crop rooted up and the irritated gardener complaining that the beans have destroyed more valuable Maltese melon seeds he had earlier planted.

Rousseau uses the story to establish two principles. The first is the familiar negative one: the idea of property acts as a limit on unregulated appropriation.[39] But this principle is accompanied by a second acknowledging that

> Our first duties are to ourselves; our primary sentiments are centered on ourselves; all our natural movements relate in the first instance to our preservation and well-being. Thus, the first sentiment of justice does not come to us from the justice we owe but from that which is due to us. (p. 97)[40]

As in the *Discourse on Inequality*, the individual in *Emile* must have something before he can grasp the idea of justice. This suggests there will be an important connection between property and moral education. The tutor encourages Emile's desire to participate in the "power and activity" of cultivation he sees around him in the countryside. He helps him plant his beans. Emile rejoices to see the first sprouts and is even happier when the tutor tells him that the investment of labor has made the crop his (p. 98). But then Emile finds that Robert has retaliated against those who ruined the melons he had planted in the same space Emile worked. The boy is able to appreciate Robert's anger because he now knows what it means to possess – or, more precisely, to be deprived of – something of one's own. But this insight does not provide a basis for discussing what constitutes legitimate ownership. Rousseau retreats from the second to the first of his principles, from justice as a method for establishing what is due, to justice as a general sense of limitation.

The garden episode includes a number of other elements that are less often discussed, perhaps because they do not mesh easily with what we expect in a discussion of property. The first is that Robert does not really own the property, which belongs to his landlord, Emile's father.[41] One might conjecture that Rousseau wants the reader to think about the difference between legal and "real" ownership, but this seems unlikely since the emphasis throughout the story is on the sense of dispossession. When Emile exclaims "But I don't have a garden!" it is not pointed out that he will inherit one. Nor is it suggested he could go cultivate another patch of land. As Robert himself tells us, "There is hardly any fallow land left. I work what my father improved. Each in turn does the same, and all the lands you see have been occupied for a long time" (p. 99).[42] There is no suggestion that this state of affairs could be modified or that an approach could be made to the real owner (for Robert avoids speaking of ownership at all). A natural right to property, we know from the *Social Contract*, exists only so long as there remains some vacant land (I, ix; p. 57). But what the mechanisms might be for mediating a social right to property we are not told. On the contrary, Emile confronts a world that is already completely *settled*, in every sense of the term.

Rousseau's story makes sense if it is read allegorically, as illustrating Emile's initiation into the symbolic world of culture, to whose laws all men are subject, rather than as a discussion of property. The experience of dispossession gives Emile a sense of himself as a person to whom justice is due. Read in this way, Emile's confrontation with a prior and non-negotiable network of relations and constraints provides a vivid reminder that social men never act in a vacuum. The end of the story is meant to reassure us that our dependence need not be painful. The tutor (here called Jean-Jacques) proposes a deal whereby Robert will sublease, as it were, a part of his garden in exchange for half Emile's crop, but the gardener rejects the bargain. Instead, he grants Emile free use of the land as long as his melons are undisturbed. As the conclusion to a story involving a young child, this is plausible enough, but as a lesson in practice it is less compelling. This reluctance to engage in specific negotiation, which would involve calculation and comparison – tools of reason, but also reminders of dependence – becomes a recurring feature of *Emile*'s argument.

Rousseau says at the end of the story that from this point "to the right of property and to exchange there is only a step, after which one must simply stop short" (p. 99).[43] This step is taken in Book III, which is devoted to instruction in the arts and sciences. Here, Emile learns about trade as a cooperative means to ensure the distribution of goods over countries very different in climate and resources. He acquires his first notions of politics at this point, viewing government solely in terms of the organization of trade as a response to general human needs. But since in this part of *Emile* the pupil's education is still governed solely by the observation of natural differences, Rousseau does not go into the legal or social consequences of commerce.

Finally, in Book IV, the tutor introduces his charge into society. Rousseau anticipates the objection that Emile has no right to participate in the affairs of the world because he is young and – more important – because "he still disposes only of himself; it is as though he disposed of nothing" (p. 249).[44] In other words, Emile has no fortune to back up his claim to status. But just when the reader expects Rousseau to get more specific about the relationship between "our important rights of property" and "that of the person," he introduces the Savoyard vicar to instruct Emile in the metaphysical order of the universe. The young man learns to contemplate and to enjoy his place within a divine scheme that answers man's psychological need for certainty. One can see this passage as an extension of Rousseau's emphasis on symbolic over material relations. Rousseau makes no mention of the notion of stewardship, for example, used by Locke in his appeal to religion as a key to the moral use of property.[45] No doubt the idea of stewardship was incompatible with the intimate reciprocity of the heart extolled by the vicar, just as the idea of a lease did not suit the easy confidence established between Emile, Robert, and Jean-Jacques.[46]

Armed by religion against the seductions of the city, Emile arrives in Paris. His urban education remains, however, at some distance from social and economic interests. To live in society is above all else to be at ease in a world of convention, but the conventions in question, the context being exclusively that of *salon* conversation, are those of taste. According to Rousseau, taste is the exercise of judgment in trivial matters. This critique of social frivolity allows Rousseau to avoid discussing practical issues: neither in good company nor in *Emile* do money and property seem to be suitable topics for conversation. Although the motives may be different, aristocratic *politesse* and the outsider's contempt for worldliness produce the same result. One might add that the appeal to aesthetic appreciation resembles Rousseau's invocation of a religious sense of order in the *"Profession de foi."* In both cases, he skips over appropriation as the basis of social differentiation in order to focus on notions of moral appropriateness within a system of symbolic representations. As in the garden story, this system is viewed only as an abstract totality. As such, it can be idealized and then dismissed as irrelevant to Emile's "practical" concerns. No real connection between property and manners can be made.

But what about property as a support for rugged independence? At the end of Book IV, Rousseau interrupts Emile's story to speak in his own person about what he would do if he were rich. Far from working to improve his property, he would use his wealth to free himself from any concern with property at all. He contrasts the frugal but free life he would lead with that of the ordinary rich man, dependent on servants for his every need. The real benefit of wealth, he suggests, is to allow us not to be inconvenienced by the presence of other people, for even when they are there to serve us, we are compelled to think about them and to be dependent on them. Since it was the permanent proximity of other people that, according to the *Discours sur l'inégalité*, made social relationships, including property and other alienating institutions, necessary in the first place, Rousseau's daydream suggests that the only truly satisfying answer to the problem of ownership is to transcend it entirely.

This answer, however, is presented as valid only for Jean-Jacques, who, unlike other people, is able to live alone, whose needs are minimal, and whose will, parodying that of Balboa, exhausts itself in make-believe conquests (p. 354). We thus return in Book V to Emile. He cannot be satisfied with the beauty of nature: he needs a mate. Nor can he be content with nature's simple bounty, for he must have the means to support his family. But Rousseau will try to minimize the difference between these two outlooks in his portrayal of the ideal woman. Sophie is a fantasy object, like nature for Jean-Jacques, but a fantasy controlled by practical considerations. According to Rousseau, women's education is dictated by men's need to know who their children are. Here is one aspect of property that cannot be transcended through aesthetic judgment or Epicurean nonchalance. The rigor of feminine virtue is also dictated by what Rousseau believes is the unbounded nature of woman's sexuality. Just as the boy's aggressiveness was curbed by learning about property rights, Sophie's desire is subjected to the rule of the patriarchal family. It is important to realize, however, that Rousseau does not emphasize Emile's authority over his wife. Rather, he stresses Sophie's submissiveness: in *Emile*, property is always a law to which one is subjected, never a basis for the extension of power. Emile may be a patriarchal husband, but the feminine wiles Rousseau so enthusiastically praises reinstitute the aesthetic mediation – not to mention the rhetoric of religious ecstasy – that guided Emile's first steps in social relationships.

What emerges in this part of the book is Rousseau's inability to integrate or to ignore the aggressive component that he sees in any act of appropriation, when he must consider it as the act of an individual. Rousseau's uneasiness about the aggressive nature of personal appropriation was what made him reluctant to acquaint Emile with property in the first place. The same anxiety about aggression intensifies in his discussion of sex, where he must deal with the unruly force of desire. In Robert's garden, Emile learns the injustice of dispossession rather than the justice of legitimate ownership. In Sophie's cottage, Rousseau finds it easier to imagine the pleasure of being seduced than the act of seduction. Rousseau emphasizes that willful self-assertion and the intimacy of mutuality are incompatible. But his attempt to evacuate aggression entirely leads to its return in different forms. It is not surprising to read in the unfinished novel *Emile et Sophie, ou les Solitaires*, which continues the couple's story, that after the death of their child (who was a girl), Sophie rebels against her condition. Emile himself loses his only link to the world of ownership when he learns that Sophie is pregnant by another man. He therefore finds it easy to adjust to enslavement by Barbary pirates. It is not Emile's will that is disruptive, and submission to what he can regard as impersonal necessity frees him from resentment.

Indeed, as long as claims to property and the subordination of things to our purposes could be viewed as an impersonal process, in history (as in *The Discourse on Inequality*) or in the establishment of a legitimate state, Rousseau could accept the violence and exploitation involved as a kind of necessity even as he condemned them on moral grounds. Indeed, a proper awareness of both aspects of property could have a tonic effect on enfeebled minds. But when the distancing effect of historical time or philosophical speculation is removed, and appropriation is considered as the result of the self's acknowledged desire and deliberate will, this double perspective is impossible to sustain. Objects of desire – and "woman" is only the last in a series, the final example that illuminates the rest – are not just things. They are always already part of a pre-existing order. Such an order embodies *another* will. That will may, in the case of a desired person (Sophie, or, in a different context, the other people whose recognition is sought in the *Discourse on Inequality*), be her or his own. In the case of inanimate things, the will may be that of another person, like Robert the gardener or a foreigner whose lands are colonized. It may be that of God, or even the uncontrolled projection of the self's own earlier will (the Savoyard vicar, in his profession of faith, and Rousseau himself, in his more ecstatic or paranoid moments, blur the difference between the two). But, whatever the case, there is no empty space: a basic characteristic of life for socialized man is that there is no unconditioned, "first" act of will. When Rousseau describes what seems to be such a gesture – that of the "first fencer" is a good example – it is not in ordinary language but in a heightened rhetoric that emphasizes its artificial character. For to disturb any pre-existing order of things is an aggressive, subversive act.

The exception, of course, is the social contract, which creates a new, legitimate basis for property by an act of will which Rousseau wants to distinguish from all forms of appropriation. By a saving fiction, the social contract "precedes" any paralyzing consideration of the property the citizens already possess or of where the people are standing. The sovereign is constituted by the contracting citizens acting in concert and only then, "extending from the subjects to the ground they occupy, comes to include both property and persons" (I, ix; p. 57).[47] Later, they may be reminded of the outsider's perspective on the property rights they have established.

In *Emile*, where Rousseau begins from the perspective of an outsider looking in, this fiction cannot be made to work. It is true that the tutor provides his pupil with an extensive education in political citizenship in the interval between his engagement and his marriage. But the summary of the *Social Contract* included in *Emile* differs in some respects from the actual text. In the summary, Rousseau states that "If the sovereign authority is founded on the right of property, this right is the one it ought to respect most" (p. 461).[48] The second part of the sentence echoes other statements in *Political Economy* and the *Social Contract* and is connected to the idea that the sovereign may not discriminate in its treatment of citizens' property. But the first part reverses the principle that the sovereign's authority rests on free agreement and only afterwards establishes the right to property. Whereas in the *Social Contract* Rousseau could praise kings who identify themselves with the country they rule as models for the game of modern politics, in *Emile* he evokes the menacing figure of Nimrod, a primitive patriarch, whose conquests set off a cycle of violent usurpations (p. 459).[49] Here, there is no room for the complicated play between noticing and overlooking facts. Nor is there room for the outsider to include himself in the generalizing process that defines the body politic. To someone like Emile, such a body remains particular. To insert himself into it would be to violate its integrity or his own. The fact that such "violations" happen all the time and that some might not even be harmful has no bearing on the issue. If the context within which it becomes possible to accept aggressive action and balance its costs and benefits is itself created by an act of violence, then no resolution of Emile's quest is possible. In Rousseau's other texts, a restless, ironic rhetoric made it possible to express – and for his reader to grasp – this traumatic insight obliquely. But Emile is a stranger to irony. He is supposed to be at one with himself and others. For this very reason, neither he nor the work that portrays him can absorb that insight.

It is thus futile for Emile to ask which kind of regime will best guarantee his rights. Emile decides not to worry about reconciling independence and belonging through ownership; instead he will focus on his inner freedom. At the start of his quest Emile expressed a desire for a small piece of property. "Give me Sophie and my field – and I shall be rich" (p. 457). In a significant choice of terms, he finally comes to speak of "some piece of land where I could be absolutely on my own" (p. 472). Rousseau's actual expression is "be absolutely mine":[50] self-possession is the only form of ownership that is entirely innocent. The "power and activity" that Emile discovered in planting his beans will be confined to his imagination.

Rousseau's extraordinary sensitivity to encroachments on personal independence, and to the rhetorical strategies employed to rationalize them, gives his discussion of property a sharp polemical force. At their best, his works are bracing and seductive in the way they make every right, every institution, appear by turns as a hammer of oppression and as a building block of security. Ironically, it is when he looks for a stable middle ground that his conceptual structure seems to collapse. This is what happens in Rousseau's *Emile*. But it is also what happened *to* Rousseau's *Emile*. It was his attempt to reconcile *philosophes* and orthodox believers, to combine the critical spirit with a positive attitude, that provoked the French authorities to condemn his work and drive him into exile. Rousseau's retreat into himself should not make us forget the historical situation in which he wrote.

Notes

One section of this chapter has appeared, in an earlier version, in *Romance Quarterly* 38 (1991): 301–8. I am grateful to Susan Staves for her suggestions in revising the work as a whole.

1   Jean-Jacques Rousseau, *The First and Second Discourses*, ed. Roger D. Masters, trans. Judith R. Masters (New York: St Martin's Press, 1964), pp. 141–2. Further references to this edition will appear in the text. The French original reads: "Le premier qui ayant enclos un terrain, s'avisa de dire, *ceci est à moi*, et trouva des gens assez simples pour le croire, fut le vrai fondateur de la société civile. Que de crimes, de guerres, de meurtres, que de misères et d'horreurs, n'eût point épargnés au Genre-humain celui qui arrachant les pieux ou comblant le fossé, eût crié à ses semblables. Gardez-vous d'écouter cet imposteur; vous êtes perdus, si vous oubliez que les fruits sont à tous, et que la Terre n'est à personne." Jean-Jacques Rousseau, *Oeuvres complètes*, ed. B. Gagnebin and M. Raymond (Paris: Gallimard, 1959–), Vol. 3, p. 164. Further references to this edition, cited as *O.C.*, will be given in the notes along with the original text of extended quotations.

2   "Car tous les droits civils étant fondés sur celui de propriété, sitôt que ce dernier est aboli aucun autre ne peut subsister. La justice ne seroit plus qu'une chimère, et le gouvernment qu'une tyrannie, et l'autorité publique n'ayant aucun fondement légitime, nul ne seroit tenu de la reconnoitre, sinon en tant qu'il y seroit contraint par la force." (*O.C.*, Vol. 3, p. 483; my translation).

3   Jean-Jacques Rousseau, *On the Social Contract, with Geneva Manuscript and Political Economy*, ed. Roger D. Masters, trans. Judith R. Masters (New York: St Martin's Press, 1978), p. 46. The quotation comes from the opening of Book I. Further references to this edition (including book and chapter references for the *Social Contract*) will be included in the text.

4   "On convient que tout ce que chacun aliène par le pacte social de sa puissance, de ses biens, de sa liberté, c'est seulement la partie de tout cela dont l'usage importe à la communauté, mais il faut convenir aussi que le Souverain seul est juge de cette importance" (*O.C.*, Vol. 3, p. 373).

5   See, for example, the chapter in the *Considerations* entitled "Système économique" (*O.C.*, Vol. 3, pp. 1002–12). A fragment from Rousseau's notes regarding a constitution for Corsica is also revealing: "Car la propriété particulière étant si foible et si dépendante, le Gouvernement n'a besoin que de peu de force et conduit pour ainsi dire les peuples avec un mouvement de doigt" (*O.C.*, Vol. 3, p. 949). Political power can be gentle *because* property does not represent an autonomous and dynamic social force.

6   James MacAdam, "Rousseau: the moral dimensions of property," in *Theories of Property. Aristotle to the Present*, ed. Anthony Parel and Thomas Flanagan (Waterloo, Ontario: Wilfred Laurier Press, 1979), pp. 181–201. This article also appears in Howard R. Cell and James I. MacAdam, *Rousseau's Response to Hobbes* (New York: Peter Lang, 1988).

7   The argument is forcefully made in Judith Shklar, *Men and Citizens* (Cambridge, UK: Cambridge University Press, 1969).

8   For Rousseau's development of this theme, see Jean Starobinski, *Le Remède dans le mal: Critique et légitimation de l'artifice à l'âge des Lumières* (Paris: Gallimard, 1989), pp. 165–208.

9   "Après avoir prouvé que l'Inégalité est à peine sensible dans l'état de Nature, et que son influence y est presque nulle, il me reste à montrer son origine, et ses progrès dans les développements de l'Esprit humain" (*O.C.*, Vol. 3, p. 162).

10 "Sitôt que les hommes eurent commencé à s'apprécier mutuellement et que l'idée de la considération fut formée dans leur esprit, chacun prétendit y avoir droit; et il ne fut plus possible d'en manquer impunément pour personne" (*O.C.*, Vol 3, p. 170). The more positive

results of mutual appreciation, love and lyricism, are discussed by Rousseau in the *Essai sur l'origine des langues*, ed. Jean Starobinski (Paris: Gallimard, 1990).

11   "Car, selon l'axiome de sage Locke, *il ne sauroit y avoir d'injure, où il n'y a point de propriété*" (*O.C.*, Vol. 3, p. 170).

12   John Locke, *An Essay concerning Human Understanding*, Book IV, Ch. iii, para. 18. The same principle is put forward by Hobbes in *Leviathan*, Book I, Ch. xv. Pierre Coste's translation follows Locke's wording. However, Rousseau may have taken his citation from Jean Barbeyrac's preface to his translation of Pufendorf's *Droit de la nature et des gens*, a work to which Rousseau frequently refers. Editors of Rousseau seem not to have noticed that, at least in the 1740 edition (London: Jean Nours), Barbeyrac in quoting Locke also replaces *injustice* with *injure* (p. xvii).

Rousseau's substitution of terms finds some support in Hobbes's *De Cive*, III, iii–iv. (Whatever direct knowledge of Hobbes Rousseau may have had would have been limited to this work.) For Hobbes, injury and injustice are almost the same thing. Both are infractions of an agreement. In the remark to this section, Hobbes defines the difference. The French translation by Hobbes's contemporary Samuel Sorbière (1649) reads: "Le nom d'injustice a une signification relative à la loi; celui d'injure a du rapport à la loi, et à une certaine personne particulière. Car ce qui est juste, est tel envers tous. Mais une injure peut toucher un autre, sans me toucher aussi." Thomas Hobbes, *Le Citoyen*, ed. Simone Goyard-Fabre (Paris: GF-Flammarion, 1982), p. 115.

13   "De la culture des terres s'ensuivit nécessairement leur partage; et de la propriété une fois reconnüe les premières règles de la justice: car pour rendre à chacun le sien, il faut que chacun puisse avoir quelque chose" (*O.C.*, Vol. 3, p. 173).

14   Victor Goldschmidt, *Anthropologie et politique. Les principes du système de Rousseau* (Paris: Vrin, 1974), p. 487.

15   "C'est le seul travail qui donnant droit au Cultivateur sur le produit de la terre qu'il a labourée, lui en donne conséquemment sur le fond" (*O.C.*, p. 173).

16   "Les hommes commençant à porter leurs veües dans l'avenir, et se voyant tous quelques biens à perdre, il n'y en avoit aucun qui n'eût à craindre pour soi la représaille des torts qu'il pouvoit faire à autrui" (*O.C.*, Vol. 3, p. 173).

17   Rousseau neglects the pastoral stage in the *Discourse* but mentions it in the *Essay on the Origin of Languages*, sections of which were originally conceived as part of the *Discourse*. For details on the relationship between the two texts, see Jean-Jacques Rousseau, *Essai sur l'origine des langues*. For Rousseau's place in the development of the "four-stage" theory of civilization, see Ronald Meek, *The Ignoble Savage* (Cambridge, UK: Cambridge University Press, 1976).

18   In a note to the *Discourse*, Rousseau speaks of the "excessive population which results from the state of nature" and that "it would not have been long before the earth, in that state, was covered with men, thus forced to remain together" (p. 226). Of course, Rousseau distinguishes between his hypothetical state of nature and the degraded situation that prevails even in such apparently "natural" situations as the wilds of America, but, even on his own description of the state of nature, it is difficult to explain such massive population growth.

19   I have modified Masters's translation here, preferring "stronger" to "strongest" for "*du plus fort*" (*O.C.*, Vol. 3, p. 176). French does not distinguish between the comparative and the superlative in these contexts, but I think the former is more faithful to Rousseau, since the superiority he describes is never absolute. It is always a relative distinction in a shifting set of binary oppositions.

20   ". . . un conflit perpétuel qui ne se terminoit que par des combats et des meurtres. . . . La Société naissante fit place au plus horrible état de guerre" (*O.C.*, Vol. 3, p. 176).

21   See also *Social Contract*, I, iii.

22   "Qui vous a donné ces alignements, leur pouvoit-on répondre; et en vertu de quoi prétendez-vous être payé à nos dépends d'un travail que nous ne vous avons point imposé? Ignorés vous qu'une multitude de vos frères périt, ou souffre du besoin de ce que vous avés de trop, et qu'il vous faloit un consentement exprès et unanime du Genre-humain pour vous appro-

prier sur la subsistance commune tout ce qui alloit au-delà de la votre?" (O.C., Vol. 3, pp. 176–7).

23 "L'établissement de la Loi et du Droit de propriété fut son premier terme; l'institution de la Magistrature le second; que le troisième et dernier fut le changement du pouvoir légitime en pouvoir arbitraire; en sorte que l'état de riche et de pauvre fut autorisé par la première Epoque, celui de puissant et de foible par la seconde, et par la troisième celui de Maître et d'Esclave, qui est le dernier degré de l'inégalité, et le terme auquel aboutissent enfin tous les autres, jusqu' à ce que de nouvelles révolutions dissolvent tout à fait le Gouvernement, ou le rapprochent de l'institution légitime" (O.C., Vol. 3, p. 187).

24 In an important essay, Louis Althusser has analyzed, from a Marxist point of view, the way conceptual gaps (décalages) function in Rousseau's political system. See "Sur le Contrat social (les décalages)," Cahiers pour l'analyse 8 (1970): 5–42. Althusser sees these gaps solely as signs of contradiction. I would also emphasize their constructive role in creating a discursive space.

25 Rousseau's article was published first in Vol. 5 of the Encyclopédie (November 1755), then separately in 1756. Whether it was written before or after the Discourse on Inequality, and whether it marks a change of position or merely serves a different purpose, are matters of dispute.

26 ". . . car que le peuple puisse refuser, ou que le souverain ne doive pas exiger, cela est indifférent quant au droit" (O.C., Vol. 3, p. 270). Here Rousseau uses the word "sovereign" to denote the supreme power in general rather than the popular assembly he describes in the Social Contract.

27 ". . . non en enlevant les thresors à leurs possesseurs, mais en ôtant à tous les moyens d'en accumuler, ni en bâtissant des hôpitaux pour les pauvres, mais en garantissant les citoyens de le devenir" (O.C., Vol. 3, p. 258).

28 "Le droit de propriété est le plus sacré de tous les droits des citoyens, et plus important à certains égards que la liberté même" (O.C., Vol. 3, p. 263).

29 ". . . soit parce qu'il tient de plus prés à la conservation de la vie; soit parce que les biens étant plus faciles à usurper et plus difficiles à défendre que la personne, on doit plus respecter ce qui se peut ravir plus aisément; soit enfin parce que la propriété est le vrai fondement de la société civile, et le vrai garant des engagemens des citoyens" (O.C., Vol. 3, p. 263).

30 Ramon M. Lemos, Rousseau's Political Philosophy: An Exposition and Interpretation (Athens, GA: University of Georgia Press, 1977), pp. 166–7.

31 ". . . les chefs savent assez que la volonté générale est toujours pour le parti le plus favorable à l'intérêt public, c'est-à-dire le plus équitable; de sorte qu'il ne faut qu'être juste pour s'assûrer de suivre la volonté générale" (O.C., Vol. 3, p. 251).

32 Jean-Jacques Rousseau, Emile, or On Education, trans. Allan Bloom (New York: Basic Books, 1979), p. 461. Further references to this edition of Emile will be included in the text. The French text is at O.C., Vol. 4, p. 841.

33 "Ce n'est pas que par cet acte la possession change de nature en changeant de mains, et devienne propriété dans celles du Souverain; Mais comme les forces de la Cité sont incomparablement plus grandes que celles d'un particulier, la possession publique est aussi dans le fait plus forte et plus irrévocable, sans être plus légitime, au moins pour les étrangers. Car l'Etat à l'égard de ses membres est maître de tous leurs biens par le contrat social, qui dans l'Etat sert de base à tous les droits; mais il ne l'est à l'égard des autres Puissances que par le droit de premier occupant qu'il tient des particuliers" (O.C., Vol. 3, p. 365).

34 "Tout homme a naturellement droit à tout ce qui lui est nécessaire; mais l'acte positif qui le rend propriétaire de quelque bien l'exclud de tout le reste. Sa part étant faite il doit s'y borner, et n'a plus aucun droit à la communauté" (O.C., Vol. 3, p. 365).

35 Rousseau's fragment, "Du bonheur public" (O.C., Vol. 3, pp. 509–15), in which public happiness is linked to a sense of estrangement, is discussed in a somewhat different way in Paul de Man, Allegories of Reading (New Haven, CT: Yale University Press, 1979), pp. 254 ff.

36 For a discussion of moraliste thought in relation to politics, see Nannerl O. Keohane, Philosophy and the State in France (Princeton, NJ: Princeton University Press, 1980).

37 ". . . que deviendra pour les autres un homme uniquement élevé pour lui" (*O.C.*, Vol. 4, p. 251).

38 Aubrey Rosenberg, in "Property, possession, and enjoyment. Woman as object, subject, and project in the *Emile*," in Jean Terrasse (ed.), *Rousseau et l'éducation: études sur l'Emile* (Sherbrooke, Québec: Naaman, 1984), pp. 102–13, wittily examines the relationship between property and possession in relation to Sophie, but does not consider ownership in general.

39 Compare Locke's remarks on the child's "love of dominion" in "Some thoughts concerning education," in John Locke, *Educational Writings*, ed. James Axtell (Cambridge, UK: Cambridge University Press, 1968), pp. 105 ff. I should note that the child in Rousseau's example is – at least at first – not the "real" Emile, but a child raised in society who has one of those "naturels violents dont la férocité se développe de bonne heure" (p. 329). According to Rousseau, more tranquil children, as well as the ideal Emile, do not need to learn about property so soon. The textual complications arising from Rousseau's method of characterization in the *Emile* would require separate discussion.

40 "Nos premiers devoirs sont envers nous; nos sentiments primitifs se concentrent en nous-mêmes; tous nos mouvements naturels se rapportent d'abord à notre conservation et à notre bien-être. Ainsi le premier sentiment de la justice ne nous vient pas de celle que nous devons, mais de celle qui nous est düe . . ." (*O.C.*, Vol. 4, p. 329).

41 The fact is noted in a different context by Mary P. Nichols, "Rousseau's novel education in the *Emile*," *Political Theory* 13 (1985): 535–58.

42 "Mais moi, je n'ai point de jardin"; "il n'y a plus guère de terre en friche. Moi, je travaille celle que mon père a bonifiée; chacun en fait autant de son côté, et toutes les terres que vous voyez sont occupées depuis longtemps" (*O.C.*, Vol. 4, p. 332).

43 ". . . de là jusqu'au droit de propriété et aux échanges il n'y a qu'un pas, après lequel il faut s'arrêter tout court" (*O.C.*, Vol. 4, p. 333).

44 ". . . il ne dispose encore que de lui-même; c'est comme si il ne disposoit de rien" (*O.C.*, Vol. 4, p. 543).

45 John Locke, *Two Treatises of Government*, ed. Peter Laslett (Cambridge, UK: Cambridge University Press, 1988; rev. edn).

46 Robert the gardener is a steward, but his role is limited to the provision of food for immediate consumption. His refusal to sublet to Emile suggests an unwillingness to consider the larger meaning of stewardship invoked by Locke. Stewardship also involves too specific a relationship with God and is too closely based on scripture to be compatible with Rousseau's natural religion, which avoids any dogma that might lead to sectarian disputes.

47 ". . . s'étendant des sujets au terrain qu'ils occupent devient à la foi réel et personnel" (*O.C.*, Vol. 3, p. 366).

48 "Si c'est sur le droit de propriété qu'est fondée l'autorité souveraine, ce droit est celui qu'elle doit le plus respecter" (*O.C.*, Vol. 4, p. 841).

49 Nimrod has traditionally been thought of as the first "king" in the Bible. See Genesis 10: 8–12; I Chronicles 1:10. Bossuet uses him as an example of untamed will in his *Discours sur l'histoire universelle*, ed. J. Truchet (Paris: Garnier-Flammarion, 1966), p. 49. He is also called a founder of cities in Diderot's article "Cité" for the *Encyclopédie*.

50 ". . . un coin de terre où je pusse être absolument mien" (*O.C.*, Vol. 4, p. 856). Bloom's translation of "*mien*" by "on my own" misses the sense of literal self-possession.

14
Noblesse oblige
Female charity in an age of sentiment

Donna T. Andrew

Margaret Georgiana, Lady Spencer was known in her life,[1] and remembered at her death,[2] as a woman of extraordinary charity.[3] Her charity was not merely local (although, as we shall see her local connections were not unimportant) but national; not merely English but international.[4] She received letters of appeal from Bologna, Cologne, and Vienna. In many ways she was an extraordinary woman, but like many women, even aristocratic women, she has found no place in the chronicle of her times. In his edition of the letters that passed between her and David Garrick, her descendant, Earl Spencer, notes the fact and comments that she "should hold a more prominent place than she has yet attained in the social history of the eighteenth century."[5] While I hope this chapter may rectify that situation, it is, in the main, not biographical; after a brief outline of her life, I will consider the many philanthropic involvements of Lady Spencer, but most especially her charity letters, and what these can tell us about the web of relationship, the nexus of gift and obligation, of property and protection, that existed at least among the more concerned members of the female upper classes in the second half of the eighteenth century.

Margaret Georgiana Spencer was born in 1737 to Stephen Poyntz, a diplomat, and Anna-Maria Mordaunt, the granddaughter of the Earl of Peterborough. One of three surviving children, she maintained close ties with her two brothers, William and Charles. At the age of 17 she married John Spencer, principal heir to his great-grandmother, Sarah, Duchess of Marlborough. It is quite clear that this was a love match,[6] albeit a very advantageous one for Lady Spencer, for her husband was one of the wealthiest young men in the kingdom.[7] Lady Spencer, in her charity notes, always referred to her husband as "My Lord," and much of the good work she did, she did in his name. For example, though the letter from a girls' orphan asylum in Parma was sent to her, she noted that "My Lord gave £40 for the dowry of one of their charges."[8] One gets the impression, however, perhaps unjustifiably, that Lady Spencer was the powerful personality in the family;[9] it was she who corresponded with Richard Rigby, the Duke of Bedford's parliamentary agent, it was she to whom Edmund Burke wrote about parliamentary debates. In the course of time, Lady Spencer had three surviving children, all of whom were to play important roles in the history of the period; her two "naughty" daughters, the flamboyant Duchess of Devonshire and her sister the Countess of Bessborough, and her son, the second Earl Spencer, first Lord of the Admiralty during the Napoleonic wars. Lady Spencer wrote frequently to all of them, nursed her daughters through their confinements, and even corresponded voluminously with her daughter-in-law, of whom she was not really very fond. All of her correspondence was carried out in her own hand, by her own efforts, in a time when it was quite usual for women of her station to have secretaries to lighten the burden of writing and responding.[10] Her correspondences are massive and, as yet, largely unread. They stretch from an exchange over almost sixty years with her closest friend, the Honorable Mrs. Howe, to one of thirty-eight years with Sir William Hamilton, English ambassador at Naples and art collector. What I wish to consider, however, is one particular branch of this correspondence, which Lady Spencer herself separated out of the general mass, roughly alphabetized and notated, and which she called her "charity" letters.[11]

At the beginning of the first A folio, there is a note in Lady Spencer's hand, which describes these as those charity letters which she keeps as "a Cordial – to remind me of my Lord's never failing Generosity and Humanity and of the earnestness with which I executed and sometimes endeavoured to imitate his benevolence." This suggests that the note was affixed some time after his death in 1783. Indeed, when the letters are examined, one finds some addressed to Lord Spencer; even before 1783, however, the great bulk of the letters are addressed to Lady Spencer herself. And while the collection is mainly of letters received by the countess, there are also miscellaneous scraps of related material included: a printed charity proposal from Jonas Hanaway to Sir Charles Whitworth, cut from a newspaper and pasted onto a larger sheet of paper, a few draft letters of response that Lady Spencer wrote, a curious genealogical table of the Browns, a local working-class family, etc. On the whole, however, these are thirty-three folios of letters, received between the late 1750s and 1814, the year of the countess's death.

Certainly Lady Spencer was not the first or only wealthy person to receive such letters. Quite the contrary. It was very common for all sorts of wealthy people (and not only aristocrats[12]) to be bombarded with this kind of appeal. However, I do not think Lady Spencer was "typical" or "ordinary" either; she would not have stood out so brightly if she had been an average benevolent lady. What I wish to argue is that while she was certainly unusual, she was not so unusual as to be aberrant, but rather that her life displays more clearly, but in the same manner, the concerns and activities of many of the more engaged philanthropists of her day. And as an added bonus, this is the only collection of begging letters I know of, that is both extant and separate. In these folios it is not the sensibilities of the twentieth-century historian that has guided the categorization of letters as charitable; that was done by the recipient herself. And this makes the collection very exciting.

Why did Lady Spencer keep these letters, and why did she keep them in this manner? There may well have been some religious motive, for Lady Spencer was a devout though not a "serious" Christian.[13] But why note, as she often did, her responses on the letters in that case? Perhaps these letters, and her notations, served as rough working files, reminding her of what she had given, allowing her to keep her giving in a rational order, introducing that kind of method to charity that was to be advocated by the group she was instrumental in organizing[14] and running, the Ladies' Charitable Society.

The relation between charity and property, between giving and having, was, and remained, of central importance, both to Lady Spencer and to much of English society. The traditional notion of beneficence was that charity was a basic obligation entailed by the ownership of property, that as God was the sole Proprietor, and men only his stewards, charity to the poor, to God's poor, was not mercy, but justice. "We are apt to take it for granted," remarked Knightly Chetwood in 1708, "that our Estates . . . are entirely at our own Disposal, legal Debts being discharg'd; but this is a great Mistake, Charity is a principal Branch of Justice. . . . we are but Stewards, not Proprietors, even when Estates are gotten by the most justifiable Means."[15] However, while these long-standing views continued to be preached, other clergymen began to rethink the relationship between charity as justice and the ownership of property. Bishop Sherlock, for example, by making the establishment and sanctity of private property one of God's primary laws, weakened the obligatory lien of charity on property: "Property is established . . . by the positive law of God; which is to us the highest Reason and Authority. . . . And to this Right of his own establishing even God himself submits." Charity then, from being a right that the dispossessed could justly demand of the possessors, was "the *free and voluntary* Gift of such as can spare from their own subsistence some Part of what they enjoy." Sherlock went on to argue that a new sort of connection existed between charity and property; rather than seeing alms-giving as an obligation incumbent on its owners, he viewed it as "the Inheritance of the Poor; it is, as I may say, their Property." What this property meant, however, was merely that "those who have a Right to this kind of Maintenance, have a Right to ask for it, that is, to beg the Charity of all well-disposed Christians."[16]

Charity, however, whether obligatory or voluntary, was commonly recognized both as an emblem of the donor's power and a mark of his responsibilities. While the rich were cognizant of the first attribute of charity, the poor were not above reminding their betters of the second. Thus one old woman whom Lady Spencer aided commented that her reward would be "a Crown of Glory wich is promised to all Good Stewards." Another correspondent remarked that "it is earnestly to be wished, that all the great would copy your example."[17] And her correspondence is a testimony to the varied sorts of claims that the lowly or those in need felt they had on the great. An unusually active and responsible donor, Lady Spencer, moved by a tangled combination of guilt and remorse, a sense of obligation and occupation as well as a desire to control and ameliorate the lives of the poor, is a fitting illustration of the complex impulses to benevolence in the second half of the eighteenth century.[18]

That this was a great age of charity was almost a cliché of the period. Often applauded, sometimes bemoaned, always contested, the major charities of eighteenth-century England were divided into two sorts: what was called public charity, that is, that dispersed by poor law officials or by churchmen, and private charity, which usually referred to the great associated, usually urban, establishments of the day: the Foundling Hospital, the Smallpox Hospital, or the Marine Society. Private charity could also include individual benevolence, though from the seventeenth century (and before) this came increasingly under criticism from those who saw it as feeding poverty rather than aiding the poor. While associated charities were organized and directed only by men, Lady Spencer was nevertheless prominent both as an important donor and for her management "advice" given behind the scenes.[19] She was also very involved in the distribution of poor law and church funds in the locales in which her family were significant, though this is an aspect of her work that I have not yet really investigated. At the same time, both sorts of public charity and even institutional private charity seemed unable to deal with a number of situations which fell outside of their purview. To these sorts of situations, requiring tact and discretion, begging letters seemed one possible solution.

Letter writing was, and is, an ambiguous business. A personal letter is an occasion to exchange experiences and ideas, to sort out thoughts and feelings, to "talk" to the absent recipient. A business letter, on the other hand, is an attempt to arrange some transaction, to achieve some satisfactory negotiation, to convince the recipient of the advisability of some course of action. The letters sent to Lady Spencer were a curious amalgam of both sorts. Though largely instrumental and thus like business letters (the main point of all these petitions or requests was to obtain some boon), many tell a story of the writer's life, his or her hard times, and the circumstances leading to the letter's composition. Most also specify why the writer chose to write to Lady Spencer, rather than to some other aristocrat or wealthy person. Many articulate this in terms of some justifiable claim they feel they can make on her, whether of service, of support, of mutual maternity, or of general humanity. Almost all present themselves as needy but worthy objects of assistance, reduced to their present circumstances by occurrences which they could not foresee or control, like a Mr. Robinson who, in his letter to Lord Spencer, notes that he was born "what is term'd a gentle-man" but on account of "unavoidable misfortunes and unfortunate accidents he is in grave want" though redeemable by a little assistance to a position of self-support and self-respect. Most tell stories of their lives in which they are the virtuous victims, down but not yet out. They are in fact just the sorts of people that J. M. Bourne, in his account of charity letters written to the East India Company of the nineteenth century, describes as "deserving."[20] But for a correspondence to be most useful to the historian, it is important to have both its ends, that is, the letters to and from both its partners. For a letter to be understood, it is necessary not only to know what the writer intended, but what the recipient understood it to intend, and how that reader responded to the intention. On the whole, in this respect, Lady Spencer's charity letters are incomplete. Very, very occasionally, she included, or rather seemed to forget to destroy, a draft of her response. Sometimes, much more commonly, she noted on the back of the letter itself what action, if any, she took. However, both of these are sporadic, and the absence of comment does not necessarily mean she refused assistance. We know this because sometimes there are follow-up letters thanking her for aid of which there is no other record. We also know that her charity files were not complete. It is not at all unusual for a writer to remind Lady Spencer of the aid she supplied several years before, though no letter exists for the earlier date, and perhaps never, in fact, existed.[21] There is also a paucity of letters for the 1750s and 1760s[22] and it is not possible to know whether this reflects the number of letters received, or the number of letters kept. I believe, however, that enough letters exist (there are more than 2,500 documents included) and these of enough variety, for piecing them together to afford us an approximation of Lady

Spencer's charitable practice and an insight into her understanding of her charitable obligations.

What follows then is a study which seeks to understand the joint creation, construction, or explanation of what it meant to be "deserving" by both those seeking charitable assistance and those they sought it from. How did letter writers explain their lives and justify their need? The stories they told were not always entirely true, but had to be approximations of the truth, of what was "believable." What kept them within the realm of plausibility, as well, was Lady Spencer's well-known practice of checking the stories she was sent, before any aid was offered. Thus the stories not only had to be "likely" but had to present a true story, albeit drawn in the most flattering fashion. What was the nature of the claims for relief that such writers made on Lady Spencer? And how did she respond to these? What sorts of requests did she recognize as legitimate, and how did she attempt to aid these proper objects? How did she decide who was unworthy of relief, and, as important, how, in a vast world of charitable solicitation, did she obtain the knowledge upon which such decisions can rationally be made?

First we must note that although almost all the correspondence under consideration takes the form of the personal letter, addressed either to Lord or Lady Spencer, there are some older forms of request and appeal also present. These are self-proclaimed petitions, whose structure is ancient and multi-purposed.[23] Here, for example, is a quite typical one, sent to Lady Spencer in December 1812 from London:

> Honoured Madam
>
>> the humble petition of Ann Hutchins humbly sheweth she is a widow in great Distress having brought up a family of 19 children but it has pleased god to call them all except one who has it not in her power to help me and through great age am unabled to help myself being now in my 78th year humbly begging that your ladyship will be pleased to pardon this Liberty and take my Diplorable situation into concideration and be pleased to make me a partaker of your ladyships benevolence through the means of the honourable society of Ladies and your petitioner as in duty bound will ever pray.

Although we can learn something even from such a stylized and formal document, the structure of the petition does not allow for full-blown appeals to sentiment, to patriotism, to religion, or whatever. The personal begging letter, crafted by educated men and women whose need had shaped and honed their eloquence, is a much more supple form of appeal, and therefore more crammed with possibilities for the historian.

Before we get to Lady Spencer's charity letters themselves, a final digression must be made. For there were also begging letters that were not sent, or not only sent, to private individuals. Throughout the eighteenth century begging letters also appear as personal advertisements in newspapers.[24] Sometimes letters to individuals were in fact only the preliminary step to such public letters. For though the returns on a letter of appeal seen by a mass audience might potentially be much greater than the restricted amount that could be expected from a single donor, there were two requisites that had first to be met. A newspaper advertisement required both an initial investment, seed money we might say, and also the use and inclusion of a "powerful" name, a name that would sanction and add respectability and veracity to the story told. Mrs. Maria Mathew, deserted by her extravagant husband and left with three small infants, asked Lady Spencer for the money to place such an advertisement, while Mrs. Sarah Jackson in a letter to Lady Spencer said that she had already gotten some support for her newspaper venture, but still needed "exalted patronage . . . on an advertisement."[25] For persons known for benevolence as well as for station possessed power, a power with which that combination endowed them. Their names were guarantors of unimpeachable authority. No wonder that someone like Lady Spencer was, as we shall see, so chary either of having her name used without her permission or even of having it known by the object relieved. Though the begging letter usually came first, sometimes the newspaper appeal preceded the letter, as in the case of John Smith, an artist who had lost the use of his right hand, and to whose published plight the Spencers responded. Smith followed up this first donation with a further request for more support, and for possible employment.[26]

But to turn finally to the begging letters themselves: who wrote them and how did they couch their appeals? One way to consider the letters is to separate those that are written by the needy for themselves and their families from those written by others on their behalf, for money, jobs, or favors. Those of the second type are well known to students of eighteenth-century England. Everyone wrote them to everyone else who might have some access to available positions, or might be willing to contribute to general subscriptions, or might know someone who had done or would do either or both. This sort of letter, written for a third party, is usually discussed under the rubric of "patronage." In this context patronage is used to describe not only the direct access of supplicant to patron, but the indirect chain of request that characterized so much of eighteenth-century donation. Often patrons were also brokers of patronage, the recipients of favor also the brokers for alms to others. For since gift- or alms-giving was both a sign of power and simultaneously conferred power on the donor, all attempted to be conduits for favor, both to serve their friends and to enhance their own authority. The next best thing to being a patron (and certainly much cheaper than so being) was having influence with one. Thus David Garrick wrote to his friends, Lord and Lady Spencer, on behalf of his old friend Mr. Moody, an army officer of fine family fallen on hard times. Moody, Garrick wrote, had spoken to him of his "frequent intentions of applying himself to you; but not having the honor and happiness to be known to you, his modesty and spirit, for he has both in a great degree, overcame his necessities and he chose rather to struggle on than run the risque of being thought too bold and presuming." Writing on his behalf, Garrick obtained assistance for his friend. On October 19, 1765, Moody wrote a grateful letter to Lord and Lady Spencer, which is endorsed "40£ a yr for life at Mr. Garrick's request." Lady Spencer herself often acted in this capacity; when she wished to assist a Mr. Lacey in finding employment, for instance, she wrote to Mrs. Pigou and asked her to use her influence with her husband, Frederick, a London gunpowder merchant, to obtain the position. When Garrick again asked a boon for another friend, a Mr. Lloyd, Lady Spencer refused, but suggested Garrick apply to the Wilmots instead.[27] This suggestion probably not only mentioned the Wilmots as the appropriate people to contact, but authorized Garrick to use Lady Spencer's name to attest to the worth of the application. Not only people of high and middle station, like Lady Spencer and David Garrick, acted as patronage brokers;

many of the letters to Lady Spencer, in support of aid for poor, worthy objects, were from people who are themselves of the lower orders or are already themselves receiving assistance from her. An example of the former is Mary Freeman, a nurse of Great Brington, Northamptonshire, who nursed a young woman, Elizabeth Jollings, through the smallpox, and now asks Lady Spencer's assistance to find work for her, "fearful she [Jollings] may not take good ways having nobody to look after or take any care of her." In another case, the housekeeper of a poor needy woman, Mrs. Ship, wrote to Lady Spencer's housekeeper, suggesting that the countess and her noble daughter the Duchess of Devonshire should assist her worthy but poverty-stricken mistress.[28] Elizabeth King, herself a pensioner at Lady Spencer's almshouse at St. Albans, similarly asked assistance for a nurse Beach and her two daughters, one of whom wanted a place in a school, as did another much more querulous and troublesome old-age pensioner, Mrs. Jackson, who asked for a job for a Mrs. Sharpless as assistant in the local Sunday school.[29] For Miss Jackson, herself a pensioner of Lady Spencer's, soliciting help for others was a psychological necessity, to convince herself both that she was still gentle, that is, a person of influence, albeit in reduced circumstances, and that there were people still worse off than she.

Sometimes Lady Spencer was asked to act as an intermediary by the needy themselves. Eliza Richmond wrote to Lady Spencer for relief, invoking the powerful names of the Marquess of Rockingham, the Countess of Northumberland, and Lady Charlotte Finch as past donors, and requested that the countess write to both the Archbishop of Canterbury and Lady Betty Germaine on her behalf, "both of whom delight in good works, but will not do any thing without some attestation." Even after a recommendation to her London banker from the Countess of Liverpool, Hammersley the banker insisted that he would only ask his friends to get Mrs. Sarah Jackson's husband a post if she could get a recommendation from "some lady of distinction." And as support for her application to the post of wet-nurse to the queen, Elizabeth Lymer asked Lady Spencer to write on her behalf, for "one word from a person of fashion would do more than a Hundred from any other person." Others asked Lady Spencer to help them win assistance from members of her family: in one case, that her son, the second Earl Spencer, should present one John Bangs to a place at his disposal in the Charterhouse; in another, Thomas Liddell pleaded that Lady Spencer "use your influence with your Darling son and his Countess" to relieve his distress.[30]

In addition to these requests for indirect aid were claims of a familiar sort, asking Lady Spencer to engage on their behalf in her role as patron. The Spencers were well-known *cognoscenti*, building a fabulous London mansion at St. James' Place, importing classical antiquities, commissioning paintings, supporting the theater and the arts generally. Thus the poet Thomas Maurice not only wrote for a subscription to his poems "Richmond Hill" and "Westminster Abbey" but also solicited her general support. Pianists, novelists, painters, and short story writers begged for Lady Spencer's patronage. There are two especially interesting requests for patronage, one from Sarah Yeates, who solicited a subscription for her novel *Eliza*, and one from Lady Camilla Robinson, who had written a memoir of the King of Poland and the late Empress of Russia, and wanted the lady's patronage. In both cases Lady Spencer sent money but would not allow her name to appear in the subscription list, saying it was "her practice not to put her name to any publication when she was totally unacquainted with the author and subject." One suspects, however, this was Lady Spencer's polite way of saying that she would not publicly support any literature which might not be of the highest moral standards of propriety. Similarly, after five years of patronage, Lady Spencer refused to further assist Dr. "Electricity" Graham, noting "that the character he had acquired precluded me from doing any thing for him by way of recommendation." More unusual perhaps were the several appeals to the countess for patronage of invention and commerce, one author noting that "Every Branch of British commerce has its adoption and glory from the care and protection of great Personages."[31]

Much more common, and perhaps closer to Lady Spencer's heart, were the many requests for clerical patronage or assistance. Lady Spencer seemed to have a soft spot in her heart for clergymen; perhaps because her brother Charles was one, perhaps because she herself was quite devout. Aged ministers, ministers ill or retired, writers of sermons, and clerical widows all applied. The Rev. Thomas Shirreff's plea was not unusual. After he had given twenty-two years of dedicated service to the Church, his patron had died, and, left with the ubiquitous clerical "quiverful" of children to support, he was in grievous need. He urged Lady Spencer to use her influence on his behalf with the Chancellor, "who has at all times a number of such things at his disposal."[32]

In one of the cleverest letters of the collection, a Miss Rebow maintained she was not writing a begging letter at all, but requesting a loan. Begging letters, she continued, "endeavour to excite your charity by representing scenes of distress"; in contrast she frankly admitted that she was not financially hard pressed. The writers of begging letters, she noted, "ask small sums" but she is after a large one. "In a word," she said, such letters are "full of compliments, which you have too much sense to be pleased with." Lady Spencer, perhaps caught by the novelty of this approach, lent her £150, which, she noted, was "never repaid." Still Miss Rebow was certainly accurate in her characterization, which only illustrates how much certain requisite elements of the structure of the begging letter were already well known.[33]

Before we consider the representations of scenes of distress, however, let us first consider the compliments. When Jane Marriott explained why she was writing for assistance to Lady Spencer, she commented: "I know of no Lady in this . . . Kingdom that has so great a name for Charity." Susan Crawford, a Leicestershire widow, started her appeal simply with "hearing of your goodness," and Lieutenant William Gore noted that "Although I have not the honour of being known to you, I am however actuated by a knowledge of your Ladyship's humane Character." The Rev. P. Touch, waxing even more eloquent, hoped his letter would find a place "in such a temple of philanthropy as your Ladyship's Heart." Miss Gorges's encomium to Lady Spencer, beginning with, "The fact is, knowing in common with all europeans your wish and your exertions to benefit the poor," was topped by the Rev. D. W. Price, who rhapsodized, "Your Fame for Charity, is well known in all Climates . . . as a Character most distinguished for Charity." Perhaps Lady Spencer *was* flattered by this, did indeed enjoy the praise and courtly posturing of these extravagant applications. For this sort of effusiveness was thought necessary by most of the letter writers, as illustrating perhaps a full recognition of Lady Spencer's gracious condescension, the proper and perhaps only return for the charity they hoped to receive. Sometimes this flattery lapsed into a silliness, which surely could have only been tiresome. Lady Spencer must have regretted her reputation when Mrs. Sarah Spence wrote her, explaining "that the amiable character you bear, is the sole reason for my troubling *you*, rather than any *other* lady of rank and fashion." Perhaps more welcome was Charles Townley's left-handed and rather unadroit compliment, when he noted that "Your Ladyship was the first woman in England, not for your Beauty, but for your excellent understanding and your amazing punctuality in business."[34]

No amount of flattery could overcome one of the greatest difficulties that some letter writers had in their bid to convince Lady Spencer to open her heart and her purse; this was the circumstance of being "unknown." A person "unknown" was one without legitimate claims, for whom nothing could, should, or would be done. Thus when William Right wrote to Lady Spencer, asking for assistance, explaining that he was a native of Northamptonshire, an orphan who had lost a leg in the Navy, Lady Spencer merely noted: "Know nothing of him and said I would do nothing." Hannah Trent, equally a stranger to the countess, acknowledged this problem: "I am well aware that our being Stranger is a strong bar against our meeting with Assistance from your Ladyship." Her suit, however, proved successful, for she was able to provide references which satisfied Lady Spencer, of her being known by someone of repute to be deserving. Knowledge of the recipient, preferably face-to-face knowledge, but personal knowledge in any case, was an essential element for relief. When Harriot Douglas wrote in 1796 of her great distress, apologizing for the absence of an address since she was hiding from her creditors, Lady Spencer noted: "Wrote word how sorry I was I could not assist her as a place of enquiry seemed purposely avoided." Similarly when a woman wrote for relief, using the name Matilda Crayfield, which she admitted was not her own but was employed because her real name would "disgrace my Relations in High Life," Lady Spencer noted that her reasons for anonymity were not sufficient, and that if she wanted her assistance she must make it possible for enquiry to be made into "the truth of the particulars" of her story. Although there is a most peculiar reference to a loan to an anonymous person early in the countess's married life, this seems never to have recurred.[35]

Most predictable, perhaps, were the letters from tenants or immediate residents of the locales in which the Spencers were the "great" family. When William Addison, a stranger, applied to Lady Spencer, he acknowledged that there were those who had "a prior and more immediate claim to consideration" than himself; Addison described them as "those who, from either some local connection or from a personal knowledge of their Misfortunes or Merits," appealed to her charity. Thomas Coker, minister of Mappowder, in a letter requesting aid to his parish, reminded the Spencers of their responsibilities "where they have Estates and property." Another clergyman, J. Clarke of Northampton, playfully suggested that as one of Lady Spencer's almoners, he had "entered upon my New and important appointment, of Treasurer and Paymaster to part of your Ladyship's irregular forces." When Richard Manning of Great Brington appealed for a trifle with which to start a business, the countess noted, "A very idle fellow who cannot be made to work," yet nevertheless she "promised him that I will double what he earns by labour for one year from this time January 1776 as far as 3sh per week." A year later, she remarked, "I have done it to the amount of above £8 but fear he is not the better for it." She also sent the rather feckless daughter-in-law of one of her husband's ex-tenants a sum of money, and made a practice of giving the graduates of her girls' school in Brington five guineas upon graduation. When Edward Clarke, a Wimbledon glazier ill with rheumatism and low on stock, asked the countess for the wherewithal to acquire what he needed, she promptly sent it. But it is not only for those who lived on or near Spencer property that she made herself responsible; when any of her brother Charles's parishioners were needy, they too called on her. Thus in 1799, a young member of the parish of North Creake, where Charles Poyntz was minister, wrote to Lady Spencer, and asked her what profession she recommended he follow. When it was agreed that he would go to sea, she not only furnished him with clothes and introductions, but for the next ten years continued to help him in his career. Lady Spencer could be stern as well as kindly, refusing aid to erring locals, especially on moral grounds. Both Charles Louch of St. Albans and John Manning (a relative of Richard's?) of Little Brington were denied assistance for sexual misconduct. As the countess informed Louch, it was "her Duty to attend as much as she can to the character of those . . . [she aids], and Mr. C. must remember her first knowledge of him was his living with a Wife he had publicly married while another Wife by whom he had many Children was still alive."[36] However, if moral character were unblemished, Lady Spencer was very open to requests from local people.

Another potent reason that writers unabashedly gave for the claims they had on the charity of the countess was in return for past services, either unpaid or paid. The largest category of unpaid services was usually described as having "served the Spencers' interests." When H. Stevens, a soldier turned shoemaker, was in need, he asked Lady Spencer for employment, noting that he had "done every thing in my Power to serve the interest from the first Moment I purchased the freedom of St. Albans which is twenty three years and which cost me Eleven Pound." When John Nutt, also from St. Albans, wanted a job as an East India Company warehouseman, he reminded Lady Spencer that he and his family had long served "the Interest of Earl Spencer." John Gutteridge, writing after the death of the first earl, made it abundantly clear exactly what "serving the interest" entailed:

> I was during the long Contested Election for Northamptonshire in the year 1768 well known and much respected by Earl Spencer, and being very active in procuring votes to his interest he more than once assured me I should never want a Friend, but alas he and the gentleman who heard his promise are now no more, but I have no doubt but that your Ladyship out of respect to his memory and on consideration of my services in his cause, and of my great age and distress will have the goodness to bestow your benevolence upon me.

Several reminded the countess not only that they had served, but at what cost and expense to themselves. Thus in an afterword to a strange, incoherent letter of request, Thomas Cowper suddenly seemed lucid and intelligible: "I think if her Grace the Duchess of Devonshire knew how things was with me Perhaps she might do something for me if she did but Remember the Great Election when I went in Danger of my Life for the Honour of her Dear Deceas'd and Noble Father." Serving the present interest of the second earl was perhaps as useful as having served his father; in 1791 one J. Whinham came in person to obtain money from the countess and sent in a note explaining that he needed assistance because "Lord Spencer Insesing of my Serving of a Single Vote last Election has lost all my friends at Gozvam Bay." A much more unusual, though even more potent, claim on Lady Spencer's purse, was the debt she owed both to the young captain and his family who were responsible for the Spencers' safe return from France after a trip abroad. Although Lady Spencer found his mother rather a trial to assist, because of her violent temper, she commented that though Mrs. Garner "did not behave very well [she] nevertheless was rewarded (on acct of her son's merit) with a pension of 80£ for life."[37]

Yet another category of supplicants were those who had claims based on the paid service they had performed for the Spencers or for their friends. Sometimes these servants had left for other jobs, sometimes been fired, sometimes retired. Sometimes this claim was so attenuated that it came from the children or relations of old family retainers. Thus when John Stevens wrote to Lady Spencer asking for a job in the customs house, he reminded her that he had been the late earl's butcher for seven years. When Matthew Nutley, Lady Spencer's agent for antiquities, fell sick in Rome, or when John Stephenson injured himself hanging bells for her, both wrote to her for assistance. Even servants who had left the employ of the Spencers called on them later, in times of need. When Tappy the coachman went to the Clives from the service of the Spencers, Lord Clive promised him a pension of £50 per annum for life. On Clive's death, his young heir refused to pay the sum, and Lady Clive said she could not afford the extra expense. As a consequence Lady Spencer took on the obligation, noting, "I allowed him £50 a year for his life," and paid for his funeral when he died almost a decade later. The need to establish a chain of obligations, and the ability to acquire "knowledge" through inheritance, as it were, are well illustrated by the case of Mary Clark, a poor woman afflicted for twenty years with palsy. In her letter, she reminded Lady Spencer that her father "had lived with her Ladyship's family when she was still Miss Poyntz," and she was rewarded, as was Mary Leete, who in her youth had worked for Lady Spencer's mother and brothers as a laundress. The only claim that William Davis had on Lady Spencer's benevolence was that she had rented his house in Bath. Although she did not accede to this request, she did note on the letter that she had "already done more than prudence can justify." Even the relations of ex-servants who had abused Lord Spencer applied in their old age for relief, and were considered and assisted. These sorts of claims were among the most powerful and certain of success.[38]

If voters and servants merited assistance, how much stronger a case had relations, or friends or acquaintances of relations. It is clear, however, that of her two families, that is, of the Poyntzes and the Spencers, it was the Poyntz family that caused her infinitely more trouble. Even very distant relatives felt that they had some right to appeal to Lady Spencer. Mrs. Elizabeth Sprigg, for example, in asking for aid, commented that she was the daughter of Mr. Poyntz Ousley, who had been Lady Spencer's father's first cousin. But far and away the most demanding and difficult were the very large brood of Mr. James Poyntz, a very distant relative, whose only real claim was the shared name. Not only did he and his wife and children receive countless favors and assistance over many, many years, but so did his grandchildren, his children's in-laws, etc. Thus, when the husband of one of the daughters of James Poyntz wrote to Lady Spencer, on June 12, 1799, to tell her of the "entire ruin" of another Poyntz in-law, he (Mr. Wright) commented:

> I am well acquainted with yr Ladyships uncommon generosity to various Branches of my Wife's Family, and have to lament that some of them have made so bad an use of it. I cannot but admit that yr Ladyship had too much reason to be tired of such repeated applications, and God knows, with what sorrow and reluctance I have ever troubled you.

Lady Spencer was clearly irritated with them, lamenting the "many honest industrious creditors" who had been ruined by the Wrights' prodigality, "while Mr. W and his family did not debar themselves of any luxury within their reach." Yet she kept sending money. Mr Wright promised, in answer to her rebuke, that he would "never, without your express commands, trouble your ladyship again." Yet he was still in receipt of her charity eight years later. One can well understand the irritation of the countess when a Mr. Cragg wrote, claiming to be her cousin, the son of an illegitimate child her brother had fathered in the West Indies. She replied: "Explained to him how egregiously he must have been misinformed – as by his age – no father, uncle or cousin of mine could have been the person he mentions and my Brothers were never in the West Indies."[39]

Those who claimed relation to the Spencers were less troublesome, by and large. An interesting case is that of Fanny Murray, an actress and the illegitimate half-sister of Lady Spencer's husband. When she appealed to him, "My Lord granted her a pension of £160 a year for her life to enable her to quit the way of life she was in, and to marry Ross the Actor. He continued at her Request 50£ a year to her [step]Father." Lady Spencer not only honored this bequest to Murray's stepfather, but aided Ross for almost a decade after his wife's death. And then there was the Spencer relation on the lam from the bailiffs, a wild companion of a relation of the first earl's in need, one of Lord Spencer's godchildren who wanted a job, and sundry others who claimed some affinity, wanted favors, were considered, and were usually aided.[40]

Friendship could be a lien on Spencer property, but it did not even have to be as close a relationship as Garrick had with the Spencers. Anna Quincy's main reason for appealing to the countess was that she was a near relation of "the late Mrs. Sibley, who experienced the Honor of your Ladyship's Friendship and Bounty." Mrs. Sibley's niece, Hannah Gwynn, asked for assistance on the same basis. And despite the fact that John Leifchild "used [her] very ungenerously," Lady Spencer lent him some money because of an earlier kindness she had shown to his mother. Eleanor Halford wrote from Paris for help, resting her case on the charity the countess's mother, Mrs. Poyntz, had given her. And, in a sort of geometric appeal, Mrs. Mary Pratt cited her own earlier kindness to a Mrs. Dodd, whose last years were spent in Lady Spencer's almshouse. And that closed the circle, for these almshouses were familial, begun by Lord Spencer's great-grandmother, Sarah Churchill.[41]

The claims we have considered so far, in that they are rooted in the obligations of property, family, employment or friendship, might be thought to be unsurprising. These are the sorts of claims that probably moved the wealthy to aid certain of the needy for a very long time before Lady Spencer's day. While it is interesting to note, perhaps, that these sorts of claims retained and perhaps increased their potency,[42] even in a commercial age, and that formal petitions still were sent, and acted upon, even in the early years of the nineteenth century, the reader asks, but what was new? Several things must be said. First of all, as we shall soon see, these were not the *only* claims made, even in letters that contained these "traditional" appeals. With begging letters, as with most attempts to convince, the more different types of reasons you could adduce for support, the more likely you were to achieve donation. Second, the continuing importance of "personal knowledge" in a world where such information was more and more unusual and hard to come by led to the need to investigate the demands of the "unknown" but potentially deserving poor, and to the creation of structures for that investigation.

Before we come to these methods of acquiring information about possible recipients of aid, let us consider some of the remaining appeals, often made in conjunction with those already discussed, sometimes given alone, but always imbuing the request with a new flavor, a touch of sentiment, of gentility under attack or of sacrifice for country. Let us consider the last, first. Although most claims are more modern, there are a few of antique character, like John Bangs, whose misfortunes were attributed to the fact that his "Ancestors lost their estate in the Civil Wars on Acct of their Loyalty to Chas I," or the Rev. Talbot Keene, five of whose cousins in addition to his father and brother were in the armed services, and all had "bled for King and Country" though in unspecified campaigns. Many others claimed their family problems to be the result of the American war. Mrs. Charlotte Skinner vas not unusual; her dead husband, an American loyalist at the outbreak of the war, had his estates promptly confiscated when he joined the British army as a surgeon. Her father too had been in the service of the Crown as a naval officer, and two of her brothers had died in the army. As late as 1813 Sarah Evans told Lady Spencer of the many years she had cared for three of her great-aunts and an old great-uncle "who lost the whole of his property in America." Perhaps if the countess had lived longer, she would have received more correspondence citing the Napoleonic wars as cause for distress; when she did, as in the case of William Gould, who had served in three naval actions under Nelson, and later lost his right arm in an explosion, she usually responded favorably. But then the countess seemed, like many at the time, to be emotionally committed to the naval service, supporting many of her young protégés as midshipmen and lieutenants, and rather antipathetic to the army, actively supporting those who wished to leave it.[43]

When a Rev. Mr. Brook wrote to Lady Spencer in 1781, on behalf of an old acquaintance of his, a Mrs. Adlam, he described her situation in great detail. She was the wife of an ex-army man who had invested badly in American property; her whole family was in dire straits, despite the fact that "they have struggled against Poverty by an industry scarcely to be equalled [exhibiting] . . . the most exemplary Patience." Mr. Brook could not contain himself, either at the moment, or later, when telling Lady Spencer about it. Although he himself was in need, having only two guineas at hand, he felt compelled to give Mrs. Adlam half a guinea: "I could not resist the poignant feelings, I suppose natural to a human heart, for her exquisite distress." This language of sensitivity, of Rousseauian sympathy, certainly found its way into the claims the letters attempted to make. Here, for example, are lines of an anonymous letter, written on behalf of Jane Sanders, perhaps by Sanders herself. Note the use of the language of sensibility to flatter and convince the countess: "To rescue modest merit from misery, to wipe the tear from the cheek of innocence, to promote the interests of the rising generation, and to encourage virtue and piety, a great part of Lady Spencer's time has been spent."[44]

Especially moving, it was thought, would be the plea to a shared maternity, that social and biological fact which could bridge ranks at a single bound. Writing from the Fleet prison, where she had just given birth, Mrs. D. Powell urged, "A Mothers feelings is the only Apology I can offer for this intrusion." A similar appeal was made by Isabella Scott to "the sensibility" of Lady Spencer, "too well acquainted with the tender duties of wife and mother, not to feel for a wretched one." And if this sort of appeal carried a powerful claim, how much more powerful was that of Ann Burke, who, portraying the "really great distresses of a fond Mother and an innocent lovely child" (it was herself and her babe to whom she was referring) prophesied that both of them "*must* be lost – unless Benevolence avert the evils that threaten us." Where Lady Spencer could ascertain the truth and worth of these mothers in distress, she tended to respond favorably, and much of her giving was, in fact, to women.[45]

How did women present themselves, so that they would appear worthy objects of such charity? Did women, perhaps, have some advantage over men, in writing such requests, and did they sometimes therefore write in lieu of them? What, beyond appeals to maternity, could be expected to reduce a rather steely character like Lady Spencer's to the melting condition of the Rev. Mr. Brook?

Perhaps the kinds of requests that I found most surprising were those on behalf of, and from, women who claimed gentle birth, that is, from those women who used the title "Lady." A most bizarre letter is one from Lord Albemarle to Mrs. Poyntz, Lady Spencer's mother, in which he asked her to use her influence with her daughter, and with a host of other charitable women of her acquaintance, to collect a sum of money so that his sister, Lady Sophia Thomas, and her five children would have an income. Lady Sophia Thomas's distress, due to the "great indiscretions" of her husband who was then in jail for debt, moved the Spencers to contribute £100 on her behalf. Lady Perrott, "related to some of the first families of Scotland," and Lady Elizabeth Pryce, imprisoned for debt in King's Bench, both appealed to Lady Spencer, and both were aided. Then there was the tragic tale of Lady Jane Flack, whose memory is preserved in the Spencer letters by a little cardboard card, on one side of which someone, probably Flack herself, had noted that she was the daughter of the late Earl of Wigtoun and now was in the millinery business. She asked potential customers to use the rear door of her home. Lady Spencer, clearly moved, wrote on the back: "Rec'd this card but knew not the deep distress of the person who wrote it & who died soon after of Want." The countess contributed handsomely to the maintenance and education of some of her orphaned children.[46]

Though aristocratic women, fallen on hard times, would have had a clear appeal for Lady Spencer, they were only the more poignant examples of a much more prevalent claim that many women made, and could creditably make and be believed. That is, a vast number of women, of all ranks and conditions, wrote to Lady Spencer, asking for relief, because they were women alone, often taken advantage of by the very men who should have been their protectors, and often left with the sole care of children, and/or aged parents. There were, of course, many widows, and those of blameless husbands whose only fault was in dying too soon, who wrote to the countess. There were as many widows, however, like Ann Spencer, the daughter of an Irish judge whose husband, Colonel Spencer, "thro' his misconduct . . . found himself obliged to dispose of his commission," died soon afterwards, and left her dependent upon her needle for income. There were old women who had outlived all friends and relations, and unmarried women, sick and alone. There were also deserted women like Maria Mathew (whom we have already noticed), whose only comment on her departed husband was, "Alas! he proved very extravagant," or M. Douglas, "betrayed into error I was deserted in an early state of pregnancy without the least provision." Even reformed prostitutes, who presented themselves as promised marriage only to be sold into harlotry, wrote Lady Spencer and were assisted.

But many women's problems sprang, they claimed, not from the absence of a male, but from the presence of an avaricious or wicked one, often a relation, whose greed and rapacity were the sole causes of their perilous condition. The misconduct of brothers-in-law, sons-in-law, and stepfathers was cited; water proved no thinner than blood, for sons and brothers and uncles were equally culpable. Thus Jane Graglia, widowed less than a year and in need, wrote that "in the early part of my life my expectations were such as would have placed me far above mediocrity, if I had not been deprived of my fraternal right by an Uncle in whose hands it was placed." This comment about Graglia's early expectations was common and significant, and one to which we shall return shortly. Relations, however, were not the only predators on unwary or powerless females. Mary Hamilton's fortune was dissipated by the insolvency of her executor, while Louisa Whitmore's mother was reduced to penury by the "Villainy of a Lawyer." Further down the social ladder, but equally in need, was the widowed Mary Palmer, reduced to begging for help because the man for whom she had been housekeeper, and who owed her two years' salary, absconded without payment.

There were also a great many married women with living husbands who wrote to Lady Spencer. This posed something of a problem, since husbands were supposed to care for and support their wives and families. And so when these women wrote, appealing for assistance, they had to explain their husbands' incapacity. A not uncommon reason given was illness or unemployment. Ann Boston wrote on behalf of herself, five children, and her husband, a laboring man in a poor state of health, as did Elizabeth Kenney, whose husband was both ill and out of work. When Chauvin Rothay applied for aid, she explained that her husband was fighting in America; when Lady Spencer found that "both herself and the man she calls her husband are young and in good health," assistance was withdrawn. Some wives found what they hoped were compelling excuses for their husbands' non-earning. Martha Rogers explained that her husband William, though working part-time at a market garden, was finishing learning the violin, while the wife of an army lieutenant argued that her husband's salary was "required to support his own State and personal Appearance." These sorts of reasons could be used, and were used by husbands themselves when they wrote to Lady Spencer, as we will see. Many wives had no excuses for their husbands, but confessed straight out that their husbands were wastrels, that they were "unfortunately married." The clergyman writing in behalf of Mrs. Starkey explained that her poverty was the result of the "Imprudence of Mr. Starkey and his extravagant mismanagement." At least two letters came from women who found themselves in compromising marital situations. The first, Mrs. Catherine Shuter, had discovered that her husband was a bigamist, and she was his second wife, and the other, Mrs. Walton, left her husband after discovering his liaison with her sister. Others had less exotic, or specific, but still trying and impoverishing marital situations to put up with – madness, separation, and being turned out of doors. This last deserves some attention, as it encapsulates several of the themes already described. Mrs. Swinton was the wife of a Norfolk gentleman who, having squandered his own large fortune, attempted to break the family entail. When Mrs. Swinton stopped him from so doing, he turned her out; this led to an appeal for assistance, and after it was given, Mrs. Swinton herself became Lady Spencer's almoner.[47]

We have seen how potent the appeal to aristocracy-on-the-rocks was; almost as powerful was the combination of "gentility" fallen on hard tines. Bourne says "it was irresistible and may be said to constitute 'influential poverty.'"[48] Here again, women were the natural agents of appeal. Women because they had less "honor" to lose, because their role was thought to allow all efforts, no matter how demeaning, to protect and preserve their families, could make such pleas with fewer mitigating reasons than could men. Thus Elizabeth Morrison noted simply that she was "a person that was tenderly brought up and [had] lived in Credit and Respectability." Mrs. Taunton described herself as a "very unhappy widow, who by family, fortune and education had reason to expect better things." The Rev. Mr. Brook advised Lady Spencer to visit Mrs. Adlam, whom he had recommended for assistance, so that she could see for herself "the neatness and order and decency in personal appearance of the genteel condition." Gentility then was a matter of manners as well as of birth, and constituted in itself a compelling claim for assistance. Eliza Clarke, who admitted that she had lost her friends by an unnamed "Indiscretion," nevertheless felt that her education "at one of the best schools this kingdom boasts of" entitled her to consideration.[49] Even men could make use of this claim; Sir Richard Murray, a poor baronet of Nova Scotia, not only relied on the cachet of his own family name, but noted that he was "married to a Lady of one of the oldest families in this Kingdom." However, when men made such applications, they had to explain or apologize. Lieutenant Gore was typical in this respect; when he wrote to Lady Spencer asking for money with which to silence his creditors, he addressed this problem directly: "I therefore hope Your Ladyship will not think it derogatory to my Character as an Officer or a Gentleman, to submit my unfortunate situation to your Ladyship's benevolent consideration, particularly when I inform you that I have an amiable wife and two darling little girls." Military men of course could explain their poverty by the demands of the profession; thus when Mr. Morris, himself in King's Bench, wrote for Charles Ravenscroft, who was also unhappily immured there, he explained his debt thus: "his ambitions, perhaps not quite inexcusable, the desire of supporting the character of an officer and of keeping company of superior rank . . . plunged him into difficulties." Lieutenant Blasfield, on the other hand, explained his poverty by the fact that he had been taken advantage of "by some base principled Man." Some male letter writers attributed their poverty to a father's amiable vice of over-generosity, or to their own "too generous conception of mankind." It is curious that only men made this sentimental excuse for poverty. Perhaps in their uncomfortable appeals to Lady Spencer, they do not wish to suggest that her charity, like theirs, was the result of such will-o'-the-wisp sentimentality. Other men excused their requests by resting on their deserts; for example, when a tenant wanted Lord Spencer to pay for his son's stay at Bedlam, he remarked that he had "reared a family of eight without friends or the Parish," or when the aged Joseph Bird wanted assistance, he remarked that he had been a reputable householder for fifty years. But fewer males applied, and their applications were on the whole more apologetic.[50]

Being gently born was presented as a tremendous handicap by the genteel. Explaining why she wrote to Lady Spencer, Lady Perrott explained that "our situation in Life precluding us from making those common applications for relief, which objects of a certain description do; we are obliged to preserve some degree of appearance." Keeping up appearances was an absolute necessity for the shabby gentility. Not only was the possibility of appeal more circumscribed and difficult for them, but their experience of poverty was more severe, it was frequently asserted by those who had known the comforts of polite society. "Indigence and Poverty is more Senceably felt by those that have lived in a Creditable Manner than by those that were born in that station," remarked Mrs. Cornfield. J. L. Bodeur supposed that since he and his wife "were born and bred up as something better than common Beggars, our case is much harder than theirs." Why did they say this and how did they support this position? Mrs. Edwards, scion of an old Norfolk family, explained that her fortune had been swallowed up by "that dreadful guelph," to which the well-born were especially liable, "a chancery suit"; Mrs. Park could do no work because she was "a martyr to irritable nerves," while Mrs. Miller simply noted that she was "deprived of doing one thing for a livelihood upon the account of my Family and being brought up with no other notions but that of a gentlewoman."[51]

For gentle people, the prime requisite, both psychological and economic, was keeping up appearances. Mrs. Garner was especially concerned lest her son know she was asking for aid, commenting to Lady Spencer that "nothing is so hard as to be forced to keep up appearances." In Miss Dodd's letter on behalf of the Weyburne family, we see a fine articulation of this need, expressed in the language of sentiment: "Born to enjoy a much happier lot," she noted, "their chief care seems to be that of smothering the outward appearance of what are easily conceived of as the *internal anguish* they feel of inexpressible distress." Many talked of the need "to keep our Misfortunes from *the World* as much as we can." That world included society, servants, and – especially – creditors. Mrs. Mary Barker noted that "i take care to pay my Rent and keep my Distress from the lower sort of People."[52]

Most applicants directly linked the need to keep up appearances with the larger difficulty of evading or fooling creditors. In a world where credit was endemic and yet unsteady, where creditors watched those in their debt for any sign of difficulty, it was incumbent on debtors to remain living at their accustomed levels, lest their creditors, fearing default, either refused to extend credit or seized the few possessions of the debtors themselves. Mrs. Nugent confessed to Lady Spencer that both she and her husband were unemployed and needy, but continued, "I would not wish to make my situation known even in the house where I live." Clearly she was worried about being evicted. When a lady agent of the countess's came to visit the family of the Rev. Mr. Perfect to investigate his claims, but missed them, Perfect wrote angrily to Lady Spencer: "If it was Curiosity alone that led this Lady to such an Enquiry," he commented, "it was a little uncharitable, as it laid open my sores to a Creditor." Mrs. Pratt explained that she was "oblig'd to keep up appearance, to gain credit for Bread." Not only were officers obliged to keep up "an appearance" but the plea was also used by their wives: "I am obliged to keep up an appearance of gentility . . . and I must not disgrace the Character of an Officer's wife." Especially hit were the old, like Mrs Elizabeth Wynne, who feared that if the tradesmen she dealt with knew her true financial situation "they would stop my credit though I hope to be better able to pay next year." This need for disclosure created a real problem: on the one hand we have already mentioned Lady Spencer's refusal to aid anyone of whom she did not have "knowledge"; on the other hand, her attempts to obtain such knowledge might in themselves lead to the financial ruin which the letters were seeking to avert.[53]

And yet neither Lady Spencer nor even the letter writers expected assistance without investigation. This was the purpose of the names that the writers always included for reference, the authority of personages who could attest to the validity of the claim. Lady Spencer was furious with Andrew McCulloch who she said "applied both to my Lord and Lord Hardwicke in my name without my leave." Names were the most valuable sort of currency, and any debasement meant a diminution of the power of their owners. A problem arose, however, when donors like Lady Spencer began doubting either that letter writers had obtained permission for their use, or that the named person acted responsibly in allowing the use of his or her name. And what of those worthy poor folks who knew no one of eminence – should they not be helped if deserving? What was needed was some investigative process to solve these problems. "Impostors are too many," noted one of the writers, "which is injurious to those in distress." Lady Spencer thought she had detected one of these impostors when a Mr. McCarthy wrote her for assistance from the Fleet. She commented: "Have reason to believe from the name that it is a Man who has long got his living by writing begging letters." While Lady Spencer could herself detect some incompetents, like this man, to separate the deserving from the frauds, she needed assistance. In order to do this she set up a network of investigators throughout Britain, to whom she could write, asking them to visit the cases under consideration, view their circumstances, speak to their neighbors, and generally get a sense of their merits. This was not an entirely new procedure: the Countess of Liverpool had used the Rev. Mr. Stephens to investigate Mrs. Sarah Jackson before recommending her to her banker; Lady Spencer employed James Traille, an apothecary of Hatton Garden, to investigate the story of Mary Barker, who wanted to set up a small business. The countess often employed Selina Trimmer to deliver aid and probably to investigate claims, like that of the injured army lieutenant who asked for help. The Rev. Mr. Meakin of Newport Pagnall also worked for her, delivering aid and probably investigating an old couple, the Lindseys. Lady Spencer also used her philanthropic colleagues as investigative agents, interesting W. M. Pitt and Lady Stanley in the appeal of a penitent prostitute.[54] However, by the 1770s, for reasons that are not at all apparent, a group of charitable women and men organized themselves into a formal organization to aid the poor, and to centralize and make more efficient the gathering of "knowledge."

The Ladies' Charitable Society, or the Society for Charitable Purposes, which began early in the 1770s, has unfortunately left only the faintest traces of a record. Mrs. Elizabeth Carter, in language that recalls Bishop Sherlock's view of charity, described her vision of its purpose: "to relieve those who are really entitled to it, and, so far as can be lawfully done, punish impostors and cheats." She later elaborated on the kinds of people she, and the society, thought were "really entitled to it": "such objects as by age and sickness are disabled from working." The reward of such charity for the donors was both spiritual and practical; Mrs. Carter described the "two people who have just interrupted me by returning their thanks for the relief which they have obtained, and which has enabled them to return to their work, which had been interrupted by sickness, which obliged them to part with every thing necessary for carrying on their business." In the course of the winter of 1774, 160 women were employed by the workrooms of the committee, sewing clothes. Problems with this make-work scheme arose even in these early days, "For the Subcommittee works up cloaths without selling them." In addition to the work committee there were two other committees, one to settle what would be done in each case, the other to double-check and review the decisions of the first. Two investigators, Mrs. Dodd and Mrs. Ducherne, were hired, for "The detection of Impostors is one of the original intentions of the Society." After some interesting manuscript reports of the early days of the society, the evidence becomes very thin until a published account of the society appeared in 1793. By this point the society confined its operations to the care of the worthy of five West End parishes, largely by the giving of clothing and bedding, and the vetting of begging letters. The employment function of the charity seemed to operate in two ways: to employ and care for the women of the lower classes, especially the old and widowed, and to employ (as managers and investigators) the needy of gentle birth. Most of the women who wrote to Lady Spencer, thanking her for the boon of the Ladies' Society, mentioned the gift of sheets and blankets. Some letters suggest that it offered small pensions. Little more is known; perhaps a search through parish records will turn up something. Another possible approach is through a prosopography of its subscribers. Although a more exhaustive investigation of its subscription list is necessary and under way, it may be enough to note that many of its subscribers also appeared as agents or patrons in begging letters to Lady Spencer.[55]

Having analyzed these letters written to Lady Spencer, what can we now say about the claims and obligations of the needy and the responses of their benefactor? We can discern the lineaments of a developing and widely understood rhetoric of need, one with enough flexibility to meet changing circumstances. The begging letter was the means for the creation of this rhetoric of need. It operated as a central conduit of exchange; the exchange of dependence for obligation, of service for care, of need for succor. Although many different ones could be and were employed by the writers, the categories were limited. Rather baldly stated, they included property, service, family, propriety, gender, and sentiment – with deserts underlying all. The language of need establishing communication between favor-asker and favor-giver was both complex and formal. While many letters were servile and sentimental, some were manly and stoic. Those that failed to master the rhetoric and simply expressed naive greed also failed to earn donations.[56] Successful writers attempted to establish connections, relationships, legitimate reasons for appeal. The ground for such successful claims was "being known" or knowable. In these letters we get a glimpse at an historical cusp, a period when personal knowledge was still a valued requisite for attention, but had been pushed to its limits; when appeals were still to individuals, but also to the anonymous readers of the press; when upper-class folk adopted middle-class forms to more scientifically and systematically direct their charity; when knowledge of circumstance was being transformed, transvalued into moral and religious worthiness. The letters demonstrate the continuing influence of Christian charity viewed as a rent upon property, yet they also reveal a new, emerging Christian charity in which only the deserving are to be aided.

Notes

1 *London Courant*, February 12, 1781: "Amidst the general reproaches, however, which such conduct [low subscription to a charity opera] in our nobility so justly merits, we are happy in the opportunity to exempt one Lady from the number, who on this, as on various other occasions, has proved herself as much distinguished for benevolence as rank – we mean LADY SPENCER, who sent for six places, and accompanied the order with a donation much above the established sum that is generally paid for them. How much is it to be lamented, as well for the credit of the affluent in this country, as the distressed abroad, that this example was not more generally followed."

2 *Gentleman's Magazine*, March 1814, p. 309. "No one was ever better formed by nature, not only to become, but to shed a grace and ornament upon the high station in which she was placed . . . and to exert the noblest prerogative which rank, and wealth confer, by giving a high example of virtue and piety, united with a proper display of splendour . . . which naturally belonged to her situation. . . . Her words and her actions bore, in their general and unfailing benevolence, the stamp of the characteristic virtue of her religion, and shewed how intimately Christian charity was blended with her manners, her feelings and her opinions. . . . Amidst the pleasures and occupations of the world, she never had forgotten the offices of benevolence and piety."

3 Mrs. Elizabeth Montagu to Mrs. Robinson, September 22, 1786; quoted in *A Lady of the Last Century*, ed. Dr. Doran (London: Richard Bentley, 1873), pp. 332–3. "The history of La Fee Bienfaisante is not half so delightful as seeing the manner in which Lady Spencer spends her day. Every moment of it is employed in some act of benevolence and charity."

4 The Marquise de Laincel wrote from Bologna, July 5, 1794, Althorp F 142; the Comtesse de Beauregard from London, April 11, 1796, Althorp F 133; an ex-French abbess, Isabella de Blankart, from Cologne, May 1803, Althorp F 133; J. Lemmer from Vienna, February 20, 1803, Althorp F 143.

5 *Letters of David Garrick and Georgiana Countess Spencer 1759–1779*, ed. Earl Spencer and Christopher Dobson (Cambridge: the Roxburgh Club, 1960), p. 2.

6 Her friend Mrs. Carter, in a letter to Mrs. Elizabeth Montagu, noted shortly after Earl Spencer's death: "I am glad poor amiable Lady Spencer has left Bath. Her heart must suffer most severely by this stroke, however long expected, which has separated her from a husband whom she loved with the fondest attachment, and who, I firmly believe, never felt for a moment the least abatement for his original esteem and affection for her." *Letters from Mrs. Elizabeth Carter to Mrs. Montagu between the years 1755 and 1800 . . .*, ed. the Rev. Montagu Pennington, 3 vols (London: F. C. and J. Rivington, 1817), Vol. 3, pp. 207–8. Some very charming and gushingly girlish letters to her childhood friend Theodora Cowper, from the period just predating her marriage, prove the affection on both sides. See Althorp F 122.

7 Ibid. "I am glad Lady Spencer has so good a jointure, she would make a noble use of the largest fortune, and I feel certain she will make thousands happy by what she has, which will certainly enable her to live both in great affluence and in a generous manner." I refer throughout this chapter to Margaret Georgiana Spencer as Lady Spencer, although for a 4-year period, 1757 to 1761, she was just Mrs. Spencer.

8 April 4, 1771, Althorp F 152.

9 Compare the earl's obituary, for example (*Gentleman's Magazine*, October 1783, pp. 980–1) with the countess's cited in note 1.

10 Nor is there any evidence that Lady Spencer followed what *The Times* of November 26, 1789 described as a widespread practice among the upper classes: "The etiquette of several families now is, to order all letters to be opened by their servants. If they contain petitions,

or relations of distress, the letters must be suppressed, and no answers sent; and thus they add insult to minds already corroded by cares and distresses."

11 In his book, *Public Life and the Propertied Englishman, 1689–1798* (Oxford: 1991), Paul Langford says that "Some aristocratic piety had its origins in middle-class life. This was true of the brand offered by the celebrated Countess Spencer, the exemplar of aristocratic female virtue." There is no explanation for the attribution of "middle-class." While it is true that one of Lady Spencer's grandfathers was a commoner, her great-grandfather was an earl. It seems to me that throughout her life she acted as one would imagine a responsible aristocrat should; that is certainly what her contemporaries said of her.

12 Thus, for example, Mrs. Montagu got similar letters; see the article by Edith Sedgwick Larson, "A measure of power: the personal charity of Elizabeth Montagu," *Studies in Eighteenth-Century Culture* 16 (1986): 197–210. John Thornton hired his own "almoner" to handle requests for assistance.

13 Although, according to Mrs. Montagu's letters, "Le Texier [the French actor] got into hot water at Lady Spencer's by reciting Voltaire's 'Dimanche' [in the spring of 1776], Lord Spencer vowing he should never enter the house again, the Frenchman adroitly contrived to reestablish his position." *Mrs. Montagu, "Queen of the Blues,"* ed. Reginald Blunt, (Boston, MA: Houghton Mifflin, 1923), Vol. 1, p. 310. By 1780, Lady Spencer had promised Le Texier "that the Duke of Devonshire, the Duchess of Devonshire, My Lord and myself would join in a subscription if one was made for him" and subsequently sent him ten guineas (October 17, 1780 to February 26, 1781, Althorp F 157). Her obituary noted that Lady Spencer was not religiously gloomy, but given to hilarity and fun.

14 Mrs. Carter and Ralph S. Walker, in his annotated notes to *James Beattie's London Diary, 1773*, said that Mrs John Pitt founded the society. Walker noted that a Miss Mary Cooper, future wife of the geologist DeLuc, was the most active member of this group, "which Mrs John Pitt formed in 1714." But the Rev. Burrows, writing to Lady Spencer, commented that "the Society will not, like old Rome, and many other Societies, fall by its own Weight, and am convinced that *You* carry Cesar, and all his fortunes" (February 24, 1774, Althorp F 134). Even in 1800, another member of the society, Mrs. Garthshore, addressed the countess as "one of our chief supports" (May 21, 1800, Althorp F 138).

15 Knightly Chetwood, Dean of Gloucester, *A Sermon preach'd before the Lord Mayor of London, the Aldermen, Sheriffs and Governours of the Several Hospitals of the City of London* (London: 1708), p. 29; see also Joseph Roper, *The Character of a Liberal Man* (London: 1734); William Lupton, *The Necessity and Measure, the Excellency and Efficacy of Works of Charity Represented* (London: 1713); Henry Layng, *A Sermon Preached before the President and Governors of the Northampton County Infirmary* (London: 1746); and Zachariah Pearce, *A Sermon before the Governors of Several Hospitals* (London: 1743).

16 Thomas Sherlock, *Several Discourses Preached at the Temple Church*, 4 vols (London: 1754), Vol. 3, pp. 108–10.

17 Mary Leete, January 29, 1808, Althorp F 143; John Bennett, October 1, 1790, Althorp F 133.

18 Lady Spencer, in her letters to Mrs. Howe, gives many reasons for her benevolence. On one occasion, she noted, "I am an Idiot about play [gambling], and make what amends I can for that Vice, by being something of a Lady Bountiful to the poor" (June 6, 1780, Althorp F 48). She also notes the comfort her charity gives her after her husband's death (March 1, 1784, Althorp F 54), the sense of occupation she finds in it (December 26, 1787, Althorp F 63), her notion that only benevolence establishes lasting local memorials (February 20, 1787, Althorp F 61), and that her charity cements her local, political influence and quiets turbulence and disaffection (April 11, 1796, Althorp F 78, and July 21, 1795, Althorp F 77).

19 See, for example, Lady Spencer's curious draft of a most detailed and peculiar letter of instruction from herself to Dr. Maxwell, the secretary and minister to the Asylum for Orphaned Girls, about how mealtimes should be conducted in the asylum (n.d., Althorp F 154).

20 Mr. Robinson, n.d., Althorp F 152. J. M. Bourne, *Patronage and Society in Nineteenth-Century England* (London: Edward Arnold, 1986).

21 There are one or two scraps of paper which note that the writer is at the door, and begs permission to speak to Lady Spencer about some important, though sensitive, issue. Perhaps this is how the initial kindness was granted, but there is no way of knowing whether or not this was so.

22 There are only 29 documents for the 1750s and 88 for the 1760s. The number of documents for the succeeding decades never fell below 260.

23 There has been relatively little attention paid to the petition in modern European history. The only published works I know that use petitions as a major source of evidence are Natalie Zemon Davis, *Fiction in the Archives* (Stanford, CA: Stanford University Press, 1987) and S. D. Mumm, "Writing for their lives: woman applicants to the Royal Literary Fund, 1840–1880," *Publishing History* 27 (1990): 27–48.

24 So, for example, Horace Walpole wrote to his man of business, Grosvenor Bedford, on July 30, 1764, enclosing three newspaper begging letters, and asking Bedford "at your leisure as you go into the City, I beg you to inquire after, and if their cases are really compassionate, to give half a guinea for me to each . . . but don't mention me" (*The Yale Edition of Horace Walpole's Correspondence*, ed. W. S. Lewis [New Haven, CT: Yale University Press, 1937–83]), Vol. 40, p. 345. I am in the middle of the beginning of a study of such newspaper advertisements. See Pat Rogers, "Pope and his subscribers," *Publishing History* 3 (1978): 7–36 for similar developments in the world of literature.

25 Mrs. Maria Mathew, July 26, 1811, Althorp F 144; Mrs. Sarah Jackson, July 7, 1808, Althorp F 142.

26 John Smith, 1772, Althorp F 155. There is also an interesting letter in this collection from a woman who advertised for a job as a companion or "as Almoner or any other work of piety and mercy which a Lady of Fortune might wish to employ her in." Lady Spencer replied to this advertisement, asking for more details, though there is no information as to whether or not she decided to employ or, in some other way, relieve her (November 29, 1809, Althorp F 156).

27 *Letters of Garrick and Countess Spencer*, ed. Spencer and Dobson, pp. 2–3, 15; October 30, 1778, Althorp F 142.

28 May 19, 1806, Althorp F 142; October 25, 1783, Althorp F 133.

29 February 2, 1800, Althorp F 142; October 3, 1788, Althorp F 140.

30 April 9, 1807, Althorp F 132; February 1796, Althorp F 143.

31 Lord Spencer was one of the Society of Dilettanti. For the Spencers' building projects see C. S. Sykes, *Private Palaces: Life in Great London Houses* (London: Chatto & Windus, 1985), pp. 171–5. When "Athenian" Stuart, the architect and designer of their mansion, died, Lady Spencer secretly financed the education of his daughter (November 9, 1801, Althorp F 156). Thomas Maurice, November 21, 1807, Althorp F 144; Matthew Crotch, pianist, June 1, 1785, Althorp F 136; J. M. Poole, novelist, May 26, 1807, Althorp F 150; C. T. Townley, painter, August 15, 1779, Althorp F 158; Sophia Troughton, short story writer, April 13, 1813, Althorp F 158; Sarah Yeates, November 18, 1797, Althorp F 164; and Lady Camilla Robinson, May 9, 1798, Althorp F 152. For more on the shady Lady Robinson, see *The Correspondence of Horace Walpole with the Countess of Upper Ossory*, 3 vols (Yale, CT: Yale University Press, 1965), Vol. 1, p. 120, note 20. Dr Graham, March 24, 1784, Althorp F 139; for more on Graham, see Roy Porter, "Mixed feelings: the Enlightenment and sexuality," in P.-G. Boucé (ed.), *Sexuality in Eighteenth-Century Britain* (Manchester: Manchester University Press, 1982), pp. 1–27. Spinning-machine inventor, July 20, 1799, Althorp F 139; and a plan to produce raw silk in England, Edward Bell, June 27, 1785, Althorp F 133.

32 See the Rev. James Meakin's letter on behalf of the Rev. Mr Cotton, April 15, 1812, Althorp F 144; the Rev. D. W. Morgan, June 16, 1783, Althorp F 145; the Rev. J. B. Pike, December 30, 1794, Althorp F 150; John Moir, sermon writer, July 3, 1788, Althorp F 145; Lady J. Townshend for Mrs. Sisson, a clergyman's widow, April 28, 1800, Althorp F 155; the Rev. Thomas Shirreff, August 26, 1806, Althorp F 155.

33 1757? Althorp F 150. Bourne expresses nicely what the begging letter is, and can tell us: "Begging letters . . . are pathetic and heart-rending, whining and cringing, hopeless and expectant, commonplace and incredible, threatening, cajoling, imploring, invoking friend-

ship and kinship, decency and honour, justice and merit, mammon and God." By the later eighteenth century, many published guides to such letter writing were available; for example, *The Compleat Letter Writer* (London: S. Crowder & H. Woodgate, 1756), George Brown, *The New and Complete English Letter Writer* (London: A. Hogg, 1770), George Hawkins, *The London Universal Letter Writer* (London: Richardson & Urquhart, 1781).

34 Jane Marriott, October 13, 1801, Althorp F 144; Susan Crawford, March 18, 1813, Althorp F 136; William Gore, June 7, 1804, Althorp F 139; the Rev. P. Touch, July 16, 1796, Althorp F 157; D. F. Gorges, July 20, 1799, Althorp F 139; the Rev. D. W. Price, March 29, 1799, Althorp F 150; Sarah Spence, November 16, 1795, Althorp F 155; C. T. Townley, July 31, 1800, Althorp F 159.

35 We have already seen Mr. Moody's hesitation to approach the Spencers, since he was unknown to them, and his use of Garrick as an intermediary. William Right, January 20, 1808, Althorp F 152; Hannah Trent, April 5, 1777, Althorp F 158; Harriot Douglas, June 25, 1796, Althorp F 146; Matilda Crayfield, July 20, 1782, Althorp F 132. In 1760 the Spencers lent £140 to someone using the initials A.L. without knowing to whom they were giving this money. Lady Spencer says the money was promptly repaid. Perhaps some letters, originally enclosed but now missing, might have explained what this was all about (Althorp F 142). See, for example, the story Bourne relates of this sort of relationship entered into by a farm laborer, John Shakespear, and Lord Moira, because they both sheltered under the same tree during a thunderstorm (*Patronage and Society*, p. 67).

36 William Addison, July 4, 1800, Althorp F 132; Thomas Coker, December 7, 1782, Althorp F 125; J. Clarke, May 5, 1804, Althorp F 137; Richard Manning, January 18, 1776, Althorp F 144; Mary Cornfield, September 24, 1774, Althorp F 136; Edward Clarke, February 8, 1783, Althorp F 135; Jefferson Miles, nineteen letters between August 26, 1799 and March 22, 1810, Althorp F 144. When John Butler, son of the Spencers' "late tenant of Nobottle," wrote for aid, Lady Spencer commented "I have promised to enquire into his character and give him a trifle if it is good" (September 28, 1800, Althorp F 134); Charles Louch, March 5, 1802, Althorp F 143; John Manning, n.d., Althorp F 144. Thomas Gisborne commented: "in the exercise of charitable and friendly regard to the neighbouring poor, women in general are exemplary." Gisborne's *An Inquiry into the Duties of the Female Sex* (London: T. Cadell, 1797) was one of the most important conduct books of the late eighteenth century.

37 H. Stevens, October 9, 1797, Althorp F 156; John Nutt, February 10, 1796, Althorp F 146; John Gutteridge, October 17, 1811, Althorp F 139; Thomas Cowper, February 1786, Althorp F 136; J. Whinham, August 1791, Althorp F 160; C T. Garner, March 5, 1780, Althorp F 138. After asking Lady Spencer to help her son to a place in a blue-coat school, Mrs. Mary Jee said: "I beg leave at the same time to observe to your Ladyship that my Husband William Jee and his late Father at St. Albans always gave their Vote to Lord Spencer and my Son when he attains his Age of Twenty one Years intends on all Occasions to do the same to the utmost of his power for your Ladyships Family" (August 31, 1805, Althorp F 142).

38 John Stevens, May 1795, Althorp F 156; Matthew Nutley, March 28, 1787, Althorp F 146; John Stephenson, April 1799, Althorp F 156; P. Tappy, February 26, 1775, November 21, 1785, Althorp F 157; Mary Clark, March 1813, Althorp F 135; Mary Leete, from June 1806 to December 1810, Althorp F 143; William Davis, August 5, 1795, Althorp F 137; Mrs. Parker, May 5 and 17, 1797, Althorp F 138. Though Lady Spencer initially refused to help her because she had behaved "extremely improperly in regard to the Spencer family, abusing My Lord Spencer with a violence and licentiousness of speech she was too much given to indulge," she did reconsider, only to find that her son had already given her a pension. See also the case of Elizabeth Roe, who asks for assistance, mentioning the fact that her late nephew, the Rev. Mr. Griffith, had been the tutor of the late Lord Henry Spencer, thereby establishing a family connection (December 26, 1809, Althorp F 152). There are innumerable requests for assistance from French and Italian servants whom the Spencers hired when abroad. Gisborne advised: "Let not your kindness to the meritorious [servant] terminate when they leave your house; but reward good conduct in them, and encourage it

in others, by subsequent acts of benevolence adapted to their circumstances" (*Inquiry*, p. 276).

39 Mrs Elizabeth Sprigg, May 22, 1758, Althorp F 156; Thomas Wright, sixty-two letters from March 10, 1788 to June 25, 1807, Althorp F 163; W. Cragg, December 28, 1787, Althorp F 136.

40 Fanny Murray's earliest letters are undated, but they were probably sent in the early 1750s and continued through November 13, 1787, Althorp F 145; Lewis Richards, n.d., Althorp F 152; Edward Lowry, the wild companion of the late Mr. Spencer, October 24, 1782, Althorp F 143; Lord Spencer's godson, John S. Parker, January 27, 1802, Althorp F 147. See also Thomas Spencer, July 7, 1808, Althorp F 156, and Mary Hamilton, November 21, 1764, Althorp F 140, both of whom claimed to be distant relations. For the story of how Earl Grey was deluged with applications for assistance from kinsmen when he became Prime Minister in 1830 see Bourne, *Patronage and Society*, p. 66.

41 Anna Quincy, November 27, 1778, Althorp F 150; Hannah Gwynn, eighteen letters between March 1, 1777 and February 24, 1813, Althorp F 139; John Leifchild, March 30, 1789, Althorp F 143; Eleanor Halford, December, 26, 1772, Althorp F 140; Mary Pratt, November 1798, Althorp F 150. "One of the central features of patronage relationships is their constant disequilibrium. Debts are never discharged. Every favour asked for and every one given created a new obligation, a future claim for reciprocation and the excuse for further solicitation. In this way, the lives of whole families and whole generations became shot through with patronage. Patronage was laid upon layer of patronage, a palimpsest of friendship, loyalty, obligation, charity, humanity, hope, ambition and service" (Bourne, *Patronage and Society*, p. 97). See also the case of Susannah Brimyard, who asked for assistance for herself and her son on the basis of the earlier kindness that Lady Spencer had shown to her father, February 20, 1811, Althorp F 133.

42 My book *Philanthropy and Police: London Charity in the Eighteenth Century* (Princeton, NJ: Princeton University Press, 1989) argues that there was a renewed call for commitment to local, personal charities in the late eighteenth century. Gisborne explained the importance of such "traditional" giving; talking of the ideal charitable woman, he said: "Her habitual insight into local events and local necessities, and her acquaintance with the characters and situations of individuals, enable her to adapt the relief which she affords to the merits and to the distress of the person assisted. They enable her, in the charitable expenditure of any specific sum, to accomplish purposes of greater and more durable utility than would have been attained in a place where she would not have enjoyed these advantages" (*Inquiry*, p. 291).

43 John Bangs, April 9, 1807, Althorp F 133; the Rev. Talbot Keene, March 11, 1794, Althorp F 142; Charlotte Skinner, October 2, 1798, Althorp F 155; Sarah Evans, March 6, 1813, Althorp F 137; William Gould, January 24, 1812, Althorp F 139. Lady Spencer got Andrew McCulloch's son a recommendation for a ship and started him on his naval career; see the letters from January 25, 1799 to June 4, 1814, Althorp F 143. She also obtained the discharge of W. Johnson from the army at the request of his mother (December 6, 1798, Althorp F 142). It must be remembered that her son was the head of the Admiralty during this period.

44 See the Rev. Mr. Brook, May 31, 1781, Althorp F 132, and an anonymous appeal for Jane Sanders, February 1783, Althorp F 132.

45 I am not trying to suggest that no appeals to maternity were made in the seventeenth century; I am sure they were. What I am trying to argue is that the language of sensibility is a new one, and one with some purchase by the later eighteenth century, even among the genteel poor. "These endowments form the glory of the female sex . . . modesty, delicacy, sympathizing sensibility, prompt and active benevolence" (Gisborne, *Inquiry*, p. 23). When a Scottish banker like Thomas Coutts could openly speak of "the peculiar sensibility of his heart" without embarrassment, we know the term has become one of importance; E. H. Coleridge, *The Life of Thomas Coutts, Banker*, 2 vols (London: John Lane, 1920), Vol. 2, p. 210. Isabella Scott, December 1782, Althorp F 154; and Ann Burke, April 21, 1794, Althorp F 134.

46 Albemarle's letter to Mrs. Poyntz, March 26, 1757, Althorp F 132; Lady Perrott, 1794, Althorp F 148; Lady Elizabeth Pryce, October 1786 to March 1791, Althorp F 150; Lady Jane Flack and her children, n.d., Althorp F 138; letter from Mrs. Jefferson about the children, January 30, 1798, Althorp F 142. After 1789 any number of French aristocrats became pensioners of Lady Spencer's.

47 For widows of blameless husbands, see Anne Jones, six letters between July 7, 1809 and December 20, 1813, Althorp F 142; and Ann Spencer, n.d., Althorp F 155; for women ill and old, see Elizabeth Robinson, July 1796, Althorp F 152, and M. Douglas, n.d. but probably early in 1780, Althorp F 137; for penitent prostitutes, see Maltilda May, 1798, Althorp F 144, and Sarah Street and an unnamed friend, January 1, 1781, Althorp F 156. For evil relations, see the following: a brother-in-law, Urania Newton, n.d., Althorp F 145; a son-in-law, Mrs Morgan, March 12, 1786, Althorp F 150; a stepfather, A. Palmer, January 13, 1809, Althorp F 146; a bad son, Margaret Nicholson, March 1787, Althorp F 145; a wicked brother, Miss Keeling, October 5, 1807, Althorp F 136; Jane Graglia, February 25, 1807, Althorp F 139; Mary Hamilton, November 21, 1764, Althorp F 140; Mrs. Whitmore, April 17, 1786, Althorp F 160; Mary Palmer, July 13, 1813, Althorp F 146; Ann Boston, January 12, 1811, Althorp F 133; Elizabeth Kenney, January 1, 1811, Althorp F 142; Chauvin Rothay, January 10–12, 1782, Althorp F 152; Martha Rogers, September 19, 1810, Althorp F 152; Mrs. Jackson, July 7, 1808, Althorp F 142. For those unfortunately married, see P. Morris, March 25, 1812, Althorp F 145; letter for Mrs. Starkey, May 31, 1788, Althorp F 156; Catherine Shuter, nineteen letters from 1757 to March 29, 1762, Althorp F 155; Mrs Walton, January 12, 1810, Althorp F 159. Mrs Sheldon's husband was mad (November 11, 1806, Althorp F 155); Mrs. Droughton was separated from hers (November 3, 1803, Althorp F 137) and Mrs. Swinton was evicted by hers (n.d. to March 24, 1812, Althorp F 156).

48 Bourne, *Patronage and Society*, pp. 57, 80.

49 Ibid., p. 80. For more on the problems of the middling poor, see Paul Langford, *A Polite and Commercial People: England 1727–1783* (Oxford: Clarendon Press, 1989), esp. pp. 76–9. Elizabeth Morrison, February 15, 1806, Althorp F 145; Mrs. Taunton, February 16, 1761, Althorp F 157; Mrs. Adlam, May 31, 1781, Althorp F 132; Eliza Clarke, n.d., Althorp F 135.

50 Sir Richard Murray, July 25, 1768, Althorp F 145; Lieutenant Gore, June 7, 1804 to September 25, 1804, Althorp F 139; Charles Ravenscroft, May 7, 1783, Althorp F 151; Lieutenant Blasfield, October 1810, Althorp F 133. Both H. Coxeter, whose "father was too free with charity" (July 13, 1761, Althorp F 136) and D. MacDonald (September 12, 1800, Althorp F 143) explain their poverty as a result of sentimental charity. This theme, so popular in the literature and drama of the day (see Sheridan's *The School for Scandal*, for example) is not widely used by Lady Spencer's correspondents. Lady Spencer seemed dubious about this sort of emotionalism. She notes of the playwright Cumberland: "He must have a good heart . . . but he has too much feeling . . . Garrick used to say he was like a Man without Skin, sensible of pain at every pore" (May 24, 1796, Althorp F 78). My thanks to Susan Staves for raising this issue. Clerical men, like military men, also claimed the need to live up to their station; see the Rev. John Moir, July 3, 1788, Althorp F 144. Edward Littleton for Bird, August 6, 1770; Joseph Bishop, September 26, 1811, Althorp F 133.

51 Lady Perrott, 1794, Althorp F 148; Mrs. Cornfield, September 24, 1774, Althorp F 136; J. L. Bodeur, n.d., Althorp F 155; Mrs. Edwards, May 23, 1797, Althorp F 137; Mrs Park, January 17, 1796, Althorp F 147; Mrs. Miller n.d., Althorp F 145.

52 Mrs. Garner, n.d., Althorp F 138; Mrs. Mary Barker, n.d, Althorp F 133.

53 Catherine Nugent, March 1813, Althorp F 146; the Rev. Mr. Perfect, February 10, 1760, Althorp F 148; Mrs. Pratt, November 25, 1798, Althorp F 150; Susanna Wilson, officer's wife, October 14, 1796, Althorp F 161; Elizabeth Wynne, October 8, 1786, Althorp F 164. Lady Spencer valued genteel reticence, too, saying of a woman aided: "She has hitherto had the Merit of being Unobtrusive": Miss J. Wayne March 18, 1801, Althorp F 160.

54 Andrew McCulloch, August 5, 1806, Althorp F 143; Mrs Pratt, November 1798, Althorp F 151; Mr. McCarthy, October 29, 1795, Althorp F 143; Countess of Liverpool, July 1809, Althorp F 142; Mary Barker, December 26, 1758, Althorp F 133; an army lieutenant, January 1803, Althorp F 143; the Lindseys, January 2, 1804, Althorp F 143; Maryan

Campion, January 1789 to May 1789, Althorp F 134. As a consequence of this investigative role, and general charitable involvement, people wrote to Lady Spencer for general information on charity, for example, on the state of charity schools throughout the nation, October 1, 1790, Althorp F 133.

55 For Mrs. Carter's comments, see *A Series of Letters between Mrs. Elizabeth Carter and Miss Catherine Talbot, from the year 1741 to 1770: To which are added, Letters from Mrs. Elizabeth Carter to Mrs. Vesey, between the years 1763 and 1787* (London: F. C. Rivington, 1808), pp. 99–110. Also see Althorp F 133 for the Rev. Burrows's letters to Lady Spencer about the early days of the society, and the letters between her and Mrs. Howe on the subject in Althorp F 43. The 1793 state of the society is to be found in *An Account of the Proceedings of the Society for Charitable Purposes*, which also contains a list of subscribers.

56 See, for example, the rather sweet letters from a young boy, whom Lady Spencer sent to school, who constantly asked for presents, especially for "a Pig, Turkey or Goose." He was reprimanded by the local doctor and told not to repeat either request, and to realize "the great distance between your Ladyships situation in life and his." If he wanted such luxuries, the doctor told him, he must procure them by his own exertions. Thomas Baker, September to December 20, 1804, Althorp F 133.

15
Defending conduct and property
The London press and the luxury debate

James Raven

For much of the period between Bernard Mandeville's *Fable of the Bees* (1714) and John Brown's *Estimate of the Manners and Principles of the Times* (1757) debate about luxury fed on what Hume described as its "very uncertain signification."[1] From the mid-1750s to the mid-1780s, however, magazines and polite tracts referred to "luxury" less as a general portmanteau term and more in relation to specific domestic objects and actions. Many interpretations of luxury remained as relativist and dependent upon circumstance as other moral concepts (particularly as many magazines borrowed liberally from ancient publications), but many writers attempted detailed and contemporary definitions of luxury in order to entertain and instruct readerships perceived as increasingly young, impressionable, female, and non-metropolitan. New representations were inspired both by changes in the literary market and by changing economic conditions, notably in domestic consumption, productivity, and landownership. Here I want to show how continuing discussion of luxury became a vehicle by which an expanding but often defensive London press examined more intently the relationship between property and conduct.

In the twenty or so London magazines of the 1750s, ranging from shortlived concoctions like Carnan's *Midwife* to solid reviews like *The Gentleman's Magazine*, most portrayals of luxury reflected a balance between its inevitability and its destructiveness. No real debate was in evidence. "Civis" in *The London Magazine* typically inveighed against the "Prevalence and Bad Effects of Luxury," warning of a "gulf of ruin" while admitting that luxury was "the daughter of commerce and promoter of trade" and "an evident token of a people's being wealthy."[2] In the same magazine, "Luxuria – victum ulciscitur Orbem," supposedly written from "Birminghamensis" in December 1755, was agitated by the growing number of these "common-place declamations against the degeneracy of the present times," and then proceeded to add to their number. "The growth of luxury," explained the writer, "is a sure prognostication of the decline of empires."[3] Both whimsy and resignation color many of these articles. Few magazine contributors emulated Hume and related luxury in any positive sense to the material progress of society. For debate to flourish and for more specific examples of luxury to be discussed, there had to be a restatement and updating both of older, apocalyptic views of luxury and of neo-Humean discussions of the advantages of luxurious activities.

During the next twenty-five years more detailed aspects of the luxury question were popularized by occasional tracts and by journals and magazines. Many contributions now accepted not only the inevitability but also the necessity of luxury, reflecting or indeed directly quoting from learned disquisitions on the history and progress of British civilization. Extracts were carried, for example, from Adam Ferguson's *An Essay on the History of Civil Society* of 1767, elaborating the argument that general luxury was a question of changing tastes developed in accordance with the new conveniences of the age. Essays and letters in *The Town and Country Magazine* (founded 1769) stressed the currency and appropriateness of a debate about luxury. In these, a variety of distinctions was attempted: between luxury as a moral or physical state and as a material object; between the luxury of non-productivity and of over-consumption; between its consequences for the individual and for the state.

The debate became a subject for journalism. The prolific publisher-author John Trusler produced several accounts of the topic. In the opening statement to his 1780 *Luxury No Political Evil, But Demonstratively Proved to be Necessary to the Preservation and Prosperity of States*, Trusler acknowledged the vitality of the debate: "The influence of Luxury on the prosperity of States, gives rise to one of those questions, on which most men have something to say; but wherein they generally disagree."[4] His defence of luxury was wide-ranging, arguing that the consumer should be left "to the luxuriance of his fancy" for states to prosper and populations to multiply, that luxury was the acceptable consequence of the material improvement of societies, and that "a desire for Luxuries begets a love of property, makes a man attentive to the preservation of his wealth . . . and will not suffer any order of men to vegetate in idleness."[5] In response, a rival publishing cleric condemned Trusler for eulogizing the economic benefits of luxury "in an Age, when both Art and Nature seem almost exhausted by the varied, ingenious Invention of new Luxuries; and are tortured, ransacked, and plundered on every side, in order to create new Appetites and Desires."[6]

The debate – as the following attempts to illustrate – centered on the search for legitimate, acceptable standards of conduct, and for careful discrimination between innocent, beneficial luxury and a pernicious luxury of excess. In 1778 *The Town and Country Magazine* carried an article by "Poplicola" ("Friend of the People") which pilloried "locusts of the state," projectors, and false traders as promoting luxury and subverting true commerce. Poplicola rehearsed familiar notions: "Wealth not acquired by the balance of trade is of no value: it seduces the merchant and artisan out of the channel of exportation: it sets them on importing and procuring luxuries for wealthy debauchees."[7] Three years later, in the same magazine, "An Admirer of Ease and Convenience" debated the advantages and disadvantages of luxury, settling for compromise and the caution to "let misers and cynics rail at imaginary luxury." Advocates of luxury insisted that it was necessary to promote industry and support labor – "the coffers of departed misers are opened, and their contents circulated." Opponents suggested that luxury "tends to the depravity of manners" and "in its ample field . . . eventually must ruin the community."[8]

Warnings of luxury had always addressed issues both of consumption and of production. Charges had ranged from excessive indolence and neglect of industry to worthless over-indulgence. A changing sociology of those accused of luxury in the second half of the century was mirrored by a greater concentration on questions of consumption and a relative decline in charges of luxury as non-productivity – charges levelled, for example, against lazy workers or indolent aristocracy. Hume's 1742 essay reflected the beginnings of this change in emphasis. As Hume concluded, "Luxury, when excessive, is the source of many ills, but is in general preferable to sloth and idleness, which wou'd commonly succeed in its place, and are more pernicious both to private persons and to the public."[9] Hume's concern remained with the avoidance of non-productivity, but, as "sloth," it was distinct from the vice of "luxury" – a common label for sloth and idleness early in the century.

New representations of consumption revealed two distinct preoccupations: the nature of the possessed and the conduct of the possessor. Practical definitions of thrift, prudence, and appropriate ownership were in great measure responses to new economic tensions brought about by new credit mechanisms, shifts in wealth distribution, new consumption patterns, and the greater economic instability resulting from war, inflation, and the expansion and diversification of domestic trade and manufacturing. Writers reformulated moral questions according to changes in personal wealth-holding and patterns of expenditure. It is now over ten years ago that A. W. Coats identified in the eighteenth century "an increasing prevalence of a 'commercial spirit' in the general literature of the time, a change which reflected the combined influence of economic progress and contemporary writers' responsiveness to the growth of a substantial new middle-class readership." He complained then (and could do so still) that "historians of literature seem much more aware of the significance of this point than historians of economics."[10] A key question concerns the discourse and literary media available to explain economic and social transformation.

Like many other eighteenth-century entrepreneurs, London booksellers[11] and magazine publishers experimented with new products and commercial techniques to supply and stimulate market demand. Faced, as a result of this, by charges of being merely entertaining and of promoting the unworthy and seditious, booksellers reaffirmed their commitment to "instruction." Traditional courtesy books were remodeled, hack writers and genteel authors were asked to submit "moral primers," and booksellers launched "improving" types of periodical, chapbook, and cheap tract. In particular, the magazine became a vehicle for up-to-the-minute essays on social issues, with publications aimed at coffee-houses, commercial and private libraries, and individual subscribers in town and country. By the end of the century over 260 periodical magazines were published in Great Britain, and a quarter of these in London. During the second half of the century, three main types of magazine can be distinguished: the critical review, the periodical essay, and the miscellany magazine. The most successful, such as *The Gentleman's Magazine* or *The London Magazine*, boasted editions of about 4,000. Many other magazines were shortlived and were issued in much smaller numbers. Many brief ventures, however, such as William Owen's *Magazine of Magazines* and many of the periodical essays, were also considerable successes.

For good commercial reasons writers were encouraged to present graphic and entertaining instruction in social proprieties and financial management. Dozens of popular pamphlets and magazine essays defined in practical terms acceptable and unacceptable methods of gaining, retaining, and deploying personal wealth. In order to be instructive, depiction became more detailed, and culprits were drawn increasingly from the same social order as the readers. In 1754 "Civis" had specifically argued that luxury did not harm the rich but only affected artisans and the poor: "its baleful influence extends even to inferior ranks of people, who vie with each other in furniture, eating, drinking and apparel."[12] During the next decade far greater attention was given to the example set by the rich in encouraging luxury amongst the working classes. Luxury was considered increasingly in relation to vices practised not by the unpropertied but by the propertied, not by the illiterate but by the literate.

In his broad examination of Smollett's fiction and voluminous non-fiction, John Sekora argued that much of Smollett's thought derived from the "ancient concept of Luxury" of which the novelist and historian was the last champion. Smollett conceived of luxury as a vice breeding extravagance, idleness, corruption, and dissoluteness in all classes.[13] The new emphasis upon fashion generated in the popular press from the 1770s, however, was concerned with a specific application of luxury. It indicted the extravagant wealthy, not those affected only by a marginal increase in their income. In the magazines, essays, letters to the editor, and the answers to some of the earliest "agony columns" outlined ideals of charity, benevolence, economy, and the proper responsibilities of wealth. These removed the application of luxury largely, if not completely, from the poor, focusing attention on the luxurious propertied.

Changing economic circumstances, especially in wartime, underpinned these revisions to the representation of luxury. The outbreak of the Seven Years' War brought a resurgence of neoclassical, often xenophobic, condemnations. One of the most famous contributions to be carried in extracts by the magazines was the Rev. John Brown's *Estimate of the Manners and Principles of the Times* (1757), itself reprinted at least a dozen times in its first year. *The London Magazine* carried such articles as "The profligacy of the present times," its author ("Britannicus") pointing out that "the time of War . . . seems the fittest to suppress Luxury," and complaining that "every village must now have a publick assembly; every handycraftsman must have his horse and country-house, and every tradesman's wife, her routs."[14] The Noble brothers, fashionable publishers and always alert to the popular market,[15] issued *The Tryal of the Lady Allurea Luxury*, in which Lady Allurea, a foreigner, is tried by a jury led by Sir Oliver Roastbeef, Bart., and charged with "corrupting the Morals of our People." Henry True-Briton testifies that Allurea Luxury arrived in Britain with the Restoration, Charles II taking her to his bed. Lord Good-Mind recalls that after letting Luxury into his house, "my old English hospitable Table was covered with nothing but Frenchified disguised Dishes." She corrupted tradesmen and merchants, told sailors to stay at home, and "used every Stratagem to corrupt, and render effeminate and cowardly, the B——h Soldiery".[16] The *Tryal* also includes a defence, but all the witnesses are discredited. Nevertheless, the arguments which are rubbished by the prosecution are those which gained respectability during the next two decades – that luxury encourages "a perpetual Circulation of Business," and that "we had neither Trade or Wealth, till she came amongst us."[17]

A similar intensification of published responses during the American war encouraged more complex debate, combining fears of economic crisis and an emphasis on material possessions, with the acceptance that certain luxury could bring benefits. Neoclassical Jeremiahs were not completely silent,[18] but the consensus of contributions to the magazines during the 1780s accepted the necessity for luxury, while demanding a variety of measures to prevent its excess. A piece on "National luxury" of 1781 decided that "luxury produces vice, and vice misery; but luxury is, notwithstanding, essentially necessary to national greatness . . . It is indeed true, that nations have been undone by luxury; but it is also true, that no nation can subsist without it."[19] A letter (by "H.B.") "to the Printer" in the same season warned of the viciousness of luxury, blaming "the monstrous size of our capital."[20] A letter signed "Voltaire" championed luxury, claiming primarily that it clothed the poor.[21] This was echoed in 1787 by a closely argued article, "On the bad consequences of national avarice," warning of national decline "if sumptuary laws were to preclude that luxury and extravagance which prevail through every rank of the community," and defining luxuries as "those necessary incentives to every laudable pursuit and useful undertaking." Of "superfluities," it claimed, "individuals would, perhaps in time, be happier without them; but the body politic, as it now is constituted, would soon shew symptoms of a hasty consumption." The author therefore suggested that the rich should be "prudently luxurious."[22] A more common argument was that the availability of new comforts was necessary to promote industry, but that sumptuary laws had to be revived as safeguards against luxury's over-development. Other writers demanded war taxation on luxuries.[23] The search was for standards of legitimate personal consumption, for justification for the purchase of decencies which went far beyond traditional concepts of the necessary. This discussion of the luxury of over-consumption in relation to property took various forms: it recharged debate about the social and political value of land, offered energetic if often contradictory responses to a consumer revolution, and examined questions of risk and the legitimacy of credit.

Discussion of land ownership was often the issue within the luxury debate most clearly associated with a "country" voice. Civic virtue and public action were shown to be founded on the ownership of land, which ensured independence and responsibility. The interests of the whole country could best be directed by those not in the pocket of the city financier and by those far removed from commercial operations based upon credit and speculation. In the view of the authors of dozens of magazine articles, property had to have a real presence, even if in the form of tradeable merchandise. A second, but no less important, issue was the change in ownership of land, a concern reflecting both increasing strains upon the retention of land and the influence of more general hostility toward new proprietors.

The thesis of an increasingly limited market in land in the second half of the eighteenth century, serving to protect the dominance of the great landholders, has been modified by evidence of a considerable turnover in small estates and by marked – if hardly surprising – regional variation.[24] Greatest land transaction and market competitiveness occurred at the level of the medium-sized properties of the gentry and smaller occupiers.[25] Even if recent research leaves the advocate of *nouveau-riche* land lust with only the pastures of the lesser gentry, these remain extremely extensive.[26] Land prices were primarily determined by demand, itself reflecting, amongst other factors, the attractiveness of government securities. One effect of the high interest rates offered on government securities during the American conflict was the lowering of land prices, making land purchase much easier for would-be small estate owners. In 1786 the

German visitor to London, Sophie von la Roche, sarcastically denied the popularity of Trusler's *Way to be Rich and Respectable*:

> But this useful English book cannot be very well known, even in its own country, as in the latest papers I saw a number of estates up for sale; it seems to me as long as paint *à la* Ninon Enclos, soap-bubbles of Venus, hair-oil of Athens, and exaggerated fashions are sought by the "ladies", as this paper reports, and as long as there are men who dodge the ban upon the coming fashion of tying shoes with laces, which threatens to ruin buckle-makers . . . so long there will be family estates on the market, and this booklet will need to go through more than five editions . . . for the nation cannot always count on a William Pitt to succeed with virtuous precepts in counteracting this irresponsible squandering.[27]

New means of supporting indebtedness, with the mortgage as a common instrument of long-term debt, did preserve many small estates, but this also heightened anxiety over retention of property and redoubled the calls against the luxury of excessive consumption. The land tax was a sore complaint and accounts were given of how the diversion of capital into taxation hindered estate improvement. Sales of land were often traumatic crises in a long family history, and resistance to sale was most famously demonstrated by the institution of trusteeships and strict settlement in an attempt to preserve contingent remainders and ensure successive resettlement.[28] As much as the loss of the financial investment in a property, landowners fought against any devaluation of land as a symbol and purveyor of social and political status and as the conspicuous emblem of leisure. The estate provided a sense of identity between generations – a true "vehicle of family purpose" as Habakkuk put it, or, as Namier observed, embodying the ultimate entitlement to citizenship.[29] Property was held in trust for future generations as the family inheritance. It was not to be squandered on personal pleasure, nor (in theory) should it have been derived from suddenly accumulated riches.

Magazine contributors gave particular attention to unexpectedly large purchases of land or sudden, spectacular improvements. Outstanding targets were the returned Anglo-Indian and new industrialist purchases like Josiah Wedgwood's Etruria Hall and Barleston Hall, Jedediah and William Strutt's Milford House and Derby and Nottingham estates, Robert Clive's homes in Berkeley Square and Shropshire, and Laurence Sulivan's Ponsborne Manor in Hertfordshire. As *The Topographer* believed, "every year produces an inundation of *new men*, that over-run almost every county in the kingdom, expell the ancient families, destroy the venerable mansions of antiquity, and place in their stead what seemeth good in their own eyes of glaring brick or ponderous stone."[30]

Property or its modification was also portrayed according to the perceived quality of its owners. Magazine ridicule of the new villa or estate owner presumed that aspirants to gentility could be identified by flourishes of obvious bad taste. Mockery was aimed at a full range of gentrifying accoutrements – zig-zag avenues (instead of the fine gladed and straight avenues of true gentility), *parterres*, absurdly placed lakes, and, most infamously, an extravagant love of classical statues, especially Cupids and Venuses. Thornton's *Connoisseur* made direct references to the designs of William and John

Romanians Can't Afford Land That Is Theirs

Special to The New York Times

GREBENIS, Romania, Feb. 6 — When the agricultural cooperative here broke up this year, most members took a few animals and retreated to their homes to await the return of their land, seized in the Communist era.

But Liviu Dobroiu, head of the defunct cooperative, had bigger plans and more money. So he bought 40 cows, and he now houses them in a stable in the old collective. Although he is a squatter, Mr. Dobroiu is one of the few farmers to have found security in Romania's agricultural sector.

"No one else is interested in this land," he said. "The former owner is dead, and anyway this land is no good for cultivation, because it's full of stones."

In spite of a year-old law returning land to dispossessed farmers, little has changed in the Romanian countryside. As of Jan. 1, cooperatives legally ceased to exist, yet in fact if not in name, they remain dominant.

Most peasants remain without property and the administrators who used to run the big farms remain in firm control.

Mr. Dobroiu took out loans from the agricultural bank to buy a tractor. But peasants rarely have enough collateral or connections to get bank loans. Nor do they have cash to buy seeds, feed, fertilizer or equipment. Economically, they are locked into collective farming.

Over 12.3 million acres have gone unsown this year, and Agriculture Minister Petre Marculescu admitted in a newspaper interview in December that the land-return law had not been carried out properly.

Viorel Pasca, a representative of the county chapter of the National Peasants Party, said, "The land is left fallow because the peasants don't know where their plots of land are, they would have no tractors to cultivate it if they did, and there was no gasoline available during the planting season

anyway."

The law provides for the restoration of up to 25 acres to farmers or their descendants whose land was incorporated into collectives. Those whose land was put into state farms are not entitled to regain their land, but they are eligible to receive profit from the farms in cash or produce.

Today, only 16,000 of over six million who reportedly have put in land claims have received deeds. Four million have documents in hand proclaiming that they own land in principle, but neither the location nor the conditions for ownership are defined.

The collectives have been transformed into so-called agricultural associations, and in fact these are the only options for farmers who need equipment and raw materials. Virtually all the members of one former collective, Saulia, for example, have joined the new association.

"I think only associations can survive, because the majority of the owners have no more than two hectares," or about five acres, said Saulia's chief engineer, Ariana Borbat.

"We offer our produce to the state, and the state helps us with subsidies," she said. "Some of our members complained we'd stolen the wheat, because we sold it to the state, but they must understand we must do what is necessary to maintain our production."

Mr. Marculescu said the Government lends equipment to associations because it can be used most efficiently on large plots. But, Mr. Pasca says, "The state does not want to recognize the right of people who lost their lands, and it certainly does not want to give up its property."

The New York Times

In Grebenis and elsewhere, most peasants still have no property.

1.1 "Romanians Can't Afford Land That Is Theirs," *New York Times*, February 12, 1992. Reproduced by kind permission of the *New York Times*.

11.1 English coffee-house, *c.* 1700. Reproduced by kind permission of Mary Evans Picture Library.

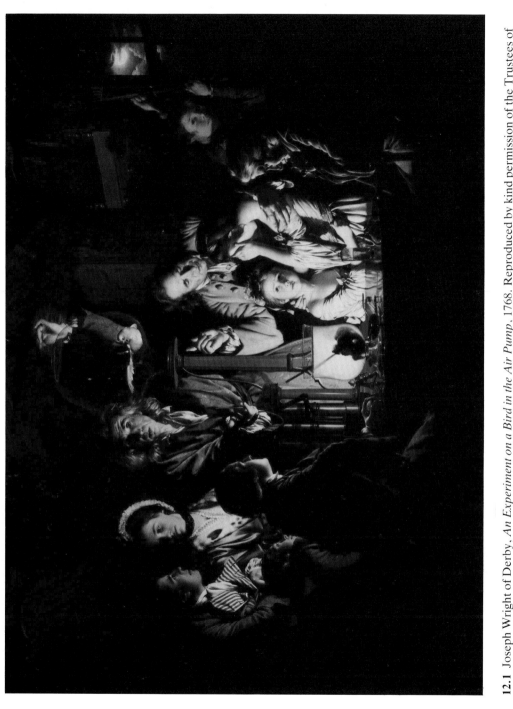

12.1 Joseph Wright of Derby, *An Experiment on a Bird in the Air Pump*. 1768. Reproduced by kind permission of the Trustees of the National Gallery, London.

12.2 John Closterman, *Anthony Ashley Cooper, 3rd Earl of Shaftesbury, and his brother the Hon. Maurice Ashley Cooper*, 1702. Reproduced by kind permission of the National Portrait Gallery, London.

14.1 Portrait of Margaret Georgiana, Lady Spencer. Reproduced by kind permission of Mary Evans Picture Library.

Lady Jane Flack

Daughter of the late Earl of Wigtown Solicitor the Countenance of the Countess of Spencer in prosecuting the Milliner's Business which for the Support of a large family of infant Children, She is under the Necessity of Carrying on (in private) not wishing to make a publick Shew of Business but to Confine her Attendance to the Nobility only — at her House N° 28 Norton Street

Portland Chapple

14.2 A cardboard card with a handwritten appeal for discreet customers for Lady Jane Flack's millinery business, found among the papers of Lady Spencer. Reproduced by kind permission of the British Library.

Recd this Card but knew not the deep distress of the person who wrote it or who died soon after of Want leaving many helpless orphans many of whom were taken care of by different persons of Rank

14.3 The reverse of the card shown in Plate 14.2; Lady Spencer notes that Lady Jane died soon after of want. Reproduced by kind permission of the British Library.

16.1 James Gillray, *Shakespeare Sacrificed – or The Offering to Avarice*. Reproduced by kind permission of the British Museum.

17.1 Eighteenth-century French post office. Reproduced by kind permission of Mary Evans Picture Library.

20.1 Robert Bakewell's New Leicester or Dishley sheep. Reproduced by kind permission of the Rural History Centre, University of Reading.

Mail-Order Mates With a Biotech Twist

Through artificial insemination, a prize bull can father thousands of cows, passing along his superior genes to herds around the world. But the technique will not work for pork farmers, because pig sperm does not stand freezing, and artificial insemination is of limited use with horses, because horse sperm can be refrigerated only briefly. But now a Gulph Mills, Pa., company that specializes in commercializing biotechnology patents is working on a method of preserving sperm that requires no refrigeration

The company, British Technology Group USA, uses a polymer gel to encapsulate the sperm. At room temperature, the polymer solidifies, immobilizing the sperm and lowering their metabolic activity. The polymer is permeable, letting oxygen in and waste products out. Because it is encapsulated in the polymer, the sperm can be sent through the mail. In the case of cows and mice — the only species for which the technology has been demonstrated so far — the sperm can survive up to 21 days

Inserted in the female, the gel melts, freeing the sperm over a period of 14 to 18 hours. Dr. Richard Gill, vice president of British Technology, said the slow melt rate could be a boon in breeding purebred dogs, because it is hard to tell precisely when the female is fertile. The window of opportunity varies by breed, generally 7 to 11 days, and natural insemination has a success rate of only about 30 percent, Dr. Gill said. With the sperm released over the course of 18 hours, the success rate should be higher. The technique is also more efficient than natural insemination, he said, because the reproductive tract of a dog is quite complex, and sperm have trouble finding their way to the ovum.

Tom Bloom

Artificial insemination puts the sperm precisely where they will be most effective, he said.

The technology was developed by a molecular biologist, Jonathan van Blerkom, for Genetic Engineering Inc., a Denver-based biotechnology company, and licensed to British Technology.

Although the animal market is easier to commercialize, the technique could eventually help human couples who have trouble conceiving because of a low sperm count, Dr. Gill said. The ejaculate would be concentrated in gel and then inserted. (It would not be a substitute for long-term storage by freezing.) But an animal version will come first — within a few months, British Technology hopes.

20.2 *New York Times*, November 15, 1991. Reproduced by kind permission of the *New York Times*.

AD OPERAM

ANGÉLIQUE MARGUERITE DUCOUDRAY.

Pensionnée et envoyée par le Roy, pour enseigner à pratiquer l'art des Accouchements dans tout le Royaume.

Gravé par J. Robert.

21.1 Portrait of Mme du Coudray, *c.* 1773. Reproduced by kind permission of The Wellcome Institute Library, London.

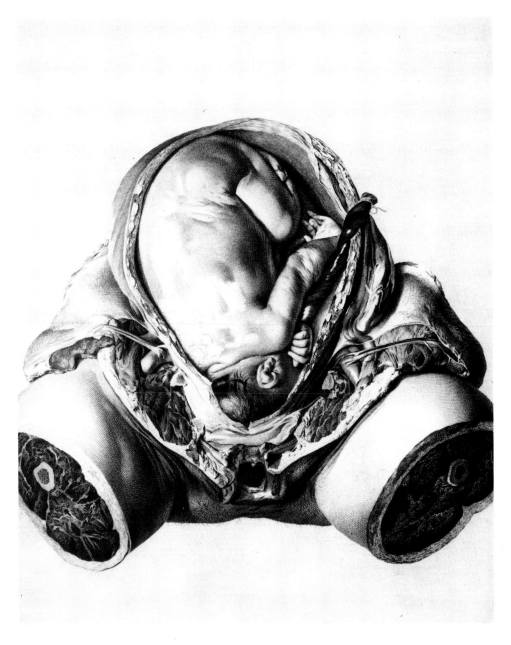

22.2 The fetus in presentation position, as illustrated by William Hunter, *The Anatomy of the Human Gravid Uterus*, Birmingham, 1774. By kind permission of the Wellcome Institute Library.

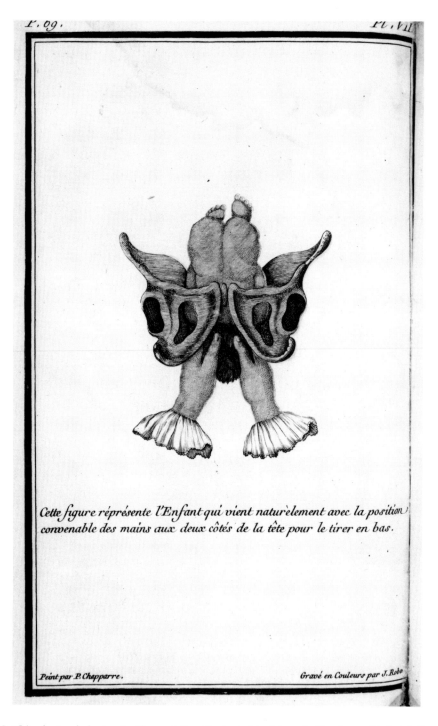

Cette figure réprésente l'Enfant qui vient naturèlement avec la position convenable des mains aux deux côtés de la tête pour le tirer en bas.

Peint par P.Chapparre.   Gravé en Couleurs par J.Robe

22.3 "L'enfant qui vient naturèlement," as illustrated by Mme du Coudray, *Abrégé de l'art des accouchements*, Paris, 1771. By kind permission of the Wellcome Institute Library, London.

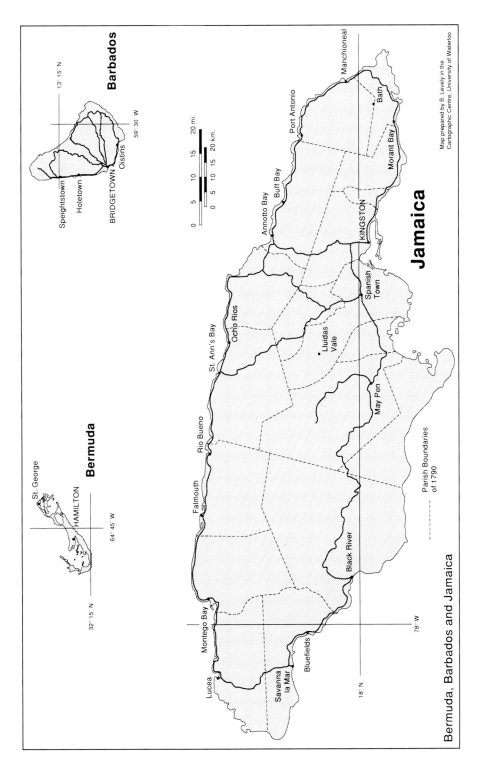

Barbados

13° 15' N

59° 30' W

Speightstown
Holetown
BRIDGETOWN
Oistins

0   5   10   15   20 mi.

0   5   10   15   20 km.

Bermuda

St. George

HAMILTON

32° 15' N

64° 45' W

Jamaica

Manchioneal
Bath
Morant Bay
Port Antonio
Buff Bay
Annotto Bay
KINGSTON
Spanish Town
Ocho Rios
St. Ann's Bay
Lluidas Vale
May Pen
Rio Bueno
Falmouth
Black River
Montego Bay
Lucea
Savanna la Mar
Bluefields

18° N

78° W

Parish Boundaries of 1790

Map prepared by B. Levely in the
Cartographic Centre, University of Waterloo

Bermuda, Barbados and Jamaica

24.1 Map showing the relative sizes of Bermuda, Barbados, and Jamaica.

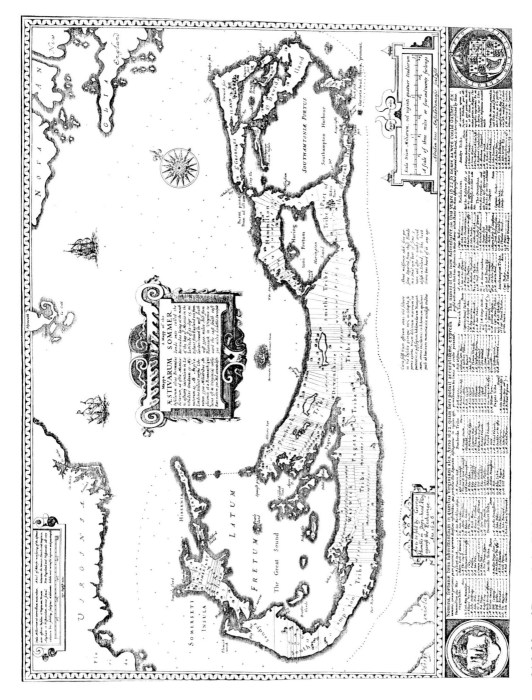

24.2 Map of Bermuda by Richard Norwood, 1622.

24.3 Map of Barbados by Richard Ligon. 1657.

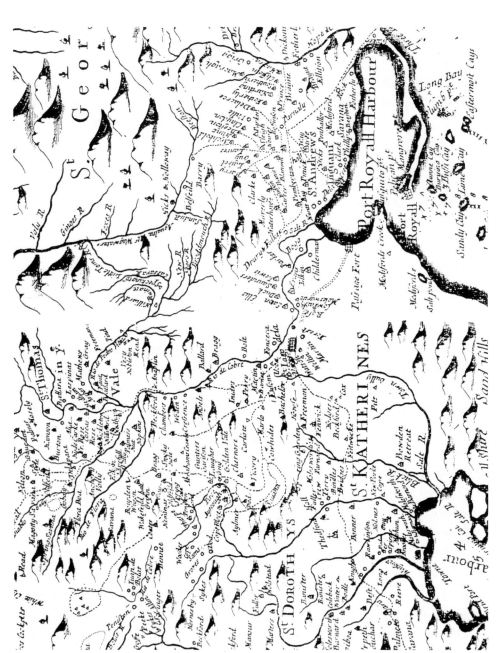

24.4 Central Jamaica by Charles Bochart and Humphrey Knollis. 1684.

Halfpenny which had achieved enormous popularity during the 1750s. Their drawings were issued in finely produced pocket-guides to the latest Gothick and Chinese.[31] Subsequent essayists associated such buildings with *parvenu* bad taste – particularly the Halfpenny Composite, which incorporated Japanese, Chinese, Indian, and High Gothick within one garden house or temple. Caricatures focused on the rejection of simplicity and its replacement by ornate bad taste. Counter-ideals were presented as "antient hospitality," neighborliness, and the proper stewardship of land and wealth.

Most attacks on *parvenu* property holders pointed malevolently to counterfeit pedigrees and false aesthetic values. The grounds of the *nouveau riche* were represented to reflect the owner – his ostentation, his newness, and his sudden transformation. He and they were vulgar and superfluous to society as well as positively destructive of the old and good. Such estates grew "trumpery shrubs" and their pretentious zig-zag avenues created the illusion of larger, more secluded grounds. The zealous collection of classical statuary was said to betray not only a sham imitation of proper elegance, but also a pathetic craving for a legitimizing tradition. Tonnish piers, pilasters, and palisades were undermining national values. Straight avenues of English oaks were being replaced by foreign, upstart convolutions, and Halfpenny zig-zaggery.

Moveable property was also featured in discussion of the luxury of over-consumption. The precise economic effects of the growth in home demand for manufactured goods are disputed, but there can be no doubt about the rapid rate of change in fashions, fueled by an increasing ability and willingness to spend on leisure and consumer goods.[32] The key variable in the support of fashion industries was not so much change in average consumption levels as change in the distribution of income and the stimulation of demand amongst the middle orders.[33] Periodical essays, particularly those in the fashionable *Town and Country Magazine* and *Lady's Magazine*, depicted a commodity fetish, assigned its origins to a new variety of contagious luxury, and identified its participants as the reckless newly wealthy. These often included caricatures of outlandishly adorned women, a version of which has been identified in early eighteenth-century "misogynist literature" as a trope by which "the agency of the acquisitive subject and the urgency of accumulation are concealed and deflected."[34] Similar depictions in the second half of the century, however, were more clearly intended to portray subtle gradations of responsibility, involving nice discrimination between categories of wealth-holders and dispersers.

As a defence against the charge of luxurious living, those supporting the consumer boom were assured not only that certain luxury was acceptable, but that very particular forms of luxury and very particular culprits were responsible for the outrages described by contemporary literature. Personal dishonesty was coupled with financial irresponsibility, a charge sustained by a continuing but extremely anxious pride in the mercantile and constitutional achievements of the last hundred years.[35] Almost without exception, writers depicted London as the crucible of fashion and the source of all vice. In the 1770s, *The Town and Country Magazine* revived old-style warnings about the growth of the capital and advised proscriptive legislation, for "in such *tempora*, can we wonder at such *mores*?"[36] "Plain country gentlemen," like Henry Mackenzie's Mr. John Homespun, serialized in *The Mirror* and *The Lounger*, contrasted the fearsome debauchery of the city with the ideal purity of the country.[37] London was the dominant center of both production and consumption. The West End was the resort of the fashionable.

The pleasure gardens and the Pantheon were the parade-ground of society. A self-perpetuating Season furnished evil example to the individual and to the rapidly growing provincial and northern cities. Trusler warned that "the several cities and large towns of this island catch the manners of the metropolis, and are vicious and extravagant, in proportion to the wealth and number of their inhabitants."[38] Alarmed essays and serialized magazine stories were appalled by London diseases spreading to the provinces, while the capital was credited with a destructive magnetism which attracted the young and ambitious away from their honest homes.

All writers guided the attack away from increased general consumption toward specified extravagant groups and individuals. This conception of luxury which identified as the true enemies of society the indolent or wasteful rich was in part derived from a growing sympathy for the poor. From Mun to Henry Fielding, economists and pamphleteers had stressed that the luxuries of the poor prevented the labor necessary for the support of both the workers and the existing structure of society. Fielding had blamed "a vast torrent of luxury" for the unrest of the poor in his 1751 *Enquiry into the Cause of the late Increase of Robbers*. In contrast, numerous later contributors, including Nathaniel Forster in his 1767 tract on prices, viewed an improved living standard even for the poor as an end in itself. Such attitudes were encouraged by distinctions made between high wages and high labor costs and an acknowledgment of the growing importance of industrial mechanization. Opposition was continued by resolute conservatives, notably William Temple of Trowbridge, Arthur Young, and those condemning high wages from fear of declining exports,[39] but by at least 1770 many economic writers – and many magazine imitators – held that the raising of living standards of even the poorest members of the community improved the prosperity of the whole of society.[40]

It was also the targeting of the rich that led discussion of the luxury of consumption from questions of wealth possession to questions about the behavior expected of the wealthy – from property to propriety. Consumption-luxury charges in the magazines were increasingly related to conduct in polite society. Almost without exception, magazine writers of the final third of the century emphasized the importance of the example set by the conduct of the propertied.

Description of the vernacular, learning, behavior, and status of the common people as "the vulgar" had been in currency since at least the fifteenth century and survived through the nineteenth century. From the late 1760s, however, the idea of "the vulgar" was increasingly linked to deviance from standards of taste. In the imaginative literature of the period, models of social propriety were advanced in accordance with the expectations of birth and rank, but "vulgarity" became less a specification of class and status than a measure of disparity between social actions and station. The new definition often complemented rather than replaced its original meaning. Clearly, as the rank assumed by the *nouveau riche* was deemed bogus, the continuance throughout this period of the older sense of the vulgar as the lower and unlettered classes underpinned the new usage.

The changing definition of vulgarity was reflected by the dictionaries, themselves competitive publications vaunting up-to-date coverage and attracting avid contemporary interest. The first edition of Bailey's dictionary in 1721 was satisfied by a double listing of "vulgar" as "trivial, low, mean," and as "the common sort of People, the

Rabble."[41] Dyche and Pardon's dictionary of 1735 introduced the idea of coarse and ungenteel, a significant transition which approached later acceptance of "vulgarity" as ungentlemanly taste or behavior.[42] At the same time, "taste" was featured in a parallel debate in popular magazines and essays. Continually updated ideas of "modishness," "the ton," and "fashion" were supplanting notions, to quote from a 1757 manual, that "good taste signify no more than ordinary accuracy in determining, in certain cases, that two distinct things are the same or of different kinds."[43]

The notion of "propriety" or "proper sense" was similarly closely bound to changing appraisals of refinement. During the final third of the eighteenth century the blush extended its domain. Delicacy demanded fewer oaths, greater personal hygiene, and the removal of new-found indecencies from public life. As Modesty expanded so the Wedgwood fig-leaves grew more capaciously, and the speeches of Shakespeare were trimmed.[44] The progress of popular journalism, from *The Connoisseur* and *The Mirror*, to *The Town and Country Magazine* and Alexander Hogg's *New Lady's Magazine*, can certainly be measured in terms of the development of "taste" and the march of delicacy. The output of Paternoster Row and Leadenhall Street established and defended politeness and elegance, defined norms of social behavior, and distinguished between the ranges of taste available. Popular guides in discrimination were sold as required reading for every educated man and woman. Changes in fashion appeared to quicken with each season, the consumer society to be out of control and spawning a "superabundancy of taste."

A public, reading about itself, was quick to appreciate cumulative judgments upon popular fads and fashions. The modish public which Steele and Addison had cultivated for their own use was as anxious to copy new style as it was to discriminate between the full compass of tastes presented by contemporary literature.[45] The eager response of magazines merely fueled desire for greater discrimination. Readers wanted to learn not only of fashion, but also of its excesses. Study of the outlandish and the grotesque would reaffirm the rules of polite behavior and present object lessons in the observance of correct taste. Once again, social norms and ideas of deviant taste were established by detailing the bad as well as the good.

The most significant development, however, was that taste was being sold. Instruction in discrimination was the basis for the popularity of dozens of magazines, novels, and practical guides from the Row, St. Paul's Churchyard, and Fleet Street. During the second half of the eighteenth century, magazine contributions and tales providing new ideas of propriety and elegant discrimination included highly successful and long-running publications. In his autobiography, Leigh Hunt recalled his early fascination with *The Connoisseur* and its witty arbitration between models of taste.[46] Collections by well-known publishers including John Bew, Thomas Hookham, Charles Stalker, and John Cooke, carried earnest advertisements for the pocket books and moral primers which formed a supportive encyclopedia of *politesse*. Such works emphasized the necessity of both manners and breeding for the preservation of the polite. In 1783, Trusler, differentiating between "Good-manners" and "Good-breeding," noted that "Good-breeding is of much larger extent than good-manners; it includes all the fashionable accomplishments; whereas good-manners is confined to our conduct and address."[47]

The key consideration in this was the producer's perception of the consumer. Just as

Wedgwood drapes were placed according to the anticipated class and sensibilities of the customer, popular literature was molded according to an expected readership. Authoritative manuals poured from the presses expounding standard spelling, correct grammar, the rules of deportment and conversation, the right mode of education, and the correct subjects for study, discussion, and emulation. The sheer volume of output is impressive. Conduct books, secretaries, even manuals of conversation, had enjoyed a long and distinguished history,[48] but now the pronunciation of words, the correct construction of a letter, and the minutiae of polite manners were addressed by a torrent of primers, pocket books, and serial magazine pieces and number books. The most notable contribution to spelling manuals was the reprinting of Thomas Dyche's classic of 1707, *A Guide to the English Tongue*, which went through sixty-four editions by 1800. His *Spelling Dictionary* of 1725 enjoyed a score of subsequent editions. George Fisher's *The Instructor* reached its sixty-eighth edition in 1800. There were many successes for schools, including John Shaw's *Methodical English Grammar: Containing Rules and Directions for speaking and writing the English Language with Propriety*, first published in 1778. Of the many guides to pronunciation, the most famous were William Perry's *Only Sure Guide to the English Tongue: or, New Pronouncing Spelling Book* of 1776, John Entick's *New Spelling Dictionary, Teaching How to Write and Pronounce the English Tongue*, which went through forty editions by 1800, and *Newbery's New Spelling Dictionary of the English Language*, issued in 1788. All these were reviewed, pirated, and debated by the magazines.

A recent study of the printed language of the late eighteenth century has persuasively argued that "civilization" was "largely a linguistic concept, establishing a terrain in which vocabulary and syntax distinguished the refined and the civilized from the vulgar and the savage."[49] As Olivia Smith shows, the new grammar books for English were offered for the middle classes and carried the obvious assumption that correct usage of English derived from the governing classes and automatically conveyed desired status, sensibilities, and standards of moral virtue. The battle for the middle-class bookshelf and classroom was a highly commercial one, however. It was fought at a furious tempo. Many contributors were little more than hack compilers or writer-booksellers with a quick appreciation of market potential. Trusler's *Principles of Politeness and of Knowing the World*, was sold as a work "translated into every European language." Between 1760 and 1769, at least twenty-two separate grammars were issued; between 1770 and 1779, at least twenty-eight; and between 1780 and 1789, at least thirty-one. Many of these titles were issued in dozens of editions. Alston's bibliography readily shows the tonnage of grammatical guides, dictionaries, and instructors in writing, letter writing, and pronunciation produced in this period.[50] Robert Lowth's *Short Introduction to English Grammar* of 1762 went through at least thirty-three English and Irish editions before 1790, John Ash's *Grammatical Institutes* of 1760 at least twenty-one. Many, of course, were destined for the schoolroom, but many also were clearly designed for the home library. The anonymous *Complete Letter-Writer* of 1755 had enjoyed eighteen London and Dublin editions by 1790.[51] Some primers and grammars were written by popular novelists and moralists. Alexander Bicknell achieved a notable success with a work which discussed and dismissed all his main rivals and provided extraordinarily detailed grammar rules.[52]

The keen competitiveness of booksellers is obvious in these publishing ventures.

Advertisements, prefaces, and commentaries in the works themselves made haste to describe the social ostracism inevitably faced by those withholding their custom. One of the earliest works of Dr. Trusler, ever an exploiter of market possibilities, was his 1766 version of Girard's *Difference Between Words*, whose title proclaimed its use "to all, who would, either, write or speak, with PROPRIETY, and, ELEGANCE."[53] Again, his work, like that of so many others, stressed the labor required to attain the necessary accomplishments: vulgarity in both learning and taste indicated a failure to endure the study of the essentials of social etiquette.[54] The emphasis of all such works was upon a uniformity of behavior and uncompromising notions of what was and was not correct. The commercial opportunities for selling indispensable knowledge were not overlooked. For the publishing industry, its writers, and its entrepreneurs, the representation of vulgarity and the indelicate provided more than just entertainment and self-justifying instruction: it could also be the safest and most profitable type of publication undertaken.

Nevertheless, in defining the vulgar and condemning the purely fashionable, popular publishers faced an embarrassing dilemma. Within the magazines, anti-fashion and anti-town contributions nestled uneasily amidst *"têtes-à-têtes,"* other city-gossip features, and accounts of the latest dresses, nosegays, coiffeurs, and cuisine. Literature itself was part of the fashion industry and supported by the leisured and the moneyed. Minerva, goddess of both arts and trade, was portrayed in magazine frontispieces as the protectress of innocence against vice.[55] She was also the symbol and name of William Lane's prolific, and many said profligate, library and novel-publishing business. The preface to *The London Magazine* in January 1771 was probably more candid than it should have been in its attempt to present itself as the polite people's favorite:

> It is not we but the publick that have made the alteration in the *London Magazine*. . . . If it calls for divinity, we give divinity; if it requires politicks, we publish politicks. If love-stories be the mode, we become historians of gallantry; and if antiquities be the fashion, we commence antiquarians. In short, as far as virtue and decorum will permit, we are whatever our readers please. Keeping a publick store-house we must fill it with commodities, for which there is demand.

The first number of Thomas Bellamy's *General Magazine*, carrying fashion advice and town gossip, could only assume a haughty bluff to justify its publication as a reformist journal. Rival magazines were worthless, claimed Bellamy: "Among the sons of literature some have proved rebellious to Virtue, and have endeavoured to lay waste her kingdom with the firebrands of licentiousness; while others have subverted her authority by satanical delusions."[56] Stalker and Hookham's weekly *Hive* opened its account with similar bluster against the "denomination of Magazines and Reviews" and offering its own judicious "weekly ramble through the republic of letters."[57]

The expansion of the reading public in the provinces also increased the sophistry of editors and authors in their treatment of country–city issues. The dual appeal of "Sylvanus Urban," fictional editor of *The Gentleman's Magazine*, was paralleled by that of The *Town and Country Magazine* two decades later. Such attention to the dangers of fashion and the isolation of specific exemplars of the ton was a direct result of the vulnerability of magazine and lighter literature to charges of frivolity and immorality.

The result was an even greater, competitive, and often desperate discrimination be-tween the acceptable and unacceptable, and the polite and impolite.

Again, the general method adopted in magazines and short tracts was to satirize specific aspects of contemporary society as a means of mixing entertainment with instruction. As Richard Cumberland put it in the introduction to his *Observer* of 1785, "to administer moral precepts through a pleasing vehicle seems now the general study of our Essayists, Dramatists and Novelists."[58] Old attacks upon vice and folly were reworked, and a dependence upon Addison and Steele was clear. Ridicule was to be aimed at identifiable men, and although popular literature was now engaging in little more than generalized caricature, the obsession remained with isolating supposedly authentic scoundrels. The alternative tradition of rumbustious, often facetiously crude burlesque, was suppressed in all but the lower end of the market. Many writers now portrayed injurious forms of luxury in order to prescribe the antidote: a gentlemanly morality of economy and benevolence, and a proper understanding of the responsi-bilities of wealth.

Two underlying concerns were supportive but distinct. The implicit definition of the gentleman was concerned with problems of both financial and social legitimacy. Periodical literature reinforced notions of the importance of active, circulating, and redeployable wealth, and attempted a layman's analysis of unacceptable behavior and its consequences. As the contribution entitled "The abuse of riches" in the 1775 *Town and Country Magazine* explained:

> The man who squanders his money with a wanton profusion, and the man who hoards it with a sordid parsimony, are equally strangers to the true use of riches. . . . Avarice and extravagance are undoubtedly the two rocks which men of fortune should, with the greatest caution, avoid; but it is a very nice point to draw the line of moderation between them.[59]

As seen, however, greatest venom was reserved for profligate waste, not selfish hoard-ing. As the range of consumer products widened, most imaginative literature insisted that expenditure could be as useless as and even more dangerous than selfish accumu-lation: "In prosperity, [the gentleman] is affable, humble, and benevolent; he regards his riches as intrusted to him for the benefit of his poor brethren, and distributes, with judgment and prudence, among them, what the thoughtless devote to their luxuries, or their lusts."[60] The charity of the gentleman would prevent non-use of riches; his economy and natural good sense, their misuse.

Similarly, the misuse of wealth and its sudden accumulation were interchangeable as cause and effect. The prosecution of *nouveaux riches* outlined the iniquities of an uneven distribution of wealth when this included large unused or misused fortunes. It served as a proof that vast inequalities in wealth-holding provided no stimulus to work and justified the sympathy for the poor expressed in so many recent articles. It was in the interests of popular writers to maintain mutually supportive arguments: fulminations against luxury and extravagance criticized the wealthy upstart by way of illustration, while attacks against the upstart depended upon concern over free spending. The work of Henry Mackenzie, to take one of the most popular magazine examples, was as anxious to identify culprits as it was to examine the crime:

In the country, it [the disease of Extravagance] will be productive of melancholy effects indeed; if suffered to spread there, it will not only embitter our lives, and spoil our domestic happiness, as at present it does mine, but, in its most violent stages, will bring our estates to market, our daughters to ruin, and our sons to the gallows . . . let all *little men* like myself, and every member of their families, be cautious of holding intercourse with the persons or families of *Dukes, Earls, Lords, Nabobs,* or *Contractors,* till they have good reason to believe that such persons and their households are in a sane and healthy state, and in no danger of communicating this dreadful disorder.[61]

Concern with the behavior of wealth-holders and property owners therefore returned to the question of the conduct of personal financial affairs. As Goldsmith wrote, "Of all the follies and absurdities which this great metropolis labours under, there is not one, I believe, at present, appears in a more glaring and ridiculous light than the pride and luxury of the middling class of people. . . . You shall see a grocer or a tallow-chandler sneak from behind the counter, clap on a laced coat and a bag, fly to the E. O. table, throw away fifty pieces with some sharping man of quality."[62]

New exemplars were found to demonstrate the dangers of over-expenditure and to stress the vigilance required to avoid both personal and national indebtedness. Quite in addition to the social concerns, moral essays repeated charges that particular business and consumer activity could promote economic instability, that credit crises affecting the whole community could originate from action by an individual, and that there was a determinable relationship between a right to a fortune and its usage. To some extent, familiarity with the national debt and share investments had eased anxieties, but it is also noticeable that concern was diverted to the use or misuse of wealth rather than to the manner of its accumulation. In imaginative literature, the traditional bogies of usury and financial swindling were made subordinate to outrage over the way in which particular individuals employed new wealth. The individual or institutional means whereby investments were made or loans for new expenditure raised were hardly discussed at all.

The gathering speed of domestic demand and industrial output did not preclude short-term or individual failure. Himalayan peaks and troughs mark the bankruptcy records of the period.[63] Opportunities for new credit arrangements and greater financial risk-taking in business and estate management explain much about why such anxiety over economic instability developed so rapidly in the late eighteenth century. Expansion in the manufacturing sector was certainly dependent upon short-term circulating capital. Tradesmen's tokens and paper-chases of negotiable transaction-bills proliferated during the second half of the century. Given the recurrence of local and national liquidity crises, the increasing availability of credit also served to swell the number of defaulters, and certainly altered the perceptions of risk-taking according to local conditions and the nature of personal credit arrangements.[64] Many periodicals, including the *London Magazine*, listed bankrupts together with births, marriages, deaths, and military promotions.

At the time, however, economic catastrophe seemed arbitrary and difficult to explain. Recurrent default stimulated a search for the reasons for failure, which, facing a mechanism largely mysterious beyond personal transactions, focused upon personal expenditure and literal conspicuous consumption. This, with new opportunities for greater risk-taking or survival on credit, emphasized personal failure as likely to bring the whole edifice of credit and confidence crashing down. Interest centered, therefore, upon the moral virtues – integrity, honesty, economy, even charity – as essentials to a structural stability mortgaged upon the discouragement of failure in others. Censure focused on the alleged financial irresponsibility of a neighbor. The temperature of the debate was further raised by assessing the legitimacy of risk by measure of conspicuous expenditure rather than of the largely unknowable investment interests of established businesses or property owners.

Even a glance at the popular magazines of the period will find the dangers of personal ruination repeated in dozens of pieces addressed to men of small fortune. Writers insisted at increasing length and with increasing examples that the extravagance of unthinking individuals could bring about not only their own ruin but that of the whole nation. Once again, the magazines deviated from contemporary intellectual approaches to the question of luxury and the national good, where Smith, for example, was arguing that private ruin did not lead to public catastrophe. In most magazine pieces the starting point for an explanation of national crisis or decline was a consideration of the state not of the national debt, but of the health of private – and identifiable – finances. Concern over the national debt was represented in popular literature as the unsophisticated and general need for economy. Much of the language – though not the examples – was derived from traditionalist tracts deploring the state of the national debt.[65] Attacks continued against the non-dispersal of fortunes and excessive thirst for riches, but by the end of the 1780s a far greater number of popular publications criticized the extravagant dissolution of wealth. Anxiety over the personal misuse of riches had further increased after the 1778 financial crisis, and attacks on misspent wealth and *nouveau-riche* extravagance were strengthened by renewed anxieties over gaming and wagering. In 1757 Brown had called gambling "the last wretched Effort of bungling and despairing Luxury."[66] In the following two decades public attention was held by a succession of gambling *causes célèbres*. The paramount concern was economic wastage, rather than the specific vices which ensured it. Speculation in stocks was credited with the deaths of good men impetuously trying to revive their fortunes. By the same token, sympathy was expressed for genuine misfortune befalling those engaged in trade. This fear of ruination from the irresponsible extravagance of a few newly rich, was featured in dozens of articles and letters. As *The London Magazine* announced in an early contribution:

> when the tables of the shopkeeper, the mechanick and artificer, are replenished with cates and dainties unbecoming their rank: their rooms furnished in a sumptuous manner, and themselves and their families appear cloathed in costly garments, much exceeding their stations in life, then it is that luxury and extravagance not only prejudices them, but detriments others of the same degree, by the frequent bankrupting, insolvencies, and shutting up of shop doors it occasions.[67]

Nearly forty years later *The Town and Country Magazine* was still warning:

> So that let a man be ever so well able to afford either magnificence or profusion in his way of living, the duty he owes the public obliges him to live within his

fortune, that he may not give encouragement to general waste, and become a means of introducing universal poverty and misery.[68]

Ultimately, it was claimed, free spending blighted the stability of the nation itself. Populist journals such as *The Town and Country Magazine* had denounced gaming as a spur to general and ruinous luxury.[69] Their conclusions were echoed by an array of essays. Cumberland believed that gaming had been integral to the fall of Rome.[70] *The Lady's Magazine* of 1780 devoted a long essay to the national effects of a legion of female gamblers. Gaming led women to sacrifice their virginity, their beauty, and their husbands' estates: "And what a race of warriors, patriots, and Britons is *poor Britain* to expect will be brought into the world from the wombs of such dissolute mothers?"[71] Where fears were expressed over luxury among the poor, it was not so much because of the increased income to the lower orders, but more because of their emulation of the bad example of the rich. Most magazine contributors agreed that if the benefits of peace and prosperity were to be available to all Englishmen, a harmony of interests between citizens had to be maintained by moderation in personal accumulation and by conduct appropriate to the responsibilities of wealth. Certainly not an egalitarian concern, it was the potential unbalancing of order which fired the debate over forces accused of destabilizing commercially based national prosperity. Many were concerned with the ease with which the poor might become uneasy and contribute, in Brown's words, to "Murmurs, Sedition, and Tumults."[72]

The illustration of socially specific personal extravagance has left an indelible mark in the history of the period. The conventional historical wisdom has been, in the words of Mingay, that by the second half of the eighteenth century, "the most likely cause of a family's downfall was now not a change of government, penal confiscation or burdensome taxation, but extravagance."[73] Habakkuk suggested that, in the eighteenth century, gambling and foreign travel were much more important claims on income and capital than earlier, less expensive obligations to hospitality and "port."[74] Despite this, the Stones' rebuttal to an "open elite" debunks, along the way, the idea that the wealthiest families collapsed because of extravagance.[75] Although we learn little about lesser estate-owners and the "parish gentry," no clear example can be found amongst the county grandees of any bankruptcy from building, gambling, or lavish living. The Stones, of course, are concerned only with one section of landed society, and land was also protected from loss by a variety of rules insulating it from commercial debts. Nevertheless, if the historical record of extravagance has to be tempered, then it makes the contemporary image all the more important. For here, surely, in popular, fashionable literature is a key source for persistent accounts of conspicuous consumption and familial decline which have partnered descriptions of the upward mobility of businessmen in the traditional view of a socially fluid, money-into-land England.

The representation of luxury and property was important in another sense. Recent studies have given new attention to the cultural constituents of class formation in this period. Leonore Davidoff and Catherine Hall's comparison of different regions of late eighteenth- and early nineteenth-century England has offered a new analysis of the ways in which "middle-class farmers, manufacturers, merchants, and professionals . . . critical of many aspects of aristocratic privilege and power, sought to translate their increasing economic weight into a moral and cultural authority. Their claim to moral superiority was at the heart of their challenge to an *earlier* aristocratic hegemony."[76] Such middle-class predominance, however, has been questioned by more high-profile accounts of the continuance of an *ancien régime*, and by charges against neo-Whiggish, economically reductive interpretations of Hanoverian Britain.[77] These two approaches cannot both be entirely right. One crucial element in the explication of an "elite hegemony" has been the interpretation of contemporary publications. Here, study of the debates pursued under the question of "luxury" undermines belief in the endurance of aristocratic domination of social conduct and organization. References to aristocratic standards and norms did not exclude middle-class self-justification. It is not difficult to argue (and has never been so) that political power within society remained with the aristocracy and the great landowners. It is undeniable that they controlled the political machine, that they were at the apex of a highly deferential society, that in many ways the development of "modern" class-consciousness in eighteenth-century Britain has been overstated. But this is far from saying that the aristocracy was the only, or even the most, dynamic force in society. If anything is clear from an examination of the relationship between property, propriety, and luxury, as perceived by an innovative popular press, it is that spokesmen and spokeswomen for a commercial society were self-confidently manipulating traditional language and images to justify new economic and social priorities. The aim of the satire and stern lectures in so many different periodicals was to reform the individual and legitimize new conduct by illustrating the minutiae of social manners and by exposing violations of continually updated notions of good taste. Luxury was both narrowed to questions of consumption and widened by the infusion of real debate. The definition of propriety became a defence for writers and booksellers eager to prove their responsibilities toward the public. A detailed illustration of vulgarity eased consciences over the double standards adopted in the discussion of fashion and the continuing consumer boom, while at the same time actually promoting another "fashion" – that of appreciating the current totems of respectability.

Notes

1   David Hume, "Of luxury," *Political Discourses* (London: 1742), p. 23.
2   *The London Magazine* (hereafter, *LM*) 23 (August 1754): 409.
3   *LM* 25 (January 1756): 15–17 (15).
4   John Trusler, *Luxury No Political Evil* (London: 1780), p. 1.
5   Ibid., pp. 4, 14, 37.
6   Rev. J. Fawel, *Observations on a Pamphlet entitled "Luxury No Political Evil"* (Wigan: 1785), p. 40.
7   "Essay on the state of the nation," *Town and Country Magazine* (hereafter, *T&C*) 10 (January 1778): 24–6 (24).
8   To the editor, "On luxury," *T&C* 13 (October 1781): 537.
9   Hume, "Of luxury," 40.
10   A. W. Coats, "The relief of poverty: attitudes to labour and economic change in England, 1660–1782," *International Review of Social History* 21 (1976): 98–115 (103).
11   I shall retain the eighteenth-century term "booksellers" for those publishing books as well as selling them.
12   *LM* 23 (August 1754): 409.

13   He cites *Humphry Clinker* (1771) as "the last major English literary work to be informed by the older sense of luxury"; John Sekora, *Luxury: The Concept in Western Thought, Eden to Smollett* (Baltimore, MD and London: Johns Hopkins University Press, 1977), p. x.

14   *LM* 27 (May 1758): 223–4 (223).

15   James Raven, "The Noble brothers and popular publishing, 1737–1789," *The Library*, 6th series, 12, 4 (December 1990): 293–345.

16   *The Tryal of the Lady Allurea Luxury* (London: 1757), pp. 6, 8, 13, 17.

17   Ibid., pp. 40, 52, 66.

18   Of several magazine examples, *T&C* 12 (February 1780): 63–5.

19   *T&C* 13 (June 1781): 318.

20   *T&C* 13 (February 1781): 67–8.

21   *T&C* 14 (January 1782): 31.

22   *T&C* 19 (September 1787): 394–6.

23   For example, "Letter to the Observer," *T&C* 10 (January 1778): 28.

24   An overview is given in Sir John Habakkuk, "The rise and fall of English landed families, 1600–1800," Part 1, *Transactions of the Royal Historical Society* (hereafter *TRHS*) 5th series, 29 (1979): 187–207; with Part 2, *TRHS*, 5th series, 30 (1980): 199–221; and Part 3, *TRHS*, 5th series, 31 (1981) : 195–217.

25   J. V. Beckett, "English landownership in the later seventeenth and eighteenth centuries: the debate and the problems," *Economic History Review* (hereafter *EcHR*), 2nd series, 30, 4 (November 1977): 567–81 (579–80); Christopher Clay, "Marriage, inheritance, and the rise of large estates in England, 1660–1815," *EcHR*, 2nd series, 21, 3 (December 1968): 503–18 (515–16).

26   Lawrence Stone and Jeanne C. Fawtier Stone, *An Open Elite? England, 1540–1880* (Oxford: Clarendon Press, 1984). It is also not yet established that the Stones' conclusions hold for the thirty-eight English counties outside their study.

27   *Sophie in London, 1786*, ed. Clare Williams (London: Jonathan Cape 1931), pp. 296–7.

28   Lloyd Bonfield, "Marriage settlements and the 'rise of great estates': The demographic aspect," *EcHR*, 2nd series, 32, 4 (November 1979): 483–93. Further comment is offered by Eileen Spring, "The family, strict settlement, and the historians," *Canadian Journal of History* 18 (1983): 379–98, and Susan Staves, *Married Woman's Separate Property in England, 1660–1833* (Cambridge, MA: Harvard University Press, 1990).

29   H. J. Habakkuk, "England," in A. Goodwin (ed.), *European Nobility in the Eighteenth Century* (London: Adam & Charles Black, 1953), pp. 1–21 (p. 2); Sir Lewis Namier, *England in the Age of the American Revolution* (London: Macmillan; New York: St Martin's Press, 1961), pp. 18–26.

30   *The Topographer, for the Year 1789* (London: 1789), p. iii.

31   William Halfpenny, alias Michael Hoare (*fl.* 1752), resided in Surrey. His first book of designs was published as early as 1722.

32   The effect of home demand upon eighteenth-century economic growth is a controversy beyond the scope of this study. For the most skeptical view, see K. Berrill, "International trade and the rate of economic growth," *EcHR*, 2nd series, 12 (1960): 351–9, and J. Mokyr, "Demand vs. supply in the Industrial Revolution," *Journal of Economic History* 37 (1977): 981–1008; and by contrast, Harold Perkin, *The Origins of Modern English Society, 1780–1880* (London: Routledge & Kegan Paul, 1969), pp. 91–6.

33   Neil McKendrick, John Brewer, and J. H. Plumb, *The Birth of a Consumer Society* (London: Europa, 1982); Louise Lippincott, *Selling Art in Georgian London: The Rise of Arthur Pond* (New Haven, CT and London: Yale University Press, 1983); Lorna Weatherill, *Consumer Behaviour and Material Culture in Britain, 1660–1760* (London and New York: Methuen, 1988).

34   Laura Brown, "Reading race and gender: Jonathan Swift," *Eighteenth-Century Studies* 23 (1990): 425–43 (428).

35   The importance of developmental, stage-led, and classical decline-and-fall notions of history to the crisis-thinking concerning trade and industry is surveyed in Ronald L. Meek, *Social Science and the Ignoble Savage* (Cambridge, UK: Cambridge University Press, 1976).

36   "On London being over-built," *T&C* 9 (July 1777): 378–9 (379).

37   Introduced in Essay 12 of *The Mirror* (1780), and continued in *The Lounger* and elsewhere throughout the decade. Both periodicals were first published in Edinburgh, but soon reprinted in London.

38   John Trusler, *The Way to be Rich and Respectable* (London: 1784; 4th edn), pp. 8–9.

39   The key texts are discussed in A. W. Coats, "Changing attitudes to labour in the mid-eighteenth century," *EcHR*, 2nd series, 11, 1 (1958): 35–51.

40   Of many statements, Thomas Mortimer [1730–1810], *The Elements of Commerce, Politics and Finances* (London: 1772); Francis Moore, *Considerations on the Exorbitant Price of Provisions* (London: 1773), and Smith's proposition in *The Wealth of Nations* that no society could prosper and be happy if a majority of its members were impoverished.

41   N[athan] Bailey, *An Universal Etymological English Dictionary* (London: 1721).

42   Thomas Dyche and William Pardon, *A New General English Dictionary: Peculiarly calculated for the Use and Improvement of Such as are unacquainted with the learned languages* (London: 1735). Cf. letter from George Selwyn to George Williams, 1763, in John Heneage Jesse, *George Selwyn and his Contemporaries*, 4 vols (London: 1843–4), Vol. 1, p. 264.

43   *A Dialogue on Taste* (London: 1757; 2nd edn), p. 4.

44   McKendrick *et al.*, *Birth of a Consumer Society*, p. 113; Roy Porter, *English Society in the Eighteenth Century* (Harmondsworth, Mx: Penguin, 1982), pp. 321–6.

45   Charles A. Knight, "Bibliography and the shape of the literary periodical in the early eighteenth century," *The Library*, 6th series, 8, 3 (September 1986): 232–48.

46   J. E. Morpurgo (ed.), *The Autobiography of Leigh Hunt* (London: Cresset Press, 1949), p. 139.

47   John Trusler, *Distinction Between Words esteemed Synonymous in the English Language Pointed Out, and the Proper Choice of them Determined: Useful to all who would either write or speak with Propriety and Elegance* (London: 1783; 2nd edn), p. 3. The contrast was not included in the 1st edn of 1766.

48   Since at least William Fulwood's letter-writer, *The Enimie of Idlenese* (1568), and Angel Day's *English Secretarie* (1586), considered in Louis B. Wright, *Middle-Class Culture in Elizabethan England* (Chapel Hill, NC: University of North Carolina Press, 1935), Ch. 5, and Katherine Gee Hornbeak, "The complete letter writer in English, 1568–1800," *Smith College Studies in Modern Languages*, 15, 3–4 (Northampton, MA: April–July 1934).

49   Olivia Smith, *The Politics of Language* (Oxford: Clarendon Press, 1984), p. vii. Cf. also Cary Macintosh, *Common and Courtly Language: The Stylistics of Social Class in Eighteenth-Century English Literature* (Philadephia, PA: University of Pennsylvania Press, 1986).

50   The most concise listing of these, with their editions, is found in R. C. Alston, *A Bibliography of the English Language from the Invention of Printing to the Year 1800* (Ilkley, Yorks.: Janus Press, 1974).

51   *The Complete Letter-Writer: or, New and Polite English Secretary* (London: 1755).

52   Alexander Bicknell, *The Grammatical Wreath; or, A Complete System of English Grammar* (London: 1790).

53   Based on Abbé Gabriel Girard, *Synonymes françois, leurs différentes significations, et le choix qu'il en faut faire pour parler avec justesse* (Geneva: 1753; 10th edn).

54   Trusler, *Distinction Between Words*, Preface.

55   As, for example, *The General Magazine* (hereafter, *GM*) 2 (1778), frontispiece, "Minerva protecting innocence against the allurements of vice."

56   *GM* 1, 6 (June 1787).

57   *The Hive: A Hebdomadel Selection of Literary Tracts* (London: 1789), "To the public."

58   Richard Cumberland, *The Observer: Being a Collection of Moral, Literary, and Familiar Essays*, 5 vols (London: 1791 [1785]; 4th edn), Vol. 1, p. 5.

59   *T&C* 7 (July 1775): 361–5 (361).

60   [Albinia Gwynn], *The Rencontre: or, Transition of a Moment*, 2 vols (reprtd Dublin: 1785; 2nd edn), Vol. 1, p. 16.

61   *The Mirror* 12 (March 6, 1779): 48.

62   Oliver Goldsmith, "Of the pride and luxury of the middling class of people," *The Bee* (1759).

63   T. S. Ashton noted that a high level of bankruptcies over a period of years was the mark of

an expanding economy; see his *An Economic History of England: The Eighteenth Century* (London: Methuen, 1955), p. 125.

64 B. L. Anderson, "Provincial aspects of the financial revolution of the eighteenth century," *Business History* 11, 1 (January 1969): 11–22.

65 This typically pointed out that a national debt which did not exist in 1688 "has intirely been since incurred": *An Address to the Landed, Trading and Funded Interests of England on the Present State of Public Affairs* (London: 1786), p. 8.

66 John Brown, *An Estimate of the Manners and Principles of the Times* (London: 1758), p. 39.

67 "Civis," *LM* 23 (1754): 410.

68 *T&C* 22 (February 1790): 64.

69 Of various examples, "Essay on gaming," *T&C* 2 (Supplement for 1770): 685–6; "Strictures on modern luxury," *T&C* 8 (July 1776): 377; "On the present rage for gaming," *T&C* 13 (June 1781): 305; "Essay on gaming," *T&C* 14 (March 1782): 124–5.

70 "On gaming," in Cumberland, *Observer*, Vol. 1, pp. 286–95 (pp. 290–1).

71 "On the practice of gaming among ladies of quality," *The Lady's Magazine* 11 (February 1780): 65–6 (66).

72 Brown, *Estimate*, p. 196.

73 G. E. Mingay, *English Landed Society in the Eighteenth Century* (London: Routledge & Kegan Paul; Toronto: University of Toronto Press, 1963), pp. 47–8.

74 Habakkuk, "English landed families," Part 1, pp. 198–9.

75 Stone and Stone, *An Open Elite?*, especially Ch. 5.

76 Leonore Davidoff and Catherine Hall, *Family Fortunes: Men and Women of the English Middle Class, 1780–1850* (London: Hutchinson, 1987), p. 30 (emphasis added).

77 J. C. D. Clark, *English Society 1688–1832: Ideology, Social Structure and Political Practice during the Ancien Régime* (Cambridge, UK: Cambridge University Press, 1985), but for a strong counter-argument, Joanna Innes, "Jonathan Clark, social history and England's 'ancien régime,'" *Past and Present* 115 (May 1987): 165–200.

Part V
Literary property

16
(Re)Writing Lear
Literary property and Dramatic Authorship

Laura J. Rosenthal

Nahum Tate's 1681 *King Lear* has become infamous in literary history as the version of Shakespeare's play in which Cordelia and Edgar marry, and Lear himself survives to give the bride away. Few now prefer Tate's play to Shakespeare's: "In Tate's alteration," Hazleton Spencer wrote, "the principle of poetic justice receives the most pitiable sacrifice in all the English drama."[1] Yet this version actually replaced Shakespeare's on stage until David Garrick's version replaced Tate's. While a few arguments about the stifling power of neoclassical principles have been offered to explain this phenomenon, critics have overall tended to share a belief in a massive aesthetic and philosophical blind spot that lasted from Tate to the middle of the nineteenth century when theaters restored the Shakespearean text in its entirety. This argument is circular, though: if we begin by positing Shakespeare as the poet for all time, then any age or culture that prefers an altered text appears populated by aesthetic deviants. The assumption of Shakespeare's eternality has buried Tate's unique contribution to the canonization of *King Lear*, as well as the historically changing relationship between literary property and dramatic authorship.

Tate's play has remained in the shadow of Shakespeare's in literary history. We call it an "adaptation." Yet Tate and his contemporaries who rewrote Shakespeare called their plays "alterations"[2] or "imitations"; the first use of the word "adaptation" as meaning the revision of a play that readers for the *Oxford English Dictionary* happened to encounter occurs in 1790.[3] Calling Tate's play an adaptation elides significant differences between Restoration revisions of Shakespeare and more recent ones. Further, Shakespeare's play itself rewrote a previous text, a play called *The True Chronicle History of King Leir and His Three Daughters*. And the anonymous author of the *King Leir* did not invent the story either, for it appears in numerous Renaissance histories, romances, and poems. Some of these retellings claim a final historical truth to the story, but the multiplicity of the story's versions makes locating a single origin impossible. Still, we always remember Tate's play as an adaptation of Shakespeare. What, finally, is the difference between Shakespeare's use of *King Leir* and Tate's use of *King Lear*? Why has one been received as an adaptation, and the other as an authentic play?

One important distinction lies in the differing conceptions of literary property inscribed in each version of this story, and the specific conceptions of literary property at the time each was written. In the world of modern authorship, a writer can own a story or a text. Perhaps academic writers understand this better than anyone else. We define the collection of texts we study with metaphors from real estate: everyone has a field or an area, and constantly risks crossing territorial boundaries. Plagiarism has become a grave violation. And while no simple linear narrative can explain the various and complex forms of dramatic authorship from Shakespeare to Tate, each wrote his *Lear* under different legal and material conditions and left different kinds of texts. Shakespeare's play was, Gerald Bentley reminds us, written for performance, not publication;[4] Shakespeare left no carefully arranged printed version with a dedication and an explanation of how he altered *Leir*. In fact, he left two substantially different versions of this play, neither authorized as the final product.[5] For Shakespeare, the story of Lear had no particular owner or specific textual origin. Yet when Tate wrote his *King Lear*, he faced Shakespeare's formidable folio, only the second (after Ben Jonson's) such collection of drama compositions. Perhaps the authority of print, which, as Julie Stone Peters has demonstrated, became a powerful force in dramatic writing during the late seventeenth century, accounts for part of the Restoration's admiration of these two dramatists.[6] Tate represents his own play specifically as a revision of Shakespeare's, and any version since Tate's necessarily responds to Shakespeare.

The first English law that located the origin of literary property in composition was the 1709 Copyright Act, and throughout the eighteenth century courts wrangled over whether to interpret this ownership as perpetual or temporary.[7] Mark Rose has argued that eighteenth-century debates over perpetual copyright produced "a twin birth, the simultaneous emergence in the discourse of the law of the proprietary author and the literary work," and that "the distinguishing characteristic of the modern author . . . is that he is a proprietor, that he is conceived as the originator and therefore the owner of a special kind of commodity, the 'work'."[8] Before the eighteenth century, authors did not generally hold the copyrights to their own texts; literary careers and literary texts changed significantly when they both entered a marketplace. Copyright law, however, cannot in itself entirely explain different forms of authorship, for it does not address the issue of how exactly a writer defines the borders between his or her own text and the text of another. If modern authors have become proprietors, then they own whatever they can copyright. But if Pope can own the copyright for his *Iliad*, what cultural and authorial position does Homer now inhabit? Does he become an owner in any sense as well? In the eighteenth century, it seems to me that authorship changed just as much for the dead as it did for the living. What characterizes modern authorship is not just the living author's position as proprietor, but the tension between legal ownership, which carries with it the taint of workmanship,[9] and the cultural authority of a status that depends upon the myth of rising above the marketplace. Writing in an emerging print culture (though one prior to the Copyright Act), Tate represented his use of Shakespeare's play as an ethical relationship between two authors. Tate not only rewrote the story of Lear in terms of his own culture, but he rewrote Shakespeare's authorship in new terms as well.

Restoration and eighteenth-century British writing has long been characterized as having a particularly uncomfortable and even obsessive relationship with the past.[10] Poets imitated Horace and Juvenal; critics insisted that drama conform to classical standards; epics and the heroic were mocked, but rarely attempted. Plagiarism became a common accusation as writers struggled more than ever to define what belonged to whom.[11] A writer's ability to own, to sell, and even to retain a continuing financial stake in his or her work clearly generated new forms of authorship and different kinds of careers. Yet the reception of Shakespeare in the Restoration and the eighteenth century demonstrates another repercussion of literary property and print culture – one we might call an "enclosure" of the text. While the origin of the King Lear story seems to have had little significance for Shakespeare, it gained a tremendous significance for Tate. No text can claim absolute originality, and dramatic texts in particular have long depended upon the reworking of earlier material and collaboration. Shakespeare and Tate each use already written texts to compose their own, yet they differ in their concern for attribution.

From a legal standpoint, the King Lear story's status as property has not changed. When Shakespeare sat down to write his version, nothing in the law could stop him from telling this old story one more time, nor could anything stop him from borrowing elements of the anonymous King Leir. Nor can the law prevent anyone now from writing this story again: the story of King Lear, as well as the texts of King Leir and Shakespeare's King Lear, has entered the public domain. Yet, from a broadly cultural instead of a strictly legal perspective, to write this story again would be an entirely different task. Writing King Lear has necessarily become an engagement with Shakespeare; "Shakespeare" – the figure created by literary history as opposed to the actual man – has become the irreducible point of the story's origin.[12] Perhaps it might be objected that no historical problem actually exists here, and that Shakespeare was simply the "strong poet" who told this story so well that all subsequent writers fall under his shadow. But if this were true, no one would have bothered to alter it in the Restoration; further, it would have been perfectly obvious all along which plays Shakespeare wrote, which has been far from the case. So while legal access to the story of Lear has not changed, the sense of its authorship has.

When Shakespeare revised *The True Chronicle of King Leir* into his own *King Lear*, the law had not yet located the origin of literary property in composition. Unlike Tate, Shakespeare probably gave little consideration to any personal advantages from selling *King Lear* to a publisher, although as a sharer in the King's Men he would have enjoyed a portion of the company's profits from any such sale. As an attached playwright, Shakespeare would have turned the rights to the play over to his company.[13] Anxious over being associated with low-status professionals, amateur playwrights "often arranged (unlike the majority of the regular professionals) to secure a fairly prompt publication of their plays" and "shrilly declared their nonprofessional status" in dedications and prefaces.[14] Attached professionals, however, usually made scant claims to their plays once they turned them over to their companies. Some did sell their plays to printers, but usually *after* their association with the company for which the play was written had ended.[15] Performance remained the playwright's primary concern.

Early print legislation was designed (successfully or not) to give the government some measure of control of publication and not to protect the property rights of writers or holders of copyrights. Printers in the Renaissance gained the right to copy only by registering texts at the Stationers' Company, and rarely do early censorship laws single out the writer for culpability. The writer, in fact, could not even hold a copyright under the law, for only members of the Stationers' Company had that right.[16] "Texts, books, and discourses really began to have authors," according to Foucault, "to the extent that authors became subject to punishment."[17] But as David Saunders and Ian Hunter insist, "liability for obscenity attaches not to the activity of *writing* but to that of *publication*" (original emphases).[18] Early printed books often bear the stamp "*cum privilegio*," signifying the printer's right to publish but not the *exclusive* right – it simply meant that the monarch's regulators had approved of the book. For theaters, the promptbook became a crucial piece of property because it was their single licensed copy that proved the company's ownership of the play and its permission to perform it.[19] Later regulations insisted upon an author's legal responsibility for potentially offensive printed books, but in the absence of an author's name the responsibility reverted to the publisher. By Elizabeth's reign, the stamp of approval becomes "*ad imprimendum solum*," and some records begin to indicate the punishment of a printer for publishing noncontroversial books.[20] Scholars have speculated that this may represent the emergence of protection from piracy.[21] Still, none of this prevented the numerous publications of plays from memorial reconstruction.

Shakespeare later became the poet through whom nature spoke, but it is not even clear that all his plays were originally received as new works in their own right. Because of the old play *The Troublesome Raigne of John King of England*, Shakespeare's *King John* did not require a separate entrance into the Stationers' Register.[22] The entries of *King Lear* tell an even more interesting story. The title-page for the 1605 *King Leir* lists no author, and describes the play as "The True Chronicle History of King Leir and his three daughters, Gonorill, Ragan, and Cordella." The 1608 version lists M. William Shakespeare as the author of "his true chronicle historie of the life and death of King Lear and his three daughters. With the unfortunate life of Edgar, sonne and heire to the Earle of Gloster, and his sullen and assumed humor of Tom of Bedlam." *Leir*'s title page adds "As it hath been diuers and sundry times enacted," while *Lear* distinguishes itself as the version "As it was plaid before the Kinges Maiestie at Whitehall vpon S. Stephans night in Christmas Holidays/ By his Maiesties Seruants vsually playing at the Globe on the Banckside."[23] The later play's title page clearly insists on its difference from the earlier: it reports that Lear dies, and that this new version includes the added plot of Edgar and Glo[uce]ster. If the consumer cannot distinguish the plays from this information, the title page adds the day and location of its performance, as well as the company. It seems that readers and publishers would not have taken *King Lear*'s status as a new, distinct play for granted and that Shakespeare's name alone was not enough to distinguish it from *Leir*. Scholars have found the entry of Shakespeare's *King Lear* into the register unusually long, and R. Crompton Rhodes even suggests that some sort of legal battle between John Wright, who owned *Leir*, and Nathanael Butter and John Busby, who entered Shakespeare's *Lear*, accounts for the entry's uncommon detail.[24] But whether or not Butter and Busby faced a legal struggle to demonstrate that Shakespeare's *Lear* actually constituted a new play and thus a distinct piece of property, the new title page indicates the necessity to distinguish *Lear* from *Leir* in detail, and perhaps even constitutes an advertisement of the second as a new and improved version of the first.

Shakespeare, though, treats the old *Leir* as if it belongs to the public domain, and neither he nor the early publishers of his plays specifically posit the writer of *Leir* as an authorial origin: Shakespeare's *Lear*, in fact, incorporates and revises a multiplicity of other texts. The *Leir* playwright remained anonymous: both the printer and whoever wrote it do not seem to have considered credit for authorship significant. Yet in some ways, Shakespeare's artistic practice resembles Tate's later alteration of *his* version. By offering two plots about familial and political deception instead of *Leir*'s one and by decentering *Leir*'s interest in female rule by balancing the daughter plot with an equally important drama about sons (which he did not invent either), Shakespeare "improves" on and competes with this earlier play. Yet Shakespeare treats neither the Lear plot nor the Gloucester plot as the individual property of a previous author; he merely retells the stories and incorporates them into his own play without attribution. Shakespeare's *Lear*, then, does not appear to us as an adaptation because our use of that term assumes a kind of literary property that Shakespeare's intertextuality does not recognize. The distinction between adaptations and non-adaptations depends upon a modern (and often artificial) system of attribution to individual authorial responsibility.

Theater companies in Shakespeare's time, however, regularly employed writers to revise old plays in the company's possession. Richard Brome reported that as part of his contract with Salisbury Court, "he hath made divers scenes in old revived plays for them and many prologues and epilogues to such plays of theirs, songs, and one Introduction at their first playing after the ceasing of the plague."[25] Printers often advertised plays as "newly revised," although some of these had not been altered. Most of Fletcher's plays that appeared in print probably had been revised in some way, although the publisher denied it. The third edition of *The Malcontent* bears a title page statement of the same kind of nonsynchronous dual authorship that characterizes many Restoration alterations of Shakespeare: "Augmented by Marston. With the additions played by the King's Majesty's servants. Written by John Webster." But as Bentley concludes, audiences seemed to have preferred novelty: theaters generally charged double for admission to a new play. As one writer put it, "They [the actors] are as crafty with an old play as bawds with old faces: the one puts on a new fresh color, the other a new face and name."[26] While Tate's *King Lear* proclaims a similar double authorship, the playwright's invocation of Shakespeare supports the value of his play as well as confesses a debt.

Private ownership, incidentally, becomes the central issue of the play in Shakespeare's revision. While Lear should have kept the kingdom as one piece of land, he instead attempts to divide it into private portions. In *Leir*, the primary dramatic tension comes from Ragan and Gonorill's jealousy of their more beautiful sister Cordella, and they plot to diminish her in the eyes of their father. But in Shakespeare's version, the division of the kingdom itself divides Cordelia from Lear and provides the central dramatic tension of the play. Lear's blindness, and the tragedy that it brings, originates in his inability to see the danger of dividing the kingdom. And in his madness he insists that all property still originates with him: "They cannot touch me for coining; I am the king himself."[27] He has lost his throne, though, and his own stamp on a coin no longer transforms it into currency. Shakespeare demonstrates

Lear's loss of authority through the loss of the power of his words as well. His rambling proclamations pass judgment on his subjects, but this only proves his madness, for his words no longer carry royal authority. He comes to prefer the company of his fool, who speaks in riddles, and Mad Tom, who speaks apparent nonsense. Gloucester eventually loses all access to texts: in his first experience of literal blindness, he must redundantly point out to Lear that he cannot read, for he has no eyes. Edmund had manipulated him earlier by the usurpation of writing, for he convinced him of Edgar's guilt through a forged note, a text whose authorship he falsifies. Royal authority in this play consists of an ability to control language and to infuse words with an extraordinary, even mystical kind of power. Indeed, Jonathan Goldberg has argued that in the Renaissance, the only "author" was the monarch.[28]

When Tate rewrites this play, however, the division of property becomes a secondary concern to the romance of Edgar and Cordelia. Tate also, however, introduces a different conception of literary property into the process of rewriting. He not only acknowledges the Shakespearean origin of his play, but he makes his revision of Shakespeare a crucial part of his audience's experience. His misogynistic prologue insists that:

> Since by mistakes your best delights are made
> (For ev'n wives can please in masquerade),
> 'Twere worth our while t'have drawn you in this day
> By a new name to our old honest play;
> But he that did this evening's treat prepare
> Bluntly resolved beforehand to declare
> Your entertainment should be most old fare,
> Yet hopes, since in rich Shakespeare's soil it grew,
> 'Twill relish yet with those whose tastes are true.[29]

Clearly it had become important to recognize Shakespeare in particular as the precursor instead of simply offering one more retelling of a very old story. Shakespeare's own process of rewriting, however, becomes invisible: by the late seventeenth century, Shakespeare had become the poet of nature. Tate describes Shakespeare's art as "creating fancy" and the play as a "heap of flowers" and an "unpolished jewel": even without specifically calling Shakespeare the poet of nature, Tate uses metaphors that so describe him. In spite of Shakespeare's own revision of *Leir* and the possibility that audiences may not have even considered Shakespeare's version a new play at all, this particular representation of Shakespeare erases any sense of *Lear* as having any origin other than Shakespeare. Tate represents himself as the refiner and the organizer, and Shakespeare as the spontaneous creator of raw material. Shakespeare, then, not only becomes an origin, but he becomes Tate's *single* origin for this play. And while Shakespeare cannot become the legal owner of *King Lear*, Tate nevertheless represents the play as Shakespeare's property. Tate encloses the story under the name of Shakespeare: instead of retelling the Lear story one more time, he self-consciously appropriates and alters a play that once belonged to Shakespeare.

As much as he represented Shakespeare as the poet of nature, though, Tate showed no interest in authenticity: he claimed, in fact, to improve on Shakespeare's effort. Alterations of Shakespeare, in fact, abound with metaphors of refinement. In her essay on "Pope's refinement," Susan Staves describes neoclassical translators as positioning themselves as "imperialists of language, appropriating for a resource-poor English language great poems for English literature."[30] Most Shakespearean alterations reveal a similar aesthetic ideology, only in this case the new playwright cultivates England's own garden. In the play's dedication, Tate details such acts of refinement: "I found the whole . . . a heap of jewels, unstrung and unpolished, yet so dazzling in their disorder that I soon perceived I had seized a treasure. 'Twas my good fortune to light on one expedient to rectify what was wanting in the regularity and probability of the tale, which was to run through the whole a love betwixt Edgar and Cordelia, that never changed word with each other in the original."[31] Others who altered Shakespearean plays made more dramatic uses of their precursor: before George Granville's *Jew of Venice* (1701), the ghost of Shakespeare appears and delivers the prologue in praise of the adapter's improvements. Before Dryden's *Troilus and Cressida*, Shakespeare's ghost declares: "I found not, but created the first Stage."[32] Dryden not only locates the origin of *Troilus and Cressida* in Shakespeare, but he represents Shakespeare as the single founder of British theater itself. Granville and Tate do not place their versions side by side with Shakespeare's as different ways into the same story; rather, they construct Shakespeare as their single origin, but at the same time *replace* his play with their own. After his own improvements, Tate's preface implies, why would anyone want to perform Shakespeare's old play any more? The betrayal, overthrow, and death of the king may have appealed to the barbaric audiences of the Renaissance, but it will no longer do for this civilized age. And while Tate describes Shakespeare's errors as aesthetic, they were inevitably also political. The king had to survive at the end of the play not because of a sense of moral and political certainty about the monarchy, but because of the lack of it.[33]

So as much as Tate's reception of *King Lear* differs from Shakespeare's reception of *Leir*, it still has little in common with the reception of Shakespeare under the modern construction of authorship. At the same time that Tate represents Shakespeare as the original owner of the story, Shakespeare does not become, as in our own age, the *perpetual* owner of the text. Yet Shakespeare's perpetual ownership under modern authorship is a cultural (and at times even ethical) construction as opposed to a legal issue: while no law prevents a writer from listing Shakespeare's mistakes or from improving on *Lear* and publishing such a play under his or her own name, such an effort would be met with ridicule if not outrage. This is, in fact, precisely the response of many modern critics to Restoration adaptations of Shakespeare.[34] Paradoxically, the decision that placed Shakespeare's plays in the public domain – that denied legal perpetual ownership – helped render the bond between Shakespeare and his works inseparable; while it recognized the unique contents of a book as a commodity, it became a commodity that would soon cease to be owned but always be attributed. Ever since it entered the public domain, *King Lear* has remained enclosed by the boundaries of Shakespeare's authorship. This law, it seems, enforced the distinction between the ancients and the moderns, and strengthened the cultural authority of the ancients by taking their copyrights out of the marketplace.

In the eighteenth century, after the Statute of Anne had passed and when authors increasingly became the proprietors of their writing, the reception of Shakespeare reveals an emerging tension between the attractions of the market for writers and the attempt to create a place of cultural authority above it. This tension itself began to create the demand for an authentic Shakespeare in print and on stage.[35] Authenticity in Shakespeare's printed plays had been an issue since the First Folio: Heminge and Condell remind their readers that while before "you were abus'd with diverse stolne, and surreptitious copies, maimed, and deformed by the frauds and stealths of iniuious imposters," now they, by contrast, offer plays "cur'd, and perfect of their limbes; and all the rest absolute in their numbers, as he conceived them."[36] When Robert Walker printed his cheap Shakespeare editions in the middle of the eighteenth century, Tonson, who held most of the copyrights, attacked his competition in a similar way, claiming that Walker's *Merry Wives* was published "in a very Mangled, Imperfect, and Incorrect manner." Tonson further appealed to consumers to protect the market itself, citing Walker's "vile Practice" as injurious to "the Fair-Trader" and threatening "the apparent Loss, if not Ruin, of the Proprietor of the Copy-Right of the said Plays."[37] But while the desire for Shakespearean authenticity may not have been created anew in the eighteenth century, never before had it drawn such serious attention. This age's editing of Shakespeare became an industry in itself, and a glance at the reception of Shakespeare by the editor Lewis Theobald will begin to show the way that newer conceptions of literary property transformed Shakespeare's authorship.[38]

Theobald distinguished his editions of Shakespeare by seeking a text closest to what he believed Shakespeare really wrote. Theobald advertised his 1740 version as "a real Restoration of the genuine Reading" and declared his "Hopes of restoring to the Publick their greatest Poet in his Original Purity . . . a Labour, that is the first Assay of the kind on any modern Author whatsoever."[39] He contrasts his project to Bentley's edition of Milton, which followed the usual practice of correcting the author's assumed errors. Theobald instead wishes "to restore corrupted Passages . . . the numerous Faults and Blemishes, purely [Shakespeare's] own, are left as they were found." Theobald represents his own edition as pioneering in its strict adherence to authenticity; this editorial principle represents the beginning of the modern practice, even if it did earn Theobald his prominent place in Pope's *Dunciad*.

The editorial goal of faithfulness to an author's original intentions both raises new possibilities of understanding texts as marketable property and resists such possibilities. First, it establishes a competitive basis on which to promote new editions. And second, unlike Tate's reception of Shakespeare, it treats *King Lear* as Shakespeare's perpetual property that no subsequent poet or editor has the right to change. At the same time, however, editorial authenticity defends itself with claims that appear to transcend the market. For Theobald (and even more so for Garrick), "Shakespeare" becomes an insistently present entity to whom readers owe a moral obligation. Foucault calls this the "author-function," which he defines as a cultural construction that critics endow with a realistic status by positing deep motives, creative powers, and a design that unifies the text.[40] The goal of the editor, director, and critic then becomes an illusionary direct access to this author-function. The conception of writing as property creates a stake in authenticity, and the stake in authenticity creates an interest in Shakespeare "the man" (i.e. the author-function): entrepreneurs throughout the eighteenth century sold slivers of Shakespeare's mulberry tree and fragments of Shakespeare's furniture, and nineteenth-century American bardolators went so far as to campaign to exhume Shakespeare's body.[41] Such artifacts promise the fantasy of an unmediated access to the poet.

In spite of his editorial innovations, however, Theobald did not consistently strive for authenticity. He represented his edition as the authentic Shakespeare, but then he also rewrote *Richard II* and *The Double Falshood; or, The Distrest Lovers*, a play "Written Originally by W. SHAKESPEARE; And now Revised and Adapted to the Stage" in 1728. For Theobald, the printed Shakespeare owed an obligation to authenticity that the performed Shakespeare did not.[42] His *Double Falshood*, though, drew fire not for its revisions, but for Theobald's questionable claim to discovering a new Shakespearean play. His contemporaries accused the editor of writing the play himself, and the contradictions of Theobald's simultaneous passion for authenticity and his alleged forgery did not escape his detractors.[43] One anonymous poem represents *The Double Falshood* as a violation against property by comparing Theobald's dramatic efforts with his former career that brought him into constant contact with questions of property:

> See Theobald leaves the lawyer's gainful train,
> To wrack with poetry his tortured brain;
> Fired or not fired, to write resolves with rage,
> And constant pores o'er Shakespeare's sacred page;
> – Then starting cries, I something will be thought,
> I'll write – then – boldly swear 'twas Shakespeare wrote.
> Strange! he in poetry no forgery fears,
> That knows so well in law he'd lose his ears.[44]

Theobald has violated the new conception of literary property by attaching Shakespeare's name – the sign for the unique author responsible for the text – to another play. On the one hand, this poem accuses Theobald of failing to recognize dramatic poetry as the same kind of property that lawyers process all the time. On the other hand, though, it represents Shakespeare's plays as a special kind of property. The fictional Theobald decides to become famous ("I something will be thought") not by writing as well as Shakespeare and thus producing an equally valuable play, but by claiming to discover a new and authentic Shakespearean text. Part of the value of *The Double Falshood*, then, does not lie in the skill of its composition or the thing itself, but in its possible attribution to Shakespeare. Further, the poem does not represent Theobald as committing forgery to get rich, but it represents him as seeking fame, respect, and rewards somewhere above a marketplace.

Competing editors and commentators, in fact, strove to place their own endeavors above the marketplace and their rivals' endeavors in the midst of it. Theobald's "Hopes of restoring to the Publick their greatest Poet in his Original Purity" represent his project as a public service rather than a commercial venture. Samuel Johnson, however, considered Theobald tainted by a desire for profit:

> Mr. Theobald, if fame be just to his memory, considered learning only as an instrument of gain, and made no further enquiry after his authour's meaning, when once he had notes sufficient to embellish his page with the expected decorations.[45]

So while Theobald represents his own work as a service to the community and the memory of Shakespeare, Johnson accuses him of ignoring such things in favor of profit. For our purposes, though, it matters less who honored Shakespeare more sincerely than it does to notice that Johnson and Theobald both edited (and wrote) for a market, yet constructed Shakespeare's authorship and their own relationship to it as things that transcend a gritty and mechanical bookselling trade. Yet Theobald paid close attention to his own property in "Shakespeare" to the point of covering up the traces of his collaboration with William Warburton. Theobald's edition, as Geoffrey Bullough has shown, benefited from correspondence with Warburton in which the latter sent numerous emendations and references to his friend. While Warburton at first did not object to Theobald's appropriations, the great success of the 1733 edition "soon made the aspiring cleric consider that he had been robbed of public notice, as well as financial profit, that his part in the preface had been insufficiently acknowledged, and that the value of his notes had been underestimated."[46] Theobald represented a collaborative effort as an act of individual editorship.

Even though literary history tends to lump David Garrick with Tate as one of the irreverent improvers of Shakespeare, Garrick actually brought the editor's desire for authenticity to the stage. When he performed *King Lear* in 1756, he emphatically defined himself against Tate. He advertised his version as using a text "with Restorations from Shakespeare." He produced *Macbeth* "the Tragedy Reviv'd as Shakespeare Wrote It" and *Antony and Cleopatra* as "Written by William Shakespeare: Fitted for the Stage by Abridging Only." Garrick apparently sensed a demand for the authentic Shakespeare on stage; altering Shakespeare's text had became a violation of the author. Garrick's performance as Lear became legendary and was, in the opinion of at least one critic, his "supreme achievement."[47] According to the *London Chronicle*, he gave such a moving performance that the women playing the parts of Regan and Goneril dissolved into tears on stage.[48] The same reporter noted that "the play received considerable improvement" by Garrick's innovation of period costumes: part of the contemporary interest in this play originated in Garrick's public negotiations between adaptation and authenticity. While Garrick's extensive revision of Tate's plays appeared in print in 1773, though, the version that he performed in 1756 only restored ten of Shakespeare's lines but cut 193 of Tate's.[49] Further, Garrick never restored Shakespeare's tragic ending or the fool.

In spite of his own rewriting of Shakespeare, though, Garrick claimed to restore Shakespeare to the stage, and he represented his own interest in authenticity as marking a respect for Shakespeare that Restoration playwrights, pandering to common tastes, lacked. This position, then, became an ethical one for Garrick: he attempted to construct his relationship with Shakespeare as a personal rather than a financial commitment. An anonymous poem in *The London Magazine*, spoken to Garrick by "the ghost of Shakespeare," demonstrates the effectiveness of this theater manager's self-representation:

> Garrick, whose voice inforces every thought,
> By whom my sentiments are noblest taught.

* * *

To thee, my great restorer, must belong
The task to vindicate my injur'd song,
To place each character in proper light,
To speak my words and do my meaning right,
To save me from a dire impending fate,
Nor yield me up to Cibber and to Tate:
Retrieve the scenes already snatched away,
Yet, take them back, nor let me fall their prey:
My genuine thoughts when by thy voice exprest,
Shall still be deemed the greatest and the best;
So by each others aid we both shall live,
I, fame to thee, thou, life to me, shalt give.[50]

Garrick could not have put it better himself. In this poem, Shakespeare expresses his gratitude to Garrick for rescuing his plays from the adapters Cibber and Tate. The ghost, in fact, charges Garrick with the ethical task of interpreting the plays to drama- tize the author's intended meaning; further, Garrick must restore the authentic Shakespearean text and rescue Shakespeare's memory from the violence of the pro- ducer's scissors. By placing these commands on the lips of the ghost of Shakespeare, the anonymous poet represents authenticity as a moral imperative to Garrick from Shakespeare himself. The person of Shakespeare (Foucault's author-function) becomes real and present (though ghostly); his appearance takes adaptation and production out of the material world of the marketplace and into the ethereal realm of the timeless.

While the ghost in *The London Magazine* praised Garrick, sometimes Shakespeare's spirit noticed the extent of Garrick's alteration and complained bitterly about it. Arthur Murphy, one of Garrick's contemporary biographers, disapproved so strongly of the playwright's alteration of *Hamlet* that he parodied it in a skit that re-creates the scene of Old Hamlet's ghost asking his son to avenge his murder, only this time Shakespeare becomes the ghost asking Garrick to avenge the murder of his text. During their exchange, Shakespeare's ghost accuses Garrick of ingratitude, specifically because Garrick made a great profit from *Hamlet* but would not retain the authentic text. Not only does this skit provide a sharp contrast to Tate's apparent confidence in his own improvements of the play, but it accuses Garrick of violating an ethical bond with the play's author. Murphy represents this obligation as ideally transcending profit, but accuses Garrick of ignoring this higher obligation in favor of the marketplace. For Murphy, Garrick's financial desires undermine his legitimacy as an author and a Shakespearean; even worse, though, Garrick's profits from this play drag *Shakespeare* into the marketplace – an offense that the bard's ghost will not witness without comment. And when Jesse Foote published this skit in his biography of Murphy, he remained true to its author: "the most important lesson that is to be drawn from this publication of the following Parody," he warned, "is intended to apply to *future violators* of the sacred pages of the immortal bard."[51] Murphy and Foote place Shakespeare above the marketplace, and they become territorial for Shakespeare, whose ghostly return implies a simultaneous interest in and place beyond the material world.

For Murphy, all of Shakespeare's plays had been enclosed: their attribution to Shakespeare and their authenticity took on an ethical dimension. Shakespeare became the "owner" of his plays, but since the real Shakespeare no longer needed to make a profit from his writing, Murphy easily transformed Shakespeare's form of ownership to an immaterial kind (and in his skit, gave him an immaterial body). All this represents Shakespeare's authorship as something that transcended the material world of profit – a construction that seems important to modern canonical authorship. While Shakespeare, being beyond material needs by Murphy's time, could inhabit this position, Garrick's authorship oscillates dangerously between his desire for profit and his moral debt to Shakespeare, between the material marketplace and the Shakespearean sphere that these writers represent as transcending the material. Murphy forgave his friend, though, and insisted that even Garrick himself came to recognize the error of cutting the gravediggers' scene from *Hamlet*; further, he apologized in Garrick's place for the passages from Tate that his friend left in his *King Lear*.[52] As canonical texts, then, Shakespeare's plays become property, but, in an unresolvable contradiction, *immaterial* property that must paradoxically transcend profit. While Shakespeare's ghost remained fairly comfortable in this situation, living authors required more complex strategies – strategies that would form the distinctly modern constructions of authorship.

In a 1752 essay, Murphy literalized the metaphor of literary enclosure by representing the imaginary (immaterial) land of Parnassus, like England itself, as carved into private portions. In this fantasy, each poet owns a piece of property that signifies his writing. The ancients already own most of the land, but "you may take in a open manner, what slips you please to graft upon your own stock, and you may transplant at pleasure, without any injury to the first possessor, provided it be seen that you remove to a proper soil, and have skill to encourage the growth."[53] Writing, then, does not consist of strictly original production, but of claiming the already written as well. This borrowing, however, has strict limits: "he who attempts to conceal where he first *found*, is considered as a mere *poacher*, who wants to vend what he had gained surreptitiously from his neighbors." In this literary landscape, most discourse is always already owned and the moderns must, for the most part, lease from the ancients. "The great Shakespeare," however,

> sat upon a cliff, looking abroad through all creation. His possessions were very near as extensive as *Homer's*, but, in some places, had not received sufficient culture.

For Tate in the Restoration, Shakespeare *was* a garden in want of weeding. But in this new episteme of authorship and literary property, an immaterial Shakespeare *owns* the luxuriant but overgrown immaterial grounds.

In spite of the scholarly tradition of transforming Shakespeare into a kind of owner of *King Lear*, though, few modern productions of the play fail to take advantage of Tate's version as well. As Doris Adler has argued, most productions at some point use Tate's ordering of scenes instead of Shakespeare's.[54] Tate's Cordelia, a romantic ingénue, has tended to dominate modern interpretations of Shakespeare's tragic heroine. Unlike a printed book, performance is so fundamentally collaborative that it can only rarely produce the illusion of control by a single individual. While scholars may purge Shakespeare's texts of many alien, non-Shakespearean elements, the collective and collaborative nature of performance tends to resist attempts to create authorial purity.

Adaptation still exists, but with the modern conception of authorship that emerged in Garrick's time it has taken a distinctly different form. Akira Kurosawa's film *Ran* has been received as an adaptation of *King Lear*. *New York Magazine* referred to it as a film "based on *King Lear* and set in sixteenth-century Japan."[55] *Asiaweek* also identified Shakespeare as the film's primary influence and calls it "a parable influenced by Shakespeare's *King Lear*,"[56] privileging the Western over the Eastern context. Yet in an interview, Kurosawa himself confirmed that while *King Lear* had a measure of influence over his film, he had not conceived of *Ran* as an adaptation of Shakespeare or even of Shakespeare's play as his primary influence.[57] But reviews of the film inevitably represent it as an adaptation: in spite of the intentions of the director and the powerful Japanese context, any resemblance to Shakespeare's story now constitutes an adaptation. Shakespeare owns it. The reviewer for *Time Magazine* admired the film so much, in fact, that he tried to extricate it from the taint of adaptation. After summarizing the plot, he comments:

> Yes, of course. *King Lear*. But wait. The great lord is called Hidetora, and he speaks in a tongue Will Shakespeare would not have recognized, inhabits a landscape unknown to the Bard. . . . We are obviously far from the place of this tragic tale's mythic birth and noble retelling, and we are far from the inert reverence of the typical movie adaptation of a classic. Indeed in *Ran* . . . we venture into a territory where the very word adaptation distorts and diminishes both intention and accomplishment. For what Akira Kurosawa has done is to reimagine *Lear*.[58]

For *Time*'s reporter, *Ran* is both an adaptation and better than an adaptation. The reviewer recognizes that to call it an adaptation diminishes it, for in a culture of literary property, originality becomes a primary value in art. And while the reporter struggles to raise *Ran* above an adaptation, he still calls Kurosawa's king a "Lear figure" and describes the sons as versions of Goneril, Regan, and Cordelia. He defines it against adaptation, but at the same time can only write about the film in terms of Shakespeare.

While Tate continues to offend some Shakespeareans, though, few object to *Ran*, or to such adaptations as *Kiss Me Kate* or *West Side Story*. But then, these do not claim to improve or to replace *Lear*. Modern adaptation in general takes the form of placing Shakespeare's story in new circumstances, such as reimagining Romeo and Juliet as teenagers from Brooklyn or Prospero as a commercial artist who escapes from his corrupt firm to a Greek island with his daughter. And while Tate's style of adaptation implicitly argues for Shakespeare as the poet "of an age," modern adaptations like *West Side Story* take a story that Shakespeare wrote but did not invent, transplant it into a culture more familiar to the adapter's own, and thus create the illusion of Shakespeare as the poet for all time.[59]

Notes

I wish to thank Susan Staves and Gary Taylor for their helpful suggestions and references.

1   Hazelton Spencer, *Shakespeare Improved* (New York: Frederick Ungar, 1927), p. 252. For a more recent and more tolerant discussion of Restoration alterations of Shakespearean

drama, see Gary Taylor, *Reinventing Shakespeare: A Cultural History from the Restoration to the Present* (Oxford: Oxford University Press, 1989), Ch. 1.

2   George R. Guffey makes this important distinction in his paper, "Framing *The Tempest*: a Restoration example of deconstructive consumption" (paper delivered at the conference on "Conceptions of Property in the Seventeenth and Eighteenth Centuries," University of California at Los Angeles: January 1990).

3. J. A. Simpson and E. S. C. Weinert (eds), *The Oxford English Dictionary* (Oxford: Clarendon Press, 1989; 2nd edn).

4   Gerald Eades Bentley, *The Profession of Dramatist in Shakespeare's Time, 1590–1642* (Princeton, NJ: Princeton University Press, 1971).

5   See Gary Taylor and Michael Warren (eds), *The Division of the Kingdom: Shakespeare's Two Versions of King Lear* (Oxford: Clarendon Press, 1983); Steven Urkowitz, *Shakespeare's Revision of King Lear* (Princeton, NJ: Princeton University Press, 1980).

6   Julie Stone Peters, *Congreve, the Drama, and the Printed Word* (Stanford, CA: Stanford University Press, 1990), especially Ch. 1. Peters explores Congreve's ambivalence to print, but also his concern for the physical appearance of his publications.

7   4 Anne, c. 19 (1709). As Peters demonstrates in *Congreve, Drama, Printed Word*, the Copyright Act benefited large, careful, and legitimate publishers the most. It also encouraged attention to quality in printing by requiring the printer to submit one good copy of each work to the public libraries (p. 57).

8   Mark Rose, "The author as proprietor: *Donaldson* v. *Becket* and the genealogy of modern authorship," *Representations* 23 (Summer 1988): 5–85 (65, 54). David Saunders and Ian Hunter in "Lessons from the 'literary': how to historicise authorship," *Critical Inquiry* 17, 3 (Spring 1991): 479–505, emphasize the importance of print. See also Linda Zionkowski, "Territorial disputes and the republic of letters: canon formation and the literary profession," *The Eighteenth Century: Theory and Interpretation* 31 (Spring 1990): 3–22; Susan Staves, "Pope's refinement," *The Eighteenth Century: Theory and Interpretation* 29 (Spring 1988): 145–63; Alvin B. Kernan, *Printing Technology, Letters, and Samuel Johnson* (Princeton, NJ: Princeton University Press, 1987); Joseph Loewenstein, "The script in the marketplace," *Representations* 12 (Fall 1985): 101–14; Martha Woodmansee, "The genius and the copyright: economic and legal conditions of the emergence of the 'Author'," *Eighteenth-Century Studies* 17, 4 (Summer 1984): 425–48.

9   See Zionkowski, "Territorial disputes," especially pp. 8–10.

10 W. J. Bate makes this classic argument in *The Burden of the Past and the English Author* (Cambridge, MA: Belknap Press, 1970).

11 In *Plagiarism and Imitation During the English Renaissance* (Cambridge, MA: Harvard University Press, 1935), Harold O. White demonstrates that plagiarism was a relatively unimportant issue in Renaissance writing and literary careers. For an example of the concern for plagiarism in the Restoration, see Gerard Langbaine, *Momus Triumphans* (1687, expanded in 1691). In his *Comparison between Two Stages* (1702), Charles Gildon also has his characters dismiss certain plays as mere plagiarisms.

12 The publication of the Lambs' *Tales from Shakespeare* exemplifies this point. What has made *Shakespeare* the origin of these tales?

13 See Bentley, *Profession of Dramatist*, especially Chs 4 and 6.

14 Ibid., p. 13.

15 Ibid., p. 266. See also Alfred W. Pollard, *Shakespeare's Fight with the Pirates and the Problems of the Transmission of his Text* (Cambridge, UK: Cambridge University Press, 1920). But as Bentley points out in his *Profession of Dramatist*, professionals who were not attached to a company often published their plays after they were performed. Marston, in fact, regularly sold his plays to printers (p. 286). The only plays that Fletcher published during his lifetime were those *not* written for the company to which he was attached; some that failed on stage appeared in print as well, although Bentley speculates that Fletcher probably did not publish these himself (p. 276). The difference between the pre-Commonwealth print culture and the late seventeenth-century one was a matter of degree.

16   See Lyman Ray Patterson, *Copyright in Historical Perspective* (Nashville, TN: Vanderbilt University Press, 1968).

17   Michel Foucault, "What is an author?" in *Textual Strategies*, ed. Josué V. Harari (Ithaca, NY: Cornell University Press, 1979), pp. 141–60 (p. 148).

18   Saunders and Hunter, "Lessons from the 'literary'," p. 487.

19   Gary Taylor, general introduction to Gary Taylor and Stanley W. Wells, *William Shakespeare: A Textual Companion* (Oxford: Clarendon Press, 1987), p. 15.

20   Pollard, *Shakespeare's Fight*, pp. 7–21.

21   Pollard makes this argument in *Shakespeare's Fight*.

22   R. Crompton Rhodes, *Shakespeare's First Folio* (New York: D. Appleton, 1923), p. 17. As A. R. Braunmuller summarizes, most scholars assume different authors for the two plays but disagree over which came first. See his introduction to William Shakespeare, *The Life and Death of King John* (Oxford: Clarendon Press, 1989).

23   Quoted by Rhodes, *Shakespeare's First Folio*, p. 20. Gary Taylor suggests that "the prominence given to Shakespeare's name . . . may reflect the bookseller's desire to distinguish this play from . . . *Leir*." See his general introduction to *William Shakespeare: A Textual Companion*, p. 35.

24   Rhodes, *Shakespeare's First Folio*.

25   Bentley (p. 257) quotes this from Ann Haaker, "The plague, the theater, and the poet," *Renaissance Drama*, new series, 1 (1968): 283–306 (305), and concludes that this statement reflects a regular practice.

26   Bentley, *Profession of Dramatist*, p. 238. See his Ch. 9, "Revision," especially pp. 239–40, 242, 256.

27   Gary Taylor and Stanley W. Wells (eds), *William Shakespeare: The Complete Works* (Oxford: Clarendon Press, 1986), scene xx, l. 83. This line appears in *The Tragedy of Lear: The Quarto Text*. In the Folio, however, Lear declares that they cannot touch him for crying.

28   Jonathan Goldberg, *James I and the Politics of Literature* (Baltimore, MD: Johns Hopkins University Press, 1983).

29   Nahum Tate, *The History of King Lear*, ed. James Black (Lincoln, NB: University of Nebraska Press, 1975), p. 5.

30   Staves, "Pope's refinement," p. 147.

31   Tate, *History of King Lear*, pp. 1–2.

32   H. T. Swedenberg (general ed.), *The Works of John Dryden* (Berkeley, CA: University of California Press, 1984), Vol. 13, p. 249.

33   Michael McKeon makes this argument about poetic justice in *The Origins of the English Novel 1600–1740* (Baltimore, MD: Johns Hopkins University Press, 1987), Ch. 1.

34   See, for example, Spencer's *Shakespeare Improved*. There are, of course, modern adaptations of Shakespeare, but the authorial claims they make are entirely different from the Restoration ones.

35   For an important consideration of this issue, see Stephen Orgel, "The authentic Shakespeare," *Representations* 21 (Winter 1988): 1–26.

36   Quoted by Rhodes, *Shakespeare's First Folio*, p. 7.

37   Quoted by Giles E. Dawson, "The copyright of Shakespeare's dramatic works," in *Studies in Honor of A. H. R. Fairchild*, ed. Charles T. Prouty (Columbia, MO: University of Missouri Press, 1946), pp. 9–35 (p. 30).

38   For a thorough study of Theobald's editing career, see Peter Seary, *Lewis Theobald and the Editing of Shakespeare* (Oxford: Clarendon Press, 1990). See also Thomas R. Lounsbury, *The Text of Shakespeare* (New York: Charles Scribner's Sons, 1906).

39   Lewis Theobald, *Shakespeare Restored (1726)* (New York: Garland Press, 1974), p. 75. For a recent study of Shakespeare editions and the issue of authenticity, see Margreta De Grazia, *Shakespeare Verbatim: The Reproduction of Authenticity and the 1790 Apparatus* (Oxford: Clarendon Press, 1991), which has appeared since this chapter was written. De Grazia calls Malone's 1790 edition of Shakespeare "the first to emphasize the principle of authenticity in treating Shakespeare's works" (p. 2). She makes a powerful case for the 1790 edition's difference from any that came before it; still, I would maintain that negotiations over authenticity

appear well before Malone. But even though Theobald raises authenticity as an issue, it is far from a settled one with him.

40 Foucault, "What is an author?" p. 149. Foucault argues that literary property led to the creation of the author-function. In his terms, I believe that Tate treated Shakespeare as a writer, while Theobald treated Shakespeare as an author.

41 F. E. Halliday, *The Cult of Shakespeare* (London: Duckworth Press, 1957), p. 119.

42 Still, Shakespearean adaptations from the eighteenth century differ from the Restoration ones in that they tend to make far fewer changes in the plot. Radical reconceptualizations such as Tate's gave way to less drastic practices, such as cutting the text for a shorter performance, eliminating characters, and suppressing passages perceived to be obscene or barbaric.

43 While modern scholars have tended to agree with Theobald's accusers, Brean S. Hammond suggests that Theobald may really have possessed a manuscript of Shakespeare and Fletcher's now-lost *Cardenio*, which he adapted as *The Double Falshood*. See "Theobald's *Double Falshood*: an 'agreeable cheat'?" *Notes and Queries* 31 (1984): 2–3. See also G. Harold Metz, "Stage history of *Cardenio–Double Falshood*," *Theatre History Studies* 6 (1986): 87–92, and Nancy A. Mace, "Fielding, Theobald, and *The Tragedy of Tragedies*," *Philological Quarterly* 66 (1987): 457–72, who argues that "the primary object of Fielding's burlesque is Lewis Theobald" (p. 457).

44 Quoted by Walter Graham (ed.), *The Double Falshood* (Cleveland, OH: Western Reserve University Bulletin, 1920), p. 10.

45 Arthur Sherbo (ed.), *Johnson on Shakespeare*, Vols 7 and 8 of *The Works of Samuel Johnson*, 15 vols (New Haven, CT: Yale University Press, 1968), Vol. 7, p. 56.

46 Geoffrey Bullough, "Theobald on Shakespeare's sources," in *Mirror up to Shakespeare: Essays in Honour of G. R. Hibbard*, ed. J. C. Gray (Toronto: University of Toronto Press, 1984), pp. 15–33 (p. 31).

47 Kalman A. Burnim, *David Garrick: Director* (Pittsburgh, PA: University of Pittsburgh Press, 1961), p. 141.

48 *London Chronicle*, May 21, 1770.

49 Harry William Pedicord, "Shakespeare, Tate, and Garrick: new light on alterations of *King Lear*," *Theatre Notebook: A Journal of the History and Technique of the British Theatre* 36 (1982): 14–21.

50 June 1750: 279.

51 Jesse Foote, *The Life of Arthur Murphy, Esq.* (London: 1811), p. 254.

52 Arthur Murphy, *The Life of David Garrick* (London: 1801).

53 *The Works of Arthur Murphy*, 7 vols (London: 1786), Vol. 5, p. 34.

54 Doris Adler, "The half-life of Tate in *King Lear*," *The Kenyon Review*, 3rd series, 7 (1985): 52–6. See also Rose A. Zimbardo, "The King and the fool: *King Lear* as self-deconstructing text," *Criticism: A Quarterly for Literature and the Arts* 32 (1990): 1–29. While Adler argues that modern performances of *King Lear* retain much from Tate, Zimbardo holds that modern readings of *King Lear* treat the play as Tate's "novelistic" version instead of Shakespeare's "emblematic 'pattern'." These essays depart from traditional arguments in their acknowledgment of the importance of Tate in our reception of *Lear*. At the same time, though, each in its own way posits an authentic and unmediated Shakespearean text to which Tate's play denies us access.

55 Wendy Goodman, "The Orient expressed," *New York Magazine* 30 (September 1985): 64.

56 Reprinted in *World Press Review* (September 1985): 56.

57 Bernard Raison, *Le Livre de Ran* (Paris: Seuil, Cahiers du Cinéma, 1985), p. 11.

58 R. Schickel, "Review of *Ran*," *Time Magazine*, December 30, 1985, p. 83.

59 For the transmission of Shakespearean drama from one generation to the next, see Taylor, *Reinventing Shakespeare*.

17
Epistolary property
Michel de Servan and the plight of letters on the eve of the French Revolution

Dena Goodman

La lumière de l'esprit peut changer de climat, mais elle est aussi impérissable que celle du soleil. Il y a deux grandes inventions: la poste qui porte presque en six semaines une découverte de l'équateur au pôle, et l'imprimerie qui la fixe à jamais.

(Diderot to Falconet)

Les pensées d'un homme sont assurément la plus incontestable des propriétés.
(Michel de Servan)

In the 1780s, an *avocat-général* from Grenoble turned his attention to the legal issues surrounding a kind of intellectual property that the general literate public as well as the literary elite were engaged in creating in tremendous volume: that constituted by letters and correspondences. Letters were the basic unit of intellectual exchange in the eighteenth century, both circulating through the postal system and being printed in various forms. Michel de Servan's reflections on the publication, circulation, and interception of letters and correspondences raise complex issues surrounding epistolary property in the changing environment of pre-Revolutionary France. That environment was a social and political world in which, for the first time since the fall of Rome, distinct public and private spheres were being articulated in relation to each other.[1] By tracing the paths of letters and Servan's reflections on them, we can see how questions of property, and of literary property in particular, were raised in the eighteenth century as a function of the new social and political relations defined by the emergence of conflicting public and private spheres.

I Public and private spheres: mapping the *ancien régime*

In recent years, historians of private life and theorists of the public sphere have given us a new understanding of how public and private spheres were differentiated over the course of the seventeenth and eighteenth centuries. The composite narrative that they provide shows a private sphere emerging first from a combination of forces: the rise of the state; increased literacy and printing; and new forms of religion that were more inward than traditional Catholicism.[2] Jürgen Habermas has argued further that the eighteenth century saw the development out of this private sphere of a new, authentic public sphere independent of and in opposition to the state: a new, literate, public sphere whose publicity was defined by the reading public.[3] By the 1780s, the experience of many French men and women was thus defined not simply by public and private spheres, but by overlapping and competing conceptions of them. There was a public sphere of the state whose subjects they were and of which they were the object; at the other end of the spectrum, there was an "intimate" private sphere increasingly identified with the family. Between these two extremes was Habermas's authentic, bourgeois public sphere, which had emerged out of the private sphere and remained private to the extent that it was the sphere of private persons using their reason publicly and critically.

If the intimate private sphere was the realm of the family, the authentic public sphere was the home of the individual. The individual was no romantic loner, however, for, as Philippe Ariès puts it, "the social 'space' liberated by the rise of the state and the decline of communal forms of sociability was occupied by the individual, who established himself – in the state's shadow, as it were – in a variety of settings." In these newly liberated spaces, beginning with the Parisian *hôtel*, institutions of sociability were developed that became the institutions of Habermas's authentic public sphere: salons, reading societies, *lycées*, and *musées*.[4] Habermas's authentic public sphere was made up of private persons gathering together to exchange ideas; private persons communicating their ideas through the public medium of print. Between the immediacy of conversation and the publicity of print, lay the epistolary networks that embodied the ambiguity of a public sphere made up of private persons.

The joining together of private persons into a public in a variety of ways constituted the great transformation of the eighteenth century. It is important to remember, however, that this new public sphere was only one of the spheres of action that defined the experience of men and women of eighteenth-century France. Their difficulty lay in navigating among these various and often conflicting spheres in the course of their daily lives. The vessels in which they traversed these rocky seas were often the letters with which they corresponded with one another.

Michel de Servan may have been the only contemporary Frenchman to reflect on the implications of private writing moving into both public spheres defined by Habermas: into the authentic public sphere of the reading public by means of print; and into the public sphere of the state by means of the post. With Servan as guide, we will be able to consider the ways in which letters and correspondences crossed the ill-defined boundaries between private and public spheres in the eighteenth century and thereby raised fundamental questions about relationships between individuals, and between the individual and the state.

II Michel de Servan: *avocat-général* of the Republic of Letters

Michel de Servan began his professional career as a lawyer, an *avocat-général* in the provincial Parlement of Grenoble. His responsibility there, as one of his biographers puts it, was to act as intermediary between two powers that were constantly at war – the king and the Parlement – for he was at once the representative of the king and an "independent organ of justice that struggled against arbitrary [power] and oppression."[5] Servan made his debut at the bar and in the Republic of Letters in the fall of 1765, at the age of 28. He was asked to give the *discours de rentrée* for the Parlement and chose as his topic: "les avantages de la vraie philosophie considérée dans ses rapports avec les devoirs du magistrat." In this speech he argued that *philosophie* was not only useful to the citizen, but indispensable to any magistrate who cared about justice, because it enabled him to develop a necessary love for humanity.[6]

Asked to give the *discours de rentrée* again the following year, Servan delivered an eloquent speech on the administration of criminal justice; its success was immediate and large. He sent a copy of the speech to the noted encyclopedist Jean le Rond d'Alembert, who called it "full of philosophy and sensitivity." D'Alembert was so impressed that he passed it around among his *philosophe* friends in Paris, including abbé André Morellet, whose translation of Cesare Beccaria's *Dei delitti e delle pene* had appeared earlier that year. Morellet then communicated his own esteem and respect for Servan to Beccaria himself.[7] Voltaire, who was already in correspondence with Servan, asked the young lawyer to send him copies of everything he wrote.[8] Servan complied the following year with a copy of his defense of a Protestant woman whose husband was trying to nullify their marriage by converting to Catholicism so that he could marry someone else. Servan went beyond the narrow terms of the case by raising the broader issue of the precarious situation of France's Protestant population and calling for reform.[9] Voltaire praised the young man for doing what no other lawyer had achieved:

> It seems to me, sir, that you are the first public man who has joined heartfelt eloquence to instructive [eloquence]; this is, it seems to me, what is missing in Chancellor d'Aguesseau; he has never spoken from the heart. He may have defended the laws, but has he ever defended humanity? You have been its protector in a speech that has no model; you make one really feel the degree to which our laws are in need of reform.[10]

Voltaire was not alone in being moved by Servan's eloquence. For once, the Parlement came down on the side of innocence, or, as the biographer Michaud writes, "*l'esprit de corps* gave eloquence its due."[11] Years later, when Jean-François de La Harpe came to write his *Cours de littérature ancienne et moderne*, which was in general a renunciation of his pre-Revolutionary philosophic views and friendships, he still singled out this pleading as "a true masterpiece of judicial eloquence, and of a purity of style that makes real connoisseurs distinguish it, in the end, as a piece worthy of the ancient masters of the art, and [one] that will never be read without admiration and even without some tears."[12] When, soon after this case was heard, Servan was sent to Versailles as part of a deputation of magistrates to present remonstrances to the king, he was offered a post as *maître des requêtes*, which he declined, preferring, according to one biographer, to preserve his honesty by steering clear of the court.[13]

In 1772, however, Servan's bubble burst. In that year he stood by his principles and challenged the public opinion that had catapulted him to fame by defending a nobleman, the comte de Suze, in his attempt to relieve himself of a voluntary obligation toward an actress who was ruining him. The count, now respectably married, was trying to have invalidated notes for cash advances that he had signed over to his mistress to the tune of 50,000 *livres*. Servan threw himself into this case with his customary passion, arguing that one cannot be bound by an immoral obligation. This time, however, he was not only on the losing side, but the object of the public's scorn. Like the most famous *cause célèbre* of the 1770s, the Morangiès Affair, this one pitted a "haughty aristocrat" against a "poor, wronged woman." "The cause of an actress against a noble was thus the cause of the people against the aristocracy, and the suit of the comte de Suze, thus taking on a political color, had to have a very great resonance throughout the country."[14] Before the case even went to trial Servan found himself the object of *libelles* and *placards*. "Pursued by calumnies and by couplets, interrupted several times in [making] his plea, [Servan] learned that his concluding remarks were going to be hissed and, quickly suppressing the last part of his indictment, he announced that both his speech and his public career were over."[15] Voltaire consoled Servan, who was now all of 35.

> You are in the flower of your age and your reputation; your name is precious to anyone who loves equity and humanity. Anywhere you find yourself, you will be on a great stage; you will instruct us on the public law of nations, instead of losing your voice [*vous enrhumer*] in taking up the cases of Dauphinois, in whom the rest of the world is only moderately interested: you will speak to the human race instead of speaking to the councillors of Grenoble. The rays of your glory will shine on Petersburg, instead of a large part of them possibly being lost in the Grésivaudan.[16]

If Servan had come out the villain in the courtroom drama, he needed only to move to a bigger stage and a more cosmopolitan audience to find his talents appreciated. Giving up a career as the man of letters of the bar, he turned his energies to a new one as the advocate of humanity in the Republic of Letters. In the words of his biographer,

> Servan profited nobly from this type of extension of power that his freedom gave him, and, making himself a sort of *avocat-général* of humanity, he dedicated himself at times to avenging innocence imprudently condemned, at times to enlightening the magistrates in order to spare them useless regrets.[17]

Freed from the limitations of the courtroom and the issues raised in it, Servan also expanded the range of his discourse beyond particular cases of guilt and innocence to larger questions of policy that arose in the public sphere. His strength as a lawyer had lain in his ability to generalize from particulars, to draw the larger issues of justice and humanity from the particular case before him, to apply, that is, the universal reason and sensitivity of a man of letters to a legal case and so to generalize its significance. He had taken private matters such as love, marriage, and pregnancy, and made public issues of them. The result was both the raising of questions of private guilt and innocence to those of public justice and injustice, and the infusing of those public questions with the sentimental power of the heart. Now he could turn things around by using his legal mind to analyze public problems directly and to suggest particular solutions to them. Not surprisingly, in 1788–9 he threw his hat into the ring in the pamphlet debates on the Estates General and related constitutional and political issues (he published eight pamphlets in 1789 alone), but he politely declined when offered the opportunity to participate directly as a representative to the Estates General. Throughout the Revolution he continued to participate in the ongoing political dialogue with a stream of pamphlets.

Between 1772, when he made his dramatic departure from the parliamentary stage, and 1789, when the whole of France became a theater to exercise the talents of lawyers and men of letters, Servan turned his attention to a variety of issues. His strong and outspoken support of Mesmerism disappointed the Parisian *philosophes*.[18] Otherwise, he was a steady and respected worker in the Enlightenment Republic of Letters, and in 1781 he was elected to the Academy of Lyon.[19] He expended his energies most often on what Michaud called "brochures of circumstance and academic discourses."[20] True to the age that shaped him, Servan had a tendency to write in response – to events, but more often to the writings of others.

Among those subjects upon which Servan chose to reflect was the legal status of letters. When he took up the question of letters, he did so as a lawyer and man of letters and in response to two publications that had stimulated him to reflect on the social, political, moral, and legal questions raised by their publication, circulation, and interception. While neither of these publications took letters as their central concern, both were of intense interest to the reading public. The first was Rousseau's *Confessions*, the first six books of which were published in 1782, four years after the author's death; the second was *De l'administration des finances*: Jacques Necker's public accounting of royal finances published in 1784, three years after his dismissal from the post of Director-General of Finances by Louis XVI.

Now, what does either of these posthumous public accountings have to do with letters?[21] From the point of view of either author, doubtless nothing at all. Thus, while Servan's essays were truly occasional pieces, taking advantage as they did of the occasion of reading another work for their impetus and justification, the issues he raised in response to them were on his own mind more than anything else. "Réflexions sur la publication des lettres de Rousseau et des lettres en général," was the final section of a pamphlet Servan published in 1783 entitled *Réflexions sur les Confessions de J.-J. Rousseau, sur le caractère et le génie de cet écrivain, sur les causes et l'étendue de son influence, enfin sur quelques principes de ses ouvrages*. Michaud describes this pamphlet as "full of ingenious insights and poor taste."[22] The following year, 1784, Servan published his *Commentaire sur un passage du livre de M. Necker, ou éclaircissements demandés à Messieurs les commis des postes, préposés à décacheter les lettres*. Taken together, the two pieces form an extended and thoughtful reflection on the legal issues surrounding letters at the end of an era that had seen the origin and development of the postal service and of the epistolary genre as the most popular form for publications of all sorts.

Why would the legal issues surrounding the circulation, publication, and interception of letters have been on Servan's mind? Because, I think, this was a logical extension of Servan's talent for and preoccupation with the public implications of private actions. He was not, moreover, alone in being concerned about such implications, as the work of Sarah Maza on other eighteenth-century lawyers demonstrates. It is we, she reminds us, and not they, who tend to impose an overly clear distinction between public and private discourse, public and private matters through our selection of the texts we choose to interpret as political. "Premodern Western societies," she explains, "distinguished not so much between intimate matters and affairs of state as between subjects of general interest and concern and those with 'particular' relevance. In such societies, a personal or intimate matter could easily be understood as a 'public' issue if its general relevance were made clear."[23] I would go even further to argue that, for Servan at least, the public implications of private matters were not incidental but central to his interests as a man of both law and letters. The centrality of this concern, moreover, put Servan in a privileged position as observer of the fundamental transformation of his society since identified by Habermas. The following analysis of Servan's two pamphlets on the subject of letters is meant to put into relief that transformation and the legal and political issues it raised.

III   Violation of epistolary property: the danger of publication

In the eighteenth century, the circulation of letters did not stop with their delivery at the addressee's door. Indeed, this was often only a first stop in a more extended journey that increased the readership of letters far beyond the literal addressee, just as books, journals, and newspapers were generally read by a much wider group than their purchasers.[24] Letters were read aloud in family groups and salons. They were copied, sometimes multiple times, and these copies, in turn, would be read in additional circles of family and friends. Still in manuscript, letters by important people could circulate further by being transcribed into newsletters such as the *Mémoires secrets* and the literary correspondences of Grimm, La Harpe, and others.

Letters also made their way into print in a number of ways. Already in the seventeenth century, editions of both letters and correspondences were a significant literary genre. The popularity of Mme de Sévigné's letters never abated over the course of the eighteenth century but continued to inspire the publication of letters and correspondences by women and men.[25] Letters could find their way into print in other ways, moreover, that were faster and less literary in their aims. Just as they peppered newsletters such as Grimm's, they were scattered throughout printed journals such as the *Mercure de France* and the *Journal Encyclopédique*. Indeed, editors depended upon letters from luminaries such as Voltaire to fill column space and attract subscribers.[26] Letters to the editor, which remain an important feature of newspapers today, were even more important for eighteenth-century journals. They served as an indicator of readership and as a way to commit readers to the journal by drawing them into it as (potential) writers as well as readers, thus engaging them actively in a dialogue over time. Letters and epistolary verse (*epîtres*) sent in by readers in the provinces both gave readers a stake in the journal (made true subscribers of them) and added the dimension of reader-to-reader correspondence that made of the editor and his journal a *bureau de correspondance* or even a *bureau de poste*.[27]

In the newspapers of the eighteenth century, the line between letters and articles was quite blurred. When newspapers called themselves *Courriers* and called their articles *dépêches*, they betrayed their origins as bureaus that received epistolary reports and then circulated them by transforming them into print and sending them out again through the post. The epistolary form of early newspapers in turn supports Alain Pagès's argument that letters are fundamentally transmitters of news, rather than feelings, more akin to the newspapers and journals that developed from them than the memoirs they came to resemble in the eighteenth century.[28] While journals and newspapers depended upon the post for both the receipt of contributions and the circulation of the finished product, they also mimicked the post, serving a mediating role between writers and readers and between readers (turned writers) and other readers modeled upon it.

There was yet another important way in which letters were transformed into print in the eighteenth century: through pamphlets. The letter was the most popular form taken by anonymous pamphlets during the French Revolution: 642 of the known anonymous pamphlets of the Revolutionary era were called "Lettre à . . .," while 209 titles began "Réponse à . . .," adding up to a minimum of 851 letter-pamphlets. Only the word "Adresse" surpassed "Lettre" as a designation of form, at 651.[29] Using a different approach, Bernard Bray has identified 475 published works whose titles indicate they are epistolary, discussed in the pages of Grimm's *Correspondance littéraire* between 1747 and 1793.[30] Pamphlets in other than epistolary form, moreover, could include epistolary material within them. There were, for example, the *mémoires judiciaires* or *factums*, which Sarah Maza has defined as "carefully crafted pamphlets, in-quarto, whose length varied from five to 200 pages, and that appeared in the context of all types of lawsuits."[31] Letters were often used as supporting documents, or *pièces justificatives*, in these judicial memoirs. In 1766, David Hume and the *philosophes* in Paris published a pamphlet made up almost entirely of letters (most of them between Hume and Rousseau) that was a sort of judicial memoir in the case of Jean-Jacques versus *le bon David* being heard in the tribunal of public opinion.[32] Open letters such as Rousseau's *Lettre à d'Alembert sur les spectacles* or Diderot's *Lettre sur les aveugles*, and fictional *mémoires*, such as Diderot's *La Religieuse*, are simply the tip of the iceberg of eighteenth-century epistolary pamphlet literature. As Servan wrote in 1783: "It's all the rage today, it's an epidemic, the publication of letters; there's not even a *factum* that isn't furnished with letters."[33]

The letter, as theorists of the epistolary genre emphasize, is one of the private genres within the range of literary expression.[34] Unlike other members of this family, however, such as private memoirs and journals, the letter is incomplete until it is read by its addressee. The necessity for circulation thus opens up the possibility of interception and misappropriation. Recently, feminist scholars have focused on the publication of letters as yet another way in which they have been misappropriated. They argue that what was identified from the outset as a peculiarly female genre because of its privacy has been repeatedly violated by men who, through publication, make it both literary and public. "Since the sixteenth century," writes Elizabeth Goldsmith,

> when the familiar letter was first thought of as a literary form, male commentators have noted that the epistolary genre seemed particularly suited to the

female voice. . . . But the new admiration for a "natural" feminine style clashed with old arguments about female virtue: to be virtuous was to be modest, self-effacing, above all not talked about, and most certainly not published. To publish a woman's letters, even if the purpose of publication was to praise female epistolary style, was in some way to violate her personal integrity.[35]

While Servan does not identify genre and gender, he does see appropriation and violation as the fate of private letters when they, by necessity, escape the control of both sender and addressee through either publication or interception.

In his essay on the publication of letters, Servan ascribes the interest of readers in published letters to their desire to find in these private writings two sorts of faults: faults of style and faults of conduct. Like a common voyeur, a man of taste will spy upon a superior writer in the hopes of catching him in a state of literary *négligée*, and like the voyeur, he will generally be disappointed: "an author no more abandons his genius [*son esprit*] than a woman her face; the letter is his reflection, as the *négligée* is her toilette."[36]

Servan was himself accused of faults of style even by his own admiring biographer, most probably for using the kind of figure just quoted. The use of such jarring, down-to-earth figures is the most striking characteristic of Servan's style and is no doubt the sort of thing that caused Michaud, too, to accuse him of poor taste. In 1816, Servan became the focus of an attack on eighteenth-century judicial rhetoric as "an abuse of figures."[37] In an analysis of his *mémoire* in defense of the comte de Suze, Gaspard Gilbert Delamalle asked the reader: "Are these the images to display in the temple of austere justice, and before a senate of grave magistrates?" Returning to the same passage pages later, he wrote: "It is not enough to reject that which is low and gross; judgment and taste must preside in the invention of figures in order to avoid affectation and exaggeration."[38]

Servan probably took the Enlightenment *élogiste* Antoine-Léonard Thomas as his rhetorical model.[39] Thomas's "Enlightenment" style elevated true nobility through striking contrasts with the common elements from which it arose, rather than by making comparisons with the noble Caesars of the past. It gave to the rhetoric of public forums such as academy, courtroom, and print the private stylistic and ethical values of salon conversation as they had developed outside of and in opposition to the court. "The secret [of good conversation]," Mlle de Scudéry had written in the seventeenth century, "is always to speak nobly of low things, [and] rather simply of elevated things."[40] Like Delamalle, Servan's early nineteenth-century biographer Portets found both the rhetoric and the doctrine of the encyclopedists distasteful. He was thus unable to see the consistency between Servan's style and his own interpretation of the charge of the Parlements under Louis XV: "to become, by means of the word [*la parole*], the sacred intermediary that united all that was inferior in the state with all that was most elevated."[41] Servan's style was both enlightened and *parlementaire*.

For Servan, the really inexcusable fault was not a lapse of style that might be an embarrassment to the writer, but the embarrassment of the addressee through exposure of his or her faults, which Servan identified as a fault of conduct. "The publication of letters," he writes, "must wound some of those who have received them;

one finds in them, in fact, responses that are very humiliating for those who have made requests."[42] Even if the name of the other party is suppressed, Servan points out, all it takes is for one person to identify him and the whole world knows. Especially in correspondences between celebrities and "obscure men who are tired of being so," you can count on the writer having a confidant, and so, by whatever means, within six months everyone knows the identity of M.*** who, "having written a ridiculous letter to M. Rousseau, received in payment this admirable response that covers him with confusion."[43] In this case Servan does not make the obvious comparison of the nobody scorned by the celebrity and a woman compromised by a man who, for example, publishes his response to a letter of hers. The analogy must be apparent to any reader of *Les Liaisons dangereuses* who recalls Madame de Tourvel's repeated attempts not to receive letters forced upon her by Valmont, or the enormity of Cécile's indiscretion in receiving and responding to those of Danceny. In the *ancien régime*, letters could compromise a woman regardless of their content.[44]

However, it is not the situation of a woman compromised by a man, but that of an obscure person writing to a famous one, and then suffering the humiliation of having the great man's belittling response to him published, that causes Servan to reach the conclusion that a letter is not the property of its author, but is owned jointly by sender and receiver.

> What! it will be said, Rousseau's letters do not belong to him? No, and I believe, barring some mistake, that a letter no more belongs to the person who receives it than to the one who writes it: it is a communal property, and neither of the two can dispose of it without the express permission of the other.[45]

Servan derives the principle of joint epistolary property from consideration of the dangers of publication, which amounts to entering Habermas's authentic public sphere. He compounds the importance of this principle by situating the publication of private letters within the context of the other public sphere, that of the French state. Since the French, he points out, do not govern themselves and have not sought their happiness in a "stormy liberty," they must at least be able to find happiness in "civil peace and the *douceurs* of society." The privacy of letters, he concludes, is obviously essential to this civil peace and quiet and therefore must not be abused.[46]

By focusing on the situation of a correspondence between persons of unequal talent, status, and power, and then placing that correspondence within the larger context of a society whose means of happiness is limited by the constitution of the state, Servan has arrived at an understanding of epistolary property that seems to violate its privacy by making it communal, but still keeps it outside the public sphere. In making his case, however, Servan does not deny that the letter remains the property of its author. That, he asserts, is incontestable, since the author "has written down his thoughts only on the condition that they will remain private, and this condition, by the very nature of the thing, must be inviolable."[47] The ambiguity of Servan's definition of epistolary property reflects that of Habermas's "public/private" sphere: the world of private persons coming together voluntarily that is instantiated in correspondence.

Because it is based upon writing that is necessarily embedded in the multiple spheres of eighteenth-century experience, Servan's theory of literary property goes beyond that of his contemporaries, most notably beyond that expressed by Denis Diderot, who, in his essay *Sur la liberté de la presse*, asserts written expression to be the property of the writer alone.[48] Diderot's interest had been in the relationship between the writer, the publisher, and the state. He was concerned to protect the author's right to sell his intellectual property without interference from either corporations or the state so as to be able to reap its full economic value in a free market. To this end he wrote: "*Laissez faire* the publisher, *laissez faire* the author. . . . Simply guarantee to the first his acquisition and his property, a condition without which the author's production will necessarily lose its just price."[49] Servan's question is entirely different and more complex because it inserts an addressee between the writer and the publisher. Servan questions whether the author is the *sole* proprietor of a letter and therefore has the right to publish it without permission of its addressee. He reasserts the position that the author does not have that right,

> because a letter is generally the interest and private concern [*le secret*] of two persons, because the thoughts of the one are intertwined with those of the other; because, if it is a response, it indicates the question; if it is a question, it can be made to divulge the response.[50]

Servan begins from a theory of literary property whose aim is to protect the rights and property of the author in an age without copyright, but then breaks new ground by assuming all letters to be parts of correspondences and therefore the property of the addressee as well as the author, and thus communal rather than strictly private.

Having established the correspondence rather than the individual letter as the primary unit of property and the subject of public law, Servan can then interpret the correspondence as a social bond between private individuals within the larger public context of the state. The correspondence becomes the mark by which civil society – Habermas's authentic public sphere – is made visible. Because individuals are of unequal power and status, it is the state's obligation to protect the privacy of letters within a correspondence in order to guarantee civil peace.

Servan's model of the state is not Diderot's Lockean *laissez-faire* model, but the French monarchy's own more active one of guarantor of public harmony. Implicitly, Servan is acknowledging the state's own representation of itself as the source of harmony among competing groups in the society of estates and orders. If, as Keith Baker explains, the monopolization of the public sphere in this way by the monarchy led to the frequently invoked notion of *le secret du roi*, then Servan was speaking the monarchy's own language in asking the state to protect *le secret des lettres*, while at the same time asserting and inserting another public sphere constituted by correspondences whose duty it was also the monarchy's to protect.[51] If politics was the king's private domain, then it was his responsibility to protect through public law the privacy of obscure citizens whose own public sphere was constituted out of the private through means of correspondence.

"According to the laws of the public trust [*la bonne foi publique*]," Servan continues,

> a *cachet* is for each individual a no less respectable *sceau* than the sovereign's own *sceau*. The latter has placed his seal on his thoughts so that his subjects may know them as himself; and the individual, by contrast, has placed his on

his [thoughts] so that no one besides himself and his correspondent may know them. These contrary effects derive from the same principle, public order.[52]

It is the publicity of seals that guarantees public order by guaranteeing what Servan calls the "respectability" of the king's thoughts as well as the privacy of the individual citizen's. Because the seal is respected, he says, so is that which it validates. The validation of the king's private thoughts transforms them into public pronouncements, while that of individuals assures that their essential privacy will be respected. The seal, which is public and universally respected, guarantees that the letter, which travels freely across the boundaries between private and public spheres, will be protected in its journey and arrive safely at its destination. It both makes the private thoughts of the king public and protects the privacy of the thoughts of individuals from publicity. Having established the parallel between the public person of the king and the private citizen, however, Servan reasserts his real concern, which is not with the sovereign, but with the sovereignty of the individual in the private sphere:

> Thus every man who with his seal seals his thoughts and his name says to you by this sacred sign: "I put my name and my thoughts in your hands, under the safeguard of the public trust; either burn my letter without reading it, or, if you read it, fulfill the obligation that my seal demands: divulge neither my thoughts nor my name, nor indicate either the one or the other in divulging your response. My letter was for you alone: your response must be for me alone. From the moment that you have placed it in my hands, it is mine more than it is yours."[53]

Servan goes on to explain the ways in which a letter, as part of a correspondence, may reveal the thoughts of its addressee. First, the person to whom one writes may determine the "tone, the cast, and the foundation" of the thoughts expressed in a letter. For example, an otherwise cautious man might adopt a rather light-hearted tone in writing to Voltaire about religion, and then suffer the consequences if Voltaire's reply to him were published. Second, the letter to which one responds can inspire a certain confidence and cause one to express the thoughts of the moment which may not, in fact, be more than that. Finally, because of the exigencies of epistolary commerce – the need often to respond immediately, without even the time to think – the thoughts one expresses in a letter may reflect one's health or psychological state more than firmly held views.[54]

All of Servan's examples suggest the kinship between epistolary writing and conversation. If, as epistolary theorists often argue, correspondence is conversation among those who are not present to each other, Servan is exploring the implications of transforming this oral medium first into writing, and then into print. In conversation, the danger of spontaneity is controlled in three ways: first, by its ephemeral nature; second, by limiting interlocutors; and, third, by the confidence that underlies the friendship between conversation partners. Written correspondence, while still spontaneous and responsive, is no longer ephemeral, and once pen has been put to paper, words and ideas can circulate infinitely through their transformation into print. *Bons mots*, of course, also circulated out of conversational circles, but the confidence upon which those circles were built operated (ideally) to place into circulation only those bits of conversation that would contribute to the reputation of the speaker.

For Servan, the significant difference between conversation and correspondence lies primarily in the different relationships between conversation partners, on the one hand, and correspondents, on the other. Servan's paradigm, remember, is of an obscure man writing to a famous one. This is not intimate correspondence, then, correspondence between friends, but the "private" correspondence of the new, literate, public sphere. If correspondence began as a sign of friendship, as conversation between friends separated by distance, then a false sense of confidence reigns when those who are not friends engage in it. It is the betrayal of this confidence through publication which Servan bemoans and which he looks to the state to restore.

The paradox of letters is that they are produced under the conditions of conversation – spontaneity, responsiveness, confidence – but then become permanent, free-standing objects. Without the letter-writer's knowledge or authorisation, the letter objectifies his or her thoughts, which then escape control and can be used against the writer. Like words (*paroles*), but unlike other written texts or documents, letters are often produced indiscreetly, and the indiscretion is now recorded. They can be used, for example, as damaging evidence in a trial. Lawyer Servan advocates legal reform that would preserve the privacy of letters and bar their use in trials.[55] He goes much further, however, in arguing that because letters are the objectification of private thoughts their legal status is a function of our understanding of intellectual property:

> The thoughts of a man are surely the most incontestable of properties; but before the invention of printing, it was the least solid: a mouse could nibble away in a week thirty years of reflections. Since [the invention of] printing, on the contrary, ideas are the most durable property; not a building on earth is more imperishable than a good work, and the most fertile soil will be buried beneath the sand before a good work is buried in oblivion.[56]

While Servan roots the notion of intellectual property in man's very being, he asserts that for all practical purposes it is a function of printing and a problem of the modern world ushered in by the printing press.

After a digression on the unauthorized publication of manuscripts (which, predictably, he compares to the public exposure of an author's nudity), Servan returns to the question of letters and their status as intellectual property. In so doing he returns again to the differences between correspondence and conversation. While earlier he had stressed implicitly the way in which correspondence resembled conversation, he now focuses on the differences between the two forms of discourse: whereas conversation is an exchange of ideas that implies the alienation of one's intellectual property in exchange for that of another, correspondence does not imply such alienation because writing is only a deposit of ideas on paper. Writing, according to Servan, is a way of defining one's thoughts as property and thus "facilitating their enjoyment." The paper on which they are written is no more than a repository for them. To print what one has written is to "assure the author of the irrevocable property of his thoughts, on the condition of ceding their usage to the public." Conversation, he continues, "is a true commerce of ideas: one gives only in order to receive equal value; and from this principle derive the rules that propriety, politeness, and even pleasure, prescribe for conversation." There are no such rules for correspondence, or written commerce, and thus the threat to intellectual property and to reputation posed by the publication of letters. Once again, it is the breakdown of reciprocity and the confidence which it generates that makes correspondence different from conversation.[57]

The main point Servan wants to make, however, is that as long as one does not alienate one's thoughts in the free, fair, and reciprocal exchange of conversation, they remain one's property, no matter if they are written or printed. Indeed, writing and publication are means of securing the intellectual property in one's ideas, not of alienating it. This is real property, Servan asserts, and often valuable. The potential consequence of such value is, of course, theft. In a note, Servan compares the theft of a man's thoughts to the theft of his purse.[58] If intellectual property is the least alienable and the most valuable kind of property a person can have, then its theft is clearly the most grievous crime. This is exactly the position Servan will take a year later in his pamphlet on the interception of letters by the postal service.

Before turning to Servan's second pamphlet concerning epistolary matters, however, let me summarize his position concerning intellectual property as it relates to the publication of letters and consider the implications of that position. "In a word," Servan concludes,

> it is an essential maxim that any writing, whatever it may be, cannot be imputed as either a fault or a crime except from the moment at which the author himself has communicated it without constraint. Until that point, it is nothing; and, in the words of M. de Voltaire, it is nothing but black applied to white.[59]

This principle, once understood, can now become the basis of the legal reform of abuses involving the violation of epistolary property ranging from the uses of letters in the courtroom to the publication of an author's letters after death, or of any letters at all without the express permission of both partners in the correspondence. Servan built his case from the assertion that letters must be understood as parts of correspondences, and thus of the public sphere of private persons. It is then the monarchy's responsibility to protect the privacy of the correspondence just as it protects members of society and maintains the security of their private lives in a state where they are limited to this private sphere that has association, communication, and publication as its own forms of publicity. The need for the protection of the laws for correspondents arises from the differences between spoken and written language and the possibility and thus necessity of guaranteeing intellectual property with the invention of printing. The law must thus be brought in to protect the intellectual property of private citizens.

In the case of letters, property rights are threatened for three reasons: first, because, as part of an epistolary exchange or correspondence, letters imply each other, so that the publication of one letter can compromise the writer of another; second, because the thoughts expressed in letters are akin to those in conversation, but are not protected by its rules of propriety and politeness; and, finally, because, as joint rather than private property, the privacy of letters cannot be secured except by the state, which alone guarantees the order of society. Indeed, Servan goes on to say, the press is such a powerful force in shaping public opinion, and public opinion such a powerful force in a monarchy, that legislation must control it. While the laws reflect public opinion in a republic, in a monarchy they are an independent authority that may conflict with public opinion. Since, Servan continues, the respect for public opinion is nothing more than deference to the opinion of the majority, it is worthy of respect. When society accepts the authority of public opinion it means that members of that society respect each other and, conversely, mutual respect means a respect for the public. It is thus the role of public law to restrict the abuse by individuals of each other so that this mutual respect will flourish. The law must "give to each man a sort of rampart that the eyes and the discourse of others cannot cross without shame [*pudeur*]."[60]

Is Servan, then, simply an opponent of intellectual freedom and freedom of the press? Is this where his reflections on the publication of letters lead him? Not exactly. And the position he finds himself in at the end is not unlike that of most enlightened opinion in the eighteenth century: in championing the right of privacy, Servan seeks protection from the state in both senses: protection by the state from the invasion of the privacy of individuals; and protection from the invasion by the state of the privacy of those same individuals. The public trust of the monarchy means that it must both respect and guarantee the privacy of its citizens in a state that limits their activity to that sphere. For Servan, this means that "in a monarchy the liberty of the press must be, to the greatest possible extent, broad with regard to things, and narrow with regard to persons."[61] The freedom of writers must be secured, but so must the privacy of individuals. The problem with the publication of letters, and of Rousseau's letters in particular, is that they expose the persons of both correspondents to the judgment of the reading public and thereby threaten both the reputations of individuals and the integrity of public opinion. It is in the public interest, therefore, to guarantee privacy. The creation of a public sphere out of the fabric of the private sphere does not, therefore, eliminate questions of privacy; rather it complicates them. The state is now in a position of having to guarantee both the privacy of individuals and the integrity and autonomy of a new public sphere created in and out of the private.

IV   Violation of *confiance*: the danger of circulation

The question of the state's role in guaranteeing the privacy of correspondence is the major focus of Servan's 1784 response to Necker's *De l'administration des finances*. Now, however, the state is not simply the neutral embodiment of the law that protects the epistolary property of individuals from each other, but also an active threat to the privacy and property of the citizens it has the responsibility of protecting. The object of Servan's attack is not really Necker, but the nefarious institution of the *Cabinet noir*: that room in the bowels of the central post office in Paris described by the historian Eugène Vaillé as "an officially organized service that stops letters, opens them with the requisite dexterity, takes a copy, reconstitutes the original letter, and can declare lost those missives [too] clumsily opened. . . . From [1633] on the *Cabinet noir* exists and is under the orders of the First Minister."[62]

Vaillé dates the origin of the French postal service itself to November 16, 1603: the date on which Henri IV commissioned his controller-general, La Varenne, to enable royal couriers to accept, to transport, and to distribute letters for the public.[63] As an institution of the state and for the public, the postal service was the creation of Henri IV and La Varenne, although it was descended from earlier messenger services, both royal and corporate. By first instituting a system of overland relays that covered the entire territory of the realm, and then taking over the administration of horse rentals, the king managed to restrict and to control freedom of overland movement and to set up the eventual control over the circulation of letters.[64] By 1608, La Varenne had been named Postmaster General by letters patent, and the French had something that fits Vaillé's definition of a postal service: "an organism assuring, according to fixed schedules and itineraries, and in the shortest amount of time, bearing in mind what was then possible, the transport of correspondences in the service not only of the state, but also of individuals, for which service the latter must pay the cost."[65]

The new postal service marked the growing power of the monarchy and its increasing control over the realm, but at the same time it was a service demanded by a growing literate and commercial public.[66] The monarchy and the public would both benefit from the creation of a unified system by means of which written and printed words could circulate with freedom and security. If this new system tightened the monarchy's control over its subjects, it also strengthened the bonds among them, and especially among those who also considered themselves citizens of a growing Republic of Letters.

The tension between state control and public service was at the very heart of the postal system, just as it was at the heart of the state itself. In Habermas's terms, this tension arose because the public defined by the monarchy as the object of its policies was at the same time an autonomous, "authentic" public that came increasingly to assert this autonomy through criticism of the state.[67] Because this tension not only persisted, but intensified as the state and its institutions grew stronger, the public increasingly demanded both better service and less control. In the case of the post, this meant demanding faster and more dependable service, on the one hand, and, on the other, absolute privacy of the letters that passed through the mails and freedom of movement for printed goods – journals in particular. Not surprisingly, too, since the public had to bear the cost directly for this service, they did everything they could to avoid paying, abusing franking privileges and resorting to diplomatic pouches and the pockets of friends whenever possible, especially when communicating across national borders.

The post can thus be seen as the focal point of a growing tension between a monarchy attempting to expand its power and hegemonic control over the state, and a literate public sphere developing at the same time out of the mass of the people. This new public both demanded services from the state and, at the same time, asserted its autonomy in relation to it. Viewed in terms of the post, this meant that the sealed letter was to circulate freely, with maximum speed and dependability, while at the same time, its contents would remain absolutely private and secure. The outside of the letter was public, its interior was private, and the seal was the mark of the confidence with which the public entrusted their private thoughts to the public servants of the state. The *Cabinet noir* was the violation of that confidence.

Before there was a public, Saint-Simon complained about the *Cabinet noir* in the privacy of his memoirs; Madame de Maintenon did so in her letters. With the ascendancy of Cardinal Dubois during the regency of the Duc d'Orléans, the scope of the *Cabinet*'s interests expanded beyond the public world of plots, spies, and diplomacy to the private sphere of intimate relations. "Much more than previously" writes Vaillé,

> an interest began to be taken in the personal affairs of highly placed personages at the court and in the city, in order to know their relations, their behavior, their private lives [*petites histoires*], and interestingly, the vicissitudes, the mysteries, the anguish, the joys, or the scandals of their love affairs. First the Regent, then Louis XV, would develop a taste for these indiscretions.[68]

In the estimation of the nineteenth-century scholar Maurice Tourneux, "Louis XV knew how to make of [the *Cabinet noir*] at the same time an instrument of political information and of scandalous revelations, and to give it an extension that it had never had until then."[69] Between the politics of the monarchy's public sphere and the intimacy of private lives lay, of course, that other public sphere of private persons using their reason together publicly. In traversing the ground from the public sphere of the state to the intimate private sphere, the monarchy found itself violating as well the autonomy of Habermas's authentic public sphere as it came into existence.[70]

If Servan was unique in raising questions of literary property in epistolary terms, he was far from alone in his opposition to the *Cabinet noir*. By the 1780s, the *Cabinet noir* was invoked as frequently as the *lettre de cachet* as a prime example of abuse of monarchical power in the eyes of the public. Vaillé documents the fact that very few issues were the subject of such unanimous complaint in the *cahiers de doléance* prepared by all three estates in 1788 for the meeting of the Estates General the following year.[71] That same year the author of a *Code national dédié aux Etats Généraux* devoted a section of his work to the "inviolable privacy [*secret*] of letters confided to the Post."[72] An anonymous pamphleteer of 1788 or '89 stated categorically that "the respect due to letters confided to the post follows necessarily from individual liberty."[73]

In the spirit of reform that marked his reign but changed little, Louis XVI had abolished the *Cabinet noir* publicly, but it continued to function nevertheless. Imagine, then, Jacques Necker's quandary when, in making his public accounting of the expenses of the royal administration in 1784, he was confronted with the postal service. Anyone so naive as not to know of the existence of the *Cabinet noir* would no doubt be confused by the rather philosophical reflections with which Necker opened his section on the secret expenses of the postal service. "He who harbors the interests of a nation," Necker began,

> he especially who does so after having himself had a hand in the conduct of its affairs, contracts, without question, great obligations. But without underestimating the extent of these obligations, there is another law that I must impose on myself: to present the most useful truths with the discretion and

the respect appropriate to each subject. I do not know if it will be found that I have fulfilled this intention, but I desire it fervently.

After having thus flown to the heights of rhetorical obfuscation, Necker then touched solid ground by pointing out that he had considered ignoring these expenses altogether – as he had three years earlier, in his *Compte rendu au roi*. This omission, however, would have amounted to the only exception to his aim of a complete accounting, and thus "seemed to me a stain on a work in which it had already been dared to treat perhaps equally delicate subjects."[74]

But how was this particular delicate subject to be handled? How was Necker to account for the expenses of a department whose very existence was not only secret, but officially denied? Necker's solution lay in referring to secret expenses without explaining what they were – and then discussing them as if everyone knew what they were. He decided to refer to the *Cabinet noir* as the "secret administration that I will abstain only from explaining or defining."[75]

Having figured out how to discuss the *Cabinet noir* so as to maintain his loyalty both to his king and to the truth, Necker went on to criticize it in no uncertain terms. The too-penetrating gaze of the king caused more problems than it solved in a country such as France, where there was no reason to fear revolution; where people were "more ardent in their feelings than profound in their thoughts"; where people "would have the habit and the need to communicate their most spontaneous feelings, and would often reveal themselves one day what they would no longer be the next." In such a country, if the king rested his gaze upon the "private language" of certain persons, or on "the confidential discourse of their friends and enemies," he was more likely to come to a false judgment than to gain any real information.[76] The interception of letters, Necker concluded, could only be useful in such a country in times of crisis. It is an extraordinary measure that, when employed in the ordinary conduct of affairs, becomes simply a weapon in the hands of malicious people.[77]

Servan's response to Necker supports the ex-minister's position, but takes it even further. The *Commentaire* takes the form of a pleading made up of two main points: that the *Cabinet noir* is good for nothing, on the one hand, and harmful to everything, on the other. This second point is specified with five complaints: the violation of property; the threat to liberty; the corruption of *moeurs*; the weakening of the king's revenues; and the degradation of his majesty through the compromising of his authority.[78] In arguing that the *Cabinet noir* is good for nothing, Servan is careful to distinguish between the legitimate activities of the postal service, which he praises at length, and the illegitimate ones, which he excoriates for roughly the same reasons as Necker had.[79] His originality lies in his discussion of the threat posed by the *Cabinet noir* to property, to liberty, and to morals. It is in this first context that Servan compares the interception of a letter to the prostitution of a young woman.

In contrast to Necker's measured and cautious prose is the vigorous rhetoric of the *avocat-général* of the Republic of Letters. Indeed, Servan's figures in this pamphlet are so graphic that the editor of his posthumous *Oeuvres* excised the best parts. The writer who had compared the reading of a famous author's private correspondence to the voyeur's glimpses of a woman in *négligée* now compares the interception of a letter to prostitution and sexual violation.

> Deign to reflect on it, Sirs, [and] this comparison between the prostitution of a young woman and the violation and the prostitution of a well-sealed letter is not absurd. . . . Because, in the end, to sell a girl is not at all to rob her; sometimes it even enriches her. But to surrender for money the thoughts of a citizen, after having taken them from the letter, like picking his snuff-box from his pocket, this can be called a clearly defined theft, a theft with *effraction* [breaking and entering], Sirs. And what breaking and entering! that of a *cachet*, of a true *sceau*, that much the more sacred for being so fragile; of a *cachet* more inviolable than the lock on a strong-box; because, after all, the lock is protected by the iron of which it is made, while the meltable wax of a *cachet* has nothing to defend it but public opinion.[80]

The image of violation runs through Servan's text and is supported by the repeated use of language that can best be described as intimate. For example, in asserting that one's thoughts constitute private property, he does not identify them with the soul, as Diderot had in *Sur la liberté de la presse*, but with "my purse, my shirt, or my doublet."[81] Building on the conception of epistolary property as being communal rather than strictly private, Servan goes on to argue that the theft of a letter is thus a violation of the property rights not just of two people, but of two friends. "Now," he explains,

> when I have put my thoughts, nicely folded and well sealed in a letter addressed to my intimate friend, if you divest the faithful postman to whom I have entrusted it of his bag, if you rob my letter by unsealing it, in good faith, do you not rob two people at once, my dear friend and me?[82]

The real intensity of Servan's plea can be seen in his treatment of the *cachet*. In his earlier essay he had already compared it with the lock on a strong-box. Indeed, commercial metaphors and images were not uncommon in that work. Now, however, the idea of violation is intensified as the letter is compared to a female body, and the intellectual property it contains to the virginity that comprises the entire value of a young woman. The *cachet* of a letter is no longer simply the equivalent of the royal *sceau*, but of the hymen that guards the girl's virginity. In the language of Servan, the gentlemen of the *Cabinet noir* are potential rapists before whose power the citizenry of France is all but helpless:

> But we, Sirs, what have we to defend ourselves from your eyes and your hands? A yielding bit of wax the thickness of a line, and two sheets of paper that a breath would carry off: voilà our keys, our strong-boxes, our walls; and this fragile deposit is a hundred miles away from us, and it is in your hands! Who could guarantee it from any danger? Only the public trust; and the ministers of the public trust themselves, its very guardians, violate it without shame![83]

Entrusting your thoughts to the post is about as safe as entrusting your daughter to a sex fiend, except that there is no alternative. The plight of the French citizen is like that of poor Suzanne Simonin, Diderot's fictional nun, who is raped first by her mother superior, and then by her confessor. Whom can you trust?[84]

Ultimately, trust, *confiance*, is what is at stake in Servan's discussion of epistolary property. *Confiance* is the characteristic that unites the two sides of the letter: its inside and outside, its private and public faces. Janet Altman has demonstrated the centrality of *confiance* and *confidence* in the epistolary novel, but Servan goes further.[85] For him, *confiance* is always endangered in correspondence in a way that it is not in conversation: first, because the letter is written; but, more importantly, because it becomes a deposit in the public trust when it leaves the hands of the writer and enters the public world of the state postal service. A further threat lurks always in the possibility of publication. While printing makes intellectual property possible, at the same time it threatens what it creates, just as the *confiance* upon which epistolary commerce is based is at the same time threatened by the means that makes correspondence possible: the post.

Confiance publique is an ambiguous term. On the one hand it refers to the "confidence of the public" – the trust that the public places in the state (thus in the state's ability to repay loans); on the other, it refers to the trustworthiness of the state as a public entity, the "public trust." *Confiance publique* is both the public trust and the expression of positive public opinion directed toward the state. In other words, both public spheres – that of the public and that of the state – are implied by the term *confiance publique*. Each time a letter is entrusted to the postal service, it is placed in the public trust, but, because of the existence of the *Cabinet noir*, it must also be defended by public opinion. The security of letters is thus a function of mutually reinforcing public spheres, of a double *confiance*. Necker, himself, had made the link between *opinion publique* and *confiance publique* in his public accountings. As Keith Baker has pointed out, Necker's experience as a banker had taught him both the importance of *la confiance publique* in financial affairs, and the way in which the English had maintained it through public accounting. The *Compte rendu* was his attempt to inspire such confidence in the French public and was criticized by the minister, Vergennes, as an appeal to public opinion. In *De l'administration des finances*, Necker had not only defended the *Compte rendu* as such an appeal, but had argued for the importance of public opinion as a political force.[86]

For Servan, the only answer to the paradoxical threats that inhere in epistolary property is public trust guaranteed by law and public opinion. Because a letter is by definition communal (public/private) rather than narrowly private (intimate), it is a matter of public concern. Because a letter is only actualized when it is received and read by its addressee, it of necessity enters the public sphere of the state, which alone can guarantee its security, even as it threatens it. The duplication of public spheres means that one – the state – must guarantee the integrity of the other, and, through it, the privacy of the individual. Conversely, the individual's letters can only be defended from violations of the public trust by public opinion.

Through an examination of the problems involved in epistolary property, Servan has come to a conception of the state as a public organ that guarantees the privacy of its citizens and their public sphere. At the same time, however, that guarantee itself depends upon the force of public opinion. The complexity of the problem stems from the uneasy coexistence of two public spheres, and the reasoning ends up circular. Freedom of thought is not possible without the protection of the state and its laws, but the state must itself become the subject of public opinion if it is to be trusted.

Not only is the state as the guarantor of public order necessary to guarantee epistolary property, but the liberty of thought which such a guarantee makes possible becomes in turn a bulwark of the state. Not only is "the faith in privacy possibly that which is most appropriate for the conservation of the union of families and [unity] among citizens, [but] its violation is the vice most capable of spreading among them hatred and disorder."[87] Indeed, Servan argues, "in the present state of our civil societies, I dare to maintain that the circulation and privacy of letters are perhaps the sole means of bringing to the attention of kings, of ministers, of bureaucrats [*hommes en place*], of men of letters, the truths of which they have such need."[88]

Servan's case for the security of the post is the same as that made twenty years earlier by the enlightened royal minister Chrétien-Guillaume de Lamoignon de Malesherbes and the *philosophe* abbé Morellet for the freedom of the press. Necker, too, had associated *confiance* with publicity in his *Compte rendu*, reversing the formula by assuring the king he could have *confiance* in his accounting because it was made public.[89] What is novel about Servan's argument is that he associates *confiance* with the security of *private* discourse because those who engage in it constitute the public. Ultimately, any simple distinction between public and private discourse dissolves, and a new relationship emerges: the responsibility of the state is both to guarantee the publicity and to secure the privacy of the public's discourse.[90]

If the state must conceive itself as a public service whose purpose is to guarantee the rights to property and privacy of its citizens in the name of public order and harmony, it can realize this goal only through further guaranteeing the intellectual freedom of its citizens by making the postal system a secure conduit of truth. This intellectual freedom is the principle of the literate public sphere – the sphere of public opinion – whose integrity and autonomy it is now the state's responsibility to protect. Servan sees in the postal service the possibility of a communication more honest and more secure than direct speech, and finds in the *Cabinet noir* a reality that is just the opposite. He calls upon the state to make possible the transparent language that had been a dream of eighteenth-century thinkers from Montesquieu through Rousseau and that would become the political aim of revolutionaries during the Terror.[91] "What would be the soul of an institution," he wonders,

> that would, as it were, give to a king eyes and ears in all parts of his domain; of an institution that would establish between the monarch and his subjects a communication as intimate as that between a father and his children while sparing the monarch the unpleasantness of importunity, and the subjects the troubles of travel and timidity? The soul of such an institution would be good faith; if you suppress this virtue, the post will be nothing more for a king than a simple matter of finance, and for the subjects a means of circulating greed in letters of exchange, or vanity in vain compliments.[92]

Ultimately, the definition of epistolary property and the means necessary to guarantee it cannot be understood except in terms of the new relations being established between the state and the citizenry. Good faith, *confiance*, the public trust – without this essential but intangible soul, neither the state nor its citizens rises above the basest of pursuits. Greed and vanity, prostitution and violation threaten the virtue of both citizens and the state entrusted to protect them. The letter, which unites private citizens with each other into an authentic, literate public sphere, and unites each with the state by means of the postal service, has for its guarantee and protection only a fragile seal, a symbolic measure that, to do its job, requires the further and universal recognition of *la confiance publique*. The meaning, importance, and security of epistolary property are grounded in this new understanding of public trust that marks the beginning of the modern world.

Notes

Research for this paper was conducted with the assistance of a Faculty Research Grant from the University of Alabama at Birmingham and a Mellon Faculty Fellowship at Harvard University. I am particularly grateful for the hospitality and assistance of the librarians of the Musée de la Poste in Paris. I am also grateful to Françoise Douay for her insights into the rhetoric and style of Servan. I would also like to thank those who took the time to read the manuscript and to offer suggestions for its revision: Suzanne Desan, Caroline Ford, Thomas Kaiser, Sarah Maza, and participants at the Clark Library Workshop and at a "Works-in-Progress" Seminar in the History Department of Louisiana State University.

1 Hannah Arendt first made this argument in *The Human Condition: A Study of the Central Dilemmas Facing Modern Man* (Chicago: University of Chicago Press, 1958).
2 Philippe Ariès, "Introduction" to *A History of Private Life*, Vol. 3, *Passions of the Renaissance*, ed. Roger Chartier, ·trans. Arthur Goldhammer (Cambridge, MA: Harvard University Press, 1989), pp. 1–11; Roger Chartier, "Epilogue," in *Passions of the Renaissance*, pp. 609–10; Jürgen Habermas, *The Structural Transformation of the Public Sphere: An Inquiry into a Category of Bourgeois Society*, trans. Thomas Burger with the assistance of Frederick Lawrence (Cambridge, MA: MIT Press, 1989), pp. 11–12. See also Dena Goodman, "Public sphere and private life: toward a synthesis of current historiographical approaches to the Old Regime," *History and Theory* 31 (1992); 1–28.
3 Habermas, *Structural Transformation*, esp. pp. 14–26, but this is the central argument of the book as a whole. See also Ariès, "Introduction," p. 8.
4 Ibid., pp. 7–8; Habermas, *Structural Transformation*, pp. 31–43.
5 Charles Prud'homme, *Michel de Servan (1737–1807): Un Magistrat réformateur* (Paris: La Société du Recueil Général des Lois et des Arrêts, 1905), pp. 7–8.
6 Ibid., p. 15. Not two year later, in January 1767, Antoine-Léonard Thomas made a similar argument in his *discours de réception* at the Académie française on the subject of "L'homme de lettres comme citoyen." See *Discours prononcés dans l'Académie française le jeudi 22 janvier 1767* (Paris: 1767).
7 Jean le Rond d'Alembert to Servan, June 15 [1766], in Antoine-Joseph-Michel de Servan, *Oeuvres choisies*, ed. X. de Portets, 4 vols (Paris: Didot l'Aîné, 1822), Vol. 1, pp. cxxxii–cxxxiii.
8 Voltaire (François-Marie Arouet) to Servan, May 9, 1766, in Voltaire, *Correspondence*, ed. Theodore Besterman, 107 vols (Geneva: Institut et Musée Voltaire, 1953–65), no. D13291.
9 Prud'homme, *Michel de Servan*, p. 21.
10 Voltaire to Servan, February 14, 1767, in Voltaire, *Correspondence*, no. D13955; here and hereafter, the translation is my own.
11 Joseph François Michaud, *Biographie universelle ancienne et moderne*, 45 vols (Paris: Delagrave, 1842–65), Vol. 39, p. 139.
12 Quoted in [Gaspard Gilbert] Delamalle, *Essai d'institutions oratoires à l'usage de ceux qui se destinent au barreau*, 2 vols (Paris: Delaunay, 1816), Vol. 2, p. 92.
13 X. de Portets, "Notice sur la vie et les ouvrages de Michel de Servan," in Servan, *Oeuvres choisies*, Vol. 1, p. xliii.
14 Prud'homme, *Michel de Servan*, pp. 30–1; Portets "Notice," pp. xlix–1. On the Morangiès

Affair and the *causes célèbres* in general, see Sarah Maza, "Le Tribunal de la nation: Les Mémoires judiciaires et l'opinion publique à la fin de l'Ancien Régime," *Annales: économies, sociétés civilisations* (January–February 1987): 73–90.

15   Michaud, *Biographie universelle*, Vol. 39, p. 139; also, Portets, "Notice," p. liii. Prud'homme's account is even more painful: "The audience was stormy. Verses were sent circulating around the hall in which the orator was ridiculed; at night posters were put up that made fun of him. At the fourth audience, Servan was warned that people were prepared to hiss at his conclusions" (*Michel de Servan*, p. 33).

16   Voltaire to Servan, February 9, 1772, in Voltaire, *Correspondence*, no. D17906.

17   Portets, "Notice," p. lv.

18   Ibid., pp. lxvii–lxxi. See also Robert Darnton, *Mesmerism and the End of the Enlightenment in France* (Cambridge, MA: Harvard University Press, 1968).

19   Prud'homme, *Michel de Servan*, p. 37.

20   Michaud, *Biographie universelle*, Vol. 39, p. 140.

21   The age of criticism was an age of public accounting, according to Reinhart Koselleck. See *Critique and Crisis: Enlightenment and the Pathogenesis of Modern Society* (Cambridge, MA: MIT Press, 1988), pp. 9–10. As Servan's pamphlets demonstrate, public accounting was, like criticism itself, an infinite process, rather than a final statement, generating accountings of the accountings by other members and self-proclaimed representatives of the public. No subject was ever closed.

22   Michaud, *Biographie universelle*, Vol. 39, p. 140.

23   Sarah Maza, "Domestic melodrama as political ideology: the case of the Comte de Sanois," *American Historical Review* 94 (December 1989): 1249–64 (1250–1).

24   On reading practices in the eighteenth century, see Roger Chartier, *Lectures et lecteurs dans la France d'Ancien Régime* (Paris: Seuil, 1987); and Roger Chartier, "The practical impact of writing," in Ariès, *Passions of the Renaissance*, pp. 111–59.

25   See Janet Gurkin Altman, "The letter book as a literary institution 1539–1789: toward a cultural history of published correspondences in France," *Yale French Studies* 71 (1986): 17–62.

26   See, for example, Jean-François Marmontel to Voltaire, [around May 25, 1758] in Marmontel, *Correspondance*, ed. John Renwick, 2 vols (Clermont-Ferrand: Université de Clermont-Ferrand, 1974).

27   For a good example of how periodicals drew in subscribers by encouraging their contributions, see Nina Rattner Gelbart, *Feminine and Opposition Journalism in Old Regime France: "Le Journal des Dames"* (Berkeley, CA: University of California Press, 1987), Ch. 1. See also Dena Goodman, "Enlightenment salons: the convergence of female and philosophic ambitions," *Eighteenth-Century Studies* 22 (Spring 1989): 329–50 (340–8).

28   Alain Pagès, "La Communication circulaire," in Jean-Louis Bonnat and Mireille Bossis, *Ecrire. Publier. Lire. Les Correspondances (Problématique et économie d'un "genre littéraire")* (Nantes: Université de Nantes, 1982), pp. 344–53.

29   This tally is based on André Martin and Gérard Walter, *Catalogue de l'histoire de la Révolution Française*, 8 vols (Paris: Imprimerie de la Bibliothèque Nationale, 1955), Vol. 4, *Ecrits de la période révolutionnaire – anonymes*. Here are some comparative figures:

Observation	496
Mémoire	333
Pétition	272
Réflexion	260
Discours	129
Histoire	31
Manifeste	21

30   Bernard Bray, "La *CL* témoin du goût pour la forme épistolaire," in *La Correspondance Littéraire de Grimm et de Meister (1754–1813)*, ed. Bernard Bray, Jochen Schlobach, and Jean Varloot (Paris: Klincksieck, 1976), pp. 213–20 (213–14).

31   Maza, "Le Tribunal de la nation," p. 75. See also Lise Andries, "Récits de survie: les

mémoires d'autodéfense pendant l'an II et l'an III," in *La Carmagnole des muses: L'Homme de lettres et l'artiste dans la Révolution*, ed. Jean-Claude Bonnet (Paris: Armand Colin, 1988), pp. 261–75.

32 *Exposé succinct de la contestation qui s'est élevée entre M. Hume et M. Rousseau avec les pièces justificatives* (Londres [Paris]: 1766). See Dena Goodman, "From private *querelle* to public *procès*: the creation of public opinion in the Hume/Rousseau affair," *Eighteenth-Century Studies* 25 (Winter 1991–2): 171–201.

33 Servan, "Réflexions sur la publication des lettres de Rousseau, et des lettres en général," *Oeuvres choisies*, Vol. 2, p. 407. On the relationship between legal and literary writing, and on those who engaged in both, see Sarah Maza, *Private Lives and Public Affairs: The Causes Célèbres of Prerevolutionary France* (Berkeley, CA: University of California Press, 1993).

34 The question of whether or not letters, since they are private writing, can be considered a literary genre at all has been hotly disputed. The debate centers around the literary status of the letters of Madame de Sévigné. "On the one hand," explains Elizabeth C. Goldsmith, "it is argued that her art derives only from her lived experience, and that she was unconcerned with literary conventions and had no pretentions to the status of an author. Other readers reply that even private letters, particularly in the seventeenth century, are written with a public in mind." Elizabeth C. Goldsmith, *Exclusive Conversations: The Art of Interaction in Seventeenth-Century France* (Philadelphia, PA: University of Pennsylvania Press, 1988), p. 114. The main combatants in this fray are Roger Duchêne, "Réalité vécue et réussite littéraire," *Revue de l'Histoire Littéraire de la France* 71 (1971): 177–94; and Bernard Bray, "L'Epistolier et son public en France au 17e siècle," *Travaux de Linguistique et de Littérature* 2 (1973): 7–17. Goldsmith notes more recent contributions to the debate as well.

35 Elizabeth C. Goldsmith, "Introduction" to *Writing the Female Voice: Essays on Epistolary Literature*, ed. Elizabeth C. Goldsmith (Boston, MA: Northeastern University Press, 1989), p. vii. See also other essays in this volume, especially those by Katherine A. Jensen and Elizabeth C. Goldsmith; and Altman, "The letter book as a literary institution."

36 Servan, *Oeuvres choisies*, Vol. 2, p. 408.

37 Delamalle, *Essais d'institutions oratoires*, Vol. 2, p. 122.

38 Ibid., pp. 163 and 171. Prud'homme notes that "Servan's style was the object of numerous polemics," following the publication of Delamalle's *Essais*. See *Michel de Servan*, pp. 63–4, note 4.

39 "At this time, the emphatic tone of the encyclopedic sect was supported by the authority of Thomas, who had made this genre fashionable," writes Portets in his "Notice," p. xxi.

40 Quoted in Daniel Gordon, "The idea of sociability in pre-revolutionary France" (PhD dissertation, University of Chicago: 1990), p. 181.

41 Portets, "Notice," p. xi.

42 Servan, *Oeuvres choisies*, Vol. 2, p. 408.

43 Ibid., pp. 408–9.

44 See Françoise Meltzer, "Laclos' purloined letter," *Critical Inquiry* 8 (Spring 1982): 515–29. For a consideration of this phenomenon in the English context, see Ruth Perry, *Women, Letters, and the Novel* (New York: AMS Press, 1980).

45 Servan, *Oeuvres choisies*, Vol. 2, p. 409.

46 Ibid. By the 1780s, "stormy" was the common modifier used to describe English politics, as Keith Michael Baker demonstrates in "Public opinion as political invention," in *Inventing the French Revolution: Essays on French Political Culture in the Eighteenth Century* (Cambridge, UK: Cambridge University Press, 1990), pp. 178–85.

47 Servan, *Oeuvres choisies*, Vol. 2, p. 409.

48 "In fact, what goods can belong to a man, if not a work of the mind, the fruit of his education alone, of his studies, of his late-night vigils, of his time, of his research, of his observations; [if not the fruit of] the happiest hours, the most beautiful moments of his life; if his own thoughts, the feelings of his heart; the most precious part of himself, that which does not perish, that which immortalizes him does not belong to him. What comparison can there be between man, the very substance of man, his soul, and the field, the meadow, the tree or the vine offered by nature equally to all and that the individual appropriates

only through cultivation, the first legitimate means of possession. Who is more within his rights than the author to dispose of what is his by gift or by sale[?]" Denis Diderot, *Sur la liberté de la presse*, ed. Jacques Proust (Paris: Editions Sociales, 1964), pp. 41–2. Note that Diderot assumes a Lockean notion of property. He also follows the line of argument of one of his own *libraires*, David, who wrote in the *Encyclopédie*: "If there is in fact anywhere on earth a free *état*, it must be that of men of letters; if there is in nature an effect of which the possessor's property cannot be disputed, it must be the productions of the mind." See "Droit de copie," in *Encyclopédie, ou Dictionnaire raisonné des sciences, des arts et des métiers*, ed. Denis Diderot and Jean le Rond d'Alembert, 35 vols (Paris, 1751–65), Vol. 5, p. 146.

49   Diderot, *Sur la liberté de la presse*, p. 50.
50   Servan, *Oeuvres choisies*, Vol. 2, p. 410.
51   Baker, "Public opinion as political invention," pp. 169–70.
52   Servan, *Oeuvres choisies*, Vol. 2, p. 410.
53   Ibid., pp. 410–11.
54   Ibid., p. 412.
55   Ibid., pp. 412–14. Servan had himself used letters in making his case for the comte de Suze in 1772.
56   Ibid., p. 415.
57   Ibid., p. 421. Servan's conception of conversation as reciprocal exchange regulated by rules of polite conduct is consistent with theories of polite conversation developed in France and England over the course of the seventeenth and eighteenth centuries. See Goldsmith, *Exclusive Conversations*; Gordon, "The idea of sociability," Ch. 3; Lawrence Klein, "The third Earl of Shaftesbury and the progress of politeness," *Eighteenth-Century Studies* 18 (1984–5): 186–214; and Lawrence Klein, "Berkeley, Shaftesbury, and the meaning of politeness," *Studies in Eighteenth-Century Culture* 16 (1986): 57–68.
58   Servan, *Oeuvres choisies*, Vol. 2, p. 422, note 1.
59   Ibid., p. 424.
60   Ibid., pp. 430–2.
61   Ibid., p. 434.
62   Eugène Vaillé, *Le Cabinet noir* (Paris: Presses Universitaires de France, 1950), pp. 52–3.
63   Eugène Vaillé, *Histoire des Postes françaises jusqu' à la Révolution* (Paris: Presses Universitaires de France, 1946), pp. 45–6.
64   Ibid., p. 41.
65   Ibid., p. 45.
66   One important manifestation of the post's role as intermediary between royal control and private enterprise lay in the circulation of gazettes. R. Moulinas has shown how the publisher of the *Courrier* headquartered in Avignon negotiated with the French Intendant des Postes in 1740 an agreement that was favorable to both parties. By using the royal post as a circulation and distribution network, the publisher was able to secure attractive and uniform subscription rates; at the same time, the monarchy could control the content of the *Courrier*, since it now had a monopoly on distribution which it could suspend at any time. The result was wide distribution of a gazette whose editor practiced self-censorship and achieved commercial success with subscription rates that undercut competitors. See "Du Rôle de la poste royale comme moyen de contrôle financier sur la diffusion des gazettes en France au XVIIIe siècle," in *Modèles et moyens de la réflexion politique au XVIIIe siècle*, 3 vols (Villeneuve-d'Ascq: Université de Lille III, 1977–9), Vol. 1, pp. 383–95. See also Jeremy D. Popkin, *News and Politics in the Age of Revolution: Jean Luzac's "Gazette de Leyde"* (Ithaca, NY: Cornell University Press, 1989), pp. 114–16.
67   Habermas, *Structural Transformation*, p. 68; see also Koselleck, *Critique and Crisis*, pp. 98–123. I should add that I do not agree with Koselleck's assessment of the move from autonomy to political criticism as hypocrisy.
68   Vaillé, *Cabinet noir*, pp. 127–8.
69   Maurice Tourneux, "Une Epave du Cabinet noir de Louis XV," *Revue de l'Histoire Littéraire de la France* 4 (1897): 35–60 (35).
70   This same ground was traversed in the opposite direction by the *libelles*. "The scandalous

tales that make up *Les Fastes de Louis XV*," Sarah Maza writes of one of the most popular of these clandestine pamphlets (published in 1782), "add up to a description of what might variously be termed the feminization, eroticization, or privatization of the public sphere under Louis XV": Sarah Maza, "The diamond necklace affair revisited (1785–1786): the case of the missing queen," in *Eroticism and the Body Politic*, ed. Lynn Hunt (Baltimore, MD: Johns Hopkins University Press, 1990), pp. 63–89 (p. 68).

71 Vaillé, *Cabinet noir*, pp. 201–7.

72 [Bosquillon], *Code national dédié aux Etats Généraux* (Geneva: 1788), pp. 209–12.

73 *Principes généraux de la constitution françoise. Ouvrage utile à tous les Députés qui forment l'Assemblée des Etats Généraux* (n.p.: n.d.), p. 15.

74 Jacques Necker, *De l'Administration des finances*, 2 vols (Paris: 1784), Vol. 2, pp. 213–14.

75 Ibid., p. 214.

76 Ibid., p. 215.

77 Ibid., p. 217.

78 Servan, *Commentaire*, pp. 16–17. The version of this text published in the *Oeuvres choisies* is quite different. Where cited passages exist in both versions I will cite both texts. In this case, I refer only to the original pamphlet because the later editor has reorganized the text to such an extent that it no longer follows the structure laid out here.

79 Ibid., pp. 67–72; and Servan, *Oeuvres choisies*, Vol. 2, pp. 462–5, note 1.

80 Servan, *Commentaire*, pp. 20–1.

81 Ibid., p. 17. Portets omits the shirt and the doublet. See note 48, above, for the quotation from Diderot.

82 Ibid., pp. 17–18.

83 Ibid., pp. 21–2. This passage loses much of its power in Portets's version, since he omits the analogy to the prostitution of a young woman that precedes it, substituting instead the example of domestic theft. See Servan, *Oeuvres choisies*, Vol. 2, pp. 476–8. Claude-Adrien Helvétius had raised the issue of public trust in relation to the post in *De l'homme* (1776): "How can one persuade the adolescent to be faithful, to be trustworthy in society, and to respect the privacy of others, when even in England the government, under even the most frivolous pretext, opens the letters of individuals and betrays the public trust." Quoted in Vaillé, *Cabinet noir*, p. 186.

84 As recent scholarship has shown, the female body was a major *topos* of pre-Revolutionary and Revolutionary pamphlet literature. See Dorinda Outram, *The Body and the French Revolution: Sex, Class and Political Culture* (New Haven, CT: Yale University Press, 1989); and Lynn Hunt, "The many bodies of Marie Antoinette: political pornography and the problem of the feminine in the French Revolution," in *Eroticism and the Body Politic*, ed. Hunt, pp. 108–30.

85 Janet Gurkin Altman, *Epistolarity: Approaches to a Form* (Columbus, OH: Ohio State University Press, 1982), Ch. 2.

86 Baker, "Public opinion as political invention," pp. 191–2. Habermas points to the *Compte rendu* as the means by which Necker opened a breach in the secrecy of the absolutist public sphere, creating for the first time a space for "a public sphere in the political realm," that is, a fully public sphere. See *Structural Transformation*, p. 69.

In "Public credit: John Law's scheme and the question of confiance", *Proceedings of the Annual Meeting of the Western Society for French History* 16 (1989): 72–81, Thomas E. Kaiser traces the problem of *confiance* in the eighteenth century to a problem with *crédit*, and sees the solution in an appeal to public opinion.

87 Servan, *Commentaire*, p. 36; and Servan, *Oeuvres choisies*, Vol. 2, p. 492.

88 Servan, *Commentaire*, p. 70; and *Oeuvres choisies*, Vol. 2, p. 465, note 1.

89 Chrétien-Guillaume de Lamoignon de Malesherbes, *Mémoires sur la librairie et sur la liberté de la presse* (1759); André Morellet, *Réflexions sur les avantages de la liberté d'écrire et d'imprimer sur les matières de l'administration* (written 1764; published 1775); Necker, "Compte rendu au roi," in *Oeuvres complètes*, 15 vols, ed. Auguste Louis de Staël-Holstein (Paris: Treuttel & Wurz, 1820), Vol. 2, p. 16. See Daniel Gordon, " 'Public opinion' and the civilizing process in France: the example of Morellet," and Jeremy Popkin, "Pamphlet journalism at the end

of the old regime," both in *Eighteenth-Century Studies* 22 (Spring 1989): 302–28 (312–17) and 351–67 (356); and Baker, "Public opinion as political invention," pp. 191–2.

90 Habermas identifies the inviolability of letters as one of the basic rights that guaranteed the functions of private people in written constitutions, such as the French. See *Structural Transformation*, p. 83. In "'Public opinion' and the civilizing process," Daniel Gordon calls attention to the way in which Morellet grounds liberty of the press on the freedom of conversation, thus also linking public and private discourse.

91 See, for example, Jean Starobinski, "Introduction" to *Montesquieu par lui-même* (Paris: Seuil, 1953); and Jean Starobinski, *Jean-Jacques Rousseau: Transparency and Obstruction*, trans. Arthur Goldhammer (Chicago: University of Chicago Press, 1988). On the revolutionaries see Lynn Hunt, *Politics, Culture. and Class in the French Revolution* (Berkeley, CA: University of California Press, 1984), pp. 44–6 and 72–4; and Hunt, "The many bodies of Marie Antoinette," p. 112.

92 Servan, *Commentaire*, pp. 71–2.

18

The bank, the press, and the "return of Nature"

On currency, credit, and literary property in the 1690s

J. S. Peters

> As paper in Holland passes for money, pamphlets with us pass for religion and policy. A bit of paper in Holland, from a man of credit, takes up goods here, pays debts there; so a pamphlet will take up fools here, make fools there.
>
> (Crowne, *City Politiques*)

Seven years after the 1688 revolution, in 1694–5, the Bank of England was founded, the Licensing Act that had controlled printing was permitted to lapse, and, in the winter, Thomas Betterton led a group of actors in revolt. "Complaining" of the "Oppression" of Christopher Rich, manager and principal beneficiary of the United Company's theatrical monopoly (Downes, p. 91), the actors succeeded in procuring a license from the king (who was likely to be sympathetic to those in revolt against tyranny) and set up a new company in the theater they rebuilt in Lincoln's Inn Fields. For the company's first production, Congreve's *Love for Love*, an "unknown Hand" sent a prologue:

> A long *Egyptian* Bondage we endur'd,
> Till Freedom, by your Justice we procur'd . . .
> Freedom's of *English* growth, I think, alone;
> What for lost *English* Freedom can attone?
> A Free-born Player loaths to be compell'd;
> Our Rulers Tyraniz'd, and We Rebell'd.
>
> (Congreve, p. 211)[1]

Like the nation seven years earlier, which had been (as Locke put it) "on the very brink of Slavery and Ruine" (*Two Treatises*, p. 137), the actors were rebelling against the tyranny of rulers in the name of freedom. We are born into that *"perfect freedom"* (which Locke had posited as the "State all Men are naturally in" [p. 269; II.4]) with the right to own property, even if, in conditions of abundance, property need not be accumulated. Our freedom, in fact, is predicated on our freedom to own and not to be owned.

Congreve's own prologue also invokes Lockean terms in his paean to the revolt:

As Nature gave the World to Man's first Age,
So from your Bounty, we receive this Stage;
The Freedom Man was born to, you've restor'd,
And to our World, such Plenty you afford,
It seems like *Eden*, fruitful of its own accord.

(Congreve, p. 213)

The rebellion is rooted in the freedom that stems from the state of nature established at the site of human origin, the freedom established in the pure and unsullied Edenic world. The actors' "First-fruit Offering" is "a Virgin Play." Here, there is no labor because nature is "fruitful of its own accord," and so (as Locke would have it) no accumulation of property. Revolt restores to the actors their prelapsarian state, before the advent of money, before the fall of language, before the alienation of the natural inheritance of freedom.

In *Love for Love*, Sir Sampson is determined to disinherit his prodigal son Valentine, whom he accuses of being a "Wit," a "Beau," of having "a Rogues face . . . a hanging look . . . a damn'd *Tyburn* face, without the benefit o' the Clergy" (p. 243; II.i.304–7). For Sir Sampson, the authority of the parent is like the authority of the absolutist monarch or of the master:

> Why Sirrah, mayn't I do what I please? Are not you my Slave? Did not I beget you? . . . Answer me that? Did you come a Voluntier into the World? Or did I beat up for you with the lawful Authority of a Parent, and press you to the service?

> (p. 244; II.i.323–32)

Valentine, however, thinking of familial relations in more Lockean terms, understands that "*Adam* had not either by natural Right of Fatherhood, or by positive Donation from God, any such Authority over his Children, or Dominion over the World" (Locke, *Two Treatises* p. 267; I.1). As Locke and those who quoted him after the 1688 revolution would have argued, Valentine has the right to revolt against this authority (which is in violation of natural law), just as the actors have the right to revolt against their "Oppress[or]," Christopher Rich.[2] Valentine knows that Sir Sampson's treatment of him is "Unnatural Usage" (p. 244; II.i.322), that the natural system he imagines once to have existed is no longer in force. When fathers prove unnatural, to revolt is only (as Valentine says) "a reasonable return of Nature" (p. 311; V.i.512).

In Valentine's revolt, he attempts to exchange poetry for his inheritance, words for money, in an economy of equivalence that is set up by his first determination to become a poet in his poverty, and carried throughout the play in a systematic metaphoric equation: "Projector[s]" and "Poet[s]" are "Mad[men]" (p. 295; IV.i.739–40); "promises" are "Debts" (p. 221; I.i.190–92); behind-the-scenes lovers show "their Reading" when they have no "ready Cash" (p. 315). Books, in *Love for Love*, belong to the impoverished underworld, that of "a worn-out Punk, with Verses in her Hand . . . as if she were carrying her Linnen to the Paper-Mill, to be converted into Folio Books" (p. 219; I.i.108, 111–12). Letters are absorbed into a system of commercial exchange; written words (appropriable and materialized) become credit instruments; literature is property. In Valentine's world, in the late seventeenth-century British cultural economy, the saleability of literature takes on new meanings in the context of the 1688 revolution, with the supplanting of a "natural" monarch with a financial-military monarch, the erosion of class and paternal authority through the establishment of money as the principal authority (William and the Bank of England are one), the repositioning of money as a great equalizer (unequal equalizer though it may be). In this context, banks and books and bills of credit and cheques and the numerous similar objects that circulate in post-1688 England in themselves concretize the historic symbolic relation between money and words.

Economic production, storage, and circulation have traditionally offered metaphors for literary and linguistic production, storage, and circulation.[3] In Greek, *sēmē* means both 'word' and 'coin' (Shell, *Money*, p. 2). New words are "coined," as in *Coriolanus*: "My lungs / Coin words till their decay" (Shakespeare, *Coriolanus*, p. 198; III.i.76–7). For Marx, reading through *Faust*, the New Testament *logos* that is the beginning of all things is both word and money (the first symbolization of commodity exchange).[4] Money and writing, both ways of signifying first the things of the world, and then the relations between things, entail the same kinds of action (they are both systems for storage and circulation); they perform similar functions (they stand in for things we cannot always carry around with us – sacks of grain, the bodies of humans in the theater of lived action); they offer portable representations of things valued (belongings, knowledge). And so, each can be conceived as inherently false and decayed representations (not the necessities of survival, not things in themselves); or, each can be seen merely as capable of corruption (devalued coinage, bad writing).

The tropes that bind the two identify the means of their parallel economies: means of production (coining, writing, imprinting, and so on); means of storage (banks, libraries, printed matter in general); means of circulation (currency, inflation and loss of value, trade, imitation); means of corruption (counterfeit, forgery, plagiarism, false attribution). In the seventeenth century no longer merely occasional metaphors, they become part of a larger conceptual structure, in which the two systems (the economic and the literate) are divided and organized in many of the same ways. Money and writing, banks and print are delayed representations of each other, homologous terms in a series of seemingly separate ways of imagining each, in which parallel grammar or thought patterns identify them: bankers and pamphleteers are both members of "a tribe . . . risen and grown up in Cromwell's time" (Clarendon, Vol. III, p. 7), belonging to a "trade" which relies upon "credit."[5] Money and literature meet in the shared realm of "economy," a literary and monetary term whose use becomes important to the seventeenth century as a way of identifying the parallel values of each.[6] The two networks of signification, that belonging to money and that belonging to print-world literature, are woven into each other.

At the end of the century, England's versions of the money/writing trope have come more insistently to carry this homologous structure. In Buckingham's *Rehearsal*, Prince Pretty-man pays Tom Thimble "in your own coyn: you give me nothing but words" (p. 22; III.i). "Words are wise men's counters," writes Hobbes, "they do but reckon by them; but they are the money of fools, that value them by the authority of . . . [any] doctor whatsoever" (p. 22). But that trope has also changed under a number of pressures; among the most important: the expansion and institutionalization of print;

the new attitudes toward (and laws surrounding) literary property (lapse of the Licensing Act, agitation for a copyright act); the development of the literary labor market; the new banking systems and systems of credit (and the printing of money and credit instruments); the development of the stock exchange; and the naturalization of "projectors."

The connection between banking and printing is even more explicit than the simple relation between money and writing. Banking both stores and reproduces capital; printing both stores and reproduces cultural knowledge (whether "objective" technical knowledge or "subjective" literary knowledge). In late seventeenth-century England, the storage and reproduction of both capital and knowledge are felt to be taking place with a troubling facility and abundance, and the figural links between money and words carry with them a new series of associations and baggage of related metaphoric and thematic habits. Sprat, in his *History of the Royal Society* (1667), refers to narratives not yet written as "ready in Bank."[7] In his *Satyr Against Wit* (1699), Sir Richard Blackmore proposes the establishment of a "Bank for Wit and Sense" to supply the "want of ready wit" with "Bills" that "Will through *Parnassus* circulate with ease" so that poets will "throng to write / Great Sums of Wit" (pp. 10–11). The words/coins trope so determinant for the century seems redundant by century's end because material conditions have institutionalized the relationship: money *is* printed words (bank notes, checks); printed words *are* commodities, items of exchange like money, because literature is property.

The network of money/book tropes that contributes to the epistemic structure is reiterated in the material link between the two economies – the economy of money and capitalist projection, and the economy of literary production and distribution.[8] During the seventeenth century, the business of publishing grew in complexity, in part because the audience increased and in part because changes in legislation meant that the market (rather than the Crown or the Stationers' Company) was regulating itself. New ways of protecting profits like congers and stock-sharing arrangements, new ways of distributing editions like trade dinners and book auctions, new ways of selling books like subscription publishing – these meant that a series of complex institutions was growing up around the book market. The developing readership, the increasing sale-ability of printed matter, suggested the extent to which publishing could be a profitable operation, and publishers began to speak of the "ownership" of "valuable copies."

In 1695, the Licensing Act, which had both helped the government in its power of censorship and protected the stationers, was allowed to lapse: printers were no longer required to register their publications.[9] Officially, literary production was the possession neither of the government, nor of the Stationers' Company, nor of individual publishers, nor of the authors, who increasingly complained about the tyranny of the booksellers: "Upon triall I find all of your *trade* are Sharpers," proclaims Dryden in a letter to Tonson (p. 80; December 1695/January 1696).

In legal terms at least, the authors finally did better than the booksellers: the protection that emerged during the first decade of the eighteenth century was not publisher copyright, but author-held copyright, established in the Copyright Act of 1710.[10] In reality, the terms of the act were almost never enforced, until the late eighteenth century, and even in the nineteenth century many continued to ignore them. Most authors sold their copyrights immediately to the booksellers. Most powerful booksellers, fortified by collective trade agreements, simply acted as if the copyrights they had always held were held in perpetuity. Printers who chose to partake of their share of the "public domain," or authors who chose to reclaim their works, were duly prosecuted. Oddly enough, despite the terms of the Act, the courts upheld the booksellers' claims against those who challenged it in litigation.

When an author sold his literary property, it was sold for good. But the author's right to sell it was confirmed, and so, at least conceptually, was the legitimacy of author-held copyright. At the same time, private banking and the use of written credit was on the increase. A sketchy outline and brief catalogue of the changes instituted by post-1688 economics might include: willingness to accept a centralized banking system not dominated by the monarchy (eventually, the Bank of England, established in part to fund William's war against Louis, in close collaboration with the Crown, but not controlled by it); a developed stock exchange (which had begun under Charles II); more projectors, but also more viable projects, than those promoted under the early Stuarts; the development of both public and private credit, with the accompanying bureaucracy that larger credit systems entailed; the proliferation of written instruments of credit available to the ordinary individual (bills of exchange, Exchequer bills, bank notes); the printing (and hence further proliferation) of credit instruments.[11]

By the Restoration, the land that Elizabeth and the early Stuarts had released (trying to raise money) was locked up. The gentry (at least the minor members of the gentry), were no longer necessarily landowners.[12] With the shift from land to foreign trade and credit, with the development of the stock exchange after the Restoration, "projectors" became central, both in the economy and in the public imagination.[13] Projectors had been around for a long time, promoting such schemes as a project for the recovery of wrecks or a tax on feather-beds (Horwitz, p. 207). But their activities boomed in the 1690s, particularly during 1692–3, just before the founding of the Bank. In 1688 there were fewer than 15 companies; but by 1695 more than 150 had been founded (Clay, Vol. II, p. 267, note). By the turn of the century, there was a developed and highly specialized profession for those dealing exclusively in money (see Clay, Vol. II, p. 276; Dickson, pp. 253–60, 424–9, 486–97). The growth in projectors accompanied other changes in credit and banking. Under Elizabeth, exchange had been a royal monopoly, but the Stuarts had had difficulty preserving control over it and, by the 1640s, it was clear that the privilege belonged to anyone who could survive market competition. Those who could do so played a growing part in government as the Crown's creditors and contractors, a role that finally resulted in the formation of the Bank of England. The initial fragmentation of financial power, in the increase in goldsmith bankers, allowed a new concentration eventually to displace the government as central financial authority, and those who had originally put pressure on the older system eventually came to control the national system on which the government was dependent.[14]

The empowerment of the merchant elite, then, accompanied the corrosion of royal prerogative and the diffusion and reconstitution of economic power.[15] And so the growth of banking could easily be associated, in the seventeenth-century popular imagination, with mercantile power and, by extension, with republicanism (although later this is modified to limited constitutional monarchism to fit the post-1688 model). The public identified national banks (during the Interregnum in particular) with the examples of those in republics or free cities: Amsterdam or Venice, for instance.[16] (After the Restoration, in spirited anti-republicanism, the same examples were used in arguments against a national bank.) And, in fact, it is precisely during the Interregnum that banking (like pamphlet literature) increases most.[17]

Private banking and the use of written credit were already growing, but the earlier seventeenth-century economy was still conceived primarily in terms of cash, not credit. The culture was one of coins and bullion. Mun, writing in the 1630s, seems surprised by the Italians and others, who "have Banks both publick and private, wherein they do assign their credits from one to another daily for very great sums . . . by writings only" (Mun, p. 17). Although, in the 1690s, remittances to finance the war were handled almost entirely by bills and drafts, Luttrell (like most) is still living in the older coin culture when he writes that there will be "a bank at Antwerp, where they will coin money to pay our army in Flanders" (p. 473; May 16, 1695). Even after deposit was well established, Pepys still keeps most of his cash at home, although he also stores some money "out" with the goldsmith, Alderman Backwell (Pepys, Vol. II, p. 76; Vol. V, p. 269 n.).

But after Charles II began issuing hand-written money orders to raise funds, as deposit began to be supplemented by "write-off" from one account to another, as something like hand-written checks began to develop between about 1630 and 1670, as goldsmith bankers began to keep "running cashes" with increasing regularity in the 1670s and 1680s and these began to be accepted as a circulating medium, the conception of money as coins and bullion seemed inadequate.[18] The remedy for too little money, claimed Sir William Petty in his *Quantulumcumque concerning Money* (1682), was to "erect a Bank, which well computed doth almost double the Effect of our coined Money: and we have in England Materials for a Bank which shall furnish Stock enough to drive the Trade of the whole Commercial World" (quoted by Richards, p. 103). And so, in 1694 the Bank of England was founded, emerging in connection with the development of the stock exchange, the boom in projectors, and changes in private banking (as well as with William's need for funds to finance the war).[19]

The fact that the Bank was, in a sense, another "project" allowed for the legitimation of the projectors and of moneylenders in general, treated less satirically at the end of the century than they had been in the earlier decades. The author of *Angliae Tutamen* (1695) writes with old-style ire that the Bank's relatively low interest rates had

> almost crush'd several sorts of Blood-suckers, mere Vermin, Usurers and Gripers, Goldsmiths, Tally-Jobbers, *Exchequer* Brokers, and Knavish Money-Scriveners, and Pawn-Brokers, with their Twenty and Thirty *per cent.*

> (p. 6)

The Bank offered interest rates that may have hurt some moneylenders, but it also naturalized moneylending, which was hardly crushed: there were more small private bankers in 1700 than there had been in 1687.[20] By the last decade of the seventeenth century, then, considerable changes had taken place both in the conception of money-lending and in the understanding of the nature of credit and the willingness to partici-pate in its expansion. All of the original £1.2 million loan that had been provided to underwrite the Bank of England was quickly subscribed (Richards, p. 148), suggesting the readiness of the English imagination for the instruments that were to be the medium of the altered understanding of credit.

Very soon after the Bank's foundation, the government tried its first experiment in issuing printed checks and printed paper money.[21] The printing of checks and the use of monetary instruments like paper money, which displaced the exclusive reliance on metal (demarcated in coin denominations) as the basis of monetary exchange, constituted a significant conceptual change, as someone like Locke understood in his ardent advocacy of a gold standard. For Locke, debased coinage (the result both of clipping and of alterations in the value of silver) destroyed the relation between the monetary instrument's identity as measure and its identity as commodity, a relation necessary to the preservation of credibility (credit) in exchange. With paper money, the relation seemed to deteriorate even further, for the material object as measure ceased to have a separate commodity value. (The value of paper as a commodity was seen as so slight, in relation to the value it measured, as to be negligible.) The transformation from coin to paper was one from monetary instrument as both measure and commodity to monetary instrument as measure alone.[22]

That the checks and bank notes of the Bank of England in the 1690s were printed differentiated them from the older treasury orders and other notes (which, as manuscripts, seemed exceptional even when their use was widespread). With the early handwritten treasury orders and other letters of this kind (those used before the late seventeenth century), the action of transferring money, even if it happened hundreds of times, seemed a single action with its own character, not one repeated mechanically and (potentially) infinitely. With written (as opposed to printed) instruments, money seemed relatively stable, insofar as each paper of credit, as an individual instrument, preserved its relation to the particular commodity-measure it represented. Printed instruments, on the other hand, indicated merely an abstract idea of metallic commodities. The printing of the first checks, then, was the definitive condition distinguishing them from letters of credit: money could now "grow" mechanically, could be easily disseminated, gave an impression of mobility, and allowed one easily to keep one's possessions on one's person. The idea of an infinitely expandable credit system, which the new paper system seemed to make possible, was both compelling and, to theorists like Locke, frightening. In the relatively circumscribed international economy of the late seventeenth century, with little experience of paper credit to examine, Locke could easily believe the gold standard to be a solution to the fluctuation of currency values. For Locke, the gold standard could redress the confusion inherent in deteriorating coinage and unreliable paper credit systems. But it was only with the printing (and hence proliferation) of credit instruments that such redress seemed necessary.

These changes, of course, colored the notion of literary property. If those printed credit documents attested to the "Ownership of money," if the pieces of paper issued by the Bank were "Bills of Property" belonging to "Proprietors,"[23] then literary property ("copy," like a printed credit instrument) was not so different from the kind on which credit was based. The banking system and the print-world literary system marked parallel paths in their treatment of property: in both cases, the creator (of capital or of words) was accorded the rights of ownership. It is not odd that the fifteen years between the lapse of the Licensing Act in 1695 and the inauguration of the Copyright Act in 1710 (the fifteen years in which literature was officially nobody's property) only strengthened the sense of literature as property. Whatever effect the changes in banking had, the lapse of authority itself helped to clarify the exact terms of the battleground over the ownership of literary property, and to codify the notion of authorship that had been developing throughout the seventeenth century. Agitation for a copyright act gave voice and terms to the long-developing idea that literature was a saleable commodity: poetry had to be owned by someone so that (as Aristotle had suggested several millennia earlier, in his apology for private property) it would have someone to take care of it.[24]

The conception of the dignity of authorship came into conflict, however, with reality.[25] The commercialization of the author at one and the same time gave and rescinded authority. The Grub Street cliché contains within it both sides of that struggle: the hack was the author as commercial commodity, slave to trade; the inventor of the hack as a character in the unfolding drama of seventeenth- and eighteenth-century authorship was the "poet" attempting to uphold the dignity of letters. To be a hack was not only to yield up one's writing as the property of another, but also to yield up oneself as property, to be owned.[26] To mock the hacks was not only a way of distinguishing oneself from those who are owned (not to be owned is to be an owner, at least of oneself), but also a way of attempting to establish a place for authors, owners both of themselves and of their works. Grub Street was clearly founded in real conditions. But it was also (through its literary version) an expression of the author's consciousness of his or her potential rights and powers, seemingly abraded, on one end, by the exploitative booksellers, and, on the other, by the underworld of scribblers willing to accept those terms and so to perpetuate the system. The Grub Street cliché, then, was not only a way of recognizing literature as a commodity, but also a way of acknowledging the battle over the problem of literary possession.

The possession of authorial property – whether by authors or by booksellers – in the last decades of the seventeenth century, made it possible to conceive of the imagination and the literature that could emerge from it as possessions, having the status of other kinds of property. This could be expressed in legal ways: authors could, for instance, get credit based on future production. It could also be expressed in more poetic ways: rather than pawning their material possessions (coats, spoons), authors could sell their imaginations. As the prologue to Vanbrugh's *The Relapse* (1696) claims, with the habitual mockery of the period:

> Of our late poets, nature few has made;
> The greatest part – are only so by trade.
> Still want of something brings the scribbling fit:
> For want of money some of 'em have writ,
> And others do't, you see – for want of wit.
>
> (*The Relapse*, p. 5)

One finds, of course, jokes about impoverished poets throughout the seventeenth century and earlier. Similarly, the aristocratic claim not to be writing for money was a seventeenth-century cliché. (One published only at the insistence of friends or to prevent the publication of a corrupt copy by a "sneaking bookseller.") But there was a not-so-subtle shift at century's end. The aristocratic claim remained a prominent feature in prefaces and dedications, but it was understood that authors wrote primarily to pay the rent.[27] However present the aristocratic claims (which endured well into the eighteenth century), the paradigm was that literature, dramatic literature included, was for sale.

Dramatic literature, however, was a special case, since it existed both on the page and in the transformed condition of performance. The most common early seventeenth-century professional theatrical structure involved professional playwrights who were contractually attached to a particular company, obliged to write for that company and (usually) no other. The playwrights, in a sense, belonged to the company. Like "props" – furniture, flats, bits of costume – they were properties of the company.[28] From time to time companies would sell texts when it seemed profitable to do so just as they would sell properties when it seemed profitable to do so.[29] But profit from texts was an occasional by-product of the theatrical enterprise, and it was difficult to conceive of the principal dramatic production – the performance – as property. To break a contract of exclusive engagement to a theatre by writing for another company might show a resistance to established commercial and labor configurations in the theatre. It might constitute a rebellion, for instance, against "the stoppage of [a playwright's] weekly means" or against "unkind carriage," but not necessarily involve the notion that dramatists have a right to own or sell their dramatic-literary productions.[30]

But the later part of the century offered a different paradigm. Desire for possession of dramatic-literary property expressed itself through control of the publication of the dramatic text: an entity with a separate existence from performance; an entity whose principal life was in its dissemination in print; an entity through which playwrights felt that they could control their intellectual labor, establishing scenic design (through stage directions), identifying entrances and exits, including scenes that had been excluded in performance, suppressing scenes ("bawdry," principally) that seemed to detract from the dignity of the work.[31] Although playwrights often acknowledged the help of the actors or the goodwill of the audience in the stage success of a production, they complained at least as often of the way the play was "mangled" by the "untimely witticisms" of a few or transformed by an actor in his cups.[32]

The idea of dramatic literature as property was based, then, on the printed word, the portable script, property of the author who belonged to no one. The hack, whether working for a publisher or working for a theater, struggled to achieve the power of authorial celebrity, which was held out as the promise of liberation in the ostensible meritocracy of the free market. The institution of Grub Street hackdom showed a redoubled effort on the part of publishers to dominate literary production during a time in which they felt their control to be threatened. It showed an attempt to gain, through different means and in a freer commercial market, the power that the Stationers' Company had once had. The configuration of playwright, publisher, and theater manager, then, changed over the course of the seventeenth century, though not unidirectionally. There was often, for instance, an overlap of actor-playwright-manager, as in the case of the actor-managers Betterton, Barry, and Verbruggen after the theater revolt, in the cases of Steele or Congreve and Vanbrugh (who were playwright-managers), or in the cases of Cibber or Garrick (who were all three) in the eighteenth century. Some successful playrights did find an alternative to theatrical power in the control and celebrity that publication could bring. For most, however, the promise seemingly enshrined in the Copyright Act was not fulfilled in either economic or social terms.

Many publishers, on the other hand, while they had lost much of the protection of a powerful Stationers' Company, gained from the freedom of the market. Although smaller publishers were often crushed by the lack of protection offered in a freer market, those (like Tonson) who could manipulate collaborations properly and establish a reputation that would attract celebrity authors, could become powerful and successful. Others (like Curll) could do quite nicely by taking advantage of the ready supply of authors, acquiring manuscripts through indirect channels, and working in ways that were perceived by author and public alike as unscrupulous. As the trade grew bigger and more complex, some publishers (their power in theory delimited by author-held copyright) grew more powerful by collaboration, not conflict, with authors. The same was true of many theater managers, who learned, over the course of the late seventeenth and the eighteenth centuries, to benefit from the ever-expanding theater audiences and to manipulate market forces not by conflict with authors, but by collaboration, using both author- and actor-celebrity to the benefit of management.[33]

Authorial power, however, even when merely theoretical, offered a conceptual change that was significant for playwrights, who (whatever their real economic power) found in the developing sense of literature as property, and in their power to manage the text, a kind of control – a control which could reinforce a tendency to privilege text over performance. The privileging of text tended to highlight the theater's fleetingness (by contrast with the permanence of the text), while it meant a greater appreciation of its power of ostensive reference, its power as medium of "presence": "*Minerva* walks upon the Stage before us, and we are more assured of the real presence of Wit when it is delivered *viva voce*," writes Congreve ("Congreve to the Reader of Incognita", December 22, 1691; *Letters*, p. 59).

The late seventeenth-century sense of the vulnerability of linguistic representation (disjoined from the animate and laboring body and from ostensive reference)[34] was paralleled in the later seventeenth-century conception of financial representation. Like many throughout the century, Hobbes (for example) was sensitive to the difference between trading the thing and trading the promise of the thing (otherwise known as credit):

> There is difference between transferring of right to the thing; and transferring, or tradition, that is, delivery of the thing itself. For the thing may be delivered together with the translation of the right; as in buying and selling with ready-money; or exchange of goods, or lands: and it may be delivered some time after.
>
> (Hobbes, p. 87)

This sensitivity ran parallel to his consciousness of the difference between the thing and the word, his consciousness that words (like credit instruments) are only "counters" (Hobbes, p. 22).

In an early recognition of the illusory status of credit, even an advocate of banking like the merchant Samuel Lambe (writing in 1657) termed paper-based credit "imaginary money."[35] Several decades later, in *Discourses on the Publick Revenues* (1698), Charles Davenant wrote: "Of all beings that have existence only in the minds of men, nothing is more fantastical and nice than Credit" (p. 151; quoted by Brewer, p. 187). The anxiety expressed here is similar to the more precise concern of those who felt, with Sir Theodore Janssen, that the practice of "giving out Notes payable to Bearer" (as he writes in his 1697 *Discourse concerning Banks*) was "liable to many Dangers and Inconveniences." In the 1740s, the historian James Ralph still understood paper money "such as Exchequer-Tallies, Bank bills and Government Securities, instead of Gold and Silver" as "fictitious wealth" (Vol. II, p. 564). The speculative fever that was, in a sense, responsible for the establishment of the Bank was simply the other side of the sense of economic instability.[36] The Bank's desire to believe that "imaginary money" (paper credit) could be expanded infinitely had run up against the public concern about the solidity of that imaginary money's foundation. The author of the *Mint and Exchequer united* (1695) wrote that the bank directors gave out "sums (*ad infinitum*) . . . which seems to be a Credit . . . never practised before by any Corporation, and almost a Fraud on the Subject."

The coinage crisis of the 1690s, with most of the coins in circulation badly clipped and with the status of the clipped coins uncertain, only underlined the fragility of the economy.[37] "It is no wonder, if the price and value of things be confounded and uncertain," wrote Locke in *Further Considerations concerning raising the Value of Money* (1695),

> when the measure itself is lost. For we have now no lawful silver money current amongst us; and therefore cannot talk nor judge right, by our present, uncertain, clipped money, of the value and price of things, in reference to our lawful, regular coin, adjusted and kept to the unvarying standard of the mint.
>
> (p. 158; quoted by Caffentzis, p. 27)

At the center of the recoinage controversy was the debate over whether silver content or "credence" gave value to money: for Locke, it was the silver that gave value to the coins; for those like Sir Richard Temple, it was credence and consensus that gave it value. As Temple wrote in 1696: "The Mony of every Country, and not the Ounce of Silver, or the intrinsick value, is the Instrument and Measure of Commerce there" (p. 4; quoted by Appleby, p. 224, and Caffentzis, p. 33). The troubled nature of monetary representation, which the recoinage debate revealed, highlighted the crisis over the more general nature of monetary representation which the issuing of paper-based credit (intended, during the 1690s, to help remedy the bullion shortage) had spurred. The "fraud" of clipping and counterfeiting (now treasonable offenses) was identified with the perceived "fraud" of paper-based credit.

Whether such credit was understood as magic or fraud, writers at the end of the century recognized and registered their anxiety that, if the new credit systems were to work, there had to be a continual revolution of exchange, or the "bubble" would explode and the hollow center be revealed. Defoe, writing somewhat later in his *Review*, was eloquent on the subject:

> Credit has made Paper pay Millions instead of Money, doubled and trebled our Specie by Circulation; Credit has brought out our Hoards, melted down our Plate, sold our Jewels to take Air for Silver, and split Stick for Gold; Credit has paid Interest for nothing, and turn'd nothing into something, Coin'd Paper into Metal, and stampt a Value upon what had no Value before.
>
> (*Defoe's Review*, p. 214; quoted by Southerne, p. 78, note)

Paper credit, like the "nonsense" of much of print-world literature, was a "nothing" that had been turned into a seeming "something" by the false stamp of value. The new systems were conceived as relying (even more than did coins) on the maintenance of the collective illusion that there was "real presence" where there was only, as Defoe would have seen it, absence, a "nothing" that "had no Value before." With no material link to sustain them, the systems would collapse (and with them, their merely apparent value) if the illusion were to collapse.

Credit became, then, like printed language simultaneously more accessible and more illusory: more could have it, but those who had it did not know what it was. Where words and credit instruments (manuscripts, coins) had seemed to have value outside any constructed system of symbolic exchange, where they had seemed to have intrinsic value or autonomous substance, words and credit instruments seemed now to have only the fragile and fleeting value that human (imaginary) symbolic systems could give them. If one stopped thinking their relations, they would cease to exist. The shift entailed a paradox: the more abundant, portable, and accessible the material (yet inanimate) instruments of exchange (paper words, paper money), the more abstract and hence illusory the systems. Locke recognized the fragility of the symbolic system when he condemned so harshly the clippers and counterfeiters: "The injury done to the public faith [by clippers and counterfeiters], in this point, is that which in clipping and false coining heightens the robbery into treason" (*Further Considerations*, p. 144; quoted by Caffentzis, p. 47).

By suggesting rhetorically the religious nature of monetary "faith," Locke underlined the connection between monetary and political fraud. The faith, once the religious faith essential to sustaining political continuity, had been shifted into the sphere where the monetary most explicitly met the symbolic. There, injury to the symbolic system was tantamount to treason, for the political-symbolic had itself changed.[38] Like the banking system and the linguistic system, the post-1688 political system was based on the collective agreement to accept an illusion. In 1660, there had been no doubt that, insofar as hereditary monarchy was legitimate, Charles II was the legitimate heir of Charles I, whether or not one felt that the Stuarts had betrayed the true heavenly King. But after the 1688 revolution, it was pure pragmatism to hold to the illusion that William and Mary were the heirs to the throne. To be a non-juror was less to be a traitor than to believe in an archaic system of idols.[39] (The identification of the idolatry of Catholicism with that of Jacobism is explicit.) To accept the legitimacy of William and Mary was less to adhere to what was perceived as a real principle of monarchic right – whatever the odd claims that James had abdicated – than to choose to attach a symbolic power to a useful political choice. (William and Mary would exclude the possibility of a Catholic heir and link England with the Dutch financial and military enterprises.) As with the systems of credit, only adherence to the illusion prevented the danger of collapse.

Not that this was the first time in English history that the ostensible rightful monarch (and the legal heir) had been pushed aside, but the Interregnum, among other things, had greatly changed the way royal authority could be conceived. William and Mary's entry into England was the first time that a revolution (no longer a usurpation) coincided with such a diminishment of royal power and such an increase in parliamentary authority.[40] It was the first time that there was no need for the kind of bloody revolutionary war in which victory could be said to be God's way of designating his chosen monarch. (William's pre-1688 military victories were useful in what they promised as strength against the French, but they had nothing to do with divine justification.) It was the first time that it was generally accepted that the choice was a popular, political, and pragmatic one rather than a divine one.[41]

In 1688, there was a sense, too, that England had not only already experienced enough financial and political upheaval, but had also experienced enough literary upheaval. Late seventeenth-century England, unlike France (and particularly when it compared itself with France), had a hard time feeling that the bulk of the century had produced a continuous literary (dramatic) production that could represent the nation. The Interregnum had divided the century in two, rupturing the political continuity which might have permitted literary continuity, and eradicating the theater (and most of the drama) for eighteen years. Where were England's Corneille, Molière, and Racine? There were Shakespeare, Jonson, and perhaps Fletcher on one end of the century. There was Dryden on the other, and perhaps Congreve, if one wanted to count a young man with a few promising comedies.[42] To have faith in the literary system was to have faith in an illusion of continuity akin to the monarchic illusion. To call on the ancients and to write progress pieces was to attempt to reclaim the points of contact in a state of discontinuity.[43] To give credence to the structure of linguistic or financial representation, to believe in monarchic or literary continuity, was to attempt to undo revolution by affirming one's ties with more radical origins, with the "nature" of a world without rupture.

The progress pieces that invented the continuity often traced it back to the Homeric golden age, in which pure song was unsullied by the decay of the word in print-world commerce. The desire that land be the foundation of money, which Defoe expressed when he wrote in 1697 that land was "the best bottom for Publick Banks" (*Essay upon Projects*, p. 67), was an attempt at an imagined return similar to that invoked in the progress pieces.[44] Agitation for a land bank was an attempt to found currency again in tangible matter, in matter that could link the economy to the "primitive" economy of the earth, the "original" of the "copies" that the money represented, the non-representational system imagined as having existed in an age of "primitive purity."[45] The sense of the illusoriness of money, and the desire to ground it in real things like land, found a parallel in the treatment by some of language, detached from the live presence of enactment and matter. If poets dreamed of a purely oral and therefore "natural" language, some philosophic writers too dreamed of a language that would have a natural status. But such languages, such systems of trade (as most writers on monetary, philosophic, or linguistic economies finally asserted) cannot involve a return, for there can be no return to a pre-representational system – no hope for a world of reals as the foundation for language, no hope for fixed commodities as the foundation for trade.[46] Humans were bound to that process of continual motion which could prevent the representational systems from collapsing, bound to the continual translation of representations (money into goods into money, words into things into words).

But that continual motion and translation could nevertheless reconstruct an idea of nature. Circulation was all. The "true philosophy" (the "natural" philosophy) of Hooke's *Micrographia* (1665), like the circulation of the blood which Harvey had discovered earlier in the century, was to begin

With the Hands and Eyes, and to *proceed* on through the Memory, to be *continued* by the Reason; nor is it to stop there, but to *come about* to the Hands and Eyes again, and so, by a *continual passage round* from one Faculty to another, it is to be maintained in life and strength, as much as the body of man is by the *circulation* of the blood.

(p. vii)

In this natural economy of representation, signs had to circulate with the same necessity as the blood, like the signs of the natural monetary economy that Hobbes imagined in 1651 when he identified money as "the blood of a commonwealth" which

passeth from man to man, within the commonwealth; and goes round about, nourishing, as it passeth, every part thereof; in so much as this concoction, is as it were the sanguification of the commonwealth: for natural blood is in like manner made of the fruits of the earth; and circulating, nourisheth by the way every member of the body of man.

(pp. 188–9)

A sign, like "the Money of the Kingdom, like the Blood in the Veins" (as Defoe reimagined them in 1690) "has its regular, circular motion, and every Member in the *Body* is warm'd and refreshed by it" (*Taxes no Charge*, p. 11; quoted by Appleby, p. 210).

Sir Sampson tells Valentine that to erase the debt the child owes the father he must return to the condition in which he was born by stripping, but Valentine responds:

My Cloaths are soon put off: – But you must also deprive me of Reason, Thought, Passions, Inclinations, Affections, Appetites, Senses, and the huge Train of Attendants that you begot along with me. . . . I am of my self, a plain easie simple Creature; and to be kept at small expence; but the Retinue that you gave me are craving and invincible.

(Congreve, p. 244; II.i.339–47)

Like most seventeenth-century writers on monetary, philosophic, or linguistic economics, Congreve understands that there is no natural self without appetites and so without a place in the artificially constructed economy of exchange, just as there is no natural economy, no natural language, and (though he would not say so explicitly) no natural monarch. Or, rather, since natural parents can be "Unnatural," the notion of the "natural" (parent, king, consumption, speech), the notion of an inevitable set of relations in a world of immanence is, for him, naive.

Revolution (England's in 1688, the actors' in 1695) may look like a return to Locke's unadulterated state of nature, a return to the Edenic Paradise of Congreve's prologue, a "reasonable return of Nature" (p. 311; V.i.512), as Valentine tells Sir Sampson. But even in Locke's state of nature there are those who violate natural law;[47] even in Congreve's "restored" Eden of the theater revolt, there is already a fallen state:

But since in *Paradise* frail Flesh gave way,
And when but two were made, both went astray;

Forbear your Wonder, and the Fault forgive, ⎫
If in our larger Family we grieve   ⎬
One falling *Adam*, and one tempted *Eve*.   ⎭
(p. 213)[48]

Congreve understands that Eden is an oxymoron, for in a place of no division, of no sin, there can be no Fall. In the same way, the live voice of the stage cannot be a return from the world of hackdom, of the buying and selling of material and appropriable words. Valentine must renounce the theatrical, along with the idea of his natural inheritance. He must acknowledge that his madness was (like his credit, like coins and words, which gull us into believing in them, even like gold and the live voice) "all Counterfeit" (p. 311; V.i.506). Only an act of grace, of the strange providence of the angelic Angelica, can bring some form of "reasonable return of Nature." But this, as Congreve knows, is a fantasy, not the way of the world, but rather part of the comic contract. Only in romance can translation (monetary, linguistic) be natural, can there be a perfect system of exchange, words for things, money for goods, representation for represented, Love for Love.

Notes

1   I have elided several lines here:

Our Taskmasters were grown such very *Jews*, ⎫
We must at length have Play'd in Wooden Shooes, ⎬
Had not your Bounty taught us to refuse.   ⎭

The issues they raise about anti-Semitism and the perception of the biblical and historical Jew, the relation of the Jew and the Dissenter, the mythic understanding of revolt are too complex to be treated in a few sentences.

Play citations, here, will give a page number followed by a semicolon, and then act, scene, and (if available) line number. All Congreve references are to the *Complete Plays* unless otherwise noted.

2   Locke would actually argue that parents do have authority, and that children who "will enjoy the *Inheritance* of their Ancestors . . . [must] submit to all the Conditions annex'd to such a Possession" (*Two Treatises*, p. 315; VI.73), but these details were not important in the public imagination, which habitually invoked Locke's arguments against Filmer's notion of patriarchy to justify its revolution.

3   Marc Shell, in *Money, Language, and Thought* (as well as in *The Economy of Literature*), offers a rich phenomenology of the intersection of money and language, arguing that money and language have always been "complementary or competing systems of tropic production and exchange" (p. 180), but that alterations in money's material forms involve shifts in the ways money is itself symbolized, and that "the new forms of metaphorization or exchanges of meaning that accompanied the new forms of economic symbolization and production were changing the meaning of meaning itself" (p. 4). Behind discussions like those of Shell are the two axes of Marxism and psychoanalysis, the discussions of the economic basis of language and the symbolization of money in, for instance, Simmel, Ferenczi, and, more recently, Goux. In *Clipped Coins, Abused Words, and Civil Government*, Caffentzis analyzes in greater detail the intersection of money and language during the historical moment I am discussing here, identifying the importance of its articulation in an era of changing monetary systems.

4   *Capital*, Vol. I., p. 180; see Shell, *Money*, pp. 106–7.

5 Clarendon refers here specifically to bankers, but the vocabulary (members of a "tribe" or "trade" relying on "credit") is common in references to bankers and projectors, writers and publishers alike. Two examples (emphasis added): for Shadwell in a defense of *The Libertine*, a critic who has attacked him "begins with the vanity of his *Tribe*. What *Tribe* that really is, it is not hard to ghess [*sic*]; but all the Poets will bear me witness it is not theirs" (Vol. III, p. 22); in *A Tale of a Tub*, Swift attacks the pamphlet "answerers" whose "Readers had need be cautious how they rely upon their *Credit*" when they indulge in kinds of writing that "is no part of their *Trade*" (p. 8).

6 "Economy" is used by critics to describe structure and proportion, principally the kind of proportion that involves using minimal means for maximal effects (as in the modern sense). Farquhar, in "A discourse upon comedy" (1702), writes: "the Scholar calls upon us for *Decorums* and *Œconnomy*" (p. 366); "All the Authorities, all the Rules of Antiquity have prov'd too weak to support the Theatre, whilst others who have dispenc'd with the Criticks, and taken a Latitude in the *Œconomy* of their Plays, have been the chief Supporters of the Stage, and the Ornament of the *Drama*" (p. 369). Of Shakespeare, Jonson, and Fletcher, he writes, "the Æconomy of their Plays was *ad libitum*, and the Extent of their Plots only limited by the Convenience of Action" (p. 380).

7 "There lye now ready in Bank, the most memorable Actions of Twenty years" (those of the Interregnum), according to Sprat. "It might certainly challenge all the Writings of past, or present Times" (p. 44).

8 Much of the last decade's critical discussion of the late seventeenth- and eighteenth-century relations among language, economics, and literature has focused on the impact of end-of-century economic change (and its accompanying ideological structures) on the development of the novel and other kinds of non-dramatic writing (with only a glance at the theater). One need only mention the many responses to Watt's *Rise of the Novel*, culminating most notably in McKeon's *Origins of the English Novel*. There are a few analyses of the role of money and finance in the theater and drama (historical, as in Milhous's account of management, or figural, as in Braverman's account of capital in *The Way of the World*). Others have examined the expansion of printing and literacy, and, in somewhat less detail, *its* impact, again paying special attention to non-dramatic forms. (See, for instance, Kernan, Kroll, the essays in Rivers, etc.) Like any historical analysis, these are focused on one issue, or a few issues, to the exclusion of crucially related issues. Few call attention to the overlap of the monetary and linguistic systems (exceptions are Caffentzis and Kroll, who notes the "neoclassical use of numismatic metaphors for the circulation of knowledge and language" [p. 14]); none investigates this overlap's special relation to the idea of the theater.

9 On the lapse and its impact on the trade, see Blagden, *Stationers' Company*, pp. 175–7. On the political background of the lapse, see Horwitz, *Parliament, Policy and Politics*. pp. 113–14, 152–3.

10 Authors with works already in print were to be allowed the right to the printing and reprinting of them for twenty-one years. From April 10, 1710 (when the Act was to go into effect), an author entering a book in the register before publication would have the right to it for fourteen years, renewable for another fourteen if the author was still alive. Authors could, of course (and most often did) sell these rights to publishers. On the Copyright Act, see Blagden, *Stationers' Company*, pp. 175–7; Kenny, "Publication," p. 312; and Feather, "The publishers and the pirates" and "Publishers and politicians."

11 On changes in credit and banking over the course of the seventeenth century, I have relied primarily on Richards and Appleby, with Dickson, Horwitz, Vilar, D. W. Jones, and Rubini offering additional perspectives. Brewer's *Sinews of Power* gives an overview of the politics underlying post-1688 economic policy and governmental structure.

12 On the shift from a land-based economy to one based on foreign trade and credit, see, for instance, Stone and Stone, *Open Elite?*, and Stone, "Social Mobility," pp. 13–22; Clay, *Economic Expansion*, Vol. I, pp. 154, 163; and Dickson (throughout). Clay describes the diversion of attention from land to other kinds of investment over the course of the seventeenth century: "Long-term mortgages from the 1620s onwards, interest bearing deposits

with goldsmith bankers from the 1650s, the bonds of the East India and other joint stock trading companies, and at the very end of the century Bank of England stock and the first of the new forms of government securities . . . all offered a significantly higher rate of return than did land. . . . In general these opportunities were perceived by investors as being sufficiently safe to divert a growing proportion of the surplus capital generated in economic activities other than agriculture away from the purchase of land" (Vol. I, p. 163).

The victory of the Bank of England over those proposing a land bank during the 1690s offers a historical particularization of the more general shift from land to money, although (of course) the story is not so simple. Rubini analyzes the politics that lay beneath that struggle, offering a corrective to the view of an absolute dichotomy between moneyed interests and landed interests, Whig and Tory. Nonetheless, he identifies concisely the perceived relation between the Bank and the anti-agrarian bourgeoisie: "The Bank of England seemed to [the country leadership] inherently anti-agrarian, too much allied with commercial interests and with the growing bourgeoisie. It appeared to be the spearhead of a financial revolution which was furthering the change from a landed to a commercial economy" ("Politics," p. 697). Brewer, too, recognizes the political assumptions of the Bank of England's opponents, who feared "its political ancestry – which was decidedly Dissenting and whig, not to say republican. . . . Their response was to try to replace the Bank of England by a Land Bank" (*Sinews of Power*, p. 153).

13 See Hoppit, "Use and abuse," p. 64–5 for a summary of the scholarly "commonplace that in eighteenth-century England all businessmen made frequent use of credit" (p. 64) and on credit's expansion in the eighteenth century. As Brewer writes: "Between the late seventeenth and late eighteenth centuries the British economy saw national integration increase, more and more subjects become involved in long-distance trade, including small producers and retailers, and inter-regional – indeed international – systems of credit develop. . . . Credit was everywhere. Contemporaries estimated that two-thirds of all transactions involved credit rather than cash" (*Sinews of Power*, pp. 183, 186). On the development of the stock exchange and the boom in projectors, see Scott and Horsefield.

14 On the increase in the number and power of goldsmith bankers, see especially Richards, *Early History of Banking*, pp. 23–131; and Clay, *Economic Expansion*, Vol. I, p. 37, Vol. II, pp. 274–5, who writes that by the 1690s the circulating notes of the goldsmith bankers may have been worth as much as £2 million (Vol. I, p. 37).

15 After 1660, as Stone writes: "The growing rôle of the leading London merchants as government creditors and contractors, culminating in the Bank of England, gave them considerable behind-the-scenes influence. As a result, foreign, military, and economic policies were increasingly conducted with an eye to the interests, and with the advice, of this merchant elite. . . . By the late seventeenth century merchants, lawyers, clergymen and officials were held in much less contempt than they had been a century earlier" (Stone, "Social mobility," p. 21).

16 See Richards (*Early History of Banking*, pp. 94–6), for instance, on proposals for the adoption of "Venetian banking methods in England" and for the establishment of "a bank in the cittie of London as is at Amsterdam."

17 Clarendon writes that bankers "were a tribe that had risen and grown up in Cromwell's time, and never were heard of before the late troubles, till when the whole trade of money had passed through the hands of the scriveners" (*Life*, Vol. III, p. 7).

18 On these events, see especially Richards, *Early History of Banking*, pp. 23–91; and Clay, *Economic Expansion*, Vol. II, pp. 274–5. By the end of the century, the goldsmiths' notes were treated as cash: "The notes of goldsmiths," wrote Chief Justice Holt in 1698, "whether they be payable to order or bearer, are always accounted by merchants as ready cash and not as bills of exchange" (quoted by Richards, *Early History of Banking*, p. 162; see also p. 49).

19 As Horwitz notes in *Parliament, Policy and Politics*, the creation of the Bank of England (like many other departures of the "financial revolution") originated in projectors' proposals (p. 207). On William's use of both the Bank and changes in taxation to finance the war, see Brewer, *Sinews of Power*.

20   On the goldsmith bankers' friendly interactions with the Bank of England, see Richards, *Early History of Banking*, esp. pp. 171–2.

21   The Bank's directors, after the first meetings, suggested three methods of keeping "running cash": "Notes payable to bearer to be endorsed," "Books or Sheets of Paper wherein their Acco[ts] to be entered," and "Notes to persons to be accomptable," the rough equivalent of bank notes, deposit books, and checks (Richards, *Early History of Banking*, p. 153). A little later, the Bank issued "Bank Bills, sealed" which were printed and usually not interest-bearing – the equivalent of regular circulating notes (ibid., pp. 156–8). Very soon after the Bank's foundation, it was decided that the notes be printed. See ibid., pp. 156–60 on the printing of paper credit instruments and for details on design and engraving. He writes: "It is probable that the very earliest promissory notes issued by the Bank were entirely written. On 31st July 1694, however, it was decided that they were to be printed and made payable to bearer" (p. 158). Although they were, for a time again, written, the printing was resumed, and "the two earliest specimens in the Bank's remarkable collection of paper money are printed, and dated 1699" (p. 158). Some notes were still written, but these were probably only experiments in new kinds of notes – notes payable to order, as opposed to the notes to bearer which "were all printed" (p. 159) – and these too were eventually printed.

22   Shell, summarizing Marx, describes the way that gold as a commodity, when transformed into paper money, "seems to use only its exchange-value as a means of purchase and to have lost its commodity-value" (Shell, *Money*, p. 108). As Marx writes in the *Contribution to the Critique of Political Economy*: "The token of value, say a piece of paper . . . *seems* to represent the value of commodities *directly*, since it appears to be not a token of gold but a token of the exchange-value which exists solely in the commodity and is merely expressed in the price. But the appearance is deceptive. The token of value is directly only a *token of price*, that is, a *token of gold*, and only indirectly a token of the value of the commodity" (p. 115).

23   Such references are common. A bank, according to Samuel Hartlib, writing in 1653, "is no other thing than the transmitting of the Ownership of money" (quoted by Richards, *Early History of Banking*, p. 106). William Paterson, in his *Brief Account of the intended Bank of England* (1694), proposes that "what Profits and Improvements can be made from the Business or Credit of the Bank, will also be divided among the Proprietors" (p. 10), account-holders who have "Bills of Property." Defoe thinks the Bank of England "Useful to the Government, and . . . Profitable to the Proprietors" (*Essay upon Projects*, p. 43; quoted by Richards, *Early History of Banking*, p. 132).

24   "What is common to the greatest number gets the least amount of care. Men pay most attention to what is their own: they care less for what is common" (Aristotle, *Politics*, p. 44; 1261b).

25   The relationship between print and the developing idea of authorship has been explored in some detail. In *Authorizing Words*, for instance, Elsky describes the ways that manuscript and print help to determine authorial identity for a number of Renaissance English writers (Bacon, Herbert, and Jonson in particular; see especially pp. 101–9, 180–96). Murray, in *Theatrical Legitimation*, discusses theatrical "authorship as material form" (pp. 23–104), examining "the epistemological transfer performed by an author's move from stage to page" (p. 16). See also Eisenstein, *Printing Press*, pp. 121–2, 153–8, 229–34, 242–3; and Kernan, *Printing Technology*, pp. 71–7, 100–2.

26   There is much to be said about self-alienation in Grub Street, and, in particular, the special place of women as property in the context of the emerging role of women as professional authors during this period. See, for instance, Gallagher on the particular self-alienation of the female hack. Again, such issues are beyond the scope of this chapter.

27   John Oldmixon, for instance, describes the needs of the hungry poets in his Dedication to *The Grove* (1700): "Fame is not the Mistress they Court: To talk of a future Reputation when a present Supply is to be rais'd wou'd to them seem Silly and Extravagant. Indeed I think they are very much to be excus'd; for a man must have little Stomach to hear of an Immortal Name, when his own puts him in mind of Mortality."

28   Bentley, in *The Professions of Dramatist and Player*, gives the fullest elaboration of the evidence that the attachment of dramatists to particular companies was the early seventeenth-century norm. He also describes in detail the performance orientation of those dramatists, and their dependence on the companies to which they belonged.

29   See Bentley, *Professions*, pp. 64–92; and Blayney, "Shakespeare's fight," for examples of the sale of texts for profit. Usually, in the early seventeenth century texts were sold only when exclusive performance no longer seemed profitable.

30   Richard Brome is defending, here, his violation of the exclusivity clause in his 1635 contract with the Queen's Men (quoted by Bentley, *Professions*, p. 115). Bentley gives, as examples, Brome's and James Shirley's disputed contracts with the company, to whom they were "oblige[d]" to "dedicate all [their] labor and plays totally unto their sole profits" (quoted p. 115). He shows that, even though Brome and Shirley decided to break their contracts by writing for another company, they generally accepted the terms of their obligations, and refrained from publishing plays that (it was understood) belonged to the Salisbury Court company (ibid., pp. 112–6, 266–71).

31   Vanbrugh, in his Preface to *The Relapse* (1696), refers to the frequent practice of taking out obscenities in print: "If there was any obscene expressions upon the stage, here they are in the print; for I have dealt fairly, I have not sunk a syllable that could (though by racking of mysteries) be ranged under that head" (p. 3).

32   Vanbrugh describes the first night of *The Relapse* (1696) in the Preface: "The fine gentleman of the play, drinking his mistress's health in Nantes brandy from six in the morning to the time he waddled on upon the stage in the evening, had toasted himself up to such a pitch of vigor, I confess I once gave Amanda for gone" (p. 4). As Zimansky comments in the note "George Powell, who played Worthy, must have given V.iv a liveliness that the printed text sadly lacks."

33   Avery and Scouten (in the Introduction to the *London Stage*) describe the 1690s as the moment in which theater management "came under the direction of proprietors whose only real interest in the enterprise was its financial success" (p. lx). Rich's regime, for instance, shows the increasing commercial savvy of the manager; the Betterton and Cibber regimes show the ways in which friendly collaboration or dramatist management could be financially beneficial. (See Milhous, "Company management," for details of company management between 1660 and 1800, and of complex systems for financing theater in the late seventeenth and eighteenth centuries.) There was, here, a kind of paradoxical double expectation. In some ways, there was less conflict between managers and playwrights, who were less invested in performance because they had power, to a certain extent, over printed versions of their plays. But in some ways there was more conflict, because the model of authorial power suggested by the Copyright Act offered playwrights an inflated sense of their right to control any manifestation of their works.

34   This issue has been much explored in historical accounts (see, for instance, Howell, "*Res et verba*"), in rhetorical analyses (see, for instance, Williamson, *Senecan Amble*), and in linguistic-philosophic discussions (see, for instance, Caffentzis, *Clipped Coins*, pp. 77–123). The most complete and convincing account of the late seventeenth-century struggle with the representational indeterminacy of language and its repercussions is that of Kroll, who, in *The Material Word*, shows the relation of the problem to a range of cultural discourses (Epicureanism, theology, and literary criticism, for instance). Kroll correctly challenges the argument of earlier critics (R. F. Jones, most centrally) that the late seventeenth-century understanding of "plain style" constituted a claim for a scientific language of perfect transparency and precise referentiality, or that there was a shift from the "Ciceronian" to the "Senecan" (Williamson and Croll). Although he may underestimate the power of the naturalist fantasy, his corrective is helpful. As he argues, the late seventeenth-century understanding of language is "indebted to Cicero's arguments about the rhetorical grounds of all knowledge" (Kroll, *Material Word*, p. 2), and "is conscious of its own artificiality" (ibid. p. 4). See Trudeau on the sixteenth-century belief in the "intrinsic value of words." The origin of much of the recent discussion is Foucault's sweeping epistemological account in *The Order of Things*, especially pp. 78–124. I am not attempting, here, to summarize the discussion, but have

tried merely to indicate its relevance to the axis of conditions I am identifying.

35　A bank, Samuel Lambe writes, "is a certain number of sufficient Men of Estates and Credit joined together in a Joint Stock, being, as it were, the General Cashkeepers or Treasurers of that Place where they are settled, letting out imaginary Money at Interest" (quoted by Richards, *Early History of Banking*, p. 99).

36　Appleby writes: "While the successful floating of the Bank of England owed much to this speculative fever, the inflation accompanying the Bank's funding only added to the impression of instability" (*Economic Thought*, pp. 261–2). But the anxiety was not unfounded, as Brewer shows in his description of the dangers that were inherent in expanding credit systems: "Overtrading was the consequence of seeking too much credit – a risk made greater by the ease with which money could be borrowed and by the habit of using short-term credit instruments like bills of exchange to raise capital. Excessive debts made traders vulnerable in a credit crisis" (*Sinews of Power*, p. 187; see also, p. 188). That credit, and bank notes in particular, were vulnerable was shown by the run on the Bank in 1696, set off by the fact that, two days earlier, money that had been clipped (by those eager to exchange the valuable silver on the foreign market) had lost currency. The sudden loss of faith in the paper notes, which had in fact been overissued, caused the run. The mint was in the process of the general recoinage of 1695–6, which had been handled badly. Full cash payment had to be suspended, with the promise of partial payment in coin, interest on the rest, a discount on notes (up to 24 percent), and full payment when coin could be gotten from the mint. The loss of the notes' credibility (the loss of them as viable credit) was only temporary, but indicated the degree of the larger cultural anxiety.

37　See Caffentzis for an extended reading of the anxiety over the clipped coins and some of the ideological issues at work in clipping and in the recoinage crisis. The recoinage debate, as Caffentzis points out, registers the loss of faith in the intrinsic value of tokens of exchange, which the use of paper money makes palpable.

38　Caffentzis comments on the importance of the recent transformation of monetary crimes into treasonable offenses, and on the relationship between the religious and the monetary in the financial state, writing: "Clearly the locale of heresy had shifted from private religious conviction to public monetary faith" (*Clipped Coins*, p. 47).

39　Brewer draws a broad portrait of the political constitution of the late seventeenth- and eighteenth-century bureaucracy when he writes that the "new officials" were "more loyal to the crown than to the king. The extreme volatility of monarchical politics in the seventeenth and early eighteenth centuries weakened attachment to individual monarchs even as it strengthened commitment to royal, mixed government" (*Sinews of Power*, p. 84). Caffentzis identifies the weakness in currency with weakness in monarchic inheritance, "when people not only lost confidence in their currency but began to link its weakness with the change from James II to William and Mary" (*Clipped Coins*, p. 174, note).

That non-jurors were tolerated is indicative, and the forms that non-juring was permitted to take suggest that it was recognized that a change in "faith" had taken place. It was understood, for instance, that clergymen and others might hesitate to swear the old Jacobean oath of allegiance in 1688, and a new oath was required in which oath-takers did not have to acknowledge William and Mary as "lawful and rightful" king and queen, but merely to swear to be "faithful and bear true allegiance" to them (Horwitz, *Parliament, Policy and Politics*, p. 21). On the debates about the oath of allegiance, see ibid, pp. 21–6.

40　Although, as Horwitz indicates (ibid., p. 14), the constitution was not fundamentally altered, the assumptions about the nature and limitations of the monarch's rule were. On the importance of parliamentary authority in the success of the revolution, and on the "stipulations" and "terms" with which William was required to accord, see ibid., pp. 8–14. The Prince "cannot take it ill," claimed William Garroway, "if we make conditions to secure ourselves for the future [to] do justice to those who sent us hither" (quoted by Horwitz, p. 12). Brewer notes that the effect of Parliament's post-revolutionary financial measures "was to end the possibility of financial independence for the crown" and describes the political ramifications: "Not even in peacetime could the monarch use his ordinary revenue 'to live of his own'. In future he had perforce to turn to parliament if he were to remain solvent. The object of securing fiscal dependency was clear: to ensure the regular calling of parliament. This, in turn, would enable the lower house to scrutinize the actions of the executive and redress the grievances of their constituents" (*Sinews of Power*, p. 145).

41 See Horwitz, *Parliament, Policy and Politics*, pp. 1–16, on the politics immediately preceding the revolution and on the public debate about who ought to have the title to the throne. It was still necessary to claim that James had "ceded," "abdicated," or "deserted" the throne (see ibid., pp. 7–10) and to cite historical precedents in asserting William's right to call a parliament after declaring himself king (p. 7). But members of Parliament found themselves speaking nonetheless of James's "demise" (p. 10), and many loyalists understood that parliamentary debate about whether William or another ought to be monarch was not much different from elective monarchy (ibid.).

42 Dryden sketches the traditional genealogy in his poem to Congreve on *The Double-Dealer* (1693):

> In easie Dialogue is *Fletcher*'s Praise:
> He mov'd the mind, but had not power to raise.
> Great *Johnson* did by strength of Judgment please:
> Yet doubling *Fletcher*'s Force, he wants his Ease. . . .
> But both to *Congreve* justly shall submit,
> One match'd in judgment, both o'er-match'd in Wit. . . .
>   Oh that your Brows my Lawrel had sustain'd,
> Well had I been Depos'd, if You had reign'd! . . .
> Heav'n that but once was Prodigal before,
> To *Shakespeare* gave as much; she cou'd not give him more.
>   (Congreve, *Complete Plays*, pp. 123–4)

43 Murray succinctly identifies the seventeenth-century consciousness of historical discontinuity (a broader version of the linguistic discontinuity delineated by Foucault), when he writes that seventeenth-century texts "openly express skepticism of the continuities of tradition, of any unbreachable laws of the past. . . . Seventeenth-century writers, especially practitioners of theatrical enterprises, turn their attention to mental and linguistic forces of reversibility, those forces focusing the critic's attention on the disruptive manifestations of desire and persuasion standing alongside the veil of historical continuity" (*Theatrical Legitimation*, p. 12).

The parallels between the ruptures in political/literary continuity and ruptures in linguistic/monetary representation highlight the extent to which both involve discontinuities not only of space but also of time. The sense of linguistic/monetary illusion is principally a problem of space, of the physical distance between speaker and recipient, between barterer and thing bartered. But it is also a problem of time, of the temporal gap between the representation (conceived as an event) and the reception of the representation, as Hobbes understands when he writes that in monetary exchange, "the thing may be delivered . . . some time after" (*Leviathan*, p. 14). One might argue that the claim for the dramatic unities, in attempting also to redress spatial and temporal discontinuities, responds to linguistic, monetary, and political crisis.

44 Rubini describes the failure of land bank schemes in the 1690s, noting the country land bank proponents' opposition to floating paper money of the kind their rival, the Bank of England, was attempting to use ("Politics," p. 713). Although by the 1690s even land bank plans recognized the need for institutionalized credit instruments, they were opposed to the extension of credit beyond the value of the land that was its foundation, not unlike those who saw the Bank of England's extension of credit beyond the original £1.2 million subscription as a form of fraud. (On proposals for a land bank and hostility between the Bank of England and the land bank advocates, see also Horwitz, *Parliament, Policy and Politics*, pp. 166–7, 177–8, 180–2; and Brewer, *Sinews of Power*, p. 153.)

45 The phrase is a common one in the last decades of the seventeenth century. For instance, Sprat urges a return to a "primitive purity" in language (*History*, p. 113). John Dennis praises Rymer's intention "to restore Tragedy to its primitive purity" (*Critical Works*, Vol. I, p. 30).

46   Brewer notes the late seventeenth-century recognition of the impossibility of return in the
      financial sphere: "Gradually the opponents of the financial revolution came to recognize that
      a reversion to earlier days was no longer possible. It was now necessary to harness and tame
      the forces of public credit, not to seek their abolition" (*Sinews of Power*, p. 154).
47   "In transgressing the law of nature, the offender declares himself to live by another rule than
      that of reason and common equity, which is that measure God has set to the actions of men"
      (Locke, *Two Treatises*, p. 10; II.8).
48   These lines refer more specifically, to the actors Joseph Williams and Susanna Mountfort,
      who, dissatisfied with Betterton's terms, returned to Rich at Drury Lane.

Works cited

Angliae Tutamen; or, the Safety of England By a Person of honour, London: for the author, 1695.
Appleby, Joyce Oldham, *Economic Thought and Ideology in Seventeenth-Century England*, Princeton:
    Princeton University Press, 1978.
Aristotle, *The Politics of Aristotle*, ed. and trans. Ernest Barker, London: Oxford University Press,
    1958.
Avery, Emmett L., Scouton, Arthur, and Van Lennep, William (eds) *The London Stage 1660–1800.
    Part I: 1660–1700*, Carbondale, IL: Southern Illinois University Press, 1965.
Bentley, Gerald Eades, *The Professions of Dramatist and Player in Shakespeare's Time, 1590–1642*,
    Princeton, NJ: Princeton University Press, 1986.
Blackmore, Sir Richard, *A Satyr Against Wit*, London: Samuel Crouch, 1700.
Blagden, Cyprian, *The Stationers' Company: A History, 1403–1959*, London: Allen & Unwin, 1960.
Blayney, Peter, "Shakespeare's fight with *what* pirates?" typescript, 1987.
Braverman, Richard, "Capital relations and the way of the world," *ELH* 52 (1985): 133–58.
Brewer, John, *The Sinews of Power: War, Money and the English State, 1688–1783*, London: Unwin
    Hyman, 1989.
Buckingham, George Villiers, Duke of, *The Rehearsal*, 3rd edn, London: Thomas Dring, 1675.
Caffentzis, Constantine George, *Clipped Coins, Abused Words, and Civil Government: John Locke's
    Philosophy of Money*, New York: Autonomedia, 1989.
Clarendon, Edward Hyde, Earl of, *The Life of Edward, earl of Clarendon . . . Written by himself*,
    Oxford: Clarendon Press, 1827.
Clay, C. G. A., *Economic Expansion and Social Change: England 1500–1700*, 2 vols, Cambridge, UK:
    Cambridge University Press, 1984.
Congreve, William, *The Complete Plays of William Congreve*, ed. Herbert Davis, Chicago: University
    of Chicago Press, 1967.
Congreve, William, *Letters and Documents*, ed. John C. Hodges, London: Macmillan, 1964.
Croll, Morris W., *Style, Rhetoric, and Rhythm*, ed. J. Max Patrick and Robert O. Evans with John
    M. Wallace and R. J. Schoeck, Princeton, NJ: Princeton University Press, 1966.
Davenant, Charles, *The Political and Commercial Works of that Celebrated Writer Charles Davenant*, ed.
    Sir Charles Whitworth, Vol. 1, London: R. Horsfield, 1771.
Defoe, Daniel [?], *Taxes no Charge*, London: R. Chiswell, 1690.
Defoe, Daniel, *Essay upon Projects*, London: printed by R. R. for Tho. Cockerill, 1697.
Defoe, Daniel, *Defoe's Review*, 7:55, ed. Arthur Wellesley Secord, facsimile of Book 17, New York:
    Columbia University Press, 1938.
Dennis, John, *The Critical Works of John Dennis*, ed. Edward Niles Hooker, 2 vols, Baltimore, MD:
    Johns Hopkins University Press, 1939–43.
Dickson, P. G. M., *The Financial Revolution in England: A Study of the Development of Public Credit,
    1688–1756*, London: Macmillan, 1967.
Downes, John, *Roscius Anglicanus*, ed. Judith Milhous and Robert D. Hume, London: Society for
    Theatre Research, 1987.
Dryden, John, *The Letters of John Dryden*, ed. Charles E. Ward, Chapel Hill, NC: Duke University
    Press, 1942.

Eisenstein, Elizabeth, *The Printing Press as an Agent of Change: Communications and Cultural Transformations in Early-Modern Europe*, Cambridge, UK: Cambridge University Press, 1979.

Elsky, Martin, *Authorizing Words: Speech, Writing, and Print in the English Renaissance*, Ithaca, NY: Cornell University Press, 1989.

Farquhar, George, "A discourse upon comedy," in *The Works of George Farquhar*, ed. Shirley Strum Kenny, 2 vols, Oxford: Clarendon Press, 1988, Vol. 2, pp. 364–86.

Feather, John, "The publishers and the pirates: British copyright law in theory and practice," *Publishing History* 22 (1987): 5–32.

Feather, John, "Publishers and politicians: the remaking of the law of copyright in Britain 1775–1842. Part I: Legal deposit and the battle of the library tax," *Publishing History* 24 (1988): 49–76.

Ferenczi, Sandor, "The ontogenesis of the interest in money," in *Sex in Psychoanalysis*, ed. Ernst Jones, New York: Basic Books, 1960, pp. 319–31.

Foucault, Michel, *The Order of Things*, London: Tavistock Publications, 1970.

Gallagher, Catherine, "Who was that masked woman? The prostitute and the playwright in the comedies of Aphra Behn," *Women's Studies* 15 (1988): 23–42.

Goux, Jean-Joseph, *Symbolic Economies After Marx and Freud*, trans. Jennifer Curtiss Gage, Ithaca, NY: Cornell University Press, 1990.

Hobbes, Thomas, *Leviathan, or the Matter, Forme and the Power of a Commonwealth Ecclesiasticall and Civil*, ed. Michael Oakshott, Oxford: Blackwell, 1946.

Hooke, Robert, *Micrographia*, London: Jo. Martin and Ja. Allestry, 1665.

Hoppit, Julian, "The use and abuse of credit in eighteenth-century England," in *Business Life and Public Policy: Essays in honour of D. C. Coleman*, ed. Neil McKendrick and R. B. Outhwaite, Cambridge, UK: Cambridge University Press, 1986, pp. 64–78.

Horsefield, S. K., *British Monetary Experiments*, Cambridge, MA: Harvard University Press, 1960.

Horwitz, Henry, *Parliament, Policy and Politics in the Reign of William III*, Manchester: Manchester University Press, 1977.

Howell, A. C., "*Res et verba*: words and things," *English Literary History* 13 (1946): 131–42.

Jones, D. W., "London merchants and the crisis of the 1690s," *Crisis and Order in English Towns 1500–1700*, ed. Peter Clark and Paul Slack, Toronto: University of Toronto Press, 1972, pp. 311–55.

Jones, Richard Foster, *Ancients and Moderns: A Study of the Rise of the Scientific Movement in Seventeenth-Century England*, St Louis: Washington University Studies, 1961, 2nd edn.

Kenny, Shirley Strum, "The publication of plays," *The London Theatre World, 1660–1800*, ed. Robert D. Hume, Carbondale and Edwardsville, IL: Southern Illinois University Press, 1980, pp. 309–36.

Kernan, Alvin, *Printing Technology, Letters & Samuel Johnson*, Princeton, NJ: Princeton University Press, 1987.

Kroll, Richard W. F., *The Material Word: Literate Culture in the Restoration and Early Eighteenth Century*, Baltimore, MD: Johns Hopkins University Press, 1991.

Lambe, Samuel, *Seasonable Observations humbly offered to His Highness the Lord Protector*, London, 1658.

Locke, John, *Two Treatises of Gov't*, ed. Peter Laslett, New York: Cambridge University Press, 1988.

Locke, John, *Further Considerations concerning raising the Value of Money*, Vol. 5, *The Works of John Locke, A New Edition, Corrected, in Ten Volumes*, London: Thomas Tegg, 1823.

Luttrell, Narcissus, *A Brief Historical Relation of State Affairs from Sept. 1678 to April 1714*, Vol. 3, Oxford: Oxford University Press, 1857.

McKeon, Michael, *The Origins of the English Novel, 1600–1740*, Baltimore, MD: Johns Hopkins University Press, 1987.

Marx, Karl, *Capital*, ed. Ernest Mandel, trans. Ben Fowkes, New York: Vintage, 1977.

Marx, Karl, *Contribution to the Critique of Political Economy*, ed. Maurice Dobb, trans. S. W. Ryazanskaya, New York: International Publishers, 1970.

Milhous, Judith, "Company management," in *The London Theatre World, 1660–1800*, ed. Robert D. Hume, Carbondale and Edwardsville, IL: Southern Illinois University Press, 1980, pp. 1–34.

Mint and Exchequer united, London [?], 1695.

Mun, Thomas, *England's Treasure by Forraign Trade*, reprtd New York: Augustus M. Kelley, 1965.

Murray, Timothy, *Theatrical Legitimation: Allegories of Genius in Seventeenth-Century England and France*, New York: Oxford University Press, 1987.

Oldmixon, John, *The Grove; or, Love's Paradice*, London: Richard Parker, 1700.

Paterson, William [?], *A Brief Account of the intended Bank of England*, London: 1694.

Pepys, Samuel, *The Diary of Samuel Pepys*, ed. Robert Latham and William Matthews, 11 vols, Berkeley and Los Angeles, CA: University of California Press, 1979–83.

Petty, Sir William, *Quantulumcumque concerning Money*, London: 1682.

Ralph, James, *The History of England: during the reigns of K. William, Q. Anne, and K. Georg. I*, London: printed by D. Browne for F. Cogan *et al.*, 1744–6.

Richards, R. D., *The Early History of Banking in England*, London: 1929; reprtd New York: Augustus M. Kelley, 1965.

Rivers, Isabel (ed.), *Books and Their Readers in Eighteenth-Century England*, Leicester: Leicester University Press, 1982.

Rubini, Dennis, "Politics and the battle for the banks, 1688–1697," *English Historical Review* 85 (1970): 693–714.

Scott, William Robert, *The Constitution and Finance of English, Scottish and Irish Joint-Stock Companies to 1720*, 3 vols, Cambridge, UK: Cambridge University Press, 1910–12.

Shadwell, Thomas, *Complete Works of Thomas Shadwell*, ed. Montague Summers, London: Fortune Press, 1927.

Shakespeare, William, *Coriolanus*, ed. Philip Brockbank in the Arden Shakespeare series, London: Methuen, 1976.

Shell, Marc, *The Economy of Literature*, Baltimore, MD: Johns Hopkins University Press, 1978.

Shell, Marc, *Money, Language, and Thought: Literary and Philosophic Economies from the Medieval to the Modern Era*, Berkeley, CA: University of California Press, 1982.

Simmel, Georg, *The Philosophy of Money*, London: Routledge & Kegan Paul, 1978.

Southerne, Thomas, *Oroonoko*, ed. Maximillian E. Novak and David Stuart Rodes, Lincoln, NB: University of Nebraska Press, 1976.

Sprat, Thomas, *The History of the Royal Society*, ed. Jackson I. Cope and Harold Whitmore Jones, St Louis: Washington University Studies, 1959.

Stone, Lawrence, "Social mobility in England 1500–1700," in *Seventeenth-century England: A Changing Culture*, Vol. 2, *Modern Studies*, ed. W. R. Owens, Totowa, NJ: Barnes & Noble, 1980, pp. 7–23.

Stone, Lawrence and Stone, Jeanne C. Fawtier, *An Open Elite? England, 1540–1880*, Oxford: Clarendon Press, 1984.

Swift, Jonathan, *A Tale of a Tub with Other Early Works 1696–1707*, ed. Herbert Davis, Oxford: Blackwell, 1957.

Temple, Sir Richard, *Some short remarks upon Mr. Lock's book in answer to Mr. Lownds*, London: Richard Baldwin, 1696.

Trudeau, Danielle, "Langue et monnaie au 16e siècle," *Stanford French Review* 7, 1 (Spring 1983): 37–55.

Vanbrugh, Sir John, *The Relapse*, ed. Curt A. Zimansky, Lincoln, NB: University of Nebraska Press, 1970.

Vilar, Pierre, *A History of Gold and Money, 1450–1920*, trans. Judith White, London: NLB, 1976.

Watt, Ian, *The Rise of the Novel*, Berkeley, CA: University of California Press, 1957.

Williamson, George, *The Senecan Amble: A Study in Prose from Bacon to Collier*, London: Faber, 1951.

19

Literary capital

Gray's "Elegy," Anna Laetitia Barbauld, and the vernacular canon

John Guillory

The renewal of interest in the history of literary property, of which this volume is evidence, has compelled us to redefine some of the most basic concepts of literary history. We now know that what we call "literature" must have been read very differently after authors began to consider their works as a kind of property, and after that redefinition of literary work was ratified by the institution of copyright law. In this chapter I would like to consider another sense in which literature might circulate as a kind of property. This secondary sense of literary property refers to the peculiar way in which one's education entitles one to "possess" literature itself, and particularly the literature of one's own country. Such possession is in an obvious way contingent upon the fact of *literacy*, but literacy is a very complex fact. The eighteenth century, for example, ushered in a momentous transition in the history of literacy, the transition from a school system primarily designed to produce literacy in the classical languages, to one designed to produce a largely vernacular literacy. The success of this transition was dependent upon a revaluation of the cultural property embodied in the works of vernacular literature, a celebration of their very accessibility to the "common reader." I will argue in this chapter that vernacular literacy is marked by a certain paradox, perhaps even a contradiction. For the vernacular canon is at once conceived to be the property of everyone in the nation, "common" property, while it remains the case that literacy itself is by no means a universal possession.

Gray's "Elegy" has a unique and quite interesting part to play in this story, as its most signal claim to fame in English literary history may well be its accessibility to the "common reader." In that sense the "Elegy" is something of a monument to vernacular literacy, despite Gray's own disdain for its popularity. The latter elitist sentiment may be reflected in the poem's unusual foregrounding of a literacy unavailable to the peasants who are ambivalently celebrated for their ignorance. The narrator, as we recall, imagines a hypothetical scene in which a future visitor to the country churchyard is conducted by a peasant to the epitaph on the narrator's tomb: "Approach and read (for thou canst read)/ The lay . . ." The parenthetical "for thou canst read" explicitly underscores the peasant's cultural deprivation, what I would describe as his lack of a certain kind of literary capital, the very capital that would allow him to "acquire" or "possess" the works of English literature. If literary property in this *other* sense is very much a concern of the poem – its "mute, inglorious Miltons" are mute after all because they are illiterate – we shall see that this concern is manifest at many levels of the "Elegy," both formally and thematically. In the pages to follow, I propose first to consider the relation between these levels in the "Elegy," in the context of vernacular literacy, and then to demonstrate how one "common reader," Anna Laetitia Barbauld, responded to the poem's anxious meditation on the paradox of literary capital.

The genre of Gray's "*Elegy*"

Gray finally called his poem an "elegy," but that generic designation may not be the most comprehensive. The "Elegy" belongs most obviously to the tradition of the locodescriptive poem, even if the location of its scene is deliberately inexact. As Samuel Johnson recognized in his comment on Sir John Denham's "Cooper's Hill," the loco-descriptive poem makes possible a style of expatiation eminently characteristic of the "Elegy":

> *Cooper's Hill* is the work that confers upon him [Denham] the rank and dignity of an original author. He seems to have been, at least among us, the author of a species of composition that may be denominated *local poetry*, of which the fundamental subject is some particular landscape to be poetically described, with the addition of such embellishments as may be supplied by historical retrospection or incidental meditation.[1]

The typical thematic variety and loose structure of poems such as "Cooper's Hill" have tended to bring compositional strategies themselves to the foreground in discussions of the genre, in particular, the "embellishment" or digression remarked by Johnson. It has been the argument of much of the best recent criticism of the genre, that of John Barrell, for example, that what Johnson calls "local poetry" derives its compositional principles from an especially fertile cross-breeding of aesthetic forms – painting and poetry – and that it would be impossible to conceive of the locodescriptive genre before the appearance in seventeenth-century England of *landscape* painting, a new genre of visual art.

In what follows I shall incorporate and respond to the argument of John Barrell, whose discussion of the topographical genre in his several books itself incorporates and responds to the work of Ralph Cohen and others. It has been Barrell's distinction to demonstrate how topographical poems in the eighteenth century organize their pictorial descriptions not in order to replicate exactly the pictorial scene of landscape painters such as Claude, but rather to produce a textual analogue for the way in which the eye moves across and into the space of the painting. Barrell argues specifically that just as in Claude "our eye is drawn to the horizon instantaneously" and then moves back to recover objects in the foreground or middleground, so in a topographical description such as we find in Thomson's *Seasons*, the relative abstraction of the initial landscape details is intended to hurry the reader along to the horizonal point, after which a more leisurely and excursive elaboration of detail is permitted.[2] On the basis of this structuring motif, Barrell argues that key landscape descriptions in topographical poetry, especially those "prospects" from the vantage of elevated terrain, depict the view as a representative image of the national order. The landscape organizes the entire social order as a harmonious totality, a construction already apparent in Denham's poem. If the significance of landscape in the eighteenth century also raises the question of *property in the land*, then one might legitimately ask what relation literary landscape figures between the national order and private property. As we shall see, this is the very problem which Gray's "Elegy" will take over from the locodescriptive genre.

In Barrell's analysis, it is crucial that the totalizing impulse can be indulged only by a radical simplification of the landscape that usually entails depopulating it of many of its residents. In the following passage, added in 1744 to Thomson's "Spring" (first published in 1728), the rural population is reduced to a metonymic trace, the "smoke" of the villages and towns on the horizon:

> Meantime you gain the height, from whose fair brow
> The bursting prospect spreads immense around;
> And, snatched o'er hill and dale, and wood and lawn,
> And verdant field, and darkening heath between,
> And villages embosomed soft in trees,
> And spiry towns by surging columns marked
> Of household smoke, your eye excursive roams --
> Wide-stretching from the Hall in whose kind haunt
> The hospitable Genius lingers still,
> To where the broken landscape, by degrees
> Ascending, roughens into rigid hills . . .
>   ("Spring," ll. 950–60)

Barrell comments on this passage: "It is of course particularly easy to see a vast prospect as a harmonious composition, if in its foreground is a landscaped park designed to organize the world beyond it into a pictorial unity from a carefully chosen station."[3] Lord Lyttelton, the gentleman addressed in Thomson's lines, views the national order from his "station," that of a nobleman, and from his estate, Hagley Park; everything beyond the park is shrunk perspectively to a margin. This effect might be described in rhetorical terms, if also redundantly, as the landscape *topos*: a totalizing pictorial representation in which the horizon or frame encloses not simply the view or "prospect" but the nation. This picture is obviously not *literally* representative, since it depicts the nation as a landscape or park, devoid of any except its most picturesque rural laborers.

The escalating valuation of landscape painting during the seventeenth and eighteenth centuries may well be sufficient to explain the fashion of pictorial description in poetry, but not to explain the totalizing drive of that description. The social investment in landscape painting's symbolic (and increasingly, monetary) value is contingent as well upon the development of gardening itself into *landscaping*, the large-scale reconstruction of estates and private parks. English gardens of the eighteenth century decline the symmetry of their French counterparts or Renaissance predecessors, which is to say that the visual principles according to which the new gardens are designed converge upon the pictorial principles of landscape painting. There are few movements in English taste more lavishly documented than the one I have just named,[4] and I will pass quickly here to what is for Barrell the crucial question of historical context: the possibility of the large-scale reconstruction projects and therefore also the possibility of a new social valuation of landscape is contingent upon the large-scale transformation of the countryside in the wake of agricultural capitalism, and in particular, as a consequence of successive waves of enclosure, agricultural "improvement," and consequent depopulation. While it is by no means the fate of every enclosed "common" land to become a private park such as Thomson describes in the passage quoted above, it is nevertheless the case that enclosure came increasingly to be associated with the *aesthetic* as well as the economic improvement of the countryside. Barrell is able to show that "the cultivated classes in England felt much more at ease, in the eighteenth and nineteenth centuries, in landscape which had been enclosed."[5] Initially, the aesthetic predeliction for landscape (and enclosed fields) may have been confined largely to the landed aristocracy, but increasingly, as Barrell argues, both enclosure and topographical poetry were taken up by the capitalist farmers and aristocratic improvers, who saw enclosure as simply agricultural improvement.[6] It follows that landscape as a representation of the *land*, the nation, also became an arena of contested self-representation for those constituencies, the landed aristocrats or capitalist farmers, whose claims to status were based equally on rural property, but on different relations to property. To this point I shall return. The central paradox of the landscape *topos* is at any rate capable of being succinctly formulated: the transformation of the "commons" into private property, the imposition of the grid of property upon the land (hedge and ha-ha), makes possible the *description* of landscape as a perspective upon the social order itself. Such a perspective represents the interests of property, but represents these interests as *universal*, and therefore as capable of expression by recourse to the rhetorical commonplace.

Here we may return to Johnson's early definition of the locodescriptive genre in order to acknowledge that what struck him as distinctive about the genre was not only its description of "some particular landscape" but the "embellishments" of "historical retrospection or incidental meditation." These embellishments have often been characterized in more or less disparaging terms as "rhetorical commonplaces," and they would appear to be a necessary constituent of the genre. The commonplaces usually turn out to be propositions of "moral philosophy," of a very general or abstract nature, and they are ordinarily *suggested by*, rather than embodied in, the details of the landscape itself. James Turner thus defines the genre as "topical in two senses: it is a response to historical events in the countryside, and it consists of topoi, traditional exercises of rhetoric."[7] But the relation between these senses of the topical is not all obvious. Barrell also remarks of much landscape description that its departure from the accurate description of real rural settings can be measured by its recourse to "rhetorical commonplaces," what Coleridge called the genre's "perpetual trick of moralizing everything."[8] So far from structuring topographical poems, then, rhetorical commonplaces tend to destructure them, and even to mar them, in the view of their detractors, with frequent lapses into banality and cliché. One may argue that what pictorial devices structure is precisely this mass of abstract, digressive material, which might otherwise degenerate into mere quotation, mere digression. But it would be more accurate to say that locodescription both invites the digressive style, and resists it by referring it continually to a "horizon" of pictorial space. The pictorial frame thus strives to counter descriptive chaos by making this chaos into a totality, a unity. If the resultant image of social harmony seems often forced or premature, that fact only registers the internal contradiction between a pictorial principle of organization and a rhetorical.

The question that emerges in the practice of the topographical genre concerns nothing less than the relation between rhetoric and what appears to be its successor in the eighteenth century, aesthetics. Barrell observes that the discourse of "aesthetics," which had previously "taken its examples mainly from rhetoric," came to concern "itself with aesthetic values chiefly as they were revealed in the contemplation of landscape."[9] One might go further than this and say that aesthetics – the familiar discourses of taste, judgment, the beautiful and the sublime – *displaced* rhetoric as the discourse within which writers meditated on questions relating to art, and that the topographical genre is one place where we can see aesthetics begin to establish its primacy over rhetoric. Raymond Williams has drawn our attention to the fact that the shift from rhetoric to aesthetics reorients the analysis of the beautiful from the activity of production to the activity of consumption:

> The replacement of the disciplines of grammar and rhetoric (which speak to the multiplicities of intention and performance) by the discipline of criticism (which speaks of effect, and only through effect to intentions and performance) is a central intellectual movement of the bourgeois period. Each kind of discipline moved, in the period of change, to a particular pole: grammar and rhetoric to writing; criticism to reading.[10]

Here it is important to recall that the discipline of rhetoric in the Renaissance is not primarily analytic but practical; the rhetoric handbooks are written as guides to writing, as a technical means of literary production.[11] Does it then follow that the ubiquitous commonplace books (*thesauri*, treasuries) which schoolchildren of the Renaissance produced, which filled the shelves of the school libraries, and upon which Renaissance writers drew to make their writing "copious," were simply replaced as resources in the discourses of the arts by the storehouse of images derived from pictorial depictions of landscape? We know that in fact the practice of keeping commonplace books continued in the schools throughout the eighteenth century. I would like to argue here for something like the survival of rhetoric in the form of those "rhetorical commonplaces" which inhabit the topographical genre itself, a genre which is at the same time uniquely allied to the new discourses of aesthetics. In a certain sense I propose only to make the modest critical gesture of re-emphasizing the rhetorical derivation of the topographical genre in relation to the pictorial. But ultimately I will suggest a somewhat larger hypothesis: that the topographical genre's use of pictorial composition reconstructs the rhetorical commonplace as the sign of a property as real as the enclosed field, namely, the "treasury" of vernacular literary works. This new form of cultural property is very urgently sought by an upwardly mobile professional class, who see it as both "common" in relation to the classical literacy which precedes it, and *private*, because it is produced and consumed as a commodity.

Complacency and commonplace in Gray's "Elegy"

Let us sketch the borders of the locodescriptive genre by considering a poem that is both more and less than topographical, Gray's "Elegy Written in a Country Churchyard." Here is the opening stanza of what is perhaps the most consistently anthologized poem in English literature:

> The curfew tolls the knell of parting day,
> The lowing herd wind slowly o'er the lea,
> The ploughman homeward plods his weary way,
> And leaves the world to darkness and to me.[12]

There is certainly no question that Gray's "Elegy" stands in the line of the topographical poem, as it proceeds directly to invoke the concept of "landscape," and situates its meditative spectator where he has a prospect of both the countryside and the social order. Yet Gray immediately withdraws the visible prospect in the next stanza ("Now fades the glimmering landscape") and gives himself over entirely to "incidental meditation" provoked by that abbreviated original prospect. In effect, Gray gives up the structuring device of moving through the landscape and generates nothing but rhetorical commonplaces, leading up to the major inductive *topos* of the poem, "The paths of glory lead but to the grave." This turning of the tables on the locodescriptive poem is apparently responsible for the "Elegy's" enduring popularity (after most topographical poetry ceases to be anthologized), as well as for the occasional criticism of its extreme "sententiousness" (a term which would have been wholly laudatory in the Renaissance). The "Elegy" can be, and has been, both praised and dismissed for the fact that it is a tissue of quotations (to use a contemporary commonplace); its phrases sound familiar even in the absence of identified pretexts, as though it were the anonymous distillation of literary sententiae. It may no longer be possible now to distinguish this effect from the effect of memorization in the classroom, since the "Elegy" has been adopted as such a school text for nearly two centuries. Hence Leslie Stephen could remark in his 1909 study, "Gray and his school": "Everyone knows [Gray's] poetry by heart. The 'Elegy' has so worked itself into the popular imagination that it includes more familiar phrases than any poem of equal length in the language."[13] That this impression of familiarity even upon the first reading is by no means simple is confirmed by the slightly reserved praise of nineteenth-century critics for the virtual inevitability of the poem; thus Edmund Gosse in 1882: "The Elegy may almost be looked upon as the typical piece of English verse, our poem of poems, not that it is the most brilliant or original or profound lyric in our language, but because it combines in more balanced perfection than any other all the qualities that go into the production of a poetical effect."[14] The total impression of an immediate but sophisticated accessibility locates the poem within a literary culture which may well now be based upon an anthology of literary clichés available to every minimally educated reader (what E. D. Hirsch calls "cultural literacy"[15]), but which in Gray's time was still based upon the practice of keeping a commonplace book.[16] Gray compiled three folio commonplace books in his lifetime, within which he transcribed and translated quotations, as well as drafts of his own poetry, including the "Elegy."[17] Wordsworth's complaint that "Gray wrote English verses as his brother Eton schoolboys wrote Latin, filching a phrase now from one author and now from another,"[18] is an accurate characterization of a compositional process mediated by a text whose significance in the process of literary production should be recognized as such. In the Renaissance the practice of keeping a common-place book reproduces the classical rhetor's device of finding (*inventio*) the topic or line of argument (*locus*) appropriate to a given, usually oral, persuasive performance. The motive of persuasion begins to recede after the successful dissemination in the sixteenth century of Erasmus's *De Copia*, with its stylistic norms adapted to written production, and its specific pedagogic injunction that schoolchildren copy down into books of blank paper selected passages from their reading. These commonplace books tended to be organized according to headings (adversity, anger, fear, God, honesty, justice) that were designed to give access to *topoi* in the Aristotelian sense, commonplaces (*koinoi topoi*) which are simply lines of argument in a typical rhetorical performance, an attempt to move or persuade an audience to some position.[19] But the practice of transcribing exemplary *topoi* eventually insures the memorability of texts or passages in whatever context of recollection, and hence the transformation of "topics" into the modern conception of indexical categories of any sort. In 1706, Locke published "A new method of a common-place book" organized around just this indexical, or post-rhetorical, principle.[20] Gray followed Locke's plan in compiling his own folio volumes.

Over the long term, then, we can observe a transformation in the purpose of the commonplace book, as the rhetorical motive is gradually displaced by a more explicitly anthological one, a motive oriented toward the *consumption* rather than the production of texts. Nevertheless it would be incorrect to suppose that this transformation entailed the disappearance of the rhetorical motive of persuasion, which lingers in the very conception of commonplaces as truths generally believed. If Gray's "Elegy" is indeed composed in much the same manner as a commonplace book, its "sententiousness" takes the strictly Aristotelian form of the enthymeme, or rhetorical syllogism, a trun-cated logic deducing the death of specific individuals from a universal mortality; it is scarcely surprising that the syllogism converges upon the exemplary classical syllogism, "All men are mortal . . ." The doubling back of the rhetorical motive upon what might be thought of as a purely anthological principle (collecting beautiful passages or works) marks the point at which the "commonplace" itself becomes synonymous with banality, or mere truism. One supposes also that the commonplace book had to be discarded as a means of literary production in order for the Romantic locodescriptive lyric to set itself against the rhetorical commonplace, or to stigmatize the effect of "sententiousness." The confusion of the rhetorical and the anthological motive in the topographical poem – the generic matrix of the Romantic lyric – underlines the semantic ambiguity of the *topos*, which was perhaps even in Aristotle an unstable sliding between a "place" in the visual memory and in a text. But we will not consider here the interesting question of to what extent this confusion continues to determine aspects of composition at the turn of the century. Suffice it to say that critical banalities about "generalization" in eighteenth-century poetry are inadequate to describe the genre-specific effects of loco-descriptive poetry, and only betray the need for an analysis of banality itself, as the new meaning of "commonplace," and thus the lexical sign of a new condition of literary production.

When Johnson comes to praise the "Elegy," he locates its power precisely in the evocation of what is "common," and the language of his praise thus functions symptomatically to register the full force and resonance of the word "common" in eighteenth-century discourse:

> In the character of his *Elegy* I rejoice to concur with the common reader, for by the common sense of readers uncorrupted with literary prejudices, after all the refinements of subtility and the dogmatism of learning, must finally be decided all claim to poetical honours. The "Churchyard" abounds with images which find a mirrour in every mind, and with sentiments to which every bosom returns an echo. The four stanzas beginning "Yet even these bones" are to me original: I have never seen the notions in any other place; yet he that reads them here persuades himself that he has always felt them. Had Gray written often thus it had been vain to blame, and useless to praise him.
>
> (Vol. III, p. 441)

The poem Johnson describes is uttered by the *Zeitgeist*, as though it were the consummate expression of a social consensus. This is not to say, however, that the social totality merely speaks its own truth through Gray (or Johnson). The "Elegy" does not abound with images which find a mirror in *every* mind. Let us eliminate from this consensus to begin with everyone who will not read the poem because he or she cannot read. What then is left of the poem's truth? Primarily its claim to a "common sense" which embraces everyone in the same way that everyone is embraced by a mortal fate. The fact of the universal mortal fate is the ground of a claim to a universal truth that does not even allow of an "original" thought unless that thought can be experienced as "always felt." This effect has been subjected to the sharpest critique by Empson in his now unavoidable sentences on the "massive calm" and "complacence" of the poem: "The truism of the reflections in the church-yard, the universality and impersonality this gives to the style, claim as if by comparison that we ought to accept the injustice of society as we do the inevitability of death."[21] The persuasiveness of the poem's truth-effect has everything to do with its style, with the peculiar force of its commonplaces in a specific linguistic form.

The tradition of Romantic criticism has been suspicious enough of the commonplaces to wonder at the source of their power, and even to trouble itself about the value of the truth which anyone might acknowledge. I. A. Richards, whose theoretical armature was mobilized to a high degree of readiness for an attack upon banality, exempts Gray's "Elegy" from this charge on the ground of its successful "tone," which he defines as "a perfect recognition of the writer's relation to the reader." Gray's flawless staging of this relation compels Richards to repeat the very terms of Johnson's praise, doubly symptomatic now for the defensiveness of the rhetoric:

> Gray's "Elegy", indeed, might stand as a supreme instance to show how powerful an exquisitely adjusted tone may be. It would be difficult to maintain that the thought in this poem is striking or original, or that its feeling is exceptional. It embodies a sequence of reflections and attitudes that under similar conditions arise readily in any contemplative mind. Their character as commonplaces, needless to say, does not make them any less important, and the "Elegy" may usefully remind us that boldness and originality are not necessities for great poetry.[22]

A footnote adds to this statement a small quibble with Johnson, denying the originality of the lines beginning "Yet even these bones." In fact, it is important for Richards to deny any originality at all to the poem in order to make the strongest possible argument for the overcoming of banality by exquisiteness of tone. But it is hard to see how this argument has not been anticipated by Johnson's gesture of merely joining a unanimous and harmonious chorus, to which indeed he already belonged. This chorus cannot be reduced to the company of "any contemplative mind"; nor can it be expanded to include all who would agree that "the paths of glory lead but to the grave" (presumably everyone). On the contrary, Johnson has already identified the social locus of "common sense" in the "common reader." If the question of tone concerns the relation of writer to reader, that relation is defined not solely by the exchange of commonplaces but, in Empson's words, as an effect of "complacence," that is, a species of pleasure. It is against this pleasure that Empson reacts with "irritation," the precisely antithetical affect ("Many people have been irritated . . . by the complacence"). The affect of complacence is produced, as Empson rightly argues, by the relation of the commonplaces as such – the continuous quotation from a kind of generalized commonplace book of eighteenth-century literary culture – to the "universality and impersonality" of the style. I would like to propose that this style is produced by the systematic linguistic normalization of quotation, a compositional method of translating, decontextualizing, and grammatically regularizing the matter of the commonplace book. In this way Gray gives the anthological commonplace a new rhetorical motive: the technique of linguistic normalization *disseminates* the commonplaces as the convergence of "common sense" with a common language. The cento of quotable quotations generates a scenario of reception (consumption) characterized by the reader's pleased recognition that "this is my truth," the truth common to all. But the pleasure of finding oneself in this common place is also founded upon the subliminal recognition that "this is my language." Johnson's figures of "mirror" and "echo" accurately track the sequence of these recognitions. The pleasure elicited in the scenario is in a sense, then, narcissistic, but it is not the pleasure of an individual's recognition of his or her individuality; rather it takes the form of the individual's pleased identification with a social group, an identification through the medium of what the reader and writer possess in common, a language.

The latter point can be extrapolated from Empson's reading of the famous "gem" stanza in Gray's "Elegy." For Empson the distinction between the rich and the poor, which governs the prospect of the social order in the poem, takes the quite specific form of an observation on the lack of *social mobility* in a particular historical form of class structure. It is only in the context of conceiving the possibility of movement above one's class that Gray's characteristic strategies of ironizing wealth or power under the shadow of death, or granting to poverty a noble pathos, become intelligible:

Gray's "Elegy" is an odd case of poetry with latent political ideas:

> Full many a gem of purest ray serene
> The dark, unfathomed caves of ocean bear;
> Full many a flower is born to blush unseen
> And waste its sweetness on the desert air.

What this means, as the context makes clear, is that eighteenth-century England had no scholarship system or *carrière ouverte aux talents*. This is stated as pathetic, but the reader is put into a mood in which one would not try to alter it. (It is true that Gray's society, unlike a possible machine society, was necessarily based on manual labour, but it might have used a man of special ability wherever he was born.) By comparing the social arrangement to Nature he makes it seem inevitable, which it was not, and gives it a dignity which was undeserved. Furthermore, a gem does not mind being in a cave and a flower prefers not to be picked; we feel that the man is like the flower, as short-lived, natural, and valuable, and this tricks us into feeling that he is better off without opportunities. The sexual suggestion of *blush* brings in the Christian idea that virginity is good in itself, and so that any renunciation is good; this may trick us into feeling it is lucky for the poor man that society keeps him unspotted from the World . . .

Many people, without being communists, have been irritated by the complacence in the massive calm of the poem, and this seems partly because they feel there is a cheat in the implied politics; the "bourgeois" themselves do not like literature to have too much "bourgeois ideology."

(Some Versions of Pastoral, pp. 4–5)

These sentences still stand in my view against all the refutations of them because they counter Gray's pathos with an equally powerful analytic performance, a triumph of reason. The elements of pathos do not survive their disarticulation. And yet the wasting of human potential, in Empson's own words, "cannot but be felt deeply," and indeed this pathos is the motive of Empson's rational critique of Gray. Empson claims both that there is too much "bourgeois ideology" in Gray's poem, and that "all the great poetic statements [of the waste of human powers]" are in a way "bourgeois," a contradiction that occasions his striking translation of the "gem" stanza into a statement about the absence of an institutional structure facilitating social mobility. What this stanza means is that eighteenth-century England had no system of *schooling* that would produce such mobility. But in fact, as historians have amply demonstrated, there was a much greater degree of social mobility in this century than in the feudal era of fixed "estates," or in the two previous transitional centuries.[23] The fact of increased upward mobility is at once an axiom of "bourgeois ideology" – that anyone can succeed – and its major source of social anxiety. Hence the continuous appropriation by the bourgeoisie of aristocratic caste traits, precisely in order to reinforce and stabilize a class structure founded upon a necessary degree of instability or fluidity. Needless to say, this functional instability of social hierarchy requires complex practical and discursive strategies in order to maintain the structure as a whole; there must be neither too little nor too much social mobility. In the same way, mobility must be valued neither too little nor too much. Gray's narrative scenario of imagining what the ignorant peasant might have been valorizes in its image of the unfound gem the process of mobility or circulation: what cannot move is waste. The poem associates the waste of human life with death itself, but that hyperbole passes over without notice the social structures blocking the realization of human potential in some *productive* accomplishment. One such structure is of course the educational system. If the poem seems devoid of specific reference to the school on its glassy surface, we need to insist upon the fact that its idealization of moral poverty is at every moment dependent upon the resources of *literacy*: there is no epitaph for the unremembered poor without access to at least this form of cultural capital. Hence Gray is forced to reveal (in an otherwise gratuitous parenthesis) that the peasant who guides the melancholy speaker to the graven epitaph which concludes the poem cannot himself read the epitaph: "Approach and read (*for thou canst read*) / The lay . . ." But this condition is perhaps already more than implicit in the poem's most famous hypothesis of a "mute, inglorious Milton."[24]

The vernacular curriculum as cultural capital

Despite its inaccuracy, Empson's identification of the school as the site at which social mobility is choked off is a perversely brilliant intuition. Eighteenth-century guardians of class structure were worried about just the mobilizing and possibly destabilizing effects of education, and they were likely to argue that the availability of knowledge had to be actively restricted. In the previous century Locke had suggested that the children of the poor should not be taught to read at all, and this opinion was simply the consensus of the educated.[25] Soame Jenyns, for example, remarks entirely seriously that ignorance "is a cordial, administered by the gracious hand of providence, of which [the poor] ought never to be deprived by an illjudged and improper education"[26] – a sentiment whose expression is only *tonally* distinct from Gray's ambivalent celebration of rural ignorance. Not until the later eighteenth century were the poor provided in any numbers with the means to acquire literacy, and then only as an adjunct to the disciplinization of their everyday life (the program, for example, of the new "monitorial" systems of basic education).[27] If knowledge is a real form of property or wealth, it is difficult to see how this property can come to be possessed by the endemically impoverished, how indeed a "mute, inglorious Milton" can ever come to write, for better or for worse. Clearly the question of social mobility, as it is raised by access to knowledge, does not refer to the poor at all, except as they represent *in extremis* a condition of deprivation that is in fact *relative* to certain other social groups. Only those in possession of some capital are in a position to acquire the knowledge that in turn signifies the possibility, at once attractive and dangerous, of upward mobility, even if this mobility is essentially enacted in the realm of the imaginary, as the imitation of upper-class behavior or educated manners; that is, as social *pretension*.

Here we may invoke the concept of a specifically symbolic or *cultural* capital to discern the motive force behind a variety of developments that traverse the market, the class structure, and the transformation of discourses. These are: the wider availability of vernacular printed matter, particularly subscription series such as the *Spectator* (discussed in Chapter 11 by Lawrence E. Klein); the establishment of quasi-educational bodies such as the literary clubs, the coffee-houses, and the lending libraries; and the rise of for-profit grammar schools and vocational academies designed for the commercial classes.[28] In this newer institutional setting, not only are professional knowledges such as accounting and surveying disseminated, but also traditional knowledges – of the classical languages and literatures – which are disseminated (usually in translation) as the sign of acquired rather than inherited capital, and as means of exhibiting status. Such social emulation of upper-class culture expresses itself not so much as antagonism toward social superiors but as a kind of embrace, the complement of that bourgeoisification of the nobility by which their revenues came to be invested more and more in trade. As soon as we look at the educational sites of social pretension, we note that the curricular form of this pretension is marked by the clear distinction of "polite letters," of linguistic knowledges, from the nascent discourses of natural philosophy, pure or applied. This distinction, which would have been meaningless in the medieval university, is articulated already in the seventeenth century in Locke's well-known critique of the Latin curriculum: "Can there be anything more ridiculous, than that a Father should waste his own Money, and his Son's time, in setting him to learn the Roman Language; when at the same time he designs him for a Trade, wherein he having no use of Latin, fails not to forget that little which he brought from School."[29] But Locke goes on to concede that a knowledge of Latin is of course the endowment of every gentleman. The vocational academies of the eighteenth century follow Locke's utilitarian principle in offering new courses in skills needful for various forms of commerce, and their rise is paralleled by a decline in the quality of the grammar schools, which had been vital institutions in the preceding two centuries, and by the ossification of the university programs patronized by bored noble progeny.[30]

Two consequences follow from this curricular reformation: first, the position of the classical languages, as the knowledge provided by the traditional curriculum, changes; but this knowledge does not suffer in the end a simple derogation in status. On the contrary, since the children of gentlemen continue to be educated in the traditional classical languages, their "useless" knowledge comes by the later eighteenth century to stand as a pure sign of their genteel status.[31] Second, there is installed in the upwardly mobile middle classes a linguistic ambivalence which takes the form of a suspicion of the classical languages as useless knowledge, but at the same time, and perhaps equally strongly, an envy of the social distinction they represent.[32] This ambivalence, as we shall see, is ultimately worked through and resolved with the entry of vernacular literature into the new, middle-class schools. The study of vernacular literature is thus at first a substitute for the study of Greek or Latin, but with the same object of producing a linguistic sign of social distinction, a distinctive language.

John Barrell helpfully surveys the outpouring of linguistic controversy in the eighteenth century and he demonstrates that "proper" or correct English is still usually conceptualized from the perspective of the gentleman: "The gentleman . . . was believed to be the only member of society who spoke a language universally intelligible; his usage was 'common,' in the sense of being neither a local dialect nor infected by the terms of any particular art."[33] Nonetheless the impetus behind the standardization of speech through the teaching of vernacular literature does not come from the landed nobility or gentry but from a much wider and more heterogenous group, which is beginning to recognize itself not just as other than aristocratic but as part of a society of "gentlemen," newly defined according to norms of behavior and educational attainments rather than blood: "For well before the 1730s it is clear that, though the gentleman may survive as the ideal of the comprehensive observer, he is no longer easily identifiable with any very considerable body of men within the society of England."[34]

Perhaps the most striking claims for the upwardly mobilizing power of vernacular literacy are put forward by the middle-class Dissenters, who had been excluded since the 1662 Act of Uniformity from teaching in the grammar schools and universities. The "Dissenting academies" which emerged as a result of that act initially merely reproduced for their constituencies the curriculum of the traditional schools, but this imitation clearly did not provide the cultural capital most desired by the commercial and professional classes who were most likely to be Dissenters in the first place. The decades-long campaign to replace Latin with vernacular texts had doubtless many determinants, but we might describe the particular moment under scrutiny as the temporary victory of linguistic ambivalence over social emulation. Just as the late medieval nobility acquired literacy, but did not care to master the scholastic curriculum of the clergy, the middling sort wished to acquire polite speech, but not necessarily a knowledge of Latin or Greek. In this way a *difference* from the aristocracy was preserved within the gradual process of cultural homogenization; and this difference expressed both a resentment against exclusions based upon class and religious belief, and a canny recognition that the dissemination of polite speech provided a cultural basis for the *dispersion* of political power. Hence the program to vernacularize the curriculum became quite urgent by mid-century, the subject of intense controversy. By the time that Thomas Sheridan writes his important polemic, *British Education: or the Source of the Disorders of Great Britain* (1756), the connection between vernacular linguistic refinement and a progressive political agenda was firmly entrenched, and took the pedagogic form in the Dissenting academies of a revival of "political oratory," or rhetoric. It was in the context of a rhetorical program whose ends are also easily recognizable as nationalistic that Sheridan, like many others, urged a syllabus of English literature:

> as models of style, Milton in the poetic, and Shakespeare in the dramatic, Swift, Addison, Dryden, and Sir William Temple (in some of his works) in prose, may be considered as truly classical, as the Virgil, Caesar, Tully, and Sallust of the Romans; nor is there any reason that they should not be handed down as such equally to the end of time . . .
>
> And shall we not endeavor to secure to future generations, entire and unchanged, their birthright in Milton, in Addison, and Swift? Or shall we put in the power of a giddy and profuse age to dissipate, or render of no value, the heaps of treasure now collected in the many excellent books written by English authors?[35]

The anxiety expressed by Sheridan is that, in the absence of an institutional form of dissemination, literary culture cannot be entrusted to preserve English works of the past; vernacular works must be revalued as equal in value to classical works and therefore worthy to be taught in the schools. But the introduction of these works into school curricula exceeded the objective of instituting a standard of grammatical speech as a credential of gentility, and discovered in the form of anthologized vernacular works the means of directing this speech toward a political objective. The rhetorical or "elocutionary" practice which emerged in the schools, the reading and thus *performing* of select texts from English literature, thus served a new rhetorical program in which rhetorical "commonplaces" in the older sense were replaced by a selection of the best of English literary works; at the same time the ability to read and quote these works performed something like the rhetorical function of the Aristotelian *topoi*. Oratory consists first of the ability to speak the standard dialect, the language of "gentlemen," and the production of this speech entailed a constant and perhaps largely tacit process of normalizing the linguistically heterogeneous works of English literature. The form of the anthology thus resembles very much the form of Gray's "Elegy"; or better, the "Elegy" is situated just where the older form of the commonplace book is absorbed into the program of the vernacular anthology.

Early vernacular anthologies such as William Enfield's frequently reprinted *Speaker* (1774), the Adamic ancestor of *The Norton Anthology*, were thus devised for use in the classroom as texts for elocution practice. What we think of as literary study – the interpretation of texts – was still confined in the schools largely to the field of biblical studies.[36] The *Speaker*, which was compiled for use in Warrington Academy, one of the more distinguished of the Dissenting academies (Joseph Priestley taught there), opens with an essay on elocution and goes on to reproduce a recognizably modern selection of English literary texts, notably different perhaps only for a greater selection of mid-century writers and the relative absence of those Restoration poets whose language was paradigmatic for the polite speech of the earlier eighteenth century. There appeared then, within and in some sense also against, the polite speech of the "gentleman" in the technical sense, a different linguistic practice, different but also the same: a "standard English" based upon the linguistically classicist norms of the language spoken originally in the Restoration court, but more and more being defined by the normative practice of the London bourgeoisie. It should be emphasized, however, that even if the middle-class academies disseminated a form of cultural capital from which certain strata of this class had been excluded by the traditional schools, that dissemination ceased at the border of property. That border might be marked in cultural terms as the gross division between the literate and the illiterate, but within the former category the distinction between classical and vernacular literacy corresponds roughly to the difference between two relations to property, to wit, entitlement, and acquisition.

Barbauld's "Warrington Academy"

That culture can be acquired *like property*, or that it is a real form of property, is scarcely surprising, but in the context of the relation between an aristocracy still in some ways ideologically hegemonic and a bourgeoisie still in the process of translating its material acquisitions into a cultural identity, the cultural value of a symbolic commodity such as vernacular literacy is still being negotiated. I would like to consider briefly here one example of this complex negotiation, carried on in part by means of allusion to the topographical genre. The example is a poem by Anna Laetitia Barbauld, called "Warrington Academy," and printed immediately after Gray's "Elegy" in Enfield's *Speaker*. Both Gray's and Barbauld's poems are included under the category of "Descriptive pieces," a genre concept inclusive of, if not derived from, the topographical poem. The "descriptive piece" develops specifically the anthological tendency of that genre. The adjacency of Barbauld's poem to Gray's does not seem to me accidental, as her poem alludes openly and quite interestingly to the "Elegy." Some lines of Barbauld's poem are also quoted at the conclusion of Enfield's dedication of the volume to John Lees, then President of Warrington Academy. The dedication boasts, as does the passage from Barbauld, of the successful careers pursued by graduates of the academy:

> In this Seminary, which was at first established, and has been uniformly conducted, on the extensive plan of providing a proper course of Instruction for young men in the most useful branches of Science and Literature, you have seen many respectable characters formed, who are now filling up their stations in society with reputation to themselves and advantage to the Public. And, while the same great object continues to be pursued, by faithful endeavours to cultivate the understandings of youth, and by a steady attention to discipline, it is hoped, that you will have the satisfaction to observe the same effects produced, and that the scene will be realized, which OUR POETESS has so beautifully described [there follow ll. 56–62 of "Warrington Academy," to be quoted below].[37]

Anna Laetitia Barbauld was the daughter of a Warrington tutor, Dr John Aiken, and in addition to being a good poet and fairly well known in her day, she was extremely possessed of that mobility by which one travels in literary circles. In her later life she was a friend of both Wordsworth and Coleridge. She produced an edition of English novelists in fifty volumes (including many women novelists) and later a companion volume to Enfield's for women readers, entitled *The Female Speaker*. I convey these accessible facts not so much to resurrect Barbauld from an undeserved obscurity, but to present her impeccable credentials in literary culture. She was very much at the vanguard of that anthologizing movement by which English literature was given a canonical form.[38] I reproduce here, then, the text of "Warrington Academy":[39]

> Mark where its simple front yon mansion rears,
> The nursery of men for future years!
> Here callow chiefs and embryo statesmen lie
> And unfledg'd poets short excursions try:
> While Mersey's gentle current, which too long
> By fame neglected, and unknown to song
> Between his rushy banks, (no poet's theme)
> Had crept inglorious, like a vulgar stream,
> Reflects th'ascending feats with conscious pride,
> And dares to emulate a classic tide.   10
> Soft music breathes along each op'ning shade,
> And sooths the dashing of his rough cascade.
> With mystic lines his sands are figured o'er,
> And circles trac'd upon the lettr'd shore.
> Beneath his willows rove th'inquiring youth,
> And court the fair majestic form of truth.
> Here nature opens all her secret springs,
> And heav'n born science plumes her eagle-wings:
> Too long had bigot rage, with malice swell'd,
> Crush'd her strong pinions, and her flight withheld: 20
> Too long to check her ardent progress strove:

So writhes the serpent round the bird of Jove;
Hangs on her flight, restrains her tow'ring wing,
Twists its dark folds, and points its venom'd sting.
Yet still (if aught aright the Muse divine)
Her rising pride shall mock the vain design;
On founding pinions yet aloft shall soar,
And thro' the azure deep untravell'd paths explore.
Where science smiles, the Muses join the train;
And gentlest arts and purest manners reign.   30
   Ye generous youth who love this studious shade,
How rich a field is to your hopes display'd!
Knowledge to you unlocks the classic page;
And virtue blossoms for a better age.
Oh golden days! oh bright unvalued hours!
What bliss (did ye but know that bliss) were yours!
With richest stores your glowing bosoms fraught,
Perception quick, and luxury of thought;
The high designs that heave the labouring soul,
Panting for fame, impatient of controul,   40
And fond enthusiastic thought, that feeds
On pictur'd tales of vast heroic deeds;
And quick affections, kindling into flame
At virtue's or their country's honour'd name;
And spirits light, to every joy in tune;
And friendship, ardent as a summer's noon;
And generous scorn of vice's venal tribe;
And proud disdain of interest's sordid bribe;
And conscious honour's quick instinctive sense;
And smiles unforc'd, and easy confidence;   50
And vivid fancy; and clear simple truth;
And all the mental bloom of vernal youth.
   How bright the scene to fancy's eye appears,
Thro' the long perspective of the distant years,
When this, this little group their country calls
From academic shades and learned halls,
To fix her laws, her spirit to sustain,
And light up glory thro' her wide domain,
Their various tastes in different arts display'd,
Like temper'd harmony of light and shade,   60
With friendly union in one mass shall blend,
And this adorn the state, and that defend.
These the sequestered shade shall cheaply please,
With learned labor, and inglorious ease;
While those, impell'd by some resistless force,
O'er seas and rocks shall urge their vent'rous course;
Rich fruits matur'd by glowing suns behold,

And China's groves of vegetable gold;
From every land the various harvest spoil,
And bear the tribute to their native soil: 70
But tell each land (while every toil they share,
Firm to sustain, and resolute to dare,)
MAN is the nobler growth our realms supply,
And SOULS are ripen'd in our northern sky.
   Some pensive creep along the shelly shore;
Unfold the silky texture of a flower,
With sharpen'd eyes inspect an hornet's sting,
And all the wonders of an insect's wing.
Some trace with curious search the hidden cause
Of nature's changes, and her various laws;   80
Untwist her beauteous web, disrobe her charms,
And hunt her to her elemental forms:
Or prove what hidden powers in herbs are found
To quench disease and cool the burning wound;
With cordial drops the fainting head sustain,
Call back the flitting soul, and still the throbs of pain.
   The patriot passion this shall strongly feel,
Ardent, and glowing with undaunted zeal;
With lips of fire shall plead his country's cause
And vindicate the majesty of laws.   90
This, cloath'd with Britain's thunder, spread alarms
Thro' the wide earth, and shake the pole with arms.
That, to the sounding lyre his deeds rehearse,
Enshrine his name in some immortal verse,
To long posterity his praise consign,
And pay a life of hardships by a line.
While others, consecrate to higher aims,
Whose hallow'd bosoms glow with purer flames,
Love in their heart, persuasion in their tongue,
With words of peace shall charm the list'ning throng,   100
Draw the dread veil that wraps th'eternal throne,
And launch our souls into the bright unknown.

"Warrington Academy" situates itself in relation to the generic tradition of Denham's "Cooper's Hill," the ur-topographical poem. The Mersey winds its way emblematically through the landscape as does the Thames in Denham's poem. In so locating her poem generically, Barbauld also declines to pastoralize her subject in the way that Gray throws a veil of decorous pathos over his depiction of the social order. Barbauld's poem lifts the pastoral scrim from Gray's pretty set, exposing behind the anachronism of its pathos certain facts, the struggle of individuals and social groups to rise. Gray's peasants of course do not struggle, but that is because they are *peasants*. The social world of the "Elegy" is archaically divided into a peasantry and what looks like the pastoral aristocrat in disguise as a peasant. The bourgeois exists in this world only as its secret *point of view*, the actual "horizon" of Gray's landscape. Barbauld's word for the condition of the social order she so firmly grasps is "emulation" (see 1.10), which here has its most exact meaning of to compete by imitation. This point is important because the opening lines express the fact of struggle in cultural terms, as the Mersey's desire to "emulate a classic tide." The Mersey not only successfully competes against its classic precursors, but puts forward its vernacular claim to "classic" status by allusively appropriating the most famous vernacular *locus classicus* of topographical poetry, an anthological commonplace in the eighteenth century:

> O could I flow like thee, and make thy stream
> My great example, as it is my theme!
> Though deep, yet clear, though gentle, yet not dull,
> Strong without rage, without ore-flowing full.

In these famous lines from "Cooper's Hill," Denham reinscribes the ancient Ciceronian *topos*, the *universum flumen* of rhetorical topics, as the topography of the Thames itself. It is well known, of course, that this topography is explicitly royalist. The effortless embodiment of the very fluidity they long for, these lines distilled for Restoration and eighteenth-century culture everything that was left of the Renaissance nobility's *sprezzatura* into a single linguistic performance, the supreme anticipation of polite speech. And what unquestionably excited so many imitations of these lines was just the way in which the language becomes the referent. To imitate them after 1660 is to celebrate the Restoration linguistic *politesse* as it stands for the Restoration polity. Yet Barbauld pointedly opposes to Denham's Thames a naturally "gentle current" which is like a "vulgar stream" only in having had no poet to sing of it ("By fame neglected, and unknown to song"), or perhaps only a "mute, inglorious Milton" to languish on its "inglorious" banks. Gray's problem of wasted talent is regrounded in the language of the ur-text of topographical poetry to foreground in Barbauld's landscape, to set beside the stream of language itself, the institution – the school – within which that language is produced as a signifier of linguistic facility, and of social mobility.

The distinction between "gentle" and "vulgar" which plays across the surface of Barbauld's setting of the scene of the academy thus activates the latent class referents of Denham's rhetoric, but in the context of the conditions giving rise to the Dissenting academies themselves:

> Here nature opens all her secret springs,
> And heav'n born science plumes her eagle-wings:
> Too long had bigot rage, with malice swell'd,
> Crush'd her strong pinions, and her flight withheld.

> Ye generous youth who love this studious shade,
> How rich a field is to your hopes display'd!
> Knowledge to you unlocks the classic page;
> And virtue blossoms for a better age.
>
> (ll.17–20, 31–4)

Barbauld alludes in the first set of lines to the laws by which Dissenters were excluded from access to the traditional educational institutions; it is perhaps only a historical irony, rather than an allusion proper, which characterizes as "bigot rage" the very idealized social arrangement Denham saw emblematized in the Thames: "strong without rage." More interesting still is Barbauld's reworking of the various tropes by means of which Gray characterizes the social deprivation of the poor, whose "rage" would mean something rather different:

> But knowledge to their eyes her ample page
> Rich with the spoils of time did ne'er unroll;
> Chill Penury repressed their noble rage,
> And froze the genial current of their soul.
>
> ("Elegy," ll. 49–52)

Barbauld's opening of the "secret springs," her unfreezing of Gray's "genial current," supplies a precise antecedent to the pronominal subjects of Gray's universalized and abstracted condition of deprivation. The subjects of "repression" in Barbauld are not the poor, after all, but a certain stratum of the middle classes. The very absence of precise reference in Gray's poem, its generalization of particular deprivations, permitted its readers to apply the concept of deprivation to their own situations. Barbauld anticipates but also qualifies Empson's reduction of the poem's generalization to the specific conditions of the educational system: "England had no scholarship system or *carrière ouverte aux talents*. This is stated as pathetic, but the reader is put into a mood in which one would not try to alter it." In fact there were many who were disposed very strongly to alter this condition. Such a motive would account for Barbauld's fierce praise of "emulation," as well as her location of Warrington Academy in the *space* of the locodescriptive poem. The foregrounding of the academy as the scene and the subject of the poem reminds us that it is *Eton* which is always just over the horizon of Gray's landscape, the poem's unacknowledged condition of production. And it is the difference between Eton and Warrington Academy which is at stake in Barbauld's reworking of the landscape *topos*.

By discarding the nostalgic pastoralism of Gray's mysteriously literate rural poet, by insisting upon the terms of the locodescriptive genre, Barbauld insists also upon the equation of knowledge with the form of property. Such property is acquired; it is not passed on like noble blood. One can only reread Gray's poem after Barbauld for the conspicuous absence from its *mise-en-scène* of the school, as the institution producing the knowledge upon which depends the pathos-effect of sympathetic identification with the peasants who will be unable to read the poem commemorating their very obscurity.[40] One sees where this irony goes at the latter end of the century, when Crabbe writes in "The Village": "Nor you, ye poor, of lettered scorn complain / To you the smoothest song is smooth in vain." Barbauld's command of the vernacular literary tradition, and of the locodescriptive genre, suggests one reason why the topographical poem was so important in the eighteenth century: it is uniquely situated between the commonplace book and the vernacular anthology; and in its merging of the anthological with the rhetorical motive, the new class of literate professionals found one way in which to stand together in a common place, a place which was, at the same time, private property.

Notes

1   Samuel Johnson, *Lives of the English Poets*, ed. George Birkbeck Hill, 3 vols (Oxford: Clarendon Press, 1905), Vol. I, p. 77.

2   John Barrell, *The Idea of Landscape and the Sense of Place 1730–1840* (Cambridge, UK: Cambridge University Press, 1972), pp. 19–20.

3   John Barrell, *An Equal Wide Survey: English Literature in History* (London: Hutchinson, 1983), p. 87.

4   For a useful general discussion of the subject, see John Dixon Hunt, *The Figure in the Landscape: Poetry, Painting and Gardening in the Eighteenth Century* (Baltimore, MD: Johns Hopkins University Press, 1976).

5   Barrell, *Idea of Landscape*, p. 32.

6   Ibid., p. 61 ff. Barrell also points out that the appreciation of landscape views was of course always confined to those with sufficient means to travel.

7   James Turner, *The Politics of Landscape: Rural Scenery and Society in English Poetry 1630–1660* (Oxford: Oxford University Press, 1979), p. 116.

8   Barrell, *Idea of Landscape*, p. 35.

9   Ibid., p. 4.

10 Raymond Williams, *Marxism and Literature* (Oxford: Oxford University Press, 1973), p. 149.

11 For a thorough discussion of the subject, see William G. Crane, *Wit and Rhetoric in the Renaissance: The Formal Basis of Elizabethan Prose Style* (New York: Columbia University Press, 1937). See also the excellent analysis of the situation of rhetoric in the Renaissance by Terence Cave, *The Cornucopian Text: Problems of Writing in the French Renaissance* (Oxford: Oxford University Press, 1979). Cave emphasizes the difference writing makes to the mnemo-technique of the Aristotelian *koinoi topoi*, and thus the importance of the common-place books as written texts.

12 One might emphasize here the significance of the fact that the "Elegy" is now frequently taught at the lower levels of the school system, as a text by means of which to introduce schoolchildren to English literature. For an interesting argument about the later history of the "Elegy" in the university see William H. Epstein, "Counter-intelligence: cold-war criticism and eighteenth-century studies," *ELH* 57 (1990): 63–9.

13 Leslie Stephen, *Hours in a Library* (London: Smith, Elder, 1909), p. 97. Stephen raises the issue to be considered here, the effect of banality: " 'The Bard' and the lines upon Eton have become so hackneyed as perhaps to acquire a certain tinge of banality."

14 Edmund Gosse, *Gray*, English Man of Letters series (New York: Harper, 1882).

15 I note that "The Elegy Written in a Country Churchyard" is an item in the list which defines E. D. Hirsch's concept of cultural literacy. See *Cultural Literacy: What Every American Needs to Know* (Boston, MA: Houghton Mifflin, 1987), p. 169. Thomas Gray's name, however, does not appear on the list.

16 The importance of the "notebook" in early modern education is stressed by R. R. Bolgar, in *The Classical Heritage and its Beneficiaries* (Cambridge, UK: Cambridge University Press, 1954), pp. 272 ff. Bolgar quotes the detailed instructions of Vives: "Make a book of blank leaves of a proper size. Divide it into certain topics, so to say, nests. In one, jot down the names of subjects of daily converse . . . in another, sententiae." For a useful discussion of commonplace books in the early modern period, see Ruth Mohl, *Milton and his Commonplace Book* (New York: Frederick Ungar, 1969), pp. 11–30.

17 A discussion of the form and contents of Gray's commonplace books may be found in Roger Martin, *Essai sur Thomas Gray* (London: Oxford University Press, 1934), pp. 187–200.

18 R. P. Gillies, *Memoires* (1851), Vol. II, p. 165, quoted in *Lives of the English Poets*, ed. Birkbeck Hill, Vol. II, p. 441.

19 See Crane, *Wit and Rhetoric*, p. 33.

20 Locke's "A new method of a common-place book, translated out of the French from the second volume of the Bibliothèque Universelle" gives a general description of the layout of the commonplace book, which is organized by an alphabetical index. The sample entries (Acheron, Aegesilaus, Aer, Aera) suggest how far Locke has moved away from the rhetorical (Aristotelian) concept of the commonplace.

21   William Empson, *Some Versions of Pastoral* (London: Chatto & Windus, 1935; New York: New Directions, 1950), p. 4.

22   A. Richards, *Practical Criticism: A Study of Literary Judgment* (New York: Harcourt, Brace, World, 1929), p. 197.

23   Roy Porter, *English Society in the Eighteenth Century* (Harmondsworth, Mx: Penguin, 1982), p. 65, cites a typical statement of Defoe's: "Men are every day starting up from obscurity to wealth." The question of social mobility is no longer simple, if it ever was, and I must therefore add the following qualification to my argument. Historians are now inclined to emphasize a disparity between the perception of upward mobility and the actual rate at which this mobility occurred. Doubtless if one confines the definition of mobility to actual examples of the bourgeoisie passing into the ranks of the nobility, the numbers of those making the move, as Lawrence Stone and Jeanne C. Fawtier Stone have demonstrated in *The Open Elite? England, 1540–1880* (Oxford: Clarendon Press, 1984), are relatively small. They bias their study by constricting their definition of the ruling elite to the landed aristocracy, and are thus able to conclude that the "perennial openness of England's landed elite to penetration by members of the newly enriched bourgeoisie is clearly no more than a hoary myth." Now this statistical revisionism is based upon what can only be an arbitrary judgment about precisely what minimum number of aristocratized bourgeois would qualify the elite as "open." Setting aside the question whether this use of statistics is not intended to confound the very possibility of a class analysis, one may at least argue that the perception of upward mobility, which was ubiquitous and even hysterical at times in the eighteenth century, is a real event with real historical consequences. For a somewhat different analysis from the Stones', see Peter Laslett's *The World We Have Lost* (New York: Charles Scribner's Sons, 1965). The perception of upward mobility is related to the demonstrable imitation of aristocratic manners by the professional and commercial middle classes and the *haute bourgeoisie*. The concept of upward mobility therefore cannot be confined to the actual expansion of the landed nobility; its site is rather the cultural homogenization of the aristocracy and the bourgeoisie. The professional middle classes were more capable of easily acquiring the knowledge and manners of the aristocracy than of acquiring vast landed capital. It is this phenomenon of "social mobility" which is crucial to the present argument.

24   That Gray's argument was a commonplace of eighteenth-century discourse is attested by Edward Young's statement in his *Conjectures on Original Composition* (1759), ed. Edith J. Moreley (London: 1918), p. 17: "Many a genius, probably, there has been, which could neither write, nor read."

25   Barrell, *An Equal Wide Survey*, p. 119.

26   See James Bowen, *A History of Western Education*, 3 vols (New York: St Martin's Press, 1972), pp. 138 ff. For a general discussion of this subject, see also John Lawson and Harold Solver, *A Social History of Education in England* (New York: Methuen, 1973), pp. 193 ff. They note that the lending libraries were initially opposed by the Anglican clergy.

27   On the matter of education for the working class, see R. K. Webb's discussion of Hannah More and the SPCK, in *The British Working-Class Reader* (New York: Augustus M. Kelley, 1971), p. 25 ff. On the monitorial system, see Karen Jones and Kevin Williamson, "The birth of the schoolroom," *Ideology and Consciousness* 6 (1979): 59–110. On the relation of the middle classes to new developments in education, see Brian Simon, *Studies in the History of Education, 1780–1870* (London: Lawrence & Wishart, 1960), pp. 107 ff.

28   Bowen, *A History of Western Education* Vol. III, pp. 138 ff.

29   John Locke, *Some Thoughts Concerning Education* (1693), in *The Educational Writings of John Locke*, ed. James L. Axtell (Cambridge, UK: Cambridge University Press, 1968), p. 268.

30   Bowen, *A History of Western Education*, Vol. III, p. 139.

31   Nicholas Hans, *New Trends in Education in the Eighteenth Century* (London: Routledge & Kegan Paul, 1951), p. 212. "By the end of the eighteenth century, classical education had become simply a sign of social prestige." Hans discusses the revival of the grammar schools and the classical curriculum in the nineteenth century as the revival of aristocratic caste traits when the social pretension of the bourgeoisie is no longer satisfied by vernacular literacy.

32   I am following here the excellent discussion of Richard D. Altick, *The English Common Reader:*

A Social History of the Mass Reading Public, 1800–1900 (Chicago: University of Chicago Press, 1957), pp. 42 ff.

33   Barrell, *An Equal Wide Survey*, p. 34.

34   Ibid., p. 36. Barrell also quotes Steele's statement to the effect that a gentleman is a "Man compleatly qualify'd as well for the Service and Good, as for the Ornament and Delight, of Society." See also the discussion beginning on p. 133; and see Lawrence Stone's comment on the effects of education in *The Open Elite?*, p. 411. For a carefully nuanced discussion of the "class of the polite," see Susan Staves, "Pope's refinement," *The Eighteenth Century: Theory and Interpretation* 29 (1988): 145–63.

35   Thomas Sheridan, *British Education: or the Source of the Disorders of Great Britain* (New York: Garland Publishing, 1970), pp. 180, 192.

36   Herbert McLachlan, *English Education under the Test Acts* (Manchester: Manchester University Press, 1931), p. 216.

37   William Enfield, *The Speaker: or Miscellaneous Pieces, Selected from the Best English Writers, and disposed under proper heads, with a view to facilitate the improvement of youth in reading and speaking* (London: Joseph Johnson, 1774). Enfield was lecturer on belles-lettres at Warrington Academy. For a discussion of the later history of *The Speaker*, see Margaret Weedon, "Jane Austen and William Enfield's *The Speaker*," *British Journal for Eighteenth-Century Studies* 11 (1988): 158–60.

38   The significance of middle-class women in this movement has been stressed by Nancy Armstrong, "Literature as women's history," *Genre* 19 (1986): 367: "Today few of us realize that many features of our standard humanities curriculum came from a curriculum designed specifically for educating polite young women who were not of the ruling class, or that the teaching of native British literature developed as a means of socializing children, the poor, and foreigners before we became a masculine profession." Barbauld was uniquely privileged in her educational opportunities (she even persuaded her father, Dr Aiken, to teach her Latin and Greek), although she was not an advocate of schools for women. She seems to have promoted instead the more unofficial instruments of literary culture, as a means of disseminating knowledge to women.

39   "Warrington Academy" appears in a slightly different form in Barbauld's collected works under the title "The invitation."

40   This is the context in which one might understand Gray's disdain for the popularity of his poem. It is as though the emergence of an exclusively vernacular literacy had erased the difference between the literate and the illiterate altogether. For a good discussion of Gray's aversion to his popular audience, see Linda Zionkowski, "Bridging the gulf between the poet and the audience in the work of Gray," *ELH* 58 (1991): 331–50.

Part VI

Reification: the invention
and institution of special
forms of property

20

Possessing Mother Nature
Genetic capital in eighteenth-century Britain

Harriet Ritvo

Once upon a time, there was a man named Robert Bakewell (1725–95), who lived on a large farm called Dishley Grange in Leicestershire, admired by his neighbors, respected by his employees, and beloved by his animals, to whom he was unusually kind. He never married, but devoted himself entirely to livestock husbandry. As a result of years of selfless and patriotic dedication, he presented to his countrymen, who demanded increasing quantities of fresh meat as a result of their burgeoning population and intermittent wars with the French, improved strains of the most important domestic species – more succulent sheep and cattle, larger cart-horses, and pigs which his friends, at least, described as "superior."[1] One of these improved strains, the New Leicester or Dishley sheep, appeared to be of such transcendent merit that it dominated British sheep-breeding for decades. The production of these distinguished creatures was not the result of lucky accident, nor even of the instinctive application of craft expertise, although Bakewell had plenty of that. More important, however, were his general ideas about how to select superior animals and then pair them so as to ensure that their desirable qualities would predictably re-emerge in their offspring and more remote descendants. Based on repeated inbreeding, Bakewell's method had still greater impact on his fellow agriculturalists than did the animals who exemplified it; together, his precepts and his example laid the foundation for the British pre-eminence in stock-breeding that lasted through the nineteenth century.

Bakewell's lifetime of service and achievement made him one of the patron saints, or at least one of the presiding geniuses, of the agricultural revolution. Like Newton and his apple or Franklin and his kite, albeit with a more restricted audience, the Leicestershire improver and his fat sheep became icons of the Enlightenment. One of his early disciples asserted that "he has absolutely struck out new lights, and not only adopted a breed of cattle and sheep, different from, and superior in many essential respects to most others, but established them in such a manner as to gain ground in every corner of Great Britain and Ireland, in consequence of their superior merit."[2] His only modern biographer began his work with the statement that "Robert Bakewell may be regarded as a man whose work assumed an importance which has not been exceeded by any agriculturalist before or since his time."[3] This assertion may smack of booster-ism, but it is consistent with the more muted claims of relatively disinterested chro-niclers. In the standard history of British livestock husbandry, Bakewell is the only individual to get his own chapter – or, indeed, to be mentioned by name in the table of contents.[4] His fireside chair, a capacious and solid wooden article, has been preserved as a trophy by the Royal Agricultural Society of England; it figured prominently under the rubric "The Agrarian Revolution: the Age of the Agricultural Improvers" in the large historical exhibition mounted to commemorate "British Food and Farming Year" in 1989.[5]

Like all legends, however, this one is open to reinterpretation, and on several levels. The heroic version of Bakewell's character and accomplishments is rooted in a heroic version of the agricultural revolution, which has itself come under increasingly ener-getic revision in recent years. That is to say, the complex of developments, embracing agricultural chemistry, crop selection and management, farm machinery and drainage techniques as well as animal husbandry, that was celebrated by eighteenth-century improvers as well as by subsequent antiquarians and historians as a great and discrete leap forward, is now frequently interpreted as part of a relatively protracted process with roots as far back as the medieval period.[6]

But the contestation of the Bakewell legend is not just an artifact of modern historio-graphy. Bakewell was a controversial figure in his own time, inspiring detractors as well as admirers; the literature of contradiction and debunking has been as persistent, if not as voluminous, as the literature of adulation. Every component of his reputation has been repeatedly challenged, beginning with the most fundamental claim: that of originality or priority. Arthur Young's widely echoed assertion that Bakewell's stock-breeding principles and techniques were "perfectly new" or at least "hitherto . . . totally neglected," coexisted with alternative stories about the creation of Bakewell's celebrated strains.[7] Sometimes these stories featured rival innovators. A shadowy predecessor named Joseph Allom was frequently named as the first improver of Leicester sheep, while a Mr. Webster of Canley was known to have done similar work with longhorn cattle, indeed, to have sold Bakewell several animals early in his career as an improver. Mr. Webster's old shepherd, it was rumored, also claimed that his master's ewes had helped found the Dishley flocks.[8] Other stories implicitly claimed that Bakewell had unfairly appropriated personal credit for accomplishments for which he was merely a synecdoche, by stressing the number of less celebrated contemporary farmers who had pursued analogous breeding strategies. Thus an eighteenth-century observer noted that the area around Dishley had "for many years abounded with intelligent and spirited breeders," and a nineteenth-century livestock historian claimed that the improvement of the longhorns "dates from the 1720s," the decade of Bakewell's birth.[9]

If Bakewell had not done it first, perhaps he had done it wrong. Critics claimed that while his principal technique, in-and-in breeding or repeated crossing within a single lineage, might produce impressive results quickly, in the long run it led to delicate health and declining vigor; that is, that it "prove[d] as destructive to flocks, as marriages of near relations to the human kind."[10] Attacks on his system led to attacks on his judgment in less theoretical matters. Bakewell viewed sheep, cattle, and pigs as machines for producing meat, and so selected them to maximize the expensive cuts and minimize the bones and innards, but sceptics alleged that the barrel shape he aimed at in breeding all species but the horse often induced an "excessive tendency to obesity [which] abates the procreative . . . powers."[11] And despite the striking changes he effected in the animals he chose for improvement, some of his strains proved to have surprisingly little staying power. Improved longhorns were fleshy, but their meat was unappealing, and as a side-effect of improvement their milk yield and prolificacy decreased dramatically; after a brief heyday, they quickly disappeared from English pastures and slaughterhouses. Bakewell was no more successful than other stock-breeders in reforming the amorphous eighteenth-century pig. Even the renowned Dishley sheep might come in retrospect to seem more a triumph of public relations than of applied science.[12]

When they had finished with Bakewell's animals, critics might move on to his character. Although he was conventionally praised for the gentleness with which he treated his animals – it was said that even his largest bulls could be led by a child – and for the hearty hospitality of his bachelor table, the counter-tradition suggested that he drove a hard bargain, that he was mean-spirited and possessive, and that his concern for profit led him to be secretive about information he should have shared. For example, when he considered his breeding rams to be past their reproductive prime, he sent them to the butcher; but to make sure that his colleagues and competitors would not attempt to reprieve them and thus gain free and unauthorized access to their carefully selected genetic material, he first infected them with "rot."[13] And he was as unwilling to part with this material in its abstract as in its concrete form; agricultural writers throughout the nineteenth century echoed contemporary complaints about "the mystery with which he . . . carried on every part of his business, and the various means which he employed to mislead the public."[14]

Damaging as such allegations might seem, however, they provoked no substantial riposte in more reverential discourse. On the contrary, they may have provided an occasion for the two traditions to converge. (Of course, these alternative commentaries also agreed that Bakewell was well worth talking about.) On the back of Bakewell's carefully preserved chair a nineteenth-century admirer carved the following inscription: "This chair was made under the direction of the Celebrated Robert Bakewell of Dishley out of a willow tree that grew on his farm. It was his favorite seat, and the back which thus records his Memory, served as a screen when seated by his fireside, calculating on the Profits, or devising some Improvement on his farm. Thousands of pounds have been known to exchange hands in the same . . ."[15] As a eulogy this may leave something to be desired, but it nevertheless suggests the source of Bakewell's enduring renown and notoriety. Whether or not his selective breeding techniques reshaped his longhorn cattle and Leicester sheep as much or as well as he and his adherents have claimed, there is no question that, on the conceptual level, they helped to restructure the whole enterprise of animal breeding.

Bakewell assumed that the qualities that defined animal excellence were inherited and that careful selection and pairing of parents would insure that their own desirable attributes were replicated or enhanced in their offspring. That is, he assumed that it was possible for the improver to redraw the conventional boundary between the sphere of nature and the sphere of agriculture. These assumptions were not necessarily inconsistent with received stockbreeding wisdom; indeed, there was no contemporary consensus about what could be inherited and how.[16] But the prevalent practices of mid-eighteenth-century husbandry were based on other assumptions, particularly the predominance of such environmental factors as climate and diet in determining the qualities of adult animals. Even at the end of the eighteenth century, the distinguished members of the Board of Agriculture devoted a great deal of attention to the effect of different grazing regimens on sheep and cattle breeds.[17] The breeders of a few kinds of luxury and sporting animals – mainly race-horses, and to a lesser extent foxhounds and greyhounds – selected and paired their stock along the lines later adopted by Bakewell, but most breeders of farm animals were less concerned with the heritable merits of individual animals.[18] What they wanted from their herds and flocks, in addition to meat or milk or wool or tallow, was a healthy and numerous progeny, not particularly distinguishable from their parents or from each other. As far as reproduction was concerned, parent animals were also essentially interchangeable. Breeding males were selected on the basis of availability and willingness to procreate; breeding females, by and large, were not selected at all. The result was a livestock population consisting mostly, at least in Bakewell's terms and those of subsequent improvers, of rather nondescript regional strains.[19]

Bakewell's system replaced fungibility with a high degree of differentiation. He assessed the reproductive potential of individual animals in subtle qualitative terms rather than in terms of simple addition. It became possible to ask "How good?" and "How reliable?," not merely "How many?" The answers to these new questions were not, however, merely qualitative; augmented quality meant augmented value, which was routinely measured in cash. Perhaps the most telling evidence of the desirability of Bakewell's stock and the prestige of his method was the amount other breeders were willing to pay for the services of his male animals, especially rams.[20] When Bakewell began renting out rams or tups in 1760, he charged 17s 6d per animal per season (this fee included as many ewes as the ram could be persuaded to serve), which can be roughly compared with bulling fees of between 6d and 1s per cow, which were standard through much of the eighteenth century; and with the stud fee of a guinea per mare advertised in 1755 by the owner of several undistinguished stallions.[21] By 1784 Bakewell was asking £100 per season for his best rams, and five years later equivalent services commanded £300–£400 per season. (His rule for bulls, once he had hit his marketing stride, was to ask half the animal's value for a season's hire.)[22]

The breathtaking steepness of this trajectory – a fourhundredfold increase within thirty years – suggests that it recorded a change in kind rather than (or as well as) a change in degree. The escalation in fees was too rapid to reflect simply the enhanced quality of the New Leicesters, striking though that was in the view of many. It also represented the entry of a whole new source of value into the price calculation. Bakewell claimed that when he sold one of his carefully bred animals, or, as in the case of stud fees, when he sold the procreative powers of one of these animals, he was selling something much more specific, more predictable, and more efficacious than mere reproduction. In effect, he was selling a template for the continued production of animals of a special type; that is, the distinction of his rams consisted not only in their constellation of personal virtues, but in their ability to pass this constellation down their family tree. They were the result of a minor act of creation, and, if skilfully managed, they could be the agents or catalysts of additional similar acts. Thus it was possible for a disciple like George Culley of Durham to transform his own flocks by hiring a ram from Bakewell each year. He began this practice in the 1760s, when Bakewell was just starting to make his reputation, and continued it even after other northern breeders had begun paying liberal fees to hire Culley rams.[23] And this redefined relation between an individual animal and its lineage was newly reciprocal as well as newly powerful. At least the best breeding animals were expected to enhance as well as merely to express and pass on the reproductive potential of their strain, a point that was emphasized by the tendency of some breeders to name lineages (often referred to as "families" or "tribes") after particularly influential or exemplary ancestors.[24]

So complete was the conceptual transformation wrought by this redefinition of an animal's worth, that at a remove of two centuries it may be difficult to recover its novelty. We now routinely take the kind of genetic property created by Bakewell and his adherents into account when pricing animals; indeed, often it is the primary, if not the only, source of value – the reason, for example, that neutered animals are not permitted to compete for most show prizes. Nor does this policy reflect a recent consensus. If the possibility of theft may be taken to indicate the presence of property, then the concept of genetic property was already firmly entrenched a hundred years ago, when the Kennel Club was formed to regulate dog showing and breeding. At least in its early years, only a few violations were considered heinous enough to be censured by the club's governing committee, but stolen kisses were definitely among them. Two cases of genetic larceny immediately occupied the committee's attention: one committed by a breeder who brought his bitch in heat to a dog show (already an infraction, since animals in that condition were officially barred) and managed to position her within the easy reach of a male champion; the other committed by a breeder whose attempts to purchase the services of a particular dog had been spurned by that animal's owner. By dint of spying, plotting, and the corruption of railway employees, he arranged for his bitch and the dog in question to spend some unsupervised moments together in a baggage compartment.[25] Although such behavior had been recognized as theft since at least the end of the eighteenth century, the Kennel Club disciplinary hearings may have represented a hardening sense of the seriousness of the offense. When Thomas Booth, one of the best-known early improvers of shorthorn cattle, was similarly imposed upon – by a tenant who put an attractive cow into the field next to one of his most distinguished bulls, thus depriving Booth not only of the stud fee but of the cost of repairing the fence – it was remarked more as an instance of ludicrous delinquency than as one of serious moral turpitude.[26]

But even this rather light-hearted acquiescence in the possibility of owning the design of an animal represented a significant shift in stockbreeders' attitudes, a shift in which the miscreant participated, since Booth, like many progressive landlords, provided the services of the more ordinary bulls to his tenants gratis. Forty years earlier, when Bakewell had instituted his policy of hiring out his best rams for the season, he encountered a great deal of resistance. In the words of David Low, Professor of Agriculture at the University of Edinburgh during the first part of the nineteenth century, "the plan was ridiculed and opposed in every way, and it was not until after the lapse of nearly a quarter of a century that he succeeded in establishing it as a regular system."[27] This resistance was probably only partly a kneejerk conservative reaction to a perceived commercial innovation. After all, although Bakewell's name was strongly associated with seasonal hiring – for example, in 1790 the engraver and naturalist Thomas Bewick illustrated "the modern practice of letting out Rams for hire by the season; which from very small beginnings, has already risen to an astonishing height" exclusively with reference to Bakewell – he was, in this case as in others, only the publicizer and standardizer, not the innovator.[28] Other breeders had rented out rams without provoking hostile commentary, and, in any case, the practice bore an obvious relation to the stud fees traditionally charged for individual services.

Nor can the criticism of seasonal hiring be blamed on Bakewell's prices; since these did not rise high enough to provoke complaints until the 1780s, when resistance to his marketing techniques had subsided. Instead, since Bakewell linked the practice of hiring with the special virtues he claimed for his stock and with his reluctance to alienate any of his best animals permanently, it is more likely that the strong initial hostility to renting rams by the season reflected a suspicion of the new notion of property embodied in Bakewell's system. Potential customers may have worried that he was selling something that should not be sold, or, to put it more skeptically, could not be sold.

His marketing strategy seemed designed to reify the somewhat intangible genetic property embodied in his animals. He formalized this strategy (and included within it his closest colleagues and rivals) in 1783, when he founded the Dishley Society. The high end breeders of New Leicester stock who composed its membership agreed to comply with an elaborate and stringent set of restrictions on their activities, including the number of rams they could let per season, when they could let them, and to whom they could let them. It was, for example, forbidden to let rams to anyone who let or sold rams at fairs or markets. (Other prohibitions included letting rams on Sundays and leaving society meetings without asking permission.) Prices were fixed, too: at least 10 guineas per ram per season to ordinary breeders, at least 40 guineas to breeders who themselves let rams, and at least 50 guineas for any ram let by Bakewell himself to anyone living within 100 miles of Dishley. In return for compliance (which was enforced by fines of up to 200 guineas) and for dues of about 100 guineas, members received privileged access to each others,' and especially to Bakewell's stock, as well as the benefits of belonging to a cartel.[29]

The Dishley Society may have been the most exclusive marketplace for highly engineered genetic material in the 1780s, but it was not the only one. Persuaded either by the sight of the improved animals, which were available for inspection at the farms of breeders and sometimes at fairs or semi-public exhibitions like the sheep-shearings sponsored by elite agriculturists, or by their promotion in the agricultural press, stockbreeders gradually accepted the notion of genetic property implicit in Bakewell's practices. Demand for this commodity consequently burgeoned, and, predictably enough, so did the supply. (This increase in supply and demand was not restricted to New Leicesters, but extended to other kinds of sheep, and to improved strains of other domesticated species, especially cattle.)[30] Once breeders proliferated, quality control became an issue. Bakewell himself had refused to give any guarantee of the quality of his stock except his own name. Not only was he loath to reveal the parentage of particular animals, but, as even his admirers have lamented for the past two centuries, he systematically concealed the breeders and the regions which had supplied his foundation stock.[31] But no one else could get away with this kind of metonymic assurance. Lesser men had to offer harder evidence.

The template that constituted the chief value of an expensive animal was a rather tenuous article, not immediately apparent to the prospective purchaser or renter. With uncomplicated animals who had not been subject to Bakewellian reconstruction, a shrewd eye and hand could assess the quality of an adult with some confidence, and make a fair guess as to the probable development of a juvenile. But such tools failed when the issue was reproductive power rather than personal charm. The two most important components of an animal's genetic endowment – the best indication of its likelihood of passing on desirable qualities to its progeny – were both functions of its lineage: purity of descent, meaning a heritage that included a preponderance of forebears with the same qualities; and prepotency, meaning a heritage sufficiently concentrated and powerful to dominate the heritage of potential mates. As stockbreeding manuals repeatedly advised, when the production of distinguished offspring was the main point, these hidden qualities could be more important than the manifest ones. The annals of husbandry included many rams, bulls, and stallions who won no prizes themselves but were celebrated "getters." As one mid-nineteenth-century cattleman put it, "We ought always to prefer a bull of high pedigree, with fair symmetry and quality, to another bull, though much superior in appearance, but of questionable pedigree."[32]

Bakewell's contemporaries would have appreciated the wisdom of this advice, although they might not have put it in the same terms, since the readers for the *Oxford English Dictionary* do not report the word "pedigree" being applied to domestic animal lineages until the first part of the nineteenth century. And difficulties of implementation would have overshadowed those of expression. The acceptance of paper pedigrees as reliable evidence of the existence, legitimacy, and value of genetic property depended on elaborate, plausible, and sustained record-keeping. Such records were hard to come by in mid-eighteenth-century Britain. Indeed, before the new and more nuanced sense of an animal's individuality implied by Bakewell's practices, they were almost inconceivable. As long as domestic animals were understood as interchangeable members of flocks and herds, they were rarely named; their reproductive history was apt to be obscure, and their genealogy impossible to trace.[33] Even the renowned imported stallions who laid the foundation for modern thoroughbred horses in the late seventeenth and early eighteenth centuries were, somewhat paradoxically, semi-anonymous, referred to only by their English ownership and their supposed country of origin: the Darley Arabian, the Godolphin Barb, the Byerley Turk. One of the most celebrated animals of the 1790s, a massive specimen of the shorthorn breed of cattle, toured simply as "the Durham ox."

Speculative reconstructions of the descent of Bakewell's own animals include such shadowy creatures as "a Westmoreland bull" and "a Canley cow," said to be the parents of the distinguished longhorn bull Twopenny, who figured prominently (and also frequently, due to Bakewell's predilection for inbreeding) in many subsequent pedigrees.[34] Although he did not publicize his animals' family trees, Bakewell needed to keep track of them for his own continuing experimental purposes. And so his breeding stock, like that of many of his contemporaries, emerged into the light of nomenclature. By the end of the eighteenth century, any well-bred animal was likely to come supplied not only with its own name, but with those of its parents. Often these names injected a little poetry into the ordinarily prosaic practice of animal husbandry. For example, their portraits proclaimed that the shorthorn Comet was the son of Favourite and Young Phoenix, and that the longhorn Garrick was the son of Shakespear and Broken Horn Beauty. None of these animals had been named by Bakewell, however, whose taste in nomenclature, as in other things, tended toward the functional: many of his sheep were identified merely by letters of the alphabet or by butchers' terms like Shoulders, Bosom, Carcass, and Campbells (hocks) that suggested their strongest marketing points.[35]

Thus the value of the most distinguished animals was ratified in language after it had been created in the breeding-pen; in a sense, it did not exist on the hoof until it had been inscribed in the record books. But though written evidence might be a necessary guarantee of genetic property, it was not sufficient. The breeders' private records were only too liable to manipulation and falsification, to the creation of genetic property in a different and more radical sense, with no help from the breeding pen. Occasionally the pedigrees of superstar animals like Comet and Garrick would be published in agricultural or sporting periodicals, which at least put a stop to their further elaboration. This practice was generalized in the breed books, really genealogical catalogues, that began to appear at the end of the eighteenth century. The preface to the first of them, the *General Stud Book* for race-horses or thoroughbreds, published in 1791, defined its purpose as "to correct the . . . encreasing evil of false and inaccurate Pedigrees;" the preface to the *General Short-Horned Herd Book* of 1822, the first such work devoted to farm livestock, noted that "it must be both the interest and the wish of every breeder to be enabled to breed with the greatest possible accuracy as to pedigrees."[36]

More was at stake in this interest and wish than merely forestalling fraud. Stud books proliferated during the nineteenth century, even for breeds in which misrepresentation could hardly be considered an issue; that is, breeds which had been little improved, and for which, therefore, the problem facing cataloguers was an absence of information rather than a plethora. For example, the secretary of the British Berkshire Pig Society assured readers of its first *Herd Book* that all the animals listed within it were "of undoubted purity," even though many of them had been included on the basis of "exceedingly short pedigrees" or "only a note"; the compiler of the first *Ayrshire Herd Book* complained that he was impeded in his labors "as hitherto names have rarely been given to animals."[37] The editors of the first *British Goat Society Herd Book* may have faced the most difficult task of all, since "the propagation of these animals has not been conducted with any regard to purity of breed" and "very few breeders . . . have kept any record of Pedigree."[38] Herculean though they may have been, however, these labors were rarely thankless. Indeed they were predictably if indirectly rewarded in cash. The editors of the second volume of the *Sussex Herd Book* complacently noted that in the six years that had passed since the appearance of the first volume in 1879, the prediction there expressed "that Sussex Cattle would come more and more into favour, has been fully borne out, and we can point with satisfaction to the greatly increased number of Animals."[39] Increased "favour" meant larger demand, and consequently higher profits for breeders.

The enhanced value that normally followed the appearance of a breed book may have been partly the result of the attendant publicity's leading to a wider appreciation of the merits of a particular kind of stock. But breed books created distinction as well as merely cataloguing it. As the establishment of individual pedigrees defined and reified the genetic endowment and capacity of individuals, group genealogies analogously defined and reified the template associated with a given breed. And this definition could work both ways. That is, if the existence of a numerous and popular breed required the compilation of a breed book, so the compilation of a breed book could imply the existence of a breed. Thus, members of the Galloway Cattle Society felt that "it was desirable to have a separate Herd Book" for their animals, even though they had probably "sprung from the same source" as the Polled Angus and Aberdeens; with similar determination, the editor of the first *Norfolk and Suffolk Red Polled Herd Book* made a point of denying the assertion that "this is but a branch of the Galloway breed naturalized here."[40] The *Oxford Down Flock Book* was both evidence and agent of its society's "special pride and boast": to have created an independent breed from the combination of two others.[41]

This literary construction of breeds could have a physical dimension. Especially for breeds that had been only loosely defined – breeds that, like many local strains of cattle, sheep, and pigs, consisted of a regional label and little else – the publication of a catalogue might encourage breeders to mate their animals within the prescribed pool and to select animals possessing the characteristics identified as most desirable. The British Goat Society offered an extreme example of this possibility when it confessed, in its first *Herd Book*, that it could not aspire to "preserve a record of pure-bred Stock," only to guide "breeders desirous of introducing fresh blood into their herds."[42] But most creation by breed book occurred on the conceptual level. Like the process of individual naming and genealogy that they repeated and multiplied, these catalogues concretized a rather abstract component of the value of the animals listed within them. As an animal's lineage enhanced and guaranteed the promise of its personal qualities, so its membership in a breed underwrote the claims of its lineage.

And although their ostensible function was straightforwardly descriptive, breed books helped to redefine the category they illustrated. After all, despite the complaints of some elitists that they were not discriminating enough, they did not list every animal proposed for inclusion.[43] Decisions to admit inevitably both reflected and reinforced the compilers' idea, not only of the nature of thoroughbred horses or shorthorn cattle, but of breed itself. By the middle of the eighteenth century, this term had become unstable. As the *Oxford English Dictionary* suggests, the use of the word "breed" to refer to a related stock of animals, along with the more or less interchangeable constellation of "race," "strain," and "variety" (the latter often carrying a scientific connotation, but no real difference in denotation), had been common at least since the late sixteenth or early seventeenth centuries. Originally what defined a breed seems to have been shared provenance and shared function, as well as some degree of physical resemblance. As late as the eighteenth century the term was often used in that sense by enlightened agriculturalists who wished to disparage unimproved animals. Thus, in 1794, a surveyor commissioned by the Board of Agriculture referred to the "original black breed" of Carmarthenshire cattle as "ill shaped and unprofitable to the pail," and to the local "breed of swine – a narrow, short, prick-eared kind."[44]

When improved animals were in question, however, animals of the same breed might have both more and less in common. Geographical contiguity was only accidental and so was close familial connection, except in breeds based on intense inbreeding, like the New Leicester sheep, or breeds where a few ancestors had been particularly appealing, such as the shorthorns, all of which were descended in one way or another from Comet.[45] What was essential, however, was the template. As one improving farmer put it, certain "varieties have been usually distinguished among farmers by the appellation of different *breeds*; as they have supposed that their distinguishing qualities are, at least, in a certain degree, transmissible to their descendants."[46] Such definitions bestowed upon breeds a newly enhanced degree both of permanence and of content.

As a result, the category represented by "breed" increased in status. And this glorification was not apparent only within the discourse of elite animal husbandry, where cynics might ascribe it to narcissism or financial interest. The consensus of enlightened agriculturalists was echoed by another discourse, which was further removed from the barn and the butcher and which lent the authority of science. Domestic animals belonged to the animal kingdom as well as to the enterprise of agriculture, and they figured prominently in the catalogues and schemata of quadrupeds voluminously produced by eighteenth-century naturalists. Indeed, because they were easy to observe and economically important, they often occupied far more than their share of space.[47] They were favored not only in terms of pages allotted, but in terms of categorical analysis.

Although eighteenth-century taxonomies differed from modern ones in many important ways, involving both form and content, they similarly consisted of a hierarchical – that is to say, increasingly inclusive – set of categories. But not every animal group, and especially not every group of domestic animals, found a place in this structure; to be included at all conveyed a measure of distinction. The smallest category conceived to represent significant differentiation was the species. Designation as a species corroborated and validated a group's separateness. In addition, since the form of hierarchy inevitably suggests increasing prestige, species possessed a kind of status that mere races, strains, or varieties lacked. Although drawing the boundary between any particular species, as well as defining "species" in general, presented, then as now, very knotty problems, pragmatic differentiations were ordinarily based on physical similarity and the production of fertile offspring.

A rigorous application of those criteria should not have privileged breeds of domestic animals. Different breeds of cattle or pigs or dogs resembled each other physically and reproduced with ease and efficiency; and in any case increased variability within species was widely recognized as one of the most frequent consequences of domestication. Nevertheless, naturalists tended to accord breeds of domestic animals the same taxonomic status as species of wild animals. Sometimes this was done tacitly. For example, in his popular *General History of Quadrupeds* (1790), Thomas Bewick presented "The Arabian Horse," "The Race-Horse," "The Hunter," "The Black Horse," and "The Common Cart Horse" in separate entries analogous to those devoted to "The Ass" and "The Zebra."[48] Following Linnaeus, George Shaw tagged many dog breeds with latinate binomials that at least sounded like the names of species; for example, the hound was *Canis sagax*, the shepherd's dog was *Canis domesticus*, and the pomeranian was *Canis pomeranus*.[49] And if the same claim could not quite be made for cat breeds, another disciple of Linnaeus presented minor feline variations as subspecies: thus, the angora cat was *Felis catus angorensis* and the tortoiseshell was *Felis catus hispanicus*.[50] The *Naturalist's Pocket Magazine* argued that treating certain kinds of domestic sheep "as varieties, does not . . . sufficiently discriminate between them. . . . To us it appears, that there is, probably, even a specific distinction."[51] Thomas Pennant, a distinguished zoologist, upped the ante still further. He referred to what were known as the wild cattle of Chillingham, an unruly strain of white animals preserved in the parks of several great houses, mostly for decoration or sport rather than for the dairy or the slaughterhouse, as *Bisontes scotici*, putting them into a separate genus or subgenus from the *Bos taurus* that grazed on ordinary British pastures.[52]

Given this ball, some agriculturalists quickly ran with it. Claims for the taxonomic reification of breeds might be made obliquely, as when Bakewell's disciple George Culley suggested that, with regard to domestic goats, "the different species . . . might be greatly improved, by the simple rule of selecting the best males and best females."[53] Or they might be made circumspectly, as with John Wilkinson's assertion that "The distinction between some [breeds] . . . has scarcely been less than the distinction between that variety and the whole species. The longer . . . these perfections have been continued, the more stability will they have acquired and the more will they partake of nature."[54] But in his comprehensive manual of farm livestock, John Lawrence distinguished directly between the genus, which included "original and distinct kinds . . . as the genus of neat cattle, of swine, of sheep," the species, which included "the most remarkable divisions of genus: as in the horse genus, the racer and the cart horse; in neat cattle, the bison and the common European species, also the long and short-horned: in sheep, the coarse and long, the fine and short woolled: in swine, the lop and prick eared."[55]

Thus the distinctions that separated breeds of domestic animals were conceptualized in terms that made them competitive with, and sometimes identical to, the impenetrable barriers that were generally held to divide wild species. The accomplishments of agricultural improvers might thus rival as well as shadow those previously wrought by nature. This implied that something very real and valuable indeed had been created, since, as one English translator of Buffon put it, "the most constant and invariable thing in Nature is the image or model allotted to each particular species."[56] And more was implied in this claim than the creation of new genetic property for stockbreeders to buy and sell, important though that was. The implicit removal of domestic animals from the natural realm into the realm of technology recorded a shift in the relation between people and their natural environment – an expansion of the territory in which people need not fear to tread.

All this may go some way toward explaining the long historical shadow cast by Robert Bakewell, even if he did not accomplish any of the things on which his legendary stature is said to depend. Whether or not he really improved the longhorns and New Leicesters, or whether anyone did, or whether they were any good after they had been improved – whether he introduced new commercial methods or merely borrowed those used by others with less effective publicists – he was both agent and symbol of a more profound, if less tangible, shift. The market in animal templates that emerged in consequence of the wide appreciation of his labors, if not of those labors themselves, depended on a reconceptualization of the kind of property that an animal constituted, which itself implied an enlargement of the appropriate sphere of cultural activity. Such reconceptualizations of the relationship between culture and nature, between people and God, tended to stir things up two hundred years ago, and they have not lost that power. And the prominence of the profit motive has usually intensified the uneasiness provoked by such boundary shifts – when humans transcend their biblically allotted role as namers to become creators. Thus it should be no surprise that many of the issues raised by Bakewell's work, and much of the energy in the debate it provoked, have resurfaced only superficially transformed in recent and continuing discussions of genetic engineering, recombinant DNA, and the patenting of engineered organisms.

Notes

I am grateful to Juliet Clutton-Brock for her comments on an earlier version of this essay.

1   H. Cecil Pawson, *Robert Bakewell, Pioneer Livestock Breeder* (London: Crosby Lockwood, 1957), pp. 65–6.
2   George Culley, *Observations on Live Stock, Containing Hints for Choosing and Improving the Best Breeds of the Most Useful Kinds of Domestic Animals* (London: 1786), p. 26.
3   Pawson, *Robert Bakewell*, p. xiii.
4   Robert Trow-Smith, *A History of British Livestock Husbandry 1700–1900* (London: Routledge & Kegan Paul, 1959).
5   *This Land is Our Land: Aspects of Agriculture in English Art*, ed. Demelza Spargo (London: Royal Agricultural Society of England, 1989), p. 41. The year 1989 was both the 150th anniversary of the first Royal Agricultural Society show and the centenary of the creation of the Ministry of Agriculture, Fisheries and Food.
6   Nicholas Russell's *Like Engend'ring Like: Heredity and Animal Breeding in Early Modern England* (Cambridge, UK: Cambridge University Press, 1986) offers the most elaborate revision of the traditional history of stockbreeding; see also John Walton, "Pedigree and the national cattle herd, *circa* 1750–1950," *Agricultural History Review* 34 (1986), Part II: 149–70, and Peter Edwards, *The Horse Trade of Tudor and Stuart England* (Cambridge, UK: Cambridge University Press, 1988).
7   Arthur Young, *A Farmer's Tour Through the East of England* (London: W. Strahan, 1771), Vol. I, p. 110, quoted in Carl Jay Bajema (ed.), *Artificial Selection and the Development of Evolutionary Theory* (Stroudsburg, PA: Hutchinson Ross, 1982), p. 29.
8   M. L. Ryder, *Sheep and Man* (London: Duckworth, 1983), p. 486; Russell, *Like Engend'ring Like*, p. 146; Thomas Barnet to Colonel Robert Fulke Greville, December 30, 1789, in Joseph Banks, *The Sheep and Wool Correspondence of Sir Joseph Banks, 1781–1820*, ed. Harold B. Carter (London: British Museum [National History] for the Library Council of New South Wales, 1979), p. 179. See also Nicholas Russell, "Who improved the eighteenth-century longhorn cow?," in *Agricultural Improvement: Medieval and Modern*, ed. Walter Minchinton (Exeter, Devon: University of Exeter Press, 1981), pp. 19–40.
9   W. Marshall, *Rural Economy of the Midland Counties* (1790), quoted in J. D. Chambers and G. E. Mingay, *The Agricultural Revolution, 1750–1880* (London: B. T. Batsford, 1966), p. 67; John Coleman and Gilbert Murray, "The longhorns," in *The Cattle of Great Britain: Being a Series of Articles on the Various Breeds of Cattle of the United Kingdom, their Management, &c.*, ed. John Coleman (London: The Field, 1875), p. 83.
10 Ambrose Blacklock, *Treatise on Sheep; with the Best Means for their Improvement, General Management. and the Treatment of their Diseases* (Glasgow: W. R. McPhun, 1838), p. 102. This reservation, it should be emphasized, was technical rather than moral. In-and-in breeding drew occasional criticism on grounds of incest, but such commentary was not taken very seriously by Bakewell and his disciples. Harriet Ritvo, *The Animal Estate: The English and Other Creatures in the Victorian Age* (Cambridge, MA: Harvard University Press, 1987), p. 67.

11 John Lawrence, *A General Treatise on Cattle, the Ox, the Sheep, and the Swine: Comprehending Their Breeding, Management, Improvement, and Diseases* (London: H. D. Symonds, 1805), p. 387.

12 David Low, *The Breeds of the Domestic Animals of the British Islands* (London: Longman, Orme, Brown, Green, & Longmans, 1842), Vol. I, p. 48; Stephen J. G. Hall and Juliet Clutton-Brock, *Two Hundred Years of British Farm Livestock* (London: British Museum [Natural History], 1989), pp. 203–4; Professor Sheldon, "Sheep," in *The Best Breeds of British Stock: A Practical Guide for Farmers and Owners of Live Stock in England and the Colonies* (London: W. Thacker, 1898), p. 110; Russell, *Like Engend'ring Like*, p. 215.

13 "Rot" was probably liver fluke rather than foot rot, as has sometimes been alleged. Pawson, *Robert Bakewell*, pp. 83–4.

14 John Saunders Sebright, *The Art of Improving the Breeds of Domestic Animals* (London: J. Harding, 1809), p. 9.

15 Spargo, *This Land is Our Land*, p. 41.

16 For scientific views, see John Farley, *Gametes and Spores: Ideas about Sexual Reproduction, 1750–1914* (Baltimore, MD: Johns Hopkins University Press, 1982), Ch. 1.

17 This is a recurrent theme in the Board of Agriculture minute book, November 27, 1798–March 18, 1805, Institute of Agricultural History and Museum of English Rural Life.

18 Harriet Ritvo, "Pride and pedigree: the evolution of the Victorian dog fancy," *Victorian Studies* 29 (1986): 230–3.

19 Ritvo, *Animal Estate*, pp. 64–6.

20 For Bakewell's bull-hiring, see James Wilson, *The Evolution of British Cattle and the Fashioning of Breeds* (London: Vinton, 1909), p. 120–1.

21 Low, *Breeds of Domestic Animals*, Vol. II, p. 67; Russell, *Like Engend'ring Like*, p. 152; newspaper clipping in John Johnson Collection of Printed Ephemera, Bodleian Library.

22 Low, *Breeds of Domestic Animals*, Vol. II, p. 67; Cadwallader John Bates, *Thomas Bates and the Kirklevington Shorthorns: A Contribution to the History of Pure Durham Cattle* (Newcastle upon Tyne: Robert Redpath, 1897), p. 40.

23 Russell, *Like Engend'ring Like*, pp. 210–11; John Sinclair, *The Code of Agriculture* (London: W. Bulmer, 1817), p. 95.

24 One of the best-known examples was the Duchess line established by Thomas Bates early in the nineteenth century. Thomas Bell and Thomas Bates, *The History of Improved Short-horn or Durham Cattle and of the Kirklevington Herd. . .* (Newcastle upon Tyne: Robert Redpath, 1871), p. 209; Hall and Clutton-Brock, *Two Hundred Years*, p. 50.

25 The Kennel Club minute book, December 1, 1874 to April 21, 1884, Kennel Club Archives.

26 William Carr, *The History of the Rise and Progress of the Killerby, Studley and Warlaby Herds of Short-horns*, quoted in Lewis Falley Allen, *History of the Short-horn: Cattle Their Origin, Progress and Present Condition* (Buffalo, NY: Lewis Falley Allen, 1874), pp. 101–2.

27 Low, *Breeds of Domestic Animals*, Vol. II, p. 67.

28 Thomas Bewick, *A General History of Quadrupeds* (Newcastle upon Tyne: T. Bewick, 1824), p. 64; Russell, *Like Engend'ring Like*, pp. 208–9.

29 Pawson, *Robert Bakewell*, pp. 72–8.

30 See, for example, John R. Walton, "The diffusion of improved sheep breeds in eighteenth- and nineteenth-century Oxfordshire," *Journal of Historical Geography* 9 (1983): 175–95, and Juliet Clutton-Brock, "British cattle in the eighteenth century," *Ark* 9 (February 1982): 55–9.

31 Many subsequent commentators have speculated about this mystery. See, for example, Hall and Clutton-Brock, *Two Hundred Years*, p. 151; Trow-Smith, *History of British Livestock Husbandry*, pp. 60–2; Russell, *Like Engend'ring Like*, pp. 208–10; Ryder, *Sheep and Man*, p. 486; for a range of suggestions.

32 William M'Combie, *Cattle and Cattle-Breeders* (Edinburgh: William Blackwood, 1867), pp. 152–3.

33 Keith Thomas attributes the practice of naming pet animals to a parallel process of individuation. *Man and the Natural World: A History of the Modern Sensibility* (New York: Pantheon, 1983), pp. 113–14.

34 Wilson, *Evolution of British Cattle*, p. 119.

35   Spargo, *This Land is Our Land*, pp. 42–3, 88; Russell, *Like Engend'ring Like*, p. 213.

36   *The General Stud Book, Containing Pedigrees of Race Horses* . . . (London: James & Charles Weatherby, 1827 [1791]; 3rd edn), Vol. I, p. iii; George Coates, *The General Short-Horned Herd-Book: Containing the Pedigrees of Short-Horned Bulls, Cows, &c. of the Imported Durham Breed* (Otley: W. Walker, 1822), p. vii.

37   *British Berkshire Herd Book* (Salisbury, Wilts: Edward Roe, 1885), Vol. I, p. vii; G. R. Vernon (comp.), *The Ayrshire Herd Book, Containing Pedigrees of Cows, Heifers, and Bulls of the Ayrshire Breed* (Ayr: Hugh Henry, 1878), Vol. I, p. v.

38   *British Goat Society Herd Book and Prize Record from 1875 to 1885*, Vol. I, Pt I (1886), p. 1.

39   *Sussex Herd Book, Containing the Names of the Breeders, the Age, and the Pedigrees of the Sussex Cattle*, Vol. II (1885), "Preface," n.p.

40   *The Galloway Herd Book, Containing Pedigrees of Pure-Bred Galloway Cattle* (Dumfries: Galloway Cattle Society, 1878), Vol. I, "Preface," n.p.; *The Norfolk and Suffolk Red Polled Herd Book*, Vol. I (1874), p. 9.

41   *Oxford Down Flock Book* (London: Oxford Down Sheep Breeders' Association, 1889), Vol. I, p. 8.

42   *British Goat Society Herd Book*, Vol. I (1886), p. 2.

43   One such elitist was Thomas Bates, who declined to list his shorthorns in the *Herd Book* after his friend and its founding editor George Coates died, on the ground that he did not want his highly bred animals flanked by mongrels. Ritvo, *Animal Estate*, pp. 61–2.

44   Charles Hassall, *General View of the Agriculture of the County of Carmarthen* (London: W. Smith, 1794), pp. 35, 37.

45   Wilson, *Evolution of British Cattle*, p. 124.

46   James Anderson, *Essays Relating to Agriculture and Rural Affairs* (Edinburgh: William Creech, 1777), Vol. II, pp. 138–9. This definition and others along the same lines did not settle the matter completely. Disagreement and confusion about the nature of breeds has persisted to the present. For the problem and the solution, see Juliet Clutton-Brock, "The definition of a breed," *Archaeozoology: Proceedings of the IIIrd International Archaeozoological Conference* (Szczecin, Poland: Agricultural Academy, 1979), Vol. I, pp. 35–44.

47   Ritvo, *Animal Estate*, p. 18.

48   Bewick, *General History*, pp. 1–23.

49   George Shaw, *General Zoology* (London: G. Kearsley, 1800), Vol. I (2), pp. 277–80.

50   Robert Kerr, *The Animal Kingdom or Zoological System, of the Celebrated Sir Charles Linnaeus; Class I. Mammalia* . . . (London: John Murray, 1792), p. 154.

51   *The Naturalist's Pocket Magazine: or, Compleat Cabinet of the Curiosities and Beauties of Nature*, Vol. VII (n.d., *c.* 1800), n.p.

52   Thomas Pennant, *History of Quadrupeds* (London: B. J. White, 1793), Vol. I, pp. 16–17.

53   George Culley, *Observations on Live Stock; Containing Hints for Choosing and Improving the Best Breeds of the Most Useful Kinds of Domestic Animals* (London: G. Wilkie & J. Robinson, 1807), p. 220.

54   John Wilkinson, *Remarks on the Improvement of Cattle, &c. in a Letter to Sir John Saunders Sebright, Bart.* (Nottingham: H. Barnet, 1820), pp. 4–5.

55   John Lawrence, *A General Treatise on Cattle, the Ox, the Sheep, and the Swine* (London: Sherwood, Gilbert, & Piper, 1808), p. 1.

56   Georges Louis Leclerc, Comte de Buffon, *Barr's Buffon. Buffon's Natural History* . . . *With Notes by the Translator* (London: H. D. Symonds, 1797), Vol. VI, p. 48.

21
Monopoly, economic thought, and the Royal African Company

Tim Keirn

The following account of the legislative and public debate surrounding the monopoly of the Royal African Company is taken from a larger project seeking to examine economic ideas and discourse during the reigns of William III and Mary, and of Anne. Given that virtually all economic literature at the end of the seventeenth century was addressed to, and attempted to inform, debates concerning the effectiveness and applicability of economic policy, this study attempts to analyze this literature within its political and legislative context.[1] The process of economic policy-making in Parliament was extremely fragmentary and usually instigated by private interest groups without government coordination (except, notably, in revenue matters). In this sense, the state's interest in economic affairs was "reactive"; it took little interest in directing economic affairs and acted only when spurred by the initiatives of interested groups and individuals from London and the provinces.[2] The reactive nature of the state, in conjunction with the rise of Parliament as the key policy-making body within government, allowed for a relatively open political culture and broad participation in the making of economic policy.

Most economic legislation during the reigns of William III and Anne, be it destined to pass or fail, was the occasion for some form of public scrutiny and debate, and evoked some form of contention and opposition.[3] The success or failure of a particular piece of legislation was a function both of parliamentary procedure and the weight and influence of constituent interests directly represented within Parliament, and also of the interplay of ideas presented by different sectional groups. Moreover, legislative – as opposed to conciliar – forms of economic policy-making called for much greater use of the press by interested parties seeking to mobilize public opinion to influence policy. It was the submitting of economic legislation which invited economic debate and instigated the interplay and transmission of economic ideas in print by agents acting as antagonists and protagonists for particular policies. Stimulated by the lapsing of the Licensing Act in 1695, and the growing politicization of English society (especially in the metropolis), the reigns of William and Anne witnessed an enormous increase in the volume of economic literature, most of which was produced in the form of polemical broadsides, short pamphlets, and "commentary" published in periodicals and newspapers.[4]

This polemical economic literature has not been examined by historians in any systematic way. Instead, most studies of early modern English economic thought have concentrated on longer works where authorship is known. The works of Barbon, Cary, Child, Davenant, Locke, and North are most frequently cited and, over time, have become the "classics," if not the "canon," of late seventeenth- and early eighteenth-century economic literature. Yet, one can question the representativeness of these works when attempting to discuss late seventeenth-century economic theory, ideology, and discourse. As Coleman has noted, one of the most important questions in the study of economic ideas is simply this: how widely were economic tracts read by contemporaries?[5] From my own perusals of the extant accounts and inventories of the libraries of some forty Augustan legislators, it is clear that these "classics" were rarely possessed by contemporary policy-makers. Yet, it is also clear that the economic ideas disseminated through the less expensive literary medium of the broadsheet, pamphlet, newspaper, and journal reached a relatively wide audience given that these publications were strategically placed in coffee-houses, posted in provincial and metropolitan markets and exchanges, and distributed within the lobbies of Parliament.[6] Indeed, longer treatises were often condensed and reprinted as broadsides to facilitate the easier dissemination of a particular argument. For example, Charles Davenant's *Reflections upon the Constitution and Management of the Trade to Africa* (1709) was reprinted in at least five different broadsheet titles, and appropriate sections of John Cary's *Essay on the State of England* (1695) were also republished during the African trade debates.[7]

Unlike historians of economic ideas, students of political discourse and ideology have discovered the importance of pamphlet and polemical literature, and consequently have recognized lower levels of discourse " 'below' the classical works we associated with canons in literature and philosophy, yet 'above' the culture of everyday life."[8] In this sense, political discourse was practiced as much by the party pamphleteer as it was by Locke or Toland.[9] The study of economic discourse (inclusive of the study of theory), and the use of "low" literature as well as "high," is as imperative for the student of economic ideas as it is for the historian of political ideas. It is through this type of economic literature that we can gain a more representative notion of the assumptions, maxims, and theories of late seventeenth-century economic thought.

Some would argue that the study of broadsides for their economic content is marred by their overtly political overtones and purposes. Yet, early modern economic thought and ideology did not evolve within an intellectual vacuum or in academic isolation. On the contrary, men like Davenant, Cary or the anonymous writers of pamphlets were not "economists" in any way close to the modern sense of the word, nor were they akin to the "political economists" of the later eighteenth century. Instead, these participants in commercial and economic debates came from a diversity of backgrounds and occupations. Schumpeter argued that the economic writers of the period could be delineated into two groups, these being "consultant administrators," who were the teachers and authors of "more or less systematic treatises," and "pamphleteers," who were "advocates or foes of a particular measure or policy" and often "cranks with pet ideas." Yet, the historical utility of this demarcation is open to question.[10] As noted, virtually all economic literature in the late seventeenth and early eighteenth centuries addressed itself to current economic policy issues and controversies which came before Parliament, the Privy Council, or the Board of Trade. Rarely, if ever, was an author concerned with advancing economic knowledge purely for its own sake. This is true even of the classic treatises of the "consultant administrators" such as Cary, Davenant, and North.[11]

Consultant administrators and pamphleteers were both advocates whose arguments and beliefs often differed only in respect of the length and style of their presentation. Unlike the twentieth-century economist who recognizes a dual obligation, "to provide scientific explanations of the 'normal' working of economic systems and to furnish 'guidance' as to the 'best' policies under any given circumstances," his late seventeenth-century precursor recognized no such obligation and discussed normative economics only insofar as it served to enhance and make more convincing his guidance on policy.[12] Occupational interest or patronage ensured that this guidance did not come impartially: in general, most participants in economic debates had a political axe to grind.[13] Given this orientation of late seventeenth-century economic writing, it seems only fitting that this discourse be studied within its contemporary political and economic context.

However, historians of economic thought have tended to shy away from contextual analysis. Generally, they have been practitioners of a vertical history of ideas, seeking to trace the origins or progress of a particular idea or argument over time, sometimes paying little attention to its contemporary context. There has been a strong tendency to create teleological narratives which seek to anticipate the liberal economics and free trade arguments of Adam Smith. Hence, there is a general inclination within the historical literature to categorize early modern authors and their economic ideas within the historically imprecise construct of contrasting "liberal" and "mercantilist" contributions to economic thought and theory.[14] Others, especially economists, who have perhaps ignored the linear tracing of the ancestry of classical economic theory, nonetheless have analyzed mercantilist writings and policies in retrospect to the body of economic knowledge found in the modern world, asking in essence if the mercantilists were "right" or "wrong."[15]

Both approaches contain elements of "presentism," either in tracing the morphology of a particular idea over time, or in juxtaposing that idea with modern viewpoints, which serve to disguise the meaning of the idea in its own historical time.[16] Historians of political ideas have argued for many years that the recovery of the context is imperative to understanding any text in a historical sense, and, in doing so, have drawn special attention to language use. Clearly, the contextual examination of language use within the study of economic ideas is fruitful, given that most previous studies of economic literature have focused predominantly on theory, disregarding other perspectives. At the end of the seventeenth century, rational assessments and normative statements concerning economics took place within convention-governed contexts, thus it is important to have some comprehension of the contemporary vocabulary of economics. The normative use of language in economic discourse must be examined, analyzing those words frequently used to describe, to evaluate (in both a positive and a negative sense), and to legitimate contemporary economic (and political) policies and practices. By doing so, we obtain better insight into how literate members of English society "understood" economics in the late seventeenth and early eighteenth centuries.[17]

Of course, one must not exaggerate the absence of contextual studies in the history of early modern economic ideas. Some do exist. Pocock and others have examined the "high" economic discourse of the period, although not all would agree with the historical reality of the neo-Machiavellian context in which this discourse has been placed.[18] Moreover, a number of studies analyze early modern economic ideas contextually within broad economic and social backgrounds which are schematic and generalized, usually viewing the development of these ideas within the broad constructs of the "rise" of a commercial/capitalist society, the market economy, or the nation-state.[19] While such constructs are perhaps useful in the long-term analysis of changes in the stock of ideas, nonetheless, in the short-term, such highly unfocused historical backgrounds often make it difficult to distinguish the ideological wood from the historical tree. Indeed, the absence of the investigation of the political and legislative context of early modern economics has led to a number of over-simplifications. For example, there has been a tendency within the current historical literature to portray a general congruence between the economic ideas and policies within "liberalism" and "mercantilism," by congregating natural law, more abstract economic theorizing, and free trade policies on the one hand, and fixed notions of wealth, unsystematic economic theorizing, and protectionist policies on the other. In turn, merchants are often exemplified as in the vanguard of liberalism; landowners and manufacturers are portrayed as the primary supporters of mercantilism. And yet the close examination of economic legislation and debate reveals that the relationship between ideology and policy is complex, and it is inaccurate to place a body of economic policies and a body of ideas under the same heading without a better understanding of the relationship between the two.[20] Indeed, one may even question the applicability of a historically recoverable division between liberal and mercantilist economic ideologies at the end of the seventeenth century, at least at the level of "low" discourse.

Examining the dispute over the monopoly of the Royal African Company allows us to tackle many of these issues. Between 1689 and 1714, Parliament debated legislation or inquired into the state of the commercial organization of the English trade to Africa in fifteen different sessions. The repetitive history of the African trade bills has ensured that a great deal of significant material on the political structure and agency of this legislation survives, and allows for the analysis of a large body of economic literature within a relatively concrete political and economic context.[21] My analysis will first entail a brief examination of both the state of the African trade in the late seventeenth century and the course of the debate in Parliament; and secondly, pursue an investigation of the economic ideas found within the literature. I hope to show that the "monopolists" and "free traders" in this debate were not arguing about different or contrasting concepts of economic ideology and thought. If the African trade issue was a conflict of ideologies, it was one of Whig and Tory and not one between mercantilism and liberalism.

The importance of the African trade in the late seventeenth century lay in its role as a provider of labor to the plantations of the West Indies. While gold had been the principal motivator of English contact with Africa since Elizabethan times, the slave trade dominated English activity on the African coast from the middle of the seventeenth century. By the 1640s, sugar was being produced with slave labor on the island of Barbados, and cultivation later spread to the Leeward Islands and Jamaica. The expansion of sugar cultivation in the West Indies led to extensive English participation in the slave trade.[22] The English slave trade grew steadily over the second half of the seventeenth century as the labor demands of sugar planters grew. In the absence of technological change, planters were increasing output by expanding their supplies of slaves above and beyond the high rate of replacement engendered by appalling levels of mortality within slave communities. Indeed, as intensive sugar cultivation exhausted soil fertility, and as the cost of maintaining slaves increased (as the sugar islands became increasingly dependent on imported building materials and foodstuffs) and the price of sugar fell (as a consequence of ever growing output), masters worked their slaves harder, treated them with greater brutality, and fed them less as the century wore on. Since the price of slaves was generally stable (or falling) during the three decades following the Restoration, these harsh entrepreneurial decisions were inculcated within the planter mentality and the increase in the demand for slaves became virtually immutable.

Between the Restoration and the end of the seventeenth century, sugar production doubled (and may have tripled) in the English Caribbean. The price of sugar in London fell by over 50 percent between 1660 and 1690 (when war began to disrupt supplies), widening the domestic market and consumption. By 1700, sugar accounted for more than 10 percent of the value of English imports and roughly 15 percent of all re-exports. Moreover, sugar imports played a vital role in the rapid growth of the outports of Bristol and Liverpool, and contributed significantly to state customs revenue.[23] The English direct trade to Africa (exporting some cloth and iron manufactures and importing small amounts of gold and ivory) was normally of little significance. Hence, the importance of the African trade was within the triangular trade plied between England, Africa, and the Americas, provisioning labor for the plantation economies, and not only for sugar cultivation in the West Indies, but also for Chesapeake tobacco and Carolina rice production.[24] Contemporaries were ever aware of the important human linkage between Africa and the plantations. The trade policy toward the former was dictated by the latter, as one pamphleteer noted:

> for that the Plantations be worth nothing to the Nation without such Hands, so consequently those who Increase and Improve the African Trade must, by carrying the greatest Numbers of Negroes thither, seem to desire the most encouragement.[25]

It was the critical importance of the plantations in the total scheme of English trade in the late seventeenth century that put great public emphasis on the state of the trade to Africa.

For most of the seventeenth century, the English organization of the African trade was "theoretically" under the auspices of an incorporated joint-stock company with an exclusive monopoly granted by patent from the Crown, although interlopers accounted for a considerable percentage of the English slave trade. In 1672, in the wake of the insolvency of the Company of Royal Adventurers of England Trading into Africa,

Charles II granted a charter of incorporation with extensive privileges to the Royal African Company. Most important was the grant of monopoly that reserved the English trade to Africa and the slave trade to the colonies solely to shareholders of the company (or to their licensees). These privileges also included the right to make war with "non-Christian Princes," the grant of Mine Royal, and the right to erect a court of judicature on the coast of Africa to assist in the suppression of interlopers (whose goods and ships the company was empowered to seize). The African Company monopoly had its origin in the royal prerogative, exploiting a loophole in the Statute of Monopolies (1624) which permitted crown patents of monopoly to towns, corporations, and companies.[26] Moreover, the early African Company was well represented by members of the peerage with close connections at the court of Charles II. James, Duke of York, served as governor of the company between 1672 and 1688 and four members of the Cabal were initial investors in the company.[27]

The Royal African Company was from its birth encumbered with debts and most likely never made a profit. At the end of the last Dutch War, the company embarked on a vigorous and costly project of rebuilding and expanding English forts and settlements in Africa beyond the means of its subscripted capital. In addition, the company suffered a serious liquidity problem in its trade to the plantations. The turnover of capital was slow given the great span of time taken in procuring, shipping, and selling a single consignment of slaves. Too often these slaves were sold to the planters on credit. These loans became increasingly difficult to redeem as planters were squeezed by falling prices and rising costs.[28] By 1690, the company had a significant percentage of its assets tied up in bad debts. It had always borrowed short on its seal to obtain trading capital and to maintain appreciation of its stock value. Yet, by 1691, the company was forced to quadruple its stock, depreciating share values. The financial status of the company continued to crumble and "the company plumbed the depths of joint-stock finance" but to little avail.[29] The bond creditors of the company became an important interest group in the ensuing trade debates. Hence, for our purposes, it is important to keep in mind that the Royal African Company was financially crippled when it first came under attack in Parliament in the 1690s. However, in political terms, the real failure of the company was in its inability to accomplish what it was primarily appointed to do – to deliver slaves. The company's peak trade came in 1687 when roughly 10,000 slaves were transported. However, this figure fell below 3,000 within two years and diminished further thereafter. Throughout the late 1680s and 1690s, the gap between the demand for slaves and the supply provided by the company widened.[30]

Political pressure to break the company's monopoly in the 1680s grew commensurate with the development of an increasingly formalized West India interest in London, consisting of absentee planters, sugar merchants, and colonial and commission agents. The late seventeenth-century process of attempting to centralize politically the colonies focused colonial political interests and social aspirations upon London, as planters sought patronage and political connections to bolster their positions of authority in the colonies. In the West Indies, this had an economic counterpart in the formation of the commission system which increasingly concentrated the economic interests of the sugar colonies upon the London produce and credit markets, and its mercantile and financial community. The commission system was the genesis of a strong economic relationship between the "plantocracy" in the islands and important London commercial groups with political connections.[31]

While in the late 1680s the West India interest was most concerned with reversing recently imposed additional duties on sugar (1685), complaints about the monopolist bottleneck in the supply of slaves also became increasingly vocal. As early as 1679, Parliament set up an investigative committee to examine allegations of the African company's "unjust" practices of seizing interloping vessels. Although no legislation arose from this committee, nonetheless the company felt threatened enough to publish a public defense of its monopoly.[32] Yet, if Davies is correct, opposition to the Royal African Company in the 1680s took the form of action and not words. It is clear that interlopers were beginning to operate widely in the 1680s and at cheaper cost, controlling perhaps one-third of the English slave trade.[33] However, while the company enjoyed a close relationship with James II, sustained political assault on the company was impossible.

The Glorious Revolution brought significant changes to the company's fortune. The onset of war increased the expenses of the company in defending its shipping and settlements from French attacks and its financial situation continued to deteriorate. At the same time, wartime disruptions to commerce and shipping reversed the secular downswing in sugar prices.[34] Higher prices encouraged planters to expand output and sugar acreage, and to clamor for more slave labor which was increasingly difficult to procure. Indeed, while the volume of the English slave trade to the Caribbean continued to expand during the period 1689–1714, prices for slaves rose sharply as the number of slaves transported proved still inadequate to meet the ever expanding labor demands of colonial planters.[35] Moreover, by 1700, interlopers were providing planters with approximately 80 percent of their slaves as the Royal African Company proved unable to enforce its monopoly, nor could it compete in what was essentially an open market.[36] Within this economic context of rising labor prices and shortages of supply, the monopoly of the Royal African Company appeared increasingly absurd.

Thus, it is not mere coincidence that the first assaults on the company's monopoly in Parliament were paralleled by the first increase in slave prices in over a quarter of a century. However, political circumstances for the Royal African Company in the 1690s had changed as significantly as had the economic context. With the departure of James II, the company no longer felt protected by the royal prerogative. "Monopoly" still retained its pejorative sense in the late seventeenth century: it was firmly tied in the public imagination to the royal prerogative, and was perceived as a threat to the liberties of both the House of Commons and the subject. The memory of Elizabethan and early Stuart abuse of the patent system was still deeply ingrained, despite the fact that Charles II and James II had been careful to restrict their use of the grant of monopoly when issuing patents.[37] However, the political tension engendered by the policies of James II, coupled with the assertiveness of the House of Commons in the aftermath of the Glorious Revolution, served only to exacerbate public and political hostility to monopoly.[38] Consequently, on the basis of the changed political climate, the African Company, and other commercial monopolies, sought to transfer the legitimacy of their monopoly privileges from the right of prerogative to statute law.[39]

In 1690, the company turned to Parliament for confirmation of its charter. This had three effects on the company: first, it provided a public and parliamentary forum for the company's critics; secondly, it forced the company to justify its monopoly in respect to its commercial record; and finally, it exposed the company to its political liabilities in a freshly invigorated partisan atmosphere. While the company's effort in 1690 failed, parliamentary confirmation would remain a primary preoccupation of the company. Already in 1690 a pattern was established. The company or its opponents would submit a petition for settlement of the trade (i.e., seeking either to confirm or destroy the company's monopoly) which would stimulate lobbying and an extensive printed response from vested interest groups. In addition to the African Company and its creditors, these groups included the West India interest, interloping slave traders, merchants of the western outports, cloth and metal manufacturers exporting to Africa, and, by the early eighteenth century, the planters of the Chesapeake. The issue would then be put into legislative committee (or sent off to the Board of Trade for further opinion) where, more often than not, it died with the adjournment of the session. Most of these proceedings were repetitious in nature and hence only a few generalizations need be made about the parliamentary course of the debate.[40]

Unlike most economic legislation during the reigns of William III and Anne, the African Company's conflict in Parliament was of a partisan nature. This did not go unnoticed by contemporaries. Defoe, writing for the company in the *Review* in 1709, noted with some wit that settling an "Exclusive Company" would be beneficial, especially:

> If it were only to have it be exclusive of such People, whose awkward Politicks have ruin'd it already: This seems natural to the Trade, but much more natural to the Contest between the Parties.[41]

Other pamphleteers made frequent reference to the contest between the parties in their contributions, stressing that the African trade issue was "to be the daily Occasion of our Coffee-house Contests and Debates."[42] Commercial conflict on the coast of Guinea was a useful literary parallel to political conflict in Westminster, and the company was portrayed in the press as affiliated with the Tories, while the interlopers were associated with the Whigs.

There seems to be little doubt that the Royal African Company was Tory in its political composition. As noted, the company had relied on the patronage of James II and had always maintained an affinity towards the Tories and to the City of London. Of the sixteen successful Tory candidates in City elections to Parliament between 1681 and 1702, fourteen held shares in the African Company.[43] Of the thirty-eight members of the company's Court of Assistants who sat in Parliament after 1689, only nine did so as Whigs.[44] Unfortunately, we have no surviving division lists for any African bill, although a careful analysis of tellers, runners, speakers, presenters, and chairmen in the *Commons Journals* and House of Lords Manuscripts, in conjunction with references to speakers found in various manuscript sources, gives at least an impressionistic view of the partisan nature of the African issue. Of thirty-one MPs known to have supported the company in this period, at least twenty-five voted consistently with the Tories. In turn, of the forty-one known to have opposed the company, a minimum of thirty-five were Whigs.[45]

In the 1690s, most of the debate in Parliament revolved around two points of contention. First, the company's opponents argued that monopoly restricted the supply of slaves to the islands and limited exports of manufactures, an argument difficult for the African Company to counter given its shrinking trading performance. The other point of contention dealt with the necessity of forts in the African trade. Here the African Company was on firmer ground. In the 1690s, most of the company's opponents accepted the necessity of forts though it was argued that these forts could be maintained by a regulated company as opposed to a joint-stock.[46] Proceeds from entry fines would support the forts, while all merchants would trade on their own account without significantly limiting the number of buyers and sellers in the trade.[47]

While parliamentary select committees in 1693/4, 1694/5, and 1695/6 pressed for bills stressing the importance of forts and the necessity of a joint-stock organization in the African trade, these measures were either defeated or stalled in the increasingly Whig-controlled Commons.[48] Thereafter, the company abandoned attempts to gain full confirmation of its charter and was willing to promote compromise bills which surrendered some of the company's privileges. In 1698 such a compromise bill was passed. Though the bill was not drawn up in direct response to a petition by the African Company, it does seem to equate with proposals submitted by the company to the Board of Trade.[49] These proposals had suggested limiting the African Company monopoly to that area between Cape Blanco and Cape Mount where "that trade consists chiefly in hides, wax, Elephants Tooth and Redwood and few Negroes . . . which can no way prejudice the Plantations." Furthermore, the proposals suggested that the separate traders pay 15 percent on their export of goods and manufactures and 15s per head on Negroes to help pay for the "high Costs and necessity of maintaining the severall Forts and Factories without which this important Trade cannot be carried on or preserved to this Nation as hath been already noted in Parliament."[50] The amended bill, which came out of committee, and eventually passed into law, reveals that the African Company had been forced to give up further ground to its opponents for the bill went far beyond their original offers of compromise. Indeed, the company lost its exclusive charter and monopoly; the trade was opened to all Englishmen willing to contribute to the maintenance of forts and factories by paying the company a duty of 10 percent on exports to and from Africa.[51]

The Act of 1698 did nothing to subvert the dominance in the slave trade which the interlopers (or "separate traders") had secured. While the company's trade did recover briefly, this was clearly a manifestation of peace, rather than of a new comparative advantage, and the gap between the separate traders continued to widen with time as the company's financial and commercial activity disintegrated after 1705. The company soon believed that the Act of 1698 had done it more harm than good by encouraging more to enter the slave trade outside the auspices of the company. Once again the African Company pursued a policy toward obtaining full reconfirmation of its monopoly privileges, attempting to remove the private trader by statutory authority. On the other hand, the separate traders sought a repeal of the 1698 Act in the belief that the 10 percent duty was a nuisance, increasing the cost of purchasing slaves, which in turn was passed on to the planters in higher prices.[52]

In 1707, the company took its case to Queen Anne who immediately referred it to the Board of Trade. The board, under Sunderland's instruction, initiated a major investigation into the state of the African trade. The board thoroughly dissected the company's books and accounts, and accused the African Company of mismanaging the proceeds of the 10 percent duty, and of masking the asset structure of the company with bad debts. However, the trade figures for slave exports provided by the separate traders came from unverifiable sources (i.e., based on oral testimony rather than on the presentation of accounts and ledgers) and these went unquestioned by the board. Indeed, the most important point in favor of the private traders was in regard to the satisfaction silently claimed by the West Indies planters. The board's report noted that the interlopers had improved the trade and "since the passing of that Act, we have not heard of any complaints from the Plantations either as to the Scarcity or excessive Prices of Negroes." The report recommended that the African trade be organized "free of monopoly" and within a regulated company.[53]

However, what is most remarkable about the board's report is the one-sided nature of its conclusions in respect to the highly subjective presentation of the proceedings. As a recent historian of the Board of Trade has noted, the board "seldom conducted an inquiry with as much prejudice as was apparent in dealing with the Royal African Company."[54] In the board's investigation, the company's evidence in support of its case was scrutinized fully, and yet the company was not allowed (as was the usual procedure in such cases) to challenge the separate traders' highly suspect figures. Indeed, as Davenant remarked: "the separate traders, by an early and close application, with the help of some political or rather fallacious computations, as to their own imaginary performances, and several groundless suggestions against the company . . . prepossessed the commissioners with such an opinion of the supposed advantages arising from a separate trade." The board made no attempt to "obtain such vouchers and adminicles from the coast of Africa or the plantations in time, as might enable them to put these matters in so clear a light." The greatest damage arising from this was that unsubstantiated figures were given authenticity by their acceptance as presentable evidence before the board, and were circulated to MPs by opponents of the company.[55] Indeed, the figures from the Board of Trade reports became the gospel in parliamentary debates in this period, and were reprinted in numerous pamphlets in support of the separate traders.[56] In 1708 and 1709, the board reported to Parliament that the trade to Africa should be open and free under a suitable proviso to preserve the forts, thus killing the African Company's attempts to procure a bill for reconfirmation of its monopoly and charter. Indeed, late in the sessions of 1708/9 and 1709/10, the Whigs initiated legislation in response to the Board of Trade's recommendations to settle a free trade to Africa.[57] This effort was halted in April 1710 when Queen Anne dissolved Parliament and brought the Tories back into her ministry.

With the return of Harley to power, the issue of the African trade was complicated by his plan for the South Sea Company. Indeed, there appear to have been strong links between the two companies. A considerable number of subscribers in the South Sea Company had at one time or another been on the Court of Assistants of the African Company.[58] The Oxford ministry was supportive of the African Company's fight against the Whigs, yet was reluctant to fully resurrect the company such that it might threaten the success of a primary commercial objective – to secure the Spanish *Asiento* for the South Sea Company.[59] The Tories did give the African Company a new lease of life and an injection of trading capital in 1712 when supporting the company's parliamentary unification with its bond creditors.[60] After 1710, the new Tory-dominated

Board of Trade rejected the former Whig board's recommendations for a free trade yet refused to guide Parliament except in simply reproducing the arguments of all interests involved. Bills were submitted both for monopoly and for a free or regulated trade right up to 1714. All died in committee. In the African and South Sea Company papers it is clear that the former company abandoned all pretenses of regaining its privileges after 1712, and saw its future as subordinate to the more dynamic and politically viable projects promoted by the Tory leadership. In the session of 1711/12, William Farrer's bill to set up a regulated African Company failed by the slimmest of margins (69–63). In 1713, Farrer and the Whigs submitted another bill which set up a "free and open" trade under "such proper Regulations" to maintain the English forts and settlements in Africa. This bill passed the Commons by a comfortable vote of 135 to 102.[61] In response, representatives of the African Company met with the South Sea Company to consider how to settle the African trade to secure to the South Sea Company "the full benefit of the *Asiento*." While the bill was considered in the Lords, representatives of the South Sea Company met with the Lord Treasurer stressing their opposition to the bill. However, they did have contingency plans aiming to have clauses added to the bill securing the collection of the 10 percent duty and maintaining their right "to trade in their Politick Capacity" if it were likely to pass. The bill died in committee in the Lords.[62] Indeed, by 1713 the African Company was concentrating its energies on gaining the subcontract for delivering slaves to the South Sea Company under the *Asiento*. This was one victory gained over the separate traders, but in the meantime the 1698 Act had expired and after 1714 the African Company would never again threaten to control the English slave trade through its monopoly.[63] In 1750, the remnants of the African Company were finally dissolved by Parliament and replaced by a regulated company, forbidden to trade as a corporate entity, and set up simply to maintain the English forts and trading factories in Africa.[64]

In turning to the literature generated by the debate, perhaps it would first be pertinent to present some "robust" quantifiable data to give some notion of the volume of ideas produced. The following figures are crude, although one assumes that the chance of survival of a particular broadsheet or pamphlet is constant. The *Eighteenth Century Short Title Catalogue* (*ECSTC*) has 106 titles within its files containing the (truncated) search terms "Royal Africa," "Africa," "Guinea," and "separate trader" (excluding those titles concerned with the East India trade debates) between the years 1700 and 1714. I have discovered an additional fifty-five tracts not on file either because they are in collections and libraries not yet integrated with the system, or simply because they were missed in the compilation of the *ECSTC* or lacked the obvious key words in their title to be picked up in my computer search. In addition, thirty-seven tracts were published in the 1690s, though admittedly the dating of many of these broadsides is difficult. This then gives us a sum total of 198 different titles between 1689 and 1714, at least 80 percent of which are one- or two-page polemical tracts.[65] The titles are split fairly evenly between those defending and those attacking the monopoly of the Royal African Company. From my research into other economic issues, it is clear that the debate surrounding the African trade generated as much literature as, if not more than, any other economic controversy during this period.

However, one should not exaggerate the significance of the volume of literature concerning the African trade as evidence of its heightened importance relative to other contemporary issues. In the 1690s, the African debate solicited a far smaller output from the press than did the legislative debates pertaining to the coinage or the East India Company monopoly. Indeed, it would appear that approximately 90 percent of the Royal African Company literature was produced in the second round of legislative attempts beginning in 1708. In the early eighteenth century, the debate on the African trade was carried on in an atmosphere where political conflict was increasingly accentuated by the formation of public opinion solicited by printers and pamphleteers. Following the expiration of the Licensing Act in 1695, there was a tremendous growth in the production of political literature, peaking just before the implementation of the Stamp Act in 1712. This explosion in the volume of political literature was both cause and effect of an increasing sense of partisan rivalry which permeated the period. Given the standards of the later eighteenth century, elections were frequent and the franchise was wide in this period. As Englishmen became more politicized, they craved more political information which was not provided impartially. Again to present some more "robust" figures: 214 tracts are to be found in the *ECSTC* file with "Sacheverell" in the title. Hence, the increase in literary interest in the African trade is not a manifestation of its importance relative to other issues, but instead reveals that the debate was imbued with the same highly politicized atmosphere which typified most controversies in the reign of Anne.[66]

The press was used both by the separate traders and the Royal African Company to influence public and parliamentary opinion. While the separate traders and planters were the principal exploiters of the medium of the press in the 1690s, the African Company utilized pamphleteers and the press to a much greater extent during the reign of Anne. Oftentimes, the company had minutes from its court meetings printed in broadsides or in the *Gazette* when it felt that the court's discussions would promote a favorable response to its cause, or publicly propagate the financial viability of the company.[67] The company also exploited the use of an expert corps of pamphleteers organized under Harley. Davenant and Defoe, who were both part of Harley's "literary entourage," wrote longer tracts in favor of the company during this period. Indeed, Davenant had opposed the monopoly of the African Company in print prior to his recruitment to the company's cause.[68] Defoe kept up a constant commentary in the *Review*, supporting the company whenever its case was put before Parliament. His *Essay upon the Trade to Africa* (1711) was directly commissioned by the African Company.[69]

The separate traders did not utilize such well-known authors in their literary assault on the company. Indeed, the Whig organization of pamphleteering in this period was more loosely structured than that of their Tory counterparts. Most of the longer tracts extant are in support of the African Company. The separate traders appear to have preferred the anonymous authors found in the "literary underworld" of the broadside to promote their message, although the African Company also utilized this abundant source of literary labor, albeit to a lesser degree.[70] The anonymous authors promoting the separate traders occasionally wielded personal attacks on the company's writers, especially Davenant, whose non-mercantile background was a special focus of criticism; he was accused of being a "Conceited Enterprizing Therist, prepar'd to assent or confute according as he is paid."[71]

Davenant's lengthy essay on the African Company was the only written effort which attempted to support the company on quantitative grounds. Davenant utilized the records not only of the customs, but of the company as well, extracting company correspondence from the African coast to portray the vicious commercial tactics of the separate traders and the Dutch.[72] However, by and large, the literature in favor of the company stressed the theoretical reasons for a monopoly. The literature of the private traders, on the other hand, was more concerned with the factual data to be presented in the dispute. Many of these writers, opposing monopoly in only a page or two, lacked sufficient space and opportunity to express their theoretical presuppositions. More to the point, they were not arguing about theory but were instead lobbying for a specific policy.

The pamphlets produced, for and against the company, closely correlated with the arguments and presentations made in Parliament. To a significant degree, the pamphlet literature simply reiterates or precedes those ideas expounded in the House or before the Board of Trade.[73] A great deal of the literature was concerned with the quantitative data surrounding the issue of free trade to Africa. The African Company, finding it difficult to justify its own monopoly through its meager commercial performance, often spent a good deal of time and energy attempting to slander and demean the quantitative material presented by the separate traders. Likewise, the opponents of the company expended appreciable amounts of paper against Davenant's accounts and, at the same time, promoted their own buoyant trade figures "authenticated" by the recognition given to them by the Board of Trade.[74] Furthermore, a great deal of the literature revolved around issues unique to the African trade, specifically addressing such points as the necessity of forts, the extent of the company's debts, and the brutal behavior (of both parties) on the African coast.[75] In addition, a significant number of pamphlets concerned themselves exclusively with the desires of a specific vested interest group. This is most notable in the cases of the merchants of the outports and the company's creditors.[76] However, since the Act of 1698 and its expiration in 1712 are often noted as significant victories for "*laissez-faire*," we should now turn to examine the structure of argument and justification for monopoly or free trade.

The company defended its privileges on the grounds that its monopoly was, in essence, natural and not a contrivance of the royal authority. The crux of its argument ran that trade necessitated a heavy investment of fixed capital for forts and settlements, and variable capital for the commercial viability of the enterprise. Since the plantations were so crucial to the economic prosperity of England, the monopolist emphasized that African trade policy should be based on attaining security rather than market flexibility, since as one pamphleteer put it: "Private Persons who are *ad libitum*, can have neither will or ability to defray a standing expense of this magnitude."[77] Others argued that an open trade diminished the state's ability to conduct economic policy, for:

> While the Trade to Africa lies open, it can never be distinctly known how nationally speaking we may be either Gainers or Losers by it. Perhaps some cunning Persons may gain considerably by commissions while, at the same time, our National Interest is sinking daily till it dwindle away to nothing at last by the cunning strategies and undermining Practices of our Foreign Competitors, before we can have sufficient time to apply a Remedy for recovery thereof.[78]

Defoe argued that a regulated company would fail to support the African trade with sufficient capital in periods of commercial flux since merchants would be motivated to contribute to the maintenance of the forts and settlements only when their short-term expectations of profit were good. He noted that if war or the necessity of increasing charges should arise:

> your Trade will decline; the more Expence, the less the Profit, the less the Trade, the more the Trade declines, the heavier this will fall, and so on, till all the Traders being discourag'd, the Payments stop. As they stop, the Forts and Factories die and decay, and where's the Security for Trade in all this?[79]

On the other hand, a joint-stock provided the necessary and constant flow of capital to the maintenance of trade, regardless of commercial fluctuation. The case was proven by constant reference to the similar experience of other nations trading in Africa: "All the European Nations . . . have from the nature and uncommon circumstances of that Trade, found it impracticable to carry it on, securely and advantageously, by any other Method, than that of a Joint-Stock, with exclusive and encouraging Privileges."[80]

Much of the defense of the monopoly of the Royal African Company was thus phrased in terms of a public-goods problem, whereby the private expenditure for forts and defense on the coast of Africa benefited the public good (vis-à-vis the promotion of the plantation trades) and as such was awarded with the privilege of monopoly. Many apologists for the company were careful to point out that this was an exception to the "General Maxim" that "Freedom of Trade" was the original right of the Subject, yet "Necessity gives the Crown a Power to Grant to any of its Subjects, Authority to get Possession by Force, and by Fortifications and Coercive Power, to get and protect the Trade." However, the 1698 African Trade Act accentuated the free rider problem inherent to public-goods issues, "giving Liberty to other Subjects, in the Nature of Lodgers and Inmates, to enter the Company's Forts at small rent," forcing them "to keep the Company's Houses in good repair for these New Guests." Shareholders in the African Company had right and property invested in these forts and settlements, which they felt to be violated by the 1698 legislation and by calls for free trade (if realized). Supporters of the company argued that their monopoly right was "equal with any Subjects' Right to his Freehold," warning that legislators: "Do unto the Company and Their Property, as you would have others do unto you, and your Estates."[81]

The case for a natural monopoly was based on two suppositions concerning the African trade: the necessity of force and of maintaining a united front. This, in turn, was a result of fears of the African people, of European competitors, and of unrestrained competition among the English themselves. Force, according to the proponents of the company, had been found essential to the trade since its European origins. The *Review* noted that the African trade "is carried meerly by Force, and you carry on your commerce as Princes make Treaties, Sword in Hand."[82] The necessity of using force was justified by reinforcing the image of black Africans as being "barbarous," threatening, and void of any entrepreneurial skill. Each author in favor of monopoly tried to outdo his antagonists in painting a more horrific spectacle of the "Barbarian" threat to English life and limbs. Defendants of the African Company published fantastic accounts of factors kidnapped in Africa who survived among the natives long enough to witness the supposed sexual depravity and cannibalism of the native population yet escaped miraculously to live and vividly tell the story.[83] However, the same authors were also keen to depict the African as rational and entrepreneurially minded when it suited their purpose to present the horrible commercial consequences of the unrestrained competition of the English separate traders. As one pamphleteer noted, when the separate traders bring

> many Ships to the Places where the Company have Forts, the Blacks who are subtle People, taking Advantage thereof, have not only lowred the Prizes of our own Commodities, but advanced the Price of Negroes from Three Pounds per Head to Twelve Pounds per Head; all which advantage the Blacks Gain, and the same is a clear Loss to England.[84]

Indeed, a similar viewpoint was stated in the *Review*: the "Natives" have "been made meer Merchants, sharp and crafty as an Exchange-Alley Stock-Jobber . . . and learn'd to put their own Price upon you . . . to the entire ruin of that Trade."[85]

However, even more threatening to the interests of the English were the European competitors on the coast. Virtually all the company's authors argued that the Dutch continued to harass the English interest in Africa, fomenting division among the natives against the company, and exploiting the differences between the separate traders to their own advantage. With jealous admiration, the *Review* noted: "The Dutch have nothing nearer their Hearts upon this Affair, than is possible to beat off the English from that Coast; and they would soon show us the Difference of the Trade, if once they had Possession of the Coast."[86] Though the company suffered marauding attacks in Gambia from the French, the company's pamphleteers were conspicuously silent in this regard, harboring instead the habitual Tory distrust and animosity toward the republican and dissenting Dutch.[87] Supporters of the African Company argued that by securing the whole trade to Africa

> we may yet put our selves into a Capacity of cutting off all other Nations, or at least making it difficult for them to get any great Number of Slaves from the Coast of Africa, the Consequence thereof must be, that then their Plantations must fall to Decay.[88]

Indeed, monopoly was exemplified as more conducive to a "positive" balance of trade since "the Increase and wealth of all states is evermore made upon the Foreigner."

Yet, of the greatest importance to the promoters of a monopoly was the necessity of maintaining a united front in Africa through the restraint of competition and self-interest. In the parliamentary debates, this was the crux of the company's argument against the separate traders, that

> it is not only the Contention between the separate Traders and the Company, but between the separate Traders and themselves vying and struggling one with another. This has made them sell to Loss, buy Extravagently, and expos'd their Folly so much, that the Negroes of Afrik Play upon them, and make a market of their Necessity.[89]

As one author put it: private traders brought on "the calamities of a National War" to the African trade.[90] Unrestrained competition was best alleviated through the united government and interests of the shareholders. Protected from the detrimental practice of underbidding, monopoly would guarantee that the trade would remain "permanent, creditable and an advantageous trade to the nation."[91] The defenders of the company were agreed that monopoly defended the national over the individual interest in trade for, as Defoe noted: "'Tis a freedom to manage the Trade for the General Good, not a freedom to insult trade."[92]

The separate traders, merchants, and planters who argued for freedom to trade into Africa did so most convincingly by pointing to the readily apparent failures of the company.[93] Nonetheless, the African Company was encompassed within the "traditional" argument against monopoly: namely, that monopoly was an odious fixture of the royal prerogative and absolute monarchy; it threatened the stature of the House of Commons and was a violation of the subject's liberty at common law to engage freely in trade. As one pamphlet stated, if the Crown had "a Power to grant liberty to some Persons to Trade and exclude others, they would have no occasion for Parliament to raise money."[94] In the 1690s, this argument was imbedded in a Whiggish conception that monopolies were vehicles for Tory patronage, and hence were a political manifestation and an artificial restraint on trade. In the press, stress was put upon the company's connections with James II, and brief slanted histories of the company focused on the role of bribes and royal mistresses in the company's origins. The metaphorical connection between the tyranny of James II and that found in the company's operations was also clearly made. Attempts by the company to enforce its monopoly through the seizure of ships and goods were portrayed as particularly brutish, writers claiming that "Masters and Seamen were Beaten, Abused and falsely Imprisoned by the Agents of the Company."[95] Monopoly was criticized as being only an artificial method by which a limited number of buyers and sellers could keep prices in their favor, supporting their own profits to the detriment of the public good. Hence the

> Limitations of Trade tend chiefly to the enriching of a few in prejudice to the general Good of a Nation subjecting it to a double tax. For such Monopolists buy the native Growths and Manufactures cheap at Home, and sell the Foreign Dear to the Subject.[96]

By limiting the number of suppliers unnaturally, this restricted the benefits of the plantations to the nation. With a virtually insatiable demand for slaves in the islands, it is not surprising that the "free-traders" felt that the number of slaves provided would increase in exact proportion to the augmenting of suppliers. As one pamphlet stated:

> Neither can there be any more danger of being over-stockt with Negroes, than that too much Sugar should be sent to England; for it is plain consequence, that with more Negroes more Goods will be produced, the more Goods the more Custom paid, and all those Commodities rendered here at home so cheap as will enable this Nation to send them abroad cheap also, to the great discouraging of the Plantation Trade of all other Nations.

It was argued time and again, that the plantations were favorable to the nation's balance of trade, stressing that since

> the Ballance is with us; if this Ballance can be augmented, if this Trade can be improv'd to a great height then surely this part of our Trade ought be indulg'd

and cherish'd and our Legislators will make it part of their Care and Concern to encourage and protect it, and to emancipate and set it free.[97]

Since increasing the supply of slaves would enhance the overall balance, then all restraints should be removed, allowing all to partake in the slave trade.

Finally, the private traders argued that there were no grounds for the company's defense of a "natural" monopoly. The necessity of force in Africa was questioned by the free-traders, who felt (by their own experience) that the trade did not necessitate heavy capital investments in forts and factories. It was argued that monopoly discouraged trade and in turn "if Forts are necessary to Trade only, as is alledged, and such Trade is not drove, there would be no Occassion to maintain those Forts."[98] Therefore, the image of the African to the separate trader was quite different from that portrayed by the monopolist. The separate traders noted that they had "seldom or never met with any Insults from the Natives, but often from the Company's Servants, and their Agents residing in the said Forts." However, by giving a favorable picture of the African, the private traders sought (like their counterparts) to justify their barbarous trade. In one pamphlet they went so far as to argue:

> I cannot but think it charitable and commendable, as well as lawful Undertaking, to buy a Slave in Guinea where the severity of his Government has subjected him to a Discipline, that Flesh and Blood can scarce go thro; and to transport him to one of our Plantations, where he retains the Name of Slave but performs only the work and Business of a Servant; without injury to himself, he becomes useful and profitable to his Master and beneficial to the Publick.[99]

Indeed, out of all the surviving pamphlets, only one criticizes the trade on moral grounds. Here, the author depicts the inherent gentleness of the African and the horrors and cruelty of the slave trade; yet, advocates a free trade with the qualification that the trade be "manag'd with more Justice and Humanity both in the first and after Buyer."[100] All in all, both the interloper and the monopolist manipulated their image of the African community to reinforce and justify their commercial activity.

Those who argued for free trade also recognized the threat of European competitors in Africa, yet through Whiggish eyes saw their primary enemy as the French, not the Dutch. One author noted: the Dutch "are so far from encroaching on us, that they show all the civil Treatment to our Traders that they can, whilst the Company's Factors oppress us to the last degree."[101] The separate traders argued that the best defense against foreign competitors was to supply the plantations readily with slaves who will

> make such an Addition of Strength to Great Britain, as will in time put us on Foot of Power superior to any of our Neighbours, all which depends on the Numbers of these useful Hands brought from Africa by the Separate Traders.[102]

Finally, like the monopolist, the separate trader was fearful of self-interest, yet found it most threatening in the guise of monopoly which had the commercial and political privileges of making a few individual interests dominant to those of the nation. In this regard, it was argued that if monopolists could have been

> persuaded to study the publick Profit more, and their private Gain less; would they be so honest as not to countenance or engage themselves in a way of Trade or Commerce, whereby the whole loseth, so particular Persons get?[103]

In the end, the greatest benefit of free trade in Africa was that competition expanded trade, captured markets, diminished the French, and consequently increased the wealth and power of the nation.

In concluding, K. G. Davies felt that *laissez-faire* in the African trade was "given its chance by one of the least ideological of all revolutions, and it won on merits that were severely practical."[104] In part, this is undeniably true. Free trade to Africa was a victory of commercial and financial forces in the 1690s which made the private trader the master of the English slave trade. It is significant that the debate effectually ended with the expiration, and not the enactment, of a piece of legislation.

However, the ideological aspects of the controversy concerning the African trade should not be ignored simply because it appears to have played no role in the conclusion of the debate. Protagonists and antagonists of the Royal African Company spent a great deal of time and effort trying to make their respective viewpoints known and to inform the policy-making process. It is significant that while one party argued for "free trade" and the other for "monopoly," clearly both sides were unwilling to abandon crucial mercantilist dogmas of the age.[105] Both groups conceived of a limited source of wealth in the trade. This was based on a finite conception of the number of potential African laborers within a context by which no technological or organizational change in sugar production was ever considered. Each group justified its activity by claiming that every African taken from the coast bettered the plantations and increased the balance of trade of Britain in respect to its neighbors. Each African was potentially a source of wealth to the Dutch or French, hence both monopolist and free-trader argued that their particular form of organization was better suited to eliminate foreign gains.

Thus, neither party attempts to justify its action by recourse to a liberal conception of the "rational individual trader" pursuing his own self-interest in an entirely free marketplace, nor did they attempt to engage in more abstract economic theorizing. The freedom to export slaves to the British plantations was a freedom reserved for the nation's subjects, not foreign competitors. Furthermore, along the hypothesis set out by Coleman, the unequivocal acceptance of the "maxim" of a balance of trade (never questioning it as theory) seems conclusive evidence that Whigs and Tories, private and company traders, all still viewed the nation's commerce, in Coleman's words, as an aggregation of bilateral, quasi-political trades all participating "in a conflict over an international cake of more of less fixed size." Hence, the economic recommendations of both groups were fixed on the achievement of certain self-interested and political aims, albeit to increase England's wealth and strength (and their own profits) relative to France or Holland. The Whigs and separate traders argued that a free trade would stymie the economic expansion of the French, while the Tories and the company argued that a monopoly would stymie that of the Dutch. It is notable that Coleman found both political parties arguing on the same principles about tariff structures within the Treaty of Utrecht, yet in this case the Whigs and their pamphleteers demanded prohibitions against the French while the Tory pens argued for free trade.[106]

Indeed, both parties in this period argued about policies and not economic theory. Apparent contradictions in policy are more easily explained by contrasts in sociopolitical postures toward France or Holland, or in attitudes toward the royal prerogative, than by differences in economic theory and ideology. Both the proponents and critics of the African Company monopoly shared in a concept that ultimately wealth could be obtained only at the expense of other European nations and the African people. They argued for free trade or monopoly simply because they felt one organization was superior in enhancing this "expence" and, at the same time, augmenting their own individual profits. It is important to keep in mind that all commentary within the debate was vested in one viewpoint or the other. Hence, men were arguing adamantly for the freedom of the individual to trade, yet did so on the premise that self-interest was evil. The monopolist argued that this evil was inherent in the cut-throat activity and resultant lowered profits and dislocation in supply evident in an "open" trade. Free-traders argued that it was most threatening in the form of monopoly where the self-interest of a few individuals could do damage to the profits of all. Both parties differed in their viewpoints as to which economic organization best restrained the excesses of self-interest. However, in their view of the individual, and their assumptions concerning the creation of wealth, the conceptions of both groups bore a likeness which was essentially mercantilist despite the fact that they were arguing over the ramifications of an essentially liberal economic policy to free trade from the confines of monopoly. Perhaps we could venture, then, that economic thought in the early eighteenth century was to a great extent developed as intellectual justification for economic activity after the fact. The actual organization of the trade to Africa by 1714 resembled that of the late eighteenth century; the ideological conceptualization was many decades removed.

Notes

1 As a result of the constitutional and financial settlements of the Glorious Revolution, the 1690s witnessed the beginnings of regular meetings of Parliament and a massive proliferation of legislation and statutory law. Consequently, state regulation of the economy was increasingly characterized by statute in contrast to the royal edict or proclamation which had been the dominant forms of economic regulation for most of the seventeenth century. See: C. G. A. Clay, *Economic Expansion and Social Change: England, 1500–1700* (Cambridge, UK: Cambridge University Press: 1984), Vol. II, pp. 203–6; J. Innes and J. Styles, "The crime wave: recent writing on crime and criminal justice in eighteenth-century England," *Journal of British Studies* (hereafter *JBS*) 25 (1986): 380–435; A. McInnes, "When was the English Revolution?", *History* 67 (1982): 377–92; H. T. Dickinson, "How revolutionary was the 'Glorious Revolution' of 1688?", *British Journal for Eighteenth-Century Studies* 11 (1988): 125–42.

2 L. Davison and T. Keirn, "The reactive state: English governance and society, 1688–1750," in L. Davison, T. Hitchcock, T. Keirn and R. B. Shoemaker (eds), *Stilling the Grumbling Hive: The Response to Social and Economic Problems in England, 1688–1750* (Stroud, Glos. and New York: Alan Sutton, and St Martin's Press, 1992), pp. xi–liv. See also J. Brewer,

The Sinews of Power: War, Money and the English State, 1688–1783 (London: Century Hutchinson, 1988), esp. Ch. 8.

3 Approximately one-half of all economic bills in this period failed to pass into law, although the failure of a piece of legislation did not necessarily mean that a bill was contentious. Bills of little interest were routinely tabled or delayed when the legislative calendar became too crowded with imperative revenue bills at the end of the parliamentary session.

4 For the importance of the press, politicization, and public opinion, see, for example, G. S. de Krey, *A Fractured Society: The Politics of London in the First Age of Party, 1688–1715* (Oxford: Clarendon Press, and New York: Oxford University Press, 1985); J. A. Downie, *Robert Harley and the Press: Propaganda and Public Opinion in the Age of Swift and Defoe* (Cambridge and New York: Cambridge University Press, 1979); W. A. Speck, "The electorate in the first age of party," in C. Jones (ed.), *Britain in the First Age of Party, 1680–1750* (London and Ronceverte, WV: Hambledon Press, 1987), pp. 45–62.

5 D. C. Coleman, "Mercantilism revisited," *Historical Journal* (hereafter *HJ*) 23 (1980): 773–91 (782).

6 For example, in the extensive manuscript collections of William Brockman and Edward Clarke, two dedicated and active MPs (representing Hythe and Taunton respectively), one finds a vast array of economic broadsides and pamphlets concerned with day-to-day legislative issues. Brockman was in the habit of making notes from committee meetings on the margins of these tracts; Clarke took the time and effort extensively to annotate and critique the arguments made in these broadsides. For Brockman, see British Library (hereafter BL) Additional MSS 42,592, and 42, 614. For Clark, see Somerset Record Office (hereafter RO), Sanford MSS; L. Davison and T. Keirn, "John Locke, Edward Clarke and the 1696 guineas legislation," *Parliamentary History* 7 (1988): 228–40.

7 See Appendix II below. Cary remarked to Locke during the legislative debates pertaining to the East India Company monopoly that treatises were inadequate for making much impact in Parliament, consequently noting that "the Managers" of the bill had reprinted parts of his *Essay on Trade* "which treated of the East India Trade, and delivered it to both Houses, where it raised objections." BL Additional MSS 5540/72, Cary to Locke, May 9, 1696.

8 D. Hollinger, "The return of the prodigal: the persistence of historical knowing," *American Historical Review* (hereafter *AHR*) 94 (1989): 610–21 (617).

9 See, for example, H. T. Dickinson, *Liberty and Property: Political Ideology in Eighteenth-Century Britain* (New York: Holmes & Meier, 1977); L. Colley and M. Goldie, "The principles and practice of eighteenth-century party," *HJ* 22 (1979): 239–46; M. Goldie, "The revolution of 1689 and the structure of political argument: an essay and an annotated bibliography of pamphlets on the allegiance controversy," *Bulletin of Research in the Humanities* 83 (1980): 473–564.

10 J. A. Schumpeter, *History of Economic Analysis* (London and Boston, MA: Allen & Unwin, 1954), pp. 159–61. Indeed many consultant administrators, such as Charles Davenant, were also pamphleteers. D. Waddell, "Charles Davenant (1656–1714) – a biographical sketch," *Economic History Review* (hereafter *EcHR*), 2nd series, 7 (1958): 279–88.

11 For example, Sir Dudley North's *Discourses upon Trade* (1691) may on first perusal appear to be devoted to the examination and communication of economic theory and principles, but on closer inspection reveals the author's preoccupation with policy recommendation to reform specific laws which "hamper Trade."

12 D. Winch, *Economics and Policy: A Historical Study* (New York: Walker Publishing, 1969), p. 19. In other words, the aim of the late seventeenth-century economic author "was simply to convince rather than to discover." T. Keirn and F. Melton, "Thomas Manley and the rate of interest debate, 1667–1672," *JBS* (1990): 147–83.

13 See W. Letwin, *The Origins of Scientific Economics: English Economic Thought, 1660–1776* (London: Methuen, 1963).

14 See, for example, J. Appleby, *Economic Thought and Ideology in Seventeenth-Century England* (Princeton, NJ: Princeton University Press, 1978); T. Cowen, "Nicholas Barbon and the origins of economic liberalism," *Research in the History of Economic Thought* 4 (1987): 67–83; L. Gomes, *Foreign Trade and the National Economy: Mercantilist and Classical Perspectives*

(Basingstoke, Hants: Macmillan, 1987), Chs 1–3; W. D. Grampp, "The liberal elements in English mercantilism," reprinted in J. J. Spengler and W. R. Allen (eds), *Essays in Economic Thought* (Chicago: Rand McNally, 1960), pp. 61–91; E. K. Hunt, *Property and Prophets: Evolution of Economic Institutions and Ideology* (New York: Harper & Row, 1986), pp. 29–34; E. A. J. Johnson, *Predecessors of Adam Smith: The Growth of British Economic Thought* (London: P. S. King, 1937); G. S. L. Tucker, *Progress and Profit in British Economic Thought, 1650–1850* (Cambridge, UK: Cambridge University Press, 1960); D. Winch, "Economic ideology as liberalism: the Appleby version," *EcHR*, 2nd series 38 (1985): 287–97.

15   For example, see, R. B. Ekelund and R. D. Tollison, *Mercantilism as a Rent-Seeking Society: Economic Regulation in Historical Perspective* (College Station, TX: Texas A & M University Press, 1981); J. M. Keynes, *The General Theory of Employment, Interest and Money* (London: Macmillan, 1936), Ch. 23; T. Hutchison, *Before Adam Smith: The Emergence of Political Economy, 1662–1776* (Oxford and New York: Blackwell, 1988); Schumpeter, *History*, Chs 3, 5, and 6.

16   Presentism being in essence, "the weird tendency of much writing . . . to be made up of what propositions in what great books remind the author of what propositions in what other great books." J. Dunn, *Political Obligation in Its Historical Context* (Cambridge, UK: Cambridge University Press, 1980), p. 15.

17   See J. G. A. Pocock, *Virtue, Commerce and History: Essays on Political Thought and History, Chiefly in the Eighteenth Century* (Cambridge and New York: Cambridge University Press, 1985), Introduction; Q. Skinner and J. Tully (eds), *Meaning and Context: Quentin Skinner and His Critics* (Cambridge, UK: Polity Press, 1988), Chs 1–3. Of course, this brazen advocacy of contextualism for the study of economic thought might strike some literary theorists and intellectual historians as being a bit "dated"! For defense of contextualism in the face of the poststructuralist critique, see Q. Skinner, "Meaning and understanding in the history of ideas," in Skinner and Tully, *Meaning and Context*, pp. 29–67; J. Appleby, "One good turn deserves another," *AHR* 94 (1989): 1326–32; Hollinger, "Return of the prodigal."

18   J. G. A. Pocock, *The Machiavellian Moment* (Princeton, NJ: Princeton University Press, 1975), Ch. 8; I. Hont, "Free trade and the economic limits to national politics: neo-Machiavellian political economy reconsidered," in J. Dunn (ed.), *The Economic Limits to Modern Politics* (Cambridge, UK: Cambridge University Press, 1990), pp. 41–120.

19   See, for example, Appleby, *Economic Thought*; Ekelund and Tollison, *Mercantilism*; Gomes, *Foreign Trade*; L. Magnusson, "Eli Heckscher, mercantilism, and the favourable balance of trade," *Scandinavian Economic History Review* (hereafter *SEcHR*) 26 (1978): 103–27; Schumpeter, *History*.

20   D. C. Coleman, "Eli Heckscher and the idea of mercantilism," reprinted in D. C. Coleman (ed.), *Revisions in Mercantilism* (London: Methuen, 1969), pp. 92–117 (p. 114).

21   Of the nine African trade bills initiated in the Commons in this period only one – the temporary African Trade Act of 1698 – was enacted into law: 9 & 10 Gul. III, c. 26. This legislation is briefly discussed in: W. R. Scott, *The Constitution and Finance of English, Scottish and Irish Joint-Stock Companies to 1720* (Cambridge, UK: Cambridge University Press, 1912), Vol. II, pp. 20–4; K. G. Davies, *The Royal African Company* (New York: Atheneum, 1970), Ch. 3; D. A. G. Waddell, "Queen Anne's government and the slave trade," *Caribbean Quarterly* 6 (1960): 7–10. The fortunes of the various bills can be followed in: *Commons Journal* (hereafter *CJ*); *Lords Journal* (hereafter *LJ*); E. Donnan (ed.), *Documents Illustrative of the History of the Slave Trade to America, 1930–35*, 4 vols (Washington, DC: Carnegie Institution of Washington, 1930–5); L. F. Stock (ed.), *Proceedings and Debates in the British Parliament Respecting North America* (Washington, DC: Carnegie Institution, 1924–41). Manuscript versions of failed African trade bills have been found at: BL Additional MSS 17, 477/9–30; Public Record Office (hereafter *PRO*) CO 388/6, February 22, 1697/8; Somerset RO, Sanford MSS DD/SF 2713. A list of the extant economic literature is provided at Appendix II below.

22   The following discussion of sugar production and the English slave trade is based on: H. M. Beckles and A. Downes, "The economics of transition to the black labor system in Barbados, 1630–1680," *Journal of Interdisciplinary History* 18 (1987): 225–48; Davies, *Royal*

African Company; R. S. Dunn, *Sugar and Slaves: The Rise of the Planter Class in the English West Indies, 1624–1713* (Chapel Hill, NC: University of North Carolina Press, for Institute of Early American History and Culture, 1972); D. W. Galenson, *Traders, Planters and Slaves: Market Behavior in Early English America* (Cambridge and New York: Cambridge University Press, 1986); J. A. Rawley, *The Trans-Atlantic Slave Trade* (New York: Methuen, 1981); D. Watts, *The West Indies: Patterns of Development, Culture and Environmental Change* (Cambridge and New York: Cambridge University Press, 1987).

23   See P. G. E. Clemens, "The rise of Liverpool, 1665–1750," *EcHR*, 2nd series, 29 (1976): 211–25; R. Davis, "English foreign trade, 1660–1700," reprinted in W. Minchinton (ed.), *The Growth of English Overseas Trade in the 17th and 18th Centuries* (London: Methuen, 1969), pp. 99–120; Rawley, *Transatlantic Slave Trade*, Chs 8–9.

24   In the 1680s, Chesapeake planters first began to exploit slave labor to cultivate tobacco and by 1710 were accounting for roughly 10 percent of the English slave trade. Davies, *Royal African Company*; H. S. Klein, *The Middle Passage: Comparative Studies in the Atlantic Slave Trade* (Princeton, NJ; Princeton University Press, 1978), pp. 122–3; S. Westbury, "Slaves of colonial Virginia: where they came from," *William and Mary Quarterly* (hereafter *W&MQ*), 3rd series, 42 (1985): 228–3.

25   *The State of the Trade to Africa between 1680 and 1707, as well under the Management of an Exclusive Company, as under that of Separate Traders . . .* (1708?), p. 1.

26   For the charter and early history of the Royal African Company, see C. T. Carr, *Select Charters of Trading Companies, 1530–1707*, Vol. 28 (London: B. Quartich, 1913, for the Selden Society), pp. 186–92; Scott, *Constitution and Finance*, Vol. II, pp. 17–35; Davies, *Royal African Company*, Intro. and Ch 1.

27   However, with the exception of the Duke of York (who remained as governor of the company until 1688), the peerage gradually dropped out of the company and were replaced by members from mercantile backgrounds. ibid., pp. 63–74.

28   Hence, planter opposition to the Royal African Company's monopoly of the slave trade was accentuated by the fact that planters owed a great deal of money – debts that might hopefully be cancelled with the company's demise.

29   For the financial troubles of the Royal African Company, see Davies, *Royal African Company*, pp. 47–96, esp. p. 85; Scott, *Constitution and Finance*, Vol. II, pp. 25–35.

30   Davies, *Royal African Company*, Appendix III; D. Galenson, "The Atlantic slave trade and the Barbados market, 1663–1723," *Journal of Economic History* (hereafter *JEH*) 42 (1982): 491–511.

31   For estate consolidation and the rise of the plantocracy, see Dunn, *Sugar and Slaves*, esp. Ch. 3. On the formation of interest groups in the colonial trades, see: S. Reagor, "The West India interest and English colonial administration, 1660–1691" (unpublished DPhil thesis, University of Oxford: 1970); A. G. Olson, *Anglo-American Politics, 1660–1775* (New York: Oxford University Press, 1973), pp. 96–105; A. G. Olson, "The Virginia merchants of London: a study in eighteenth-century interest-group politics," *W&MQ*, 3rd series, 40 (1983): 363–88. See also K. G. Davies, "The origins of the commission system in the West India trade," *Transactions of the Royal Historical Society* (hereafter *TRHS*), 5th series, 2 (1952): 79–98; R. Dunn, "Imperial pressures on Massachusetts and Jamaica, 1675–1700," in A. G. Olson and R. M. Brown (eds), *Anglo-American Political Relations, 1675–1775* (New Brunswick, NJ: Rutgers University Press, 1970), pp. 52–75.

32   *Certain Considerations Relating to the Royal African Company* (1680).

33   Davies, *Royal African Company*, pp. 106–8, 113–18, Appendix III; Galenson, *Traders*, Table 1.5 and Ch. 2; Watts, *West Indies*, Table 8.7.

34   London sugar prices had doubled since the pre-war lows of the mid-1680s. Watts, *West Indies*, Tables 6.4 and 6.5.

35   See ibid., Table 8.7; Davies, *Royal African Company*, Appendices III and IV; Galenson, *Traders*, esp. Table 1.5 and Ch. 2.

36   This "open market" was closed to foreign slave traders by the Navigation Acts, although a considerable volume of illicit slave trading did take place, mainly by Dutch traders, with little local official interference. The Royal African Company's problems in enforcing its

monopoly were especially acute in the sugar islands, where local common law courts, unlike the Vice-Admiralty courts, ruled unfavorably on the attempts of company factors to seize the cargoes of interlopers. Davies, *Royal African Company*, pp. 100–22.

37 In popular mythology, the abuse of monopolies was portrayed as a primary cause of the Civil War. Charles II and James II were careful not to exploit exemptions within the Statute of Monopolies and did not use their prerogative to grant monopolies to corporations for fiscal gain, although the patent system was used to promote political patronage. Later Stuart industrial patents were careful to provide sole use to a particular invention (for a limited period), but without excluding others from producing the same article by other methods. In general, exclusive monopoly rights were granted only in the case of a handful of commercial patents of incorporation to attract sufficient amounts of capital into especially high-risk ventures of long-distance trades, lying outside the normal orbit of English diplomatic and military influence. See C. MacLeod, *Inventing the Industrial Revolution: The English Patent System, 1660–1800* (Cambridge and New York: Cambridge University Press, 1988), Chs 1–2; Davies, *Royal African Company*, Ch. 2.

38 The major monopolies case of the *East India Company* v. *Sandys* (1684) served further to connect the evils of monopoly with the abuses of the prerogative as Lord Chief Justice Jeffreys upheld the royal prerogative to grant monopolies to foreign trading companies, despite the well-publicized abuses perpetrated by the East India Company against fellow subjects interloping in the Asian trade. See *A Brief Account of the Great Oppressions and Injuries which the Managers of the East India Company have Acted on the Lives, Liberties and Estates of Their Fellow Subjects* (1691?).

39 While the loophole within the Statute of Monopolies which exempted companies and corporations from the prohibition on monopoly was questioned, the right of Parliament to sanction specific monopolies was not. Thus, Parliament set up a number of new monopolies in the reigns of William III and Anne to assist in the funding of the National Debt (noting the cases of the Bank, South Sea, and New and United East India Companies), where the notion of monopoly generated relatively little public opposition.

40 African trade petitions and bills were submitted in the following sessions: 1689/90, 1690, 1690/1, 1693/4, 1694/5, 1695/6, 1696/7, 1697/8, 1707/8, 1708/9, 1709/10, 1710/11, 1711/12, 1713, and 1714. The African Company had previously sought parliamentary confirmation of its charter in 1672, but legislation to such effect died with the end of the parliamentary session.

41 Daniel Defoe, *The Review*, ed. Arthur Wellesley Secord (New York: Columbia University Press, for the Facsimile Text Society edn, 1938), February 24, 1709, p. 569. See also T. Keirn, "Daniel Defoe and the Royal African Company," *Historical Research* 61 (1988): 243–7.

42 *A True State of the Present Difference between the Royal African Company and the Separate Traders by a True Lover of His Country* (1710).

43 Davies, *Royal African Company*, pp. 67, 104; de Krey, *Fractured Society*, pp. 25–9.

44 See Table 21.1 below.

45 See Tables 21.2a and 21.2b. Whig-sponsored legislation also removed or liberalized the trading monopolies of the Old East India Company (1698) and the Russia Company (1699). See G. Cherry, "The development of the English free trade movement in Parliament, 1689–1702," *Journal of Modern History* (hereafter *JMH*) 25 (1953): 103–19; H. Horwitz, "The East India trade, the politicians and the constitution: 1689–1702," *JBS* 17, 2 (1978): 1–18; J. M. Price, *The Tobacco Adventure to Russia* (Philadelphia, PA: American Philosophical Society, 1961). For the public connection of these issues with the African trade, see *An Apology for the English Nation: That It Is as much the Interest for the English Nation, that the Trades to the East-Indies and Africk should Be as Free as that to Spain* (1695?).

46 "Regulated companies" such as the Levant Company had exclusive control of their particular trades, and yet permitted all Englishmen to engage in these trades after payment of a moderate entry fine. Trade was done on private account, avoiding the pernicious means of licensing as so often practiced by the joint-stock trades. Consequently, these regulated companies were not usually described as "monopolies" because with private trading they could not corporately control or restrict sales (and inflate prices) and entry fines were not

normally seen as restricting one's "liberty to trade." The Hamburg Company proved to be an exception to the rule. In the highly competitive German cloth trade, the entry fine, coupled with various obtrusive administrative requirements, proved to be a nuisance and a "restriction" on trade. The company's monopoly was abolished by statute in 1689. See 1 Gul. & Mary, c. 32; *Reasons Humbly Offered against the Continuation of a General Liberty for Exporting the Woollen Manufactures of this Kingdom by Foreigners, into the Privileges of the Merchant Adventurer of England* (1693).

47   Compare, for example, *Reasons Showing that the Trade to Guinea on the Coast of Africa Cannot Be Preserved without Forts and Castles, and the Best and Surest Way to Maintain Them Is by a Joynt-Stock* (1696?) in Robert Harley's papers (at BL Harleian MS 7310/201) with *Reasons for Establishing the African Trade under a Regulated Company* (1709).

48   These committees were chaired by Robert Harley and the Tories John Hungerford and Colonel John Granville respectively, all of whom were supporters of the Royal African Company. *CJ*, XI, pp. 113–14, 233–4, 498; BL Harleian MS 7310/195–8, 207–35, 241–2. See also *The British Interest on the Coast of Africa Consider'd, with the Interest of other Europeans, and the Politicks They Used for Carrying on that Trade* (1710?) which is dedicated to Hungerford.

49   PRO, CO 388/6/71; *CJ*, XII, p. 99.

50   BL Sloane MSS 2902, f. 88.

51   9 & 10 Gul. III, c. 26. In response to interest-group pressure, the export of redwood for dyeing textiles was to pay only 5 percent; the export of slaves was exempted from duty. However, the opponents of the company failed to achieve their demand to pay only 5 percent on all exports and imports. Huntington Library, Ellesmere MSS 9610. Petitions against the African Company were received from the merchants and planters of Virginia, Maryland, Jamaica, and the "Cariby Islands," and from textile interests in Bristol, London, Wiltshire, and Somerset. *CJ*, XII, pp. 120–1, 125, 133, 185; HMC, *House of Lords MSS* new series, III, pp. 243–4.

52   The 10 percent duty was essentially no different from the much-hated monopolist practice of licensing private trade. *Prince Butlers Queries, Relating to the Bill for Settling the Trade to Africa* (1699).

53   BL Additional MSS 14,034/92. The board's proceedings can be followed in PRO CO 389/20; PRO CO 388/11.

54   I. K. Steele, *Politics of Colonial Policy: The Board of Trade in Colonial Administration, 1696–1720* (Oxford: Clarendon Press, 1968), p. 127. The Whig Ministry had no love for the African Company, who, as Lord Treasurer Godolphin remarked, have "been managed from a great many years by a pack of knaves . . . who cheated all their adventurers." H. L. Snyder (ed.), *The Marlborough–Godolphin Correspondence* (Oxford: Clarendon Press, 1975), Vol. II, p. 1139.

55   Charles Davenant, *Reflections Upon the Constitution and Management of the Trade to Africa*, reprinted in Sir Charles Whitworth (ed.), *The Political and Commercial Works of Charles Davenant* (1771), Vol. V, pp. 96–8.

56   See, for example, *The State of the Trade to Africa between 1680 and 1707 . . . Whereby It Appears the Separate Adventurers Have Improv'd that Trade to the Benefit of Great Britain at least One Million a Year* (1708?).

57   *CJ*, XVI, pp. 163, 167, 324, 339.

58   *A List of the Names of the Corporation of the Governor and Company of Merchants of Great Britain Trading to the South-Seas, and other Parts of America and for Encouraging the Fishery* (1714).

59   For Harley, the South Sea Company, and the *Asiento*, see: J. Carswell, *The South Sea Bubble* (Stanford, CA: Stanford University Press, 1960), Ch. 3; C. A. Palmer, *Human Cargoes: The British Slave Trade to Spanish America, 1700–1739* (Urbana, IL: University of Illinois Press, 1981); J. G. Sperling, "The division of 25 May 1711, on an amendment to the South Sea Bill: a note on the reality of parties in the age of Anne", *HJ* 4 (1961): 191–202.

60   10 Anne, c. 34; PRO T 70/88/296–7; Buckinghamshire RO, Verney Papers, reel 54, January 3, 1712.

61   *CJ*, XVII, pp. 252, 389; PRO T 70/101/141.

62   BL Additional MSS 22,495, fos 60, 65–6. See also Historical Manuscripts Commission (hereafter HMC), *House of Lords Mss*, new series, X, pp. 178–90.

63   Shortly after the failure of the 1713 bill, the South Sea Company solicited proposals from

both the African Company and the separate traders to provide slaves for the *Asiento*. The contract was granted to the African Company. However, by the spring of 1714, the African and South Sea Companies began to fall out over disputed debts and the former company's attempt to restrain the latter "from contracting for Negroes elsewhere than with that company." In 1714, the African Company did unsuccessfully attempt to secure a bill resurrecting its monopoly. BL Additional MSS 25,495, fos 66–9, 76, 83–5, 159; PRO T 70/88/388; *CJ*, XVII, p. 636.

64 In 1730, with no 10 percent revenue from which to maintain these forts, the African Company received a small parliamentary subsidy which was not renewed after 1744. Rawley, *Trans-Atlantic Slave Trade*, pp. 163–4.

65 Based on searches in: the British, Goldsmiths, Guildhall, and Lincoln's Inn Libraries in London; the Bodleian Library in Oxford; the Chetham, Ryland, and Public Libraries in Manchester; the Kress Library in Cambridge (MA); and the Clark and Sutro Libraries in California. Furthermore, some tracts were discovered within manuscript collections in the PRO, British Library, and various county record offices.

66 The increase in published contributions to the African trade debates was paralleled in trend by an increase in the number of petitions presented to Parliament, both for and against the African Company monopoly; e.g. 10 petitions submitted in 1698; 26 petitions received in 1709. *CJ*, XII and XVI.

67 See, for example, PRO T 70/88/7; *Gazette*, July 25, 1705; *At a General Court of the Adventurers of the Royal African Company of England, Held the 18th Day of September, 1706* (1706).

68 Comparing Davenant's views "On the plantation trade" in the *Discourses on the Public Revenue* with *Reflections upon the Constitution and Management of the Trade to Africa*. Both are reprinted in Whitworth, *Works of Charles Davenant*. See also Waddell, "Charles Davenant."

69 See Keirn, "Defoe."

70 The company's Court Assistants often had "*Cases*" or "*Reasons*" drawn up, printed, and circulated; e.g. on July 28, 1713, 500 copies of the "*Proposals*" were sent out to be drawn up and printed and then circulated in the Lords. PRO T 70/88/407.

71 *Some Remarks on a Pamphlet Call'd Reflections, on the Constitution . . .* (1709).

72 Davenant, *Reflections*, Parts I and II.

73 Indeed, the African Company went to considerable efforts to stay abreast of debates both in Parliament and in print. Members were often "desired to make Application to Their Friends in the Houses, and informe them of the Reasonableness of the Company's Case." PRO T 70/101/24. Petitions, pamphlets, and proposed bills were discussed in detail amongst the company's Court of Assistants (or within special subcommittees arranged to oversee the company's parliamentary affairs), who considered and outlined measured responses in the form of petitions to Parliament (or direct to Harley) or in the production of pamphlets answering and refuting the printed arguments of their opponents. See, for example, PRO T 70/88 fos 282, 320, and 335; BL Loan 29/289/79–81; *An Answer to the Reasons against an African Company Humbly Submitted* (1711); *Remarks upon Some Queries Handed about by the Separate Traders to Africa* (1711?).

74 *Seasonable Animadversions, on All the Papers and Pamphlets Lately Printed on Behalf of the Separate Traders to Africa . . .* (1710); *The African Company's Account of the Exports for the African Trade Prov'd to be Wrong Stated and Erroneous* (1711?).

75 See, for example, *The Argument Touching Security Necessary to Be Given for Carrying on the African Trade, Demonstrated to Be Groundless and Ridiculous* (1711?); *A Defense of the African Company's Creditors* (1713); *The Case of John Leadstone, A Private Trader Residing in Africa* (1711?).

76 Certainly, the whole debate was structured upon the integrated motivations of various interest groups. However, the outports and creditors were the most conspicuous proponents of views narrowly confined to their own specific interest. As the Bristol MP Robert Yates noted to Harley: "Since the merchants of London have already gott the trade to severall parts of the world exclusive; it will be very severe on the outports to be further excluded." BL Loan 29/289/75. See also: *A Letter from a Merchant in Bristol . . .* (1711); *The Case of the African Company's Creditors* (1712?).

77   *The Case of the Royal African Company of England* (1694).

78   [Davenant], *Several Arguments Proving that our Trade to Africa Cannot Be Preserved and Carried on Effectually by any Other Method, than that of a Considerable Joint-Stock, with Exclusive Privileges* (1709?).

79   *The Review*, February 22, 1709.

80   *A Memorial Touching the Nature and Present State of the Trade to Africa* (1709).

81   *Trade: An Essay* (1712?); *An Explanation of the African-Company's Property in the Sole Trade to Africa* . . . (1712). See also G. Anderson and R. D. Tollison, "Apologiae for chartered monopolies in foreign trade, 1600–1800," *History of Political Economy* (hereafter *HPE*) 15 (1983): 549–66.

82   "Dear Experiment has taught us, in the African Trade, that it is in no way to be carried on but by Force, for a mere Correspondencee with the Natives as Merchants, is as impracticable as it would be if they were a Nation of Horses." *The Review*, February 19, 1712.

83   See, for example, R.B., *The English Acquisitions in Guinea and East-India* (1708) , pp. 50–7.

84   *Some Considerations on the late Act of Parliament, for Settling the Trade to Africa* (1709?), p. 4.

85   *The Review*, February 19, 1712.

86   *The Review*, March 12, 1708.

87   This excessive criticism of the Dutch was characteristic of Tory ideology during the period. The French, on the other hand, were equally as odious to the Whigs, representing an economic threat in the guise of absolute monarchy and popery. See *A Short and True Account of the Importance and Necessity of Settling the African Trade* . . . (1711); D. C. Coleman, "Politics and economics in the age of Anne," in D. C. Coleman and A. H. John (eds), *Trade, Government and Economy* (London: Weidenfeld & Nicolson, 1976), pp. 187–211.

88   W. Cleland, *Some Observations Shewing the Danger of Losing the Trade of the Sugar Colonies* (1714), p. 8.

89   *The Review*, February 24, 1709.

90   *Reasons for Settlement of the Trade to Africa in a Joynt-Stock* . . . (1711?). Indeed, it was this "national war" (in conjunction with the shipping losses engendered by international conflict at sea) which acted as an explanatory device for the African Company to account for its commercial failings, e.g. *An Explanation of the African-Company's Property in the Sole Trade to Africa* . . . (1712).

91   Davenant, *Reflections*, p. 137.

92   *The Review*, February 24, 1709.

93   See, for example, *An Account of the Number of Negroes Delivered into the Islands of Barbadees, Jamaica and Antego* . . . (1709?).

94   *Considerations Concerning the African-Companies Petition* (1698).

95   *The Case of Edmond Harrison, William Dockwra, John Thrale, and Thomas Jones of London* . . . (1695?).

96   *Companies in Joint-Stock Unnecessary and Inconvenient* (1691), p. 1.

97   *Remarks on the African Company's Memorial* (1709), p. 3; *Considerations upon the Trade to Guinea* (1708), p. 5.

98   *The Argument Touching Security Necessary to Be Given for Carrying on the Trade* . . . (1711?), p. 1. Those opponents of the company who still felt that forts were necessary in the trade argued that the African Company could be divested of its property for the public good. "When the Common Interest of the Whole Nation requires the departing from a private Property upon having an Equivalent for it, the Legislative Power may, without any hardship, provide for the good of the Publick, by removing the nusance . . . giving the private Proprietors full Value of what they take from them." *A Second Letter to a Member of Parliament, Relating to the Settling the Trade to Africa* (1710?), p. 1.

99   *Considerations upon the Trade to Guinea* (1708), pp. 29–30.

100 *A Letter from a Merchant at Jamaica to a Member of Parliament in London, Touching the African Trade* (1709), p. 13.

101 *An Answer to a Paper Called Short Remarks on the African Trade* (1711).

102 *Considerations, Touching the Bill for Settling the Trade to Africa* (1698?).

103 *Considerations upon the Trade to Guinea* (1708), p. 4.

104 Davies, *African Company*, p. 152.

105 By mercantilism, I refer to the set of characteristics enumerated by Coleman: the contemporary acceptance of a maxim of a balance of trade, the use of economic means to achieve political ends, and the conceptualization of trade as a "conflict over a cake seen as fixed in size." Coleman, "Mercantilism revisited."

106 Coleman, "Politics."

APPENDIX I

Politics and the African Company

Table 21.1 Members of the Royal African Company's Court of Assistants who served in the House of Commons, 1689–1714

Assistants	Tenure		Constituency	Party
	Company	Parliament		
Sir Benjamin Bathurst	1689[b1] 1690–5 1700	1702–4[b]	New Romney	Tory
William Betts	1704 1706	1710–11 1713–14[a]	Weymouth Melcombe Regis	Whig
Robert Bristow	1695–6	1698–1701	Winchelsea	Whig
John Burton	1702–3 1705–7	1701	Great Yarmouth	Tory
Sir John Cass	1705–8	1713–14	London	Tory
Sir Peter Colleton	1688–90[b]	1689–94[b]	Bossiney	Whig
Edward Colston	1689–90[2] 1691[b]	1710–13	Bristol	Tory
Sir Thomas Cooke	1690–2 1701–2 1703–4[1] 1705–9	1690–5 1698–1705	Colchester	Tory
Sir Francis Dashwood	1693–5 1697–1700 1704 1706–7 1709–12	1708–13	Winchelsea	Whig
Sir Samuel Dashwood	1689[b] 1692–3 1698–9 1701–3 1705	1690–5[b]	London	Tory
Stephen Evance	1692–3 1696 1703 1707 1710	1690–8	Bridgport	Whig
Sir John Fleet	1693–4 1697–8[1] 1699–1702 1704	1690–1705	London	Tory
Sir John Germaine	1709 1711–12	1713–14[a]	Morpeth	Whig
Charles Godolphin	1690–1	1689–1701[b]	Helston	Mixed
Frederick Herne	1698–9	1699–1714	Dartmouth	Tory
Sir Nathaniel Herne	1701–2	1698–1713	Dartmouth	Tory
John Hopkins	1700–1	1710–14[a]	St Ives	Whig
Edward Jeffreys	1702	1702–5 1708–13	Marlborough Brecon	Tory

Assistants	Tenure		Constituency	Party
	Company	Parliament		
Sir Jeffrey Jeffreys	1692–8[b]	1690–8	Brecon	Tory
		1700–9		
John Jeffreys	1690–1	1690–8	Radnorshire	Tory
	1693	1700–2	Marlborough	
		1702–5	Breconshire	
		1705–7	Marlborough	
William Johnson	1689[b]	1689–1714[a]	Aldeburgh	Tory
John Lade	1712	1713–14[a]	Southwark	Tory
Sir John Mathewes	1683–4[b]	1689[b]	Evesham	Tory
John Mead	1707	1710–13	Sudbury	Tory?
Arthur Moore	1709–10	1695–1700	Great Grimsby	Tory
		1701–14[a]		
Sir John Morgan	1689[b]	1689–93[b]	Herefordshire	Tory
	1700			
Sir Benjamin Newland	1682–4[b]	1689–99[b]	Southampton	Mixed
John Nicholson	1698–1704	1698–1700	Great Yarmouth	Tory
	1705–6[1]	1701–8		
	1707–10			
John Pery	1693–4[b]	1690–1700	New Shoreham	Tory
	1698–9	1702–5		
Sir William Pritchard	1699–1700	1690–5[b]	London	Tory
	1704	1702–5		
Gabriel Roberts	1695–1701	1713–14[a]	Marlborough	Tory
Edward Rudge	1690–5[b]	1690–5[b]	Evesham	Whig
John Rudge	1697–1701	1698–1701	Evesham	Whig
		1702–14[a]		
Samuel Shepheard (senior)	1695–8	1700–1	Newport (Wight)	Mixed
		1705–8	London	
Sir William Stevens	1690–1[b]	1698–95[b]	Newport (Wight)	Tory?
Sir William Turner	1691[b]	1690–1	London	Tory
Sir John Verney	1691–2[b]	1710–14[a]	Buckinghamshire	Tory
Sir William Withers	1697–8	1708–13	London	Tory
	1706			
	1707–9[1]			

Key
[a] Served prior to 1689.
[b] Served after 1714.
[1] Served as Sub-Governor of the Royal African Company.
[2] Served as Deputy Governor of the Royal African Company.

Sources
I. F. Burton, P. J. W. Riley, and E. Rowlands, *Political Parties in the Reigns of William III and Anne: The Evidence of Division Lists* (London: Athlone Press, special supplement of the Bulletin of the Institute of Historical Research, 1698).
K. G. Davies, *The Royal African Company* (New York: Atheneum, 1960).
G. S. de Krey, *A Fractured Society: The Politics of London in the First Age of Party, 1688–1715* (Oxford: Clarendon Press, and New York: Oxford University Press, 1985).
B. D. Henning (ed.), *The House of Commons, 1660–1690*, 3 vols (London: Secker & Warburg, for the History of Parliament Trust, 1983).
H. Horwitz, *Parliament, Policy and Politics in the Reign of William III* (New York: University of Delaware Press, 1977).
Official Return of Members of the House of Commons.
Public Record Office (PRO), London, Treasury Papers, T 70/82–8, Royal African Company minute books.
R. Sedgwick (ed.), *The House of Commons, 1715–1754*, 2 vols (London: HMSO, for the History of Parliament Trust, 1970).
H. Snyder, "Party configurations in the early eighteenth-century House of Commons," *Bulletin of the Institute of Historical Research* V (1972): 38–72.

Table 21.2a Members of the House of Commons moving in favor of the Royal African Company, 1689–1714

MP	Session	Action	Constituency	Party
Alex. Abercromby	1708/9	T	Banffshire	Tory
Francis Annesley	1710/11	C	Westbury	Tory
	1711/12	B		
John Arnold	1693/4	S	Southwark	Whig
Sir James Bateman	1713	T	Ilchester	Mixed
	1713	S		
Sir George Beaumont	1713	T	Leicester	Tory
Robert Benson	1709/10	P	York	Tory
Peregrine Bertie	1708/9	S	Boston	Tory
Thomas Blofield	1696/7	B	Norwich	Tory
Sir John Bolles	1693/4	S	Lincoln	Tory
William Bromley	1709	S	Oxford University	Tory
Henry Campion	1713	T	Bossiney	Tory
	1714	T	Sussex	
William Campion	1696/7	T	Seaford	Whig
John Conyers	1695/6	P	East Grinstead	Tory
	1713[1]	T		
Sir Robert Cotton	1693/4	S	Cambridgeshire	Mixed
William Culliford	1696/7	B	Corfe Castle	Mixed
Paul Docminique	1711/12	T	Gatton	Mixed
	1713	T		
Edmund Duncomb	1713	T	Appleby	Tory
Heneage Finch	1713	T	Surrey	Tory
Col. Henry Goldwell	1693/4	S	Bury St. Edmunds	Tory
John Granville	1695/6	C	Plymouth	Tory
Sir Christ. Hales	1713	T	Coventry	Tory
Col. George Hamilton	1713	S	Fife	Tory
Anthony Hammond	1698	S	Cambridge University	Tory
Simon Harcourt	1696/7	C	Abingdon	Tory
Robert Harley	1693/4	C	New Radnor	Tory/Country
John Hungerford	1694/5	C	Scarborough	Tory
	1711	S		
Archibald Hutcheson	1714	T	Hastings	Mixed
Christopher Musgrave	1690/1	P	Westmorland	Tory
Samuel Ogle	1696/7	T	Berwick	Whig
Gabriel Roberts	1714	S	Marlborough	Tory
Sir Richard Temple	1708/9	S	Buckingham	Tory
Sir William Trumbull	1697/8	P	Oxford University	Tory
Henry Vincent (senior)	1708/9	T	Truro	Tory
John Ward	1708	P	London	Tory
William Withers	1711/12	T	London	Tory

[1] or Thomas Conyers (Durham, Tory)

Key
B Member of committee to draw up bill for the Royal African Company.
C Chairman of committee for the Royal African Company.
P Presenter of bill/petition for the Royal African Company.
S Speech or comment made for the Royal African Company.
T Teller for the Royal African Company.

Sources
See Table 20.2b.

Table 21.2a Members of the House of Commons moving in favor of the Royal African Company, 1689–1714

MP	Session	Action	Constituency	Party
Alex. Abercromby	1708/9	T	Banffshire	Tory
Francis Annesley	1710/11	C	Westbury	Tory
	1711/12	B		
John Arnold	1693/4	S	Southwark	Whig
Sir James Bateman	1713	T	Ilchester	Mixed
	1713	S		
Sir George Beaumont	1713	T	Leicester	Tory
Robert Benson	1709/10	P	York	Tory
Peregrine Bertie	1708/9	S	Boston	Tory
Thomas Blofield	1696/7	B	Norwich	Tory
Sir John Bolles	1693/4	S	Lincoln	Tory
William Bromley	1709	S	Oxford University	Tory
Henry Campion	1713	T	Bossiney	Tory
	1714	T	Sussex	
William Campion	1696/7	T	Seaford	Whig
John Conyers	1695/6	P	East Grinstead	Tory
	1713[1]	T		
Sir Robert Cotton	1693/4	S	Cambridgeshire	Mixed
William Culliford	1696/7	B	Corfe Castle	Mixed
Paul Docminique	1711/12	T	Gatton	Mixed
	1713	T		
Edmund Duncomb	1713	T	Appleby	Tory
Heneage Finch	1713	T	Surrey	Tory
Col. Henry Goldwell	1693/4	S	Bury St. Edmunds	Tory
John Granville	1695/6	C	Plymouth	Tory
Sir Christ. Hales	1713	T	Coventry	Tory
Col. George Hamilton	1713	S	Fife	Tory
Anthony Hammond	1698	S	Cambridge University	Tory
Simon Harcourt	1696/7	C	Abingdon	Tory
Robert Harley	1693/4	C	New Radnor	Tory/ Country
John Hungerford	1694/5	C	Scarborough	Tory
	1711	S		
Archibald Hutcheson	1714	T	Hastings	Mixed
Christopher Musgrave	1690/1	P	Westmorland	Tory
Samuel Ogle	1696/7	T	Berwick	Whig
Gabriel Roberts	1714	S	Marlborough	Tory
Sir Richard Temple	1708/9	S	Buckingham	Tory
Sir William Trumbull	1697/8	P	Oxford University	Tory
Henry Vincent (senior)	1708/9	T	Truro	Tory
John Ward	1708	P	London	Tory
William Withers	1711/12	T	London	Tory

[1] or Thomas Conyers (Durham, Tory)

Key
B Member of committee to draw up bill for the Royal African Company.
C Chairman of committee for the Royal African Company.
P Presenter of bill/petition for the Royal African Company.
S Speech or comment made for the Royal African Company.
T Teller for the Royal African Company.

Table 21.2b Continued

MP	Session	Action	Constituency	Party
Samuel Shepheard (junior)	1713/14	T	Cambridge	Mixed
	1714	T		
Sir Charles Turner	1709/10	P	King's Lynn	Whig
Sir Thomas Vernon	1690/1	B	London	Mixed
John Ward	1708/9	C	London	Whig
	1709/10	B		
Robert Yates	1708/9	B	Bristol	Whig
	1709/10	B		
Sir Walter Yonge	1695/6	T	Honiton	Whig

Key
B Member of committee to draw up bill against the Royal African Company.
C Chairman of committee against the Royal African Company.
P Presenter of bill/petition against the Royal African Company.
S Speech or comment made against the Royal African Company.
T Teller against the Royal African Company.

Sources: actions made for/against the Royal African Company.
Bodleian Library, Rawlinson MS D.174. Hammond papers.
Bodleian Library, Rawlinson MS A.312. Pepys papers.
British Library, Additional MSS 22,459, South Sea Company Papers.
British Library, Harleian MSS 7310, Robert Harley's Committee Notes: 1693–4.
British Library, Loan MSS 29/35 and 29/289, Portland Loan, Harley family papers.
Buckinghamshire Record Office, Verney Papers, 1709–12.
CJ, vols X–XVII.
Historical Manuscripts Commission, *House of Lords MSS*, new series, vols III and X.
Henry L. Snyder (ed.), *The Marlborough–Godolphin Correspondence* (Oxford: Oxford University Press, 1975), Vol. II, p. 1139.

Sources: Political Background
I. F. Burton, P. W. J. Riley, and E. Rowlands, *Political Parties in the Reigns of William III and Anne: The Evidence of Division Lists* (London: Athlone Press, special supplement 7 of the Bulletin of the Institute of Historical Research, 1968).
G. S. de Krey, *A Fractured Society: The Politics of London in the First Age of Party: 1688–1715* (Oxford: Clarendon Press, 1985).
B. D. Henning, *The House of Commons: 1660–1690*, 3 vols (London: HMSO for the History of Parliament Trust, 1983).
G. Holmes, *British Politics in the Reign of Anne* (London: Macmillan, 1967).
H. Horwitz, *Parliament, Policy and Politics in the Reign of King William III* (Manchester: Manchester University Press, 1977).
S. Lambert, *Bills and Acts: Legislative Procedure in Eighteenth-Century England* (Cambridge, UK: Cambridge University Press, 1971).
T. K. Moore and H.. Horwitz, "Who runs the house? Aspects of parliamentary organization in the later seventeenth century," *Journal of Modern History* 43 (1971): 205–27.
R. Sedgwick, *The House of Commons: 1715–1754*, 2 vols (London: HMSO, 1970).
H. L. Snyder, "Party configurations in the early eighteenth-century House of Commons," *Bulletin on the Institute of Historical Research* 45 (1972): 37–72.

APPENDIX II

Economic literature and the African trade 1689–1714

Abbreviations

anti/pro in opposition/favour of the African Company monopoly
BL   British Library
G   Goldsmiths Library, University of London
H   L. W. Hanson, *Contemporary Printed Sources for British and Irish Economic History, 1701–1750* (Cambridge, UK: Cambridge University Press, 1963)
Hogg   P. Hogg, *The African Slave Trade and Its Suppression: A Classified and Annotated Bibliography of Books, Pamphlets, and Periodical Articles* (London: Frank Cass, 1973).
K   *Catalogue of the Kress Library of Business and Economics* (Boston, MA, 1940).
K–G   *Kress-Goldsmiths Library Catalogue.*
K.S.   *Catalogue of the Kress Library of Business and Economics: A Supplement* (Boston, MA: 1956)
LI   Lincolns Inn Library, London
Moore   J. R. Moore, *A Checklist of the Writings of Daniel Defoe* (Hamden, CT: Archon, 1971)
MP   Free Public Library, Manchester
S   Sutro Library, California State University Library, San Francisco
W   Donald Wing (ed.), *Short-Title Catalogue of Books Printed in England, Scotland, Ireland, Wales and British America and of English Books in other Countries: 1641–1700*, 3 vols (New York: Columbia University Press, 1945–1951)

Further reading

B., R., *The English Acquisitions in Guinea and East-India* (1708) [BL 795.a.51; pro].

Blaney, Jo., *A Letter to the Committee of the Honourable House of Commons, upon the African Trade* (1709) [2 pp.; G.4536; H.1021; anti].

Bleau, Robert, *A Letter from One of the Royal African-Company's Chief Agents on the African Coasts* (1714?) [2 pp.; K-G5128.3; H.2008; anti].

Cary, John, *A Discourse of the Advantage of the African Trade to This Nation, Extracted from an Essay on Trade* (1696?) [4 pp.; BL 816.m.11(7); Harleian MS 7310/181; extracts from *Essay on the State of England*; anti].

[Chamberlein, Hugh], *Some Short Remarks, on Two Pamphlets Lately Printed; the One Entituled Considerations upon the Trade to Guinea; the Other Entituled Proposals for Raising a New Company, for Carrying on the Trades of Africa and the Spanish-West-Indies, Under the Title of the United-Company* (1709?) [4 pp. BL 8223.e.4(26); G.4558; H.1041; Hogg 1006; pro].

Cleland, William, *The Present State of the Sugar Plantations Consider'd: But more Especially that of the Island of Barbados* (1713) [J.Morphew; 30 pp.; BL 1391.b.2; H.1904; also a 1714 edn; pro].

Cleland, William, *Some Observations Shewing the Danger of Losing the Trade of the Sugar Colonies* (1714) [15 pp.; BL 104.i.33; H.2016; Hogg 1035; pro].

Coke, Roger, *Reflections upon the East-Indy and Royal African Companies with Animadversions, Concerning the Naturalization of Foreigners* (1695) [G.3076; K.1874; W.C4980; anti].

Coke, Roger, *A Reply to an Answer from a Friend, to the Apology for the English Nation, that the Trade to the East-Indies and Africa Should Be Free* (1692) [7 pp.; BL 1481.c.33(6); K.1786; anti].

Davenant, Charles, *A Clear Demonstration, from Points of Fact, that the Recovery, Preservation and Improvement of Britain's Share of the Trade to Africa; Is Wholly Owing to the Industry, Care and Application of the Royal-African-Company* (1709) [4 pp.; BL 8223.e.4(27); H.1029; extracts from *Reflections*; another similar edition at BL 8223.e.4(32); pro].

Davenant, Charles, *A Proposal for Settling the Trade to Africa, in either of the Methods after Mentioned* (1710) [BL 8223.e.4(31); H.1039; extracts from *Reflections*; pro].

Davenant, Charles, *Reflections upon the Constitution and Management of the Trade to Africa* (1709) [J. Morphew; 3 pts; 140 pp.; BL 712.m.1(19); H.1045; Hogg 1001; pro].

Davenant, Charles, *Several Arguments Proving that Our Trade to Africa Cannot Be Preserved and Carried on Effectually by any Other Method, than that of a Considerable Joint-Stock, with Exclusive Privileges* (1709?) [4 pp.; BL l474.dd.22(7); H.1046; Hogg 1009; extracts from *Reflections*; another similar edition at BL 816.m.11(11); pro].

Davenant, Charles, *Several Reasons Proving that Our Trade to Africa Cannot Be Preserved and Carried On Effectually by any Other Method, than that of a Considerable Joint-Stock . . .* (1712?) [4 pp.; BL 8223.e.4(9); H.1046; extracts from *Reflections*; pro].

Davenant, Charles, *Some Objections against Settling the Trade to Africa, in any of the Open Methods Proposed by the Separate-Traders, and Particularly that of a Regulated Company, Like the Present Russia Company* (1709) [G.4545; H.1055; extracts from *Reflections*; pro].

Defoe, Daniel, *A Brief Account of the Present State of the African Trade* (1713) [J. Baker; 55pp.; BL T.807(5); H.1870A; Moore 263; pro].

Defoe, Daniel, *An Essay upon the Trade to Africa* (1711) [48pp.; BL T.806(1); H.1353; Moore 210; Hogg 1024; pro].

Littleton, Edward, *The Groans of the Plantations or a True Account of Their Grievous and Xtreme Sufferings by the Heavy Impositions upon Sugar and other Hardships* (1689) [M. Clerk; 35pp.; BL 1391.d.3; K.1700; W.L2578; also a 1698 edn at G.3519; anti].

T., D. [Dalby, Sir Thomas], *Considerations on the Trade of Africa, Humbly Offer'd to the Honourable House of Commons, in Behalf of the Bill Now before Them* (1698?) [3pp.; G.5852(215); K.S2035; W.T3; Hogg 991; pro].

Thomas, Sir Dalby, *An Historical Account of the Rise and Growth of the West-India Collonies, and of the Great Advantages They Are to England, in Respect to Trade* (1690) [J. Hindmarsh; 53 pp.; BL 1061.g.25; G.2815; K.1749; W.T961; Hogg 981; anti].

Wilkinson, William, *An Answer to a Paper, Lately Printed and Published by the African-Company* (1695?) [BL 8223.e.I(178); anti].

Wilkinson, William, *An Answer to the Book Written by the Guiney Company in Their Own Defence, for the Management of Their Trade in Africa* (1690) [4 pp.; BL 816.m.11(36); W.W2254; Hogg 983; anti].

Wilkinson, William, *The Case of William Wilkinson Late Commander of the Ship Henry and William of London, 1685* (1690) [BL 816.m.11(34); W.W2255; anti].

Wilkinson, William, *Systema Africanum: Or, a Treatise Discovering the Intrigues and Arbitrary Proceedings of the Guinea Company* (1690) [26 pp.; G.2814; K.1751; W.W2256; Hogg 982; anti].

An Abstract of Several Cases Relating to the Trade to Africa (1714) [2 pp.; BL 23.c.6(82); K.S2010; H.2010; anti].

An Abstract of the Case of the Royal African Company of England (1714?) [2 pp.; LI m.103(41); pro].

An Abstract of the Charter and Large Privileges, Granted by the States-General of the United Netherlands, to the Dutch-African and West-India-Company; Dated the 26 of September, 1674 (1710) [LI M.103(39); H.1148; also a 1713 edn; pro].

An Account of the Ballance of the African Company's Books, Given in to the Lords Commissioners of Trade, by the Said Company and by that Board Reported to the House of Commons in the year 1709 (1712) [G.4869; H.1593; anti].

An Account of the Number of Negroes Delivered into the Islands of Barbadees, Jamaica, and Antego, from the year 1698 to 1708, since the Trade Was Open'd . . . (1709?) [K.S2423; H.1022; Hogg 1000; anti].

An Account of the Ships Employed in the African Trade, from the Ports of London and Bristol, Belonging to the Separate Traders to Africa with the Value of the Said Ships and Cargoes and the Number of Negroes Usually Carried by the Said Ships (1713) [LI m.103(45); K.S.2514; H.1869; pro].

An Act for the Better Improvement of the Trade to Africa, by Establishing a Regulated Company (1708) [7pp.; G.4483; anti].

An Address Relating to the African Company to be Presented to Her Majesty (1711) [2pp.; BL 8223.e.4(16); K.S.2537; H.1349; Hogg 1026; anti].

The African Companies Considerations on the Late Act of Parliament for Settling the Trade to Africa, Answer'd Paragraph by Paragraph (1709) [BL 8223.e.4(23); H.919; Hogg 1012; anti].

The African Company's Account of the Exports for the African Trade Prov'd to Be Wrong Stated and Erroneous (1711?) [K.S.2515; H.1588; anti].

The African Company's Property to the Forts and Settlements in Guinea Consider'd; and the Necessity of Establishing the Trade in a Regulated Company, Demonstrated (1709?) [Bodleian; H.1024; anti].

The African Trade in No Danger of Being Lost Otherwise than by the Designs of the Company (1711) [G.4687; H.1350; anti].

Amendments Humbly Proposed to the Bill for Settling the Trade to Africa, with the Reasons Thereof (1698) [K.S2028; anti].

The Anatomy of the African Company's Scheme for Carrying on That Trade in a Joint-Stock Exclusive, on the Foot of New Subscriptions (1710?) [2 pp.; K–G 4607.0–1; anti].

The Answer of the Generality of the Creditors of the Royal African Company, to the Observations of the Separate-Traders; On the Bill for Making Effectual Their Agreement with the Company (1712) [2 pp.; G.4872; H.1595; pro].

An Answer to a Paper Call'd Particulars against the Bill for an Open Trade to Africa: with Some Presidents Touching the Laying Open Foreign Trades, by Act of Parliament (1713) [G.4996; H.1887; anti].

An Answer to a Paper Called Short Remarks on the African Trade (1711) [K.S2516; anti].

An Answer to Several Pretended Arguments, Proving, that Our Trade to Africa Cannot be Preserved and Carried on Effectually by any other Method than that of a Considerable Joint-Stock with Exclusive Privileges (1710? and 1714?) [3 pp.; LI m.103(2); K.S1254; H.1149; 2 versions; anti].

An Answer to the Objections to the Bill for a Free Trade to Africa, Particularly as It Relates to the Late Act, to Enable the African Company to Compound with Their Creditors (1711?) [2 pp.; K–G 4721.3; anti].

An Answer to the Reasons against an African Company Humbly Submitted (1711) [31 pp.; BL 1029.e.20(9); H.1360; Hogg 1021; pro].

An Answer to the Separate Trader's Feigned Great Trade for Eighty Thousand Negroes, in Thirteen Years; Tis Most Evident, and a Much More Reasonable Calculation (1712) [BL 8223.e.4(3); pro].

An Apology for the English Nation: That It Is as much the Interest for the English Nation, that the Trades to the East-Indies and Africk should Be as Free as that to Spain (1695?) [4 pp., K.S 1831]

The Appellants Case (1669?) [K.S1669; anti].

The Argument Touching Security Necessary to Be Given for Carrying on the African Trade, Demonstrated to Be Groundless and Ridiculous (1711?) [G.4689; H. 1351; anti].

Arthur Zouch, His Case, in Relation to the Royal African Company's Proceedings against Him, as a Criminal, with Their Servant Henry Bishop (1707) [BL. L.R.404.n.5(81); H.789; anti].

The Barbados Petition, Relating to the African Trade (1710) [G.4603; pro].

A Bill for Establishing the Trade to Africa Free and Open to All Her Majesty's Subjects of Great Britain, and the Plantations (1713?) [3 pp.; K–G5049.9; anti].

A Bill for Establishing the Trade to Africa, in a Regulated Company (1712) [4 pp.; Bodleian; K–G 4607.0–10; H.1597; anti].

A Bill for Making Effectual Some Agreement, as Shall Be Made between the Royal-African-Company of England, and Their Creditors (1712) [BL L.23.c.7(74); H;1592; pro].

A Bill for the Relief of the Creditors of the Royal African Company (1710?) [4 pp.; K–G 4607.011; pro].

A Brief Narrative of the Royal-African Company's Proceedings with Their Creditors the Last Year; with Some Rules and Restrictions, They are Willing to Submit to, by a Bill in Parliament (1710) [2 pp.; BL 8233.e.4(30); H.1150; pro].

The British Interest on the Coast of Africa Consider'd, with the Interest of Other Europeans, and the Politicks They Used for Carrying on that Trade (1710?) [BL 8223.e.24; H.911; pro].

The Case between the African Company and the People of England (1692) [2 pp.; BL Harleian MS 7310/189; LI m.103(4); H. 913; W.C854; Hogg 984; anti].

The Case between the African Company and the People of England, Briefly Laid Open in Some Considerations upon the Said Company's Petition (1708?) [2 pp.; LI m.103(29); H.912; anti].

The Case of About One Thousand African-Creditors Now United with the Company, by Virtue of the Late Act of Parliament (1713) [G.4999; H.1871; pro].

The Case of Edmond Harrison, William Dockwra, John Thrale, and Thomas Jones of London, Merchants; and Their Partners (1695?) [BL 816.m.11(8); anti].

The Case of John Leadstone, a Private Trader Residing in Africa (1711?) [K.S2518; H.1872; anti].

The Case of Sir John and Mr. Charles Crisp, Grandsons of Sir Nicholas Crisp, in relation to the Forts and Castles of Africa (1710?) [BL 8223.e.4(22); K.S2434; H.1151; anti].

The Case of the African Company's Creditors (1712?) [G.4875; H.1594; pro].

The Case of the African Company's Property to the Trade and Settlements in Africa, Justly Distinguished (1713) [BL 1887.b.60(31); H.1873; pro].

The Case of the Appellants to the Royal African Company William Dockwra, Mr and Mrs Roger Langden, Richard Dickerson (1704) [BL Cup.645.b.11(29); anti].

The Case of the Bond Creditors of the Royal African Company (1709) [K.S2428; H.1025; pro].

The Case of the City of Bristol, and All the Outports in Respect to Trade, Especially to that of Africa (1713?) [LI m.103(69); K.S2521; H.1874; anti].

The Case of the Clothiers, Serge-Makers, Dyers, etc. in Relation to the Bill for Settling the Trade to Africa (1698?) [BL G.5852(207); anti].

The Case of the Creditors of the African Company, and of the Company United with Them (1713) [Bodleian; H.1875; pro].

The Case of the Creditors of the Royal African Company (1711?) [BL 8223.e.4120); K.S2522; H.1877: pro].

The Case of the Creditors of the Royal African Company, Now Incorporated with the Said Company Humbly Represented to the Honourable the House of Commons (1713) [Bodleian; H.1876; pro].

The Case of the Late African Company (1694) [4 pp.; BL Harleian MS 7310/1; K.S1802; anti].

The Case of the National Traders to Africa (1713) [LI m.103(28); K.S2524; H.1878; anti].

The Case of the Present Merchants, Now Trading to Barbary (1696?) [K.S1924; anti].

The Case of the Royal African Company (1709) [4 pp.; BL 816.m.11(14); H. 1027; Hogg 1003; pro].

The Case of the Royal African Company (1710) [2 pp.; BL 8223.e.4(18); H. 1026; pro].

The Case of the Royal African Company and of the Plantations (1714) [3 pp.; BL 8223.e.1(171): LI m.103(7); H.2011; Hogg 1034; pro].

The Case of the Royal African Company and Their Creditors as to the Prosecution by the Queen for Albert's Debt (1711?) [LI m.103(66); H.1352; pro].

The Case of the Royal African Company of England (1694) [BL 1474.dd.22(3); LI m.103(1); W.C1161; Hogg 986; pro].

The Case of the Separate Traders to Africa (1708) [4 pp.; LI m.103(3); H.1028; Hogg 996: anti].

The Case of the Woollen Manufacturers of the Western Counties, Particularly Cornwall and Devon: As Relates to the Trade to Africa (1713) [2pp.; K-G 5003.5; H.1880; anti].

A Collection of Papers Relating to the Trade to Africa (1712?) [62 pp.; BL 104.h.60; H.1589; Hogg 1029; anti].

*Companies in Joint-Stock Unnecessary and Inconvenient (1691) [4pp.; G.2876: same author as *Free, Regulated Trade, Particularly to India*, anti].

Considerations Concerning the African Companies Petition (1698) [Harleian MS 7310/260; W.C5908a; anti].

Considerations Humbly Offer'd to the Honourable House of Commons, by the Planters, and Others, Trading to Our British Plantations, in Relation to the African Company's Petition, Now before This Honourable House (1709?) [BL 1474.dd.22(4); H.1030; Hogg 1007; anti].

Considerations Humbly Offered to the Honourable House of Commons, by the Planters, in Relation to the Bill to Settle the Trade to Africa (1698) [BL 816.m.11(17); K.S1993; Hogg 993; anti].

Considerations on the Bill for Settling the Trade to Africa, Humbly Offered to the Lords Spiritual and Temporal in Parliament Assembled, in Behalf of the Plantations (1698) [3 pp.; BL L.R. 305.a.7(13); anti].

Considerations Relating to the African Bill (1698?) [BL 816.m.11(18); K.S2036; W.C5913; anti].

Considerations, Touching the Bill for Settling the Trade to Africa (1698?) [3 pp.; L.R.305.a.7(13); anti].

Considerations Upon the Trade to Guinea (1708) [30 pp.; G.4480; H.914; Hogg 999; anti].

Copy of the Royal African Company's Letter to the Mayor, Aldermen and Common-Council of the City of Bristol, Dated London, the 26th February, 1712/13 (1713) [K-G 5049.15; H.1881; pro].

A Defense of the African Company's Creditors (1713) [LI m.103(32); H.1882; pro].

A Detection of the Gross Falsities which the Separate Traders to Africa Endeavour to Impose on the Publick, by a Printed Order, Intituled, An Account of the Ships Imployed in the African Trade, etc. (1712?) [2 pp.; Sutro A4:88 (Banks); H.1870; pro].

An Explanation of the African Company's Property in the Sole Trade to Africa, Making Their Right Equal with Any Subject's Right to Freehold (1712) [14 pp.; BL 1029.e.20(10); H.1590; pro].

An Extract of a Letter from the Coast of Africa, Receiv'd the 16th of March 1710/11 (1711) [LI m.103(37); H.1354; pro].

Extract Out of the Report of the Lords Commissioners of Trade, Laid before the House of Commons in 1708/9 (1711?) [3 pp.; BL L.23.c.7(73); K.S2530; H.1884; anti].

Extracts of Divers Passages Relating to Exclusive Joint-Stock Companies, Taken from Monsieur De Witt's Treatise of the True Interest and Political Maxims of Holland and West-Friesland Published by the Authority of the States General, and Translated into English in the Year 1702 (1713?) [BL 1474.dd.22(6): H.1883; anti].

The Falsities of Private Traders to Africa Discover'd, and the Mischiefs They Occasion Demonstrated: and an Account of the Settlements on that Coast Purchased, Built and Now Possest by the Company (1708) [4pp.; BL 8223.e.4(12); pro].

A Few Remarks Proper to Be Regarded in the Establishment of the African Trade (1709?) [H.1031; pro].

A Few Remarks Recommended to the Consideration of the Creditors of the Royal African Company (1712) [BL 816.m.11(32); H.1596; pro].

A Few Remarks upon the Royal African Company, in Respect to Their Trade and Settlements (1713) [2 pp.; K G5042.2; H.1885; pro].

A Full Answer to All the Objections to the Bill for Establishing the Trade to Africa in a Regulated Company (1712) [LI m.103(39); K.S2529; H.1601; anti].

At a General Court of the Adventurers of the Royal African Company of England, Held the 27th Day of March, 1701 . . . (1701) [BL 816.m.11(38); pro].

At a General Court of the Adventurers of the Royal African Company of England, Held the 13th Day of December, 1702. . . (1702?) [BL 816.m.11(39); pro].

At a General Court of the Adventurers of the Royal African Company of England, Held the 1st Day of June, 1704 . . . (1704) [BL 916.m.11(40); pro].

At a General Court of the Adventurers of the Royal African Company of England, Held the 26th Day of June, 1706 . . . (1706) [BL 816.m.11(41); pro].

At a General Court of the Adventurers of the Royal African Company of England, Held the 18th Day of September, 1706. . . (1706) [BL 816.m.1(42); pro].

Heads of Proposals for a More Beneficial and Equal Establishment of a Regulated Company, to Carry on the Trade of Africa, or Guiny (1698?) [BL Harleian MS 7310/203; K.S1704; W.H1286; anti].

Henry Bishop's Case in Relation to the Royal African Company's Proceedings against Him (1707) [LI m.103(26); H.790; anti].

The Humble Petition of Several Planters, and Other Inhabitants of Your Majesty's Island of Barbadoes (1710) [BL 816.m.18(31); H.1371; pro].

The Improvement of the African Trade farther Demonstrated by Separate Traders, in Answer to a Scurrilous Paper, Call'd, the Falsities of Private Traders Discovered (1708) [BL 8223.e.4(13); K.S2404; H.916; Hogg 998; anti].

John Chidley's Vindication of Himself from Slander and Calumny Cast Upon Him, in the Sixth and Seventh Pages of a Book, Entitled Reflections upon the Constitution and Management of the Trade to Africa (1709) [16 pp.; BL T.1593(9); H.1048; anti].

A Joint-Letter from the Most Considerable Proprietors of the Island of Barbadoes to Colonel Richard Scot, Colonel Robert Stewart, Richard Bate, Patrick Mein, and Thomas Fullerton, Esqs; . . . for Having the Trade to Africa Carried on by a Company of Sufficient Joint-Stock; Together with Their Reasons Subjoin'd (1709) [BL 816.m.5(147); H.1035; pro].

A Letter from a Merchant at Jamaica to a Member of Parliament in London, Touching the African Trade (1709) [A. Baldwin; BL 104.h.40; H. 1032; pro].

A Letter from a Merchant in Bristol, Touching the Trade to Africa, as It Relates to the Out-Ports of Great Britain (1711) [2 pp.; K.S2538; H.1355; Hogg 1022; anti].

A Letter to a Member of Parliament Concerning the African Trade (1709) [3 pp.; BL 8223.e.4(35); LI m.103; H.1033; Hogg 1010; anti].

A Letter to a Member of Parliament, Setting Forth the Trade to Africa (1709) [3 pp.; LI m.103(61); H.1034; pro].

A Letter to a Member of Parliament Touching the African Trade (1711?) [2 pp.; G.4705; H.1356; anti].

A Letter to a Separate Trader to Africa (1714?) [LI m.103(10); pro].

A List of the Forts and Castles which the African Company Pretend to Have, with the Number of Men and

Guns which They Say Are There; and also the Number of Men and Guns that Really Are in Each Fort and Castle; and the True Nature of the Guns, and What Sort of Buildings the Forts and Castles Are (1698) [BL 816.m.11(22); anti].

A Memorial on Behalf of the Royal-African-Company, Relating to Their Proposal Lately Given in to the Honourable House of Commons; for the Better Establishment of that Trade: Together with Their Said Proposal Subjoin'd (1710) [3 pp.; BL 816.m.11(45); H.1153; pro].

A Memorial Touching the Nature and Present State of the Trade to Africa (1709) [7 pp.; G.4550; H.1036; Hogg 1008; pro].

Mr. Phipps' Speech to a Committee of the Honourable House of Commons, Concerning the African Trade, 27 March 1712 (1712) [16pp.; BL 8245.a.43; H.1591; pro].

Objections to the Bill for Establishing the Trade to Africa in a Regulated Company (1712) [G.4887; H.1599; pro].

Observations on D.T.'s Considerations on the Trade to Africa, Humbly Offered to the Honourable House of Commons, Relating to the Bill Now before Them (1698) [3 pp.; K.S2064; anti].

Particulars Wherein the Bill for Laying the Trade to Africa Free and Open, Takes Away and Destroys the Property of the African-Company and Their Creditors, Now United by an Act Passed in the Last Session of Parliament (1713) [BL L.23.c.7(98); LI m.103(44); H.1886; pro].

A Plain Account of the Loss, This Nation Has Sustain'd, by Laying Open the Trade to Africa (1712) [G.4683; H.1357; Hogg 1028; pro].

The Planters Objections to the Bill Intitled, a Bill for Establishing the Trade to Africa, Free and Open to All Her Majesty's Subjects of Great Britain, and the Plantations (1713) [BL L.23.c.7(8); H.1888; pro].

Precedents Relating to the Establishing of Foreign Trade and Repealing Monopolies (1712) [BL 8223.e.9(11); K.S2544; H.1602; anti].

The Present Case of the African Trade Truly Stated, with Reasons for the Bill for Establishing the Same Now Depending (1713) [BL 1887.b.60(41); K.S2545; H.1889; anti].

The Present State of the African Trade Truly Stated, with Reason for the Bill for Establishing the Same Now Depending (1711) [G.4547; anti].

The Present State of the Royal African Company (1713) [Bodleian; H.1890; pro].

Prince Butlers Queries, Relating to the Bill for Settling the Trade to Africa, in a Joint-Stock Company, etc. as the Company Propose (1699) [A. Baldwin; 2 pp.; K./S.2127; W.P.3480; anti].

Property Derived under Charters and Grants from the Crown of England not Inferior to Property Derived under Grants from the Subjects of England (1713?) [LI m.103(11); H.1891; pro].

A Proposal Agreed unto for the Effectual Support, and Carrying on the Trade to Africa (1712) [BL 816.m.11(4); H.1358; pro].

A Proposal for Settling the Trade to Africa, Wherein the Ends Prosessed to Be Aimed at, Both by the Separated Traders, and the Company; and also by the North Britains, Out-Ports and Plantations, and Likewise by the Manufacturers are Effectually Provided for (1713) [LI m.103(49); H.1892; also a 1714 edn; pro].

Proposals for Raising a New Company for Carrying on the Trades of Africa and the Spanish West Indies under the Title of the United Company (1709) [J. Morphew; 13 pp.; G.4552; H.1040; anti].

Proposals Humbly Offered to the Honourable House of Commons, for Enlarging and Protecting the Trade to Africa (1712?) [BL 8223.e.4(5); H.1587; anti].

Proposals Humbly Offer'd to the Honourable House of Commons, for the Inlargement and More Effectual Carrying On the Trade to Africa, for the Support of Our Plantations and Improvement of Our British Manufactures (1709?) [2 pp.; K–G 4560.12; anti].

Reasons against Confirming the Charter to the African Company by Act of Parliament (1711) [BL Cup.651.e. (206); K.S2549; Hogg 1018; anti].

Reasons against Establishing an African Company at London, Exclusive to the Plantations, and All the Out-Ports, and Other Subjects of Great Britain (1711) [2 pp.; BL 816.m.11(3); H.1359; Hogg 1019; anti].

Reasons against Establishing an African Company by Act of Parliament, Humbly Offered to Consideration (1711?) [BL Cup 651.e.206; anti].

Reasons against Selling the Trade to Africa, or any Part thereof, in a Company with Joynt Stock Exclusive of Others (1707?) [K.S.2317; anti].

Reasons against the Bill for the Better Improvements of the Trade to Africa by Establishing a Regulated-Company (1709) [G.4553; H.1042; pro].

Reasons against the Regulating Bill (1712) [Bodleian; H.1598; pro].

Reasons for Establishing the African Trade under a Regulated Company (1709) [2 pp.; G.4554; H.1043; anti].

Reasons for Making the Duties Easie upon the Trade to Africa (1698) [BL 816.m.11(31); K.S2072; pro].

Reasons for Settlement of the Trade to Africa in a Joynt-Stock, with the Arguments of the Separate-Traders against It, Answer'd (1711?) [BL L.23.c.6(89); H.1361; pro].

Reasons for Vesting the Settlements on the Coast of Africa in the Crown: and the Dangers of an Exclusive Company Demonstrated (1712?) [2 pp.; Sutro A5:9 (Banks); Bodleian; K.S. 2552; H.1044; anti].

Reasons Humbly Offered by the Merchants and Traders to Guiney and the West-Indies, against the Bill for Settling the Trade to Africa (1698) [BL G.5852(217); Hogg 994; anti].

Reasons Humbly Offered, for Confirming the Royal-African-Company's Charter by Parliament to Such Persons Who Are Willing to Become Adventurers in That Trade (1711?) [2 pp.; BL 816.m.11; H.1362; Hogg 1017; pro].

Reasons Humbly Offered for Repealing a Clause in the Act for Settling the Trade to Africa, by which Foreign Copper Bars May Be Exported from England (1698) [3 pp.; G.3509; anti].

Reasons Humbly Offered in Behalf of the Plantations, against the Bill for Settling the Trade to Africa (1698) [BL G.5852; K.S2080; Hogg 992; anti].

Reasons Humbly Offer'd to the Honourable the Commons of England Assembled in Parliament, Shewing the Great Loss that Accrues to Their Majesties in Their Revenue, and Their Subjects Both at Home and in Their Plantations Abroad, by the African Company's Ingrossing the Sole Trade of Africa Confining It to the Narrow Joynt Stock of Little More than One Hundred Thousand Pounds, Excluding All Other Their Majesties Subjects Both at Home and Abroad to Their Great Detriment and Threatned Ruine (1694?) [BL 1890.e.4(96); anti].

Reasons Showing that the Trade to Guinea on the Coast of Africa Cannot be Preserved without Forts and Castles, and the Best and Surest Way to Maintain Them Is By a Joynt-Stock (1696?) [BL Harleian MS 7310/201; pro].

Reflections on the Separate Trades Proceedings, in Opposition to the Settlement of the African Trade (1711) [BL 816.m.11(9); H.1363; pro].

Remarks on the African Company's Memorial (1709) [G.4886; anti].

Remarks on the Bill for Relief of the Creditors of the Royal African Company (1711?) [K-G 4721.12; anti].

Remarks upon Some Queries Handed about by the Separate Traders to Africa (1711?) [BL 816.m.11(6); H.1603; pro].

Resolutions of a General Court of the Adventurers of the Royal African Company, Held on Thursday the 26th of February, 1712/13 (1713) [Bodleian; H.1893; pro].

The Royal African-Company, and Separate Traders Agree (1712?) [G.4892; H.1605; pro].

The Royal African Company of England, Appellants (1709) [BL Cup 645.b.11(40); H.393; pro].

The Scandalous Political Arithmetick (as They Term It) of the Private Traders Detected (1708) [MP; H.917; pro].

Seasonable Animadversions, on All the Papers and Pamphlets Lately Printed on Behalf of the Separate Traders to Africa . . . as Pretended Arguments against Establishing and Carrying on the Trade to Africa, upon the Foot of an Exclusive Joint-Stock (1710) [7 pp.; BL 8223.e.4(38); H.1154; Hogg 1015; pro].

A Scheme, by which 'tis Humbly Conceived the Trade to Africa Will Be Most Effectually Preserved, Carried on to the Utmost Extent, and Secured for after Ages, to the Great Benefit of This Kingdom, and the Plantations and Colonies thereunto Belonging (1711?) [2 pp.; K-G 4721.10; anti].

A Scheme for an Additional Stock to the Royal African Company by Subscription. Read and Agreed to in a General Court the 18th of February 1713/14 (1714) [3 pp.; BL 8233.e.4(19); pro].

The Scheme Humbly Proposed to the Honourable House of Commons, for the Effectual Support, and Carrying on the Trade to Africa (1711?) [Bodleian; H.1364; anti].

A Second Letter to a Member of Parliament, Relating to the Settling the Trade to Africa (1710?) [BL 8223.e.4(14); K.S2566; H.1155; anti].

The Separate-Traders Queries, or Rather Clamours, against the Bill of the Royal African-Company's Creditors, Proved to Be Malicious, Groundless and False (1712?) [BL 8233.e.4(7); H.1604; pro].

The Separate Traders Scheme for Carrying on the Trade to Africa (1710) [BL 8223.e.4(2); H.1156: Hogg 1023; anti].

Several Informations of the Evil Practices of Mr Chidley, Late Evidence against the R. A. C. (1709?) [MP; H.1049; pro].

A Short Account of the Present State of the Trade to Africa, Humbly Offered to the Consideration of the Parliament (1709) [LI m.102(50); H.1051; pro].

A Short and True Account of the Importance and Necessity of Settling the African Trade This Present Session of Parliament . . . (1711) [4 pp.; G.4684; H.1365; Hogg 1020; pro].

Short Remarks on the Bill for a Free Trade to Africa (1713?) [Bodleian; H.1894; pro].

Short Remarks Relating to the African Trade (1711) [BL 816.m.11(47); H.1366; pro].

Some Considerations Humbly Offered, against Granting the Sole Trade to Guiny from Cape Blanco to Cape Lopez, to a Company with a Joint Stock, Exclusive of Others (1696?) [2 pp.; BL 816.m.11(19); K.S1792; Hogg 990; anti].

Some Considerations Humbly Offered to Demonstrate How Prejudicial It Would be to the English Plantations, Revenues of the Crown, the Navigation and General Good of This Kingdom, that the Sole Trade for Negroes Should Be Granted to a Company with a Joynt-Stock Exclusive to All Others (1698?) [2 pp.; K.S2083; anti].

Some Considerations on the Late Act of Parliament, for Settling the Trade to Africa (1709?) [BL 1474.dd.22(5); H.918; Hogg 1011; pro].

Some Considerations Relating to the Trade to Guiny (1695?) [2 pp.; BL 1474.dd.22(2); K.S1714; Hogg 989; anti].

Some further Objections Humbly Offer'd to the Consideration of the Legislature, against the Bill, for Establishing the Trade to Africa in a Regulated Company (1712) [BL 8223.e.4(42); H.1600; anti].

Some General Reflections Humbly Offered by John Chidley, in Vindication of Himself, from the Calumnies which the African Company Have Endeavoured to Throw upon Him, in Two Late Papers, Whereof They Dispersed Several Copies, Even in the Lobby of the House of Commons (1709?) [K-G 4560.4; H.1050; anti].

Some Observations on Extracts Taken Out of the Report from the Lords Commissioners for Trade and Plantations (1708) [4 pp.; BL 516.m.18(14); K-G4491.2; H.915; pro].

Some Observations on the Bill, for Making Effectual Such Agreement as Shall Be Made between the African Company of England and Their Creditors (1711?) [2 pp.; K-G 4721.15; anti].

Some Queries Relating to the Bill for Making Effectual Such Agreement, as Shall Be Made between the African Company and Their Creditors (1711?) [K.S2513; anti].

Some Queries Relating to the Present Dispute about the Trade to Africa (1711?) [BL 816.m.11(5); K.S2563; H.1368; anti].

Some Remarks on a False and Scurrilous Libel, Intituled, The Case of the National Traders to Africa (1713) [LI M.102(36); H.1879; pro].

Some Remarks on a Pamphlet Call'd, Reflections, on the Constitution and Management of the Trade to Africa (1709) [32 pp.; BL T.1990(12); H.1047; Hogg 1002; anti].

Some Short and Necessary Observations Proper to Be Considered, in the Settlement of the African Trade (1711) [2 pp.; LI m.103(27); H.1369; Hogg 1016; pro].

A Specimen of the Falsehoods, Absurdities and Contradictions Contained in Some Late Papers, Published by the Separate Traders to Africa (1711) [2 pp.; G.4718; H.1370; pro].

The Specious, but Fallacious Insinuations of the Separate Traders to Africa, under the Title of a Regulated Company Are Invented (1709) [2 pp.; G.4547; H.1052; pro].

The State of the Trade to Africa between 1680 and 1707, as Well under the Management of an Exclusive Company as under that of Separate Traders, Impartially Considered, with Regard to Matter of Fact and Demonstration; Whereby It Appears the Separate Adventurers Have Improv'd that Trade to the Benefit of Great-Britain at least One Million a Year (1708?) [4 pp.; LI m.103(53); K.S2418; Hogg 995: anti].

A Supplement to the Royal-African-Company's Memorial Touching the Nature and Present-State of the Trade to Africa (1709) [MP; H.1037; pro].

Trade: An Essay; Explaining the General Maxim, that Freedom of Trade Is the Original Right of the Subject, and Coeval with the Constitution, and Cannot in Any Part Be Disposed of by the Crown (1712?) [2 pp.; Sutro A4:79(Banks); anti].

That the Trade to Africa, Is Only Manageable by an Incorporated Company and a Joynt Stock, Demonstrated in a Letter to a Member of the Present House of Commons, by a Gentleman in the City (1690) [7 pp.; BL 816.m.11(35); PRO SP 32/3/42; W.T841; pro].

A True Account of Eight Years Exports of the Royal African Company, and Eight Years Exports of the Separate Traders (1711) [BL 816.m.11(48); H.1372; pro].

A True Account of the Forts and Castles Belonging to the Royal African Company, upon the Gold Coast in Africa with the Number of Men, and Guns, the Nature of the Said Forts and Castles, and the Guns Planted on Them, as Taken from Sundry Persons Very Lately Come from Thence (1698) [BL 816.m.11(23); K.S2088; pro].

A True State of the Present Difference between the Royal African Company and the Separate Traders by a True Lover of His Country (1710) [40 pp.; G4605; H.1157; Hogg 1014; the personal copy of Narcissus Luttrell; anti].

The Unavoidable Consequences of a Trade to Africa, in a Regulated Company as Proposed by the Separate Traders, Demonstrated (1712?) [BL 8223.e.4(6); H.1606; pro].

A View of the State of the Trade to Africa (1708) [15 pp.; BL 1029.e.20(6); K S2420 H 920].

22
Delivering the goods
Patriotism, property, and the midwife mission of Mme du Coudray

Nina Rattner Gelbart

Mme du Coudray was a most extraordinary Frenchwoman of the eighteenth century (born 1715, died 1794), a midwife pensioned by two successive kings to travel throughout the realm teaching illiterate peasant women how to deliver babies safely. Several things make her remarkable: that she functioned as a kind of royal ambassadress on a mandated mission, first for Louis XV, then for Louis XVI; that she spent twenty-five years on this arduous ambulatory teaching expedition, traveling by carriage, overcoming constant obstacles, and giving her course in more than forty cities, thus training between 5,000 and 10,000 young women to become "*sages-femmes*"; that she produced an illustrated textbook on delivery, thus entering the almost exclusively male world of medical print culture and claiming the right to *see* in the totally male world of the "medical gaze"; that she used original, life-size obstetrical models of her own invention for demonstrations, hundreds of which were made by her and distributed in the regions where she taught; and that, in an unprecedented inversion of the social and medico-political order, she instructed male surgeons in the art of childbirth, male disciple-demonstrators who would perpetuate her teachings by giving refresher courses on her mannequins in each region after her departure (Plate 22.1).

But this crusader, this secular saint of sorts, propeled by a profound sense of mission, was a personal enigma. I have spent the last many years trying to piece together her puzzle, her story. Yes, as Virginia Woolf remarked, writing lives is the devil! Biography is dangerous, presumptuous, because we know so little, because we feel our subject's self remains somehow always submerged. This turns out to be especially so in my case, for Mme du Coudray was an activist, a woman of the instrumental world who sacrificed all to her calling, who revealed next to nothing of her private life in her letters, who made no home the center of her activity, who had no resting place where I might find her "inwardness"or "bridge her silences."[1] Her life was literally a journey, a quest plot, a roadshow; the whole country was her stage. This woman, who undertook a perilous and lonely odyssey on the roads of France in middle age, fascinated me all the more because of her sense of privacy. A public figure, a celebrity, a consummate performer, she was nonetheless ungenerous, begrudging me any glimpse behind her masks. I could scarce know the dancer from the dance.

Historians-turned-biographers often have trouble maintaining objectivity in dealing with the conflicts and contradictions in their subjects. I was naturally attracted to Mme du Coudray as a feminist heroine. Her very choice of the profession of midwifery seemed revelatory: devotion to the service of other women, to restoring some dignity in that moment of their lives most fraught with panic and peril. So I started out looking for qualities in Mme du Coudray that I considered "admirable," and reacting with disappointment to others that seemed to dishonor her. I wished to deliver, rescue, memorialize her, give her witness, create her myth. I wondered, with another writer of biographies, whether "the political usefulness of her story" might not be undermined by the "more ambiguous, potentially subverting, reality."[2] For this courageous, risk-taking woman was also self-serving and ingratiating. She was at once principled and calculating. Her vocation linked her to the lying-in women she served and taught, but her success and fame put an unbridgeable chasm between her and them. This paradox of the singular woman, whose story seems exemplary yet has moot meaning beyond its own idiosyncratic self, has been aptly summed up by Caroline Heilbrun: "Exceptional women are the chief imprisoners of non-exceptional women, simultaneously proving that any woman could do it and assuring, in their uniqueness among men, that no other woman will."[3] Mme du Coudray reached what Heilbrun has called a level of achievement not excusable in a female self,[4] and doubtless because of this she recognized no debt to other women, agreeing that her thousands of students accept a subordinate position in the hierarchy of medical practitioners. This was more than mollifying rhetoric. Like Florence Nightingale, this queen bee wanted no stardom for her disciples.[5] She could be compassionate and gentle, but also bossy and managerial, knowing she had a great accomplishment to her credit. She was, after all, determined to make it in a man's world, to do brave and important things, to take risks, to be autonomous. Of course there was much posturing, self-aggrandizement, exaggeration, but she did effectively woo her audience and she did succeed through her dazzling self-presentation and her understanding of the *ancien régime* on its own terms. In many ways she challenged her society, but she knew how to neutralize her threat, how to play a precarious game without antagonizing the men in power, how to disarm those who perceived as a menace the intrusion of a woman into the public sphere. An examination of her practical and rhetorical strategies shows how she conceived and manipulated her moment, how she navigated with alacrity across an allegedly polarized cultural terrain, how she permeated the boundaries of male and female spheres, how she divided her loyalties. And with time I have come to accept just how divided these loyalties were.

I want to illustrate this by examining some multiple and even conflicting notions of property that underlie and explain Mme du Coudray's beliefs and behaviors. First, since contemporaries viewed the body as national property, her mission was fueled by populationist politics, by the notion of female bodies as breeders for the state, of newborn bodies as belonging to the *patrie*. Second, she was fiercely protective of the special kinds of property she created. She recognized and exploited her popular midwifery manual as valuable literary property and demanded government support for all five editions. Still more aggressively, she made enormous numbers of obstetrical mannequins and sold them for profit. Medical teaching and props were seen by Mme du Coudray as products, commodities for which there was now a government-created market, and she was very skilled at selling her expertise to these new consumers. Finally, there is an interesting sense in which Mme du Coudray took possession of a problem and made it her own. Surgeons and male accoucheurs had not mobilized to remedy the situation she devoted over a quarter of a century to solving. It took the initiative of this bold, indefatigable woman, who then, quite legitimately, defended her rights to her work as her property, her rights to the ownership of her mission. And she insisted on passing her mission with its accompanying pension on to her "heir," in her case a (probably fabricated) "niece." It was the state that created her mission, but she assumed proprietary control, and believed in her exclusive right to possess, enjoy, and dispose of it.

Let us examine first the notion of the body, especially that of the female peasant, as somehow coming under the ownership or at least the stewardship, management, "use-rights," of the state. Michel Foucault has called this the "biopolitics" of the body, its placement in organic communication with the social body whose regular fecundity it was supposed to ensure. By the mid-1750s France was convinced it had a severe crisis, that its population was shrinking dramatically. Married women, the French state now declared, were morally obliged to guarantee the life of children, were patriotically bound to perform the public function of producing citizens. Sex and reproductivity began to be taken into account, administered, indeed, policed. The "ordered maximization" of life-forces was now seen to be useful, even essential for the state's welfare. The regime began to concern itself intensely with birth and death rates, life-expectancy, patterns of fertility. The collective sexual behavior of France's subjects became a political concern; subjects as individual persons seemed to matter less as attention focused increasingly on "population," a term used in connection with taxes, soldiers, and labor capacity. Now, instead of stressing the death penalty, the right of seizure, of "taking life," those in power sought to ensure, sustain, and multiply life. The propagation of the human species became an urgent matter, for it was feared France, and hence the earth, would soon be depleted, would become a wasteland. The administration of life came under the sphere of government control and intervention, the body was valorized and took on an entirely new political importance to the state. It became impossible to talk about the body without talking about power.[6]

The reproductive capacity of the country poor was targeted as the main area of surveillance. Because peasants lived at subsistence level, their lives governed by necessity rather than choice, they could not be self-managing or self-possessed, could not on their own understand healthy breeding as their civic responsibility.[7] For political purposes the state therefore appropriated the control that the rural poor did not have over themselves. Their preservation and conservation became necessary; their offspring would ensure the future of the nation, indeed of the human race. Children came to be discussed almost as commodities, building blocks of the state's prosperity, their health intimately related to that of the economic and social fabric. They were, literally, the "enfants de la patrie." The waste of babies became a kind of public crime, a form of lèse-majesté.

The management of the health and fecundity of rural France, its "medicalization," was, by the end of the century, taken over by the Société Royale de Médecine, a vast network of doctors corresponding, reporting, supervising, analyzing, compiling statistics, and treating.[8] But decades earlier, when France was in the midst of the humiliating Seven Years War, Mme du Coudray had volunteered to tackle the problem head-on and single-handedly. She meant to mobilize the whole countryside in an effort to make childbirth safer and more productive. In this she would become the trusted agent of the populationist government.

La Michodière was the intendant of Auvergne when Mme du Coudray came to his attention for her success teaching free midwifery classes to peasant women near Clermont Ferrand. He had since 1757 been in correspondence with Voltaire regarding the whole question of whether France was really experiencing a population crisis. An increased number of French subjects, he was sure, would make for a more prosperous nation, furnishing higher tax revenues and more military manpower.[9] It was for this reason that he supported Mme du Coudray, spoke of her in glowing terms at Versailles, and got the king, his controller-general, and other ministers of state excited about what she was doing. She was soon commissioned to teach "throughout the realm," as the king's *brevet* stipulated, without being harassed or troubled in any way. Provision was even made for her to grant her own certificates to those she trained, thus empowering her to create a sort of emergency squad and short-circuiting the usual pattern of midwives' serving as apprentices and then being tested by a jury of doctors and surgeons. This kind of attention and entitlement to a female practitioner was entirely unprecedented.

It must be recalled that those to whom Mme du Coudray addressed her teaching, the provincial poor, were in the habit of watching the majority of their infants die, as Olwen Hufton has pointed out.[10] Husbands, of course, had unlimited sexual access to their wives, conception was frequent and nearly always unwelcome, and the birth of an infant was commonly followed by its death and burial. Such mortality, though surely emotionally wrenching, was considered a matter of course. Hufton has described in detail the upheavals in the lives of peasant families in eighteenth-century France, the catastrophe of pregnancy – which put the women temporarily out of commission – and of birth – which presented yet another mouth to feed in families that could not even provide enough for the father, instead sending him out on the road to earn money if he could, but at least to "eat away from home." The simple fact is, then, that while increasing the population was the goal of the state, it was not necessarily the wish of the "breeder" families. The protest over rampant infant mortality, in other words, was not coming from the tiny victims' parents at all, but from the elites in power, who saw the citizens of France as national property. Increasing the population was thus a political, not a humanitarian, policy.

The state propagated this view of women as property, to be managed, administered, husbanded with the same sort of care that a farmer gave his land and cattle. Officials implementing the royal will even claimed they needed to upgrade the view of wives so that they would be taken as seriously as livestock, for it was the perception of the elite that peasants did not value the mothers of their children or the children themselves sufficiently, in fact, nowhere near as much as their "owned" things. Rural animals seemed to be getting better medical attention than rural people. The subdelegate of Ribemont, near Soisson, implied a link between wives and beasts when he reported to his superior in 1760 that in his countryside, when it came to birthing of any kind, "shepherds are the most experienced, and often in difficult [human] deliveries it is to them that one has recourse."[11] From Champagne in 1772 came a lament that parishioners "cared more about their cows when they wanted to drop their calves, than about their wives when they had to give birth."[12] A handbook on childbirth by the accoucheur Augier DuFot in 1775 stated baldly the woeful ignorance of fathers, their intense loyalty to their herds at the expense of their families.[13] In Tours in the late 1770s, the inspector in charge of delivery, trying to raise money for midwifery instruction, wrote of the peasants to the intendant: "You know better than I their character. If it were to train a veterinarian, the hope of having a man who could forestall or prevent mortality in their cattle would bring them to donate all that was asked without repugnance. But to save their wives, it's another matter entirely. One lost, another found."[14]

It was even eventually decided that veterinarians should be taught human obstetrics, on the facile assumption that this would be merely an additional twist to the mechanical birthing skills they had already acquired. In 1780 the Ecole Royale Vétérinaire d'Alfort began offering courses in midwifery. The king in his goodness, it was explained, wanted to make this innovation, because veterinarians often dwelt and worked in remote rural areas where medical practitioners and even trained midwives were unavailable. The king was soon convinced that animal doctors could do human obstetrics and "really were in a fit state to render the services hoped of them."[15] Mme du Coudray herself was the first to teach these courses in midwifery at the royal veterinary school in 1780. She was by then 65 years old and it is probably fair to say that birthing was now even more of a business for her than it had been two decades earlier when she first undertook her mission.

Was Mme du Coudray motivated by sympathy for women, or did she merely subscribe to the patriarchal state's view of mothers as things to be manipulated? Evidence suggests that at the start of her public career she cared quite deeply for her female flock. Her book *Abrégé de l'art des accouchements*, first published in 1759, is full of sensitivity for the plight of mothers. Indeed, she claimed that "compassion made me an author," that listening to the stories and the sufferings of the women of Auvergne had moved her to do all she could to lighten their load.[16] The peasant women around Clermont, whose husbands were away as seasonal migrants for as much as nine months a year, developed into strong matriarchs. They were able, determined women, not dependent or pathetic.[17] Yet motherhood took a terrible toll on them, delivery often leaving them with some lifelong painful or even crippling deformity. It may have been precisely the strength and perseverance of these women that first inspired Mme du Coudray; given her own character, she would have identified with such fighters. And her very determination to teach thousands of young women a profession shows a sense of solidarity with other women. They need not all be victims of their reproductive processes, she seemed to be saying. Many could learn a trade, a livelihood, the art of midwifery, and could practice it for profit. They could learn to read and write if they did not know how already. They could improve the lives of other women, and do something vital for humanity. Thus Mme du Coudray ennobled women's work; she seemed not to think of women as helpless, pitiful, or disorderly by nature.

Whereas often in texts the male medical establishment tended to treat peasant women as "other," Mme du Coudray empathized and was consequently able to mediate between the two. She never saw her job as "taming," "subduing," or "civilizing" them. She spoke sometimes of the "disgust" a city person might experience in some of their poor hovels, and she occasionally complained about the "*peu d'intelligence*" of some of her students. In the margin of some annotated instructions, she commented that it was not easy to mold their minds, to bend their wills.[18] But the fact remains that she worked tirelessly with and for them. She found them worthy of her attention, her instruction, her help, her inspiration, her very life. Never did she talk of them as idle or morally depraved, as unruly or threatening. She managed even to work with some of their "superstitions" – she did not use this judgmental term – allowing them to cling to relics if it comforted them during birthing, for example. Her focus on understanding these women is notable. Peasant husbands are conspicuous for their absence in Mme du Coudray's textbook and letters. It was the women she taught, the laboring women in the fields, around whose hard farmwork at harvest time she had to schedule her courses, so that she did not further complicate their already difficult lives with conflicting demands. Communicating with them was her mission, and she did it on many levels. The book was there for those who could read. The illustrations were added for those who could not. The months of lessons, recitations, and demonstrations on the mannequin or "machine" were for both. Inept, slovenly, unreliable persons who had previously done this work had been blamed for France's depopulation, and Mme du Coudray, who felt such criticism to be justified, would now redeem her profession. She wanted in fact to distinguish her fresh new group of midwives from the older untrained matrons with their variety of failings. In contrast to these ignorant old crones – Mme du Coudray did not hesitate to condemn them as harshly as men did – her graduates would be young, newly trained, unspoiled by prejudices, guided, shaped, and molded by her from scratch.

She succeeded admirably, miraculously even, in communicating her enthusiasm and warmth. Male observers commented often on her charisma, the way she reached and charmed classes of over 100 women at a time. LeNain, intendant of Moulins, marvelled at the very beginning of her ambulatory teaching odyssey that she had, already then, the natural "talent to make herself loved."[19] She seemed able to inspire an intense loyalty in her students, many of whom stayed in touch with her for years. Even much later, in the 1770s, observers reported how triumphant her good students felt at the completion of the class, how devastated those who failed because they might have personally disappointed her.[20] She remained involved with numerous former students, getting them supplies, pleading at their trials, lending them small sums, and even toward the end of her life sacrificing 500 of her 8,000 *livres* retirement pension as an annual salary for one of them.

But that is only half the story. The very scope of Mme du Coudray's ambition necessarily and increasingly privileged efficiency over personal attention. Whatever Mme du Coudray's connection with her students and however sympathetic her book, the obstetrical mannequin itself encouraged a rote approach to women in labor, and to delivery. This objectified pelvis, on which the students practiced daily, was part of an almost mechanical routine, and did contribute to a reductive view of the female in labor as a puzzle of parts to be dexterously realigned. In Poitier in 1765 the intendant had articulated this. Mme du Coudray's students, he said, "know how to deliver like a cobbler knows how to make shoes. That is all that is required."[21] Years of traveling and teaching the mechanism of midwifery (it was in these words that Mme du Coudray referred to her lessons to male surgeon-demonstrators) had made it almost automatic. In France the metaphor of the body as a machine, inherited from Descartes, had perhaps stripped it of much of its emotional baggage. That she referred to her invention always as her "machine" too suggests her tendency to reduce birthing women to things, commodities. Indeed, there appears to be no sense of outrage, no subtext of protest in Mme du Coudray's letters from Alfort, where she complied entirely with the king's wishes to make childbirth part of the province of veterinarians, to liken human mothers to so many cows.

A brief comment on Mme du Coudray's *Abrégé* illustrations is in order here, for with their outstretched waiting hands, they very much emphasize the midwife's focus and claim on the new child, rather than any attachment to the mother. Such images have meaning within a larger cultural climate of reproductive politics, coded messages, political signs, moral injunctions, but it is not always easy to decode them. The midwife's illustrations might seem in some ways a quite daring, even feminist addition to her book. It is true that by the very presentation of such pictures in a text for women, Mme du Coudray took a bold step and asserted their right to *see*, to partake of the medical gaze, to behold rather than simply be beheld. Some men, in fact, reacted quite violently to her inclusion of images in her new edition, as if the visual were a realm exclusively theirs.[22] It is also true that her images show a certain respect for women and are much more decorous than those in male texts which gratuitously feature breasts and external genitalia, or emphasize sensuality, or display the woman, *agonistes*, as dead meat (Plate 22.2).[23] On the other hand, however, Mme du Coudray's pictures negate the mother, render her invisible, with their X-ray-like technique. The fetus becomes primary, almost autonomous. Except for the pelvic bone cavity, there is no reference to the pregnant mother, who is absent. Some of this is attributable, of course, to the necessary schematization of diagrammatic illustrations; the baby in its various positions is, after all, the point of these representations. But in some of Mme du Coudray's pictures we could forget entirely that this fetus is dependent for its life, not on empty space as depicted, but on its mother's body, on her uterus and bloodstream, to support it. We have a kind of denial of the womb. So in a way this imagery reinforces and serves the patriarchal system. Making the mother's body transparent, erasing it in order to view the fetus, should be understood as a political act.[24] It represents intervention in a private matter, surveillance, and potential social control. It is a kind of circumventing of parental authority. And the baby is highlighted by a color print process, a new technique that cost the midwife considerable expense (see below, p. 476). The fetus in these images is developed, a person already, all pink and alive and ready to be born and to serve. The baby can then become the property of another, whose hands are there waiting to claim it (Plate 22.3). Thus, Mme du Coudray's illustrations suggest that she was able to establish her vast control over childbirthing only by working within the system of political and medical patriarchy, only by agreeing to function as an agent of the state. She was, it seems, more of a patriot than a feminist.

I want now to turn to the "business" side of Mme du Coudray's mission. We have seen that to a considerable extent she played into the government's view of female subjects as state property, of babies as national goods. But at least as interesting is the way she conceived of her own work as hers, as her goods, and insisted that the king and his ministers recognize her property rights. These two facets of her story were of course inextricably intertwined.

Because Mme du Coudray was pensioned by the state to undertake her mission – the king issued her royal *brevets* in 1759, 1767, and 1774 (and one to her *survivante* niece in 1785) – she believed she had certain rights of ownership. Earlier, before her celebrity, she had functioned in the private sphere, although even then she was aggressive and exacting. In 1745 she seems to have been one of several who spearheaded a group of forty midwives to sign a petition demanding better education, and requesting a course in anatomy from the Paris Faculty of Medicine. This was an attempt to cement a new alliance with the physicians of the capital, because the surgeons were disparaging midwives' apprentices by accusing them of ignorance and refusing to examine them or admit them to practice.[25] Mme du Coudray and her group of petitioners had a strong sense of work identity and camaraderie. They banded together also to defend against unlicensed or inadequately trained matrons their sole right to practice. We know too that Mme du Coudray commanded a high price for teaching her art to apprentices. One contract from 1751 shows her charging 300 *livres* for three years of training an aspirant, whereas other midwives often passed on their expertise for much less money and even for free, and occasionally threw in room and board.[26] So Mme du Coudray had a healthy sense of the usefulness, importance, and financial worth of her profession long before she ventured into the public sphere, long before she could boast, as she loved to do, that "it is the king who pays me."[27]

Once she became the "national midwife" and undertook what she saw as political service, however, she got an approbation and royal privilege for her textbook, thus "going public" with her knowledge in exchange for the protection of her literary property. She also approached the Royal Academy of Surgery and got from them a certificate of approval for her mannequin.[28] She hoped, her letters of that period make clear, to receive a "*traitement*" or monetary reward for this ingenious invention. These were her props. They shored her up, enhanced her impact, improved her act. She aspired, in other words, already then, to have her talent and public-spirited initiative translate into financial recompense, her honor into rewards, her good works into property, in French her "*bien*" into "*biens*." She would continue to make such claims, to see payment as her due, throughout her mission. She had, after all, taken possession of a problem and literally devoted her life to traveling and solving it. She saw herself as an emancipated commercial female, entirely deserving of her hard-earned royal pension.

What is curious, however, is that Mme du Coudray had little interest in material goods, in actual property. They did not fit into her life-style. She was a nomad, with no base, no home. From 1760 to 1783 she roamed the countryside, taking along with her in a carriage "the little I possess."[29] What she wanted was enough to continue her mission in a dignified and comfortable way. During her sojourning she had, on occasion, been reduced to borrowing money, even to struggling in strange towns without wood or candles. Once, in Bourges, she had actually been forced into a kind of hibernation because her funds did not suffice to buy her light and heat.[30] Far from trying to accumulate a fortune, she wanted more simply to be permanently protected from such indignities, to be able to finance her mission and never be subject to such humiliation. As time went on she became understandably preoccupied with securing her old age, providing for her retirement ("*assurer mon sort*"), and with passing on her reputation and her pension to her niece. The possessions, the property Mme du Coudray valued were not homes and furnishings. The latter would have been encumbrances and the former would have been of no use to a committed traveler. But she did value the salary that made possible her work, the papers and references attesting to how much she had been appreciated, and the occasional objects given to her by towns and cities where she taught – a silver *cafetière* here, a plaque there – in gratitude for her instruction and inspiration. She also wished for the intangibles, for fame, glory, and immortality, which she felt she richly merited, but which were always linked in her mind to tangible recompense. She wanted her work to be regarded as a "monument to humanity"[31] for centuries to come. This in part explains why she did not train other women to teach. She was recognized by the men she impressed as a totally exceptional female, "unique," "extraordinary," a "phenomenon."[32] Her singularity pleased her, indeed fueled her, and she experienced as a violation of her self, of her property, any pecuniary damages or threats to her autonomous reputation. She knew she was doing something of vital importance. Nobody, however highborn, was going to rob her of that recognition. Once, when she felt the Controller-General's moral and financial support waning, she made a trip to Paris to toot her own horn. She returned triumphant, boasting to a friend that she had "ruled like a queen over the ministers of state."[33]

There is in her correspondence some interesting linguistic slippage that at first muddles but ultimately illuminates the relationship of the female body and the body politic, of birthing to power, of life to profit. Values, of course, are ratified in language, and an examination of Mme du Coudray's numerous letters, most of which were instrumental (or at least contained a long section on the business of midwifery), shows that her words often had both descriptive and evaluative functions.

Her self-presentation was bold, never apologetic. It was her job, she told all her correspondents, to spread the "*bien de l'humanité*." This catchphrase recurs repeatedly in her letters, often three or four times in a single missive. "*Biens*" in French can mean both good and goods, both blessings, betterment, and good works, on the one hand, and property, possessions, assets, on the other. Its moral meaning, according to the contemporary *Encyclopédie*, was thus "equivocal."[34] These *biens de l'humanité* were argued to be "*intéressant*," another word described in the same source as having "varied . . . simple and figurative meanings"[35] signifying both worthy (as a cause) and financially attractive. "*Intérêt*," a word that comes up repeatedly in Mme du Coudray's correspondence, she used to mean her service to the *patrie*, but also her due, her share, her stake, her benefit. She spoke of her work being "*cher*," which again has both senses of dear, that is, cherished and beloved, but also estimable, worth considerable cost. It was worth, in fact, a great "*prix*," sometimes even a "*prix infini*," again suggesting both a moral and economic value. "*Bienveillance*" and "*humanité*" were of course both cornerstones of Enlightenment discourse, and Mme du Coudray exploited that language to the hilt. The *Encyclopédie* defined "*humanité*" as "a sentiment of benevolence [*bienveillance*] for all that blazes only in the hearts of large, sensitive souls. This noble and sublime enthusiasm is tormented by the suffering of others and by the need to give them solace; it would traverse the universe to abolish . . . misfortune."[36] All of this makes the notion of the "*bien de l'humanité*" polyvalent. Mme du Coudray indeed voyaged, if not through the universe, at least through all of France. She was surely teaching midwifery because of her own humanity, and for the good of humanity, but she was also, as she never ceased to remind her populationist supporters, by delivering the babies, quite literally *delivering the goods.*

From the beginning Mme du Coudray had made it clear that her time was money, that anything or anyone who obstructed her or delayed her travels was squandering funds and wasting something *"cher au bien de l'humanité."*[37] She would threaten that she had to report all reasons for her "inaction" to the authorities.[38] Already in 1764 one of her male facilitators explained that she absolutely counted on profits from her book and machines, that it would be a kind of "larceny" to deprive her of those sales.[39] For the first few years the various provinces themselves financed her voyages and courses, but in 1767 the king awarded her a new *brevet*, stipulating an annual pension of 8,000 *livres* from the royal treasury, and a guaranteed income at retirement. Mme du Coudray was overwhelmed by this generosity which only enhanced her sense of self-importance. An observer wondered if, now that her future was provided for, her zeal might cool down, because before she had had to continually prove her worth, whereas now it was being assumed.[40] She, however, could be said to have had a policy of reinvestment, using the new financial security not to slacken her pace but to make her teaching still more effective. She invented a costly supplement for her "machine," a set of sacs and sponges filled with liquids to represent blood and the breaking of the amniotic waters to make the demonstration for her students more realistic. Not only was she forever perfecting her mannequin – even making special side-trips to inspect rival products for anything she might learn and copy from the competition[41] – but she spent nearly half of her pension one year to finance the twenty-six illustrations for the second edition of her *Abrégé* in 1769. These plates were made with the newest technology, a process of color engraving discovered only a few years earlier which had hardly been used at all in anatomical pictures and never in obstetrical representations. She wished, with her bright pink images, to be original, striking, to make her mission "perpetual" and "luminous."[42] Her work, then, was her property, her capital, and she did all she could to make it steady, solid, secure, to guarantee it against erosion.

She stressed that her teaching of surgeon-demonstrators, who were to give refresher courses after her departure, would produce *"les plus grands Biens possible."*[43] To any cities that seemed not to appreciate her sufficiently, she boasted of *"le bien que je fais a l'humanité."*[44] She even impressed Marie Antoinette's mother, the Empress Maria Theresa, who persuaded her to jump the border into the Austrian Netherlands and give a course in Ypres, and who financed a Flemish version of the *Abrégé*. Several of the provinces offered money prizes to Mme du Coudray's best students, but while she approved of such incentives at first, she eventually came to argue that their effect was divisive and that the money would be better spent instead on copies of her textbooks for all students.[45] While in Rennes in the 1770s she became increasingly concerned with *"biens," "petits intérêts," "gratifications,"* etc., pushing the intendant to accept her offer of *"un Bien dont j'étais sûre que vous sentiriez tout le prix."*[46] *"Bien"* in all its significations seems to have been her favorite word, and she used it liberally. On August 24, 1775, for example, having just been given a handsome gift by the city of Nantes and about to move on to Brittany, she wrote ahead to the intendant that she hoped the "Bretons seront aussi reconnaissants des *Bien*faits que vous allez leur procurer que le sont les Normands. Je partirai de cette province *bien* satisfaite d'y avoir apporter un *Bien* qu'ils on sçu si *bien* apprécier"[47] (emphases added). She stressed more than ever that her teaching was hers, her possession, her property, that anyone trained by her and receiving her certificate must work on "*la machine que j'ai inventé*," must instruct according to "*ma méthode*."[48] Every letter linked her humanitarian work with her profit. As she told the intendant of La Rochelle, to perpetuate the *bien de l'humanité*" . . . "it will be necessary that you purchase the model for the phantoms . . . I await a prompt response to the proposition of the model."[49] Meanwhile the letters of recommendation and references which she was accumulating were also valuable currency. They were always sent to the Controller-General of Finance in the capital who supervised the payments for her work and they were, in her words, of a "*prix infini*" for they attested to her greatness and thus guaranteed her remuneration.

She had carefully trained the young surgeon, M. Coutanceau, who had assisted her and was now married to her niece, to demand his deserved royal gratification without flinching. The next generation must see things as clearly as she did. Once when his payment was late, he wrote insisting that he be paid, determined not to allow any dangerous precedent of accepting delay.[50] She coached her niece – an impressive woman in her own right who inherited Mme du Coudray's pension and would go on to found the maternity hospital in Bordeaux – to do the same. It was not begging, it was claiming their due. It was not cooptation, but forcing the regime to respect the terms of its bargain. When Mme Coutanceau felt inadequately recompensed, she wrote to the intendant of Guienne: "I cannot remain silent about my desire to obtain from you a certain sign that you are satisfied with the zealous manner in which I always instruct my students."[51] After the outbreak of the Revolution, Mme Coutanceau went to Paris to address the National Assembly. She argued that her aunt had saved the life of the leader Lafayette, and that the work both women had done for midwifery and for "*la classe des mères si intéressante pour l'état*" could therefore never be separated from politics or from military glory.[52] Their work of conservation of servants for the state was at least as important to the *patrie* as the work of conquest.

I would suggest in closing that even Mme du Coudray's assertive portrait itself, with its frontal optic engagement, makes a kind of claim, or at the very least testifies to her highly developed sense of self-possession, to her theatricality.[53] She proudly exhibits herself, decked out, to the public gaze, plays to the crowd, presents herself to be beheld, works her power on the audience, holds her spectators captive, casts her spell on them, controls them and makes them hers. Mme du Coudray's portrait, with its motto, *Ad Operam*, even shames her passive beholders to attention. "To work," she says. That is her challenge. She will win recognition for *her* labors, she will make France populous and prosperous, and the accomplishment will be known to posterity as hers.

What, then, can be said of Mme du Coudray, with her proprietary zeal on the one hand and her acquiescence in patriarchal views on the other? For all her autonomy and courage, she did endorse the position that women's productions, their reproduction, could rightfully be claimed and consumed by the state. Babies for her were national goods, commodities. It is no accident that her dealings were always with the Controller-General of Finance, that her attitude toward her mission was necessarily mercenary. In her text, Mme du Coudray mentioned only male authors; either she did not know of the few but quite impressive earlier obstetrical texts by women, or she did not wish to seek ancestral help among females. Hers was a mechanical approach to the body, not a sentimental one. It differed hardly at all from the attitude of male anatomists. Women, she said, had to "suffer the approaches of their men." This was hardly a lusty, romantic view of reproductive relations, but rather a resigned acceptance of them as a necessary evil, part of the lot of women, just as mothering was part of their obligation to the state. So Mme du Coudray took on a soldiering mission. She was assertive, willful, a tough-minded administrator as much as a care-giving saint.

What are the true power relations here? Mme du Coudray felt relatively little solidarity with other practitioners, either professionally or as a woman. The petition of 1745 was indeed a banding together, but the perceived menace was other women practicing illegally. In fact, this queen bee midwife passed on little of her own sense of individual worth to other women, neither her students nor her patients, because she saw herself as so unique and superior. She did not insist that other women be demonstrators. She participated fully in the training of veterinarians to do childbirth. She worked, in short, to secure her own status and control, totally within the system of male dominance. Indeed, she sought the endorsement and approval of men in power, without which her own stardom could never have been achieved. Both the state and the medical establishment were rigidly patriarchal. Her role as a traditional midwife would have been terribly restricted, her opportunities hopelessly limited. So she created a role for herself that was entirely new, unprecedented, and therefore limitless. She could write the script, and perform it, and claim it as hers. And she did. But because she accepted no women as equals or as professional heirs (except her niece), she lost an opportunity to provide for other women a truly autonomous sphere. Her niece was to feel this acutely, and she compensated by being much less aggressive on the national level but much more determined to safeguard the turf of midwifery for women, to create a sexual division of labor that would guarantee women a field of practice, a field where men would not be able to compete because they would have no training, no competence.[54] Mme Coutanceau, then, had a much more gendered conception of professional property. But that is another story.[55]

Notes

1   Leon Edell, *Writing Lives: Principia Biographica* (New York: W. W. Norton, 1984), pp.16–19. I discuss these problems in much more depth in a forthcoming special issue of *French Historical Studies* on biography.

2   Carol Ascher, Louise De Salvo, and Sara Ruddick (eds), *Between Women: Biographers, Novelists, Critics, Teachers and Artists Write about their Work on Women* (Boston, MA: Beacon Press, 1984), "Introduction."

3   Carolyn G. Heilbrun, *Writing a Woman's Life* (New York: W. W. Norton, 1988), p. 81.

4   Ibid., p. 23.

5   Florence Nightingale was notorious for refusing to support the feminist cause. See Mary Poovey, *Uneven Developments: The Ideological Work of Gender* (Chicago: University of Chicago Press, 1988); and Lois A. Monteiro, "On separate roads: Florence Nightingale and Elizabeth Blackwell," *Signs* 9 (Spring 1984): 520–33.

6   Michel Foucault, *The History of Sexuality*, Vol. I, *An Introduction*, trans. Robert Hurley (New York: Pantheon Books, 1978); Frances M. Feinerman, "Population and prosperity" (PhD dissertation, University of Illinois, Chicago Circle: 1981); Camille Bloch, *L'Assistance et l'état en France à la veille de la Révolution* (Paris: Alphonse Picard et fils, 1908); Dorinda Outram,

The Body and the French Révolution. Sex, Class and Political Culture (New Haven, CT and London: Yale University Press, 1989), esp. pp. 25–68; Lynn Hunt, *Eroticism and the Body Politic* (Baltimore; MD: Johns Hopkins University Press, 1991). I would also like to acknowledge the helpful comments made by Monica Green on an earlier version of this chapter.

7   See William Coleman, "Health and hygiene in the *Encyclopédie*: A medical doctrine for the bourgeoisie," *Journal of the History of Medicine* 29 (1974): 339–421; Ludmilla Jordanova, "Guarding the body politic: Volney's *Catéchisme* of 1793," in Francis Barker (ed.), *1789: Reading, Writing and Revolution* (Colchester, Essex: University of Essex Press, 1982), pp. 12–22.

8   Jean-Pierre Goubert (ed.), *La Médicalisation de la société française 1770–1830* (Waterloo Ont.: Historical Reflections Press, 1982).

9   Theodore Besterman (ed.), *Voltaire's Correspondence: Complete Works of Voltaire* (Geneva and Oxford: Voltaire Foundation, 1968–77), letters D7420 and D7516.

10 Olwen Hufton, *The Poor of Eighteenth-Century France* (Oxford: Oxford University Press, 1974).

11 Georges Meynier, *Un cours provinciale d'accouchements au 18e siècle (Généralité de Soisson)* (Paris: 1899), pp. 14–15.

12 Bloch, *L'Assistance*, p. 246.

13 Augier DuFot, *Catéchisme sur l'art des accouchements pour les sages-femmes de la campagne* (Soisson: 1775), "Discours preliminaire," p. xv.

14 Jocelyne Leymarie-Couturier, *Histoire de la fondation de l'Ecole de sages-femmes de Bordeaux* (Bordeaux: thèse, 18 mars 1987), 57.

15 *Almanac vétérinaire* (Paris: an. VII; 3rd edn.), pp. 32–3.

16 Le Boursier du Coudray, Marguerite Angélique, *Abrégé de l'art des accouchements* (Paris: 1759).

17 Olwen Hufton, "Women and the family economy in 18th-century France," *French Historical Studies* 9, 1 (Spring 1975): 1–22.

18 Mme du Coudray made such comments during her teaching in Le Mans, Angers, and Tours.

19 LeNain, *Mémoire sur les cours publics d'accouchements faits à Moulins par Mme du Coudray* (s.l.n.d.).

20 Intendants and subdelegates and reporters to the various provincial *Affiches* and *Gazettes* commented constantly on Mme du Coudray's power and skill, and the devotion of her students.

21 Archives Departementales (henceforth AD) d'Ille-et-Vilaine, C1326, fol. 6.

22 See, for example, Jean Le Bas, *Précis de doctrine sur l'art d'accoucher* (Paris: 1779), pp. x–xiii.

23 For an interesting discussion of this question in British obstetrics, see L. J. Jordanova, "Gender, generation and science: William Hunter's obstetrical atlas," in W. F. Bynum and Roy Porter (eds), *William Hunter and the Eighteenth-Century Medical World* (Cambridge, UK: Cambridge University Press, 1985), pp. 385–412.

24 See Rosalind Pollack Petchesky, "Fetal images: the power of visual culture in the politics of reproduction," *Feminist Studies* 13, 2 (Summer 1987): 263–92.

25 Ecoles de Médecine – Commentaires de la Faculté, vol. XX, 953–74. The petition is in Archives Nationales, Minutier Central (henceforth AN, MC) XV 640 (29 juin) 1745.

26 AN, MC – depouillement 1751. These are notarial documents. I have examined about fifty apprenticeship contracts made during that year with midwives.

27 AD d'Indre-et-Loire, C355.

28 Both are reprinted in Mme du Coudray's *Abrégé*.

29 AD de la Gironde, C3302.

30 AD du Cher, C319, fol. 58.

31 This phrase runs throughout the correspondence.

32 Such words were used by doctors, surgeons, royal ministers, intendants, town syndics, parish priests, and students. See a compilation of reactions to du Coudray's teaching in *Lettre d'un citoyen, amateur du bien public . . .* (Paris: 1777).

33 AD des Vosges, 1C43, fol. 63.

34 Diderot and d'Alembert, *Encyclopédie*, Vol.II, pp. 243–4.

35 Ibid., Vol. VIII, p. 818.

36 Ibid., p. 348.

37   This term recurs throughout the correspondence.

38   AD d'Indre-et-Loire C355.

39   AD de la Gironde (Angoulème letters), C3302, fol. 6.

40   Archives Nationales (henceforth AN) O^{1}111, fol. 226.

41   For example, Mme du Coudray traveled to Metz where a different kind of mannequin was being displayed and sold.

42   On color print process, see Gautier de Montdorge, *L'Art d'imprimer les tableaux traité d'après les écrits, les opérations et les instructions verbales de J. C. LeBlon* (Paris: 1756).

43   AD du Doubs, 1C599.

44   The city of Amiens needed to be so reminded, as did Bourges on several occasions.

45   AD de la Seine Maritime, C95, fol. 45. For a full discussion of how this textbook was deployed, see my "Books and the birthing business: the midwife manuals of Mme du Coudray," in Dena Goodman and Elizabeth Goldsmith, eds, *Going Public: Women and Publishing in Early Modern France*, forthcoming.

46   AD d'Ille et Vilaine, C1326, fol. 19.

47   Ibid., fol. 21

48   AD d'Ille et Vilaine, C1328, fol. 83.

49   AD de la Charente-Maritime, DC 10, fol. 28.

50   AD d'Ille et Vilaine, C1326.

51   AD de la Gironde, C3304, fol. 75.

52   AN, F^{16} 936.

53   An interesting treatment of portraiture during this period can be found in Michael Fried, *Absorption and Theatricality: Painting and Beholder in the Age of Diderot* (Berkeley, CA: University of California Press, 1980), pp. 109–15.

54   For a fine analysis of midwifery in historical perspective and of the sexual division of labor in health care see Monica Green, "Women's medical practice and, health care in medieval Europe," *Signs* 14, 2 (1989): 434–73.

55   For an overview of Mme du Coudray's travels, see my "Midwife to a Nation: Mme du Coudray serves France," in Hilary Marland, ed., *The Art of Midwifery: Early Modern Midwives in Europe* (London, Routledge, 1993), pp. 131–51. A fuller discussion of all these matters and of Mme du Coudray's remarkable niece, will be found in the biography I am presently completing.

23
Property in office under the
ancien régime
The case of the stockbrokers

David D. Bien

Almost by definition the stockbrokers (*agents de change*) were in one of the most modern of *ancien régime* occupations. But one could hardly have guessed it. Because they owned venal offices and privilege, the agents de change were part of the ubiquitous order that was widely called feudal before it was destroyed. The story of the stockbrokers illustrates features of that old order, its connection to a state that continued to find it useful until 1789, and some surprisingly modern practices and ideas concerning property that were intrinsic to pre-revolutionary "feudalism." After a review of the status of venal officeholding in the 1770s and 1780s, the agents de change will be worth a close look.

It appears that the regime of privilege, venal offices, and corps before the Revolution was distinctively French, the byproduct of a relatively advanced and developed economy. Like all states, that of France was chronically short of funds in the early modern period. Unlike the absolutisms of Eastern Europe, however, and like England, the French state could engage in credit operations – it had subjects whose wealth it could borrow. But because absolutist and lacking a national representative body that could levy taxes and guarantee loans, French kings by themselves, as individuals, had a poor credit rating. Their financial problem was circular: they repudiated debts and were often bankrupt, lenders would then advance new funds only at high rates of interest, and in turn those high rates, consuming a larger and larger share of revenues, contributed heavily to the coming of the next bankruptcy. When three-fifths of government expenditure went on debt service in one form or another, the high interest rate mattered. Still, the situation might have been worse. Over several centuries successive governments discovered ways to subsist by "expedients" that hardened into a system. French kings found intermediaries whose credit rating with the public was higher than their own. When those intermediaries (individuals and corps) did some of the borrowing for the king, the state's interest rate was lower and bankruptcies less frequent. In the end nothing actually solved the problem, which was structural, and the effect of borrowing through intermediaries reinforced localism and privilege. But the regime, after all, did survive until 1789, which it might not have done without a curious system of indirect borrowing.

That system included different kinds of bodies with varying privileges – clergy, provincial estates, municipalities, guilds – but venal offices grouped into corps were its largest single part. A brief description of how that part of the system worked may provide the background for understanding the stockbrokers' story.[1] The sale of offices, known since the sixteenth century, proceeded by sophisticated practices that ministers developed in the long search for credit. Offices, distinctive because a property kings could actually create, found purchasers who were interested variously in an office's functions (real or nominal), or its revenues (large or small), or the privileges it gave (tax exemptions, sometimes ennoblement, sometimes nothing when the revenues were large). The calculation of finance ministers in interaction with the market of buyers fixed the office's price at a level depending also on economic circumstances, war, and so on. To sell offices on the broad scale that governments had in mind, however, it was essential that acquirers be able to borrow some or all of the price. To this end it was a great help that the law defined an office as if it were land, that is, an immovable property (*immeuble*). Its owner could sell or bequeath it, and also borrow against it by loans that were, in effect, perpetual mortgages. The government did what it could to help. In receipts acknowledging payment for the office, the *trésorier des parties casuelles* specified the names of lenders, the exact amounts lent, and the nature of the privileged lien each creditor held on the proceeds of the office should it be sold. With this assurance – copies of the receipts were permanently recorded in the government's registers – lenders were satisfied to advance money against a somewhat peculiar collateral, that is, offices whose commercial value depended in part on what privileges were considered to be worth. The result of these practices in the end was the existence of more and more offices that entered into the royal debt – everyone understood that offices could be eliminated only if their owners were reimbursed. And the debt represented by offices drew on a wider network of lenders than is obvious at first glance: by selling offices, the king in effect borrowed directly from his officers and indirectly from many others who lent their funds to the officers.

Once sold, except for turnover and other fees, offices did not automatically supply fresh resources. But there were ways to make their owners add substantially to their capital investments at intervals. The favored technique was called *augmentations de gages*. *Gages* were annual payments assigned to many offices as a kind of interest on the capital. To augment the gages was not to express the king's generosity by raising the rate he was paying, but rather to demand that the holder place in his office additional funds on which the new gages would be the interest. For offices without gages the same effect was achieved by raising the level of the fees that the officer could collect from clients, the enhanced income then constituting the interest on the new capital advance. Demands for fresh capital, however, came usually in times of war or economic troubles, that is, exactly when some of the officers were in financial distress themselves and unable to find immediately the money the government required. The result was a growing tendency for the government to deal with whole corps rather than with their individual members. The state needed the money urgently, and it lacked the administrative capacity to track down recalcitrants and to listen to all the excuses, good or bad, that individuals advanced for not paying right away. It was better to negotiate with (and sometimes threaten) the spokesman of the corps for a lump sum payment, and then to leave the details of its collection to the members themselves. Within the corps, governance was by officials chosen in general assemblies by majority vote, and the corps had both incentive and the means to impose discipline on dissident colleagues better than the state could have done it. In the end this collective responsibility probably reinforced corporatism and privilege, but there is no doubt that it brought in money to the government faster.

The final step in building the system of credit on venal offices came when corps began to substitute collective loans for those of the individual members. In these cases the corps itself took the new gages or the pooled proceeds of increased fees, and instead of dividing them among the membership, assigned the money to pay the interest on bonds that it sold to the public. The capital from this operation went to the king, and the corps, counting on the king's more or less good promise of new gages or higher fees, undertook the obligation to pay the interest to its creditors. In these arrangements there was something for everyone. The king received the money he sought in full and promptly. The corps used a collective credit to supplement the personal credit of various members who were in financial difficulty during wars. The risks from establishing the collective debt were mitigated for the members by the introduction of limited liability: the member on entering the corps signed an agreement to share equally with all his colleagues in taking responsibility for the corporate debt, but only up to the value of his office and any gages still owing to him. His other, personal property was not subject to seizure to pay the corporate debt, and on his leaving office all further obligation was transferred to his successor. The purchasers of the *rentes* that the corps sold also found several advantages. The corps provided them a solid collateral for their capital in the pooled value of all its members' offices. And within the corps investors saw men of some wealth who had a stake in maintaining their own investments in office, and who were collectively responsible for meeting the interest payments on the corps' borrowing. Although financial problems might arise (when the king did not pay the corps, or paid too little, or paid very late), they were problems for the corps but not its creditors. In such situations the officers met in assembly and voted to assess the membership the sums needed to make up what was owing to the corps' creditors. The mechanisms of self-governance and collective responsibility in corps worked well to supply money for the king and security for outside investors who would have been reluctant to entrust their funds to the king directly.

The credit of the officers, individually and collectively, was usually good and, as already noted, through these men and bodies the king could borrow at low rates. How large was the debt represented by offices, and what did it actually cost? Several bureaux did research on the subject in the early 1770s and an administrator analyzed the evidence in 1779 for Necker (and for us, since his *mémoire* survives).[2] The administrator was particularly well placed to understand the situation. Francis-Joseph Harvouin was an insider in the world of finance. To prepare his report he had at hand materials from two large surveys made in 1771 to learn the likely yield of a new tax on offices. The *centième denier* called for a 1 percent annual levy and a $4^3/5$ percent turnover fee based on the capital value of an office. The officer who wanted to make the payment and to protect his property had now to declare its worth. Most elected to do so, and a mass of evaluations arrived at the Bureau des Parties casuelles where clerks set to work on them. They assembled the documents, and drew up lists of offices and the capital they represented for each *généralité*. Next the lists were sent on to the Bureau des Etats du Roy for systematic comparison with others, showing how much in gages was being paid. Finally, Harvouin himself examined registers of the parties casuelles, for the years 1773 through 1776, to find what portion of those gages the officers paid back to the king in the form of taxes and fees. At the end there emerged figures for overall capital investment and net gages.

The report set out a remarkable story. Harvouin began by calculating the theoretical rate of interest on the largest group of offices, nearly 50,000 of them, with a stated worth of 481 million *livres*. The annual state payment in gages and augmentations de gages for the use of that capital, listed at 9.7 million *livres*, was thus about 2 percent of the capital. That sum, however, was an exaggeration. It could be reduced to 8.6 million right off by the royal tax on incomes (the two *vingtièmes* with the 20 percent surcharge on the first). Then came other deductions, for the *centième denier* of course but as well for the entry and turnover fees that varied by types of office ("*casuels*" and "*à survivance*" or "*héréditaire*"). After subtracting again, Harvouin could show that the state's real outlay for those offices should not have exceeded 3.7 million each year, or 3/4 of 1 percent on the capital. The actual payment was not quite that low – some officers were not paying the centième denier, and the mutation fees fell below their estimated yield during the Maupeou-Terray years when offices did not change hands as often as expected. Even so, when adjusted for that, and when a few previously excluded offices were added in, the rate rose only a little. The literal "bottom line" of the financial analysis was that the king paid only a shade over 1 percent on the capital of 600.7 million *livres*, invested in 51,009 offices.

Harvouin did, however, leave something out of the equation. A believer in the system, he wanted to present it in a favorable light to his superior, and he was also a financial administrator working in the terms and framework of royal budgeting. One or both of the two facts may explain why he neglected to discuss the *droits* or fees that the public paid to many of the officers directly. That revenue was one the officers counted on to supplement their gages, or in some cases even to replace them altogether. But the fees, to the officers an addition to income and to the public a kind of hidden taxation, held little interest for the king and his agents. Unlike gages, which were paid from, and visibly lessened, the regular tax revenues, the fees reached the officers almost unnoticed by the state, in what could seem private transactions. Only theoretically were they a royal income – capitalized and borrowed against, alienated probably for ever, they did not ordinarily appear on the king's books or enter into the routine calculations of his budget. The range was wide, but on average the fees would seem to have raised the income from office to something between 2 percent and 3 percent of the capital. Offices created more recently, or those in finance receiving a percentage (*taxations*) of assured revenues, did better than the others. Still, the return was quite low in most cases. And what Harvouin saw, and appreciated, was a capital debt of 600 million that cost the king only 1 percent from his own regular revenues.

The point, then, is that the debt represented by offices was indispensable, large, and lasting. Together with the rest of the debt resting on privilege, it was perhaps one-third of the total royal debt. And even though hostility to privilege was rising in the late eighteenth century, venality of office retained its advocates. Harvouin was of course one of them. The financier's defense of the structure is not surprising, since he had a personal stake in its benefits. Through offices Harvouin had found both profits and standing. His place of *receveur-général* (receiver of direct taxes) was lucrative, at least for a time, and the one he acquired in the Grande Chancellerie in 1749 had made him a nobleman after twenty years' service, or non-service because the office required no work at all. What he stressed when writing to Necker in 1779, however, was not that, but the practical advantage of venality for the state. Offices, Harvouin explained, provided the least "onerous" of public loans. Unlike the rentes sold by the king to the public directly, rentes whose rates were necessarily set at levels advantageous to the *rentiers* and, once sold, produced no further revenue, offices cost little in interest and were "resources . . . offering endlessly new yields that serve to nourish the state every day."[3] Thus, it was unthinkable to reimburse existing offices, and the old structure should not be touched.

But Harvouin was no mere defender of the past. With an eye on the present he went on to describe the fresh opportunities that were available. The thing was to know how to use the inherited system correctly, treating venal officers with care as he believed Louis XIII and Louis XIV had done, and never humiliating them by periodic suppressions of offices and revocations of privileges in the manner of Louis XV. In fact, only good could come from preserving "in the nation the taste for acquiring [offices]." Imagine, the financier wrote, that the government needed 100 million *livres* and chose to raise the sum not through rentes, whose annual cost Harvouin calculated at something over 7 percent, but by selling new offices. For the fresh capital the state would have to pay new gages running to 4 percent or 5 percent each year, but the net outlay in cash was less than it seemed: 2 of the possibly 5 million would be returned to the king each year in taxes and fees. Thus, if the interest on capital obtained by creating new offices cost more than the government was currently paying on the old ones, 3 percent overall instead of 1 percent, the price was still far below that for rentes.[4] For Harvouin the old ways were best, and his prescription for the ailments of state finance was not only to conserve the old order, but to extend it.

Who was listening? Few in government would have admitted it if they were, for the official rhetoric was opposed to Harvouin's views. The language of ministers and formal documents designed for public consumption, especially the preambles to *édits*, was hostile to privilege. Calonne said as much to the Assembly of Notables, and his rival, Necker, put the idea into his widely distributed writings. Ministers who could agree on little else projected a common image of the reformist state that would contain private and selfish interests in the interest of society as a whole. Such fine sentiments, however, did not and probably could not dictate all practice, for the inexorable pressures of budgets and deficits would not permit it. A harsher financial reality meant that almost no possible resource could be overlooked. And in the archives, assembled not for historians but for use by financial administrators, there were many examples of the resources that lay in offices and privileges. There, in the unprinted record, insiders could see beyond the well-known words of admired reformers, the Sullys and Colberts, and realize that no matter what they said, the ablest of past ministers were distinguished less by their having rejected the system than by their greater care and skill in applying it. No doubt, the late eighteenth-century administrators were sincere in wanting to control and diminish privilege. But whatever their preferences, they were hardheaded men responsible above all for directing the state. They would do what they had to.

In the 1780s signs appear that the government was prepared to follow Harvouin's suggestion. Calonne's clerks scoured the archives for old *édits* creating offices that had never been sold. Such édits could still be useful. Registered in Parlement long before, they raised in the present no new questions calling for discussion and publicity. From a creation in the chancellerie at Perpignan in 1715, eleven unfilled offices were "found" and marketed in 1785 and 1787. With a similar office discovered at Pau, the twelve offices of *secrétaire du roi* brought in 960,000 *livres*. The place of *chevalier d'honneur*, unsold since its creation in 1702 in the Bureau des Finances at Rouen, yielded 20,000 *livres* in 1785, and the next year a purchaser paid 30,000 *livres* to acquire the office of *greffier en chef* that had lain idle in the Chambre des Comptes de Lorraine for sixty-four years.[5] The sale of scattered older offices, however, although interesting or revealing a tendency and state of mind, was relatively small change for the government, certainly nothing on the scale needed to resolve the difficulties of the budget. To find funds in larger amounts, the trick was to locate new sources of revenue. The old hands in the *contrôle général* had to know where economic activities of various kinds were expanding and susceptible to being tapped by the government. Generally the administrators' understanding of the economy was sophisticated and the use of the knowledge imaginative. Having identified a new revenue or an older one that was growing, the government could decide not to add it to annual income but instead to capitalize and to borrow against it immediately. Assigned to officers as the interest on a fresh capital advance, the new source of income then provided an instant resource worth twenty times its annual amount if the interest was at 5 percent or thirty-three times the revenue if we use Harvouin's formula (3 percent) for the net annual cost of new offices. The evidence is fairly good for various offices; among them, the agents de change in Paris. The stockbrokers will illustrate several of the themes described so far.

Agents de change

Efforts by the government to use the agents de change had not been a great success in the past. This must have been disappointing, because the financial possibilities inherent in brokerage would seem to have been large. The brokers' functions should have generated an income to support an important credit structure. With the office purchasers acquired the exclusive right to handle wholesale transactions in beverages and cloth goods, and to the negotiation of all paper and notes, private and commercial as well as those issued by and for the state. Successive statutes and regulations (1638, 1706, 1714) formed the officers into corps having monthly meetings, electing sindics and other officials, administering a common fund, and applying to members a corporate discipline of the kind that the state approved and could use.[6] But unfortunately the offices possessed other features that had limited their fees and, thus, their use by the state, keeping the price at a fairly low level and preventing collective financial action by the owners. First, the functions that the édits reserved to these officers were too broad and diffuse for the monopoly over their exercise to be guaranteed. Although at intervals the government tried to police the market and to protect the agents' exclusive rights, the frequency with which it had to restate those rights and to fine interlopers suggests the ineffectiveness of the effort. In 1714, responding to the agents' most recent complaint about encroachments that reduced their emoluments to "very little," the administration understood and cut its capital demand for new gages by one-half.[7] The second problem had to do with the workings of the corporation itself. Its regulations provided for establishing a fund from a fixed share (25 percent) of the members' commissions and fees. There, in theory, was a regular corporate revenue that might pay the interest on collective borrowing for the king, but in fact the fund never existed. Because the clients of the agents de change were then usually merchants and business-men and, as such, entitled to absolute secrecy in their dealings, the agents' books which might have revealed those dealings were closed. It followed that no one could actually verify how much each officer owed to the common fund, and none paid. Hence the corporation had no *"bourse commune"* and could sustain no collective debt.[8] For that reason, and in the absence of effective guarantees for rights and revenues, the offices went at a fairly modest price when sold at all.

The most serious attempt to market the offices came during the War of the Spanish Succession. Adding gages at 5 percent and new privileges, the government then created 116 for quick sale. Two *traitants*, who took the offices in repayment of their own financial advances to the Crown, did their best to dispose of them, but not a single purchaser was willing to pay 10,000 *livres* for any of ninety-six established in the provinces. It was better in Paris where there was more business, but even there the twenty offices designed to sell at 60,000 *livres* had to be subdivided into first forty, and then sixty, to lower the price for each. In 1714, with no more than thirty-seven Parisian offices actually occupied, the total yield to the government had been a little under 750,000, a sum the government reimbursed to the holders in 2 percent securities in 1723. When no buyers appeared that year to take new offices, created this time without attribution of gages or personal privileges but purchasable in depreciated paper, the government simply gave up. It designated persons to exercise the functions on commis-sion, with no capital advance required, and contented itself with the fees paid at each entry into the positions that had ceased to be offices at all.[9]

That was still the situation sixty years later. Nevertheless, an evolution was under way that would at last give the places a greater value. The changes were of varying kinds, one being institutional and another economic. The state took steps to define and to narrow what its agents de change were to do: it concentrated their activities more exclusively on the negotiation of public securities, and also strengthened the effort to reserve that activity to these officials alone. Already in 1705 and 1713 the government, seeking to sell the offices, insisted that its *fermiers-traitants* should go through the agents de change when negotiating their semi-public notes. Then, with the creation of the Bourse in 1720, an institutional mechanism appeared for applying at least some discipline to the larger financial community. Rules for the stock exchange, set down in 1724 and episodically renewed, with small modifications, until the 1780s, made it mandatory that all trading in paper issued by or for the government take place there. Although anyone was free to enter the Bourse to deal in private paper and mer-chandise, only the agents de change had the right to handle the exchange of public securities and notes. Each transaction involving public paper required the intervention of two agents (one each for the buyer and seller) who split a commission of one-quarter of 1 percent on the value exchanged. By the 1770s the agents de change had a special location set aside for them at the Bourse, and they were at last distinguished from the ubiquitous "*courtiers*" or wholesale merchants who crowded into the other sections. New rules governed also the agents' recruitment and the procedure for arranging transactions.[10] The greater specialization and control, incomplete though the control always was, nonetheless gave the promise of reserving an economic sphere to the agents de change at the very time when that sphere was expanding. With the development of business, a certain democratization of investment, and the government's chronic need for short-term credit, the trade in government paper became active. And reinforcing the long-term trend was the sharp rise in speculation at the end of the *ancien régime*. The frenzied trade in proliferating stocks of state-chartered companies and in government paper of all kinds was carried on in an atmosphere evoking the era of John Law or New York in the 1920s. Securities and paper turned over rapidly as many bought "on the margin," traded in "futures," and generally gambled on the rise or fall in short-term prices.[11] Some gained, some lost, but the consistent winners were of course the stock-brokers. It was a good time to be an agent de change.

The opportunity for the state was clear, and Calonne seized it in 1786. Unable then to float public loans, he approached the companies involved in finance, the agents de change, first. After a discussion that must have been rather one-sided – the agents de change said later it involved the outright threat to fire and replace them – the decision was made to re-establish the sixty unsold offices created in 1723. A royal declaration (March 19, 1786) implemented the decision.[12] As usual, the government rooted the announced purpose for selling the offices in public utility: the investment would give the agents de change "a more solid consideration" and reassure the public at a time when the volume of trading was already large and becoming larger. Unstated but more relevant for the state was the office's high price, now set at 100,000 livres, not to mention fees of about 6,000 that each new officer would henceforth pay at entry. For his capital the purchaser was to receive gages at 4 percent (raised to $4^1/_2$ percent in September when Calonne made several small concessions to speed delivery of the cash).[13] The declaration renewed generally all privileges and emoluments of the office, and specifically restated the exclusive right to negotiate royal and public obligations.

The operation was a success. Thirty-three of the fifty agents de change who had been exercising the functions on commission found the money and paid up, and registers for the revenus casuels show that all the rest of the offices were sold quickly, in 1786 and 1787. In 1786, then, one more corps of venal officers came into existence, and in the process the state obtained 6 million badly needed *livres*. And the price it paid was even better than Harvouin predicted for newly created offices – after deducting fees and taxes, the effective interest was only 2.2 percent.[14]

But the story was not over. Two years later it was Loménie de Brienne's turn to play a role. In a maneuver worthy of Richelieu or Mazarin, he managed to end the payment of interest altogether. What he knew was that the price the government had received, although high, was nonetheless a compromise, and that the offices were proving to be lucrative. Purchased at 100,000 *livres*, they were already worth 180,000 to 190,000 on the open market.[15] When Brienne went back to the corps in the late spring of 1788, he had leverage in the form of an offer from an old-style traitant. Speaking for a group of financiers, Luciani proposed establishing more officers to enjoy the expanding revenues. His plan was for the government to suppress and to reimburse the 60 existing offices, and to re-create them plus another 60 to give 120 at the same price of 100,000 livres each. The effect of doubling the number of offices would have been to raise the capital investment from 6 million to 12 million, and the financiers offered then to handle the new sale themselves, advancing immediately 1 million *livres* toward the additional 6 that the scheme yielded. The government also considered two scaled-down proposals. Each assumed an end to payments of gages (270,000 *livres* annually) and the creation of forty additional offices. In the one case, the new offices sold at the current official price of 100,000 *livres* would have brought in 4 million in fresh capital. The other plan left the total capital where it was, at 6 million, and simply divided that sum among 100 offices rather than 60. The reduction in the investment by the existing officers would supposedly compensate them for the loss of their gages. In the end Brienne, who was negotiating simultaneously with the agents de change, bypassed Luciani and his colleagues to make his deal with the corps directly. The agents de change met and, told to choose between renouncing the gages agreed on in 1786 or accepting the creation of new offices which would share in their other revenues, they decided to give up their gages.[16] From mid-1788, then, the 6 million *livres* secured from them in 1786 cost the government nothing in interest, and its revenus casuels continued to profit from the higher entry fees and capitation tax that the proprietors of the now expensive venal offices paid.

Could the government have had more in 1788? Might Brienne have raised new capital through the offices in that year? Possibly so, but the hour was late, events moving swiftly toward the larger bankruptcy that smaller operations could no longer put off. Anyway, the government obtained something in the spring, a trophy in the form of diminished annual payments that, showing the government's intent to cut expenses, might help to restore public confidence and the state's credit. And beyond that, there would have been a risk in selling more of these particular offices at the time. Everyone knew that the stockbrokers' profits depended heavily on the current craze for speculation, and to sell new offices of that type in 1788 was certain to implicate the government further in the supposedly secret and sinister dealings so passionately condemned by moralists and the popular imagination. Brienne, therefore, settled for what seemed possible and reasonable.

The story has an epilogue that is interesting too, for in the Revolution it was possible to state various unspecified but important ideas that underlay the earlier transactions and negotiations. In 1790 the agents de change, having recently heard much talk about the sacred rights of property, remembered the one they had lost. Together they decided on an effort to recover the gages they relinquished in 1788. Their petition to the National Assembly told how they were twice victimized, first by the "absolute will" of Calonne when he disguised as a creation of offices what they said was really a forced loan, and again by the "minister-despot" Brienne who, after promising at first to protect them, took away the legitimate interest on that loan. Their renunciation of the gages, the agents de change now insisted, was not given freely, and simple equity required that the present revolutionary government pay the back interest on money its *ancien régime* predecessor borrowed. How unjust, they said, to have mistreated men who had made such efforts to aid the king in difficult times!

An outraged administrator, however, took a quite different view of the matter. From

Gérard-Maurice Turpin, who was working for the Treasury in 1790, came a heated response.[17] Turpin was one of those bureaucrats whose career and ideas linked the old regime and the new. Although he once held a venal office himself, as *contrôleur-général des restes* in the Chambre des Comptes with commission to act also in the Royal Council, he was no admirer of privilege and venality. In the office his job had been to oversee repayment of sums found owing by tax collectors after verification of their accounts, a task that evidently gave him a strong feel for pure administration and royal power. He was not like Harvouin, the financier so comfortable with the ways of the *ancien régime* and, as receveur-général, the very type of venal office-holder whom Turpin investigated regularly for the king. Turpin, by contrast, adjusted easily to the new principles of the Revolution, and served in the Treasury without a break until 1806.[18] Answering the agents de change in 1790, he denounced their morals and logic in a lengthy and scathing *mémoire*. In it he regretted the financial necessity that had ever led the king to be involved in selling privilege to such persons, or indeed to anyone:

> No one is ignorant of the fact that charges, offices, guild memberships, privileges owe their origin and existence to the needs of the state alone. To the sovereign it would have been far more satisfying to have justice administered to his people free of charge; to have imposed no obstacles to the liberty of their commerce, industry, and talents, to the exercise of their professions, to progress in the arts and trades.

As for the agents de change in particular, Turpin continued, how absurd for them to demand arrears of gages when they should never have had gages in the first place. The rapid rise in the market price of their offices was abundant proof that it was they who had taken advantage of the king. Far from having come to his aid, they had in fact blackmailed him. As extortioners they deserved nothing now or then.

Underneath a good deal of fairly humorless rhetoric about greed (which he opposed), Turpin went on to set out the legal basis for royal action in such affairs. The king's power was complete. In 1786 the king owed no interest because he did not borrow money at all. Instead, he sold a right – the exclusive privilege of acting as broker in certain transactions – that was always his to dispose of whenever he wished. The king had been absolutely free to do anything, free to have no agents de change, or to establish the functions and have them exercised by non-officers who were replaceable at will, or to create and sell offices – with or without gages. Before 1786 the agents de change owned nothing, had no vested rights in their positions, and could have been fired at a moment's notice. In 1786, then, rather than lending the king money, they purchased a property which was the office and the monopoly of a function that went with it. Using the standard analogy for such cases, Turpin said that property in office was the same as a house, and, he asked rhetorically, could one imagine purchasing a house, taking possession of it, living in it, and then expecting to receive perpetual interest on the capital one had paid to acquire it? The obvious answer was, no – with the original transfer of the property the transaction was complete. Although the king sometimes decided to give gages to judicial officers when their emoluments were negligible, he did not have to do so, and he never paid gages to the other *officiers ministériels*. The agents de change had made no loan, had no automatic right to receive interest, and, except that they were entitled to reimbursement if the king decided to suppress their offices, had no legal rights against the royal will.

Turpin's assertion was bold and clear, but perhaps more theoretical than practical. Conveniently suited to a state trying to escape mountainous debt in 1790, it did not describe well the realities of 1786. For that the agents de change are the better source.[19] Their advance to the king was of course a loan, they wrote, and it did entitle them to interest. The government knew that was true at the time, and also knew why. The king's own law, the declaration establishing the offices, had stated in the usual way that as property the offices were *immeubles*, and it specifically invited the purchasers to borrow the capital, establishing privileged liens and mortgages on the new property as needed. The Act provided that creditors who lent some or all of the price to purchasers should receive their money first when the office was sold or reimbursed, and that those creditors could get a court order and even force the sale of the office if their interest was unpaid. On the strength of those guarantees the agents de change borrowed the money to buy the offices, as their receipts from the state would show. The office was now the surety for dowries and the other funds the officer had tapped when himself borrowing money to purchase it. Everyone knew the officers counted on the gages at $4^1/_2$ percent to pay most of the interest on their own borrowing at 5 percent. And from the negotiations the government was well aware that the gages were an integral part of the deal, that without them the purchasers would not have taken the offices or would not have paid so much for them. All parties understood that the credit arrangements were essential and interlocking. Everything depended on mutual respect for what the agents de change called the "formal contract" that sealed the purchase and assured the safety of their money. Because they in turn had creditors, the agents de change were properly the creditors of the king. No doubt the royal will was strong, but when the king made a contract, he in fact had no right to change or to violate it.

Now, what is interesting, beyond the opposing ideas themselves, is how little of all this became public before 1789. It appears that the only item in print at the time was the corps' "voluntary" decision to renounce its gages in 1788. Passions ran high, but before the Revolution both sides had a stake in quiet compromise and preserving the system. No battles in court, no pamphlets. And, in spite of what was said later, each party had obtained something. The government got capital, in the end interest-free because the mania for speculation generated such large revenues for the offices. The agents de change gained not only the continuation of their monopoly over certain lucrative fees, but a new security in operating it – to end it the government after 1786 would have had to find 6 million *livres* to reimburse their offices, which of course was unlikely. Clearly there was tension between the officers and the administration, but before 1789 it remained beneath the surface. Whatever Turpin thought then, he did not say it publicly. The two parties coexisted under the *ancien régime* within a system whose constraints were effective because all the participants required the confidence and credit of a wider public. The deal they struck and subsequent changes in it had to be made on terms and in a style that reassured others. Neither side could afford then to act on legalisms or the logic of a theory.

What, then, does the example of the stockbrokers illustrate about the system of borrowing through offices? Not everything, of course. The brokers had not yet contracted collective loans.[20] But the other features were there: the government's manufacturing of a kind of artificial immovable property (with the privilege intrinsic to it); loans secured on that property, like mortgages; the new officers invoking the wide network of lenders on whom they and the state depended; the ministers' use of the self-governing corps as negotiating partner in their search for inexpensive credit. A sense of the crucial role of credit ran through everything, and the stockbrokers' arguments reveal the general, if tacit, understandings that best explain a whole system's survival. The need not to alarm lenders and investors locked the state into the regime of corps and privileges, a regime the state itself had created and continued to depend on. Showing that continuing dependence is one of the most interesting aspects of this story. Even in 1786, only three years away from the Revolution, the government sold new offices, and in 1788, on its very eve, was threatening to do so again. Ideas of reform notwithstanding, the old order operated actively to the end, as no doubt it had to.

In a wide-ranging volume on the history of property, how to conclude this chapter? Specialists in British or other histories may discover here a distinctively French property, and will draw their own conclusions from the contrast it suggests with the property they know better. My own speculation at the finish, not really a conclusion, is confined to French history and involves wondering what was the legacy of venal office-holding. What, if any, meaning did it have for later development? The most striking fact in venal office-holding is, I suppose, the modernity of a regime that historians used to call feudal.[21] Within the old order, practices of impersonal investment developed strongly, and the results were impressive. Investments of all kinds in and through offices may have reached 800 million *livres*. The total state debt resting on privileges in one form or another (including those of the clergy, provincial estates, and guilds) ran well over 1 billion *livres*: that is, a sum more than twice as large as annual state revenues. In August 1789, however, the *ancien régime* disappeared, destroyed almost overnight, and with it went not only privilege but the places for large investments. The fate of the money is probably not important. Generally investors were repaid: the unlucky ones held the *assignats* they received too long, until their value evaporated in the inflation through the mid-1790s; others used assignats to purchase true immeubles, that is, land (the *biens nationaux*). In neither case did the released capital seem to transform anything. The more significant inheritance from the *ancien régime* lay elsewhere, very likely in the habits of impersonal investment that it had spread so widely. Simple investment was of course nothing new, but the number of investors expanded exponentially in the eighteenth century. By the tens of thousands individuals grew accustomed to lending for a return through the system of venal office-holding. Widows, never-married women, guardians of young children, artisans and sometimes domestics, wealthier bourgeois and nobles, many kinds of people put sums, large and small, into offices and corps. The system seems to have contributed to a considerable democratization of investment prior to 1789. Almost certainly land, the true immeuble, would have been insufficient by itself to have done the same thing, to condition a large society to lending and impersonal investment. And it is easy to imagine that the habits carried across the 1790s, to find expression again after 1800. Through the nineteenth century France continued to have a relatively dense and wealthy population, a rich agriculture, and an active trade. With the growth of banking and the mobilization of French capital for heavy investment in "infrastructure" (canals, railroads), much was new in nineteenth-century development. But not everything, for the nineteenth century was to build on a culture of investment passed down to it from the eighteenth.

Notes

1   What follows summarizes parts of D. Bien, "Offices, corps, and a system of state credit: the uses of privilege under the *ancien régime*," in *The Political Culture of the Old Regime*, ed. Keith Baker, Vol. I of *The French Revolution and the Creation of Modern Political Culture* (Oxford: 1987), pp. 89–114.

2   Bibliothèque Nationale (hereafter BN), Mss fr. 14084, "Mémoire sur l'Etat actuel (1779) des offices tant casuels qu'à survivance (Par M. Harvouin, Receveur Général)."

3   Ibid., f. 12.

4   Ibid., ff. 13–14.

5   Archives Nationales (hereafter AN), P3744–6, annual registers of trésoriers des revenus casuels, 1785–7.

6   Except as noted, all the printed official documentation (édits, arrêts, règlements) for the agents de change comes from AN, AD$_{XI}$1. See édit, December 1638; *Statuts et Reglemens pour les Conseillers Agens de Banque, Change, Commerce et Finance de la Ville de Paris, créez par Edit du mois de décembre 1705*; *Reglement des Quarante Conseillers du Roy Agens de Banque, Change . . .* October 2, 1714.

7   *Edit du Roy, Qui attribue des Augmentations de Gages aux Agens de Change à Paris*, May 1713; *Déclaration du Roy . . .* July 13, 1714. See also, among other printed documents, the arrêt du conseil of April 10, 1706 and the déclaration of September 3, 1709.

8   The bourse commune based on the shares of fees, appearing in 1638 regulations, was omitted from the statutes of 1706 and 1714. The one in 1706 referred to the secrets of negotiations that cannot be revealed.

9   *Edit du Roy, Portant création de cent seize Offices d'Agens de Change*, December 1705; *Edit du Roy, Portant suppression des Charges d'Agens de Change créez pour les Provinces . . .*, May 1707; *Résultat du Conseil*, August 25, 1708; *Edit du Roy, Portant suppression des vingt offices d'Agens de Change à Paris . . . Et création de quarante autres pareils Offices . . .*, August 1708; *Déclaration du Roy*, September 3, 1709; *Edit du Roy, Portant création de vingt nouvelles Charges d'Agens de Change à Paris*, November 1714; *Edit du Roi, Portant suppression . . . et Création de soixante nouveaux Offices d'Agens de Change, Banque et Commerce . . .*, January 1723; and five arrêts du conseil of February 23, 1706, August 30, 1720, May 17, 1721, August 4, 1723, September 24, 1724.

10   Edits of December 1705 and May 1713, cited in notes 7 and 9 above; *Ordonnance de Sa Majesté . . .* July 20, 1720 (creating Bourse); four printed arrêts du conseil, September 24, 1724, December 22, 1733 (citing another important arrêt of February 26, 1726), March 30, 1774, November 26, 1781 (contains new règlement for corps); two *Ordonnances*, enforcing the company's rules and monopoly, made by the Lieutenant Général de Police de Paris, February 11, 1727, July 17, 1736; *Règlement que Sa Majesté veut et entend être gardé et observé par les Agens de Change de la ville de Paris . . .*, September 5, 1784.

11   The printed arrêt du conseil of August 7, 1785, issued to forbid abusive negotiations, referred to the "inordinate speculation," the dangers of trading in futures, and the "infinity of insidious maneuvers" being made to rig the market. The arrêt of October 2, 1785, even while trying to quiet fears and to insist that there was no threat to royal credit that would affect solid, non-speculating investors, spoke of the current "madness of speculation." See also the arrêt du conseil of September 22, 1786. The best known among the many pamphlets evoking and criticizing the financial activity is comte de Mirabeau, *Dénonciation de l'agiotage à l'Assemblée des Notables*, 1787. See also Herbert Lüthy, *La banque protestante en France, de la révocation de l'Edit de Nantes à la Révolution*, 2 vols (Paris: 1959–61), Vol. 2; Jean Bouchary, *Les manieurs d'argent à Paris à la fin du XVIIIe siècle*, 3 vols (Paris: 1939–43).

12   *Déclaration du Roi, Concernant l'établissement des Offices d'Agens de Change, créés pour la ville de Paris, par Edit de Janvier 1723.*

13 *Arrêt du Conseil*, September 10, 1786, and *Lettres Patentes du Roi, Qui ordonnent que les gages des Offices d'Agent de Change de Paris . . . leur seront payés sur le pied du denier vingt, avec la retenue du Dixième seulement . . .* January 28, 1787 (in New York Public Library collection). The agents de change had asked for a full 5 percent, but Calonne, by imposing the 10 percent withholding tax, granted only 4$^{1}/_{2}$ percent.

14 Information on purchases from AN, P3745–6 (revenus casuels) and H1456, no. 139, *Mémoire pour les agens de change, de la ville de Paris, en réponse à des observations du contrôleur des bons d'état* (s.l.n.d. [1790]), p. 4. The figure for the net annual cost to the government (132,000 *livres* on a capital of 6 million) appears in AD$_{XI}$ 58, *Mémoire à l'Assemblée Nationale pour les Agens de change de la ville de Paris* (1790), p. 9.

15 AN, H^1 1456, no. 156, mémoire by Turpin, l'agent du Trésor public, addressed "Au Roi, et à nos seigneurs de son conseil." The rapporteur of the comité d'agriculture et de commerce referred in passing to a lower price of 150,000 *livres* during a debate (March 27, 1791) in the Assemblée Nationale, *Archives parlementaires*, ed. J. Mavidal, E. Laurent, *et al.*, series I, 1787–99, 82 vols (Paris: 1879–1913), Vol. 24, p. 405.

16 AN, H^1 1456, no. 128, "Rapport de la demande formée par les agens de change"; no. 129, draft arrêt accepting company's offer to relinquish gages; no. 131, note on alternate offers of financiers; no. 152, "soumission, 26 mai 1788" [signed, Luciani]; no. 155, délibération of compagnie des Agens de Change, April 24, 1788. For the agents' description of the events, AD$_{XI}$ 58, *Mémoire à l'Assemblée Nationale . . .* (1790).

17 Cited in note 13 above.

18 For Turpin, see J. F. Bosher, *French Finances, 1770–1795. From Business to Bureaucracy* (Cambridge, UK: Cambridge University Press, 1970), pp. 115, 242; Michel Bruguière, *Gestionnaires et profiteurs de la Révolution. L'administration des finances françaises de Louis XVI à Bonaparte* (Paris: O. Orban, 1986), pp. 288–9.

19 See their *mémoires* from 1790, cited in note 14 above.

20 In the Grande Chancellerie of Paris 300 secrétaires du roi owning 36 million *livres* in offices had jointly borrowed another 24 million for the king. See D. Bien, "The secrétaires du roi: absolutism, corps, and privilege under the *ancien régime*," *Vom ancien régime zur französischen revolution. Forschungen und perspektiven*, ed. A. Cremer (Göttingen: Vandenhoeck und Ruprecht, 1978), pp. 153–68.

21 If feudalism is taken to mean what it meant in the Middle Ages, that is, the private ownership of public function (rather than a mode of production or simply domination by an agrarian elite), the eighteenth-century French order was in fact feudal.

Part VII
The property of empire

24
Property and propriety
Land tenure and slave property in the creation of a British West Indian plantocracy, 1612–1740

Michael Craton

Sine Justicia Magna Regna nil aliud sunt quam Magna Latrocinia:
The best Common-wealths, without the due current of Law and Justice, are no other than open Robberies.

> (Augustine, quoted by John Jennings, Clerk of the
> Barbadian Assembly, in his preface to the Acts, 1654)

Law is as the Soul in Government, that giveth it Life and Form, and is certainly the last Guard, as well of the King's Prerogative, as of the Peoples Darlings, Liberty and Property.

> (William Rawlin, in "Epistle dedicatory" to
> Laws of Barbados, 1699)

. . . this brief Narrative is an Instance and undeniable Proof, that *Liberty* and *Property* are the great Motives that induce Subjects to be faithful, or fight for the Glory of their Prince; and that an Encroachment on these is a sure Sign of a Sickly State, that is on the Decline, and hasting to be lost.

> (Charles Leslie, *A New Account of Jamaica* [1739], p. 83)

However diverse were the motives, aims, and beliefs of those who founded the earliest English colonies overseas, all concurred in the convenient myth that they were occupying extensions of sovereign territory, and that this allowed them to implant an English society and institutions which had already demonstrated an effective adaptability throughout the British Isles, the Celtic natives notwithstanding. For the settlers and their patrons alike, the forms of land grant and tenure, and the creation of a system of law and order to guarantee them and settle disputes, were of critical importance in establishing an effective socioeconomic structure. For the settlers, the reconstitution of local government on the English model – including its pragmatic dichotomy between appointed and unpaid gentlemen JPs and juries of male freeholders – was more or less taken for granted. But the creation of an autonomous elective assembly with rights similar to those of the English House of Commons was regarded as most vital of all, not so much to ensure that socioeconomic and political standing would continue to be measured by the holding of land, as to guarantee that local statute laws would reflect local needs, conditions, and priorities.

Such concerns applied to all the North American settlement colonies, but they had special force when and where labor-intensive plantations became established, above all in the Caribbean. In place of the problems of dealing with inimical indigenes (being initially uninhabited or lightly peopled) these colonies soon had to face the legal, political, and socioeconomic problems posed by the fact that black African slaves and their descendants, a steadily increasing number of them of mixed race and nominally free, constituted an overwhelming majority of each colony's population. As much as the need for a protective economic system, and for military and naval protection from enemies within and without, the sustaining of the foundation myth that English overseas colonies were transplanted fragments of English people and their institutions, particularly in relation to the holding of land, self-legislation, and the definition of property in persons, therefore helps to explain both the peculiar development of the British West Indian colonies and why they remained loyal to the British Crown even as the mainland colonies fought for their independence.

Given that all English settlement colonies overseas were basically transplantations of English society and English systems of law, courts, and representative institutions, four main variables determined the slight but growing variations between the colonies, and their deviations from the original English model. These were the different terms, principles, and rules under which the colonies were granted; the different initial and later social composition of each settlement; the turbulent political events and changes that occurred in the metropolis over the foundation period, particularly the conflict between the Stuart kings and Parliament, the Commonwealth era, the Restoration, the "Glorious Revolution," and the Hanoverian Settlement; and the local factors, mainly geographical, that led to important socioeconomic readjustments.

English overseas colonization began at a critical phase in the transition from the medieval to the modern world, speeding that transition in the process. As far as land tenure and social status in England were concerned, the principle that no land was held but of a lord had faded as completely as that of absolute serfdom. Gradually, feudal services had been commuted, even the lowliest tenants had become more secure in their tenancies, and lands might more easily be bought, sold, and passed on through inheritance. But vestiges of feudalism remained deeply ingrained – in the continuing importance of the manorial unit, in the legal forms of tenure, and in the continuing concepts that there was no such thing as absolute freehold, and that all land was held ultimately of the sovereign. Overseas colonization, on the one hand, offered the conditions of freer land and looser tenures such as had resulted from the demographic disaster of the Black Death in the fourteenth century, and the opportunities for speculation and upward social mobility for an emergent bourgeoisie that had first been offered by the secularization of church lands at the Reformation. But on the other hand, it also encouraged a backward-looking Anglo-Scottish monarchy, and its client aristocracy, to revert to a version of the tenurial feudalism that had characterized the extension of royal authority, from southern England to the north and west, and across the narrow sea to the Irish Pale, and from the Scottish lowlands into the highlands and islands.

Such a dichotomy or ambivalence can be traced in the different forms of early colonial charter. Whether they were ambitious courtiers like Grenville, Raleigh, or Gorges, companies of adventurers such as those who founded Virginia, Bermuda, or Providence, or groups of religious and political dissidents like the Pilgrim Fathers, all applicants were prepared to accept royal suzerainty in return for a share of the royal prerogatives; in other words, it was an acceptance of the royal claim to the land as the basis for their own viceregal privileges and subordinate tenure. Yet the preferred wording of the royal grants in respect of the tenure was that already hallowed in English practice: "In free and common socage as of our manor of East Greenwich in the County of Kent." Contrary to the assertion by Charles M. Andrews that this had nothing to do specifically with either East Greenwich or the County of Kent as such, its preference in the American colonies over alternative forms (such as of the king's manors of Windsor or Hampton Court in England, or of Carregrotion, Trim, or Limerick in Ireland) surely was a calculated reference to the type of late medieval tenurial system found, among other places, in Kent, along with a hint of the peculiar "liberties, franchises and immunities" associated with the ancient Kentish custom of gavelkind. Not only did "free and common socage" in the Kentish manner indicate that the land was free of all liabilities other than a nominal quit-rent, but it could be freely bought, sold, and inherited, and might not even be subject to "fines" and "reliefs" when changing hands. Moreover, by inference, the form of tenure might be argued to favor the kind of "partible inheritance" more suitable than primogeniture to areas of much available land, since Kentish gavelkind, among other things, allowed lands "to descend to all the sons and heirs of the nearest degree together."[1]

The "East Greenwich" formula left the grant of lands in the hands of the charter grantees, who could, as in England, use the land for themselves like a feudal demesne, assign it in common to the settlers, sub-grant it to individuals on leases of various kinds, or alienate it by grant, sale, or bequest, either in "fee simple" or in "fee tail" (that is, entail). The range of land tenures in the charter colonies was thus from the beginning much like those in England, with virtual freeholds being at least as common. The alternative extreme, however, was a reversion to a type of purely feudal land grant found throughout Norman England and lingering on in the northern and western marches, the virtually autonomous tenancy-in-chief granted to favored individuals, retained in the formula "in capite, as of the county palatine and bishopric of Durham."[2] Such a seigneurial and viceregal grant, with its military flavor so suitable in theory to vast colonial marchlands, was especially congenial to the first two Stuart kings, with their Scottish background, reactionary political views, and importunate favorites, and to aristocratic courtiers eager to establish an anachronistic overseas feudal estate, or to profit from the huge tracts of land claimed by the Crown with little or no expense or even effort on their own part.

Elements of the feudal seignory were strong in the Elizabethan grants to Grenville and Raleigh, and the proprietary system actually reached its fullest development – in a progressively less obviously feudalistic form – after the Restoration; in the grants to Lords Fairfax, Berkeley, and Carteret, the eight Proprietors of Carolina, William Penn, James Oglethorpe, and the Georgia trustees.[3] But the Durham palatinate model was essentially an early Stuart device, found in the grants on Long Island, Newfoundland, the American mainland and in the Lesser Antilles to Stirling, Calvert, Carlisle, Montgomery-Pembroke, Heath, and Kirke (1621–37).[4] In the West Indies, geographical ignorance led to the overlapping grants of the "Caribbees" to Lords Carlisle and Pembroke, decreed in favor of the former in 1629.[5] Yet, while the Carlisle patent provided for many settlers a convenient authorization and legal protection for grants of land, in return for the proprietor's right to appoint officials and collect quit-rents, it conflicted from the beginning with the interests of independent commercial colonial promoters, and settlers with practical access and prior claims to land, who resented the impositions and pretensions of aristocratic absentees and their local delegates – and pretty soon came to prefer direct crown rule to proprietorial exploitation.

This outcome was conditioned and complicated by the intertwining of colonial affairs with the political, social, and economic turmoil in the metropole from 1629 to 1689, or 1715. At the most generic level this represented a dynamic phase in the evolution of "possessive individualism," the development of commercial capitalism, and the emergence to predominance of a capitalistic bourgeois class – in Britain uniquely reinforced from the aristocracy and nobility as well as from below.[6] To the extent that these trends facilitated the development of colonial economies and strengthened representative colonial assemblies, they were welcomed by at least the dominant settlers in the colonies. Yet, almost paradoxically, the parliamentary and Cromwellian interregnum in England saw the institution of a more aggressive imperialism far from congenial to individual, and individualistic, colonies; an assertion of the imperialistic function of the English Parliament, the imposition of protectionst economic policies initially targeting the Dutch, and the initiation of ideological and expansionist wars embroiling colonies in conflicts with Spain and France as well as Holland.

By and large, the colonials welcomed the Stuart Restoration for the opportunities for reconciliation and renegotiation which it offered, and for the prospect of legitimizing a maturing socioeconomic order. But ambivalence and conflict continued as long as the Stuarts ruled, only gradually resolving themselves, as a peripheral result of the institution of "constitutional monarch" with the accession of William and Mary, Anne, and the Hanoverians, by the provision of more effective systems of economic, naval, and military protection, and, above all, by the initiation of the quarter-century of "Walpole's Peace" between 1713 and 1739.[7]

The early evolution of the English West Indian colonies under the influences of the external factors considered above and the considerable variations in local conditions, is best illustrated through a brief sequential account of developments in the three salient early colonies: Bermuda from 1612 to 1684, Barbados from 1625 to about 1700, and Jamaica from 1655 to 1740 (Plate 24.1).

Claimed in competition with Spain in 1609, uninhabited Bermuda was first granted as a subordinate part of Virginia to a syndicate of nineteen London-based investors in 1612.[8] These "adventurers" sponsored the first shiploads of settlers, some 500 in all, who were distributed over the most fertile central parts of the mini-archipelago. Loosely organized into "tribes" named for the chief investors, the first inhabitants were set to build fortifications and work the land in common, under the almost absolute authority of a sort of lieutenant-governor chosen by the adventurers. The most notable achievement of this phase was the first survey of the island, made by the remarkable Richard Norwood – indicating the need to know precisely the shape and extent of the land before it could be properly apportioned and developed.[9]

The apparent potential of Bermuda as distinct from Virginia, and the need for a more formal organization along with more capital, led to the formation of the separate Bermuda or Somers Island Company in 1615. Though Bermudian land provided the main equity for the shareholders, this was almost quintessentially a bourgeois commercial enterprise, run by absentee proprietors much like the "undertakers" in the Irish "plantations." Of the 118 original shareholders, by Henry Wilkinson's computation, 5 were noblemen (of whom the adventurous puritan Earl of Warwick was much the most influential), 18 knights (including the ubiquitous Thomas Smith and puritan lobbyist Edwin Sandys), 14 "gentlemen," and the remainder almost all City merchants. No fewer than 21 of the non-noble shareholders were at some time Members of Parliament.[10]

By the 1615 charter, local authority was delegated to a governor and his chosen council, who were to promulgate laws consonant with English law and establish common law courts like those in England. There was also a presumption that local government would be an amalgam of quasi-manorial and parochial custom on the evolving English model. By Norwood's second survey, Bermuda was divided into eight tribes (analogous to English parishes, though not declared to be such until 1679),[11] each made up of some fifty narrow lots stretching from sea to sea of about 20 acres apiece and including a glebe for a church and its minister – with the eastern quarter of the colony reserved to the Company to raise the general running expenses. Lands were allocated to each shareholder according to his investment, at £12. 10s per unit, with a limit of fifteen to each. The grants were in "free socage," but in fact were very close to absolute freeholds since quit-rents were never exacted during the Company period, and there was an active and complex trade in shares – that is, in Bermudian land – from the very beginning.[12]

Few of the original shareholders ever visited the colony, however, their holdings being mainly managed by younger family members or other resident agents, leased, or, in course of time, sold, to the more successful landless settlers. Initially, the majority of the inhabitants were indentured servants, sharecroppers, or tenants on short leases. But the small size of the holdings, the limited amount of total land, and the failure of Bermuda to establish a lasting plantation system while at the same time acquiring a considerable number of slaves, meant that though there was considerable early upward mobility and the creation of a marked social hierarchy based on land and the control of labor, this was relatively soon fixed in the founding families. Wilkinson, with his unrivalled awareness of the genealogical roots of Bermudian class-divisions, noted that while by the mid-seventeenth century there were no more than a half-dozen persons besides the Governor titled "Esquire," there were at least ten times that number warranting the gentlemanly prefix "Mister," bearing virtually all the surnames dominant in later Bermudian history. The remainder of the whites were yeomanly "goodmen" or simply servants, while slaves already constituted more than a quarter of the population.[13]

The Bermudian Assembly proudly dates itself from 1620, just one year after that of Virginia. It was first called by Governor Nathaniel Butler, who also instituted the courts of petty sessions in the separate tribes, presided over by bailiffs much like English local JPs.[14] The earliest Bermudian Assembly, with two elected burgesses from each of the tribes, met in the main church in combined session with the governor and council, like that of Virginia. Though the very first Acts passed did include measures in the burgesses' own interest, such as the preservation of boundary marks and the control of indentured servants, the assembly was clearly intended to be little more than a rubber stamp for the governor's policies. But with the evolution of a local landowning class increasingly concerned with questions of social control and at odds with an absentee company felt to be exploitative, the elective assembly became gradually more assertive.

Tensions heightened during the English Civil Wars on religious as well as sociopolitical grounds. The Company was responsible for appointing ministers as well as governors, and the puritan influence in its council insured that these tended to be of a Nonconformist persuasion. Such latitude was unimportant before Bermudian local government became fixed in the parochial mode and before the Laudian reforms in England forced parish clergy into greater conformity. But the developing conflict in England was reflected in Bermuda by the growing division between Independent preachers and their congregations, who rejected most secular obligations, and those landowners who favored a regular parochial system as the basis of their own sociopolitical position – through the vestries, the militia, the petty sessions courts, and representation in the assembly.

The chief Independents were exiled to Eleuthera between 1647 and 1649, and when news of the execution of Charles I reached Bermuda, Royalist landowners from "the country" and the militia which they monopolized took over the government and proclaimed King Charles II.[15] Although the Commonwealth reasserted its authority in the 1650s and most of the Independents returned, the Restoration saw a steady increase in the power of the chief inhabitants through the assembly and a concomitant decline in the power and authority of the Company, which culminated in the takeover of the colony by the Crown in 1684. However, this process produced a local slaveholding landowning class under imperial auspices which differed in crucial respects from that which evolved in Barbados and Jamaica. The Somers Island Company faded for economic as much as for political reasons, for tiny Bermuda, after some years of legislated parity in the production of tobacco, inevitably failed as a plantation colony in competition with Virginia once that colony (freed of company control in 1625) began to utilize its huge potential. Those Bermudians who had come to monopolize the land – many of them through purchase from the shareholders of a declining company – reinforced their power through turning to the maritime activities for which Bermuda was far more suited: shipbuilding, whaling, salt-raking in the Turks and Caicos Islands, trading, and privateering. They became, in fact, more a modest bourgeois oligarchy, though with a vested interest in the imperial system nonetheless.[16]

Barbados, like Bermuda, was uninhabited when the English arrived, and while also a very small island, had the advantage of being immensely fertile once its dense tropical woodlands were cleared. First claimed for the English Crown in 1625, it was initially settled in competition by shiploads of servants and would-be smallholders financed by the Anglo-Dutch entrepreneur Sir William Courteen and his associates, and by other adventurers authorized by James Hay, Earl of Carlisle, under the terms of a proprietary patent granted in 1627 – including a syndicate of London merchants awarded a block of 10,000 acres, a tenth of the island.[17] In order to counter the courtly influence of Carlisle, Courteen encouraged the rival proprietary claim of the Earl of Pembroke. But the proprietorial dispute, which confused development for over fifty years and has clouded much subsequent scholarship, should really be regarded as no more than one element in a three-sided conflict between quasi-feudal absentee magnates and mercantile investors over who owned the island, and between both of these and the actual settlers, who needed protection and capital, but wanted tax-free land of their own and political self-determination. Similarly, the confused political history of the colony's first forty years, which most earlier writers saw simply in terms of an extension of the conflict in England between "Roundheads" and "Cavaliers," should rather be seen mainly in local terms: as a function of the socioeconomic and therefore political revolution that was a consequence of the shift from smallholdings growing tobacco and cotton largely with white indentured servants, to large plantations producing sugar with the labor of African slaves.[18]

Like the Bermudian adventurers, the initial investors in Barbados clearly expected to develop the colony as an overseas estate worked by dependent laborers. But the overlapping claims of the two main principals and the convenience of making subleases or even selling land rather than developing it directly through managers, coupled with the will to ownership and ingenuity of the settlers, meant that the governors whom the rival proprietors appointed were unable either to inhibit an active market in land from the beginning, or to deflect the demand for a legislative assembly representing all landholders.

Carlisle's charter promised that the Barbadian settlers would be "as free as they who were born in England," and also "freely, quietly, and peaceably, to have and possess all the liberties, franchises and privileges of this kingdom, and to use and enjoy them as liege people of England." In the context of Stuart England in 1628 this scarcely guaranteed them either freehold tenure or true representative government. The charter, however, did more specifically authorize Carlisle (or his deputy) to enact laws "with the Consent, Assent and Approbation of the freeholders . . . or the greater part of them thereunto be called."[19]

The situation clearly hinged on the settlers' claim to be freeholders, and the attitude of the proprietor can clearly be traced in Carlisle's Instructions to his governors. In 1634, Governor Henry Hawley was instructed to make no grants save in leasehold for a maximum of seven years' term, renewable, and in no case for longer than the grantee's lifetime. Besides quit-rents, all lessees were to pay dues to the governor and tithes to the clergy, and lands were to be forfeited for the neglect of any of these terms, the neglect of cultivation, or the failure to provide an indentured servant for every 10 acres granted. Carlisle further instructed Hawley in 1636 to order all landholders to take out new patents, to pay "fines" on taking over bought or inherited land, and to pay an annual tax of "the fifth part of ye peoples Labours" – amounting typically to 20 pounds of clean cotton for each man, woman, or male child living on the land. This was the substance of the settlers' later claim that the Proprietors had exerted a "Transcendente Authoritie" which had subjected them "to slavery worse than villany."[20]

Deteriorating political conditions in England, the death of the first Lord Carlisle, and the reality of conditions in distant Barbados, however, ensured that Governor Hawley was neither willing nor able to impose quasi-feudal land tenures. When the second Lord Carlisle appointed the more pliant Henry Huncks in his place, Hawley moved to obtain the support of the puritan Earl of Warwick (who had personally bought out Pembroke's interest in Barbados), summoned the first Barbadian Assembly (1639), and had it elect him governor on the promise of a more liberal land policy and self-legislation. As an earnest of this, Hawley had the assembly pass an Act "for settling the estates and titles of the inhabitants," and set up an Alienation Court, charged with the function of settling land disputes.[21]

The authority of Carlisle and the king was still enough to reinstate Huncks for a year or so, but the political conflagration in England allowed Barbados to develop along its own lines at the very same time that the most enterprising and best-funded planters were learning the cultivation and processing of sugar from the Dutch. Vincent T. Harlow entitled the second chapter of his *History of Barbados* on the period 1641–50 "Barbados as an independent state," though the title of the second chapter of Richard Dunn's *Sugar and Slaves* might be a better alternative: "Barbados: the rise of the planter class."[22]

A crucial figure throughout this period was the neutralist Governor Philip Bell, a former governor of Bermuda. Officially appointed by Carlisle though with the approbation of Lord Warwick and the Committee of Trade and Plantations, Bell established the Anglican Church, but also decreed the cessation of proprietary dues, completed the organization of parish government and the system of courts, chose a council representing the most substantial islanders, regularized the assembly and granted it the power of initiating legislation. Among the crucial pieces of legislation passed during Bell's tenure was that which reaffirmed Hawley's land grant act and added the proviso that "those who were in quiet possession of land granted to them by former governors or by virtue of conveyance or other acts in law, should be confirmed in it either in part or in whole, or it should otherwise descend, or be confirmed to their heirs forever." As to the civil war in England, Bell reported of the Barbadians in 1645 that

> it pleased god so to unite all their minds and harts together, that every parish declared themselves resolutely for the maintenance of their peace and present government; and to admitt of noe alterationes or new commissiones from either side . . . for against the kinge we are resolved never to be, and without the freindeshipe of the perliament and free trade of London ships we are not able to subsist.[23]

During the 1640s, many new planters settled in Barbados; not just displaced Royalists as the older books averred, but also more or less apolitical gentry on the make, most with sound mercantile connections, such as John and Peter Colleton, Thomas Kendall, Thomas Modyford, Daniel Searle, Humphrey Walrond, and Lord Willoughby of Parham. In the island, they joined already well-established planters such as Christopher Codrington, James Drax, James Holdip, and John Yeamans in the competitive rush to control land, labor, and local political power. This is the phase of which Richard Ligon (who accompanied Thomas Modyford to Barbados in 1647) gave such an invaluable account in his *True and Exact History of the Island of Barbados*, published in 1657 (Plate 24.2). Ligon described an island in which almost all land was already patented, though not all yet cleared, where the acreage in smallholdings growing tobacco and cotton was fast being outstripped by large sugar estates, and black slaves already outnumbered white indentured servants (and were thought even more likely to rebel). In other respects, it was virtually a "Little England" in the Tropics. "They Govern there by the Lawes of England, for all Criminall, Civill, Martiall, Eccleslasticall and Maritime affairs," wrote Ligon.

> This law is administered by a Governour, and ten of his Councill, for Courts of ordinary Justice, in Civill causes, which divide the land in four Circuits; Justices of the Peace, Constables, Churchwardens and Tithing-men: five sessions a year, for tryall of Criminall causes, and all Appeals from inferiour Courts, in Civill causes. And when the Governour pleases to call an Assembly, for the supream Court of all, for the last Appeales, for the making of new Lawes, and abolishing old, according to occasion, in the nature of the Parliament of *England*, and accordingly consists of the Governour, as Supream, his Councill, in nature of the Peers, and two Burgesses chosen by every Parish for the rest. The island is divided into eleven Parishes. No Tithes paid to the Minister, but a yearly allowance of a pound of Tobacco, upon an acre of every man's land, besides certain Church-duties, of Mariages, Christenings and Burials.[24]

When King Charles I was executed, Lord Willoughby assumed the governorship on the authority of the exiled Charles II, and the Barbadian legislature declared for the king against the Parliament in England. But the essential issue was not royalism but Barbadian independence against a metropolitan legislature claiming imperial powers, including the right to forbid colonies trading where they willed. This seemed particularly to threaten the commerce with the Dutch, on whom the development of the Barbadian sugar industry had depended, as well as the general right of the Barbadian plantocracy to enact laws controlling their land and labor. As the English Parliament passed the Navigation Act against the Dutch, and the parliamentary authorities declared an embargo on Barbadian trade and organized an expedition under Sir George Ayscue to reduce rebellious colonies in the West Indies, Willoughby, with the support of his council and assembly, issued on February 18, 1651 the remarkable document usually called the Barbadian Declaration of Independence. Anticipating the more celebrated American Declaration by 125 years, it proclaimed self-legislation as the birthright of all freeborn Englishmen, implied the principle of no taxation without representation, and accused the Westminster Parliament of usurpation.[25]

Though the Barbadians were not eager to fight, Ayscue was not strong enough to risk a pitched battle on land and merely blockaded Barbados for three months. Pragmatic moderates, notably Thomas Modyford, effected a deal and Willoughby surrendered under generous terms on January 11, 1652. The Articles of Surrender guaranteed liberty of conscience and the Barbadian constitution, including the right of the assembly to approve all taxation. An amnesty was declared, and the restitution of all goods of Barbadians seized in England promised. The embargo was lifted and free trade with all friendly nations pledged – though this was compromised by the Anglo-Dutch War and the terms of the Navigation Act.[26]

Between March 1652 and July 1654, George Ayscue and his successor as governor, Daniel Searle, saw through the Barbadian legislature no fewer than 102 Acts which, collected by John Jennings the clerk of the Barbadian Assembly and printed in London, are the earliest surviving set of Barbadian laws – almost the foundation code of the Barbadian plantocracy.[27] Of the eight Acts signed by Ayscue, by far the most important was that which declared the Carlisle patent void, while guaranteeing quiet possession to all landowners holding patents from previous governors, legal conveyances, or tenure by legislative Acts. Despite the terms of the amnesty, one of Ayscue's Acts specifically expelled Lord Willoughby from Barbados, an action gaining legislative approval presumably because Willoughby claimed the leasehold of Carlisle's proprietary rights to the island. Except for the act affirming the subscription of Barbados to the English parliamentary document called the Engagement, these were the only Acts relating directly to the recent political strife.

The 94 Acts signed by Governor Searle not only confirmed the status quo in Barbados but entrenched the planters' power in respect of their concerns about land and the control of labor. One Act reaffirmed the parochial system of local government, while two others established that ranks in the militia would be strictly geared to socioeconomic standing. Field officers were to hold at least 100 acres of land, captains 50, lieutenants 25, and ensigns 15 – though exceptions were, interestingly, made for "substantial and confiding Merchants and Store-house keepers" in Bridgetown. The other ranks of the "trained bands" and militia cavalry were to be filled by white freemen aged 16 to 60, whether they held property or not. The military purpose of the militia was not stated, but the many laws concerning the regulation and policing of "Negroes," and the even greater number relating to "Servants," strongly suggest that it was as much for the control of the laboring population as a defence against foreign enemies.[28] As far as land was concerned, Acts were passed against encroachment on boundaries through the cutting down of trees, for the proper registration of title deeds, for the facilitation of transfers through sale and bequest, and for the more efficient management of the property of married women. Besides this, the Chancery court, where many land cases were adjudged, was reconstituted, and an Act concerning powers of attorney facilitated the increasing number of property transactions that were being made outside the island.[29]

Fittingly, the Interregnum saw the increase of the power of the Barbadian planters through their local parliament, and their political gains and growing wealth through sugar production enabled them to override and actually profit from the adjustments which followed the Stuart Restoration in 1660. Predictably, Lord Willoughby was reinstated by Charles II as governor and granted compensation for the remaining seven years of his lease from Lord Carlisle, but the Barbadian plantocracy was quite able to negotiate favorable terms with the new regime. The basis of this agreement was that the king would assume the proprietorship of Barbados himself, but confirm all land tenures and the rights of the assembly in return for a permanent revenue for his administration of the island. Originally appointed in April 1661, but delayed by the negotiations which allowed him to keep his personal proprietorship of Surinam, Governor Willoughby arrived in Barbados in August 1663. Immediately he met with the council and assembly in plenary session and obtained the permanent grant of $4\frac{1}{2}$ percent duty on all exports, on the understanding that the king had purchased all proprietary rights, that all proprietary dues were immediately cancelled, and that all existing land titles were good "in spite of existing defects, in free and common socage of the Crown, on payment of a yearly grain of Indian corn, if demanded" – that is, in virtually absolute freehold, without even the obligation of an annual quit-rent. As soon as the agreement was signed and sealed, Willoughby set sail for the other "Caribbee Isles" to make identical arrangements.[30]

That the planters of the Lesser Antilles soon quarrelled with the misappropriation of the $4^{1}/_{2}$ percent duty – a tedious wrangle that continued for almost two centuries – indicated their growing pretensions and congenital dislike of direct taxation, rather than a general dissatisfaction with the principle of Crown Colony rule under the Old Representative System. A study of the first major compilation of Barbadian laws after that by Jennings in 1654, made by William Rawlin in 1699, shows that the plantocracy had not only retained the basic principles of the earlier code, but considerably extended and greatly refined it as the apparatus of their socioeconomic and political power. This was particularly notable in the comprehensive Act for the conveyancing of estates, originally enacted in 1661 as part of the Restoration Settlement, and other Acts regarding land and real estate, in the comprehensive Act for Governing Negroes dating from 1688, and other Acts relating to slaves and servants, which, as we shall see, all set models for the other plantation colonies.[31]

This structure of plantocratic laws accurately reflected the completion of the complex socioeconomic and political revolution that began, or was speeded, once Barbados switched to the monocultural production of sugar on large quasi-industrial estates. As Richard S. Dunn has best shown, this was a process which, among other things, saw the total number of landholdings fall from 5,000 in 1650 to 3,000 in 1680, the number of estates over 200 acres rise from 50 to 150, and the percentage of the total land area represented by large estates rise from 40 to 80 percent. The same 30-year period saw the percentage of Negro slaves in the total population rise from under 50 to over 70 percent, and an even greater decline in the absolute number of white indentured servants than in the number of white smallholders. By 1680, from figures sent back to England by Governor Atkins, the top 175 planters (less than 7 percent of all property-owners) not only owned 53 percent of the land and 54 percent of the slaves and white servants, but also monopolized all the public offices.[32] These factors together accounted for the fact that while Barbados had become economically "saturated" and socially fixed, and remained one of the most densely populated areas of the world, it steadily exported its surplus white population throughout the rest of plantation America – ineffectually or temporarily to Surinam and St Lucia, more effectively to the Leeward Islands, Virginia, and South Carolina, but most notably of all, to what was to become by far the most important British sugar colony, Jamaica.[33]

Twenty-five times larger than Barbados, and 400 times the size of Bermuda, Jamaica was the first British colony acquired by conquest as a result of state policy. Seized by an expedition under Admiral Penn and General Venables in 1655 as a kind of consolation prize after the failure to capture Santo Domingo, the large undeveloped island was not cleared of the Spanish until the year of Charles II's Restoration. Taken over by the Crown from its Cromwellian founders in the face of Spanish opposition, it was presumably thought too rich or difficult a possession to award to favorite courtiers or mercantile syndicates, and therefore developed as a state enterprise, without the burdens and complications of proprietary or company owner-ship. Their gratitude for the protection of the Crown, and habitual (if disingenuous)

expressions of loyalty, though, did not prevent the founding settlers and their descendants claiming special privileges by an imagined right of conquest, and vigorously
opposing the Crown's representatives in a successful quest to establish a plantocracy at
least as powerful as that of Barbados.[34]

The actual conquest of Jamaica was a raggle-taggle affair. The invading forces, some
5,000 Cromwellian veterans augmented by 2,000 eager but untrained surplus poor
whites from Barbados and the Leewards, greatly outnumbered the total population of
the island. But unused to the terrain, inadequately supplied, and sickly, they were
beleaguered in three regimental "quarters" of southern Jamaica, roaming the woods for
wild cattle and desperately growing provisions under the command of their officers.
Those who survived and stayed, however, augmented by a trickle of recruits in the first
five years, formed the founding nucleus of Jamaican planters – with most of the officers
(whom the last Cromwellian governor termed, with some exaggeration, "men of good
Familys" exiled by Cromwell for jealousy)[35] being the first landholders, and most of the
labor provided by the other ranks of the disbanded army.

The first formal land grants were made and an embryonic civil government established by the transitional governor, Edward D'Oyley (1657–61), a more formal
structure was put in place by Lord Windsor, the first fully civilian governor (though he
stayed less than three months, in 1662), and a prototypical plantocratic system
initiated by the Barbadian "planter-governor," Thomas Modyford, between 1664 and
1671. D'Oyley was instructed to ensure that a large area of the island be reserved as a
royal demesne, which implied at least a two-tier system of land allocation, and was also
empowered to set up courts and pass laws "not repugnant" to those of England, with
the help of a council of twelve, elected by the army officers, chief planters, and other
substantial white inhabitants.

Governor Windsor, though he found only 3,000 whites and 500 blacks settled in
Jamaica, carried a commission and instructions that were much more detailed and
precise. Besides a council, he was empowered to call an Assembly, "according to the
Custome of our Plantacons, to make Lawes and uppon Eminent Necessityes to leavy
Moneys, as shall be most conduceable to the Honour and Advantage of our Crown and
the good & wellfare of our Subjects, provided they be not repugnant to any of our
Lawes of England," and that such laws "shall be in force for two yeares and noe longer
unless they shall be approved and continued by us." This body first met in January
1664, during the regime of Windsor's Deputy-Governor, Charles Lyttelton, with five
members from Jamaica's only two towns, and one each from 15 sparsely settled and
scattered country districts, passing laws which included one dividing the island into
fifteen "precincts" or parishes, as well as others concerning the raising of revenue.[36]

As to the allocation of land, Windsor's instructions retained traces of the Stuarts'
predilection for feudal forms. The Governor was authorized to confirm all existing land
tenures, but 400,000 acres was to be set aside, one-fourth in each of the four quarters of
Jamaica, as a royal demesne "as for a Mark of our Soveraignty in and over" the island.
Lord Windsor himself, as a kind of tenant-in-chief, was granted 50,000 acres, with the
authority to allot land in free and common socage at a rent which he and his Council
should decide. Much more important than this was the provision for headright land to
new settlers, who were promised 30 acres for every man, woman, and child, free,
indentured, and slave, whom they brought to the island.[37]

Thomas Modyford, who arrived in Jamaica in July 1664 with the first half of about 1,700 displaced Barbadian small planters and their servants, was both the developer and chief beneficiary of this new system. The previous scheme with a separate royal demesne was scrapped in favor of crown land grants under quit-rent tenure for all persons who would plant within five years, giving all planters the chance to patent virtually freehold land in proportion to the number of persons in their "family" of actual relatives and dependent laborers. A land registry was established on the Barbadian model, and a pre-emptive rush began which within a decade saw nearly all the plantable land in Jamaica nominally alienated. As Richard Dunn has computed, the four chief members of the Modyford clan patented at least 21,218 acres throughout Jamaica, of which Sir Thomas and his son claimed over 9,000. In order to forestall complaints, the governor pointed out to the Council of Trade and Plantations that since in addition to his actual family, he owned 400 slaves and servants, he was legally entitled to 12,000 acres.[38]

The freewheeling Modyford also encouraged the freebooters (at least until Charles II signed the Treaty of Madrid with Spain in 1670), and was directly involved in the trade in slaves – both through the chartered Royal African Company and by unlicensed "interlopers." The former activity, of which Henry Morgan, later Lieutenant-Governor and Vice-Admiralty judge, was the most famous exponent, generated considerable wealth for lateral transfer into Jamaican plantations, while the latter provided a growing, if scarcely cheap, workforce for the labor-intensive production of sugar.[39]

A typical early "planter" ran cattle and grew cocoa, cotton, tobacco, and indigo as well as some sugar, all on a modest scale, with the labor of the few white servants and black slaves he could afford. But with land being readily available and almost free, and while the price of sugar remained high and the cost of slaves, "utensils," and borrowing money relatively low, the graduation toward owning a sizeable sugar plantation – the essential generator of socioeconomic and political power – could be as short as a single lifetime. The process was also, of course, expedited at every stage by better than average access to capital resources, whether through buccaneering, direct involvement in trade, good mercantile connections, or canny dynastic alliances. In truly exceptional cases, such as that of Henry Morgan, even an indentured servant might become a rich plantocrat, if hardy and long-lived, clever or rapacious, and lucky enough.[40]

Modyford's efforts to attract new and substantial settlers as well as capital to Jamaica were moderately successful, so that by 1673 there were said to be 17,000 persons in Jamaica (a quarter of the population of Barbados), of whom 4,000 were white men, 2,000 white women, 1,700 white children, and 9,500 black slaves. There were approximately 500 estates, some of them huge, though no more than 150 were sugar plantations, with 44 planters holding 1,000 or more acres, and 16 holding 2,000 or more.[41] During his regime, Governor Modyford firmly established the parochial system of local government, though some of the parishes, up to four times the size of Barbados, were almost unpeopled, and it was a century or more before all had parish churches and parsons. Modyford also almost completed the structure of the island's courts.[42] By his commission he was empowered to select his own council rather than have it elected as formerly, while at the same time he moved to make the assembly more truly representative of the planter class throughout the island – though with some representation for the mercantile element in the towns. Though council and assembly were thus nominally separated, Modyford's choice of the most substantial of his fellow planters for his council ensured that there was little tension between the two bodies, only minor differences between "town" and "country" interests in the assembly, and that the laws passed were essentially plantocratic. This is borne out by the earliest extant compilation of Jamaican laws, made by Charles Harper in 1684, which demonstrated almost exact parallels with Barbados.[43]

The full evolution of a Jamaican plantocracy was not achieved, though, without a protracted and complex constitutional struggle with the imperial government, lasting until 1728, just as the full extension of the Jamaican sugar plantation system was delayed by setbacks, natural disasters, and the resolute opposition of the Maroons, who controlled the mountainous and forested interior of the island until the end of the 1730s.[44]

As in all the American colonies, the constitutional conflict concerned the relative rights of the Crown and imperial Parliament on the one hand, and the colonists and their representative assembly on the other. In the Jamaican case, the principles debated mainly revolved around the status of conquered colonies rather than those peacefully settled; but in reality, as in Barbados, the conflict came down to a simple trade-off between the allocation of a permanent revenue to the administration and the granting of the right of virtual self-legislation to the colonial assembly.

The lordly and contemptuous non-planter Governor Vaughan was disgusted by the pretensions of the Jamaican assembly encouraged by Governors Modyford and Lynch, and his successor Lord Carlisle (no relation to the former proprietor of the Caribbees) arrived in Jamaica in 1678 not only with a list of approved nominees for the council and a raft of ready-made Jamaican laws, but with instructions to relegate the assembly to the status of the Irish Parliament, as constituted by the terms of Poyning's Law. The issue was soon joined, with Samuel Long, Speaker of the Assembly (grandfather of the great planter-historian Edward Long), and William Beeston (later a popular planter-governor and first of the great absentee planter lobbyists) vigorously putting the plantocratic case. This was that as freeborn and voluntary settlers they had carried with them all their rights and privileges as Englishmen, including the common law, and all statutes in operation when they migrated. From these claims it followed that in the absence of colonial representation in an imperial parliament, they owed allegiance to the monarch through his governor, but had the right to legislate for themselves, especially in regard to Jamaica's special conditions and needs. In addition, they claimed special rights in Jamaica by virtue of being "the conquerors of the land."[45]

On the contrary, the imperial lawyers argued (as was maintained by the landmark Jamaican case of *Blankard* v. *Galdy* in 1694) that whereas,

> where the English people gained territory by discovery and settlement "all the Laws in Force in England, are in force there"; but in the case of a conquered country such as Jamaica, the laws of England were not operative "until declared so by the Conqueror and his Successor. . . . In such cases where the Laws are rejected or silent, the conquered Country shall be governed according to the Rule of Natural Equity."[46]

By the most extreme interpretation, this implied not only that the Jamaican colonists had no automatic right to representative government or even the common law, but that they might be ruled directly by the Crown. Nor was the reference to "natural Equity" an unintentional pun, for it was no accident that the colonial courts of Chancery – so vital for the adjudication of real estate – almost everywhere consisted of the colonial governor and his council sitting as judges.[47]

Yet the extreme imperial position had no more chance of asserting itself than had the Stuarts the likelihood of winning their long-running battles with their Parliaments at home. What gave the Jamaican assembly the whip-hand in the contest was the inability of the imperial government to back up its constitutional demands with financial allocations, and the utter dependence of the governors on the assembly for raising and granting the revenue necessary for running the colonial administration. In 1678, Carlisle was forced to agree to the amendments made by the assembly to his laws and pass them for the normal two years, in return for a two years' revenue grant; and when in 1681 the assembly first departed from the custom of short-term Acts to approve a seven years' grant of revenue, the chief island laws were reciprocally confirmed for a seven-year term. Two years later, still during the second term of the pro-planter Governor Lynch, when the assembly generously decided to grant revenue for twenty-one years, the principal laws (including the previous batch) were confirmed for a similar period. Finally, in 1728, during the temporary regime of the planter President of the Council, John Ayscough, the assembly voted the administration a permanent revenue, in return for a grant of all the rights, privileges, and immunities already enjoyed by the legislatures of the "non-conquered" colonies.[48]

These were in fact critical years for Jamaica in every respect. In the 1690s, an earthquake totally destroyed Port Royal, an epidemic of lethal malaria swept the island, and a French invasion devastated the eastern settlements. By 1700, the white population had actually fallen below 2,000, and though it made great strides in the years of European peace following Queen Anne's War, the extension of the plantations was hampered by the depredations of the Maroons. These descendants of the "Spanish Negroes" who had resisted the original English incursion had been greatly augmented by runaway slaves, of whom the "Coromantees," already expert musketeers in their native Ashanti, were the most formidable opponents. Sporadic but bloody wars throughout the 1730s – in which white casualties greatly outnumbered those of the Maroons and, uniquely in the annals of war, the wounded were outnumbered by the dead – placed a huge strain on the parochial militia system and the Jamaican treasury.[49]

But sheer numbers, and the inexorable capitalist dynamic of the plantation system (for by 1740, Jamaica contained 10,000 whites and 100,000 slaves, and there were some 400 sugar plantations)[50] eventually told. In 1738 and 1739, the two chief Maroon communities were persuaded to sign peace treaties with the regime. Though ostensibly made between equal belligerents, with the Maroons becoming allies of the regime, granted lands in perpetuity, and promised a large degree of political autonomy, these were in fact trickily unequal agreements, ensuring that the Maroons would gradually be subsumed within the plantocratic system, and lose their independent polity and way of life. Perhaps the best (or worst) example of this process was the way in which the Maroon heroine Nanny and her clan were treated by the regime. The warrior chieftainess and her followers were allocated land on the forested slopes of the Blue Mountains, but the form of the grant was that of a normal colonial patent. Nanny and her household – who may have had pre-1655 or even Amerindian antecedents – were fictitiously said to have "transported themselves and their slaves into our said Island," and to be therefore eligible for land at the usual rate of 30 acres a head. By this formula not only was Nanny seemingly made a recipient of the bounty of the Crown but, more subtly, the idea was conveyed that Jamaica had had no native inhabitants when "conquered" by the English.[51]

As John Austin and other distinguished positivist theorists have argued, a prevailing system of law can be said to serve and define, that is, to signify, the dominant elements in the social order. If law is not quite simply the will of the sovereign, a society is its law.[52] What then, briefly, was the corpus of law which signified the British West Indian plantocracies once they had established themselves, especially in the key respects of property in land and the control of labor?

In the case of land, the West Indian planters inherited a rich and useful array of customs, common laws and statutes from the mother country, which required minimal adaptation, augmentation, and refinement in the colonies. In respect of imposing harsh working conditions on servants and other employees, requiring at least commuted services from tenants with less than freeholds, and imposing a general requirement to work on all landless men by the threat of vagrancy, they also had ample models from the metropole. Only in their pressing need to define the necessary Negro laborers as chattel slaves (while at the same time attempting to police and punish them as if they were persons) were the British West Indian planters forced into inventing new law, or at least to borrowing from ancient times and other legal traditions – in a way that was in due course to be regarded as anachronistic, as well as oppressive and illogical, by all but the planters themselves.[53]

As we have already suggested, throughout the American colonies the method of land grant and tenure, labor and military obligations, the systems of local government, and even household structure, owed much to English feudal and manorial traditions. Yet even before any English persons settled overseas, these traditions had already been greatly modified, in respect of the growth of individual property rights, the extension of practical freehold tenure, a freeing of restrictions on the purchase, sale and inheritance of all real estate, and a steady, if still incomplete, loosening of the bonds that tied individuals to one master, to one locality, or to a permanent rank in the social order. Thus, according to different local conditions, colonial settlers could use English law and custom selectively: either to sustain or revert to an earlier system, or to hasten the process of change already begun.

The essential difference between old and new world was expressed in the inscription on a colonial token (perhaps intentionally advertising colonization) dated 1647: "In Virginia land free and labour scarce; in England land scarce and labour plenty."[54] But for the plantation and island colonies this motto had different implications than for those settlements farther north. For the northern mainland colonies, conditions invited the formation of a society of small farmers, ruggedly independent, close-family oriented, and relatively democratic, socially static but geographically mobile. Such a people naturally adhered to a system of land law favoring the traditions of partible inheritance and the rejection of all binding forms of tenancy, having a particular disinclination for sharecropping arrangements. The common law was valued for the ways in which it defended individual property rights against quasi-feudal magnates, corporations, or even the Crown itself, and local statute law developed this individualistic trend.[55]

Early island and southern mainland conditions favored lands worked in common, and binding tenancies, but this was soon followed by the creation of small plantations strongly rooted in the English rural seigneurial family-household tradition – that "World We Have Lost" of which Peter Laslett writes.[56] The subsequent establishment of larger, more labor-intensive sugar plantations, the "saturation" of the islands initially settled and the extension of the plantation system from island to island, provided chances of rapid upward mobility for a fortunate few. But it also widened social divisions, first by the depression of white "servants" from fictional family members into a virtual helot class, and then by the substitution for them of black slaves, regarded by the white landowners as outside the social order altogether.

The wealth which sugar could generate – far greater than the profits which could be derived from an English country estate – and the successful sugar planters' almost inevitable connections with merchants and bankers, determined that they became a bourgeois ruling class. But there were aristocratic counter-attractions and influences. Not only did the sugar plantation system fix a planter's fortune in a particular unit (or set of units) of land, but, however meanly born, he inherited the tradition that he was no more than a capitalist entrepreneur unless he and his family were linearly rooted in the land they owned. This explains why West Indian planters always favored single over partible inheritance, preferred primogeniture, but (given the great mortality of the colonies) were quite prepared to accept female heirs, gave more rights to widows than was common in England, and were far more inclined to entail their estates than were North Americans. They were also, in a more exaggerated way than their English equivalents, active marriage-brokers and dynasts, and, as a notable species of nouveaux riches, ingenious inventors of fictitious genealogies.[57]

In all the above respects, West Indian planters simply had to follow established English legal customs and precedents in their useful variation, or adopt existing English statutes. This explains the concern of the early colonists to assert that they carried with them English legal custom, the common law, and English statutes operative before their own legislatures came into being, as well as their concurrence with the imperial authorities in having an English system of common law courts established from the very beginning. Even some colonial statutes, such as those dealing with the organization of the local courts, show little or no differences in principle from English models. Other colonial Acts, however, did show substantial deviations from the beginning, and once the plantocracies established themselves in each colony, the laws they enacted became ever more nakedly self-serving, whether or not they risked running foul of the principle of non-repugnancy to English laws.

The essential founding Acts for the West Indian plantocracies were those which set up the system of courts and asserted the principles on which they followed English models and practice, those which enumerated the English laws which continued to apply in the colonies and why they did so, and, the critical third stage, those which guaranteed and justified the practice of self-legislation in return for granting a permanent revenue to the Crown.[58] Before this process was completed, colonial statutes, as befitted their mixed provenance, illustrated the different or mutual interests of the Crown through the governor and council, or the settlers represented in the assembly.

Thus, Acts encouraging settlement by generous land grants and guarding landholdings against misappropriation, encroachment and trespass, giving freeholders authority within the parochial system, and guaranteeing labor by fixing the terms of indenture and policing the servants and slaves, were interleaved with those aimed at ensuring the efficient collection of quit-rents by the Crown, and imposing upon often reluctant planters and their servants the obligations of building and maintaining roads and bridges and serving in the militia.[59]

Yet once the plantocracies were entrenched, colonial Acts, first subtly then ever more boldly, were framed in the interests of the ruling class. Even such Acts as those laying down the principles of the conveyancing of real estate which essentially followed English practice had tacked to them clauses which liberally served special local conditions and needs. Such a case were the Barbadian Conveyancing Acts of 1661, 1669, and 1670, which included clauses to protect landholdings called in question as a result of the Interregnum, to facilitate deeds contracted outside Barbados, to safeguard the interests of widows, and to establish the generous principle that valid title resided in all lands held in quiet possession for a mere five years.[60]

Once crown land was almost entirely distributed, or its allocation had fallen firmly under the control of the local ruling class, laws naturally placed less emphasis on the encouragement of new settlers, and became more concerned with discouraging land speculation, absenteeism, and the non-development of patented land, and with guaranteeing a sufficient proportion of white servants to manage estates and police the slaves. Quit-rent Acts had always been notoriously ineffectual, but they now became concerned less with the raising of revenue than with the resumption of undeveloped lands by the Crown. This was both to augment the reservoir of patentable lands for the more active and successful local planters, and to prevent undeveloped land from falling into the hands of squatting smallholders or, even worse, becoming refuges for runaway slaves and bands of Maroons. Similarly, the Deficiency Laws, which required a certain proportion of white servants in relation to the number of slaves on pain of fines for non-observance, though almost as ineffectual as the quit-rent Acts in their main objective, had several clear plantocratic purposes: not just to provide more effective controls against the slave majority, but to enlarge that class of lesser whites without which the planters had no pretensions to dominate a colonial society from which they had excluded black slaves by law.[61]

Such local legislation was aimed in part against the increasing menace of planter absenteeism, though on this issue the local laws were bound to be ambivalent. From the beginning, colonial legislation had fulfilled the need to facilitate transactions in real estate from abroad, and the metropolitan business involved in trading, making advances, loans and, above all, mortgages. Subsequent Acts seeking to penalize planters who forsook the West Indies for English estates or closer involvement in metropolitan commerce, ran uncomfortably counter to these. But in due course, even the local legislatures were bound to acknowledge that much of the tide of absenteeism was involuntary or, in the situation, inevitable, and were therefore moved to pass laws that tried to slow the process by protecting absentee as well as resident planters against proceedings for debt, bankruptcy, and foreclosure. Naturally, some of these enactments invoked the criticisms of English lawyers representing countervailing interests, as did the Acts passed in all the plantation colonies arbitrarily, if almost certainly ineffectually, decreeing a limit – normally 10 percent – on the interest chargeable on West Indian accounts.[62]

One type of enactment very much in the planters' favor on which metropolitan lawyers did comment positively was that which accompanied the issuing of land grant patents with a procedure for formal surveys, and which regularized, recorded, and registered property deeds and all dealings in real estate. All of the plantation colonies had a formal registry with a salaried registrar at least a century before such existed in England itself. As Charles Harper described the Jamaican system in 1684, incoming settlers

> take an Order from the Governor for so much [land]: This Order is directed to a legal, sworn Surveyor, and by him returned to the Clerk of the Pattents, who by direction of the King's Attorney, draws the Pattent and affixes the Plat on it; this at Sealing day is Sealed, and afterwards enrolled in the Office of Enrolments; for all which the Surveyor and his Clerk have as in the Act for fees.

"Nor are Purchasers here incumbred with bad Titles," proudly noted Harper, the clerk of the Jamaican Assembly, in another work in the same year, "for that Register (so much wished for in England) is here established where all Conveyances being acknowledged are to be enroll'd within three months, if the Cognisers inhabit here."[63]

Other local Acts, however, were far more bluntly selfish, even evoking negative comments from lawyers in an England where similar interests were similarly served, and the normal practice was to turn a blind eye to colonial legislation where metropolitan interests and susceptibilities were not directly infringed. Some of the most blatant cases were private Acts, such as those passed on behalf of individual Jamaican planters, ostensibly for the improvement of communications and the economy at large. These, for example, allowed individual planters to circumvent restrictions on the size of landholdings, to have aqueducts built across less powerful neighbors' lands, to have roads built at the public expense simply to serve their own inland estates, or even to erect tollgates, wharves, or markets for their private emolument.[64]

Of the many general Acts which blatantly signified the planters' interests, one kind was perhaps the most significant and aroused most widespread comment throughout the American colonies, as well as in England. This was the set of Acts passed in several West Indian colonies declaring that Negro slaves were not just chattel property but should be regarded for legal purposes as real estate. The reason for this was that while estates could be entailed and kept in being through the normal processes of bequest, slaves as chattel property could not be entailed and might easily be sold apart from the estate for which they were the essential labor force – for example, in cases of intestacy, female inheritance, or wardship. The effect of the Acts was to fix the slave populations on the land which depended upon them, except in the cases where the planters specifically decreed otherwise – though a rider was added in the Barbados case at least, that the Act did not prevent slaves being still regarded as chattels in cases of debt.[65]

Several of the slaves-as-real-estate laws did remain in operation into slavery's last years. This not only pointed up the plantocratic imperative to reify the slave workforce and treat slaves as legal pawns, and the necessity of self-legislation in order to do so.

It also illustrated the essential illogicality and contradictions inherent in the West Indian slave system, not least the willingness of the imperial authorities – including the Crown lawyers – to allow slavery to exist in the colonies though long fallen into disuse, or outlawed, at home. In other words, the corpus of slave laws was not only essential to the British West Indian plantocratic structure, it was also that structure's foundational weakness.

In the absence of clear documentation and contemporary discussion, no one is now able to know with certainty what were the immediate models of the British West Indian slave laws. The very first British slave laws have disappeared, some no doubt destroyed because the planters did not want such a close scrutiny as might reveal a rooting in outmoded English forms of bondage, or, perhaps even more "repugnant," in the Roman civil law and foreign slave codes, namely those of the Spanish, Portuguese, or Dutch. Besides this, perhaps as a consequence, West Indian planters passed slave laws only to the degree that they were absolutely necessary, preferring the far more effective, and less easily questioned, operation of pragmatic custom. Nonetheless, a whole corpus of slave laws was passed in due course in each colony, and a careful analysis, in particular of the more ingenuous preambles, does disclose a derivation both from Roman civil law principles and those of ancient English serfdom.[66]

Medieval English practice was, indeed, generally agreeable to the early West Indian settlers in trying to attach laborers to their new plantations. Bermudian tenants, as we have seen, commonly worked much like the freer types of manorial bondsmen, for half-shares or less. Hilary Beckles too has cogently argued that Barbadian white servants were not only less free (and worse treated) than any English farm laborers at that time, but that their obligation to labor (if not, strictly, their persons) was a marketable commodity.[67] In the case of the least free of all white laborers in the West Indies, that is, those "rebel" Irish and Scots rounded up in Cromwell's wars, the later victims of Monmouth's Rebellion, and those unfortunates "Barbadoed" from English jails, the principles of the generic European law of slavery dating from Roman times were already implicitly applied, that is, that captives in war and criminals could be virtually treated as chattel slaves.

In another respect, however, Roman law principles sometimes worked to the benefit of persons whom the earliest English settlers attempted to enslave, that is, the Amerindian natives. English settlers quite readily enslaved Amerindians whom they could plausibly regard as war captives, or even transgressors against the law of nature, though they generally found it most convenient to ship them to a different colony – such as happened to the captives in King Philip's war who were transported to Bermuda and Barbados in the 1670s. Those Amerindians, however, who could claim to be free natives of the soil and thus subjects of the English king or state, persons not already slaves elsewhere, or guilty of either unnatural practices or defeat in war (admittedly a fulsome list of provisos), were, by the same generic principles, not subject to enslavement. These, rather than the general unsuitability of Amerindians as praedial laborers, were the reasons why certain Arawakans enslaved by Barbadian planters were freed on the orders of the English Council of State in a famous case in 1656.[68]

No such provisions could free those half-million Africans carried to the British West Indies before 1740, whose servile labor was so vital to the sugar plantations. "Whereas the Priviledges of England are So universally Extensive as not to admit of the Least thing called Slavery," wrote a Bermudian lawyer ignorant of grammar as of logic, but certain of what he wanted, in 1730,

> Occasioned the making of such Laws for the preservation of every Individual Subject in his or their Lives, Estates and Indisputable Rights and properties; But here in his majesties Colonies and plantations in America the cases and Circumstances of things are wonderfully altered, for the very kindred nay sometimes even the Parents of these unfortunate Creatures (upon the coasts of Affrica) Expose their own Issue to perpetual Bondage and Slavery by Selling them unto your majesties Subjects trading there and from thence are brought to these and other your majesties Settlements in America and consequently purchased by the Inhabitants thereof, they being for the Brutishness of their Nature no otherwise valued or Esteemed amongst us than as our goods and Chattels or other personal Estates.[69]

Given such unashamed self-interest in a colony that had many slaves but few lawyers and fewer plantations, it is not surprising to discover the tortuous ingenuity and effort that went into the creation of the slave codes in the true sugar colonies: to define property in slaves, permanently to fix them, their progeny, and descendants in their status and location, to guard against their will to run away, rebel, or commit acts of theft or violence, as far as possible to prevent them having property, family, or a culture truly their own, and only incidentally, late in the process, and under pressure from outside philanthropists, showing any concern to ensure that they had minimal standards of food and clothing, were protected against the most savage types of oppression, and were promised the benefits of the masters' religion.[70]

The British West Indian planters never constituted a single homogenous type. Quite apart from inevitable differences of character, health, and luck, they varied, more or less, in respect to social background, initial access to money and political influence, the extent of land and local political power acquired, dynastic history, and, perhaps most critical of all, the degree of commitment to the islands which were the source of their wealth. Nor were the plantocracies established in different West Indian colonies ever identical, varying according to the context and terms of their foundation, the size, climate, topography, and soils of each island, and, above all, the speed and completeness of the achievement of a sugar monoculture. This made for a clear distinction between the neat, complete, well-ordered and comparatively modest Barbadian model, and the much richer, more expansive and flamboyant, but never quite finished, Jamaican model – not to mention the plantocratic variations developed in the islands taken over in 1763, and the colonies acquired in the very last French wars, which are outside the scope of the present chapter.[71] Yet all British West Indian planters and the plantocracies they constructed were involved in the same basic enterprise in the same global contexts, copied and learned from each other, and gravitated toward a socioeconomic and political ideal form and style. Most important, they all depended for their evolution as a class upon the effective exploitation of undeveloped tropical land and black slave labor. Thus, following up on the evidence and arguments already deployed, it should be possible in conclusion to propose some rounding generalizations and, in particular, to decide whether the British West Indian planters did in fact create a distinctive, fully formed, and lasting class.

The essential plantocratic ideology was quasi-aristocratic, a set of attitudes, a culture, drawn from the possession of land and the control over its labor force. It derived from the mother country, though only a minority of the founding planters were "to the manor born." There was, in fact, a spectrum of original planter types; from those of noble families who also had initial wealth, through those with "gentle" antecedents but no inherited money, and those with new money but of obscure social origin, to almost completely self-made men (and women) to whom the plantations themselves were the sole fount of wealth and status. Dynastic engineering, however, was a necessary concomitant to the preservation and extension of socioeconomic power, and an increasingly tight and homogenous network of families evolved among the owners of estates, as land, money, and title intermarried.

Though a thorough typology of early British West Indian planters is a worthy project still to be undertaken, it is probably permissible to propose four or five basic categories, with the most dynamic and significant individuals being those who combined several, if not all, of the different typological characteristics, and who, by choice or lack of it, committed themselves to making the West Indies their home.

Foremost of West Indian "planters" were those noble adventurers and courtiers who became involved in the plantations as a natural extension of their privileged position in the ambit of the Crown. Even if, like Lord Willoughby of Parham, they became directly involved in the colonies, they were more interested in proprietorships than in single plantations (though they might own many), and took it for granted that they were natural candidates to be the king's viceroys.

In the second rank were those gentlemen of squirearchical background like the Codringtons, Modyfords, Stapletons, Warners, and Colletons, who committed themselves to the colonies in order to rescue or augment their family fortunes. These filled the upper ranks of the colonial administrations, as much by their gentlemanly training as by natural right, but, having extensive holdings and expansive ideas, were rarely involved in the day-to-day management of individual estates, or permanently committed to a single island.[72]

A third important category were those planters, like the Noells, Poveys, Draxes, Lascelles, and Beckfords, who brought investment capital, good mercantile connections, and perhaps lobbying influence, rather than title and gentle birth, to become further enriched through the development of the plantations. While some family members might be directly involved in plantation affairs, the ownership of plantations was best managed from England, and the interests of England-based planters were rarely limited to a single colony.[73]

The majority of the resident planters were recruited from a fourth category: persons of questionably gentle, yeoman, or more obscure social provenance, who made their start and fortunes in the islands – however much they or their descendants tended to exaggerate the distinction of their social origins. Some, like the Pinneys or the Morgans, began as servants, petty traders, or privateers; others, like the Prices, Barretts, Dawkinses, Barhams, or Tharps, were survivors of those who claimed to be the first "conquerors" of Jamaica. But nearly all were essentially self-made men, beginning as tenants and graduating to smallholders, pen-keepers and perhaps modest sugar producers, and thus laying the groundwork for their descendants to become major sugar producers and slave-owners, with, in the most successful cases, a whole network of estates. Such persons and families, like those whose names dot Richard Ford's 1674 map of Barbados or Bochart and Knollis's Jamaican map of 1684, tended to confine their interests to a single island, though in the earliest years they might, like Cary Helyar, Henry Morgan, and perhaps Francis Price, have moved from Barbados to Jamaica, seeking to improve their chances along with the general extension of the plantation system.[74]

To this category of upwardly mobile planters should also be added a final formative type, that of the would-be planters at any stage of the process. There was hardly a white person on the socioeconomic ladder who did not strive to climb, rung by rung, into the planter class; from the meanest indentured servant once his time had expired, through the Scots bookkeepers and managers under scarcely less onerous contracts, to the privileged but land-poor overseers and attorneys. Such aspirants included even the collateral members of the upper reaches of white society, the doctors, lawyers, clergymen-teachers, and merchants in town. The aspirations, the occupational investment, of all such persons – who, of course, always outnumbered the actual planters – was an important invisible support of the plantocratic system.[75]

As has been suggested already, perhaps the most significant of all early planters was the "planter-governor" Thomas Modyford (1620–79), who not only combined in himself several of the types of early planter, but was one of the most influential founders of the plantocratic system, in both Barbados and Jamaica.[76] Thomas Modyford's outstanding career and achievements, though, even his very popularity with his fellow planters, showed up and anticipated the essential flaws in the plantocratic system. To Barbadian and Jamaican planters alike, Modyford rejoiced in the title of the Planter-Governor, but it proved difficult for him to wear both hats at the same time, and impossible for later governors even to claim such interchangeable headgear. All planters, in fact, were torn between irreconcilable opposites. First of these was that while they were dependent on the Crown as the ultimate source of land and the provider of protection, they were yet compelled by their interests to set up an assembly which was bound to confront any assertions of imperial authority. Thus they were forced into the absurdity of claiming to be a landed aristocracy and professing loyalty to the Crown, while at the same time indulging in republican rhetoric.

Secondly, while the planters were drawn toward an aristocratic life-style and ethos by the imperatives of landownership and the control of labor, and affected a spirit of *noblesse oblige*, they were at the same time driven by the commercial profit motive, and by the perceived necessity to regard slaves as less than human beings. Some English noblemen, unlike the French, were able to reconcile the contradictions between landowning and commerce, but few were able to bridge the gap between the conditions of English rural life and the crude realities of slave plantation production; conversely, few persons with the kind of background or temperament that made it possible to exploit Negroes as chattel laborers in the cause of profit, could effectively make the transition to English country gentleman.

Moreover, the very transition to Jamaica which Modyford spearheaded was part of a steady process of economic extension and intensification. Just as the slave sugar plantation first supplanted the quasi-manorial system of smallholdings in Barbados, so the expansion of sugar production to other islands and the quest for efficiencies of scale under increased competition made for a more crudely exploitative system, and progressively widened the gap between the gentlemanly ideal of landowning and the management of dependent labor and the harsh industrial reality of the fully developed slave plantation system. Modyford himself was praised for being the "most considerable" Jamaican planter and "the ablest and most upright" judge in the white men's court, but was not notable for humanity when it came to managing slaves. Jamaica, in fact, had the character of a crude frontier area from the beginning, compared with settled Barbados, where even the great early sugar magnate Henry Drax could still refer to his servants and slaves as his "family" in 1670. But the process of intensification in the search for efficiency led to an increasingly standard level of practice – best represented perhaps in the widely circulated *Essay on Plantership* by the Antiguan planter Samuel Martin (1750), in which sugar production was no more than an industrial business, and slaves regarded as little more than animate industrial machines.[77]

The response of most planters who found the stink of the sugar factory and the realities of Negro slavery too oppressive was to distance themselves as far as possible from the sordid source of their wealth. Besides, there were other motives which encouraged planters to become absentees. From the earliest times, the planters who succeeded most, and most rapidly, were those who retained good metropolitan mercantile connections, and under the later conditions of expansion and intensification, as the history of the Pinney family fortune conclusively illustrates, it became as vital to have a strong metropolitan base as to have efficient managers on the spot.[78] Many families, such as the Jamaican Barretts, had different branches of a large family in England and Jamaica, and nearly all male members of absentee planter families spent at least part of their adult lives directly managing their West Indian plantations. But contrary to most accounts, there were at least as many resident planters whose fortunes evaporated through bad mercantile connections and extravagant dissipation as there were absentee planters milking their distant estates in order to keep up a pretentious life-style in England. In course of time, moreover, as plantation profits declined, fewer owners of West Indian property retained any option but to stay in England and attempt to diversify their fortunes, leaving their plantations and slaves in the hands of peripatetic bookkeepers, hard-grafting managers, and attorneys.[79]

Barbados was relatively less affected by the absentee problem than was Jamaica. Since Barbadian plantations were modest-sized, relatively few Barbadian planters, like the majority of the landowners of Bermuda, were ever wealthy enough to become absentees. But many families were also encouraged to stay by the very conditions that allowed Barbados to become known as "the civilized island" or "Little England": a comparatively large white population well distributed throughout the island; a comprehensive and effective system of law and order; small, well-organized parishes with a full complement of parsons; and an adequate system of local schools.[80] Perhaps a quarter of Barbadian plantations were absentee-owned in 1700, but this increased to no more than a third by the end of the eighteenth century. For Jamaica, that proportion had already been exceeded by 1740, and by 1800 it was almost two-thirds. Even Edward Long, the most eloquent proponent of an ideal resident Jamaican plantocracy, and owner of one of the richest plantations in Clarendon parish, spent the years 1769–1813, the greater part of his long life, living in England off the income from his estate and from the fruits of his absentee tenure of the judgeship of the Jamaican Vice-Admiralty court.[81]

Even more than Charles Leslie's substantial account of 1740, Edward Long's three-volume *History of Jamaica* (1774) illustrates the contradictions between plantocratic loyalism and "republican" independentism, between the ideal of a white society and the cruder realities, between pride in the English legal heritage and the planters' demand to make laws for themselves, and between the need for royal authority in the granting of land and the planters' will to have its subsequent disposal entirely in their own hands. But both books, even less intentionally, reveal that the most critical contradiction of all – and ultimately the chief impediment to the forming of a lasting plantocracy – concerned the legal questions surrounding the planters' claim to hold property in their slaves.[82]

To make Negroes into chattels when Britons no longer could be slaves was probably the most compelling reason for the British West Indian planters to have independent legislatures of their own, since (as Lord Mansfield was to decree in 1772) "so high an act of dominion" required nothing less than a "positive law."[83] There was something of an irony in the fact that the rights of property had become a sacred principle of English jurisprudence in parallel with the gradual process whereby property in persons, or even in a person's labor, had become outlawed. Yet the undeniable fading out of slavery in English custom and common law was an embarrassment when at the same time the West Indian planters wanted the benefit of all those English laws and customs which guaranteed the rights of possession and transmission of real estate in general. In addition, the planters had ever to tread carefully, that the principles on which they justified slavery in their statutes – derived without acknowledgment mainly from ancient principles of Roman law – were not held to be repugnant to current English law, and thus disallowed.

The chief contradictions in British West Indian slave laws, however, were internal to the laws themselves. The basic laws defined slaves as property – whether chattel or real estate – yet the slave codes included many other laws which treated slaves as persons, not things, particularly in respect of committing crimes. Even if these were not intrinsically illogical and inoperable (for how could a thing commit a crime any more than it could own property, let alone be brought to court as a person to stand normal trial?), the laws compounded the situation by proposing systems of punishment so flexible and relativistic as to make a mockery of absolute justice. One polar example was that on the one side a white person could never be punished with the normal penalties for murder for killing a slave, while on the other a slave might be put to death in barbaric fashion for even offering violence to a white. Even more ridiculous perhaps was the sliding scale of punishment in the laws concerning slave marronage (running away). A free white person harboring a runaway would be severely fined, whereas a white indentured servant would be physically punished and serve extra time, and a free black person lose his freedom or even be put to death. The runaway slave, however, being valuable property, would simply be given corporal punishment, albeit of a savage kind (including, in some islands, the loss of a foot for repeated offences). A slave who died during "justified punishment" was not the victim of murder, and if one was killed while running away or resisting arrest, the owner received monetary compensation from the colonial treasury.[84]

Even had there been far more resident whites in the British West Indies, they could not have created a true society while the corpus of social laws was so untuned to natural justice or equity, and where the majority of people were treated as chattels, even of a sentient type. In course of time, the white plantocracy would be forced to accept, albeit unconsciously, that they were merely the dominant component in a creolized "slave society," including free colored persons as well as the black slave majority, in which customary practice was at least as determinant as formal laws.[85] But such problems were merely inherent in Barbados in 1680 or Jamaica in 1740, when the plantocracies were only just established and asserting their rule, and the sugar plantation system as a whole had not yet reached its apogee. The basic injustices as well as the intrinsic contradictions of the slave system at large, were inevitably and irresistibly only to surface once sugar plantations and sugar plantocracies started to decline, and the age of Enlightenment promoted the ending of slavery on rational economic as well as humanistic grounds. At this time, the last defenders of the old plantocratic ideology were to be driven back into the tortured logic and scarcely concealed private agonies discernible in the works of Bryan Edwards, Elie Moreau de St Méry, and Thomas Jefferson.[86]

Notes

1   Charles M. Andrews, *The Colonial Period of American History*, 4 vols (New Haven, CT: Yale University Press, 1934–8, Vol. I, pp. 86–7; Theodore F. T. Plucknett, *A Concise History of the Common Law* (Boston, MA: Little, Brown, 1956 [1929]; 5th edn), pp. 516–74; Frederick G. Kempin, Jr, *Legal History: Law and Social Change* (Englewood Cliffs, NJ: Prentice-Hall, 1959), pp. 55–70; Alan Harding, *A Social History of English Law* (Harmondsworth, Mx: Penguin, 1966).

2   Andrews, *Colonial Period*, Vol. I, p. 86, note 1; Vol. II, pp. 199–240, 282–5; Plucknett, *Common Law*, pp. 521–74.

3   Andrews, *Colonial Period*; Vol. II, pp. 199–240. Samuel Lucas, *Charters of the Old English Colonies in America* (London: Parker, 1850).

4   Andrews, *Colonial Period*, Vol. II, p. 202, note 3, pp. 274–324.

5   James A. Williamson, *The Caribbee Islands under the Proprietary Patents* (London: Oxford University Press, 1926); Vincent T. Harlow, *A History of Barbados, 1625–1685* (New York: Negro Universities Press, 1969 [1926]).

6   Crawford B. Macpherson, *The Political Theory of Possessive Individualism: Hobbes to Locke* (Oxford: Clarendon Press, 1964); John G. A. Pocock, "British history: a plea for a new subject," *Journal of Modern History* 47 (1975): 601–28; Immanuel Wallerstein, *The Modern World System, Vol. II Mercantilism and the Consolidation of the European World Economy, 1600–1750* Vol. II, (New York: Academic Press, 1980).

7   Angus Calder, *Revolutionary Empire: The Rise of the English-Speaking Empires from the Fifteenth Century to the 1780s* (London: Jonathan Cape, 1981); Kenneth R. Andrews, *Trade, Plunder, and Settlement: Maritime Enterprise and the Genesis of the British Empire, 1480–1630* (Cambridge and New York: Cambridge University Press, 1984).

8   John H. Lefroy, *Memorials of the Discovery and Early Settlement of the Bermudas or Somers Islands, 1515–1685*, 2 vols (Toronto: Toronto University Press, 1981 [1879]; 3rd edn); Vernon A. Ives (ed.), *The Rich Papers: Letters from Bermuda, 1615–1646* (Toronto and Buffalo: Toronto University Press for the Bermuda National Trust, 1984); Henry C. Wilkinson, *The Adventurers of Bermuda: A History of the Island from its Discovery until the Dissolution of the Somers Island Company in 1684* (Oxford: Oxford University Press, 1958 [1933]; 2nd edn); Andrews, *Colonial Period*, Vol. II, pp. 214–48; Wesley Frank Craven, "An introduction to the history of

Bermuda," *William and Mary Quarterly* 17 (1937): 176–215, 317–62, 437–65, and 18 ((1938): 13–63; Cyril O. Packwood, *Chained on the Rock: Slavery in Bermuda* (Bermuda: Baxters, 1975).

9   Wilkinson. *Adventurers of Bermuda*, p. 68 note, pp. 108–10, 241–5. For West Indian surveying in general, see Barry W. Higman, *Jamaica Surveyed: Plantation Maps and Plans of the Eighteenth and Nineteenth Centuries* (Kingston: Institute of Jamaica, 1988), pp. 19–79.

10   Wilkinson, *Adventurers in Bermuda*, pp. 77–95.

11   Answers to queries from Council of Trade and Plantations, July 15, 1679, Lefroy, *Memorials of the Bermudas*, Vol. II, p. 430.

12   Wilkinson, *Adventurers of Bermuda*, pp. 77–95. Wilkinson cites Beverly W. Bond, Jr, *The Quit-Rent System in the American Colonies* (New Haven, CT: Yale University Press, 1919), pp. 15, 109, 131, and Andrews, *Colonial Period* Vol. I, pp. 86–7.

13   Wilkinson, *Adventurers of Bermuda*, pp. 96–9. The first blacks in Bermuda were apparently a family of "Spanish Negroes" brought in around 1617 to instruct the settlers in growing cassava, maize, and tobacco. Initially free, they may have been later enslaved. The first slaves were captives from the Spaniards and Portuguese around 1620, and were used to work company lands. They were augmented by many others similarly acquired and by the natural increase which the healthy climate encouraged. As a majority of the white inhabitants became engaged in maritime activities and spurned manual labor, the slaves fulfilled agricultural needs in Bermuda, as well as being employed at the salt pans in the Turks and Caicos Islands and in the most menial maritime tasks. The slave population of Bermuda rose from a quarter to a third of the total between 1650 and 1680, not reaching a half until the mid-eighteenth century. Packwood, *Chained on the Rock*, pp. 1–116.

14   Wilkinson, *Adventurers of Bermuda*, pp. 138–41. Grand and petty juries were also established very early on. Once formed, the Bermudian legal structure was almost frozen in its original English model for two hundred years or more, in a simpler form than most of the West Indian colonies because of the colony's small size and population. In 1827, the Bermudian courts consisted of a Chancery court composed of the governor and council, who also sat as a Court of Error to hear appeals from all the island courts. There was a common law court of General Assize, with a chief justice and two associates, which sat twice yearly, and a court of Quarter Sessions to deal with lesser cases. There was, inevitably, an active Vice-Admiralty court, and officially also courts of Exchequer and Ordinary, though they rarely sat. John Henry Howard, *The Laws of the British Colonies in the West Indies and other Parts of America concerning Real and Personal Property . . . with a View of the Constitution of Each Colony*, 2 vols (London: 1827; rptd Westport, CT: Negro Universities Press, 1970), pp. 363–4.

15   Wilkinson, *Adventurers of Bermuda*, pp. 246–80.

16   Ibid., pp. 281–384; Henry C. Wilkinson, *Bermuda in the Old Empire, 1684–1784* (London and New York: Oxford University Press, 1950).

17   For the early history of Barbados, see Jerome S. Handler, *A Guide to Source Materials for the Study of Barbados History, 1627–1834* (Carbondale, IL: Southern Illinois University Press, 1971); David Watts, *The West Indies: Patterns of Development, Culture and Economic Change since 1492* (Cambridge and New York: Cambridge University Press, 1987); Robert Schomburgk, *The History of Barbados* (London: 1848); Williamson, *Caribbee Islands*; Harlow, *Barbados, 1625–1685*; Andrews, *Colonial Period* Vol. II, pp. 241–73; Archibald P. Thornton, *West-India Policy under the Restoration* (Oxford: Clarendon Press, 1956); Richard S. Dunn, *Sugar and Slaves: The Rise of the Plantation Class in the English West Indies, 1624–1713* (New York: Norton, 1972); Gary Puckrein, *Little England: Plantation Society and Anglo-Barbadian Politics, 1627–1700* (New York: New York University Press, 1984); Hilary McD. Beckles, *White Servitude and Black Slavery in Barbados, 1627–1715* (Knoxville, TN: University of Tennessee Press, 1989).

18   For example, N. Darnell Davis, *Cavaliers and Roundheads of Barbados, 1650 to 1652* (Georgetown, British Guiana: 1887); Schomburgk, *Barbados*; Harlow, *Barbados, 1625–1685*.

19   Schomburgk, *Barbados*, p. 261; Fitzroy Augier, Shirley Gordon, Douglas Hall, and Mary Reckord, *The Making of the West Indies* (London: Longman Caribbean, 1960), p. 41.

20   John Poyer, *The History of Barbados* (London: 1808), pp. 30–1; Williamson, *Caribbee Islands*, pp. 23–87; Harlow, *Barbados, 1625–1686*, pp. 1–25. The precise form of the earliest grants of lands in Barbados remains obscure compared with Jamaica after 1660. A useful compilation

of the total annual grants allocated between 1628 and 1638, though, was given in *Memoirs of the First Settlement of the Island of Barbados* (London: 1743; rptd Barbados: 1891). This shows that the average size of grant, excluding the original 10,000 acres granted in 1628 to certain London merchants, was 96½ acres, and that by 1638, 132 square miles, or 80 percent of Barbados, had been distributed. Some of the land, if not all, was allocated by headright, at the rate of 10 acres per dependent white servant – the so-called "ten-acre men" needed for militia purposes.

Table 24.1 Average size of land grants in Barbados, 1628–37

Years		Grants	Acreage	Average	Cumulative total
1628	Merchants +	64	16,400	100	16,400
1629		140	15,871	113	32,272
1630		45	14,235	316	46,507
1631		31	2,749	89	49,256
1632		63	4,138	66	53,394
1633		20	905	45	54,299
1634		64	3,511	55	57,810
1635		106	9,055	85	66,865
1636		98	9,810	100	76,675
1637		139	7,604	55	84,279

The above figures are quoted in Richard Pares, *Merchants and Planters* (Cambridge, UK: Cambridge University Press, and the Economic History Review, 1960), p. 57.

21   Harlow, *Barbados*, p. 17; Schomburgk, *Barbados*, p. 267.
22   Pares, *Merchants and Planters*, pp. 26–48; Dunn, *Sugar and Slaves*, pp. 46–83.
23   Quoted in J. Harry Bennett, "The English Caribbees, 1642–1646," *William and Mary Quarterly*, 3rd series, 24 (1967): 367–73.
24   Richard Ligon, *A True and Exact History of the Island of Barbados* (London: 1657)), pp. 100–1. In due course, Barbados had the most complete system of courts, very closely modeled on England, but with extra courts for special local conditions. As J. H. Howard reported in 1827, "The courts for the administration of civil justice in Barbadoes, are the court of Chancery [consisting of the governor and council], the court of Exchequer, five courts of Common Pleas, the court of Ordinary, the court of Admiralty, the court of Error, and the court of Escheat. Besides these general courts, there is, by a local act, a power vested in the governor to appoint a special court of Merchants and Mariners; as also a court to take cognizance of cases of persons about to quit the island in debt. For the administration of criminal justice, the courts are the court of Grand Session, the court of Quarter Sessions, a court for the trial of slaves, and the Admiralty Sessions." Howard, *Laws of the British Colonies*, pp. 95–101.
25   It is quoted in full in Schomburgk, *Barbados*, pp. 706–8.
26   The terms of the surrender are given in [John Jennings] *Acts and Statutes of the Island of Barbados Made and Enacted since the Reducement of the Same, unto the Authority of the Commonwealth of England . . .* (London: William Bentley, 1654), pp. 1–4.
27   Ibid.
28   Ibid., Acts numbered 29, 35, 59, 73, 99; 48, 50, 62; 5–12, 30, 39, 72, 81, 86.
29   Ibid., Acts numbered 28, 41–6. Parallel Acts concerned penalties for allowing animals to stray across property lines, and against human vagrants who threatened social order and discipline in a more general sense.
30   Thornton, *West-India Policy*, pp. 36–7; Williamson, *Caribbee Islands*, pp. 180–214; F. G. Spurdle, *Early West Indian Government* (Palmerston, NZ: n.d.), pp. 12–20.
31   [William Rawlin] *The Laws of Barbados, Collected in One Volume by William Rawlin, of the Middle Temple, London, Esquire, and now Clerk of the Assembly of the Said Island* (London: 1699).

32 Dunn, *Sugar and Slaves*, pp. 46–116; Watts, *West Indies since 1492*, table 7.5, p. 311.

33 Dunn, *Sugar and Slaves*, pp. 111–16.

34 For the early history of English Jamaica, see S. A. G. Taylor, *The Western Design: An Account of Cromwell's Expedition to the Caribbean* (Kingston: Institute of Jamaica, 1965); Agnes M. Whitson, *The Constitutional History of Jamaica, 1664–1729* (Manchester: Manchester University Press, 1929); Andrews, *Colonial Period*, Vol. III, pp. 1–34; Thornton, *West-India Policy*, pp. 22–123; Michael Craton and James Walvin, *A Jamaican Plantation: The History of Worthy Park, 1670–1970* (Toronto: Toronto University Press, 1970), pp. 12–70; Dunn, *Sugar and Slaves*, pp. 149–87.

35 Thornton, *West-India Policy*, p. 42.

36 Lord Windsor's Instructions, March 21, 1662, Public Record Office, London, CO 324/1, 37–56; Thornton, *West-India Policy*, p. 52; Craton and Walvin, *Jamaican Plantation*, p. 20.

37 Thornton, *West-India Policy*, p. 53.

38 Analysis of index to Jamaican land patents, 1661–1826, Jamaican Archives, Spanish Town, file 1 B/11, in Dunn, *Sugar and Slaves*, p. 154. *Calendar of State Papers, Colonial, America and West Indies*, Vol. VII, 1674, no. 1236. Governor Thomas Lynch, besides being almost as generous to himself with land grants as Modyford had been, was an even greater speculator in land. As Richard Dunn computed, Lynch "took out 10 patents for 6,040 acres, but in addition he bought 26,744 acres from other landholders and sold 11,346 acres, so that he ended with 21,438 acres, acquired in 59 separate transactions between 1662 and 1684." Dunn, *Sugar and Slaves*, p. 167.

39 C. R. Williams, "Thomas Modyford, planter-governor of Barbados and Jamaica, 1620–1679" (PhD thesis University of Kentucky: 1979); E. A. Cruikshank, *Sir Henry Morgan: His Life and Times* (Toronto: Macmillan, 1935).

40 See, for example, the early history of the Price family in Craton and Walvin, *Jamaican Plantation*, and of the Helyars in J. Harry Bennett, "Cary Helyar," *William and Mary Quarterly*, 3rd series, 21 (1964): 53–76, and Dunn, *Sugar and Slaves*, pp. 212–22, 321–3.

41 Dunn, *Sugar and Slaves*, p. 155; Watts, *West Indies since 1492*, p. 311.

42 By the mid-eighteenth century, principal courts in Jamaica were the Supreme Court, three courts of assize for what became the counties of Surrey, Middlesex, and Cornwall (1756), and "divers inferior courts of Common Pleas," one for each parish. Besides this, there were island courts of Chancery, Error, Vice-Admiralty and Ordinary. Howard, *Laws of the British Colonies*, pp. 27–33.

43 [Charles Harper] *The Laws of Jamaica Passed by the Assembly and Confirmed by his Majesty's Council, April 17, 1684* (London: 1684). Modyford, in fact, had such a good rapport with the Jamaican planters – who in any case dominated the council – that he found it unnecessary to call the assembly regularly.

44 For the constitutional struggle, see Whitson, *Constitutional History, 1664–1729*; Thornton, *West-India Policy*; Spurdle, *Early West Indian Government*. For the Jamaican Maroons, H. Orlando Patterson, "Slavery and slave revolts: a socio-historical analysis of the First Maroon War, Jamaica, 1755–1740," in Richard Price (ed.), *Maroon Societies: Rebel Slave Communities in the Americas* (New York: Doubleday, 1973); Michael Craton, *Testing the Chains: Resistance to Slavery in the British West Indies* (Ithaca, NY: Cornell University Press, 1982), pp. 61–96.

45 Howard, *Laws of the British Colonies*, pp. 19–26.

46 Richard B. Morris, *Studies in the History of American Law: With Special Reference to the Seventeenth and Eighteenth Centuries* (New York: Columbia University Press, 1930), pp. 83–4, citing 2 Salk., 411 (1694).

47 As J. H. Howard said of the Jamaican Chancery Court in 1827, it "is composed of the governor or president of the council, with four or more members of the council, and the opinion of the majority is the decision. The court derives its authority from the king's commission, and the judges are supposed to have all the authority of the chancellor of England, except in cases wholly inapplicable to the colony. . . . The practice of this court professes to conform to that of the court of Chancery in England, except where it may be altered by local laws, or special rules of their own. There are above a hundred of these rules

prescribed by the court itself, written in a book kept by the registrar, often not at all known to persons practising in the profession. . . . Many of the early orders are rude and uncouth, some very obscure, and others ludicrous; the latter ones, as far as they go, are generally wise and useful." Howard, *Laws of the British Colonies*, pp. 96–7.

48   The actual act was 1 Geo. II, c. 1, "An Act for granting a Revenue to His Majesty, his Heirs and Successors, for the Support of the Government of this Island; and for reviving and perpetuating the Acts and Laws thereof." Ibid., p. 46. As Spurdle wrote, "Onwards from 1728 each new Jamaican law simply followed the normal course of having to take the chance of confirmation or otherwise in England. Thus, though the details might differ, the result was practically the same: the cream of Jamaican laws gained permanent confirmation; a great many others, being indifferently regarded in England, were allowed simply to 'lie by' and a few, being seriously objected to, were disallowed." *Early West Indian Government*, pp. 31–2.

49   Craton, *Testing the Chains*, pp. 81–7.

50   Watts, *West Indies since 1492*, p. 311; Michael Craton, *Searching for the Invisible Man: Slaves and Plantation Life in Jamaica* (Cambridge, MA: Harvard University Press, 1978), p. 34.

Table 24.2 Frequency distribution of landholdings in Jamaica, 1670 and 1754

Acres	1670	%	1754	%
0–99	384	53	263	16
100–499	234	33	566	35
500–999	55	8	303	19
1000–1999	34	5	253	16
2000–4999	11	2	153	10
5000–9999	2	0.8	52	3
10,000–22,999	0		9	0.5
Total	720		1599	

Richard B. Sheridan, *Sugar and Slavery* (Baltimore, MD: Johns Hopkins University Press, 1974), p. 219; *Calendar of State Papers, Colonial, America and West Indies, 1669–74*, pp. 99–103. Note that in 1670, the 42.5 percent of the land in units of more than 1,000 acres was held in only 47 units, or 8 percent of the total, whereas in 1754, 77.8 percent of the land was held in 467 such parcels – 29.5 percent of the total. Whereas the number of landholdings of less than 100 acres had actually fallen from 384 to 263, those over 500 acres (which included virtually all the sugar plantations) had risen from 102 to 770. Multiple holdings, of course, determined that the actual number of substantial planters was considerably less than the 1,336 landholdings over 100 acres in 1754.

51   Jamaican Archives, Spanish Town, Patents, 1741, Craton, *Testing the Chains*, p. 94. The same principle probably explains why Leeward Island planters (most notably Sir William Young, governor of St Vincent) were at pains to stress the African rather than the Amerindian antecedents of the so-called Black Caribs of St Vincent.

52   W. Jethro Brown, *The Austinian Theory of Law* (London: John Murray, 1912); George L. Haskins, "Law and colonial society," in David H. Flaherty (ed.), *Essays in the History of Early American Law* (Chapel Hill, NC: University of North Carolina Press, 1969 [1957]), pp. 41–52; Mark de Wolfe Howe (ed.), *Holmes–Laski Letters: The Correspondence of Justice Holmes and Harold Laski*, 2 vols (Cambridge, MA: Harvard University Press, 1953).

53   David Brion Davis, *The Problem of Slavery in Western Culture* (Ithaca, NY: Cornell University Press, 1966).

54   Quoted in Andrews, *Colonial Period*, Vol. I, p. 57, note 1.

55   Morris, *Studies in American Law*, pp. 9–17, 69–125; Zechariah Chafee, Jr, "Colonial courts and the common law" (1952), Julius Goebel, Jr, "King's law and local custom in

seventeenth-century New England" (1931), Richard B. Morris, "Massachusetts and the common law: the declaration of 1646" (1925), and George L. Haskins, "The beginnings of partible inheritance in the American colonies" (1941), all in David H. Flaherty, *Essays in Early American Law* (Chapel Hill, NC: University of North Carolina Press, 1969), pp. 53–82, 83–120, 135–46, 204–44.

56 Peter Laslett, *The World We Have Lost* (London: Methuen, 1965).

57 See the later history of the Prices, including the almost certainly spurious early genealogy contributed to *Burke's Peerage*, in Craton and Walvin, *A Jamaican Plantation*. Also, for example, Jeanette Marks, *The Family of the Barretts: A Colonial Romance* (New York: Macmillan, 1938). For partible inheritance, primogeniture, and women's rights in early America, see Morris, *Studies in American Law*, pp. 126–200.

58 For the Acts setting up the court system in Barbados, see Act No. 29 of 1652 in Jennings, *Acts of Barbados*, re-enacted after the Restoration as 1 Car. II, August 29, 1661, Howard, *Laws of the British Colonies*, pp. 105–7. The Jamaican Permanent Revenue Act of 1 Geo. II, c. 1, dated April 10, 1728, already cited, is in ibid., p. 46. For a later but full "Act to declare how much of the Laws of England are practicable within the Bahama Islands," see 40 Geo. III, c. 2 of 1799, ibid., pp. 341–4. This last Act includes the telling preamble: "Whereas the common law of England is the best birthright of Englishmen, and of their descendants, but, nevertheless, is not in all respects applicable to the circumstances and condition of new and distant colonies . . . be it therefore declared, That the common law of England, in all cases where the same hath not been altered by any of the acts or statutes hereinafter enumerated, or by any act or acts of assembly of these islands, except so much thereof as hath relation to the ancient feudal tenures, to outlawries in civil suits, to the wager of law or of batail, appeals of felony, writs of attaint, and ecclesiastical matters, is, and of right ought to be, in full force within these islands, as the same now is in that part of Great Britain called England."

59 Such early Acts can be seen in Lefroy, *Memorials* (Bermuda, 1620–84), Jennings, *Acts and Statutes* (Barbados, 1652–4), and Harper, *Laws* (Jamaica, 1683–4).

60 Barbados Acts of 2 Car. II, September 27, 1661, 9 Car. II, May 24, 1669, and 11 Car. II, August 11, 1670 – which last refers to a local Act as early as September 11, 1649; Howard, *Laws of the British Colonies*, pp. 107–9, 112–16.

61 For a series of later quit-rent Acts, see Jamaican Acts of 2 Anne, c. 7, November 2, 1703, 6 Geo. II c. 7 (1733), and 9 Geo. III c. 9, December 31, 1768; ibid., pp. 42–3, 50, 60–2.

62 For perhaps the standard 10 percent Act, see Barbados Act 8 Car. II, April 29, 1668; Howard, *Laws of the British Colonies*, pp. 111–12. Montserrat in 1735 passed legislation reducing the permissible interest from 10 to 8 percent, and Antigua in 1838 even more ambitiously (though at a time of generally falling interest rates, from 10 to 6 percent. Ibid., pp. 450, 414.

63 [Charles Harper] *Laws of Jamaica, 1684*, p. xii; *Laws of Jamaica, 1683*, Preface. To the first statement, Harper added the interesting note about Jamaican tenures by crown patent: "The Tenant holds as in Common Socage, pays a half-penny per Acre, is to serve in Arms, &c."

64 See, for example, for the activities of the grandee Sir Charles Price (1708–72), Craton and Walvin, *A Jamaican Plantation*, pp. 71–94.

65 See the Barbados Acts of 8 Car. II, April 29, 1668, and 12 Car. II, January 29, 1672, and the apparently countervailing 39 Geo. III of July 30, 1799; Howard, *Laws of the British Colonies*, pp. 112, 116–17, 139–40. Also see the Nevis Acts "for ascertaining Lands, as also affixing Slaves, Coppers, &c. to the Freehold," 32 Car. II, February 8, 1681, and "for making the Negroes, Coppers, Mills, and Stills of Intestates' Estates, Chattels," 10 Wm. & Mary, October 22, 1700, and the Grenada Act "to make Slaves, Cattle, Horses, Mules, Asses, Coppers, Stills and Plantation Utensils real Estate of Inheritance, and declaring Widows dowable of them, as of Lands and Tenements," 7 Geo. III, April 29, 1767; ibid., pp. 498–500, 161–3.

66 Elsa Goveia, *The West Indian Slave Laws of the Eighteenth Century* (Barbados: Caribbean University Press, 1970). The Act No. 12 of the second session of the Bermudian Assembly

(1622) "to restrayne the insolencies of the Negroes," is claimed to be "the first law anywhere in English specifically dealing with Blacks." Packwood, *Chained on the Rock*, p. 7; Lefroy, *Memorials of the Bermudas*, Vol. I, pp. 308–11; Craven, "Introduction" (1937), p. 362. The first Barbadian Slave Act almost certainly dates from the first Assembly called by the Bermudian Philip Bell in 1639, but details have long disappeared, so that the earliest extant law is that signed by Searle in 1652. An order of the Barbadian governor in council as early as 1636, however, decreed that "Negroes and Indians that came here to be sold, should serve for Life, unless a Contract was before made to the contrary." Dunn, *Sugar and Slaves*, pp. 224–9; Acts Nos 48, 50, 62, Jennings, *Acts and Statutes of Barbados* (1654).

67   Most recently in "The concept of white slavery in the English Caribbean during the early seventeenth century," in the present volume. Also, Hilary McD. Beckles, "The English parliamentary debate on 'white slavery' in Barbados, 1659," *Barbados Museum and Historical Society* 36, 4 (1985): 344–52; Hilary McD. Beckles, *White Servitude and Black Slavery* (Knoxville, TN: University of Tennessee Press, 1989).

68   Dunn, *Sugar and Slaves*, pp. 224–8.

69   Preamble to "An Act for the Security of the Subject to prevent the forfeiture of Life and Estate on Killing a Negro or other Slave" (1730), in Michael Craton, James Walvin, and David Wright (eds), *Slavery, Abolition and Emancipation: Black Slaves and the British Empire, A Thematic Documentary* (London: Longman, 1976), p. 68.

70   Goveia, *Slave Laws*; "A Statement of the Laws that at present subsist in the West India Islands respecting Negro Slaves, Prepared by John Reeves, Clerk to the Committee," *British Sessional Papers, Commons, Accounts and Papers*, 1789, XXVI, 646a, quoted in Craton, Walvin, and Wright, *Slavery, Abolition and Emancipation*, pp. 181–90; Howard, *Laws of the British Colonies, passim*.

71   Lowell J. Ragatz, *The Fall of the Planter Class in the British Caribbean, 1763–1833* (Washington, DC: American Historical Association, 1928); John R. Ward, *British West Indian Slavery, 1750–1834: The Process of Amelioration* (Oxford: Clarendon Press, 1988).

72   Vincent T. Harlow, *Christopher Codrington* (Oxford: Clarendon Press, 1928); Williams, "Modyford"; J. R. V. Johnstone, "The Stapleton sugar plantations in the Leeward Islands," *Bulletin of the John Rylands Library* 48 (1965–6): 175–206; Aucher Warner, *Sir Thomas Warner, Pioneer of the West Indies* (London: West India Committee, 1933).

73   Pares, *Merchants and Planters*; David W. Galenson, *Traders, Planters and Slaves: Market Behaviour in Early English America* (Cambridge and New York: Cambridge University Press, 1986); N. Zahedieh, "Trade, plunder, and economic development in early English Jamaica, 1655–89," *Economic History Review*, 2nd series, 39 (1986): 205–22; Alexander Boyd, *England's Wealthiest Son: A Study of William Beckford* (London: Centaur, 1962).

74   Richard Pares, *A West India Fortune* (London and New York: Longman Green, 1950); Craton and Walvin, *A Jamaican Plantation*; J. Harry Bennett, "William Whaley, Planter of seventeenth-century Jamaica," *Agricultural History* 40 (1966): 113–23; Dunn, *Sugar and Slaves*, pp. 212–23; Richard B. Sheridan, "The rise of a colonial gentry: a case study of Antigua, 1730–1775," *Economic History Review* 13, 3 (1961): 342–57.

75   Elsa Goveia, *Slave Society in the British Leeward Islands at the End of the Eighteenth Century* (New Haven, CT: Yale University Press, 1965); Edward K. Brathwaite, *The Development of Creole Society in Jamaica, 1770–1820* (Oxford: Clarendon Press, 1971); Douglas G. Hall, *In Miserable Slavery: Thomas Thistlewood in Jamaica, 1750–86* ((London: Macmillan, 1989).

76   Thomas Modyford (1620–79), son of the Lord Mayor of Exeter, enjoyed excellent family, mercantile, and political connections. Related both to the wealthy Colletons of his native Devon (a county noted for its conservative gentry) and to George Monck (made Lord Albemarle for engineering the Restoration), he was able to put up £7,000 to purchase and develop half a 500-acre estate on his arrival in Barbados in 1647. Ever the planter first, he was a political opportunist. Colonel of the militia, he was largely responsible for the surrender of Barbados to Ayscue in 1652, and was made Searle's successor as governor by the Council of State early in 1660. Briefly imprisoned by the ultra-Royalists at the Restoration, he was soon back as Speaker of the Assembly under Willoughby, was one of the thirteen Barbadians made baronets by Charles II, and was appointed Governor of Jamaica

over several noble contenders in 1664. Largest slave owner as well as landholder in Jamaica, and great encourager of the slave trade, Modyford was sacked for supporting the buccaneers against the Spaniards and, with Henry Morgan, sent to England in ostensible disgrace in 1671. Both were soon back in Jamaica, though, Morgan being Lieutenant Governor and Vice-Admiralty judge, Modyford (despite no special training) Chief Justice and commission agent for the Royal African Company. When he died at the age of 59, his fellow planters had inscribed on his tombstone in Spanish Town churchyard the apparently sincere encomium:

> MISTAKE NOT READER, FOR HERE LYES NOT ONELY THE DECEASED BODY OF THE HONORABLE SIR THOMAS MODYFORD BARONETT, BUT EVEN THE SOULE AND LIFE OF ALL JAMAICA, WHO FIRST MADE IT WHAT IT NOW IS. HERE LYES THE BEST AND LONGEST GOVERNOUR, THE MOST CONSIDERABLE PLANTER, THE ABLEST AND MOST UPRIGHT JUDGE THIS ISLAND EVER INJOYED.

See Williams, "Modyford"; Williamson, *Caribbee Islands*; Dunn, *Sugar and Slaves*, pp. 68–9, 159.

77 Henry Drax, "Instructions I would have observed by Mr. Richard Harwood in the management of my plantation," British Museum, Rawlinson MSS A 348, fol. 7, quoted also in William Belgrove, *A Treatise upon Husbandry or Planting* (Boston, MA: 1755); Puckrein, *Little England*, pp. 78–80. Richard B. Sheridan, "Samuel Martin, innovating sugar planter of Antigua, 1750–1776," *Agricultural History* 34 (1960): 129–39.

78 Pares, *A West India Fortune, passim*.

79 Frank W. Pitman, *The Development of the British West Indies, 1700–1763* (New Haven, CT: Yale University Press, 1917); Douglas G. Hall, "Absentee proprietorship in the British West Indies to about 1850," *Jamaican Historical Review* 4 (1964): 15–35; Clare Taylor, "The journal of an absentee proprietor, Nathaniel Phillips of Slebech," *Journal of Caribbean History* 18 (1984): 67–82; Ward, *British West Indian Slavery*.

80 Karl Watson, *The Civilized Island, Barbados: A Social History, 1750–1816* (Barbados: K. Watson, 1979).

81 *Dictionary of National Biography*, ed. L. Stephen and S. Lee (Oxford: Oxford University Press, 1917), Vol. XII, pp. 100–1.

82 Charles Leslie, *A New and Exact Account of Jamaica* (London: 1740); Edward Long, *The History of Jamaica*, 3 vols (London: 1774).

83 "*Somerset* v. *Stewart*, June 1772," in Craton, Walvin, and Wright, *Slavery, Abolition and Emancipation* pp. 169–70; James Walvin, *Black and White: The Negro and English Society, 1555–1945* (Harmondsworth, Mx: Penguin, 1973), pp. 117–31; F. O. Shyllon, *Black People in Britain, 1555–1833* (London and New York: Oxford University Press, for the Institute of Race Relations, 1977), pp. 10–38.

84 Goveia, *Slave Laws*; Goveia, *Slave Society in the Leewards*.

85 For the development of this idea, see an essay which is in some ways parallel to the present one, Michael Craton, "Reluctant Creoles: the planters' world in the British West Indies," in Bernard Bailyn and Philip D. Morgan (eds), *Strangers Within the Realm: Cultural Margins of the First British Empire* (Chapel Hill, NC: University of North Carolina Press, for the Institute of Early American History and Culture, Williamsburg, VA, 1991).

86 David Brion Davis, *The Problem of Slavery in the Age of Revolution, 1770–1833* (Ithaca, NY: Cornell University Press, 1975), pp. 164–212.

25
Parliament and property rights in the late eighteenth-century British Empire

P. J. Marshall

Eighteenth-century political ideology, for long a subject which attracted little scholarly interest and even some disdain, has been illuminated in recent years by some extremely distinguished writing. "Whiggism" has been shown to be a house with many mansions, which have been separately identified and given labels, such as "court" and "country," "true," vulgar" and "scientific," "republican" or "liberal."[1] Sophisticated analysis has revealed the scope for conflict between those adhering to different strands of Whiggism in Britain, or in revolutionary America, and, above all, between Whiggism in Britain and America as a whole. Yet even the most sensitive probing still encounters solid strata of common beliefs which united Whigs of all shades of opinion. Doctrines about property seem to have been one of the areas in which no substantial disagreement existed. The security guaranteed to property rights was universally considered to be one of the glories of any British system of government. Blackstone's maxim that "The public good is in nothing more essentially interested than in the protection of every individual's property rights"[2] was taken as a universal truth. Nevertheless, as this chapter will try to show, in the later eighteenth century, from the 1760s to the 1790s, many people of British origin, not only in the American colonies but also in the West Indies, Canada, and India, were to complain that their property rights were far from secure. Americans ultimately came to see their resistance to Britain as the necessary defence of their property.

Since British opinion did not accept that property rights were in any danger, on this issue at least, Anglo-American conflict does not fit easily into a framework of different versions of Whig doctrine. What seem in fact to have been involved were differences of perspective rather than of principle. This chapter will argue that the British Parliament came to view property rights with an imperial perspective, which aroused deep misgivings among Americans and others.

Virtually all shades of opinion, both in Britain and the colonies, believed that property, with the wide connotations classically accorded to it by Locke of life and liberty as well as "estate," was a right that could be alienated only by consent. An Act of the properly constituted legislature was taken to be consent. At this point disagreement of course began. British opinion regarded an Act of the British Parliament as consent for the whole empire; those who lived in a British colony argued that property could be transferred only by consent of the appropriate colonial legislature. A second area of contention can be identified, again arising from the application of an agreed principle. It was accepted that British people everywhere were in general entitled to have questions of property regulated by the common law. Colonial British subjects stood by what they saw as their right to the full common law and nothing but the common law. British legal authorities were, however, inclined to doubt whether all aspects of the common law were applicable to the colonies, and by the 1760s they were also raising questions about the property rights of peoples of non-British origin recently incorporated into the empire. Was subjecting such people to what was for them an alien common law compatible with guaranteeing to them proper security of property? Most notably in the case of Canada and Bengal, British legislators decided to extend recognition to other systems of property law. This was in accordance with an old established principle that conquered peoples retained their laws unless the conqueror explicitly decreed otherwise, but these decisions were much resented by communities of British origin living overseas, who claimed the common law as their birthright.

In asserting a power to dispose of property throughout the empire and to recognize alien systems of law, the British Parliament was not establishing new principles. It could, however, be argued that Parliament was breaking through what had come to be accepted as customary limitations on its power.[3] Eighteenth-century parliaments had shown little inclination to extend their authority over colonial property and they had not concerned themselves with systems of property rights overseas. Parliament of course passed much legislation affecting property in Britain itself, but it did this through a mass of specific local and private Acts, employing a quasi-judicial procedure in which the immediate involvement of the interested parties through representation on or before the committees was very evident.[4] The evolution of the law affecting property in general terms was largely a matter determined by the courts.[5] In legislating for the empire between the 1760s and the 1790s Parliament showed a boldness in handling property rights which arguably it was not to show over domestic property until the 1830s, the decade in which parliamentary franchises, borough charters, and ecclesiastical property were all regulated by statute.

Close parliamentary engagement in colonial matters began in the mid-eighteenth century. In earlier periods colonial affairs had been largely within the domain of the executive government, using the instruments of the royal prerogative. By the 1760s in particular this was no longer acceptable. What the British political elite believed to be its new worldwide responsibilities were now to be met by vigorous use of parliamentary powers whose theoretical existence could not be questioned. The use of these powers was to be guided by principles, such as scrupulous respect for property rights, which were presumed to be universally acceptable. If it were helpful to invent a new category, it could be suggested that a generation of what might be termed "imperial" Whigs had emerged in Britain. What marked such people was not new or distinctive beliefs, but their confidence both in the powers which they possessed and the principles on which they acted. They were to find that their confidence was misplaced. The principles might indeed be acceptable, but the application of them on an imperial scale was not.

Whigs with an imperial view were opposed by other Whigs whose vision was much more local and particular. The events leading to the American Revolution were only the most spectacular episode in a much wider conflict.

In the second half of the eighteenth century the British Parliament passed a series of Acts that had important consequences for property rights all over the world. In 1778 Parliament in London passed an Act repealing two Acts of Queen Anne's reign which had prevented Irish Catholics from acquiring an interest in certain Irish estates.[6] This was the counterpart of a much more important Act of the Irish Parliament, which put Catholics for all practical purposes on a level with Protestants in their rights to hold and acquire property. In the 1760s the British Parliament passed a number of Acts which many people in the West Indies and North America interpreted as granting without their consent a portion of their property to the Crown through the payment of stamp duties or other forms of taxation. An Act of 1774 significantly altered what the citizens of Massachusetts generally regarded as their most important piece of collective property, the charter of 1691.[7] A series of Acts regulated the affairs of another great chartered body, the East India Company. An Act of 1774 laid down that in the new British province of Quebec in "matters of controversy relating to property and civil rights, resort should be had to the laws of Canada."[8] An Act of 1781 made certain provisions about property in Bengal. For instance, "The rights and authorities of fathers of families and masters of families" were to be protected under British rule, "according as the same might have been exercised by the Gentu or Mahommedan law."[9] Pitt's India Act of 1784 included a provision for redressing the "rights and privileges" of *zamindars* and other "native landholders."[10] Rights to hold property in slaves in Britain were probed in a series of court cases, while Parliament passed Acts regulating the slave trade in 1788 and 1789[11] and came close to abolishing the trade altogether. Property in slaves in the colonies was not formally under attack, but no one could doubt that such an attack was imminent.

Parliament's ambitious use of its power to regulate property was widely contested. The Thirteen Colonies of course carried their resistance to the point of armed rebellion and secession from the empire. In the British West Indies white society was generally outraged by the prospect of losing its property in slaves, but had little scope for resistance. The recognition of property rights defined by French law in Quebec also aroused bitter contention and was much resented by British migrants to Canada who claimed that they were being deprived of their birth right to property defined by English law. Even Englishmen in India made similar complaints. What could be presented as a particularly blatant violation of charter rights, the reforms that would have been imposed on the East India Company by Fox's India Bill of 1783, was the pretext for the great British domestic political crisis that led to the fall of the Fox–North coalition and the triumph of Pitt.

Opposition on such a scale might seem to imply a systematic disregard of colonial property rights in Britain. This was certainly not the case. Security of property was taken to be the distinguishing feature of the empire. Wherever British authority was established, it was assumed that it would take security of property with it. The French planters in the West Indian islands annexed in 1763 would, the Board of Trade believed, be turned into loyal citizens of the British Empire by guarantees of their property. "Experience shows that the possession of property is the best security for a due obedience and submission to government."[12] The new British regime in Quebec, the crown law officers recommended in 1766, should give the king's "new subjects," that is, the French, security for "their lives, libertys, and propertys with more certainty than in former times."[13] British rule in India would bring about a revolution by instituting security of property for the first time in India's history. The great majority of eighteenth-century opinion was convinced of the iniquity of what was called "oriental despotism," which was assumed to deprive everyone of secure possession. A committee of the House of Commons reported in 1773 that Indian law courts gave little "protection or security" to the subject; "the despotic principle of government rendered them the instrument of power rather than of justice."[14] From the beginning of its rule the East India Company instructed its servants to ensure "the security of the persons and properties of the native inhabitants."[15] The Permanent Settlement of the revenues was, in the words of its most distinguished interpreter, to provide "a rule of property for Bengal."[16] Restrictions on property rights of Irish Catholics, embodied in the penal laws, had become totally discredited with all sections of opinion in the British Parliament by the time they were repealed in 1778. "It was the clear opinion of every body," wrote Burke, "that property ought to have the same security and freedom in every part of the British dominions . . . in point of property all Mankind ought to be upon a level. On this great fundamental point you must have observed a perfect concurrence in all political and all religious parties. . . . Without those Sentiments Whiggism would be nothing more than the name of a faction."[17] The favorite nostrum of those who sought a gradual relaxation of slavery was to train slaves for future freedom by giving them possession of their own property. "Their little properties should be secured to them" and "Nothing would more humanize slaves and improve their condition, than their acquiring a property in their wives and families," wrote James Ramsay in 1784.[18]

Whatever British authority may have intended, colonial Americans quickly diagnosed acts of the British Parliament after the ending of the Seven Years War as a dire threat to property. This was said explicitly by the assemblies of Connecticut and Massachusetts in their protests against the Stamp Act.[19] As John P. Reid has recently demonstrated, virtually every grievance identified by the colonies could be defined as either the endangering or the loss of a property right. Not only was taxation levied by a parliament in which the Americans claimed not to be represented an invasion of property, but so too was any apparent limitation on the right to be tried by a jury of one's peers.[20] At every stage in the controversy to 1776 and beyond, Americans claimed to be defending property rights. To the New York Sons of Liberty the sale of the East India Company's tea in 1773 would mean "that we should have no property that we may call our own, and we may bid adieu to American liberty."[21] The Massachusetts Government Bill of 1774 with its revisions of the colony's charter was an obvious property issue. The Massachusetts Council saw a threat to its charter in 1770 as evidence of "how uncertain is every man's liberty and property, and even his very life."[22] In opposing the Massachusetts Bill in the House of Commons Sir George Savile asked "whether this is a property. Whether a charter is property. Whether religion, law, anything that belongs is a property?"[23] The opposition in the House of Lords protested at the way in which Massachusetts had been deprived of its "rights" in the "Election of Councillors, Magistrates, and Judges, and in the Return of Jurors, which they derive from their Charter."[24]

The majorities who voted in the British Parliament for the Stamp Act, the Massachusetts Government Act, or any of the other pieces of legislation which the Americans diagnosed as assaults on property almost certainly regarded themselves as no less committed than their critics to the sanctity of property throughout the empire. It is likely that they all subscribed to Blackstone's famous dictum: "So great moreover is the regard of the law for private property, that it will not authorize the least violation of it; no, not even for the general good of the whole community. . . . In vain may it be urged that the good of the individual ought to yield to that of the community; for it would be dangerous to allow any private man, or even any public tribunal, to be the judge of the common good." There was, however, one authority which could take away property. "The legislature alone can, and indeed frequently does, interpose and compel the individual to acquiesce," after "ordering a full indemnification and equivalent."[25]

In theory there was nothing new about British legislation affecting property in the colonies. In 1700, for instance, the Board of Trade had presented a bill to the House of Lords that would have brought all colonial charters under regulation. The bill made no progress, but the Board of Trade continued to press at intervals for legislation cancelling chartered rights, just as it pressed for parliamentary taxation of the colonies. The Stamp Act was not a new proposal and there seems to have been no serious questioning in Britain in the debates of 1764 or 1765 of the right of Parliament to tax. Nevertheless, whatever the theoretical precedents, the scale on which the British Parliament exercised its powers in the 1760s over what were conceived to be colonial property rights was entirely new. A moderate supporter of the colonial cause, who was prepared to concede that the British Parliament did possess sovereign power over the empire, still argued in 1758 that were Parliament to use this power to revise colonial charters it would be establishing "a precedent that will endanger the constitution of the whole British empire." Realistically, however, he recognized that a ministry determined on such a measure would almost certainly be able to carry it through Parliament.[26]

In the first half of the eighteenth century ministers had shown little inclination to bring such matters before the House. By the 1760s such inhibitions were fast disappearing. The regulation of the colonies had become an essential part of "the common good" and only Parliament was thought to be fully capable of providing proper regulations. The rapid acceleration of colonial trade had coincided with the great world wars in which Britain had sent huge fleets and armies overseas to protect its own commercial interests and to cripple those of France and Spain. It was a common assumption that wealth derived from worldwide trade provided the vital increment that enabled Britain to hold its own against much more populous adversaries. Secure property rights were the foundation on which the commercial prosperity of the British Empire rested. For Britain to adopt a predatory attitude to the wealth of its colonies would be totally self-defeating. But the stakes were very high. Property rights pushed to the point where colonies appeared to be unwilling to accept imperial coordination of vital matters such as trade and defence or to make a proper contribution to the common war effort would undermine the empire and ultimately bring ruin to all its parts. There must be an accommodation between individual right and the common good. Only what was now being seen as the imperial Parliament could make an accommodation that would ensure justice to all the parties.

Thomas Whately put this view in his pamphlet defending the Stamp Act:

The *British* empire in *Europe* and in *America* is still the same power: its subjects in both are still the same people; and all equally participate in the adversity or prosperity of the whole. Partial advantages that opposed the general good, would finally be detrimental to the particulars who enjoyed them: the mother country would suffer, if she tyrannized over her colonies: the colonies would decline, if they distressed their mother country; for each is equally important to the other, and mutual benefits, mutual necessity cement their connexion. It is an indisputable consequence of their being thus one nation, that they must be govern'd by the same supreme authority, be subject to one executive power in the King, to one legislative power in the parliament of *Great Britain*.[27]

In the early stages of the controversy government spokesmen insisted that the colonies were virtually represented in Parliament and thus consented to the accommodations being made between private rights and the public good. This line of argument made no converts across the Atlantic and was tacitly abandoned for unadorned statements about the sovereignty of Parliament throughout the whole empire. Pitt alone of major politicians insisted that "there is no such thing, *no idea in this constitution, as a supreme power operating upon property.*"[28] In the Commons Blackstone was less cautious about Parliament's right to take away property than he had been in the *Commentaries*. He described the power of legislation as inevitably involving an "Exertion of power over property."[29] Lord Mansfield denied "the proposition that parliament takes no man's property without his consent: it frequently takes private property without making what the owner thinks a compensation."[30] In disposing of the chartered rights of Massachusetts in 1774, government spokesmen insisted that public need must prevail. "Necessary for the preservation of the state that it should be done," Jeremiah Dyson, a respected constitutional expert, is reported to have said. "Private rights. Can that be a subject of consideration for the legislature, who are now considering at large, for the British empire at large," he added.[31] For North a charter could not be allowed "to subsist longer than it is found beneficial for the public."[32]

Debates about the authority of Parliament over the chartered rights of the shareholders of the East India Company ran parallel to debates about its authority to dispose of property rights in the American colonies. As the Company suddenly emerged as the effective ruler of a huge territorial domain in Bengal, its right to enjoy the rewards of conquest and to conduct its affairs without public intervention was called into question. Legal opinion considered that the Company had property rights in the grants made to it by Indian rulers, but that, as it was a corporation of British subjects, the rights must be subject to the sovereignty of the king in Parliament. The doctrine that emerged held that the Company had a dual function, acting both for itself and for the public interest. The public interest in India was defined by a series of acts of Parliament, which extracted payments for the state or laid down regulations to ensure effective management of the Company both at home and in its new Indian government. The Regulating Act of Lord North of 1773 or the India Act of Pitt of 1784 were the most comprehensive of many pieces of Indian legislation in this period. The Company, supported by opposition groups in Parliament, fought a rearguard action against legislative interference, arguing that its chartered rights should not be invaded. On each occasion government spokesmen insisted on the priority of the public interest.

On this issue even Chatham accepted that, although "Too much tenderness . . . cannot be used in touching charters, without absolute necessity," "the supreme controlling power of Parliament" could not be denied.[33] To the question "What right has the House of Commons to enquire into, and to judge of, property either acquired or possessed in the East Indies?" an opposition MP replied: "I hold it as the first principle of this constitution that there can be no sovereign power, whatever, the execution of which is not amenable to the representatives of the people."[34]

The debate on India reached its apogee in 1783 over Fox's India Bill. The bill's opponents saw it as an outrageous assault on property. If the bill became law, "Not a corporation of the kingdom, not a charter, not the great charter of our liberties, not a deed, not a contract, not a document, not a security, no species of property, can be safe," intoned John Wilkes.[35] The majority of the bill's exponents defended it on the usual grounds that such a piece of legislation was necessary to protect the public interest in India from the Company's mismanagement. One of the bill's defenders, however, widened the debate to bring in an issue that had been implicit in discussion of India for some years. Chartered rights were, Burke insisted in his great speech on the bill, accountable not only by the standard of the public good of Britain as a whole, but by the standard of the good of the people over whom the Company ruled. The Company must of course be accountable to Parliament. Parliament "alone is capable of comprehending the magnitude of the object" and Parliament alone could provide the remedy, which would be "a real chartered security for the *rights of men*, cruelly violated under that charter." No charter could possibly be allowed to survive if, like the Company's charter, it had become the means of "destroying an empire, and of cruelly oppressing and tyrannizing over millions of men."[36] Burke returned to this theme in his speeches against Warren Hastings. He explained to the House of Lords in his opening of the impeachment in 1788 that in the way in which the Company exercised its chartered rights in India it was doubly "responsible to the high justice of this kingdom." In the first place, it was accountable to Parliament for its privileges under its British charter. Secondly, it was accountable to the Mughal emperor who had given it another charter, the *diwani* of Bengal, under which it was bound to "observe the laws, rights, usages and customs of the natives, and to pursue their benefit in all things." Since the Mughal emperor could no longer enforce the terms of the charter, its enforcement also became the duty of the British Parliament.[37]

In the debate over the chartered rights of the East India Company, Burke had widened the criteria for parliamentary intervention over property rights. To the common good or the national interest, he had added the good of the people subject to those property rights. For him this was a matter of the highest principle. The security of property rights had no standing if it contravened "the great end for which God alone has vested power in any man," that is, the good of those subjected to that power.[38] Those who began to question property rights associated with slavery used much the same approach.

The status of slaves as property within the British Empire was defined by Acts of colonial legislatures. The main issue for legislation was whether slaves were to be considered as real estate, to be inherited with the plantation, or as chattels, which could be sold off separately to satisfy debts. The tendency in individual colonies during the eighteenth century seems to have been toward defining slaves as real estate.[39] The

British Privy Council evidently concurred with this view, instructing the new colony of Georgia to adopt it.[40] Whether slavery had any basis in English or Scottish law was a theoretical proposition, periodically debated but invariably decided in the negative. Ingenious attempts to depict slavery as an extension of villeinage carried little conviction. The major issue that concerned British courts was whether colonial slavery was a status that could be enforced in Britain. An opinion of the law officers in 1729 stated that slaves were not made free when brought to England. It was, however, said to be "the constant practice of Justices of the Peace in England . . . to enlarge all persons who demand the magistrate's protection from the tyranny of slave holders."[41] The issue was not definitively resolved by Lord Mansfield's famous judgement in Somerset's case in 1772. He advised that the whole question should be referred to Parliament. In the meanwhile, he apparently did not intend to bring about the automatic release of the 14,000 or 15,000 slaves whom he believed to be resident in Britain. In a later judgment he explained that the issue decided in Somerset's case had only been "that there was no right in the master to take the slave and carry him abroad."[42] Nevertheless, the publicity generated by Somerset's case and the much less equivocal Scottish case of *Knight* v. *Wedderburn* of 1778 seems to have convinced slaveholders that only slaves who acquiesced in their condition could safely be brought to Britain.

Whatever may have been the case in Britain itself, the security of property in slaves in British colonies seemed to be absolute. The Privy Council had never disallowed a colonial slave law. Indeed as late as 1770 and 1774 it was disallowing laws limiting the slave trade as prejudicial to "a very important branch of British commerce."[43] A number of Acts of the British Parliament could be cited which specifically recognized property in slaves in the colonies; for instance, an Act of 1732 which included "Negroes" among "hereditaments and real estates" for the purposes of recovering debts.[44] Even the most bitter critics of the slave trade and slavery were not inclined to dispute that, judged simply in terms of positive law, slaveholders in the colonies had a property in their slaves.

Public debate in the eighteenth century was ostensibly not about the right to hold slaves as property in the colonies but about the right to trade in them. The questions could not, however, be kept separate. Questions about the right to trade in slaves ultimately involved questions about the legitimacy of property in slaves.

Parliament's right to regulate trade could not be doubted. West Indian planters and merchants trading with Africa, however, pointed out in numerous petitions that interference in the slave trade would involve a massive invasion of private property valued at many millions of pounds. For instance, they claimed, not unreasonably, that the government had actively promoted the sale of land for new plantations in the islands ceded by France in 1763, but that new plantations would only develop if slaves could be imported in large quantities. Were the slave trade to be abolished, faith would be broken with the purchasers. Petitions against abolishing the slave trade did their best to demolish any claims that the public good would be served by abolition. Instead they painted a grim picture of loss, not only to the West Indies, but to British ports, shipping, and manufactures. Abolitionists might try to argue that West Indian agriculture and African trade would flourish without the slave trade, but their case lacked conviction. They had no alternative but to insist, as Burke was doing on India, that Parliament must use its authority over private property, not solely or even substantially in the interests of Britain, but in the interest of Africans and in accordance with a higher law than that which recognized property in slaves.

The cruelty of every aspect of the trade, not only the horrors of the middle passage but also the devastation said to be inflicted on Africa by the manner in which slaves were taken by raids and by war, were the issues on which the abolitionists took their stand. If their case was established, then Parliament must act to do justice to Africans. In a much admired petition the University of Cambridge expressed its hope that "the legislature will cease to support a traffick replete with misery and oppression and that it will readily extend its protection to the Africans, the most injured and defenceless of our fellow creatures."[45] William Wilberforce tried to turn the property argument round. The House should act to give Africans a secure property in themselves, since in Africa there was "no protecting legislation to defend this their only sort of property in the same manner that the rights of property are maintained by the legislature of every civilized country."[46]

Beyond arguments about the cruelty involved in the slave trade, abolitionists tried to prove that, regardless of the state of positive human law, slaves could never be legitimate property. For some this meant elaborate inquiries about the right of African rulers to sell their subjects or their prisoners. Were the slaves that the British merchants bought in African ports either criminals justly sentenced into slavery or prisoners taken in just wars? Even if this was so, was this any justification for regarding the children of slaves as the property of the purchaser? Others cut through these complications with simpler and more radical solutions. To treat a man as the property of another was to violate the rights of man and the law of God. Wesley was quite clear about this. Slaves were not legitimate property, they were "stolen goods." Those who bought them had no right to them. "Every purchaser of a slave is in contradiction to the original inherent rights of mankind."[47] Granville Sharp used the analogy of "contraband." A slave cargo should be forfeit.[48] Burke used similar arguments. "The African trade was in his opinion an absolute robbery." Planters and merchants could have no claim to compensation were it to be abolished. Those who engaged in a trade were entitled to the protection of Parliament, so long as their operations were conducted on "such principles of equity and humanity as deserved their sanction." When commerce became "an evil, a disgrace to the state," protection must be withdrawn.[49]

The debate on the slave trade had inevitably turned into a debate on slavery and the case for rejecting slaves as property had been clearly articulated. But virtually no one was as yet prepared to argue that planters should lose their property rights over slaves already in the Caribbean. Even James Ramsay was prepared to concede that "In whatsoever manner the planter has acquired his slaves, no person intends to disturb him in the quiet possession."[50] There was indeed what seems to have been an increasing body of opinion that believed that Parliament had no right to interfere with property within the West Indian colonies, however suspect its origins might be in theory. The Lord Chancellor, Lord Thurlow, made a distinction in 1792 between regulating trade and "an attempt to legislate in this country for the regulation of the West Indian islands internally, which he stated to be perfectly new and unprecedented."[51] The Chancellor's memory seems to have been imperfect: in the 1760s Parliament had shown few inhibitions about attempting "internal" colonial regulation. On the other hand, his statement reflects what seems to be a new caution about asserting parliamentary sovereignty throughout the empire. Such caution helped property in slaves to survive in the British Empire for another forty years.

From the 1760s to the 1790s Parliament, for all its undoubted reverence for property rights, had intervened substantially in questions affecting the property of British subjects in the American colonies, or trading with India or with Africa. In doing so it had provoked protests that it was undermining the security of property. The right of the British Parliament to signify consent throughout the empire had been contested and the sanctity of chartered rights and of property in slaves had been asserted. In response some powerful doctrines had been proclaimed: the sovereignty of Parliament, its duty to protect those who were suffering from abuses of property rights and, by implication, that the positive laws defining property might be overridden by such higher considerations as the common good and "the rights of man."

Beyond general questions about the security of property there was also much debate about the nature of the law that regulated property throughout the empire. In the mid-eighteenth century the English common law did not apply in certain dominions of the Crown. Scotland had its own legal system, as did the Channel Islands and Minorca. English law had been established in Ireland; and where British communities had settled in the Caribbean, on the American mainland, and even in the East India Company's settlements, they had in theory taken the laws of England with them. Precisely what they had taken was a complex matter. Lawyers tried to establish a distinction, derived from Coke's famous judgment of 1608 in Calvin's case, between colonies of settlement and colonies of conquest. In reality it was difficult to designate British colonies in this way and the precedents tended to be inconclusive. The outline was, however, relatively clear. The British Privy Council insisted that the "law of England as such" had not been introduced into any colony, but that "English law was a standard with which, all things being equal, there must be a compliance."[52] The full complexity of the common law was not deemed suitable for colonial societies and laws appropriate to local conditions would be accepted. But in its supervision of colonial legislation relating to property, the Privy Council was usually quick to disallow what it saw as any substantial deviation from the principles of English law. It saw its duty as maintaining "the rights and property of your Majestys subjects" against what it believed to be often irresponsible and self-interested colonial legislatures.[53] Much of its solicitude was undoubtedly for the property of British merchants and other British creditors, which was often thought to be at risk, as, for instance, in the bankruptcy laws disallowed for Virginia and Massachusetts.[54] But the Privy Council clearly believed that the property of citizens of the colonies as well as the property of citizens of Great Britain was entitled to the protection which it afforded by applying the criteria of English law to colonial legislation.

British officials might have intended that there should be only a qualified adoption of the common law in the colonies, but the colonists themselves appear by the mid-eighteenth century to have aimed at a very full adoption and to have succeeded in attaining it. Lawyers became increasingly professionalized and English legal texts were imported in large quantities. A more or less uniform common law system, close to that of England, seems to have been applied throughout the colonies.[55] In general, colonial opinion equated the common law with the rights of Englishmen and saw any British attempt to restrict its full application or to impose law derived from any other source as a very serious threat. In 1765 John Adams published a *Dissertation* congratulating Americans on having escaped from the clutches of the "canon" or the "feudal" law, but warning them to be vigilant in the future.[56] Greater prominence given to the Vice-Admiralty Courts after 1763 stimulated suspicion about the civil law procedures used in those courts. Samuel Adams worried about the way in which he believed that English judges were generally tending to resort to "the civil law . . . to the prejudice of the common law, the consequence of which will prove fatal to the happy constitution."[57]

Americans in particular looked to the common law as a guarantee that they held their landed property, as Blackstone described Englishmen as having done since 1660, "by one universal tenure of free and common socage."[58] The colonists were content, John Adams wrote, to hold their lands from the king, but not from "mesne or subordinate lords."[59] Jefferson regarded "absolute right" as "the basis or groundwork of the common law." Like Blackstone he considered it to be a survival of Saxon liberty; it had been transplanted to America, which had never been "conquered by William the Norman."[60]

Although it has been suggested that the exploitation of rents and other revenues from great estates was actually increasing in many colonies during the eighteenth century, the ideal of the American as an independent freeholder was a very powerful one. The suspicions of those who subscribed to this ideal were aroused by evidence that British authority was countenancing alien legal systems with very different arrangements for property. At the Peace of Paris of 1763 Britain acquired Grenada and Quebec, two former French colonies where considerable French populations remained after the conquest. It was assumed at first that rapid British immigration would soon turn these colonies into predominantly British communities. The laws of England were therefore promised in the 1763 proclamation establishing the new colonies. British planters and capital flowed into Grenada, but British subjects remained only a tiny minority in Quebec, where it became clear that any rapid introduction of English civil law would cause serious social dislocation. It was for Lord Mansfield one of the "fundamental maxims that a country conquer'd keeps her own law, till the conqueror expressly gives new."[61] In this spirit successive governments moved cautiously toward measures to preserve the use of French civil law in Quebec. The enacting of such measures finally took place in Lord North's Quebec Act of 1774. "The laws of Canada" were then recognized as "the rule and decision" in matters of "property and civil rights."[62]

The Quebec Act aroused much criticism. The provisions in favor of French civil law were seen by many as yet another assault on property rights. The British minority was said to have invested its capital in the new colony on the understanding that it would be protected by English law. "No merchant thinks he is armed to protect his property," according to Burke, "if he is not armed with English law."[63] The objections to the Custom of Paris which was used in Canada were said to be its complexity and obscurity, the seigneurial dues attached to land, and, according to Adam Smith, the continuing rights of the seigneur, which "necessarily embarrasses alienation."[64] Much was made of the fact that civil cases would not be heard by juries. To all these objections government spokesmen replied that it was the duty of Parliament to safeguard the interests of the French Canadian majority in the new colony. Edward

Thurlow, then the Attorney General, warned that Englishmen in an increasingly diverse empire now could not expect to carry the laws of England with them wherever they went.[65] Lord Mansfield said the same in his judgment in *Campbell* v. *Hall* in the same year. The inhabitants of newly conquered territories immediately became the king's "subjects" and were assured of his protection. British subjects going there had no special status. "An Englishman in Minorca or the Isle of Man, or the plantations, has no distinct right from the natives while he continues there."[66]

The East India Company's new empire in Bengal raised questions of the rights of conquered peoples and of British subjects who lived among them in an even more acute form than was the case in Quebec. Since early in the eighteenth century, cases involving Indians who resided in the trading settlements of the East India Company were judged according to English law administered by the Company's courts. There was, however, never any intention that English law should apply beyond the old settlement of Calcutta when the Company extended its rule over the whole of Bengal after 1765. Instead, the Company gradually placed the indigenous system of justice under its control, creating new courts under European judges, who administered what they liked to believe to be Hindu or Muslim law, based on codifications which were shot through with European conceptions. Modern scholars believe that Indian jurisprudence was fundamentally distorted by British interpolations and interpretations of it,[67] but to contemporaries the administration of justice in Bengal under the Company seemed to be a triumph of benevolent conservatism, guaranteeing to the "natives" their laws and customs and therefore their property.

In Canada the British minority had been obliged to accept the French civil law. In Bengal, however, it was unthinkable that Mansfield's dictum that Englishmen had "no distinct right from the natives" could be extended to make Englishmen submit to Indian law. English law remained in force for British subjects, and for Indians within the old settlements. In Calcutta a new Supreme Court was established in 1774. It was the activities of this court that brought questions of property rights in India to Parliament's attention. In 1781 the House of Commons considered petitions against the court. British residents in Bengal had complained "to the great guardians of the liberties and properties of British subjects" that they were being deprived of "certain rights inherent to Englishmen," especially the right of trial by jury in civil cases.[68] On this the House took no action. It did, however, respond to a petition from the East India Company alleging that the Supreme Court was trying to extend its powers outside Calcutta and to bring certain categories of Indians under its jurisdiction. A bill devised by Burke was passed, which defined the Supreme Court's competence and stipulated that cases involving the property rights of the mass of the population of Bengal were not within its jurisdiction, but were to be determined by the Company's courts, using Indian law.[69]

Between the 1760s and the 1790s Parliament had been responsible for a flurry of colonial legislation. By the end of the century it was walking more warily and was evidently inclined to limit its imperial commitments. It renounced its right to levy colonial taxation in 1778.[70] Pitt's 1784 India Act was the last attempt directly to intervene in Indian administration by statute. The Permanent Settlement and other major administrative changes were to be enacted by the Governor General and Council in India. By the 1790s Parliament was observing a self-denying ordinance against intervention in the internal affairs of West Indian colonies,[71] although it was of course in due time to resume unfinished business on the slave trade and slavery.

Parliament's deep involvement in colonial affairs in the thirty years or so from the 1760s to the 1790s is very much in accordance with the findings of recent studies that have shown how heavily involved it was in domestic legislation. The traditional view of the House of Commons as an inefficient and unsystematic legislative body is undergoing revision.[72] Yet the scale and scope of colonial legislation seem to have gone somewhat beyond what was considered appropriate for domestic matters. The problems of an expanding empire were real enough, but it seems inescapable that the House's willingness to deal with so many colonial bills reflects something of a self-confident imperial mentality. The assumption, for instance, that an eighteenth-century House of Commons was an appropriate body to try to regulate Indian property rights is, to say the least, a bold one.

A certain breadth of vision had been shown in the way in which the House tried to tackle colonial issues. In the 1760s men like Whately were envisaging empire as some kind of union. Attempts to ensure the survival of French or Indian property systems, even at the expense of the common law for local British communities, were not ignoble. But breadth of vision was accompanied by a self-confidence which brought its own nemesis over America. Yet it is not difficult to see why British MPs may have underestimated the difficulties they faced in legislating for the American colonies. They believed that they and the colonists shared common objectives and values. The findings of this chapter suggest that they were not necessarily mistaken. On India and slavery British people showed that they too could speak the language of the rights of man. Ideas of property carried much the same connotations on both sides of the Atlantic. Both sides agreed on the crucial importance of safeguarding property rights and that this meant that the individual could only be deprived of his property by the consent of his representatives. Both sides also agreed that the arrangements for property embodied in the common law were superior to any other. By the mid-eighteenth century anything that could be interpreted as an assault on colonial property rights by the agents of royal government was scarcely conceivable. To the British, parliamentary taxation was a completely different matter and posed no threat to the essential security of property. Americans saw things differently. An empire broke on the inability of British MPs to accept that their confidence in their capacity to determine the common good of an empire could not be accepted across the Atlantic. Imperial-minded Whigs were defeated by the tenacity with which other Whigs defended what were not essentially different concepts of property but the right of their own legislatures to be the guardians of those concepts.

Notes

My colleagues Dr Stephen Conway and Dr J. P. Parry have kindly read drafts of this chapter and made many valuable comments on them.

1   For a sample of this abundant literature, see J. G. A. Pocock, *The Machiavellian Moment* (Princeton, NJ: Princeton University Press, 1975) and "The varieties of whiggism from exclusion to reform," *Virtue, Commerce and History* (Cambridge, UK: Cambridge University Press, 1985), pp. 215–310; H. T. Dickinson, *Liberty and Property* (New York: Hymes and Meier, 1977); B. Bailyn, *Ideological Origins of the American Revolution* (Cambridge, MA:

Harvard University Press, 1967); G. S. Wood, *The Creation of the American Republic 1776–87* (Chapel Hill, NC: University of North Carolina Press, 1969).

2   *Commentaries on the Laws of England*, I.i.iii.

3   See the discussion in Jack P. Greene, *Peripheries and Center* (Athens, GA: University of Georgia Press, 1986), pp. 55–76.

4   W. S. Holdsworth, *History of English Law*, Vol. XI (London: Methuen, 1938), pp. 325–6; O. C. Williams, *The Historical Development of Private Bill Procedure and Standing Orders in the House of Commons*, 2 vols (London: HMSO, 1948–9), pp. 30–4.

5   D. Lieberman, *The Province of Legislation Determined* (Cambridge, UK: Cambridge University Press, 1989), pp. 72–3.

6   18 Geo. III, c. 61.

7   14 Geo. III, c. 45.

8   14 Geo. III, c. 83.

9   21 Geo. III, c. 70.

10 24 Geo. III, c. 25.

11 28 Geo. III, c. 54; 29 Geo. III, c. 66.

12 *Acts of the Privy Council of England: Colonial Series*, ed. W. L. Grant and J. Munro, 6 vols (Hereford: HMSO, 1908–12), Vol. IV, p. 591.

13 *Statutes, Treaties and Documents of the Canadian Constitution*, ed. W. P. M. Kennedy (Toronto: 1930; 2nd edn), p. 65.

14 *Reports from Committees of the House of Commons*, 12 vols (London: 1803–6), Vol. IV, p. 325.

15 *Fort William–India House Correspondence*, Vol. VI, *1770–2* (New Delhi: 1960), p. 82.

16 R. Guha, *A Rule of Property for Bengal* (Paris and The Hague: Mouton, 1963).

17 *The Correspondence of Edmund Burke*, 10 vols (Cambridge, UK: Cambridge University Press, 1958–78), Vol. III, ed. G. Gutteridge, pp. 455–6.

18 *Essay on the Treatment and Conversion of African Slaves in the British Sugar Colonies* (London: 1784), pp. 284–5.

19 *Prologue to Revolution: Sources and Documents on the Stamp Act Crisis*, ed. E. S. Morgan (Chapel Hill, NC: University of North Carolina Press, 1959), pp. 55–6.

20 John R. Reid, *The Constitutional History of the American Revolution: The Authority of Rights* (Madison, WI: University of Wisconsin Press, 1986).

21 *English Historical Documents*, Vol. X, *American Colonial Documents to 1776*, ed. M. Jensen (London: University of Oxford Press, 1955), p. 777.

22 Letter to W. Bollan, October 30, 1770, *Massachusetts Historical Society Collections*, series 6, Vol. IX (1897): 226.

23 *The Proceedings and Debates of the British Parliaments Respecting North America*, ed. R. C. Simmons and P. D. G. Thomas, 6 vols (Millwood, NY: Krauss International Publications, 1982–), Vol. IV, p. 317.

24 Ibid., p. 417.

25 *Commentaries on the Laws of England*, I.i.iii.

26 This was the opinion of Richard Jackson, April 24, 1758, *The Papers of Benjamin Franklin*, ed. L. W. Labaree, W. B. Willcox *et al.* (New Haven, CT: Yale University Press, 1959–), Vol. VIII, p. 26.

27 *The Regulations Lately Made Concerning the Colonies and the Taxes Imposed upon them Considered* (London: 1765), pp. 39–40.

28 *Proceedings and Debates*, Vol. V, p. 278.

29 Ibid., Vol. II, p. 148.

30 Ibid., p. 130.

31 Ibid., Vol. IV, p. 316.

32 Ibid., p. 266.

33 *Correspondence of William Pitt, Earl of Chatham*, ed. W. S. Pringle and J. H. Taylor, 4 vols (London: 1838), Vol. IV, p. 276.

34 Speech of Sir William Meredith, May 10, 1773, *Parliamentary History of England from the Norman Conquest in 1066 to the year 1806*, ed. W. Cobbett, 36 vols (London: 1806–20), Vol. XVII, pp. 859–60.

35 *Parliamentary History*, Vol. XXIV, p. 20.

36   *Writings and Speeches of Edmund Burke*, ed. P. J. Marshall (Oxford: Clarendon Press, 1981), Vol. V, pp. 385–6, 448.

37   *Works of the Right Hon. Edmund Burke*, 8 vols (London: 1854–90), Vol. VII, pp. 20–1.

38   Cited by P. J. Marshall in *The Impeachment of Warren Hastings* (London: Oxford University Press, p. 186.

39   See selections from colonial slave laws, *House of Commons Sessional Papers of the Eighteenth Century*, ed. S. Lambert, 145 vols (Wilmington, DE: Scholarly Resources, 1975), Vol. LXX.

40   *Acts of the Privy Council*, Vol. V, p. 40.

41   Granville Sharp, *A Representation of the Injustice and Dangerous Tendency of Tolerating Slavery . . . in England* (London: 1769), p. 7.

42   *A Complete Collection of State Trials*, ed. T. B. and T. J. Howell, 34 vols (London: 1816–26), Vol. XX; *A Letter of Philo-Africanus upon Slavery* (London: 1788), pp. 38–9; J. Walvin, *Black and White: the Negro and English Society 1555–1945* (London: Allen Lane, 1973).

43   *Acts of the Privy Council*, Vol. V, pp. 287–8, 399.

44   5 Geo. II, c. 7.

45   *Journals of the House of Commons*, Vol. XLIII, p. 212.

46   *Parliamentary History*, Vol. XXVIII, p. 43.

47   John Wesley, "Thoughts upon slavery," in *The Works of John Wesley*, 14 vols (London: 1872), Vol. IX, p. 79.

48   Sharp, *A Representation*, p.75.

49   *Parliamentary History*, Vol. XXVIII, pp. 96–7.

50   *Objections to the Abolition of the Slave Trade with Answers* (London: 1788; 2nd edn), p. 10.

51   *Parliamentary History*, Vol. XXIX, p. 1354.

52   J. H. Smith, *Appeals to the Privy Council from the American Plantations* (New York: 1950), pp. 525, 656. See also the material in *Select Documents on the Constitutional History of the British Empire and Commonwealth*, Vols II, *The Classical Period of the British Empire, 1689–1783*, ed. F. Madden and D. Fieldhouse (Westport, CT: Greenwood Press, 1985–), pp. 191–270.

53   Ibid., pp. 257–8.

54   *Acts of the Privy Council*, Vol. IV, pp. 389, 563.

55   W. E. Nelson, "The American Revolution and the emergence of the modern doctrines of federalism and conflict of laws," in *Law in Colonial Massachusetts. Publications of* The Historical Society of Massachusetts , Vol. 62 (1984), pp. 421–2; S. N. Katz, "The problem of a colonial legal history," in *Colonial British America*, ed. J. P. Greene and J. R. Pole (Baltimore, MD: The Johns Hopkins University Press, 1984), p. 476.

56   *The Papers of John Adams*, ed. R. J. Taylor, 8 vols to date (Cambridge, MA: Harvard University Press, 1977–), Vol. I, pp. 111–28.

57   *The Writings of Samuel Adams*, ed. H. A. Cushing, 4 vols (New York: 1904–8), Vol. II, p. 235.

58   *Commentaries on the Laws of England*, II.vi.ii.

59   *John Adams Papers*, Vol. I, p. 118.

60   Thomas Jefferson, "Draft instructions to the Virginia delegates" [July 1774], in *The Papers of Thomas Jefferson*, ed. J. P. Boyd *et al.* (Princeton, NJ: Princeton University Press, 1950–), Vol. I, pp. 132–3.

61   *The Grenville Papers*, ed. W. J. Smith, 4 vols (London: 1852–3), Vol. II, pp. 476–7.

62   14 Geo. III, c. 83, sec. 8.

63   *Proceedings and Debates*, Vol. V, p. 208.

64   Adam Smith, *An Inquiry into the Nature and Causes of the Wealth of Nations*, ed. R. H. Cambell, A. S. Skinner, and W. B. Todd, 2 vols (Oxford: Clarendon Press, 1976), IV.vii.b. See also Maseres's evidence, *Proceedings and Debates*, Vol. V, pp. 22–4.

65   Ibid., Vol. IV, p. 459.

66   *State Trials*, Vol. XX, p. 323.

67   J. D. M. Derrett, *Religion, Law and the State in India* (New York: Free Press, 1968).

68   *Commons Journals*, Vol. XXXVIII, p. 97.

69   21 Geo. III, c. 70.

70   18 Geo. III, c. 12.

71   D. J. Murray, *The West Indies and the Development of Colonial Government 1801–34* (Oxford: Clarendon Press, 1965), pp. 1–4.

72   For a recent statement, see J. Innes, "Parliament and the shaping of eighteenth-century English social policy," *Transactions of the Royal Historical Society*, 5th series, 40 (1990): 63–92.

26
Coerced indigenous labor and free mestizo peasantry
A property-rights, rent-seeking view of colonial Paraguay

Mario Pastore

Introduction

What forces accounted for the rise and fall of indigenous slavery, serfdom, internment, and contract labor, as well as for the eventual predominance of a free mestizo peasantry in colonial Paraguay?

The early colonial economy of Paraguay was characterized by Spanish enslavement of American Indians. However, enslavement contributed to indigenous depopulation, which led the Crown to outlaw indigenous slavery and replace it in the mid-sixteenth century by two versions of a form of serfdom, the *encomienda yanacona* or *originaria*, which in reality disguised the earlier slavery, and the *encomienda de la mita*, more akin to European serfdom. *Yanaconas* or *originarios* lived in the houses and on the farms and – later – ranches of their masters, serving them continuously in all sorts of tasks. Those subject to the *mita* took turns rendering their masters specified labor services in shifts of a given duration per year (see below). They were – from the 1580s onwards – increasingly confined to segregated towns, the first of which were mostly founded by Franciscan missionaries. "Town Indians" were also subject to the *mandamientos*, a state-run contract labor system which rented out indigenous laborers to Spaniards for relatively short, specified tasks.[1]

Both the bonded and the still free indigenous population had declined noticeably by the 1630s and continued to fall thereafter despite entrustment and confinement to towns, founded also by Jesuit missionaries after 1610. Alongside the relatively larger estates which Spaniards now worked with still diminishing supplies of both types of encomienda labor, the stagnating Franciscan missions and the still struggling Jesuit missions, a progressively more important mestizo, Guarani-speaking free peasantry began to proliferate. Paraguay's encomenderos or would-be encomenderos, Jesuit priests, and – beginning in the 1630s – Brazilian slave raiders competed for indigenous laborers and the resulting political and military conflicts characterized the remainder of the seventeenth century and the first part of the eighteenth.

The indigenous population of the Jesuit missions began to grow fairly rapidly after the middle of the seventeenth century, as it was successively freed from the slave raids and the labor services required by the encomienda mitaria. That of Franciscan missions – which was subject to the encomienda – also began to rise, but much later, as the middle of the eighteenth century approached, and comparatively more slowly. Nevertheless, privately held encomiendas did not now regain their past importance, even after large numbers of indigenous people became potentially available for entrustment following the Jesuits' expulsion in 1767. Private encomiendas increasingly reverted to the Crown, but remained legal until just after the turn of the century, and in practice persisted until the end of the colonial period.

The free mestizo peasantry, on the other hand, flourished, under the impulse of population growth and the transformation of some former Jesuit mission dwellers into peasants. Family farms spread in particularly rapid fashion in the last four decades of colonial rule, after the Bourbons liberalized – in the 1770s most notably – international trade restrictions imposed by the Hapsburgs in the previous century. As population and immigration increased, free land became progressively more scarce, the lands of the *pueblos de indios* were encroached upon by strangers, and sharecroppers and landless peasants appeared. The indigenous towns, unlike the encomienda, were not abolished during the colonial period and persisted beyond independence until the middle of the nineteenth century.

Any set of stylized economic facts must be seen through the prism of a certain body of economic theory and interpreted in terms of that theory. I will approach the problem neoclassically; that is, I will attempt to account for the stylized facts as behavior arising from constrained maximization. Since I seek to explain property rights on laborers and the institutional structure that evolved to enforce them, as well as the manner in which one set of property rights and enforcement institutions evolved into another, property rights will be determined endogenously and changes in property rights will result from changes in parameters. However, once a particular set of property rights and enforcement institutions has appeared, it becomes a behavioral constraint, part of the datum within which agents maximize. More precisely, the rise and decline of indigenous labor coercion will be seen to have resulted from the rent-seeking behavior of individuals and the state subject to changing relative factor prices and transaction costs constraints.

The chapter is organized as follows: the first section describes in more detail the evolution of indigenous enslavement, encomiendas, segregated towns, and mandamientos, as well as of the mestizo free peasantry; the second reviews some property rights and rent-seeking notions that will help conceptualize the described phenomena; the third uses these notions to interpret the evidence presented; the fourth shows that refutable implications derived from the theoretical scheme are consistent with the historical record and that historical evidence not utilized to derive the theoretical scheme may be interpreted in terms of it without difficulty; and the fifth draws conclusions.

I   Indigenous slaves, serfs, and the small free mestizo peasantry in Paraguay

Pre-Columbian indigenous people of the area with which we are concerned commonly practiced slavery and other forms of labor coercion, though at a much lower scale than Spaniards subsequently did. Tropical forest dwellers, the indigenous people of the Parana–Paraguay river basin were similar in many respects to those still living in the Amazon river basin. These wage war not for possession of forest land, which is abundant, but for the capture of slaves and wives. Groups tend to split once they reach a certain size and, rather than fighting over the land, the new groups simply move on to a previously unoccupied part of the forest. Forms of state are usually very simple, but more complex ones tend to appear where there are *varzeas* (very fertile land silted by periodic river floods), because it becomes necessary to exclude competing groups from them. The state then taxes the excluded inland groups for the right of access to the fertile river banks. Something similar seems to have occurred in the highlands of Mexico and Peru, where more complex forms of state and labor coercion also seem to have arisen earlier when the scarcity of land first made itself felt.[2]

Spaniards did not enslave the indigenous people of the area immediately after arriving. Instead, while they were still seeking to reach Peru from the east and southeast, they sought to obtain without coercion the Indian goods and labor services they needed to attempt the journey. To this effect they formed mutually beneficial – though shifting – alliances with the Guarani-speaking, neolithic Carios of the Asunción area and against the nomadic, more warlike Guaycurú tribes that blocked the westward way and for long had harassed the Carios. These alliances were cemented in the customary indigenous manner; that is, by trade as well as by the polygamous marital unions of Cario women to Spanish men.[3] From these Spanish-Cario "marriages" arose a mestizo population, about which more will be said later, and kinship ties between Spaniards, Carios, and their mestizo offspring. Kinship had mediated the exchange of voluntary, reciprocal labor services among indigenous tribes and the *cuñadazgo* initially served the same purpose for Spaniards and Carios.[4]

The joint westward military expeditions through the Chaco to Peru produced numerous captives that were divided up as slaves among the Spaniards and their Cario allies. These expeditions not only required the support of indigenous warriors but had to be outfitted and called for porters as well. Indigenous women became particularly valuable to Spaniards in this connection, because they had customarily been responsible for agriculture and other heavy chores. Pressed by the need to reach Peru from the east before other Peninsulars did so from the west the Spaniards quickly turned the *cuñadazgo* into a vehicle for coercively exacting progressively greater amounts of labor from their Cario "relatives," male and female. They came to use their "wives" as slaves, exchanging them freely among themselves for clothing, horses, etc. These increased exactions were responsible for some early indigenous uprisings against the Spaniards, among them that of 1539, led by Cario women.[5]

Once Peru was reached from the west, it became clear to Spaniards in the River Plate that the eastern route was more costly and would not be used; they now turned their energies to extending the conquest and colonization of the area around Asunción and began openly to raid friendly indigenous communities for slaves. It did not appear to matter that mineral resources seemed to be lacking and that no commodities suitable for export had yet been found. These raids (*malocas* or *rancheadas*) sought women in particular, for reasons already explained, and formally stretched until 1555.[6] Indigenous slaves were used domestically and were exported to São Vicente, on the Atlantic coast, where they were sold to Portuguese sugar-cane producers.[7] The Spaniards' former indigenous allies reacted against these raids with a generalized resistance (bloodily repressed), and by taking flight, as well as in other ways.[8]

Intermarriage with Spaniards, enslavement (in particular, the drastically altered sex ratio to which the enslavement of women led), resistance, flight, and European diseases rapidly lowered the indigenous population, a fact which royal officials had come to expect from previous experience elsewhere in the New World. Royal officials pressed to do away with enslavement and institute the encomiendas, a system which would protect free indigenous vassals from enslavement, and which they finally managed to impose in 1556. That year the provincial governor assigned in encomiendas mitarias 27,000 able-bodied, adult males (the equivalent of a population of 100,000) among a fraction of the Spaniards in Asunción.[9] Those who did not receive encomiendas, sorely disappointed by what they said was favoritism in their granting, set out for other areas where unentrusted indigenous settlements were known to exist, the Guairá area east of Asunción most notably, and where the same process as in Asunción was then repeated.

The encomienda mitaria required those subject to it to take turns providing their masters with specified labor services for a period of time that by the early seventeenth century had been reduced to two months per year. An encomendero was allowed to hold an encomienda grant for the remainder of his life and to bequeath it to one generation or, in very unusual circumstances, to two consecutive generations of his or her descendants (that is, always less than the perpetual grant to which encomenderos aspired). The encomienda was said to have become "vacant" at the end of the stipulated period, if the beneficiary died without heirs, or if he abandoned the encomienda. A vacant encomienda escheated (reverted) to the Crown, which could reassign it to another worthy Spaniard of its choice if it so desired.[10] The Crown could also assign encomiendas to the Church or to royal officials in pursuit of public aims.

Indios de la mita were also subject to the *congregación*, a policy that involved their resettlement, concentration, and internment in segregated towns (pueblos de indios) to which only encomenderos and a few additional persons could have access.[11] These towns were often – though not always – located near the Spaniards' own towns, and were then referred to as *fronteros*. Two supervisory layers governed the indigenous population of these towns, one Spanish, the other indigenous. The first layer included the temporal supervision of a lay Spanish town overseer and the religious supervision of a priest who imparted Catholic instruction to the American Indians confined to them. The second layer consisted of a Spanish-imposed, relatively privileged indigenous hierarchy more elaborate than the one that characterized indigenous communities of this area prior to the conquest.[12] The presence of this hierarchy, conversely, meant that town dwellers enjoyed a measure of self-government, though its extent was more circumscribed than what they had enjoyed in pre-Columbian times. As in the case of Spanish towns, indigenous towns were governed by *cabildos*. Under the direction of both supervisory layers, town dwellers were supposed to provide for their own sustenance and that of their overseers by laboring collectively on the fairly large amounts of land the colonial administration assigned to the towns, although these lands were clearly less extensive than those indigenous communities had previously roamed over and considered theirs. Town dwellers collectively owned the lands with which their town had been endowed and could not alienate them.[13] Similarly, town dwellers could trade only with those allowed access to the towns, in particular, royal officials and their encomendero(s).

Entrustment of the indigenous population and its confinement to towns could, and did in fact, take place independently of one another, especially in the beginning, and the privately undertaken founding of indigenous towns eventually became the responsibility of the religious orders. Thus, while the first encomiendas were granted in the 1550s and some indigenous towns were founded by private Spaniards, the first permanent indigenous towns were not founded until the 1580s, by Franciscan missionaries.[14]

"Recalcitrant" indigenous people who had waged war against the Spaniards or who, after 1556, had refused to submit to entrustment, could be forced to do so in "just wars" which the Spaniards waged to that effect. These slaves were kept under close supervision in the homes and farms of the Spaniards and following the first repartimientos in the mid-sixteenth century came to be regarded as belonging to another encomienda, the encomienda yanacona, later known as the originaria.[15] Like the encomiendas mitarias, the yanaconas or originarias could not legally be traded at will; they had to revert to the Crown before it reassigned them to another Spaniard. The encomienda yanacona thus disguised and prolonged indigenous slavery, but in a restricted form, since yanaconas could not legally be sold or rented. In practice, however, trades and rentals did take place.

Apart from the labor services they owed their encomendero under the encomienda mitaria, those confined to towns were also subjected to the mandamientos, a state-run system of contract labor by which indigenous laborers were rented out to private entrepreneurs who needed them for specified tasks of limited duration. Mandamientos furnished Spaniards with the indigenous laborers they needed to build and man vessels to transport yerba mate downriver to Asunción, as well as for other commercial activities. Indigenous laborers received a legally established maximum wage from their employers for the tasks they performed under the mandamientos, but they had to turn over half of it to the town's "treasury." The state could also use laborers from indigenous towns to build and repair roads, bridges, forts, and public buildings.[16] When demand for labor increased, the number of indigenous laborers that were sent out under the mandamientos increased as well. Since many of those indigenous laborers did not return to their towns of origin the population remaining in indigenous towns decreased permanently. The colonial administration appointed a special supervisor (*alcalde de sacas*) to enforce mandated extraction ceilings and to insure that indigenous laborers on mandamiento assignments returned to their towns.[17]

The "new" system of the encomiendas did not work well, for reasons that contemporaries attributed to the incentive system built into the encomiendas. Specifically mentioned were the facts that the grant was not perpetual, that it could be held only for the lifetime of the grantee and of one or two generations of his or her descendants, and that encomenderos could not freely trade or rent their encomiendas. Encomenderos shifted indigenous serfs from the encomienda mitaria to the encomienda yanacona or exceeded the terms of mandamientos, to which end they bribed the Spanish corregidores of indigenous towns if necessary. Encomenderos also evaded rendering the military service to which their grant obliged them by purchasing government offices conferring exemption from that responsibility.[18] For these and other reasons the indigenous population continued to decline. By the early seventeenth century it had been reduced to a fraction of its original size and both forms of the encomiendas had declined noticeably, despite the fact that much of the indigenous population had been confined to towns.[19] Three successive sets of royal ordinances of the late sixteenth and early seventeenth centuries noted the abuses and legislated against them.[20]

Real reprieve for the Guarani, however, did not come until after the Jesuits began to found missions in the Guairá region east of Asunción in the 1610s, with indigenous people already entrusted to Spaniards, a fact which later was to serve as the excuse for disputes between Paraguayans and Jesuits.[21] However, raids by Portuguese enslavers forced the relocation of the original Spanish settlements and Jesuit missions from Guairá to areas farther west and southwest, respectively. The displaced Spanish settlements moved within the jurisdiction of Asunción, paying a high price for the privilege. The Jesuits resettled in an area astride the Parana and Uruguay rivers, which became the Jesuit missions' *locus classicus*. The pursuing Portuguese *bandeiras*, however, were decisively defeated in the mid-seventeenth century by Jesuit-led indigenous armies which the missionaries had trained and furnished with firearms. Between 1660 and 1680, and in recognition of their success, the Crown exempted the Jesuit missions from the encomienda.[22] Henceforth, the tribute that indigenous people owed the king was paid by Jesuits not in kind but in cash, which they obtained by selling yerba mate in the regional market. Initially, Jesuit-supervised teams of indigenous laborers gathered yerba mate in far-off royally owned lands, but the operation was very costly in terms of human life and the Jesuits eventually set up plantations in the missions themselves, to reduce the loss of indigenous lives that the gathering of yerba mate involved.[23] Attempts by encomenderos to extend the encomienda to Jesuit mission towns, observed at this time, generally failed.[24] Thereafter, the indigenous population of Jesuit missions grew despite periodic bouts of the plague.

Outside the Jesuit missions the indigenous population had declined notably by the 1630s, and continued to decline thereafter – though more slowly – even though by this time it had for the most part been confined to towns. Encomenderos can now be observed to attempt to extend the encomiendas to mestizos and to introduce African slaves, but they were generally unsuccessful, because of legal regulations and the deliberate hindering of the colony's export trade, respectively. Only in the mid-eighteenth century did the indigenous population of Franciscan missions begin to rise, very slowly.

The remainder of the seventeenth and the early eighteenth centuries were marked by economic contraction and absence of immigration. As the indigenous people now "reduced" to towns vacated the lands they had occupied, family farms owned by mestizo, Guarani-speaking peasant proprietors spread over them. Resulting conflicts between Paraguayans and Jesuits over indigenous labor came to a head in the so-called Comuneros Revolt of the first third of the eighteenth century, supposedly a prelude to the independence movement of the early nineteenth century.

Following the Bourbonic liberalization of trade restrictions of the 1770s in particular, production of yerba maté in the north, tobacco in the east, and cattle for the yerba industry in the south and southeast, all increased.[25] Correspondingly, the land market became more active: land prices rose, land rents, tenant-farming, and landless peasants appeared, and the frontier was pushed farther out.[26] There was migration to the more rapidly growing yerba and cattle-ranching areas of the north from the southern mission towns abandoned by the recently expelled Jesuits, for example, as well as among immigrants who had come from outside the province.[27] Higher tobacco output grown typically by the small peasantry as a cash crop and initially encouraged by the establishment of the royal tobacco monopoly, led to an increase of the small peasantry and, therefore, of the land frontier. Furthermore, strangers (*forasteros*) increasingly encroached on the lands of the pueblos de indios during this period. As land prices rose, wages rose as well, partly because the Bourbonic reforms encouraged the development of manufacturing and agricultural state enterprises whose demand for indigenous labor revived a seventeenth-century colonial administration policy to grant no new encomiendas and to force vacant ones to revert to the Crown.[28] The greater domestic and foreign demand and the greater derived demand for land and labor helped expand the land frontier, and while it introduced a certain concentration of land and greater social differentiation, it also increased the relative importance of small peasant proprietors.

The system continued to function along these lines for the remainder of the colonial period. The Spanish Crown finally abolished the encomiendas as a legal institution in 1803, and an early national government reiterated their abolition in 1812, after Independence. However, the pueblos de indios outlived the colonial period and persisted until the middle of the nineteenth century.[29]

Now that we have described in more detail the phenomena to be explained, let us briefly discuss some basic elements of the economic theory of property rights and then attempt to substantiate the introduction's contention that the observed forms of property rights on labor and land resulted from public and private rent-seeking subject to the constraints of relative factor endowments and positive transaction costs.

II Property rights, factor proportions, and public finances

The major questions that need to be accounted for may be conceptualized within a property rights, rent-seeking framework. The preceding review made it clear that these phenomena are: first, the early enslavement of indigenous people by Spaniards; second, indigenous depopulation which led to slavery's being replaced by the encomiendas and the mandamientos, producing still further indigenous depopulation; third, the rise of a free mestizo peasantry; and fourth, the abolition of serfdom. Let us now consider a property rights and rent-seeking framework that will help us think about these changes.

In general, scarce resources will generate rents that will accrue to their owners so long as property rights are well delineated and enforced.[30] On the other hand, should property rights be poorly delineated and/or enforced, the resources will be over-exploited and the rents that would otherwise have accrued to their owners will dissipate along many margins.[31] The prospect of capturing rents that will otherwise dissipate will provide incentives to delineate and enforce property rights over scarce resources. The delineation and enforcement of property rights will internalize the formerly existing externalities.[32] Delineation and enforcement of property rights may be carried out by individuals or, if the coercion necessary for enforcement is subject to economies of scale, by a specialized institution such as the state, which will edge out competing private associations. The state will perform these and other functions such as resolving disputes over rights among its constituents, defending constituents' rights from outside threats, and solving the free rider problem usually entailed here, all in exchange for revenue derived from the rents that will accrue to owners of scarce resources.

All other things being equal, one would expect to find relatively better defined and enforced property rights over comparatively more scarce factors for which costs of measuring and monitoring rights are relatively lower.[33] Conversely, one would expect to find property rights over relatively more abundant resources to be comparatively imprecisely delineated or poorly enforced, *ceteris paribus*. Property rights will be comparatively better delineated and enforced, therefore, as resources become sufficiently scarce relative to the costs of measuring and monitoring rights. This holds for any factor of production. Should labor be scarce relative to land, we would expect property rights in labor to be better delineated and enforced than property rights in land. Conversely, should land be comparatively more scarce vis-à-vis labor, we would expect property rights in land to be comparatively more precisely delineated. A change in relative factor scarcity and, therefore, in relative factor prices, will raise the rate of return to delineating and enforcing property rights in the comparatively more scarce factor, and comparatively more resources will consequently be devoted to this task. Should labor be initially more scarce by contrast to land, property rights over laborers may be expected to be more clearly delineated and enforced; however, population growth will render land progressively more scarce in relative terms and, therefore, one would expect interest in coercing laborers to decrease progressively at the same time that interest in defining and enforcing property rights on land increases.[34]

1

Property rights in labor may be vested in the laborers themselves or in persons other than the laborers. Conversely, well-defined and enforced property rights in labor – whether vested in the laborers themselves or in their owners – will prevent dissipation of labor rent. Should property rights in labor be vested in the laborers themselves as well as enforced, and labor markets be competitive, laborers will capture the earnings that their factor's relative scarcity justifies, because the marginal product of labor and the wage will equalize. On the other hand, it is obvious that if property rights in labor are vested in persons other than the laborers, the aim is to channel away from the laborers themselves the rents that in a free labor market would have accrued to them; that is, to seek to lower the price of labor to "employers" and alter the distribution of income that would have obtained had the laborer and the owner of labor been the same person and competition been perfect.[35] In order to depress the wage rate below the marginal product of labor, competition (among employers for laborers and vice versa) will have to be hindered; this will require that the freedom of movement of the laborer be reduced to some degree, as otherwise the laborer could migrate in search of the highest wage; in turn, reducing the freedom of movement of the laborer will require, for example, his tying to the land, to other men, or both.[36] Labor coercion will, in addition, force the laborers off the labor supply curve that would characterize their labor leisure choice if this were free, leading laborers to furnish a larger labor input than they would have provided voluntarily at every wage rate.[37] The shifted labor supply curve retains its positive slope, implying that bonded laborers will move along their coerced labor supply curve in response to material incentives. We would expect to observe, therefore, that systems of coerced labor would include incentive structures to induce laborers to increase effort. In turn, this means that coerced laborers will – in general – be capable of owning property, since their rights to enjoy the material incentives offered them will have to be somehow recognized. In turn, this will have several implications for the capacity of coerced laborers to accumulate wealth, derive an income from it, and spend that income. Whether they spend the income on consumer goods or on repurchasing their freedom need not concern us at this stage.

Tying laborers will require some type of coercion to be applied, which implies that an unequal distribution of coercive power must exist between the laborers and those who keep them under subjection. Whether the required coercion is applied by individuals, the state, or both, its ultimate aim must be to appropriate the difference between the marginal product of labor and the wage rate that will obtain in what now must be regarded as an imperfectly competitive labor market. Should individuals and the state jointly apply the required coercion, one would expect to observe some arrangement by which individuals and the state will share the benefits of labor coercion. Labor coercion sanctioned by the state, therefore, may also be thought of as a public finance system.[38]

State regulation creates economic rents which may raise the rate of return to resources above what they would earn under competitive conditions and which the state may tax to obtain revenues in excess of what it could have collected in an unregulated market. In effect, the state and private entrepreneurs share the rents that these regulations create, the division of the rents depending on the bargaining power of the parties. Therefore, state regulation will be both demanded and supplied. Because rent-creating legislation is valuable, private entrepreneurs will spend resources lobbying the government for it. Whether contractual or predatory, the government will have incentives to sell rent-creating regulation at prices that reflect its position as a price-discriminating monopolist, because the sale will increase government revenues. That both contract and predatory governments may be consistent with labor coercion is clear from the historical record of the Americas, but which is more likely to sanction labor coercion is not as clear. The welfare loss is greater than that implied in the standard monopoly analysis, which does not take into account the cost of resources devoted by private entrepreneurs to lobbying the government or, we may add, by the government to price discrimination.[39] Clearly, then, some free men benefit more from coercing labor than do others, and they may consequently be expected to feel differently toward the regulatory system required to keep slavery in place, an attitude which one would expect to be reflected somehow in their political opinions and activities regarding the role of the state in preserving or abolishing labor coercion.

Now, for there to be incentives to define more precisely property rights in laborers, particularly in agricultural settings, labor must be relatively scarce vis-à-vis land or, conversely, land must be abundant by contrast with labor, which is why agricultural labor coercion is generally associated with relative land abundance.[40] Relative land abundance, however, is neither a necessary nor a sufficient condition for the rise of some form of labor coercion. It is not a necessary condition because so long as the gap between the marginal product of labor and the subsistence needs of labor is relatively large, serfdom may obtain even though free land may have disappeared, as happened in the Russian Ukraine in the eighteenth century.[41] Nor is it a sufficient condition because – as will be seen in detail below – land abundance may result in a small free peasantry.[42] In either case, state intervention in some form will be required to enforce a property-rights system on laborers. However, what share of the actual coercion required to enforce a form of labor coercion is applied by private and what by public agents is not clear. The particular case being examined here suggests that much of the actual coercion necessary to enslave American Indians was applied by private entrepreneurs, state sanction being merely formal. Domar suggested that in the case of serfdom the state must intervene to abolish the right of laborers to move, doing so by tying laborers to landowners, which causes competition among employers to cease.[43] However, what share of the necessary coercion is privately applied and what share is applied by the government is again unclear. Finally, under land abundance, the peasantry arises because the state intervenes to preserve the right of the laborers to move, causing competition to persist. In this case, Domar asserts, even if the state restricts the right to own land to a certain group of individuals, so long as competition is not restricted, land abundance will result in a class of landowners and a class of free wage laborers or sharecroppers, not in labor coercion.[44] How much coercion the state is willing to apply we will assume will depend on the rate of return to the state on the application of coercion.

2

Examining the African experience, Thomas and Bean noticed the clear link between slave hunting and depopulation. They suggested that enslaving was analogous to fishing in open-access fisheries and that depopulation could be likened to the depletion of fish stocks that ensues in that case, the classic problem studied by the economic theory of common property resources.[45] It may be reasonable to think, therefore, that the indigenous depopulation that accompanied Spanish enslavement of American Indians may be similarly consistent with the theory of common property resources, and that it may be attributed in part to the same causes. Moreover, if the consequences of enslaving are consistent with what the theory of common property resources predicts will happen to commonly owned resources, it is reasonable to think that observed responses to the over-exploitation of a common property resource like labor may be similarly consistent with policy measures which economists specializing in natural resource management recommend to prevent depletion of the resource and dissipation of its rents. The congregación, encomiendas, and mandamientos, therefore, could be viewed in this light. One may expect the encomiendas and mandamientos, in particular, to have a dual aim: one, resource conservation and, two, appropriation of the resource's rent. Finally, it is similarly reasonable to think that the chosen policies' prospective success or failure may be analyzed *ex ante* in terms of the same theory.

3

Consider now the free peasantry.[46] Its rise may be accounted for in terms of a simplified model which captures the essential characteristics of the scenario we are considering, the extreme scarcity of labor relative to land. For simplicity we may imagine that labor is homogeneous and that property rights in labor have emerged and are vested in the laborers themselves. Land, on the other hand, is infinitely abundant, equally fertile everywhere, and initially unowned. The model may or may not abstract from capital. In either case, the abundance of land reduces the number of factors by one so that the model will, in effect, be one- or two-factor, respectively.

Assume for the moment that the only two factors of production are labor and land. Being scarce, labor will fetch a price; being abundant, land will not fetch a price, nor will it earn rent, provided we abstract any locational advantages. Under these conditions, and so long as private property rights are well defined and enforced, a free, small peasantry will arise. This result follows from implicit assumptions about the nature of the technology of production and of property-rights delineation and enforcement: for reasons that Ricardo elucidated years ago, given that land is both evenly fertile and abundant in supply, the marginal product of labor will be constant and equal to its average product; the production function will therefore be a straight line out of the origin and the labor demand curve derived from it will be horizontal. Under these conditions, output will be a function of the supply of labor alone and will increase or decrease as the labor supply shifts right or left. Techniques of production will – since labor is the scarce factor and land the abundant one – economize on the use of labor but not on the use of land. That is, given the labor supply and technologically determined labor/land ratios, land inputs will be automatically determined.

Since the marginal product of labor equals the average product and given that competition equates them both to the wage rate, total output will equal the wage bill and all output will accrue to the laborers themselves. By the same logic that we envision all final output belonging to the laborers, we can envision the laborers holding – if labor and land are complementary in production – private property rights in the land they cultivate. Although techniques of production will tend to be land-intensive, peasants will have no incentive to accumulate more land than they can work alone or with the help of their families. In addition to being owned by those who work them, therefore, farms will tend to be small and fairly equal in size. The nature of property rights in labor determines the land tenure system, not the other way around.

For as long as land remains abundant, land rent will be zero. Landowners, therefore, will not hire laborers, nor will laborers hire themselves out to landowners for less than they can earn working land of their own, which under the assumed conditions they can readily obtain; consequently, land will be worked by individual proprietors without the help of hired labor. Since we are abstracting from locational advantages, von Thunian rents will not arise, nor will a market in land. Neither would we expect to observe a wage labor force or sharecropping, since both presuppose that land has become scarce. Property rights in commodities will be vested in the laborers, and the exchange of commodities, if it exists, will take place according to their labor content. The same goes for the means of production. Thus, although private property in land has arisen, so long as land remains abundant exchange proceeds as Smith had visualized it in his

"early and rude" state of society preceding stock accumulation and land appropriation.[47] The number of peasant holdings will grow with the peasant population which,
ceteris paribus, may be expected to be a direct function of the difference between peasant
output and the peasantry's subsistence requirements, among other variables.

The preceding results clearly depend on property rights being enforced at zero cost.
In reality, however, enforcing property rights is costly and, in particular, requires that
coercion be applied. In all but the simpler societies the coercion necessary for the
enforcement of property rights requires a state, whose degree of complexity will vary
with the nature of the property rights system. Without enforcement by the state the free
peasantry that will arise in response to free competition and land abundance is not
likely to persist, no matter how violence potential is distributed among peasants. An
uneven distribution of coercive capabilities among the peasants may lead some of them
to attempt to enslave or enserf others, for the purpose of appropriating some portion of
the difference between the marginal product of labor and the subsistence requirements
of labor. Should the distribution of coercive capabilities among the peasants be initially
equal it will tend to become unequal, because incentives will exist for peasants to
innovate the technology of coercion for the purpose of appropriating some of the labor
rents of those that do not.

Whether the social structure that will arise to apply the coercion required to defend
property rights under conditions of land abundance will be a predatory or a contract
state, however, is not clear. Early political philosophers like Locke thought that land
abundance would lead to a small peasantry and a representative democracy. On the
other hand, we have already made reference to modern anthropological evidence from
Amazonia which suggests that – while land abundance does tend to yield something
akin to a small peasantry – only very simple forms of political organization tend to arise
in such a setting. Forms of political organization sufficiently complex to be called a
state tend to arise only when land becomes comparatively scarce, to exclude others
from the scarce land. In their more advanced expressions these tend to resemble
predatory states rather than contract states. Whatever form of state arises, the state
may be supported from revenues levied on labor income but not on land rent.

4

Assume now that land is of uneven fertility or, alternatively, that while being evenly
fertile it is not infinitely abundant. In fact, both instances are equivalent, as Wicksteed
first demonstrated. Let us preserve the distinction for expository purposes. Should land
be unevenly fertile, intramarginal land will yield rent, which may be taxed to protect
property rights on land up to the margin. Extramarginal land remains unowned.

Population growth in a closed economy context where land is evenly fertile will
eventually lead to land scarcity. Alternatively, in an open economy context land scarcity
may result from population growth or an increase in foreign demand for land-intensive
goods that raises their prices and causes land rent to appear. There will now be reasons
for landlords to hire laborers or for sharecropping to arise rather than for coercing of
labor, but again, whether or not competitive conditions prevail will depend on the state,
which even here could reduce labor mobility if the differences between the marginal
product of labor and the subsistence requirement of laborers are large enough.

III Interpreting the evidence

1

One can gain insight into the initial conditions Spaniards encountered by recalling that abundant, evenly fertile land yielding no rent leads to a peasantry, and that differentially fertile land yielding rent leads to greater differentiation in the social and political structure. Analogously, under conditions of land abundance such as obtain in the Amazonian forests, population growth leads to competition that can be resolved fairly peacefully by the spread of small population groups throughout the available forest land, for reasons similar to those discussed above. Abundant resources earn no rent and, therefore, do not justify defining property rights, defending these rights, or resolving disputes over them, which will tend not to arise anyway. Groups need not compete militarily or otherwise for the abundant resource. Thus, land abundance and the associated lack of competition will reduce the need for a military force and a legal apparatus aimed at protecting property rights and resolving disputes between competing claimants to them. The virtual absence of the state observed under these conditions is consistent with the findings of game theory that "wealth maximizing individuals will usually find it worthwhile to cooperate with other players when the play is repeated, when they possess complete information about other players' past performance, and when there are small numbers of players."[48] That wars – to the extent they exist – should be waged for the capture of slaves and wives would appear to be consistent with the fact that labor is relatively scarce relative to land.

Incentives exist for more complex forms of state and, consequently, taxation to arise where land is not evenly fertile everywhere and, therefore, yields a differential rent, or where land is of even quality but population growth has given rise to locational rents. In both cases, the state arises to curtail entry, which prevents resource over-use and rent dissipation. Evidently, the first condition, uneven fertility, applies to communities that had settled on the varzeas, such as the Carios. Access to varzeas may be purchased with valuable goods, slaves, or labor services, in which case we would expect trade and labor coercion to be known to indigenous dwellers of varzeas and forests.

Pre-Columbian Paraguay may be viewed as a particular case of the varzea-forest setting described above.

2

Such a varzea-forest setting as was just described was precisely the setting on which mercantilist Spanish colonization of Paraguay imposed itself. Generally regarded until recently as a system of government intervention to artificially create balance of trade surpluses, mercantilism is again being thought of nowadays as the fiscal system of predatory states which – unconstrained by their constituents – freely use their discriminating monopolist position to raise revenue by selling rent-creating regulation at prices reflecting their ability to price-discriminate among regulation demanders. The theory of the single-ruler, revenue-maximizing, predatory state is put forth by North.[49] An application cast in rent-seeking terms is Baysinger, Tollison, and Ekelund's analysis of French and British mercantilism. Spanish mercantilism may be viewed in similar fashion.

Isabel and Ferdinand's *de facto* appropriation of the natural and labor resources of America by right of conquest was lawfully sanctioned by a papal bull, which the Crown obtained by assuming the Church's responsibility for converting the aboriginal Americans to Catholicism.[50] As their proprietor, the Crown could utilize those assets for its own profit, i.e. it could try to maximize the discounted future stream of net income that they could yield. To that effect the Crown could assume the risks of conquering, colonizing, and exploiting the resources, hiring individuals under a wage contract, monitoring their activities, and so on. Alternatively, the Crown could cede its rights over these resources to private entrepreneurs in exchange for either a lump sum payment or a share of the profits that they would derive from exploiting them. Whether or not it did so would depend on the Crown's attitude toward risk, its access to information about conquest opportunities vis-à-vis those of individuals, and its ability to monitor agents. Even if conquistadors were subject to greater risk than the Crown, under information asymmetry and costly monitoring, it would have been in the Crown's interest to share profits with conquistadors rather than employing them under a salary contract or selling off conquest rights to them for a lump sum payment. That is, it would have been in the Crown's interest to choose to share profits with conquistadors if the latter could obtain information about conquest opportunities relatively more effectively than the Crown, and if the Crown's monitoring of its agents' actions were comparatively costly. It has also been argued that riskiness to conquistadors "would have made it irrational for the Crown to sell off conquest rights for a lump-sum payment and not share in the returns, assuming the returns are sufficiently detectable."[51]

The conquest and colonization of America, therefore, may be seen as a joint venture between the Spanish state and private entrepreneurs. To make it worthwhile for private entrepreneurs to risk their resources in pursuit of royal ends of discovery, conquest, and colonization the Crown established a system of incentives that permitted the individuals in question to obtain a portion of the rents that these resources could produce. The Crown's share usually took the form of a tax payment, which in the case of mineral ores was the royal fifth, 20 percent of the refined metal. Crown associates obtained the residual.

The expected rate of return of investment was higher in the more densely populated highlands of Mexico and Peru, because there lay deposits of precious metals in scarce supply in Europe, a relatively large indigenous population with a highly evolved division of labor, a relatively high agricultural and artisanal labor productivity, and systems of public finance and labor coercion which had supported fairly large state and religious bureaucracies before Columbus and which were easily adapted to Spanish aims.

In the American lowlands, on the other hand, there appeared to be no deposits of precious metals. While land was abundant, the indigenous population was sparse, its labor productivity was comparatively much lower and, consequently, population groups were much smaller, nomadic or semi-nomadic, and more thinly spread. Taxation could produce sufficient revenues to sustain only a very simple form of state and religious organization, and revenues could not increase without substantial – and, therefore, costly – modification of indigenous social structures.

Under these circumstances one would have expected privately and publicly owned resources to flow toward the highlands and away from the lowlands, which is in fact what happened. However, to defend the more profitable areas of its domains from encroachment by competing rivals, both indigenous and European, Spain needed to settle the frontier areas and had to offer its agents sufficient incentives to induce them to do so. In the frontier region we are considering there were no precious metals, land was relatively abundant, and the relatively scarce resource was the indigenous labor force. Consequently, land had little or no value; only labor could, in general, produce rents.[52] Therefore, it was necessary to introduce some system of property rights in the scarce labor factor so designed that it would allow part of the rents that would have accrued to indigenous laborers had they remained free to be channeled toward the Crown's peninsular vassals. Thus, inducing Spanish colonists to remain in the frontiers implied some form of labor market regulation by coercion, since only by curtailing labor mobility could the wage rate and the marginal product of labor be made to diverge and the difference be appropriated by non-laborers.

3

It is easily understandable, therefore, that the Crown should have initially allowed indigenous enslavement to take place. The conquest itself had resulted in military confrontations which yielded captives that Spaniards and their local indigenous allies shared among themselves. Furthermore, once it was clear that Peru would be reached through Panama and the Pacific coast, it was to be expected that Spaniards in Asunción should have turned their attention to enslaving American Indians, their former allies included, even if the slaves thus obtained could produce only goods to be consumed by the Spaniards locally: hopes that mines would be found in the Rio de la Plata area remained alive, and even if that search proved futile in the end, past experience suggested that an agricultural commodity for export might still be produced if slave labor were to be available. Finally, the tax revenues which the Crown obtained from enslavement helped support royal officials in the area and defend the colony.

The enslavement of American Indians, however, had deleterious public finance implications which past experience elsewhere in the New World had already made evident to the Crown; although Spaniards were supposed to pay the Crown a head tax per indigenous slave they captured or bought from other indigenous people, free American Indians also owed the Crown a tax for the protection that it presumably afforded them; American Indians were – after all – free vassals of the Crown. The negative long-term effects of the enslavement-induced decline of the free indigenous population and the consequent shrinking of the potential tax base, therefore, could soon be expected to offset the short-term public finance advantages the Crown derived from indigenous enslavement, as it already had in regions conquered earlier.

Thus, as the *Adelantados* (individuals the Crown had authorized to undertake the conquest of Spanish America) completed their task, the Crown sought – and found – ways to amend the terms of the *capitulaciones* (contracts) it had signed with them specifying the conditions on which the conquest would be conducted and the manner in which the proceeds would be divided. Invariably, the Crown curtailed the Adelantados' political and economic powers sooner or later and ultimately replaced them by salaried officers of the royal bureaucracy designated by the king. This political struggle was a necessary prelude to the economic struggle for control of the indigenous labor force, which hinged on imposing the encomienda. Control of land was secondary and, therefore, the struggle was less concerned with it. This suggests that once the conquest of a certain region was secured, the Crown invariably sought to change the original distribution of rents in its favor by imposing the encomiendas, which achieved this aim in a manner that will become clear below.

4

When closely looked at, it becomes apparent that the encomiendas were more than a system of coercively extracting indigenous labor services. Actually, they were a tax-farming scheme by which the Crown exchanged royal grants of indigenous labor services for some form of compensation. The Crown farmed out to "worthy Spaniards" the right to collect for themselves in labor services the tax which indigenous people owed the Crown and which royal officials would otherwise have had to collect.[53] In exchange, these encomenderos committed themselves to pay certain taxes to the royal treasury, to render military service to defend the colony and, in addition, to protect, convert, and acculturate their indigenous charges as well.[54] That the encomienda was a transaction may be seen from the fact that its terms were clearly specified in a legally binding contract which was recognized by colonial courts.

The encomiendas helped the Crown attain this aim as follows: as was said before, being vassals of the Crown indigenous people deserved its protection, for which they had to pay the king a tax. However, in the region of concern to us American Indians were much less able to pay taxes than in other regions of the Spanish American Empire, because of their comparatively lesser degree of agricultural development and practically non-existent commerce. While in the regions of comparatively more developed agriculture and trade the colonial administration could profitably tax indigenous production, obtaining revenues in kind and in money, in those where these activities were comparatively less developed the costs of collecting taxes in kind frequently exceeded their value. Collecting taxes was an unprofitable undertaking owing to high transaction cost: local auction markets for agricultural produce were relatively thin, revenues in kind were perishable, and the high cost of transportation by land and water made it difficult to transport revenues to other regions of America or to Spain, where they might be more advantageously auctioned off.

Private Spanish colonists in Paraguay, on the contrary, could devote the output of indigenous agriculture to more profitable use than could the Crown. Not only could they consume *in situ* the provisions indigenous people furnished, but they could also raise indigenous labor productivity significantly if they could subject the indigenous labor force to a more disciplined work regime. Output per head could increase even more if they could set indigenous laborers to work with iron tools, which the laborers themselves recognized to be superior to stone tools and sought eagerly. By permitting serfdom to be imposed, therefore, it was possible to increase both output and taxable income.

In addition to agreeing to pay the king certain taxes, encomenderos committed themselves to help defend the colony against external and internal enemies. In this way the Crown saved itself the expenses of supporting a specialized military force to defend the colony from external and internal threats, costs which, given the colony's location on both the Indian and Portuguese frontiers, were not negligible and could be quite high. The cost of tax collection to the Crown also decreased, since there were fewer encomenderos than there were indigenous tributaries.

All of the functions encomenderos undertook to discharge were formal obligations of the Church that the Crown had committed itself to carry out in exchange for receiving from the Pope the right to colonize the newly discovered lands.

The encomienda, consequently, was but a particular case of tax-farming to which the Crown resorted to increase its revenues and reduce its expenditures, that is, to maximize its fiscal resources. That this should have involved turning free vassals of the Crown into serfs involved some inventive ideological justification, but nothing that went beyond the capabilities of Crown ideologues.

5

In conjunction with the congregación, the encomiendas also served the purpose of reducing the depletion of indigenous labor, a scarce resource that Spaniards were exploiting as if it had been an abundant one because they could in fact regard it as if it were a common pool resource.

That the problem of indigenous depopulation, insofar as it was induced by enslavement, can be thought of in terms of the economic theory of common property resources is suggested by the consistency between the observed phenomenon and the predictions of the theory as well as by the fact that the Crown's attempt to cope with it involved the choice of policy measures similar to those favored by economists to reduce over-use of commonly owned resources.

In the face of indigenous depopulation and its negative implications for public finances, the Crown declared indigenous slavery illegal except in cases of "just wars"; that is, it denied individuals the right to appropriate by force indigenous labor power without royal authority. In other words, the Crown reaffirmed its property rights in the indigenous labor force.[55] Secondly, the Crown not only outlawed the damaging rancheadas, but segregated Spaniards and American Indians subject to the mita, requiring each of them to live in towns of their own, apart from one another. Concomitantly, the Crown allowed only selected individuals for a fee to obtain licenses authorizing them to use the labor services of indigenous people under specified conditions.[56] Only the encomenderos, the town supervisor, and the priest who was supposed to Christianize the residents could have access to Indian towns. Third, by comparison with what was required of indigenous slaves, the Crown reduced the length of time and the range of labor services that indigenous people subject to the mita were obliged to render to their masters. As time went on, furthermore, the Crown progressively curtailed the length of required labor obligations, which was reduced from around six months in the mid-sixteenth century to two months early in the seventeenth century. Thus, the terms of the original encomiendas, granted in the mid-sixteenth century, were much more onerous than those of the encomienda early in the seventeenth century.[57] At the same time that the congregación reduced to towns many indigenous communities, it also curtailed their freedom to move about; that is, it accomplished the double aim of protecting indigenous people from Spaniards, thus reducing the depopulation caused by enslavement and pathogens, and restricting their freedom of movement, a necessary condition for extracting some of the labor rents.

Measures like the assignment of property rights in laborers to licensed trustees, the imposition of limits on the number of indigenous laborers that could be made to work at any one time, and the appointment of alcaldes de sacas are too similar to those that would be imposed to restrict access to fisheries to be coincidental and, generally speaking, their stated intention was the same, i.e., eliminating the dissipation of rents. In this particular case, arrangements to reduce the dissipation of rents also aimed at making it possible for the state to appropriate a larger fraction of labor rents as well. Many of the features of the encomienda and the congregación can be more fully appreciated when viewed in this light.

The behavior of the indigenous population once it was confined to segregated towns to which unauthorized Spaniards were denied access suggests that enslavement may account for a portion of the variation in population. Though still subject to periodic bouts of epidemics, it appears that the population of indigenous towns recovered faster the less varied and less onerous the labor services they were expected to render. Thus, the rate of decrease of the indigenous population slowed down after the indigenous people subject to the encomienda mitaria were confined to towns. In the Jesuit missions, where they were exempted from the encomienda, the indigenous population actually grew, even though these missions continued to have contact with Spaniards.

6

That a small mestizo peasantry should have emerged and eventually predominated over the forms of coerced indigenous labor that preceded it implies that the previously cited mechanisms of coercion were not applied to mestizos and that, on the contrary, their rights were well defined and enforced. In fact, when their fathers so recognized them and the governor concurred, mestizos were exempt from the encomienda, and the courts enforced the exemption. Due to the absence of Spanish immigration, mestizos actually occupied many of the positions of *criollos*, Indies-born children of Spaniards, although public office and encomiendas continued to be preferentially assigned to Spaniards and criollos. Thus, following the original distribution of encomiendas in Asunción, Spaniards as well as their mestizo offspring left for areas to the north and east, where there were relatively large concentrations of still unentrusted indigenous people who could be subjected to the encomienda mitaria or, if they refused, enslaved. Once the still unentrusted population disappeared, however, the population, by now mostly mestizo, had to rely on their own labor and the still abundant land for a livelihood; that is, they became peasants. As the scarcity of indigenous laborers became even more pronounced and the encomiendas stagnated, encomenderos attempted to entrust mestizos but they were unsuccessful because mestizos were legally ineligible for subjection and the colonial courts enforced that exemption. Thus, it was the government's intervention to enforce property rights that allowed a free peasantry to remain free when economic forces would have led to its bonding. As the population grew and foreign demand for Paraguay's exports increased, following the Bourbonic reforms in particular, lands became scarcer, rent on land emerged, and the land frontier was pushed farther out by family farms.

IV   Is the analysis robust?

There are at least two possible ways of increasing our confidence that the analysis is robust. The first requires that we derive from the model refutable implications consistent with the historical record. The second requires that we be able to interpret events not previously referred to in terms of the model. Let us consider each of these two tests.

In the model we have presented, changes in relative prices of productive factors result in changes in the profitability of delineating and enforcing property rights over them. We saw that this notion is consistent with the fact that the indigenous population's decline, by increasing the relative price of labor, furnished incentives for indigenous slavery to be substituted by the encomienda and mandamientos. Conversely, once the population began to increase, the importance of labor force coercion declined and that of free labor increased. Now, as the indigenous population declined and the scarcity of labor relative to land increased, the increase in the price of labor relative to land should have given rise not only to a change in the profitability of different property rights sets but to a change in production techniques as well. Those previously considered efficient should have been displaced by others which more intensively utilized the relatively abundant and, therefore, cheaper factor. In particular, we would have expected a fall in the relative importance of activities that used labor relatively intensively and an increase in the relative importance of activities that used land relatively intensively. In turn, these changes should have reflected themselves in the structure of production and exports; goods produced by techniques less intensive in labor and more intensive in land should have begun to predominate. As will be seen below, this is exactly what we observe.

Until the 1570s, the economy was based exclusively on indigenous agriculture. Cattle raising, relatively less labor-intensive than agriculture, was practically non-existent. All production was for local consumption. However, beginning in the late 1560s and the early 1570s interest in cattle raising increased. In turn, the expansion of cattle raising was linked to the founding of new cities, the expansion of the regional market and, eventually, to the development of foreign trade. The structure of exports, which were initially made up mostly of cereals, sugar, and wines, began to change toward the early part of the seventeenth century. The early exports, which presupposed a relatively labor-intensive agriculture, began by the 1630s to be overtaken by yerba maté, which did not require cultivation and could be harvested from trees that grew spontaneously in forests northeast of Asunción. We conclude, then, that at least one implication of the model is consistent with the evidence.

In addition, differences in relative labor endowments made themselves felt in the choice of technique and of product in different sectors of the yerba industry. Thus, Paraguayans, who continuously complained of the scarcity of indigenous labor, produced for the most part caa-virá, or "yerba de palos," a variety that required less processing, and never developed yerba mate plantations. The Jesuit missions, however, where the labor was more abundant, were known for producing a variety of yerba that required more labor-intensive processing (caá-mirí), and also developed plantations.

The analysis must also be able to account in terms of the model for features of Paraguay's colonial economy other than those so far described. At least two such instances may be mentioned. First, that on the one hand, as the encomiendas stagnated early in the seventeenth century, the Crown should have exempted the Jesuit missions from the encomiendas and should have refused several requests by encomenderos to cancel that exemption, while in the late eighteenth century it should have expelled the missionaries; and second, that in the eighteenth century, as population grew, land rents appeared, and foreign trade increased, the Crown should have granted no new encomiendas, should have retaken possession of those whose terms had ended, and should have substituted for the militia a semi-professional army paid for out of revenues derived from taxation of foreign trade and land rents. Let me take these two instances one at a time.

The indigenous population of Jesuit mission towns grew rapidly from their inception. By contrast, that of Franciscan missions did not begin to grow until the mid-eighteenth century and then only very slowly. Furthermore, under the direction of their Jesuit mentors, the missions contributed effectively to defense and, in addition, paid their taxes in money, punctually to boot. When indigenous people were congregated in missions under Jesuit oversight, segregated from Spaniards, and exempted from the encomienda, the stock of indigenous labor yielded much higher returns than it did when confined to towns founded by Franciscans, less isolated from Spaniards, and subjected to the encomienda. The Crown had no reason, then, to yield to encomenderos and reimpose the encomienda on indigenous dwellers in Jesuit missions, and did not.[58] On the other hand, when the Crown was able to resolve the boundary problems it had with its Portuguese neighbor to the east, the Jesuit missions' usefulness was decreased. It is perhaps no accident that few years separated the expulsion of the Jesuits and the signing of the Treaty of San Ildefonso between Spain and Portugal, which settled the frontiers in the area under discussion. Clearly, however, the Crown's decision to expel the Jesuits from its domains may not alone, perhaps not even principally, be attributed to decreased defense needs.

Second, in a period of rising wages, as the Crown granted no new encomiendas, reclaimed the encomiendas it had leased out, and put the remaining indigenous population to work in state enterprises, the encomenderos' contribution to defense decreased and the Crown's share of defense duties increased concomitantly. A new military organization had therefore to replace the old, and the system by which the colonial administration obtained contributions to defense from individuals in exchange for grants of labor was scrapped. In its stead, by the military reform of 1801 the Crown created a semi-professional army remunerated mostly in money, not in labor or land, or in both.

For the above reasons, private encomiendas declined but they persisted for nearly as long as Spanish rule lasted. That it may have lingered on beyond its formal abolition in 1803 is suggested by the fact that when Paraguayans declared independence, one of their first measures was to reiterate that the encomiendas had been abolished, a measure by which they hoped to eliminate privileges as well as to increase the supply of labor and slow down wage increases, even if only slightly.

V Conclusion

The case studied here suggests that whether slavery or serfdom arose under conditions of relative labor scarcity vis-à-vis land hinged on the degree to which the state enforced property rights, which in turn depended on the rate of return to the state of investing its scarce resources in that activity as compared to others. In Paraguay, indigenous slavery emerged when the single-ruler, revenue-maximizing, predatory mercantilist state, in order to provide incentives for private agents to settle this poor frontier colony, did not enforce its private property rights over the labor of indigenous people and allowed them to be regarded as a common property resource. Exploitation by private entrepreneurs of Crown-owned indigenous labor along common property resource lines led to the depletion of the resource and the dissipation of rents that should have accrued to the Crown. As the resource became more scarce and, therefore, more valuable, and to prevent further depletion and rent dissipation, the Crown sought to regulate the exploitation of Indian labor by means of the encomienda and the congregación. These regulatory institutions were similar to schemes for managing open access fisheries. They were intended to curtail access to the resource and reduce the dissipation of the rents it could yield to the Crown. However, the system did not work well until it became clear that indigenous people could better contribute to colonial defense and crown coffers when gathered in Jesuit missions than when entrusted to encomenderos. Only then were they exempted from the encomiendas. The growth of the mestizo population legally exempt from the encomiendas in time made labor relatively more abundant and land comparatively more scarce, a tendency that was exacerbated when the Bourbonic reforms increased foreign trade and immigration. As land and foreign trade replaced labor as the state's predominant source of tax revenues, the Crown abandoned the encomiendas in favor of other institutional arrangements by which the state sought to provide defense and obtain revenues. The systems of indigenous labor coercion were nothing but mercantilism's system of monopolies as they applied to the labor market.

Notes

This chapter was written while I visited the Department of Economics and the Center in Political Economy, Washington University in St Louis, and the Department of Economics at Miami University, Oxford, Ohio. An early version was presented in 1990 at the workshop on "The property of empire" of the NEH seminar on the Consumption of Property, Center for Seventeenth- and Eighteenth-Century Studies, University of California, Los Angeles; the University of Costa Rica, San José; Washington University's Political Economy symposium; and Miami University's Economics Department colloquium. A version closer to the current one was presented at the Indiana University Economic History symposium and the Cliometrics Society meeting, Bloomington, Indiana, in April and May of 1991, respectively. For their comments and suggestions, I thank Stanley Engerman, Evsey Domar, Branislava Susnik, Luis Galeano, Luis Campos, Jerry Cooney, Héctor Pérez Brignoli, Douglass North, John Nye, David Felix, and Elyce Rotella, as well as many other colleagues. Remaining deficiencies are my responsibility.

1   The name *yanacona* came to Paraguay with some of the men who escaped the repression that followed Pizarro's revolts in Peru, and was used in the early years of the colonial period. It later yielded to the term *originario*, which was used to refer to American Indians "outside their town of origin." Mita comes from *mit'a*, Qechua for "turn." *Mandamiento* (from *mandar*

= "to send," "to order") was known as *coatequitl, alquilaje,* or *repartimientos* in other regions of the Spanish American Empire. See Garavaglia, *Mercado interno y economía colonial,* pp. 272 and 303.

2   See Carneiro, "A theory of the origins of the state." References to the link between relative land scarcity, property rights in land and labor, and the financing of the state in Mexico may be found in Caso, "Land tenure among the ancient Mexicans," and Florescano, *Estructura y Problemas Agrarios de México, 1500–1821.* For Peru see Ramírez, "Indian and Spanish conceptions of land tenure in Perú, 1500–1800."

3   The Carios valued iron tools highly, and quickly substituted them for their own stone instruments. As far as the early polygamy of Spaniards is concerned, documents of the period speak of each Spaniard having an average of ten to fourteen indigenous wives and characterize the scenario as "Mohammed's Paradise." See Susnik, *El indio colonial del Paraguay,* Vol. I and, for the significance of exogamy to indigenous peoples of the area, Clastres, "Indépendence et exogamie: structure et dynamique des sociétés indiennes de la forêt tropicale."

4   From the Spanish, *cuñado, cuñada* = "brother-in-law," "sister-in-law."

5   For the resistance by the Guarani see Susnik, *El indio colonial,* C. Pastore, *La lucha por la tierra en el Paraguay,* and Necker, "La réaction des Indiens Guarani à la Conquête espagnole du Paraguay," and *Indiens Guarani et Chamanes franciscains.*

6   Susnik, *El indio colonial,* Vol. I.

7   See Rivarola Paoli, *La economía colonial,* p. 91.

8   See Necker, "La réaction" and *Indiens Guarani,* for a chronology of Indian uprisings against Spanish attempts to impose slavery and the encomiendas.

9   See Susnik, *El indio colonial,* Vol. I.

10 An encomienda was a temporary grant of specified, restricted labor services; it was not a land grant, nor did it necessarily imply a separate (simultaneous or subsequent) such grant. In fact, the most profitable use of encomienda labor did not require the ownership of any land at all. Encomenderos could use the indigenous laborers they were assigned to extract yerba maté from royally owned land by paying a fee for the privilege of so doing. In general, however, output cannot be produced with labor alone and, therefore, encomenderos also tended to receive grants of land, but as a result of a separate grant.

11 On the congregación see Ots Capdequí, *Instituciones sociales de la América Española en el período colonial,* pp. 62–9.

12 Its members were exempted from paying the tribute.

13 See C. Pastore, *La lucha* and Susnik, *El indio colonial.*

14 For the early founding of Indian towns by private Spaniards, see Azara, *Descripción historia.* Typically, Franciscan missionaries would found a town and then, after a period of time, would leave it in the hands of a member of the secular priesthood and go to found another town elsewhere. Margarita Durán Estragó, *Presencia Franciscana en el Paraguay: 1538–1824,* pp. 93–164.

15 Silvio Zavala, *Orígenes de la colonización en el Río de la Plata.*

16 See Garavaglia, *Mercado interno y economía colonial,* p. 309.

17 See Velázquez, "Caracteres de la encomienda paraguaya en los siglos XVII y XVIII," p. 143.

18 James S. Saeger, "Survival and abolition: the eighteenth-century Paraguayan encomienda," p. 74.

19 Adalberto López, "Shipbuilding in sixteenth-century Asunción del Paraguay," quotes sources suggesting that the indigenous population was reduced to one-tenth of its original numbers by the early sixteenth century. A more conservative estimate is given by Juan Carlos Garavaglia in *Mercado interno y economía colonial,* in which he suggests a 50 percent reduction.

20 For the ordinances see Julio César Chaves, "Las ordenanzas de Ramírez de Velasco, Hernandarias y Alfaro," pp. 107–20.

21 For the funding of the first Spanish towns and Jesuit missions in the Guayra see Ramón I. Cardozo, *La antiqua provincia del Guairá y Villa Rica del Espíritu Santo.*

22 See Garavaglia, *Economía, sociedad, y regiones,* p. 141.

22 See Garavaglia, *Economía, sociedad, y regiones*, p. 141.

23 Alberto Armani, *Ciudad de Dios y Ciudad del Sol. El "estado" jesuita de los guaranies (1609–1769)*.

24 See Thomas de Krüger, "Asunción y su área de influencia en la época colonial," p. 41.

25 See Garavaglia, *Mercado interno y economía colonial* pp. 353–79, and *Economía, sociedad y regiones*, pp. 193–260. See also Jerry W. Cooney, "The yerba mate and cattle frontier of Paraguay, 1776–1811: social, economic, and political impact," and "Bureaucrats, growers, and defense: the royal tobacco monopoly of Paraguay." For the late eighteenth-century boom see Jerry W. Cooney, "An ignored aspect of the viceroyalty of the Río de la Plata."

26 Direct evidence of the appearance of land rents can first be found around the 1780s.

27 See René Ferrer de Arréllaga, *Un siglo de expansión colonizadora: los orígenes de Concepción* for internal migration; Jerry W. Cooney, "Foreigners in the intendencia of Paraguay," for the – by local standards – relatively large immigration that was observed.

28 For some of the state enterprises see Jerry W. Cooney, "A colonial naval industry: the fabrica de cables of Paraguay," and "Paraguayan astilleros and the Platine merchant marine, 1796–1806," and for the escheating of the encomienda to the Crown see Saeger, "Survival and abolition," p. 77.

29 See M. H. Pastore, "State-led industrialization or predatory public rent-seeking? The economic development of Paraguay, 1850–1870."

30 See Ronald Coase, "The problem of social cost."

31 For the argument that resources will be overexploited see H. Scott Gordon, "The economic theory of a common property resource: the fishery." For the argument that dissipation will occur among many margins see Steven N. S. Cheung, "The structure of a contract and the theory of a non-exclusive resource."

32 See Harold Demsetz, "Toward a theory of property rights," and A. Alchian and H. Demsetz, "The property rights paradigm."

33 For the original statement regarding the importance of measurement in delineating and enforcing property rights see Yoram Barzel, "Measurement costs and the organization of markets."

34 See Douglass C. North and Robert P. Thomas, *The Rise of the Western World*.

35 Conspicuous consumption may be said to be an alternative motive for demanding slaves, but it has been found to be an unimportant factor in the antebellum US South. See A. Conrad and J. R. Meyer, *The Economics of Slavery and Other Studies in Econometric History*, and Robert Fogel and Stanley Engerman, *The Reinterpretation of American Economic History*, pp. 311–41.

36 Laborers tied to the land are less mobile than slaves. Therefore, slavery can be more efficient than systems of labor coercion that tie the laborer to the land. See Robert Evans, Jr, "Some notes on coerced labor." Other possible ways of curtailing labor mobility include, for example, the military draft, impediments to the free flow of individuals through national borders, and restriction on settlement outside of specified areas, such as the homelands of South Africa.

37 See Stanley Engerman, "Some considerations relating to property rights in man," in particular p. 46.

38 See J. R. Hicks, *A Theory of Economic History*.

39 The welfare loss, therefore, will be larger than is implied in the standard monopoly analysis. See Gordon Tullock, "The welfare costs of tariffs, monopolies, and theft."

40 For the reasons why labor coercion and land abundance would tend to be connected see Evsey Domar, "The causes of slavery or serfdom, an hypothesis." For other contributing factors see David Feeny, "The decline of property rights in man in Thailand, 1800–1913."

41 As reported by Domar, "The causes."

42 For an explanation of why competition results in a small free peasantry when a regime of free land exists see Domar, "The causes." For the statement that this result will not persist unless the state enforces the property rights that arose as Domar suggested, see M. H. Pastore, "La hipótesis de Domar sobre las causas de la servidumbre o la esclavitud y una colonia hispanoamericana: contraste y reformulación," available in English as "State-led

industrialization: the evidence on Paraguay, 1832–1870," *Journal of Latin American Studies* (May 1994): 295–324.

43   See Domar, "The causes," p. 20.

44   See ibid.

45   See Robert P. Thomas and Richard Bean, "The fishers of men: the profits of the slave trade." In ocean fishing, high costs of measurement and enforcement do not permit private property rights to be delineated over fish stocks, which therefore become a common property resource. The number of fishermen is greater than the optimal and fishermen fish until the average (not marginal) product of labor and capital is equal to the sum of the rate of return on capital and the rate of remuneration to labor. The industry will be characterized by the periodic depletion of fishing banks and the dissipation of the rents that the stock of fish could otherwise produce.

46   The following discussion owes much to Evsey Domar's "The causes of slavery or serfdom," and Douglass C. North's "A framework for analyzing the state in economic history."

47   The system so far closely resembles Adam Smith's "early and rude state of society" in which, Adam Smith asserted, it will be true that "If it takes twice the labor to kill a beaver as it does to kill a deer, one beaver will exchange for two deer" and, in addition, "the whole produce of labor belongs to the laborer." If Smith is said to have had a labor theory of value for pre-capitalist societies, Locke may be said to have had a labor theory of property rights. Conversely, it may be said that the Smith labor theory of value simultaneously defines the property rights over commodities as well as their rate of exchange. See also K. Marx, *Capital*, Vol. I, p. 768.

48   North, *Institutions, Institutional Change, and Economic Performance*, p. 12.

49   North, "A framework for analyzing the state in economic history."

50   Pope Alexander VI's bull of 1493. By the "Patronato Real" the Crown also agreed to collect the ecclesiastical tithe in exchange for two-ninths of the proceeds.

51   See Ronald W. Batchelder and Nicolás Sanchez, "The encomienda and the maximizing imperialist: an interpretation of Spanish imperialism in the Americas," p. 11.

52   Land does not become a scarce resource until very late in the colonial period. Historians can find no archival evidence that land parcels were rented until the 1760s.

53   See C. Pastore, *La lucha*, p. 12.

54   The taxes in question were the "media anata" and the "año de demora." See James S. Saeger, "Survival and abolition."

55   The Crown, however, ended up allowing indigenous enslavement in cases of "just war," which provided a loophole for those wishing to disregard the prohibition against enslavement, even though the waging of just wars required previous government approval.

56   That worthy individuals alone could receive encomiendas was a way of discriminating in the sale of the grant.

57   See R. de la Fuente Machaín, *El gobernador Domingo Martínez de Irala*.

58   The following report of November 7, 1715 from the Royal Treasurer to the Crown regarding the wisdom of subordinating the Jesuit missions to the authority of the Spanish colonial administration is clear on the effects that such a measure was anticipated to have, overall as well as on fiscal revenues: "Such great injury as may result from changing the governance of those Indians, putting Spanish governors and judges to rule them, that there is not the slightest doubt of the risk to which those settlements, where such a [large] number of Indians dwell, would be exposed . . . it being worthy of all attention that, if for any accident the said Indians became restless, they would abandon the missions . . . even if none of this were to happen and the Spaniards could quietly and peacefully begin to govern . . . given the known poverty of those lands and the tribute . . . which each Indian contributes to His Majesty, the Treasurer would not expect much of an increase in Royal revenues, given how general is the covetousness, especially in those parts, of those who come to govern, who only care for their own interests . . . a bull will be issued to the Audiencia ordering it not to allow any change in the government which for such a long time said Indian settlements have had." de Krüger, "Asunción y su área," p. 41.

References

Alchian, Armen and Demsetz, Harold (1973) "The property rights paradigm," *Journal of Economic History* 33, 1 (March): 16–27.

Armani, Alberto (1986) *Ciudad de Dios y Ciudad del Sol. El "estado" jesuita de los guaraníes (1609–1769)* (Mexico: Fondo de Cultura Económica).

Azara, Félix de (1847) *Descripción e historia del Paraguay y del Río de la Plata* in *Biblioteca Indiana. Viajes por la América del Sur*, Vol. II (Madrid: Editorial Aguilar, 1962).

Barzel, Yoram (1982) "Measurement costs and the organization of markets," *Journal of Law and Economics* 25, 1: 27–48.

Batchelder, Ronald W. and Sanchez, Nicolás (1988) "The encomienda and the maximizing imperialist: an interpretation of Spanish imperialism in the Americas" (working paper 501, Department of Economics, University of California at Los Angeles).

Baysinger, B., Ekelund, R. B., and Tollison, R. J. (1981) "Mercantilism as a rent-seeking society," in J. M. Buchanan (ed.), *Towards a Theory of the Rent-Seeking Society* (College Station, TX: Texas A & M University Press).

Cardozo, Ramón I. (1938) *La antigua provincia del Guairá y Villa Rica del Espíritu Santo* (Buenos Aires: J. Menéndez).

Carneiro, Robert (1970) "A theory of the origin of the state," *Science* 169 (August): 733–8.

Caso, A. (1963) "Land tenure among the ancient Mexicans," *American Anthropologist* 65, 4 (August): 862–78.

Chaves, Julio César (1969–70) "Las ordenanzas de Ramírez de Velasco, Hernandarias y Alfar," *Historia Paraguaya* 113: 107–20.

Cheung, Steven N. S. (1970) "The structure of a contract and the theory of a non-exclusive resource," *Journal of Law and Economics* 13 (1970): 49–70.

Clastres, Pierre (1974) "Indépendence et exogamie: structure et dynamique des sociétés indiennes de la forêt tropicale," in *La Société contre l'état* (Paris: Editions du Minuit), pp. 43–68.

Coase, Ronald (1960) "The problem of social cost," *Journal of Law and Economics* 3, 1 (October): 1–44.

Conrad, A. and Meyer, J. R. (1964) *The Economics of Slavery and Other Studies in Econometric History* (Chicago: Aldine).

Cooney, Jerry W. (1977) "An ignored aspect of the viceroyalty of the Río de la Plata," *Intercambio Internacional* 2, 1 (January): 10–13.

Cooney, Jerry, W. (1979) "A colonial naval industry: the fabrica de cables of Paraguay," *Revista de historia de América* 87 (January–June): 105–26.

Cooney, Jerry W. (1980) "Paraguayan astilleros and the Platine merchant marine, 1796–1806," *The Historian* 43 (November): 55–74.

Cooney, Jerry W. (1982–3) "Foreigners in the intendencia of Paraguay," *The Americas* 3 (January): 333–58.

Cooney, Jerry W. (1987a) "The yerba mate and cattle frontier of Paraguay, 1776–1811: social, economic, and political impact" (unpublished paper).

Cooney, Jerry W. (1987b) "Bureaucrats, growers, and defense: the royal tobacco monopoly of Paraguay" (unpublished paper).

De la Fuente Machaín, R. (1939) *El gobernador Domingo Martínez de Irala* (Buenos Aires: Librería y editorial "La Facultad").

Demsetz, Harold (1967) "Toward a theory of property rights," *American Economic Review* 57: 347–59.

Domar, Evsey (1970) "The causes of slavery or serfdom: an hypothesis," *Journal of Economic History* 30, 1 (March) 18–32.

Durán Estragó, Margarita (1987) *Presencia Franciscana en el Paraguay: 1553–1824* (Asunción: Universidad Católica).

Engerman, Stanley (1973) "Some considerations relating to property rights in man," *Journal of Economic History* 33, 1 (March): 43–65.

Evans, Robert, Jr, (1970) "Some notes on coerced labor," *Journal of Economic History* 30: 861–6.

Feeny, David (1989) "The decline of property rights in man in Thailand, 1800–1913," *Journal of*

Economic History 49, 2 (June): 285–96.

Ferrer de Arréllaga, René (1985) *Un siglo de expansión colonizadora: los orígenes de Concepción* (Asunción: Editorial Historia).

Florescano, Enrique (1971) *Estructura y Problemas Agrarios de México, 1500–1821* (Mexico: Secretaría de Educación Pública).

Fogel, Robert and Engerman, Stanley (1971) *The Reinterpretation of American Economic History* (New York: Harper & Row).

Gandía, Enrique de (1939) *Francisco de Alfaro y la condición social de los indios* (Buenos Aires: Librería y editorial "El Ateneo").

Garavaglia, Juan Carlos (1983) *Mercado interno y economía colonial. Tres siglos de historia de la verba mate* (Mexico: Editorial Grijalbo).

Garavaglia, Juan Carlos (1987) *Economía, sociedad, y regiones* (Buenos Aires: Ediciones de la Flor).

Gordon, H. Scott (1954) "The economic theory of a common property resource: the fishery," *Journal of Political Economy* 62: 124–42.

Hicks, J. R. (1969) *A Theory of Economic History* (Oxford: Oxford University Press).

Krüger, Thomas de (1978) "Asunción y su área de influencia en la época colonial," *Estudios Paraguayos* 6, 2: 33–44.

López, Adalberto (1975) "Shipbuilding in sixteenth-century Asunción del Paraguay," *Mariner's Mirror* 61, 1 (February): 59–85.

López, Adalberto (1976) *The Revolt of the Comuneros, 1721–1735: A Study in the Colonial History of Paraguay* (Cambridge, MA: Schenkman).

Maeder, E. J. and Bolsi, A. S. (1974) "La población de las misiones guaraniés entre 1702 y 1767," *Estudios Paraguayos* 2, 1: 111–37.

Martins, F. A. and Martins, R. B. (1983) "Slavery in a non-export economy: nineteenth-century Minas Gerais revisited," *Hispanic American Historical Review* 63: 537–68.

Marx, Karl (1983) *Capital*, Vol. 1 (New York: International Publishers).

Necker, Louis (1974) "La réaction des Indiens Guarani à la Conquête espagnole du Paraguay, un des facteurs de la colonisation de l'Argentine à la fin de XVIe siècle," *Bulletin de la Société Suisse des Américanistes* 38: 71–80.

Necker, Louis (1979) *Indiens Guarani et Chamanes franciscains. Les Premières réductions du paraguay (1580–1800)* (Paris: Editions Anthropos).

North, Douglass C. (1979) "A framework for analyzing the state in economic history," *Explorations in Economic History* 16 (July): 249–59. Also in North (1981), Ch. 3.

North, Douglass C. (1981) *Structure and Change in Economic History* (New York: Norton).

North, Douglass C. (1990) *Institutions, Institutional Change and Economic Performance* (Cambridge, UK: Cambridge University Press).

North, D. C. and Thomas, R. P. (1973) *The Rise of the Western World* (Cambridge, UK: Cambridge University Press).

Ots Capdequí, José M. (1934) *Instituciones sociales de la América Española en el período colonial* (La Plata, Argentina: Universidad de la Plata).

Pastore, Carlos (1972) *La lucha por la tierra en el Paraguay* (Montevideo: Editorial Antequera).

Pastore, Mario Héctor (1990a) "La hipótesis de Domar sobre las causas de la servidumbre o la esclavitud y una colonia hispanoamericana: contraste y reformulación," *Revista de Historia Económica* (Madrid) 8, 3 (Otoño): 575–89.

Pastore, Mario Héctor (1990b) "State-led industrialization or predatory public rent-seeking? The economic development of Paraguay, 1850–1870" (paper presented at session on Latin American industrialization, International Economic History Congress, Louvain, Belgium: August 1990).

Ramírez, Susan (1989) "Indian and Spanish conceptions of land tenure in Peru, 1500–1800," (unpublished paper, DePaul University, Chicago, IL, 8 January 1989).

Rivarola Paoli, Juan Bautista (1986) *La economía colonial* (Asunción: published by the author).

Saeger, James Schofield (1981) "Survival and abolition: the eighteenth-century Paraguayan encomienda," *The Americas* 28 (July): 59–85.

Susnik, Branislava (1965) *El indio colonial del Paraguay*, Vol. I, *El guaraní colonial* (Asunción: Museo Etnográfico "Andrés Barbero").

Thomas, Robert P. and Bean, Richard (1974) "The fishers of men: the profits of the slave trade," *Journal of Economic History* 34: 885–914.

Tullock, Gordon, "The welfare costs of tariffs, monopolies, and theft," *Western Economic Journal* 5, 3 (June): 224–32.

Velázquez, Rafael Eladio (1972) "La población del Paraguay en 1682," *Revista Paraguaya de sociología* 9, 24 (May–August): 128–48.

Velázquez, Rafael Eladio (1982) "Caracteres de la encomienda paraguaya en los siglos XVII y XVIII," *Historia Paraguaya* 19: 115–63.

White, Richard Alan (1978) *Paraguay's Autonomous Revolution, 1810–1840* (Albuquerque, NM: University of New Mexico Press).

Zavala, Silvio (1977) *Orígenes de la colonización en el Río de la Plata* (Mexico: El Colegio Nacional).

27

The concept of "white slavery" in the English Caribbean during the early seventeenth century

Hilary Beckles

The early success of the English colonial enterprise in the West Indies between 1625 and 1650 depended heavily on the importation of large numbers of servile laborers. Before the mid-1640's most workers were recruited as indentured servants from the British Isles; slaves from West Africa, already widely in use in the Spanish and Portuguese colonies, remained a small minority. The social composition of Barbados, the leading English colony in this period, reflects the servant majority in the labor force (see Table 27.1). It is also important to note that the plantation system of cultivation was already in place before 1645 when the advent of the sugar industry revolutionized the economy, resulting in a massive importation of African slaves. By the mid-1650s, blacks outnumbered whites in the colony, and slavery became the principal labor institution.

The purpose of this chapter is to illustrate the sociolegal and economic aspects of the relationship between white servitude and black slavery in this early period of English settlement. It contends that the demands of plantation agriculture under frontier conditions led to the restructuring of the traditional form of indentured servitude. As planters, under market pressures, abandoned the pre-capitalist, moral-paternalistic ideological superstructure of traditional servitude, a colonial form of "near slavery" emerged, a form more compatible with the needs of capital accumulation.

English planters, unlike the Iberians discussed by Mario Pastore in Chapter 26, were not directly familiar with slave relations in the production of agricultural commodities. It was common practice in Britain for farmers to hire labor by the year for agricultural and artisanal work. They possessed, however, a highly developed market concept of labor in which property rights were an integral part. In the West Indies planters quickly perceived their contracted servants in terms of productive capital, and emphasized that the hiring of servants was an investment with market-determined property values. Their sensitivity to colonial and global economic forces in the accumulation of wealth was the basis of this development. They allowed market forces to determine the type of labor used, as well as the nature of its use. The shift from a white to a black labor regime between 1645 and 1680 was primarily a response to market forces, but some of the important structures and relations necessary for slavery were already established; they were further developed as the intensification of resource exploitation became necessary during the early years of sugar production because of massive capital outlay and high recurrent cost in that industry.[1]

Unlike the Spanish settlements in the Greater Antilles, Barbados and the Leewards were not densely populated with Indians who could be reduced to chattel slavery. The islands were part of the wider survival network of the Caribs who inhabited the Lesser Antilles. The Caribs (like the European invaders) were a militant and imperial people who were in the process of establishing their hegemony in the eastern Caribbean. Du Tertre, the French missionary who was familiar with the Caribs, noted that they possessed an innate contempt for servitude which drove them to launch a full-scale war against the Europeans. They won some battles and killed a large number of whites, but eventually over the seventeenth and eighteenth centuries they were defeated and eliminated by Anglo-French and Dutch military pressures.[2]

To clear the very forested land and initiate production, English colonists, therefore, looked outward for a labor supply. Like the French in the New World they looked first to their homeland. The slave trade from Africa was not fully established in the early seventeenth century, and was a virtual monopoly of the Iberians and the Dutch. The price of slave labor from Africa was prohibitively expensive and the English were not managerially prepared for black slavery as an institution, which made the dependence on British labor more complete. The most logical step, therefore, was to demand labor from England under temporary indenture, not for a year, but for anything between three and ten years. The planters would pay the passage and feed, clothe, and shelter

Table 27.1 Labour structure of fifteen pre-sugar plantations in Barbados, 1639–43

Year	Owner	Acres	Servants	Slaves
1639	Thomas Hethersall	100	7	–
1640	Samuel Andrews	200	10	–
1640	Henry Hawley	300	28	–
1640	Lancelot Pace	360	17	–
1640	William Woodhouse	150	26	–
1640	Captain Skeete	–	26	–
1641	Colonel Drax	225	4	22
1641	Lancelot Pace	426	20	–
1642	Gerald Hawtaine	124	4	2
1642	Thomas Rous	60	8	–
1643	Alexander Lindsay	60	2	4
1643	Christopher Moulropp	250	6	12
1643	James Holdip	200	29	–
1643	Captain Perkins	200	5	6
1643	John Friesenborch	26	2	5
	Totals	2,681	194	51

Source Deeds and inventories of Barbados, Barbados Archives, RB 3/1, ff. 15, 55–77, 237, 290, 316, 418, 729, 946. Also R. Dunn, *Sugar and Slaves: The Rise of the Planter Class in the English West Indies, 1624–1715* (New York: 1972), p. 68.

the servants in return for their labor. At the end of the indenture the servant would be given a "freedom due" of £10 or a piece of land. Such practices were legitimate and acceptable within the labor tradition of English society.

In 1638, Peter Hay noted that "a plantation in this place [Barbados] is worth nothing unless there be a good store of hands upon it." These hands were shipped out from Britain, and white workers under indenture became the "mainstay of the colony." In 1645, George Downing wrote to John Winthrop, governor of Massachusetts:

> A man that will settle there [West Indies] must looke to procure servants, which if you could gett out of England for 6, or 8 or 9 yeares time, only paying their passages, or at the most but some smale above it, it would do very well, for so . . . [you] shall be able to doe something upon a plantation.[3]

The mercantile interests had been prominent in the councils of the English imperial state from the 1620s, and well-established merchants, such as Thomas Povey, Martin Noell, Andrew Riccard, and Maurice Thompson, all had West Indian investments and were therefore prepared to assist the colonists with a large supply of indentured servants.[4]

The spread of sugar production throughout the West Indies demanded not only large sums of capital and technology, but also a considerable flow of labor with varying degrees of skill, from common field laborers to highly specialized artisans. By seventeenth-century standards, the plantation was a sophisticated production unit, demanding a labor force more complex than, say, an English estate. The grinding, boiling, curing, refining, and distilling processes of sugar manufacture demanded industrial machinery which had to be assembled, maintained, and at times modified. This meant that a labor force with basic literacy and a familiarity with advanced industrial technology was necessary. In the early phase of sugar production, planters claimed that these qualities were rare in most Africans, and when they were present, thought it politically necessary to suppress or to eradicate them. As a result, they became heavily dependent on white indentured servants to make the critical transition to sugar production.

In this period, servants brought to the colonies skills which were adapted to meet the planters' demands. Their emergence from a rapidly developing technological society made them suitable. The importation of servants was conceived of not only in terms of labor inputs, but also as injections of technology. A sample of 1,808 servants who registered for servitude in Barbados at Bristol (see Table 27.2) can be used as an indication of the qualitative nature of the labor force being attracted by Barbadian planters. When compared with Virginia, a tobacco colony, Barbados attracted more skilled workers in the period.

The majority of planters found indentured servants qualitatively adequate for sugar production. The result was a very large increase in the demand for servants during the sugar boom of the late 1640s and early 1650s. The Civil War in England was critical in releasing large numbers of laborers, and between 1645 and 1650 at least 8,000 servants joined the labor force in the West Indies. By 1652, some 12,000 servants were employed in Barbados sugar production. Governor Jonathan Atkins noted that, during the period of early sugar production, indentured servants "did most of the work on the plantation"; these "poor tradesmen and artificers" from the British Isles were critical to

Table 27.2 Servants shipped to Barbados and Virginia from Bristol, 1654–60

Date	Barbados (1)			Virginia		
	No.	No. skilled	% skilled	No.	No. skilled	% skilled
1654	16	14	87.5	35	5	14.2
1655	115	53	46.0	78	24	30.7
1656	158	68	43.0	102	49	48.0
1657	371	225	60.6	80	44	55.0
1658	415	149	35.9	151	56	37.0
1659	494	268	54.2	156	90	57.6
1660	239	142	59.4	149	87	58.3
Totals	1,808	919	50.8	751	355	47.2

Source Tolzey Book of Indentures, 1654–86, Bristol Records Office, England. See for an analysis of English indentured migrants to the Americas, D. Galenson, "The social origins of some early Americans," *William and Mary Quarterly* 36, 2 (1979): 264–87; also D. Galenson, " 'Middling people' of 'common sorts?' The social origins of some early Americans, re-examined," *William and Mary Quarterly* 36 (July 1978): 449–541; M. Campbell, "Social origins of some early Americans," in J. M. Smith (ed.), *Seventeenth-Century America* (Chapel Hill, NC: University of North Carolina Press, 1959), pp. 1–27.

the development of the sugar industry in the colony.[5] In 1655, one observer noted that in spite of the large number of African slaves on the island, the

> custom of all merchants trading thither is to bring as many men and women [from Britain] as they can. No sooner doth a ship come to anchor than the Islanders go aboard enquiring what servants they can buy . . . these servants planteth, weedeth and manureth their ground all by hand in which lieth their estates.[6]

Seventeenth-century Englishmen were familiar with the institution of indentured servitude; indeed they conceived it to be essential to the organization of agricultural labor. Within the socioeconomic organization of society it was a popular and legitimate institution. It grew out of the feudal system of apprenticeship, and was characterized by the establishment of a contractual agreement with mutual obligations, not moral but legal, between master and servant. Yet in the formative period of West Indian colonization the system evolved quite differently in its functions and forms of legitimation. Contemporary observers described it as "white slavery" and referred to indentured servants as "white niggers."[7] Certainly the institution, as it developed in the early English West Indies, resembled chattel slavery more than the traditional English servitude, and the forces which enhanced this development were said to be specific to the nature of early plantation economy.

Pioneer Barbadian planters quite freely bought, sold, gambled away, mortgaged, taxed as property, and alienated in wills their indentured servants. These practices were governed not by English labor customs and traditions, but by a loosely defined concept – "the custom of the Country" – which was the law and deciding force in the colonies before a comprehensive master-and-servant code was established in 1661.[8] Through the manipulation of this concept, early Barbadian planters developed a system of white servitude which was peculiarly New World, and in many ways came remarkably close to the "ideal type" of chattel slavery which later became associated with the African experience.

Historians have generally agreed, however, that the central feature which distinguished white indentured servitude from black slavery was that, unlike the slave, it was the servant's indentured time (contracted labor power) which was marketed and not the servant's self. It should be pointed out, nonetheless, that it was this very issue of the "servant's time" which distinguished English from West Indian servitude. Unlike the English master, the West Indian planter on purchasing a servant obtained by the "custom of the country" total control over the servant, that is, not only his or her laboring hours, but also the non-laboring hours. The servant was accountable to the master for the total time embraced under the indenture. The result was that servants could not legally leave their plantations without a pass signed by the master: thus the total control of mobility so characteristic of black slavery was directly applicable to white servants. Also, planters were keen to demonstrate that the servant was not a free person under contractual obligations, but primarily a capital investment with property characteristics.

Though the servant's market value was usually determined primarily by the length of unexpired servitude, planters developed other methods of property valuation, whereby the resale values of some servants were quite independent of remaining indentured time. Common in Barbados was a method which evaluated bodies rather than time. Equiano, an ex-slave, wrote in his autobiography in relation to slaves, "I have often seen slaves . . . in different islands, put into scales and weighed and then sold, from three pence to six pence a pound." This practice was also used to value some white servants. Richard Ligon's descriptive account of such a transaction in Barbados during the 1640s is very informative. On this occasion, a young female was being bartered for a pig. The parties to the transaction obtained the scales and weighed both the pig and the servant for their relative value. According to Ligon, "the price was set at a groat [four pence] a pound for the hogs flesh, and six pence for the woman's flesh." Furthermore, Ligon admitted in dismay, here "'tis an ordinary thing" to sell servants and "in exchange receive any commodities that are in the island." The planters acting under the "custom of the country" merely continued what the merchants had started – dealing with their servants as a species of property.[9]

The development of West Indian servitude was the outgrowth of a complex mixture of economic and social forces operating within the construction of the agricultural systems. The early Barbadians, like other English colonists dependent on tobacco and cotton production, found that depression in the markets for those products threatened not only capital accumulation, but the very future of English Caribbean colonization. There were two fundamental responses by the planters to this sense of economic stagnation and the unsatisfactory utilization of indentured labor. A significant number emigrated from the West Indies, taking their servants, to the mainland colonies, particularly Virginia and Maryland. Those who stayed behind began to reappraise the relationship between capital accumulation and labor organization. These planters developed a more market-oriented conception of labor and its function as capital. Engerman made an interesting correlation between production, productivity levels, and the establishment of property rights in labor. He stated: "It is clear, that the allocation of property rights in man could affect the measured level of output in the economy. The slave owner is able to obtain higher output from his labor force than might be obtained where labor is free, because of the ability to manipulate the supply of labor available." The Barbados planters, by establishing property rights in servants under indenture, were able to maximize output with the available technology and land. By this process, these planters were able to accumulate capital in order to survive the crises in the tobacco and cotton markets between 1628 and 1640, and finally to make the leap into high-cost sugar production with black slave labor.[10]

On pre-sugar plantations, capital investment in indentured labor was the second largest single outlay, next to the investment in land. The most effective method by which a wide range of economic functions could be attached to indentured servants was to establish by the "custom of the island" their use as a form of alienable property. Since servants represented in this period the most liquid form of capital on the plantation, planters wanting to raise small amounts of money on a short-term basis could achieve this by selling servant stock on the open market, thereby increasing significantly the cashflow level on the commodity markets. The use of labor as property with all the market functions of such is the common feature of chattel slavery wherever it has been found. The early Barbadian planters, by using white servants as property on the market, therefore, laid down the basic prerequisite for slavery to develop.

Despite doubts expressed by some historians, the deeds of Barbados contain much direct evidence to show that the sales of servants were not simply transference of their labor services. Two historians of Barbados, A. E. Smith and V. T. Harlow, thought only the labor services of servants were being sold.[11] Harlow, however, in his history of Barbados, was intrigued by the wording and the implications of some deeds by which indentured servants were sold, especially in the nature of the "rights" and "title" being transferred. He concluded, though, that these related not to the servant's self as property, as with black slaves, but to the servant's labor services. One Barbados deed reads as follows:

> I, William Marshall of the Island aforesaid [Barbados] Merchant, do by these present, assign, sett and order, all my right, title, and interest of one maide servant, by the name Alice Skinner, for the full term of four years from ye day of her arrival in this island, unto Mr. Richard Davis, or his assigns.[12]

Also illustrative is the wording of a 1640 deed of sale between Richard Atkinson and John Batt. In this instance, Atkinson offered his "body" for six years as collateral in a commercial transaction with Batt. The agreement was that Batt would advance a cash loan to Atkinson, repayable in installments over one year. The deed stated that in case of his financial default "It shall bee for the said John Batt, or his assigns, to take the body of me Richard Atkinson, servant for the terme of six yeares without further trouble or suite of lawe."[12]

Barbadian deeds, wills, and property inventories all yield evidence on the transfer of ownership of servants. These documents show that in plantation accounts, sales, and government investigations into property values, indentured servants were categorized as property, like cattle, slaves, and fixed assets. For example, when the governor's estate agents appraised "all such good cattle and chattel as are now upon the Plantation" of George Bulkeley, on June 12, 1640, the report was itemized as follows:

livestock (valued at 42,000 pounds of cotton), kitchen utensils, household stuffs (valued at 1,125 pounds of cotton), and nine servants (valued at 3,120 pounds of cotton).[13] Servants were not only tied to the plantation as an integral component of its capital assets, but were also disposed of with the estate as it changed ownership, either by sale or by will. During negotiations for the sale of a plantation the seller would present an appraisal of its capital value. These appraisals gave detailed itemizations of every asset to be sold with the land, with their current value. Servants were generally listed as alienable property in these inventories. For example, when Three Houses Plantation in Barbados was sold by Captain Henry Hawley to Captain Francis Skeete on June 19, 1640, the "goods and chattel" attached to the land in sale were 40 sows, 160 pigs, 2 hogs, 1 horse, 6 donkeys, and 28 servants, valued at 12,000, 5,150, 3,000, 750, 3,600, and 7,350 pounds of cotton respectively.[14]

The inclusion of servants as chattels to be alienated in property transactions illustrates how Barbadian planters imposed market functions on indentured servants as they did on their African slaves. The government of the colony also recognized the market functions of indentured servants as alienable property. Magistrates and tax officials frequently confiscated indentured servants in order to recover tax arrears, or to pay the debts of the deceased. For example, on April 7, 1647, the Provost Marshal of Barbados gave a local constable an order to "seize and attach any of ye cotton, tobacco, servants, plantacon, or other goods or estate, whs'over belonging to the children of Capt. William Rayley deceased . . . to be resold to meet the debt owed by the deceased to Mr. Alexander Lindsay."[15]

Like the tax officers, individuals preferred to reclaim debts by obtaining indentured servants; they could either be quickly sold for cash or a commodity, or easily put to work. There was, therefore, a widespread preference for indentured servants as a short-term capital investment, more than for African slaves, who were seen as problematic, in that they had to be trained into productive roles.

Servants were also used as integral parts of the commercial and financial structure. Planters commonly used them as property security in mortgage agreements. In March 1647, John Wiseman, Barbados planter, was in debt to the value of 500 pounds of cotton to William Russell. In order to satisfy Russell, Wiseman had to mortgage his "plantation and servants" until the agreed repayment date was fixed.[16] The placing of indentured servants on 2- to 5-year mortgages was common; individuals preferred to use servants as property guarantees in such agreements. The logical market extension of such a system was the use of indentured servants as a form of currency accepted by all and legitimized by local law and custom. Some individuals insisted that payment in transactions be made not in sterling but in servants, while others made payment in servants a material element of contracts. In 1644, Thomas Applewhaite, a Barbados planter, bought a 200-acre plantation in the parish of St Thomas and St George; the seller required payment to be made with twenty-five indentured servants.[17]

All these functions were part of a wider system of property and possessory relations in human beings developed in the colonies, a system corresponding to plantation production and legitimized by its legal-custom superstructure. In most analyses of property, the concept of appropriation appears central across a wide range of social relations. The total appropriation of a person's social and productive capacity by another in any set of social relations implied the formation of ownership and rights system in that person. Furthermore, the ultimate proof of the existence of property rights in persons lies in whether those rights and titles can be alienated. Torrance argued that "appropriated rights which are enjoyed by individuals through inheritance . . . will be called the property of the individual . . . as they are alienable free property."[18] In Barbados, indentured servants, like slaves, were bequeathed and inherited by wills, and no one questioned the legality of this method of property alienation. For example, the will of John Daulton, April 15, 1656, declared: "I give and bequeath unto my daughters Emillie Daulton and Joan Daulton . . . my estate whatsoever, and goods and chattels, commodities, merchandizes, servants . . . upon it."[19] No system of slavery could function effectively unless property rights were not only defended but also alienable, especially within the family through the inheritance mechanism.

Some have argued that because servants had rights against maltreatment, their status was fundamentally different from that of slaves. Smith, for instance, has argued that, whether property or not, indentured servants were Christian and they were white, hence they were protected by their right to complain to magistrates. He made much of this right of servants to complain to local magistrates over maltreatment, and implied that its existence undermined the conception of them as property. It is true that some constraints prevented masters from using their servants fully as chattel slaves. For example, servants were protected under law in areas such as property ownership, sexual abuse, parenthood, marriage, and family. Slaves could not own property, they had no legal recourse in case of sexual violation, and their marital and family relations were not legally recognized.

Nevertheless, property systems usually have rules against the misuse or maltreatment of many kinds of property and penalties for violation of those rules. Earlier English law, for instance, had many sanctions against "waste" in real property (for example, rules against cutting trees in a forest), and we are all familiar with statutory prohibitions against cruelty to animals or modern environmental regulations prohibiting wide varieties of "abuses" by owners.

The nuisance rules Robert Gordon discussed in Chapter 5 can also be considered constraints on owners' powers to use their own property. So the existence of remedies against "misuse" or "abuse" of a particular kind of property is not evidence of the impossibility of owning that kind of property. Engerman quite correctly observed that even in societies in which slavery existed and was held morally defensible, both law and custom recognized that man was a rather peculiar form of property. Slave codes to regulate treatment by masters were widespread and there were more legal constraints on the behavior of slaves than on other forms of property. (Barbados eventually had both slave and servant codes, although not until 1661, when the numerical economic significance of servants in the society was rapidly diminishing.)

That indentured servants had some formal rights against mistreatment, however significant from the perspective of legal theory, did not necessarily mean that servants were able to exercise those rights very effectively in practice. For more powerful than the servants, the council, assembly, and judiciary – the political apparatus of the planters' hegemony – were not very interested in enforcement. For example, in 1640 when two Barbados servants lodged complaints with the local magistrates against their master, Captain Thomas Stanhope, for maltreatment, they were adjudged malicious and publicly flogged, thus weakening any threat to the planters' right to treat their property as they wished within the wide limits of the "custom of the country."[20] Planters expected such decisions from the judiciary and held the view that since they paid a property tax on their servants, their disposal and use of them was no concern of the wider community.

Constraints of class, race, and culture played an important part in the development of the particular forms of indentured servitude in Barbados. Both the planter class and the imperial government would have had great difficulty in legitimizing the reduction of indentured servants to chattel slaves. Indeed, the history of the English people was popularly conceived to be characterized primarily by the gradual freeing of lower orders, and this was identified in the seventeenth century as an important area of progress. Furthermore, most servants came to the West Indies voluntarily, and would have objected to such a development. Their use as property had already created a political crisis in the white community, as evidenced by the aborted servant insurrections of 1634 and 1647.[21]

Nonetheless, it was clear before the 1661 Masters and Servants Act, and especially in the period before 1647, that both servants and slaves were used as property; slaves, however, were seen, like animals, as permanent and self-reproductive. The controversy initiated by Oscar and Mary Handlin's well-known essay on the origins of slavery in English America is directly relevant to this period of West Indian history, since it was at Barbados that the English developed their first expansive slave system in the New World. It is now difficult to accept their argument that the English in the early West Indies were innately prejudiced against blacks, who were a small minority in the pre-sugar era.[22] The evidence, however, does support their other argument that the masters, in terms of the market use of labor, did not significantly distinguish in this formative period between servants under indenture and blacks. While the blacks served indefinitely and the servants for periods of three to ten years, what was common to both was their property status. Though this status was in itself insufficient to allow for a definition of the servant as slave, added with other features, blacks clearly became slaves. For example, the blacks' status was involuntary and self-reproductive; in addition, non-pecuniary returns, such as sociosexual benefits (including rape and other forms of physical assault) could be obtained from slaves without legal penalties, whereas servants could not be used in these ways.[23]

There is one instance where servant complaints reached the highest levels of imperial government, and became the basis of the first parliamentary debate on white bondage, and its relation to black slavery within the empire. On the evening of March 24, 1659, two petitions, "which leaped over the heads of about four score others," were presented to the Commons Grand Committee of Grievances on behalf of seventy-three political prisoners "sold into slavery in Barbados" by the major-generals after the Salisbury uprising of March 1654. One petition was preferred on behalf of a man called Rivers, another called Foyle and seventy others; the other petition by a man called Rowland Thomas. All the petitioners had been sold in Barbados as the "goods and chattel" of the leading West Indian merchant Martin Noell – under the Protector's instructions. The debate in Parliament was recorded by one member, Sir Thomas Burton, in his diary for the Interregnum (hereinafter cited as *Diary*), and has been reproduced by Leo Stock in his 1920s edition of parliamentary discussions on North America in the early colonial period (hereinafter cited as Stock). The petition of Foyle and Rivers was published as a pamphlet in 1659 to obtain popular support against the arbitrary shipping of the working class to the sugar colonies by both the West Indian merchants and the state.[24] Received as indentured servants by the sugar planters on 10-year contracts, and in some cases for life, the political prisoners were quickly absorbed into the many occupations on the various plantations with their African counterparts. They were kept "grinding at the mills, attending the furnaces and digging in the scorching land."[25]

The interregnum debate was charged with emotion, nationalism, racism, and political pragmatism (this last, an early expression of bourgeois political rationality). The basic question which underlay the debate was this: if the history of the English nation was chiefly characterized by the gradual freeing of the lower orders, so lately and so notably advanced by the Revolution, was it possible to legitimize the development of a form of "near enslavement" of white labor in the colonies? For the first time politicians discussed the fate of bonded white laborers in the plantations. In the debate, many commoners articulated their views on black slavery, white supremist ideology, the embryonic concept of "human rights," the limitations of party-political conflict, and the need for white consciousness at the colonial frontier.

During the debate, the question was often posed whether or not the Revolution was producing a flow of "white slaves" to Barbados – the "sugar machine of the Indies." Having fought for the consolidation of bourgeois freedom, many commoners wondered if in the process they were institutionalizing white working-class "slavery." Foyle and Rivers, the petitioners, claimed that on their arrival at Barbados, the captain sold "the generality of them to most inhuman and barbarous persons for 1,500 pounds of sugar a piece, more or less according to their working faculties, as the goods and chattels of Mr. Martin Noell" (*Diary*, p. 256). The petitioners then documented some of the realities of Barbadian servitude during the sugar revolution. They noted how they were commonly "bought and sold still from one planter to another, attached as horses and beasts for the debt of their masters, whipped at the whipping post for their master's pleasure, and many other ways made miserable beyond expression or Christian imagination" (*Diary*, pp. 256–7). What the petitioners wanted to know was, by what "authority so great a breach is made upon the free people of England . . . by merchants that deal in slaves and souls of men" (*Diary*, p. 257)?

Martin Noell, the West Indian merchant with significant Barbadian property interests, was called upon to give evidence concerning this trade "in the bodies and souls of men" from which he had clearly profited. Naturally, Noell was very defensive and constructed a mild apologetic image of Barbadian servitude. In the previous year he had sold a small cargo of prisoners in Barbados for £100, the legality of which Parliament also wanted to discuss. He told the Commons: "I abhor the thoughts of setting 100*l* upon any man's person. It is false and scandalous . . . the work is hard but . . . not so hard as is represented to you. It [Barbados] is a place as grateful to you for trade as any part of the world" (*Diary*, pp. 258–9). Parliament was not convinced by Noell's defence. Nevertheless, most members took the view of one Colonel Clarke that they should be careful even in dealing with Cavaliers like the prisoners, for in the final instance they were Englishmen, and the Revolution had been fought to defend the "human rights" of all Englishmen. This dichotomy ran throughout the debate. Colonel White argued that the Cavaliers got what they deserved, for which he would not be apologetic; nevertheless, he insisted, "if every justice may commit a man [to colonial bondage] because he cannot give a good account of himself," it would certainly be a practice "against the free-born people of England" (*Diary*, p. 262).

Several members voiced distress at the condition to which the prisoners had apparently been reduced and worried that their fate represented a significant threat to the liberties of Englishmen. Sir Henry Vane was firm in his conviction that the issue of "white slavery" in Barbados transcended party politics, and was basically one of "human rights" and individual liberty. He replied to one Colonel Birch, "I do not look on this business as a Cavalierish business; but as a matter that concerns the liberty of the free-born people of England . . . to be used in this barbarous manner . . . and sold there for 100*l*" (*Diary*, pp. 262–3). Sir John Lenthall was not concerned at this time with the question of nationalism but with the contradictory elements in what was their liberation movement. In full awareness of the ambiguity in the debate, he hoped "it is not the effect of our war to make merchandise of men . . . we are the freest people in the world" (Stock, p. 256). Lenthall wanted all English servants removed from the field gangs of Barbadian sugar estates, leaving such work only for blacks and Irishmen. In this he got the full support of one Mr Boscawen, who noted with much clarity and less emotionalism, "I am as much against the Cavalier party as any man in these walls . . . but you have Paul's case before you. A Roman ought not to be beaten . . . or our lives will be as cheap as those of negroes" (*Diary*, p. 268). Boscawen was able to inject this comparison with the blacks into the debate with conviction because he had vested interests in the early Jamaica venture, and was fully aware of the nature of slave usage in the West Indies. One Mr Gewen wanted not only a full debate of the issue, but also an investigation into Barbadian indentured servitude. After Boscawen's interjection, he protested, "I would not have men sold like bullocks and horses. The selling of a man is an offence of a high nature" (Stock, p. 260). Like Boscawen, Gewen was specific in his meaning if not in his language: "white slavery" was the issue of controversy, "black slavery" was a unanimous assumption of the House. Sir Arthur Haslerigge was moved to tears by the plight of these servants – "sold into slavery amongst beasts" (*Diary*, p. 271). In his view, that white men should be forced to labor in gangs with Africans represented heresy that Charles I would himself find undignified.

On the other hand, there were the political pragmatists, the hardliners, who saw it as strictly a party-political issue devoid of the moral-humanist outpouring of fellow commoners. This group was led by one Major Knight. In his view the prisoners were sent to labor for anti-revolutionary activities, which was only politically expedient, and since Parliament had no control over the sugar planters' use of them, the debate was pointless. He got to his feet and argued, "I move to reject the petitions, for if you sit twelve months you will not have time to hear all petitions from Cavaliers. What will you do with the Scots taken at Dunbar, and at Durham and Worcester? Many of them were sent to Barbadoes" (*Diary*, p. 270). The debate went on until 3.00 a.m.; at which point some moved to adjourn for an hour, others until the following day. The Chair made no comment and rose. On the afternoon of March 30, Sarjeant-at-Law Wylde moved to reintroduce the debate. He stated that the issue was of paramount importance in that the selling of white men to Barbadian planters as slaves is "noised abroad as if the Secretary of State could enslave, and had enslaved, the people of England at his pleasure" (Stock, p. 258). The news had certainly leaked out and was publicized throughout Europe. The Venetian ambassador to London reported that the secretary of state gave regular orders to recruit people at random for the Barbadian sugar plantations. He noted in 1656 how he saw some 1,200 people collected from the streets of London put on board a ship for Barbados.[26] The debate continued until early morning and ended with no result as formerly. The House rose at 1.00 a.m. The petitioners were not freed.

Between 1659 and 1662, the Commons supported plans to set up an African trading company. This was established in 1663 as the Company of Royal Adventurers trading into Africa. When this company was declared bankrupt, the Commons supported plans to establish another, which was formed in 1672 as the Royal African Company. Discussion of the "human rights" and liberty of the West Indian labor force did not take place in Parliament for another 150 years. Then it was not "Capitalism and Servitude" but "Capitalism and Slavery," but the precedent for the pattern and the nature of debate was already established.

The rise of the plantation system, like the development of white "proto-slavery," preceded the emergence of "sugar and black slavery." The demands of commodity production had the effect of creating a new form of servitude out of the old institution, one which was more suitable to the property requirements of the early planters. This subject has gone largely unresearched because of the greater involvement of African slave labor and Asian indentured labor in plantation development in the West Indies. Much work has been done on the servant trade and the displacement of servant labor by black slaves particularly on the mainland colonies, but the property nature of early West Indian servitude on the plantations is still in need of researchers.

What our inquiry into indentured servitude does suggest, however, is the folly of assuming that the categories of "owner" and "owned" have been borrowed from nature or of assuming that "persons" own "things." The bundles of rights to one's own labor power and of rights to the labor power of others have been, and still are, extraordinarily various. They may be arranged along continua of one sort or another, but it is surprisingly difficult to draw bright lines between those with full personal autonomy and those without it. Our inquiry has also illustrated the power of legal systems to reify, indeed, the power of one legal system to reify even persons whose race, language, and culture were the same as those of the legislators and judges who did the reifying. To lose out in a battle where control of the legal rules of property is at stake, may, then, be to lose crucial aspects of personhood itself.

Notes

1   See H. Gemery and J. Hogendorn, "The Atlantic slave trade: a tentative model," *Journal of African History* 15, 2 (1974): 223–5; R. Bean and R. Thomas, "The fishers of men: the profits of the slave trade," *Journal of Economic History* 34, 4 (1974): 885–914; F. C. Innes, "The pre-sugar era of European settlement in Barbados," *Journal of Caribbean History* 1 (1970): 17–20; R. C. Batie, "Why sugar? Economic cycles and the changing of staples in the English and French Antilles, 1624–54," *Journal of Caribbean History* 8–9 (1979): 7–9; H. Beckles and A. Downes, "The economics of transition to the black labor system in Barbados, 1630–1680," *Journal of Interdisciplinary History* 18, 2 (1987): 225–47.

2   H. Beckles, *A History of Barbados: from Amerindian Settlement to Nation-State* (Cambridge, UK:

Cambridge University Press, 1990), pp. 1–6; C. Jesse, "Du Tertre and Labat on seventeenth-century slave life in the French Antilles," *Caribbean Quarterly* 7, 3 (1961): 137.

3   Cited in R. Dunn, *Sugar and Slaves: The Rise of the Planter Class in the English West Indies, 1624–1715* (New York: 1972), p. 52.

4   A. P. Thornton, *West Indian Policy under the Restoration* (Oxford: Clarendon Press, 1956), p. 6; M. Ashley, *Financial and Commercial Policy under the Cromwellian Protectorate* (London: Oxford University Press, 1934), pp. 10–82.

5   Egerton MS 2395, f. 632, British Library; Public Record Office (hereafter PRO), London, *Calendar of State Papers, colonial series (hereafter CSPC)*1574–1660, p. 446; Governor Jonathan Atkins to the Lords of Trade and Plantations, October 26, 1680, PRO, *CSPC* 1677–80, No. 1558.

6   Francis Barrington to Sir John Barrington, June 5, 1655, Historical Manuscript Commission, London, report 7/572a.

7   See F. Cass, *Memoirs of Père Labat, 1693–1705* (London: 1970), p. 125; "A description of Barbados, 1667", PRO, CO 1/31, no. 170; A. E. Smith, *Colonists in Bondage: White Servitude and Convict Labor in America, 1607–1776* (New York: 1971), p. 309; V. T. Harlow, *A History of Barbados, 1625–1685* (Oxford: Clarendon Press, 1926), p. 293; E. Williams, *Capitalism and Slavery* (London: André Deutsch, 1975), p. 18.

8   "An Act for the ordaining of rights between masters and servants," in Richard Hall (ed.), Manuscript Laws of Barbados, PRO, CO 30/1, no. 30.

9   P. Edwards (ed.), *Equiano's Travels* (London: Heinemann, 1967), pp. 71, 171; R. Ligon, *A True and Exact History of Barbados* (London: 1657), p. 59; N. Foster, *A Briefe Relation of the Late Horrid Rebellion Acted in the Island of Barbados* (London: 1650), pp. 243–5.

10 See S. Engerman, "Some considerations relating to property rights in man," *Journal of Economic History* 33, 1 (1976): 48.

11 See Smith, *Colonists in Bondage*, p. 233; Harlow, *A History of Barbados*, p. 293.

12 Deed of William Marshall, Barbados Archives, RB, 3/2, f. 47. Deed of John Batt, December 14, 1640, Royal Commonwealth Society Archives, London, Davis MSS, box 2.

13 Inventory of George Bulkeley, June 12, 1640, Barbados Archives RB, 3/1, f. 14.

14 Inventory of Henry Hawley, June 19, 1640, Barbados Archives, RB, 3/1, f.14.

15 V. T. Harlow (ed.), *Colonising Expeditions to the West Indies and Guiana, 1623–1667* (London: Hakluyt Society, 1924), p. 28. Order of the Provost Marshal, April 7, 1647, Barbados Archives, RB, 3/2, f. 70.

16 Deed of William Russell, Barbados Archives, March 1647, 3/2, f. 53.

17 Deed of Thomas Applewhaite, July 1644, Barbados Archives, RB, 3/1, f. 536.

18 J. Torrance, *Estrangement, Alienation, and Exploitation* (New York: Columbia University Press, 1977), pp. 163–5.

19 Will of John Daulton, April 15, 1656, Barbados Archives, RB, 6/13, f. 134.

20 Cited in "Pages from the early history of Barbados, 1627–1652," British Library, London, MS 1865, C9 (68).

21 See H. Beckles, "Rebels and reactionaries: the political responses of white laborers to planter-class hegemony in seventeenth-century Barbados," *Journal of Caribbean History* 15 (1981): 1–20; also H. Beckles, "A 'riotious and unruly lot': Irish indentured servants and freeman in the English West Indies, 1644–1713," *William and Mary Quarterly* 47 (October 1990): 505–20.

22 Oscar Handlin and Mary Handlin, "Origins of the southern labor system," *William and Mary Quarterly* 7 (1950): 220–1; Oscar Handlin, *Race and Nationality in American Life* (Boston, MA: Little, Brown, 1957), pp. 1–26.

23 See Dunn, *Sugar and Slaves*, pp. 226–30.

24 Thomas Burton, *Parliamentary Diary, 1656–1659* (London: 1828), Vol. 4, pp. 252–307; Leo Stock (ed.), *Proceedings and Debates in the British Parliament Respecting North America* (Washington, DC: Carnegie Institution, 1924–41), Vol. 1 (1924), pp. 247–73.

25 A. B. Ellis, "White slaves and bondservants in the plantations," *The Argosy*, May 6, 1893.

26 Francisco Giavarnia, March 3, 1656, PRO, *Calendar of State Papers*, Venetian series, 1655–6, pp. 184, 209, 309.

Index

Lyttleton, Charles 508

MacAdam, James 255–6, 262
Machiavelli, Niccolo 62
Mackenzie, Henry 307, 312–13
Macnaghten, Edward, Lord
    119–11
Macpherson, C. B. 3, 146
Magazine of Magazines 303
Magna Carta, and due process
    rights 1, 2–3, 127
Maine, Henry 147
Maitland, F. W. 122, 132
Malcoomson, A. P. W. 203
Malesherbes, C.-G. de
    Lamoignan de 358
Malone, Edmund 337 n.39
Malthus, Thomas 56, 63
mandamientos 545, 546, 549–50,
    551, 554, 563
Mandeville, Bernard 54, 301
manners, politics of *see* politeness
Manning v. *Burgess* 115
Mansfield, William Murray, 1st
    Earl
    and colonial legislation 521,
        540–1
    and commercial law 5, 104,
        105, 129, 145, 150–2, 155
    and equity of redemption 117
    and property 129, 153, 535
    and slavery 637
    and testator's intent 152–3
market
    credit 99
    and labor system 572–3
    in land 305–6
    and poverty 49, 54, 55, 56–7
    regulation 68, 71–3
    and reward for labor 18, 27–8,
        30, 31, 33–4
    see also labor market
marriage
    and dowry 172–3, 176
    and property rights of children
        6, 205–6, 214
    and property rights of widow
        177–8
    and property rights of wife 175
    and sexuality 166–7
Married Woman's Property and
    Earnings Acts 102
Marshall, Peter J. 15, 16, 530–42
Marshall, T. H. 63
Marston, John Westland 336
    n.15
Martin, Benjamin 245
Martin, Samuel 520
Marx, Karl
    and domestic labor 29
    and exchange value 382 n.23

and labor theory of value 24,
    25, 62–3
and poverty 54
and private property 161
and productive capacity 24–5
and workmanship ideal 3,
    24–5, 26–7, 30, 34
Marxism
    and Chartist movement 65
    and rural industrialization 70,
        78
    and workmanship ideal 24–7
masculinity, and independence
    196
Massachusetts Government Act,
    1774 533–4, 535
Massinger, Philip 197
Masters and Servants Act, 1661
    580
Maurice, Thomas 281
Maza, Sarah 344, 345
Medcalf v. *Hall* 157 n.41
Medick, Hans 70
Mellor v. *Lees* 116
membership
    and "misteries" 4, 73–5
    rights of property in 64, 67–70,
        73, 74, 75, 83
    and rural industrialization
        75–81, 82
Mendels, Franklin 70
Mensch, Elizabeth 101
mercantilism
    and common property 97
    and early modern economics
        429–30, 444–5
    in Locke 46, 48
    Spanish 557–8, 565
    and West Indies interest 574
    and workhouse labor 48–50
    see also commerce, and law
Meredith, Sir Richard 536
mestizos, Paraguay 547, 550,
    551, 562, 565
Meynier, Georges 470–1
Michaud, Joseph François 341–3,
    346
Michodière, Jean Baptiste
    François de la 470
middle class
    and civil society 130
    and franchise 63–4
    growth in consumption 303,
        307, 315–16
    and inheritance 125
    and judiciary 133
    and taste and behaviour 310,
        313, 398
    and upward mobility 10,
        315–16, 400–2, 407, 409 n.23

midwifery, skills 12–13, 18,
    467–74
Mill, John Stuart 132, 146
Millar, John 146, 150, 246
Milldam Acts, America 100
Mingay, G. E. 315
Mirror, The 307, 309
"mistery" of labor associations 4,
    67, 73–5
mobility, social
    and colonization 498, 501, 514,
        518–19
    and commercial society 315
    and Gray's "Elegy" 10, 397–8,
        399–402, 406
modernity, and commerce
    221–31
Modyford, Thomas 504, 505,
    508–10, 519–20
Molesworth, Robert 223
monarchy
    absolute 161, 163–4, 442
    and colonial land tenure 499
    constitutional 63, 130, 500
    and monopoly 431–3, 442, 445
    and Parliament 376–7
    and public sphere 348–9,
        352–8
money
    cash and paper 6, 9, 99,
        370–1, 374–7
    and equity of redemption 117,
        120
    and Glorious Revolution 367
    in Locke 36 n.4, 371, 375–6
    and moneyed interest 221–31,
        242
    nouveaux riches and luxury
        306–7
    and words 366–8
monopoly
    class 26
    natural 440, 443
    profession as 12, 17–18
    and Royal African Company
        12, 17, 427, 430, 431–7,
        439–45
    and Spanish Crown 551, 565
Montagu, Edward Wortley 200
Montagu, Elizabeth 294 n.3, 296
    n.13
Montagu, Lady Mary Wortley
    200
Montesquieu, Charles de
    Secondat 91 n.70, 144
    and depopulation 164–5
    and women 5, 161–2, 167
morality, and art 235–8, 242–3,
    248–9
Morellet, André 341, 358